EVERYMAN'S LIBRARY

EVERYMAN,
I WILL GO WITH THEE,
AND BE THY GUIDE,
IN THY MOST NEED
TO GO BY THY SIDE

G. K. CHESTERTON

THE
EVERYMAN
CHESTERTON

EDITED AND INTRODUCED
BY IAN KER

EVERYMAN'S LIBRARY
Alfred A. Knopf   New York   London   Toronto

337

THE EVERYMAN
CHESTERTON

———

C O N T E N T S

CONTENTS

INTRODUCTION

Making a selection from the works of any writer obviously involves the editor in critical judgments. When the writer in question is as prolific and multi-talented as Chesterton, and so engaged in the controversies of his own day, the task is that much harder. So much he wrote is of the highest quality yet so much remains relatively unknown. For that reason I have chosen in this anthology to emphasize the lesser known Chesterton. Of course I might have reprinted his well-known novels – *The Napoleon of Notting Hill* and *The Man who was Thursday* – but they are already available in many editions, and it is arguable that they are not his best works. The purpose of this collection is, first, to introduce readers to the rich treasury of his other work and, second, to show that much of that work is at least as good as the more famous stories and poems, fine though these are, and often better.

There is a close parallel here between Chesterton and a nineteenth-century writer, like him pre-eminently a controversialist and convert to Catholicism, and that is John Henry Newman. Chesterton, of course, was a professional journalist, but Newman edited two periodicals and one of his best literary works was *The Tamworth Reading Room* (1841), a collection of seven lengthy commissioned letters to *The Times*, a slim publication of fifty pages and one of his two satirical masterpieces. Then again, both writers' main output lay in non-fiction prose, but both published fiction and verse, including two innovative novels and two long poems that were immensely popular in their time and which still resonate with religious believers, although neither the novels nor the poems could be called, except by uncritical enthusiasts, major works. Thus, just as Newman's *Loss and Gain* (1848) introduced a new kind of introspective self-questioning into the English novel, while Chesterton's nightmarish fantasy *The Man who was Thursday* anticipated the sinister world of Kafka; so too, Newman's *The Dream of Gerontius* (1865) was the second most widely-read work on death and the future life after Tennyson's *In Memoriam* in an age preoccupied with death, as well as inspiring Elgar's great oratorio, while Chesterton's immensely popular *The Ballad of the White Horse* inspired soldiers in the trenches during the First World War, as well as the famously terse leader in *The Times* during the Second World War which quoted two verses from it after the disastrous fall of Crete. But, whereas Newman has come to be recognized as a major literary figure to be ranked with his contemporaries, Carlyle, Ruskin and Arnold, Chesterton, seen principally as the author of *The Man who was Thursday*, *The Napoleon of Notting Hill*, *The Ballad of the White Horse*, and the Father Brown stories, is unsurprisingly dismissed as a minor writer. But this selection claims, on the contrary, that, just as Newman's great works are his non-fictional prose writings, so too is that true of Chesterton. The Chesterton, then, of this anthology is the successor of Newman and the other great Victorian 'sages', as they have been called.

Chesterton in fact used the word of himself when he wrote that as 'the sage, the sayer of things' he was 'forced' in the age in which he lived 'to pretend to be something else, a minor poet or novelist'.[1] Chesterton felt that one reason why he was not 'able to be a novelist' was that he always had been 'and presumably always shall be a journalist'. Not that he is the least self-deprecatory about this, since it was the 'serious or even solemn' part of him that made him a journalist. He was not a serious novelist simply because of incapacity, but 'because I really like to see ideas or notions wrestling naked, as it were, and not dressed up in a masquerade as men and women'. The truth was that he was not really interested in the imaginative creation of real fictional characters that was the work of a novelist: 'But I could be a journalist because I could not help being a controversialist.'[2] Nor was he in the least deprecatory about the profession of journalism, writing that what was apparently 'ephemeral journalism' can be 'eternal journalism'.[3] But he knew he was no novelist: 'The novelist can do something very splendid which I cannot do at all – something that may well be much more splendid than theorizing or thinking; he can call up living souls out of the void ...'[4] But there are two exceptions to this depreciation of his fiction: *The Man who was Thursday*, which takes the form of a nightmare in which no one turns out to be what he seems to be, and the Father Brown detective stories, in which the only character who can be known to the reader is the detective himself. And so it is not surprising that these are Chesterton's most successful attempts at fiction. This selected volume, therefore, contains a substantial number of the Father Brown stories which are self-contained in themselves, although nothing from the novel, from which it is hardly possible to make selections and which anyway, as I have already indicated, is not in my view one of Chesterton's major works, let alone a work that would justify its inclusion in its entirety. As a self-confessedly minor poet, Chesterton's verse is represented here by a handful of his best poems, but to make selections from *The Ballad of the White Horse* – a work of 'first-rate journalistic balladry' in T. S. Eliot's words[5] – would be almost as awkward as attempting to select from one of the novels.

Chesterton's posthumously published *Autobiography* (1936) has been strangely neglected by his biographers and critics. And yet it is surely a classic of autobiography in the same class as Newman's *Apologia pro Vita sua* and Ruskin's *Praeterita*. There are many delightful vignettes in this book which radiates Chesterton's joyful humour, but to include them all here would mean a somewhat fragmentary and disconnected selection. I have therefore selected only the first two chapters, the best part of the autobiography, with their marvellous insights into childhood.

Chesterton's critical masterpiece *Charles Dickens*, published in 1906, one of the classics of literary criticism, is one of his half-dozen or so major works, possibly his greatest. It is unusual for a literary critic to be at his best when writing about writers of the immediately preceding generation, but Chesterton is at his best when writing about the Victorians. For Chesterton, Dickens was the English literary response to the French Revolution, who gave expression to the idea of equality and liberty. No writer had ever '*encouraged* his characters so much' – they were like 'spoilt children. They shake the house like heavy and shouting schoolboys; they smash the story to pieces like so much furniture.' The fundamental democratic doctrine was that 'all men are interesting', so that when Dickens tried to create dull characters 'he could not keep them dull'. Like Chesterton, Dickens knew what it was 'to feel a joy so vital and violent that only impossible characters can express that'. He also understood the immense seriousness of humour, that 'exhilaration is ... a mystical fact; that exhilaration can be infinite, like sorrow; that a joke can be so big that it breaks the roof of the stars. By simply going on being absurd, a thing can become godlike; there is but one step from the ridiculous to the sublime.'[6]

Unlike contemporary intellectuals like Shaw and Wells, with their contempt for the masses, Chesterton like Dickens was 'spiritually at one with the poor, that is, with the great mass of mankind'. Dickens understood, for instance, that there were 'no pleasures like the pleasures of the poor'. No other writer had 'ever come so near the quick nerve of happiness as his descriptions of the rare extravagances of the poor'. Unlike the so-called 'philanthropists', he had 'sympathy with the poor in the Greek and literal sense; he suffered with them mentally; for the things that irritated them were the things that irritated him. He did not pity the people, or even champion the people, or even merely love the people; in this matter he was the people.'[7]

It is a typically Chestertonian paradox that lies at the heart of his study – or rather celebration – of Dickens: the fact that while Dickens despised the Middle Ages, he 'loved whatever good things the Middle Ages left behind', such as Christmas, and loathed 'the smug and stingy philosophy' of Utilitarianism, the 'exclusive creation' of progressive nineteenth-century England. On Dickens had 'descended the real tradition of "Merry England", and not upon the pallid mediaevalists who thought they were reviving it': 'The Pre-Raphaelites, the Gothicists, the admirers of the Middle Ages, had in their subtlety and sadness the spirit of the present day. Dickens had in his buffoonery and bravery the spirit of the Middle Ages. He was much more mediaeval in his attacks on mediaevalism than they were in their defences of it.' For he himself 'supposed the Middle Ages to have consisted of tournaments and torture-chambers, he supposed himself to be a brisk man of the manufacturing age, almost a Utilitarian'. In fact, 'He cared as little for mediaevalism as the mediaevals did.' Again, Dickens had no time for the religion of the Middle Ages – when he came across it in Europe 'he simply called it an old-world superstition, and sat looking at it like a moonlit ruin' – and yet, just as Catholicism believed that 'any man could be a saint if he chose', so Dickens believed in the 'encouraging of any body to be any thing'. His desire too was that his characters 'may have life, and that they may have it more abundantly'. Dickens even unconsciously understood the Catholic concept of the 'holy fool', all his 'great characters' being 'great fools', indeed specifically 'holy' fools. Dickens understood the precept that we must 'suffer fools' – but suffer them 'gladly'.[8]

Chesterton's second most important work of literary criticism was *The Victorian Age in Literature* (1913), the best pages of which are on the great Victorian 'sages', particularly Newman and Arnold, and of course on Dickens. Newman is brilliantly depicted as 'a man at once of abnormal energy and abnormal sensibility: nobody without that combination could have written the *Apologia*. If he sometimes seemed to skin his enemies alive, it was because he himself lacked a skin.' And Chesterton hailed Newman's satirical masterpiece, *Lectures on the Present Position of Catholics in England* (1851), with the very Chestertonian compliment that the book contained 'something grander than humour, there is fun'. But Newman's satirical 'triumphs' were those also 'of a highly sensitive man: a man must feel insults before he can so insultingly and splendidly avenge them. He is a naked man, who carries a naked sword.' His method as a controversialist is defined with beautiful precision and succinctness: 'The quality of his logic is that of a long but passionate patience, which waits until he has fixed all corners of an iron trap.'[9]

Chesterton wickedly suggests that Arnold's answer to the 'priggishness and provinciality' of bourgeois Victorian England – 'culture', that is, 'the disinterested play of the mind through the sifting of the best books and authorities' – was in fact 'a man, whose name was Matthew Arnold'. Nevertheless, Arnold 'happened to know certain things' that other Victorian 'sages' like Carlyle did not know – such as that 'England was a part of Europe'. Chesterton brilliantly analyses Arnold's critical method, his 'patient unravelling of the tangled Victorian ideas, as if they were matted hair under a comb'. He turned his method of 'laborious lucidity into a peculiarly exasperating form of satire and controversy', with his 'smile of heart-broken forbearance, as of the teacher in an idiot school, that was enormously insulting'. But Arnold's dogma-less religion is dissected with deadly irony – 'He would embalm the body that it might often be revisited by the soul – or souls.'[10] What Arnold 'knew' Dickens 'tasted' and 'felt'. Travelling on the French railways, he 'noticed that this eccentric nation provided him with wine that he could drink and sandwiches he could eat', while 'remembering the ghastly sawdust-eating waiting-rooms of the North English railways': 'Matthew Arnold could have told him that this was but a part of the general thinning down of European civilization in these islands at the edge of it . . .'[11]

Orthodoxy (1908), the first of Chesterton's two apologetic classics, celebrates 'the thrilling romance of Orthodoxy'. Far from orthodox Christianity being 'something heavy, humdrum, and safe', 'There never was anything so perilous or so exciting as orthodoxy. . . . It was the equilibrium of a man behind madly rushing horses, seeming to stoop this way and to sway that . . .' The orthodox Christian Church 'swerved to left and right, so exactly as to avoid enormous obstacles. . . . The orthodox Church never took the tame course or accepted the conventions; the orthodox Church was never respectable. . . . It is always easy to let the age have its head; the difficult thing is to keep one's own. . . . To have fallen into any one of the fads . . . would indeed have been obvious and tame. But to have avoided them all has been one whirling adventure; and in my vision the heavenly chariot flies thundering through the ages, the dull heresies sprawling and prostrate, the wild truth reeling but erect.'[12]

The threat to orthodox Christianity from so-called liberal theology was actually 'definitely illiberal' and would 'bring tyranny into the world'. A liberal clergyman 'always means a man who wishes at least to diminish the number of miracles; it never means a man who wishes to increase that number. It always means a man who is free to disbelieve that Christ came out of His grave; it never means a man who is free to believe that his own aunt came out of her grave.' To deny 'the liberty of God' to work miracles is hardly 'a triumph of the liberal idea' but rather 'leaves nothing free in the universe'. Again, liberal theologians believe that religions teach the same things, albeit in different 'rites and forms'. But the Christian saint is the diametrical opposite of the Buddhist saint who 'always has his eyes shut, while the Christian saint always has them very wide open. The Buddhist saint has a sleek and harmonious body, but his eyes are heavy and sealed with sleep. The medi-aeval saint's body is wasted to its crazy bones, but his eyes are frightfully alive.' The reason is that the Buddhist 'is looking with a peculiar intentness inwards. The Christian is staring with a frantic intentness outwards.' In Buddhism 'God is inside man', and consequently 'man is always inside himself'; but because Christianity believes that 'God transcends man, man has transcended himself'. Nor is there anything 'liberal' in substituting monotheism for Trinitarian Christianity which sees God as 'a society': 'The *heart* of humanity, especially of European humanity, is certainly much more satisfied by the strange hints and symbols that gather round the Trinitarian idea, the image of a council at which mercy pleads as well as justice...' For 'it is not well for God to be alone' as in Islam. Nor, again, is there anything 'liberal' in believing that salvation is 'inevitable', that 'existence ... must end up in a certain way' as in Buddhism, as opposed to the Christian idea that 'exist-ence is a *story*, which may end up in any way'. As for 'liberal' 'attempts to diminish or to explain away the divinity of Christ', what is certain is this divinity is 'terribly revolutionary'. And here Chestertonian paradox rises to an extraordinary theo-logical intensity and penetration in the most daring passage in all Chesterton's writings:

Christianity is the only religion on earth that has felt that omnipotence made God incomplete. Christianity alone has felt that God, to be wholly God, must have been a rebel as well as a king. Alone of all creeds, Christianity has added courage to the virtues of the Creator. For the only courage worth calling courage must necessarily mean that the soul passes a breaking point – and does not break ... But in that terrific tale of the Passion there is a distinct emotional sugges-tion that the author of all things (in some unthinkable way) went not only through agony, but through doubt. It is written, 'Thou shalt not tempt the Lord thy God.' No: but the Lord thy God may tempt Himself; and it seems as if this was what happened in Gethsemane. In a garden Satan tempted man: and in a garden God tempted God. He passed in some superhuman manner through our human horror of pessimism. When the world shook and the sun was wiped out of heaven, it was not at the crucifixion, but at the cry from the cross: the cry which confessed that God was forsaken of God.

Chesterton boasts that there has never been 'another god who has himself been in revolt'; and atheists will never find another god 'who ever uttered their isolation', for there is 'only one religion in which God seemed for an instant to be an atheist'.[13]

This God-man that Chesterton encounters in the Gospels is not the stereotyped Jesus of popular imagination:

There I found an account, not in the least of a person with his hair parted in the middle or his hands clasped in appeal, but of an extraordinary being with lips of thunder and acts of lurid decision, flinging down tables, casting out devils, passing with the wind from mountain isolation to a sort of dreadful demagogy; a being who often acted like an angry god – and always like a god. Christ had even a literary style of his own, not to be found, I think, elsewhere; it consists of an almost furious use of the *a fortiori*. His 'how much more' is piled one upon another like castle upon castle in the clouds. The diction ... used by Christ is quite curiously gigantesque; it is full of camels leaping through needles and mountains hurled into the sea.

And Chesterton ends the book with a no less startling Christ:

The tremendous figure which fills the Gospels ... never concealed His tears ... Yet He concealed something. ... He never restrained His anger. ... Yet He restrained something. I say it with reverence; there was in that shattering personality a thread that must be called shyness. There was something that He hid from all men when He went up a mountain to pray. There was something that He covered constantly by abrupt silence or impetuous isolation. There was some one thing that was too great for God to show us when He walked upon our earth; and I have sometimes fancied that it was His mirth.[14]

In his other great apologetic classic *The Everlasting Man* (1925), Chesterton similarly challenges the post-Christian imagination to see Christianity as though for the first time. First of all, he points out that Christianity rests on a 'single paradox', namely, that 'the hands that had made the sun and stars were too small to reach the huge heads of the cattle'. 'It would be vain to attempt to say anything adequate, or anything new, about the change which this conception of a deity born like an outcast or even an outlaw had upon the whole conception of law and its duties to the poor and outcast.' Then there is the grown-up Christ of the Gospels, who is actually very different from the stereotype of Jesus as the 'most merciful and humane lover of humanity' who has been obscured by the Church's 'repellant dogmas'. That, insists Chesterton, 'is ... very nearly the reverse of the truth'.

The truth is that it is the image of Christ in the churches that is almost entirely mild and merciful. It is the image of Christ in the Gospels that is a good many other things as well. The figure in the Gospels does indeed utter in words of almost heart-breaking beauty his pity for our broken hearts. But they are very far from being the only sort of words that he utters. Nevertheless they are almost the only kind of words that the Church in its popular imagery ever represents him as uttering. The popular imagery is inspired by a perfectly sound popular instinct. The mass of the poor are broken, and the mass of the people are poor, and for the mass of mankind the main thing is to carry the conviction of the incredible compassion of God. . . . In any case there is something appalling, something that makes the blood run cold, in the idea of having a statue of Christ in wrath.

Contrary to the popular image, there was nothing 'meek and mild' about Jesus the exorcist: 'It is much more like the tone of a very business-like lion-tamer or a strong-minded doctor dealing with a homicidal maniac.' The truth is that the real Christ of the Gospels was 'actually ... more strange and terrible than the Christ of the Church'. While the Jesus of popular conception was 'a made-up figure' totally unlike the 'strolling carpenter's apprentice' who 'said calmly and almost carelessly, like one looking over his shoulder: "Before Abraham was, I am." '[15]

Jesus is popularly thought of as essentially a teacher, but Chesterton points to 'the persistent suggestion that he has not really come to teach' – but rather 'to die'. But of his death by crucifixion Chesterton refuses to speak – for 'if there be any sound that can produce a silence, we may surely be silent about the end and the extremity; when a cry was driven out of that darkness in words dreadfully distinct and dreadfully unintelligible, which man shall never understand in all the eternity they have purchased for him; and for one annihilating instant an abyss that is not for our thoughts had opened even in the unity of the absolute; and God had been forsaken of God'.[16] Paradox here reaches an imaginative power that is unequalled in his writings.

Chesterton ends the book by again inviting his readers to look afresh at Christianity by realizing that the Gospel when originally preached really was *good news*, even if it is no longer *news*. The Gospel was 'nothing less than the loud assertion that this mysterious maker of the world has visited his world in person'. It was literally 'a piece of good news; or news that seems too good to be true': 'It declares that really ... there did walk into the world this original invisible being; about whom the thinkers make theories and the mythologists hand down myths; the Man Who Made the World.' The pagan priests had no 'sensational secret like what those running messengers of the Gospel had to say. Nobody else except those messengers has any Gospel; nobody else has any good news; for the simple reason that nobody else has any news.' Ages after the first announcement of the good news, the runners are still running: 'They have not lost the speed and momentum of messengers; they have hardly lost, as it were, the wild eyes of witnesses.' He sympathized with Jews and Moslems who regard this alleged 'incredible interruption ... a blow that broke the very backbone of history' as 'blasphemy; a blasphemy that might shake the world. But it did not shake the world; it steadied the world.'[17]

In *St Thomas Aquinas* (1923), the sequel to his *St Francis of Assisi* (1923), Chesterton explains that both saints 'were really doing the same thing. One of them was doing it in the world of the mind and the other in the world of the worldly.' The 'popular poetry of St Francis and the almost rationalistic prose of St Thomas' both contributed to 'the development of the supreme doctrine, which was also the dogma of all dogmas'. Both saints were 'doing the same great work; one in the study and the other in the street': 'St Francis, for all his love of animals, saved us from being Buddhists; and ... St Thomas, for all his love of Greek philosophy, saved us from being Platonists. But it is best to say the truth in its simplest form; that they both reaffirmed the Incarnation, by bringing God back to earth.' Francis's 'readiness ... to learn from the flowers or the birds', far from anticipating 'the Pagan renaissance', instead pointed back to the New Testament and forward to 'the Aristotelian realism of the *Summa* of St Thomas Aquinas'. By 'humanizing divinity', Francis was not 'paganizing divinity', since 'the humanizing of divinity is actually the strongest and starkest and most incredible dogma in the Creed': 'St Francis was becoming more like Christ, and not merely more like Buddha, when he considered the lilies of the field or the fowls of the air; and St Thomas was becoming more of a Christian, and not merely more of an Aristotelian, when he insisted that God and the image of God had come in contact through matter with a material world.' These two saints were 'in the most exact sense of the term, Humanists; because they were insisting on the immense importance of the human being', because they were 'strengthening that staggering doctrine of Incarnation'.[18]

The whole Thomist system rested on 'one huge and simple idea', that of what Thomas called in Latin *Ens*, unfortunately translated by the English word 'being', which, Chesterton complained, 'has a wild and woolly sort of sound', whereas *Ens* 'has a sound like the English word *End*': 'It is final and even abrupt; it is nothing except itself.' And it was upon 'this sharp pin-point of reality' that 'There *is* an Is', that Thomas had reared 'the whole cosmic system of Christendom'. Thomas was not 'ashamed' to say that his reason was 'fed' by his senses, and that as far as his reason was concerned he felt 'obliged to treat all this reality as real'. For him there was 'this primary idea of a central common sense that is nourished by the five senses'. As 'one of the great liberators of the human intellect', he 'reconciled religion with reason ... expanded it towards experimental science ... insisted that the senses were the windows of the soul and that the reason had a divine right to feed upon facts, and that it was the business of the Faith to digest the strong meat of the toughest and most practical of pagan philosophies'.[19]

The only expertise that the hero of Chesterton's Father Brown stories possesses is his intimate knowledge of the human heart, a knowledge he acquires from his religion, in two ways. First, there is his belief in original sin and the human capacity for evil. It is precisely because of his own sins as a human being that he can understand another's sins. He rejects the science of criminology because to him criminals are friends, not strangers, because they are fellow human beings. Instead of trying to observe the suspected criminal from the outside, Father Brown tries to get inside, or rather tries to *be* the criminal. The other source of his knowledge of the human heart is his work as a priest, not only through hearing confessions but also through his pastoral experience of mixing with all kinds of people.

Because it is impossible in a detective story to have normal fictional characterization, since every character has to be a suspect *except* the detective, this means that the one character who can be a character in his own right is the detective. And this is certainly true in the case of Father Brown, who is very much the mouthpiece of the author. Thus Father Brown, who never displays any special spiritual powers that Protestant readers would associate with priestcraft, emphasizes that Catholicism and Catholic theology are entirely consonant with common sense and reason, while it is false religions that dabble in the mysterious and occult. Like Chesterton, Father Brown regularly employs paradoxes, insisting, for instance, that all genuine religion is materialistic. Chesterton's views on capitalism and socialism are also those of Father Brown.

Chesterton's extraordinary ingenuity in the plots he constructs – he is surely the most ingenious of detective-story writers – may not exceed the bounds of possibility, but it certainly detracts from the realism of the stories. In this he follows in the footsteps of the inventor of the detective story, Edgar Allan Poe. But there is another important influence, that of Conan Doyle whose Sherlock Holmes is a character in his own right, like Dr Watson his confidant, and unlike Poe's detective Auguste Dupin and his confidant. Like Conan Doyle, too,

INTRODUCTION

Chesterton invests the most prosaic of London scenes with romance. As one who began life as an art student and painter rather than writer, he has no difficulty in evoking the kind of scene and atmosphere that a mystery story requires, being particularly good at describing light and sky.

In the Father Brown stories, then, Chesterton makes his own distinctive contribution to detective fiction, and, although they are not among his major writings, they will no doubt continue to be the most popular.

This selection concludes with Chesterton's two most brilliant nonsense and satirical poems, as well as his best-known serious poems (with the one exception noted at the beginning of this introduction).

Ian Ker

NOTES

Except where otherwise stated, all references are to the Ignatius Press *Collected Works of G. K. Chesterton*.
1 A. L. Maycock, ed., *The Man who was Orthodox: A Selection from the Uncollected Writings of G. K. Chesterton* (London: Dennis Robinson, 1963), 163.
2 *Autobiography*, 276–7.
3 J. P. de Fonseka, ed., *G. K. C. as M. C.: Being a Collection of Thirty-Seven Introductions* (London: Methuen, 1929), 77.
4 *Illustrated London News*, xxxiv. 88.
5 *The Tablet*, 20 June 1936.
6 *Charles Dickens*, 46–7, 49–50.
7 Ibid, 61, 68, 138, 191.
8 Ibid, 89, 131–2, 138, 147, 187–8.
9 *The Victorian Age in Literature*, 440–41.
10 Ibid, 452–4.
11 Ibid, 457.
12 *Orthodoxy*, 305–6.
13 Ibid, 330–33, 336, 340–41, 342–3.
14 Ibid, 351, 365–6.
15 *The Everlasting Man*, 169, 187, 189, 193, 196, 198.
16 Ibid, 204, 207, 212.
17 Ibid, 266–7, 269.
18 *St Thomas Aquinas*, 426–8, 432–3.
19 Ibid, 429–31, 517–18, 529.

SELECT BIBLIOGRAPHY

CONLON, D. J., *G. K. Chesterton: The Critical Judgments: Part 1, 1900–1937* (Antwerp: Antwerp Studies in English Literature, 1976).

CONLON, D. J., ed., *G. K. Chesterton: A Half Century of Views* (Oxford: Oxford University Press, 1987).

KER, IAN, *The Catholic Revival in English Literature, 1845–1961*, ch. 4 (Notre Dame, Indiana: University of Notre Dame Press, 2003).

KER, IAN, *G. K. Chesterton: A Biography* (Oxford: Oxford University Press, 2011).

NICHOLS, AIDAN O. P., *G. K. Chesterton, Theologian* (London: Darton, Longman and Todd, 2009).

ODDIE, WILLIAM, *Chesterton and the Romance of Orthodoxy: The Making of GKC 1874–1908* (Oxford: Oxford University Press, 2008).

WARD, MAISIE, *Gilbert Keith Chesterton* (London: Sheed and Ward, 1944).

WARD, MAISIE, *Return to Chesterton* (London: Sheed and Ward, 1952).

CHRONOLOGY

DATE	AUTHOR'S LIFE	LITERARY CONTEXT
1870		Death of Dickens.
		Newman: *Grammar of Assent.*
		Froude's *History of England* completed.
		D. G. Rossetti: *Poems.*
1871		Darwin: *The Descent of Man.*
		Arnold: *Friendship's Garland.*
		Ruskin: *Fors Clavigera* (to 1884).
		Eliot: *Middlemarch* (to 1872).
		Carroll: *Through the Looking-Glass.*
		MacDonald: *At the Back of the North Wind.*
		Swinburne: *Songs Before Sunrise.*
1872		Butler: *Erewhon.*
		Winwood Reade: *The Martyrdom of Man.*
1873		Newman: *The Idea of a University.*
		Arnold: *Literature and Dogma.*
		Mill: *Autobiography.*
1874	Born 29 May at 23 Sheffield Terrace, Campden Hill, London.	
1875	Birth of Cecil Chesterton.	Eliot: *Daniel Deronda* (to 1876).
		Trollope: *The Way We Live Now.*
		Browning: *Aristophanes' Apology.*
1876		Spencer: *Principles of Sociology* (to 1896).
		Trollope: *The Prime Minister.*
1877		Lear: *Laughable Lyrics.*
		Patmore: *The Unknown Eros.*
1878		Hardy: *The Return of the Native.*
		Swinburne: *Poems and Ballads: second series.*
1879		Meredith: *The Egoist.*
		Browning: *Dramatic Idyls.*
1880		Trollope: *The Duke's Children.*
		Tennyson: *Ballads and Other Poems.*

Franco-Prussian War (to 1871). Elementary Education Act. Civil Service in England thrown open to competitive examination. Doctrine of papal infallibility. Italy annexes Papal States.

Paris Commune suppressed. Wilhelm I of Prussia declared German Emperor at Versailles; Bismarck becomes Chancellor. Third Republic created in France. In Britain Trades Union Act gives protection to Union funds and strengthens their legal status. Meeting of Stanley and Livingstone at Ujiji.

Secret ballot at elections imposed by law.

Disraeli prime minister (to 1880), following aggressive imperial and military policy in South Africa, the Balkans and the Mediterranean. Factory Act. First Impressionist exhibition in Paris.
Trial by Jury: first of the Gilbert and Sullivan operas produced by D'Oyley Carte (to 1896). Public Health Act.

Queen Victoria Empress of India. Disraeli buys shares in Suez Canal. 'Bulgarian Atrocities' massacre of Christians by Moslems in Serbia. Telephone patented by Alexander Graham Bell.
Russo-Turkish War (to 1878). Edison's phonograph.

Congress of Berlin settles Eastern Question. Second Afghan War (to 1880). First electric street lighting in London. William Booth founds Salvation Army.
Zulu War.

Liberals win majority in general election; Gladstone prime minister. First Boer War (to 1881).

DATE	AUTHOR'S LIFE	LITERARY CONTEXT
1881		Death of Carlyle.
		Froude: *Reminiscences* (of Carlyle).
		James: *The Portrait of a Lady.*
		Shorthouse: *John Inglesant.*
		C. Rossetti: *A Pageant and Other Poems.*
1882		Stevenson: *New Arabian Nights.*
		Death of Emerson.
1883		Nietzsche: *Thus Spake Zarathustra* (to 1892).
		Manning: *The Eternal Priesthood.*
		Meredith: *Poems and Lyrics of the Joy of Earth.*
1884		Tolstoy: *What I believe.*
		Huysmans: *Against Nature.*
		Twain: *Huckleberry Finn.*
1885		Meredith: *Diana of the Crossways.*
		Pater: *Marius the Epicurean.*
		Zola: *Germinal.*
1886		Ruskin: *Praeterita* (to 1889).
		Stevenson: *The Strange Case of Dr Jekyll and Mr Hyde.*
		George Moore: *Confessions of a Young Man.*
1887	Enters St Paul's School.	Browning: *Parleyings with Certain People of Importance in Their Day.*
		Maupassant: *Le Horla.*
1888		Kipling: *Plain Tales from the Hills.*
		Hardy: *Wessex Tales.*
		Morris: *A Dream of John Ball.*
1889		Death of Browning.
		Ibsen's *The Doll's House* opens in London.
		Shaw: *Fabian Essays in Socialism.*
		Wallace: *Darwinism.*
		Jerome: *Three Men in a Boat.*
1890	Founding of Junior Debating Club.	Death of Newman.
1891		Wilde: *The Picture of Dorian Gray*; *The Soul of Man Under Socialism.*
		Gissing: *New Grub Street.*
		Morris: *News from Nowhere.*

CHRONOLOGY

DATE	AUTHOR'S LIFE	LITERARY CONTEXT
1891 *cont.*		Hardy: *Tess of the d'Urbervilles.* Shaw: *The Quintessence of Ibsenism.* Holmes: *Over the Tea-Cups.*
1892	Leaves St Paul's School.	Death of Tennyson and Whitman. Doyle: *The Adventures of Sherlock Holmes.* Wilde: *Lady Windermere's Fan.*
1893	Enters University College, London to study art at the Slade School.	T. H. Huxley: *Evolution and Ethics.* S. & B. Webb: *History of Trade Unionism.* Blatchford: *Merrie England.* Francis Thompson: 'The Hound of Heaven'.
1894		Shaw: *Arms and the Man.* Kipling: *The Jungle Book.* Morris: *The Wood beyond the World.* *The Yellow Book* launched in Britain (to 1897), with Aubrey Beardsley as art editor.
1895	Leaves University College, London without any qualifications. Begins work at Redway's publishers.	Wilde: *The Importance of Being Earnest; An Ideal Husband.* Hardy: *Jude the Obscure.* Wells: *The Time Machine.*
1896	Moves to Fisher Unwin publishers. Meets Blogg family in Bedford Park.	Beerbohm: *The Works of Max Beerbohm.* Housman: *A Shropshire Lad.*
1897		James: *What Maisie Knew.* Stoker: *Dracula.* Shaw: *The Devil's Disciple.* S. & B. Webb: *Industrial Democracy.* Havelock Ellis: *Studies in the Psychology of Sex* (to 1928).
1898	Engaged to Frances Blogg.	Wilde: *The Ballad of Reading Gaol.* Wells: *The War of the Worlds.* James: *The Turn of the Screw.*
1899		Tolstoy: *Resurrection.*
1900	Begins reviewing for *The Speaker.* Meets Hilaire Belloc. *Greybeards at Play. The Wild Knight.* Begins writing for *The Daily News.*	Death of Ruskin. Freud: *The Interpretation of Dreams.* Conrad: *Lord Jim.*

CHRONOLOGY

Gladstone forms fourth administration.

Independent Labour Party formed under Keir Hardy. Second Irish Home Rule Bill is passed by the House of Commons but defeated in the Lords. Government brings in troops to break miners' strike. First Matabele War (to 1894).

Gladstone resigns, having split the Liberal Party over Home Rule. Alfred Harmsworth and his brother buy the *London Evening News* and, two years later, the *Daily Mail*, beginning the creation of modern mass-market journalism. Dreyfus case begins in France.

Salisbury forms Unionist ministry (to 1902), with Joseph Chamberlain as Colonial Secretary. Rhodesia founded. Jameson Raid on the Transvaal. Freud's *Studien über Hysterie* inaugurates psychoanalysis. Wilde's trial and imprisonment. First Promenade Concert. Lumière brothers patent cinematograph. X-rays discovered by Röntgen. Marconi demonstrates radio transmission.
Second Matabele War (to 1897). Sudan War (to 1899).

Queen Victoria's Diamond Jubilee. After a century of expansion the British Empire covers one fifth of the globe, home to one quarter of the world's population. Destruction of Benin City (West Africa) by British. Thomson discovers the electron. Aspirin marketed.

Death of Gladstone. First German Navy Law (2nd in 1900): arms race with Britain begins. Britain and France clash in the Sudan (Fashoda incident). Britain granted 99-year lease on Hong Kong by Chinese government. Strike of Amalgamated Society of Engineers (the strongest union) is defeated. Curies discover radium.
Second Boer War (to 1902).
Keir Hardy and Richard Bell become first two Labour MPs. Boer women and children confined in concentration camps – a policy reversed the following year after public outcry in Britain. First Zeppelin flight. First agricultural tractor. Planck's quantum theory.

DATE	AUTHOR'S LIFE	LITERARY CONTEXT
1901	Marries Frances Blogg. *The Defendant.*	Wells: *Anticipations*; *The First Men in the Moon.* Kipling: *Kim.*
1902	*Twelve Types.*	Belloc: *The Path to Rome.* Conrad: *Heart of Darkness.* Doyle: *The Hound of the Baskervilles.*
1903	Columnist on *The Daily News.* Controversy with Robert Blatchford. *Robert Browning.* Meets Father John O'Connor.	Wells: *Mankind in the Making.* Shaw: *Man and Superman.* Butler: *The Way of All Flesh.*
1904	*G. F. Watts. The Napoleon of Notting Hill.*	James: *The Golden Bowl.* Wells: *The Food of the Gods.* Barrie: *Peter Pan.*
1905	*The Club of Queer Trades. Heretics.* 'Our Notebook' columnist on *The Illustrated London News.*	Shaw: *Major Barbara.* Wells: *A Modern Utopia.* Forster: *Where Angels Fear to Tread.* Wilde: *De Profundis.*
1906	*Charles Dickens.*	Galsworthy: *The Man of Property.* Kipling: *Puck of Pook's Hill.*
1907		Gosse: *Father and Son.* Belloc: *Cautionary Tales.*
1908	*The Man who was Thursday.* Suicide of Knollys Blogg. *All Things Considered. Orthodoxy. Varied Types.*	Bennett: *The Old Wives' Tale.* Forster: *A Room with a View.*
1909	*George Bernard Shaw.* Chestertons move from Overstrand Mansions, Battersea, to Overroads, Beaconsfield, Buckinghamshire. *Tremendous Trifles.*	Kipling: *Actions and Reactions.* Wells: *Tono-Bungay.*
1910	*The Ball and the Cross. What's Wrong with the World. Alarms and Discussions. William Blake.*	Saki: *Reginald in Russia.* . Bennett: *Clayhanger.*
1911	*Appreciations and Criticisms of the Works of Charles Dickens. The Innocence of Father Brown. The Ballad of the White Horse.* Belloc and Cecil Chesterton found *The Eye-Witness.* 'Lepanto'. Public debate with George Bernard Shaw.	Conrad: *Under Western Eyes.* Saki: *The Chronicles of Clovis.* Beerbohm: *Zuleika Dobson.*

CHRONOLOGY

DATE	AUTHOR'S LIFE	LITERARY CONTEXT
1912	*Manalive.* The *New Witness*, successor to *The Eye-Witness*, under Cecil Chesterton's editorship denounces the Marconi scandal. *A Miscellany of Men.*	Jung: *The Psychology of the Unconscious.* Belloc: *The Servile State.* De la Mare: *The Listeners.* E. Marsh (ed.): *Georgian Poetry* (5 vols, to 1922).
1913	Resigns as regular Saturday columnist on *The Daily News*. *The Victorian Age in Literature.* Cecil Chesterton found guilty of criminal libel. *Magic.*	Shaw: *Pygmalion.* Lawrence: *Sons and Lovers.* Proust: *Du côté de chez Swann.* Fournier: *Le Grand Meaulnes.*
1914	*The Flying Inn. The Wisdom of Father Brown. The Barbarism of Berlin.* Falls seriously ill.	Joyce: *Dubliners.* Hardy: *Satires of Circumstance.*
1915	*Poems.* Recovers from life-threatening illness. *The Crimes of England.*	Woolf: *The Voyage Out.* Ford: *The Good Soldier.* Lawrence: *The Rainbow.* Buchan: *The Thirty-Nine Steps.*
1916	*Divorce versus Democracy.* Temporary editor of *The New Witness* in the absence of Cecil Chesterton on military service.	Joyce: *A Portrait of the Artist as a Young Man.*
1917	*Lord Kitchener.* Cecil Chesterton marries 'Keith' Jones. *A Short History of England. Utopia of Usurers and other essays.*	Kipling: *A Diversity of Creatures.* Yeats: *The Wild Swans at Coole.*
1918	Founds the New Witness League. Visits Ireland. Death of Cecil Chesterton.	Spengler: *The Decline of the West* (to 1923). Strachey: *Eminent Victorians.* Knox: *A Spiritual Aeneid.* Hopkins: *Poems.* Brooke: *Collected Poems.* Wodehouse: *Piccadilly Jim.*
1919	*Irish Impressions.*	Keynes: *The Economic Consequences of the Peace.* Shaw: *Heartbreak House.* Beerbohm: *Seven Men.*

CHRONOLOGY

HISTORICAL EVENTS

The *Titanic* sinks. First Balkan War. Marconi scandal: Liberal ministers accused of insider trading.

Second Balkan War. *The New Statesman* founded by the Webbs and Bernard Shaw.

Assassination of Jean Jaurès, French Socialist leader. Assassination of Archduke Franz Ferdinand and his wife in Sarajevo. Outbreak of World War I. First battle of Ypres. Home Rule Act passed but implementation delayed for duration of war.
Second battle of Ypres. First Zeppelin air raid on London. Gallipoli landings. Sinking of the *Lusitania*. Asquith forms coalition with Conservatives. Einstein's general theory of relativity.

Easter Rising in Ireland. Battle of Verdun. Naval battle of Jutland. General conscription introduced in Britain. Armoured tanks first used in the battle of the Somme (July-Nov). Asquith resigns; Lloyd George becomes prime minister (to 1922), splitting the Liberal Party.
February Revolution in Russia. Abdication of Nicholas II. Bolshevik (October) Revolution. Assassination of the Tsar and his family. Civil war in Russia and Ukraine (to 1921). United States declares war on Germany. Third battle of Ypres (Paschendaele: July-Nov). Heavy bomber raids on London. British Mandate in Palestine (to 1948); Balfour Declaration promises Palestine to the Jews.
President Wilson's Fourteen Points for world peace presented to Congress (Jan). Russia withdraws from World War I (March). Allies intervene in Russian Civil War (Aug). Final Allied push to German border (Oct). Collapse of Habsburg empire. German revolution; abdication of Kaiser Wilhelm II; Weimar Republic established. Armistice (11 November). Lloyd George's Coalition government is returned to power after general election (Dec). Women over 30 obtain the vote in Britain.
Treaty of Versailles: punitive financial and territorial measures imposed on Germany. Short-lived Soviet republics in Hungary and Bavaria. 'Comintern' (Third International) founded in Moscow. 'Red Scare' begins in US. Nazi Party formed in Germany and Fascist Party in Italy. Irish War of Independence (to 1921). Dismantling of Ottoman empire. Amritsar massacre in India. Nancy Astor first woman MP. Alcock and Brown make first non-stop flight across Atlantic. Widespread strikes in Britain: 35 million working days lost.

DATE	AUTHOR'S LIFE	LITERARY CONTEXT
1920	The Chestertons visit the Holy Land. *The Uses of Diversity. The New Jerusalem.*	Wells: *The Outline of History.* Belloc: *Europe and the Faith.* Bury: *The Idea of Progress.* Owen: *Poems.* Pound: *Canzoni.*
1921	The Chestertons in America for lecture tour.	Russell: *The Analysis of Mind.* Hašek: *The Good Soldier Svejk* (to 1923).
1922	*Eugenics and other Evils. What I Saw in America.* The Chestertons move to Top Meadow, Beaconsfield. Chesterton received into Roman Catholic Church. *The Man who Knew too much.*	Joyce: *Ulysses.* T. S. Eliot: *The Waste Land.* Mansfield: *The Garden Party.* Woolf: *Jacob's Room.* Wells: *A Short History of the World.*
1923	*The New Witness* ceases publication. *Fancies versus Fads. St Francis of Assisi.*	Shaw: *Saint Joan.* Huxley: *Antic Hay.* Masefield: *Collected Poems.*
1924		Ford: *Some Do Not . . .* Forster: *A Passage to India.* Mann: *The Magic Mountain.*
1925	*G. K.'s Weekly* begins publication. *Tales of the Long Bow. The Everlasting Man. William Cobbett.*	Woolf: *Mrs Dalloway.* Kafka: *The Trial.* Fitzgerald: *The Great Gatsby.* Belloc: *The Cruise of the Nona.* Coulton: *The Medieval Village.*
1926	Lectures in Spain. *The Incredulity of Father Brown.* The Distributist League founded. Frances Chesterton received into Roman Catholic Church. Arrival of Dorothy Collins as secretary. *The Outline of Sanity.*	Kafka: *The Castle.* Kipling: *Debits and Credits.* Christie: *The Murder of Roger Ackroyd.*
1927	*The Catholic Church and Conversion.* The Chestertons and Dorothy Collins visit Poland. *The Return of Don Quixote. Collected Poems. The Judgement of Dr Johnson.* Public debate with Shaw. *Robert Louis Stevenson.*	Knox: *The Belief of Catholics; The Three Taps.* Russell: *Why I am not a Christian.* Dunne: *An Experiment with Time.* Woolf: *To the Lighthouse.* Mauriac: *Thérèse Desqueyroux.*
1928	*Generally Speaking: A Book of Essays.*	Lawrence: *Lady Chatterley's Lover.* Waugh: *Decline and Fall.* Maugham: *Ashenden.* Belloc: *Belinda.* Sassoon: *Memoirs of a Fox-Hunting Man.*

CHRONOLOGY

HISTORICAL EVENTS

League of Nations founded; US does not join. Churchill controversially orders aerial bombardment of rebel tribes in Iran. Threat of general strike forces Lloyd George to abandon military intervention in Russia. Prohibition in US (to 1933). American women win voting rights.

Irish Free State established. Marie Stopes opens first birth control clinic in London. New Economic Policy introduced in Russia. Warren Harding US president. Charlie Chaplin: *The Kid.*
Mussolini's march on Rome; forms Fascist government. Stalin becomes Secretary of the Communist Party Central Committee. Russia becomes USSR. Irish Civil War (to 1923). Fall of Lloyd George's Coalition government; Bonar Law forms Conservative ministry.

German hyperinflation. When Germans default on war reparations, French occupy Ruhr Valley (to 1925).

First Labour (minority) government in Britain, with Ramsay MacDonald as prime minister (Jan). Conservative election victory (Oct): Baldwin prime minister. Britian recognizes USSR. Death of Lenin. Failure of Hitler's Munich *putsch.* Dawes Plan (to 1929) eases reparations crisis. Surrealist manifesto. Locarno Pact guarantees existing Franco-German frontier. Churchill returns Britain to the pre-war Gold Standard. Miners' strike. Scopes 'Monkey' Trial in Dayton, Tennessee. Hitler: *Mein Kampf* (vol. 1).

Miners' strike (May–Nov). General Strike (4–12 May). Germany admitted to League of Nations. Television demonstrated by J. L. Baird.

Trades Disputes and Trade Union Act: sympathetic strikes and mass picketing made illegal. Trotsky expelled from the Communist Party. BBC founded. *The Jazz Singer* – first 'talkie'.

Kellogg-Briand Pact, outlawing war and providing for peaceful settlement of disputes. First Five Year Plan in USSR. Stalin *de facto* dictator and object of nationwide cult. Suffrage in Britain extended to women over 21. Fleming discovers Penicillin.

DATE	AUTHOR'S LIFE	LITERARY CONTEXT
1929	Controversy with G. G. Coulton. *The Poet and the Lunatics.* The Chestertons and Dorothy Collins stay in Rome, where Chesterton meets Mussolini and Pope Pius IX. *The Thing. G.K.C. as M.C.*	Shaw: *The Apple Cart.* Graves: *Goodbye to All That.* Hemingway: *A Farewell to Arms.* Yeats: *The Winding Stair.* Bernanos: *La Joie.*
1930	Elected first president of the Detection Club. *Four Faultless Felons.* Second American lecture tour. *The Resurrection of Rome. Come to Think of it ... A Book of Essays.*	Freud: *Civilization and its Discontents.* T. S. Eliot: *Ash Wednesday.* Pritchett: *The Spanish Virgin and Other Stories.*
1931	The Chestertons and Dorothy Collins return to England. *All is Grist: A Book of Essays.*	
1932	*Chaucer. Sidelights.* The Chestertons attend International Eucharistic Congress in Dublin. *Christendom in Dublin.*	Russell: *Education and the Social Order.* Knox: *Broadcast Minds.* A. Huxley: *Brave New World.* Waugh: *Black Mischief.* Greene: *Stamboul Train.* Mauriac: *Le Noeud de vipères.*
1933	*All I Survey: A Book of Essays. St Thomas Aquinas.*	Wells: *The Shape of Things to Come.* Maugham: *Ah King.* Coward: *Private Lives*; *Design for Living.* Sayers: *Murder Must Advertise.*
1934	Taken ill while on holiday in Italy. *Avowals and Denials.*	Wodehouse: *Thank You, Jeeves*; *Right Ho, Jeeves.* Waugh: *A Handful of Dust.* Orwell: *Burmese Days.* Sayers: *The Nine Tailors.* Christie: *Murder on the Orient Express.* Priestley: *English Journey.*
1935	*The Scandal of Father Brown.* The Chestertons and Dorothy Collins holiday in France and Spain. Controversy with G. G. Coulton. *The Well and the Shallows.*	Greene: *England Made Me.* Isherwood: *Mr Norris Changes Trains.*
1936	The Chestertons and Dorothy Collins holiday in France. *As I was Saying: A Book of Essays.* Death of Chesterton on 14 June. *Autobiography.*	Orwell: *Keep the Aspidistra Flying.* Auden: *Look Stranger!.* C. S. Lewis: *The Allegory of Love.* Bernanos: *Journal d'un curé de campagne.* Mauriac: *Vie de Jésu.*

CHRONOLOGY

Wall Street Crash: beginning of worldwide Depression. Second minority Labour government under MacDonald. Forcible collectivization of agriculture in USSR. Briand proposes a union of European nations. Lateran Treaty establishes independent state of the Vatican.

Allies evacuate Rhineland. Gandhi's civil disobedience campaign in India. First Round Table Conference between Britain and India. First football world cup.

Trade Unions refuse to accept MacDonald's budgetary cuts: he splits the Labour Party, forming a National Government to balance budget (to 1935). Britain abandons the Gold Standard. 'Red Terror': persecution of the Catholic Church in Republican Spain (to 1936).
UK unemployment peaks at over 2,900,000, around 23% of the workforce. Clashes between Hunger Marchers and police in London. Oswald Mosley founds British Union of Fascists. Nazis largest party in German Reichstag. Lausanne conference: German war reparations suspended indefinitely by allies and repudiated by Hitler in 1933. Geneva conference on disarmament (to 1934). Famine in Ukraine (to 1934). Cockcroft and Walton split the atom.

Hitler becomes German Chancellor. First concentration camps in Germany. Germany and Japan leave League of Nations. Dollfuss right-wing dictator in Austria. Franklin Concordat between Holy See and German Reich, guaranteeing the rights of the Catholic Church in Germany and almost immediately violated. Roosevelt elected US president: announces 'New Deal' for economic recovery.
Death of President Hindenburg; Hitler becomes German Führer. 'Night of the Long Knives': Hitler purges his opponents. Churchill warns against German rearmament. Dollfuss assassinated by Nazis. Comintern calls for formation of Popular Front (left-wing alliances) against Fascism. Murder of Kirov (Dec) gives Stalin pretext for launching his 'Great Terror' in which millions die.

Nuremberg Laws in Germany debar Jews from public life. MacDonald retires and is replaced by Baldwin. Government of India Act allows limited self-government.

Popular Front win election in Spain, prompting Fascist military coup and Spanish Civil War (to 1939). Popular Front win French election; Léon Blum becomes first socialist prime minister. Hitler marches into demilitarized Rhineland. Rome-Berlin Axis signed. Death of George V and accession of Edward VIII; abdication crisis; George VI becomes king. Jarrow March. BBC begins television broadcasts.

THE
EVERYMAN
CHESTERTON

AUTOBIOGRAPHY

I

HEARSAY EVIDENCE

Bowing down in blind credulity, as is my custom, before mere authority and the tradition of the elders, superstitiously swallowing a story I could not test at the time by experiment or private judgment, I am firmly of opinion that I was born on the 29th of May, 1874, on Campden Hill, Kensington; and baptized according to the formularies of the Church of England in the little church of St George opposite the large Waterworks Tower that dominated that ridge. I do not allege any significance in the relation of the two buildings; and I indignantly deny that the church was chosen because it needed the whole water-power of West London to turn me into a Christian.

Nevertheless, the great Waterworks Tower was destined to play its part in my life, as I shall narrate on a subsequent page; but that story is connected with my own experiences, whereas my birth (as I have said) is an incident which I accept, like some poor ignorant peasant, only because it has been handed down to me by oral tradition. And before we come to any of my own experiences, it will be well to devote this brief chapter to a few of the other facts of my family and environment which I hold equally precariously on mere hearsay evidence. Of course what many call hearsay evidence, or what I call human evidence, might be questioned in theory, as in the Baconian controversy or a good deal of the Higher Criticism. The story of my birth might be untrue. I might be the long-lost heir of The Holy Roman Empire, or an infant left by ruffians from Limehouse on a door-step in Kensington, to develop in later life a hideous criminal heredity. Some of the sceptical methods applied to the world's origin might be applied to my origin, and a grave and earnest enquirer come to the conclusion that I was never born at all. But I prefer to believe that common sense is something that my readers and I have in common; and that they will have patience with a dull summary of the facts.

I was born of respectable but honest parents; that is, in a world where the word 'respectability' was not yet exclusively a term of abuse, but retained some dim philological connection with the idea of being respected. It is true that even in my own youth the sense of the word was changing; as I remember in a conversation between my parents, in which it was used with both implications. My father, who was serene, humorous and full of hobbies, remarked casually that he had been asked to go on what was then called The Vestry. At this my mother, who was more swift, restless and generally Radical in her instincts, uttered something like a cry of pain; she said, 'Oh, Edward, don't! You will be so respectable! We never have been respectable yet; don't let's begin now.' And I remember my father mildly replying, 'My dear, you present a rather alarming picture of our lives, if you say that we have never for one single instant been respectable.' Readers of *Pride and Prejudice* will perceive that there was something of Mr Bennet about my father; though there was certainly nothing of Mrs Bennet about my mother.

Anyhow, what I mean here is that my people belonged to that rather old-fashioned English middle class; in which a business man was still permitted to mind his own business. They had been granted no glimpse of our later and loftier vision, of that more advanced and adventurous conception of commerce, in which a business man is supposed to rival, ruin, destroy, absorb and swallow up everybody else's business. My father was a Liberal of the school that existed before the rise of Socialism; he took it for granted that all sane people believed in private property; but he did not trouble to translate it into private enterprise. His people were of the sort that were always sufficiently successful; but hardly, in the modern sense, enterprising. My father was the head of a hereditary business of house agents and surveyors, which had already been established for some three generations in Kensington; and I remember that there was a sort of local patriotism about it and a little reluctance in the elder members, when the younger first proposed that it should have branches outside Kensington. This particular sort of unobtrusive pride was very characteristic of this sort of older business men. I remember that it once created a comedy of cross-purposes, which could hardly have occurred unless there had been some such secret self-congratulation upon any accretion of local status. The incident is in more ways than one a glimpse of the tone and talk of those distant days.

My grandfather, my father's father, was a fine-looking old man with white hair and beard and manners that had something of that rounded solemnity that went with the old-fashioned customs of proposing toasts and sentiments. He kept up the ancient Christian custom of singing at the dinner-table, and it did not seem incongruous when he sang 'The Fine Old English Gentleman' as well as more pompous songs of the period of Waterloo and Trafalgar. And I may remark in passing that, having lived to see Mafeking Night[1] and the later Jingo lyrics, I have retained a considerable respect for those old and pompous patriotic songs. I rather fancy it was better for the tradition of the English tongue to hear such rhetorical lines as these, about Wellington[2] at the deathbed of William the Fourth,

> For he came on the Angel of Victory's wing
> But the Angel of Death was awaiting the King,

than to be entirely satisfied with howling the following lines, heard in all music-halls some twenty years afterwards:

> And when we say we've always won
> And when they ask us how it's done
> We proudly point to every one
> Of England's soldiers of the Queen.

I cannot help having a dim suspicion that dignity has something to do with style; but anyhow the gestures, like the songs, of my grandfather's time and type had a good deal to do with dignity. But, used as he was to ceremonial manners, he must have been a good deal mystified by a strange gentleman who entered the office and, having conferred with my father briefly on business, asked in a hushed voice if he might have the high privilege of being presented to the more ancient or ancestral head of the firm. He then approached my grandfather as if the old gentleman had been a sort of shrine, with profound bows and reverential apostrophes.

'You are a Monument,' said the strange gentleman, 'Sir, you are a Landmark.'

My grandfather, slightly flattered, murmured politely that they had certainly been in Kensington for some little time.

---

1 The night of jubilation in Britain at the relief on 17 May 1900 of the besieged city in the Boer War.
2 The Duke of Wellington, victor at the Battle of Waterloo.

'You are an Historical Character,' said the admiring stranger. 'You have changed the whole destiny of Church and State.'

My grandfather still assumed airily that this might be a poetical manner of describing a successful house-agency. But a light began to break on my father, who had thought his way through all the High Church and Broad Church movements and was well-read in such things. He suddenly remembered the case of 'Westerton *versus* Liddell', in which a Protestant churchwarden prosecuted a parson for one of the darker crimes of Popery, possibly wearing a surplice.

'And I only hope,' went on the stranger firmly, still addressing the Protestant Champion, 'that the services at the Parish Church are now conducted in a manner of which you approve.'

My grandfather observed in a genial manner that he didn't care how they were conducted. These remarkable words of the Protestant Champion caused his worshipper to gaze upon him with a new dawn of wonder, when my father intervened and explained the error, pointing out the fine shade that divides Westerton and Chesterton. I may add that my grandfather, when the story was told, always used to insist that he had added to the phrase 'I don't care how they're conducted,' the qualifying words (repeated with a grave motion of the hand) 'provided it is with reverence and sincerity.' But I grieve to say that sceptics in the younger generation believed this to have been an afterthought.

The point is, however, that my grandfather was pleased, and not really very much amazed, to be called a monument and a landmark. And that was typical of many middle-class men, even in small businesses, in that remote world. For the particular sort of British bourgeoisie of which I am speaking has been so much altered or diminished, that it cannot exactly be said to exist today. Nothing quite like it at least can be found in England; nothing in the least like it, I fancy, was ever found in America. One peculiarity of this middle class was that it really was a class and it really was in the middle. Both for good and evil, and certainly often to excess, it was separated both from the class above it and the class below. It knew far too little of the working classes, to the grave peril of a later generation. It knew far too little even of its own servants. My own people were always very kind to servants; but in the class as a whole there was neither the coarse familiarity in work, which belongs to democracies and can be seen in the clamouring and cursing housewives of the Continent, nor the remains of a feudal friendliness such as lingers in the real aristocracy. There was a sort of silence and embarrassment. It was illustrated in another hearsay anecdote, which I may here add to the anecdote of the Protestant Champion. A lady of my family went to live in a friend's house in the friend's absence; to be waited on by a sort of superior servant. The lady had got it fixed in her head that the servant cooked her own meals separately, whereas the servant was equally fixed on the policy of eating what was left over from the lady's meals. The servant sent up for breakfast, say, five rashers of bacon; which was more than the lady wanted. But the lady had another fixed freak of conscience common in the ladies of the period. She thought nothing should be wasted; and could not see that even a thing consumed is wasted if it is not wanted. She ate the five rashers and the servant consequently sent up seven rashers. The lady paled a little, but followed the path of duty and ate them all. The servant, beginning to feel that she too would like a little breakfast, sent up nine or ten rashers. The lady, rallying all her powers, charged at them with her head down, and swept them from the field. And so, I suppose, it went on; owing to the polite silence between the two social classes. I dare not think how it ended. The logical conclusion would seem to be that the servant starved and the lady burst. But I suppose that, before they reached that point, some communications had been opened even between two people living on two floors of the same house. But that was certainly the weak side of that world; that it did not extend its domestic confidence to domestic servants. It smiled and felt superior when reading of old-world vassals who dined below the salt, and continued to feel equally superior to its own vassals, who dined below the floor.

But however we may criticize the old middle class, and however heartily we may join in those immortal words of the Song of the Future, which are said to run:

> Class-conscious we are, class-conscious we'll be;
> Till our foot's on the necks of the bourgeoisie,

it has a right to historical justice; and there are other points to remember. One point is that it was partly the real 'culture conquests' of this stratum of the middle class, and the fact that it really was an educated class, that made it unduly suspicious of the influence of servants. It attached rather too much importance to spelling correctly; it attached enormous importance to speaking correctly. And it did spell and speak correctly. There was a whole world in which nobody was any more likely to drop an *h* than to pick up a title. I early discovered, with the malice of infancy, that what my seniors were really afraid of was any imitation of the intonation and diction of the servants. I am told (to quote another hearsay anecdote) that about the age of three or four, I screamed for a hat hanging on a peg, and at last in convulsions of fury uttered the awful words, 'If you don't give it me, I'll say 'at.' I felt sure that would lay all my relations prostrate for miles around.

And this care about education and diction, though I can see much to criticize in it now, did really have its good side. It meant that my father knew all his English literature backwards, and that I knew a great deal of it by heart, long before I could really get it into my head. I knew pages of Shakespeare's blank verse without a notion of the meaning of most of it; which is perhaps the right way to begin to appreciate verse. And it is also recorded of me that, at the age of six or seven, I tumbled down in the street in the act of excitedly reciting the words,

> Good Hamlet, cast this nighted colour off,
> And let thine eye look like a friend on Denmark,
> Do not for ever with thy veiléd lids
> Seek for thy noble father in the dust,[1]

at which appropriate moment I pitched forward on my nose.

What is perhaps even less appreciated is that the particular class I mean was not only cut off from what are called the lower classes, but also quite as sharply from what are called the upper classes. Since then we may say, with all graceful apologies, that this class has split up into the two great sections of the Snobs and the Prigs. The first are those who want to get into Society; the second are those who want to get out of Society, and into Societies. I mean Vegetarian Societies and Socialist Colonies and things of that sort. But the people I mean were not cranks, and, what is more, they were not snobs. There were plenty of people in their time, of

---

1 *Hamlet* I.ii.68–71, which Chesterton misquotes from memory, substituting 'this' for 'thy' in the first line.

course, who were snobbish; but those I mean were really a class apart. They never dreamed of knowing the aristocracy except in business. They had, what has since become almost incredible in England, a pride of their own.

For instance, almost all that district of Kensington was and is laid out like a chart or plan to illustrate Macaulay's Essays. Of course we read Macaulay's Essays; and in our simple isolation, often even believed them. We knew all the great names of the Whig aristocrats who had made the Revolution[1] (and incidentally their own fortunes) and those names were written conspicuously all over the Kensington estates. Every day we passed Holland House,[2] that opened its hospitality to Macaulay, and the statue of Lord Holland inscribed with the boast that he was the nephew of Fox and the friend of Grey.[3] The street opposite where we came to live bore the name of Addison; the street of our later sojourn the name of Warwick,[4] the step-son of Addison. Beyond was a road named after the house of Russell,[5] to the south another with the name of Cromwell. Near us, on our original perch in Campden Hill, was the great name of Argyll.[6] Now all these names thrilled me like trumpets, as they would any boy reading Macaulay. But it never so much as crossed my mind that we should ever know any people who bore them, or even especially want to. I remember making my father laugh very much by telling him of the old Scots ballad with the line,

There fell about a great dispute between Argyle and Airlie.[7]

For he knew, as a house-agent, that Lord Airlie's house was actually quite close to Argyll Lodge; and that nothing was more

1 The 'Glorious Revolution' of 1688 overthrew James II, replacing him with William of Orange.
2 The residence of Henry Richard Fox, 3rd baron Holland and centre of the Whig circle of politicians and writers presided over by his uncle Charles James Fox (1749–1806), leader of the Whigs and opponent of the Tory William Pitt the Younger.
3 Lord Grey who succeeded Fox as leader of the Whig party and whose administration passed the 1832 Reform Bill and abolished slavery.
4 Edward Henry Rich, 7th Earl of Warwick (1698–1721).
5 The earls and dukes of Bedford.
6 Archibald Campbell, 8th Earl of Argyll (1607–61), led the opposition in Scotland to Charles I and was executed by Charles II.
7 James Ogilvy, created Earl of of Airlie in 1639, joined the Marquess of Montrose in support of Charles I in Scotland.

likely than that there might fall about a great dispute, directly affecting his own line of business. He knew the old Duke of Argyll in purely business relations, and showed me a letter from him as a curiosity; but to me it was like a delightful curiosity in a museum. I no more thought of expecting McCallum More[1] to come in any way into my own social existence, than I expected Graham of Claverhouse[2] to ride up on his great black horse to the front-door, or Charles the Second to drop in to tea. I regarded the Duke living at Argyll Lodge as an historical character. My people were interested in an aristocracy because it was still an historical thing. The point is worth mentioning, because it is exactly this difference, whether for good or evil, that justifies a fight or feud of which I shall have to write on a later page. Long afterwards, I had the luck to figure in a political row about the Sale of Peerages; and many said that we were wasting our energies in denouncing it. But we were not. The treatment of a title did make a difference; and I am just old enough to be able to measure the difference it has really made. If, regarding Lord Lorne with historical respect, I had been introduced to an unknown Lord Leatherhead, I should have respected him also as something historical. If I were to meet him now, I should know he might be any pawnbroker from any gutter in Europe. Honours have not been sold; they have been destroyed.

One considerable family connected with the family business, merely in the way of business, may be worth mentioning for quite other reasons. The firm was, and indeed still is, agent for the large Phillimore Estate then owned by two brothers who both played considerable public parts; Admiral Phillimore who died long ago and Lord Justice Phillimore, one of the most famous of the modern English judges, who died more recently. We had nothing to do with such people, nor tried to, though I remember more than one quite independent testimony to the magnanimity of the old Admiral. But I mention this vague background of the great Kensington Estate for another reason. For the name of Phillimore was destined in a strange and double and rather ironic fashion, to be entwined with my subsequent adventures in life. The Admiral I never saw; but

1 'Whom the Southern call the Duke of Argyll.' Walter Scott, *Rob Roy*, ch. 9.
2 Graham of Claverhouse, John Graham of Claverhouse, Viscount Dundee (*c.* 1649–89), the scourge of the rebellious Covenanters and supporter of the Stuart cause in Scotland.

his son,[1] who must have been a child of about my own age, I was long afterwards to know and love and lose, as a friend and an ally in a cause which would then have seemed fantastically far away from our boyhoods. And the Judge I was destined to see sitting on the seat of judgment, and to give evidence before him on behalf of my brother,[2] who stood in the dock at the Old Bailey and was found guilty of patriotism and public spirit.

My mother's family had a French surname; though the family, as I knew it by experience as well as tradition, was entirely English in speech and social habit. There was a sort of family legend that they were descended from a French private soldier of the Revolutionary Wars, who had been a prisoner in England and remained there; as some certainly did. But on the other side my mother came of Scottish people, who were Keiths from Aberdeen; and for several reasons, partly because my maternal grandmother long survived her husband and was a very attractive personality, and partly because of a certain vividness in any infusion of Scots blood or patriotism, this northern affiliation appealed strongly to my affections; and made a sort of Scottish romance in my childhood. But her husband, my maternal grandfather whom I never saw, must have been an interesting person too; and something of an historical type, if not an historical character. He had been one of the old Wesleyan lay-preachers and was thus involved in public controversy, a characteristic which has descended to his grandchild. He was also one of the leaders of the early Teetotal movement; a characteristic which has not. But I am quite sure there was a great deal in him, beyond anything that is implied in mere public speaking or teetotalism. I am quite sure of it, because of two casual remarks he made; which are indeed the only two remarks I ever heard of him making. Once, when his sons were declaiming against

---

1 J. S. Phillimore, professor of Greek at Glasgow University, a friend of Chesterton and Belloc and a convert to Catholicism, was a regular contributor to the *New Witness* (see next note).

2 Cecil Chesterton edited the *New Witness*, which battled against political corruption, until his death in the First World War, when his brother succeeded him. In 1913 Cecil was sued for criminal libel by Godfrey Isaacs, a Jewish business man at the centre of the Marconi scandal. He was found guilty but only fined and not sent to prison because he had acted honestly if misguidedly and without malice. Chesterton's gloss on the verdict and the severe lecture Lord Justice Phillimore gave to the defendant is somewhat disingenuous.

mode and convention in the manner of all liberal youth, he said abruptly, 'Ah, they talk a lot about fashion; but fashion is civiliza-tion.' And in the other case, the same rising generation was lightly tossing about that pessimism which is only possible in the happy time of youth. They were criticizing the General Thanksgiving in the Prayer-Book, and remarking that a good many people have very little reason to be thankful for their creation. And the old man, who was then so old that he hardly ever spoke at all, said suddenly out of his silence, 'I should thank God for my creation if I knew I was a lost soul.'

Of the other side of my family I may say more when I come to my own memories; but I put this side of the matter first because there is so much more of it that I have received only at secondhand. And this is the part of the book which is forced to be biography and cannot be autobiography. It deals with the things that were just behind me and merely threw their shadows on my earliest path; the things I saw in reflection rather than reality. Of these there were more on my mother's side; especially that historical interest in the house of Keith, which was mixed up with my general historical interest in things like the house of Argyll. But on my father's side also there were legends; the nearest and most eminent figure being that Captain Chesterton, who was famous in his day as a reformer of prisons. He was a friend of Dickens, and, I suspect, himself some-thing of a Dickens character. But indeed these first memories and rumours suggest that there were a good many Dickens characters in the days of Dickens. I am far from denying the inference; that a good many Dickens characters are humbugs. It would not be fair to say all I have said in praise of the old Victorian middle class, without admitting that it did sometimes produce pretty hollow and pompous imposture. A solemn friend of my grandfather used to go for walks on Sunday carrying a prayer-book, without the least intention of going to church. And he calmly defended it by saying, with uplifted hand, 'I do it, Chessie, as an example to others.' The man who did that was obviously a Dickens character. And I am disposed to think that, in being a Dickens character, he was in many ways rather preferable to many modern characters. Few modern men, however false, would dare to be so brazen. And I am not sure he was not really a more genuine fellow than the modern man who says vaguely that he has doubts or hates sermons, when he only wants to go and play golf. Hypocrisy itself was more sincere. Anyhow, it was more courageous.

What I can but call a Great Gusto breathed out of that epoch; something now only remembered in the rich and rollicking quotation of Swiveller and Micawber. But the point is that the savour of it could then be found in scores of quite worthy and obscure people; certainly much more worthy than the blatantly Pecksniffian person with the prayer-book; and much more obscure than the eccentric but efficient, and even eminent, prison governor and reformer. To use a trade term of the period, this indescribable sort of relish was by no means only a gentlemen's relish. It was the effect, I think, of that popular humour, which is still perhaps our only really popular institution, working upon the remains of the rhetoric of the eighteenth-century orators, and the almost equally rhetorical rhetoric of the nineteenth-century poets, like Byron and Moore. Anyhow, it was evidently common to countless common or average people, and rather specially to commercial clerks. The clerk came afterwards to figure rather as a mere cheap Cockney with clipped speech; a sort of broken English that seems broken by accident; chipped rather than clipped. But there was a race that really dealt in periods as rounded as Christmas platters and punchbowls. My father told me of a fellow clerk of his youth, or boyhood, who took leave of the tavern or chop-house with a stately message of thanks, which he delivered in a big booming voice, before stalking into the street, 'Tell Mrs Bayfield that the steak was excellent; the potatoes done to a turn; in short a dinner fit for an Emperor.' Is not that exactly like 'F.B.' in the moments when Thackeray was most Dickensian? From the same remote source, I recall another quite Dickensian scene; a bland, round-faced little man in spectacles, the sort that is always chaffed anywhere; and a fellow clerk named Carr, of more mysterious humours; both ghosts from my father's time of apprenticeship. At intervals the more sombre clerk would call out across the office, 'Mr Hannay!' The round face, bright with its smile and spectacles, would bob up with never-failing freshness and expectation: 'Yes, Mr Carr.' Then Mr Carr would fix him with a sphinx-like visage and say in hollow but resounding tones, 'Boundless Space!' And then Mr Carr would turn more briskly to the other clerks, shaking his head, and repeating in a hopeless tone, 'He can't grasp it!' I do not know what

either of them would have thought of the idea of Professor Einstein
entering the office and avenging Mr Hannay on Mr Carr, by
suggesting that space is not boundless at all. The point is that there
is this element of pomp and ritual about jokes; even about practical
jokes; indeed even about practical deceptions. It was known in
humbler walks, among mountebanks and even monstrosities, as
well Dickens knew; and there was something as stately about the
cheap-jacks demanding money as the orators demanding fame.
One of my own earliest memories is of looking from a balcony
above one of the big residential roads of a watering-place, and
seeing a venerable party with white hair solemnly taking off a
white hat as he walked down the centre of the street, and saying
to nobody in particular in the loud voice of a lecturer, 'When I first
came into Cannon Street – I beg your pardon, Cannon Place . . .'
a performance which he repeated every day, always falling into
the same error to be followed by the same apology. This gave me,
I know not why, enormous pleasure; partly, I think, from the
feeling that a gigantic clockwork doll had been added to what
Mr Maurice Baring[1] calls the puppet-show of memory. But his
importance here is that the rest of his speech seemed all the more
polished and faultless for that one strangely recurrent fault; and it
always ended with a beautiful peroration, about recalling in the
distant future, and in the hour of death, 'the kindness I have met
with in Cannon Place'. Later, I remember the same seaside paths
paraded by a yet more loquacious public character wearing cap
and gown, I fear with but little academic authority; but I think he
marked a much later stage, because he was acrid and antagonistic,
and appealed to his audience by calling them hypocrites and
whited sepulchres; which had the curious effect upon that very
English crowd of causing them to throw pennies into his mortar-
board. But in the earlier stage which concerns me here, a glow of
convivial courtesy covered everything; and the wing of friendship
could never moult a feather. The amazing patience of our populace then went with a certain pomp, but it was a pompous geniality; and even their jeers were still jovial. Their mockery and their
heroism still remain, heaven knows; but they no longer thus combine in the mock heroic. But anybody who heard, or heard of, the

1 Maurice Baring (1874–1945), a successful novelist, was a convert to Catholicism and a
close friend of Chesterton.

men I mention, will be certain to his dying day that Dick Swiveller[1] did say, 'When he who adores thee has left but the name – in case of letters or parcels,' or that the poor usher at the party did whisper to each lady in turn, 'Had I a heart for falsehood framed I ne'er could injure you.' There was a glow in it; not to be copied by sparks, even when they really sparkle. The world is less gay for losing that solemnity.

Another real Victorian virtue, not to be discredited by many imaginary Victorian virtues, belongs not so much to my generation as to my father's and grandfather's, or at least, if I was specially lucky, to my father and grandfather. It should, therefore, be mentioned in this place, if it is illustrated by incidents within my own memory. My own people in any case had a strict standard of commercial probity; but I fancy the standard was stricter in all that more stolid commercial class than in a later time, when the notion of success was mixed up not only with cynicism but with a queer sort of piratical romance. The change may be felt, as in the word 'respectable', in the very atmosphere of certain words. The favourite modern ideal in morals and even in religion, especially the religion popularized in the papers for millions of modern business men, is the word 'adventure'. The most menacing monster in morals, for the business men of my old middle class, was branded with the title of 'adventurer'. In later times, I fancy, the world has defended some pretty indefensible adventurers by implying the glamour of adventure. Anyhow, this is not merely my own belated opinion in an age of reaction. It was the opinion of the best even of the old optimists and orthodox economists, who lived when the change was beginning, and believed they were living in an age of reform. My own father and uncles were entirely of the period that believed in progress, and generally in new things, all the more because they were finding it increasingly difficult to believe in old things; and in some cases in anything at all. But though as Liberals they believed in progress, as honest men they often testified to deterioration.

I remember my father telling me how much he had begun to be pestered by great swarms of people wanting private commissions upon transactions, in which they were supposed to represent

1 A character in Dickens's *Old Curiosity Shop* (1840).

another interest. He mentioned it not only with the deepest disgust, but more or less as if it were a novelty as well as a nuisance. He was himself in the habit of meeting these unpleasant people with a humorously simulated burst of heartiness and even hilarity; but it was the only sort of occasion on which his humour might be called grim and even ferocious. When the agent, bargaining for some third party, hinted that an acceptable trifle would smooth the negotiations, he would say with formidable geniality, 'Oh, certainly! certainly! So long as we are all friends and everything is open and above-board! I am sure your principals and employers will be delighted to hear from me that I'm paying you a small –' He would then be interrupted with a sort of shriek of fear and the kind diplomatic gentleman would cover his tracks as best he could in terror. 'And doesn't that prove to you,' said my father with innocent rationalism, 'the immorality of such a proposal?'

My Uncle Sidney, who was his partner in the business, was a more unanswerable witness, because a more unwilling witness. My father was very universal in his interests and very moderate in his opinions; he was one of the few men I ever knew who really listened to argument; moreover, he was more traditional than many in the liberal age; he loved many old things, and had especially a passion for the French cathedrals and all the Gothic architecture opened up by Ruskin in that time. It was not quite so inconceivable that he might admit another side to modern progress. But my uncle was the very reverse of a *laudator temporis acti*.[1] He was one of those sensitive and conscientious men, very typical of the modern world, who had the same scrupulous sense of the duty of accepting new things, and sympathizing with the young, that older moralists may have had about preserving old things and obeying the elders. I remember him assuring me quite eagerly of the hopeful thoughts aroused in him by the optimistic official prophecies of the book called *Looking Backwards*;[2] a rather ironical title, seeing that the one thing forbidden to such futurists was Looking Backwards. And the whole philosophy, afterwards sublimated by the genius of Mr Wells, was the duty of Looking Forwards. My uncle, much more than my father, was this scrupulously sanguine sort of man; and the last man in the world to hold any

1 Praiser of time past.
2 Edward Bellamy's *Looking Backwards* (1888) was a Utopian romance set in the year 2000.

brief for the good old times. But he was also a quite transparently truthful man; and I remember him telling me, with that wrinkle of worry in his brow, which confessed his subconscious and sensitive anxiety, 'I'm bound to confess that commercial morality has got steadily worse through my lifetime.'

Of course I admit, or rather I boast, that in anything like sympathy with any such Utopia, such individuals were in advance of the times. But I boast much more that, in the great modern growth of high finance, they were behind the times. The class as a whole was, indeed, dangerously deaf and blind upon the former question of economic exploitation; but it was relatively more vigilant and sensitive upon the latter question of financial decency. It never occurred to these people that anybody could possibly admire a man for being what we call 'daring' in speculation, any more than a woman for being what we call 'daring' in dress. There was something of the same atmospheric change in both cases. The absence of social ambition had a great deal to do with it. When the restrictions really were stuffy and stupid, they were largely those of ignorance; but this was nothing like so evil and ruinous as the ignorance of the real wrongs and rights of the working classes. Heaven knows, it is even possible that in some cases the reader knows, that I am no admirer of the complacent commercial prosperity of England in the nineteenth century. At the best it was an individualism that ended by destroying individuality; an industrialism which has done nothing except poison the very meaning of the word industry. At the worst it turned at last into a vulgar victory of sweating and swindling. I am only pointing out a particular point about a particular group or class, now extinct; that if they were ignorant of, or often indifferent to the sweating, they were really indignant at the swindling. In the same way, few will accuse me of Puritanism; but I think it due to the Puritan tradition to say that certain notions of social sobriety did have something to do with delaying the full triumph of flashy finance and the mere antics of avarice. Anyhow, there has been a change from a middle class that trusted a business man to look after money because he was dull and careful, to one that trusts a business man to get more money because he is dashing and worldly. It has not always asked itself for whom he would get more money, or whose money he would get.

I know well I was very fortunate in my own family. But even

those less fortunate were not subject to the special evils now commonly labelled Victorian. Indeed, in the modern sense, Victorian was not at all Victorian. It was a period of increasing strain. It was the very reverse of solid respectability; because its ethics and theology were wearing thin throughout. It may have been orderly compared with what came after; but not compared with the centuries that came before. It sometimes boasted of being domestic; but the Englishman's home was not half so domestic as that of the horrid foreigner; the profligate Frenchman. It was the age when the Englishman sent all his sons to boarding-school and sent all his servants to Coventry. I cannot imagine why anybody ever said that the Englishman's house was his castle; since he was one of the few Europeans who did not even own his house; and his house was avowedly a dull box of brick, of all the houses the least like a castle. Above all, so far from being stiff with orthodox religion, it was almost the first irreligious home in all human history. Theirs was the first generation that ever asked its children to worship the hearth without the altar. This was equally true, whether they went to church at eleven o'clock, with more decent thoroughness than the gay deceiver with the prayer-book, or were reverently agnostic or latitudinarian, as was much of my own circle. For the most part, it was family life stripped of its festivals and shrines and private cults, which had been its poetry in the past. It was a joke to talk of the heavy father's heavy furniture, and call the chairs and tables his household gods. It was the fact that he was the first man, for whom there were no household gods but only furniture.

That was the duller side; but there has been even more exaggeration about the darker side. I mean that modern novelists and others have started a trick of writing as if the old middle-class home was almost always a private lunatic asylum, with the lunatic in charge; as in the case of the exceedingly Mad Hatter who inhabited Hatter's Castle. This is a grotesque exaggeration; there were parents with this savage degree of selfishness; I recall not many more than three of them in the whole of our old social circle; but the wrong associations are attached even to them. A few of them may have been religious fanatics. I remember one, who locked up his daughters like prisoners; and one of them said to me, 'You see he thinks nobody else can think at all, except himself and Herbert Spencer.' I remember another who was an extreme Radical, a champion of liberty everywhere except at home. The point is of some historic importance. Tyrants, religious or irreligious, turn up anywhere. But this type of tyrant was the product of the precise moment when a middle-class man still had children and servants to control; but no longer had creeds or guilds or kings or priests or anything to control him. He was already an anarchist to those above him; but still an authoritarian to those below. But he was an abnormal fellow anyhow; and none of my people bore the least resemblance to him.

What Puritanic element there was in this forgotten society must certainly be allowed for as a part of the picture. It was mostly, among my people, a rather illogical disapproval of certain forms of luxury and expenditure. Their tables would groan under far grander dinners than many aristocrats eat today. But they had, for instance, a fixed feeling that there was something rather raffish about taking a cab. It was probably connected with their sensitive pride about not aping the aristocracy. I can remember my grandfather, when he was nearly eighty and able to afford any number of cabs, standing in the pouring rain while seven or eight crowded omnibuses went by; and afterwards whispering to my father (in a hushed voice lest the blasphemy be heard by the young), 'If three more omnibuses had gone by, upon my soul I think I should have taken a cab.' In the matter of driving about in cabs, I cannot claim to have kept the family escutcheon unspotted, or to have lived up to the high standard of my sires. But in the matter of their motive for not doing so, I am disposed to defend them, or at least to say that they are much misunderstood. They were the last descendants of Mrs Gilpin, who told the chaise to stop a few doors from her house, lest the neighbours should think her proud. I am not sure that she was not a healthier person than the smart lady who will be seen in anybody's Rolls Royce, lest the neighbours should think her humble.

Such, so far as I know it, was the social landscape in which I first found myself; and such were the people among whom I was born. I am sorry if the landscape or the people appear disappointingly respectable and even reasonable, and deficient in all those unpleasant qualities that make a biography really popular. I regret that I have no gloomy and savage father to offer to the public gaze as the true cause of all my tragic heritage; no pale-faced and partially poisoned mother whose suicidal instincts have cursed me with the temptations of the artistic temperament. I regret that there was nothing in the range of our family much more racy than a remote and mildly impecunious uncle; and that I cannot do my duty as a true modern, by cursing everybody who made me whatever I am. I am not clear about what that is; but I am pretty sure that most of it is my own fault. And I am compelled to confess that I look back to that landscape of my first days with a pleasure that should doubtless be reserved for the Utopias of the Futurist. Yet the landscape, as I see it now, was not altogether without a visionary and symbolic character. And among all the objects in that landscape, I find myself returning at the last to those which I mentioned first. In one way and another, those things have come to stand for so many other things, in the acted allegory of a human existence; the little church of my baptism and the waterworks, the bare, blind, dizzy tower of brick that seemed, to my first upward starings, to take hold upon the stars. Perhaps there was something in the confused and chaotic notion of a tower of water; as if the sea itself could stand on one end like a water-spout. Certainly later, though I hardly know how late, there came into my mind some fancy of a colossal water-snake that might be the Great Sea Serpent, and had something of the nightmare nearness of a dragon in a dream. And, over against it, the small church rose in a spire like a spear; and I have always been pleased to remember that it was dedicated to St George.

II
THE MAN WITH THE GOLDEN KEY

THE VERY first thing I can ever remember seeing with my own eyes was a young man walking across a bridge. He had a curly moustache and an attitude of confidence verging on swagger. He carried in his hand a disproportionately large key of a shining yellow metal and wore a large golden or gilded crown. The bridge he was crossing sprang on the one side from the edge of a highly perilous mountain chasm, the peaks of the range rising fantastically in the distance; and at the other end it joined the upper part of the tower of an almost excessively castellated castle. In the castle tower there was one window, out of which a young lady was looking. I cannot remember in the least what she looked like; but I will do battle with anyone who denies her superlative good looks.

To those who may object that such a scene is rare in the home life of house-agents living immediately to the north of Kensington High Street, in the later seventies of the last century, I shall be compelled to admit, not that the scene was unreal, but that I saw it through a window more wonderful than the window in the tower; through the proscenium of a toy-theatre constructed by my father; and that (if I am really to be pestered about such irrelevant details) the young man in the crown was about six inches high and proved on investigation to be made of cardboard. But it is strictly true to say that I saw him before I can remember seeing anybody else; and that, so far as my memory is concerned, this was the sight on which my eyes first opened in this world. And the scene has to me a sort of aboriginal authenticity impossible to describe; something at the back of all my thoughts; like the very back-scene of the theatre of things. I have no shadow of recollection of what the young man was doing on the bridge, or of what he proposed to do with the key; though a later and wearier knowledge of literature and legend hints to me that he was not improbably going to release the lady from captivity. It is a not unamusing detail of psychology that, though I can remember no other characters in the story, I do remember noting that the crowned gentleman had a moustache and no beard, with a vague inference that there was another crowned gentleman who had a beard as well. We may safely guess, I imagine, that the bearded one was by way of being a wicked king; and we should not need much more converging evidence to convict him of having locked up the lady in the tower. All the rest is gone; scenes, subject, story, characters; but that one scene glows in my memory like a glimpse of some incredible paradise; and, for all I know, I shall still remember it when all other memory is gone out of my mind.

Apart from the fact of it being my first memory, I have several reasons for putting it first. I am no psychologist, thank God; but if psychologists are still saying what ordinary sane people have always said – that early impressions count considerably in life – I recognize a sort of symbol of all that I happen to like in imagery and ideas. All my life I have loved edges; and the boundary-line that brings one thing sharply against another. All my life I have loved frames and limits; and I will maintain that the largest wilderness looks larger seen through a window. To the grief of all grave dramatic critics, I will still assert that the perfect drama must strive to rise to the higher ecstasy of the peep-show. I have also a pretty taste in abysses and bottomless chasms and everything else that emphasizes a fine shade of distinction between one thing and another; and the warm affection I have always felt for bridges is connected with the fact that the dark and dizzy arch accentuates the chasm even more than the chasm itself. I can no longer behold the beauty of the princess; but I can see it in the bridge that the prince crossed to reach her. And I believe that in feeling these things from the first, I was feeling the fragmentary suggestions of a philosophy I have since found to be the truth. For it is upon that point of truth that there might perhaps be a quarrel between the more material psychologists and myself. If any man tells me that I only take pleasure in the mysteries of the window and the bridge because I saw these models of them when I was a baby, I shall take the liberty of telling him that he has not thought the thing out. To begin with, I must have seen thousands of other things before as well as after; and there must have been an element of selection and some reason for selection. And, what is still more obvious, to date the occasion does not even begin to deal with the fact. If some laborious reader of little books on child-psychology cries out to me in glee and cunning, 'You only like romantic things like toy-theatres because your father showed you a toy-theatre in your childhood,' I shall reply with gentle and Christian patience, 'Yes, fool, yes. Undoubtedly your explanation is, in that sense, the true one. But what you are saying, in your witty way, is simply that I associate these things with happiness because I was so happy. It does not even begin to consider the question of why I was so happy. Why should looking through a square hole, at yellow paste-board, lift anybody into the seventh heaven of happiness at any time of life? Why should it specially do so at that time of life? That is the psychological fact that you have to explain; and I have never seen any sort of rational explanation.'

I apologize for this parenthesis; and for mentioning child-psychology or anything else that can bring a blush to the cheek. But it happens to be a point on which I think some of our psycho-analysts display rather unblushing cheek. I do not wish my remarks confused with the horrible and degrading heresy that our minds are merely manufactured by accidental conditions, and therefore have no ultimate relation to truth at all. With all possible apologies to the free-thinkers, I still propose to hold myself free to think. And anybody who will think for two minutes will see that this thought is the end of all thinking. It is useless to argue at all, if all our conclusions are warped by our conditions. Nobody can correct anybody's bias, if all mind is all bias.

The interlude is now over, thank you; and I will proceed to the more practical relations between my memory and my story. And it will first be necessary to say something about memory itself; and the reliability of such stories. I have begun with this fragment of a fairy play in a toy-theatre, because it also sums up most clearly the strongest influences upon my childhood. I have said that the toy-theatre was made by my father; and anybody who has ever tried to make such a theatre or mount such a play, will know that this alone stands for a remarkable round of crafts and accomplishments. It involves being in much more than the common sense the stage carpenter, being the architect and the builder and the draughtsman and the landscape-painter and the story-teller all in one. And, looking back on my life, and the relatively unreal and indirect art that I have attempted to practise, I feel that I have really lived a much narrower life than my father's.

His mere name, of course, is enough to recall wider memories. One of my first memories is playing in the garden under the care of a girl with ropes of golden hair; to whom my mother afterwards called out from the house, 'You are an angel'; which I was disposed to accept without metaphor. She is now living in Vancouver as Mrs Kidd; and she and her sister had more to do with enlivening my early years than most. Since then, I have met what used to be called the wits of the age; but I have never known wittier conversation. Among my first memories also are those seascapes that were blue flashes to boys of my generation; North Berwick with the cone of green hill that seemed like the hill absolute; and a French seaside associated with little girls, the daughters of my father's old friend Mawer Cowtan, whom I shall not forget. But indeed I had a whole background of cousins; Tom Gilbert (my godfather, who gave me his last and my first name) had a large family of daughters, and my uncle Sidney a large family of sons; and they all still move in my memory almost like a male and female chorus in a great Greek play. The eldest of the boys, the one whom I once knew best, was killed with my brother in the Great War; but many of the others, I am glad to say, are still friends as well as relations. All these are memorable memories; but they do not resolve that first individual speculation about memory itself. The girl with the yellow hair is an early memory, in the sense in which some of the others have inevitably become later memories, at once expanded and effaced.

Really, the things we remember are the things we forget. I mean that when a memory comes back sharply and suddenly, piercing the protection of oblivion, it appears for an instant exactly as it really was. If we think of it often, while its essentials doubtless remain true, it becomes more and more our own memory of the thing rather than the thing remembered. I had a little sister who died when I was a child. I have little to go on; for she was the only subject about which my father did not talk. It was the one dreadful sorrow of his abnormally happy and even merry existence; and it is strange to think that I never spoke to him about it to the day of his death. I do not remember her dying; but I remember her falling off a rocking-horse. I know, from experience of bereavements only a little later, that children feel with exactitude, without a word of explanation, the emotional tone or tint of a house of mourning. But in this case, the greater catastrophe must somehow have become confused and identified with the smaller one. I always felt it as a tragic memory, as if she had been thrown by a real horse and killed. Something must have painted and repainted the picture in my mind; until I suddenly became conscious about the age of eighteen that it had become the picture of Amy Robsart lying at the foot of the stairs, flung down by Varney and another villain.[1] This is the real difficulty about remembering anything; that we have remembered too much – for we have remembered too often.

I will take another example of this psychological trick, though it involves the anticipation of much later events in my life. One of these glimpses of my own prehistoric history is a memory of a long upper room filled with light (the light that never was on sea or land) and of somebody carving or painting with white paint the deal head of a hobby-horse; the head almost archaic in its simplification. Ever since that day my depths have been stirred by a wooden post painted white; and even more so by any white horse in the street; and it was like meeting a friend in a fairytale to find myself under the sign of the White Horse at Ipswich on the first day of my honeymoon. But for that very reason, this image has remained and memory has constantly returned to it; and I have even done my best to deface and spoil the purity of the White Horse by writing an interminable ballad about it. A man does not generally manage to forget his wedding-day; especially such a highly comic wedding-day as mine. For the family remembers against me a number of now familiar legends, about the missing of trains, the losing of luggage, and other things counted yet more eccentric. It is alleged against me, and with perfect truth, that I stopped on the way to drink a glass of milk in one shop and to buy a revolver with cartridges in another. Some have seen these as singular wedding-presents for a bridegroom to give to himself; and if the bride had known less of him, I suppose she might have fancied that he was a suicide or a murderer or, worst of all, a teetotaller. They seemed to me the most natural things in the world. I did not buy the pistol to murder myself or my wife; I never was really modern. I bought it because it was the great adventure of my youth, with a general

1 In Walter Scott's novel, *Kenilworth* (1821).

notion of protecting her from the pirates doubtless infesting the
Norfolk Broads, to which we were bound; where, after all, there
are still a suspiciously large number of families with Danish names.
I shall not be annoyed if it is called childish; but obviously it was
rather a reminiscence of boyhood, and not of childhood. But the
ritual consumption of the glass of milk really was a reminiscence of
childhood. I stopped at that particular dairy because I had always
drunk a glass of milk there when walking with my mother in my
infancy. And it seemed to me a fitting ceremonial to unite the two
great relations of a man's life. Outside the shop there was the figure
of a White Cow as a sort of pendant to the figure of the White
Horse; the one standing at the beginning of my new journey and
the other at the end. But the point is here that the very fact of these
allegories having been acted over again, at the stage of marriage
and maturity, does in a sense transform them, and does in some
sense veil even while it invokes the original visions of the child. The
sign of the White Horse has been repainted, and only in that sense
painted out. I do not so much remember it as remember remembering it. But if I really want to be realistic about those remote
days, I must scratch around till I find something not too much
blunted to scratch me; something sufficiently forgotten to be
remembered. I make the experiment at this moment as I write.
Searching for those lost surroundings, I recall for the first time, at
this moment, that there was another shop, next to the milk-shop,
which had some mysterious charm for my childhood; and then
I recall that it was an oil and colour shop, and they sold gold paint
smeared inside shells; and there was a sort of pale pointed chalks
I have been less familiar with of late. I do not think here of
the strong colours of the common paint-box, like crimson-lake
and prussian-blue, much as I exulted and still exult in them. For
another boy called Robert Louis Stevenson has messed about with
my colours upon that sort of palette; and I have grown up to enjoy
them in print as well as in paint. But when I remember that these
forgotten crayons contained a stick of 'light-red', seemingly a more
commonplace colour, the point of that dull red pencil pricks me as
if it could draw red blood.

From this general memory about memory I draw a certain inference. What was wonderful about childhood is that anything in it
was a wonder. It was not merely a world full of miracles; it was a

miraculous world. What gives me this shock is almost anything
I really recall; not the things I should think most worth recalling.
This is where it differs from the other great thrill of the past, all
that is connected with first love and the romantic passion; for that,
though equally poignant, comes always to a point; and is narrow
like a rapier piercing the heart, whereas the other was more like a
hundred windows opened on all sides of the head.

I have made here a sort of psychological experiment in memory.
I have tried to think of the things I forget adjoining the things I
remember; and in the childish case, though they are without form,
I am sure they are of the same tint. I have long remembered the
milk-shop; I have only just remembered the oil-shop; I have no
notion at all about the next shop to the oil-shop. I am sure it was
a shop shining with the same lost light of morning; because it was in
the same street under the same sky. I have no notion on what street
the row of windows in the long uplifted room looked out, when the
white horse head was carved. But I feel in a flash that it was a happy
street; or, if we must be pedantic, a street in which I should have
been happy. Now it is not like that with even the happiest hours of
the later things called love-affairs. I have already mentioned how
my honeymoon began before the White Cow of my childhood; but
of course I had in my time been myself a calf, not to say a moon
calf, in the sort of calf-love that dances in the moonshine long
before the honeymoon. Those day-dreams also are wrecks of something divine; but they have the colour of sunset rather than the
broad daylight. I have walked across wide fields at evening and
seen, as a mere distant dot in a row of houses, one particular
window and just distinguishable head; and been uplifted as with
roaring trumpets as if by the salute of Beatrice.[1] But it did not, and
does not, make me think the other windows and houses were all
almost equally interesting; and that is just what the glimpse of the
baby's wonderland does. We have read countless pages about love
brightening the sun and making the flowers more flamboyant; and
it is true in a sense; but not in the sense I mean. It changes the
world; but the baby lived in a changeless world; or rather the man
feels that it is he who has changed. He has changed long before he
comes near to the great and glorious trouble of the love of woman;

1 Dante's beloved.

and that has in it something new and concentrated and crucial; crucial in the true sense of being as near as Cana to Calvary. In the later case, what is loved becomes *instantly* what may be lost.

My point here is that we can test the childish mood by thinking, not only of what was there, but of what must have been there. I think of the backs of houses of which I saw only the fronts; the streets that stretched away behind the streets I knew; the things that remained round the corner; and they still give me a thrill. One of the sports of the imagination, a game I have played all my life, was to take a certain book with pictures of old Dutch houses, and think not of what was in the pictures but of all that was out of the pictures, the unknown corners and side-streets of the same quaint town. The book was one my father had written and illustrated himself, merely for home consumption. It was typical of him that, in the Pugin period he had worked at Gothic illumination; but when he tried again, it was in another style of the dark Dutch renaissance, the grotesque scroll-work that suggests woodcarving more than stone-cutting. He was the sort of man who likes to try everything once. This was the only book he ever wrote; and he never bothered to publish it.

My father might have reminded people of Mr Pickwick, except that he was always bearded and never bald; he wore spectacles and had all the Pickwickian evenness of temper and pleasure in the humours of travel. He was rather quiet than otherwise, but his quietude covered a great fertility of notions; and he certainly liked taking a rise out of people. I remember, to give one example of a hundred such inventions, how he gravely instructed some grave ladies in the names of flowers; dwelling especially on the rustic names given in certain localities. 'The country people call them Sailors' Pen-knives,' he would say in an offhand manner, after affecting to provide them with the full scientific name, or, 'They call them Bakers' Bootlaces down in Lincolnshire, I believe'; and it is a fine example of human simplicity to note how far he found he could safely go in such instructive discourse. They followed him without revulsion when he said lightly, 'Merely a sprig of wild bigamy.' It was only when he added that there was a local variety known as Bishop's Bigamy, that the full depravity of his character began to dawn on their minds. It was possibly this aspect of his unfailing amiability that is responsible for an entry I find in an ancient minute-book, of mock trials conducted by himself and his brothers; that Edward Chesterton was tried for the crime of Aggravation. But the same sort of invention created for children the permanent anticipation of what is profoundly called a Surprise. And it is this side of the business that is relevant here.

His versatility both as an experimentalist and a handy man, in all such matters, was amazing. His den or study was piled high with the stratified layers of about ten or twelve creative amusements; water-colour painting and modelling and photography and stained glass and fretwork and magic lanterns and mediaeval illumination. I have inherited, or I hope imitated, his habit of drawing; but in every other way I am emphatically an unhandy man. There had been some talk of his studying art professionally in his youth; but the family business was obviously safer; and his life followed the lines of a certain contented and ungrasping prudence, which was extraordinarily typical of him and all his blood and generation. He never dreamed of turning any of these plastic talents to any mercenary account, or of using them for anything but his own private pleasure and ours. To us he appeared to be indeed the Man with the Golden Key, a magician opening the gates of goblin castles or the sepulchres of dead heroes; and there was no incongruity in calling his lantern a magic-lantern. But all this time he was known to the world, and even the next-door neighbours, as a very reliable and capable though rather unambitious business man. It was a very good first lesson in what is also the last lesson of life; that in everything that matters, the inside is much larger than the outside. On the whole I am glad that he was never an artist. It might have stood in his way in becoming an amateur. It might have spoilt his career; his private career. He could never have made a vulgar success of all the thousand things he did so successfully.

If I made a generalization about the Chestertons, my paternal kinsfolk (which may be dangerous, for there are a lot of them still alive), I should say that they were and are extraordinarily English. They have a perceptible and prevailing colour of good nature, of good sense not untinged with dreaminess, and a certain tranquil loyalty in their personal relations which was very notable even in one, like my brother Cecil,[1] who in his public relations was

1 See note 2, p. 13.

supremely pugnacious and provocative. I think this sort of sleepy sanity rather an English thing; and in comparison it may not be entirely fanciful to suppose there was something French, after all, in the make-up of my mother's family; for, allowing for the usual admixture, they ran smaller in stature, often darker in colouring, tough, extraordinarily tenacious, prejudiced in a humorous fashion and full of the fighting spirit. But whatever we may guess in such matters (and nobody has yet done anything but guess about heredity) it was for another purpose that I mentioned the savour of something racial about such a stock. English in so many things, the Chestertons were supremely English in their natural turn for hobbies. It is an element in this sort of old English business man which divides him most sharply from the American business man, and to some extent from the new English business man, who is copying the American. When the American begins to suggest that 'salesmanship can be an art', he means that an artist ought to put all his art into his salesmanship. The old-fashioned Englishman, like my father, sold houses for his living but filled his own house with his life.

A hobby is not a holiday. It is not *merely* a momentary relaxation necessary to the renewal of work; and in this respect it must be sharply distinguished from much that is called sport. A good game is a good thing, but it is not the same thing as a hobby; and many go golfing or shooting grouse because this is a concentrated form of recreation; just as what our contemporaries find in whisky is a concentrated form of what our fathers found diffused in beer. If half a day is to take a man out of himself, or make a new man of him, it is better done by some sharp competitive excitement like sport. But a hobby is not half a day but half a life-time. It would be truer to accuse the hobbyist of living a double life. And hobbies, especially such hobbies as the toy-theatre, have a character that runs parallel to practical professional effort, and is not merely a reaction from it. It is not merely taking exercise; it is doing work. It is not merely exercising the body instead of the mind, an excellent but now largely a recognized thing. It is exercising the rest of the mind; now an almost neglected thing. When Browning, that typical Victorian, says that he likes to know a butcher paints and a baker writes poetry, he would not be satisfied with the statement that a butcher plays tennis or a baker golf. And my father and uncles, also typical Victorians of the sort that followed Browning, were all marked in varying degrees by this taste for having their own tastes. One of them gave all his spare time to gardening and has somewhere in the horticultural records a chrysanthemum named after him, dating from the first days when chrysanthemums came to us from the islands of the Rising Sun. Another travelled in an ordinary commercial fashion, but made a most amazing collection of cranks and quacks, fitted to fill a far better memoir than this, whom he had met in his wanderings, and with whom he had argued and sympathized and quoted Browning and George MacDonald,[1] and done I fancy not a little good, for he was himself a most interesting man; above all, interesting because he was interested. But in my own household, as I have said, it was not a question of one hobby but a hundred hobbies, piled on top of each other; and it is a personal accident, or perhaps a personal taste, that the one which has clung to my memory through life is the hobby of the toy-theatre. In any case, watching such work has made one great difference to my life and views to this day.

I cannot do much, by the standard of my nursery days. But I have learned to love seeing things done; not the handle that ultimately causes them to be done, but the hand that does them. If my father had been some common millionaire owning a thousand mills that made cotton, or a million machines that made cocoa, how much smaller he would have seemed. And this experience has made me profoundly sceptical of all the modern talk about the necessary dullness of domesticity; and the degrading drudgery that only has to make puddings and pies. Only to make things! There is no greater thing to be said of God Himself than that He makes things. The manufacturer cannot even manufacture things; he can only pay to have them manufactured. And (in the same way) I am now incurably afflicted with a faint smile, when I hear a crowd of frivolous people, who could not make anything to save their lives, talking about the inevitable narrowness and stuffiness of the Victorian home. We managed to make a good many things in our Victorian home which people now buy at insane prices from Art and Craft Shops; the sort of shops that have quite as much craft as art. All the things that happened in the house, or were in any sense

1 George MacDonald (1824–1905) was pre-eminently a writer of children's stories who greatly influenced Chesterton.

done on the premises, linger in my imagination like a legend; and as much as any, those connected with the kitchen or the pantry. Toffee still tastes nicer to me than the most expensive chocolates which Quaker millionaires sell by the million; and mostly because we made toffee for ourselves.

No. 999 in the vast library-catalogue of the books I have never written (all of them so much more brilliant and convincing than the books that I have written) is the story of a successful city man who seemed to have a dark secret in his life; and who was eventually discovered by the detectives still playing with dolls or tin soldiers or some undignified antic of infancy. I may say with all modesty that I am that man, in everything except his solidity of repute and his successful commercial career. It was perhaps even more true, in that sense, of my father before me; but I for one have never left off playing, and I wish there were more time to play. I wish we did not have to fritter away on frivolous things, like lectures and literature, the time we might have given to serious, solid and constructive work like cutting out cardboard figures and pasting coloured tinsel upon them. When I say this, I come to the third reason for taking the toy-theatre as a text; and it is one about which there will be much misunderstanding, because of the repetitions and the stale sentiment that have somehow come to cling to it. It is one of those things that are always misunderstood, because they have been too often explained.

I am inclined to contradict much of the modern Cult of the Child at Play. Through various influences of a recent and rather romantic culture, the Child has become rather the Spoilt Child. The true beauty has been spoilt by the rather unscrupulous emotion of mature persons, who have themselves lost much of their sense of reality. The worst heresy of this school is that a child is concerned only with make-believe. For this is interpreted in the sense, at once sentimental and sceptical, that there is not much difference between make-believe and belief. But the real child does not confuse fact and fiction. He simply likes fiction. He acts it, because he cannot as yet write it or even read it; but he never allows his moral sanity to be clouded by it. To him no two things could possibly be more totally contrary than playing at robbers and stealing sweets. No possible amount of playing at robbers would ever bring him an inch nearer to thinking it is really right to rob. I saw the distinction perfectly clearly when I was a child; I wish I saw it half as clearly now. I played at being a robber for hours together at the end of the garden; but it never had anything to do with the temptation I had to sneak a new paint-box out of my father's room. I was not *being* anything false; I was simply writing before I could write. Fortunately, perhaps, for the condition of the back-garden, I early transferred my dreams to some rude resemblance to writing; chiefly in the form of drawing straggling and sprawling maps of fabulous countries, inhabited by men of incredible shapes and colours and bearing still more incredible names. But though I might fill the world with dragons, I never had the slightest real doubt that heroes ought to fight with dragons.

I must stop to challenge many child-lovers for cruelty to children. It is quite false to say that the child dislikes a fable that has a moral. Very often he likes the moral more than the fable. Adults are reading their own more weary mockery into a mind still vigorous enough to be entirely serious. Adults like the comic *Sandford and Merton*. Children liked the real *Sandford and Merton*.[1] At least I know I liked it very much, and felt the heartiest faith in the Honest Farmer and the Noble Negro. I venture to dwell on the point if only in parenthesis: for on this also there is a current misunderstanding. Indeed there is what may be called a current cant; and none the less so because it is a cant against cant. It is now so common as to be conventional to express impatience with priggish and moralizing stories for children; stories of the old-fashioned sort that concern things like the sinfulness of theft; and as I am recalling an old-fashioned atmosphere, I cannot refrain from testifying on the psychology of the business.

Now I must heartily confess that I often adored priggish and moralizing stories. I do not suppose I should gain a subtle literary pleasure from them now; but that is not the point in question. The men who denounce such moralizings are men; they are not children. But I believe multitudes would admit their early affection for the moral tale, if they still had the moral courage. And the reason is perfectly simple. Adults have reacted against such morality, because they know that it often stands for immorality.

1 Thomas Day (1748–89), was the author of the children's book *The History of Sandford and Merton* with its message that many can be made good by instruction and the appeal to reason.

They know that such platitudes have been used by hypocrites and pharisees, by cunning or perversion. But the child knows nothing about cunning or perversion. He sees nothing but the moral ideals themselves, and he simply sees that they are true. Because they are.

There is another blunder made by the modern cynic about the moralizing story-teller. The former always imagines that there is an element of corruption, in his own cynical manner, about the idea of reward, about the position of the child who can say, as in Stevenson's verses, 'Every day when I've been good, I get an orange after food.' To the man made ignorant by experience this always appears as a vulgar *bribe* to the child. The modern philosopher knows that it would require a very large bribe indeed to induce *him* to be good. It therefore seems to the modern philosopher what it would seem to the modern politician to say, 'I will give you fifty thousand pounds when you have, on some one definite and demonstrated occasion, kept your word.' The solid price seems something quite distinct from the rare and reluctant labour. But it does not seem like that to the child. It would not seem like that to the child, if the Fairy Queen said to the Prince, 'You will receive the golden apple from the magic tree when you have fought the dragon.' For the child is not a Manichee. He does not think that good things are in their nature separate from being good. In other words, he does not, like the reluctant realist, regard goodness as a bad thing. To him the goodness and the gift and the golden apple, that is called an orange, are all parts of one substantial paradise and naturally go together. In other words, he regards himself as normally on amiable terms with the natural authorities; not normally as quarrelling or bargaining with them. He has the ordinary selfish obstacles and misunderstandings; but he does not, in his heart, regard it as odd that his parents should be good to him, to the extent of an orange, or that he should be good to them, to the extent of some elementary experiments in good behaviour. He has no sense of being corrupted. It is only we, who have eaten the forbidden apple (or orange) who think of pleasure as a bribe.

My main purpose here, however, is to say this. To me my whole childhood has a certain quality, which may be indescribable but is not in the least vague. It is rather more definite than the difference between pitch dark and daylight, or between having a toothache and not having a toothache. For the sequel of the story, it is necessary to attempt this first and hardest chapter of the story: and I must try to state somehow what I mean by saying that my own childhood was of quite a different kind, or quality, from the rest of my very undeservedly pleasant and cheerful existence.

Of this positive quality the most general attribute was clearness. Here it is that I differ, for instance, from Stevenson, whom I so warmly admire; and who speaks of the child as moving with his head in a cloud. He talks of the child as normally in a dazed day-dream, in which he cannot distinguish fancy from fact. Now children and adults are both fanciful at times; but that is not what, in my mind and memory, distinguishes adults from children. Mine is a memory of a sort of white light on everything, cutting things out very clearly, and rather emphasizing their solidity. The point is that the white light had a sort of wonder in it, as if the world were as new as myself; but not that the world was anything but a real world. I am much more disposed now to fancy that an apple-tree in the moonlight is some sort of ghost or grey nymph; or to see the furniture fantastically changing and crawling at twilight, as in some story of Poe or Hawthorne. But when I was a child I had a sort of confident astonishment in contemplating the apple-tree as an apple-tree. I was sure of it, and also sure of the surprise of it; as sure, to quote the perfect popular proverb, as sure as God made little apples. The apples might be as little as I was; but they were solid and so was I. There was something of an eternal morning about the mood; and I liked to see a fire lit more than to imagine faces in the firelight. Brother Fire, whom St Francis loved, did seem more like a brother than those dream-faces which come to men who have known other emotions than brotherhood. I do not know whether I ever, as the phrase goes, cried for the moon; but I am sure that I should have expected it to be solid like some colossal snowball; and should always have had more appetite for moons than for mere moonshine. Only figures of speech can faintly express the fact; but it was a fact and not a figure of speech. What I said first about the toy-theatre may be urged in contradiction, and as an example of delight in a mere illusion.

In that case, what I said first about the toy-theatre will be entirely misunderstood. In fact, there was in that business nothing of an

illusion or of a disillusion. If this were a ruthless realistic modern
story, I should of course give a most heartrendering account of how
my spirit was broken with disappointment, on discovering that the
prince was only a painted figure. But this is not a ruthless realistic
modern story. On the contrary, it is a true story. And the truth is
that I do not remember that I was in any way deceived or in any
way undeceived. The whole point is that I did like the toy-theatre
even when I knew it was a toy-theatre. I did like the cardboard
figures, even when I found they were of cardboard. The white light
of wonder that shone on the whole business was not any sort of
trick; indeed the things that now shine most in my memory were
many of them mere technical accessories; such as the parallel sticks
of white wood that held the scenery in place; a white wood that is
still strangely mixed in my imaginative instincts with all the holy
trade of the Carpenter. It was the same with any number of other
games or pretences in which I took delight; as in the puppet-show
of Punch and Judy. I not only knew that the figures were made of
wood, but I wanted them to be made of wood. I could not imagine
such a resounding thwack being given except by a wooden stick on
a wooden head. But I took the sort of pleasure that a primitive man
might have taken in a primitive craft, in seeing that they were
carved and painted into a startling and grimacing caricature of
humanity. I was pleased that the piece of wood was a face; but I was
also pleased that the face was a piece of wood. That did not mean
that the drama of wood, like the other drama of cardboard, did
not reveal to me real ideas and imaginations, and give me glorious
glimpses into the possibilities of existence. Of course the child did
not analyse himself then; and the man cannot analyse him now.
But I am certain he was not merely tricked or trapped. He enjoyed
the suggestive function of art exactly as an art critic enjoys it; only
he enjoyed it a jolly sight more. For the same reason I do not think
that I myself was ever very much worried about Santa Claus,
or that alleged dreadful whisper of the little boy that Father
Christmas 'is only your father'. Perhaps the word 'only' would
strike all children as the *mot juste*.

My fixed idolatry of Punch and Judy illustrated the same fact
and the same fallacy. I was not only grateful for the fun, but I came
to feel grateful for the very fittings and apparatus of the fun; the
four-cornered tower of canvas with the one square window at the

top, and everything down to the minimum of conventional and obviously painted scenery. Yet these were the very things I ought to have torn and rent in rage, as the trappings of imposture, if I had really regarded the explanation as spoiling the experience. I was pleased, and not displeased, when I discovered that the magic figures could be moved by three human fingers. And I was right; for those three human fingers are more magical than any magic figures; the three fingers which hold the pen and the sword and the bow of the violin; the very three fingers that the priest lifts in benediction as the emblem of the Blessed Trinity. There was no conflict between the two magics in my mind.

I will here sum up in four statements, which will look very like puzzles upon this page. I can assure the reader that they have a relevance to the ultimate upshot of this book. Having littered the world with thousands of essays for a living, I am doubtless prone to let this story stray into a sort of essay; but I repeat that it is not an essay but a story. So much so, that I am here employing a sort of device from a detective story. In the first few pages of a police novel, there are often three or four hints rather to rouse curiosity than allay it; so that the curate's start of recognition, the cockatoo's scream in the night, the burnt blotting-paper or the hasty avoidance of the subject of onions, is exhibited in the beginning though not explained until the end. So it is with the dull and difficult interlude of this chapter, a mere introspection about infancy which is not introspective. The patient reader may yet discover that these dark hints have something to do with the ensuing mystery of my misguided existence, and even with the crime that comes before the end. Anyhow, I will set them down here without discussion of anything which they foreshadow.

First; my life unfolded itself in the epoch of evolution; which really only means unfolding. But many of the evolutionists of that epoch really seemed to mean by evolution the unfolding of what is not there. I have since, in a special sense, come to believe in development; which means the unfolding of what is there. Now it may seem both a daring and a doubtful boast, if I claim that in my childhood I was all there. At least, many of those who knew me best were quite doubtful about it. But I mean that the distinctions I make here were all there; I was not conscious of them but I contained them. In short, they existed in infancy in the condition called implicit;

though they certainly did not then express themselves in what is commonly called implicit obedience.

Second; I knew, for instance, that pretending is not deceiving. I could not have defined the distinction if it had been questioned; but that was because it had never occurred to me that it could be questioned. It was merely because a child understands the nature of art, long before he understands the nature of argument. Now it is still not uncommon to say that images are idols and that idols are dolls. I am content to say here that even dolls are not idols, but in the true sense images. The very word images means things necessary to imagination. But not things contrary to reason; no, not even in a child. For imagination is almost the opposite of illusion.

Third; I have noted that I enjoyed Punch and Judy as a drama and not a dream; and indeed the whole extraordinary state of mind I strive to recapture was really the very reverse of a dream. It was rather as if I was more wide-awake then than I am now, and moving in broader daylight, which was to our broad daylight what daylight is to dusk. Only, of course, to those seeing the last gleam of it through the dusk, the light looks more uncanny than any darkness. Anyhow, it looks quite different; of that I am absolutely and solidly certain; though in such a subjective matter of sensation there can be no demonstration. What was the real meaning of that difference? I have some sort of notion now; but I will not mention it at this stage of the story.

Fourth; it will be quite natural, it will also be quite wrong, to infer from all this that I passed a quite exceptionally comfortable childhood in complete contentment; or else that my memory is merely a sundial that has only marked the sunny hours. But that is not in the least what I mean; that is quite a different question. I was often unhappy in childhood like other children; but happiness and unhappiness seemed of a different texture or held on a different tenure. I was very often naughty in childhood like other children; and I never doubted for a moment the moral of all the moral tales; that, as a general principle, people ought to be unhappy when they have been naughty. That is, I held the whole idea of repentance and absolution implicit but not unfolded in my mind. To add to all this, I was by no means unacquainted with pain, which is a pretty unanswerable thing; I had a fair amount of toothache and especially earache; and few can bemuse themselves into regarding earache as a form of epicurean hedonism. But here again there is a difference. For some unaccountable reason, and in some indescribable way, the pain did not leave on my memory the sort of stain of the intolerable or mysterious that it leaves on the mature mind. To all these four facts I can testify; exactly as if they were facts like my loving a toy gun or climbing a tree. Their meaning, in the murder or other mystery, will appear later.

For I fear I have prolonged preposterously this note on the nursery; as if I had been an unconscionable time, not dying but being born, or at least being brought up. Well, I believe in prolonging childhood; and I am not sorry that I was a backward child. But I can only say that this nursery note is necessary if all the rest is to be anything but nonsense; and not even nursery nonsense. In the chapters that follow, I shall pass to what are called real happenings, though they are far less real. Without giving myself any airs of the adventurer or the globe-trotter, I may say I have seen something of the world; I have travelled in interesting places and talked to interesting men; I have been in political quarrels often turning into faction fights, I have talked to statesmen in the hour of the destiny of states; I have met most of the great poets and prose writers of my time; I have travelled in the track of some of the whirlwinds and earthquakes in the ends of the earth; I have lived in houses burned down in the tragic wars of Ireland; I have walked through the ruins of Polish palaces left behind by the Red Armies;[1] have heard talk of the secret signals of the Ku Klux Klan upon the borders of Texas; I have seen the fanatical Arabs come up from the desert to attack the Jews in Jerusalem. There are many journalists who have seen more of such things than I; but I have been a journalist and I have seen such things; there will be no difficulty in filling other chapters with such things; but they will be unmeaning, if nobody understands that they still mean less to me than Punch and Judy on Campden Hill.

In a word; I have never lost the sense that this was my real life; the real beginning of what should have been a more real life; a lost experience in the land of the living. It seems to me that when I came out of the house and stood on that hill of houses, where the roads

1 A reference to the Polish–Soviet War of 1919–21.

sank steeply towards Holland Park, and terraces of new red houses could look out across a vast hollow and see far away the sparkle of the Crystal Palace (and seeing it was a juvenile sport in those parts), I was subconsciously certain then, as I am consciously certain now, that there was the white and solid road and the worthy beginning of the life of man; and that it is man who afterwards darkens it with dreams or goes astray from it in self-deception. It is only the grown man who lives a life of make-believe and pretending; and it is he who has his head in a cloud.

At this time, of course, I did not even know that this morning light could be lost; still less about any controversies as to whether it could be recovered. So far the disputes of that period passed over my head like storms high up in air; and as I did not foresee the problem I naturally did not foresee any of my searches for a solution. I simply looked at the procession in the street as I looked at the processions in the toy-theatre; and now and then I happened to see curious things, two-pence coloured rather than a penny plain, which were worthy of the wildest pageants of the toy-theatre. I remember once walking with my father along Kensington High Street, and seeing a crowd of people gathered by a rather dark and narrow entry on the southern side of that thoroughfare. I had seen crowds before; and was quite prepared for their shouting or shoving. But I was not prepared for what happened next. In a flash a sort of ripple ran along the line and all these eccentrics went down on their knees on the public pavement. I had never seen people play any such antics except in church; and I stopped and stared. Then I realized that a sort of little dark cab or carriage had drawn up opposite the entry; and out of it came a ghost clad in flames. Nothing in the shilling paint-box had ever spread such a conflagration of scarlet, such lakes of lake; or seemed so splendidly likely to incarnadine the multitudinous sea. He came on with all his glowing draperies like a great crimson cloud of sunset, lifting long frail fingers over the crowd in blessing. And then I looked at his face and was startled with a contrast; for his face was dead pale like ivory and very wrinkled and old, fitted together out of naked nerve and bone and sinew; with hollow eyes in shadow; but not ugly; having in every line the ruin of great beauty. The face was so extraordinary that for a moment I even forgot such perfectly scrumptious scarlet clothes.

We passed on; and then my father said, 'Do you know who that was? That was Cardinal Manning.'[1]

Then one of his artistic hobbies returned to his abstracted and humorous mind; and he said,

'He'd have made his fortune as a model.'

---

1 Henry Edward Manning (1808–92), Cardinal Archbishop of Westminster, a convert to Catholicism like Newman but unlike him an Ultramontane or extreme papalist, was an early promoter of social justice and influenced Pope Leo XIII's *Rerum Novarum* (1891) which laid the foundations of Catholic social teaching.

CHARLES DICKENS

I
THE DICKENS PERIOD

Much of our modern difficulty, in religion and other things, arises merely from this: that we confuse the word 'indefinable' with the word 'vague'. If some one speaks of a spiritual fact as 'indefinable' we promptly picture something misty, a cloud with indeterminate edges. But this is an error even in commonplace logic. The thing that cannot be defined is the first thing; the primary fact. It is our arms and legs, our pots and pans, that are indefinable. The indefinable is the indisputable. The man next door is indefinable, because he is too actual to be defined. And there are some to whom spiritual things have the same fierce and practical proximity; some to whom God is too actual to be defined.

But there is a third class of primary terms. There are popular expressions which every one uses and no one can explain; which the wise man will accept and reverence, as he reverences desire or darkness or any elemental thing. The prigs of the debating club will demand that he should define his terms. And, being a wise man, he will flatly refuse. This first inexplicable term is the most important term of all. The word that has no definition is the word that has no substitute. If a man falls back again and again on some such word as 'vulgar' or 'manly', do not suppose that the word means nothing because he cannot say what it means. If he could say what the word means he would say what it means instead of saying the word. When the Game Chicken (that fine thinker) kept on saying to Mr Toots, 'It's mean. That's what it is – it's mean,' he was using language in the wisest possible way. For what else could he say? There is no word for mean except mean. A man must be very mean himself before he comes to defining meanness. Precisely because the word is indefinable, the word is indispensable.

In everyday talk, or in any of our journals, we may find the loose but important phrase, 'Why have we no great men today? Why have we no great men like Thackeray, or Carlyle, or Dickens?' Do not let us dismiss this expression, because it appears loose or arbitrary. 'Great' does mean something, and the test of its actuality is to be found by noting how instinctively and decisively we do apply it to some men and not to others; above all, how instinctively and decisively we do apply it to four or five men in the Victorian era, four or five men of whom Dickens was not the least. The term is found to fit a definite thing. Whatever the word 'great' means, Dickens was what it means. Even the fastidious and unhappy who cannot read his books without a continuous critical exasperation, would use the word of him without stopping to think. They feel that Dickens is a great writer even if he is not a good writer. He is treated as a classic; that is, as a king who may now be deserted, but who cannot now be dethroned. The atmosphere of this word clings to him; and the curious thing is that we cannot get it to cling to any of the men of our own generation. 'Great' is the first adjective which the most supercilious modern critic would apply to Dickens. And 'great' is the last adjective that the most supercilious modern critic would apply to himself. We dare not claim to be great men, even when we claim to be superior to them.

Is there, then, any vital meaning in this idea of 'greatness' or in our laments over its absence in our own time? Some people say, indeed, that this sense of mass is but a mirage of distance, and that men always think dead men great and live men small. They seem to think that the law of perspective in the mental world is the precise opposite to the law of perspective in the physical world. They think that figures grow larger as they walk away. But this theory cannot be made to correspond with the facts. We do not lack great men in our own day because we decline to look for them in our own day; on the contrary, we are looking for them all day long. We are not, as a matter of fact, mere examples of those who stone the prophets and leave it to their posterity to build their sepulchres. If the world would only produce our perfect prophet, solemn, searching, universal, nothing would give us keener pleasure than to build his sepulchre. In our eagerness we might even bury him alive. Nor is it true that the great men of the Victorian era were not called great in their own time. By many they were called great from the first. Charlotte Brontë held this heroic language about Thackeray. Ruskin held it about Carlyle. A definite school regarded Dickens as a great man from the first days of his fame: Dickens certainly belonged to this school.

In reply to this question, 'Why have we no great men today?' many modern explanations are offered. Advertisement, cigarette-smoking, the decay of religion, the decay of agriculture, too much humanitarianism, too little humanitarianism, the fact that people are educated insufficiently, the fact that they are educated at all, all these are reasons given. If I give my own explanation, it is not for its intrinsic value; it is because my answer to the question, 'Why have we no great men?' is a short way of stating the deepest and most catastrophic difference between the age in which we live and the early nineteenth century; the age under the shadow of the French Revolution, the age in which Dickens was born.

The soundest of the Dickens critics, a man of genius, Mr George Gissing,[1] opens his criticism by remarking that the world in which Dickens grew up was a hard and cruel world. He notes its gross feeding, its fierce sports, its fighting and foul humour, and all this he summarizes in the words hard and cruel. It is curious how different are the impressions of men. To me this old English world seems infinitely less hard and cruel than the world described in Gissing's own novels. Coarse external customs are merely relative, and easily assimilated. A man soon learnt to harden his hands and harden his head. Faced with the world of Gissing, he can do little but harden his heart. But the fundamental difference between the beginning of the nineteenth century and the end of it is a difference simple but enormous. The first period was full of evil things, but it was full of hope. The second period, the *fin de siècle*, was even full (in some sense) of good things. But it was occupied in asking what was the good of good things. Joy itself became joyless; and the fighting of Cobbett was happier than the feasting of Walter Pater. The men of Cobbett's day were sturdy enough to endure and inflict brutality; but they were also sturdy enough to alter it. This 'hard and cruel' age was, after all, the age of reform. The gibbet stood up black above them; but it was black against the dawn.

This dawn, against which the gibbet and all the old cruelties stood out so black and clear, was the developing idea of liberalism, the French Revolution. It was a clear and a happy philosophy. And only against such philosophies do evils appear evident at all. The optimist is a better reformer than the pessimist; and the man who

1 George Gissing (1857–1903), novelist, chiefly known for his *New Grub Street* (1891), published *Charles Dickens* in 1898.

believes life to be excellent is the man who alters it most. It seems a paradox, yet the reason of it is very plain. The pessimist can be enraged at evil. But only the optimist can be surprised at it. From the reformer is required a simplicity of surprise. He must have the faculty of a violent and virgin astonishment. It is not enough that he should think injustice distressing; he must think injustice *absurd*, an anomaly in existence, a matter less for tears than for a shattering laughter. On the other hand, the pessimists at the end of the century could hardly curse even the blackest thing; for they could hardly see it against its black and eternal background. Nothing was bad, because everything was bad. Life in prison was infamous – like life anywhere else. The fires of persecution were vile – like the stars. We perpetually find this paradox of a contented discontent. Dr Johnson takes too sad a view of humanity, but he is also too satisfied a Conservative. Rousseau takes too rosy a view of humanity, but he causes a revolution. Swift is angry, but a Tory. Shelley is happy, and a rebel. Dickens, the optimist, satirizes the Fleet, and the Fleet is gone. Gissing, the pessimist, satirizes Suburbia, and Suburbia remains.

Mr Gissing's error, then, about the early Dickens period we may put thus: in calling it hard and cruel he omits the wind of hope and humanity that was blowing through it. It may have been full of inhuman institutions, but it was full of humanitarian people. And this humanitarianism was very much the better (in my view) because it was a rough and even rowdy humanitarianism. It was free from all the faults that cling to the name. It was, if you will, a coarse humanitarianism. It was a shouting, fighting, drinking philanthropy – a noble thing. But, in any case, this atmosphere was the atmosphere of the Revolution; and its main idea was the idea of human equality. I am not concerned here to defend the egalitarian idea against the solemn and babyish attacks made upon it by the rich and learned of today. I am merely concerned to state one of its practical consequences. One of the actual and certain consequences of the idea that all men are equal is immediately to produce very great men. I would say superior men, only that the hero thinks of himself as great, but not as superior. This has been hidden from us of late by a foolish worship of sinister and exceptional men, men without comradeship, or any infectious virtue. This type of Caesar does exist. There is a great man who makes every man feel small. But the real great man is the man who makes every man feel great.

The spirit of the early century produced great men, because it believed that men were great. It made strong men by encouraging weak men. Its education, its public habits, its rhetoric, were all addressed towards encouraging the greatness in everybody. And by encouraging the greatness in everybody, it naturally encouraged superlative greatness in some. Superiority came out of the high rapture of equality. It is precisely in this sort of passionate unconsciousness and bewildering community of thought that men do become more than themselves. No man by taking thought can add one cubit to his stature; but a man may add many cubits to his stature by not taking thought. The best men of the Revolution were simply common men at their best. This is why our age can never understand Napoleon. Because he was something great and triumphant, we suppose that he must have been something extraordinary, something inhuman. Some say he was the Devil; some say he was the Superman. Was he a very, very bad man? Was he a good man with some greater moral code? We strive in vain to invent the mysteries behind that immortal mask of brass. The modern world with all its subtleness will never guess his strange secret; for his strange secret was that he was very like other people.

And almost without exception all the great men have come out of this atmosphere of equality. Great men may make despotisms; but democracies make great men. The other main factory of heroes besides a revolution is a religion. And a religion again, is a thing which, by its nature, does not think of men as more or less valuable, but of men as all intensely and painfully valuable, a democracy of eternal danger. For religion all men are equal, as all pennies are equal, because the only value in any of them is that they bear the image of the King. This fact has been quite insufficiently observed in the study of religious heroes. Piety produces intellectual greatness precisely because piety in itself is quite indifferent to intellectual greatness The strength of Cromwell was that he cared for religion. But the strength of religion was that it did not care for Cromwell; did not care for him, that is, any more than for anybody else. He and his footman were equally welcomed to warm places in the hospitality of hell. It has often been said, very truly, that

religion is the thing that makes the ordinary man feel extraordinary; it is an equally important truth that religion is the thing that
makes the extraordinary man feel ordinary.

Carlyle killed the heroes; there have been none since his time.
He killed the heroic (which he sincerely loved) by forcing upon
each man this question: 'Am I strong or weak?' To which the
answer from any honest man whatever (yes, from Caesar or
Bismarck) would certainly be 'weak'. He asked for candidates for
a definite aristocracy, for men who should hold themselves consciously above their fellows. He advertised for them, so to speak;
he promised them glory; he promised them omnipotence. They
have not appeared yet. They never will. For the real heroes of
whom he wrote had appeared out of an ecstasy of the ordinary.
I have already instanced such a case as Cromwell. But there is no
need to go through all the great men of Carlyle. Carlyle himself
was as great as any of them; and if ever there was a typical child of
the French Revolution, it was he. He began with the wildest hopes
from the Reform Bill, and although he soured afterwards, he had
been made and moulded by those hopes. He was disappointed with
Equality; but Equality was not disappointed with him. Equality is
justified of all her children.

But we, in the post-Carlylean period, have become fastidious
about great men. Every man examines himself, every man examines his neighbours, to see whether they or he quite come up to
the exact line of greatness. The answer is, naturally, 'No'. And
many a man calls himself contentedly 'a minor poet' who would
then have been inspired to be a major prophet. We are hard to
please and of little faith. We can hardly believe that there is such
a thing as a great man. They could hardly believe there was such a
thing as a small one. But we are always praying that our eyes may
behold greatness, instead of praying that our hearts may be filled
with it. Thus, for instance, the Liberal party (to which I belong)
was, in its period of exile, always saying, 'O for a Gladstone!' and
such things. We were always asking that it might be strengthened
from above, instead of ourselves strengthening it from below, with
our hope and our anger and our youth. Every man was waiting for
a leader. Every man ought to be waiting for a chance to lead. If a
god does come upon the earth, he will descend at the sight of the
brave. Our prostrations and litanies are of no avail; our new moons

and our sabbaths are an abomination. The great man will come when all of us are feeling great, not when all of us are feeling small. He will ride in at some splendid moment when we all feel that we could do without him.

We are then able to answer in some manner the question, 'Why have we no great men?' We have no great men chiefly because we are always looking for them. We are connoisseurs of greatness, and connoisseurs can never be great; we are fastidious, that is, we are small. When Diogenes[1] went about with a lantern looking for an honest man, I am afraid he had very little time to be honest himself. And when anybody goes about on his hands and knees looking for a great man to worship, he is making sure that one man at any rate shall not be great. Now, the error of Diogenes is evident. The error of Diogenes lay in the fact that he omitted to notice that every man is both an honest man and a dishonest man. Diogenes looked for his honest man inside every crypt and cavern; but he never thought of looking inside the thief. And that is where the Founder of Christianity found the honest man; He found him on a gibbet and promised him Paradise. Just as Christianity looked for the honest man inside the thief, democracy looked for the wise man inside the fool. It encouraged the fool to be wise. We can call this thing sometimes optimism, sometimes equality; the nearest name for it is encouragement. It had its exaggerations – failure to understand original sin, notions that education would make all men good, the childlike yet pedantic philosophies of human perfectibility. But the whole was full of a faith in the infinity of human souls, which is in itself not only Christian but orthodox; and this we have lost amid the limitations of a pessimistic science. Christianity said that any man could be a saint if he chose; democracy, that any man could be a citizen if he chose. The note of the last few decades in art and ethics has been that a man is stamped with an irrevocable psychology, and is cramped for perpetuity in the prison of his skull. It was a world that expected everything of everybody. It was a world that encouraged anybody to be anything. And in England and literature its living expression was Dickens.

We shall consider Dickens in many other capacities, but let us put this one first. He was the voice in England of this humane

1 Greek Cynic philosopher (412 or 404–323 BC).

intoxication and expansion, this encouraging of anybody to be anything. His best books are a carnival of liberty, and there is more of the real spirit of the French Revolution in *Nicholas Nickleby* than in *The Tale of Two Cities*. His work has the great glory of the Revolution, the bidding of every man to be himself; it has also the revolutionary deficiency: it seems to think that this mere emancipation is enough. No man *encouraged* his characters so much as Dickens. 'I am an affectionate father,' he says, 'to every child of my fancy.' He was not only an affectionate father, he was an over-indulgent father. The children of his fancy are spoilt children. They shake the house like heavy and shouting schoolboys; they smash the story to pieces like so much furniture. When we moderns write stories our characters are better controlled. But, alas! our characters are rather easier to control. We are in no danger from the gigantic gambols of creatures like Mantalini and Micawber. We are in no danger of giving our readers too much Weller or Wegg. We have not got it to give. When we experience the ungovernable sense of life which goes along with the old Dickens sense of liberty, we experience the best of the revolution. We are filled with the first of all democratic doctrines, that all men are interesting; Dickens tried to make some of his people appear dull people, but he could not keep them dull. He could not make a monotonous man. The bores in his books are brighter than the wits in other books.

I have put this position first for a defined reason. It is useless for us to attempt to imagine Dickens and his life unless we are able at least to imagine this old atmosphere of a democratic optimism – a confidence in common men. Dickens depends upon such a comprehension in a rather unusual manner, a manner worth explanation, or at least remark.

The disadvantage under which Dickens has fallen, both as an artist and a moralist, is very plain. His misfortune is that neither of the two last movements in literary criticism has done him any good. He has suffered alike from his enemies, and from the enemies of his enemies. The facts to which I refer are familiar. When the world first awoke from the mere hypnotism of Dickens, from the direct tyranny of his temperament, there was, of course, a reaction. At the head of it came the Realists, with their documents, like Miss Flite. They declared that scenes and types in Dickens were wholly

impossible (in which they were perfectly right), and on this rather
paradoxical ground objected to them as literature. They were not
'like life', and there, they thought, was an end of the matter. The
realist for a time prevailed. But Realists did not enjoy their victory
(if they enjoyed anything) very long. A more symbolic school of
criticism soon arose. Men saw that it was necessary to give a much
deeper and more delicate meaning to the expression 'like life'.
Streets are not life, cities and civilizations are not life, faces even
and voices are not life itself. Life is within, and no man hath seen
it at any time. As for our meals, and our manners, and our daily
dress, these are things exactly like sonnets; they are random symbols of the soul. One man tries to express himself in books, another
in boots, both probably fail. Our solid houses and square meals are
in the strict sense fiction. They are things made up to typify our
thoughts. The coat a man wears may be wholly fictitious; the movement of his hands may be quite unlike life.

This much the intelligence of men soon perceived. And by this
much Dickens's fame should have greatly profited. For Dickens is
'like life' in the truer sense, in the sense that he is akin to the living
principle in us and in the universe; he is like life, at least in this
detail, that he is alive. His art is like life, because, like life, it cares for
nothing outside itself, and goes on its way rejoicing. Both produce
monsters with a kind of carelessness, like enormous by-products;
life producing the rhinoceros, and art Mr Bunsby. Art indeed
copies life in not copying life, for life copies nothing. Dickens's art
is like life because like life, it is irresponsible, because, like life, it is
incredible.

Yet the return of this realization has not greatly profited Dickens,
the return of romance has been almost useless to this great romantic. He has gained as little from the fall of the realists as from their
triumph; there has been a revolution, there has been a counter
revolution, there has been no restoration. And the reason of this
brings us back to that atmosphere of popular optimism of which
I spoke. And the shortest way of expressing the more recent neglect
of Dickens is to say that for our time and taste he exaggerates the
wrong thing.

Exaggeration is the definition of art. That both Dickens and the
Moderns understood. Art is, in its inmost nature, fantastic. Time
brings queer revenges, and while the realists were yet living, the art

of Dickens was justified by Aubrey Beardsley.[1] But men like Aubrey Beardsley were allowed to be fantastic, because the mood which they overstrained and overstated was a mood which their period understood. Dickens overstrains and overstates a mood our period does not understand. The truth he exaggerates is exactly this old Revolution sense of infinite opportunity and boisterous brotherhood. And we resent his undue sense of it, because we ourselves have not even a due sense of it. We feel troubled with too much where we have too little; we wish he would keep it within bounds. For we are all exact and scientific on the subjects we do not care about. We all immediately detect exaggeration in an exposition of Mormonism or a patriotic speech from Paraguay. We all require sobriety on the subject of the sea-serpent. But the moment we begin to believe a thing ourselves, that moment we begin easily to overstate it; and the moment our souls become serious, our words become a little wild. And certain moderns are thus placed towards exaggeration. They permit any writer to emphasize doubts for instance, for doubts are their religion, but they permit no man to emphasize dogmas. If a man be the mildest Christian, they smell 'cant'; but he can be a raving windmill of pessimism, and they call it 'temperament'. If a moralist paints a wild picture of immorality, they doubt its truth, they say that devils are not so black as they are painted. But if a pessimist paints a wild picture of melancholy, they accept the whole horrible psychology, and they never ask if devils are as blue as they are painted.

It is evident, in short, why even those who admire exaggeration do not admire Dickens. He is exaggerating the wrong thing. They know what it is to feel a sadness so strange and deep that only impossible characters can express it: they do not know what it is to feel a joy so vital and violent that only impossible characters can express that. They know that the soul can be so sad as to dream naturally of the blue faces of the corpses of Baudelaire: they do not know that the soul can be so cheerful as to dream naturally of the blue face of Major Bagstock. They know that there is a point of depression at which one believes in Tintagiles: they do not know that there is a point of exhilaration at which one believes in Mr Wegg.... For every mood there is an appropriate impossibility –

1 Aubrey Beardsley (1872–98), illustrator and writer, was notoriously the leading artist of *fin-de-siècle* decadence.

a decent and tactful impossibility – fitted to the frame of mind. Every train of thought may end in an ecstasy, and all roads lead to Elfland. But few now walk far enough along the street of Dickens to find the place where the cockney villas grow so comic that they become poetical. People do not know how far mere good spirits will go. For instance, we never think (as the old folk-lore did) of good spirits reaching to the spiritual world. We see this in the complete absence from modern, popular supernaturalism of the old popular mirth. We hear plenty today of the wisdom of the spiritual world; but we do not hear, as our fathers did, of the folly of the spiritual world, of the tricks of the gods, and the jokes of the patron saints. Our popular tales tell us of a man who is so wise that he touches the supernatural . . . but they never tell us (like the popular tales of the past) of a man who was so silly that he touched the supernatural, like Bottom the Weaver. We do not understand the dark and transcendental sympathy between fairies and fools. We understand a devout occultism, an evil occultism, a tragic occultism, but a farcical occultism is beyond us. Yet a farcical occultism is the very essence of *The Midsummer Night's Dream*. It is also the right and credible essence of 'The Christmas Carol'. Whether we understand it depends upon whether we can understand that exhilaration is not a physical accident, but a mystical fact; that exhilaration can be infinite, like sorrow; that a joke can be so big that it breaks the roof of the stars. By simply going on being absurd, a thing can become godlike; there is but one step from the ridiculous to the sublime.

Dickens was great because he was immoderately possessed with all this; if we are to understand him at all we must also be moderately possessed with it. We must understand this old limitless hilarity and human confidence, at least enough to be able to endure it when it is pushed a great deal too far. For Dickens did push it too far; he did push the hilarity to the point of incredible character-drawing; he did push the human confidence to the point of unconvincing sentimentalism. . . . There is plenty to carp at in this man if you are inclined to carp; you may easily find him vulgar if you cannot see that he is divine; and if you cannot laugh with Dickens, undoubtedly you can laugh at him.

I believe myself that this braver world of his will certainly return; for I believe that it is bound up with the realities, like morning and the spring. But for those who beyond remedy regard it as an error, I put this appeal before any other observations on Dickens. First let us sympathize, if only for an instant, with the hopes of the Dickens period, with that cheerful trouble of change. If democracy has disappointed you, do not think of it as a burst bubble, but at least as a broken heart, an old love-affair. Do not sneer at the time when the creed of humanity was on its honeymoon; treat it with the dreadful reverence that is due to youth. For you, perhaps, a drearier philosophy has covered and eclipsed the earth. The fierce poet of the Middle Ages[1] wrote, 'Abandon hope, all ye who enter here', over the gates of the lower world. The emancipated poets of today have written it over the gates of this world. But if we are to understand the story which follows, we must erase that apocalyptic writing, if only for an hour. We must re-create the faith of our fathers, if only as an artistic atmosphere. If, then, you are a pessimist, in reading this story, forgo for a little the pleasures of pessimism. Dream for one mad moment that the grass is green. Unlearn that sinister learning that you think so clear; deny that deadly knowledge that you think you know. Surrender the very flower of your culture; give up the very jewel of your pride; abandon hopelessness, all ye who enter here.

1 Dante, *Inferno*, III.9.

II

THE BOYHOOD OF DICKENS

CHARLES DICKENS was born at Landport, in Portsea, on 7 February 1812. His father was a clerk in the Navy Pay-office, and was temporarily on duty in the neighbourhood. Very soon after the birth of Charles Dickens, however, the family moved for a short period to Norfolk Street, Bloomsbury, and then for a long period to Chatham, which thus became the real home, and for all serious purposes, the native place of Dickens. The whole story of his life moves like a Canterbury pilgrimage along the great roads of Kent.

John Dickens, his father, was, as stated, a clerk; but such mere terms of trade tell us little of the tone or status of a family. Browning's father (to take an instance at random) would also be described as a clerk and a man of the middle class; but the Browning family and the Dickens family have the colour of two different civilizations. The difference cannot be conveyed merely by saying that Browning stood many strata above Dickens. It must be conveyed that Browning belonged to that section of the middle class which tends (in the small social sense) to rise; the Dickenses to that section which tends in the same sense to fall. If Browning had not been a poet, he would have been a better clerk than his father, and his son probably a better and richer clerk than he. But if they had not been lifted in the air by the enormous accident of a man of genius, the Dickenses, I fancy, would have appeared in poorer and poorer places, as inventory clerks, as caretakers, as addressers of envelopes, until they melted into the masses of the poor.

Yet at the time of Dickens's birth and childhood this weakness in their worldly destiny was in no way apparent; especially it was not apparent to the little Charles himself. He was born and grew up in a paradise of small prosperity. He fell into the family, so to speak, during one of its comfortable periods, and he never in those early days thought of himself as anything but as a comfortable middle-class child, the son of a comfortable middle-class man. The father whom he found provided for him, was one from whom comfort drew forth his most pleasant and reassuring qualities, though not perhaps his most interesting and peculiar. John Dickens seemed, most probably, a hearty and kindly character, a little florid of speech, a little careless of duty in some details, notably in the detail of education. His neglect of his son's mental training in later and more trying times was a piece of unconscious selfishness which remained a little acrimoniously in his son's mind through life. But even in this earlier and easier period what records there are of John Dickens give out the air of a somewhat idle and irresponsible fatherhood. He exhibited towards his son that contradiction in conduct which is always shown by the too thoughtless parent to the too thoughtful child. He contrived at once to neglect his mind, and also to over-stimulate it.

There are many recorded tales and traits of the author's infancy, but one small fact seems to me more than any other to strike the note and give the key to his whole strange character. His father found it more amusing to be an audience than to be an instructor; and instead of giving the child intellectual pleasure, called upon him, almost before he was out of petticoats, to provide it. Some of the earliest glimpses we have of Charles Dickens show him to us perched on some chair or table singing comic songs in an atmosphere of perpetual applause. So, almost as soon as he can toddle, he steps into the glare of the footlights. He never stepped out of it until he died. He was a good man, as men go in this bewildering world of ours, brave, transparent, tender-hearted, scrupulously independent and honourable; he was not a man whose weaknesses should be spoken of without some delicacy and doubt. But there did mingle with his merits all his life this theatrical quality, this atmosphere of being shown off – a sort of hilarious self-consciousness. His literary life was a triumphal procession; he died drunken with glory. And behind all this nine years' wonder that filled the world, behind his gigantic tours and his ten thousand editions, the crowded lectures and the crashing brass, behind all the thing we really see is the flushed face of a little boy singing music-hall songs to a circle of aunts and uncles. And this precocious pleasure explains much, too, in the moral way. Dickens had all his life the faults of the little boy who is kept up too late at night. The boy in such a case exhibits a psychological paradox; he is a little too irritable because he is a little too happy. Dickens was always a little too irritable because he was a little too happy. Like the over-wrought child in society, he was splendidly sociable, and yet suddenly quarrelsome. In all the practical relations of his life he was what the child is in the last hours of an evening party, genuinely delighted, genuinely delightful, genuinely affectionate and happy, and yet in some strange way fundamentally exasperated and dangerously close to tears.

There was another touch about the boy which made his case more peculiar, and perhaps his intelligence more fervid; the touch of ill-health. It could not be called more than a touch, for he suffered from no formidable malady and could always through life endure a great degree of exertion, even if it was only the exertion of walking violently all night. Still the streak of sickness was sufficient to take him out of the common unconscious life of the community of boys; and for good or evil that withdrawal is always a matter of deadly importance to the mind. He was thrown back perpetually upon the pleasures of the intelligence, and these began to burn in his head like a pent and painful furnace. In his own unvaryingly vivid way he has described how he crawled up into an unconsidered garret, and there found, in a dusty heap, the undying literature of England. The books he mentions chiefly are *Humphrey Clinker* and *Tom Jones*. When he opened those two books in the garret he caught hold of the only past with which he is at all connected, the great comic writers of England of whom he was destined to be the last.

It must be remembered (as I have suggested before) that there was something about the county in which he lived, and the great roads along which he travelled that sympathized with and stimulated his pleasure in this old picaresque literature. The groups that came along the road, that passed through his town and out of it, were of the motley laughable type that tumbled into ditches or beat down the doors of taverns under the escort of Smollett and Fielding. In our time the main roads of Kent have upon them very often a perpetual procession of tramps and tinkers unknown on the quiet hills of Sussex; and it may have been so also in Dickens's boyhood. In his neighbourhood were definite memorials of yet older and yet greater English comedy. From the height of Gads-hill at which he stared unceasingly there looked down upon him the monstrous

ghost of Falstaff, Falstaff who might well have been the spiritual
father of all Dickens's adorable knaves, Falstaff the great mountain
of English laughter and English sentimentalism, the great, healthy,
humane English humbug, not to be matched among the nations.

At this eminence of Gads-hill Dickens used to stare even as a
boy with the steady purpose of some day making it his own. It is
characteristic of the consistency which underlies the superficially
erratic career of Dickens that he actually did live to make it his
own. The truth is that he was a precocious child, precocious not
only on the more poetical but on the more prosaic side of life. He
was ambitious as well as enthusiastic. No one can ever know what
visions they were that crowded into the head of the clever little brat
as he ran about the streets of Chatham or stood glowering at Gads-
hill. But I think that quite mundane visions had a very considerable
share in the matter. He longed to go to school (a strange wish), to
go to college, to make a name, nor did he merely aspire to these
things; the great number of them he also expected. He regarded
himself as a child of good position just about to enter on a life of
good luck. He thought his home and family a very good spring-
board or jumping-off place from which to fling himself to the positions which he desired to reach. And almost as he was about to
spring the whole structure broke under him, and he and all that
belonged to him disappeared into a darkness far below.

Everything had been struck down as with the finality of a thunderbolt. His lordly father was a bankrupt, and in the Marshalsea
prison. His mother was in a mean home in the north of London,
wildly proclaiming herself the principal of a girls' school, a girls'
school to which nobody would go. And he himself, the conqueror
of the world and the prospective purchaser of Gads-hill, passed
some distracted and bewildering days in pawning the household
necessities to Fagins in foul shops, and then found himself somehow or other one of a row of ragged boys in a great dreary factory,
pasting the same kinds of labels on to the same kinds of blacking-
bottles from morning till night.

Although it seemed sudden enough to him, the disintegration
had, as a matter of fact, of course, been going on for a long time. He
had only heard from his father dark and melodramatic allusions to
a 'deed' which, from the way it was mentioned, might have been
a claim to the crown or a compact with the devil, but which was in

truth an unsuccessful documentary attempt on the part of John Dickens to come to a composition with his creditors. And now, in the lurid light of his sunset, the character of John Dickens began to take on those purple colours which have made him under another name absurd and immortal. It required a tragedy to bring out this man's comedy. So long as John Dickens was in easy circumstances, he seemed only an easy man, a little long and luxuriant in his phrases, a little careless in his business routine. He seemed only a wordy man, who lived on bread and beef like his neighbours; but as bread and beef were successively taken away from him, it was discovered that he lived on words. For him to be involved in a calamity only meant to be cast for the first part in a tragedy. For him blank ruin was only a subject for blank verse. Henceforth we feel scarcely inclined to call him John Dickens at all; we feel inclined to call him by the name through which his son celebrated this preposterous and sublime victory of the human spirit over circumstances. Dickens, in *David Copperfield*, called him Wilkins Micawber. In his personal correspondence he called him the Prodigal Father.

Young Charles had been hurriedly flung into the factory by the more or less careless good-nature of James Lamert, a relation of his mother's; it was a blacking factory, supposed to be run as a rival to Warren's by another and 'original' Warren, both practically conducted by another of the Lamerts. It was situated near Hungerford Market. Dickens worked there drearily, like one stunned with disappointment. To a child excessively intellectualized, and at this time, I fear, excessively egotistical, the coarseness of the whole thing – the work, the rooms, the boys, the language – was a sort of bestial nightmare. Not only did he scarcely speak of it then, but he scarcely spoke of it afterwards. Years later, in the fullness of his fame, he heard from Forster[1] that a man had spoken of knowing him. On hearing the name, he somewhat curtly acknowledged it, and spoke of having seen the man once. Forster, in his innocence, answered that the man said he had seen Dickens many times in a factory by Hungerford Market. Dickens was suddenly struck with a long and extraordinary silence. Then he invited Forster, as his best friend, to a particular interview, and, with every appearance of difficulty and distress, told him the whole story for the first and

1 John Forster (1812–76), journalist and professional biographer, is best known for his life of Dickens.

the last time. A long while after that he told the world some part of the matter in the account of Murdstone and Grinby's in *David Copperfield*. He never spoke of the whole experience except once or twice, and he never spoke of it otherwise than as a man might speak of hell.

It need not be suggested, I think, that this agony in the child was exaggerated by the man. It is true that he was not incapable of the vice of exaggeration, if it be a vice. There was about him much vanity and a certain virulence in his version of many things. Upon the whole, indeed, it would hardly be too much to say that he would have exaggerated any sorrow he talked about. But this was a sorrow with a very strange position in Dickens's life; it was a sorrow he did not talk about. Upon this particular dark spot he kept a sort of deadly silence for twenty years. An accident revealed part of the truth to the dearest of all his friends. He then told the whole truth to the dearest of all his friends. He never told anybody else. I do not think that this arose from any social sense of disgrace; if he had it slightly at the time, he was far too self-satisfied a man to have taken it seriously in after life. I really think that his pain at this time was so real and ugly that the thought of it filled him with that sort of impersonal but unbearable shame with which we are filled, for instance, by the notion of physical torture, of something that humiliates humanity. He felt that such agony was something obscene. Moreover there are two other good reasons for thinking that his sense of hopelessness was very genuine. First of all, this starless outlook is common in the calamities of boyhood. The bitterness of boyish distresses does not lie in the fact that they are large; it lies in the fact that we do not know that they are small. About any early disaster there is a dreadful finality; a lost child can suffer like a lost soul.

It is currently said that hope goes with youth, and lends to youth its wings of a butterfly; but I fancy that hope is the last gift given to man, and the only gift not given to youth. Youth is pre-eminently the period in which a man can be lyric, fanatical, poetic; but youth is the period in which a man can be hopeless. The end of every episode is the end of the world. But the power of hoping through everything, the knowledge that the soul survives its adventures, that great inspiration comes to the middle-aged; God has kept that good wine until now. It is from the backs of the elderly gentlemen that the wings of the butterfly should burst. There is nothing that so much mystifies the young as the consistent frivolity of the old. They have discovered their indestructibility. They are in their second and clearer childhood, and there is a meaning in the merriment of their eyes. They have seen the end of the End of the World.

First, then, the desolate finality of Dickens's childish mood makes me think it was a real one. And there is another thing to be remembered. Dickens was not a saintly child after the style of Little Dorrit or Little Nell. He had not, at this time at any rate, set his heart wholly upon higher things, even upon things such as personal tenderness or loyalty. He had been, and was, unless I am very much mistaken, sincerely, stubbornly, bitterly ambitious. He had, I fancy, a fairly clear idea previous to the downfall of all his family's hopes of what he wanted to do in the world, and of the mark that he meant to make there. In no dishonourable sense, but still in a definite sense, he might, in early life, be called worldly; and the children of this world are in their generation infinitely more sensitive than the children of light. A saint after repentance will forgive himself for a sin; a man about town will never forgive himself for a *faux pas*. There are ways of getting absolved for murder; there are no ways of getting absolved for upsetting the soup. This thin-skinned quality in all very mundane people is a thing too little remembered; and it must not be wholly forgotten in connection with a clever, restless lad who dreamed of a destiny. That part of his distress which concerned himself and his social standing was among the other parts of it the least noble; but perhaps it was the most painful. For pride is not only, as the modern world fails to understand, a sin to be condemned; it is also (as it understands even less) a weakness to be very much commiserated. A very vitalizing touch is given in one of his own reminiscences. His most unendurable moment did not come in any bullying in the factory or any famine in the streets. It came when he went to see his sister Fanny take a prize at the Royal Academy of Music. 'I could not bear to think of myself – beyond the reach of all such honourable emulation and success. The tears ran down my face. I felt as if my heart were rent. I prayed when I went to bed that night to be lifted out of the humiliation and neglect in which I was. I never had suffered so much before. There was no envy in this.' I do not think that there was, though the poor little wretch could hardly have been blamed if there had been. There was only a furious sense of frustration; a spirit like a wild beast in a cage. It was only a small matter in the external and obvious sense; it was only Dickens prevented from being Dickens.

If we put these facts together, that the tragedy seemed final, and that the tragedy was concerned with the supersensitive matters of the ego and the gentleman, I think we can imagine a pretty genuine case of internal depression. And when we add to the case of the internal depression the case of the external oppression, the case of the material circumstances by which he was surrounded, we have reached a sort of midnight. All day he worked on insufficient food at a factory. It is sufficient to say that it afterwards appeared in his works as Murdstone and Grinby's. At night he returned disconsolately to a lodging-house for such lads, kept by an old lady. It is sufficient to say that she appeared afterwards as Mrs Pipchin. Once a week only he saw anybody for whom he cared a straw; that was when he went to the Marshalsea prison, and that gave his juvenile pride, half manly and half snobbish, bitter annoyance of another kind. Add to this, finally, that physically he was always very weak and never very well. Once he was struck down in the middle of his work with sudden bodily pain. The boy who worked next to him, a coarse and heavy lad named Bob Fagin, who had often attacked Dickens on the not unreasonable ground of his being a 'gentleman', suddenly showed that enduring sanity of compassion which Dickens had destined to show so often in the characters of the common and unclean. Fagin made a bed for his sick companion out of the straw in the work-room, and filled empty blacking-bottles with hot water all day. When the evening came, and Dickens was somewhat recovered, Bob Fagin insisted on escorting the boy home to his father. The situation was as poignant as a sort of tragic farce. Fagin in his wooden-headed chivalry would have died in order to take Dickens to his family; Dickens in his bitter gentility would have died rather than let Fagin know that his family were in the Marshalsea. So these two young idiots tramped the tedious streets, both stubborn, both suffering for an idea. The advantage certainly was with Fagin, who was suffering for a Christian compassion, while Dickens was suffering for a pagan pride. At last Dickens flung off his friend with desperate farewell and thanks, and dashed up the steps of a strange house on the Surrey side. He knocked and rang as Bob Fagin, his benefactor and his incubus, disappeared round the corner. And when the servant came to open the door, he asked, apparently with gravity, whether Mr Robert Fagin lived there. It is a strange touch. The immortal Dickens woke in him for an instant in that last wild joke of that weary evening. Next morning, however, he was again well enough to make himself ill again, and the wheels of the great factory went on. They manufactured a number of bottles of Warren's Blacking, and in the course of the process they manufactured also the greatest optimist of the nineteenth century.

This boy who dropped down groaning at his work, who was hungry four or five times a week, whose best feelings and worst feelings were alike flayed alive, was the man on whom two generations of comfortable critics have visited the complaint that his view of life was too rosy to be anything but unreal. Afterwards, and in its proper place, I shall speak of what is called the optimism of Dickens, and of whether it was really too cheerful or too smooth. But this boyhood of his may be recorded now as a mere fact. If he was too happy, this was where he learnt it. If his school of thought was a vulgar optimism, this is where he went to school. If he learnt to whitewash the universe, it was in a blacking factory that he learnt it.

As a fact, there is no shred of evidence to show that those who have had sad experiences tend to have a sad philosophy. There are numberless points upon which Dickens is spiritually at one with the poor, that is, with the great mass of mankind. But there is no point in which he is more perfectly at one with them than in showing that there is no kind of connection between a man being unhappy and a man being pessimistic. Sorrow and pessimism are indeed, in a sense, opposite things, since sorrow is founded on the value of something, and pessimism upon the value of nothing. And in practice we find that those poets or political leaders who come from the people, and whose experiences have really been searching and cruel, are the most sanguine people in the world. These men out of the old agony are always optimists; they are sometimes offensive optimists. A man like Robert Burns, whose father (like Dickens's father) goes bankrupt, whose whole life is a struggle against miserable external powers and internal weaknesses yet more miserable – a man whose life begins grey and ends black –

Burns does not merely sing about the goodness of life, he positively rants and cants about it. Rousseau, whom all his friends
and acquaintances treated almost as badly as he treated them –
Rousseau does not grow merely eloquent, he grows gushing and
sentimental, about the inherent goodness of human nature.
Charles Dickens, who was most miserable at the receptive age
when most people are most happy, is afterwards happy when all
men weep. Circumstances break men's bones; it has never been
shown that they break men's optimism. These great popular
leaders do all kinds of desperate things under the immediate
scourge of tragedy. They become drunkards; they become demagogues; they become morpho-maniacs. They never become pessimists. Most unquestionably there are ragged and unhappy men
whom we could easily understand being pessimists. But as a matter
of fact they are not pessimists. Most unquestionably there are
whole dim hordes of humanity whom we should promptly pardon
if they cursed God. But they don't. The pessimists are aristocrats
like Byron; the men who curse God are aristocrats like Swinburne.
But when those who starve and suffer speak for a moment, they
do not profess merely an optimism, they profess a cheap optimism;
they are too poor to afford a dear one. They cannot indulge in any
detailed or merely logical defence of life; that would be to delay
the enjoyment of it. These higher optimists, of whom Dickens was
one, do not approve of the universe; they do not even admire the
universe; they fall in love with it. They embrace life too close to
criticize or even to see it. Existence to such men has the wild
beauty of a woman, and those love her with most intensity who
love her with least cause.

III
THE YOUTH OF DICKENS

THERE are popular phrases so picturesque that even when they are intentionally funny they are unintentionally poetical. I remember, to take one instance out of many, hearing a heated Secularist in Hyde Park apply to some parson or other the exquisite expression, 'a sky-pilot'. Subsequent inquiry has taught me that the term is intended to be comic and even contemptuous; but in that first freshness of it I went home repeating it to myself like a new poem. Few of the pious legends have conceived so strange and yet celestial a picture as this of the pilot in the sky, leaning on his helm above the empty heavens, and carrying his cargo of souls higher than the loneliest cloud. The phrase is like a lyric of Shelley. Or, to take another instance from another language, the French have an incomparable idiom for a boy playing truant: 'Il fait l'école buis-sonnière' – he goes to the bushy school, or the school among the bushes. How admirably thin accidental expression, 'the bushy school' (not to be lightly confounded with the Art School at Bushey) – how admirably this 'bushy school' expresses half the modern notions of a more natural education! The two words express the whole poetry of Wordsworth, the whole philosophy of Thoreau, and are quite as good literature as either.

Now, among a million of such scraps of inspired slang there is one which describes a certain side of Dickens better than pages of explanation. The phrase, appropriately enough, occurs at least once in his works, and that on a fitting occasion. When Job Trotter is sent by Sam on a wild chase after Mr Perker, the solicitor, Mr Perker's clerk condoles with Job upon the lateness of the hour, and the fact that all habitable places are shut up. 'My friend,' says Mr Perker's clerk, 'you've got the key of the street.' Mr Perker's clerk, who was a flippant and scornful young man, may perhaps be pardoned if he used this expression in a flippant and scornful sense; but let us hope that Dickens did not. Let us hope that Dickens saw the strange, yet satisfying, imaginative justice of the words; for

Dickens himself had, in the most sacred and serious sense of the term, the key of the street. When we shut out anything, we are shut out of that thing. When we shut out the street, we are shut out of the street. Few of us understand the street. Even when we step into it, we step into it doubtfully, as into a house or room of strangers. Few of us see through the shining riddle of the street, the strange folk that belong to the street only – the street-walker or the street arab, the nomads who, generation after generation, have kept their ancient secrets in the full blaze of the sun. Of the street at night many of us know even less. The street at night is a great house locked up. But Dickens had, if ever man had, the key of the street. His earth was the stones of the street; his stars were the lamps of the street; his hero was the man in the street. He could open the inmost door of his house – the door that leads into that secret passage which is lined with houses and roofed with stars.

This silent transformation into a citizen of the street took place during those dark days of boyhood, when Dickens was drudging at the factory. Whenever he had done drudging, he had no other resource but drifting, and he drifted over half London. He was a dreamy child, thinking mostly of his own dreary prospects. Yet he saw and remembered much of the streets and squares he passed. Indeed, as a matter of fact, he went the right way to work unconsciously to do so. He did not go in for 'observation', a priggish habit; he did not look at Charing Cross to improve his mind or count the lamp-posts in Holborn to practise his arithmetic. But unconsciously he made all these places the scenes of the monstrous drama in his miserable little soul. He walked in darkness under the lamps of Holborn, and was crucified at Charing Cross. So for him ever afterwards these places had the beauty that only belongs to battlefields. For our memory never fixes the facts which we have merely observed. The only way to remember a place for ever is to live in the place for an hour; and the only way to live in the place for an hour is to forget the place for an hour. The undying scenes we can all see if we shut our eyes are not the scenes that we have stared at under the direction of guide-books; the scenes we see are the scenes at which we did not look at all – the scenes in which we walked when we were thinking about something else – about a sin, or a love-affair, or some childish sorrow. We can see the background now because we did not see it then. So Dickens did not stamp these places on his mind; he stamped his mind on these places. For him ever afterwards these streets were mortally romantic; they were dipped in the purple dyes of youth and its tragedy, and rich with irrevocable sunsets.

Herein is the whole secret of that eerie realism with which Dickens could always vitalize some dark or dull corner of London. There are details in the Dickens descriptions – a window, or a railing, or the keyhole of a door – which he endows with demoniac life. The things seem more actual than things really are. Indeed, that degree of realism does not exist in reality: it is the unbearable realism of a dream. And this kind of realism can only be gained by walking dreamily in a place; it cannot be gained by walking observantly. Dickens himself has given a perfect instance of how these nightmare minutiæ grew upon him in his trance of abstraction. He mentions among the coffee-shops into which he crept in those wretched days one in St Martin's Lane, 'of which I only recollect that it stood near the church, and that in the door there was an oval glass plate with "COFFEE ROOM" painted on it, addressed towards the street. If I ever find myself in a very different kind of coffee-room now, but where there is such an inscription on glass, and read it backwards on the wrong side, MOOR EEFFOC (as I often used to do then in a dismal reverie), a shock goes through my blood.' That wild word, 'Moor Eeffoc', is the motto of all effective realism; it is the masterpiece of the good realistic principle – the principle that the most fantastic thing of all is often the precise fact. And that elvish kind of realism Dickens adopted everywhere. His world was alive with inanimate objects. The date on the door danced over Mr Grewgious's, the knocker grinned at Mr Scrooge, the Roman on the ceiling pointed down at Mr Tulkinghorn, the elderly armchair leered at Tom Smart – these are all mooreeffocish things. A man sees them because he does not look at them.

And so the little Dickens Dickensized London. He prepared the way for all his personages. Into whatever cranny of our city his characters might crawl, Dickens had been there before them. However wild were the events he narrated as outside him, they could not be wilder than the things that had gone on within. However queer a character of Dickens might be, he could hardly be queerer than Dickens was. The whole secret of his after-writings is sealed up in those silent years of which no written word remains. Those

years did him harm perhaps, as his biographer, Forster, has
thoughtfully suggested, by sharpening a certain fierce individualism in him which once or twice during his genial life flashed like a
half-hidden knife. He was always generous; but things had gone
too hardly with him for him to be always easy-going. He was always
kind-hearted; he was not always good-humoured. Those years may
also, in their strange mixture of morbidity and reality, have
increased in him his tendency to exaggeration. But we can scarcely
lament this in a literary sense; exaggeration is almost the definition
of art – and it is entirely the definition of Dickens's art. Those years
may have given him many moral and mental wounds, from which
he never recovered. But they gave him the key of the street.

There is a weird contradiction in the soul of the born optimist.
He can be happy and unhappy at the same time. With Dickens the
practical depression of his life at this time did nothing to prevent
him from laying up those hilarious memories of which all his books
are made. No doubt he was genuinely unhappy in the poor place
where his mother kept school. Nevertheless it was there that he
noticed the unfathomable quaintness of the little servant whom he
made into the Marchioness. No doubt he was comfortless enough
at the boarding-house of Mrs Roylance; but he perceived with a
dreadful joy that Mrs Roylance's name was Pipchin. There seems
to be no incompatibility between taking in tragedy and giving out
comedy; they are able to run parallel in the same personality. One
incident which he described in his unfinished 'autobiography', and
which he afterwards transferred almost verbatim to David Copperfield, was peculiarly rich and impressive. It was the inauguration
of a petition to the King for a bounty, drawn up by a committee
of the prisoners in the Marshalsea, a committee of which Dickens's
father was the president, no doubt in virtue of his oratory, and also
the scribe no doubt in virtue of his genuine love of literary flights.

'As many of the principal officers of this body as could be got
into a small room without filling it up, supported him in front of
the petition; and my old friend, Captain Porter (who had washed
himself to do honour to so solemn an occasion), stationed himself
close to it, to read it to all who were unacquainted with its contents.
The door was then thrown open, and they began to come in in a
long file; several waiting on the landing outside, while one entered,
affixed his signature, and went out. To everybody in succession

Captain Porter said, "Would you like to hear it read?" If he weakly showed the least disposition to hear it, Captain Porter in a loud sonorous voice gave him every word of it. I remember a certain luscious roll he gave to such words as "Majesty – Gracious Majesty – Your Gracious Majesty's unfortunate subjects – Your Majesty's well-known munificence", as if the words were something real in his mouth and delicious to taste: my poor father meanwhile listening with a little of an author's vanity and contemplating (not severely) the spike on the opposite wall. Whatever was comical or pathetic in this scene, I sincerely believe I perceived in my corner, whether I demonstrated it or not, quite as well as I should perceive it now. I made out my own little character and story for every man who put his name to the sheet of paper.'

Here we see very plainly that Dickens did not merely look back in after days and see that these humours had been delightful. He was delighted at the same moment that he was desperate. The two opposite things existed in him simultaneously, and each in its full strength. His soul was not a mixed colour like grey and purple, caused by no component colour being quite itself. His soul was like a shot silk of black and crimson, a shot silk of misery and joy.

Seen from the outside, his little pleasures and extravagances seem more pathetic than his grief. Once the solemn little figure went into a public-house in Parliament Street, and addressed the man behind the bar in the following terms – 'What is your very best – the VERY best ale a glass?' The man replied, 'Twopence.' 'Then,' said the infant, 'just draw me a glass of that, if you please, with a good head to it.' 'The landlord,' says Dickens, in telling the story, 'looked at me in return over the bar from head to foot with a strange smile on his face; and instead of drawing the beer looked round the screen and said something to his wife, who came out from behind it with her work in her hand and joined him in surveying me. . . . They asked me a good many questions as to what my name was, how old I was, where I lived, how I was employed, etc., etc. To all of which, that I might commit nobody, I invented appropriate answers. They served me with the ale, though I suspect it was not the strongest on the premises; and the landlord's wife, opening the little half-door, and bending down, gave me a kiss.' Here he touches that other side of common life which he was chiefly to champion; he was to show that there is no ale like the ale of a poor man's festival, and no pleasures like the pleasures of the poor. At other places of refreshment he was yet more majestic. 'I remember,' he says, 'tucking my own bread (which I had brought from home in the morning) under my arm, wrapt up in a piece of paper like a book, and going into the best dining-room in Johnson's Alamode Beef House in Clare Court, Drury Lane, and magnificently ordering a small plate of *à-la-mode* beef to eat with it. What the waiter thought of such a strange little apparition coming in all alone I don't know; but I can see him now staring at me as I ate my dinner, and bringing up the other waiter to look. I gave him a halfpenny, and I wish, now, that he hadn't taken it.'

For the boy individually the prospect seemed to be growing drearier and drearier. This phrase indeed hardly expresses the fact; for, as he felt it, it was not so much a run of worsening luck as the closing in of a certain and quiet calamity like the coming on of twilight and dark. He felt that he would die and be buried in blacking. Through all this he does not seem to have said much to his parents of his distress. They who were in prison had certainly a much jollier time than he who was free. But of all the strange ways in which the human being proves that he is not a rational being, whatever else he is, no case is so mysterious and unaccountable as the secrecy of childhood. We learn of the cruelty of some school or child-factory from journalists; we learn it from inspectors, we learn it from doctors, we learn it even from shame-stricken schoolmasters and repentant sweaters; but we never learn it from the children; we never learn it from the victims. It would seem as if a living creature had to be taught, like an art of culture, the art of crying out when it is hurt. It would seem as if patience were the natural thing; it would seem as if impatience were an accomplishment like whist. However this may be, it is wholly certain that Dickens might have drudged and died drudging, and buried the unborn Pickwick, but for an external accident.

He was, as has been said, in the habit of visiting his father at the Marshalsea every week. The talks between the two must have been a comedy at once more cruel and more delicate than Dickens ever described. Meredith might picture the comparison between the child whose troubles were so childish, but who felt them like a damned spirit, and the middle-aged man whose trouble was final ruin, and who felt it no more than a baby. Once, it would appear, the boy broke down altogether – perhaps under the unbearable buoyancy of his oratorical papa – and implored to be freed from the factory – implored it, I fear, with a precocious and almost horrible eloquence. The old optimist was astounded – too much astounded to do anything in particular. Whether the incident had really anything to do with what followed cannot be decided, but ostensibly it had not. Ostensibly the cause of Charles's ultimate liberation was a quarrel between his father and Lamert, the head of the factory. Dickens the elder (who had at last left the Marshalsea) could no doubt conduct a quarrel with the magnificence of Micawber; the result of this talent, at any rate, was to leave Mr Lamert in a towering rage. He had a stormy interview with Charles, in which he tried to be good-tempered to the boy, but could hardly master his tongue about the boy's father. Finally he told him he must go, and with every observance the little creature was solemnly expelled from hell.

His mother, with a touch of strange harshness, was for patching up the quarrel and sending him back. Perhaps, with the fierce feminine responsibility, she felt that the first necessity was to keep the family out of debt. But old John Dickens put his foot down here – put his foot down with that ringing but very rare decision with which (once in ten years, and often on some trivial matter) the weakest man will overwhelm the strongest woman. The boy was miserable; the boy was clever; the boy should go to school. The boy went to school; he went to the Wellington House Academy, Mornington Place. It was an odd experience for any one to go from the world to a school, instead of going from school to the world. Dickens, we may say, had his boyhood after his youth. He had seen life at its coarsest before he began his training for it, and knew the worst words in the English language probably before the best. This odd chronology, it will be remembered, he retained in his semi-autobiographical account of the adventures of David Copperfield, who went into the business of Murdstone and Grinby's before he went to the school kept by Dr Strong. David Copperfield, also, went to be carefully prepared for a world that he had seen already. Outside *David Copperfield*, the records of Dickens at this time reduce themselves to a few glimpses provided by accidental companions of his schooldays, and little can be deduced from them about his personality beyond a general impression of sharpness and, perhaps, of bravado, of bright eyes and bright speeches. Probably the young creature was recuperating himself for his misfortunes, was making the most of his liberty, was flapping the wings of that wild spirit that had just not been broken. We hear of things that sound suddenly juvenile after his maturer troubles, of a secret language sounding like mere gibberish, and of a small theatre, with paint and red fire, such as that which Stevenson loved. It was not an accident that Dickens and Stevenson loved it. It is a stage unsuited for psychological realism; the cardboard characters cannot analyse each other with any effect. But it is a stage almost divinely suited for making surroundings, for making that situation and background which belongs peculiarly to romance. A toy-theatre, in fact, is the opposite of private theatricals. In the latter you can do anything with the people if you do not ask much from the scenery; in the former you can do anything in scenery if you do not ask much from the people. In a toy-theatre you could hardly manage a modern dialogue on marriage, but the Day of Judgment would be quite easy.

After leaving school, Dickens found employment as a clerk to Mr Blackmore, a solicitor, as one of those inconspicuous underclerks whom he afterwards turned to many grotesque uses. Here, no doubt, he met Lowten and Swiveller, Chuckster and Wobbler, in so far as such sacred creatures ever had embodiments on this lower earth. But it is typical of him that he had no fancy at all to remain a solicitor's clerk. The resolution to rise which had glowed in him even as a dawdling boy, when he gazed at Gads-hill, which had been darkened but not quite destroyed by his fall into the factory routine, which had been released again by his return to normal boyhood and the boundaries of school, was not likely to content itself now with the copying out of agreements. He set to work, without any advice or help, to learn to be a reporter. He worked all day at law, and then all night at shorthand. It is an art which can only be effected by time, and he had to effect it by over-time. But learning the thing under every disadvantage, without a teacher, without the possibility of concentration or complete mental force, without ordinary human sleep, he made himself one of the most rapid reporters then alive. There is a curious contrast between the casualness of the mental training to which his parents and others subjected him and the savage seriousness of the training to which he subjected himself. Somebody once asked old John Dickens where his son Charles was educated. 'Well, really,' said the great creature, in his spacious way, 'he may be said – ah – to have educated himself.' He might indeed.

This practical intensity of Dickens is worth our dwelling on, because it illustrates an elementary antithesis in his character, or what appears as an antithesis in our modern popular psychology. We are always talking about strong men against weak men; but Dickens was not only both a weak man and a strong man, he was a very weak man and also a very strong man. He was everything that we currently call a weak man; he was a man hung on wires; he was a man who might at any moment cry like a child; he was so sensitive to criticism that one may say that he lacked a skin; he was so nervous that he allowed great tragedies in his life to arise only out of nerves. But in the matter where all ordinary strong men are miserably weak – in the matter of concentrated toil and clear purpose and unconquerable worldly courage – he was like a straight sword. Mrs Carlyle, who in her human epithets often hit the right nail so that it rang, said of him once, 'He has a face made of steel.' This was probably felt in a flash when she saw, in some social crowd, the clear, eager face of Dickens cutting through those near him like a knife. Any people who had met him from year to year would each year have found a man weakly troubled about his worldly decline; and each year they would have found him higher up in the world. His was a character very hard for any man of slow and placable temperament to understand; he was the character whom anybody can hurt and nobody can kill.

When he began to report in the House of Commons he was still only nineteen. His father, who had been released from his prison a short time before Charles had been released from his, had also become, among many other things, a reporter. But old John Dickens could enjoy doing anything without any particular aspiration after doing it well. But Charles was of a very different temper. He was, as I have said, consumed with an enduring and almost angry thirst to excel. He learnt shorthand with a dark self-devotion as if it were a sacred hieroglyph. Of this self-instruction, as of everything else, he has left humorous and illuminating phrases. He describes how, after he had learnt the whole exact alphabet, 'there then appeared a procession of new horrors, called arbitrary characters – the most despotic characters I have ever known; who insisted, for instance, that a thing like the beginning of a cobweb meant "expectation", and that a pen-and-ink skyrocket stood for "disadvantageous" '. He concludes, 'It was almost heartbreaking.' But it is significant that somebody else, a colleague of his, concluded, 'There never *was* such a shorthand writer.'

Dickens succeeded in becoming a shorthand writer; succeeded in becoming a reporter; succeeded ultimately in becoming a highly effective journalist. He was appointed as a reporter of the speeches in Parliament, first by *The True Sun*, then by *The Mirror of Parliament*, and last by *The Morning Chronicle*. He reported the speeches very well, and if we must analyse his internal opinions, much better than they deserved. For it must be remembered that this lad went into the reporters' gallery full of the triumphant Radicalism which was then the rising tide of the world. He was, it must be confessed, very little overpowered by the dignity of the Mother of Parliaments: he regarded the House of Commons much as he regarded the House of Lords, as a sort of venerable joke. It was, perhaps, while he watched, pale with weariness from the reporters' gallery, that there sank into him a thing that never left him, his unfathomable contempt for the British Constitution. Then perhaps he heard from the Government benches the immortal apologies of the Circumlocution Office. 'Then would the noble lord or right honourable gentleman, in whose department it was to defend the Circumlocution Office, put an orange in his pocket, and make a regular field-day of the occasion. Then would he come down to that house with a slap upon the table and meet the honourable gentleman foot to foot. Then would he be there to tell that honourable gentleman that the Circumlocution Office was not only blameless in this matter, but was commendable in this matter, was extollable to the skies in this matter. Then would he be there to tell that honourable gentleman that although the Circumlocution Office was invariably right, and wholly right, it never was so right as in this matter. Then would he be there to tell the honourable gentleman that it would have been more to his honour, more to his credit, more to his good taste, more to his good sense, more to half the dictionary of common places if he had left the Circumlocution Office alone and never approached this matter. Then would he keep one eye upon a coach or crammer from the Circumlocution Office below the bar, and smash the honourable gentleman with the Circumlocu-tion Office account of this matter. And although one of two things always happened; namely, either that the Circumlocution Office had nothing to say, and said it, or that it had something to say of which the noble lord or right honourable gentleman blundered one half and forgot the other; the Circumlocution Office was always voted immaculate by an accommodating majority.' We are now generally told that Dickens has destroyed these abuses, and that this is no longer a true picture of public life. Such, at any rate, is the Circumlocution Office account of this matter. But Dickens as a good Radical would, I fancy, much prefer that we should continue his battle than that we should celebrate his triumph; espe-cially when it has not come. England is still ruled by the great Barnacle family. Parliament is still ruled by the great Barnacle trinity – the solemn old Barnacle, who knew that the Circumlocu-tion Office was a protection, the sprightly young Barnacle who knew that it was a fraud, and the bewildered young Barnacle who knew nothing about it. From these three types our Cabinets are still exclusively recruited. People talk of the tyrannies and anoma-lies which Dickens denounced as things of the past like the Star Chamber. They believe that the days of the old stupid optimism and the old brutal indifference are gone for ever. In truth, this very belief is only the continuance of the old stupid optimism and the old brutal indifference. We believe in a free England and a pure England, because we still believe in the Circumlocution Office account of this matter. Undoubtedly our serenity is wide-spread. We believe that England is really reformed, we believe that Eng-land is really democratic, we believe that English politics are free from corruption. But this general satisfaction of ours does not show that Dickens has beaten the Barnacles. It only shows that the Barn-acles have beaten Dickens.

It cannot be too often said, then, that we must read into young Dickens and his works this old Radical tone towards institutions. That tone was a sort of happy impatience. And when Dickens had to listen for hours to the speech of the noble lord in defence of the Circumlocution Office, when, that is, he had to listen to what he regarded as the last vapourings of a vanishing oligarchy, the impatience rather predominated over the happiness. His incur-ably restless nature found more pleasure in the wandering side of journalism. He went about wildly in post-chaises to report political meetings for the *Morning Chronicle*. 'And what gentlemen they were to serve,' he exclaimed, 'in such things at the old *Morning Chronicle*. Great or small it did not matter. I have had to charge for half a dozen breakdowns in half a dozen times as many miles. I have had to charge for the damage of a great-coat from the drippings of a blazing wax candle, in writing through the smallest hours of the night in a swift flying carriage and pair.' And again, 'I have often transcribed for the printer from my shorthand notes important public speeches in which the strictest accuracy was required, and a mistake in which would have been to a young man severely compromising, writing on the palm of my hand, by the light of a dark lantern, in a post-chaise and four, galloping through a wild country and through the dead of the night, at the then surprising rate of fifteen miles an hour.' The whole of Dickens's life goes with the throb of that nocturnal gallop. All its real wildness shot through with an imaginative wickedness he afterwards uttered in the drive of Jonas Chuzzlewit through the storm.

All this time, and indeed from a time of which no measure can be taken, the creative part of his mind had been in a stir or even a fever. While still a small boy he had written for his own amusement some sketches of queer people he had met; notably, one of his uncle's barbers, whose principal hobby was pointing out what Napoleon ought to have done in the matter of military tactics. He had a notebook full of such sketches. He had sketches not only of persons, but of places, which were to him almost more personal than persons. In the December of 1833 he published one of these fragments in the *Old Monthly Magazine*. This was followed by nine others in the same paper, and when the paper (which was a romantically Radical venture, run by a veteran soldier of Bolivar) itself collapsed, Dickens continued the series in the *Evening Chronicle*, an off-shoot of the morning paper of the same name. These were the pieces afterwards published and known as the *Sketches by Boz*; and with them Dickens enters literature. He also enters upon many things about this time; he enters manhood, and among other things marriage. A friend of his on the *Chronicle*, George Hogarth, had several daughters. With all of them Dickens appears to have been on terms of great affection. This sketch is wholly literary, and I do not feel it necessary to do more than touch upon such incidents as his marriage, just as I shall do no more than touch upon the tragedy that ultimately overtook it. But it may be suggested here that the final misfortunes were in some degree due to the circumstances attending the original action. A very young man fighting his way, and excessively poor, with no memories for years past that were not monotonous and mean, and with his strongest and most personal memories quite ignominious and unendurable, was suddenly thrown into the society of a whole family of girls. I think it does not overstate his weakness, and I think it partly constitutes his excuse, to say that he fell in love with all of them. As sometimes happens in the undeveloped youth, an abstract femininity simply intoxicated him. And again, I think we shall not be mistakenly accused of harshness if we put the point in this way; that by a kind of accident he got hold of the wrong sister. In what came afterwards he was enormously to blame. But I do not think that his was a case of cold division from a woman whom he had once seriously and singly loved. He had been bewildered in a burning haze, I will not say even of first love, but of first flirtations. His wife's sisters stimulated him before he fell in love with his wife; and they continued to stimulate him long after he had quarrelled with her for ever. This view is strikingly supported by all the details of his attitude towards all the other members of the sacred house of Hogarth. One of the sisters remained, of course, his dearest friend till death. Another who had died, he worshipped as a saint, and he always asked to be buried in her grave. He was married on 2 April 1836. Forster remarks that a few days before the announcement of their marriage in *The Times*, the same paper contained another announcement that on the 31st would be published the first number of a work called *The Posthumous Papers of the Pickwick Club*. It is the beginning of his career.

The *Sketches*, apart from splendid splashes of humour here and there, are not manifestations of the man of genius. We might almost say that this book is one of the few books by Dickens which would not, standing alone, have made his fame. And yet standing alone it did make his fame. His contemporaries could see a new spirit in it, where we, familiar with the larger fruits of that spirit, can only see a continuation of the prosaic and almost wooden wit of the comic books of that day. But in any case we should hardly look in the man's first book for the fullness of his contribution to letters.

Youth is almost everything else, but it is hardly ever original. We read of young men bursting on the old world with a new message. But youth in actual experience is the period of imitation and even of obedience. Subjectively its emotions may be furious and head-long; but its only external outcome is a furious imitation and a headlong obedience. As we grow older we learn the special thing we have to do. As a man goes on towards the grave he discovers gradually a philosophy he can really call fresh, a style he can really call his own, and as he becomes an older man he becomes a newer writer. Ibsen, in his youth, wrote almost classic plays about vikings; it was in his old age that he began to break windows and throw fireworks. The only fault, it was said, of Browning's first poems was that they had 'too much beauty of imagery, and too little wealth of thought'. The only fault, that is, of Browning's first poems, was that they were not Browning's.

In one way, however, the *Sketches by Boz* do stand out very sym-bolically in the life of Dickens. They constitute in a manner the dedication of him to his especial task; the sympathetic and yet exaggerated painting of the poorer middle class. He was to make men feel that this dull middle class was actually a kind of elf-land. But here, again, the work is rude and undeveloped; and this is shown in the fact that it is a great deal more exaggerative than it is sympathetic. We are not, of course, concerned with the kind of people who say that they wish that Dickens was more refined. If those people are ever refined it will be by fire. But there is in this earliest work, an element which almost vanished in the later ones, an element which is typical of the middle classes in England, and which is in a more real sense to be called vulgar. I mean that in these little farces there is a trace, in the author as well as in the characters, of that petty sense of social precedence, that hub-bub of little unheard of oligarchies, which is the only serious sin of the bourgeoisie of Britain. It may seem pragmatical, for example, to instance such a rowdy farce as the story of Horatio Sparkins, which tells how a tuft-hunting family entertained a rhetorical youth think-ing he was a lord, and found he was a draper's assistant. No doubt they were very snobbish in thinking that a lord must be eloquent; but we cannot help feeling that Dickens is almost equally snobbish in feeling it so very funny that a draper's assistant should be elo-quent. A free man, one would think, would despise the family quite as much if Horatio had been a peer. Here, and here only, there is just a touch of the vulgarity, of the only vulgarity of the world out of which Dickens came. For the only element of lowness that there really is in our populace is exactly that they are full of superiorities and very conscious of class. Shades, imperceptible to the eyes of others, but as hard and haughty as a Brahmin caste, separate one kind of charwoman from another kind of charwoman. Dickens was destined to show with inspired symbolism all the immense virtues of the democracy. He was to show them as the most humorous part of our civilization; which they certainly are. He was to show them as the most promptly and practically compassionate part of our civilization; which they certainly are. The democracy has a hundred exuberant good qualities; the democracy has only one outstanding sin – it is not democratic.

IV
THE PICKWICK PAPERS

...In PICKWICK, and, indeed, in Dickens, generally it is in the details that the author is creative, it is in the details that he is vast. The power of the book lies in the perpetual torrent of ingenious and inventive treatment; the theme (at least at the beginning) simply does not exist. The idea of Tupman, the fat lady-killer, is in itself quite dreary and vulgar; it is the detailed Tupman, as he is developed, who is unexpectedly amusing. The idea of Winkle, the clumsy sportsman, is in itself quite stale; it is, as he goes on repeating himself, that he becomes original. We hear of men whose imagination can touch with magic the dull facts of our life, but Dickens's yet more indomitable fancy could touch with magic even our dull fiction. Before we are halfway through the book the stock characters of dead and damned farces astonish us like splendid strangers. . . .

In *The Pickwick Papers* Dickens sprang suddenly from a comparatively low level to a very high one. To the level of *Sketches by Boz* he never afterwards descended. To the level of *The Pickwick Papers* it is doubtful if he ever afterwards rose. *Pickwick*, indeed, is not a good novel, but it is not a bad novel, for it is not a novel at all. In one sense, indeed, it is something nobler than a novel, for no novel with a plot and a proper termination could emit that sense of everlasting youth – a sense as of the gods gone wandering in England. This is not a novel, for all novels have an end; and *Pickwick*, properly speaking, has no end – he is equal unto the angels. The point at which, as a fact, we find the printed matter terminates is not an end in any artistic sense of the word. Even as a boy I believed there were some more pages that were torn out of my copy, and I am looking for them still. The book might have been cut short anywhere else. It might have been cut short after Mr Pickwick was released by Mr Nupkins, or after Mr Pickwick was fished out of the water, or at a hundred other places. And we should still have known that this was not really the story's end.

We should have known that Mr Pickwick was still having the same
high adventures on the same high roads. As it happens, the book
ends after Mr Pickwick has taken a house in the neighbourhood
of Dulwich. But we know he did not stop there. We know he broke
out, that he took again the road of the high adventures; we know
that if we take it ourselves in any acre of England, we may come
suddenly upon him in a lane.

But this relation of *Pickwick* to the strict form of fiction demands
a further word, which should indeed be said in any case before the
consideration of any or all of the Dickens tales. Dickens's work is
not to be reckoned in novels at all. Dickens's work is to be reckoned
always by characters, sometimes by groups, oftener by episodes,
but never by novels. You cannot discuss whether *Nicholas Nickleby*
is a good novel, or whether *Our Mutual Friend* is a bad novel.
Strictly, there is no such novel as *Nicholas Nickleby*. There is no such
novel as *Our Mutual Friend*. They are simply lengths cut from the
flowing and mixed substance called Dickens – a substance of which
any given length will be certain to contain a given proportion of
brilliant and of bad stuff. You can say, according to your opinions,
'the Crummles part is perfect', or 'the Boffins are a mistake', just
as a man watching a river go by him could count here a floating
flower, and there a streak of scum. But you cannot artistically
divide the output into books. The best of his work can be found in
the worst of his works. *The Tale of Two Cities* is a good novel; *Little
Dorrit* is not a good novel. But the description of 'The Circumlocution Office' in *Little Dorrit* is quite as good as the description of
'Tellson's Bank' in *The Tale of Two Cities*. *The Old Curiosity Shop* is
not so good as *David Copperfield*, but Swiveller is quite as good as
Micawber. Nor is there any reason why these superb creatures, as
a general rule, should be in one novel any more than another.
There is no reason why Sam Weller, in the course of his wanderings, should not wander into *Nicholas Nickleby*. There is no reason
why Major Bagstock, in his brisk way, should not walk straight
out of *Dombey and Son* and straight into *Martin Chuzzlewit*. To this
generalization some modification should be added. *Pickwick* stands
by itself, and has even a sort of unity in not pretending to unity.
David Copperfield, in a less degree, stands by itself, as being the only
book in which Dickens wrote of himself; and *The Tale of Two Cities*
stands by itself as being the only book in which Dickens slightly

altered himself. But as a whole, this should be firmly grasped, that the units of Dickens, the primary elements, are not the stories, but the characters who affect the stories – or, more often still, the characters who do not affect the stories.

This is a plain matter; but, unless it be stated and felt, Dickens may be greatly misunderstood and greatly underrated. For not only is his whole machinery directed to facilitating the self-display of certain characters, but something more deep and more un-modern still is also true of him. It is also true that all the *moving* machinery exists only to display entirely *static* character. Things in the Dickens story shift and change only in order to give us glimpses of great characters that do not change at all. If we had a sequel of Pickwick ten years afterwards, Pickwick would be exactly the same age. We know he would not have fallen into that strange and beautiful second childhood which soothed and simplified the end of Colonel Newcome. Newcome, throughout the book, is in an atmosphere of time: Pickwick, throughout the book, is not. This will probably be taken by most modern people as praise of Thackeray and dispraise of Dickens. But this only shows how few modern people understand Dickens. It also shows how few understand the faiths and the fables of mankind. The matter can only be roughly stated in one way. Dickens did not strictly make a literature; he made a mythology.

For a few years our corner of Western Europe has had a fancy for this thing we call fiction; that is, for writing down our own lives or similar lives in order to look at them. But though we call it fiction, it differs from older literatures chiefly in being less fictitious. It imitates not only life, but the limitations of life; it not only reproduces life, it reproduces death. But outside us, in every other country, in every other age, there has been going on from the beginning a more fictitious kind of fiction. I mean the kind now called folklore, the literature of the people. Our modern novels, which deal with men as they are, are chiefly produced by a small and educated section of the society. But this other literature deals with men greater than they are – with demi-gods and heroes; and that is far too important a matter to be trusted to the educated classes. The fashioning of these portents is a popular trade, like ploughing or bricklaying; the men who made hedges, the men who made ditches, were the men who made deities. Men could not elect their kings, but they could elect their gods. So we find ourselves faced with a fundamental contrast between what is called fiction and what is called folklore. The one exhibits an abnormal degree of dexterity operating within our daily limitations; the other exhibits quite normal desires extended beyond those limitations. Fiction means the common things as seen by the uncommon people. Fairy tales mean the uncommon things as seen by the common people.

As our world advances through history towards its present epoch, it becomes more specialist, less democratic, and folklore turns gradually into fiction. But it is only slowly that the old elfin fire fades into the light of common realism. For ages after our characters have dressed up in the clothes of mortals they betray the blood of the gods. Even our phrascology is full of relics of this. When a modern novel is devoted to the bewilderments of a weak young clerk who cannot decide which woman he wants to marry, or which new religion he believes in, we still give this knock-kneed cad the name of 'the hero' – the name which is the crown of Achilles. The popular preference for a story with 'a happy ending' is not, or at least was not, a mere sweet-stuff optimism; it is the remains of the old idea of the triumph of the dragon-slayer, the ultimate apotheosis of the man beloved of heaven.

But there is another and more intangible trace of this fading supernaturalism – a trace very vivid to the reader, but very elusive to the critic. It is a certain air of endlessness in the episodes, even in the shortest episodes – a sense that, although we leave them, they still go on. Our modern attraction to short stories is not an accident of form; it is the sign of a real sense of fleetingness and fragility; it means that existence is only an impression, and, perhaps, only an illusion. A short story of today has the air of a dream; it has the irrevocable beauty of a falsehood; we get a glimpse of grey streets of London or red plains of India, as in an opium vision; we see people – arresting people with fiery and appealing faces. But when the story is ended, the people are ended. We have no instinct of anything ultimate and enduring behind the episodes. The moderns, in a word, describe life in short stories because they are possessed with the sentiment that life itself is an uncommonly short story, and perhaps not a true one. But in this elder literature, even in the comic literature (indeed, especially in the comic literature), the reverse is true. The characters are felt to be fixed things of which we have fleeting glimpses; that is, they are felt to be divine. Uncle Toby is talking for ever, as the elves are dancing for ever. We feel that whenever we hammer on the house of Falstaff, Falstaff will be at home. We feel it as a Pagan would feel, that, if a cry broke the silence after ages of unbelief, Apollo would still be listening in his temple. These writers may tell short stories, but we feel they are only parts of a long story. And herein lies the peculiar significance, the peculiar sacredness even, of penny dreadfuls and the common printed matter made for our errand-boys. Here in dim and desperate forms, under the ban of our base culture, stormed at by silly magistrates, sneered at by silly schoolmasters, – here is the old popular literature still popular; here is the unmistakable voluminousness, the thousand and one tales of Dick Deadshot, like the thousand and one tales of Robin Hood. Here is the splendid and static boy, the boy who remains a boy through a thousand volumes and a thousand years. Here in mean alleys and dim shops shadowed and shamed by the police, mankind is still driving its dark trade in heroes. And elsewhere, and in all other ages, in braver fashion, under cleaner skies, the same eternal tale-telling goes on, and the whole mortal world is a factory of immortals.

Dickens was a mythologist rather than a novelist; he was the last of the mythologists, and perhaps the greatest. He did not always manage to make his characters men, but he always managed, at the least, to make them gods. They are creatures like Punch or Father Christmas. They live statically, in a perpetual summer of being themselves. It was not the aim of Dickens to show the effect of time and circumstance upon a character; it was not even his aim to show the effect of a character on time and circumstance. It is worth remark, in passing, that whenever he tried to describe change in a character, he made a mess of it, as in the repentance of Dombey or the apparent deterioration of Boffin. It was his aim to show character hung in a kind of happy void, in a world apart from time – yes, and essentially apart from circumstance, though the phrase may seem odd in connection with the godlike horse-play of *Pickwick*. But all the Pickwickian events, wild as they often are, were only designed to display the greater wildness of souls, or sometimes merely to bring the reader within touch, so to speak, of that wildness. The author would have fired Mr Pickwick out of a cannon to get him to Wardle's by Christmas; he would have taken the roof

off to drop him into Bob Sawyer's party. But once put Pickwick at
Wardle's, with his punch and a group of gorgeous personalities,
and nothing will move him from his chair. Once he is at Sawyer's
party, he forgets how he got there; he forgets Mrs Bardell and all
his story. For the story was but an incantation to call up a god, and
the god (Mr Jack Hopkins) is present in divine power. Once the
great characters are face to face, the ladder by which they climbed
is forgotten and falls down, the structure of the story drops to
pieces, the plot is abandoned, the other characters deserted at
every kind of crisis; the whole crowded thoroughfare of the tale is
blocked by two or three talkers, who take their immortal ease as if
they were already in Paradise. For they do not exist for the story;
the story exists for them; and they know it.

To every man alive, one must hope, it has in some manner happened that he has talked with his more fascinating friends round a
table on some night when all the numerous personalities unfolded
themselves like great tropical flowers. All fell into their parts as in
some delightful impromptu play. Every man was more himself
than he had ever been in this vale of tears. Every man was a beautiful caricature of himself. The man who has known such nights will
understand the exaggerations of *Pickwick*. The man who has not
known such nights will not enjoy *Pickwick* nor (I imagine) heaven.
For, as I have said, Dickens is, in this matter, close to popular religion, which is the ultimate and reliable religion. He conceives an
endless joy; he conceives creatures as permanent as Puck or Pan –
creatures whose will to live aeons upon aeons cannot satisfy. He is
not come, as a writer, that his creatures may copy life and copy its
narrowness; he is come that they may have life, and that they may
have it more abundantly. It is absurd indeed that Christians should
be called the enemies of life because they wish life to last for ever;
it is more absurd still to call the old comic writers dull because they
wished their unchanging characters to last for ever. Both popular
religion, with its endless joys, and the old comic story, with its endless jokes, have in our time faded together. We are too weak to
desire that undying vigour. We believe that you can have too much
of a good thing – a blasphemous belief, which at one blow wrecks
all the heavens that men have hoped for. The grand old defiers of
God were not afraid of an eternity of torment. We have come to
be afraid of an eternity of joy. It is not my business here to take

sides in this division between those who like life and long novels and those who like death and short stories; my only business is to point out that those who see in Dickens's unchanging characters and recurring catchwords a mere stiffness and lack of living movement miss the point and nature of his work. His tradition is another tradition altogether; his aim is another aim altogether to those of the modern novelists who trace the alchemy of experience and the autumn tints of character. He is there, like the common people of all ages, to make deities; he is there, as I have said, to exaggerate life in the direction of life. The spirit he at bottom celebrates is that of two friends drinking wine together and talking through the night. But for him they are two deathless friends talking through an endless night and pouring wine from an inexhaustible bottle.

This, then, is the first firm fact to grasp about *Pickwick* – about *Pickwick* more than about any of the other stories. It is, first and foremost, a supernatural story. Mr Pickwick was a fairy. So was old Mr Weller. This does not imply that they were suited to swing in a trapeze of gossamer; it merely implies that if they had fallen out of it on their heads they would not have died. But, to speak more strictly, Mr Samuel Pickwick is not the fairy; he is the fairy prince; that is to say, he is the abstract wanderer and wonderer, the Ulysses of comedy; the half-human and half-elfin creature – human enough to wander, human enough to wonder, but still sustained with that merry fatalism that is natural to immortal beings – sustained by that hint of divinity which tells him in the darkest hour that he is doomed to live happily ever afterwards. He has set out walking to the end of the world, but he knows he will find an inn there.

And this brings us to the best and boldest element of originality in *Pickwick*. It has not, I think, been observed, and it may be that Dickens did not observe it. Certainly he did not plan it; it grew gradually, perhaps out of the unconscious part of his soul, and warmed the whole story like a slow fire. Of course it transformed the whole story also; transformed it out of all likeness to itself. About this latter point was waged one of the numberless little wars of Dickens. It was a part of his pugnacious vanity that he refused to admit the truth of the mildest criticism. Moreover, he used his inexhaustible ingenuity to find an apologia that was generally an afterthought. Instead of laughingly admitting, in answer to criticism, the glorious improbability of Pecksniff, he retorted with a sneer, clever and very unjust, that he was not surprised that the Pecksniffs should deny the portrait of Pecksniff. When it was objected that the pride of old Paul Dombey breaks as abruptly as a stick, he tried to make out that there had been an absorbing psychological struggle going on in that gentleman all the time, which the reader was too stupid to perceive. Which is, I am afraid, rubbish. And so, in a similar vein, he answered those who pointed out to him the obvious and not very shocking fact that our sentiments about Pickwick are very different in the second part of the book from our sentiments in the first; that we find ourselves at the beginning setting out in the company of a farcical old fool, if not a farcical old humbug, and that we find ourselves at the end saying farewell to a fine old English merchant, a monument of genial sanity. Dickens answered with the same ingenious self-justification as in the other cases – that surely it often happened that a man met us first arrayed in his more grotesque qualities, and that fuller acquaintance unfolded his more serious merits. This, of course, is quite true; but I think any honest admirer of *Pickwick* will feel that it is not an answer. For the fault in *Pickwick* (if it be a fault) is a change not in the hero but in the whole atmosphere. The point is not that Pickwick turns into a different kind of man; it is that *The Pickwick Papers* turns into a different kind of book. And however artistic both parts may be, this combination must, in strict art, be called inartistic. A man is quite artistically justified in writing a tale in which a man as cowardly as Bob Acres becomes a man as brave as Hector. But a man is not artistically justified in writing a tale which begins in the style of *The Rivals* and ends in the style of the *Iliad*. In other words, we do not mind the hero changing in the course of a book; but we are not prepared for the author changing in the course of the book. And the author did change in the course of this book. He made, in the midst of this book, a great discovery, which was the discovery of his destiny, or, what is more important, of his duty. That discovery turned him from the author of *Sketches by Boz* to the author of *David Copperfield*. And that discovery constituted the thing of which I have spoken – the outstanding and arresting original feature in *The Pickwick Papers*.

Pickwick, I have said, is a romance of adventure, and Samuel Pickwick is the romantic adventurer. So much is indeed obvious. But the strange and stirring discovery which Dickens made was this

– that having chosen a fat old man of the middle classes as a good thing of which to make a butt, he found that a fat old man of the middle classes is the very best thing of which to make a romantic adventurer. *Pickwick* is supremely original in that it is the adventures of an old man. It is a fairy tale in which the victor is not the youngest of the three brothers, but one of the oldest of their uncles. The result is both noble and new and true. There is nothing which so much needs simplicity as adventure. And there is no one who so much possesses simplicity as an honest and elderly man of business. For romance he is better than a troop of young troubadours; for the swaggering young fellow anticipates his adventures, just as he anticipates his income. Hence both the adventures and the income, when he comes up to them, are not there. But a man in late middle age has grown used to the plain necessities, and his first holiday is a second youth. A good man, as Thackeray said with such thorough and searching truth, grows simpler as he grows older. Samuel Pickwick in his youth was probably an insufferable young coxcomb. He knew then, or thought he knew, all about the confidence tricks of swindlers like Jingle. He knew then, or thought he knew, all about the amatory designs of sly ladies like Mrs Bardell. But years and real life have relieved him of this idle and evil knowledge. He has had the high good luck in losing the follies of youth to lose the wisdom of youth also. Dickens has caught, in a manner at once wild and convincing, this queer innocence of the afternoon of life. The round, moon-like face, the round, moon-like spectacles of Samuel Pickwick move through the tale as emblems of a certain spherical simplicity. They are fixed in that grave surprise that may be seen in babies; that grave surprise which is the only real happiness that is possible to man. Pickwick's round face is like a round and honourable mirror, in which are reflected all the fantasies of earthly existence; for surprise is, strictly speaking, the only kind of reflection. All this grew gradually on Dickens. It is odd to recall to our minds the original plan, the plan of the Nimrod Club, and the author who was to be wholly occupied in playing practical jokes on his characters. He had chosen (or somebody else had chosen) that corpulent old simpleton as a person peculiarly fitted to fall down trap-doors, to shoot over butter slides, to struggle with apple-pie beds, to be tipped out of carts and dipped into horse-ponds. But Dickens, and Dickens only, discovered as he went on how fitted the fat old man was to rescue ladies, to defy tyrants, to dance, to leap to experiment with life, to be a *deus ex machinâ* and even a knight errant. Dickens made this discovery. Dickens went into the Pickwick Club to scoff, and Dickens remained to pray.

Molière and his marquises are very much amused when M. Jourdain, the fat old middle-class fellow, discovers with delight that he has been talking prose all his life. I have often wondered whether Molière saw how in this fact M. Jourdain towers above them all and touches the stars. He has the freshness to enjoy a fresh fact, the freshness to enjoy even an old one. He can feel that the common thing prose is an accomplishment like verse; and it is an accomplishment like verse; it is the miracle of language. He can feel the subtle taste of water, and roll it on his tongue like wine. His simple vanity and voracity, his innocent love of living, his ignorant love of learning, are things far fuller of romance than the weariness and foppishness of the sniggering cavaliers. When he consciously speaks prose, he unconsciously thinks poetry. It would be better for us all if we were as conscious that supper is supper or that life is life, as this true romantic was that prose is actually prose. M. Jourdain is here the type, Mr Pickwick is elsewhere the type, of this true and neglected thing, the romance of the middle classes. It is the custom in our little epoch to sneer at the middle classes. Cockney artists profess to find the bourgeoisie dull; as if artists had any business to find anything dull. Decadents talk contemptuously of its conventions and its set tasks; it never occurs to them that conventions and set tasks are the very way to keep that greenness in the grass and that redness in the roses - which they have lost for ever. Stevenson, in his incomparable *Lantern Bearers*, describes the ecstasy of a schoolboy in the mere fact of buttoning a dark lantern under a dark great-coat. If you wish for that ecstasy of the schoolboy, you must have the boy; but you must also have the school. Strict opportunities and defined hours are the very outline of that enjoyment. A man like Mr Pickwick has been at school all his life, and when he comes out he astonishes the youngsters. His heart, as that acute psychologist, Mr Weller, points out, had been born later than his body. It will be remembered that Mr Pickwick also, when on the escapade of Winkle and Miss Allen, took immoderate pleasure in the performances of a dark lantern which was not dark enough, and was nothing but a nuisance to everybody. His soul also was with Stevenson's boys on the grey sands of Haddington, talking in the dark by the sea. He also was the league of the *Lantern Bearers*. Stevenson, I remember, says that in the shops of that town they could purchase 'penny Pickwicks (that remarkable cigar)'. Let us hope they smoked them, and that the rotund ghost of Pickwick hovered over the rings of smoke.

Pickwick goes through life with that god-like gullibility which is the key to all adventures. The greenhorn is the ultimate victor in everything; it is he that gets the most out of life. Because Pickwick is led away by Jingle, he will be led to the White Hart Inn, and see the only Weller cleaning boots in the courtyard. Because he is bamboozled by Dodson and Fogg, he will enter the prison house like a paladin, and rescue the man and the woman who have wronged him most. His soul will never starve for exploits or excitements who is wise enough to be made a fool of. He will make himself happy in the traps that have been laid for him; he will roll in their nets and sleep. All doors will fly open to him who has a mildness more defiant than mere courage. The whole is unerringly expressed in one fortunate phrase – he will be always 'taken in'. To be taken in everywhere is to see the inside of everything. It is the hospitality of circumstance. With torches and trumpets, like a guest, the greenhorn is taken in by Life. And the sceptic is cast out by it.

V

THE GREAT POPULARITY

THERE is one aspect of Charles Dickens which must be of interest even to that subterranean race which does not admire his books. Even if we are not interested in Dickens as a great event in English literature, we must still be interested in him as a great event in English history. If he had not his place with Fielding and Thackeray, he would still have his place with Wat Tyler[1] and Wilkes;[2] for the man led a mob. He did what no English statesman, perhaps, has really done; he called out the people. He was popular in a sense of which we moderns have not even a notion. In that sense there is no popularity now. There are no popular authors today.... A man reading the Dickens novel wished that it might never end. Men read a Dickens story six times because they knew it so well.... In short, the Dickens novel was popular, not because it was an unreal world, but because it was a real world; a world in which the soul could live. The modern 'shocker' at its very best is an interlude in life. But in the days when Dickens's work was coming out in serial, people talked as if real life were itself the interlude between one issue of *Pickwick* and another.

In reaching the period of the publication of *Pickwick*, we reach this sudden apotheosis of Dickens. Henceforward he filled the literary world in a way hard to imagine. Fragments of that huge fashion remain in our daily language; in the talk of every trade or public question are embedded the wrecks of that enormous religion. Men give out the airs of Dickens without even opening his books; just as Catholics can live in a tradition of Christianity without having looked at the New Testament.... There are no modern Bumbles and Pecksniffs, no modern Gamps and Micawbers. Mr Rudyard Kipling (to take an author of a higher type than those before mentioned) is called, and called justly, a popular author; that is to say, he is widely read, greatly enjoyed, and highly

1 Leader of the Peasants' Revolt or Great Rising of 1381.
2 John Wilkes (1727–97), radical journalist and politician.

remunerated; he has achieved the paradox of at once making poetry and making money. But let any one who wishes to see the difference try the experiment of assuming the Kipling characters to be common property like the Dickens characters. Let any one go into an average parlour and allude to Strickland as he would allude to Mr Bumble, the Beadle. Let any one say that somebody is 'a perfect Learoyd', as he would say 'a perfect Pecksniff'. Let any one write a comic paragraph for a halfpenny paper, and allude to Mrs Hawksbee instead of to Mrs Gamp. He will soon discover that the modern world has forgotten its own fiercest booms more completely than it has forgotten this formless tradition from its fathers. The mere dregs of it come to more than any contemporary excitement; the gleaning of the grapes of *Pickwick* is more than the whole vintage of *Soldiers Three*. There is one instance, and I think only one, of an exception to this generalization; there is one figure in our popular literature which would really be recognized by the populace. Ordinary men would understand you if you referred currently to Sherlock Holmes. Sir Arthur Conan Doyle would no doubt be justified in rearing his head to the stars, remembering that Sherlock Holmes is the only really familiar figure in modern fiction. But let him droop that head again with a gentle sadness, remembering that if Sherlock Holmes is the only familiar figure in modern fiction, Sherlock Holmes is also the only familiar figure in the Sherlock Holmes tales. Not many people could say offhand what was the name of the owner of Silver Blaze, or whether Mrs Watson was dark or fair. But if Dickens had written the Sherlock Holmes stories, every character in them would have been equally arresting and memorable. A Sherlock Holmes would have cooked the dinner for Sherlock Holmes; a Sherlock Holmes would have driven his cab. If Dickens brought in a man merely to carry a letter, he had time for a touch or two, and made him a giant. Dickens not only conquered the world, he conquered it with minor characters. Mr John Smauker, the servant of Mr Cyrus Bantam, though he merely passes across the stage, is almost as vivid to us as Mr Samuel Weller, the servant of Mr Samuel Pickwick. The young man with the lumpy forehead, who only says 'Esker' to Mr Podsnap's foreign gentleman, is as good as Mr Podsnap himself. They appear only for a fragment of time, but they belong to eternity. We have them only for an instant, but they have us for ever.

In dealing with Dickens, then, we are dealing with a man whose public success was a marvel and almost a monstrosity. And here I perceive that my friend, the purely artistic critic, primed with Flaubert and Turgenev, can contain himself no longer. He leaps to his feet, upsetting his cup of cocoa, and asks contemptuously what all this has to do with criticism. 'Why begin your study of an author,' he says, 'with trash about popularity? . . . The people like bad literature. If your object is to show that Dickens was good literature, you should rather apologize for his popularity, and try to explain it away. You should seek to show that Dickens's work was good literature, although it was popular. Yes, that is your task, to prove that Dickens was admirable, although he was admired!'

I ask the artistic critic to be patient for a little and to believe that I have a serious reason for registering this historic popularity. To that we shall come presently. But as a manner of approach I may perhaps ask leave to examine this actual and fashionable statement, to which I have supposed him to have recourse – the statement that the people likes bad literature, and even likes literature because it is bad. This way of stating the thing is an error, and in that error lies matter of much import to Dickens and his destiny in letters. The public does not like bad literature. The public likes a certain kind of literature and likes that kind of literature even when it is bad better than another kind of literature even when it is good. Nor is this unreasonable; for the line between different types of literature is as real as the line between tears and laughter; and to tell people who can only get bad comedy that you have some first-class tragedy is as irrational as to offer a man who is shivering over weak warm coffee a really superior sort of ice. . . .

Dickens stands first as a defiant monument of what happens when a great literary genius has a literary taste akin to that of the community. For this kinship was deep and spiritual. Dickens was not like our ordinary demagogues and journalists. Dickens did not write what the people wanted. Dickens wanted what the people wanted. And with this was connected that other fact which must never be forgotten, and which I have more than once insisted on, that Dickens and his school had a hilarious faith in democracy and thought of the service of it as a sacred priesthood. Hence there was this vital point in his popularism, that there was no condescension in it. The belief that the rabble will only read rubbish can be read between the lines of all our contemporary writers, even of those writers whose rubbish the rabble reads. . . . The only difference lies between those writers who will consent to talk down to the people, and those writers who will not consent to talk down to the people. But Dickens never talked down to the people. He talked up to the people. He approached the people like a deity and poured out his riches and his blood. This is what makes the immortal bond between him and the masses of men. He had not merely produced something they could understand, but he took it seriously, and toiled and agonized to produce it. They were not only enjoying one of the best writers, they were enjoying the best he could do. His raging and sleepless nights, his wild walks in the darkness, his notebooks crowded, his nerves in rags, all this extraordinary output was but a fit sacrifice to the ordinary man. He climbed towards the lower classes. He panted upwards on weary wings to reach the heaven of the poor.

His power, then, lay in the fact that he expressed with an energy and brilliancy quite uncommon the things close to the common mind. But with this mere phrase, the common mind, we collide with a current error. Commonness and the common mind are now generally spoken of as meaning in some manner inferiority and the inferior mind; the mind of the mere mob. But the common mind means the mind of all the artists and heroes; or else it would not be common. Plato had the common mind; Dante had the common mind; or that mind was not common. Commonness means the quality common to the saint and the sinner, to the philosopher and the fool; and it was this that Dickens grasped and developed. In everybody there is a certain thing that loves babies, that fears death, that likes sunlight: that thing enjoys Dickens. . . . And when I say that everybody understands Dickens I do not mean that he is suited to the untaught intelligence. I mean that he is so plain that even scholars can understand him.

The best expression of the fact, however, is to be found in noting the two things in which he is most triumphant. In order of artistic value, next after his humour, comes his horror. And both his humour and his horror are of a kind strictly to be called human; that is, they belong to the basic part of us, below the lowest roots of our variety. His horror for instance is a healthy churchyard horror, a fear of the grotesque defamation called death; and this every man has, even if he also has the more delicate and depraved fears that come of an evil spiritual outlook. . . . In a word, Dickens does, in the exact sense, make the flesh creep; he does not, like the decadents, make the soul crawl. And the creeping of the flesh on being reminded of its fleshly failure is a strictly universal thing which we can all feel, while some of us are as yet uninstructed in the art of spiritual crawling. In the same way the Dickens mirth is a part of man and universal. All men can laugh at broad humour, even the subtle humorists. Even the modern *flâneur*, who can smile at a particular combination of green and yellow, would laugh at Mr Lammle's request for Mr Fledgeby's nose. In a word – the common things are common – even to the uncommon people.

These two primary dispositions of Dickens, to make the flesh creep and to make the sides ache, were a sort of twins of his spirit; they were never far apart and the fact of their affinity is interestingly exhibited in the first two novels.

Generally he mixed the two up in a book and mixed a great many other things with them. As a rule he cared little if he kept six stories of quite different colours running in the same book. The effect was sometimes similar to that of playing six tunes at once. He does not mind the coarse tragic figure of Jonas Chuzzlewit crossing the mental stage which is full of the allegorical pantomime of Eden, Mr Chollop and the *Watertoast Gazette*, a scene which is as much of a satire as *Gulliver*, and nearly as much of a fairy tale. He does not mind binding up a rather pompous sketch of prostitution in the same book with an adorable impossibility like Bunsby. But *Pickwick* is so far a coherent thing that it is coherently comic and consistently rambling. And as a consequence his next book was, upon the whole, coherently and consistently horrible. As his natural turn for terrors was kept down in *Pickwick*, so his natural turn for joy and laughter is kept down in *Oliver Twist*. In *Oliver Twist* the smoke of the thieves' kitchen hangs over the whole tale, and the shadow of Fagin falls everywhere. The little lamp-lit rooms of Mr Brownlow and Rose Maylie are to all appearance purposely kept subordinate, a mere foil to the foul darkness without. It was a strange and appropriate accident that Cruikshank and not 'Phiz' should have illustrated this book. There was about Cruikshank's art a kind of cramped energy which is almost the definition of the criminal mind. His drawings have a dark strength: yet he does not only draw morbidly, he draws meanly. In the doubled-up figure and frightful eyes of Fagin in the condemned cell there is not only a baseness of subject; there is a kind of baseness in the very technique of it. It is not drawn with the free lines of a free man; it has the half-witted secrecies of a hunted thief. It does not look merely like a picture of Fagin; it looks like a picture by Fagin. Among these dark and detestable plates there is one which has with a kind of black directness, the dreadful poetry that does inhere in the story, stumbling as it often is. It represents Oliver asleep at an open window in the house of one of his humaner patrons. And outside the window, but as big and close as if they were in the room, stand Fagin and the foul-faced Monk, staring at him with dark monstrous visages and great white wicked eyes, in the style of the simple devilry of the draughtsman. The very *naïveté* of the horror is horrifying: the very woodenness of the two wicked men seems to make them worse than mere men who are wicked. But this picture of big devils at the window-sill does express, as has been suggested above, the thread of poetry in the whole thing; the sense, that is, of the thieves as a kind of army of devils compassing earth and sky crying for Oliver's soul and besieging the house in which he is barred for safety. In this matter there is, I think, a difference between the author and the illustrator. In Cruikshank there was surely something morbid; but, sensitive and sentimental as Dickens was, there was nothing morbid in him. He had, as Stevenson had, more of the mere boy's love of suffocating stories of blood and darkness; of skulls, of gibbets, of all the things, in a word, that are sombre without being sad. There is a ghastly joy in remembering our boyish reading about Sikes and his flight; especially about the voice of that unbearable pedlar which went on in a monotonous and maddening sing-song, 'will wash out grease-stains, mud-stains, blood-stains', until Sikes fled almost screaming. For this boyish mixture of appetite and repugnance there is a good popular phrase, 'supping on horrors'. Dickens supped on horrors as he supped on Christmas pudding. He supped on horrors because he was an optimist and could sup on anything. There was no saner or simpler schoolboy than Traddles, who covered all his books with skeletons.

Oliver Twist had begun in Bentley's *Miscellany*, which Dickens edited in 1837. It was interrupted by a blow that for the moment broke the author's spirit and seemed to have broken his heart. His wife's sister, Mary Hogarth, died suddenly. To Dickens his wife's family seems to have been like his own; his affections were heavily committed to the sisters, and of this one he was peculiarly fond. All his life, through much conceit and sometimes something bordering on selfishness, we can feel the redeeming note of an almost tragic tenderness; he was a man who could really have died of love or sorrow. He took up the work of *Oliver Twist* again later in the year, and finished it at the end of 1838. His work was incessant and almost bewildering. In 1838 he had already brought out the first number of *Nicholas Nickleby*. But the great popularity went booming on; the whole world was roaring for books by Dickens, and more books by Dickens, and Dickens was labouring night and day like a factory....

Nicholas Nickleby is the most typical perhaps of the tone of his earlier works. It is in form a very rambling, old-fashioned romance, the kind of romance in which the hero is only a convenience for the frustration of the villain. Nicholas is what is called in theatricals a stick. But any stick is good enough to beat a Squeers with. That strong thwack, that simplified energy is the whole object of such a story; and the whole of this tale is full of a kind of highly picturesque platitude. The wicked aristocrats, Sir Mulberry Hawk, Lord Verisopht and the rest are inadequate versions of the fashionable profligate. But this is not (as some suppose) because Dickens in his vulgarity could not comprehend the refinement of patrician vice. There is no idea more vulgar or more ignorant than the notion that a gentleman is generally what is called refined. The error of the Hawk conception is that, if anything, he is too refined. Real aristocratic blackguards do not swagger and rant so well. A real fast baronet would not have defined Nicholas in the tavern with so much oratorical dignity. A real fast baronet would probably have been choked with apoplectic embarrassment and said nothing at all. But Dickens read into this aristocracy a grandiloquence and a natural poetry which, like all melodrama, is really the precious jewel of the poor.

But the book contains something which is much more Dickensian. It is exquisitely characteristic of Dickens that the truly great achievement of the story is the person who delays the story. Mrs Nickleby, with her beautiful mazes of memory, does her best to prevent the story of Nicholas Nickleby from being told. And she does well. There is no particular necessity that we should know

what happens to Madeline Bray. There is a desperate and crying
necessity that we should know that Mrs Nickleby once had a foot-
boy who had a wart on his nose and a driver who had a green shade
over his left eye. If Mrs Nickleby is a fool, she is one of those fools
who are wiser than the world. She stands for a great truth which
we must not forget; the truth that experience is not in real life a
saddening thing at all. The people who have had misfortunes are
generally the people who love to talk about them. Experience is
really one of the gaieties of old age, one of its dissipations. Mere
memory becomes a kind of debauch. Experience may be disheartening to those who are foolish enough to try to co-ordinate it
and to draw deductions from it. But to those happy souls, like Mrs
Nickleby, to whom relevancy is nothing, the whole of their past life
is like an inexhaustible fairyland. Just as we take a rambling walk
because we know that a whole district is beautiful, so they indulge
a rambling mind because they know that a whole existence is
interesting. A boy does not plunge into his future more romantically and at random, than they plunge into their past.

Another gleam in the book is Mr Mantalini. Of him, as of all the
really great comic characters of Dickens, it is impossible to speak
with any critical adequacy. Perfect absurdity is a direct thing, like
physical pain, or a strong smell. A joke is a fact. However indefensible it is it cannot be attacked. However defensible it is it cannot be
defended. That Mr Mantalini should say in praising the 'outline' of
his wife, 'The two Countesses had no outlines, and the Dowager's
was a demd outline', – this can only be called an unanswerable
absurdity. . . . Dickens has greatly suffered with the critics precisely
through this stunning simplicity in his best work. The critic is called
upon to describe his sensations while enjoying Mantalini and
Micawber, and he can no more describe them than he can describe
a blow in the face. Thus Dickens, in this self-conscious, analytical
and descriptive age, loses both ways. He is doubly unfitted for the
best modern criticism. His bad work is below that criticism. His
good work is above it.

But gigantic as were Dickens's labours, gigantic as were the exactions from him, his own plans were more gigantic still. He had the
type of mind that wishes to do every kind of work at once; to do
everybody's work as well as its own. There floated before him a
vision of a monstrous magazine, entirely written by himself. It is

true that when this scheme came to be discussed, he suggested that other pens might be occasionally employed; but, reading between the lines, it is sufficiently evident that he thought of the thing as a kind of vast multiplication of himself, with Dickens as editor opening letters, Dickens as leader-writer writing leaders, Dickens as reporter reporting meetings, Dickens as reviewer reviewing books, Dickens, for all I know, as office-boy opening and shutting doors. This serial, of which he spoke to Messrs Chapman and Hall, began and broke off and remains as a colossal fragment bound together under the title of *Master Humphrey's Clock*. One characteristic thing he wished to have in the periodical. He suggested an Arabian Nights of London, in which Gog and Magog, the giants of the city, should give forth chronicles as enormous as themselves. He had a taste for these schemes or frameworks for many tales. He made and abandoned many; many he half-fulfilled. I strongly suspect that he meant Major Jackman, in 'Mrs Lirriper's Lodgings' and 'Mrs Lirriper's Legacy', to start a series of studies of that lady's lodgers, a kind of history of No. 81, Norfolk Street, Strand. 'The Seven Poor Travellers' was planned for seven stories; we will not say seven poor stories. Dickens had meant, probably, to write a tale for each article of 'Somebody's Luggage': he only got as far as the hat and the boots. This gigantesque scale of literary architecture, huge and yet curiously cosy, is characteristic of his spirit, fond of size and yet fond of comfort. He liked to have story within story, like room within room of some labyrinthine but comfortable castle. In this spirit he wished *Master Humphrey's Clock* to begin, and to be a big frame or bookcase for numberless novels. The clock started; but the clock stopped.

In the prologue by Master Humphrey reappear Mr Pickwick and Sam Weller, and of that resurrection many things have been said, chiefly expressions of a reasonable regret. Doubtless they do not add much to their author's reputation, but they add a great deal to their author's pleasure. It was ingrained in him to wish to meet old friends. All his characters are, so to speak, designed to be old friends; in a sense every Dickens character is an old friend, even when he first appears. He comes to us mellow out of many implied interviews, and carries the firelight on his face. Dickens was simply pleased to meet Pickwick again, and being pleased, he made the old man too comfortable to be amusing.

But *Master Humphrey's Clock* is now scarcely known except as the shell of one of the well-known novels. *The Old Curiosity Shop* was published in accordance with the original *Clock* scheme. Perhaps the most typical thing about it is the title. There seems no reason in particular, at the first and most literal glance, why the story should be called after the Old Curiosity Shop. Only two of the characters have anything to do with such a shop, and they leave it for ever in the first few pages. It is as if Thackeray had called the whole novel of *Vanity Fair* 'Miss Pinkerton's Academy'. It is as if Scott had given the whole story of *The Antiquary* the title of 'The Hawes Inn'. But when we feel the situation with more fidelity we realize that this title is something in the nature of a key to the whole Dickens romance. His tales always started from some splendid hint in the streets. And shops, perhaps the most poetical of all things, often set off his fancy galloping. Every shop, in fact, was to him the door of romance. Among all the huge serial schemes of which we have spoken, it is a matter of wonder that he never started an endless periodical called 'The Street', and divided it into shops. He could have written an exquisite romance called 'The Baker's Shop'; another called 'The Chemist's Shop'; another called 'The Oil Shop', to keep company with *The Old Curiosity Shop*. Some incomparable baker he invented and forgot. Some gorgeous chemist might have been. Some more than mortal oil-man is lost to us for ever. This Old Curiosity Shop he did happen to linger by: its tale he did happen to tell.

Around Little Nell, of course, a controversy raged and rages; some implored Dickens not to kill her at the end of the story: some regret that he did not kill her at the beginning. To me the chief interest in this young person lies in the fact that she is an example, and the most celebrated example of what must have been, I think, a personal peculiarity, perhaps a personal experience of Dickens. There is, of course, no paradox at all in saying that if we find in a good book a wildly impossible character it is very probable indeed that it was copied from a real person. This is one of the commonplaces of good art crticism. For although people talk of the restraints of fact and the freedom of fiction, the case for most artistic purposes is quite the other way. Nature is as free as air: art is forced to look probable. There may be a million things that do happen, and yet only one thing that convinces us as likely to happen. Out of a million possible things there may be only one appropriate thing. I fancy, therefore, that many stiff, unconvincing characters are copied from the wild freak-show of real life. And in many parts of Dickens's work there is evidence of some peculiar affection on his part for a strange sort of little girl; a little girl with a premature sense of responsibility and duty; a sort of saintly precocity. Did he know some little girl of this kind? Did she die, perhaps, and remain in his memory in colours too ethereal and pale? In any case there are a great number of them in his works. Little Dorrit was one of them, and Florence Dombey with her brother, and even Agnes in infancy; and, of course, Little Nell. And, in any case, one thing is evident; whatever charm these children may have they have not the charm of childhood. They are not little children: they are 'little mothers'. The beauty and divinity in a child lie in his not being worried, not being conscientious, not being like Little Nell. Little Nell has never any of the sacred bewilderment of a baby. She never wears that face, beautiful but almost half-witted, with which a real child half understands that there is evil in the universe.

As usual, however, little as the story has to do with the title, the splendid and satisfying pages have even less to do with the story. Dick Swiveller is perhaps the noblest of all the noble creations of Dickens. He has all the overwhelming absurdity of Mantalini, with the addition of being human and credible, for he knows he is absurd. His high-falutin is not done because he seriously thinks it right and proper, like that of Mr Snodgrass, nor is it done because he thinks it will serve his turn, like that of Mr Pecksniff, for both these beliefs are improbable; it is done because he really loves high-falutin, because he has a lonely literary pleasure in exaggerative language. Great draughts of words are to him like great draughts of wine – pungent and yet refreshing, light and yet leaving him in a glow. In unerring instinct for the perfect folly of a phrase he has no equal, even among the giants of Dickens. 'I am sure,' says Miss Wackles, when she had been flirting with Cheggs, the market-gardener, and reduced Mr Swiveller to Byronic renunciation, 'I am sure I'm very sorry if—' 'Sorry,' said Mr Swiveller, 'sorry in the possession of a Cheggs!' The abyss of bitterness is unfathomable. Scarcely less precious is the pose of Mr Swiveller when he imitates the stage brigand. After crying, 'Some wine here! Ho!' he hands the flagon to himself with profound humility, and receives it haughtily. Perhaps the very best scene in the book is that between Mr Swiveller and the single gentleman with whom he endeavours to remonstrate for having remained in bed all day: 'We cannot have single gentlemen coming into the place and sleeping like double gentlemen without paying extra. . . . An equal amount of slumber was never got out of one bed, and if you want to sleep like that you must pay for a double-bedded room.' His relations with the Marchioness are at once purely romantic and purely genuine; there is nothing even of Dickens's legitimate exaggerations about them. A shabby, larky, good-natured clerk would, as a matter of fact, spend hours in the society of a little servant girl if he found her about the house. It would arise partly from a dim kindliness, and partly from that mysterious instinct which is sometimes called, mistakenly, a love of low company – that mysterious instinct which makes so many men of pleasure find something soothing in the society of uneducated people, particularly uneducated women. It is the instinct which accounts for the otherwise unaccountable popularity of barmaids.

And still the pot of that huge popularity boiled. In 1841 another novel was demanded, and *Barnaby Rudge* supplied. It is chiefly of interest as an embodiment of that other element in Dickens, the picturesque or even the pictorial. Barnaby Rudge, the idiot with his rags and his feathers and his raven, the bestial hangman, the blind mob – all make a picture, though they hardly make a novel. One touch there is in it of the richer and more humorous Dickens, the boy-conspirator, Mr Sim Tappertit. But he might have been treated with more sympathy – with as much sympathy, for instance, as Mr Dick Swiveller; for he is only the romantic guttersnipe, the bright boy at the particular age when it is most fascinating to found a secret society and most difficult to keep a secret. And if ever there was a romantic guttersnipe on earth it was Charles Dickens. *Barnaby Rudge* is no more an historical novel than Sim's secret league was a political movement; but they are both beautiful creations. When all is said, however, the main reason for mentioning the work here is that it is the next bubble in the pot, the next thing that burst out of that whirling, seething head. The tide of it rose and smoked and sang till it boiled over the pot of Britain and poured over all America. In the January of 1842 he set out for the United States.

VI
DICKENS AND AMERICA

THE ESSENTIAL of Dickens's character was the conjunction of common sense with uncommon sensibility. The two things are not, indeed, in such an antithesis as is commonly imagined. Great English literary authorities, such as Jane Austen and Mr Chamberlain, have put the word 'sense' and the word 'sensibility' in a kind of opposition to each other. But not only are they not opposite words: they are actually the same word. They both mean receptiveness or approachability by the facts outside us. To have a sense of colour is the same as to have a sensibility to colour. A person who realizes that beef-steaks are appetizing shows his sensibility. A person who realizes that moonrise is romantic shows his sense. But it is not difficult to see the meaning and need of the popular distinction between sensibility and sense, particularly in the form called common sense. Common sense is a sensibility duly distributed in all normal directions; sensibility has come to mean a specialized sensibility in one. This is unfortunate, for it is not the sensibility that is bad, but the specializing; that is, the lack of sensibility to everything else. A young lady who stays out all night to look at the stars should not be blamed for her sensibility to starlight, but for her insensibility to other people. A poet who recites his own verses from ten to five with the tears rolling down his face should decidedly be rebuked for his lack of sensibility – his lack of sensibility to those grand rhythms of the social harmony, crudely called manners. For all politeness is a long poem, since it is full of recurrences. This balance of all the sensibilities we call sense; and it is in this capacity that it becomes of great importance as an attribute of the character of Dickens.

Dickens, I repeat, had common sense and uncommon sensibility. That is to say, the proportion of interests in him was about the same as that of an ordinary man, but he felt all of them more excitedly. This is a distinction not easy for us to keep in mind, because we hear today chiefly of two types, the dull man who likes ordinary things mildly, and the extraordinary man who likes extraordinary things wildly. But Dickens liked quite ordinary things; he merely made an extraordinary fuss about them. His excitement was sometimes like an epileptic fit; but it must not be confused with the fury of the man of one idea or one line of ideas. He had the excess of the eccentric, but not the defects, the narrowness. Even when he raved like a maniac he did not rave like a monomaniac. He had no particular spot of sensibility or spot of insensibility: he was merely a normal man minus a normal self-command. He had no special point of mental pain or repugnance, like Ruskin's horror of steam and iron, or Mr Bernard Shaw's permanent irritation against romantic love. He was annoyed at the ordinary annoyances: only he was more annoyed than was neces-sary. He did not desire strange delights, blue wine or black women with Baudelaire, or cruel sights east of Suez with Mr Kipling. He wanted what a healthy man wants, only he was ill with wanting it. To understand him, in a word, we must keep well in mind the med-ical distinction between delicacy and disease. Perhaps we shall comprehend it and him more clearly if we think of a woman rather than a man. There was much that was feminine about Dickens, and nothing more so than this abnormal normality. A woman is often, in comparison with a man, at once more sensitive and more sane.

This distinction must be especially remembered in all his quarrels. And it must be most especially remembered in what may be called his great quarrel with America, which we have now to approach. The whole incident is so typical of Dickens's attitude to everything and anything, and especially of Dickens's attitude to anything political, that I may ask permission to approach the matter by another, a somewhat long and curving avenue.

Common sense is a fairy thread, thin and faint, and as easily lost as gossamer. Dickens (in large matters) never lost it. Take, as an example, his political tone or drift throughout his life. His views, of course, may have been right or wrong; the reforms he supported may have been successful or otherwise: that is not a matter for this book. But if we compare him with the other men that wanted the same things (or the other men that wanted the other things) we feel a startling absence of cant, a startling sense of humanity as it is, and of the eternal weakness. He was a fierce democrat, but in his best vein he laughed at the cocksure Radical of common life, the red-faced man who said, 'Prove it!' when anybody said anything. He fought for the right to elect: but he would not whitewash elections. He believed in Parliamentary government; but he did not, like our contemporary newspapers, pretend that Parliament is something much more heroic and imposing than it is. He fought for the rights of the grossly oppressed Nonconformists; but he spat out of his mouth the unction of that too easy seriousness with which they oiled everything, and held up to them like a horrible mirror the foul fat face of Chadband. He saw that Mr Podsnap thought too little of places outside England. But he saw that Mrs Jellaby thought too much of them. In the last book he wrote he gives us, in Mr Honeythunder, a hateful and wholesome picture of all the Liberal catchwords pouring out of one illiberal man. But perhaps the best evidence of this steadiness and sanity is the fact that, dogmatic as he was, he never tied himself to any passing dogma; he never got into any *cul de sac* of civic or economic fanaticism; he went down the broad road of the Revolution.... He was not even a politician of any kind. He was simply a man of very clear, airy judgment on things that did not inflame his private temper, and he perceived that any theory that tried to run the living State entirely on one force and motive was probably nonsense. Whenever the Liberal philosophy had embedded in it something hard and heavy and lifeless, by an instinct he dropped it out. He was too romantic, perhaps, but he would have to do only with real things. He may have cared too much about Liberty. But he cared nothing about *Laissez Faire*.

Now, among many interests of his contact with America this interest emerges as infinitely the largest and most striking, that it gave a final example of this queer, unexpected coolness and candour of his, this abrupt and sensational rationality. Apart altogether from any question of the accuracy of his picture of America, the American indignation was particularly natural and inevitable. For the large circumstances of the age must be taken into account. At the end of the previous epoch the whole of our Christian civilization had been startled from its sleep by trumpets to take sides in a bewildering Armageddon, often with eyes still misty. Germany and Austria found themselves on the side of the old order, France and America on the side of the new. England, as at the Reformation, took up eventually a dark middle position, maddeningly difficult to define. She created a democracy, but she kept an aristocracy: she reformed the House of Commons, but left the magistracy (as it is still) a mere league of gentlemen against the world. But underneath all this doubt and compromise there was in England a great and perhaps growing mass of dogmatic democracy; certainly thousands, probably millions expected a Republic in fifty years. And for these the first instinct was obvious. The first instinct was to look across the Atlantic to where lay a part of ourselves already Republican, the van of the advancing English on the road to liberty. Nearly all the great Liberals of the nineteenth century enormously idealized America. On the other hand, to the Americans, fresh from their first epic of arms, the defeated mother country, with its coronets and county magistrates, was only a broken feudal keep.

So much is self-evident. But nearly halfway through the nineteenth century there came out of England the voice of a violent satirist. In its political quality it seemed like the half-choked cry of the frustrated republic. It had no patience with the pretence that England was already free, that we had gained all that was valuable from the Revolution. It poured a cataract of contempt on the so-called working compromises of England, on the oligarchic cabinets, on the two artificial parties, on the government offices, on the JPs, on the vestries, on the voluntary charities. This satirist was Dickens, and it must be remembered that he was not only fierce, but uproariously readable. He really damaged the things he struck at, a very rare thing. He stepped up to the grave official of the vestry, really trusted by the rulers, really feared like a god by the poor, and he tied round his neck a name that choked him; never again now can he be anything but Bumble. He confronted the fine old English gentleman who gives his patriotic services for nothing as a local magistrate, and he nailed him up as Nupkins, an owl in open day. For to this satire there is literally no answer; it cannot be denied that a man like Nupkins can be and is a magistrate, so long as we adopt the amazing method of letting the rich man of a district actually be the judge in it. We can only avoid the vision of the fact by shutting our eyes, and imagining the nicest rich man we can think of, and that, of course, is what we do. But Dickens, in this matter, was merely realistic; he merely asked us to look on Nupkins, on the wild, strange thing that we had made. Thus Dickens seemed to see England not at all as the country where freedom slowly broadened down from precedent to precedent, but as a rubbish heap of seventeenth-century bad habits abandoned by everybody else. That is, he looked at England almost with the eyes of an American democrat.

And so, when the voice, swelling in volume, reached America and the Americans, the Americans said, 'Here is a man who will hurry the old country along, and tip her kings and beadles into the sea. Let him come here, and we will show him a race of free men such as he dreams of, alive upon the ancient earth. Let him come here and tell the English of the divine democracy towards which he drives them. There he has a monarchy and an oligarchy to make game of. Here is a republic for him to praise.' It seemed, indeed, a very natural sequel, that having denounced undemocratic England as the wilderness, he should announce democratic America as the promised land. Any ordinary person would have prophesied that as he had pushed his rage at the old order almost to the edge of rant, he would push his encomium of the new order almost to the edge of cant. Amid a roar of republican idealism, compliments, hope, and anticipatory gratitude, the great democrat entered the great democracy. He looked about him; he saw a complete America, unquestionably progressive, unquestionably self-governing. Then, with a more than American coolness, and a more than American impudence, he sat down and wrote *Martin Chuzzlewit*. That tricky and perverse sanity of his had mutinied again. Common sense is a wild thing, savage, and beyond rules; and it had turned on them and rent them.

The main course of action was as follows; and it is right to record it before we speak of the justice of it. When I speak of his sitting down and writing *Martin Chuzzlewit*, I use, of course, an elliptical expression. He wrote the notes of the American part of *Martin Chuzzlewit* while he was still in America; but it was a later decision presumably that such impressions should go into a book, and it was little better than an afterthought that they should go into *Martin Chuzzlewit*. Dickens had an uncommonly bad habit (artistically speaking) of altering a story in the middle as he did in the case of *Our Mutual Friend*. And it is on record that he only sent young Martin to America because he did not know what else to do with him, and because (to say truth) the sales were falling off. But the first action, which Americans regarded as an equally hostile one, was the publication of *American Notes*, the history of which should first be given. His notion of visiting America had come to him as a very vague notion, even before the appearance of *The Old Curiosity Shop*. But it had grown in him through the whole ensuing period in the plaguing and persistent way that ideas did grow in him and live with him. He contended against the idea in a certain manner. He had much to induce him to contend against it. Dickens was by this time not only a husband, but a father, the father of several children, and their existence made a difficulty in itself. His wife, he said, cried whenever the project was mentioned. But it was a point in him that he could never, with any satisfaction, part with a project. He had that restless optimism, that kind of nervous optimism, which would always tend to say 'Yes'; which is stricken with an immortal repentance, if ever it says 'No'. The idea of seeing America might be doubtful, but the idea of not seeing America was dreadful. 'To miss this opportunity would be a sad thing,' he says. '. . . God willing, I think it *must* be managed somehow!' It was managed somehow. First of all he wanted to take his children as well as his wife. Final obstacles to this fell upon him, but they did not frustrate him. A serious illness fell on him; but that did not frustrate him. He sailed for America in 1842.

He landed in America, and he liked it. . . . it is due to him, as well as to the great country that welcomed him, that his first good impression should be recorded, and that it should be 'considered independently of any modification it afterwards underwent'. But the modification it afterwards underwent was, as I have said above, simply a sudden kicking against cant, that is, against repetition. He was quite ready to believe that all Americans were free men. He would have believed it if they had not all told him so. He was quite prepared to be pleased with America. He would have been pleased with it if it had not been so much pleased with itself. The 'modification' his view underwent did not arise from any modification of America as he first saw it. His admiration did not change because America changed. It changed because America did not change. The Yankees enraged him at last, not by saying different things, but by saying the same things. They were a republic; they were a new and vigorous nation; it seemed natural that they should say so to a famous foreigner first stepping on to their shore. But it seemed maddening that they should say so to each other in every car and drinking saloon from morning till night. It was not that the Americans in any way ceased from praising him. It was rather that they went on praising him. It was not merely that their praises of him sounded beautiful when he first heard them. Their praises of themselves sounded beautiful when he first heard them. That democracy was grand, and that Charles Dickens was a remarkable person, were two truths that he certainly never doubted to his dying day. But, as I say, it was a soulless repetition that stung his sense of humour out of sleep; it woke like a wild beast for hunting, the lion of his laughter. He had heard the truth once too often. He had heard the truth for the nine hundred and ninety-ninth time, and he suddenly saw that it was falsehood.

It is true that a particular circumstance sharpened and defined his disappointment. He felt very hotly, as he felt everything, whether selfish or unselfish, the injustice of the American piracies of English literature, resulting from the American copyright laws. He did not go to America with any idea of discussing this; when, some time afterwards, somebody said that he did, he violently rejected the view as only describable 'in one of the shortest words in the English language'. But his entry into America was almost triumphal; the rostrum or pulpit was ready for him; he felt strong enough to say anything. He had been most warmly entertained by many American men of letters ... and in his consequent glow of confidence he stepped up to the dangerous question of American copyright. He made many speeches attacking the American law and theory of the matter as unjust to English writers and to American readers. The effect appears to have astounded him. 'I believe there is no country,' he writes, 'on the face of the earth where there is less freedom of opinion on any subject in reference to which there is a broad difference of opinion than in this. There! I write the words with reluctance, disappointment, and sorrow; but I believe it from the bottom of my soul.... The notion that I, a man alone by myself in America, should venture to suggest to the Americans that there was one point on which they were neither just to their own countrymen nor to us, actually struck the boldest dumb! ... every man who writes in this country is devoted to the question, and not one of them *dares* to raise his voice and complain of the atrocious state of the law. . . . The wonder is that a breathing man can be found with temerity enough to suggest to the Americans the possibility of their having done wrong. I wish you could have seen the faces that I saw down both sides of the table at Hartford when I began to talk about Scott. I wish you could have heard how I gave it out. My blood so boiled when I thought of the monstrous injustice that I felt as if I were twelve feet high when I thrust it down their throats.'

That is almost a portrait of Dickens. We can almost see the erect little figure, its face and hair like a flame.

For such reasons, among others, Dickens was angry with America. But if America was angry with Dickens, there were also reasons for it. I do not think that the rage against his copyright speeches was, as he supposed, merely national insolence and self-satisfaction. America is a mystery to any good Englishman; but I think Dickens managed somehow to touch it on a queer nerve. There is one thing, at any rate, that must strike all Englishmen who have the good fortune to have American friends; that is, that while there is no materialism so crude or so material as American materialism, there is also no idealism so crude or so ideal as American idealism. America will always affect an Englishman as being soft in the wrong place and hard in the wrong place; coarse exactly where all civilized men are delicate, delicate exactly where all grown-up men are coarse. Some beautiful ideal runs through these people, but it runs aslant. The only existing picture in which the thing I mean has been embodied is in Stevenson's *Wrecker*, in the blundering delicacy of Jim Pinkerton. America has a new delicacy, a coarse, rank refinement. But there is another way of embodying the idea, and that is to say this – that nothing is more likely than that the Americans thought it very shocking in Dickens, the divine author, to talk about being done out of money. Nothing would be more American than to expect a genius to be too high-toned for trade. It is certain that they deplored his selfishness in the matter; it is probable that they deplored his indelicacy. A beautiful young dreamer, with flowing brown hair, ought not to be even conscious of his copyrights. For it is quite unjust to say that the Americans worship the dollar. They really do worship intellect – another of the passing superstitions of our time.

If America had then this Pinkertonian propriety, this new, raw

sensibility, Dickens was the man to rasp it. He was its precise opposite in every way. The decencies he did respect were old-fashioned
and fundamental. On top of these he had that lounging liberty and
comfort which can only be had on the basis of very old conventions,
like the carelessness of gentlemen and the deliberation of rustics.
He had no fancy for being strung up to that taut and quivering
ideality demanded by American patriots and public speakers. And
there was something else also, connected especially with the question of copyright and his own pecuniary claims. Dickens was not
in the least desirous of being thought too 'high-souled' to want his
wages, nor was he in the least ashamed of asking for them. Deep
in him (whether the modern reader likes the quality or no) was a
sense very strong in the old Radicals – very strong especially in the
old English Radicals – a sense of personal *rights*, one's own rights
included, as something not merely useful but sacred. He did not
think a claim any less just and solemn because it happened to be
selfish; he did not divide claims into selfish and unselfish, but into
right and wrong. It is significant that when he asked for his money,
he never asked for it with that shamefaced cynicism, that sort of
embarrassed brutality, with which the modern man of the world
mutters something about business being business or looking after
number one. He asked for his money in a valiant and ringing voice,
like a man asking for his honour. While his American critics were
moaning and sneering at his interested motives as a disqualifica-
tion, he brandished his interested motives like a banner. 'It is nothing to them,' he cries in astonishment, 'that, of all men living, I am
the greatest loser by it' (the Copyright Law). 'It is nothing that
I have a claim to speak and be heard.' The thing they set up as a
barrier he actually presents as a passport. They think that he, of all
men, ought not to speak because he is interested. He thinks that
he, of all men, ought to speak because he is wronged.

But this particular disappointment with America in the matter
of the tyranny of its public opinion was not merely the expression of the fact that Dickens was a typical Englishman; that is, a
man with a very sharp insistence upon individual freedom. It also
worked back ultimately to that larger and vaguer disgust of which
I have spoken – the disgust at the perpetual posturing of the people
before a mirror. The tyranny was irritating, not so much because
of the suffering it inflicted on the minority, but because of the awful

glimpses that it gave of the huge and imbecile happiness of the majority. The very vastness of the vain race enraged him, its immensity, its unity, its peace. He was annoyed more with its contentment than with any of its discontents. The thought of that unthinkable mass of millions, every one of them saying that Washington was the greatest man on earth, and that the Queen lived in the Tower of London, rode his riotous fancy like a nightmare. But to the end he retained the outlines of his original republican ideal and lamented over America not as being too Liberal, but as not being Liberal enough. Among others, he used these somewhat remarkable words: 'I tremble for a Radical coming here, unless he is a Radical on principle, by reason and reflection, and from the sense of right. I fear that if he were anything else he would return home a Tory. . . . I say no more on that head for two months from this time, save that I do fear that the heaviest blow ever dealt at liberty will be dealt by this country, in the failure of its example on the earth.'

We are still waiting to see if that prediction has been fulfilled; but nobody can say that it has been falsified.

He went west on the great canals; he went south and touched the region of slavery; he saw America superficially indeed, but as a whole. And the great mass of his experience was certainly pleasant, though he vibrated with anticipatory passion against slave-holders, though he swore he would accept no public tribute in the slave country (a resolve which he broke under the pressure of the politeness of the south), yet his actual collisions with slavery and its upholders were few and brief. In these he bore himself with his accustomed vivacity and fire, but it would be a great mistake to convey the impression that his mental reaction against America was chiefly, or even largely, due to his horror at the negro problem. Over and above the cant of which we have spoken, the weary rush of words, the chief complaint he made was complaint against bad manners; and on a large view his anti-Americanism would seem to be more founded on spitting than on slavery. When, however, it did happen that the primary morality of man-owning came up for discussion, Dickens displayed an honourable impatience. One man, full of anti-abolitionist ardour, button-holed him and bombarded him with the well-known argument in defence of slavery, that it was not to the financial interest of a slave-owner to damage

or weaken his own slaves. Dickens, in telling the story of this interview, writes as follows: 'I told him quietly that it was not a man's
interest to get drunk, or to steal, or to game, or to indulge in any
other vice; but he *did* indulge in it for all that. That cruelty and
the abuse of irresponsible power were two of the bad passions
of human nature, with the gratification of which considerations of
interest or of ruin had nothing whatever to do. . . .' It is hardly
possible to doubt that Dickens, in telling the man this, told him
something sane and logical and unanswerable. But it is perhaps
permissible to doubt whether he told it to him quietly.

He returned home in the spring of 1842, and in the later part of
the year his *American Notes* appeared, and the cry against him that
had begun over copyright swelled into a roar in his rear. Yet when
we read the *Notes* we can find little offence in them, and, to say
truth, less interest than usual. They are no true picture of America,
or even of his vision of America, and this for two reasons. First, that
he deliberately excluded from them all mention of that copyright
question which had really given him his glimpse of how tyrannical
a democracy can be. Second, that here he chiefly criticizes America
for faults which are not, after all, especially American. For example, he is indignant with the inadequate character of the prisons,
and compared them unfavourably with those in England. But it
was a mere accident that American gaols were inferior to English.
There was and is nothing in the American spirit to prevent their
effecting all the reforms of Tracey and Chesterton, nothing to prevent their doing anything that money and energy and organization
can do. America might have (for all I know, does have) a prison
system cleaner and more humane and more efficient than any
other in the world. And the evil genius of America might still
remain – everything might remain that makes Pogram or Chollop
irritating or absurd. And against the evil genius of America
Dickens was now to strike a second and a very different blow.

In January, 1843, appeared the first number of the novel called
Martin Chuzzlewit. The earlier part of the book and the end, which
have no connection with America or the American problem, in any
case require a passing word. But except for the two gigantic gro-
tesques on each side of the gateway of the tale, Pecksniff and Mrs
Gamp, *Martin Chuzzlewit* will be chiefly admired for its American
excursion. It is a good satire embedded in an indifferent novel. Mrs

Gamp is, indeed, a sumptuous study, laid on in those rich, oily, almost greasy colours that go to make the English comic characters, that make the very diction of Falstaff fat, and quaking with jolly degradation. Pecksniff also is almost perfect, and much too good to be true. The only other thing to be noticed about him is that here, as almost everywhere else in the novels, the best figures are at their best when they have least to do. Dickens's characters are perfect as long as he can keep them out of his stories. Bumble is divine until a dark and practical secret is entrusted to him – as if anybody but a lunatic would entrust a secret to Bumble. Micawber is noble when he is doing nothing; but he is quite unconvincing when he is spying on Uriah Heep, for obviously neither Micawber nor any one else would employ Micawber as a private detective. Similarly, while Pecksniff is the best thing in the story, the story is the worst thing in Pecksniff. His plot against old Martin can only be described by saying that it is as silly as old Martin's plot against him. His fall at the end is one of the rare falls of Dickens. Surely it was not necessary to take Pecksniff so seriously. Pecksniff is a merely laughable character; he is so laughable that he is lovable. Why take such trouble to unmask a man whose mask you have made transparent? Why collect all the characters to witness the exposure of a man in whom none of the characters believe? Why toil and triumph to have the laugh of a man who was only made to be laughed at?

But it is the American part of *Martin Chuzzlewit* which is our concern, and which is memorable. It has the air of a great satire; but if it is only a great slander, it is still great. His serious book on America was merely a squib, perhaps a damp squib. In any case, we all know that America will survive such serious books. But his fantastic book may survive America. It may survive America as *The Knights* has survived Athens. *Martin Chuzzlewit* has this quality of great satire that the critic forgets to ask whether the portrait is true to the original, because the portrait is so much more important than the original. Who cares whether Aristophanes correctly describes Kleon, who is dead, when he so perfectly describes the demagogue, who cannot die? Just as little, it may be, will some future age care whether the ancient civilization of the west, the lost cities of New York and St Louis, were fairly depicted in the colossal monument of Elijah Pogram. For there is much more in the American episodes

than their intoxicating absurdity; there is more than humour in the
young man who made the speech about the British Lion, and said,
'I taunt that lion. Alone I dare him'; or in the other man who told
Martin that when he said that Queen Victoria did not live in the
Tower of London he 'fell into an error not uncommon among his
countrymen'. He has his finger on the nerve of an evil which was
not only in his enemies, but in himself. The great democrat has
hold of one of the dangers of democracy. The great optimist con-
fronts a horrible nightmare of optimism. Above all, the genuine
Englishman attacks a sin that is not merely American, but English
also. The eternal, complacent iteration of patriotic half-truths; the
perpetual buttering of one's self all over with the same stale butter;
above all, the big defiances of small enemies, or the very urgent
challenges to very distant enemies; the cowardice so habitual and
unconscious that it wears the plumes of courage – all this is an
English temptation as well as an American one. *Martin Chuzzlewit*
may be a caricature of America. America may be a caricature of
England. But in the gravest college, in the quietest country house
of England, there is the seed of the same essential madness that fills
Dickens's book, like an asylum, with brawling Chollops and raving
Jefferson Bricks. That essential madness is the idea that the good
patriot is the man who feels at ease about his country. This notion
of patriotism was unknown in the little pagan republics where our
European patriotism began. It was unknown in the Middle Ages.
In the eighteenth century, in the making of modern politics, a
'patriot' meant a discontented man. It was opposed to the word
'courtier', which meant an upholder of present conditions. In all
other modern countries, especially in countries like France and Ireland, where real difficulties have been faced, the word 'patriot'
means something like a political pessimist. This view and these
countries have exaggerations and dangers of their own; but the
exaggeration and danger of England is the same as the exaggeration and danger of *The Water-Toast Gazette*. The thing which is
rather foolishly called the Anglo-Saxon civilization is at present
soaked through with a weak pride. It uses great masses of men not
to procure discussion but to procure the pleasure of unanimity; it
uses masses like bolsters. It uses its organs of public opinion not to
warn the public, but to soothe it. It really succeeds not only in
ignoring the rest of the world, but actually in forgetting it. And

when a civilization really forgets the rest of the world – lets it fall as something obviously dim and barbaric – then there is only one adjective for the ultimate fate of that civilization, and that adjective is 'Chinese'.

Martin Chuzzlewit's America is a mad-house: but it is a mad-house we are all on the road to. For completeness and even comfort are almost the definitions of insanity. The lunatic is the man who lives in a small world but thinks it is a large one: he is the man who lives in a tenth of the truth, and thinks it is the whole. The madman cannot conceive any cosmos outside a certain tale or conspiracy or vision. Hence the more clearly we see the world divided into Saxons and non-Saxons, into our splendid selves and the rest, the more certain we may be that we are slowly and quietly going mad. The more plain and satisfying our state appears, the more we may know that we are living in an unreal world. For the real world is not satisfying. The more clear become the colours and facts of Anglo-Saxon superiority, the more surely we may know we are in a dream. For the real world is not clear or plain. The real world is full of bracing bewilderments and brutal surprises. Comfort is the blessing and the curse of the English, and of Americans of the Pogram type also. With them it is a loud comfort, a wild comfort, a screaming and capering comfort; but comfort at bottom still. For there is but an inch of difference between the cushioned chamber and the padded cell.

VII
DICKENS AND CHRISTMAS

IN THE July of 1844 Dickens went on an Italian tour, which he afterwards summarized in the book called *Pictures from Italy*. They are, of course, very vivacious, but there is no great need to insist on them considered as Italian sketches; there is no need whatever to worry about them as a phase of the mind of Dickens when he travelled out of England. He never travelled out of England. There is no trace in all these amusing pages that he really felt the great foreign things which lie in wait for us in the south of Europe, the Latin civilization, the Catholic Church, the art of the centre, the endless end of Rome. His travels are not travels in Italy, but travels in Dickensland. He sees amusing things; he describes them amusingly. But he would have seen things just as good in a street in Pimlico, and described them just as well. Few things were racier even in his raciest novel, than his description of the marionette play of the death of Napoleon. Nothing could be more perfect than the figure of the doctor, which had something wrong with its wires, and hence 'hovered about the couch and delivered medical opinions in the air'. Nothing could be better as a catching of the spirit of all popular drama than the colossal depravity of the wooden image of 'Sir Uudson Low'. But there is nothing Italian about it. Dickens would have made just as good fun, indeed just the same fun, of a Punch and Judy show performing in Long Acre or Lincoln's Inn Fields.

Dickens uttered just and sincere satire on Plornish and Podsnap; but Dickens was as English as any Podsnap or any Plornish. He had a hearty humanitarianism, and a hearty sense of justice to all nations, so far as he understood it. But that very kind of humanitarianism, that very kind of justice, were English. He was the Englishman of the type that made Free Trade, the most English of all things, since it was at once calculating and optimistic. He respected catacombs and gondolas, but that very respect was English. He wondered at brigands and volcanoes, but that very wonder was English. The very conception that Italy consists of these things was an English conception. The root things he never understood, the Roman legend, the ancient life of the Mediterranean, the world-old civilization of the vine and olive, the mystery of the immutable Church. He never understood these things, and I am glad he never understood them: he could only have understood them by ceasing to be the inspired cockney that he was, the rousing English Radical of the great Radical age in England. That spirit of his was one of the things that we have had which were truly national. All other forces we have borrowed especially those which flatter us most. Imperialism is foreign, socialism is foreign, militarism is foreign, education is foreign, strictly even Liberalism is foreign. But Radicalism was our own; as English as the hedge-rows.

Dickens abroad, then, was for all serious purposes simply the Englishman abroad; the Englishman abroad is for all serious purposes, simply the Englishman at home. Of this generalization one modification must be made. Dickens did feel a direct pleasure in the bright and busy exterior of the French life, the clean caps, the coloured uniforms, the skies like blue enamel, the little green trees, the little white houses, the scene picked out in primary colours, like a child's picture-book. This he felt, and this he put (by a stroke of genius) into the mouth of Mrs Lirriper, a London landlady on a holiday: for Dickens always knew that it is the simple and not the subtle who feel differences; and he saw all his colours through the clear eyes of the poor. And in thus taking to his heart the streets, as it were, rather than the spires of the Continent, he showed beyond question that combination of which we have spoken – of common sense with uncommon sensibility. For it is for the sake of the streets and shops and the coats and hats, that we should go abroad; they are far better worth going to see than the castles and cathedrals and Roman camps. For the wonders of the world are the same all over the world, at least all over the European world. Castles that throw valleys in shadow, minsters that strike the sky, roads so old that they seem to have been made by the gods, these are in all Christian countries. The marvels of man are at all our doors. A labourer hoeing turnips in Sussex has no need to be ignorant that the bones of Europe are the Roman roads. A clerk living in Lambeth has no need not to know that there was a Christian art exuberant in the thirteenth century; for only across the river he can see the live stones of the Middle Ages surging together towards the stars. But exactly the things that do strike the traveller as extraordinary are the ordinary things, the food, the clothes, the vehicles; the strange things are cosmopolitan, the common things are national and peculiar. Cologne spire is lifted on the same arches as Canterbury; but the thing you cannot see out of Germany is a German beer-garden. There is no need for a Frenchman to go to look at Westminster Abbey as a piece of English architecture; it is not in the special sense, a piece of English architecture. But a hansom cab is a piece of English architecture; a thing produced by the peculiar poetry of our cities, a symbol of a certain reckless comfort which is really English; a thing to draw a pilgrimage of the nations. The imaginative Englishman will be found all day in a *café*; the imaginative Frenchman in a hansom cab.

This sort of pleasure Dickens took in the Latin life; but no deeper kind. And the strongest of all possible indications of his fundamental detachment from it can be found in one fact. A great part of the time that he was in Italy he was engaged in writing 'The Chimes', and such Christmas tales, tales of Christmas in the English towns, tales full of fog and snow and hail and happiness.

Dickens could find in any street divergences between man and man deeper than the divisions of nations. His fault was to exaggerate differences. He could find types almost as distinct as separate tribes of animals in his own brain and his own city, those two homes of a magnificent chaos. The only two southerners introduced prominently into his novels, the two in *Little Dorrit*, are popular English foreigners, I had almost said stage foreigners. Villainy is, in English eyes, a southern trait, therefore one of the foreigners is villainous. Vivacity is, in English eyes, another southern trait, therefore the other foreigner is vivacious. But we can see from the outlines of both that Dickens did not have to go to Italy to get them. While poor panting millionaires, poor tired earls and poor God-forsaken American men of culture are plodding about Italy for literary inspiration, Charles Dickens made up the whole of that Italian romance (as I strongly suspect) from the faces of two London organ-grinders.

In the sunlight of the southern world, he was still dreaming of the firelight of the north. Among the palaces and the white campanili, he shut his eyes to see Marylebone and dreamed a lovely dream of chimney-pots. He was not happy, he said, without streets. The very foulness and smoke of London were lovable in his eyes and fill his Christmas tales with the vivid vapour. In the clear skies of the south he saw afar off the fog of London like a sunset cloud and longed to be in the core of it.

This Christmas tone of Dickens, in connection with his travels, is a matter that can only be expressed by a parallel with one of his other works. Much the same that has here been said of his *Pictures from Italy*, may be said about his *Child's History of England*; with the difference that while the *Pictures from Italy* do in a sense add to his fame the *History of England* in almost every sense detracts from it. But the nature of the limitation is the same. What Dickens was travelling in distant lands, that he was travelling in distant ages; a sturdy, sentimental English Radical with a large heart and a narrow mind. He could not help falling into that besetting sin or weakness of the modern progressive, the habit of regarding the contemporary questions as the eternal questions and the latest word as the last. . . . He could not help seeing the remotest peaks lit up by the raging bonfire of his own passionate political crisis. . . . He lived in an eternal present like all simple men. It is indeed *A Child's History of England*; but the child is the writer and not the reader.

But Dickens, in his cheapest cockney utilitarianism, was not only English, but unconsciously historic. Upon him descended the real tradition of 'Merry England', and not upon the pallid mediaevalists who thought they were reviving it. The Pre-Raphaelites, the Gothicists, the admirers of the Middle Ages, had in their subtlety and sadness the spirit of the present day. Dickens had in his buffoonery and bravery the spirit of the Middle Ages. He was much more mediaeval in his attacks on mediaevalism than they were in their defences of it. It was he who had the things of Chaucer, the love of large jokes and long stories and brown ale and all the white roads of England. Like Chaucer he loved story within story, every man telling a tale. Like Chaucer he saw something openly comic in men's motley trades. Sam Weller would have been a great gain to the Canterbury Pilgrimage and told an admirable story. Rossetti's Damozel would have been a great bore, regarded as too fast by the Prioress and too priggish by the Wife of Bath. It is said that in the somewhat sickly Victorian revival of feudalism which was called 'Young England', a nobleman hired a hermit to live in his grounds. It is also said that the hermit struck for more beer. Whether this anecdote be true or not, it is always told as showing a collapse from the ideal of the Middle Ages to the level of the present day. But in the mere act of striking for beer the holy man was very much more 'mediaeval' than the fool who employed him.

It would be hard to find a better example of this than Dickens's great defence of Christmas. In fighting for Christmas he was fighting for the old European festival, Pagan and Christian, for that trinity of eating, drinking and praying which to moderns appears irreverent, for the holy day which is really a holiday. He had himself the most babyish ideas about the past. He supposed the Middle Ages to have consisted of tournaments and torture-chambers, he supposed himself to be a brisk man of the manufacturing age, almost a Utilitarian. But for all that he defended the mediaeval feast which was going out against the Utilitarianism which was coming in. He could only see all that was bad in Mediaevalism. But he fought for all that was good in it. And he was all the more really in sympathy with the old strength and simplicity because he only knew that it was good and did not know that it was old. He cared as little for mediaevalism as the mediaevals did. He cared as much as they did for lustiness and virile laughter and sad tales of good lovers and pleasant tales of good lovers. He would have been very much bored by Ruskin and Walter Pater if they had explained to him the strange sunset tints of Lippi and Botticelli. He had no pleasure in looking on the dying Middle Ages. But he looked on the living Middle Ages, on a piece of the old uproarious superstition still unbroken; and he hailed it like a new religion. The Dickens character ate pudding to an extent at which the modern mediaevalists turned pale. They would do every kind of honour to an old observance, except observing it. They would pay to a Church feast every sort of compliment except feasting.

And (as I have said) as were his unconscious relations to our European past, so were his unconscious relations to England. He imagined himself to be, if anything, a sort of cosmopolitan; at any rate to be a champion of the charms and merits of continental lands against the arrogance of our island. But he was in truth very much more a champion of the old and genuine England against that comparatively cosmopolitan England which we have all lived to see. And here again the supreme example is Christmas. Christmas is, as I have said, one of numberless old European feasts of which the essence is the combination of religion with merry-making. But among those feasts it is also especially and distinctively English in the style of its merry-making and even in the style of its religion. For the character of Christmas (as distinct, for instance, from the continental Easter) lies chiefly in two things: first on the terrestrial side the note of comfort rather than the note of brightness; and on the spiritual side, Christian charity rather than Christian ecstasy. And comfort is, like charity, a very English instinct. Nay, comfort is, like charity, an English merit; though our comfort may and does degenerate into materialism, just as our charity may and does degenerate into laxity and make-believe.

This ideal of comfort belongs peculiarly to England; it belongs peculiarly to Christmas; above all, it belongs pre-eminently to Dickens. And it is astonishingly misunderstood. It is misunderstood by the continent of Europe; it is, if possible, still more misunderstood by the English of today. On the Continent the restaurateurs provide us with raw beef, as if we were savages; yet old English cooking takes as much care as French. And in England has arisen a parvenu patriotism which represents the English as everything but English; as a blend of Chinese stoicism, Latin militarism, Prussian rigidity, and American bad taste. And so England, whose fault is gentility and whose virtue is geniality, England with her tradition of the great gay gentlemen of Elizabeth, is represented to the four quarters of the world (as in Mr Kipling's religious poems) in the enormous image of a solemn cad. And because it is very difficult to be comfortable in the suburbs, the suburbs have voted that comfort is a gross and material thing. Comfort, especially this vision of Christmas comfort, is the reverse of a gross or material thing. It is far more poetical, properly speaking, than the Garden of Epicurus. It is far more artistic than the Palace of Art. It is more artistic because it is based upon a contrast, a contrast between the fire and wine within the house and the winter and the roaring rains without. It is far more poetical, because there is in it a note of defence, almost of war; a note of being besieged by the snow and hail; of making merry in the belly of a fort. The man who said that an Englishman's house is his castle said much more than he meant. The Englishman thinks of his house as something fortified, and provisioned, and his very surliness is at root romantic. And this sense would naturally be strongest in wild winter nights, when the lowered portcullis and the lifted drawbridge do not merely bar people out, but bar people in. The Englishman's house is most sacred, not merely when the King cannot enter it, but when the Englishman cannot get out of it.

This comfort, then, is an abstract thing, a principle. The English poor shut all their doors and windows till their rooms reek like the Black Hole. They are suffering for an idea. Mere animal hedonism would not dream, as we English do, of winter feasts and little rooms, but of eating fruit in large and idle gardens. Mere sensuality would desire to please all its senses. But to our good dreams this dark and dangerous background is essential; the highest pleasure we can imagine is a defiant pleasure, a happiness that stands at bay. The word 'comfort' is not indeed the right word, it conveys too much of the slander of mere sense; the true word is 'cosiness', a word not translatable. One, at least, of the essentials of it is smallness, smallness in preference to largeness, smallness for smallness' sake. The merry-maker wants a pleasant parlour, he would not give twopence for a pleasant continent. In our difficult time, of course, a fight for mere space has become necessary. Instead of being greedy for ale and Christmas pudding we are greedy for mere air, an equally sensual appetite. In abnormal conditions this is wise; and the illimitable veldt is an excellent thing for nervous people. But our fathers were large and healthy enough to make a thing humane, and not worry about whether it was hygienic. They were big enough to get into small rooms.

Of this quite deliberate and artistic quality in the close Christmas chamber, the standing evidence is Dickens in Italy. He created these dim firelit tales like little dim red jewels, as an artistic necessity, in the centre of an endless summer. Amid the white cities of Tuscany he hungered for something romantic, and wrote about a rainy Christmas. Amid the pictures of the Uffizi he starved for something beautiful, and fed his memory on London fog. His feeling for the fog was especially poignant and typical. In the first of his Christmas tales, the popular 'Christmas Carol', he suggested the very soul of it in one simile, when he spoke of the dense air, suggesting that 'Nature was brewing on a large scale'. This sense of the thick atmosphere as something to eat or drink, something not only solid but satisfactory, may seem almost insane, but it is no exaggeration of Dickens's emotion. We speak of a fog 'that you could cut with a knife'. Dickens would have liked the phrase as suggesting that the fog was a colossal cake. He liked even more his own phrase of the Titanic brewery, and no dream would have given him a wilder pleasure than to grope his way to some such tremendous vats and drink the ale of the giants.

There is a current prejudice against fogs, and Dickens, perhaps, is their only poet. Considered hygienically, no doubt this may be more or less excusable. But, considered poetically, fog is not undeserving, it has a real significance. We have in our great cities abolished the clean and sane darkness of the country. We have outlawed night and sent her wandering in wild meadows; we have lit eternal watch-fires against her return. We have made a new cosmos, and as a consequence our own sun and stars. And as a consequence also, and most justly, we have made our own darkness. Just as every lamp is a warm human moon, so every fog is a rich human nightfall. If it were not for this mystic accident we should never see darkness, and he who has never seen darkness has never seen the sun. Fog for us is the chief form of that outward pressure which compresses mere luxury into real comfort. It makes the world small, in the same spirit as in that common and happy cry that the world is small, meaning that it is full of friends. The first man that emerges out of the mist with a light is for us Prometheus, a saviour bringing fire to men. He is that greatest and best of all men, greater than the heroes, better than the saints, Man Friday. Every rumble of a cart, every cry in the distance, marks the heart of humanity beating undaunted in the darkness. It is wholly human; man toiling in his own cloud. If real darkness is like the embrace of God, this is the dark embrace of man.

In such a sacred cloud the tale called 'The Christmas Carol' begins, the first and most typical of all his Christmas tales. It is not irrelevant to dilate upon the geniality of this darkness, because it is characteristic of Dickens that his atmospheres are more important than his stories. The Christmas atmosphere is more important than Scrooge, or the ghosts either; in a sense, the background is more important than the figures. The same thing may be noticed in his dealings with that other atmosphere (besides that of good humour), which he excelled in creating, an atmosphere of mystery and

wrong, such as that which gathers round Mrs Clennam, rigid in
her chair, or old Miss Havisham, ironically robed as a bride. Here
again the atmosphere altogether eclipses the story, which often
seems disappointing in comparison. The secrecy is sensational; the
secret is tame. The surface of the thing seems more awful than
the core of it. It seems almost as if these grisly figures, Mrs Chadband and Mrs Clennam, Miss Havisham and Miss Flite, Nemo and
Sally Brass, were keeping something back from the author as well
as from the reader. When the book closes we do not know their real
secret. They soothed the optimistic Dickens with something less
terrible than the truth. The dark house of Arthur Clennam's childhood really depresses us; it is a true glimpse into that quiet street
in hell, where live the children of that unique dispensation which
theologians call Calvinism and Christians devil-worship. But some
stranger crime had really been done there, some more monstrous
blasphemy or human sacrifice than the suppression of some silly
document advantageous to the silly Dorrits. Something worse than
a common tale of jilting lay behind the masquerade and madness
of the awful Miss Havisham. Something worse was whispered by
the misshapen Quilp to the sinister Sally in that wild, wet summer-
house by the river, something worse than the clumsy plot against
the clumsy Kit. These dark pictures seem almost as if they were
literally visions; things, that is, that Dickens saw but did not
understand.

And as with his backgrounds of gloom, so with his backgrounds
of good-will, in such tales as 'The Christmas Carol'. The tone of
the tale is kept throughout in a happy monotony, though the tale
is everywhere irregular and in some places weak. It has the same
kind of artistic unity that belongs to a dream. A dream may begin
with the end of the world and end with a tea party; but either
the end of the world will seem as trivial as a tea-party or that tea-
party will be as terrible as the day of doom. The incidents change
wildly; the story scarcely changes at all. 'The Christmas Carol' is
a kind of philanthropic dream, an enjoyable nightmare, in which
the scenes shift bewilderingly and seem as miscellaneous as the
pictures in a scrap-book, but in which there is one constant state
of the soul, a state of rowdy benediction and a hunger for human
faces. The beginning is about a winter day and a miser; yet the
beginning is in no way bleak. The author starts with a kind of

happy howl; he bangs on our door like a drunken carol singer; his style is festive and popular; he compares the snow and hail to philanthropists who 'come down handsomely'; he compares the fog to unlimited beer. Scrooge is not really inhuman at the beginning any more than he is at the end. There is a heartiness in his inhospitable sentiments that is akin to humour and therefore to humanity; he is only a crusty old bachelor, and had (I strongly suspect) given away turkeys secretly all his life. The beauty and the real blessing of the story do not lie in the mechanical plot of it, the repentance of Scrooge, probable or improbable; they lie in the great furnace of real happiness that glows through Scrooge and everything round him; that great furnace, the heart of Dickens. Whether the Christmas visions would or would not convert Scrooge, they convert us. Whether or no the visions were evoked by real Spirits of the Past, Present, and Future, they were evoked by that truly exalted order of angels who are correctly called High Spirits. They are impelled and sustained by a quality which our contemporary artists ignore or almost deny, but which in a life decently lived is as normal and attainable as sleep, positive, passionate, conscious joy. The story sings from end to end like a happy man going home; and, like a happy and good man, when it cannot sing it yells. It is lyric and exclamatory from the first exclamatory words of it. It is strictly a Christmas Carol.

Dickens, as has been said, went to Italy with this kindly cloud still about him, still meditating on Yule mysteries. Among the olives and the orange-trees he wrote his second great Christmas tale, 'The Chimes', at Genoa in 1844, a Christmas tale only differing from 'The Christmas Carol' in being fuller of the grey rains of winter and the north. 'The Chimes' is, like the 'Carol', an appeal for charity and mirth, but it is a stern and fighting appeal: if the other is a Christmas carol, this is a Christmas war-song. In it Dickens hurled himself with even more than his usual militant joy and scorn into an attack upon a cant, which he said made his blood boil. This cant was nothing more nor less than the whole tone taken by three-quarters of the political and economic world towards the poor. It was a vague and vulgar Benthamism with a rollicking Tory touch in it. It explained to the poor their duties with a cold and coarse philanthropy unendurable by any free man. It had also at its command a kind of brutal banter, a loud good humour which

Dickens sketches savagely in Alderman Cute. He fell furiously on all their ideas: the cheap advice to live cheaply, the base advice to live basely, above all, the preposterous primary assumption that the rich are to advise the poor and not the poor the rich. There were and are hundreds of these benevolent bullies. Some say that the poor should give up having children, which means that they should give up their great virtue of sexual sanity. Some say that they should give up 'treating' each other, which means that they should give up all that remains to them of the virtue of hospitality. Against all of this Dickens thundered very thoroughly in 'The Chimes'. It may be remarked in passing that this affords another instance of a confusion already referred to, the confusion whereby Dickens supposed himself to be exalting the present over the past, whereas he was really dealing deadly blows at things strictly peculiar to the present. Embedded in this very book is a somewhat useless interview between Trotty Veck and the church bells, in which the latter lecture the former for having supposed (why, I don't know) that they were expressing regret for the disappearance of the Middle Ages. There is no reason why Trotty Veck or any one else should idealize the Middle Ages, but certainly he was the last man in the world to be asked to idealize the nineteenth century, seeing that the smug and stingy philosophy, which poisons his life through the book, was an exclusive creation of that century. But, as I have said before, the fieriest mediaevalist may forgive Dickens for disliking the good things the Middle Ages took away, considering how he loved whatever good things the Middle Ages left behind. It matters very little that he hated old feudal castles when they were already old. It matters very much that he hated the New Poor Law while it was still new.

The moral of this matter in 'The Chimes' is essential. Dickens had sympathy with the poor in the Greek and literal sense; he suffered with them mentally; for the things that irritated them were the things that irritated him. He did not pity the people, or even champion the people, or even merely love the people; in this matter he was the people. He alone in our literature is the voice not merely of the social substratum, but even of the subconsciousness of the substratum. He utters the secret anger of the humble. He says what the uneducated only think, or even only feel, about the educated. And in nothing is he so genuinely such a voice as in this fact of his fiercest mood being reserved for methods that are counted scientific and progressive. Pure and exalted atheists talk themselves into believing that the working classes are turning with indignant scorn from the churches. The working classes are not indignant against the churches in the least. The things the working classes really are indignant against are the hospitals. The people has no definite disbelief in the temples of theology. The people has a very fiery and practical disbelief in the temples of physical science. The things the poor hate are the modern things, the rationalistic things – doctors, inspectors, poor law guardians, professional philanthropy. They never showed any reluctance to be helped by the old and corrupt monasteries. They will often die rather than be helped by the modern and efficient workhouse. Of all this anger, good or bad, Dickens is the voice of an accusing energy. When, in 'The Christmas Carol', Scrooge refers to the surplus population, the Spirit tells him, very justly, not to speak till he knows what the surplus is and where it is. The implication is severe but sound. When a group of superciliously benevolent economists look down into the abyss for the surplus population, assuredly there is only one answer that should be given to them; and that is to say, 'If there is a surpus, you are a surplus.' And if any one were ever cut off, they would be. If the barricades went up in our streets and the poor became masters, I think the priests would escape, I fear the gentlemen would; but I believe the gutters would be simply running with the blood of philanthropists.

Lastly, he was at one with the poor in this chief matter of Christmas, in the matter, that is, of special festivity. There is nothing on which the poor are more criticized than on the point of spending large sums on small feasts; and though there are material difficulties, there is nothing in which they are more right. It is said that a Boston paradox-monger said, 'Give us the luxuries of life and we will dispense with the necessities.' But it is the whole human race that says it, from the first savage wearing feathers instead of clothes to the last costermonger having a treat instead of three meals.

The third of his Christmas stories, 'The Cricket on the Hearth', calls for no extensive comment, though it is very characteristic. It has all the qualities which we have called dominant qualities in his Christmas sentiment. It has cosiness, that is the comfort that depends upon a discomfort surrounding it. It has a sympathy with the poor, and especially with the extravagance of the poor; with what may be called the temporary wealth of the poor. It has the sentiment of the hearth, that is, the sentiment of the open fire being the red heart of the room. That open fire is the veritable flame of England, still kept burning in the midst of a mean civilization of stoves. But everything that is valuable in 'The Cricket on the Hearth' is perhaps as well expressed in the title as it is in the story. The tale itself, in spite of some of those inimitable things that Dickens never failed to say, is a little too comfortable to be quite convincing. 'The Christmas Carol' is the conversion of an anti-Christmas character. 'The Chimes' is a slaughter of anti-Christmas characters. 'The Cricket', perhaps, fails for lack of this crusading note. For everything has its weak side, and when full justice has been done to this neglected note of poetic comfort, we must remember that it has its very real weak side. The defect of it in the work of Dickens was that he tended sometimes to pile up the cushions until none of the characters could move. He is so much interested in effecting his state of static happiness that he forgets to make a story at all. His princes at the start of the story begin to live happily ever afterwards. We feel this strongly in *Master Humphrey's Clock*, and we feel it sometimes in these Christmas stories. He makes his characters so comfortable that his characters begin to dream and drivel. And he makes his reader so comfortable that his reader goes to sleep.

The actual tale of the carrier and his wife sounds somewhat sleepily in our ears; we cannot keep our attention fixed on it, though we are conscious of a kind of warmth from it as from a great wood fire. We know so well that everything will soon be all right that we do not suspect when the carrier suspects, and are not frightened when the gruff Tackleton growls. The sound of the Christmas festivities at the end come fainter on our ears than did the shout of the Cratchits or the bells of Trotty Veck. All the good figures that followed Scrooge when he came growling out of the fog fade into the fog again.

VIII
THE TIME OF TRANSITION

Dickens was back in London by the June of 1845. About this time he became the first editor of *The Daily News*, a paper which he had largely planned and suggested, and which, I trust, remembers its semi-divine origin. That his thoughts had been running, as suggested in the last chapter, somewhat monotonously on his Christmas domesticities, is again suggested by the rather singular fact that he originally wished *The Daily News* to be called *The Cricket*. Probably he was haunted again with his old vision of a homely, tale-telling periodical such as had broken off in *Master Humphrey's Clock*. About this time, however, he was peculiarly unsettled. Almost as soon as he had taken the editorship he threw it up; and having only recently come back to England, he soon made up his mind to go back to the Continent. In the May of 1846 he ran over to Switzerland and tried to write *Dombey and Son* at Lausanne. Tried to, I say, because his letters are full of an angry impotence. He could not get on. He attributed this especially to his love of London and his loss of it, 'the absence of streets and numbers of figures. . . . *My* figures seem disposed to stagnate without crowds about them.' But he also, with shrewdness, attributed it more generally to the laxer and more wandering life he had led for the last two years, the American tour, the Italian tour, diversified, generally speaking, only with slight literary productions. His ways were never punctual or healthy, but they were also never unconscientious as far as work was concerned. If he walked all night he could write all day. But in this strange exile or interregnum he did not seem able to fall into any habits, even bad habits. A restlessness beyond all his experience had fallen for a season upon the most restless of the children of men.

It may be a mere coincidence: but this break in his life very nearly coincided with the important break in his art. *Dombey and Son*, planned in all probability some time before, was destined to be the last of a quite definite series, the early novels of Dickens.

The difference between the books from the beginning up to *Dombey*, and the books from *David Copperfield* to the end may be hard to state dogmatically, but is evident to every one with any literary sense. Very coarsely, the case may be put by saying that he diminished, in the story as a whole, the practice of pure caricature. Still more coarsely it may be put in the phrase that he began to practise realism. If we take Mr Stiggins, say, as a clergyman depicted at the beginning of his literary career, and Mr Crisparkle, say, as a clergyman depicted at the end of it, it is evident that the difference does not merely consist in the fact that the first is a less desirable clergyman than the second. It consists in the nature of our desire for either of them. The glory of Mr Crisparkle partly consists in the fact that he might really exist anywhere, in any country town into which we may happen to stray. The glory of Mr Stiggins wholly consists in the fact that he could not possibly exist anywhere except in the head of Dickens. Dickens has the secret recipe of that divine dish. In some sense, therefore, when we say that he became less of a caricaturist we mean that he became less of a creator. That original violent vision of all things which he had seen from his boyhood began to be mixed with other men's milder visions and with the light of common day. He began to understand and practise other than his own mad merits; began to have some movement towards the merits of other writers, towards the mixed emotion of Thackeray, or the solidity of George Eliot. And this must be said for the process; that the fierce wine of Dickens could endure some dilution. On the whole, perhaps, his primal personalism was all the better when surging against some saner restraints. Perhaps a flavour of strong Stiggins goes a long way. Perhaps the colossal Crummles might be cut down into six or seven quite credible characters. For my own part, for reasons which I shall afterwards mention, I am in real doubt about the advantage of this realistic education of Dickens. I am not sure that it made his books better; but I am sure it made them less bad. He made fewer mistakes undoubtedly; he succeeded in eliminating much of the mere rant or cant of his first books; he threw away much of the old padding, all the more annoying, perhaps, in a literary sense, because he did not mean it for padding, but for essential eloquence. But he did not produce anything actually better than Mr Chuckster. But then there is nothing better than Mr Chuckster. Certain works of art, such as the Venus of Milo, exhaust our aspiration. Upon the whole this may, perhaps, be safely said of the transition. Those who have any doubt about Dickens can have no doubt of the superiority of the later books. Beyond question they have less of what annoys us in Dickens. But do not, if you are in the company of any ardent adorers of Dickens (as I hope for your sake you are) do not insist too urgently and exclusively on the splendour of Dickens's last works, or they will discover that you do not like him.

Dombey and Son is the last novel in the first manner: *David Copperfield* is the first novel in the last. The increase in care and realism in the second of the two is almost startling. Yet even in *Dombey and Son* we can see the coming of a change, however faint, if we compare it with his first fantasies such as *Nicholas Nickleby* or *The Old Curiosity Shop*. The central story is still melodrama, but it is much more tactful and effective melodrama. Melodrama is a form of art, legitimate like any other, as noble as farce, almost as noble as pantomime. The essence of melodrama is that it appeals to the moral sense in a highly simplified state, just as farce appeals to the sense of humour in a highly simplified state. Farce creates people who are so intellectually simple as to hide in packing-cases or pretend to be their own aunts. Melodrama creates people so morally simple as to kill their enemies in Oxford Street, and repent on seeing their mother's photograph. The object of the simplification in farce and melodrama is the same, and quite artistically legitimate, the object of gaining a resounding rapidity of action which subtleties would obstruct. And this can be done well or ill. The simplified villain can be a spirited charcoal sketch or a mere black smudge. Carker is a spirited charcoal sketch: Ralph Nickleby is a mere black smudge. The tragedy of Edith Dombey teems with unlikelihood, but it teems with life. That Dombey should give his own wife censure through his own business manager is impossible, I will not say in a gentleman, but in a person of ordinary sane self-conceit. But once having got the inconceivable trio before the footlights, Dickens gives us good ringing dialogue, very different from the mere rants in which Ralph Nickleby figures in the unimaginable character of a rhetorical money-lender. And there is another point of technical improvement in this book over such books as *Nicholas Nickleby*. It has not only a basic idea, but a good basic idea. There is a real artistic opportunity in the conception of a solemn and selfish man of affairs, feeling for his male heir, his first and last emotion, mingled of a thin flame of tenderness and a strong flame of pride. But with all these possibilites, the serious episode of the Dombeys serves ultimately only to show how unfitted Dickens was for such things, how fitted he was for something opposite.

The incurable poetic character, the hopelessly non-realistic character of Dickens's essential genius could not have a better example than the story of the Dombeys. For the story itself is probable; it is the treatment that makes it unreal. In attempting to paint the dark pagan devotion of the father (as distinct from the ecstatic and Christian devotion of the mother) Dickens was painting something that was really there. This is no wild theme, like the wanderings of Nell's grandfather, or the marriage of Gride. A man of Dombey's type would love his son as he loves Paul. He would neglect his daughter as he neglects Florence. And yet we feel the utter unreality of it all, while we feel the utter reality of monsters like Stiggins or Mantalini. Dickens could only work in his own way, and that way was the wild way. We may almost say this: that he could only make his characters probable if he was allowed to make them impossible. Give him licence to say and do anything, and he could create beings as vivid as our own aunts and uncles. Keep him to likelihood and he could not tell the plainest tale so as to make it seem likely. The story of *Pickwick* is credible, although it is not possible. The story of Florence Dombey is incredible although it is true.

An excellent example can be found in the same story Major Bagstock is a grotesque, and yet he contains touch after touch of Dickens's quiet and sane observation of things as they are. He was always most accurate when he was most fantastic. Dombey and Florence are perfectly reasonable, but we simply know that they do not exist. The Major is mountainously exaggerated, but we all feel that we have met him at Brighton. Nor is the rationale of the paradox difficult to see; Dickens exaggerated when he had found a real truth to exaggerate. It is a deadly error (an error at the back of much of the false placidity of our politics) to suppose that lies are told with excess and luxuriance, and truths told with modesty and restraint. Some of the most frantic lies on the face of life are told with modesty and restraint; for the simple reason that only modesty and restraint will save them. Many official declarations

are just as dignified as Mr Dombey, because they are just as fictitious. On the other hand, the man who has found a truth dances
about like a boy who has found a shilling; he breaks into extravagances, as the Christian churches broke into gargoyles. In one
sense truth alone can be exaggerated; nothing else can stand the
strain. The outrageous Bagstock is a glowing and glaring exaggeration of a thing we have all seen in life – the worst and most dangerous of all its hypocrisies. For the worst and most dangerous
hypocrite is not he who affects unpopular virtue, but he who affects
popular vice. The jolly fellow of the saloon bar and the racecourse
is the real deceiver of mankind; he has misled more than any false
prophet, and his victims cry to him out of hell. The excellence of
the Bagstock conception can best be seen if we compare it with the
much weaker and more improbable knavery of Pecksniff. It would
not be worth a man's while, with any worldly object, to pretend to
be a holy and high-minded architect. The world does not admire
holy and high-minded architects. The world does admire rough
and tough old army men who swear at waiters and wink at women.
Major Bagstock is simply the perfect prophecy of that decadent
jingoism which corrupted England of late years. England has been
duped, not by the cant of goodness, but by the cant of badness.
It has been fascinated by a quite fictitious cynicism, and reached
that last and strangest of all impostures in which the mask is as
repulsive as the face.

Dombey and Son provides us with yet another instance of this
general fact in Dickens. He could only get to the most solemn emotions adequately if he got to them through the grotesque. He could
only, so to speak, really get into the inner chamber by coming down
the chimney, like his own most lovable lunatic in *Nicholas Nickleby*.
A good example is such a character as Toots. Toots is what none
of Dickens's dignified characters are, in the most serious sense, a
true lover. He is the twin of Romeo. He has passion, humility, self-
knowledge, a mind lifted into all magnanimous thoughts, everything that goes with the best kind of romantic love. His excellence
in the art of love can only be expressed by the somewhat violent
expression that he is as good a lover as Walter Gay is a bad one.
Florence surely deserved her father's scorn if she could prefer Gay
to Toots. It is neither a joke nor any kind of exaggeration to say
that in the vacillations of Toots, Dickens not only came nearer to

the psychology of true love than he ever came elsewhere, but nearer than any one else ever came. To ask for the loved one, and then not to dare to cross the threshhold, to be invited by her, to long to accept, and then to lie in order to decline, these are the funny things that Mr Toots did, and that every honest man who yells with laughter at him has done also. For the moment, however, I only mention this matter as a pendant case to the case of Major Bagstock, an example of the way in which Dickens had to be ridiculous in order to begin to be true. His characters that begin solemn end futile; his characters that begin frivolous end solemn in the best sense. His foolish figures are not only more entertaining than his serious figures, they are also much more serious. The Marchioness is not only much more laughable than Little Nell; she is also much more of all that Little Nell was meant to be; much more really devoted, pathetic, and brave. Dick Swiveller is not only a much funnier fellow than Kit, he is also a much more genuine fellow, being free from that slight stain of 'meekness', or the snobbishness of the respectable poor, which the wise and perfect Chuckster wisely and perfectly perceived in Kit. Susan Nipper is not only more of a comic character than Florence; she is more of a heroine than Florence any day of the week. In *Our Mutual Friend* we do not, for some reason or other, feel really very much excited about the fall or rescue of Lizzie Hexam. She seems too romantic to be really pathetic. But we do feel excited about the rescue of Miss Podsnap, because she is, like Toots, a holy fool; because her pink nose and pink elbows, and candid outcry and open indecent affections do convey to us a sense of innocence helpless among human dragons, of Andromeda tied naked to a rock. Dickens had to make a character humorous before he could make it human; it was the only way he knew, and he ought to have always adhered to it. Whether he knew it or not, the only two really touching figures in *Martin Chuzzlewit* are the Misses Pecksniff. Of the things he tried to treat unsmilingly and grandly we can all make game to our heart's content. But when once he has laughed at a thing it is sacred for ever.

Dombey, however, means first and foremost the finale of the early Dickens. It is difficult to say exactly in what it is that we perceive that the old crudity ends here, and does not reappear in *David Copperfield* or in any of the novels after it. But so certainly it is. In detached scenes and characters, indeed, Dickens kept up his farcical note almost or quite to the end. But this is the last farce; this is the last work in which a farcical licence is tacitly claimed, a farcical note struck to start with. And in a sense his next novel may be called his first novel. But the growth of this great novel, *David Copperfield*, is a thing very interesting, but at the same time very dark, for it is a growth in the soul. We have seen that Dickens's mind was in a stir of change; that he was dreaming of art, and even of realism. Hugely delighted as he invariably was with his own books, he was humble enough to be ambitious. He was even humble enough to be envious. In the matter of art, for instance, in the narrower sense, of arrangement and proportion in fictitious things, he began to be conscious of his deficiency, and even, in a stormy sort of way, ashamed of it; he tried to gain completeness even while raging at any one who called him incomplete. And in this matter of artistic construction, his ambition (and his success too) grew steadily up to the instant of his death. The end finds him attempting things that are at the opposite pole to the frank formlessness of *Pickwick*. His last book, *The Mystery of Edwin Drood*, depends entirely upon con-struction, even upon a centralized strategy. He staked everything upon a plot; he who had been the weakest of plotters, weaker than Sim Tappertit. He essayed a detective story, he who could never keep a secret; and he has kept it to this day. A new Dickens was really being born when Dickens died.

And as with art, so with reality. He wished to show that he could construct as well as anybody. He also wished to show that he could be as accurate as anybody. And in this connection (as in many others) we must recur constantly to the facts mentioned in connection with America and with his money-matters. We must recur, I mean, to the central fact that his desires were extravagant in quantity, but not in quality; that his wishes were excessive, but not eccentric. It must never be forgotten that sanity was his ideal, even when he seemed almost insane. It was thus with his literary aspirations. He was brilliant; but he wished sincerely to be solid. Nobody out of an asylum could deny that he was a genius and an unique writer; but he did not wish to be an unique writer, but an universal writer. Much of the manufactured pathos or rhetoric against which his enemies quite rightly rail, is really due to his desire to give all sides of life at once, to make his book a cosmos instead of a tale. He was sometimes really vulgar in his wish to be a literary Whiteley, an universal provider. Thus it was that he felt about realism and truth to life. Nothing is easier than to defend Dickens as Dickens, but Dickens wished to be everybody else. Nothing is easier than to defend Dickens's world as a fairyland, of which he alone has the key; to defend him as one defends Maeterlinck, or any other original writer. But Dickens was not content with being original, he had a wild wish to be true. He loved truth so much in the abstract that he sacrificed to the shadow of it his own glory. He denied his own divine originality, and pretended that he had plagiarized from life. He disowned his own soul's children, and said he had picked them up in the street.

And in this mixed and heated mood of anger and ambition, vanity and doubt, a new and great design was born. He loved to be romantic, yet he desired to be real. How if he wrote of a thing that was real and showed that it was romantic? He loved real life; but he also loved his own way. How if he wrote his own real life, but wrote it in his own way? How if he showed the carping critics who doubted the existence of his strange characters, his own yet stranger existence? How if he forced these pedants and unbelievers to admit that Weller and Pecksniff, Crummles and Swiveller, whom they thought so improbably wild and wonderful, were less wild and wonderful than Charles Dickens? What if he ended the quarrels about whether his romances could occur, by confessing that his romance had occurred?

For some time past, probably during the greater part of his life, he had made notes for an autobiography. I have already quoted an admirable passage from these notes, a passage reproduced in *David Copperfield*, with little more alteration than a change of proper names – the passage which describes Captain Porter and the debtors' petition in the Marshalsea. But he probably perceived at last what a less keen intelligence must ultimately have perceived, that if an autobiography is really to be honest it must be turned into a work of fiction. If it is really to tell the truth, it must at all costs profess not to. No man dare say of himself, over his own name, how badly he has behaved. No man dare say of himself, over his own name, how well he has behaved. Moreover, of course a touch of fiction is almost always essential to the real conveying of fact, because fact, as experienced, has a fragmentariness which is bewildering at first hand and quite blinding at second hand. Facts have at least to be sorted into compartments and the proper head and tail given back to each. The perfection and pointedness of art are a sort of substitute for the pungency of actuality. Without this selection and completion our life seems a tangle of unfinished tales, a heap of novels, all volume one. Dickens determined to make one complete novel of it.

For though there are many other aspects of *David Copperfield*, this autobiographical aspect is, after all, the greatest. The point of the book is that, unlike all the other books of Dickens, it is concerned with quite common actualities, but it is concerned with them warmly and with the war-like sympathies. It is not only both realistic and romantic; it is realistic because it is romantic. It is human nature described with the human exaggeration. We all know the actual types in the book; they are not like the turgid and preternatural types elsewhere in Dickens. They are not purely poetic creations like Mr Kenwigs or Mr Bunsby. We all know that they exist. We all know the stiffnecked and humorous old-fashioned nurse, so conventional and yet so original, so dependent and yet so independent. We all know the intrusive step-father, the abstract strange male, coarse, handsome, sulky, successful, a breaker-up of homes. We all know the erect and sardonic spinster, the spinster who is so mad in small things and so sane in great ones. We all know the cock of the school; we all know Steerforth, the creature whom the gods love and even the servants respect. We know his poor and aristocratic mother, so proud, so gratified, so desolate. We know the Rosa Dartle type, the lonely woman in whom affection itself has stagnated into a sort of poison.

But while these are real characters they are real characters lit up with the colours of youth and passion. They are real people romantically felt; that is to say, they are real people felt as real people feel them. They are exaggerated, like all Dickens's figures: but they are not exaggerated as personalities are exaggerated by an artist; they are exaggerated as personalities are exaggerated by their own friends and enemies. The strong souls are seen through the glorious haze of the emotions that strong souls really create. We have Murdstone as he would be to a boy who hated him; and rightly, for a boy would hate him. We have Steerforth as he would be to a boy who adored him; and rightly, for a boy would adore him. It may be that if these persons had a mere terrestrial existence, they appeared to other eyes more insignificant. It may be that Murdstone in common life was only a heavy business man with a human side that David was too sulky to find. It may be that Steerforth was only an inch or two taller than David, and only a shade or two above him in the lower middle classes; but this does not make the book less true. In cataloguing the facts of life the author must not omit that massive fact, illusion.

When we say the book is true to life we must stipulate that it is especially true to youth: even to boyhood. All the characters seem a little larger than they really were, for David is looking up at them. And the early pages of the book are in particular astonishingly vivid. Parts of it seem like fragments of our forgotten infancy. The dark house of childhood, the loneliness, the things half understood, the nurse with her inscrutable sulks and her more inscrutable tenderness, the sudden deportations to distant places, the seaside and its childish friendships, all this stirs in us when we read it, like something out of a previous existence. Above all, Dickens has excellently depicted the child enthroned in that humble circle which only in after years he perceives to have been humble. Modern and cultured persons, I believe, object to their children seeing kitchen company or being taught by a woman like Peggotty. But surely it is more important to be educated in a sense of human dignity and equality than in anything else in the world. And a child who has once had to respect a kind and capable woman of the lower classes will respect the lower classes for ever. The true way to overcome the evil in class distinctions is not to denounce them as revolutionists denounce them, but to ignore them as children ignore them.

The early youth of David Copperfield is psychologically almost as good as his childhood. In one touch especially Dickens pierced the very core of the sensibility of boyhood; it was when he made David more afraid of a manservant than of anybody or anything else. The lowering Murdstone, the awful Mrs Steerforth are not so alarming to him as Mr Littimer, the unimpeachable gentleman's gentleman. This is exquisitely true to the masculine emotions, especially in their undeveloped state. A youth of common courage does not fear anything violent, but he is in mortal fear of anything correct. This may or may not be the reason that so few female writers understand their male characters, but this fact remains: that the more sincere and passionate and even headlong a lad is the more certain he is to be conventional. The bolder and freer he seems the more the traditions of the college or the rules of the club will hold him with their gyves of gossamer; and the less afraid he is of his enemies the more cravenly he will be afraid of his friends. Herein lies indeed the darkest peril of our ethical doubt and chaos. The fear is that as morals become less urgent, manners will become more so; and men who have forgotten the fear of God will retain the fear of Littimer. We shall merely sink into a much meaner bondage. For when you break the great laws, you do not get liberty; you do not even get anarchy. You get the small laws.

The sting and strength of this piece of fiction, then, do (by a rare accident) lie in the circumstance that it was so largely founded on fact. *David Copperfield* is the great answer of a great romancer to the realists. David says in effect: 'What! you say that the Dickens tales are too purple really to have happened! Why, this is what happened to me, and it seemed the most purple of all. You say that the Dickens heroes are too handsome and triumphant! ... You say the Dickens villains are too black! Why, there was no ink in the devil's ink-stand black enough for my own step-father when I had to live in the same house with him. The facts are quite the other way to what you suppose. This life of grey studies and half tones, the absence of which you regret in Dickens, is only life as it is looked at. This life of heroes and villains is life as it is lived. The life a man knows best is exactly the life he finds most full of fierce certainties and battles between good and ill – his own. Oh yes, the life we do not care about may easily be a psychological comedy. Other people's lives may easily be human documents. But a man's own life is always a melodrama.'

There are other effective things in *David Copperfield*; they are not all autobiographical, but they nearly all have this new note of quietude and reality. Micawber is gigantic; an immense assertion of the truth that the way to live is to exaggerate everything. But of him I shall have to speak more fully in another connection. Mrs Micawber, artistically speaking, is even better. She is very nearly the best thing in Dickens. Nothing could be more absurd, and at the same time more true, than her clear argumentative manner of speech as she sits smiling and expounding in the midst of ruin. What could be more lucid and logical and unanswerable than her statement of the prolegomena of the Medway problem, of which the first step must be to 'see the Medway', or of the coal-trade, which required talent and capital. 'Talent Mr Micawber has. Capital Mr Micawber has not.' It seems as if something should have come at last out of so clear and scientific an arrangement of the ideas. Indeed if (as has been suggested) we regard *David Copperfield* as an unconscious defence of the poetic view of life, we might regard Mrs Micawber as an unconscious satire on the logical view of life. She sits as a monument of the hopelessness and helplessness of reason in the face of this romantic and unreasonable world.

As I have taken *Dombey and Son* as the book before the transition, and *David Copperfield* as typical of the transition itself, I may perhaps take *Bleak House* as the book after the transition, and so complete the description. *Bleak House* has every characteristic of his new realistic culture. Dickens never now, as in his early books, revels in the parts he likes and scamps the parts he does not, after the manner of Scott. He does not, as in previous tales, leave his heroes and heroines mere walking gentlemen and ladies with nothing at all to do but walk: he expends upon them at least ingenuity. By the expedients (successful or not) of the self-revelation of Esther or the humorous inconsistencies of Rick, he makes his younger figures if not lovable at least readable. Everywhere we see this tighter and more careful grip. He does not, for instance, when he wishes to denounce a dark institution, sandwich it in as a mere episode in a rambling story of adventure, as the debtors' prison is embedded in the body of Pickwick or the low Yorkshire school in the body of Nicholas Nickleby. He puts the Court of Chancery in the centre of the stage, a sombre and sinister temple, and groups round it in artistic relation decaying and fantastic figures, its offspring and its satirists. An old dipsomaniac keeps a rag and bone shop, type of futility and antiquity, and calls himself the Lord Chancellor. A little mad old maid hangs about the courts on a forgotten or imaginary lawsuit, and says with perfect and pungent irony, 'I am expecting a judgment shortly. On the Day of Judgment.' Rick and Ada and Esther are not mere strollers who have strayed into the court of law, they are its children, its symbols, and its victims. The righteous indignation of the book is not at the red heat of anarchy, but at the white heat of art. Its anger is patient and plodding, like some historic revenge. Moreover, it slowly and carefully creates the real psychology of oppression. The endless formality, the endless unemotional urbanity, the endless hope deferred, these things make one feel the fact of injustice more than the madness of Nero. For it is not the activeness of tyranny that maddens, but its passiveness. We hate the deafness of the god more than his strength. Silence is the unbearable repartee.

Again we can see in this book strong traces of an increase in social experience. Dickens, as his fame carried him into more fashionable circles, began really to understand something of what is strong and what is weak in the English upper class. Sir Leicester Dedlock is a far more effective condemnation of oligarchy than the ugly swagger of Sir Mulberry Hawk, because pride stands out more plainly in all its impotence and insolence as the one weakness of a good man, than as one of the million weaknesses of a bad one. Dickens, like all young Radicals, had imagined in his youth that aristocracy rested upon the hardness of somebody; he found, as we all do, that it rests upon the softness of everybody. It is very hard not to like Sir Leicester Dedlock, not to applaud his silly old speeches, so foolish, so manly, so genuinely English, so disastrous to England. It is true that the English people love a lord, but it is not true that they fear him; rather, if anything, they pity him; there creeps into their love something of the feeling they have towards a baby or a black man. In their hearts they think it admirable that Sir Leicester Dedlock should be able to speak at all. And so a system, which no iron laws and no bloody battles could possibly force upon a people, is preserved from generation to generation by pure, weak good-nature.

In *Bleak House* occurs the character of Harold Skimpole, the character whose alleged likeness to Leigh Hunt has laid Dickens open to so much disapproval. Unjust disapproval, I think, as far as fundamental morals are concerned. In method he was a little clamorous and clumsy, as, indeed, he was apt to be. But when he said that it was possible to combine a certain tone of conversation taken from a particular man with other characteristics which were not meant to be his, he surely said what all men who write stories know. A work of fiction often consists in combining a pair of whiskers seen in one street with a crime seen in another. He may quite possibly have really meant only to make Leigh Hunt's light philosophy the mask for a new kind of scamp, as a variant on the pious mask of Pecksniff or the candid mask of Bagstock. He may never once have had the unfriendly thought, 'Suppose Hunt

behaved like a rascal!' he may have only had the fanciful thought,
'Suppose a rascal behaved like Hunt!'

But there is a good reason for mentioning Skimpole especially.
In the character of Skimpole, Dickens displayed again a quality
that was very admirable in him – I mean a disposition to see things
sanely and to satirize even his own faults. He was commonly occupied in satirizing the Gradgrinds, the economists, the men of
Smiles and Self-Help. For him there was nothing poorer than their
wealth, nothing more selfish than their self-denial. And against
them he was in the habit of pitting the people of a more expansive
habit – the happy Swivellers and Micawbers, who, if they were
poor, were at least as rich as their last penny could make them. He
loved that great Christian carelessness that seeks its meat from
God. It was merely a kind of uncontrollable honesty that forced
him into urging the other side. He could not disguise from himself
or from the world that the man who began by seeking his meat from
God might end by seeking his meat from his neighbour, without
apprising his neighbour of the fact. He had shown how good irresponsibility could be; he could not stoop to hide how bad it could
be. He created Skimpole; and Skimpole is the dark underside of
Micawber.

In attempting Skimpole he attempted something with a great
and urgent meaning. He attempted it, I say; I do not assert that he
carried it through. As has been remarked, he was never successful
in describing psychological change; his characters are the same
yesterday, today, and for ever. And critics have complained very
justly of the crude villainy of Skimpole's action in the matter of
Joe and Mr Bucket. Certainly Skimpole had no need to commit a
clumsy treachery to win a clumsy bribe; he had only to call on Mr
Jarndyce. He had lost his honour too long to need to sell it.

The effect is bad; but I repeat that the aim was great. Dickens
wished, under the symbol of Skimpole, to point out a truth which
is perhaps the most terrible in moral psychology. I mean the fact
that it is by no means easy to draw the line between light and heavy
offence. He desired to show that there are no faults, however
kindly, that we can afford to flatter or to let alone; he meant that
perhaps Skimpole had once been as good a man as Swiveller. If
flattered or let alone, our kindliest fault can destroy our kindliest
virtue. A thing may begin as a very human weakness, and end as a

very inhuman weakness. Skimpole means that the extremes of evil are much nearer than we think. A man may begin by being too generous to pay his debts, and end by being too mean to pay his debts. For the vices are very strangely in league, and encourage each other. A sober man may become a drunkard through being a coward. A brave man may become a coward through being a drunkard. That is the thing Dickens was darkly trying to convey in Skimpole – that a man might become a mountain of selfishness if he attended only to the Dickens virtues. There is nothing that can be neglected; there is no such thing (he meant) as a peccadillo.

I have dwelt on this consciousness of his because, alas, it had a very sharp edge for himself. Even while he was permitting a fault originally small to make a comedy of Skimpole, a fault originally small was making a tragedy of Charles Dickens. For Dickens also had a bad quality, not intrinsically very terrible, which he allowed to wreck his life. He also had a small weakness that could sometimes become stronger than all his strengths. His selfishness was not, it need hardly be said, the selfishness of Gradgrind; he was particularly compassionate and liberal. Nor was it in the least the selfishness of Skimpole. He was entirely self-dependent, industrious, and dignified. His selfishness was wholly a selfishness of the nerves. Whatever his whim or the temperature of the instant told him to do must be done. He was the type of man who would break a window if it would not open and give him air. And this weakness of his had, by the time of which we speak, led to a breach between himself and his wife which he was too exasperated and excited to heal in time. Everything must be put right, and put right at once, with him. If London bored him, he must go to the Continent at once; if the Continent bored him, he must come back to London at once. If the day was too noisy, the whole household must be quiet; if night was too quiet, the whole household must wake up. Above all, he had this supreme character of the domestic despot – that his good temper was, if possible, more despotic than his bad temper. When he was miserable (as he often was, poor fellow), they only had to listen to his railings. When he was happy they had to listen to his novels. All this, which was mainly mere excitability, did not seem to amount to much; it did not in the least mean that he had ceased to be a clean-living and kind-hearted and quite honest man. But there was this evil about it – that he did not resist his little weakness at all; he pampered it as Skimpole pampered his. And it separated him and his wife. A mere silly trick of temperament did everything that the blackest misconduct could have done. A random sensibility, started about the shuffling of papers or the shutting of a window, ended by tearing two clean, Christian people from each other, like a blast of bigamy or adultery.

IX
LATER LIFE AND WORKS

I HAVE deliberately in this book mentioned only such facts in the life of Dickens as were, I will not say significant (for all facts must be significant, including the million facts that can never be mentioned by anybody), but such facts as illustrated my own immediate meaning. I have observed this method consistently and without shame because I think that we can hardly make too evident a chasm between books which profess to be statements of all the ascertainable facts, and books which (like this one) profess only to contain a particular opinion or a summary deducible from the facts. . . . No catalogue, of course, can contain all the facts even of five minutes; every catalogue, however long and learned, must be not only a bold, but, one may say, an audacious selection. But if a great many facts are given, the reader gains a blurred belief that all the facts are being given. In a professedly personal judgment it is therefore clearer and more honest to give only a few illustrative facts, leaving the other obtainable facts to balance them. For thus it is made quite clear that the thing is a sketch, an affair of a few lines.

It is as well, however, to make at this point a pause sufficient to indicate the main course of the later life of the novelist. And it is best to begin with the man himself, as he appeared in those last days of popularity and public distinction. Many are still alive who remember him in his after-dinner speeches, his lectures, and his many public activities; as I am not one of these, I cannot correct my notions with that flash of the living features without which a description may be subtly and entirely wrong. Once a man is dead, if it be only yesterday, the new-comer must piece him together from descriptions really as much at random as if he were describing Caesar or Henry II. Allowing, however, for this inevitable falsity, a figure vivid and a little fantastic, does walk across the stage of Forster's *Life*.

Dickens was of a middle size and his vivacity and relative physical insignificance probably gave rather the impression of small size; certainly of the absence of bulk. In early life he wore, even for that epoch, extravagant clusters of brown hair and in later years, a brown moustache and a fringe of brown beard (cut like a sort of broad and bushy imperial) sufficiently individual in shape to give him a faint air as of a foreigner. His face had a peculiar tint or quality which is hard to describe even after one has contrived to imagine it. It was the quality which Mrs Carlyle felt to be, as it were metallic, and compared to clear steel. It was, I think, a sort of pale glitter and animation, very much alive and yet with something deathly about it, like a corpse galvanized by a god. His face (if this was so) was curiously a counterpart of his character. For the essence of all Dickens's character was that it was at once tremulous and yet hard and sharp, just as the bright blade of a sword is tremulous and yet hard and sharp. He vibrated at every touch and yet he was indestructible; you could bend him, but you could not break him. Brown of hair and beard, somewhat pale of visage (especially in his later days of excitement and ill-health) he had quite exceptionally bright and active eyes; eyes that were always darting about like brilliant birds to pick up all the tiny things of which he made more, perhaps, than any novelist has done; for he was a sort of poetical Sherlock Holmes. The mouth behind the brown beard was large and mobile, like the mouth of an actor; indeed he was an actor, in many things too much of an actor. In his lectures, in later years, he could turn his strange face into any of the innumerable mad masks that were the faces of his grotesque characters. He could make his face fall suddenly into the blank inanity of Mrs Raddle's servant, or swell, as if to twice its size, into the apoplectic energy of Mr Serjeant Buzfuz. But the outline of his face itself, from his youth upwards, was cut quite delicate and decisive and in repose, and in its own keen way, may even have looked effeminate.

The dress of the comfortable classes during the later years of Dickens was, compared with ours, somewhat slipshod and somewhat gaudy. It was the time of loose pegtop trousers of an almost Turkish oddity, of large ties, of loose short jackets and of loose long whiskers. Yet even this expansive period, it must be confessed, considered Dickens a little too flashy or, as some put it, too Frenchified in his dress. Such a man would wear velvet coats and wild waistcoats that were like incredible sunsets; he would wear those old white hats of an unnecessary and startling whiteness. He did not mind being seen in sensational dressing-gowns; it is said he had his portrait painted in one of them. All this is not meritorious; neither is it particularly discreditable; it is a characteristic only, but an important one. He was an absolutely independent and entirely self-respecting man. But he had none of that old lusty, half-dignified English feeling upon which Thackeray was so sensitive; I mean the desire to be regarded as a private gentleman, which means at bottom the desire to be left alone. This again is not a merit; it is only one of the milder aspects of aristocracy. But meritorious or not, Dickens did not possess it. He had no objection to being stared at, if he were also admired. . . . Nor had he the dull desire to 'get on' which makes men die contented as inarticulate Under-Secretaries of State. He did not desire success so much as fame, the old human glory, the applause and wonder of the people. Such he was as he walked down the street in his Frenchified clothes, probably with a slight swagger.

His private life consisted of one tragedy and ten thousand comedies. By one tragedy I mean one real and rending moral tragedy – the failure of his marriage. He loved his children dearly, and more than one of them died; but in sorrows like these there is no violence and above all no shame. The end of life is not tragic like the end of love. And by the ten thousand comedies I mean the whole texture of his life, his letters, his conversation, which were one incessant carnival of insane and inspired improvisation. So far as he could prevent it, he never permitted a day of his life to be ordinary. There was always some prank, some impetuous proposal, some practical joke, some sudden hospitality, some sudden disappearance. It is related of him (I give one anecdote out of a hundred) that in his last visit to America, when he was already reeling as it were under the blow that was to be mortal, he remarked quite casually to his companions that a row of painted cottages looked exactly like the painted shops in a pantomime. No sooner had the suggestion passed his lips than he leapt at the nearest doorway and in exact imitation of the clown in the harlequinade, beat conscientiously with his fist, not on the door (for that would have burst the canvas scenery of course), but on the side of the doorpost. Having done this he lay down ceremoniously across the doorstep for the owner to fall over him if he should come rushing out. He then got up gravely and went on his way. His whole life was full of such unexpected energies, precisely like those of the pantomime clown. Dickens had indeed a great and fundamental affinity with the landscape, or rather housescape, of the harlequinade. He liked high houses, and sloping roofs, and deep areas. But he would have been really happy if some good fairy of the eternal pantomime had given him the power of flying off the roofs and pitching harmlessly down the height of the houses and bounding out of the areas like an india-rubber ball. The divine lunatic in *Nicholas Nickleby* comes nearest to his dream. I really think Dickens would rather have been that one of his characters than any of the others. With what excitement he would have struggled down the chimney. With what ecstatic energy he would have hurled the cucumbers over the garden wall.

His letters exhibit even more the same incessant creative force. His letters are as creative as any of his literary creation. His shortest postcard is often as good as his ablest novel; each one of them is spontaneous; each one of them is different. He varies even the form and shape of the letter as far as possible; now it is in absurd French; now it is from one of his characters; now it is an advertisement for himself as a stray dog. All of them are very funny; they are not only very funny, but they are quite as funny as his finished and published work. This is the ultimately amazing thing about Dickens; the amount there is of him. He wrote, at the very least, sixteen thick important books packed full of original creation. And if you had burnt them all he could have written sixteen more, as a man writes idle letters to his friend.

In connection with this exuberant part of his nature there is another thing to be noted, if we are to make a personal picture of him. Many modern people, chiefly women, have been heard to object to the Bacchic element in the books of Dickens, that celebration of social drinking as a supreme symbol of social living, which those books share with almost all the great literature of mankind, including the New Testament. Undoubtedly there is an abnormal amount of drinking in a page of Dickens, as there is an abnormal amount of fighting, say, in a page of Dumas. If you reckon up the beers and brandies of Mr Bob Sawyer, with the care of an arithmetician and the deductions of a pathologist, they rise alarmingly like a rising tide at sea. Dickens did defend drink clamorously, praised it with passion, and described whole orgies of it with enormous gusto. Yet it is wonderfully typical of his prompt and impatient nature that he himself drank comparatively little. He was the type of man who could be so eager in praising the cup that he left the cup untasted. It was a part of his active and feverish temperament that he did not drink wine very much. But it was a part of his humane philosophy, of his religion, that he did drink wine. To healthy European philosophy wine is a symbol; to European religion it is a sacrament. Dickens approved it because it was a great human institution, one of the rites of civilization, and this it certainly is. The teetotaller who stands outside it may have perfectly clear ethical reasons of his own, as a man may have who stands outside education or nationality, who refuses to go to a University or to serve in an Army. But he is neglecting one of the great social things that man has added to nature. The teetotaller has chosen a most unfortunate phrase for the drunkard when he says that the drunkard is making a beast of himself. The man who drinks ordinarily makes nothing but an ordinary man of himself. The man who drinks excessively makes a devil of himself. But nothing connected with a human and artistic thing like wine can bring one nearer to the brute life of nature. The only man who is, in the exact and literal sense of the words, making a beast of himself is the teetotaller.

The tone of Dickens towards religion, though like that of most of his contemporaries, philosophically disturbed and rather historically ignorant, had an element that was very characteristic of himself. He had all the prejudices of his time. He had, for instance, that dislike of defined dogmas, which really means a preference for unexamined dogmas. He had the usual vague notion that the whole of our human past was packed with nothing but insane Tories. He had, in a word, all the old Radical ignorances which went along with the old Radical acuteness and courage and public spirit. But this spirit tended, in almost all the others who held it, to a specific dislike of the Church of England; and a disposition to set the other sects against it, as truer types of inquiry, or of individualism. Dickens had a definite tenderness for the Church of England. He might have even called it a weakness for the Church of England, but he had it. Something in those placid services, something in that reticent and humane liturgy pleased him against all the tendencies of his time; pleased him in the best part of himself, his virile love of charity and peace. Once, in a puff of anger at the

Church's political stupidity (which is indeed profound), he left it for a week or two and went to an Unitarian Chapel; in a week or two he came back. This curious and sentimental hold of the English Church upon him increased with years. In the book he was at work on when he died he describes the Minor Canon, humble, chivalrous, tender-hearted, answering with indignant simplicity the froth and platform righteousness of the sectarian philanthropist. He upholds Canon Crisparkle and satirizes Mr Honeythunder. Almost every one of the other Radicals, his friends, would have upheld Mr Honeythunder and satirized Canon Crisparkle.

I have mentioned this matter for a special reason. It brings us back to that apparent contradiction or dualism in Dickens to which, in one connection or another, I have often adverted, and which, in one shape or another, constitutes the whole crux of his character. I mean the union of a general wildness approaching lunacy, with a sort of secret moderation almost amounting to mediocrity. Dickens was, more or less, the man I have described – sensitive, theatrical, amazing, a bit of a dandy, a bit of a buffoon. Nor are such characteristics, whether weak or wild, entirely accidents or externals. He had some false theatrical tendencies integral in his nature. For instance, he had one most unfortunate habit, a habit that often put him in the wrong, even when he happened to be in the right. He had an incurable habit of explaining himself. This reduced his admirers to the mental condition of the authentic but hitherto uncelebrated little girl who said to her mother, 'I think I should understand if only you wouldn't explain.' Dickens always would explain. It was a part of that instinctive publicity of his which made him at once a splendid democrat and a little too much of an actor. He carried it to the craziest lengths. He actually printed, in *Household Words*, an apology for his own action in the matter of his marriage. That incident alone is enough to suggest that his external offers and proposals were sometimes like screams heard from Bedlam. Yet it remains true that he had in him a central part that was pleased only by the most decent and the most reposeful rites, by things of which the Anglican Prayer-book is very typical. It is certainly true that he was often extravagant. It is most certainly equally true that he detested and despised extravagance.

The best explanation can be found in his literary genius. His literary genius consisted in a contradictory capacity at once to entertain and to deride – very ridiculous ideas. If he is a buffoon, he is laughing at buffoonery. His books were in some ways the wildest on the face of the world. Rabelais did not introduce into Paphlagonia or the Kingdom of the Coqcigrues satiric figures more frantic and misshapen than Dickens made to walk about the Strand and Lincoln's Inn. But for all that, you come, in the core of him, on a sudden quietude and good sense. Such, I think, was the core of Rabelais, such were all the far-stretching and violent satirists. This is a point essential to Dickens, though very little comprehended in our current tone of thought. Dickens was an immoderate jester, but a moderate thinker. He was an immoderate jester because he was a moderate thinker. What we moderns call the wildness of his imagination was actually created by what we moderns call the tameness of his thought. I mean that he felt the full insanity of all extreme tendencies, because he was himself so sane; he felt eccentricities, because he was in the centre. We are always, in these days, asking our violent prophets to write violent satires; but violent prophets can never possibly write violent satires. In order to write satire like that of Rabelais – satire that juggles with the stars and kicks the world about like a football – it is necessary to be one's self temperate, and even mild. . . .

I have mentioned his religious preference merely as an instance of this interior moderation. To say, as some have done, that he attacked Nonconformity is quite a false way of putting it. It is clean across the whole trend of the man and his time to suppose that he could have felt bitterness against any theological body as a theological body; but anything like religious extravagance, whether Protestant or Catholic, moved him to an extravagance of satire. And he flung himself into the drunken energy of Stiggins, he piled up to the stars the 'verbose flights of stairs' of Mr Chadband, exactly because his own conception of religion was the quiet and impersonal Morning Prayer. It is typical of him that he had a peculiar hatred for speeches at the grave-side.

An even clearer case of what I mean can be found in his political attitude. He seemed to some an almost anarchic satirist. He made equal fun of the systems which reformers made war on, and of the instruments on which reformers relied. He made no secret of his feeling that the average English premier was an accidental ass. In two superb sentences he summed up and swept away the whole

British constitution: 'England, for the last week, has been in an awful state. Lord Coodle would go out, Sir Thomas Doodle wouldn't come in, and there being no people in England to speak of except Coodle and Doodle, the country has been without a government.' He lumped all cabinets and all government offices together, and made the same game of them all. He created his most staggering humbugs, his most adorable and incredible idiots, and set them in the highest thrones of our national system. To many moderate and progressive people, such a satirist seemed to be insulting heaven and earth, ready to wreck society for some mad alternative, prepared to pull down St Paul's, and on its ruins erect a gory guillotine. Yet, as a matter of fact, this apparent wildness of his came from his being, if anything, a very moderate politician. It came, not at all from fanaticism, but from a rather rational detachment. He had the sense to see that the British constitution was not democracy, but the British constitution. It was an artificial system – like any other, good in some ways, bad in others. His satire of it sounded wild to those that worshipped it; but his satire of it arose not from his having any wild enthusiasm against it, but simply from his not having, like every one else, a wild enthusiasm for it. Alone, as far as I know, among all the great Englishmen of that age, he realized the thing that Frenchmen and Irishmen understand. I mean the fact that popular government is one thing, and representative government another. He realized that representative government has many minor disadvantages, one of them being that it is never representative. He speaks of his 'hope to have made every man in England feel something of the contempt for the House of Commons that I have'. He says also these two things, both of which are wonderfully penetrating as coming from a good Radical in 1855, for they contain a perfect statement of the peril in which we now stand, and which may, if it please God, sting us into avoiding the long vista at the end of which one sees so clearly the dignity and the decay of Venice – 'I am hourly strengthened,' he says, 'in my old belief, that our political aristocracy and our tuft-hunting are the death of England. In all this business I don't see a gleam of hope. As to the popular spirit, it has come to be so entirely separated from the Parliament and the Government, and so perfectly apathetic about them both, that I seriously think it a most portentous sign.' And he says also this: 'I really am serious in

thinking – and I have given as painful consideration to the subject
as a man with children to live and suffer after him can possibly give
it – that representative government is become altogether a failure
with us, that the English gentilities and subserviences render the
people unfit for it, and the whole thing has broken down since the
great seventeenth-century time, and has no hope in it.'

These are the words of a wise and perhaps melancholy man, but
certainly not of an unduly excited one. It is worth noting, for
instance, how much more directly Dickens goes to the point than
Carlyle did, who noted many of the same evils. But Carlyle fancied
that our modern English government was wordy and long-winded
because it was democratic government. Dickens saw, what is
certainly the fact, that it is wordy and long-winded because it is aristocratic government, the two most pleasant aristocratic qualities
being a love of literature and an unconsciousness of time. But all
this amounts to the same conclusion of the matter. Frantic figures
like Stiggins and Chadband were created out of the quietude of
his religious preference. Wild creations like the Barnacles and the
Bounderbys were produced in a kind of ecstasy of the ordinary, of
the obvious in political justice. His monsters were made out of his
level and his moderation, as the old monsters were made out of
the level sea.

Such was the man of genius we must try to imagine; violently
emotional, yet with a good judgment; pugnacious, but only when
he thought himself oppressed; prone to think himself oppressed,
yet not cynical about human motives. He was a man remarkably
hard to understand or to reanimate. He almost always had reasons
for his action; his error was that he always expounded them. Sometimes his nerve snapped; and then he was mad. Unless it did so he
was quite unusually sane.

Such a rough sketch at least must suffice us in order to summarize his later years. Those years were occupied, of course, in two
main additions to his previous activities. The first was the series of
public readings and lectures which he now began to give systematically. The second was his successive editorship of *Household Words*
and of *All the Year Round*. He was of a type that enjoys every new
function and opportunity. He had been so many things in his life,
a reporter, an actor, a conjurer, a poet. As he had enjoyed them
all, so he enjoyed being a lecturer, and enjoyed being an editor. It

is certain that his audiences (who sometimes stacked themselves so thick that they lay flat on the platform all round him) enjoyed his being a lecturer. It is not so certain that the sub-editors enjoyed his being an editor. But in both connections the main matter of importance is the effect on the permanent work of Dickens himself. The readings were important for this reason, that they fixed, as if by some public and pontifical pronouncement, what was Dickens's interpretation of Dickens's work. Such a knowledge is mere tradition, but it is very forcible. My own family has handed on to me, and I shall probably hand on to the next generation, a definite memory of how Dickens made his face suddenly like the face of an idiot in impersonating Mrs Raddle's servant, Betsy. This does serve one of the permanent purposes of tradition; it does make it a little more difficult for any ingenious person to prove that Betsy was meant to be a brilliant satire on the over-cultivation of the intellect.

As for his relation to his two magazines, it is chiefly important, first for the admirable things that he wrote in the magazines himself (one cannot forbear to mention the inimitable monologue of the waiter in 'Somebody's Luggage'), and secondly for the fact that in his capacity of editor he made one valuable discovery. He discovered Wilkie Collins. Wilkie Collins was the one man of unmistakable genius who has a certain affinity with Dickens; an affinity in this respect, that they both combine in a curious way a modern and cockney and even commonplace opinion about things with a huge elemental sympathy with strange oracles and spirits and old nights. There were no two men in Mid-Victorian England, with their top-hats and umbrellas, more typical of its rationality and dull reform; and there were no two men who could touch them at a ghost-story. No two men would have more contempt for superstitions; and no two men could so create the superstitious thrill. Indeed, our modern mystics make a mistake when they wear long hair or loose ties to attract the spirits. The elves and the old gods when they revisit the earth really go straight for a dull top-hat. For it means simplicity, which the gods love.

Meanwhile his books, appearing from time to time, while as brilliant as ever, bore witness to that increasing tendency to a more careful and responsible treatment which we have remarked in the transition which culminated in *Bleak House*. His next important book, *Hard Times*, strikes an almost unexpected note of severity.

The characters are indeed exaggerated, but they are bitterly and deliberately exaggerated; they are not exaggerated with the old unconscious high spirits of Nicholas Nickleby or Martin Chuzzlewit. Dickens exaggerates Bounderby because he really hates him. He exaggerated Pecksniff because he really loved him. *Hard Times* is not one of the greatest books of Dickens; but it is perhaps in a sense one of his greatest monuments. It stamps and records the reality of Dickens's emotion on a great many things that were then considered unphilosophical grumblings, but which since have swelled into the immense phenomenon of the socialist philosophy. To call Dickens a Socialist is a wild exaggeration; but the truth and peculiarity of his position might be expressed thus: that even when everybody thought that Liberalism meant individualism he was emphatically a Liberal and emphatically not an individualist. Or the truth might be better still stated in this manner: that he saw that there was a secret thing, called humanity, to which both extreme socialism and extreme individualism were profoundly and inexpressibly indifferent, and that this permanent and presiding humanity was the thing he happened to understand; he knew that individualism is nothing and non-individualism is nothing but the keeping of the commandment of man. He felt, as a novelist should, that the question is too much discussed as to whether a man is in favour of this or that scientific philosophy; that there is another question, whether the scientific philosophy is in favour of the man. That is why such books as *Hard Times* will remain always a part of the power and tradition of Dickens. He saw that economic systems are not things like the stars, but things like the lamp-posts, manifestations of the human mind, and things to be judged by the human heart.

Thenceforward until the end his books grow consistently graver and, as it were, more responsible; he improves as an artist if not always as a creator. *Little Dorrit* (published in 1857) is at once in some ways so much more subtle and in every way so much more sad than the rest of his work that it bores Dickensians and especially pleases George Gissing. It is the only one of the Dickens tales which could please Gissing, not only by its genius, but also by its atmosphere. There is something a little modern and a little sad, something also out of tune with the main trend of Dickens's moral feeling, about the description of the character of Dorrit as actually and finally weakened by his wasting experiences, as not lifting any cry above the conquered years. It is but a faint fleck of shadow. But the illimitable white light of human hopefulness, of which I spoke at the beginning, is ebbing away, the work of the revolution is growing weaker everywhere; and the night of necessitarianism cometh when no man can work. For the first time in a book by Dickens perhaps we really do feel that the hero is forty-five. Clennam is certainly very much older than Mr Pickwick.

This was indeed only a fugitive grey cloud; he went on to breezier operations. But whatever they were, they still had the note of the later days. They have a more cautious craftsmanship; they have a more mellow and a more mixed human sentiment. Shadows fell upon his page from the other and sadder figures out of the Victorian decline. A good instance of this is his next book, *The Tale of Two Cities* (1859). In dignity and eloquence it almost stands alone among his books by Dickens. But it also stands alone among the books by Dickens in this respect, that it is not entirely by Dickens. It owes its inspiration avowedly to the passionate and cloudy pages of Carlyle's *French Revolution*. And there is something quite essentially inconsistent between Carlyle's disturbed and half-sceptical transcendentalism and the original school and spirit to which Dickens belonged, the lucid and laughing decisiveness of the old convinced and contented Radicalism. Hence the genius of Dickens cannot save him, just as the great genius of Carlyle could not save him from making a picture of the French Revolution, which was delicately and yet deeply erroneous. Both tend too much to represent it as a mere elemental outbreak of hunger or vengeance; they do not see enough that it was a war for intellectual principles, even for intellectual platitudes. We, the modern English, cannot easily understand the French Revolution, because we cannot easily understand the idea of bloody battle for pure common sense; we cannot understand comon sense in arms and conquering. In modern England common sense appears to mean putting up with existing conditions. For us a practical politician really means a man who can be thoroughly trusted to do nothing at all; that is where his practicality comes in. The French feeling – the feeling at the back of the Revolution – was that the more sensible a man was, the more you must look out for slaughter.

In all the imitators of Carlyle, including Dickens, there is an obscure sentiment that the thing for which the Frenchmen died must have been something new and queer, a paradox, a strange idolatry. But when such blood ran in the streets, it was for the sake of a truism; when those cities were shaken to their foundations, they were shaken to their foundations by a truism.

I have mentioned this historical matter because it illustrates these later and more mingled influences which at once improve and as it were perplex the later work of Dickens. For Dickens had in his original mental composition capacities for understanding this cheery and sensible element in the French Revolution far better than Carlyle. The French Revolution was, among other things, French, and, so far as that goes, could never have a precise counterpart in so jolly and autochthonous an Englishman as Charles Dickens. But there was a great deal of the actual and unbroken tradition of the Revolution itself in his early radical indictments; in his denunciations of the Fleet Prison there was a great deal of the capture of the Bastille. There was, above all, a certain reasonable impatience which was the essence of the old Republican, and which is quite unknown to the Revolutionist in modern Europe. The old Radical did not feel exactly that he was 'in revolt'; he felt if anything that a number of idiotic institutions had revolted against reason and against him. Dickens, I say, had the revolutionary idea, though an English form of it, by clear and conscious inheritance; Carlyle had to rediscover the Revolution by a violence of genius and vision. If Dickens, then, took from Carlyle (as he said he did) his image of the Revolution, it does certainly mean that he had forgotten something of his own youth and come under the more complex influences of the end of the nineteenth century. His old hilarious and sentimental view of human nature seems for a moment dimmed in *Little Dorrit*. His old political simplicity has been slightly disturbed by Carlyle.

I repeat that this graver note is varied, but it remains a graver note. We see it struck, I think, with particular and remarkable success in *Great Expectations* (1860–61). This fine story is told with a consistency and quietude of individuality which is rare in Dickens. But so far had he travelled along the road of a heavier reality, that he even intended to give the tale an unhappy ending, making Pip lose Estella for ever; and he was only dissuaded from it by the robust romanticism of Bulwer Lytton. But the best part of the tale

— the account of the vacillations of the hero between the humble life to which he owes everything, and the gorgeous life from which he expects something, touch a very true and somewhat tragic part of morals; for the great paradox of morality (the parodox to which only the religions have given an adequate expression) is that the very vilest kind of fault is exactly the most easy kind. We read in books and ballads about the wild fellow who might kill a man or smoke opium, but who would never stoop to lying or cowardice or to 'anything mean'. But for actual human beings opium and slaughter have only occasional charm; the permanent human temptation is the temptation to be mean. The one standing probability is the probability of becoming a cowardly hypocrite. The circle of the traitors is the lowest of the abyss, and it is also the easiest to fall into. That is one of the ringing realities of the Bible, that it does not make its great men commit grand sins; it makes its great men (such as David and St Peter) commit small sins and behave like sneaks.

Dickens has dealt with this easy descent of desertion, this silent treason, with remarkable accuracy in the account of the indecisions of Pip. It contains a good suggestion of that weak romance which is the root of all snobbishness: that the mystery which belongs to patrician life excites us more than the open, even the indecent virtues of the humble. Pip is keener about Miss Havisham, who may mean well by him, than about Joe Gargery, who evidently does. All this is very strong and wholesome; but it is still a little stern. *Our Mutual Friend*, 1864, brings us back a little into his merrier and more normal manner; some of the satire, such as that upon Veneering's election, is in the best of his old style, so airy and fanciful, yet hitting so suddenly and so hard. But even here we find the fuller and more serious treatment of psychology; notably in the two facts that he creates a really human villain, Bradley Headstone, and also one whom we might call a really human hero, Eugene, if it were not that he is much too human to be called a hero at all. It has been said (invariably by cads) that Dickens never described a gentleman; it is like saying that he never described a zebra. A gentleman is a very rare animal among human creatures, and to people like Dickens, interested in all humanity, not a supremely important one. But in Eugene Wrayburn he does, whether consciously or not, turn that accusation with a vengeance. For he not only describes a gentleman but describes the inner weakness and peril that belong to a gentleman, the devil that is always rending the entrails of an idle and agreeable man. In Eugene's purposeless pursuit of Lizzie Hexam, in his yet more purposeless torturing of Bradley Headstone, the author has marvellously realized that singular empty obstinacy that drives the whims and pleasures of a leisured class. He sees that there is nothing that such a man more stubbornly adheres to, than the thing that he does not particularly want to do. We are still in serious psychology.

His last book represents yet another new departure, dividing him from the chaotic Dickens of days long before. His last book is not merely an attempt to improve his power of construction in a story: it is an attempt to rely entirely on that power of construction. It not only has a plot, it is a plot. *The Mystery of Edwin Drood*, 1870, was in such a sense, perhaps, the most ambitious book that Dickens ever attempted. It is, as every one knows, a detective story, and certainly a very successful one, as is attested by the tumult of discussion as to its proper solution. In this, quite apart from its unfinished state, it stands, I think, alone among the author's works. Elsewhere, if he introduced a mystery, he seldom took the trouble to make it very mysterious. *Our Mutual Friend* was finished, but if only half of it were readable, I think any one could see that John Rokesmith was John Harman. *Bleak House* is finished, but if it were only half finished I think any one would guess that Lady Dedlock and Nemo had sinned in the past. *Edwin Drood* is not finished; for in the very middle of it Dickens died.

He had altogether overstrained himself in a last lecturing tour in America. He was a man in whom any serious malady would naturally make very rapid strides; for he had the temper of an irrational invalid. I have said before that there was in his curious character something that was feminine. Certainly there was nothing more entirely feminine than this, that he worked because he was tired. Fatigue bred in him a false and feverish industry, and his case increased, like the case of a man who drinks to cure the effects of drink. He died in 1870; and the whole nation mourned him as no public man has ever been mourned; for prime ministers and princes were private persons compared with Dickens. He had been a great popular king, like a king of some more primal age whom his people could come and see, giving judgment under an oak tree.

He had in essence held great audiences of millions, and made proclamations to more than one of the nations of the earth. His obvious omnipresence in every part of public life was like the omnipresence of the sovereign. His secret omnipresence in every house and hut of private life was more like the omnipresence of a deity. Compared with that popular leadership all the fusses of the last forty years are diversions in idleness. Compared with such a case as his it may be said that we play with our politicians, and manage to endure our authors. We shall never have again such a popularity until we have again a people.

He left behind him this almost sombre fragment, *The Mystery of Edwin Drood*. As one turns it over the tragic element of its truncation mingles somewhat with an element of tragedy in the thing itself; the passionate and predestined Landless, or the half maniacal Jasper carving devils out of his own heart. The workmanship of it is very fine; the right hand has not only not lost, but is still gaining its cunning. But as we turn the now enigmatic pages the thought creeps into us again which I have suggested earlier, and which is never far off the mind of a true lover of Dickens. Had he lost or gained by the growth of technique and probability in his later work? His later characters were more like men; but were not his earlier characters more like immortals? He has become able to perform a social scene so that it is possible at any rate; but where is that Dickens who once performed the impossible? Where is that young poet who created such majors and architects as Nature will never dare to create? Dickens learnt to describe daily life as Thackeray and Jane Austen could describe it; but Thackeray could not have thought such a thought as Crummles; and it is painful to think of Miss Austen attempting to imagine Mantalini. After all, we feel there are many able novelists; but there is only one Dickens, and whither has he fled?

He was alive to the end. And in this last dark and secretive story of Edwin Drood he makes one splendid and staggering appearance, like a magician saying farewell to mankind. In the centre of this otherwise reasonable and rather melancholy book, this grey story of a good clergyman and the quiet Cloisterham Towers, Dickens has calmly inserted one entirely delightful and entirely insane passage. I mean the frantic and inconceivable epitaph of Mrs Sapsea, that which describes her as 'the reverential wife' of Thomas Sapsea, speaks of her consistency in 'looking up to him', and ends with the words, spaced out so admirably on the tombstone, 'Stranger pause. And ask thyself this question, Canst thou do likewise? If not, with a blush retire.' Not the wildest tale in *Pickwick* contains such an impossibility as that; Dickens dare scarcely have introduced it, even as one of Jingle's lies. In no human churchyard will you find that invaluable tombstone; indeed, you could scarcely find it in any world where there are churchyards. You could scarcely have such immortal folly as that in a world where there is also death. Mr Sapsea is one of the golden things stored up for us in a better world.

Yes, there were many other Dickenses: a clever Dickens, an industrious Dickens, a public-spirited Dickens; but this was the great one. This last outbreak of insane humour reminds us wherein lay his power and his supremacy. The praise of such beatific buffoonery should be the final praise, the ultimate word in his honour. The wild epitaph of Mrs Sapsea should be the serious epitaph of Dickens.

X
THE GREAT DICKENS CHARACTERS

ALL CRITICISM tends too much to become criticism of criticism; and the reason is very evident. It is that criticism of creation is so very staggering a thing. We see this in the difficulty of criticizing any artistic creation. We see it again in the difficulty of criticizing that creation which is spelt with a capital C. The pessimists who attack the Universe are always under this disadvantage. They have an exhilarating consciousness that they could make the sun and moon better; but they also have the depressing consciousness that they could not make the sun and moon at all. A man looking at a hippopotamus may sometimes be tempted to regard a hippopotamus as an enormous mistake; but he is also bound to confess that a fortunate inferiority prevents him personally from making such mistakes. It is neither a blasphemy nor an exaggeration to say that we feel something of the same difficulty in judging of the very creative element in human literature. And this is the first and last dignity of Dickens; that he was a creator. He did not point out things, he made them. We may disapprove of Mr Guppy, but we recognize him as a creation flung down like a miracle out of an upper sphere; we can pull him to pieces, but we could not have put him together. We can destroy Mrs Gamp in our wrath, but we could not have made her in our joy. Under this disadvantage any book about Dickens must definitely labour. Real primary creation (such as the sun or the birth of a child) calls forth not criticism, not appreciation, but a kind of incoherent gratitude. This is why most hymns about God are bad; and this is why most eulogies on Dickens are bad. The eulogists of the divine and of the human creator are alike inclined to appear sentimentalists because they are talking about something so very real. In the same way love-letters always sound florid and artificial because they are about something real.

Any chapter such as this chapter must therefore in a sense be inadequate. There is no way of dealing properly with the ultimate greatness of Dickens, except by offering sacrifice to him as a god; and this is opposed to the etiquette of our time. But something can perhaps be done in the way of suggesting what was the quality of this creation. But even in considering its quality we ought to remember that quality is not the whole question. One of the god-like things about Dickens is his quantity, his quantity as such, the enormous output, the incredible fecundity of his invention. I have said a moment ago that not one of us could have invented Mr Guppy. But even if we could have stolen Mr Guppy from Dickens we have still to confront the fact that Dickens would have been able to invent another quite inconceivable character to take his place. Perhaps we could have created Mr Guppy; but the effort would certainly have exhausted us; we should be ever afterwards wheeled about in a bath-chair at Bournemouth.

Nevertheless there is something that is worth saying about the quality of Dickens. At the very beginning of this review I remarked that the reader must be in a mood, at least, of democracy. To some it may have sounded irrelevant; but the Revolution was as much behind all the books of the nineteenth century as the Catholic religion (let us say) was behind all the colours and carving of the Middle Ages. Another great name of the nineteenth century will afford an evidence of this; and will also bring us most sharply to the problem of the literary quality of Dickens.

Of all these nineteenth-century writers there is none, in the noblest sense, more democratic than Walter Scott. As this may be disputed, and as it is relevant, I will expand the remark. There are two rooted spiritual realities out of which grow all kinds of democratic conception or sentiment of human equality. There are two things in which all men are manifestly and unmistakably equal. They are not equally clever or equally muscular or equally fat, as the sages of the modern reaction (with piercing insight) perceive. But this is a spiritual certainty, that all men are tragic. And this again, is an equally sublime spiritual certainty, that all men are comic. No special and private sorrow can be so dreadful as the fact of having to die. And no freak or deformity can be so funny as the mere fact of having two legs. Every man is important if he loses his life; and every man is funny if he loses his hat, and has to run after it. And the universal test everywhere of whether a thing is popular, of the people, is whether it employs vigorously these extremes of the tragic and the comic. Shelley, for instance, was an aristocrat, if ever there was one in this world. He was a Republican, but he was not a democrat: in his poetry there is every perfect quality except this pungent and popular stab. For the tragic and the comic you must go, say, to Burns, a poor man. And all over the world, the folk literature, the popular literature, is the same. It consists of very dignified sorrow and very undignified fun. Its sad tales are of broken hearts; its happy tales are of broken heads.

These, I say, are two roots of democratic reality. But they have in more civilized literature, a more civilized embodiment or form. In literature such as that of the nineteenth century the two elements appear somewhat thus. Tragedy becomes a profound sense of human dignity. The other and jollier element becomes a delighted sense of human variety. The first supports equality by saying that all men are equally sublime. The second supports equality by observing that all men are equally interesting.

In this democratic aspect of the interest and variety of all men, there is, of course, no democrat so great as Dickens. But in the other matter, in the idea of the dignity of all men, I repeat that there is no democrat so great as Scott. This fact, which is the moral and enduring magnificence of Scott, has been astonishingly over-looked. His rich and dramatic effects are gained in almost every case by some grotesque or beggarly figure rising into a human pride and rhetoric. The common man, in the sense of the paltry man, becomes the common man in the sense of the universal man. He declares his humanity. For the meanest of all the modernities has been the notion that the heroic is an oddity or variation, and that the things that unite us are merely flat or foul. The common things are terrible and startling, death, for instance, and first love: the things that are common are the things that are not commonplace. Into such high and central passions the comic Scott character will suddenly rise. Remember the firm and almost stately answer of the preposterous Nicol Jarvie when Helen Macgregor seeks to brow-beat him into condoning lawlessness and breaking his bourgeois decency. That speech is a great monument of the middle class. Molière made M. Jourdain talk prose; but Scott made him talk poetry. Think of the rising and rousing voice of the dull and glut-tonous Athelstane when he answers and overwhelms De Bracy. Think of the proud appeal of the old beggar in *The Antiquary* when

he rebukes the duellists. Scott was fond of describing kings in disguise. But all his characters are kings in disguise. He was, with all
his errors, profoundly possessed with the old religious conception,
the only possible democratic basis, the idea that man himself is a
king in disguise.

In all this Scott, though a Royalist and a Tory, had in the strangest way, the heart of the Revolution. For instance, he regarded
rhetoric, the art of the orator, as the immediate weapon of the
oppressed. All his poor men make grand speeches, as they did in
the Jacobin Club, which Scott would have so much detested. And
it is odd to reflect that he was, as an author, giving free speech to
fictitious rebels while he was, as a stupid politician, denying it
to real ones. But the point for us here is this: that all this popular
sympathy of his rests on the graver basis, on the dark dignity of
man. 'Can you find no way?' asks Sir Arthur Wardour of the beggar
when they are cut off by the tide. 'I'll give you a farm . . . I'll make
you rich.' . . . 'Our riches will soon be equal,' says the beggar, and
looks out across the advancing sea.

Now, I have dwelt on this strong point of Scott because it is
the best illustration of the one weak point of Dickens. Dickens had
little or none of this sense of the concealed sublimity of every separate man. Dickens's sense of democracy was entirely of the other
kind; it rested on the other of the two supports of which I have
spoken. It rested on the sense that all men were wildly interesting
and wildly varied. When a Dickens character becomes excited
he becomes more and more himself. He does not, like the Scott
beggar, turn more and more into man. As he rises he grows more
and more into a gargoyle or grotesque. He does not, like the fine
speaker in Scott, grow more classical as he grows more passionate,
more universal as he grows more intense. The thing can only be
illustrated by a special case. Dickens did more than once, of course,
make one of his quaint or humble characters assert himself in a
serious crisis or defy the powerful. There is, for instance, the quite
admirable scene in which Susan Nipper (one of the greatest of
Dickens's achievements) faces and rebukes Mr Dombey. But it is
still true (and quite appropriate in its own place and manner) that
Susan Nipper remains a purely comic character throughout her
speech, and even grows more comic as she goes on. She is more
serious than usual in her meaning, but not more serious in her style.

Dickens keeps the natural diction of Nipper, but makes her grow
more Nipperish as she grows more warm. But Scott keeps the natural diction of Baillie Jarvie, but insensibly sobers and uplifts that
style until it reaches a plain and appropriate eloquence. This plain
and appropriate eloquence was (except in a few places at the end
of *Pickwick*) almost unknown to Dickens. Whenever he made comic
characters talk sentiment comically, as in the instance of Susan, it
was a success, but an avowedly extravagant success. Whenever he
made comic characters talk sentiment seriously it was an extravagant failure. Humour was his medium; his only way of approaching
emotion. Wherever you do not get humour, you get unconscious
humour.

As I have said elsewhere in this book Dickens was deeply and
radically English; the most English of our great writers. And there
is something very English in this contentment with a grotesque
democracy; and in this absence of the eloquence and elevation of
Scott. The English democracy is the most humorous democracy in
the world. The Scotch democracy is the most dignified, while the
whole abandon and satiric genius of the English populace come
from its being quite undignified in every way. A comparison of the
two types might be found, for instance, by putting a Scotch Labour
Leader like Mr Keir Hardie alongside an English Labour Leader
like Mr Will Crooks. Both are good men, honest, and responsible
and compassionate; but we can feel that the Scotchman carries
himself seriously and universally, the Englishman personally and
with an obstinate humour. Mr Keir Hardie wishes to hold up his
head as Man, Mr Crooks wishes to follow his nose as Crooks. Mr
Keir Hardie is very like a poor man in Walter Scott. Mr Crooks is
very like a poor man in Dickens.

Dickens then had this English feeling of a grotesque democracy.
By that is more properly meant a vastly varying democracy. The
intoxicating variety of men – that was his vision and conception
of human brotherhood. And certainly it is a great part of human
brotherhood. In one sense things can only be equal if they are
entirely different. Thus, for instance, people talk with a quite
astonishing gravity about the inequality or equality of the sexes; as
if there could possibly be any inequality between a lock and a key.
Wherever there is no element of variety, wherever all the items
literally have an identical aim, there is at once and of necessity

inequality. A woman is only inferior to man in the matter of being not so manly; she is inferior in nothing else. Man is inferior to woman in so far as he is not a woman; there is no other reason. And the same applies in some degree to all genuine differences. It is a great mistake to suppose that love unites and unifies men. Love diversifies them, because love is directed towards individuality. The thing that really unites men and makes them like to each other is hatred. Thus, for instance, the more we love Germany the more pleased we shall be that Germany should be something different from ourselves, should keep her own ritual and conviviality and we ours. But the more we hate Germany the more we shall copy German guns and German fortifications in order to be armed against Germany. The more modern nations detest each other the more meekly they follow each other; for all competition is in its nature only a furious plagiarism. As competition means always similarity, it is equally true that similarity always means inequality. If everything is trying to be green, some things will be greener than others; but there is an immortal and indestructible equality between green and red. Something of the same kind of irrefutable equality exists between the violent and varying creations of such a writer as Dickens. They are all equally ecstatic fulfilments of a separate line of development. It would be hard to say that there could be any comparison or inequality, let us say between Mr Sapsea and Mr Elijah Pogram. They are both in the same difficulty; they can neither of them contrive to exist in this world; they are both too big for the gate of birth.

Of the high virtue of this variation I shall speak more adequately in a moment; but certainly this love of mere variation (which I have contrasted with the classicism of Scott) is the only intelligent statement of the common case against the exaggeration of Dickens. This is the meaning, the only sane or endurable meaning, which people have in their minds when they say that Dickens is a mere caricaturist. They do not mean merely that Uncle Pumblechook does not exist. A fictitious character ought not to be a person who exists; he ought to be an entirely new combination, an addition to the creatures already existing on the earth. They do not mean that Uncle Pumblechook could not exist; for on that obviously they can have no knowledge whatever. They do not mean that Uncle Pumblechook's utterances are selected and arranged so as to bring out his essential Pumblechookery; to say that is simply to say that he occurs in a work of art. But what they do really mean is this, and there is an element of truth in it. They mean that Dickens nowhere makes the reader feel that Pumblechook has any kind of fundamental human dignity at all. It is nowhere suggested that Pumblechook will some day die. He is felt rather as one of the idle and evil fairies, who are innocuous and yet malignant, and who live for ever because they never really live at all. This dehumanized vitality, this fantasy, this irresponsibility of creation, does in some sense truly belong to Dickens. It is the lower side of his hilarious human variety. But now we come to the higher side of his human variety, and it is far more difficult to state.

Mr George Gissing, from the point of view of the passing intellectualism of our day, has made (among his many wise tributes to Dickens) a characteristic complaint about him. He has said that Dickens, with all his undoubted sympathy for the lower classes, never made a working man, a poor man, specifically and highly intellectual. An exception does exist, which he must at least have realized – a wit, a diplomatist, a great philosopher. I mean, of course, Mr Weller. Broadly, however, the accusation has a truth, though it is a truth that Mr Gissing did not grasp in its entirety. It is not only true that Dickens seldom made a poor character what we call intellectual; it is also true that he seldom made any character what we call intellectual. Intellectualism was not at all present to his imagination. What was present to his imagination was character – a thing which is not only more important than intellect, but is also much more entertaining. When some English moralists write about the importance of having character, they appear to mean only the importance of having a dull character. But character is brighter than wit, and much more complex than sophistry. The whole superiority of the democracy of Dickens over the democracy of such a man as Gissing lies exactly in the fact that Gissing would have liked to prove that poor men could instruct themselves and could instruct others. It was of final importance to Dickens that poor men could amuse themselves and could amuse him. He troubled little about the mere education of that life; he declared two essential things about it – that it was laughable, and that it was livable. The humble characters of Dickens do not amuse each other with epigrams; they amuse each other with themselves. The

present that each man brings in hand is his own incredible personality. In the most sacred sense and in the most literal sense of the
phrase, he 'gives himself away'. Now, the man who gives himself
away does the last act of generosity; he is like a martyr, a lover, or
a monk. But he is also almost certainly what we commonly call
a fool.

The key of the great characters of Dickens is that they are all
great fools. There is the same difference between a great fool and
a small fool as there is between a great poet and a small poet. The
great fool is a being who is above wisdom rather than below it. That
element of greatness of which I spoke at the beginning of this book
is nowhere more clearly indicated than in such characters. A man
can be entirely great while he is entirely foolish. We see this in the
epic heroes, such as Achilles. Nay, a man can be entirely great
because he is entirely foolish. We see this in all the great comic
characters of all the great comic writers of whom Dickens was the
last. Bottom the Weaver is great because he is foolish; Mr Toots is
great because he is foolish. The thing I mean can be observed, for
instance, in innumerable actual characters. Which of us has not
known, for instance, a great rustic? – a character so incurably characteristic that he seemed to break through all canons about
cleverness or stupidity; we do not know whether he is an enormous
idiot or an enormous philosopher; we know only that he is enormous, like a hill. These great, grotesque characters are almost
entirely to be found where Dickens found them – among the poorer
classes. The gentry only attain this greatness by going slightly mad.
But who has not known an unfathomably personal old nurse? Who
has not known an abysmal butler? The truth is that our public life
consists almost exclusively of small men. Our public men are small
because they have to prove that they are in the commonplace interpretation clever, because they have to pass examinations, to learn
codes of manners, to imitate a fixed type. It is in private life that
we find the great characters. They are too great to get into the
public world. It is easier for a camel to pass through the eye of a
needle than for a great man to enter into the kingdoms of the earth.
The truly great and gorgeous personality, he who talks as no one
else could talk and feels with an elementary fire, you will never find
this man on any cabinet bench, in any literary circle, at any society
dinner. Least of all will you find him in artistic society; he is utterly

unknown in Bohemia. He is more than clever, he is amusing. He is more than successful, he is alive. You will find him stranded here and there in all sorts of unknown positions, almost always in unsuccessful positions. You will find him adrift as an impecunious commercial traveller like Micawber. You will find him but one of a batch of silly clerks, like Swiveller. You will find him as an unsuccessful actor, like Crummles. You will find him as an unsuccessful doctor, like Sawyer. But you will always find this rich and reeking personality where Dickens found it – among the poor. For the glory of this world is a very small and priggish affair, and these men are too large to get in line with it. They are too strong to conquer.

It is impossible to do justice to these figures because the essential of them is their multiplicity. The whole point of Dickens is that he not only made them, but made them by myriads; that he stamped his foot, and armies came out of the earth. But let us, for the sake of showing the true Dickens method, take one of them, a very sublime one, Toots. It affords a good example of the real work of Dickens, which was the revealing of a certain grotesque greatness inside an obscure and even unattractive type. It reveals the great paradox of all spiritual things; that the inside is always larger than the outside.

Toots is a type that we all know as well as we know chimney-pots. And of all conceivable human figures he is apparently the most futile and the most dull. He is the blockhead who hangs on at a private school, overgrown and underdeveloped. He is always backward in his lessons, but forward in certain cheap ways of the world; he can smoke before he can spell. Toots is a perfect and pungent picture of the wretched youth. Toots has, as this youth always has, a little money of his own; enough to waste in a semi-dissipation he does not enjoy, and in a gaping regard for sports in which he could not possibly excel. Toots has, as this youth always has, bits of surreptitious finery, in his case the incomparable ring. In Toots, above all, is exactly rendered the central and most startling contradiction; the contrast between a jauntiness and a certain impudence of the attire, with the profound shame and sheepishness of the visage and the character. In him, too, is expressed the larger contrast between the external gaiety of such a lad's occupations, and the infinite, disconsolate sadness of his empty eyes. This is

Toots; we know him, we pity him, and we avoid him. Schoolmasters deal with him in despair or in a heart-breaking patience. His family is vague about him. His low-class hangers-on (like the Game Chicken) lead him by the nose. The very parasites that live on him despise him. But Dickens does not despise him. Without denying one of the dreary details which make us avoid the man, Dickens makes him a man whom we long to meet. He does not gloss over one of his dismal deficiencies, but he makes them seem suddenly like violent virtues that we would go to the world's end to see. Without altering one fact, he manages to alter the whole atmosphere, the whole universe of Toots. He makes us not only like, but love, not only love, but reverence this little dunce and cad. The power to do this is a power truly and literally to be called divine.

For this is the very wholesome point. Dickens does not alter Toots in any vital point. The thing he does alter is us. He makes us lively where we were bored, kind where we were cruel, and above all, free for an universal human laughter where we were cramped in a small competition about that sad and solemn thing, the intellect. His enthusiasm fills us, as does the love of God, with a glorious shame; after all, he has only found in Toots what we might have found for ourselves. He has only made us as much interested in Toots as Toots is in himself. He does not alter the proportions of Toots; he alters only the scale; we seem as if we were staring at a rat risen to the stature of an elephant. Hitherto we have passed him by; now we feel that nothing could induce us to pass him by; that is the nearest way of putting the truth. He has not been whitewashed in the least; he has not been depicted as any cleverer than he is. He has been turned from a small fool into a great fool. We know Toots is not clever; but we are not inclined to quarrel with Toots because he is not clever. We are more likely to quarrel with cleverness because it is not Toots. All the examinations he could not pass, all the schools he could not enter, all the temporary tests of brain and culture which surrounded him shall pass, and Toots shall remain like a mountain.

It may be noticed that the great artists always choose great fools rather than great intellectuals to embody humanity. Hamlet does express the aesthetic dreams and the bewilderments of the intellect; but Bottom the Weaver expresses them much better. In the same manner Toots expresses certain permanent dignities in human nature more than any of Dickens's more dignified characters can do it. For instance, Toots expresses admirably the enduring fear, which is the very essence of falling in love. When Toots is invited by Florence to come in, when he longs to come in, but still stays out, he is embodying a sort of insane and perverse humility which is elementary in the lover.

There is an apostolic injunction to suffer fools gladly. We always lay the stress on the word 'suffer', and interpret the passage as one urging resignation. It might be better, perhaps, to lay the stress upon the word 'gladly', and make our familiarity with fools a delight, and almost a dissipation. Nor is it necessary that our pleasure in fools (or at least in great and godlike fools) should be merely satiric or cruel. The great fool is he in whom we cannot tell which is the conscious and which the unconscious humour; we laugh with him and laugh at him at the same time. An obvious instance is that of ordinary and happy marriage. A man and a woman cannot live together without having against each other a kind of everlasting joke. Each has discovered that the other is a fool, but a great fool. This largeness, this grossness and gorgeousness of folly is the thing which we all find about those with whom we are in intiniate contact; and it is the one enduring basis of affection, and even of respect. When we know an individual named Tomkins, we know that he has succeeded where all others have failed; he has succeeded in being Tomkins. Just so Mr Toots succeeded; he was defeated in all scholastic examinations, but he was the victor in that visionary battle in which unknown competitors vainly tried to be Toots.

If we are to look for lessons, here at least is the last and deepest lesson of Dickens. It is in our own daily life that we are to look for the portents and the prodigies. This is the truth, not merely of the fixed figures of our life; the wife, the husband, the fool that fills the sky. It is true of the whole stream and substance of our daily experience; every instant we reject a great fool merely because he is foolish. Every day we neglect Tootses and Swivellers, Guppys and Joblings, Simmerys and Flashers. Every day we lose the last sight of Jobling and Chuckster, the Analytical Chemist, or the Marchioness. Every day we are missing a monster whom we might easily love, and an imbecile whom we should certainly admire. This is the real gospel of Dickens; the inexhaustible opportunities offered by the liberty and the variety of man. Compared with this life, all public life, all fame, all wisdom, is by its nature cramped and cold and small. For on that defined and lighted public stage men are of necessity forced to profess one set of accomplishments, to rise to one rigid standard. It is the utterly unknown people, who can grow in all directions like an exuberant tree. It is in our interior lives that we find that people are too much themselves. It is in our private life that we find people intolerably individual, that we find them swelling into the enormous contours, and taking on the colours of caricature. Many of us live publicly with featureless public puppets, images of the small public abstractions. It is when we pass our own private gate, and open our own secret door, that we step into the land of the giants.

XI

ON THE ALLEGED OPTIMISM
OF DICKENS

IN ONE of the plays of the decadent period, an intellectual
expressed the atmosphere of his epoch by referring to Dickens
as 'a vulgar optimist'. I have in a previous chapter suggested something of the real strangeness of such a term. After all, the main
matter of astonishment (or rather of admiration) is that optimism
should be vulgar. In a world in which physical distress is almost the
common lot, we actually complain that happiness is too common.
In a world in which the majority is physically miserable we actually
complain of the sameness of praise; we are bored with the abun-
dance of approval. When we consider what the conditions of the
vulgar really are, it is difficult to imagine a stranger or more splendid tribute to humanity than such a phrase as vulgar optimism. It
is as if one spoke of 'vulgar martyrdom' or 'common crucifixion'.

First, however, let it be said frankly that there is a foundation for
the charge against Dickens which is implied in the phrase about
vulgar optimism. It does not concern itself with Dickens's confidence in the value of existence and the intrinsic victory of virtue;
that is not optimism but religion. It is not concerned with his habit
of making bright occasions bright, and happy stories happy, that
is not optimism, but literature. Nor is it concerned even with his
peculiar genius for the description of an almost bloated joviality;
that is not optimism, it is simply Dickens. With all these higher variations of optimism I deal elsewhere. But over and above all these
there is a real sense in which Dickens laid himself open to the
accusation of a vulgar optimism, and I desire to put the admission
of this first, before the discussion that follows. Dickens did have a
disposition to make his characters at all costs happy, or, to speak
more strictly, he had a disposition to make them comfortable rather
than happy. He had sort of literary hospitality; he too often treated
his characters as if they were his guests. From a host is always
expected, and always ought to be expected as long as human civilization is healthy, a strictly physical benevolence, if you will, a kind

of coarse benevolence. Food and fire and such things should always be the symbols of the man entertaining men; because they are the things which all men beyond question have in common. But something more than this is needed from the man who is imagining and making men, the artist, the man who is not receiving men, but rather sending them forth.

As I shall remark in a moment in the matter of the Dickens villains, it is not true that he made every one thus at home. But he did do it to a certain wide class of incongruous characters; he did it to all who had been in any way unfortunate. It had indeed its origin (a very beautiful origin) in his realization of how much a little pleasure was to such people. He knew well that the greatest happiness that has been known since Eden is the happiness of the unhappy. So far he is admirable. And as long as he was describing the ecstasy of the poor, the borderland between pain and pleasure, he was at his highest. Nothing that has ever been written about human delights, no Earthly Paradise, no Utopia has ever come so near the quick nerve of happiness as his descriptions of the rare extravagances of the poor; such an admirable description, for instance, as that of Kit Nubbles taking his family to the theatre. For he seizes on the real source of the whole pleasure; a holy fear. Kit tells the waiter to bring the beer. And the waiter, instead of saying, 'Did you address that language to me,' said, 'Pot of beer, sir; yes, sir.' That internal and quivering humility of Kit is the only way to enjoy life or banquets; and the fear of the waiter is the beginning of dining. People in this mood 'take their pleasures sadly'; which is the only way of taking them at all.

So far Dickens is supremely right. As long as he was dealing with such penury and such festivity his touch was almost invariably sure. But when he came to more difficult cases, to people who for one reason or another could not be cured with one good dinner, he did develop this other evil, this genuinely vulgar optimism of which I speak. And the mark of it is this: that he gave the characters a comfort that had no especial connection with themselves; he threw comfort at them like alms. There are cases at the end of his stories in which his kindness to his characters is a careless and insolent kindness. He loses his real charity and adopts the charity of the Charity Organization Society; the charity that is not kind, the charity that is puffed up, and that does behave itself unseemly.

At the end of some of his stories he deals out his characters a kind of out-door relief.

I will give two instances. The whole meaning of the character of Mr Micawber is that a man can be always almost rich by constantly expecting riches. The lesson is a really important one in our sweeping modern sociology. We talk of the man whose life is a failure; but Micawber's life never is a failure, because it is always a crisis. We think constantly of the man who if he looked back would see that his existence was unsuccessful; but Micawber never does look back; he always looks forward, because the bailiff is coming tomorrow. You cannot say he is defeated, for his absurd battle never ends; he cannot despair of life, for he is so much occupied in living. All this is of immense importance in the understanding of the poor; it is worth all the slum novelists that ever insulted democracy. But how did it happen, how could it happen, that the man who created this Micawber could pension him off at the end of the story and make him a successful colonial mayor? Micawber never did succeed, never ought to succeed; his kingdom is not of this world. But this is an excellent instance of Dickens's disposition to make his characters grossly and incongruously comfortable. There is another instance in the same book. Dora, the first wife of David Copperfield, is a very genuine and amusing figure; she has certainly far more force of character than Agnes. She represents the infinite and divine irrationality of the human heart. What possessed Dickens to make her such a dehumanized prig as to recommend her husband to marry another woman? One could easily respect a husband who after time and development made such a marriage, but surely not a wife who desired it. If Dora had died hating Agnes we should know that everything was right, and that God would reconcile the irreconcilable. When Dora dies recommending Agnes we know that everything is wrong, at least if hypocrisy and artificiality and moral vulgarity are wrong. There, again, Dickens yields to a mere desire to give comfort. He wishes to pile up pillows round Dora; and he smothers her with them, like Othello.

This is the real vulgar optimism of Dickens; it does exist, and I have deliberately put it first. Let us admit that Dickens's mind was far too much filled with pictures of satisfaction and cosiness and repose. Let us admit that he thought principally of the pleasures of the oppressed classes; let us admit that it hardly cost him any artistic pang to make out human beings as much happier than they are. Let us admit all this, and a curious fact remains.

For it was this too easily contented Dickens, this man with cushions at his back and (it sometimes seems) cotton wool in his ears, it was this happy dreamer, this vulgar optimist who alone of modern writers did really destroy some of the wrongs he hated and bring about some of the reforms he desired. Dickens did help to pull down the debtors' prisons; and if he was too much of an optimist he was quite enough of a destroyer. Dickens did drive Squeers out of his Yorkshire den; and if Dickens was too contented, it was more than Squeers was. Dickens did leave his mark on parochialism, on nursing, on funerals, on public executions, on workhouses, on the Court of Chancery. These things were altered; they are different. It may be that such reforms are not adequate remedies; that is another question altogether. The next sociologists may think these old Radical reforms quite narrow or accidental. But such as they were, the old radicals got them done; and the new sociologists cannot get anything done at all. And in the practical doing of them Dickens played a solid and quite demonstrable part; that is the plain matter that concerns us here. If Dickens was an optimist he was an uncommonly active and useful kind of optimist. If Dickens was a sentimentalist he was a very practical sentimentalist.

And the reason of this is one that goes deep into Dickens's social reform, and like every other real and desirable thing, involves a kind of mystical contradiction. If we are to save the oppressed, we must have two apparently antagonistic emotions in us at the same time. We must think the oppressed man intensely miserable, and at the same time intensely attractive and important. We must insist with violence upon his degradation; we must insist with the same violence upon his dignity. For if we relax by one inch the one assertion, men will say he does not need saving. And if we relax by one inch the other assertion, men will say he is not worth saving. The optimists will say that reform is needless. The pessimists will say that reform is hopeless. We must apply both simultaneously to the same oppressed man; we must say that he is a worm and a god; and we must thus lay ourselves open to the accusation (or the compliment) of transcendentalism. This is, indeed, the strongest argument for the religious conception of life. If the dignity of man is an earthly dignity we shall be tempted to deny his earthly degradation. If it is a heavenly dignity we can admit the earthly degradation with all the candour of Zola. If we are idealists about the other world we can be realists about this world. But that is not here the point. What is quite evident is that if a logical praise of the poor man is pushed too far, and if a logical distress about him is pushed too far, either will involve wreckage to the central paradox of reform. If the poor man is made too admirable he ceases to be pitiable; if the poor man is made too pitiable he becomes merely contemptible. There is a school of smug optimists who will deny that he is a poor man. There is a school of scientific pessimists who will deny that he is a man.

Out of this perennial contradiction arises the fact that there are always two types of the reformer. The first we may call for convenience the pessimistic, the second the optimistic reformer. One dwells upon the fact that souls are being lost; the other dwells upon the fact that they are worth saving. Both, of course, are (so far as that is concerned) quite right, but they naturally tend to a difference of method, and sometimes to a difference of perception. The pessimistic reformer points out the good elements that oppression has destroyed; the optimistic reformer, with an even fiercer joy, points out the good elements that it has not destroyed. It is the case for the first reformer that slavery has made men slavish. It is the case for the second reformer that slavery has not made men slavish. The first describes how bad men are under bad conditions. The second describes how good men are under bad conditions. Of the first class of of writers, for instance, is Gorky. Of the second class of writers is Dickens.

But here we must register a real and somewhat startling fact. In the face of all apparent probability, it is certainly true that the optimistic reformer reforms much more completely than the pessimistic reformer. People produce violent changes by being contented, by being far too contented. The man who said that 'revolutions are not made with rose-water' was obviously inexperienced in practical human affairs. Men like Rousseau and Shelley do make revolutions, and do make them with rose-water; that is, with a too rosy and sentimental view of human goodness. Figures that come before and create convulsion and change (for instance, the central figure of the New Testament) always have the air of walking in an unnatural sweetness and calm. They give us their peace ultimately in blood and battle and division; not as the world giveth give they unto us.

Nor is the real reason of the triumph of the too-contented reformer particularly difficult to define. He triumphs because he keeps alive in the human soul an invincible sense of the thing being worth doing, of the war being worth winning, of the people being worth their deliverance. I remember that Mr William Archer,[1] some time ago, published in one of his interesting series of interviews, an interview with Mr Thomas Hardy. That powerful writer was represented as saying, in the course of the conversation, that he did not wish at the particular moment to define his position with regard to the ultimate problem of whether life itself was worth living. There are, he said, hundreds of remediable evils in this world. When we have remedied all these (such was his argument), it will be time enough to ask whether existence itself under its best possible conditions is valuable or desirable. Here we have presented, with a considerable element of what can only be called unconscious humour, the plain reason of the failure of the pessimist as a reformer. Mr Hardy is asking us, I will not say to buy a pig in a poke; he is asking us to buy a poke on the remote chance of there being a pig in it. When we have for some few frantic centuries tortured ourselves to save mankind, it will then be 'time enough' to discuss whether they can possibly be saved. When, in the case of infant mortality, for example, we have exhausted ourselves with the earth-shaking efforts required to save the life of every individual baby, it will then be time enough to consider whether every individual baby would not have been happier dead. We are to remove mountains and bring the millennium, because then we can have a quiet moment to discuss whether the millennium is at all desirable. Here we have the low-water mark of the impotence of the sad reformer. And here we have the reason of the paradoxical triumph of the happy one. His triumph is a religious triumph; it rests upon his perpetual assertion of the value of the human soul and of human daily life. It rests upon his assertion that human life is enjoyable because it is human. And he will never admit, like so many compassionate pessimists, that human life ever ceases to be human. He does not merely pity the lowness of men; he feels an insult to

1 William Archer (1856–1924), drama critic and translator of Ibsen.

their elevation. Brute pity should be given only to the brutes. Cruelty to animals is cruelty and a vile thing; but cruelty to a man is not cruelty, it is treason. Tyranny over a man is not tyranny, it is rebellion, for man is royal. Now, the practical weakness of the vast mass of modern pity for the poor and the oppressed is precisely that it is merely pity; the pity is pitiful, but not respectful. Men feel that the cruelty to the poor is a kind of cruelty to animals. They never feel that it is injustice to equals; nay, it is treachery to comrades. This dark, scientific pity, this brutal pity, has an elemental sincerity of its own; but it is entirely useless for all ends of social reform. Democracy swept Europe with the sabre when it was founded upon the Rights of Man. It has done literally nothing at all since it has been founded only upon the wrongs of man. Or, more strictly speaking, its recent failure has been due to its not admitting the existence of any rights or wrongs, or indeed of any humanity. Evolution (the sinister enemy of revolution) does not especially deny the existence of God; what it does deny is the existence of man. And all the despair about the poor, and the cold and repugnant pity for them, has been largely due to the vague sense that they have literally relapsed into the state of the lower animals.

A writer sufficiently typical of recent revolutionism – Gorky – has called one of his books by the eerie and effective title *Creatures that Once were Men*. That title explains the whole failure of the Russian revolution. And the reason why the English writers, such as Dickens, did with all their limitations achieve so many of the actual things at which they aimed, was that they could not possibly have put such a title upon a human book. Dickens really helped the unfortunate in the matters to which he set himself. And the reason is that across all his books and sketches about the unfortunate might be written the common title, 'Creatures that Still are Men'.

There does exist, then, this strange optimistic reformer; the man whose work begins with approval and yet ends with earthquake. Jesus Christ was destined to found a faith which made the rich poorer and the poor richer; but even when He was going to enrich them, He began with the phrase, 'Blessed are the poor'. The Gissings and the Gorkys say, as an universal literary motto, 'Cursed are the poor'. Among a million who have faintly followed Christ in this divine contradiction, Dickens stands out especially. He said, in all his reforming utterances, 'Cure poverty'; but he said in all his actual descriptions, 'Blessed are the poor'. He described their happiness, and men rushed to remove their sorrow. He described them as human, and men resented the insults to their humanity. It is not difficult to see why, as I said at an earlier stage of this book, Dickens's denunciations have had so much more practical an effect than the denunciations of such a man as Gissing. Both agreed that the souls of the people were in a kind of prison. But Gissing said that the prison was full of dead souls. Dickens said that the prison was full of living souls. And the fiery cavalcade of rescuers felt that they had not come too late.

Of this general fact about Dickens's descriptions of poverty there will not, I suppose, be any serious dispute. The dispute will only be about the truth of those descriptions. It is clear that whereas Gissing would say, 'See how their poverty depresses the Smiths or the Browns,' Dickens says, 'See how little, after all, their poverty can depress the Cratchits.' No one will deny that he made a special feature a special study of the subject of the festivity of the poor. We will come to the discussion of the veracity of these scenes in a moment. It is here sufficient to register in conclusion of our examination of the reforming optimist, that Dickens certainly was such an optimist, and that he made it his business to insist upon what happiness there is in the lives of the unhappy. His poor man is always a Mark Tapley, a man the optimism of whose spirit increases if anything with the pessimism of his experience. It can also be registered as a fact equally solid and quite equally demonstrable that this optimistic Dickens did effect great reforms.

The reforms in which Dickens was instrumental were indeed, from the point of view of our sweeping social panaceas, special and limited. But perhaps, for that reason especially, they afford a compact and concrete instance of the psychological paradox of which we speak. Dickens did definitely destroy – or at the very least help to destroy – certain institutions; he destroyed those institutions simply by describing them. But the crux and peculiarity of the whole matter is this, that, in a sense, it can really be said that he described these things too optimistically. In a real sense, he described Dotheboys Hall as a better place than it is. In a real sense, he made out the workhouse as a pleasanter place than it can ever be. For the chief glory of Dickens is that he made these places interesting; and the chief infamy of England is that it has made these places dull. Dulness was the one thing that Dickens's genius could never succeed in describing; his vitality was so violent that he could not introduce into his books the genuine impression even of a moment of monotony. If there is anywhere in his novels an instant of silence, we only hear more clearly the hero whispering with the heroine, the villain sharpening his dagger, or the creaking of the machinery that is to give out the god from the machine. He could splendidly describe gloomy places, but he could not describe dreary places. He could describe miserable marriages, but not monotonous marriages. It must have been genuinely entertaining to be married to Mr Quilp. This sense of a still incessant excitement he spreads over every inch of his story, and over every dark tract of his landscape. His idea of a desolate place is a place where any-thing can happen; he has no idea of that desolate place where noth-ing can happen. This is a good thing for his soul, for the place where nothing can happen is hell. But still, it might reasonably be main-tained by the modern mind that he is hampered in describing human evil and sorrow by this inability to imagine tedium, this dulness in the matter of dulness. For, after all, it is certainly true that the worst part of the lot of the unfortunate is the fact that they have long spaces in which to review the irrevocability of their doom. It is certainly true that the worst days of the oppressed man are the nine days out of ten in which he is not oppressed. This sense of sickness and sameness Dickens did certainly fail or refuse to give. When we read such a description as that excellent one – in detail – of Dotheboys Hall, we feel that, while everything else is accurate, the author does, in the words of the excellent Captain Nares in Stevenson's *Wrecker*, 'draw the dreariness rather mild'. The boys at Dotheboys were, perhaps, less bullied, but they were certainly more bored. For, indeed, how could any one be bored with the society of so sumptuous a creature as Mr Squeers? Who would not put up with a few illogical floggings in order to enjoy the conversa-tion of a man who could say, 'She's a rum 'un is Natur'. . . . Natur', is more easier conceived than described.' The same principle applies to the workhouse in *Oliver Twist*. We feel vaguely that neither Oliver nor any one else could be entirely unhappy in the presence of the purple personality of Mr Bumble. The one thing he did not describe in any of the abuses he denounced was the soul-destroying potency of routine. He made out the bad school, the bad parochial system, the bad debtors' prison as very much jollier and more exciting than they may really have been. In a sense, then, he flattered them; but he destroyed them with the flattery. By making Mrs Gamp delightful he made her impossible. He gave every one an interest in Mr Bumble's existence; and by the same act gave every one an interest in his destruction. It would be difficult to find a stronger instance of the utility and energy of the method which we have, for the sake of argument, called the method of the optimistic reformer. As long as low Yorkshire schools were entirely colourless and dreary, they continued quietly tolerated by the public, and quietly intolerable to the victims. So long as Squeers was dull as well as cruel he was permitted; the moment he became amusing as well as cruel he was destroyed. As long as Bumble was merely inhuman he was allowed. When he became human, humanity wiped him out. For in order to do these great acts of justice we must always realize not only the humanity of the oppressed, but even the humanity of the oppressor. The satirist had, in a sense, to create the images in the mind before, as an iconoclast, he could destroy them. Dickens had to make Squeers live before he could make him die.

In connection with the accusation of vulgar optimism, which I have taken as a text for this chapter, there is another somewhat odd thing to notice. Nobody in the world was ever less optimistic than Dickens in his treatment of evil or the evil man. When I say optimistic in this matter I mean optimism, in the modern sense, of an attempt to whitewash evil. Nobody ever made less attempt to whitewash evil than Dickens. Nobody black was ever less white than Dickens's black. He painted his villains and lost characters more black than they really are. He crowds his stories with a kind of villain rare in modern fiction – the villain really without any 'redeeming point'. There is no redeeming point in Squeers, or in Monks, or in Ralph Nickleby, or in Bill Sikes, or in Quilp, or in Brass, or in Mr Chester, or in Mr Pecksniff, or in Jonas Chuzzlewit, or in Carker, or in Uriah Heep, or in Blandois, or in a hundred more. So far as the balance of good and evil in human characters is concerned, Dickens certainly could not be called a vulgar optimist. His emphasis on evil was melodramatic. He might be called a vulgar pessimist.

Some will dismiss this lurid villainy as a detail of his artificial romance. I am not inclined to do so. He inherited, undoubtedly, this unqualified villain as he inherited so many other things, from the whole history of European literature. But he breathed into the blackguard a peculiar and vigorous life of his own. He did not show any tendency to modify his blackguardism in accordance with the increasing considerateness of the age; he did not seem to wish to to make his villain less villainous; he did not wish to imitate the analysis of George Eliot, or the reverent scepticism of Thackeray. And all this works back, I think, to a real thing in him, that he wished to have an obstreperous and incalculable enemy. He wished to keep alive the idea of combat, which means, of necessity, a combat against something individual and alive. I do not know whether, in the kindly rationalism of his epoch, he kept any belief in a personal devil in his theology, but he certainly created a personal devil in every one of his books.

A good example of my meaning can be found, for instance, in such a character as Quilp. Dickens may, for all I know, have had originally some idea of describing Quilp as the bitter and unhappy cripple, a deformity whose mind is stunted along with his body. But if he had such an idea, he soon abandoned it. Quilp is not in the least unhappy. His whole picturesqueness consists in the fact that he has a kind of hellish happiness, an atrocious hilarity that makes him go bounding about like an india-rubber ball. Quilp is not in the least bitter; he has an unaffected gaiety, an expansiveness, an universality. He desires to hurt people in the same hearty way that a good-natured man desires to help them. He likes to poison people with the same kind of clamorous camaraderie with which an honest man likes to stand them drink. Quilp is not in the least stunted in mind; he is not in reality even stunted in body – his body, that is, does not in any way fall short of what he wants it to do. His smallness gives him rather the promptitude of a bird or the precipitance of a bullet. In a word, Quilp is precisely the devil of the Middle Ages; he belongs to that amazingly healthy period when even the lost spirits were hilarious.

This heartiness and vivacity in the villains of Dickens is worthy of note because it is directly connected with his own cheerfulness. This is a truth little understood in our time, but it is a very essential one. If optimism means a general approval, it is certainly true that the more a man becomes an optimist the more he becomes a melancholy man. If he manages to praise everything, his praise will develop an alarming resemblance to a polite boredom. He will say that the marsh is as good as the garden; he will mean that the garden is as dull as the marsh. He may force himself to say that emptiness is good, but he will hardly prevent himself from asking what is the good of such good. This optimism does exist – this optimism which is more hopeless than pessimism – this optimism which is the very heart of hell. Against such an aching vacuum of joyless approval there is only one antidote – a sudden and pugnacious belief in positive evil. This world can be made beautiful again by beholding it as a battlefield. When we have defined and isolated the evil thing, the colours come back into everything else. When evil things have become evil, good things, in a blazing apocalypse, become good. There are some men who are dreary because they do not believe in God; but there are many others who are dreary because they do not believe in the devil. The grass grows green again when we believe in the devil, the roses grow red again when we believe in the devil.

No man was more filled with the sense of this bellicose basis of all cheerfulness than Dickens. He knew very well the essential truth, that the true optimist can only continue an optimist so long as he is discontented. For the full value of this life can only be got by fighting; the violent take it by storm. And if we have accepted everything, we have missed something – war. This life of ours is a very enjoyable fight, but a very miserable truce. And it appears strange to me that so few critics of Dickens or of other romantic writers have noticed this philosophical meaning in the undiluted villain. The villain is not in the story to be a character; he is there to be a danger – a ceaseless, ruthless, and uncompromising menace, like that of wild beasts or the sea. For the full satisfaction of the sense of combat, which everywhere and always involves a sense of equality, it is necessary to make the evil thing a man; but it is not always necessary, it is not even always artistic, to make him a mixed and probable man. In any tale, the tone of which is at all symbolic, he may quite legitimately be made an aboriginal and infernal energy. He must be a man only in the sense that he must have a wit and will to be matched with the wit and will of the man chiefly fighting. The evil may be inhuman, but it must not be impersonal, which is almost exactly the position occupied by Satan in the theological scheme.

But when all is said, as I have remarked before, the chief fountain in Dickens of what I have called cheerfulness, and some prefer to call optimism, is something deeper than a verbal philosophy. It is, after all, an incomparable hunger and pleasure for the vitality and the variety, for the infinite eccentricity of existence. And this word 'eccentricity' brings us, perhaps, nearer to the matter than any other. It is, perhaps, the strongest mark of the divinity of man that he talks of this world as 'a strange world', though he has seen no other. We feel that all there is is eccentric, though we do not know what is the centre. This sentiment of the grotesqueness of the universe ran through Dickens's brain and body like the mad blood of the elves. He saw all his streets in fantastic perspectives, he saw all his cockney villas as top heavy and wild, he saw every man's nose twice as big as it was, and every man's eyes like saucers. And this was the basis of his gaiety – the only real basis of any philosophical gaiety. This world is not to be justified as it is justified by the mechanical optimists; it is not to be justified as the best of all possible worlds. Its merit is not that it is orderly and explicable; its merit is that it is wild and utterly unexplained. Its merit is precisely that none of us could have conceived such a thing, that we should have rejected the bare idea of it as miracle and unreason. It is the best of all impossible worlds.

XII
A NOTE ON THE FUTURE OF DICKENS

THE HARDEST thing to remember about our own time, of course, is simply that it is a time; we all instinctively think of it as the Day of Judgment. But all the things in it which belong to it merely as this time will probably be rapidly turned upside down; all the things that can pass will pass. It is not merely true that all old things are already dead; it is also true that all new things are already dead; for the only undying things are the things that are neither new nor old. The more you are up with this year's fashion, the more (in a sense) you are already behind next year's. Consequently, in attempting to decide whether an author will, as it is cantly expressed, live, it is necessary to have very firm convictions about what part, if any part, of man is unchangeable. And it is very hard to have this if you have not a religion or, at least, a dogmatic philosophy.

The equality of men needs preaching quite as much as regards the ages as regards the classes of men. To feel infinitely superior to a man in the twelfth century is just precisely as snobbish as to feel infinitely superior to a man in the Old Kent Road. There are differences between the man and us, there may be superiorities in us over the man; but our sin in both cases consists in thinking of the small things wherein we differ when we ought to be confounded and intoxicated by the terrible and joyful matters in which we are at one. But here again the difficulty always is that the things near us seem larger than they are, and so seem to be a permanent part of mankind, when they may really be only one of its parting modes of expression. Few people, for instance, realize that a time may easily come when we shall see the great outburst of Science in the nineteenth century as something quite as splendid, brief, unique, and ultimately abandoned, as the outburst of Art at the Renaissance. Few people realize that the general habit of fiction, of telling tales in prose, may fade, like the general habit of the ballad, of telling tales in verse, has for the time faded. Few people realize that reading and writing are only arbitrary, and perhaps temporary sciences, like heraldry.

The immortal mind will remain, and by that writers like Dickens will be securely judged. That Dickens will have a high place in permanent literature there is, I imagine, no prig surviving to deny. But though all prediction is in the dark, I would devote this chapter to suggesting that his place in nineteenth-century England will not only be high, but altogether the highest. At a certain period of his contemporary fame, an average Englishman would have said that there were at that moment in England about five or six able and equal novelists. He could have made a list, Dickens, Bulwer Lytton, Thackeray, Charlotte Brontë, George Eliot, perhaps more. Forty years or more have passed and some of them have slipped to a lower place. Some would now say that the highest platform is left to Thackeray and Dickens; some to Dickens, Thackeray, and George Eliot; some to Dickens, Thackeray, and Charlotte Brontë. I venture to offer the proposition that when more years have passed and more weeding has been effected, Dickens will dominate the whole England of the nineteenth century; he will be left on that platform alone.

I know that this is an almost impertinent thing to assert, and that its tendency is to bring in those disparaging discussions of other writers in which Mr Swinburne brilliantly embroiled himself in his suggestive study of Dickens. But my disparagement of the other English Novelists is wholly relative and not in the least positive. It is certain that men will always return to such a writer as Thackeray, with his rich emotional autumn, his feeling that life is a sad but sacred retrospect, in which at least we should forget nothing. It is not likely that wise men will forget him. So, for instance, wise and scholarly men do from time to time return to the lyrists of the French Renaissance, to the delicate poignancy of Du Bellay: so they will go back to Thackeray. But I mean that Dickens will bestride and dominate our time as the vast figure of Rabelais dominates Du Bellay, dominates the Renaissance and the world.

Let me put a negative reason first. The particular things for which Dickens is condemned (and justly condemned) by his critics, are precisely those things which have never prevented a man from being immortal. The chief of them is the unquestionable fact that he wrote an enormous amount of bad work. This does lead to a man being put below his place in his own time: it does not affect his permanent place, to all appearance, at all. Shakespeare, for instance, and Wordsworth wrote not only an enormous amount of bad work, but an enormous amount of enormously bad work. Humanity edits such writers' works for them. Virgil was mistaken in cutting out his inferior lines; we would have undertaken the job. Moreover in the particular case of Dickens there are special reasons for regarding his bad work, as in some sense, irrelevant. So much of it was written, as I have previously suggested, under a kind of general ambition that had nothing to do with his special genius; an ambition to be a public provider of everything, a warehouse of all human emotions. He held a kind of literary day of judgment. He distributed bad characters as punishments and good characters as rewards. My meaning can be best conveyed by one instance out of many. The character of the kind old Jew in *Our Mutual Friend* (a needless and unconvincing character) was actually introduced because some Jewish correspondent complains that the bad old Jew in *Oliver Twist* conveyed the suggestion that all Jews were bad. The principle is so light-headedly absurd that it is hard to imagine any literary man submitting to it for an instant. If ever he invented a bad auctioneer he must immediately balance him with a good auctioneer; if he should have conceived an unkind philanthropist, he must on the spot, with whatever natural agony and toil, imagine a kind philanthropist. The complaint is frantic; yet Dickens, who tore people in pieces for much fairer complaints, liked this complaint of his Jewish correspondent. It pleased him to be mistaken for a public arbiter: it pleased him to be asked (in a double sense) to judge Israel. All this is so much another thing, a non-literary vanity, that there is much less difficulty than usual in separating it from his serious genius: and by his serious genius, I need hardly say, I mean his comic genius. Such irrelevant ambitions as this are easily passed over, like the sonnets of great statesmen. We feel that such things can be set aside, as the ignorant experiments of men otherwise great, like the politics of Professor Tyndall or the philosophy of Professor Haeckel. Hence, I think, posterity will not care that Dickens has done bad work, but will know that he has done good.

Again, the other chief accusation against Dickens was that his characters and their actions were exaggerated and impossible.

But this only meant that they were exaggerated and impossible as compared with the modern world and with certain writers (like Thackeray or Trollope) who were making a very exact copy of the manners of the modern world. Some people, oddly enough, have suggested that Dickens has suffered or will suffer from the change of manners. Surely this is irrational. It is not the creators of the impossible who will suffer from the process of time: Mr Bunsby can never be any more impossible than he was when Dickens made him. The writers who will obviously suffer from time will be the careful and realistic writers; the writers who have observed every detail of the fashion of this world which passeth away. It is surely obvious that there is nothing so fragile as a fact, that a fact flies away quicker than a fancy. A fancy will endure for two thousand years. For instance, we all have fancy for an entirely fearless man, a hero: and the Achilles of Homer still remains. But exactly the thing we do not know about Achilles is how far he was possible. The realistic narrators of time are all forgotten (thank God) so we cannot tell whether Homer slightly exaggerated or wildly exaggerated or did not exaggerate at all, the personal activity of a Mycenaean captain in battle: for the fancy has survived the facts. So the fancy of Podsnap may survive the facts of English commerce; and no one will know whether Podsnap was possible, but only know that he is desirable, like Achilles.

The positive argument for the permanence of Dickens comes back to the thing that can only be stated and cannot be discussed: creation. He made things which nobody else could possibly make. He made Dick Swiveller in a very different sense from that in which Thackeray made Colonel Newcome. Thackeray's creation was observation: Dickens's was poetry, and is therefore permanent. But there is one other test that can be added. The immortal writer, I conceive, is commonly he who does something universal in a special manner. I mean that he does something interesting to all men in a way in which only one man or one land can do. Other men in that land, who do only what other men in other lands are doing as well, tend to have a great reputation in their day and to sink slowly into a second or a third or a fourth place. A parallel from war will make the point clearer. I cannot think that any one will doubt that although Wellington and Nelson were always bracketed, Nelson will steadily become more important and

Wellington less. For the fame of Wellington rests upon the fact that he was a good soldier in the service of England, exactly as twenty similar men were good soldiers in the service of Austria or Prussia or France. But Nelson is the symbol of a special mode of attack, which is at once universal and yet specially English, the sea. Now Dickens is at once as universal as the sea and as English as Nelson. Thackeray and George Eliot and the other great figures of that great England, were comparable to Wellington in this, that the kind of thing they were doing – realism, the acute study of intellectual things, numerous men in France, Germany and Italy were doing as well or better than they. But Dickens was really doing something universal, yet something that no one but an Englishman could do. This is attested by the fact that he and Byron are the men who, like pinnacles, strike the eye of the continent. The points would take long to study: yet they may take only a moment to indicate. No one but an Englishman could have filled his books at once with a furious caricature and with a positively furious kindness. In more central countries, full of cruel memories of political change, caricature is always inhumane. No one but an Englishman could have described the democracy as consisting of free men, but yet of funny men. In other countries where the democratic issue has been more bitterly fought, it is felt that unless you describe a man as dignified you are describing him as a slave. This is the only final greatness of a man; that he does for all the world what all the world cannot do for itself. Dickens, I believe, did it.

The hour of absinthe is over. We shall not be much further troubled with the little artists who found Dickens too sane for their sorrows and too clean for their delights. But we have a long way to travel before we get back to what Dickens meant; and the passage is along a rambling English road, a twisting road such as Mr Pickwick travelled. But this at least is part of what he meant: that comradeship and serious joy are not interludes in our travel; but that rather our travels are interludes in comradeship and joy, which through God shall endure for ever. The inn does not point to the road; the road points to the inn. And all roads point at last to an ultimate inn, where we shall meet Dickens and all his characters: and when we drink again it shall be from the great flagons in the tavern at the end of the world.

THE VICTORIAN AGE
IN LITERATURE

I

THE VICTORIAN COMPROMISE AND
ITS ENEMIES

THE PREVIOUS literary life of this country had left vigorous many old forces in the Victorian time, as in our time. Roman Britain and Mediaeval England are still not only alive but lively; for real development is not leaving things behind, as on a road, but drawing life from them, as from a root. Even when we improve we never progress. For progress, the metaphor from the road, implies a man leaving his home behind him: but improvement means a man exalting the towers or extending the gardens of his home. The ancient English literature was like all the several literatures of Christendom, alike in its likeness, alike in its very unlikeness. Like all European cultures, it was European; like all European cultures, it was something more than European. A most marked and unmanageable national temperament is plain in Chaucer and the ballads of Robin Hood; in spite of deep and sometimes disastrous changes of national policy, that note is still unmistakable in Shakespeare, in Johnson and his friends, in Cobbett, in Dickens. It is vain to dream of defining such vivid things; a national soul is as indefinable as a smell, and as unmistakable. I remember a friend who tried impatiently to explain the word 'mistletoe' to a German, and cried at last, despairing, 'Well, you know holly – mistletoe's the opposite!' I do not commend this logical method in the comparison of plants or nations. But if he had said to the Teuton, 'Well, you know Germany – England's the opposite' – the definition, though fallacious, would not have been wholly false. England, like all Christian countries, absorbed valuable elements from the forests and the rude romanticism of the North; but, like all Christian countries, it drank its longest literary draughts from the classic fountains of the ancients: nor was this (as is so often loosely thought) a matter of the mere 'Renaissance'. The English tongue and talent of speech did not merely flower suddenly into the gargantuan polysyllables of the great Elizabethans; it had always been full of the popular Latin of the Middle Ages. But whatever balance of blood and racial idiom one allows, it is really true that the only suggestion that gets near the Englishman is to hint how far he is from the German. The Germans, like the Welsh, can sing perfectly serious songs perfectly seriously in chorus: can with clear eyes and clear voices, join together in words of innocent and beautiful personal passion, for a false maiden or a dead child. The nearest one can get to defining the poetic temper of Englishmen is to say that they couldn't do this even for beer. They can sing in chorus, and louder than other Christians: but they must have in their songs something, I know not what, that is at once shamefaced and rowdy.... Compare, for example, the rants of Shakespeare with the rants of Victor Hugo. A piece of Hugo's eloquence is either a serious triumph or a serious collapse: one feels the poet is offended at a smile. But Shakespeare seems rather proud of talking nonsense: I never can read that rousing and mounting description of the storm, where it comes to –

Who take the ruffian billows by the top, curling their monstrous heads, and *hanging* them with deafening clamour in the slippery clouds

without seeing an immense balloon rising from the ground, with Shakespeare grinning over the edge of the car, and saying, 'You can't stop me: I am above reason now.' That is the nearest we can get to the general national spirit, which we have now to follow through one brief and curious but very national episode.

Three years before the young queen was crowned, William Cobbett was buried at Farnham. It may seem strange to begin with this great neglected name, rather than the old age of Wordsworth or the young death of Shelley. But to any one who feels literature as human, the empty chair of Cobbett is more solemn and significant than the throne. With him died the sort of democracy that was a return to Nature, and which only poets and mobs can understand. After him Radicalism is urban – and Toryism suburban. Going through green Warwickshire, Cobbett might have thought of the crops and Shelley of the clouds. But Shelley would have called Birmingham what Cobbett called it – a hell-hole. Cobbett was one with after Liberals in the ideal of Man under an equal law, a citizen of no mean city. He differed from after Liberals in strongly affirming that Liverpool and Leeds are mean cities.

It is no idle Hibernianism to say that towards the end of the eighteenth century the most important event in English history happened in France. It would seem still more perverse, yet it would be still more precise, to say that the most important event in English history was the event that never happened at all – the English Revolution on the lines of the French Revolution. Its failure was not due to any lack of fervour or even ferocity in those who would have brought it about: from the time when the first shout went up for Wilkes to the time when the last Luddite fires were quenched in a cold rain of rationalism, the spirit of Cobbett, of rural republicanism, of English and patriotic democracy, burned like a beacon. The revolution failed because it was foiled by another revolution; an aristocratic revolution, a victory of the rich over the poor. It was about this time that the common lands were finally enclosed; that the more cruel game laws were first established; that England became finally a land of landlords instead of common landowners. I will not call it a Tory reaction; for much of the worst of it (especially of the land-grabbing) was done by Whigs; but we may certainly call it Anti-Jacobin. Now this fact, though political, is not only relevant but essential to everything that concerned literature. The upshot was that though England was full of the revolutionary ideas, nevertheless there was no revolution. And the effect of this in turn was that from the middle of the eighteenth century to the middle of the nineteenth the spirit of revolt in England took a wholly literary form. In France it was what people did that was wild and elemental; in England it was what people wrote. It is a quaint comment on the notion that the English are practical and the French merely visionary, that we were rebels in arts while they were rebels in arms.

... There never were, I think, men who gave to the imagination so much of the sense of having broken out into the very borderlands of being, as did the great English poets of the romantic or revolutionary period; than Coleridge in the secret sunlight of the Antarctic, where the waters were like witches' oils; than Keats looking out of those extreme mysterious casements upon that ultimate sea....

This trend of the English Romantics to carry out the revolutionary idea not savagely in works, but very wildly indeed in words, had several results; the most important of which was this. It started English literature after the Revolution with a sort of bent towards independence and eccentricity, which in the brighter wits became individuality, and in the duller ones, Individualism. English Romantics, English Liberals, were not public men making a republic, but poets, each seeing a vision. The lonelier version of liberty was a sort of aristocratic anarchism in Byron and Shelley; but though in Victorian times it faded into much milder prejudices and much more *bourgeois* crotchets, England retained from that twist a certain odd separation and privacy. England became much more of an island than she had ever been before. There fell from her about this time, not only the understanding of France or Germany, but to her own long and yet lingering disaster, the understanding of Ireland. She had not joined in the attempt to create European democracy; nor did she, save in the first glow of Waterloo, join in the counter-attempt to destroy it. The life in her literature was still, to a large extent, the romantic liberalism of Rousseau, the free and humane truisms that had refreshed the other nations, the return to Nature and to natural rights. But that which in Rousseau was a creed, became in Hazlitt a taste and in Lamb little more than a whim. These latter and their like form a group at the beginning of the nineteenth century of those we may call the Eccentrics: they gather round Coleridge and his decaying dreams or linger in the tracks of Keats and Shelley and Godwin; Lamb with his bibliomania and creed of pure caprice, the most unique of all geniuses; Leigh Hunt with his Bohemian impecuniosity; Landor with his tempestuous temper, throwing plates on the floor; Hazlitt with his bitterness and his low love affair; even that healthier and happier Bohemian, Peacock. With these, in one sense at least, goes De Quincey. He was, unlike most of these embers of the revolutionary age in letters, a Tory ... But he had nothing in common with that environment. It remained for some time as a Tory tradition, which balanced the cold and brilliant aristocracy of the Whigs. It lived on the legend of Trafalgar; the sense that insularity was independence; the sense that anomalies are as jolly as family jokes; the general sense that old salts are the salt of the earth. It still lives in some old songs about Nelson or Waterloo, which are vastly more pompous and vastly more sincere than the cockney cocksureness of later Jingo lyrics. But it is hard to connect De Quincey with it; or, indeed, with anything else. De Quincey would certainly have been a happier man, and almost certainly a better man, if he had got drunk on toddy with Wilson, instead of getting calm and clear (as he himself describes) on opium, and with no company but a book of German metaphysics. But he would hardly have revealed those wonderful vistas and perspectives of prose, which permit one to call him the first and most powerful of the decadents: those sentences that lengthen out like nightmare corridors, or rise higher and higher like impossible eastern pagodas. He was a morbid fellow, and far less moral than Burns; for when Burns confessed excess he did not defend it. But he has cast a gigantic shadow on our literature, and was as certainly a genius as Poe. Also he had humour, which Poe had not. And if any one still smarting from the pinpricks of Wilde or Whistler, wants to convict them of plagiarism in their 'art for art' epigrams, he will find most of what they said said better in *Murder as One of the Fine Arts*.

One great man remains of this elder group, who did their last work only under Victoria; he knew most of the members of it, yet he did not belong to it in any corporate sense. He was a poor man and an invalid, with Scotch blood and a strong, though perhaps only inherited, quarrel with the old Calvinism; by name Thomas Hood. Poverty and illness forced him to the toils of an incessant jester; and the revolt against gloomy religion made him turn his wit, whenever he could, in the direction of a defence of happier and humaner views. In the long great roll that includes Homer and Shakespeare, he was the last great man who really employed the pun. His puns were not all good (nor were Shakespeare's), but the best of them were a strong and fresh form of art. The pun is said to be a thing of two meanings; but with Hood there were three meanings, for there was also the abstract truth that would have been there with no pun at all. The pun of Hood is underrated, like the 'wit' of Voltaire, by those who forget that the words of Voltaire were not pins, but swords. In Hood at his best the verbal neatness only gives to the satire or the scorn a ring of finality such as is given by rhyme. For rhyme does go with reason, since the aim of both is to bring things to an end. The tragic necessity of puns tautened and hardened Hood's genius; so that there is always a sort of shadow of that sharpness across all his serious poems, falling like the shadow of a sword. 'Sewing at once with a double thread a shroud as well as a shirt' – 'We thought her dying when she slept, and sleeping when she died' – 'Oh God, that bread should be so dear and flesh and blood so cheap' – none can fail to note in these a certain fighting discipline of phrase, a compactness and point which was well trained in lines like 'A cannon-ball took off his legs, so he laid down his arms.' In France he would have been a great epigrammatist, like Hugo. In England he is a punster.

There was nothing at least in this group I have loosely called the Eccentrics that disturbs the general sense that all their generation was part of the sunset of the great revolutionary poets. This fading glamour affected England in a sentimental and, to some extent, a snobbish direction; making men feel that great lords with long curls and whiskers were naturally the wits that led the world. But it affected England also negatively and by reaction; for it associated such men as Byron with superiority, but not with success. The English middle classes were led to distrust poetry almost as much as they admired it. They could not believe that either vision at the one end or violence at the other could ever be practical. They were deaf to that great warning of Hugo: 'You say the poet is in the clouds; but so is the thunderbolt.' Ideals exhausted themselves in the void; Victorian England, very unwisely, would have no more to do with idealists in politics. And this, chiefly, because there had been about these great poets a young and splendid sterility; since the pantheist Shelley was in fact washed under by the wave of the world, or Byron sank in death as he drew the sword for Hellas.

The chief turn of nineteenth-century England was taken about the time when a footman at Holland House opened a door and announced 'Mr Macaulay'. Macaulay's literary popularity was representative and it was deserved; but his presence among the great Whig families marks an epoch. He was the son of one of the first 'friends of the negro', whose honest industry and philanthropy were darkened by a religion of sombre smugness, which almost makes one fancy they loved the negro for his colour, and would have turned away from red or yellow men as needlessly gaudy. But his wit and his politics (combined with that dropping of the Puritan tenets but retention of the Puritan tone which marked his class and generation) lifted him into a sphere which was utterly opposite to that from which he came. This Whig world was exclusive; but it was not narrow. It was very difficult for an outsider to get into it; but if he did get into it he was in a much freer atmosphere than any other in England. Of those aristocrats, the Old Guard of the eighteenth century, many denied God, many defended Bonaparte, and nearly all sneered at the Royal Family. Nor did wealth or birth make any barriers for those once within this singular Whig world. The platform was high, but it was level. Moreover the upstart nowadays pushes himself by wealth: but the Whigs could choose their upstarts. . . . For the fundamental fact of early Victorian history was this; the decision of the middle classes to employ their new wealth in backing up a sort of aristocratical compromise, and not (like the middle class in the French Revolution) insisting on a clean sweep and a clear democratic programme. It went along with the decision of the aristocracy to recruit itself more freely from the middle class. It was then also that Victorian 'prudery' began: the great lords yielded on this as on Free Trade. These two decisions have made the doubtful England of today; and Macaulay is typical of them; he is the *bourgeois* in Belgravia. The alliance is marked by his great speeches for Lord Grey's Reform Bill: it is marked even more significantly in his speech against the Chartists. Cobbett was dead.

Macaulay makes the foundation of the Victorian age in all its very English and unique elements: its praise of Puritan politics and abandonment of Puritan theology; its belief in a cautious but perpetual patching up of the Constitution; its admiration for industrial wealth. But above all he typifies the two things that really make the Victorian Age itself, the cheapness and narrowness of its conscious formulae; the richness and humanity of its unconscious tradition. There were two Macaulays, a rational Macaulay who was generally wrong, and a romantic Macaulay who was almost invariably right. All that was small in him derives from the dull parliamentarism of men like Sir James Mackintosh; but all that was great in him has much more kinship with the festive antiquarianism of Sir Walter Scott.

As a philosopher he had only two thoughts; and neither of them is true. The first was that politics, as an experimental science, must go on improving, along with clocks, pistols or penknives, by the mere accumulation of experiment and variety. He was, indeed, far too strong-minded a man to accept the hazy modern notion that the soul in its highest sense can change: he seems to have held that religion can never get any better and that poetry rather tends to get worse. But he did not see the flaw in his political theory; which is that unless the soul improves with time there is no guarantee that the accumulations of experience will be adequately used. Figures do not add themselves up; birds do not label or stuff themselves; comets do not calculate their own courses; these things are done by the soul of man. And if the soul of man is subject to other laws, is liable to sin, to sleep, to anarchism or to suicide, then all sciences including politics may fall as sterile and lie as fallow as before man's reason was made. Macaulay seemed sometimes to talk as if clocks produced clocks, or guns had families of little pistols, or a penknife littered like a pig. The other view he held was the more or less utilitarian theory of toleration; that we should get the best butcher whether he was a Baptist or a Muggletonian and the best soldier, whether he was a Wesleyan or an Irvingite. The compromise worked well enough in an England Protestant in bulk; but Macaulay ought to have seen that it has its limitations. A good butcher might be Baptist; he is not very likely to be a Buddhist. A good soldier might be a Wesleyan; he would hardly be a Quaker. For the rest, Macaulay was concerned to interpret the seventeenth century in terms of the triumph of the Whigs as champions of public rights; and he upheld this one-sidedly but not malignantly in a style of rounded and ringing sentences, which at its best is like steel and at its worst like tin.

This was the small conscious Macaulay; the great unconscious Macaulay was very different. His noble enduring quality in our literature is this: that he truly had an abstract passion for history; a warm, poetic and sincere enthusiasm for great things as such; an ardour and appetite for great books, great battles, great cities, great men. He felt and used names like trumpets. The reader's greatest joy is in the writer's own joy, when he can let his last phrase fall like a hammer on some resounding name like Hildebrand or Charlemagne, on the eagles of Rome or the pillars of Hercules. As with Walter Scott, some of the best things in his prose and poetry are the surnames that he did not make. And it is remarkable to notice that this romance of history, so far from making him more partial or untrustworthy, was the only thing that made him moderately just. His reason was entirely one-sided and fanatical. It was his imagination that was well-balanced and broad. He was monotonously certain that only Whigs were right; but it was necessary that Tories should at least be great, that his heroes might have foemen worthy of their steel. . . . That is exactly where Macaulay is great; because he is almost Homeric. The whole triumph turns upon mere names; but men are commanded by names. So his poem on the Armada is really a good geography book gone mad; one sees the map of England come alive and march and mix under the eye.

The chief tragedy in the trend of later literature may be expressed by saying that the smaller Macaulay conquered the larger. Later men had less and less of that hot love of history he had inherited from Scott. They had more and more of that cold science of self-interests which he had learnt from Bentham.

The name of this great man, though it belongs to a period before the Victorian, is, like the name of Cobbett, very important to it. In substance Macaulay accepted the conclusions of Bentham; though he offered brilliant objections to all his arguments. In any case the soul of Bentham (if he had one) went marching on . . . and in the central Victorian movement it was certainly he who won. John Stuart Mill was the final flower of that growth. He was himself fresh and delicate and pure; but that is the business of a flower. Though he had to preach a hard rationalism in religion, a hard competition in economics, a hard egoism in ethics, his own soul had all that silvery sensitiveness that can be seen in his fine portrait by Watts. . . . There was about Mill even a sort of embarrassment; he exhibited all the wheels of his iron universe rather reluctantly, like a gentleman in trade showing ladies over his factory. There shone in him a beautiful reverence for women, which is all the more touching because, in his department, as it were, he could only offer them so dry a gift as the Victorian Parliamentary Franchise.

Now in trying to describe how the Victorian writers stood to each other, we must recur to the very real difficulty noted at the beginning; the difficulty of keeping the moral order parallel with the chronological order. For the mind moves by instincts, associations, premonitions and not by fixed dates or completed processes. Action and reaction will occur simultaneously: or the cause actually be found after the effect. Errors will be resisted before they have been properly promulgated: notions will be first defined long after they are dead. It is no good getting the almanac to look up moonshine; and most literature in this sense is moonshine. Thus Wordsworth shrank back into Toryism, as it were, from a Shelleyan extreme of pantheism as yet disembodied. Thus Newman took down the iron sword of dogma to parry a blow not yet delivered, that was coming from the club of Darwin. For this reason no one can understand tradition, or even history, who has not some tenderness for anachronism.

Now for the great part of the Victorian era the utilitarian tradition which reached its highest in Mill held the centre of the field; it was the philosophy in office, so to speak. It sustained its march of codification and inquiry until it had made possible the great victories of Darwin and Huxley and Wallace. If we take Macaulay at the beginning of the epoch and Huxley at the end of it, we shall find that they had much in common. They were both square-jawed, simple men, greedy of controversy but scornful of sophistry, dead to mysticism but very much alive to morality; and they were both very much more under the influence of their own admirable rhetoric than they knew. Huxley, especially, was much more a literary than a scientific man. It is amusing to note that when Huxley was charged with being rhetorical, he expressed his horror of 'plastering the fair face of truth with that pestilent cosmetic, rhetoric', which is itself about as well-plastered a piece of rhetoric as Ruskin himself could have managed. The difference that the period had developed can best be seen if we consider this: that while neither was of a spiritual sort, Macaulay took it for granted that common sense required some kind of theology, while Huxley took it for granted that common sense meant having none. Macaulay, it is said, never talked about his religion: but Huxley was always talking about the religion he hadn't got.

But though this simple Victorian rationalism held the centre, and in a certain sense *was* the Victorian era, it was assailed on many sides, and had been assailed even before the beginning of that era. The rest of the intellectual history of the time is a series of reactions against it, which come wave after wave. They have succeeded in shaking it, but not in dislodging it from the modern mind. The first of these was the Oxford Movement; a bow that broke when it had let loose the flashing arrow that was Newman. The second reaction was one man; without teachers or pupils – Dickens. The third reaction was a group that tried to create a sort of new romantic Protestantism, to pit against both Reason and Rome – Carlyle, Ruskin, Kingsley, Maurice – perhaps Tennyson. Browning also was at once romantic and Puritan; but he belonged to no group, and worked against materialism in a manner entirely his own. Though as a boy he bought eagerly Shelley's revolutionary poems, he did not think of becoming a revolutionary poet. He concentrated on the special souls of men; seeking God in a series of private interviews. Hence Browning, great as he is, is rather one of the Victorian novelists than wholly of the Victorian poets. From Ruskin, again, descend those who may be called the Pre-Raphaelites of prose and poetry.

It is really with this rationalism triumphant, and with the romance of these various attacks on it, that the study of Victorian literature begins and proceeds. Bentham was already the prophet of a powerful sect; Macaulay was already the historian of an historic party, before the true Victorian epoch began. The middle classes were emerging in a state of damaged Puritanism. The upper classes were utterly pagan. Their clear and courageous testimony remains in those immortal words of Lord Melbourne,[1] who had led the young queen to the throne and long stood there as her protector. 'No one has more respect for the Christian religion than I have; but really, when it comes to intruding it into private life—' What was pure paganism in the politics of Melbourne became a sort of mystical cynicism in the politics of Disraeli; and is well mirrored in his novels — for he was a man who felt at home in mysteries. With every allowance for aliens and eccentrics and all the accidents that must always eat the edges of any systematic circumference, it may still be said that the Utilitarians held the fort.

Of the Oxford Movement what remains most strongly in the Victorian Epoch centres round the challenge of Newman, its one great literary man. But the movement as a whole had been of great significance in the very genesis and make up of the society: yet that significance is not quite easy immediately to define. It was certainly not aesthetic ritualism; scarcely one of the Oxford High Churchmen was what we should call a Ritualist. It was certainly not a conscious reaching out towards Rome: except on a Roman Catholic theory which might explain all our unrests by that dim desire. It knew little of Europe, it knew nothing of Ireland, to which any merely Roman Catholic revulsion would obviously have turned. In the first instance, I think, the more it is studied, the more

[1] Whig prime minister under Queen Victoria.

it would appear that it was a movement of mere religion as such. It was not so much a taste for Catholic dogma, but simply a hunger for dogma. For dogma means the serious satisfaction of the mind. Dogma does not mean the absence of thought, but the end of thought. It was a revolt against the Victorian spirit in one particular aspect of it; which may roughly be called (in cosy and domestic Victorian metaphor) having your cake and eating it too. It saw that the solid and serious Victorians were fundamentally frivolous – because they were fundamentally inconsistent.

A man making the confession of any creed worth ten minutes' intelligent talk, is always a man who gains something and gives up something. So long as he does both he can create; for he is making an outline and a shape. Mohamet created, when he forbade wine but allowed five wives: he created a very big thing, which we have still to deal with. The first French Republic created, when it affirmed property and abolished peerages; France still stands like a square, four-sided building which Europe has besieged in vain. The men of the Oxford Movement would have been horrified at being compared either with Moslems or Jacobins. But their sub-conscious thirst was for something that Moslems and Jacobins had and ordinary Anglicans had not: the exalted excitement of consis-tency. If you were a Moslem you were not a Bacchanal. If you were a Republican you were not a peer. And so the Oxford men, even in their first and dimmest stages, felt that if you were a Churchman you were not a Dissenter. The Oxford Movement was, out of the very roots of its being, a rational movement; almost a rationalist movement. In that it differed sharply from the other reactions that shook the Utilitarian compromise; the blinding mysticism of Carlyle, the mere manly emotionalism of Dickens. It was an appeal to reason: reason said that if a Christian had a feast day he must have a fast day too. Otherwise, all days ought to be alike; and this was that very Utilitarianism against which their Oxford Move-ment was the first and most rational assault.

This idea, even by reason of its reason, narrowed into a sort of sharp spear, of which the spear blade was Newman. It did forget many of the other forces that were fighting on its side. But the movement could boast, first and last, many men who had this eager dogmatic quality; Keble, who spoilt a poem in order to recognize a doctrine; Faber who told the rich, almost with taunts, that God sent the poor as eagles to strip them, Froude who, with Newman announced his return in the arrogant motto of Achilles. But the greater part of all this happened before what is properly our period; and in that period Newman, and perhaps Newman alone, is the expression and summary of the whole school. It was certainly in the Victorian Age, and after his passage to Rome, that Newman claimed his complete right to be in any book on modern English literature. This is no place for estimating his theology: but one point about it does clearly emerge. Whatever else is right, the theory that Newman went over to Rome to find peace and an end of argument, is quite unquestionably wrong. He had far more quarrels after he had gone over to Rome. But, though he had far more quarrels, he had far fewer compromises: and he was of that temper which is tortured more by compromise than by quarrel. He was a man at once of abnormal energy and abnormal sensibility: nobody without that combination could have written the *Apologia*. If he sometimes seemed to skin his enemies alive, it was because he himself lacked a skin. In this sense his *Apologia* is a triumph far beyond the ephemeral charge on which it was founded; in this sense he does indeed (to use his own expression) vanquish not his accuser but his judges. Many men would shrink from recording all their cold fits and hesitations and prolonged inconsistencies. I am sure it was the breath of life to Newman to confess them, now that he had done with them for ever. His *Lectures on the Present Position of English Catholics*, practically preached against a raging mob, rise not only higher but happier, and his instant unpopularity increases. There is something grander than humour, there is fun, in the very first lecture about the British Constitution as explained to a meeting of Russians. But always his triumphs are the triumphs of a highly sensitive man: a man must feel insults before he can so insultingly and splendidly avenge them. He is a naked man, who carries a naked sword. The quality of his literary style is so successful that it succeeds in escaping definition. The quality of his logic is that of a long but passionate patience, which waits until he has fixed all corners of an iron trap. But the quality of his moral comment on the age remains what I have said: a protest of the rationality of religion as against the increasing irrationality of mere Victorian comfort and compromise. So far as the present purpose is concerned, his protest died with him: he left few imitators and (it may easily be conceived) no successful imitators. The suggestion of him lingers on in the exquisite Elizabethan perversity of Coventry Patmore; and has later flamed out from the shy volcano of Francis Thompson. Otherwise (as we shall see in the parallel case of Ruskin's Socialism) he has no followers in his own age: but very many in ours.

The next group of reactionaries or romantics or whatever we elect to call them, gathers roughly around one great name. Scotland, from which had come so many of those harsh economists who made the first Radical philosophies of the Victorian Age, was destined also to fling forth (I had almost said to spit forth) their fiercest and most extraordinary enemy. The two primary things in Thomas Carlyle were his early Scotch education and his later German culture. The first was in almost all respects his strength; the latter in some respects his weakness. As an ordinary lowland peasant, he inherited the really valuable historic property of the Scots, their independence, their fighting spirit, and their instinctive philosophic consideration of men merely as men. But he was not an ordinary peasant. If he had laboured obscurely in his village till death, he would have been yet locally a marked man; a man with a wild eye, a man with an air of silent anger; perhaps a man at whom stones were sometimes thrown. A strain of disease and suffering ran athwart both his body and his soul. In spite of his praise of silence, it was only through his gift of utterance that he escaped madness. But while his fellow-peasants would have seen this in him and perhaps mocked it, they would also have seen something which they always expect in such men, and they would have got it: vision, a power in the mind akin to second sight. Like many ungainly or otherwise unattractive Scotchmen, he was a seer. By which I do not mean to refer so much to his transcendental rhapsodies about the World-soul or the Nature-garment or the Mysteries and Eternities generally, these seem to me to belong more to his German side and to be less sincere and vital. I mean a real power of seeing things suddenly, not apparently reached by any process; a grand power of guessing. He *saw* the crowd of the new States General, Danton with his 'rude flattened face', Robespierre peering mistily through his spectacles. He *saw* the English charge at Dunbar. He *guessed* that Mirabeau, however dissipated and diseased, had something sturdy inside him. He *guessed* that Lafayette, however brave and victorious, had nothing inside him. He supported the lawlessness of Cromwell, because across two centuries he almost physically *felt* the feebleness and hopelessness of the moderate Parliamentarians. He said a word of sympathy for the universally vituperated Jacobins of the Mountain, because through thick veils of national prejudice and misrepresentation, he felt the impossibility of the Gironde. He was wrong in denying to Scott the power of being inside his characters: but he really had a good deal of that power himself. It was one of his innumerable and rather provincial crotchets to encourage prose as against poetry. But, as a matter of fact, he himself was much greater considered as a kind of poet than considered as anything else; and the central idea of poetry is the idea of guessing right, like a child.

He first emerged, as it were, as a student and disciple of Goethe. The connection was not wholly fortunate. With much of what Goethe really stood for he was not really in sympathy; but in his own obstinate way, he tried to knock his idol into shape instead of choosing another. He pushed further and further the extravagances of a vivid but very unbalanced and barbaric style, in the praise of a poet who really represented the calmest classicism and the attempt to restore a Hellenic equilibrium in the mind. It is like watching a shaggy Scandinavian decorating a Greek statue washed up by chance on his shores. And while the strength of Goethe was a strength of completion and serenity, which Carlyle not only never found but never even sought, the weaknesses of Goethe were of a sort that did not draw the best out of Carlyle. The one civilized element that the German classicists forgot to put into their beautiful balance was a sense of humour. And great poet as Goethe was, there is to the last something faintly fatuous about his half sceptical, half sentimental self-importance; a Lord Chamberlain of teacup politics; an earnest and elderly flirt; a German of the Germans. Now Carlyle had humour; he had it in his very style; but it never got into his philosophy. His philosophy largely remained a heavy Teutonic idealism, absurdly unaware of the complexity of things; as when he perpetually repeated (as with a kind of flat-footed stamping) that people ought to tell the truth; apparently supposing, to quote Stevenson's phrase, that telling the truth is as easy as blind hookey. Yet, though his general honesty is unquestionable, he was by no means one of those who will give up a fancy under the shock of a fact. If by sheer genius he frequently guessed right, he was not the kind of man to admit easily that he had guessed wrong. His version of Cromwell's filthy cruelties in Ireland, or his impatient slurring over the most sinister riddle in the morality of Fredrick the Great – these passages are, one must frankly say, disingenuous. But it is, so to speak, a generous disingenuousness; the heat and momentum of sincere admirations, not the shuffling fear and flattery of the constitutional or patriotic historian. It bears most resemblance to the incurable prejudices of a woman.

For the rest there hovered behind all this transcendental haze a certain presence of old northern paganism; he really had some sympathy with the vast vague gods of that moody but not unmanly Nature-worship which seems to have filled the darkness of the North before the coming of the Roman Eagle or the Christian Cross. This he combined, allowing for certain sceptical omissions, with the grisly Old Testament God he had heard about in the black Sabbaths of his childhood; and so promulgated (against both Rationalists and Catholics) a sort of heathen Puritanism: Protestantism purged of its evidences of Christianity.

His great and real work was the attack on Utilitarianism: which did real good, though there was much that was muddled and dangerous in the historical philosophy which he preached as an alternative. It is his real glory that he was the first to see clearly and say plainly the great truth of our time; that the wealth of the state is not the prosperity of the people. Macaulay and the Mills and all the regular run of the Early Victorians, took it for granted that if Manchester was getting richer, we had got hold of the key to comfort and progress. Carlyle pointed out (with stronger sagacity and humour than he showed on any other question) that it was just as true to say that Manchester was getting poorer as that it was getting richer: or, in other words, that Manchester was not getting richer at all, but only some of the less pleasing people in Manchester. In this matter he is to be noted in connection with national developments much later; for he thus became the first prophet of the Socialists. *Sartor Resartus* is an admirable fantasia; *The French Revolution* is, with all its faults, a really fine piece of history; the lectures on Heroes contain some masterly sketches of personalities. But I think it is in *Past and Present*, and the essay on *Chartism*, that Carlyle achieves the work he was chosen by gods and men to achieve; which possibly might not have been achieved by a happier or more healthy-minded man. He never rose to more deadly irony than in such *macabre* descriptions as that of the poor woman proving her sisterhood with the rich by giving them all typhoid fever; or that perfect piece of *badinage* about 'Overproduction of Shirts'; in which he imagines the aristocrats claiming to be quite clear of this offence. 'Will you bandy accusations, will you accuse *us* of over-production? We take the Heavens and the Earth to witness that we have produced nothing at all. . . . He that accuses us of producing, let him show himself. Let him say what and when.' And he never wrote so sternly and justly as when he compared the 'divine sorrow' of Dante with the 'undivine sorrow' of Utilitarianism, which had already come down to talking about the breeding of the poor and to hinting at infanticide. This is a representative quarrel; for if the Utilitarian spirit reached its highest point in Mill, it certainly reached its lowest point in Malthus.

One last element in the influence of Carlyle ought to be mentioned; because it very strongly dominated his disciples – especially Kingsley, and to some extent Tennyson and Ruskin. Because he frowned at the cockney cheerfulness of the cheaper economists, they and others represented him as a pessimist, and reduced all his azure infinities to a fit of the blues. But Carlyle's philosophy, more carefully considered, will be found to be dangerously optimist rather than pessimist. As a thinker Carlyle is not sad, but recklessly and rather unscrupulously satisfied. For he seems to have held the theory that the good could not be definitely defeated in this world; and that everything in the long run finds its right level. It began with what we may call the 'Bible of History' idea: that all human affairs and politics were a clouded but unbroken revelation of the divine. Thus any enormous and unaltered human settlement – as the Norman Conquest or the secession of America – we must suppose to be the will of God. It lent itself to picturesque treatment; and Carlyle and the Carlyleans were above all things picturesque. It gave them at first a rhetorical advantage over the Catholic and other older schools. They could boast that their Creator was still creating; that he was in Man and Nature, and was not hedged round in a Paradise or imprisoned in a pyx. They could say their God had not grown too old for war: that He was present at Gettysburg and Gravelotte as much as at Gibeon and Gilboa. I do not mean that they literally said these particular things: they are what

I should have said had I been bribed to defend their position. But they said things to the same effect: that what manages finally to happen, happens for a higher purpose. Carlyle said the French Revolution was a thing settled in the eternal councils to be; and therefore (and not because it was right) attacking it was 'fighting against God'. And Kingsley even carried the principle so far as to tell a lady she should remain in the Church of England mainly because God had put her there. But in spite of its superficial spirituality and encouragement, it is not hard to see how such a doctrine could be abused. It practically comes to saying that God is on the side of the big battalions – or at least, of the victorious ones. Thus a creed which set out to create conquerors would only corrupt soldiers; corrupt them with a craven and unsoldierly worship of success: and that which began as the philosophy of courage ends as the philosophy of cowardice. If, indeed, Carlyle were right in saying that right is only 'rightly articulated' might, men would never articulate or move in any way. For no act can have might before it is done: if there is no right, it cannot rationally be done at all. This element, like the Anti-Utilitarian element, is to be kept in mind in connection with after developments: for in this Carlyle is the first cry of Imperialism, as (in the other case) of Socialism: and the two babes unborn who stir at the trumpet are Mr Bernard Shaw and Mr Rudyard Kipling. Kipling also carries on from Carlyle the concentration on the purely Hebraic parts of the Bible. The fallacy of this whole philosophy is that if God is indeed present at a modern battle, He may be present not as on Gilboa but Golgotha.

Carlyle's direct historical worship of strength and the rest of it was fortunately not very fruitful; and perhaps lingered only in Froude the historian. Even he is more an interruption than a continuity. Froude develops rather the harsher and more impatient moral counsels of his master than like Ruskin the more romantic and sympathetic. He carries on the tradition of Hero Worship: but carries far beyond Carlyle the practice of worshipping people who cannot rationally be called heroes. In this matter that eccentric eye of the seer certainly helped Carlyle: in Cromwell and Frederick the Great there was at least something self-begotten, original or mystical; if they were not heroes they were at least demigods or perhaps demons. But Froude set himself to the praise of the Tudors, a much lower class of people; ill-conditioned prosperous people who merely waxed fat and kicked. Such strength as Henry VIII had was the strength of a badly trained horse that bolts, not of any clear or courageous rider who controls him. There is a sort of strong man mentioned in Scripture who, because he masters himself, is more than he that takes a city. There is another kind of strong man (known to the medical profession) who cannot master himself; and whom it may take half a city to take alive. But for all that he is a low lunatic, and not a hero; and of that sort were too many of the heroes whom Froude attempted to praise. A kind of instinct kept Carlyle from over-praising Henry VIII; or that highly cultivated and complicated liar, Queen Elizabeth. Here, the only importance of this is that one of Carlyle's followers carried further that 'strength' which was the real weakness of Carlyle. I have heard that Froude's life of Carlyle was unsympathetic; but if it was so it was a sort of parricide. For the rest, like Macaulay, he was a picturesque and partisan historian: but, like Macaulay (and unlike the craven scientific historians of today) he was not ashamed of being partisan or of being picturesque. Such studies as he wrote on the Elizabethan seamen and adventurers, represent very triumphantly the sort of romance of England that all this school was attempting to establish; and link him up with Kingsley and the rest.

Ruskin may be very roughly regarded as the young lieutenant of Carlyle in his war on Utilitarian Radicalism: but as an individual he presents many and curious divergences. In the matter of style, he enriched English without disordering it. And in the matter of religion (which was the key of this age as of every other) he did not, like Carlyle, set up the romance of the great Puritans as a rival to the romance of the Catholic Church. Rather he set up and worshipped all the arts and trophies of the Catholic Church as a rival to the Church itself. None need dispute that he held a perfectly tenable position if he chose to associate early Florentine art with a Christianity still comparatively pure, and such sensualities as the Renaissance bred with the corruption of a Papacy. But this does not alter, as a merely artistic fact, the strange air of ill-ease and irritation with which Ruskin seems to tear down the gargoyles of Amiens or the marbles of Venice, as things of which Europe is not worthy; and take them away with him to a really careful museum, situated dangerously near Clapham. Many of the great men of that generation, indeed, had a sort of divided mind; an ethical headache which was literally a 'splitting headache'; for there was a schism in the sympathies. When these men looked at some historic object, like the Catholic Church or the French Revolution, they did not know whether they loved or hated it most. Carlyle's two eyes were out of focus, as one may say, when he looked at democracy: he had one eye on Valmy and the other on Sedan. In the same way, Ruskin had a strong right hand that wrote of the great mediaeval minsters in tall harmonies and traceries as splendid as their own; and also, so to speak, a weak and feverish left hand that was always fidgeting and trying to take the pen away – and write an evangelical tract about the immorality of foreigners. Many of their contemporaries were the same. The sea of Tennyson's mind was troubled under its serene surface. The incessant excitement of Kingsley, though romantic and attractive in many ways, was a great deal more like Nervous Christianity than Muscular Christianity. It would be quite unfair to say of Ruskin that there was any major inconsistency between his mediaeval tastes and his very unmediaeval temper: and minor inconsistencies do not matter in anybody. But it is not quite unfair to say of him that he seemed to want all parts of the Cathedral except the altar.

As an artist in prose he is one of the most miraculous products of the extremely poetical genius of England. The length of a Ruskin sentence is like that length in the long arrow that was boasted of by the drawers of the long bow. He draws, not a cloth-yard shaft but a long lance to his ear: he shoots a spear. But the whole goes light as a bird and straight as a bullet. There is no Victorian writer before him to whom he even suggests a comparison, technically considered, except perhaps De Quincey; who also employed the long rich rolling sentence that, like a rocket, bursts into stars at the end. But De Quincey's sentences, as I have said, have always a dreamy and insecure sense about them, like the turret on toppling turret of some mad sultan's pagoda. Ruskin's sentence branches into brackets and relative clauses as a straight strong tree branches into boughs and bifurcations, rather shaking off its burden than merely adding to it. It is interesting to remember that Ruskin wrote some of the best of these sentences in the attempt to show that he did understand the growth of trees, and that nobody else did – except Turner, of course. It is also (to those acquainted with his perverse and wild rhetorical prejudices) even more amusing to remember that if a Ruskin sentence (occupying one or two pages of small print) does not remind us of the growth of a tree, the only other thing it does remind of is the triumphant passage of a railway train.

Ruskin left behind him in his turn two quite separate streams of inspiration. The first and more practical was concerned, like Carlyle's *Chartism*, with a challenge to the social conclusions of the orthodox economists. He was not so great a man as Carlyle, but he was a much more clear-headed man; and the point and stab of his challenge still really stands and sticks, like a dagger in a dead man. He answered the theory that we must always get the cheapest labour we can, by pointing out that we never do get the cheapest labour we can, in any matter about which we really care twopence. We do not get the cheapest doctor. We either get a doctor who charges nothing or a doctor who charges a recognized and respectable fee. We do not trust the cheapest bishop. We do not allow admirals to compete. We do not tell generals to undercut each other on the eve of a war. We either employ none of them or we employ all of them at an official rate of pay. All this was set out in the strongest and least sentimental of his books, *Unto this Last*; but many suggestions of it are scattered through *Sesame and Lilies*, *The Political Economy of Art*, and even *Modern Painters*. On this side of his soul Ruskin became the second founder of Socialism. The argument was not by any means a complete or unconquerable weapon, but I think it knocked out what little remained of the brains of the early Victorian rationalists. It is entirely nonsensical to speak of Ruskin as a lounging aesthete, who strolled into economics, and talked sentimentalism. In plain fact, Ruskin was seldom so sensible and logical (right or wrong) as when he was talking about economics. He constantly talked the most glorious nonsense about landscape and natural history, which it was his business to understand. Within his own limits, he talked the most cold common sense about political economy, which was no business of his at all.

On the other side of his literary soul, his mere unwrapping of the wealth and wonder of European art, he set going another influence, earlier and vaguer than his influence on Socialism. He represented what was at first the Pre-Raphaelite School in painting, but afterwards a much larger and looser Pre-Raphaelite

School in poetry and prose. The word 'looser' will not be found unfair if we remember how Swinburne and all the wildest friends of the Rossettis carried this movement forward. They used the mediaeval imagery to blaspheme the mediaeval religion. Ruskin's dark and doubtful decision to accept Catholic art but not Catholic ethics had borne rapid or even flagrant fruit by the time that Swinburne, writing about a harlot, composed a learned and sympathetic and indecent parody on the Litany of the Blessed Virgin.

With the poets I deal in another part of this book; but the influence of Ruskin's great prose touching art criticism can best be expressed in the name of the next great prose writer on such subjects. That name is Walter Pater: and the name is the full measure of the extent to which Ruskin's vague but vast influence had escaped from his hands. Pater's eventual leaning towards Rome would not have pleased Ruskin at all; but it is surely fair to say of the mass of his work that its moral tone is neither Puritan nor Catholic, but strictly and splendidly Pagan. In Pater we have Ruskin without the prejudices, that is, without the funny parts. I may be wrong, but I cannot recall at this moment a single passage in which Pater's style takes a holiday or in which his wisdom plays the fool. Newman and Ruskin were as careful and graceful stylists as he. Newman and Ruskin were as serious, elaborate, and even academic thinkers as he. But Ruskin let himself go about railways. Newman let himself go about Kingsley. Pater cannot let himself go for the excellent reason that he wants to stay: to stay at the point where all the keenest emotions meet, as he explains in the splendid peroration of *The Renaissance*. The only objection to being where all the keenest emotions meet is that you feel none of them.

In this sense Pater may well stand for a substantial summary of the aesthetes, apart from the purely poetical merits of men like Rossetti and Swinburne. Like Swinburne and others he first attempted to use mediaeval tradition without trusting it. These people wanted to see Paganism *through* Christianity: because it involved the incidental amusement of seeing through Christianity itself. They not only tried to be in all ages at once (which is a very reasonable ambition, though not often realized), but they wanted to be on all sides at once: which is nonsense. Swinburne tries to question the philosophy of Christianity in the metres of a Christmas carol: and Dante Rossetti tries to write as if he were Christina

Rossetti. Certainly the almost successful summit of all this attempt is Pater's superb passage on the Monna Lisa; in which he seeks to make her at once a mystery of good and a mystery of evil. The philosophy is false; even evidently false, for it bears no fruit today. There never was a woman, not Eve herself in the instant of temptation, who could smile the same smile as the mother of Helen and the mother of Mary. But it is the high-water mark of that vast attempt at an impartiality reached through art: and no other mere artist ever rose so high again.

Apart from this Ruskinian offshoot through Pre-Raphaelitism into what was called Aestheticism, the remains of the inspiration of Carlyle fill a very large part in the Victorian life, but not strictly so large a part in the Victorian literature. Charles Kingsley was a great publicist: a popular preacher; a popular novelist; and (in two cases at least) a very good novelist. His *Water Babies* is really a breezy and roaring freak; like a holiday at the seaside – a holiday where one talks natural history without taking it seriously. Some of the songs in this and other of his works are very real songs: notably, 'When all the World is Young, Lad', which comes very near to being the only true defence of marriage in the controversies of the nineteenth century. But when all this is allowed, no one will seriously rank Kingsley, in the really literary sense on the level of Carlyle or Ruskin, Tennyson or Browning, Dickens or Thackeray: and if such a place cannot be given to him, it can be given even less to his lusty and pleasant friend, Tom Hughes, whose personality floats towards the frankness of the *Boy's Own Paper*; or to his deep, suggestive metaphysical friend Maurice, who floats rather towards *The Hibbert Journal*. The moral and social influence of these things is not to be forgotten; but they leave the domain of letters. The voice of Carlyle is not heard again in letters till the coming of Kipling and Henley.

One other name of great importance should appear here, because it cannot appear very appropriately anywhere else: the man hardly belonged to the same school as Ruskin and Carlyle, but fought many of their battles, and was even more concentrated on their main task – the task of convicting liberal *bourgeois* England of priggishness and provinciality. I mean, of course, Matthew Arnold. Against Mill's 'liberty' and Carlyle's 'strength' and Ruskin's 'nature', he set up a new presence and entity which he called 'culture', the disinterested play of the mind through the sifting of the best books and authorities. Though a little dandified in phrase, he was undoubtedly serious and public-spirited in intention. He sometimes talked of culture almost as if it were a man, or at least a church (for a church has a sort of personality): some may suspect that culture was a man, whose name was Matthew Arnold. But Arnold was not only right but highly valuable. If we have said that Carlyle was a man that saw things, we may add that Arnold was chiefly valuable as a man who knew things. Well as he was endowed intellectually, his power came more from information than intellect. He simply happened to know certain things, that Carlyle didn't know, that Kingsley didn't know, that Huxley and Herbert Spencer didn't know: that England didn't know. He knew that England was a part of Europe: and not so important a part as it had been the morning after Waterloo. He knew that England was then (as it is now) an oligarchical State, and that many great nations are not. He knew that a real democracy need not live and does not live in that perpetual panic about using the powers of the State, which possessed men like Spencer and Cobden. He knew a rational minimum of culture and common courtesy could exist and did exist throughout large democracies. He knew the Catholic Church had been in history 'the Church of the multitude': he knew it was not a sect. He knew that great landlords are no more a part of the economic law than nigger-drivers: he knew that small owners could and did prosper. He was not so much the philosopher as the man of the world; he reminded us that Europe was a society while Ruskin was treating it as a picture gallery. He was a sort of Heaven-sent courier. His frontal attack on the vulgar and sullen optimism of Victorian utility may be summed up in the admirable sentence, in which he asked the English what was the use of a train taking them quickly from Islington to Camberwell, if it only took them 'from a dismal and illiberal life in Islington to a dismal and illiberal life in Camberwell?'

His attitude to that great religious enigma round which all these great men were grouped as in a ring, was individual and decidedly curious. He seems to have believed that an 'Historic Church', that is, some established organization with ceremonies and sacred books, etc., could be perpetually preserved as a sort of vessel to contain the spiritual ideas of the age, whatever those ideas might happen to be. He clearly seems to have contemplated a melting away of the doctrines of the Church and even of the meaning of the words: but he thought a certain need in man would always be best satisfied by public worship and especially by the great religious literatures of the past. He would embalm the body that it might often be revisited by the soul – or souls. . . . But while Arnold would loosen the theological bonds of the Church, he would not loosen the official bonds of the State. You must not disestablish the Church: you must not even leave the Church: you must stop inside it and think what you choose. Enemies might say that he was simply trying to establish and endow Agnosticism. It is fairer and truer to say that unconsciously he was trying to restore Paganism: for this State Ritualism without theology, and without much belief, actually was the practice of the ancient world. Arnold may have thought that he was building an altar to the Unknown God; but he was really building it to Divus Caesar.

As a critic he was chiefly concerned to preserve criticism itself; to set a measure to praise and blame and support the classics against the fashions. It is here that it is specially true of him, if of no writer else, that the style was the man. The most vital thing he invented was a new style: founded on the patient unravelling of the tangled Victorian ideas, as if they were matted hair under a comb. He did not mind how elaborately long he made a sentence, so long as he made it clear. He would constantly repeat whole phrases word for word in the same sentence, rather than risk ambiguity by abbreviation. His genius showed itself in turning this method of a laborious lucidity into a peculiarly exasperating form of satire and controversy. Newman's strength was in a sort of stifled passion, a dangerous patience of polite logic and then: 'Cowards! if I advanced a step you would run away: it is not you I fear. *Di me terrent, et Jupiter hostis.*' If Newman seemed suddenly to fly into a temper, Carlyle seemed never to fly out of one. But Arnold kept a smile of heart-broken forbearance, as of the teacher in an idiot school, that was enormously insulting. One trick he often tried with success. If his opponent had said something foolish, like 'the destiny of England is in the great heart of England', Arnold would repeat the phrase again and again until it looked more foolish than it really was. Thus he recurs again and again to 'the British College of Health in the New Road' till the reader wants to rush out and burn the place down. Arnold's great error was that he sometimes thus wearied us of his own phrases, as well as of his enemies'.

These names are roughly representative of the long series of protests against the cold commercial rationalism which held Parliament and the schools through the earlier Victorian time, in so far as those protests were made in the name of neglected intellect, insulted art, forgotten heroism and desecrated religion. But already the Utilitarian citadel had been more heavily bombarded on the other side by one lonely and unlettered man of genius.

The rise of Dickens is like the rising of a vast mob. This is not only because his tales are indeed as crowded and populous as towns: for truly it was not so much that Dickens appeared as that a hundred Dickens characters appeared. It is also because he was the sort of man who has the impersonal impetus of a mob: what Poe meant when he truly said that popular rumour, if really spontaneous, was like the intuition of the individual man of genius. Those who speak scornfully of the ignorance of the mob do not err as to the fact itself; their error is in not seeing that just as a crowd is comparatively ignorant, so a crowd is comparatively innocent. It will have the old and human faults; but it is not likely to specialize in the special faults of that particular society: because the effort of the strong and successful in all ages is to keep the poor out of society. If the higher castes have developed some special moral beauty or grace, as they occasionally do (for instance, mediaeval chivalry), it is likely enough, of course, that the mass of men will miss it. But if they have developed some perversion or over emphasis, as they much more often do (for instance, the Renaissance poisoning), then it will be the tendency of the mass of men to miss that too. The point might be put in many ways; you may say if you will that the poor are always at the tail of the procession, and that whether they are morally worse or better depends on whether humanity as a whole is proceeding towards heaven or hell. When humanity is going to hell, the poor are always nearest to heaven.

Dickens was a mob – and a mob in revolt; he fought by the light of nature; he had not a theory, but a thirst. If anyone chooses to offer the cheap sarcasm that his thirst was largely a thirst for milk-punch, I am content to reply with complete gravity and entire contempt that in a sense this is perfectly true. His thirst was for things as humble, as human, as laughable as that daily bread for which we cry to God. He had no particular plan of reform; or, when he had, it was startlingly petty and parochial compared with the deep, confused clamour of comradeship and insurrection that fills all his narrative. It would not be gravely unjust to him to compare him to his own heroine, Arabella Allen, who 'didn't know what she did like', but who (when confronted with Mr Bob Sawyer) 'did know what she didn't like'. Dickens did know what he didn't like. He didn't like the unrivalled Happiness which Mr Roebuck praised; the economic laws that were working so faultlessly in Fever Alley; the wealth that was accumulating so rapidly in Bleeding Heart yard. But, above all, he didn't like the *mean* side of the Manchester philosophy: the preaching of an impossible thrift and an intolerable temperance. He hated the implication that because a man was a miser in Latin he must also be a miser in English. And this meanness of the Utilitarians had gone very far – infecting many finer minds who had fought the Utilitarians. In the *Edinburgh Review*, a thing like Malthus could be championed by a man like Macaulay.

The twin root facts of the revolution called Dickens are these: first, that he attacked the cold Victorian compromise; second, that he attacked it without knowing he was doing it – certainly without knowing that other people were doing it. He was attacking something which we will call Mr Gradgrind. He was utterly unaware (in any essential sense) that any one else had attacked Mr Gradgrind. All the other attacks had come from positions of learning or cultured eccentricity of which he was entirely ignorant, and to which, therefore (like a spirited fellow), he felt a furious hostility. Thus, for instance, he hated the Little Bethel to which Kit's mother went: he hated it simply as Kit hated it. Newman could have told him it was hateful, because it had no root in religious history; it was not even a sapling sprung of the seed of some great human and heathen tree: it was a monstrous mushroom that grows in the moonshine and dies in the dawn. Dickens knew no more of religious history than Kit; he simply smelt fungus, and it stank. Thus, again, he hated that insolent luxury of a class counting itself a comfortable exception to all mankind; he hated it as Kate Nickleby hated a Sir Mulberry Hawke – by instinct. Carlyle could have told him that all the world was full of that anger against the impudent fatness of the few. But when Dickens wrote about Kate Nickleby, he knew about as much of the world – as Kate Nickleby. He did write *The Tale of Two Cities* long afterwards; but that was when he had been instructed by Carlyle. His first revolutionism was as private and internal as feeling sea-sick. Thus, once more, he wrote against Mr Gradgrind long before he created him. In 'The Chimes', conceived in quite his casual and charitable season, with 'The Christmas Carol' and the 'Cricket on the Hearth', he hit hard at the economists. Ruskin, in the same fashion, would have told him that the worst thing about the economists was that they were not economists: that they missed many essential things even in economics. But Dickens did not know whether they were economics or not: he only knew that they wanted hitting. Thus, to take a last case out of many, Dickens travelled in a French railway train, and noticed that this eccentric nation provided him with wine that he could drink and sandwiches he could eat, and manners he could tolerate. And remembering the ghastly sawdust-eating waiting-rooms of the North English railways, he wrote that rich chapter in 'Mugby Junction'. Matthew Arnold could have told him that this was but a part of the general thinning down of European civilization in these islands at the edge of it; that for two or three thousand years the Latin society has learnt how to drink wine, and how not to drink too much of it. Dickens did not in the least understand the Latin society: but he did understand the wine. If (to prolong an idle but not entirely false metaphor) we have called Carlyle a man who saw and Arnold a man who knew, we might truly call Dickens a man who tasted, that is, a man who really felt. In spite of all the silly talk about his vulgarity, he really had, in the strict and serious sense, good taste. All real good taste is gusto – the power of appreciating the presence – or the absence – of a particular and positive pleasure. He had no learning; he was not misled by the label on the bottle – for that is what learning largely meant in his time. He opened his mouth and shut his eyes and saw what the Age of Reason would give him. And, having tasted it, he spat it out.

I am constrained to consider Dickens here among the fighters; though I ought (on the pure principles of Art) to be considering him in the chapter which I have allotted to the story-tellers. But we should get the whole Victorian perspective wrong, in my opinion at least, if we did not see that Dickens was primarily the most successful of all the onslaughts on the solid scientific school; because he did not attack from the standpoint of extraordinary faith, like Newman; or the standpoint of extraordinary detachment or serenity, like Arnold; but from the standpoint of quite ordinary and quite hearty dislike. To give but one instance more, Matthew Arnold, trying to carry into England constructive educational schemes which he could see spread like a clear railway map all over the continent, was much badgered about what he really thought was *wrong* with English middle-class education. Despairing of explaining to the English middle class the idea of high and central public instruction, as distinct from coarse and hole-and-corner private instruction, he invoked the aid of Dickens. He said the English middle-class school was the sort of school where Mr Creakle sat, with his buttered toast and his cane. Now Dickens had probably never seen any other kind of school – certainly he had never understood the systematic State Schools in which Arnold had learnt his lesson. But he saw the cane and the buttered toast, and he *knew* that it was all wrong. In this sense, Dickens, the great romanticist, is truly the great realist also. For he had no abstractions: he had nothing except realities out of which to make a romance.

With Dickens, then, re-arises that reality with which I began and which (curtly, but I think not falsely) I have called Cobbett. In dealing with fiction as such, I shall have occasion to say wherein Dickens is weaker and stronger than that England of the eighteenth century: here it is sufficient to say that he represents the return of Cobbett in this vital sense; that he is proud of being the ordinary man. No one can understand the thousand caricatures by Dickens who does not understand that he is comparing them all with his own common sense. Dickens, in the bulk, liked the things that Cobbett had liked; what is perhaps more to the point, he hated the things that Cobbett had hated; the Tudors, the lawyers, the leisurely oppression of the poor. Cobbett's fine fighting journalism had been what is nowadays called 'personal', that is, it supposed human beings to be human. But Cobbett was also personal in the less satisfactory sense; he could only multiply monsters who were exaggerations of his enemies or exaggerations of himself. Dickens was personal in a more godlike sense; he could multiply persons. He could create all the farce and tragedy of his age over again, with creatures unborn to sin and creatures unborn to suffer. That which had not been achieved by the fierce facts of Cobbett, the burning dreams of of Carlyle, the white-hot proofs of Newman, was really or very nearly achieved by a crowd of impossible people. In the centre stood that citadel of atheist industrialism: and if indeed it has ever been taken, it was taken by the rush of that unreal army.

II

THE GREAT VICTORIAN NOVELISTS

THE VICTORIAN novel was a thing entirely Victorian; quite unique and suited to a sort of cosiness in that country and that age. But the novel itself, though not merely Victorian, is mainly modern. No clear-headed person wastes his time over definitions, except where he thinks his own definition would probably be in dispute. I merely say, therefore, that when I say 'novel', I mean a fictitious narrative (almost invariably, but not necessarily, in prose) of which the essential is that the story is not told for the sake of its naked pointedness as an anecdote, or for the sake of the irrelevant landscapes and visions that can be caught up in it, but for the sake of some study of the difference between human beings. There are several things that make this mode of art unique. One of the most conspicuous is that it is the art in which the conquests of woman are quite beyond controversy. The proposition that Victorian women have done well in politics and philosophy is not necessarily an untrue proposition; but it is a partisan proposition. I never heard that many women, let alone men, shared the views of Mary Wollstonecraft ... They did, undoubtedly, flock to Mrs Eddy; but it will not be unfair to that lady to call her following a sect, and not altogether unreasonable to say that such insane exceptions prove the rule. Nor can I at this moment think of a single modern woman writing on politics or abstract things, whose work is of undisputed importance; except perhaps Mrs Sidney Webb, who settles things by the simple process of ordering about the citizens of a state, as she might the servants in a kitchen. There has been, at any rate, no writer on moral or political theory that can be mentioned, without seeming comic, in the same breath with the great female novelists. But when we come to the novelists, the women have, on the whole, equality; and certainly, in some points, superiority. Jane Austen is as strong in her own way as Scott is in his. But she is, for all practical purposes, never weak in her own way – and Scott very often is. Charlotte Brontë dedicated *Jane Eyre* to the author of *Vanity Fair*.

I should hesitate to say that Charlotte Brontë's is a better book than Thackeray's, but I think it might well be maintained that it is a better story. All sorts of inquiring asses (equally ignorant of the old nature of woman and the new nature of the novel) whispered wisely that George Eliot's novels were really written by George Lewes. I will cheerfully answer for the fact that, if they had been written by George Lewes, no one would ever have read them. Those who have read his book on Robespierre will have no doubt about my meaning. I am no idolater of George Eliot; but a man who could concoct such a crushing opiate about the most exciting occasion in history certainly did not write *The Mill on the Floss*. This is the first fact about the novel, that it is the introduction of a new and rather curious kind of art; and it has been found to be peculiarly feminine, from the first good novel by Fanny Burney to the last good novel by Miss May Sinclair. The truth is, I think, that the modern novel is a new thing; not new in its essence (for that is a philosophy for fools), but new in the sense that it lets loose many of the things that are old. It is a hearty and exhaustive overhauling of that part of human existence which has always been the woman's province, or rather kingdom; the play of personalities in private, the real difference between Tommy and Joe. It is right that womanhood should specialize in individuals, and be praised for doing so; just as in the Middle Ages she specialized in dignity and was praised for doing so. People put the matter wrong when they say that the novel is a study of human nature. Human nature is a thing that even men can understand. Human nature is born of the pain of a woman; human nature plays at peep-bo when it is two and at cricket when it is twelve; human nature earns its living and desires the other sex and dies. What the novel deals with is what women have to deal with; the differentiations, the twists and turns of this eternal river. The key of this new form of art, which we call fiction, is sympathy. And sympathy does not mean so much feeling with all who feel, but rather suffering with all who suffer. And it was inevitable, under such an inspiration, that more attention should be given to the awkward corners of life than to its even flow. The very promising domestic channel dug by the Victorian women, in books like *Cranford*, by Mrs Gaskell, would have got to the sea, if they had been left alone to dig it. They might have made domesticity a fairyland. Unfortunately another idea, the idea of imitating men's cuffs and collars and documents, cut across this purely female discovery and destroyed it.

It may seem mere praise of the novel to say it is the art of sympathy and the study of human variations. But indeed, though this is a good thing, it is not universally good. We have gained in sympathy; but we have lost in brotherhood. Old quarrels had more equality than modern exonerations. Two peasants in the Middle Ages quarrelled about their two fields. But they went to the same church, served in the same semi-feudal militia; and had the same morality, whichever might happen to be breaking it at the moment. The very cause of their quarrel was the cause of their fraternity; they both liked land. But suppose one of them a teetotaller who desired the abolition of hops on both farms; suppose the other a vegetarian who desired the abolition of chickens on both farms: and it is at once apparent that a quarrel of quite a different kind would begin; and that in that quarrel it would not be a question of farmer against farmer, but of individual against individual. This fundamental sense of human fraternity can only exist in the presence of positive religion. Man is merely man only when he is seen against the sky. If he is seen against any landscape, he is only a man of that land. If he is seen against any house, he is only a house-holder. Only where death and eternity are intensely present can human beings fully feel their fellowship. Once the divine darkness against which we stand is really dismissed from the mind (as it was very nearly dismissed in the Victorian time) the differences between human beings become overpoweringly plain; whether they are expressed in the high caricatures of Dickens or the low lunacies of Zola.

This can be seen in a sort of picture in the Prologue of the *Canterbury Tales*; which is already pregnant with the promise of the English novel. The characters there are at once graphically and delicately differentiated; the Doctor with his rich cloak, his careful meals, his coldness to religion; the Franklin, whose white beard was so fresh that it recalled the daisies, and in whose house it snowed meat and drink; the Summoner, from whose fearful face, like a red cherub's, the children fled, and who wore a garland like a hoop; the Miller with his short red hair and bagpipes and brutal head, with which he could break down a door; the Lover who was as sleepless as a nightingale; the Knight, the Cook, the Clerk of

Oxford. Pendennis or the Cook, M. Mirabolarit, are nowhere so vividly varied by a few merely verbal strokes. But the great difference is deeper and more striking. It is simply that Pendennis would never have gone riding with a cook at all. Chaucer's knight rode with a cook quite naturally; because the thing they were all seeking together was as much above knighthood as it was above cookery. Soldiers and swindlers and bullies and outcasts, they were all going to the shrine of a distant saint. To what sort of distant saint would Pendennis and Colonel Newcome and Mr Moss and Captain Costigan and Ridley the butler and Bayham and Sir Barnes Newcome and Laura and the Duchess d'Ivry and Warrington and Captain Blackball and Lady Kew travel, laughing and telling tales together?

The growth of the novel, therefore, must not be too easily called an increase in the interest in humanity. It is an increase in the interest in the things in which men differ; much fuller and finer work had been done before about the things in which they agree. And this intense interest in variety had its bad side as well as its good; it has rather increased social distinctions in a serious and spiritual sense. Most of the oblivion of democracy is due to the oblivion of death. But in its own manner and measure, it was a real advance and experiment of the European mind, like the public art of the Renaissance or the fairyland of physical science explored in the nineteenth century. It was a more unquestionable benefit than these: and in that development women played a peculiar part, English women especially, and Victorian women most of all.

It is perhaps partly, though certainly not entirely, this influence of the great women writers that explains another very arresting and important fact about the emergence of genuinely Victorian fiction. It had been by this time decided, by the powers that had influence (and by public opinion also, at least in the middle class sense), that certain verbal limits must be set to such literature. The novel must be what some would call pure and others would call prudish; but what is not, properly considered, either one or the other: it is rather a more or less business proposal (right or wrong) that every writer shall draw the line at literal physical description of things socially concealed. It was originally merely verbal; it had not, primarily, any dream of purifying the topic or the moral tone. Dickens and Thackeray claimed very properly the right to deal with shameful passions and suggest their shameful culminations; Scott sometimes dealt with ideas positively horrible – as in that grand Glenallan tragedy which is as appalling as the *Oedipus* or the *Cenci*. None of these great men would have tolerated for a moment being talked to (as the muddle-headed amateur censors talk to artists today) about 'wholesome' topics and suggestions 'that cannot elevate'. They had to describe the great battle of good and evil and they described both; but they accepted a working Victorian compromise about what should happen behind the scenes and what on the stage. Dickens did not claim the licence of diction Fielding might have claimed in repeating the senile ecstasies of Gride (let us say) over his purchased bride: but Dickens does not leave the reader in the faintest doubt about what sort of feelings they were; nor is there any reason why he should. Thackeray would not have described the toilet details of the secret balls of Lord Steyne: he left that to Lady Cardigan. But no one who had read Thackeray's version would be surprised at Lady Cardigan's. But though the great Victorian novelists would not have permitted the impudence of the suggestion that every part of their problem must be wholesome and innocent in itself, it is still tenable (I do not say it is certain) that by yielding to the Philistines on this verbal compromise, they have in the long run worked for impurity rather than purity. In one point I do certainly think that the Victorian Bowdlerism did pure harm. This is the simple point that, nine times out of ten, the coarse word is the word that condemns an evil and the refined word the word that excuses it. A common evasion, for instance, substitutes for the word that brands self-sale as the essential sin, a word which weakly suggests that it is no more wicked than walking down the street. The great peril of such soft mystifications is that extreme evils (they that are abnormal even by the standard of evil) have a very long start. Where ordinary wrong is made unintelligible, extraordinary wrong can count on remaining more unintelligible still; especially among those who live in such an atmosphere of long words. . . .

This reticence, right or wrong, may have been connected with the participation of women with men in the matter of fiction. It is an important point: the sexes can only be coarse separately. It was certainly also due, as I have already suggested, to the treaty between the rich *bourgeoisie* and the old aristocracy, which both had to make, for the common and congenial purpose of keeping the

English people down. But it was due much more than this to a general moral atmosphere in the Victorian Age. It is impossible to express that spirit except by the electric bell of a name. It was latitudinarian, and yet it was limited. It could be content with nothing less than the whole cosmos: yet the cosmos with which it was content was small. It is false to say it was without humour: yet there was something by instinct unsmiling in it. It was always saying solidly that things were 'enough'; and proving by that sharpness (as of the shutting of a door) that they were not enough. It took, I will not say its pleasures, but even its emancipations, sadly. Definitions seem to escape this way and that in the attempt to locate it as an idea. But every one will understand me if I call it George Eliot.

I begin with this great woman of letters for both the two reasons already mentioned. She represents the rationalism of the old Victorian Age at its highest. She and Mill are like two great mountains at the end of that long, hard chain which is the watershed of the Early Victorian time. They alone rise high enough to be confused among the clouds – or perhaps confused among the stars. They certainly were seeking truth, as Newman and Carlyle were; the slow slope of the later Victorian vulgarity does not lower their precipice and pinnacle. But I begin with this name also because it emphasizes the idea of modern fiction as a fresh and largely a female thing. The novel of the nineteenth century was female; as fully as the novel of the eighteenth century was male. It is quite certain that no woman could have written *Roderick Random*. It is not quite so certain that no woman could have written *Esmond*. The strength and subtlety of woman had certainly sunk deep into English letters when George Eliot began to write.

Her originals and even her contemporaries had shown the feminine power of fiction as well or better than she. Charlotte Brontë, understood along her own instincts, was as great; Jane Austen was greater. The latter comes into our present consideration only as that most exasperating thing, an ideal unachieved. It is like leaving an unconquered fortress in the rear. No woman later has captured the complete common sense of Jane Austen. She could keep her head, while all the after women went about looking for their brains. She could describe a man coolly; which neither George Eliot nor Charlotte Brontë could do. She knew what she knew, like a sound

dogmatist: she did not know what she did not know – like a sound
agnostic. But she belongs to a vanished world before the great
progressive age of which I write.

One of the characteristics of the central Victorian spirit was a
tendency to substitute a certain more or less satisfied seriousness
for the extremes of tragedy and comedy. This is marked by a certain change in George Eliot; as it is marked by a certain limitation
or moderation in Dickens. Dickens was the People, as it was in the
eighteenth century and still largely is, in spite of all the talk for and
against Board School Education: comic, tragic, realistic, free-
spoken, far looser in words than in deeds. It marks the silent
strength and pressure of the spirit of the Victorian middle class that
even to Dickens it never occurred to revive the verbal coarseness
of Smollett or Swift. The other proof of the same pressure is the
change in George Eliot. She was not a genius in the elemental sense
of Dickens; she could never have been either so strong or so soft.
But she did originally represent some of the same popular realities:
and her first books (at least as compared with her latest) were full
of sound fun and bitter pathos. Mr Max Beerbohm has remarked
(in his glorious essay called 'Ichabod', I think), that Silas Marner
would not have forgotten his miserliness if George Eliot had written of him in her maturity. I have a great regard for Mr Beerbohm's
literary judgments; and it may be so. But if literature means anything more than a cold calculation of the chances, if there is in it,
as I believe, any deeper idea of detaching the spirit of life from the
dull obstacles of life, of permitting human nature really to reveal
itself as human, if (to put it shortly) literature has anything on earth
to do with being *interesting* – then I think we would rather have a
few more Marners than that rich maturity that gave us the analysed
dust-heaps of *Daniel Deronda*.

In her best novels there is real humour, of a cool sparkling sort;
there is a strong sense of substantial character that has not yet
degenerated into psychology; there is a great deal of wisdom,
chiefly about women; indeed there is almost every element of
literature except a certain indescribable thing called *glamour*; which
was the whole stock-in-trade of the Brontës, which we feel in
Dickens when Quilp clambers amid rotten wood by the desolate
river; and even in Thackeray when Esmond with his melancholy
eyes wanders like some swarthy crow about the dismal avenues of

Castlewood. Of this quality (which some have called, but hastily, the essential of literature) George Eliot had not little but nothing. Her air is right and intellectually even exciting; but it is like the air of a cloudless day on the parade at Brighton. She sees people clearly, but not through an atmosphere. And she can conjure up storms in the conscious, but not in the subconscious mind.

It is true (though the idea should not be exaggerated) that this deficiency was largely due to her being cut off from all those conceptions that had made the fiction of a Muse; the deep idea that there are really demons and angels behind men. Certainly the increasing atheism of her school spoilt her own particular imaginative talent: she was far less free when she thought like Ladislaw than when she thought like Casaubon. It also betrayed her on a matter specially requiring common sense; I mean sex. There is nothing that is so profoundly false as rationalist flirtation. Each sex is trying to be both sexes at once; and the result is a confusion more untruthful than any conventions. This can easily be seen by comparing her with a greater woman who died before the beginning of our present problem. Jane Austen was born before those bonds which (we are told) protected woman from truth, were burst by the Brontës or elaborately united by George Eliot. Yet the fact remains that Jane Austen knew much more about men than either of them. Jane Austen may have been protected from truth: but it was precious little of truth that was protected from her. When Darcy, in finally confessing his faults, says, 'I have been a selfish being all my life, in practice *though not in theory*,' he gets nearer to a complete confession of the intelligent male than ever was even hinted by the Byronic lapses of the Brontës' heroes or the elaborate exculpations of George Eliot's. Jane Austen, of course, covered an infinitely smaller field than any of her later rivals; but I have always believed in the victory of small nationalities.

The Brontës suggest themselves here; because their superficial qualities, the qualities that can be seized upon in satire, were in this an exaggeration of what was, in George Eliot, hardly more than an omission. There was perhaps a time when Mr Rawjester was more widely known than Mr Rochester. And certainly Mr Rochester (to adopt the diction of that other eminent country gentleman, Mr Darcy) was simply individualistic not only in practice, but in theory. Now any one may be so in practice: but a man who is simply individualistic in theory must merely be an ass. Undoubtedly the Brontës exposed themselves to some misunderstanding by thus perpetually making the masculine creature much more masculine than he wants to be. Thackeray (a man of strong though sleepy virility) asked in his exquisite plaintive way: 'Why do our lady novelists make the men bully the women?' It is, I think, unquestionably true that the Brontës treated the male as an almost anarchic thing coming in from outside nature; much as people on this planet regard a comet. Even the really delicate and sustained comedy of Paul Emanuel is not quite free from this air of studying something alien. The reply may be made that the women in men's novels are equally fallacious. The reply is probably just.

What the Brontës really brought into fiction was exactly what Carlyle brought into history; the blast of the mysticism of the North. They were of Irish blood settled on the windy heights of Yorkshire; in that country where Catholicism lingered latest, but in a superstitious form; where modern industrialism came earliest and was more superstitious still. The strong winds and sterile places, the old tyranny of barons and the new and blacker tyranny of manufacturers, has made and left that country a land of barbarians. All Charlotte Brontë's earlier work is full of that sullen and unmanageable world; moss-troopers turned hurriedly into miners; the last of the old world forced into supporting the very first crudities of the new. In this way Charlotte Brontë represents the Victorian settlement in a special way. The early Victorian Industrialism is to George Eliot and to Charlotte Brontë, rather as the Late Victorian Imperialism would have been to Mrs Humphry Ward[1] in the centre of the empire ... The real strength there is in characters like Robert Moore, when he is dealing with anything except women, is the romance of industry in its first advance: a romance that has not remained. On such fighting frontiers people always exaggerate the strong qualities the masculine sex does possess, and always add a great many strong qualities that it does not possess. That is, briefly, all the reason in the Brontës on this special subject: the rest is stark unreason. It can be most clearly seen in that sister of Charlotte Brontë's who has achieved the real feat of remaining as a great woman rather than a great writer.

1 Mrs Humphry Ward (1851–1920), novelist, best known for her novel of religious crisis. *Robert Elsmere* (1888).

There is really, in a narrow but intense way, a tradition of Emily Brontë: as there is a tradition of St Peter or Dr Johnson. People talk as if they had known her, apart from her works. She must have been something more than an original person; perhaps an origin. But so far as her written works go she enters English letters only as an original person – and rather a narrow one. Her imagination was sometimes superhuman – always inhuman. *Wuthering Heights* might have been written by an eagle. She is the strongest instance of these strong imaginations that made the other sex a monster: for Heathcliffe fails as a man as catastrophically as he succeeds as a demon. I think Emily Brontë was further narrowed by the broadness of her religious views; but never, of course, so much as George Eliot.

In any case, it is Charlotte Brontë who enters Victorian literature. The shortest way of stating her strong contribution is, I think, this: that she reached the highest romance through the lowest realism. . . . She set out with herself, with her own dingy clothes, and accidental ugliness, and flat, coarse, provincial household; and forcibly fused all such muddy materials into a spirited fairytale. If the first chapter on the home and school had not proved how heavy and hateful *sanity* can be, there would really be less point in the insanity of Mr Rochester's wife – or the not much milder insanity of Mrs Rochester's husband. She discovered the secret of hiding the sensational in the commonplace: and *Jane Eyre* remains the best of her books (better even than *Villette*) because while it is a human document written in blood, it is also one of the best blood-and-thunder detective stories in the world.

But while Emily Brontë was as unsociable as a storm at midnight, and while Charlotte Brontë was at best like that warmer and more domestic thing, a house on fire – they do connect themselves with the calm of George Eliot, as the forerunners of many later developments of the feminine advance. Many forerunners (if it comes to that) would have felt rather ill if they had seen the things they foreran. This notion of a hazy anticipation of after history has been absurdly overdone: as when men connect Chaucer with the Reformation; which is like connecting Homer with the Syracusan Expedition. But it is to some extent true that all these great Victorian women had a sort of unrest in their souls. And the proof of it is that (after what I will claim to call the healthier time of Dickens and Thackeray) it began to be admitted by the great Victorian men. If there had not been something in that irritation, we should hardly have had to speak in these pages of *Diana of the Crossways* or of *Tess of the D'Urbervilles*. To what this strange and very local sex war has been due I shall not ask, because I have no answer. That it was due to votes or even little legal inequalities about marriage, I feel myself here too close to realities even to discuss. My own guess is that it has been due to the great neglect of the military spirit by the male Victorians. The woman felt obscurely that she was still running her mortal risk, while the man was not still running his. But I know nothing about it; nor does anybody else.

In so short a book on so vast, complex and living a subject, it is impossible to drop even into the second rank of good authors, whose name is legion; but it is impossible to leave that considerable female force in fiction which has so largely made the very nature of the modern novel, without mentioning two names which almost brought that second rank up to the first rank. They were at utterly opposite poles. The one succeeded by being a much mellower and more Christian George Eliot; the other succeeded by being a much more mad and unchristian Emily Brontë. But Mrs Oliphant and the author calling herself 'Ouida' both forced themselves well within the frontier of fine literature. *The Beleaguered City* is literature in its highest sense, the other works of its author tend to fall into fiction in its best working sense. Mrs Oliphant was infinitely saner in that city of ghosts than the cosmopolitan Ouida ever was in any of the cities of men. Mrs Oliphant would never have dared to discover, either in heaven or hell, such a thing as a hairbrush with its back encrusted with diamonds. But though Ouida was violent and weak where Mrs Oliphant might have been mild and strong, her own triumphs were her own. She had a real power of expressing the senses through her style; of conveying the very heat of blue skies or the bursting of palpable pomegranates. And just as Mrs Oliphant transfused her more timid Victorian tales with a true and intense faith in the Christian mystery – so Ouida, with infinite fury and infinite confusion of thought, did fill her books with Byron and the remains of the French Revolution. In the track of such genius there has been quite an accumulation of true talent as in the children's tales of Mrs Ewing, the historical tales of Miss Yonge, the tales of Mrs Molesworth, and so on. On a general review I do not think I have been wrong in taking the female novelists first. I think they gave its special shape, its temporary twist, to the Victorian novel.

Nevertheless it is a shock (I almost dare to call it a relief) to come back to the males. It is the more abrupt because the first name that must be mentioned derives directly from the mere maleness of the Sterne and Smollett novel. I have already spoken of Dickens as the most homely and instinctive, and therefore probably the heaviest, of all the onslaughts made on the central Victorian satisfaction. There is therefore the less to say of him here, where we consider him only as a novelist: but there is still much more to say than can even conceivably be said. Dickens, as we have stated, inherited the old comic, rambling novel from Smollett and the rest. Dickens, as we have also stated, consented to expurgate that novel. But when all origins and all restraints have been defined and allowed for, the creature that came out was such as we shall not see again. Smollett was coarse; but Smollett was also cruel. Dickens was frequently horrible; he was never cruel. The art of Dickens was the most exquisite of arts: it was the art of enjoying everybody. Dickens, being a very human writer, had to be a very human being; he had his faults and sensibilities in a strong degree; and I do not for a moment maintain that he enjoyed everybody in his daily life. But he enjoyed everybody in his books; and everybody has enjoyed everybody in those books even till today. His books are full of baffled villains stalking out or cowardly bullies kicked downstairs. But the villains and the cowards are such delightful people that the reader always hopes the villain will put his head through a side window and make a last remark; or that the bully will say one thing more, even from the bottom of the stairs. The reader really hopes this; and he cannot get rid of the fancy that the author hopes so too. I cannot at the moment recall that Dickens ever killed a comic villain, except Quilp, who was deliberately made even more villainous than comic. There can be no serious fears for the life of Mr Wegg in the muckcart; though Mr Pecksniff fell to be a borrower of money, and Mr Mantalini to turning a mangle, the human race has the comfort of thinking they are still alive: and one might have the rapture of receiving a begging letter from Mr Pecksniff, or even of catching Mr Mantalini collecting the washing, if one always lurked about on Monday mornings. This sentiment (the true artist will be relieved to hear) is entirely unmoral. Mrs Wilfer deserved death much more than Mr Quilp, for she had succeeded in poisoning family life persistently, while he was (to say the least of it) intermittent in his domesticity. But who can honestly say he does not hope Mrs Wilfer is still talking like Mrs Wilfer – especially if it is only in a book? This is the artistic greatness of Dickens, before and after which there is really nothing to be said. He had the power of creating people, both possible and impossible, who were simply precious and priceless people; and anything subtler added to that truth really only weakens it.

The mention of Mrs Wilfer (whom the heart is loth to leave) reminds one of the only elementary ethical truth that is essential in the study of Dickens. That is that he had broad or universal sympathies in a sense totally unknown to the social reformers who wallow in such phrases. Dickens (unlike the social reformers) really did sympathize with every sort of victim of every sort of tyrant. He did truly pray for *all* who are desolate and oppressed. If you try to tie him to any cause narrower than that Prayer Book definition, you will find you have shut out half his best work. If, in your sympathy for Mrs Quilp, you call Dickens the champion of downtrodden woman, you will suddenly remember Mr Wilfer, and find yourself unable to deny the existence of downtrodden man. If in your sympathy for Mr Rouncewell you call Dickens the champion of a manly middle-class Liberalism against Chesney Wold, you will suddenly remember Stephen Blackpool – and find yourself unable to deny that Mr Rouncewell might be a pretty insupportable cock on his own dunghill. If in your sympathy for Stephen Blackpool you call Dickens a Socialist (as does Mr Pugh), and think of him as merely heralding the great Collectivist revolt against Victorian Individualism and Capitalism, which seemed so clearly to be the crisis at the end of this epoch – you will suddenly remember the agreeable young Barnacle at the Circumlocution Office: and you will be unable, for very shame, to assert that Dickens would have trusted the poor to a State Department. Dickens did not merely believe in the brotherhood of men in the weak modern way; he was the brotherhood of men, and knew it was a brotherhood in sin as well as in aspiration. And he was not only larger than the old factions he satirized; he was larger than any of our great social schools that have gone forward since he died.

The seemingly quaint custom of comparing Dickens and Thackeray existed in their own time; and no one will dismiss it with entire disdain who remembers that the Victorian tradition was domestic and genuine, even when it was hoodwinked and unworldly. There must have been some reason for making this imaginary duel between two quite separate and quite amiable acquaintances. And there is, after all, some reason for it. It is not, as was once cheaply said, that Thackeray went in for truth, and Dickens for mere caricature. There is a huge accumulation of truth, down to the smallest detail, in Dickens: he seems sometimes a mere mountain of facts. Thackeray, in comparison, often seems quite careless and elusive; almost as if he did not quite know where all his characters were. There is a truth behind the popular distinction; but it lies much deeper. Perhaps the best way of stating it is this: that Dickens used reality, while aiming at an effect of romance; while Thackeray used the loose language and ordinary approaches of romance, while aiming at an effect of reality. It was the special and splendid business of Dickens to introduce us to people who would have been quite incredible if he had not told us so much truth about them. It was the special and not less splendid task of Thackeray to introduce us to people whom we knew already. Paradoxically, but very practically, it followed that his introductions were the longer of the two. When we hear of Aunt Betsy Trotwood, we vividly envisage everything about her, from her gardening gloves to her seaside residence, from her hard, handsome face to her tame lunatic laughing at the bedroom window. It is all so minutely true that she must be true also. We only feel inclined to walk round the English coast until we find that particular garden and that particular aunt. But when we turn from the aunt of Copperfield to the uncle of Pendennis, we are more likely to run round the coast trying to find a watering-place where he isn't than one where he is. The moment one sees Major Pendennis, one sees a hundred Major Pendennises. It is not a matter of mere realism. Miss Trotwood's bonnet and gardening tools and cupboard full of old-fashioned bottles are quite as true in the materialistic way as the Major's cuffs and corner table and toast and newspaper. Both writers are realistic: but Dickens writes realism in order to make the incredible credible. Thackeray writes it in order to make us recognize an old friend. Whether we shall be pleased to meet the old friend is quite another matter: I think we should be better pleased to meet Miss Trotwood, and find, as David Copperfield did, a new friend, a new world. But we recognize Major Pendennis even when we avoid him. Henceforth Thackeray can count on our seeing him from his wig to his well-blacked boots whenever he chooses to say 'Major Pendennis paid a call'. Dickens, on the other hand, had to keep up an incessant excitement about his characters; and no man on earth but he could have kept it up.

It may be said, in approximate summary, that Thackeray is the novelist of memory – of our memories as well as his own. Dickens seems to expect all his characters, like amusing strangers arriving at lunch: as if they gave him not only pleasure, but surprise. But Thackeray is everybody's past – is everybody's youth. Forgotten friends flit about the passages of dreamy colleges and unremembered clubs; we hear fragments of unfinished conversations, we see faces without names for an instant, fixed for ever in some trivial grimace: we smell the strong smell of social cliques now quite incongruous to us; and there stir in all the little rooms at once the hundred ghosts of oneself.

For this purpose Thackeray was equipped with a singularly easy and sympathetic style, carved in slow soft curves where Dickens hacked out his images with a hatchet. There was a sort of avuncular indulgence about his attitude; what he called his 'preaching' was at worst a sort of grumbling, ending with the sentiment that boys will be boys and that there's nothing new under the sun. He was not really either a cynic or a *censor morum*; but (in another sense than Chaucer's) a gentle pardoner: having seen the weaknesses he is sometimes almost weak about them. He really comes nearer to exculpating Pendennis or Ethel Newcome than any other author, who saw what he saw, would have been. The rare wrath of such men is all the more effective; and there are passages in *Vanity Fair* and still more in *The Book of Snobs*, where he does make the dance of wealth and fashion look stiff and monstrous, like a Babylonian masquerade. But he never quite did it in such a way as to turn the course of the Victorian Age.

It may seem strange to say that Thackeray did not know enough of the world; yet this was the truth about him in large matters of the philosophy of life, and especially of his own time. He did not know the way things were going: he was too Victorian to understand the Victorian epoch. He did not know enough ignorant people to have heard the news. In one of his delightful asides he imagines two little clerks commenting erroneously on the appearance of Lady Kew or Sir Brian Newcome in the Park, and says: 'How should Jones and Brown, who are not, *vous comprenez, du monde*, understand these mysteries?' But I think Thackeray knew quite as little about Jones and Brown as they knew about Newcome and Kew; his world was *le monde*. Hence he seemed to take it for granted that the Victorian compromise would last; while Dickens (who knew his Jones and Brown) had already guessed that it would not. Thackeray did not realize that the Victorian platform was a moving platform. To take but one instance, he was a Radical like Dickens; all really representative Victorians, except perhaps Tennyson, were Radicals. But he seems to have thought of all reform as simple and straightforward and all of a piece; as if Catholic Emancipation, the New Poor Law, Free Trade and the Factory Acts and Popular Education were all parts of one almost self-evident evolution of enlightenment. Dickens, being in touch with the democracy, had already discovered that the country had come to a dark place of divided ways and divided counsels. In *Hard Times* he realized Democracy at war with Radicalism; and became, with so incompatible an ally as Ruskin, not indeed a Socialist, but certainly an anti-Individualist. In *Our Mutual Friend* he felt the strength of the new rich, and knew they had begun to transform the aristocracy, instead of the aristocracy transforming them. He knew that Veneering had carried off Twemlow in triumph. He very nearly knew what we all know today: that, so far from it being possible to plod along the progressive road with more votes and more Free Trade, England must either sharply become very much more democratic or as rapidly become very much less so.

There gathers round these two great novelists a considerable group of good novelists, who more or less mirror their mid-Victorian mood. Wilkie Collins may be said to be in this way a lesser Dickens and Anthony Trollope a lesser Thackeray. Wilkie Collins is chiefly typical of his time in this respect: that while his moral and religious conceptions were as mechanical as his carefully constructed fictitious conspiracies, he nevertheless informed the latter with a sort of involuntary mysticism which dealt wholly with the darker side of the soul. For this was one of the most peculiar of the problems of the Victorian mind. The idea of the supernatural was perhaps at as low an ebb as it had ever been – certainly much lower than it is now. But in spite of this, and in spite of a certain ethical cheeriness that was almost *de rigueur* – the strange fact remains that the only sort of supernaturalism the Victorians allowed to their imaginations was a sad supernaturalism. They might have ghost stories, but not saints' stories. They could trifle with the curse or unpardoning prophecy of a witch, but not with the pardon of a priest. They seem to have held (I believe erroneously) that the supernatural was safest when it came from below. When we think (for example) of the uncountable riches of religious art, imagery, ritual and popular legend that has clustered round Christmas through all the Christian ages, it is a truly extraordinary thing to reflect that Dickens (wishing to have in 'The Christmas Carol' a little happy supernaturalism by way of a change) actually had to make up a mythology for himself. Here was one of the rare cases where Dickens, in a real and human sense, did suffer from the lack of culture. For the rest, Wilkie Collins is these two elements: the mechanical and the mystical; both very good of their kind. He is one of the few novelists in whose case it is proper and literal to speak of his 'plots'. He was a plotter; he went about to slay Godfrey Ablewhite as coldly and craftily as the Indians did. But he also had a sound though sinister note of true magic; as in the repetition of the two white dresses in *The Woman in White*; or of the dreams with their double explanations in *Armadale*. His ghosts do walk. They are alive; and walk as softly as Count Fosco, but as solidly. Finally, *The Moonstone* is probably the best detective tale in the world.

Anthony Trollope, a clear and very capable realist, represents rather another side of the Victorian spirit of comfort; its leisureliness, its love of detail, especially of domestic detail; its love of following characters and kindred from book to book and from generation to generation. Dickens very seldom tried this latter experiment, and then (as in *Master Humphrey's Clock*) unsuccessfully; those magnesium blazes of his were too brilliant and glaring to be indefinitely prolonged. But Thackeray was full of it; and we often feel that the characters in *The Newcomes* or *Philip* might legitimately complain that their talk and tale are being perpetually interrupted and pestered by people out of other books. Within his narrower limits, Trollope was a more strict and masterly realist than Thackeray, and even those who would call his personages 'types' would admit that they are as vivid as characters. It was a bustling but a quiet world that he described: politics before the coming of the Irish and the Socialists; the Church in the lull between the Oxford Movement and the modern High Anglican energy. And it is notable in the Victorian spirit once more that though his clergymen are all of them real men and many of them good men, it never really occurs to us to think of them as the priests of a religion.

Charles Reade may be said to go along with these; and Disraeli and even Kingsley; not because these three very different persons had anything particular in common, but because they all fell short of the first rank in about the same degree. Charles Reade had a kind of cold coarseness about him, not morally but artistically, which keeps him out of the best literature as such: but he is of importance to the Victorian development in another way; because he has the harsher and more tragic note that has come later in the study of our social problems. He is the first of the angry realists. Kingsley's best books may be called boys' books. There is a real though a juvenile poetry in *Westward Ho!* and though that narrative, historically considered, is very much of a lie, it is a good, thundering honest lie. There are also genuinely eloquent things in *Hypatia*, and a certain electric atmosphere of sectarian excitement that Kingsley kept himself in, and did know how to convey. He said he wrote the book in his heart's blood. This is an exaggeration, but there is a truth in it; and one does feel that he may have relieved his feelings by writing it in red ink. As for Disraeli, his novels are able and interesting considered as everything except novels, and are an important contribution precisely because they are written by an alien who did not take our politics so seriously as Trollope did. They are important again as showing those later Victorian changes which men like Thackeray missed. Disraeli did do something towards revealing the dishonesty of our politics – even if he had done a good deal towards bringing it about.

Between this group and the next there hovers a figure very hard to place; not higher in letters than these, yet not easy to class with them; I mean Bulwer Lytton. He was no greater than they were; yet somehow he seems to take up more space. He did not, in the ultimate reckoning, do anything in particular: but he was a figure; rather as Oscar Wilde was later a figure. You could not have the Victorian Age without him. And this was not due to wholly superficial things like his dandyism, his dark, sinister good looks and a great deal of the mere polished melodrama that he wrote. There was something in his all-round interests; in the variety of things he tried; in his half-aristocratic swagger as poet and politician, that made him in some ways a real touchstone of the time. It is noticeable about him that he is always turning up everywhere and that he brings other people out, generally in hostile spirit. His Byronic and almost Oriental ostentation was used by the young Thackeray as something on which to sharpen his new razor of Victorian common sense. His pose as a dilettante satirist inflamed the execrable temper of Tennyson, and led to those lively comparisons to a bandbox and a lion in curlpapers. He interposed the glove of warning and the tear of sensibility between us and the proper ending of *Great Expectations*. Of his own books, by far the best are the really charming comedies about *The Caxtons* and *Kenelm Chillingly*; none of his other works have a high literary importance now; with the possible exception of *A Strange Story*; but his *Coming Race* is historically interesting as foreshadowing those novels of the future which were afterwards such a weapon of the Socialists. Lastly, there was an element indefinable about Lytton, which often is in adventurers; which amounts to a suspicion that there was something in him after all. It rang out of him when he said to the hesitating Crimean Parliament. 'Destroy your Government and save your army.'

With the next phase of Victorian fiction we enter a new world; the later, more revolutionary, more continental, freer but in some ways weaker world in which we live today. The subtle and sad change that was passing like twilight across the English brain at this time is very well expressed in the fact that men have come to mention the great name of Meredith in the same breath as Mr Thomas Hardy. Both writers, doubtless, disagreed with the orthodox religion of the ordinary English village. Most of us have disagreed with that religion until we made the simple discovery that it does not exist. But in any age where ideas could be even feebly disentangled from each other, it would have been evident at once that Meredith and Hardy were, intellectually speaking, mortal enemies. They were much more opposed to each other than Newman was to Kingsley; or than Abelard was to St Bernard. But then they collided in a sceptical age, which is like colliding in a London fog. There can never be any clear controversy in a sceptical age.

Nevertheless both Hardy and Meredith did mean something; and they did mean diametrically opposite things. Meredith was perhaps the only man in the modern world who has almost had the high honour of rising out of the low estate of a Pantheist into the high estate of a Pagan. A Pagan is a person who can do what hardly any person for the last two thousand years could do: a person who can take Nature naturally. It is due to Meredith to say that no one outside a few of the great Greeks has ever taken Nature so naturally as he did. And it is also due to him to say that no one ... ever took Nature so unnaturally as it was taken in what Mr Hardy has had the blasphemy to call Wessex Tales. This division between the two points of view is vital; because the turn of the nineteenth century was a very sharp one; by it we have reached the rapids in which we find ourselves today.

Meredith really is a Pantheist. You can express it by saying that God is the great All: you can express it much more intelligently by saying that Pan is the great god. But there is some sense in it, and the sense is this: that some people believe that this world is sufficiently good at bottom for us to trust ourselves to it without very much knowing why. It is the whole point in most of Meredith's tales that there is something behind us that often saves us when we understand neither it nor ourselves. He sometimes talked mere intellectualism about women: but that is because the most brilliant brains can get tired. ... Those who can see Meredith's mind in that are with those who can see Dickens's mind in Little Nell. Both were chivalrous pronouncements on behalf of oppressed females: neither has any earthly meaning as ideas.

But what Meredith did do for women was not to emancipate them (which means nothing) but to express them, which means a great deal. And he often expressed them right, even when he expressed himself wrong. Take, for instance, that phrase so often quoted: 'Woman will be the last thing civilized by man.' Intellectually it is something worse than false; it is the opposite of what he was always attempting to say. So far from admitting any equality in the sexes, it logically admits that a man may use against a woman any chains or whips he has been in the habit of using against a tiger or a bear. He stood as the special champion of female dignity: but I cannot remember any author, Eastern or Western, who has so calmly assumed that man is the master and woman merely the material, as Meredith really does in this phrase. Any one who knows a free woman (she is generally a married woman) will immediately be inclined to ask two simple and catastrophic questions, first: 'Why should woman be civilized?' and, second: 'Why, if she is to be civilized, should she be civilized by man?' In the mere intellectualism of the matter, Meredith seems to be talking the most brutal sex mastery . . . Now why is it that we all really feel that this Meredithian passage is not so insolently masculine as in mere logic it would seem? I think it is for this simple reason: that there is something about Meredith making us feel that it is not woman he disbelieves in, but civilization. It is a dark undemonstrated feeling that Meredith would really be rather sorry if woman were civilized by man – or by anything else. When we have got that, we have got the real Pagan – the man that does believe in Pan.

It is proper to put this philosophic matter first, before the aesthetic appreciation of Meredith, because with Meredith a sort of passing bell has rung and the Victorian orthodoxy is certainly no longer safe. Dickens and Carlyle, as we have said, rebelled against the orthodox compromise: but Meredith has escaped from it. Cosmopolitanism, Socialism, Feminism are already in the air; and Queen Victoria has begun to look like Mrs Grundy. But to escape from a city is one thing: to choose a road is another. The freethinker who found himself outside the Victorian city, found himself also in the fork of two very different naturalistic paths. One of them went upwards through a tangled but living forest to lonely but healthy hills: the other went down to a swamp. Hardy went down to botanize in the swamp, while Meredith climbed towards the sun. Meredith became, at his best, a sort of daintily dressed Walt Whitman: Hardy became a sort of village atheist brooding and blaspheming over the village idiot. It is largely because the freethinkers, as a school, have hardly made up their minds whether they want to be more optimist or more pessimist than Christianity that their small but sincere movement has failed.

For the duel is deadly; and any agnostic who wishes to be anything more than a Nihilist must sympathize with one version of nature or the other. The God of Meredith is impersonal; but he is often more healthy and kindly than any of the persons. That of Thomas Hardy is almost made personal by the intense feeling that he is poisonous. Nature is always coming in to save Meredith's women; Nature is always coming in to betray and ruin Hardy's. It has been said that if God had not existed it would have been necessary to invent Him. But it is not often, as in Mr Hardy's case, that it is necessary to invent Him in order to prove how unnecessary (and undesirable) He is. But Mr Hardy is anthropomorphic out of sheer atheism. He personifies the universe in order to give it a piece of his mind. But the fight is unequal for the old philosophical reason: that the universe had already given Mr Hardy a piece of *its* mind to fight with. One curious result of this divergence in the two types of sceptic is this: that when these two brilliant novelists break down or blow up or otherwise lose for a moment their artistic self-command, they are both equally wild, but wild in opposite directions. Meredith shows an extravagance in comedy which, if it were not so complicated, every one would call broad farce. But Mr Hardy has the honour of inventing a new sort of game, which may be called the extravagance of depression. The placing of the weak lover and his new love in such a place that they actually see the black flag announcing that Tess has been hanged is utterly inexcusable in art and probability; it is a cruel practical joke. But it is a practical joke at which even its author cannot brighten up enough to laugh.

But it is when we consider the great artistic power of these two writers, with all their eccentricities, that we see even more clearly that free-thought was, as it were, a fight between finger-posts. For it is the remarkable fact that it was the man who had the healthy and manly outlook who had the crabbed and perverse style; it was the man who had the crabbed and perverse outlook who had the healthy and manly style. The reader may well have complained of paradox when I observed above that Meredith, unlike most neo-Pagans, did in his way take Nature naturally. It may be suggested, in tones of some remonstrance, that things like 'though pierced by the cruel acerb' or 'thy fleeting-ness is bigger in the ghost', or 'her grabbling grey she eyes askant', or 'sheer film of the surface awag' are not taking Nature naturally. And this is true of Meredith's style, but it is not true of his spirit; nor even, apparently, of his serious opinions. In one of the poems I have quoted he actually says of those who live nearest to that Nature he was always praising –

> Have they but held her laws and nature dear,
> They mouth no sentence of inverted wit;

which certainly was what Meredith himself was doing most of the time. But a similar paradox of the combination of plain tastes with twisted phrases can also be seen in Browning. Something of the same can be seen in many of the cavalier poets. I do not understand it: it may be that the fertility of a cheerful mind crowds everything, so that the tree is entangled in its own branches; or it may be that the cheerful mind cares less whether it is understood or not; as a man is less articulate when he is humming than when he is calling for help.

Certainly Meredith suffers from applying a complex method to men and things he does not mean to be complex; nay, honestly admires for being simple. The conversations between Diana and Redworth fail of their full contrast because Meredith can afford the twopence for Diana coloured, but cannot afford the penny for Redworth plain. Meredith's ideals were neither sceptical nor finnicky: but they can be called insufficient. He had, perhaps, over and above his honest Pantheism two convictions profound enough to be called prejudices. He was probably of Welsh blood, certainly of Celtic sympathies, and he set himself more swiftly though more subtly than Ruskin or Swinburne to undermining the enormous complacency of John Bull. He also had a sincere hope in the strength of womanhood, and may be said, almost without hyperbole, to have begotten gigantic daughters. He may yet suffer for his chivalric interference as many champions do. I have little doubt that when St George had killed the dragon he was heartily afraid of the princess. But certainly neither of these two vital enthusiasms touched the Victorian trouble. The disaster of the modern English is not that they are not Celtic, but that they are not English. The tragedy of the modern woman is not that she is not allowed to follow man, but that she follows him far too slavishly. This conscious and theorizing Meredith did not get very near his problem and is certainly miles away from ours. But the other Meredith was a creator; which means a god. That is true of him which is true of so different a man as Dickens, that all one can say of him is that he is full of good things. A reader opening one of his books feels like a schooolboy opening a hamper which he knows to have somehow cost a hundred pounds. He may be more bewildered by it than by an ordinary hamper; but he gets the impression of a real richness of thought; and that is what one really gets from such riots of felicity as *Evan Harrington* or *Harry Richmond*. His philosophy may be barren, but he was not. And the chief feeling among those that enjoy him is a mere wish that more people could enjoy him too.

I end here upon Hardy and Meredith; because this parting of the ways to open optimism and open pessimism really was the end of the Victorian peace. There are many other men, very nearly as great, on whom I might delight to linger: on Shorthouse,[1] for instance, who in one way goes with Mrs Browning or Coventry Patmore. I mean that he has a wide culture, which is called by some a narrow religion. When we think what even the best novels about cavaliers have been (written by men like Scott or Stevenson) it is a wonderful thing that the author of *John Inglesant* could write a cavalier romance in which he forgot Cromwell but remembered Hobbes. But Shorthouse is outside the period in fiction in the same sort of way in which Francis Thompson is outside it in poetry. He did not accept the Victorian basis. He knew too much.

There is one more matter that may best be considered here, though briefly: it illustrates the extreme difficulty of dealing with the Victorian English in a book like this, because of their eccentricity; not of opinions, but of character and artistic form. There are several great Victorians who will not fit into any of the obvious categories I employ; because they will not fit into anything, hardly into the world itself. Where Germany or Italy would relieve the monotony of mankind by paying serious respect to an artist, or a scholar, or a patriotic warrior, or a priest – it was always the instinct of the English to do it by pointing out a Character. Dr Johnson has faded as a poet or a critic, but he survives as a Character. Cobbett is neglected (unfortunately) as a publicist and pamphleteer, but he is remembered as a Character. Now these people continued to crop up through the Victorian time; and each stands so much by himself that I shall end these pages with a profound suspicion that I have forgotten to mention a Character of gigantic dimensions. Perhaps the best example of such eccentrics is George Borrow;[2] who sympathized with unsuccessful nomads like the gipsies while every one else sympathized with successful nomads like the Jews; who had a genius like the west wind for the awakening of wild and casual friendships and the drag and attraction of the roads. But whether

1 Joseph Shorthouse (1834–1903), author of the historical novel *John Inglesant* (1881).
2 George Borrow (1803–81), author of the picaresque travel book *The Bible in Spain* (1843).

George Borrow ought to go into the section devoted to philosophers, or the section devoted to novelists, or the section devoted to liars, nobody else has ever known, even if he did.

But the strongest case of this Victorian power of being abruptly original in a corner can be found in two things: the literature meant merely for children and the literature meant merely for fun. It is true that these two very Victorian things often melted into each other (as was the way of Victorian things), but not sufficiently to make it safe to mass them together without distinction. Thus there was George Macdonald, a Scot of genius as genuine as Carlyle's; he could write fairy-tales that made all experience a fairy-tale. He could give the real sense that every one had the end of an elfin thread that must at last lead them into Paradise. It was a sort of optimist Calvinism. But such really significant fairy-tales were accidents of genius. Of the Victorian Age as a whole it is true to say that it did discover a new thing; a thing called Nonsense. It may be doubted whether this thing was really invented to please children. Rather it was invented by old people trying to prove their first childhood, and sometimes succeeding only in proving their second. But whatever else the thing was, it was English and it was individual. Lewis Carroll gave mathematics a holiday: he carried logic into the wild lands of illogicality. Edward Lear, a richer, more romantic and therefore more truly Victorian buffoon, improved the experiment. But the more we study it, the more we shall, I think, conclude that it reposed on something more real and profound in the Victorians than even their just and exquisite appreciation of children. It came from the deep Victorian sense of humour.

It may appear, because I have used from time to time the only possible phrases for the case, that I mean the Victorian Englishman to appear as a blockhead, which means an unconscious buffoon. To all this there is a final answer: that he was also a conscious buffoon – and a successful one. He was a humorist; and one of the best humorists in Europe. That which Goethe had never taught the Germans, Byron did manage to teach the English – the duty of not taking him seriously. . . . They had largely forgotten both art and arms: but the gods had left them laughter.

But the final proof that the Victorians were alive by this laughter can be found in the fact they could manage and master for a moment even the cosmopolitan modern theatre. They could contrive to put *The Bab Ballads* on the stage. To turn a private name into a public epithet is a thing given to few: but the word 'Gilbertian' will probably last longer than the name Gilbert.

It meant a real Victorian talent; that of exploding unexpectedly and almost, as it seemed, unintentionally. Gilbert made good jokes by the thousand; but he never (in his best days) made the joke that could possibly have been expected of him. This is the last essential of the Victorian. Laugh at him as a limited man, a moralist, conventionalist, an opportunist, a formalist. But remember also that he was really a humorist; and may still be laughing at you.

III
THE GREAT VICTORIAN POETS

WHAT WAS really unsatisfactory in Victorian literature is something much easier to feel than to state. It was not so much a superiority in the men of other ages to the Victorian men. It was a superiority of Victorian men to themselves. The individual was unequal. Perhaps that is why the society became unequal: I cannot say. They were lame giants; the strongest of them walked on one leg a little shorter than the other. A great man in any age must be a common man, and also an uncommon man. Those that are only uncommon men are perverts and sowers of pestilence. But somehow the great Victorian man was more and less than this. He was at once a giant and a dwarf. When he has been sweeping the sky in circles infinitely great, he suddenly shrivels into something indescribably small. There is a moment when Carlyle turns suddenly from a high creative mystic to a common Calvinist. There are moments when George Eliot turns from a prophetess into a governess. There are also moments when Ruskin turns into a governess, without even the excuse of sex. But in all these cases the alteration comes as a thing quite abrupt and unreasonable. We do not feel this acute angle anywhere in Homer or in Virgil or in Chaucer or in Shakespeare or in Dryden; such things as they knew they knew. It is no disgrace to Homer that he had not discovered Britain; or to Virgil that he had not discovered America; or to Chaucer that he had not discovered the solar system; or to Dryden that he had not discovered the steam-engine. But we do most frequently feel, with the Victorians, that the very vastness of the number of things they know illustrates the abrupt abyss of the things they do not know. We feel, in a sort of way, that it *is* a disgrace to a man like Carlyle when he asks the Irish why they do not bestir themselves and reforest their country: saying not a word about the soaking up of every sort of profit by the landlords which made that and every other Irish improvement impossible. We feel that it *is* a disgrace to a man like Ruskin when he says, with a solemn visage, that building in iron is ugly and unreal, but that the weightiest objection is that there is no mention of it in the Bible; we feel as if he had just said he could find no hair-brushes in Habakkuk. We feel that it *is* a disgrace to a man like Thackeray when he proposes that people should be forcibly prevented from being nuns, merely because he has no fixed intention of becoming a nun himself. We feel that it *is* a disgrace to a man like Tennyson, when he talks of the French revolutions, the huge crusades that had re-created the whole of his civilization, as being 'no graver than a schoolboy's barring out'. We feel that it *is* a disgrace to a man like Browning to make spluttering and spiteful puns about the names Newman, Wiseman,[1] and Manning.[2] We feel that it *is* a disgrace to a man like Newman when he confesses that for some time he felt as if he couldn't come in to the Catholic Church, because of that dreadful Mr Daniel O'Connell,[3] who had the vulgarity to fight for his own country. We feel that it *is* a disgrace to a man like Dickens, when he makes a blind brute and savage out of a man like St Dunstan; it sounds as if it were not Dickens talking but Dombey. We feel it *is* a disgrace to a man like Swinburne, when he had a Jingo fit and calls the Boer children in the concentration camps 'Whelps of treacherous dams whom none save we have spared to starve and slay': we feel that Swinburne, for the first time, really has become an immoral and indecent writer. All this is a certain odd provincialism peculiar to the English in that great century: they were in a kind of pocket; they appealed to too narrow a public opinion; I am certain that no French or German men of the same genius made such remarks. Renan was the enemy of the Catholic Church; but who can imagine Renan writing of it as Kingsley or Dickens did? Taine was the enemy of the French Revolution; but who can imagine Taine talking about it as Tennyson or Newman talked? Even Matthew Arnold, though he saw this peril and prided himself on escaping it, did not altogether escape it. There must be (to use an Irishism) something shallow in the depths of any man who talks about the *Zeitgeist* as if it were a living thing.

1 Nicholas Wiseman (1802–65), cardinal, first Archbishop of Westminster in the restored Roman Catholic hierarchy.
2 See note 1, p. 43.
3 Daniel O'Connell (1775–1847), Irish political leader, known as the Liberator, who fought for Catholic emancipation.

But this defect is very specially the key to the case of the two great Victorian poets, Tennyson and Browning; the two spirited or beautiful tunes, so to speak, to which the other events marched or danced. It was especially so of Tennyson, for a reason which raises some of the most real problems about his poetry. Tennyson, of course, owed a great deal to Virgil. There is no question of plagiarism here; a debt to Virgil is like a debt to Nature. But Tennyson was a provincial Virgil. In such passages as that about the schoolboy's barring out he might be called a suburban Virgil. I mean that he tried to have the universal balance of all the ideas at which the great Roman had aimed: but he hadn't got hold of all the ideas to balance. Hence his work was not a balance of truths, like the universe. It was a balance of whims; like the British Constitution. It is intensely typical of Tennyson's philosophical temper that he was almost the only Poet Laureate who was not ludicrous. It is not absurd to think of Tennyson as tuning his harp in praise of Queen Victoria: that is, it is not absurd in the same sense as Chaucer's harp hallowed by dedication to Richard II or Wordsworth's harp hallowed by dedication to George IV is absurd. Richard's court could not properly appreciate either Chaucer's daisies or his 'devotion'. George IV would not have gone pottering about Helvellyn in search of purity and the simple annals of the poor. But Tennyson did sincerely believe in the Victorian compromise; and sincerity is never undignified. He really did hold a great many of the same views as Queen Victoria, though he was gifted with a more fortunate literary style. If Dickens is Cobbett's democracy stirring in its grave, Tennyson is the exquisitely ornamental extinguisher on the flame of the first revolutionary poets. England has settled down; England has become Victorian. The compromise was interesting, it was national and for a long time it was successful: there is still a great deal to be said for it. But it was as freakish and unphilosophic, as arbitrary and untranslatable, as a beggar's patched coat or a child's secret language. Now it is here that Browning had a certain odd advantage over Tennyson; which has, perhaps, somewhat exaggerated his intellectual superiority to him. Browning's eccentric style was more suitable to the poetry of a nation of eccentrics; of people for the time being removed far from the centre of intellectual interests. The hearty and pleasant task of expressing one's intense dislike of something one doesn't understand is much more poetically achieved by saying, in a general way 'Grrr – you swine!' than it is by laboured lines such as 'the red fool-fury of the Seine'. We all feel that there is more of the man in Browning here; more of Dr Johnson or Cobbett. Browning is the Englishman taking himself wilfully, following his nose like a bulldog, going by his own likes and dislikes. We cannot help feeling that Tennyson is the Englishman taking himself seriously – an awful sight. One's memory flutters unhappily over a certain letter about the Papal Guards written by Sir Willoughby Patterne. It is here chiefly that Tennyson suffers by that very Virgilian loveliness and dignity of diction which he put to the service of such a small and anomolous national scheme. Virgil had the best news to tell as well as the best words to tell it in. His world might be sad; but it was the largest world one could live in before the coming of Christianity. If he told the Romans to spare the vanquished and to war down the mighty, at least he was more or less well informed about who *were* mighty and who *were* vanquished. But when Tennyson wrote verses like –

> Of freedom in her regal seat,
> Of England; not the schoolboy heat,
> The blind hysterics of the Celt

he quite literally did not know one word of what he was talking about; he did not know what Celts are, or what hysterics are, or what freedom was, or what regal was or even of what England was – in the living Europe of that time.

His religious range was very much wider and wiser than his political; but here also he suffered from treating as true universality a thing that was only a sort of lukewarm local patriotism. Here also he suffered by the very splendour and perfection of his poetical powers. He was quite the opposite of the man who cannot express himself; the inarticulate singer who dies with all his music in him. He had a great deal to say; but he had much more power of expression than was wanted for anything he had to express. He could not think up to the height of his own towering style.

For whatever else Tennyson was, he was a great poet; no mind that feels itself free, that is, above the ebb and flow of fashion, can feel anything but contempt for the later effort to discredit him in that respect. It is true that, like Browning and almost every other

Victorian poet, he was really two poets. But it is just to him to insist that in his case (unlike Browning's) both the poets were good. The first is more or less like Stevenson in metre; it is a magical luck or skill in the mere choice of words. 'Wet sands marbled with moon and cloud' – 'Flits by the sea-blue bird of March' – 'Leafless ribs and iron horns' – 'When the long dun wolds are ribbed with snow' – in all these cases one word is the keystone of an arch which would fall into ruin without it. But there are other strong phrases that recall not Stevenson but rather their common master, Virgil – 'Tears from the depths of some divine despair' – 'There is fallen a splendid tear from the passion-flower at the gate' – 'Was a great water; and the moon was full' – 'God made Himself an awful rose of dawn'. These do not depend on a word but on an idea: they might even be translated. It is also true, I think, that he was first and last a lyric poet. He was always best when he expressed himself shortly. In long poems he had an unfortunate habit of eventually saying very nearly the opposite of what he meant to say. I will take only two instances of what I mean. In the *Idylls of the King*, and in *In Memoriam* (his two sustained and ambitious efforts), particular phrases are always flashing out the whole fire of the truth; the truth that Tennyson meant. But owing to his English indolence, his English aristocratic irresponsibility, his English vagueness in thought, he always managed to make the main poem mean exactly what he did not mean. Thus, these two lines which simply say that

> Lancelot was the first in tournament,
> But Arthur mightiest in the battle-field

do really express what he meant to express about Arthur being after all 'the highest, yet most human too; not Lancelot, nor another'. But as his hero is actually developed, we have exactly the opposite impression; that poor old Lancelot, with all his faults, was much more of a man than Arthur. He was a Victorian in the bad as well as the good sense; he could not keep priggishness out of long poems. Or again, take the case of *In Memoriam*. I will quote one verse (probably incorrectly) which has always seemed to me splendid, and which does express what the whole poem should express – but hardly does.

> That we may lift from out of dust
> A voice as unto him that hears

> A cry above the conquered years
> To one that with us works, and trust.

The poem should have been a cry above the conquered years. It might well have been that if the poet could have said sharply at the end of it, as a pure piece of dogma, 'I've forgotten every feature of the man's face: I know God holds him alive.' But under the influence of the mere leisurely length of the thing, the reader *does* rather receive the impression that the wound has been healed only by time; and that the victor hours *can* boast that this is the man that loved and lost, but all he was is overworn. This is not the truth; and Tennyson did not intend it for the truth. It is simply the result of the lack of something militant, dogmatic and structural in him: whereby he could not be trusted with the trail of a very long literary process without entangling himself like a kitten playing cat's-cradle.

Browning, as above suggested, got on much better with eccentric and secluded England because he treated it as eccentric and secluded; a place where one could do what one liked. To a considerable extent he did do what he liked; arousing not a few complaints; and many doubts and conjectures as to why on earth he liked it. Many comparatively sympathetic persons pondered upon what pleasure it could give any man to write *Sordello* or rhyme 'end-knot' to 'offend not'. Nevertheless he was no anarchist and no mystagogue; and even where he was defective, his defect has commonly been stated wrongly. The two chief charges against him were a contempt for form unworthy of an artist, and a poor pride in obscurity. The obscurity is true, though not, I think, the pride in it; but the truth about this charge rather rises out of the truth about the other. The other charge is not true. Browning cared very much for form; he cared very much for style. You may not happen to like his style; but he did. To say that he had not enough mastery over form to express himself perfectly like Tennyson or Swinburne is like criticising the griffin of a mediaeval gargoyle without even knowing that it is a griffin; treating it as an infantile and unsuccessful attempt at a classical angel. A poet indifferent to form ought to mean a poet who did not care what form he used as long as he expressed his thoughts. He might be a rather entertaining sort of poet; telling a smoking-room story in blank verse or writing a hunting-song in the Spenserian stanza; giving a realistic analysis of infanticide in a series of triolets; or proving the truth of Immortality in a long string of limericks. Browning certainly had no such indifference. Almost every poem of Browning, especially the shortest and most successful ones, was moulded or graven in some special style, generally grotesque, but invariably deliberate. In most cases whenever he wrote a new song he wrote a new kind of song. The new lyric is not only of a different metre, but of a different shape. No one, not even Browning, ever wrote a poem in the same style as that horrible one beginning 'John, Master of the Temple of God', with its weird choruses and creepy prose directions. No one, not even Browning, ever wrote a poem in the same style as *Pisgah-sights*. No one, not even Browning, ever wrote a poem in the same style as *Time's Revenges*, no one, not even Browning, ever wrote a poem in the same style as *Meeting at Night* and *Parting at Morning*. No one, not even Browning, ever wrote a poem in the same style as *The Flight of the Duchess*, or in the same style as *A Grammarian's Funeral*, or in the same style as *A Star*, or in the same style as that astounding lyric which begins abruptly 'Some people hang pictures up'. These metres and manners were not accidental; they really do suit the sort of spiritual experiment Browning was making in each case. Browning, then, was not chaotic; he was deliberately grotesque. But there certainly was, over and above this grotesqueness, a perversity and irrationality about the man which led him to play the fool in the middle of his own poems; to leave off carving gargoyles and simply begin throwing stones. His curious complicated puns are an example of this: Hood had used the pun to make a sentence or a sentiment especially pointed and clear. In Browning the word with two meanings seems to mean rather less, if anything, than the word with one. It also applies to his trick of setting himself to cope with impossible rhymes. It may be fun, though it is not poetry, to try rhyming to ranunculus; but even the fun presupposes that you *do* rhyme to it; and I will affirm, and hold under persecution, that 'Tommy-make-room-for-your-uncle-us' does not rhyme to it.

The obscurity, to which he must in a large degree plead guilty, was, curiously enough, the result rather of the gay artist in him than the deep thinker. It is patience in the Browning students; in Browning it was only impatience. He wanted to say something comic and energetic and he wanted to say it quick. And, between his artistic skill in the fantastic and his temperamental turn for the abrupt, the idea sometimes flashed past unseen. But it is quite an error to suppose that these are the dark mines containing his treasure. The two or three great and true things he really had to say he generally managed to say quite simply. Thus he really did want to say that God had indeed made man and woman one flesh; that the sex relation was religious in this real sense that even in our sin and despair we take it for granted and expect a sort of virtue in it. The feelings of the bad husband about the good wife, for instance, are about as subtle and entangled as any matter on this earth; and Browning really had something to say about them. But he said it in some of the plainest and most unmistakable words in all literature; as lucid as a flash of lightning. 'Pompilia, will you let them murder me?' Or again, he did really want to say that death and such moral terrors were best taken in a military spirit; he could not have said it more simply than: 'I was ever a fighter; one fight more, the best and the last'. He did really wish to say that human life was unworkable unless immortality were implied in it every other moment; he could not have said it more simply: 'leave Now for dogs and apes! Man has For ever'. The obscurities were not merely superficial, but often covered quite superficial ideas. He was as likely as not to be most unintelligible of all in writing a compliment in a lady's album. I remember in my boyhood (when Browning kept us awake like coffee) a friend reading out the poem about the portrait to which I have already referred, reading it in that rapid dramatic way in which this poet must be read. And I was profoundly puzzled at the passage where it seemed to say that the cousin disparaged the picture, 'while John scorns ale'. I could not think what this sudden teetotalism on the part of John had to do with the affair, but I forgot to ask at the time and it was only years afterwards that, looking at the book, I found it was 'John's corns ail', a very Browningesque way of saying he winced. Most of Browning's obscurity is of that sort – the mistakes are almost as quaint as misprints – and the Browning student, in that sense, is more a proof reader than a disciple. For the rest his real religion was of the most manly, even the most boyish sort. He is called an optimist; but the word suggests a calculated contentment which was not in the least one of his vices. What he really was was a romantic. He offered the cosmos as an adventure rather than a scheme. He did not explain evil, far less explain it away: he enjoyed defying it. He was a troubadour even in theology and metaphysics: like the *Jongleurs de Dieu* of St Francis.[1] He may be said to have serenaded heaven with a guitar, and even, so to speak, tried to climb there with a rope ladder. Thus his most vivid things are the red-hot little love lyrics, or rather, little love dramas. He did one really original and admirable thing: he managed the real details of modern love affairs in verse, and love is the most realistic thing in the world. He substituted the street with the green blind for the faded garden of Watteau, and the 'blue spirt of a lighted match' for the monotony of the evening star.

Before leaving him it should be added that he was fitted to deepen the Victorian mind, but not to broaden it. With all his Italian sympathies and Italian residence, he was not the man to get Victorian England out of its provincial rut: on many things Kingsley himself was not so narrow. His celebrated wife was wider and wiser than he in this sense; for she was, however one-sidedly, involved in the emotions of central European politics. She defended Louis Napoleon[2] and Victor Emmanuel;[3] and intelligently, as one conscious of the case against them both. As to why it now seems simple to defend the first Italian King, but absurd to defend the last French Emperor – well the reason is sad and simple. It is concerned with certain curious things called success and failure, and I ought to have considered it under the heading of *The Book of Snobs*. But Elizabeth Barrett, at least, was no snob: her political poems have rather an impatient air, as if they were written, and even published, rather prematurely – just before the fall of her idol. These old political poems of hers are too little read today; they are amongst the most sincere documents on the history of the times, and many modern blunders could be corrected by the reading of them. And Elizabeth Barrett had a strength really rare among women poets; the strength of the phrase. She excelled in her sex, in epigram, almost as much as Voltaire in his. Pointed phrases like: 'Martyrs by the pang without the palm' – or 'Incense to sweeten a crime and myrrh to embitter a curse', these expressions, which are witty after the old fashion of the conceit, came quite freshly and spontaneously to her quite modern mind. But the

1 Minstrels for God, name given to followers of St Francis of Assisi.
2 Emperor Napoleon III (1852–70), nephew and heir of Napoleon Bonaparte.
3 Victor Emmanuel II, king of Italy (1861–78).

first fact is this, that these epigrams of hers were never so true as when they turned on one of the two or three pivots on which contemporary Europe was really turning. She is by far the most European of all the English poets of that age; all of them, even her own much greater husband, look local beside her. Tennyson and the rest are nowhere. Take any positive political fact, such as the final fall of Napoleon. Tennyson wrote these profoundly foolish lines –

> He thought to quell the stubborn hearts
> of oak
> Madman!

as if the defeat of an English regiment were a violation of the laws of Nature. Mrs Browning knew no more facts about Napoleon, perhaps, than Tennyson did; but she knew the truth. Her epigram on Napoleon's fall is in one line

> And kings crept out again to feel the sun.

Tallyrand would have clapped his horrible old hands at that. Her instinct about the statesman and the soldier was very like Jane Austen's instinct for the gentleman and the man. It is not unnoticeable that as Miss Austen spent most of her life in a village, Miss Barrett spent most of her life on a sofa. The godlike power of guessing seems (for some reason I do not understand) to grow under such conditions. Unfortunately Mrs Browning was like all the other Victorians in going a little lame, as I have roughly called it, having one leg shorter than the other. But her case was, in one sense, extreme. She exaggerated both ways. She was too strong and too weak, or (as a false sex philosophy would express it), too masculine and too feminine. I mean that she hit the centre of weakness with almost the same emphatic precision with which she hit the centre of strength. She could write finally of the factory wheels 'grinding life down from its mark' a strong and strictly true observation. Unfortunately she could also write of Euripides 'with his droppings of warm tears'. She could write in *A Drama of Exile*, a really fine exposition, touching the later relation of Adam and the animals: unfortunately the tears were again turned on at the wrong moment at the main; and the stage direction commands a silence, only broken by the dropping of angel's tears. How much noise is made by angel's tears? Is it a sound of emptied buckets, or of garden hoses, or of mountain cataracts? That is the sort of question which Elizabeth Barrett's extreme love of the extreme was always tempting people to ask. Yet the question, as asked, does her a heavy historical injustice; we remember all the lines in her work which were weak enough to be called 'womanly', we forget the multitude of strong lines that are strong enough to be called 'manly'; lines that Kingsley or Henley would have jumped for joy to print in proof of their manliness. She had one of the peculiar talents of true rhetoric, that of a powerful concentration. As to the critic who thinks her poetry owed anything to the great poet who was her husband, he can go and live in the same hotel with the man who can believe that George Eliot owed anything to the extravagant imagination of Mr George Henry Lewes.[1] So far from Browning inspiring or interfering, he did not in one sense interfere enough. Her real inferiority to him in literature is that he was consciously while she was unconsciously absurd.

It is natural, in the matter of Victorian moral change, to take Swinburne as the next name here. He is the only poet who was also, in the European sense, on the spot; even if, in the sense of the Gilbertian song, the spot was barred. He also knew that something rather crucial was happening to Christendom; he thought it was getting unchristened. It is even a little amusing, indeed, that these two Pro-Italian poets almost conducted a political correspondence in rhyme. Mrs Browning sternly reproached those who had ever doubted the good faith of the King of Sardinia, whom she acclaimed as being truly a king. Swinburne, lyrically alluding to her as 'Sea-eagle of English feather', broadly hinted that the chief blunder of that wild fowl had been her support of an autocratic adventurer: 'calling a crowned man royal, that was no more than a king'. But it is not fair, even in this important connection, to judge Swinburne by *Songs Before Sunrise*. They were songs before a sunrise that has never turned up. Their dogmatic assertions have for a long time past stared starkly at us as nonsense. As, for instance, the phrase 'Glory to Man in the Highest, for man is the master of things'; after which there is evidently nothing to be said, except that it is not true. But even where Swinburne had his greater grip, as in that grave and partly just poem *Before a Crucifix*, Swinburne,

1 George Henry Lewes (1817–78), versatile writer, best known as George Eliot's 'partner'.

the most Latin, the most learned, the most largely travelled of the Victorians, still knows far less of the facts than even Mrs Browning. The whole of the poem, *Before a Crucifix*, breaks down by one mere mistake. It imagines that the French or Italian peasants who fell on their knees before the Crucifix did so because they were slaves. They fell on their knees because they were free men, probably owning their own farms. Swinburne could have found round about Putney plenty of slaves who had no crucifixes: but only crucifixions.

When we come to ethics and philosophy, doubtless we find Swinburne in full revolt, not only against the temperate idealism of Tennyson, but against the genuine piety and moral enthusiasm of people like Mrs Browning. But here again Swinburne is very English, nay, he is very Victorian, for his revolt is illogical. For the purposes of intelligent insurrection against priests and kings, Swinburne ought to have described the natural life of man, free and beautiful, and proved from this both the noxiousness and the needlessness of such chains. Unfortunately Swinburne rebelled against Nature first and then tried to rebel against religion for doing exactly the same thing that he had done. His songs of joy are not really immoral; but his songs of sorrow are. But when he merely hurls at the priest the assertion that flesh is grass and life is sorrow, he really lays himself open to the restrained answer, 'So I have ventured, on various occasions, to remark'. When he went forth, as it were, as the champion of pagan change and pleasure, he heard uplifted the grand choruses of his own *Atalanta*, in his rear, refusing hope.

The splendid diction that blazes through the whole of that drama, that still dances exquisitely in the more lyrical *Poems and Ballads*, makes some marvellous appearances in *Songs Before Sunrise*, and then mainly falters and fades away, is, of course, the chief thing about Swinburne. The style is the man; and some will add that it does not, thus unsupported, amount to much of a man. But the style itself suffers some injustice from those who would speak thus. The views expressed are often quite foolish and often quite insincere; but the style itself is a manlier and more natural thing than is commonly made out. It is not in the least languorous or luxurious or merely musical and sensuous, as one would gather from both the eulogies and the satires, from the conscious and the unconscious imitations. On the contrary, it is a sort of fighting and profane parody of the Old Testament; and its lines are made of short

English words like the short Roman swords. The first line of one of his finest poems, for instance, runs, 'I have lived long enough to have seen one thing, that love hath an end'. In that sentence only one small 'e' gets outside the monosyllable. Through all his interminable tragedies, he was fondest of lines like –

> If ever I leave off to honour you
> God give me shame; I were the worst churl born.

The dramas were far from being short and dramatic; but the words really were. Nor was his verse merely smooth; except his very bad verse, like 'the lilies and languors of virtue, to the raptures and roses of vice', which both in cheapness of form and foolishness of sentiment, may be called the worst couplet in the world's literature. In his real poetry (even in the same poem) his rhythm and rhyme are as original and ambitious as Browning; and the only difference between him and Browning is, not that he is smooth and without ridges, but that he always crests the ridge triumphantly and Browning often does not –

> On thy bosom though many a kiss be,
> There are none such as knew it of old.
> Was it Alciphron once or Arisbe,
> Male ringlets or feminine gold,
> That thy lips met with under the statue
> Whence a look shot out sharp after thieves
> From the eyes of the garden-god at you
> Across the fig-leaves.

Look at the rhymes in that verse, and you will see they are as stiff a task as Browning's: only they are successful. That is the real strength of Swinburne – a style. It was a style that nobody could really imitate; and least of all Swinburne himself, though he made the attempt all through his later years. He was, if ever there was one, an inspired poet. I do not think it the highest sort of poet. And you never discover who is an inspired poet until the inspiration goes.

With Swinburne we step into the circle of that later Victorian influence which was very vaguely called Aesthetic. Like all human things, but especially Victorian things, it was not only complex but confused. Things in it that were at one on the emotional side were flatly at war on the intellectual. In the section of the painters, it was the allies or pupils of Ruskin, pious, almost painfully exact, and copying mediaeval details rather for their truth than their beauty. In the section of the poets it was pretty loose, Swinburne being the leader of the revels. But there was one great man who was in both sections, a painter and a poet, who may be said to bestride the chasm like a giant. It is in an odd and literal sense true that the name of Rossetti is important here, for the name implies the nationality. I have loosely called Carlyle and the Brontës the romance from the North; the nearest to a general definition of the Aesthetic movement is to call it the romance from the South. It is that warm wind that had never blown so strong since Chaucer, standing in his cold English April, had smelt the spring in Provence. The Englishman has always found it easier to get inspiration from the Italians than from the French; they call to each other across that unconquered castle of reason. Browning's *Englishman in Italy*, Browning's *Italian in England*, were both happier than either would have been in France. Rossetti was the Italian in England, as Browning was the Englishman in Italy; and the first broad fact about the artistic revolution Rossetti wrought is written when we have written his name. But if the South lets in warmth or heat, it also lets in hardness. The more the orange tree is luxuriant in growth, the less it is loose in outline. And it is exactly where the sea is slightly warmer than marble that it looks slightly harder. This, I think, is the one universal power behind the Aesthetic and Pre-Raphaelite movements, which all agreed in two things at least: strictness in the line and strength, nay violence, in the colour.

Rossetti was a remarkable man in more ways than one; he did not succeed in any art; if he had he would probably never have been heard of. It was his happy knack of half failing in both the arts that has made him a success. If he had been as good a poet as Tennyson, he would have been a poet who painted pictures. If he had been as good a painter as Burne-Jones, he would have been a painter who wrote poems. It is odd to note on the very threshold of the extreme art movement that this great artist largely succeeded by not defining his art. His poems were too pictorial. His pictures were too poetical. That is why they really conquered the cold satisfaction of the Victorians, because they did mean something, even if it was a small artistic thing.

Rossetti was one with Ruskin, on the one hand, and Swinburne on the other, in reviving the decorative instinct of the Middle Ages.

While Ruskin, in letters only, praised that decoration Rossetti and his friends repeated it. They almost made patterns of their poems. That frequent return of the refrain which was foolishly discussed by Professor Nordau was, in Rossetti's case, of such sadness as sometimes to amount to sameness. The criticism on him, from a mediaeval point of view, is not that he insisted on a chorus, but that he could not insist on a jolly chorus. Many of his poems were truly mediaeval, but they would have been even more mediaeval if he could ever have written such a refrain as 'Tally Ho!' or even 'Tooral-ooral' instead of 'Tall Troy's on fire'. With Rossetti goes, of course, his sister, a real poet, though she also illustrated that Pre-Raphaelite's conflict of views that covered their coincidence of taste. Both used the angular outlines, the burning transparencies, the fixed but still unfathomable symbols of the great mediaeval civilization; but Rossetti used the religious imagery (on the whole) irreligiously, Christina Rossetti used it religiously but (on the whole) so to make it seem a narrower religion.

One poet, or, to speak more strictly, one poem, belongs to the same general atmosphere and impulse as Swinburne; the free but languid atmosphere of later Victorian art. But this time the wind blew from hotter and heavier gardens than the gardens of Italy. Edward Fitzgerald, a cultured eccentric, a friend of Tennyson, produced what professed to be a translation of the Persian poet Omar, who wrote quatrains about wine and roses and things in general. Whether the Persian original, in its own Persian way, was greater or less than this version I must not discuss here, and could not discuss anywhere. But it is quite clear that Fitzgerald's work is much too good to be a good translation. It is as personal and creative a thing as ever was written; and the best expression of a bad mood, a mood that may, for all I know, be permanent in Persia, but was certainly at this time particularly fashionable in England. In the technical sense of literature it is one of the most remarkable achievements of that age; as poetical as Swinburne and far more perfect. In this verbal sense its most arresting quality is a combination of something haunting and harmonious that flows by like a river or a song, with something else that is compact and pregnant like a pithy saying picked out in rock by the chisel of some pagan philosopher. It is at once a tune that escapes and an inscription that remains. Thus, alone among the reckless and romantic verses that first rose in Coleridge or Keats, it preserves something also of the wit and civilization of the eighteenth century. Lines like 'a Muezzin from the tower of darkness cries', or 'Their mouths are stopped with dust' are successful in the same sense as 'Pinnacled dim in the intense inane' or 'Through verdurous glooms and winding mossy ways'. But –

> Indeed, indeed, repentance oft before
> I swore; but was I sober when I swore?

is equally successful in the same sense as –

> Damn with faint praise, assent with civil leer
> And without sneering teach the rest to sneer.

It thus earned a right to be considered the complete expression of that scepticism and sensual sadness into which later Victorian literature was more and more falling away: a sort of bible of unbelief. For a cold fit had followed the hot fit of Swinburne, which was of a feverish sort: he had set out to break down without having, or even thinking he had, the rudiments of rebuilding in him; and he effected nothing national even in the way of destruction. The Tennysonians still walked past him as primly as a young ladies' school – the Browningites still inked their eyebrows and minds in looking for the lost syntax of Browning; while Browning himself was away looking for God, rather in the spirit of a truant boy from their school looking for birds' nests. The nineteenth-century sceptics did not really shake the respectable world and alter it, as the eighteenth-century sceptics had done; but that was because the eighteenth-century sceptics were something more than sceptics, and believed in Greek tragedies, in Roman laws, in the Republic. The Swinburnian sceptics had nothing to fight for but a frame of mind; and when ordinary English people listened to it, they came to the conclusion that it was a frame of mind they would rather hear about than experience. But these later poets did, so to speak, spread their soul in all the empty spaces; weaker brethren, disappointed artists, unattached individuals, very young people, were sapped or swept away by these songs; which, so far as any particular sense in them goes, were almost songs without words. It is because there is something which is after all indescribably manly, intellectual, firm about Fitzgerald's way of phrasing the pessimism that he towers above the slope that was tumbling down to the decadents. But it is still pessimism, a thing unfit for a white man; a thing like opium, that may often be a poison and sometimes a medicine, but never a food for us, who are driven by an inner command not only to think but to live, not only to live but to grow, and not only to grow but to build.

And, indeed, we see the insufficiency of such sad extremes even in the next name among the major poets; we see the Swinburnian parody of mediaevalism, the inverted Catholicism of the decadents, struggling to get back somehow on its feet. The aesthetic school had, not quite unjustly, the name of mere dilettanti. But it is fair to say that in the next of them, a workman and a tradesman, we already feel something of that return to real issues leading up to the real revolts that broke up Victorianism at last. In the mere art of words, indeed, William Morris carried much further than Swinburne, or Rossetti the mere imitation of stiff mediaeval ornament. The other mediaevalists had their modern moments; which were (if they had only known it) much more mediaeval than their mediaeval moments. Swinburne could write –

> We shall see Buonaparte the bastard
> Kick heels with his throat in a rope.

One has an uneasy feeling that William Morris would have written something like –

> And the kin of the ill king Bonaparte
> Hath a high gallows for all his part.

Rossetti could, for once in a way, write poetry about a real woman and call her 'Jenny'. One has a disturbed suspicion that Morris would have called her 'Jehanne'.

But all that seems at first more archaic and decorative about Morris really arose from the fact that he was more virile and real than either Swinburne or Rossetti. It arose from the fact that he really was, what he so often called himself, a craftsman. He had enough masculine strength to be tidy: that is, after the masculine manner, tidy about his own trade. If his poems were too like wall-papers, it was because he really could make wallpapers. He knew that lines of poetry ought to be in a row, as palings ought to be in a row; and he knew that neither palings nor poetry look any the worse for being simple or even severe. In a sense Morris was all the more creative because he felt the hard limits of creation as he would have felt them if he were not working in words but in wood; and if he was unduly dominated by the mere conventions of the mediaevals, it was largely because they were (whatever else they were) the very finest fraternity of free workmen the world is ever likely to see.

The very things that were urged against Morris are in this sense part of his ethical importance; part of the more promising and wholesome turn he was half unconsciously giving to the movement of modern art. His hazier fellow-Socialists blamed him because he made money; but this was at least in some degree because he made other things to make money: it was part of the real and refreshing fact that at last an aesthete had appeared who could make something. If he was a capitalist, at least he was what later capitalists cannot or will not be – something higher than a capitalist, a tradesman. As compared with aristocrats like Swinburne or aliens like Rossetti, he was vitally English and vitally Victorian. He inherits some of that paradoxical glory which Napoleon gave reluctantly to a nation of shopkeepers. He was the last of that nation; he did not go out golfing: like that founder of the artistic shopman, Samuel Richardson, 'he kept his shop, and his shop kept him'. The importance of his Socialism can easily be exaggerated. Among other lesser points, he was not a socialist; he was a sort of Dickensian anarchist. His instinct for titles was always exquisite. It is part of his instinct of decoration: for on a page the title always looks important and the printed mass of matter a mere dado under it. And no one had ever nobler titles than *The Roots of the Mountains* or *The Wood at the End of the World*. The reader feels he hardly need read the fairy-tale because the title is so suggestive. But, when all is said, he never chose a better title than that of his social Utopia, *News from Nowhere*. He wrote it while the last Victorians were already embarked on their bold task of fixing the future – of narrating today what has happened tomorrow. They named their books by cold titles suggesting straight corridors of marble – titles like *Looking Backward*. But Morris was an artist as well as an anarchist. *News from Nowhere* is an irresponsible title; and it is an irresponsible book. It does not describe the problem solved; it does not describe wealth either wielded by the State or divided equally among the citizens. It simply describes an undiscovered country where every one feels good-natured all day. That he could even dream so is his true dignity as a poet. He was the first of the Aesthetes to smell mediaevalism as a smell of the morning; and not as a mere scent of decay. . . .

ORTHODOXY

I
INTRODUCTION IN DEFENCE OF EVERYTHING ELSE

THE ONLY possible excuse for this book is that it is an answer to a challenge. Even a bad shot is dignified when he accepts a duel. When some time ago I published a series of hasty but sincere papers, under the name of 'Heretics', several critics for whose intellect I have a warm respect (I may mention specially Mr G. S. Street[1]) said that it was all very well for me to tell everybody to affirm his cosmic theory, but that I had carefully avoided support-ing my precepts with example. 'I will begin to worry about my philosophy,' said Mr Street, 'when Mr Chesterton has given us his.' It was perhaps an incautious suggestion to make to a person only too ready to write books upon the feeblest provocation. But after all, though Mr Street has inspired and created this book, he need not read it. If he does read it, he will find that in its pages I have attempted in a vague and personal way, in a set of mental pictures rather than in a series of deductions, to state the philosophy in which I have come to believe. I will not call it my philosophy; for I did not make it. God and humanity made it; and it made me.

I have often had a fancy for writing a romance about an English yachtsman who slightly miscalculated his course and discovered England under the impression that it was a new island in the South Seas. I always find, however, that I am either too busy or too lazy to write this fine work, so I may as well give it away for the purposes of philosophical illustration. There will probably be a general impression that the man who landed (armed to the teeth and talk-ing by signs) to plant the British flag on that barbaric temple which turned out to be the Pavilion at Brighton,[2] felt rather a fool. I am

1 G. S. Street (1867–1936), critic, journalist and novelist, wrote in *The Outlook*, 17 June 1905: 'I shall not begin to worry about my philosophy of life until Mr Chesterton discloses his.'
2 The Royal Pavilion, the exotic oriental work of the designer John Nash. was completed between 1815 and 1822 as a seaside residence for the Prince Regent, the future King George IV (1820–30).

not here concerned to deny that he looked a fool. But if you imagine that he felt a fool, or at any rate that the sense of folly was
his sole or his dominant emotion, then you have not studied with
sufficient delicacy the rich romantic nature of the hero of this tale.
His mistake was really a most enviable mistake; and he knew it, if
he was the man I take him for. What could be more delightful than
to have in the same few minutes all the fascinating terrors of going
abroad combined with all the humane security of coming home
again? What could be better than to have all the fun of discovering
South Africa without the disgusting necessity of landing there?
What could be more glorious than to brace one's self up to discover
New South Wales and then realize, with a gush of happy tears, that
it was really old South Wales. This at least seems to me the main
problem for philosophers, and is in a manner the main problem of
this book. How can we contrive to be at once astonished at the
world and yet at home in it? How can this queer cosmic town, with
its many-legged citizens, with its monstrous and ancient lamps,
how can this world give us at once the fascination of a strange town
and the comfort and honour of being our own town?

   To show that a faith or a philosophy is true from every standpoint would be too big an undertaking even for a much bigger book
than this; it is necessary to follow one path of argument; and this
is the path that I here propose to follow. I wish to set forth my faith
as particularly answering this double spiritual need, the need for
that mixture of the familiar and the unfamiliar which Christendom
has rightly named romance. For the very word 'romance' has in it
the mystery and ancient meaning of Rome. Any one setting out to
dispute anything ought always to begin by saying what he does not
dispute. Beyond stating what he proposes to prove he should always
state what he does not propose to prove. The thing I do not propose
to prove, the thing I propose to take as common ground between
myself and any average reader, is this desirability of an active and
imaginative life, picturesque and full of a poetical curiosity, a life
such as western man at any rate always seems to have desired. If a
man says that extinction is better than existence or blank existence
better than variety and adventure, then he is not one of the ordinary people to whom I am talking. If a man prefers nothing I can
give him nothing. But nearly all people I have ever met in this western society in which I live would agree to the general proposition

that we need this life of practical romance; the combination of something that is strange with something that is secure. We need so to view the world as to combine an idea of wonder and an idea of welcome. We need to be happy in this wonderland without once being merely comfortable. It is *this* achievement of my creed that I shall chiefly pursue in these pages.

But I have a peculiar reason for mentioning the man in a yacht, who discovered England. For I am that man in a yacht. I discovered England. I do not see how this book can avoid being egotistical; and I do not quite see (to tell the truth) how it can avoid being dull. Dulness will, however, free me from the charge which I most lament; the charge of being flippant. Mere light sophistry is the thing that I happen to despise most of all things, and it is perhaps a wholesome fact that this is the thing of which I am generally accused. I know nothing so contemptible as a mere paradox; a mere ingenious defence of the indefensible. If it were true (as has been said) that Mr Bernard Shaw lived upon paradox, then he ought to be a mere common millionaire; for a man of his mental activity could invent a sophistry every six minutes. It is as easy as lying; because it is lying. The truth is, of course, that Mr Shaw is cruelly hampered by the fact that he cannot tell any lie unless he thinks it is the truth. I find myself under the same intolerable bondage. I never in my life said anything merely because I thought it funny; though of course, I have had ordinary human vainglory, and may have thought it funny because I had said it. It is one thing to describe an interview with a gorgon or a griffin, a creature who does not exist. It is another thing to discover that the rhinoceros does exist and then take pleasure in the fact that he looks as if he didn't. One searches for truth, but it may be that one pursues instinctively the more extraordinary truths. And I offer this book with the heartiest sentiments to all the jolly people who hate what I write, and regard it (very justly, for all I know) as a piece of poor clowning or a single tiresome joke.

For if this book is a joke it is a joke against me. I am the man who with the utmost daring discovered what had been discovered before. If there is an element of farce in what follows, the farce is at my own expense; for this book explains how I fancied I was the first to set foot in Brighton and then found I was the last. It recounts my elephantine adventures in pursuit of the obvious. No one can think my case more ludicrous than I think it myself; no reader can accuse me here of trying to make a fool of him: I am the fool of this story, and no rebel shall hurl me from my throne. I freely confess all the idiotic ambitions of the end of the nineteenth century. I did, like all other solemn little boys, try to be in advance of the age. Like them I tried to be some ten minutes in advance of the truth. And I found that I was eighteen hundred years behind it. I did strain my voice with a painfully juvenile exaggeration in uttering my truths. And I was punished in the fittest and funniest way, for I have kept my truths: but I have discovered, not that they were not truths, but simply that they were not mine. When I fancied that I stood alone I was really in the ridiculous position of being backed up by all Christendom. It may be, Heaven forgive me, that I did try to be original; but I only succeeded in inventing all by myself an inferior copy of the existing traditions of civilized religion. The man from the yacht thought he was the first to find England; I thought I was the first to find Europe. I did try to found a heresy of my own; and when I had put the last touches to it, I discovered that it was orthodoxy.

It may be that somebody will be entertained by the account of this happy fiasco. It might amuse a friend or an enemy to read how I gradually learnt from the truth of some stray legend or from the falsehood of some dominant philosophy, things that I might have learnt from my catechism – if I had ever learnt it. There may or may not be some entertainment in reading how I found at last in an anarchist club or a Babylonian temple what I might have found in the nearest parish church. If any one is entertained by learning how the flowers of the field or the phrases in an omnibus, the accidents of politics or the pains of youth came together in a certain order to produce a certain conviction of Christian orthodoxy, he may possibly read this book. But there is in everything a reasonable division of labour. I have written the book, and nothing on earth would induce me to read it.

I add one purely pedantic note which comes, as a note naturally should, at the beginning of the book. These essays are concerned only to discuss the actual fact that the central Christian theology (sufficiently summarized in the Apostles' Creed) is the best root of energy and sound ethics. They are not intended to discuss the very fascinating but quite different question of what is the present seat of authority for the proclamation of that creed. When the word 'orthodoxy' is used here it means the Apostles' Creed, as understood by everybody calling himself Christian until a very short time ago and the general historic conduct of those who held such a creed. I have been forced by mere space to confine myself to what I have got from this creed; I do not touch the matter much disputed among modern Christians, of where we ourselves got it. This is not an ecclesiastical treatise but a sort of slovenly autobiography. But if any one wants my opinions about the actual nature of the authority, Mr G. S. Street has only to throw me another challenge, and I will write him another book.

II
THE MANIAC

... THE MAN who begins to think without the proper first principles goes mad; he begins to think at the wrong end. And
for the rest of these pages we have to try and discover what is the
right end. But we may ask in conclusion, if this be what drives men
mad, what is it that keeps them sane? By the end of this book I hope
to give a definite, some will think a far too definite, answer. But for
the moment it is possible in the same solely practical manner to
give a general answer touching what in actual human history keeps
men sane. Mysticism keeps men sane. As long as you have mystery
you have health; when you destroy mystery you create morbidity.
The ordinary man has always been sane because the ordinary
man has always been a mystic. He has permitted the twilight. He
has always had one foot in earth and the other in fairyland. He has
always left himself free to doubt his gods; but (unlike the agnostic
of today) free also to believe in them. He has always cared more
for truth than for consistency. If he saw two truths that seemed to
contradict each other, he would take the two truths and the contradiction along with them. His spiritual sight is stereoscopic, like his
physical sight: he sees two different pictures at once and yet sees all
the better for that. Thus he has always believed that there was such
a thing as fate, but such a thing as free will also. Thus he believed
that children were indeed the kingdom of heaven, but nevertheless
ought to be obedient to the kingdom of earth. He admired youth
because it was young and age because it was not. It is exactly this
balance of apparent contradictions that has been the whole buoyancy of the healthy man. The whole secret of mysticism is this: that
man can understand everything by the help of what he does not
understand. The morbid logician seeks to make everything lucid,
and succeeds in making everything mysterious. The mystic allows
one thing to be mysterious, and everything else becomes lucid. The
determinist makes the theory of causation quite clear, and then
finds that he cannot say 'if you please' to the housemaid. The

Christian permits free will to remain a sacred mystery; but because of this his relations with the housemaid become of a sparkling and crystal clearness. He puts the seed of dogma in a central darkness; but it branches forth in all directions with abounding natural health. As we have taken the circle as the symbol of reason and madness, we may very well take the cross as the symbol at once of mystery and of health. Buddhism is centripetal, but Christianity is centrifugal: it breaks out. For the circle is perfect and infinite in its nature; but it is fixed for ever in its size; it can never be larger or smaller. But the cross, though it has at its heart a collision and a contradiction, can extend its four arms for ever without altering its shape. Because it has a paradox in its centre it can grow without changing. The circle returns upon itself and is bound. The cross opens its arms to the four winds; it is a signpost for free travellers.

Symbols alone are of even a cloudy value in speaking of this deep matter; and another symbol from physical nature will express sufficiently well the real place of mysticism before mankind. The one created thing which we cannot look at is the one thing in the light of which we look at everything. Like the sun at noonday, mysticism explains everything else by the blaze of its own victorious invisibility. Detached intellectualism is (in the exact sense of a popular phrase) all moonshine; for it is light without heat, and it is secondary light, reflected from a dead world. But the Greeks were right when they made Apollo the god both of imagination and of sanity; for he was both the patron of poetry and the patron of healing. Of necessary dogmas and a special creed I shall speak later. But that transcendentalism by which all men live has primarily much the position of the sun in the sky. We are conscious of it as of a kind of splendid confusion; it is something both shining and shapeless, at once a blaze and a blur. But the circle of the moon is as clear and unmistakable, as recurrent and inevitable, as the circle of Euclid on a blackboard. For the moon is utterly reasonable; and the moon is the mother of lunatics and has given to them all her name.

III

THE SUICIDE OF THOUGHT

W
HAT we suffer from today is humility in the wrong place.
... Modesty has moved from the organ of ambition. Modesty
has settled upon the organ of conviction; where it was never meant
to be. A man was meant to be doubtful about himself, but undoubt-
ing about the truth; this has been exactly reversed. Nowadays the
part of a man that a man does assert is exactly the part he ought
not to assert – himself. The part he doubts is exactly the part he
ought not to doubt – the Divine Reason. Huxley[1] preached a
humility content to learn from Nature. But the new sceptic is so
humble that he doubts if he can even learn. Thus we should be
wrong if we had said hastily that there is no humility typical of our
time. The truth is that there is a real humility typical of our time;
but it so happens that it is practically a more poisonous humility
than the wildest prostrations of the ascetic. The old humility was
a spur that prevented a man from stopping; not a nail in his boot
that prevented him from going on. For the old humility made a
man doubtful about his efforts, which might make him work
harder. But the new humility makes a man doubtful about his aims,
which will make him stop working altogether.

At any street corner we may meet a man who utters the frantic
and blasphemous statement that he may be wrong. Every day one
comes across somebody who says that of course his view may not
be the right one. Of course his view must be the right one, or it is
not his view. We are on the road to producing a race of men too
mentally modest to believe in the multiplication table. We are in
danger of seeing philosophers who doubt the law of gravity as
being a mere fancy of their own. Scoffers of old time were too
proud to be convinced; but these are too humble to be convinced.
The meek do inherit the earth; but the modern sceptics are too

1 Thomas Huxley (1825–95), biologist and disciple of Darwin.

meek even to claim their inheritance. It is exactly this intellectual helplessness which is our second problem.

The last chapter has been concerned only with a fact of observation: that what peril of morbidity there is for man comes rather from his reason than his imagination. It was not meant to attack the authority of reason; rather it is the ultimate purpose to defend it. For it needs defence. The whole modern world is at war with reason; and the tower already reels.

The sages, it is often said, can see no answer to the riddle of religion. But the trouble with our sages is not that they cannot see the answer; it is that they cannot even see the riddle. They are like children so stupid as to notice nothing paradoxical in the playful assertion that a door is not a door. The modern latitudinarians speak, for instance, about authority in religion not only as if there were no reason in it, but as if there had never been any reason for it. Apart from seeing its philosophical basis, they cannot even see its historical cause. Religious authority has often, doubtless, been oppressive or unreasonable; just as every legal system (and especially our present one) has been callous and full of a cruel apathy. It is rational to attack the police; nay, it is glorious. But the modern critics of religious authority are like men who should attack the police without ever having heard of burglars. For there is a great and possible peril to the human mind: a peril as practical as burglary. Against it religious authority was reared, rightly or wrongly, as a barrier. And against it something certainly must be reared as a barrier, if our race is to avoid ruin.

That peril is that the human intellect is free to destroy itself. Just as one generation could prevent the very existence of the next generation, by all entering a monastery or jumping into the sea, so one set of thinkers can in some degree prevent further thinking by teaching the next generation that there is no validity in any human thought. It is idle to talk always of the alternative of reason and faith. Reason is itself a matter of faith. It is an act of faith to assert that our thoughts have any relation to reality at all. If you are merely a sceptic, you must sooner or later ask yourself the question, 'Why should *anything* go right; even observation and deduction? Why should not good logic be as misleading as bad logic? They are both movements in the brain of a bewildered ape?' The young sceptic says, 'I have a right to think for myself.' But the old sceptic, the complete sceptic, says, 'I have no right to think for myself. I have no right to think at all.'

There is a thought that stops thought. That is the only thought that ought to be stopped. That is the ultimate evil against which all religious authority was aimed. It only appears at the end of decadent ages like our own: and already Mr H. G. Wells has raised its ruinous banner; he has written a delicate piece of scepticism called 'Doubts of the Instrument'.[1] In this he questions the brain itself, and endeavours to remove all reality from all his own assertions, past, present, and to come. But it was against this remote ruin that all the military systems in religion were originally ranked and ruled. The creeds and the crusades, the hierarchies and the horrible persecutions were not organized, as is ignorantly said, for the suppression of reason. They were organized for the difficult defence of reason. Man, by a blind instinct, knew that if once things were wildly questioned, reason could be questioned first. The authority of priests to absolve, the authority of popes to define the authority, even of inquisitors to terrify: these were all only dark defences erected round one central authority, more undemonstrable, more supernatural than all – the authority of a man to think. We know now that this is so; we have no excuse for not knowing it. For we can hear scepticism crashing through the old ring of authorities, and at the same moment we can see reason swaying upon her throne. In so far as religion is gone, reason is going. For they are both of the same primary and authoritative kind. They are both methods of proof which cannot themselves be proved. And in the act of destroying the idea of Divine authority we have largely destroyed the idea of that human authority by which we do a long-division sum. With a long and sustained tug we have attempted to pull the mitre off pontifical man; and his head has come off with it.

Lest this should be called loose assertion, it is perhaps desirable, though dull, to run rapidly through the chief modern fashions of thought which have this effect of stopping thought itself. Materialism and the view of everything as a personal illusion have some such effect; for if the mind is mechanical, thought cannot be very exciting, and if the cosmos is unreal, there is nothing to think about. But in these cases the effect is indirect and doubtful. In some cases

1 H. G. Wells read a paper on 'Scepticism of the Instrument' to the Oxford Philosophical Society in 1903.

it is direct and clear; notably in the case of what is generally called evolution.

Evolution is a good example of that modern intelligence which, if it destroys anything, destroys itself. Evolution is either an innocent scientific description of how certain earthly things came about; or, if it is anything more than this, it is an attack upon thought itself. If evolution destroys anything, it does not destroy religion but rationalism. If evolution simply means that a positive thing called an ape turned very slowly into a positive thing called a man, then it is stingless for the most orthodox; for a personal God might just as well do things slowly as quickly, especially if, like the Christian God, he were outside time. But if it means anything more, it means that there is no such thing as an ape to change, and no such thing as a man for him to change into. It means that there is no such thing as a thing. At best, there is only one thing, and that is a flux of everything and anything. This is an attack not upon the faith, but upon the mind; you cannot think if there are no things to think about. You cannot think if you are not separate from the subject of thought. Descartes said, 'I think; therefore I am.' The philosophic evolutionist reverses and negatives the epigram. He says, 'I am not; therefore I cannot think.'

Then there is the opposite attack on thought: that urged by Mr H. G. Wells when he insists that every separate thing is 'unique', and there are no categories at all. This also is merely destructive. Thinking means connecting things, and stops if they cannot be connected. It need hardly be said that this scepticism forbidding thought necessarily forbids speech; a man cannot open his mouth without contradicting it. Thus when Mr Wells says (as he did somewhere), 'All chairs are quite different', he utters not merely a misstatement, but a contradiction in terms. If all chairs were quite different, you could not call them 'all chairs'.

Akin to these is the false theory of progress, which maintains that we alter the test instead of trying to pass the test. We often hear it said, for instance, 'What is right in one age is wrong in another.' This is quite reasonable, if it means that there is a fixed aim, and that certain methods attain at certain times and not at other times. If women, say, desire to be elegant, it may be that they are improved at one time by growing fatter and at another time by growing thinner. But you cannot say that they are improved by ceasing to wish to be elegant and beginning to wish to be oblong. If the stand-ard changes, how can there be improvement, which implies a standard? Nietzsche started a nonsensical idea that men had once sought as good what we now call evil; if it were so, we could not talk of surpassing or even falling short of them. How can you over-take Jones if you walk in the other direction? You cannot discuss whether one people has succeeded more in being miserable than another succeeded in being happy. It would be like discussing whether Milton was more puritanical than a pig is fat.

It is true that a man (a silly man) might make change itself his object or ideal. But as an ideal, change itself becomes unchange-able. If the change-worshipper wishes to estimate his own progress, he must be sternly loyal to the ideal of change; he must not begin to flirt gaily with the ideal of monotony. Progress itself cannot pro-gress. It is worth remark, in passing, that when Tennyson, in a wild and rather weak manner, welcomed the idea of infinite alteration in society, he instinctively took a metaphor which suggests an imprisoned tedium. He wrote –

> Let the great world spin for ever down the ringing
> grooves of change.[1]

He thought of change itself as an unchangeable groove; and so it is. Change is about the narrowest and hardest groove that a man can get into.

The main point here, however, is that this idea of a fundamental alteration in the standard is one of the things that make thought about the past or future simply impossible. The theory of a com-plete change of standards in human history does not merely deprive us of the pleasure of honouring our fathers; it deprives us even of the more modern and aristocratic pleasure of despising them.

This bald summary of the thought-destroying forces of our time would not be complete without some reference to pragmatism; for though I have here used and should everywhere defend the pragmatist method as a preliminary guide to truth, there is an extreme application of it which involves the absence of all truth whatever. My meaning can be put shortly thus. I agree with the pragmatists that apparent objective truth is not the whole matter;

1 *Locksley Hall*, l. 182.

that there is an authoritative need to believe the things that are necessary to the human mind. But I say that one of those necessities precisely is a belief in objective truth. The pragmatist tells a man to think what he must think and never mind the Absolute. But precisely one of the things that he must think is the Absolute. This philosophy, indeed, is a kind of verbal paradox. Pragmatism is a matter of human needs; and one of the first of human needs is to be something more than a pragmatist. Extreme pragmatism is just as inhuman as the determinism it so powerfully attacks. The determinist (who, to do him justice, does not pretend to be a human being) makes nonsense of the human sense of actual choice. The pragmatist, who professes to be specially human, makes nonsense of the human sense of actual fact.

To sum up our contention so far, we may say that the most characteristic current philosophies have not only a touch of mania, but a touch of suicidal mania. The mere questioner has knocked his head against the limits of human thought; and cracked it. This is what makes so futile the warnings of the orthodox and the boasts of the advanced about the dangerous boyhood of free thought. What we are looking at is not the boyhood of free thought; it is the old age and ultimate dissolution of free thought. It is vain for bishops and pious bigwigs to discuss what dreadful things will happen if wild scepticism runs its course. It has run its course. It is vain for eloquent atheists to talk of the great truths that will be revealed if once we see free thought begin. We have seen it end. It has no more questions to ask; it has questioned itself. You cannot call up any wilder vision than a city in which men ask themselves if they have any selves. You cannot fancy a more sceptical world than that in which men doubt if there is a world. It might certainly have reached its bankruptcy more quickly and cleanly if it had not been feebly hampered by the application of indefensible laws of blasphemy or by the absurd pretence that modern England is Christian. But it would have reached the bankruptcy anyhow. Militant atheists are still unjustly persecuted; but rather because they are an old minority than because they are a new one. Free thought has exhausted its own freedom. It is weary of its own success. If any eager freethinker now hails philosophic freedom as the dawn, he is only like the man in Mark Twain who came out wrapped in blankets to see the sun rise and was just in time to see it set. If any frightened curate still says that it will be awful if the darkness of free thought should spread, we can only answer him in the high and powerful words of Mr Belloc, 'Do not, I beseech you, be troubled about the increase of forces already in dissolution. You have mistaken the hour of the night: it is already morning.' We have no more questions left to ask. We have looked for questions in the darkest corners and on the wildest peaks. We have found all the questions that can be found. It is time we gave up looking for questions and began looking for answers.

But one more word must be added. At the beginning of this preliminary negative sketch I said that our mental ruin has been wrought by wild reason, not by wild imagination. A man does not go mad because he makes a statue a mile high, but he may go mad by thinking it out in square inches. Now, one school of thinkers has seen this and jumped at it as a way of renewing the pagan health of the world. They see that reason destroys; but Will, they say, creates. The ultimate authority, they say, is in will, not in reason. The supreme point is not why a man demands a thing, but the fact that he does demand it. I have no space to trace or expound this philosophy of Will. It came, I suppose, through Nietzsche, who preached something that is called egoism. That, indeed, was simple-minded enough; for Nietzsche denied egoism simply by preaching it. To preach anything is to give it away. First, the egoist calls life a war without mercy, and then he takes the greatest possible trouble to drill his enemies in war. To preach egoism is to practise altruism. But however it began, the view is common enough in current literature. The main defence of these thinkers is that they are not thinkers; they are makers. They say that choice is itself the divine thing. Thus Mr Bernard Shaw has attacked the old idea that men's acts are to be judged by the standard of the desire of happiness. He says that a man does not act for his happiness, but from his will. He does not say, 'Jam will make me happy', but 'I want jam'. And in all this others follow him with yet greater enthusiasm. Mr John Davidson,[1] a remarkable poet, is so passionately excited about it that he is obliged to write prose. He publishes

1 John Davidson (1857–1909), to whom T. S. Eliot acknowledged a debt for his use of urban imagery and colloquial idiom, between 1901 and 1908 wrote blank verse 'Testaments' expounding a materialistic philosophy which is described in his introduction to *The Theatrocrat God and Mammon* (1907).

a short play with several long prefaces. This is natural enough in Mr Shaw, for all his plays are prefaces: Mr Shaw is (I suspect) the only man on earth who has never written any poetry. But that Mr Davidson (who can write excellent poetry) should write instead laborious metaphysics in defence of this doctrine of will, does show that the doctrine of will has taken hold of men. Even Mr H. G. Wells has half spoken in its language; saying that one should test acts not like a thinker, but like an artist, saying, 'I *feel* this curve is right', or 'that line *shall* go thus'. They are all excited; and well they may be. For by this doctrine of the divine authority of will, they think they can break out of the doomed fortress of rationalism. They think they can escape.

But they cannot escape. This pure praise of volition ends in the same break up and blank as the mere pursuit of logic. Exactly as complete free thought involves the doubting of thought itself, so the acceptance of mere 'willing' really paralyses the will. Mr Bernard Shaw has not perceived the real difference between the old utilitarian test of pleasure (clumsy, of course, and easily misstated) and that which he propounds. The real difference between the test of happiness and the test of will is simply that the test of happiness is a test and the other isn't. You can discuss whether a man's act in jumping over a cliff was directed towards happiness; you cannot discuss whether it was derived from will. Of course it was. You can praise an action by saying that it is calculated to bring pleasure or pain to discover truth or to save the soul. But you cannot praise an action because it shows will; for to say that is merely to say that it is an action. By this praise of will you cannot really choose one course as better than another. And yet choosing one course as better than another is the very definition of the will you are praising.

The worship of will is the negation of will. To admire mere choice is to refuse to choose. If Mr Bernard Shaw comes up to me and says, 'Will something', that is tantamount to saying, 'I do not mind what you will', and that is tantamount to saying, 'I have no will in the matter'. You cannot admire will in general, because the essence of will is that it is particular. A brilliant anarchist like Mr John Davidson feels an irritation against ordinary morality, and therefore he invokes will – will to anything. He only wants humanity to want something. But humanity does want something. It wants ordinary morality. He rebels against the law and tells us to will something or anything. But we have willed something. We have willed the law against which he rebels.

All the will-worshippers, from Nietzsche to Mr Davidson, are really quite empty of volition. They cannot will, they can hardly wish. And if any one wants a proof of this, it can be found quite easily. It can be found in this fact: that they always talk of will as something that expands and breaks out. But it is quite the opposite. Every act of will is an act of self-limitation. To desire action is to desire limitation. In that sense every act is an act of self-sacrifice. When you choose anything, you reject everything else. That objection, which men of this school used to make to the act of marriage, is really an objection to every act. Every act is an irrevocable selection and exclusion. Just as when you marry one woman you give up all the others, so when you take one course of action you give up all the other courses. If you become King of England, you give up the post of Beadle in Brompton. If you go to Rome, you sacrifice a rich suggestive life in Wimbledon. It is the existence of this negative or limiting side of will that makes most of the talk of the anarchic will-worshippers little better than nonsense. For instance, Mr John Davidson tells us to have nothing to do with 'Thou shalt not'; but it is surely obvious that 'Thou shalt not' is only one of the necessary corollaries of 'I will'. 'I will go to the Lord Mayor's Show, and thou shalt not stop me.' Anarchism adjures us to be bold creative artists, and care for no laws or limits. But it is impossible to be an artist and not care for laws or limits. Art is limitation; the essence of every picture is the frame. If you draw a giraffe, you must draw him with a long neck. If, in your bold creative way, you hold yourself free to draw a giraffe with a short neck, you will really find that you are not free to draw a giraffe. The moment you step into the world of facts, you step into a world of limits. You can free things from alien or accidental laws, but not from the laws of their own nature. You may, if you like, free a tiger from his bars; but do not free him from his stripes. Do not free a camel of the burden of his hump: you may be freeing him from being a camel. Do not go about as a demagogue, encouraging triangles to break out of the prison of their three sides. If a triangle breaks out of its three sides, its life comes to a lamentable end. Somebody wrote a work called 'The Loves of the Triangles'; I never read it, but I am sure that if triangles ever were loved, they were loved for being triangular. This is certainly the case with all artistic creation, which is in some ways the most decisive example of pure will. The artist loves his limitations: they constitute the *thing* he is doing. The painter is glad that the canvas is flat. The sculptor is glad that the clay is colourless.

In case the point is not clear, an historic example may illustrate it. The French Revolution was really an heroic and decisive thing, because the Jacobins willed something definite and limited. They desired the freedoms of democracy, but also all the vetoes of democracy. They wished to have votes and *not* to have titles. . . . Therefore they have created something with a solid substance and shape, the square social equality and peasant wealth of France. But since then the revolutionary or speculative mind of Europe has been weakened by shrinking from any proposal because of the limits of that proposal. Liberalism has been degraded into liberality. Men have tried to turn 'revolutionize' from a transitive to an intransitive verb. The Jacobin could tell you not only the system he would rebel against, but (what was more important) the system he would *not* rebel against, the system he would trust. But the new rebel is a sceptic, and will not entirely trust anything. He has no loyalty; therefore he can never be really a revolutionist. And the fact that he doubts everything really gets in his way when he wants to denounce anything. For all denunciation implies a moral doctrine of some kind; and the modern revolutionist doubts not only the institution he denounces, but the doctrine by which he denounces it. Thus he writes one book complaining that imperial oppression insults the purity of women, and then he writes another book (about the sex problem) in which he insults it himself. He curses the Sultan because Christian girls lose their virginity, and then curses Mrs Grundy[1] because they keep it. As a politician, he will cry out that war is a waste of life, and then, as a philosopher, that all life is waste of time. A Russian pessimist will denounce a policeman for killing a peasant, and then prove by the highest philosophical principles that the peasant ought to have killed himself. A man denounces marriage as a lie, and then denounces aristocratic profligates for treating it as a lie. He calls a flag a bauble, and then blames the oppressors of Poland or Ireland because they take away that bauble. The man of this school goes first to a political meeting,

[1] A character in Thomas Morton's play *Speed the Plough* (1798), who personifies the tyranny of conventional propriety.

where he complains that savages are treated as if they were beasts; then he takes his hat and umbrella and goes on to a scientific meeting, where he proves that they practically are beasts. In short, the modern revolutionist, being an infinite sceptic, is always engaged in undermining his own mines. In his book on politics he attacks men for trampling on morality; in his book on ethics he attacks morality for trampling on men. Therefore the modern man in revolt has become practically useless for all purposes of revolt. By rebelling against everything he has lost his right to rebel against anything.

It may be added that the same blank and bankruptcy can be observed in all fierce and terrible types of literature, especially in satire. Satire may be mad and anarchic, but it presupposes an admitted superiority in certain things over others; it presupposes a standard. When little boys in the street laugh at the fatness of some distinguished journalist, they are unconsciously assuming a standard of Greek sculpture. They are appealing to the marble Apollo. And the curious disappearance of satire from our literature is an instance of the fierce things fading for want of any principle to be fierce about. Nietzsche had some natural talent for sarcasm: he could sneer, though he could not laugh; but there is always something bodiless and without weight in his satire, simply because it has not any mass of common morality behind it. He is himself more preposterous than anything he denounces. But, indeed, Nietzsche will stand very well as the type of the whole of this failure of abstract violence. The softening of the brain which ultimately overtook him was not a physical accident. If Nietzsche had not ended in imbecility, Nietzscheism would end in imbecility. Thinking in isolation and with pride ends in being an idiot. Every man who will not have softening of the heart must at last have softening of the brain.

This last attempt to evade intellectualism ends in intellectualism, and therefore in death. The sortie has failed. The wild worship of lawlessness and the materialist worship of law end in the same void. Nietzsche scales staggering mountains, but he turns up ultimately in Tibet. He sits down beside Tolstoy in the land of nothing and Nirvâna. They are both helpless – one because he must not grasp anything, and the other because he must not let go of anything. The Tolstoyan's will is frozen by a Buddhist instinct that all special actions are evil. But the Nietzscheite's will is quite equally frozen by his view that all special actions are good; for if all special actions are good, none of them are special. They stand at the cross-roads, and one hates all the roads and the other likes all the roads. The result is – well, some things are not hard to calculate. They stand at the cross-roads. . . .

IV
THE ETHICS OF ELFLAND

WHEN the business man rebukes the idealism of his office-boy, it is commonly in some such speech as this: 'Ah, yes, when one is young, one has these ideals in the abstract and these castles in the air; but in middle age they all break up like clouds, and one comes down to a belief in practical politics, to using the machinery one has and getting on with the world as it is.' Thus, at least, venerable and philanthropic old men now in their honoured graves used to talk to me when I was a boy. But since then I have grown up and have discovered that these philanthropic old men were telling lies. What has really happened is exactly the opposite of what they said would happen. They said that I should lose my ideals and begin to believe in the methods of practical politicians. Now, I have not lost my ideals in the least; my faith in fundamentals is exactly what it always was. What I have lost is my old childlike faith in practical politics. I am still as much concerned as ever about the Battle of Armageddon; but I am not so much concerned about the General Election. As a babe I leapt up on my mother's knee at the mere mention of it. No; the vision is always solid and reliable. The vision is always a fact. It is the reality that is often a fraud. As much as I ever did, more than I ever did, I believe in Liberalism. But there was a rosy time of innocence when I believed in Liberals.

I take this instance of one of the enduring faiths because, having now to trace the roots of my personal speculation, this may be counted, I think, as the only positive bias. I was brought up a Liberal, and have always believed in democracy, in the elementary liberal doctrine of a self-governing humanity. If any one finds the phrase vague or threadbare, I can only pause for a moment to explain that the principle of democracy, as I mean it, can be stated in two propositions. The first is this: that the things common to all men are more important than the things peculiar to any men. Ordinary things are more valuable than extraordinary things; nay, they are more extraordinary. Man is something more awful than men; something more strange. The sense of the miracle of humanity itself should be always more vivid to us than any marvels of power, intellect, art, or civilization. The mere man on two legs, as such, should be felt as something more heartbreaking than any music and more startling than any caricature. Death is more tragic even than death by starvation. Having a nose is more comic even than having a Norman nose.

This is the first principle of democracy: that the essential things in men are the things they hold in common, not the things they hold separately. And the second principle is merely this: that the political instinct or desire is one of these things which they hold in common. Falling in love is more poetical than dropping into poetry. The democratic contention is that government (helping to rule the tribe) is a thing like falling in love, and not a thing like dropping into poetry. It is not something analogous to playing the church organ, painting on vellum, discovering the North Pole (that insidious habit), looping the loop, being Astronomer Royal, and so on. For these things we do not wish a man to do at all unless he does them well. It is, on the contrary, a thing analogous to writing one's own love-letters or blowing one's own nose. These things we want a man to do for himself, even if he does them badly. I am not here arguing the truth of any of these conceptions; I know that some moderns are asking to have their wives chosen by scientists, and they may soon be asking, for all I know, to have their noses blown by nurses. I merely say that mankind does recognize these universal human functions, and that democracy classes government among them. In short, the democratic faith is this: that the most terribly important things must be left to ordinary men themselves – the mating of the sexes, the rearing of the young, the laws of the state. This is democracy; and in this I have always believed.

But there is one thing that I have never from my youth up been able to understand. I have never been able to understand where people got the idea that democracy was in some way opposed to tradition. It is obvious that tradition is only democracy extended through time. It is trusting to a consensus of common human voices rather than to some isolated or arbitrary record. The man who quotes some German historian against the tradition of the Catholic Church, for instance, is strictly appealing to aristocracy. He is

appealing to the superiority of one expert against the awful authority of a mob. It is quite easy to see why a legend is treated, and
ought to be treated, more respectfully than a book of history. The
legend is generally made by the majority of people in the village,
who are sane. The book is generally written by the one man in the
village who is mad. . . . If we attach great importance to the opinion
of ordinary men in great unanimity when we are dealing with daily
matters, there is no reason why we should disregard it when we
are dealing with history or fable. Tradition may be defined as an
extension of the franchise. Tradition means giving votes to the most
obscure of all classes, our ancestors. It is the democracy of the dead.
Tradition refuses to submit to the small and arrogant oligarchy of
those who merely happen to be walking about. All democrats
object to men being disqualified by the accident of birth; tradition
objects to their being disqualified by the accident of death. Democracy tells us not to neglect a good man's opinion, even if he is our
groom; tradition asks us not to neglect a good man's opinion, even
if he is our father. I, at any rate, cannot separate the two ideas of
democracy and tradition; it seems evident to me that they are the
same idea. We will have the dead at our councils. The ancient
Greeks voted by stones; these shall vote by tombstones. It is all quite
regular and official, for most tombstones, like most ballot papers,
are marked with a cross.

   I have first to say, therefore, that if I have had a bias, it was always
a bias in favour of democracy, and therefore of tradition. Before
we come to any theoretic or logical beginnings I am content to
allow for that personal equation; I have always been more inclined
to believe the ruck of hard-working people than to believe that
special and troublesome literary class to which I belong. I prefer
even the fancies and prejudices of the people who see life from the
inside to the clearest demonstrations of the people who see life from
the outside. I would always trust the old wives' fables against the
old maids' facts. As long as wit is mother wit it can be as wild as it
pleases.

   Now, I have to put together a general position, and I pretend to
no training in such things. I propose to do it, therefore, by writing
down one after another the three or four fundamental ideas which
I have found for myself, pretty much in the way that I found them.
Then I shall roughly synthesize them, summing up my personal

philosophy or natural religion; then I shall describe my startling discovery that the whole thing had been discovered before. It had been discovered by Christianity. But of these profound persuasions which I have to recount in order, the earliest was concerned with this element of popular tradition. And without the foregoing explanation touching tradition and democracy I could hardly make my mental experience clear. As it is, I do not know whether I can make it clear, but I now propose to try.

My first and last philosophy, that which I believe in with unbroken certainty, I learnt in the nursery. I generally learnt it from a nurse; that is, from the solemn and star-appointed priestess at once of democracy and tradition. The things I believed most then, the things I believe most now, are the things called fairy tales. They seem to me to be the entirely reasonable things. They are not fantasies: compared with them other things are fantastic. Compared with them religion and rationalism are both abnormal, though religion is abnormally right and rationalism abnormally wrong. Fairyland is nothing but the sunny country of common sense. It is not earth that judges heaven, but heaven that judges earth; so for me at least it was not earth that criticized elfland, but elfland that criticized the earth. I knew the magic beanstalk before I had tasted beans; I was sure of the Man in the Moon before I was certain of the moon. This was at one with all popular tradition. Modern minor poets are naturalists, and talk about the bush or the brook; but the singers of the old epics and fables were supernaturalists, and talked about the gods of brook and bush. That is what the moderns mean when they say that the ancients did not 'appreciate Nature', because they said that Nature was divine. Old nurses do not tell children about the grass, but about the fairies that dance on the grass; and the old Greeks could not see the trees for the dryads.

But I deal here with what ethic and philosophy come from being fed on fairy tales. If I were describing them in detail I could note many noble and healthy principles that arise from them. There is the chivalrous lesson of *Jack the Giant Killer*; that giants should be killed because they are gigantic. It is a manly mutiny against pride as such. . . . There is the lesson of *Cinderella*, which is the same as that of the Magnificat – *exaltavit humiles*. There is the great lesson of *Beauty and the Beast*; that a thing must be loved *before* it is loveable.

There is the terrible allegory of the *Sleeping Beauty*, which tells how the human creature was blessed with all birthday gifts, yet cursed with death; and how death also may perhaps be softened to a sleep. But I am not concerned with any of the separate statutes of elfland, but with the whole spirit of its law, which I learnt before I could speak, and shall retain when I cannot write. I am concerned with a certain way of looking at life, which was created in me by the fairy tales, but has since been meekly ratified by the mere facts.

It might be stated this way. There are certain sequences or developments (cases of one thing following another), which are, in the true sense of the word, reasonable. They are, in the true sense of the word, necessary. Such are mathematical and merely logical sequences. We in fairyland (who are the most reasonable of all creatures) admit that reason and that necessity. For instance, if the Ugly Sisters are older than Cinderella, it is (in an iron and awful sense) *necessary* that Cinderella is younger than the Ugly Sisters. There is no getting out of it. Haeckel may talk as much fatalism about that fact as he pleases: it really must be. If Jack is the son of a miller, a miller is the father of Jack. Cold reason decrees it from her awful throne: and we in fairyland submit. If the three brothers all ride horses, there are six animals and eighteen legs involved: that is true rationalism, and fairyland is full of it. But as I put my head over the hedge of the elves and began to take notice of the natural world, I observed an extraordinary thing. I observed that learned men in spectacles were talking of the actual things that happened – dawn and death and so on – as if *they* were rational and inevitable. They talked as if the fact that trees bear fruit were just as *necessary* as the fact that two and one trees make three. But it is not. There is an enormous difference by the test of fairyland; which is the test of the imagination. You cannot *imagine* two and one not making three. But you can easily imagine trees not growing fruit; you can imagine them growing golden candlesticks or tigers hanging on by the tail. These men in spectacles spoke much of a man named Newton, who was hit by an apple, and who discovered a law. But they could not be got to see the distinction between a true law, a law of reason, and the mere fact of apples falling. If the apple hit Newton's nose, Newton's nose hit the apple. That is a true necessity: because we cannot conceive the one occurring without the other. But we can quite well conceive the apple not falling on his nose; we can fancy it flying ardently through the air to hit some other nose, of which it had a more definite dislike. We have always in our fairy tales kept this sharp distinction between the science of mental relations, in which there really are laws, and the science of physical facts, in which there are no laws, but only weird repetitions. We believe in bodily miracles, but not in mental impossibilities. We believe that a Beanstalk climbed up to heaven; but that does not at all confuse our convictions on the philosophical question of how many beans make five.

Here is the peculiar perfection of tone and truth in the nursery tales. The man of science says, 'Cut the stalk, and the apple will fall'; but he says it calmly, as if the one idea really led up to the other. The witch in the fairy tale says, 'Blow the horn, and the ogre's castle will fall'; but she does not say it as if it were something in which the effect obviously arose out of the causes. Doubtless she has given the advice to many champions, and has seen many castles fall, but she does not lose either her wonder or her reason. She does not muddle her head until it imagines a necessary mental connection between a horn and a falling tower. But the scientific men do muddle their heads, until they imagine a necessary mental connection between an apple leaving the tree and an apple reaching the ground. They do really talk as if they had found not only a set of marvellous facts, but a truth connecting those facts. They do talk as if the connection of two strange things physically connected them philosophically. They feel that because one incomprehensible thing constantly follows another incomprehensible thing the two together somehow make up a comprehensible thing. Two black riddles make a white answer.

In fairyland we avoid the word 'law'; but in the land of science they are singularly fond of it. Thus they will call some interesting conjecture about how forgotten folks pronounced the alphabet, Grimm's Law. But Grimm's Law is far less intellectual than *Grimms' Fairy Tales*. The tales are, at any rate, certainly tales; while the law is not a law. A law implies that we know the nature of the generalization and enactment; not merely that we have noticed some of the effects. If there is a law that pick-pockets shall go to prison, it implies that there is an imaginable mental connection between the idea of prison and the idea of picking pockets. And we know what the idea is. We can say why we take liberty from a man who takes liberties. But we cannot say why an egg can turn into a chicken any more than we can say why a bear could turn into a fairy prince. As *ideas*, the egg and the chicken are further off from each other than the bear and the prince; for no egg in itself suggests a chicken, whereas some princes do suggest bears. Granted, then, that certain transformations do happen, it is essential that we should regard them in the philosophic manner of fairy tales, not in the unphilo- sophic manner of science and the 'Laws of Nature'. When we are asked why eggs turn to birds or fruits fall in autumn, we must answer exactly as the fairy godmother would answer if Cinderella asked her why mice turned to horses or her clothes fell from her at twelve o'clock. We must answer that it is *magic*. It is not a 'law', for we do not understand its general formula. It is not a necessity, for though we can count on it happening practically, we have no right to say that it must always happen. It is no argument for un- alterable law (as Huxley fancied) that we count on the ordinary course of things. We do not count on it; we bet on it. We risk the remote possibility of a miracle as we do that of a poisoned pancake or a world-destroying comet. We leave it out of account, not because it is a miracle, and therefore an impossibility, but because it is a miracle, and therefore an exception. All the terms used in the science books, 'law', 'necessity', 'order', 'tendency', and so on, are really unintellectual, because they assume an inner synthesis, which we do not possess. The only words that ever satisfied me as describing Nature are the terms used in the fairy books, 'charm', 'spell', 'enchantment'. They express the arbitrariness of the fact and its mystery. A tree grows fruit because it is a *magic* tree. Water runs downhill because it is bewitched. The sun shines because it is bewitched.

I deny altogether that this is fantastic or even mystical. We may have some mysticism later on; but this fairy-tale language about things is simply rational and agnostic. It is the only way I can express in words my clear and definite perception that one thing is quite distinct from another; that there is no logical connection between flying and laying eggs. It is the man who talks about 'a law' that he has never seen who is the mystic. Nay, the ordinary scientific man is strictly a sentimentalist. He is a sentimentalist in this essential sense, that he is soaked and swept away by mere associations. He has so often seen birds fly and lay eggs that he feels as if there must be some dreamy, tender connection between the two ideas, whereas there is none. A forlorn lover might be unable to dissociate the moon from lost love; so the materialist is unable to dissociate the moon from the tide. In both cases there is no connection, except that one has seen them together. A sentimentalist might shed tears at the smell of apple-blossom, because, by a dark association of his own, it reminded him of his boyhood. So the materialist professor (though he conceals his tears) is yet a sentimentalist, because, by a dark association of his own, apple-blossoms remind him of apples. But the cool rationalist from fairyland does not see why, in the abstract, the apple tree should not grow crimson tulips; it sometimes does in his country.

This elementary wonder, however, is not a mere fancy derived from the fairy tales; on the contrary, all the fire of the fairy tales is derived from this. Just as we all like love tales because there is an instinct of sex, we all like astonishing tales because they touch the nerve of the ancient instinct of astonishment. This is proved by the fact that when we are very young children we do not need fairy tales: we only need tales. Mere life is interesting enough. A child of seven is excited by being told that Tommy opened a door and saw a dragon. But a child of three is excited by being told that Tommy opened a door. Boys like romantic tales; but babies like realistic tales – because they find them romantic. In fact, a baby is about the only person, I should think, to whom a modern realistic novel could be read without boring him. This proves that even nursery tales only echo an almost pre-natal leap of interest and amazement. These tales say that apples were golden only to refresh the forgotten moment when we found that they were green. They make rivers run with wine only to make us remember, for one wild moment, that they run with water. I have said that this is wholly reasonable and even agnostic. And, indeed, on this point I am all for the higher agnosticism; its better name is Ignorance. We have all read in scientific books, and, indeed, in all romances, the story of the man who has forgotten his name. This man walks about the streets and can see and appreciate everything; only he cannot remember who he is. Well, every man is that man in the story. Every man has forgotten who he is. One may understand the cosmos, but never the ego; the self is more distant than any star. Thou shalt love the Lord thy God; but thou shalt not know thyself. We are all under the same mental calamity; we have all forgotten our names. We have all forgotten what we really are. All that we call common sense and rationality and practicality and positivism only means that for certain dead levels of our life we forget that we have forgotten. All that we call spirit and art and ecstasy only means that for one awful instant we remember that we forget.

But though (like the man without memory in the novel) we walk the streets with a sort of half-witted admiration, still it is admiration. It is admiration in English and not only admiration in Latin. The wonder has a positive element of praise. This is the next milestone to be definitely marked on our road through fairyland. I shall speak in the next chapter about optimists and pessimists in their intellectual aspect, so far as they have one. Here I am only trying to describe the enormous emotions which cannot be described. And the strongest emotion was that life was as precious as it was puzzling. It was an ecstasy because it was an adventure; it was an adventure because it was an opportunity. The goodness of the fairy tale was not affected by the fact that there might be more dragons than princesses; it was good to be in a fairy tale. The test of all happiness is gratitude; and I felt grateful, though I hardly knew to whom. Children are grateful when Santa Claus puts in their stockings gifts of toys or sweets. Could I not be grateful to Santa Claus when he put in my stockings the gift of two miraculous legs? We thank people for birthday presents of cigars and slippers. Can I thank no one for the birthday present of birth?

There were, then, these two first feelings, indefensible and indisputable. The world was a shock, but it was not merely shocking; existence was a surprise, but it was a pleasant surprise. In fact, all my first views were exactly uttered in a riddle that stuck in my brain from boyhood. The question was, 'What did the first frog say?' And the answer was, 'Lord, how you made me jump!' That says succinctly all that I am saying. God made the frog jump; but the frog prefers jumping. But when these things are settled there enters the second great principle of the fairy philosophy.

Any one can see it who will simply read *Grimms' Fairy Tales* or the fine collections of Mr Andrew Lang.[1] For the pleasure of pedantry I will call it the Doctrine of Conditional Joy. Touchstone talked of much virtue in an 'if'; according to elfin ethics all virtue

1 Andrew Lang (1844–1912) is best known for his collections of fairy tales, each volume being named after a different colour.

is in an 'if'. The note of the fairy utterance always is, 'You may live in a palace of gold and sapphire, *if* you do not say the word "cow" '; or 'You may live happily with the King's daughter, *if* you do not show her an onion'. The vision always hangs upon a veto. All the dizzy and colossal things conceded depend upon one small thing withheld. All the wild and whirling things that are let loose depend upon one thing that is forbidden. Mr W. B. Yeats, in his exquisite and piercing elfin poetry, describes the elves as lawless; they plunge in innocent anarchy on the unbridled horses of the air –

> Ride on the crest of the dishevelled tide,[1]
> And dance upon the mountains like a flame.

It is a dreadful thing to say that Mr W. B. Yeats does not understand fairyland. But I do say it. He is an ironical Irishman, full of intellectual reactions. He is not stupid enough to understand fairyland. Fairies prefer people of the yokel type like myself; people who gape and grin and do as they are told. Mr Yeats reads into elfland all the righteous insurrection of his own race. But the lawlessness of Ireland is a Christian lawlessness, founded on reason and justice. The Fenian is rebelling against something he understands only too well; but the true citizen of fairyland is obeying something he does not understand at all. In the fairy tale an incomprehensible happiness rests upon an incomprehensible condition. A box is opened, and all evils fly out. A word is forgotten, and cities perish. A lamp is lit, and love flies away. A flower is plucked, and human lives are forfeited. An apple is eaten, and the hope of God is gone.

This is the tone of fairy tales, and it is certainly not lawlessness or even liberty, though men under a mean modern tyranny may think it liberty by comparison. People out of Portland Gaol might think Fleet Street free; but closer study will prove that both fairies and journalists are the slaves of duty. Fairy godmothers seem at least as strict as other godmothers. Cinderella received a coach out of Wonderland and a coachman out of nowhere, but she received a command – which might have come out of Brixton – that she should be back by twelve. Also, she had a glass slipper; and it cannot be a coincidence that glass is so common a substance in folk-lore. This princess lives in a glass castle, that princess on a glass

1 The line from Yeats's play *The Land of Heart's Desire* actually begins 'Run on the top. . . .'

hill; this one sees all things in a mirror; they may all live in glass houses if they will not throw stones. For this thin glitter of glass everywhere is the expression of the fact that the happiness is bright but brittle, like the substance most easily smashed by a housemaid or a cat. And this fairy-tale sentiment also sank into me and became my sentiment towards the whole world. I felt and feel that life itself is as bright as the diamond, but as brittle as the window-pane; and when the heavens were compared to the terrible crystal I can remember a shudder. I was afraid that God would drop the cosmos with a crash.

Remember, however, that to be breakable is not the same as to be perishable. Strike a glass, and it will not endure an instant; simply do not strike it, and it will endure a thousand years. Such, it seemed, was the joy of man, either in elfland or on earth; the happiness depended on *not doing something* which you could at any moment do and which, very often, it was not obvious why you should not do. Now, the point here is that to me this did not seem unjust. If the miller's third son said to the fairy, 'Explain why I must not stand on my head in the fairy palace,' the other might fairly reply, 'Well, if it comes to that, explain the fairy palace.' If Cinderella says, 'How is it that I must leave the ball at twelve?' her godmother might answer, 'How is it that you are going there till twelve?' If I leave a man in my will ten talking elephants and a hundred winged horses, he cannot complain if the conditions partake of the slight eccentricity of the gift. He must not look a winged horse in the mouth. And it seemed to me that existence was itself so very eccentric a legacy that I could not complain of not understanding the limitations of the vision when I did not understand the vision they limited. The frame was no stranger than the picture. The veto might well be as wild as the vision; it might be as startling as the sun, as elusive as the waters, as fantastic and terrible as the towering trees.

For this reason (we may call it the fairy godmother philosophy) I never could join the young men of my time in feeling what they called the general sentiment of *revolt*. I should have resisted, let us hope, any rules that were evil, and with these and their definition I shall deal in another chapter. But I did not feel disposed to resist any rule merely because it was mysterious. Estates are sometimes held by foolish forms, the breaking of a stick or the payment of a peppercorn: I was willing to hold the huge estate of earth and heaven by any such feudal fantasy. It could not well be wilder than the fact that I was allowed to hold it at all. At this stage I give only one ethical instance to show my meaning. I could never mix in the common murmur of that rising generation against monogamy, because no restriction on sex seemed so odd and unexpected as sex itself. To be allowed, like Endymion,[1] to make love to the moon and then to complain that Jupiter kept his own moons in a harem seemed to me (bred on fairy tales like Endymion's) a vulgar anti-climax. Keeping to one woman is a small price for so much as seeing one woman. To complain that I could only be married once was like complaining that I had only been born once. It was incommensurate with the terrible excitement of which one was talking. It showed, not an exaggerated sensibility to sex, but a curious insensibility to it. A man is a fool who complains that he cannot enter Eden by five gates at once. Polygamy is a lack of the realization of sex; it is like a man plucking five pears in mere absence of mind. The aesthetes touched the last insane limits of language in their eulogy on lovely things. The thistledown made them weep; a burnished beetle brought them to their knees. Yet their emotion never impressed me for an instant, for this reason, that it never occurred to them to pay for their pleasure in any sort of symbolic sacrifice. Men (I felt) might fast forty days for the sake of hearing a blackbird sing. Men might go through fire to find a cowslip. Yet these lovers of beauty could not even keep sober for the blackbird. They would not go through common Christian marriage by way of recompense to the cowslip. Surely one might pay for extraordinary joy in ordinary morals. Oscar Wilde said that sunsets were not valued because we could not pay for sunsets. But Oscar Wilde was wrong; we can pay for sunsets. We can pay for them by not being Oscar Wilde.

Well, I left the fairy tales lying on the floor of the nursery, and I have not found any books so sensible since. I left the nurse guardian of tradition and democracy, and I have not found any modern type so sanely radical or so sanely conservative. But the matter for important comment was here: that when I first went out into the mental atmosphere of the modern world, I found that the modern world was positively opposed on two points to my nurse and to the

[1] The shepherd prince, who falls in love with Cynthia the moon.

nursery tales. It has taken me a long time to find out that the modern world is wrong and my nurse was right. The really curious thing was this: that modern thought contradicted this basic creed of my boyhood on its two most essential doctrines. I have explained that the fairy tales founded in me two convictions; first, that this world is a wild and startling place, which might have been quite different, but which is quite delightful; second, that before this wildness and delight one may well be modest and submit to the queerest limitations of so queer a kindness. But I found the whole modern world running like a high tide against both my tendernesses; and the shock of that collision created two sudden and spontaneous sentiments, which I have had ever since and which, crude as they were, have since hardened into convictions.

First, I found the whole modern world talking scientific fatalism; saying that everything is as it must always have been, being unfolded without fault from the beginning. The leaf on the tree is green because it could never have been anything else. Now, the fairy-tale philosopher is glad that the leaf is green precisely because it might have been scarlet. He feels as if it had turned green an instant before he looked at it. He is pleased that snow is white on the strictly reasonable ground that it might have been black. Every colour has in it a bold quality as of choice; the red of garden roses is not only decisive but dramatic, like suddenly spilt blood. He feels that something has been *done*. But the great determinists of the nineteenth century were strongly against this native feeling that something had happened an instant before. In fact, according to them, nothing ever really had happened since the beginning of the world. Nothing ever had happened since existence had happened; and even about the date of that they were not very sure.

The modern world as I found it was solid for modern Calvinism, for the necessity of things being as they are. But when I came to ask them I found they had really no proof of this unavoidable repetition in things except the fact that the things were repeated. Now, the mere repetition made the things to me rather more weird than more rational. It was as if, having seen a curiously shaped nose in the street and dismissed it as an accident, I had then seen six other noses of the same astonishing shape. I should have fancied for a moment that it must be some local secret society. So one elephant having a trunk was odd; but all elephants having trunks looked like a plot. I speak here only of an emotion, and of an emotion at once stubborn and subtle. But the repetition in Nature seemed sometimes to be an excited repetition, like that of an angry schoolmaster saying the same thing over and over again. The grass seemed signalling to me with all its fingers at once; the crowded stars seemed bent upon being understood. The sun would make me see him if he rose a thousand times. The recurrences of the universe rose to the maddening rhythm of an incantation, and I began to see an idea.

All the towering materialism which dominates the modern mind rests ultimately upon one assumption; a false assumption. It is supposed that if a thing goes on repeating itself it is probably dead; a piece of clockwork. People feel that if the universe was personal it would vary; if the sun were alive it would dance. This is a fallacy even in relation to known fact. For the variation in human affairs is generally brought into them, not by life, but by death; by the dying down or breaking off of their strength or desire. A man varies his movements because of some slight element of failure or fatigue. He gets into an omnibus because he is tired of walking; or he walks because he is tired of sitting still. But if his life and joy were so gigantic that he never tired of going to Islington, he might go to Islington as regularly as the Thames goes to Sheerness. The very speed and ecstasy of his life would have the stillness of death. The sun rises every morning. I do not rise every morning; but the variation is due not to my activity, but to my inaction. Now, to put the matter in a popular phrase, it might be true that the sun rises regularly because he never gets tired of rising. His routine might be due, not to a lifelessness, but to a rush of life. The thing I mean can be seen, for instance, in children, when they find some game or joke that they specially enjoy. A child kicks his legs rhythmically through excess, not absence, of life. Because children have abounding vitality, because they are in spirit fierce and free, therefore they want things repeated and unchanged. They always say, 'Do it again'; and the grown-up person does it again until he is nearly dead. For grown-up people are not strong enough to exult in monotony. But perhaps God is strong enough to exult in monotony. It is possible that God says every morning, 'Do it again' to the sun; and every evening, 'Do it again' to the moon. It may not be automatic necessity that makes all daisies alike; it may be that God makes every daisy separately, but has never got tired of making them. It may be that He has the eternal appetite of infancy; for we have sinned and grown old, and our Father is younger than we. The repetition in Nature may not be a mere recurrence; it may be a theatrical *encore*. Heaven may *encore* the bird who laid an egg. If the human being conceives and brings forth a human child instead of bringing forth a fish, or a bat, or a griffin, the reason may not be that we are fixed in an animal fate without life or purpose. It may be that our little tragedy has touched the gods, that they admire it from their starry galleries, and that at the end of every human drama man is called again and again before the curtain. Repetition may go on for millions of years, by mere choice, and at any instant it may stop. Man may stand on the earth generation after generation, and yet each birth be his positively last appearance.

This was my first conviction; made by the shock of my childish emotions meeting the modern creed in mid-career. I had always vaguely felt facts to be miracles in the sense that they are wonderful: now I began to think them miracles in the stricter sense that they were *wilful*. I mean that they were, or might be, repeated exercises of some will. In short, I had always believed that the world involved magic: now I thought that perhaps it involved a magician. And this pointed a profound emotion always present and sub-conscious; that this world of ours has some purpose; and if there is a purpose, there is a person. I had always felt life first as a story: and if there is a story there is a story-teller.

But modern thought also hit my second human tradition. It went against the fairy feeling about strict limits and conditions. The one thing it loved to talk about was expansion and largeness. Herbert Spencer[1] would have been greatly annoyed if any one had called him an imperialist, and therefore it is highly regrettable that nobody did. But he was an imperialist of the lowest type. He popularized this contemptible notion that the size of the solar system ought to overawe the spiritual dogma of man. Why should a man surrender his dignity to the solar system any more than to a whale? If mere size proves that man is not the image of God, then a whale may be the image of God; a somewhat formless image; what one might call an impressionist portrait. It is quite futile to argue that

1 Herbert Spencer (1820–1903), evolutionary philosopher and friend of George Eliot.

man is small compared to the cosmos; for man was always small compared to the nearest tree. But Herbert Spencer, in his headlong imperialism, would insist that we had in some way been conquered and annexed by the astronomical universe. He spoke about men and their ideals exactly as the most insolent Unionist talks about the Irish and their ideals. He turned mankind into a small nationality. And his evil influence can be seen even in the most spirited and honourable of later scientific authors; notably in the early romances of Mr H. G. Wells. Many moralists have in an exaggerated way represented the earth as wicked. But Mr Wells and his school made the heavens wicked. We should lift up our eyes to the stars from whence would come our ruin.

But the expansion of which I speak was much more evil than all this. I have remarked that the materialist, like the madman, is in prison; in the prison of one thought. These people seemed to think it singularly inspiring to keep on saying that the prison was very large. The size of this scientific universe gave one no novelty, no relief. The cosmos went on for ever, but not in its wildest constellation could there be anything really interesting; anything, for instance, such as forgiveness or free will. The grandeur or infinity of the secret of its cosmos added nothing to it. It was like telling a prisoner in Reading gaol that he would be glad to hear that the gaol now covered half the county. The warder would have nothing to show the man except more and more long corridors of stone lit by ghastly lights and empty of all that is human. So these expanders of the universe had nothing to show us except more and more infinite corridors of space lit by ghastly suns and empty of all that is divine.

In fairyland there had been a real law; a law that could be broken, for the definition of a law is something that can be broken. But the machinery of this cosmic prison was something that could not be broken; for we ourselves were only a part of its machinery. We were either unable to do things or we were destined to do them. The idea of the mystical condition quite disappeared; one can neither have the firmness of keeping laws nor the fun of breaking them. The largeness of this universe had nothing of that freshness and airy outbreak which we have praised in the universe of the poet. This modern universe is literally an empire; that is, it was vast, but it is not free. One went into larger and larger windowless rooms, rooms big with Babylonian perspective; but one never found the smallest window or a whisper of outer air.

Their infernal parallels seemed to expand with distance; but for me all good things come to a point, swords for instance. So finding the boast of the big cosmos so unsatisfactory to my emotions I began to argue about it a little; and I soon found that the whole attitude was even shallower than could have been expected. According to these people the cosmos was one thing since it had one unbroken rule. Only (they would say) while it is one thing it is also the only thing there is. Why, then, should one worry particularly to call it large? There is nothing to compare it with. It would be just as sensible to call it small. A man may say, 'I like this vast cosmos, with its throng of stars and its crowd of varied creatures.' But if it comes to that why should not a man say, 'I like this cosy little cosmos, with its decent number of stars and as neat a provision of live stock as I wish to see'? One is as good as the other; they are both mere sentiments. It is mere sentiment to rejoice that the sun is larger than the earth; it is quite as sane a sentiment to rejoice that the sun is no larger than it is. A man chooses to have an emotion about the largeness of the world: why should he not choose to have an emotion about its smallness?

It happened that I had that emotion. When one is fond of anything one addresses it by diminutives, even if it is an elephant or a life-guardsman. The reason is, that anything, however huge, that can be conceived of as complete, can be conceived of as small. If military moustaches did not suggest a sword or tusks a tail, then the object would be vast because it would be immeasurable. But the moment you can imagine a guardsman you can imagine a small guardsman. The moment you really see an elephant you can call it 'Tiny'. If you can make a statue of a thing you can make a statuette of it. These people professed that the universe was one coherent thing; but they were not fond of the universe. But I was frightfully fond of the universe and wanted to address it by a diminutive. I often did so; and it never seemed to mind. Actually and in truth I did feel that these dim dogmas of vitality were better expressed by calling the world small than by calling it large. For about infinity there was a sort of carelessness which was the reverse of the fierce and pious care which I felt touching the pricelessness and the peril of life. They showed only a dreary waste; but I felt a sort of sacred thrift. For economy is far more romantic than extravagance. To them stars were an unending income of half-pence; but I felt about the golden sun and the silver moon as a schoolboy feels if he has one sovereign and one shilling.

These subconscious convictions are best hit off by the colour and tone of certain tales. Thus I have said that stories of magic alone can express my sense that life is not only a pleasure but a kind of eccentric privilege. I may express this other feeling of cosmic cosi-ness by allusion to another book always read in boyhood, *Robinson Crusoe*, which I read about this time, and which owes its eternal vivacity to the fact that it celebrates the poetry of limits, nay, even the wild romance of prudence. Crusoe is a man on a small rock with a few comforts just snatched from the sea: the best thing in the book is simply the list of things saved from the wreck. The great-est of poems is an inventory. Every kitchen tool becomes ideal because Crusoe might have dropped it in the sea. It is a good exer-cise, in empty or ugly hours of the day, to look at anything, the coal-scuttle or the bookcase, and think how happy one could be to have brought it out of the sinking ship on to the solitary island. But it is a better exercise still to remember how all things have had this hair-breadth escape: everything has been saved from a wreck. Every man has had one horrible adventure: as a hidden untimely birth he had not been, as infants that never see the light. Men spoke much in my boyhood of restricted or ruined men of genius: and it was common to say that many a man was a Great Might-Have-Been. To me it is a more solid and startling fact that any man in the street is a Great Might-Not-Have-Been.

But I really felt (the fancy may seem foolish) as if all the order and number of things were the romantic remnant of Crusoe's ship. That there are two sexes and one sun, was like the fact that there were two guns and one axe. It was poignantly urgent that none should be lost; but somehow, it was rather fun that none could be added. The trees and the planets seemed like things saved from the wreck: and when I saw the Matterhorn I was glad that it had not been overlooked in the confusion. I felt economical about the stars as if they were sapphires (they are called so in Milton's Eden): I hoarded the hills. For the universe is a single jewel, and while it is a natural cant to talk of a jewel as peerless and priceless, of this jewel it is literally true. This cosmos is indeed without peer and without price: for there cannot be another one.

Thus ends, in unavoidable inadequacy, the attempt to utter the unutterable things. These are my ultimate attitudes towards life; the soils for the seeds of doctrine. These in some dark way I thought before I could write, and felt before I could think: that we may proceed more easily afterwards, I will roughly recapitulate them now. I felt in my bones; first, that this world does not explain itself. It may be a miracle with a supernatural explanation; it may be a conjuring trick, with a natural explanation. But the explanation of the conjuring trick, if it is to satisfy me, will have to be better than the natural explanations I have heard. The thing is magic, true or false. Second, I came to feel as if magic must have a meaning, and meaning must have some one to mean it. There was something personal in the world, as in a work of art; whatever it meant it meant violently. Third, I thought this purpose beautiful in its old design, in spite of its defects, such as dragons. Fourth, that the proper form of thanks to it is some form of humility and restraint: we should thank God for beer and Burgundy by not drinking too much of them. We owed, also, an obedience to whatever made us. And last, and strangest, there had come into my mind a vague and vast impression that in some way all good was a remnant to be stored and held sacred out of some primordial ruin. Man had saved his good as Crusoe saved his goods: he had saved them from a wreck. All this I felt and the age gave me no encouragement to feel it. And all this time I had not even thought of Christian theology.

THE FLAG OF THE WORLD

W HEN I was a boy there were two curious men running about who were called the optimist and the pessimist. I constantly used the words myself, but I cheerfully confess that I never had any very special idea of what they meant. The only thing which might be considered evident was that they could not mean what they said; for the ordinary verbal explanation was that the optimist thought this world as good as it could be, while the pessimist thought it as bad as it could be. Both these statements being obviously raving nonsense, one had to cast about for other explanations. An optimist could not mean a man who thought everything right and nothing wrong. For that is meaningless; it is like calling everything right and nothing left. Upon the whole, I came to the conclusion that the optimist thought everything good except the pessimist, and that the pessimist thought everything bad, except himself. It would be unfair to omit altogether from the list the mysterious but suggestive definition said to have been given by a little girl, 'An optimist is a man who looks after your eyes, and a pessimist is a man who looks after your feet.' I am not sure that this is not the best definition of all. There is even a sort of allegorical truth in it. For there might, perhaps, be a profitable distinction drawn between that more dreary thinker who thinks merely of our contact with the earth from moment to moment, and that happier thinker who considers rather our primary power of vision and of choice of road.

But this is a deep mistake in this alternative of the optimist and the pessimist. The assumption of it is that a man criticizes this world as if he were house-hunting, as if he were being shown over a new suite of apartments. If a man came to this world from some other world in full possession of his powers he might discuss whether the advantage of midsummer woods made up for the disadvantage of mad dogs, just as a man looking for lodgings might balance the presence of a telephone against the absence of a sea view. But no man is in that position. A man belongs to this world before he begins to ask if it is nice to belong to it. He has fought for the flag, and often won heroic victories for the flag long before he has ever enlisted. To put shortly what seems the essential matter, he has a loyalty long before he has any admiration.

In the last chapter it has been said that the primary feeling that this world is strange and yet attractive is best expressed in fairy tales. The reader may, if he likes, put down the next stage to that bellicose and even jingo literature which commonly comes next in the history of a boy. We all owe much sound morality to the penny dreadfuls. Whatever the reason, it seemed and still seems to me that our attitude towards life can be better expressed in terms of a kind of military loyalty than in terms of criticism and approval. My acceptance of the universe is not optimism, it is more like patriotism. It is a matter of primary loyalty. The world is not a lodging-house at Brighton, which we are to leave because it is miserable. It is the fortress of our family, with the flag flying on the turret, and the more miserable it is the less we should leave it. The point is not that this world is too sad to love or too glad not to love; the point is that when you do love a thing, its gladness is a reason for loving it, and its sadness a reason for loving it more. All optimistic thoughts about England and all pessimistic thoughts about her are alike reasons for the English patriot. Similarly, optimism and pessimism are alike arguments for the cosmic patriot.

Let us suppose we are confronted with a desperate thing – say Pimlico. If we think what is really best for Pimlico we shall find the thread of thought leads to the throne or the mystic and the arbitrary. It is not enough for a man to disapprove of Pimlico: in that case he will merely cut his throat or move to Chelsea. Nor, certainly, is it enough for a man to approve of Pimlico: for then it will remain Pimlico, which would be awful. The only way out of it seems to be for somebody to love Pimlico: to love it with a transcendental tie and without any earthly reason. If there arose a man who loved Pimlico, then Pimlico would rise into ivory towers and golden pinnacles; Pimlico would attire herself as a woman does when she is loved. For decoration is not given to hide horrible things: but to decorate things already adorable. A mother does not give her child a blue bow because he is so ugly without it. A lover does not give a girl a necklace to hide her neck. If men loved Pimlico as mothers love children, arbitrarily, because it is *theirs*, Pimlico in a year or two might be fairer than Florence. Some readers will say that this is a mere fantasy. I answer that this is the actual history of mankind. This, as a fact, is how cities did grow great. Go back to the darkest roots of civilization and you will find them knotted round some sacred stone or encircling some sacred well. People first paid honour to a spot and afterwards gained glory for it. Men did not love Rome because she was great. She was great because they had loved her.

The eighteenth-century theories of the social contract have been exposed to much clumsy criticism in our time; in so far as they meant that there is at the back of all historic government an idea of content and co-operation, they were demonstrably right. But they really were wrong in so far as they suggested that men had ever aimed at order or ethics directly by a conscious exchange of interests. Morality did not begin by one man saying to another, 'I will not hit you if you do not hit me'; there is no trace of such a transaction. There *is* a trace of both men having said, 'We must not hit each other in the holy place.' They gained their morality by guarding their religion. They did not cultivate courage. They fought for the shrine, and found they had become courageous. They did not cultivate cleanliness. They purified themselves for the altar, and found that they were clean. The history of the Jews is the only early document known to most Englishmen, and the facts can be judged sufficiently from that. The Ten Commandments which have been found substantially common to mankind were merely military commands; a code of regimental orders, issued to protect a certain ark across a certain desert. Anarchy was evil because it endangered the sanctity. And only when they made a holy day for God did they find they had made a holiday for men.

If it be granted that this primary devotion to a place or thing is a source of creative energy, we can pass on to a very peculiar fact. Let us reiterate for an instant that the only right optimism is a sort of universal patriotism. What is the matter with the pessimist? I think it can be stated by saying that he is the cosmic anti-patriot. And what is the matter with the anti-patriot? I think it can be stated, without undue bitterness, by saying that he is the candid friend. And what is the matter with the candid friend? There we strike the rock of real life and immutable human nature.

I venture to say that what is bad in the candid friend is simply that he is not candid. He is keeping something back – his own gloomy pleasure in saying unpleasant things. He has a secret desire to hurt, not merely to help. This is certainly, I think, what makes a certain sort of anti-patriot irritating to healthy citizens. I do not speak (of course) of the anti-patriotism which only irritates feverish stockbrokers and gushing actresses; that is only patriotism speaking plainly. A man who says that no patriot should attack the Boer War until it is over is not worth answering intelligently; he is saying that no good son should warn his mother off a cliff until she has fallen over it. But there is an anti-patriot who honestly angers honest men, and the explanation of him is, I think, what I have suggested: he is the uncandid candid friend; the man who says, 'I am sorry to say we are ruined,' and is not sorry at all. And he may be said, without rhetoric, to be a traitor; for he is using that ugly knowledge which was allowed him to strengthen the army, to discourage people from joining it. Because he is allowed to be pessimistic as a military adviser he is being pessimistic as a recruiting sergeant. Just in the same way the pessimist (who is the cosmic anti-patriot) uses the freedom that life allows to her counsellors to lure away the people from her flag. Granted that he states only facts, it is still essential to know what are his emotions, what is his motive. It may be that twelve hundred men in Tottenham are down with small-pox; but we want to know whether this is stated by some great philosopher who wants to curse the gods, or only by some common clergyman who wants to help the men.

The evil of the pessimist is, then, not that he chastises gods and men, but that he does not love what he chastises – he has not this primary and supernatural loyalty to things. What is the evil of the man commonly called an optimist? Obviously, it is felt that the optimist, wishing to defend the honour of this world, will defend the indefensible. He is the jingo of the universe; he will say, 'My cosmos, right or wrong.' He will be less inclined to the reform of things; more inclined to a sort of front-bench official answer to all attacks, soothing every one with assurances. He will not wash the world, but whitewash the world. All this (which is true of a type of optimist) leads us to the one really interesting point of psychology, which could not be explained without it.

We say there must be a primal loyalty to life: the only question is, shall it be a natural or a supernatural loyalty? If you like to put it so, shall it be a reasonable or an unreasonable loyalty? Now, the extraordinary thing is that the bad optimism (the whitewashing, the weak defence of everything) comes in with the reasonable optimism. Rational optimism leads to stagnation: it is irrational optimism that leads to reform. Let me explain by using once more the parallel of patriotism. The man who is most likely to ruin the place he loves is exactly the man who loves it with a reason. The man who will improve the place is the man who loves it without a reason. If a man loves some feature of Pimlico (which seems unlikely), he may find himself defending that feature against Pimlico itself. But if he simply loves Pimlico itself, he may lay it waste and turn it into the New Jerusalem. I do not deny that reform may be excessive; I only say that it is the mystic patriot who reforms. Mere jingo self-contentment is commonest among those who have some pedantic reason for their patriotism. The worst jin-goes do not love England, but a theory of England. If we love England for being an empire, we may overrate the success with which we rule the Hindoos. But if we love it only for being a nation, we can face all events: for it would be a nation even if the Hindoos ruled us. Thus also only those will permit their patriotism to falsify history whose patriotism depends on history. A man who loves England for being English will not mind how she arose. But a man who loves England for being Anglo-Saxon may go against all facts for his fancy. He may end (like Carlyle . . .) by maintaining that the Norman Conquest was a Saxon Conquest. He may end in utter unreason – because he has a reason. A man who loves France for being military will palliate the army of 1870. But a man who loves France for being France will improve the army of 1870. This is exactly what the French have done, and France is a good instance of the working paradox. Nowhere else is patriotism more purely abstract and arbitrary; and nowhere else is reform more drastic and sweeping. The more transcendental is your patriotism, the more practical are your politics.

Perhaps the most everyday instance of this point is in the case of women; and their strange and strong loyalty. Some stupid people started the idea that because women obviously back up their own people through everything, therefore women are blind and do not see anything. They can hardly have known any women. The same women who are ready to defend their men through thick and thin are (in their personal intercourse with the man) almost morbidly lucid about the thinness of his excuses or the thickness of his head. A man's friend likes him but leaves him as he is: his wife loves him and is always trying to turn him into somebody else. Women who are utter mystics in their creed are utter cynics in their criticism. Thackeray expressed this well when he made Pendennis's mother, who worshipped her son as a god, yet assume that he would go wrong as a man. She underrated his virtue, though she overrated his value. The devotee is entirely free to criticize; the fanatic can safely be a sceptic. Love is not blind; that is the last thing that it is. Love is bound; and the more it is bound the less it is blind.

This at least had come to be my position about all that was called optimism, pessimism, and improvement. Before any cosmic act of reform we must have a cosmic oath of allegiance. A man must be interested in life, then he could be disinterested in his views of it. 'My son give me thy heart'; the heart must be fixed on the right thing: the moment we have a fixed heart we have a free hand. I must pause to anticipate an obvious criticism. It will be said that a rational person accepts the world as mixed of good and evil with a decent satisfaction and a decent endurance. But this is exactly the attitude which I maintain to be defective. It is, I know, very common in this age; it was perfectly put in those quiet lines of Matthew Arnold which are more piercingly blasphemous than the shrieks of Schopenhauer –

> Enough we live: – and if a life,
> With large results so little rife,
> Though bearable, seem hardly worth
> This pomp of worlds, this pain of birth.[1]

I know this feeling fills our epoch, and I think it freezes our epoch. For our Titanic purposes of faith and revolution, what we need is not the cold acceptance of the world as a compromise, but some way in which we can heartily hate and heartily love it. We do not want joy and anger to neutralize each other and produce a surly contentment; we want a fiercer delight and a fiercer discontent. We have to feel the universe at once as an ogre's castle, to be stormed, and yet as our own cottage, to which we can return at evening.

No one doubts that an ordinary man can get on with this world:

1 *Resignation*, ll. 261–4.

but we demand not strength enough to get on with it, but strength enough to get it on. Can he hate it enough to change it, and yet love it enough to think it worth changing? Can he look up at its colossal good without once feeling acquiescence? Can he look up at its colossal evil without once feeling despair? Can he, in short, be at once not only a pessimist and an optimist, but a fanatical pessimist and a fanatical optimist? Is he enough of a pagan to die for the world, and enough of a Christian to die to it? In this combination, I maintain, it is the rational optimist who fails, the irrational optimist who succeeds. He is ready to smash the whole universe for the sake of itself.

I put these things not in their mature logical sequence, but as they came: and this view was cleared and sharpened by an accident of the time. Under the lengthening shadow of Ibsen, an argument arose whether it was not a very nice thing to murder one's self. Grave moderns told us that we must not even say 'poor fellow', of a man who had blown his brains out, since he was an enviable person, and had only blown them out because of their exceptional excellence. . . . In all this I found myself utterly hostile to many who called themselves liberal and humane. Not only is suicide a sin, it is the sin. It is the ultimate and absolute evil, the refusal to take an interest in existence; the refusal to take the oath of loyalty to life. The man who kills a man, kills a man. The man who kills himself, kills all men; as far as he is concerned he wipes out the world. His act is worse (symbolically considered) than any rape or dynamite outrage. For it destroys all buildings: it insults all women. The thief is satisfied with diamonds; but the suicide is not: that is his crime. He cannot be bribed, even by the blazing stones of the Celestial City. The thief compliments the things he steals, if not the owner of them. But the suicide insults everything on earth by not stealing it. He defiles every flower by refusing to live for its sake. There is not a tiny creature in the cosmos at whom his death is not a sneer. When a man hangs himself on a tree, the leaves might fall off in anger and the birds fly away in fury: for each has received a personal affront. Of course there may be pathetic emotional excuses for the act. There often are for rape, and there almost always are for dynamite. But if it comes to clear ideas and the intelligent meaning of things, then there is much more rational and philosophic truth in the burial at the crossroads and the stake driven through the body, than in Mr Archer's suicidal automatic machines. There is a meaning in burying the suicide apart. The man's crime is different from other crimes – for it makes even crimes impossible.

About the same time I read a solemn flippancy by some free-thinker: he said that a suicide was only the same as a martyr. The open fallacy of this helped to clear the question. Obviously a suicide is the opposite of a martyr. A martyr is a man who cares so much for something outside him, that he forgets his own personal life. A suicide is a man who cares so little for anything outside him, that he wants to see the last of everything. One wants something to begin: the other wants everything to end. In other words, the martyr is noble, exactly because (however he renounces the world or execrates all humanity) he confesses this ultimate link with life; he sets his heart outside himself: he dies that something may live. The suicide is ignoble because he has not this link with being: he is a mere destroyer; spiritually, he destroys the universe. And then I remembered the stake and the crossroads, and the queer fact that Christianity had shown this weird harshness to the suicide. For Christianity had shown a wild encouragement of the martyr. Historic Christianity was accused, not entirely without reason, of carrying martyrdom and asceticism to a point, desolate and pessimistic. The early Christian martyrs talked of death with a horrible happiness. They blasphemed the beautiful duties of the body: they smelt the grave afar off like a field of flowers. All this has seemed to many the very poetry of pessimism. Yet there is the stake at the crossroads to show what Christianity thought of the pessimist.

This was the first of the long train of enigmas with which Christianity entered the discussion. And there went with it a peculiarity of which I shall have to speak more markedly, as a note of all Christian notions, but which distinctly began in this one. The Christian attitude to the martyr and the suicide was not what is so often affirmed in modern morals. It was not a matter of degree. It was not that a line must be drawn somewhere, and that the self-slayer in exaltation fell within the line, the self-slayer in sadness just beyond it. The Christian feeling evidently was not merely that the suicide was carrying martyrdom too far. The Christian feeling was furiously for one and furiously against the other: these two things that looked so much alike were at opposite ends of heaven and hell.

One man flung away his life; he was so good that his dry bones could heal cities in pestilence. Another man flung away life; he was so bad that his bones would pollute his brethren's. I am not saying this fierceness was right; but why was it so fierce?

Here it was that I first found that my wandering feet were in some beaten track. Christianity had also felt this opposition of the martyr to the suicide: had it perhaps felt it for the same reason? Had Christianity felt what I felt, but could not (and cannot) express – this need for a first loyalty to things, and then for a ruinous reform of things? Then I remembered that it was actually the charge against Christianity that it combined these two things which I was wildly trying to combine. Christianity was accused, at one and the same time, of being too optimistic about the universe and of being too pessimistic about the world. The coincidence made me suddenly stand still.

An imbecile habit has arisen in modern controversy of saying that such and such a creed can be held in one age but cannot be held in another. Some dogma, we are told, was credible in the twelfth century, but is not credible in the twentieth. You might as well say that a certain philosophy can be believed on Mondays, but cannot be believed on Tuesdays. You might as well say of a view of the cosmos that it was suitable to half-past three, but not suitable to half-past four. What a man can believe depends upon his philosophy, not upon the clock or the century. If a man believes in unalterable natural law, he cannot believe in any miracle in any age. If a man believes in a will behind law, he can believe in any miracle in any age. Suppose, for the sake of argument, we are concerned with a case of thaumaturgic healing. A materialist of the twelfth century could not believe it any more than a materialist of the twentieth century. But a Christian Scientist of the twentieth century can believe it as much as a Christian of the twelfth century. It is simply a matter of a man's theory of things. Therefore in dealing with any historical answer, the point is not whether it was given in our time, but whether it was given in answer to our question. And the more I thought about when and how Christianity had come into the world, the more I felt that it had actually come to answer this question.

It is commonly the loose and latitudinarian Christians who pay quite indefensible compliments to Christianity. They talk as if there had never been any piety or pity until Christianity came, a point on which any mediaeval would have been eager to correct them. They represent that the remarkable thing about Christianity was that it was the first to preach simplicity or self-restraint, or inwardness and sincerity. They will think me very narrow (whatever that means) if I say that the remarkable thing about Christianity was that it was the first to preach Christianity. Its peculiarity was that it was peculiar, and simplicity and sincerity are not peculiar, but obvious ideals for all mankind. Christianity was the answer to a riddle, not the last truism uttered after a long talk. Only the other day I saw in an excellent weekly paper of Puritan tone this remark, that Christianity when stripped of its armour of dogma (as who should speak of a man stripped of his armour of bones), turned out to be nothing but the Quaker doctrine of the Inner Light. Now, if I were to say that Christianity came into the world specially to destroy the doctrine of the Inner Light, that would be an exaggeration. But it would be very much nearer to the truth. The last Stoics, like Marcus Aurelius, were exactly the people who did believe in the Inner Light. Their dignity, their weariness, their sad external care for others, their incurable internal care for themselves, were all due to the Inner Light, and existed only by that dismal illumination. Notice that Marcus Aurelius insists, as such introspective moralists always do, upon small things done or undone; it is because he has not hate or love enough to make a moral revolution. He gets up early in the morning, just as our own aristocrats living the Simple Life get up early in the morning; because such altruism is much easier than stopping the games of the amphitheatre or giving the English people back their land. Marcus Aurelius is the most intolerable of human types. He is an unselfish egoist. An unselfish egoist is a man who has pride without the excuse of passion. Of all conceivable forms of enlightenment the worst is what these people call the Inner Light. Of all horrible religions the most horrible is the worship of the god within. Any one who knows any body knows how it would work; any one who knows any one from the Higher Thought Centre knows how it does work. That Jones shall worship the god within him turns out ultimately to mean that Jones shall worship Jones. Let Jones worship the sun or moon, anything rather than the Inner Light; let Jones worship cats or crocodiles, if he can find any in his street, but not the god within.

Christianity came into the world firstly in order to assert with violence that a man had not only to look inwards, but to look outwards, to behold with astonishment and enthusiasm a divine company and a divine captain. The only fun of being a Christian was that a man was not left alone with the Inner Light, but definitely recognized an outer light, fair as the sun, clear as the moon, terrible as an army with banners.

All the same, it will be as well if Jones does not worship the sun and moon. If he does, there is a tendency for him to imitate them; to say, that because the sun burns insects alive, he may burn insects alive. He thinks that because the sun gives people sun-stroke, he may give his neighbour measles. He thinks that because the moon is said to drive men mad, he may drive his wife mad. This ugly side of mere external optimism had also shown itself in the ancient world. About the time when the Stoic idealism had begun to show the weaknesses of pessimism, the old nature worship of the ancients had begun to show the enormous weaknesses of optimism. Nature worship is natural enough while the society is young, or, in other words, Pantheism is all right as long as it is the worship of Pan. But Nature has another side which experience and sin are not slow in finding out, and it is no flippancy to say of the god Pan that he soon showed the cloven hoof. The only objection to Natural Religion is that somehow it always becomes unnatural. A man loves Nature in the morning for her innocence and amiability, and at nightfall, if he is loving her still, it is for her darkness and her cruelty. He washes at dawn in clear water as did the Wise Man of the Stoics, yet, somehow at the dark end of the day, he is bathing in hot bull's blood, as did Julian the Apostate. The mere pursuit of health always leads to something unhealthy. Physical nature must not be made the direct object of obedience; it must be enjoyed, not worshipped. Stars and mountains must not be taken seriously. If they are, we end where the pagan nature worship ended. Because the earth is kind, we can imitate all her cruelties. Because sexuality is sane, we can all go mad about sexuality. Mere optimism had reached its insane and appropriate termination. The theory that everything was good had become an orgy of everything that was bad.

On the other side our idealist pessimists were represented by the old remnant of the Stoics. Marcus Aurelius and his friends had really given up the idea of any god in the universe and looked only to the god within. They had no hope of any virtue in nature, and hardly any hope of any virtue in society. They had not enough interest in the outer world really to wreck or revolutionize it. They did not love the city enough to set fire to it. Thus the ancient world was exactly in our own desolate dilemma. The only people who really enjoyed this world were busy breaking it up; and the virtuous people did not care enough about them to knock them down. In this dilemma (the same as ours) Christianity suddenly stepped in and offered a singular answer, which the world eventually accepted as *the* answer. It was the answer then, and I think it is the answer now.

This answer was like the slash of a sword; it sundered; it did not in any sense sentimentally unite. Briefly, it divided God from the cosmos. That transcendence and distinctness of the deity which some Christians now want to remove from Christianity, was really the only reason why any one wanted to be a Christian. It was the whole point of the Christian answer to the unhappy pessimist and the still more unhappy optimist. As I am here only concerned with their particular problem, I shall indicate only briefly this great metaphysical suggestion. All descriptions of the creating or sustaining principle in things must be metaphorical, because they must be verbal. Thus the pantheist is forced to speak of God *in* all things as if he were in a box. Thus the evolutionist has, in his very name, the idea of being unrolled like a carpet. All terms, religious and irreligious, are open to this charge. The only question is whether all terms are useless, or whether one can, with such a phrase, cover a distinct *idea* about the origin of things. I think one can, and so evidently does the evolutionist, or he would not talk about evolution. And the root phrase for all Christian theism was this, that God was a creator, as an artist is a creator. A poet is so separate from his poem that he himself speaks of it as a little thing he has 'thrown off'. Even in giving it forth he has flung it away. This principle that all creation and procreation is a breaking off is at least as consistent through the cosmos as the evolutionary principle that all growth is a branching out. A woman loses a child even in having a child. All creation is separation. Birth is as solemn a parting as death.

It was the prime philosophic principle of Christianity that this divorce in the divine act of making (such as severs the poet from the poem or the mother from the new-born child) was the true description of the act whereby the absolute energy made the world. According to most philosophers, God in making the world enslaved it. According to Christianity, in making it, He set it free. God had written, not so much a poem, but rather a play; a play he had planned as perfect, but which had necessarily been left to human actors and stage-managers, who had since made a great mess of it. I will discuss the truth of this theorem later. Here I have only to point out with what a startling smoothness it passed the dilemma we have discussed in this chapter. In this way at least one could be both happy and indignant without degrading one's self to be either a pessimist or an optimist. On this system one could fight all the forces of existence without deserting the flag of existence. One could be at peace with the universe and yet be at war with the world. St George could still fight the dragon, however big the monster bulked in the cosmos, though he were bigger than the mighty cities or bigger than the everlasting hills. If he were as big as the world he could yet be killed in the name of the world. St George had not to consider any obvious odds or proportions in the scale of things, but only the original secret of their design. He can shake his sword at the dragon, even if it is everything; even if the empty heavens over his head are only the huge arch of its open jaws.

And then followed an experience impossible to describe. It was as if I had been blundering about since my birth with two huge and unmanageable machines, of different shapes and without apparent connection – the world and the Christian tradition. I had found this hole in the world: the fact that one must somehow find a way of loving the world without trusting it; somehow one must love the world without being worldly. I found this projecting feature of Christian theology, like a sort of hard spike, the dogmatic insistence that God was personal, and had made a world separate from Himself. The spike of dogma fitted exactly into the hole in the world – it had evidently been meant to go there – and then the strange thing began to happen. When once these two parts of the two machines had come together, one after another, all the other parts fitted and fell in with an eerie exactitude. I could hear bolt after bolt over all the machinery falling into its place with a kind of click of relief. Having got one part right, all the other parts were repeating that rectitude, as clock after clock strikes noon. Instinct after instinct was answered by doctrine after doctrine.

Or, to vary the metaphor, I was like one who had advanced into a hostile country to take one high fortress. And when that fort had fallen the whole country surrendered and turned solid behind me. The whole land was lit up, as it were, back to the first fields of my childhood. All those blind fancies of boyhood which in the fourth chapter I have tried in vain to trace on the darkness, became suddenly transparent and sane. I was right when I felt that roses were red by some sort of choice: it was the divine choice. I was right when I felt that I would almost rather say that grass was the wrong colour than say it must by necessity have been that colour: it might verily have been any other. My sense that happiness hung on the crazy thread of a condition did mean something when all was said: it meant the whole doctrine of the Fall. Even those dim and shapeless monsters of notions which I have not been able to describe, much less defend, stepped quietly into their places like colossal caryatides of the creed. The fancy that the cosmos was not vast and void, but small and cosy, had a fulfilled significance now, for anything that is a work of art must be small in the sight of the artist; to God the stars might be only small and dear, like diamonds. And my haunting instinct that somehow good was not merely a tool to be used, but a relic to be guarded, like the goods from Crusoe's ship – even that had been the wild whisper of something originally wise, for, according to Christianity, we were indeed the survivors of a wreck, the crew of a golden ship that had gone down before the beginning of the world.

But the important matter was this, that it entirely reversed the reason for optimism. And the instant the reversal was made it felt like the abrupt ease when a bone is put back in the socket. I had often called myself an optimist, to avoid the too evident blasphemy of pessimism. But all the optimism of the age had been false and disheartening for this reason, that it had always been trying to prove that we fit in to the world. The Christian optimism is based on the fact that we do *not* fit in to the world. I had tried to be happy by telling myself that man is an animal, like any other which sought its meat from God. But now I really was happy, for I had learnt that man is a monstrosity. I had been right in feeling all things as odd, for I myself was at once worse and better than all things. The optimist's pleasure was prosaic, for it dwelt on the naturalness of everything; the Christian pleasure was poetic, for it dwelt on the unnaturalness of everything in the light of the supernatural. The modern philosopher had told me again and again that I was in the right place, and I had still felt depressed even in acquiescence. But I had heard that I was in the *wrong* place, and my soul sang for joy, like a bird in spring. The knowledge found out and illuminated forgotten chambers in the dark house of infancy. I knew now why grass had always seemed to me as queer as the green beard of a giant, and why I could feel homesick at home.

VI
THE PARADOXES OF CHRISTIANITY

T HE REAL trouble with this world of ours is not that it is an unreasonable world, nor even that it is a reasonable one. The commonest kind of trouble is that it is nearly reasonable, but not quite. Life is not an illogicality; yet it is a trap for logicians. It looks just a little more mathematical and regular than it is; its exactitude is obvious, but its inexactitude is hidden; its wildness lies in wait. I give one coarse instance of what I mean. Suppose some mathematical creature from the moon were to reckon up the human body; he would at once see that the essential thing about it was that it was duplicate. A man is two men, he on the right exactly resembling him on the left. Having noted that there was an arm on the right and one on the left, a leg on the right and one on the left, he might go further and still find on each side the same number of fingers, the same number of toes, twin eyes, twin ears, twin nostrils and even twin lobes of the brain. At last he would take it as a law; and then, where he found a heart on one side, would deduce that there was another heart on the other. And just then, where he most felt he was right, he would be wrong.

It is this silent swerving from accuracy by an inch that is the uncanny element in everything. It seems a sort of secret treason in the universe. An apple or an orange is round enough to get itself called round, and yet is not round after all. The earth itself is shaped like an orange in order to lure some simple astronomer into calling it a globe. A blade of grass is called after the blade of a sword, because it comes to a point; but it doesn't. Everywhere in things there is this element of the quiet and incalculable. It escapes the rationalists, but it never escapes till the last moment. From the grand curve of our earth it could easily be inferred that every inch of it was thus curved. It would seem rational that as a man has a brain on both sides, he should have a heart on both sides. Yet scientific men are still organizing expeditions to find the North Pole, because they are so fond of flat country. Scientific men are also still organizing expeditions to find a man's heart; and when they try to find it, they generally get on the wrong side of him.

Now, actual insight or inspiration is best tested by whether it guesses these hidden malformations or surprises. If our mathematician from the moon saw the two arms and the two ears, he might deduce the two shoulder-blades and the two halves of the brain. But if he guessed that the man's heart was in the right place, then I should call him something more than a mathematician. Now, this is exactly the claim which I have since come to propound for Christianity. Not merely that it deduces logical truths, but that when it suddenly becomes illogical, it has found, so to speak, an illogical truth. It not only goes right about things, but it goes wrong (if one may say so) exactly where the things go wrong. Its plan suits the secret irregularities, and expects the unexpected. It is simple about the simple truth; but it is stubborn about the subtle truth. It will admit that a man has two hands, it will not admit (though all the Modernists wail to it) the obvious deduction that he has two hearts. It is my only purpose in this chapter to point this out; to show that whenever we feel there is something odd in Christian theology, we shall generally find that there is something odd in the truth.

I have alluded to an unmeaning phrase to the effect that such and such a creed cannot be believed in our age. Of course, anything can be believed in any age. But, oddly enough, there really is a sense in which a creed, if it is believed at all, can be believed more fixedly in a complex society than in a simple one. If a man finds Christianity true in Birmingham, he has actually clearer reasons for faith than if he had found it true in Mercia. For the more complicated seems the coincidence, the less it can be a coincidence. If snowflakes fell in the shape, say, of the heart of Midlothian, it might be an accident. But if snowflakes fell in the exact shape of the maze at Hampton Court, I think one might call it a miracle. It is exactly as of such a miracle that I have since come to feel of the philosophy of Christianity. The complication of our modern world proves the truth of the creed more perfectly than any of the plain problems of the ages of faith. It was in Notting Hill and Battersea that I began to see that Christianity was true. This is why the faith has that elaboration of doctrines and details which so much distresses those who admire Christianity without believing

in it. When once one believes in a creed, one is proud of its complexity, as scientists are proud of the complexity of science. It shows
how rich it is in discoveries. If it is right at all, it is a compliment
to say that it's elaborately right. A stick might fit a hole or a stone
a hollow by accident. But a key and a lock are both complex. And
if a key fits a lock, you know it is the right key.

But this involved accuracy of the thing makes it very difficult to
do what I now have to do, to describe this accumulation of truth.
It is very hard for a man to defend anything of which he is entirely
convinced. It is comparatively easy when he is only partially convinced. He is partially convinced because he has found this or that
proof of the thing, and he can expound it. But a man is not really
convinced of a philosophic theory when he finds that something
proves it. He is only really convinced when he finds that everything proves it. And the more converging reasons he finds pointing
to this conviction, the more bewildered he is if asked suddenly to
sum them up. Thus, if one asked an ordinary intelligent man, on
the spur of the moment, 'Why do you prefer civilization to savagery?' he would look wildly round at object after object, and
would only be able to answer vaguely, 'Why, there is that bookcase
... and the coals in the coal-scuttle ... and pianos ... and policemen.' The whole case for civilization is that the case for it is complex. It has done so many things. But that very multiplicity of proof
which ought to make reply overwhelming makes reply impossible.

There is, therefore, about all complete conviction a kind of huge
helplessness. The belief is so big that it takes a long time to get it
into action. And this hesitation chiefly arises, oddly enough, from
an indifference about where one should begin. All roads lead to
Rome; which is one reason why many people never get there. In the
case of this defence of the Christian conviction I confess that I
would as soon begin the argument with one thing as another;
I would begin it with a turnip or a taximeter cab. But if I am to be
at all careful about making my meaning clear, it will, I think,
be wiser to continue the current arguments of the last chapter,
which was concerned to urge the first of these mystical coincidences, or rather ratifications. All I had hitherto heard of Christian
theology had alienated me from it. I was a pagan at the age of
twelve, and a complete agnostic by the age of sixteen; and I cannot
understand any one passing the age of seventeen without having

asked himself so simple a question. I did, indeed, retain a cloudy reverence for a cosmic deity and a great historical interest in the Founder of Christianity. But I certainly regarded Him as a man; though perhaps I thought that, even in that point, He had an advantage over some of His modern critics. I read the scientific and sceptical literature of my time – all of it, at least, that I could find written in English and lying about; and I read nothing else; I mean I read nothing else on any other note of philosophy. The penny dreadfuls which I also read were indeed in a healthy and heroic tradition of Christianity; but I did not know this at the time. I never read a line of Christian apologetics. I read as little as I can of them now. It was Huxley and Herbert Spencer and Bradlaugh[1] who brought me back to orthodox theology. They sowed in my mind my first wild doubts of doubt. Our grandmothers were quite right when they said that Tom Paine[2] and the freethinkers unsettled the mind. They do. They unsettled mine horribly. The rationalist made me question whether reason was of any use whatever; and when I had finished Herbert Spencer I had got as far as doubting (for the first time) whether evolution had occurred at all. . . . I was in a desperate way.

This odd effect of the great agnostics in arousing doubts deeper than their own might be illustrated in many ways. I take only one. As I read and re-read all the non-Christian or anti-Christian accounts of the faith, from Huxley to Bradlaugh, a slow and awful impression grew gradually but graphically upon my mind – the impression that Christianity must be a most extraordinary thing. For not only (as I understood) had Christianity the most flaming vices, but it had apparently a mystical talent for combining vices which seemed inconsistent with each other. It was attacked on all sides and for all contradictory reasons. No sooner had one rationalist demonstrated that it was too far to the east than another demonstrated with equal clearness that it was much too far to the west. No sooner had my indignation died down at its angular and aggressive squareness than I was called up again to notice and condemn its enervating and sensual roundness. In case any reader has not come across the thing I mean, I will give such instances as I remember at random of this self-contradiction in the sceptical attack. I give four or five of them; there are fifty more.

1 Charles Bradlaugh (1833–91), freethinker.
2 Tom Paine (1737–1809), author of *The Age of Reason*, a Deist attack on Christianity.

Thus, for instance, I was much moved by the eloquent attack on Christianity as a thing of inhuman gloom; for I thought (and still think) sincere pessimism the unpardonable sin. Insincere pessimism is a social accomplishment, rather agreeable than otherwise; and fortunately nearly all pessimism is insincere. But if Christianity was, as these people said, a thing purely pessimistic and opposed to life, then I was quite prepared to blow up St Paul's Cathedral. But the extraordinary thing is this. They did prove to me in Chapter I (to my complete satisfaction) that Christianity was too pessimistic; and then, in Chapter II, they began to prove to me that it was a great deal too optimistic. One accusation against Christianity was that it prevented men, by morbid tears and terrors, from seeking joy and liberty in the bosom of Nature. But another accusation was that it comforted men with a fictitious providence, and put them in a pink-and-white nursery. One great agnostic asked why Nature was not beautiful enough, and why it was hard to be free. Another great agnostic objected that Christian optimism, 'the garment of make-believe woven by pious hands', hid from us the fact that Nature was ugly, and that it was impossible to be free. One rationalist had hardly done calling Christianity a nightmare before another began to call it a fool's paradise. This puzzled me; the charges seemed inconsistent. Christianity could not at once be the black mask on a white world, and also the white mask on a black world. The state of the Christian could not be at once so comfortable that he was a coward to cling to it, and so uncomfortable that he was a fool to stand it. If it falsified human vision it must falsify it one way or another; it could not wear both green and rose-coloured spectacles. I rolled on my tongue with a terrible joy, as did all young men of that time, the taunts which Swinburne hurled at the dreariness of the creed –

> Thou hast conquered, O pale Galilaean, the world has
>   grown grey with Thy breath.[1]

But when I read the same poet's accounts of paganism (as in *Atalanta*), I gathered that the world was, if possible, more grey before the Galilaean breathed on it than afterwards. The poet maintained, indeed, in the abstract, that life itself was pitch dark.

1 *Hymn to Proserpine*, l. 35, which Chesterton misquotes, substituting 'with' for 'from'.

And yet, somehow, Christianity had darkened it. The very man who denounced Christianity for pessimism was himself a pessimist. I thought there must be something wrong. And it did for one wild moment cross my mind that, perhaps, those might not be the very best judges of the relation of religion to happiness who, by their own account, had neither one nor the other.

It must be understood that I did not conclude hastily that the accusations were false or the accusers fools. I simply deduced that Christianity must be something even weirder and wickeder than they made out. A thing might have these two opposite vices; but it must be a rather queer thing if it did. A man might be too fat in one place and too thin in another; but he would be an odd shape. At this point my thoughts were only of the odd shape of the Christian religion; I did not allege any odd shape in the rationalistic mind.

Here is another case of the same kind. I felt that a strong case against Christianity lay in the charge that there is something timid, monkish, and unmanly about all that is called 'Christian', especially in its attitude towards resistance and fighting. The great sceptics of the nineteenth century were largely virile. Bradlaugh in an expansive way, Huxley, in a reticent way, were decidedly men. In comparison, it did seem tenable that there was something weak and over patient about Christian counsels. The Gospel paradox about the other cheek, the fact that priests never fought, a hundred things made plausible the accusation that Christianity was an attempt to make a man too like a sheep. I read it and believed it, and if I had read nothing different, I should have gone on believing it. But I read something very different. I turned the next page in my agnostic manual, and my brain turned upside down. Now I found that I was to hate Christianity not for fighting too little, but for fighting too much. Christianity, it seemed, was the mother of wars. Christianity had deluged the world with blood. I had got thoroughly angry with the Christian, because he never was angry. And now I was told to be angry with him because his anger had been the most huge and horrible thing in human history; because his anger had soaked the earth and smoked to the sun. The very people who reproached Christianity with the meekness and non-resistance of the monasteries were the very people who reproached it also with the violence and valour of the Crusades. It was the fault of poor old Christianity (somehow or other) both that Edward the Confessor did not fight and that Richard Coeur de Leon did. The Quakers (we were told) were the only characteristic Christians; and yet the massacres of Cromwell ... were characteristic Christian crimes. What could it all mean? That was this Christianity which always forbade war and always produced wars? What could be the nature of the thing which one could abuse first because it would not fight, and second because it was always fighting? In what world of riddles was born this monstrous murder and this monstrous meekness? The shape of Christianity grew a queerer shape every instant.

I take a third case; the strangest of all, because it involves the one real objection to the faith. The one real objection to the Christian religion is simply that it is one religion. The world is a big place, full of very different kinds of people. Christianity (it may reasonably be said) is one thing confined to one kind of people; it began in Palestine, it has practically stopped with Europe. I was duly impressed with this argument in my youth, and I was much drawn towards the doctrine often preached in Ethical Societies – I mean the doctrine that there is one great unconscious church of all humanity founded on the omnipresence of the human conscience. Creeds, it was said, divided men; but at least morals united them. The soul might seek the strangest and most remote lands and ages and still find essential ethical common sense. It might find Confucius under Eastern trees, and he would be writing 'Thou shalt not steal'. It might decipher the darkest hieroglyphic on the most primeval desert, and the meaning when deciphered would be 'Little boys should tell the truth'. I believed this doctrine of the brotherhood of all men in the possession of a moral sense, and I believe it still – with other things. And I was thoroughly annoyed with Christianity for suggesting (as I supposed) that whole ages and empires of men had utterly escaped this light of justice and reason. But then I found an astonishing thing. I found that the very people who said that mankind was one church from Plato to Emerson were the very people who said that morality had changed altogether, and that what was right in one age was wrong in another. If I asked, say, for an altar, I was told that we needed none, for men our brothers gave us clear oracles and one creed in their universal customs and ideals. But if I mildly pointed out that one of men's universal customs was to have an altar, then my agnostic teachers turned clean round and told me that men had always been in darkness and the superstitions of savages. I found it was their daily taunt against Christianity that it was the light of one people and had left all others to die in the dark. But I also found that it was their special boast for themselves that science and progress were the discovery of one people, and that all other peoples had died in the dark. Their chief insult to Christianity was actually their chief compliment to themselves, and there seemed to be a strange unfairness about all their relative insistence on the two things. When considering some pagan or agnostic, we were to remember that all men had one religion; when considering some mystic or spiritualist, we were only to consider what absurd religions some men had. We could trust the ethics of Epictetus, because ethics had never changed. We must not trust the ethics of Bossuet, because ethics had changed. They changed in two hundred years, but not in two thousand.

This began to be alarming. It looked not so much as if Christianity was bad enough to include any vices, but rather as if any stick was good enough to beat Christianity with. What again could this astonishing thing be like which people were so anxious to contradict, that in doing so they did not mind contradicting themselves? I saw the same thing on every side. I can give no further space to this discussion of it in detail; but lest any one supposes that I have unfairly selected three accidental cases I will run briefly through a few others. Thus, certain sceptics wrote that the great crime of Christianity had been its attack on the family; it had dragged women to the loneliness and contemplation of the cloister, away from their homes and their children. But, then, other sceptics (slightly more advanced) said that the great crime of Christianity was forcing the family and marriage upon us; that it doomed women to the drudgery of their homes and children, and forbade them loneliness and contemplation. The charge was actually reversed. Or, again, certain phrases in the Epistles or the marriage service, were said by the anti-Christians to show contempt for woman's intellect. But I found that the anti-Christians themselves had a contempt for woman's intellect; for it was their great sneer at the Church on the Continent that 'only women' went to it. Or again, Christianity was reproached with its naked and hungry habits; with its sackcloth and dried peas. But the next minute

Christianity was being reproached with its pomp and its ritualism; its shrines of porphyry and its robes of gold. It was abused for being too plain and for being too coloured. Again Christianity had always been accused of restraining sexuality too much, when Bradlaugh the Malthusian discovered that it restrained it too little. It is often accused in the same breath of prim respectability and of religious extravagance. Between the covers of the same atheistic pamphlet I have found the faith rebuked for its disunion, 'One thinks one thing, and one another', and rebuked also for its union, 'It is difference of opinion that prevents the world from going to the dogs.' In the same conversation a freethinker, a friend of mine, blamed Christianity for despising Jews, and then despised it himself for being Jewish.

I wished to be quite fair then, and I wish to be quite fair now; and I did not conclude that the attack on Christianity was all wrong. I only concluded that if Christianity was wrong, it was very wrong indeed. Such hostile horrors might be combined in one thing, but that thing must be very strange and solitary. There are men who are misers, and also spendthrifts; but they are rare. There are men sensual and also ascetic; but they are rare. But if this mass of mad contradictions really existed, quakerish and bloodthirsty, too gorgeous and too thread-bare, austere, yet pandering preposterously to the lust of the eye, the enemy of women and their foolish refuge, a solemn pessimist and a silly optimist, if this evil existed then there was in this evil something quite supreme and unique. For I found in my rationalist teachers no explanation of such exceptional corruption. Christianity (theoretically speaking) was in their eyes only one of the ordinary myths and errors of mortals. *They* gave me no key to this twisted and unnatural badness. Such a paradox of evil rose to the stature of the supernatural. It was, indeed, almost as supernatural as the infallibility of the Pope. An historic institution, which never went right, is really quite as much of a miracle as an institution that cannot go wrong. The only explanation which immediately occurred to my mind was that Christianity did not come from heaven, but from hell. Really, if Jesus of Nazareth was not Christ, He must have been Antichrist.

And then in a quiet hour a strange thought struck me like a still thunderbolt. There had suddenly come into my mind another explanation. Suppose we heard an unknown man spoken of by many men. Suppose we were puzzled to hear that some men said he was too tall and some too short; some objected to his fatness, some lamented his leanness; some thought him too dark, and some too fair. One explanation (as has been already admitted) would be that he might be an odd shape. But there is another explanation. He might be the right shape. Outrageously tall men might feel him to be short. Very short men might feel him to be tall. Old bucks who are growing stout might consider him insufficiently filled out; old beaux who were growing thin might feel that he expanded beyond the narrow lines of elegance. Perhaps Swedes (who have pale hair like tow) called him a dark man, while negroes considered him distinctly blonde. Perhaps (in short) this extraordinary thing is really the ordinary thing; at least the normal thing, the centre. Perhaps, after all, it is Christianity that is sane and all its critics that are mad – in various ways. I tested this idea by asking myself whether there was about any of the accusers anything morbid that might explain the accusation. I was startled to find that this key fitted a lock. For instance, it was certainly odd that the modern world charged Christianity at once with bodily austerity and with artistic pomp. But then it was also odd, very odd, that the modern world itself combined extreme bodily luxury with an extreme absence of artistic pomp. The modern man thought Becket's robes too rich and his meals too poor. But then the modern man was really exceptional in history; no man before ever ate such elaborate dinners in such ugly clothes. The modern man found the church too simple exactly where modern life is too complex; he found the church too gorgeous exactly where modern life is too dingy. The man who disliked the plain fasts and feasts was mad on *entrées*. The man who disliked vestments wore a pair of preposterous trousers. And surely if there was any insanity involved in the matter at all it was in the trousers, not in the simply falling robe. If there was any insanity at all, it was in the extravagant *entrées*, not in the bread and wine.

I went over all the cases, and I found the key fitted so far. The fact that Swinburne was irritated at the unhappiness of Christians and yet more irritated at their happiness was easily explained. It was no longer a complication of diseases in Christianity, but a complication of diseases in Swinburne. The restraints of Christians saddened him simply because he was more hedonist than a

healthy man should be. The faith of Christians angered him
because he was more pessimist than a healthy man should be. In
the same way the Malthusians by instinct attacked Christianity;
not because there is anything especially anti-Malthusian about
Christianity, but because there is something a little anti-human
about Malthusianism.

Nevertheless it could not, I felt, be quite true that Christianity
was merely sensible and stood in the middle. There was really an
element in it of emphasis and even frenzy which had justified the
secularists in their superficial criticism. It might be wise, I began
more and more to think that it was wise, but it was not merely
worldly wise; it was not merely temperate and respectable. Its fierce
crusaders and meek saints might balance each other; still, the crusaders were very fierce and the saints were very meek, meek beyond
all decency. Now, it was just at this point of the speculation that
I remembered my thoughts about the martyr and the suicide. In
that matter there had been this combination between two almost
insane positions which yet somehow amounted to sanity. This was
just such another contradiction; and this I had already found to be
true. This was exactly one of the paradoxes in which sceptics found
the creed wrong; and in this I had found it right. Madly as Christians might love the martyr or hate the suicide, they never felt these
passions more madly than I had felt them long before I dreamed
of Christianity. Then the most difficult and interesting part of the
mental process opened, and I began to trace this idea darkly
through all the enormous thoughts of our theology. The idea was
that which I had outlined touching the optimist and the pessimist; that we want not an amalgam or compromise, but both things
at the top of their energy; love and wrath both burning. Here I shall
only trace it in relation to ethics. But I need not remind the reader
that the idea of this combination is indeed central in orthodox
theology. For orthodox theology has specially insisted that Christ
was not a being apart from God and man, like an elf, nor yet a
being half human and half not, like a centaur, but both things at
once and both things thoroughly, very man and very God. Now let
me trace this notion as I found it.

All sane men can see that sanity is some kind of equilibrium;
that one may be mad and eat too much, or mad and eat too
little. Some moderns have indeed appeared with vague versions of

progress and evolution which seeks to destroy the μέσον or balance of Aristotle. They seem to suggest that we are meant to starve progressively, or to go on eating larger and larger breakfasts every morning for ever. But the great truism of the μέσον remains for all thinking men, and these people have not upset any balance except their own. But granted that we have all to keep a balance, the real interest comes in with the question of how that balance can be kept. That was the problem which Paganism tried to solve: that was the problem which I think Christianity solved and solved in a very strange way.

Paganism declared that virtue was in a balance; Christianity declared it was in a conflict: the collision of two passions apparently opposite. Of course they were not really inconsistent; but they were such that it was hard to hold simultaneously. Let us follow for a moment the clue of the martyr and the suicide; and take the case of courage. No quality has ever so much addled the brains and tangled the definitions of merely rational sages. Courage is almost a contradiction in terms. It means a strong desire to live taking the form of a readiness to die. 'He that will lose his life, the same shall save it', is not a piece of mysticism for saints and heroes. It is a piece of everyday advice for sailors or mountaineers. It might be printed in an Alpine guide or a drill book. This paradox is the whole principle of courage, even of quite earthly or quite brutal courage. A man cut off by the sea may save his life if he will risk it on the precipice. He can only get away from death by continually stepping within an inch of it. A soldier surrounded by enemies, if he is to cut his way out, needs to combine a strong desire for living with a strange carelessness about dying. He must not merely cling to life, for then he will be a coward, and will not escape. He must not merely wait for death, for then he will be a suicide, and will not escape. He must seek his life in a spirit of furious indifference to it; he must desire life like water and yet drink death like wine. No philosopher, I fancy, has ever expressed this romantic riddle with adequate lucidity, and I certainly have not done so. But Christianity has done more: it has marked the limits of it in the awful graves of the suicide and the hero, showing the distance between him who dies for the sake of living and him who dies for the sake of dying. And it has held up ever since above the European lances the banner of the mystery of chivalry: the Christian courage, which is a disdain of death; not the Chinese courage, which is a disdain of life.

And now I began to find that this duplex passion was the Christian key to ethics everywhere. Everywhere the creed made a moderation out of the still crash of two impetuous emotions. Take, for instance, the matter of modesty, of the balance between mere pride and mere prostration. The average pagan, like the average agnostic, would merely say that he was content with himself, but not insolently self-satisfied, that there were many better and many worse, that his deserts were limited, but he would see that he got them. In short, he would walk with his head in the air; but not necessarily with his nose in the air. This is a manly and rational position, but it is open to the objection we noted against the com-promise between optimism and pessimism – the 'resignation' of Matthew Arnold. Being a mixture of two things, it is a dilution of two things; neither is present in its full strength or contributes its full colour. This proper pride does not lift the heart like the tongue of trumpets; you cannot go clad in crimson and gold for this. On the other hand, this mild rationalist modesty does not cleanse the soul with fire and make it clear like crystal; it does not (like a strict and searching humility) make a man as a little child, who can sit at the feet of the grass. It does not make him look up and see mar-vels; for Alice must grow small if she is to be Alice in Wonderland. Thus it loses both the poetry of being proud and the poetry of being humble. Christianity sought by this same strange expedient to save both of them.

It separated the two ideas and then exaggerated them both. In one way Man was to be haughtier than he had ever been before; in another way he was to be humbler than he had ever been before. In so far as I am Man I am the chief of creatures. In so far as I am *a* man I am the chief of sinners. All humility that had meant pessimism, that had meant man taking a vague or mean view of his whole destiny – all that was to go. We were to hear no more the wail of Ecclesiastes that humanity had no pre-eminence over the brute, or the awful cry of Homer that man was only the saddest of all the beasts of the field. Man was a statue of God walk-ing about the garden. Man had pre-eminence over all the brutes; man was only sad because he was not a beast, but a broken god. The Greek had spoken of men creeping on the earth, as if clinging to it. Now Man was to tread on the earth as if to subdue it. Christianity thus held a thought of the dignity of man that could only be expressed in crowns rayed like the sun and fans of peacock plumage. Yet at the same time it could hold a thought about the abject smallness of man that could only be expressed in fasting and fantastic submission, in the grey ashes of St Dominic and the white snows of St Bernard. When one came to think of *one's self*, there was vista and void enough for any amount of bleak abnegation and bitter truth. There the realistic gentleman could let himself go – as long as he let himself go at himself. There was an open playground for the happy pessimist. Let him say anything against himself short of blaspheming the original aim of his being; let him call himself a fool and even a damned fool (though that is Calvinistic); but he must not say that fools are not worth saving. He must not say that a man, *quâ* man, can be valueless. Here, again in short, Christianity got over the difficulty of combining furious opposites, by keeping them both, and keeping them both furious. The Church was positive on both points. One can hardly think too little of one's self. One can hardly think too much of one's soul.

Take another case: the complicated question of charity, which some highly uncharitable idealists seem to think quite easy. Charity is a paradox, like modesty and courage. Stated baldly, charity certainly means one of two things – pardoning unpardonable acts, or loving unlovable people. But if we ask ourselves (as we did in the case of pride) what a sensible pagan would feel about such a subject, we shall probably be beginning at the bottom of it. A sensible pagan would say that there were some people one could forgive, and some one couldn't: a slave who stole wine could be laughed at; a slave who betrayed his benefactor could be killed, and cursed even after he was killed. In so far as the act was pardonable, the man was pardonable. That again is rational, and even refreshing; but it is a dilution. It leaves no place for a pure horror of injustice, such as that which is a great beauty in the innocent. And it leaves no place for a mere tenderness for men as men, such as is the whole fascination of the charitable. Christianity came in here as before. It came in startlingly with a sword, and clove one thing from another. It divided the crime from the criminal. The criminal we must forgive unto seventy times seven. The crime we must not forgive at all. It was not enough that slaves who stole wine inspired partly anger and partly kindness. We must be much more angry with theft than before, and yet much kinder to thieves than before. There was room for wrath and love to run wild. And the more I considered Christianity, the more I found that while it had established a rule and order, the chief aim of that order was to give room for good things to run wild.

Mental and emotional liberty are not so simple as they look. Really they require almost as careful a balance of laws and conditions as do social and political liberty. The ordinary aesthetic anarchist who sets out to feel everything freely gets knotted at last in a paradox that prevents him feeling at all. He breaks away from home limits to follow poetry. But in ceasing to feel home limits he has ceased to feel the *Odyssey*. He is free from national prejudices and outside patriotism. But being outside patriotism he is outside *Henry V.* Such a literary man is simply outside all literature: he is more of a prisoner than any bigot. For if there is a wall between you and the world, it makes little difference whether you describe yourself as locked in or as locked out. What we want is not the universality that is outside all normal sentiments; we want the universality that is inside all normal sentiments. It is all the difference between being free from them, as a man is free from a prison, and being free of them as a man is free of a city. I am free from Windsor Castle (that is, I am not forcibly detained there), but I am by no means free of that building. How can man be approximately free of fine emotions, able to swing them in a clear space without breakage or wrong? *This* was the achievement of this Christian paradox of the parallel passions. Granted the primary dogma of the war between divine and diabolic, the revolt and ruin of the world, their optimism and pessimism, as pure poetry, could be loosened like cataracts.

St Francis, in praising all good, could be a more shouting optimist than Walt Whitman. St Jerome, in denouncing all evil, could paint the world blacker than Schopenhauer. Both passions were free because both were kept in their place. The optimist could pour out all the praise he liked on the gay music of the march, the golden trumpets, and the purple banners going into battle. But he must not call the fight needless. The pessimist might draw as darkly as he chose the sickening marches or the sanguine wounds. But he must not call the fight hopeless. So it was with all the other moral problems, with pride, with protest, and with compassion. By defining its main doctrine, the Church not only kept seemingly inconsistent things side by side, but, what was more, allowed them to break out in a sort of artistic violence otherwise possible only to anarchists. Meekness grew more dramatic than madness. Historic Christianity rose into a high and strange *coup de théâtre* of morality – things that are to virtue what the crimes of Nero are to vice. The spirits of indignation and of charity took terrible and attractive forms, ranging from that monkish fierceness that scourged like a dog the first and greatest of the Plantagenets,[1] to the sublime pity of St Catherine,[2] who, in the official shambles,[3] kissed the bloody head of the criminal. Poetry could be acted as well as composed. This heroic and monumental manner in ethics has entirely vanished with supernatural religion. They, being humble, could parade themselves: but we are too proud to be prominent. Our ethical teachers write reasonably for prison reform; but we are not likely to see Mr Cadbury,[4] or any eminent philanthropist, go into Reading Gaol and embrace the strangled corpse before it is cast into the quicklime. Our ethical teachers write mildly against the power of millionaires; but we are not likely to see Mr Rockefeller, or any modern tyrant, publicly whipped in Westminster Abbey.

Thus, the double charges of the secularists, though throwing nothing but darkness and confusion on themselves, throw a real light on the faith. It *is* true that the historic Church has at once emphasized celibacy and emphasized the family; has at once (if one may put it so) been fiercely for having children and fiercely for not having children. It has kept them side by side like two strong colours, red and white, like the red and white upon the shield of St George. It has always had a healthy hatred of pink. It hates that combination of two colours which is the feeble expedient of the philosophers. It hates that evolution of black into white which is tantamount to a dirty grey. In fact, the whole theory of the Church on virginity might be symbolized in the statement that white is a

1 King Henry II (1154–89) did public penance after the murder, at which he had connived, of St Thomas à Becket, the Archbishop of Canterbury.
2 Catherine of Siena (1347–80) comforted Nicholas di Toldo in prison and accompanied him to the scaffold.
3 Slaughterhouse.
4 George Cadbury (1839–1922), cocoa manufacturer and philanthropist.

colour: not merely the absence of a colour. All that I am urging here can be expressed by saying that Christianity sought in most of these cases to keep two colours coexistent but pure. It is not a mixture like russet or purple; it is rather like a shot silk, for a shot silk is always at right angles, and is in the pattern of the cross.

So it is also, of course, with the contradictory charges of the anti-Christians about submission and slaughter. It *is* true that the Church told some men to fight and others not to fight; and it *is* true that those who fought were like thunderbolts and those who did not fight were like statues. All this simply means that the Church preferred to use its Supermen and to use its Tolstoyans. There must be *some* good in the life of battle, for so many good men have enjoyed being soldiers. There must be *some* good in the idea of non-resistance, for so many good men seem to enjoy being Quakers. All that the Church did (so far as that goes) was to prevent either of these good things from ousting the other. They existed side by side. The Tolstoyans, having all the scruples of monks, simply became monks. The Quakers became a club instead of becoming a sect. Monks said all that Tolstoy says; they poured out lucid lamentations about the cruelty of battles and the vanity of revenge. But the Tolstoyans are not quite right enough to run the whole world; and in the ages of faith they were not allowed to run it. The world did not lose . . . the banner of Joan the Maid. And sometimes this pure gentleness and this pure fierceness met and justified their juncture; the paradox of all the prophets was fulfilled, and, in the soul of St Louis, the lion lay down with the lamb. But remember that this text is too lightly interpreted. It is constantly assured, especially in our Tolstoyan tendencies, that when the lion lies down with the lamb the lion becomes lamb-like. But that is brutal annexation and imperialism on the part of the lamb. That is simply the lamb absorbing the lion instead of the lion eating the lamb. The real problem is – Can the lion lie down with the lamb and still retain his royal ferocity? *That* is the problem the Church attempted; *that* is the miracle she achieved.

This is what I have called guessing the hidden eccentricities of life. This is knowing that a man's heart is to the left and not in the middle. This is knowing not only that the earth is round, but knowing exactly where it is flat. Christian doctrine detected the oddities of life. It not only discovered the law, but it foresaw the exceptions.

Those underrate Christianity who say that it discovered mercy; any one might discover mercy. In fact every one did. But to discover a plan for being merciful and also severe — *that* was to anticipate a strange need of human nature. For no one wants to be forgiven for a big sin as if it were a little one. Any one might say that we should be neither quite miserable nor quite happy. But to find out how far one *may* be quite miserable without making it impossible to be quite happy — that was a discovery in psychology. Any one might say, 'Neither swagger nor grovel'; and it would have been a limit. But to say, 'Here you can swagger and there you can grovel' — that was an emancipation.

This was the big fact about Christian ethics; the discovery of the new balance. Paganism had been like a pillar of marble, upright because proportioned with symmetry. Christianity was like a huge and ragged and romantic rock, which, though it sways on its pedestal at a touch, yet, because its exaggerated excrescences exactly balance each other, is enthroned there for a thousand years. In a Gothic cathedral the columns were all different, but they were all necessary. Every support seemed an accidental and fantastic support; every buttress was a flying buttress. So in Christendom apparent accidents balanced. Becket wore a hair shirt under his gold and crimson, and there is much to be said for the combination; for Becket got the benefit of the hair shirt while the people in the street got the benefit of the crimson and gold. It is at least better than the manner of the modern millionaire, who has the black and the drab outwardly for others, and the gold next his heart. But the balance was not always in one man's body as in Becket's; the balance was often distributed over the whole body of Christendom. Because a man prayed and fasted on the Northern snows, flowers could be flung at his festival in the Southern cities; and because fanatics drank water on the sands of Syria, men could still drink cider in the orchards of England. This is what makes Christendom at once so much more perplexing and so much more interesting than the Pagan empire; just as Amiens Cathedral is not better but more interesting than the Parthenon. If any one wants a modern proof of all this, let him consider the curious fact that, under Christianity, Europe (while remaining a unity) has broken up into individual nations. Patriotism is a perfect example of this deliberate balancing of one emphasis against another emphasis. The instinct of the

Pagan empire would have said, 'You shall all be Roman citizens, and grow alike; let the German grow less slow and reverent; the Frenchman less experimental and swift.' But the instinct of Christian Europe says, 'Let the German remain slow and reverent, that the Frenchman may the more safely be swift and experimental. We will make an equipoise out of these excesses. The absurdity called Germany shall correct the insanity called France.'

Last and most important, it is exactly this which explains what is so inexplicable to all the modern critics of the history of Christianity. I mean the monstrous wars about small points of theology, the earthquakes of emotion about a gesture or a word. It was only a matter of an inch; but an inch is everything when you are balancing. The Church could not afford to swerve a hair's breadth on some things if she was to continue her great and daring experiment of the irregular equilibrium. Once let one idea become less powerful and some other idea would become too powerful. It was no flock of sheep the Christian shepherd was leading, but a herd of bulls and tigers, of terrible ideals and devouring doctrines, each one of them strong enough to turn to a false religion and lay waste the world. Remember that the Church went in specifically for dangerous ideas; she was a lion tamer. The idea of birth through a Holy Spirit, of the death of a divine being, of the forgiveness of sins, or the fulfilment of prophecies, are ideas which, any one can see, need but a touch to turn them into something blasphemous or ferocious. The smallest link was let drop by the artificers of the Mediterranean, and the lion of ancestral pessimism burst his chain in the forgotten forests of the north. Of these theological equalizations I have to speak afterwards. Here it is enough to notice that if some small mistake were made in doctrine, huge blunders might be made in human happiness. A sentence phrased wrong about the nature of symbolism would have broken all the best statues in Europe. A slip in the definitions might stop all the dances; might wither all the Christmas trees or break all the Easter eggs. Doctrines had to be defined within strict limits, even in order that man might enjoy general human liberties. The Church had to be careful, if only that the world might be careless.

This is the thrilling romance of Orthodoxy. People have fallen into a foolish habit of speaking of orthodoxy as something heavy, humdrum, and safe. There never was anything so perilous or so exciting as orthodoxy. It was sanity: and to be sane is more dramatic than to be mad. It was the equilibrium of a man behind madly rushing horses, seeming to stoop this way and to sway that, yet in every attitude having the grace of statuary and the accuracy of arithmetic. The Church in its early days went fierce and fast with any warhorse; yet it is utterly unhistoric to say that she merely went mad along one idea, like a vulgar fanaticism. She swerved to left and right, so exactly as to avoid enormous obstacles. She left on one hand the huge bulk of Arianism, buttressed by all the worldly powers to make Christianity too worldly. The next instant she was swerving to avoid an orientalism, which would have made it too unworldly. The orthodox Church never took the tame course or accepted the conventions; the orthodox Church was never respectable. It would have been easier to have accepted the earthly power of the Arians. It would have been easy, in the Calvinistic seventeenth century, to fall into the bottomless pit of predestination. It is easy to be a madman: it is easy to be a heretic. It is always easy to let the age have its head; the difficult thing is to keep one's own. It is always easy to be a modernist; as it is easy to be a snob. To have fallen into any of those open traps of error and exaggeration which fashion after fashion and sect after sect set along the historic path of Christendom – that would indeed have been simple. It is always simple to fall; there are an infinity of angles at which one falls, only one at which one stands. To have fallen into any one of the fads from Gnosticism to Christian Science would indeed have been obvious and tame. But to have avoided them all has been one whirling adventure; and in my vision the heavenly chariot flies thundering through the ages, the dull heresies sprawling and prostrate, the wild truth reeling but erect.

VII
THE ETERNAL REVOLUTION

THE FOLLOWING propositions have been urged: First, that some faith in our life is required even to improve it; second, that some dissatisfaction with things as they are is necessary even in order to be satisfied; third, that to have this necessary content and necessary discontent it is not sufficient to have the obvious equilibrium of the Stoic. For mere resignation has neither the gigantic levity of pleasure nor the superb intolerance of pain. There is a vital objection to the advice merely to grin and bear it. The objection is that if you merely bear it, you do not grin. Greek heroes do not grin: but gargoyles do – because they are Christian. And when a Christian is pleased, he is (in the most exact sense) fright-fully pleased; his pleasure is frightful. Christ prophesied the whole of Gothic architecture in that hour when nervous and respectable people (such people as now object to barrel organs) objected to the shouting of the gutter-snipes of Jerusalem. He said, 'If these were silent, the very stones would cry out.' Under the impulse of His spirit arose like a clamorous chorus the façades of the mediaeval cathedrals, thronged with shouting faces and open mouths. The prophecy has fulfilled itself: the very stones cry out.

If these things be conceded, though only for argument, we may take up where we left it the thread of the thought of the natural man, called by the Scotch (with regrettable familiarity), 'The Old Man'. We can ask the next question so obviously in front of us. Some satisfaction is needed even to make things better. But what do we mean by making things better? Most modern talk on this matter is a mere argument in a circle – that circle which we have already made the symbol of madness and of mere rationalism. Evolution is only good if it produces good; good is only good if it helps evolution. The elephant stands on the tortoise, and the tor-toise on the elephant.

Obviously, it will not do to take our ideal from the principle in nature; for the simple reason that (except for some human or divine theory), there is no principle in nature. For instance, the cheap anti-democrat of today will tell you solemnly that there is no equality in nature. He is right, but he does not see the logical addendum. There is no equality in nature; also there is no inequality in nature. Inequality, as much as equality, implies a standard of value. To read aristocracy into the anarchy of animals is just as sentimental as to read democracy into it. Both aristocracy and democracy are human ideals: the one saying that all men are valuable, the other that some men are more valuable. But nature does not say that cats are more valuable than mice; nature makes no remark on the subject. She does not even say that the cat is enviable or the mouse pitiable. We think the cat superior because we have (or most of us have) a particular philosophy to the effect that life is better than death. But if the mouse were a German pessimist mouse, he might not think that the cat had beaten him at all. He might think he had beaten the cat by getting to the grave first. Or he might feel that he had actually inflicted frightful punishment on the cat by keeping him alive. Just as a microbe might feel proud of spreading a pestilence, so the pessimistic mouse might exult to think that he was renewing in the cat the torture of conscious existence. It all depends on the philosophy of the mouse. You cannot even say that there is victory or superiority in nature unless you have some doctrine about what things are superior. You cannot even say that the cat scores unless there is a system of scoring. You cannot even say that the cat gets the best of it unless there is some best to be got.

We cannot, then, get the ideal itself from nature, and as we follow here the first and natural speculation, we will leave out (for the present) the idea of getting it from God. We must have our own vision. But the attempts of most moderns to express it are highly vague.

Some fall back simply on the clock: they talk as if mere passage through time brought some superiority; so that even a man of the first mental calibre carelessly uses the phrase that human morality is never up to date. How can anything be up to date? – a date has no character. How can one say that Christmas celebrations are not suitable to the twenty-fifth of a month? What the writer meant, of course, was that the majority is behind his favourite minority – or in front of it. Other vague modern people take refuge in material metaphors; in fact, this is the chief mark of vague modern people.

Not daring to define their doctrine of what is good, they use physical figures of speech without stint or shame, and, what is worst of all, seem to think these cheap analogies are exquisitely spiritual and superior to the old morality. Thus they think it intellectual to talk about things being 'high'. It is at least the reverse of intellectual; it is a mere phrase from a steeple or a weathercock. 'Tommy was a good boy' is a pure philosophical statement, worthy of Plato or Aquinas. 'Tommy lived the higher life' is a gross metaphor from a ten-foot rule.

This, incidentally, is almost the whole weakness of Nietzsche, whom some are representing as a bold and strong thinker. No one will deny that he was a poetical and suggestive thinker; but he was quite the reverse of strong. He was not at all bold. He never put his own meaning before himself in bald abstract words: as did Aristotle and Calvin, and even Karl Marx, the hard, fearless men of thought. Nietzsche always escaped a question by a physical metaphor, like a cheery minor poet. He said, 'beyond good and evil', because he had not the courage to say, 'more good than good and evil', or, 'more evil than good and evil'. Had he faced his thought without metaphors, he would have seen that it was nonsense. So, when he describes his hero, he does not dare to say, 'the purer man', or 'the happier man', or 'the sadder man', for all these are ideas; and ideas are alarming. He says 'the upper man', or 'over man', a physical metaphor from acrobats or alpine climbers. Nietzsche is truly a very timid thinker. He does not really know in the least what sort of man he wants evolution to produce. And if he does not know, certainly the ordinary evolutionists, who talk about things being 'higher', do not know either.

Then again, some people fall back on sheer submission and sitting still. Nature is going to do something some day; nobody knows what, and nobody knows when. We have no reason for acting, and no reason for not acting. If anything happens it is right: if anything is prevented it was wrong. Again, some people try to anticipate nature by doing something, by doing anything. Because we may possibly grow wings they cut off their legs. Yet nature may be trying to make them centipedes for all they know.

Lastly, there is a fourth class of people who take whatever it is that they happen to want, and say that that is the ultimate aim of evolution. And these are the only sensible people. This is the only really healthy way with the word evolution, to work for what you want, and to call *that* evolution. The only intelligible sense that progress or advance can have among men, is that we have a definite vision, and that we wish to make the whole world like that vision. If you like to put it so, the essence of the doctrine is that what we have around us is the mere method and preparation for something that we have to create. This is not a world, but rather the material for a world. God has given us not so much the colours of a picture as the colours of a palette. But he has also given us a subject, a model, a fixed vision. We must be clear about what we want to paint. This adds a further principle to our previous list of principles. We have said we must be fond of this world, even in order to change it. We now add that we must be fond of another world (real or imaginary) in order to have something to change it to.

We need not debate about the mere words evolution or progress: personally I prefer to call it reform. For reform implies form. It implies that we are trying to shape the world in a particular image; to make it something that we see already in our minds. Evolution is a metaphor from mere automatic unrolling. Progress is a metaphor from merely walking along a road – very likely the wrong road. But reform is a metaphor for reasonable and determined men: it means that we see a certain thing out of shape and we mean to put it into shape. And we know what shape.

Now here comes in the whole collapse and huge blunder of our age. We have mixed up two different things, two opposite things. Progress should mean that we are always changing the world to suit the vision. Progress does mean (just now) that we are always changing the vision. It should mean that we are slow but sure in bringing justice and mercy among men: it does mean that we are very swift in doubting the desirability of justice and mercy: a wild page from any Prussian sophist makes men doubt it. Progress should mean that we are always walking towards the New Jerusalem. It does mean that the New Jerusalem is always walking away from us. We are not altering the real to suit the ideal. We are altering the ideal: it is easier.

Silly examples are always simpler; let us suppose a man wanted a particular kind of world; say, a blue world. He would have no cause to complain of the slightness or swiftness of his task; he might toil for a long time at the transformation; he could work away (in every sense) until all was blue. He could have heroic adventures; the putting of the last touches to a blue tiger. He could have fairy dreams; the dawn of a blue moon. But if he worked hard, that high-minded reformer would certainly (from his own point of view) leave the world better and bluer than he found it. If he altered a blade of grass to his favourite colour every day, he would get on slowly. But if he altered his favourite colour every day, he would not get on at all. If, after reading a fresh philosopher, he started to paint everything red or yellow, his work would be thrown away: there would be nothing to show except a few blue tigers walking about, specimens of his early bad manner. This is exactly the position of the average modern thinker. It will be said that this is avowedly a preposterous example. But it is literally the fact of recent history. The great and grave changes in our political civilization all belonged to the early nineteenth century, not to the later. They belonged to the black and white epoch when men believed fixedly in Toryism, in Protestantism, in Calvinism, in Reform, and not unfrequently in Revolution. And whatever each man believed in he hammered at steadily, without scepticism: and there was a time when the Established Church might have fallen, and the House of Lords nearly fell. It was because Radicals were wise enough to be constant and consistent; it was because Radicals were wise enough to be Conservative. But in the existing atmosphere there is not enough time and tradition in Radicalism to pull anything down. There is a great deal of truth in Lord Hugh Cecil's[1] suggestion (made in a fine speech) that the era of change is over, and that ours is an era of conservation and repose. But probably it would pain Lord Hugh Cecil if he realized (what is certainly the case) that ours is only an age of conservation because it is an age of complete unbelief. Let beliefs fade fast and frequently, if you wish institutions to remain the same. The more the life of the mind is unhinged, the more the machinery of matter will be left to itself. The net result of all our political suggestions, Collectivism, Tolstoyanism, NeoFeudalism, Communism, Anarchy, Scientific Bureaucracy – the plain fruit of all of them is that the Monarchy and the House of Lords will remain. The net result of all the new religions will be that the Church of England will not

1 Lord Hugh Cecil (1869–1956), Conservative politician.

(for heaven knows how long) be disestablished. It was Karl Marx, Nietzsche, Tolstoy, Cunninghame Graham,[1] Bernard Shaw and Auberon Herbert,[2] who between them, with bowed gigantic backs, bore up the throne of the Archbishop of Canterbury.

We may say broadly that free thought is the best of all the safeguards against freedom. Managed in a modern style the emancipation of the slave's mind is the best way of preventing the emancipation of the slave. Teach him to worry about whether he wants to be free, and he will not free himself. Again, it may be said that this instance is remote or extreme. But, again, it is exactly true of the men in the streets around us. It is true that the negro slave, being a debased barbarian, will probably have either a human affection of loyalty, or a human affection for liberty. But the man we see every day – the worker in Mr Gradgrind's[3] factory, the little clerk in Mr Gradgrind's office – he is too mentally worried to believe in freedom. He is kept quiet with revolutionary literature. He is calmed and kept in his place by a constant succession of wild philosophies. He is a Marxian one day, a Nietzscheite the next day, a Superman (probably) the next day; and a slave every day. The only thing that remains after all the philosophies is the factory. The only man who gains by all the philosophies is Gradgrind. It would be worth his while to keep his commercial helotry supplied with sceptical literature. And now I come to think of it, of course, Gradgrind is famous for giving libraries. He shows his sense. All modern books are on his side. As long as the vision of heaven is always changing, the vision of earth will be exactly the same. No ideal will remain long enough to be realized, or even partly realized. The modern young man will never change his environment; for he will always change his mind.

This, therefore, is our first requirement about the ideal towards

1 R. B. Cunninghame Graham (1852–1936), traveller, writer, anti-imperialist and social reformer.
2 Auberon Herbert (1838–1906), libertarian philosopher, about whom Chesterton wrote: 'Herbert Spencer really went as far as he could in the direction of individualism, just as Karl Marx went as far as he could in the direction of Socialism. He left only the gallant and eccentric Auberon Herbert to go one step further; and practically propose that we should abolish the police; and merely insure ourselves against fire and accident' (*Illustrated London News*, 15 February 1936).
3 Thomas Gradgrind, a character in Dickens's *Hard Times* who insists on hard facts and nothing but hard facts.

which progress is directed; it must be fixed. Whistler used to make many rapid studies of a sitter; it did not matter if he tore up twenty portraits. But it would matter if he looked up twenty times, and each time saw a new person sitting placidly for his portrait. So it does not matter (comparatively speaking) how often humanity fails to imitate its ideal; for then all its old failures are fruitful. But it does frightfully matter how often humanity changes its ideal; for then all its old failures are fruitless. The question therefore becomes this: How can we keep the artist discontented with his pictures while preventing him from being vitally discontented with his art? How can we make a man always dissatisfied with his work, yet always satisfied with working? How can we make sure that the portrait painter will throw the portrait out of window instead of taking the natural and more human course of throwing the sitter out of window?

A strict rule is not only necessary for ruling; it is also necessary for rebelling. This fixed and familiar ideal is necessary to any sort of revolution. Man will sometimes act slowly upon new ideas; but he will only act swiftly upon old ideas. If I am merely to float or fade or evolve, it may be towards something anarchic; but if I am to riot, it must be for something respectable. This is the whole weakness of certain schools of progress and moral evolution. They suggest that there has been a slow movement towards morality, with an imperceptible ethical change in every year or at every instant. There is only one great disadvantage in this theory. It talks of a slow movement towards justice; but it does not permit a swift movement. A man is not allowed to leap up and declare a certain state of things to be intrinsically intolerable. To make the matter clear, it is better to take a specific example. Certain of the idealistic vegetarians, such as Mr Salt, say that the time has now come for eating no meat; by implication they assume that at one time it was right to eat meat, and they suggest (in words that could be quoted) that some day it may be wrong to eat milk and eggs. I do not discuss here the question of what is justice to animals. I only say that whatever is justice ought, under given conditions, to be prompt justice. If an animal is wronged, we ought to be able to rush to his rescue. But how can we rush if we are, perhaps, in advance of our time? How can we rush to catch a train which may not arrive for a few centuries? How can I denounce a man for skinning cats, if he is only now what I may possibly become in drinking a glass of milk? A splendid and insane Russian sect ran about taking all the cattle out of all the carts. How can I pluck up courage to take the horse out of my hansom-cab, when I do not know whether my evolution-ary watch is only a little fast or the cabman's a little slow? Suppose I say to a sweater, 'Slavery suited one stage of evolution.' And sup-pose he answers, 'And sweating suits this stage of evolution.' How can I answer if there is no eternal test? If sweaters can be behind the current morality, why should not philanthropists be in front of it? What on earth is the current morality, except in its literal sense – the morality that is always running away?

Thus we may say that a permanent ideal is as necessary to the innovator as to the conservative; it is necessary whether we wish the king's orders to be promptly executed or whether we only wish the king to be promptly executed. The guillotine has many sins, but to do it justice there is nothing evolutionary about it. The favourite evolutionary argument finds its best answer in the axe. The Evolutionist says, 'Where do you draw the line?' the Revolu-tionist answers, 'I draw it *here*: exactly between your head and body.' There must at any given moment be an abstract right and wrong if any blow is to be struck; there must be something eternal if there is to be anything sudden. Therefore for all intelligible human purposes, for altering things or for keeping things as they are, for founding a system for ever, as in China, or for altering it every month as in the early French Revolution, it is equally necessary that the vision should be a fixed vision. This is our first requirement.

When I had written this down, I felt once again the presence of something else in the discussion: as a man hears a church bell above the sound of the street. Something seemed to be saying, 'My ideal at least is fixed; for it was fixed before the foundations of the world. My vision of perfection assuredly cannot be altered; for it is called Eden. You may alter the place to which you are going; but you cannot alter the place from which you have come. To the orthodox there must always be a case for revolution; for in the hearts of men God has been put under the feet of Satan. In the upper world hell once rebelled against heaven. But in this world heaven is rebelling against hell. For the orthodox there can always be a revolution; for a revolution is a restoration. At any instant you may strike a blow for the perfection which no man has seen since

Adam. No unchanging custom, no changing evolution can make the original good any thing but good. Man may have had concubines as long as cows have had horns: still they are not a part of him if they are sinful. Men may have been under oppression ever since fish were under water; still they ought not to be, if oppression is sinful. The chain may seem as natural to the slave, or the paint to the harlot, as does the plume to the bird or the burrow to the fox; still they are not, if they are sinful. I lift my prehistoric legend to defy all your history. Your vision is not merely a fixture: it is a fact.' I paused to note the new coincidence of Christianity: but I passed on.

I passed on to the next necessity of any ideal of progress. Some people (as we have said) seem to believe in an automatic and impersonal progress in the nature of things. But it is clear that no political activity can be encouraged by saying that progress is natural and inevitable; that is not a reason for being active, but rather a reason for being lazy. If we are bound to improve, we need not trouble to improve. The pure doctrine of progress is the best of all reasons for not being a progressive. But it is to none of these obvious comments that I wish primarily to call attention.

The only arresting point is this: that if we suppose improvement to be natural, it must be fairly simple. The world might conceivably be working towards one consummation, but hardly towards any particular arrangement of many qualities. To take our original simile: Nature by herself may be growing more blue; that is, a process so simple that it might be impersonal. But Nature cannot be making a careful picture made of many picked colours, unless Nature is personal. If the end of the world were mere darkness or mere light it might come as slowly and inevitably as dusk or dawn. But if the end of the world is to be a piece of elaborate and artistic chiaroscuro, then there must be design in it, either human or divine. The world, through mere time, might grow black like an old picture, or white like an old coat; but if it is turned into a particular piece of black and white art – then there is an artist.

If the distinction be not evident, I give an ordinary instance. We constantly hear a particularly cosmic creed from the modern humanitarians; I use the word humanitarian in the ordinary sense, as meaning one who upholds the claims of all creatures against those of humanity. They suggest that through the ages we have been growing more and more humane, that is to say, that one after another, groups or sections of beings, slaves, children, women, cows, or what not, have been gradually admitted to mercy or to justice. They say that we once thought it right to eat men (we didn't); but I am not here concerned with their history, which is highly unhistorical. As a fact, anthropophagy is certainly a decadent thing, not a primitive one. It is much more likely that modern men will eat human flesh out of affectation than that primitive man ever ate it out of ignorance. I am here only following the outlines of their argument, which consists in maintaining that man has been progressively more lenient, first to citizens, then to slaves, then to animals, and then (presumably) to plants. I think it wrong to sit on a man. Soon, I shall think it wrong to sit on a horse. Eventually (I suppose) I shall think it wrong to sit on a chair. That is the drive of the argument. And for this argument it can be said that it is possible to talk of it in terms of evolution or inevitable progress. A perpetual tendency to touch fewer and fewer things might – one feels, be a mere brute unconscious tendency, like that of a species to produce fewer and fewer children. This drift may be really evolutionary, because it is stupid.

Darwinism can be used to back up two mad moralities, but it cannot be used to back up a single sane one. The kinship and competition of all living creatures can be used as a reason for being insanely cruel or insanely sentimental; but not for a healthy love of animals. On the evolutionary basis you may be inhumane, or you may be absurdly humane; but you cannot be human. That you and a tiger are one may be a reason for being tender to a tiger. Or it may be a reason for being as cruel as the tiger. It is one way to train the tiger to imitate you, it is a shorter way to imitate the tiger. But in neither case does evolution tell you how to treat a tiger reasonably, that is, to admire his stripes while avoiding his claws.

If you want to treat a tiger reasonably, you must go back to the garden of Eden. For the obstinate reminder continued to recur: only the supernatural has taken a sane view of Nature. The essence of all pantheism, evolutionism, and modern cosmic religion is really in this proposition: that Nature is our mother. Unfortunately, if you regard Nature as a mother, you discover that she is a stepmother. The main point of Christianity was this: that Nature is not our mother: Nature is our sister. We can be proud of her beauty, since we have the same father; but she has no authority over us; we have to admire, but not to imitate. This gives to the typically Christian pleasure in this earth a strange touch of lightness that is almost frivolity. Nature was a solemn mother to the worshippers of Isis and Cybele. Nature was a solemn mother to Wordsworth or to Emerson. But Nature is not solemn to Francis of Assisi or to George Herbert. To St Francis, Nature is a sister, and even a younger sister: a little, dancing sister, to be laughed at as well as loved.

This, however, is hardly our main point at present; I have admitted it only in order to show how constantly, and as it were accidentally, the key would fit the smallest doors. Our main point is here, that if there be a mere trend of impersonal improvement in Nature, it must presumably be a simple trend towards some simple triumph. One can imagine that some automatic tendency in biology might work for giving us longer and longer noses. But the question is, do we want to have longer and longer noses? I fancy not; I believe that we most of us want to say to our noses, 'thus far, and no farther; and here shall thy proud point be stayed': we require a nose of such length as may ensure an interesting face. But we cannot imagine a mere biological trend towards producing interesting faces; because an interesting face is one particular arrangement of eyes, nose, and mouth, in a most complex relation to each other. Proportion cannot be a drift: it is either an accident or a design. So with the ideal of human morality and its relation to the humanitarians and the anti-humanitarians. It is conceivable that we are going more and more to keep our hands off things: not to drive horses; not to pick flowers. We may eventually be bound not to disturb a man's mind even by argument; not to disturb the sleep of birds even by coughing. The ultimate apotheosis would appear to be that of a man sitting quite still, nor daring to stir for fear of disturbing a fly, nor to eat for fear of incommoding a microbe. To so crude a consummation as that we might perhaps unconsciously drift. But do we want so crude a consummation? Similarly, we might unconsciously evolve along the opposite or Nietzschean line of development – superman crushing superman in one tower of tyrants until the universe is smashed up for fun. But do we want the universe smashed up for fun? Is it not quite clear that what we really hope for is one particular management and proposition of these two things; a certain amount of restraint and respect, a certain amount of energy and mastery? If our life is ever really as beautiful as a fairy-tale, we shall have to remember that all the beauty of a fairy-tale lies in this: that the prince has a wonder which just stops short of being fear. If he is afraid of the giant, there is an end of him; but also if he is not astonished at the giant, there is an end of the fairy-tale. The whole point depends upon his being at once humble enough to wonder, and haughty enough to defy. So our attitude to the giant of the world must not merely be increasing delicacy or increasing contempt: it must be one particular proportion of the two – which is exactly right. We must have in us enough reverence for all things outside us to make us tread fearfully on the grass. We must also have enough disdain for all things outside us, to make us, on due occasion, spit at the stars. Yet these two things (if we are to be good or happy) must be combined, not in any combination, but in one particular combination. The perfect happiness of men on the earth (if it ever comes) will not be a flat and solid thing, like the satisfaction of animals. It will be an exact and perilous balance; like that of a desperate romance. Man must have just enough faith in himself to have adventures, and just enough doubt of himself to enjoy them.

This, then, is our second requirement for the ideal of progress. First, it must be fixed; second, it must be composite. It must not (if it is to satisfy our souls) be the mere victory of some one thing swallowing up everything else, love or pride or peace or adventure; it must be a definite picture composed of these elements in their best proportion and relation. I am not concerned at this moment to deny that some such good culmination may be, by the constitution of things, reserved for the human race. I only point out that if this composite happiness is fixed for us it must be fixed by some mind; for only a mind can place the exact proportions of a composite happiness. If the beatification of the world is a mere work of nature, then it must be as simple as the freezing of the world, or the burning up of the world. But if the beatification of the world is not a work of nature but a work of art, then it involves an artist. And here again my contemplation was cloven by the ancient voice which said, 'I could have told you all this a long time ago. If there is any certain progress it can only be my kind of progress, the progress towards a complete city of virtues and dominations where righteousness and peace contrive to kiss each other. An impersonal force might be leading you to a wilderness of perfect flatness or a peak of perfect height. But only a personal God can possibly be leading you (if, indeed, you are being led) to a city with just streets and architectural proportions, a city in which each of you can contribute exactly the right amount of your own colour to the many coloured coat of Joseph.'

Twice again, therefore, Christianity had come in with the exact answer that I required. I had said, 'The ideal must be fixed,' and the Church had answered, 'Mine is literally fixed, for it existed before anything else.' I said secondly, 'It must be artistically combined, like a picture'; and the Church answered, 'Mine is quite literally a picture, for I know who painted it.' Then I went on to the third thing, which, as it seemed to me, was needed for an Utopia or goal of progress. And of all the three it is infinitely the hardest to express. Perhaps it might be put thus: that we need watchfulness even in Utopia, lest we fall from Utopia as we fell from Eden.

We have remarked that one reason offered for being a progressive is that things naturally tend to grow better. But the only real reason for being a progressive is that things naturally tend to grow worse. The corruption in things is not only the best argument for being progressive; it is also the only argument against being conservative. The conservative theory would really be quite sweeping and unanswerable if it were not for this one fact. But all conservatism is based upon the idea that if you leave things alone you leave them as they are. But you do not. If you leave a thing alone you leave it to a torrent of change. If you leave a white post alone it will soon be a black post. If you particularly want it to be white you must be always painting it again; that is, you must be always having a revolution. Briefly, if you want the old white post you must have a new white post. But this which is true even of inanimate things is in a quite special and terrible sense true of all human things. An almost unnatural vigilance is really required of the citizen because of the horrible rapidity with which human institutions grow old. It is the custom in passing romance and journalism to talk of men suffering under old tyrannies. But, as a fact, men have almost always suffered under new tyrannies; under tyrannies that had been public liberties hardly twenty years before. Thus England went mad with joy over the patriotic monarchy of Elizabeth; and then (almost immediately afterwards) went mad with rage in the trap of the tyranny of Charles the First. So, again, in France the monarchy became intolerable, not just after it had been tolerated, but just after it had been adored. The son of Louis the well-beloved was Louis the guillotined. So in the same way in England in the nineteenth century the Radical manufacturer was entirely trusted as a mere tribune of the people, until suddenly we heard the cry of the Socialist that he was a tyrant eating the people like bread. So again, we have almost up to the last instant trusted the newspapers as organs of public opinion. Just recently some of us have seen (not slowly, but with a start) that they are obviously nothing of the kind. They are, by the nature of the case, the hobbies of a few rich men. We have not any need to rebel against antiquity; we have to rebel against novelty. It is the new rulers, the capitalist or the editor, who really hold up the modern world. There is no fear that a modern king will attempt to override the constitution; it is more likely that he will ignore the constitution and work behind its back; he will take no advantage of his kingly power; it is more likely that he will take advantage of his kingly powerlessness, of the fact that he is free from criticism and publicity. For the king is the most private person of our time. It will not be necessary for any one to fight again against the proposal of a censorship of the press. We do not need a censorship of the press. We have a censorship by the press.

This startling swiftness with which popular systems turn oppressive is the third fact for which we shall ask our perfect theory of progress to allow. It must always be on the look out for every privilege being abused, for every working right becoming a wrong. In this matter I am entirely on the side of the revolutionists. They are really right to be always suspecting human institutions; they are right not to put their trust in princes nor in any child of man. The chieftain chosen to be the friend of the people becomes the enemy of the people; the newspaper started to tell the truth now exists to prevent the truth being told. Here, I say, I felt that I was really at last on the side of the revolutionary. And then I caught my breath again: for I remembered that I was once again on the side of the orthodox.

Christianity spoke again and said: 'I have always maintained that men were naturally backsliders; that human virtue tended of its own nature to rust or to rot; I have always said that human beings as such go wrong, especially happy human beings, especially proud and prosperous human beings. This eternal revolution, this suspicion sustained through centuries, you (being a vague modern) call the doctrine of progress. If you were a philosopher you would call it, as I do, the doctrine of original sin. You may call it the cosmic advance as much as you like; I call it what it is – the Fall.'

I have spoken of orthodoxy coming in like a sword; here I confess it came in like a battle-axe. For really (when I came to think of it) Christianity is the only thing left that has any real right to question the power of the well-nurtured or the well-bred. I have listened often enough to Socialists, or even to democrats, saying that the physical conditions of the poor must of necessity make them mentally and morally degraded. I have listened to scientific men (and there are still scientific men not opposed to democracy) saying that if we give the poor healthier conditions vice and wrong will disappear. I have listened to them with a horrible attention, with a hideous fascination. For it was like watching a man energetically sawing from the tree the branch he is sitting on. If these happy democrats could prove their case, they would strike democracy dead. If the poor are thus utterly demoralized, it may or may not be practical to raise them. But it is certainly quite practical to disfranchise them. If the man with a bad bedroom cannot give a good vote, then the first and swiftest deduction is that he shall give no vote. The governing class may not unreasonably say: 'It may take us some time to reform his bedroom. But if he is the brute you say, it will take him very little time to ruin our country. Therefore we will take your hint and not give him the chance.' It fills me with horrible amusement to observe the way in which the earnest Socialist industriously lays the foundation of all aristocracy, expatiating blandly upon the evident unfitness of the poor to rule. It is like listening to somebody at an evening party apologizing for entering without evening dress, and explaining that he had recently been intoxicated, had a personal habit of taking off his clothes in the street, and had, moreover, only just changed from prison uniform. At any moment, one feels, the host might say that really, if it was as bad as that, he need not come in at all. So it is when the ordinary Socialist, with a beaming face, proves that the poor, after their smashing experiences, cannot be really trustworthy. At any moment the rich may say, 'Very well, then, we won't trust them,' and bang the door in his face. On the basis of Mr Blatchford's view

of heredity and environment, the case for the aristocracy is quite
overwhelming. If clean homes and clean air make clean souls, why
not give the power (for the present at any rate) to those who
undoubtedly have the clean air? If better conditions will make the
poor more fit to govern themselves, why should not better conditions already make the rich more fit to govern them? On the
ordinary environment argument the matter is fairly manifest. The
comfortable class must be merely our vanguard in Utopia.

Is there any answer to the proposition that those who have had
the best opportunities will probably be our best guides? Is there
any answer to the argument that those who have breathed clean
air had better decide for those who have breathed foul? As far as
I know, there is only one answer, and that answer is Christianity.
Only the Christian Church can offer any rational objection to a
complete confidence in the rich. For she has maintained from the
beginning that the danger was not in man's environment, but in
man. Further, she has maintained that if we come to talk of a dangerous environment, the most dangerous environment of all is the
commodious environment. I know that the most modern manufacture has been really occupied in trying to produce an abnormally large needle. I know that the most recent biologists have been
chiefly anxious to discover a very small camel. But if we diminish
the camel to his smallest, or open the eye of the needle to its largest
– if, in short, we assume the words of Christ to have meant the very
least that they could mean, His words must at the very least mean
this – that rich men are not very likely to be morally trustworthy.
Christianity even when watered down is hot enough to boil all
modern society to rags. The mere minimum of the Church would
be a deadly ultimatum to the world. For the whole modern world is
absolutely based on the assumption, not that the rich are necessary
(which is tenable), but that the rich are trustworthy, which (for a
Christian) is not tenable. You will hear everlastingly, in all discussions about newspapers, companies, aristocracies, or party politics,
this argument that the rich man cannot be bribed. The fact is, of
course, that the rich man is bribed; he has been bribed already.
That is why he is a rich man. The whole case for Christianity
is that a man who is dependent upon the luxuries of this life is
a corrupt man, spiritually corrupt, politically corrupt, financially
corrupt. There is one thing that Christ and all the Christian saints

have said with a sort of savage monotony. They have said simply that to be rich is to be in peculiar danger of moral wreck. It is not demonstrably un-Christian to kill the rich as violators of definable justice. It is not demonstrably un-Christian to crown the rich as convenient rulers of society. It is not certainly un-Christian to rebel against the rich or to submit to the rich. But it is quite certainly un-Christian to trust the rich, to regard the rich as more morally safe than the poor. A Christian may consistently say, 'I respect that man's rank, although he takes bribes.' But a Christian cannot say, as all modern men are saying at lunch and breakfast, 'a man of that rank would not take bribes'. For it is a part of Christian dogma that any man in any rank may take bribes. It is a part of Christian dogma; it also happens by a curious coincidence that it is a part of obvious human history. When people say that a man 'in that position' would be incorruptible, there is no need to bring Christianity into the discussion. . . . In the best Utopia, I must be prepared for the moral fall of any man in any position at any moment; especially for my fall from my position at this moment.

Much vague and sentimental journalism has been poured out to the effect that Christianity is akin to democracy, and most of it is scarcely strong or clear enough to refute the fact that the two things have often quarrelled. The real ground upon which Christianity and democracy are one is very much deeper. The one specially and peculiarly un-Christian idea is the idea of Carlyle – the idea that the man should rule who feels that he can rule. Whatever else is Christian, this is heathen. If our faith comments on government at all, its comment must be this – that the man should rule who does *not* think that he can rule. Carlyle's hero may say, 'I will be king'; but the Christian saint must say 'Nolo episcopari.'[1] If the great paradox of Christianity means anything, it means this – that we must take the crown in our hands, and go hunting in dry places and dark corners of the earth until we find the one man who feels himself unfit to wear it. Carlyle was quite wrong; we have not got to crown the exceptional man who knows he can rule. Rather we must crown the much more exceptional man who knows he can't.

Now, this is one of the two or three vital defences of working democracy. The mere machinery of voting is not democracy,

1 I do not wish to be bishop.

though at present it is not easy to effect any simpler democratic method. But even the machinery of voting is profoundly Christian in this practical sense – that it is an attempt to get at the opinion of those who would be too modest to offer it. It is a mystical adventure; it is specially trusting those who do not trust themselves. That enigma is strictly peculiar to Christendom. There is nothing really humble about the abnegation of the Buddhist; the mild Hindoo is mild, but he is not meek. But there is something psychologically Christian about the idea of seeking for the opinion of the obscure rather than taking the obvious course of accepting the opinion of the prominent. To say that voting is particularly Christian may seem somewhat curious. To say that canvassing is Christian may seem quite crazy. But canvassing is very Christian in its primary idea. It is encouraging the humble; it is saying to the modest man, 'Friend, go up higher.' Or if there is some slight defect in canvassing, that is in its perfect and rounded piety, it is only because it may possibly neglect to encourage the modesty of the canvasser.

Aristocracy is not an institution: aristocracy is a sin; generally a very venial one. It is merely the drift or slide of men into a sort of natural pomposity and praise of the powerful, which is the most easy and obvious affair in the world.

It is one of the hundred answers to the fugitive perversion of modern 'force' that the promptest and boldest agencies are also the most fragile or full of sensibility. The swiftest things are the softest things. A bird is active, because a bird is soft. A stone is helpless, because a stone is hard. The stone must by its own nature go downwards, because hardness is weakness. The bird can of its nature go upwards, because fragility is force. In perfect force there is a kind of frivolity, an airiness that can maintain itself in the air. Modern investigators of miraculous history have solemnly admitted that a characteristic of the great saints is their power of 'levitation'. They might go further; a characteristic of the great saints is their power of levity. Angels can fly because they can take themselves lightly. This has been always the instinct of Christendom, and especially the instinct of Christian art. Remember how Fra Angelico represented all his angels, not only as birds, but almost as butterflies. Remember how the most earnest mediaeval art was full of light and fluttering draperies, of quick and capering feet. It was the one

thing that the modern Pre-Raphaelites could not imitate in the real
Pre-Raphaelites. Burne-Jones could never recover the deep levity
of the Middle Ages. In the old Christian pictures the sky over every
figure is like a blue or gold parachute. Every figure seems ready
to fly up and float about in the heavens. The tattered cloak of
the beggar will bear him up like the rayed plumes of the angels.
But the kings in their heavy gold and the proud in their robes of
purple will all of their nature sink downwards, for pride cannot rise
to levity or levitation. Pride is the downward drag of all things into
an easy solemnity. One 'settles down' into a sort of selfish seriousness; but one has to rise to a gay self-forgetfulness. A man 'falls'
into a brown study; he reaches up at a blue sky. Seriousness is not
a virtue. It would be a heresy, but a much more sensible heresy, to
say that seriousness is a vice. It is really a natural trend or lapse into
taking one's self gravely, because it is the easiest thing to do. It is
much easier to write a good *Times* leading article than a good joke
in *Punch*. For solemnity flows out of men naturally; but laughter is
a leap. It is easy to be heavy: hard to be light. Satan fell by the force
of gravity.

Now, it is the peculiar honour of Europe since it has been Christian that while it has had aristocracy it has always at the back of
its heart treated aristocracy as a weakness – generally as a weakness that must be allowed for. If any one wishes to appreciate this
point, let him go outside Christianity into some other philosophical
atmosphere. Let him, for instance, compare the classes of Europe
with the castes of India. There aristocracy is far more awful,
because it is far more intellectual. It is seriously felt that the scale
of classes is a scale of spiritual values; that the baker is better than
the butcher in an invisible and sacred sense. But no Christianity,
not even the most ignorant or perverse, ever suggested that a
baronet was better than a butcher in that sacred sense. No Christianity, however ignorant or extravagant, ever suggested that a
duke would not be damned. In pagan society there may have been
(I do not know) some such serious division between the free man
and the slave. But in Christian society we have always thought the
gentleman a sort of joke, though I admit that in some great crusades and councils he earned the right to be called a practical joke.
But we in Europe never really and at the root of our souls took

aristocracy seriously. It is only an occasional non-European alien
... who can even manage for a moment to take aristocracy seriously. It may be a mere patriotic bias, though I do not think so, but
it seems to me that the English aristocracy is not only the type,
but is the crown and flower of all actual aristocracies; it has all the
oligarchical virtues as well as all the defects. It is casual, it is kind,
it is courageous in obvious matters; but it has one great merit that
overlaps even these. The great and very obvious merit of the
English aristocracy is that nobody could possibly take it seriously.

In short, I had spelled out slowly, as usual, the need for an equal
law in Utopia; and, as usual, I found that Christianity had been
there before me. The whole history of my Utopia has the same
amusing sadness. I was always rushing out of my architectural study
with plans for a new turret only to find it sitting up there in the
sunlight, shining, and a thousand years old. For me, in the ancient
and partly in the modern sense, God answered the prayer, 'Prevent
us, O Lord, in all our doings.' Without vanity, I really think there
was a moment when I could have invented the marriage vow (as
an institution) out of my own head; but I discovered, with a sigh,
that it had been invented already. But, since it would be too long
a business to show how, fact by fact and inch by inch, my own
conception of Utopia was only answered in the New Jerusalem,
I will take this one case of the matter of marriage as indicating the
converging drift, I may say the converging crash of all the rest.

When the ordinary opponents of Socialism talk about impossibilities and alterations in human nature they always miss an important distinction. In modern ideal conceptions of society there are
some desires that are possibly not attainable: but there are some
desires that are not desirable. That all men should live in equally
beautiful houses is a dream that may or may not be attained. But
that all men should live in the same beautiful house is not a dream
at all; it is a nightmare. That a man should love all old women is
an ideal that may not be attainable. But that a man should regard
all old women exactly as he regards his mother is not only an un-
attainable ideal, but an ideal which ought not to be attained. I do
not know if the reader agrees with me in these examples; but I will
add the example which has always affected me most. I could never
conceive or tolerate any Utopia which did not leave to me the

liberty for which I chiefly care, the liberty to bind myself. Complete anarchy would not merely make it impossible to have any discipline or fidelity; it would also make it impossible to have any fun. To take an obvious instance, it would not be worth while to bet if a bet were not binding. The dissolution of all contracts would not only ruin morality but spoil sport. Now betting and such sports are only the stunted and twisted shapes of the original instinct of man for adventure and romance, of which much has been said in these pages. And the perils, rewards, punishments, and fulfilments of an adventure must be real, or the adventure is only a shifting and heartless nightmare. If I bet I must be made to pay, or there is no poetry in betting. If I challenge I must be made to fight, or there is no poetry in challenging. If I vow to be faithful I must be cursed when I am unfaithful, or there is no fun in vowing. You could not even make a fairy tale from the experiences of a man who, when he was swallowed by a whale, might find himself at the top of the Eiffel Tower, or when he was turned into a frog might begin to behave like a flamingo. For the purpose even of the wildest romance results must be real; results must be irrevocable. Christian marriage is the great example of a real and irrevocable result; and that is why it is the chief subject and centre of all our romantic writing. And this is my last instance of the things that I should ask, and ask imperatively, of any social paradise; I should ask to be kept to my bargain, to have my oaths and engagements taken seriously; I should ask Utopia to avenge my honour on myself.

All my modern Utopian friends look at each other rather doubtfully, for their ultimate hope is the dissolution of all special ties. But again I seem to hear, like a kind of echo, an answer from beyond the world. 'You will have real obligations, and therefore real adventures when you get to my Utopia. But the hardest obligation and the steepest adventure is to get there.'

VIII
THE ROMANCE OF ORTHODOXY

IT IS customary to complain of the bustle and strenuousness of our epoch. But in truth the chief mark or our epoch is a profound laziness and fatigue; and the fact is that the real laziness is the cause of the apparent bustle. Take one quite external case; the streets are noisy with taxicabs and motorcars; but this is not due to human activity but to human repose. There would be less bustle if there were more activity, if people were simply walking about. Our world would be more silent if it were more strenuous. And this which is true of the apparent physical bustle is true also of the apparent bustle of the intellect. Most of the machinery of modern language is labour-saving machinery; and it saves mental labour very much more than it ought. Scientific phrases are used like scientific wheels and piston-rods to make swifter and smoother yet the path of the comfortable. Long words go rattling by us like long railway trains. We know they are carrying thousands who are too tired or too indolent to walk and think for themselves. It is a good exercise to try for once in a way to express any opinion one holds in words of one syllable. If you say 'The social utility of the indeterminate sentence is recognized by all criminologists as a part of our socio-logical evolution towards a more humane and scientific view of punishment', you can go on talking like that for hours with hardly a movement of the grey matter inside your skull. But if you begin 'I wish Jones to go to gaol and Brown to say when Jones shall come out', you will discover, with a thrill of horror, that you are obliged to think. The long words are not the hard words, it is the short words that are hard. There is much more metaphysical subtlety in the word 'damn' than in the word 'degeneration'.

But these long comfortable words that save modern people the toil of reasoning have one particular aspect in which they are espe-cially ruinous and confusing. This difficulty occurs when the same long word is used in different connections to mean quite different things. Thus, to take a well-known instance, the word 'idealist' has one meaning as a piece of philosophy and quite another as a piece of moral rhetoric. In the same way the scientific materialists have had just reason to complain of people mixing up 'materialist' as a term of cosmology with 'materialist' as a moral taunt. So, to take a cheaper instance, the man who hates 'progressives' in London always calls himself a 'progressive' in South Africa.

A confusion quite as unmeaning as this has arisen in connection with the word 'liberal' as applied to religion and as applied to politics and society. It is often suggested that all Liberals ought to be freethinkers, because they ought to love everything that is free. You might just as well say that all idealists ought to be High Churchmen, because they ought to love everything that is high. You might as well say that Low Churchmen ought to like Low Mass, or that Broad Churchmen ought to like broad jokes. The thing is a mere accident of words. In actual modern Europe a freethinker does not mean a man who thinks for himself. It means a man who, having thought for himself, has come to one particular class of conclusions, the material origin of phenomena, the impossibility of miracles, the improbability of personal immortality and so on. And none of these ideas are particularly liberal. Nay, indeed almost all these ideas are definitely illiberal, as it is the purpose of this chapter to show.

In the few following pages I propose to point out as rapidly as possible that on every single one of the matters most strongly insisted on by liberalizers of theology their effect upon social practice would be definitely illiberal. Almost every contemporary proposal to bring freedom into the church is simply a proposal to bring tyranny into the world. For freeing the church now does not even mean freeing it in all directions. It means freeing that peculiar set of dogmas loosely called scientific, dogmas of monism, of pantheism, or of Arianism, or of necessity. And every one of these (and we will take them one by one) can be shown to be the natural ally of oppression. In fact, it is a remarkable circumstance (indeed not so very remarkable when one comes to think of it) that most things are the allies of oppression. There is only one thing that can never go past a certain point in its alliance with oppression – and that is orthodoxy. I may, it is true, twist orthodoxy so as partly to justify a tyrant. But I can easily make up a German philosophy to justify him entirely.

Now let us take in order the innovations that are the notes of the new theology or the modernist church. We concluded the last chapter with the discovery of one of them. The very doctrine which is called the most old-fashioned was found to be the only safeguard of the new democracies of the earth. The doctrine seemingly most unpopular was found to be the only strength of the people. In short, we found that the only logical negation of oligarchy was in the affirmation of original sin. So it is, I maintain, in all the other cases.

I take the most obvious instance first, the case of miracles. For some extraordinary reason, there is a fixed notion that it is more liberal to disbelieve in miracles than to believe in them. Why, I cannot imagine, nor can anybody tell me. For some inconceivable cause a 'broad' or 'liberal' clergyman always means a man who wishes at least to diminish the number of miracles; it never means a man who wishes to increase that number. It always means a man who is free to disbelieve that Christ came out of His grave; it never means a man who is free to believe that his own aunt came out of her grave. It is common to find trouble in a parish because the parish priest cannot admit that St Peter walked on water; yet how rarely do we find trouble in a parish because the clergyman says that his father walked on the Serpentine? And this is not because (as the swift secularist debater would immediately retort) miracles cannot be believed in our experience. It is not because 'miracles do not happen', as in the dogma which Matthew Arnold recited with simple faith. More supernatural things are *alleged* to have happened in our time than would have been possible eighty years ago. Men of science believe in such marvels much more than they did; the most perplexing, and even horrible, prodigies of mind and spirit are always being unveiled in modern psychology. Things that the old science at least would frankly have rejected as miracles are hourly being asserted by the new science. The only thing which is still old-fashioned enough to reject miracles is the New Theology. But in truth this notion that it is 'free' to deny miracles has nothing to do with the evidence for or against them. It is a lifeless verbal prejudice of which the original life and beginning was not in the freedom of thought, but simply in the dogma of materialism. The man of the nineteenth century did not disbelieve in the Resurrection because his liberal Christianity allowed him to doubt it. He disbelieved in it because his very strict materialism did not allow him to believe it. Tennyson, a very typical nineteenth-century man, uttered one of the instinctive truisms of his contemporaries when he said that there was faith in their honest doubt.[1] There was indeed. Those words have a profound and even a horrible truth. In their doubt of miracles there was a faith in a fixed and godless fate; a deep and sincere faith in the incurable routine of the cosmos. The doubts of the agnostic were only the dogmas of the monist.

Of the fact and evidence of the supernatural I will speak afterwards. Here we are only concerned with this clear point; that in so far as the liberal idea of freedom can be said to be on either side in the discussion about miracles, it is obviously on the side of miracles. Reform or (in the only tolerable sense) progress means simply the gradual control of matter by mind. A miracle simply means the swift control of matter by mind. If you wish to feed the people, you may think that feeding them miraculously in the wilderness is impossible – but you cannot think it illiberal. If you really want poor children to go to the seaside, you cannot think it illiberal that they should go there on flying dragons; you can only think it unlikely. A holiday, like Liberalism, only means the liberty of man. A miracle only means the liberty of God. You may conscientiously deny either of them, but you cannot call your denial a triumph of the liberal idea. The Catholic Church believed that man and God both had a sort of spiritual freedom. Calvinism took away the freedom from man, but left it to God. Scientific materialism binds the Creator Himself; it chains up God as the Apocalypse chained the devil. It leaves nothing free in the universe. And those who assist this process are called the 'liberal theologians'.

This, as I say, is the lightest and most evident case. The assumption that there is something in the doubt of miracles akin to liberality or reform is literally the opposite of the truth. If a man cannot believe in miracles there is an end of the matter; he is not particularly liberal, but he is perfectly honourable and logical, which are much better things. But if he can believe in miracles, he is certainly the more liberal for doing so; because they mean first, the freedom of the soul, and secondly, its control over the tyranny of circumstance. Sometimes this truth is ignored in a singularly naïve way, even by the ablest men. For instance, Mr Bernard Shaw speaks

1 'There lives more faith in honest doubt, / Believe me, than in half the creeds' (*In Memoriam*, xcvi, 11–12).

with hearty old-fashioned contempt for the idea of miracles, as if they were a sort of breach of faith on the part of nature: he seems strangely unconscious that miracles are only the final flowers of his own favourite tree, the doctrine of the omnipotence of will. Just in the same way he calls the desire for immortality a paltry selfishness, forgetting that he has just called the desire for life a healthy and heroic selfishness. How can it be noble to wish to make one's life infinite and yet mean to wish to make it immortal? No, if it is desirable that man should triumph over the cruelty of nature or custom, then miracles are certainly desirable; we will discuss afterwards whether they are possible.

But I must pass on to the larger cases of this curious error; the notion that the 'liberalizing' of religion in some way helps the liberation of the world. The second example of it can be found in the question of pantheism – or rather of a certain modern attitude which is often called immanentism, and which often is Buddhism. But this is so much more difficult a matter that I must approach it with rather more preparation.

The things said most confidently by advanced persons to crowded audiences are generally those quite opposite to the fact; it is actually our truisms that are untrue. Here is a case. There is a phrase of facile liberality uttered again and again at ethical societies and parliaments of religion: 'the religions of the earth differ in rites and forms, but they are the same in what they teach'. It is false; it is the opposite of the fact. The religions of the earth do *not* greatly differ in rites and forms; they do greatly differ in what they teach. It is as if a man were to say, 'Do not be misled by the fact that the *Church Times* and the *Freethinker* look utterly different, that one is painted on vellum and the other carved on marble, that one is triangular and the other hectagonal; read them and you will see that they say the same thing.' The truth is, of course, that they are alike in everything except in the fact that they don't say the same thing. An atheist stockbroker in Surbiton looks exactly like a Swedenborgian[1] stockbroker in Wimbledon. You may walk round and round them and subject them to the most personal and offensive study without seeing anything Swedenborgian in the hat

[1] Emanuel Swedenborg (1688–1772), Swedish visionary, who claimed that he had been given divine authority to reinterpret the Scriptures, and whose followers included William Blake.

or anything particularly godless in the umbrella. It is exactly in their souls that they are divided. So the truth is that the difficulty of all the creeds of the earth is not as alleged in this cheap maxim: that they agree in meaning, but differ in machinery. It is exactly the opposite. They agree in machinery; almost every great religion on earth works with the same external methods, with priests, scriptures, altars, sworn brotherhoods, special feasts. They agree in the mode of teaching; what they differ about is the thing to be taught. Pagan optimists and Eastern pessimists would both have temples, just as Liberals and Tories would both have newspapers. Creeds that exist to destroy each other both have scriptures, just as armies that exist to destroy each other both have guns.

The great example of this alleged identity of all human religions is the alleged spiritual identity of Buddhism and Christianity. Those who adopt this theory generally avoid the ethics of most other creeds, except, indeed, Confucianism, which they like because it is not a creed. But they are cautious in their praises of Mahometanism, generally confining themselves to imposing its morality only upon the refreshment of the lower classes. They seldom suggest the Mahometan view of marriage (for which there is a great deal to be said), and towards Thugs and fetish worshippers their attitude may even be called cold. But in the case of the great religion of Gautama they feel sincerely a similarity.

Students of popular science ... are always insisting that Christianity and Buddhism are very much alike, especially Buddhism. This is generally believed, and I believed it myself until I read a book giving the reasons for it. The reasons were of two kinds: resemblances that meant nothing because they were common to all humanity, and resemblances which were not resemblances at all. The author solemnly explained that the two creeds were alike in things in which all creeds are alike, or else he described them as alike in some point in which they are quite obviously different. Thus, as a case of the first class, he said that both Christ and Buddha were called by the divine voice coming out of the sky, as if you would expect the divine voice to come out of the coal-cellar. Or, again, it was gravely urged that these two Eastern teachers, by a singular coincidence, both had to do with the washing of feet. You might as well say that it was a remarkable coincidence that they both had feet to wash. And the other class of similarities were those which simply were not similar. Thus this reconciler of the two religions draws earnest attention to the fact that at certain religious feasts the robe of the Lama is rent in pieces out of respect, and the remnants highly valued. But this is the reverse of a resemblance, for the garments of Christ were not rent in pieces out of respect, but out of derision; and the remnants were not highly valued except for what they would fetch in the rag shops. It is rather like alluding to the obvious connection between the two ceremonies of the sword: when it taps a man's shoulder, and when it cuts off his head. It is not at all similar for the man. These scraps of puerile pedantry would indeed matter little if it were not also true that the alleged philosophical resemblances are also of these two kinds, either proving too much or not proving anything. That Buddhism approves of mercy or of self-restraint is not to say that it is specially like Christianity; it is only to say that it is not utterly unlike all human existence. Buddhists disapprove in theory of cruelty or excess because all sane human beings disapprove in theory of cruelty or excess. But to say that Buddhism and Christianity give the same philosophy of these things is simply false. All humanity does agree that we are in a net of sin. Most of humanity agrees that there is some way out. But as to what is the way out, I do not think that there are two institutions in the universe which contradict each other so flatly as Buddhism and Christianity.

Even when I thought, with most other well-informed, though unscholarly, people, that Buddhism and Christianity were alike, there was one thing about them that always perplexed me; I mean the startling difference in their type of religious art. I do not mean in its technical style of representation, but in the things that it was manifestly meant to represent. No two ideals could be more opposite than a Christian saint in a Gothic cathedral and a Buddhist saint in a Chinese temple. The opposition exists at every point; but perhaps the shortest statement of it is that the Buddhist saint always has his eyes shut, while the Christian saint always has them very wide open. The Buddhist saint has a sleek and harmonious body, but his eyes are heavy and sealed with sleep. The mediaeval saint's body is wasted to its crazy bones, but his eyes are frightfully alive. There cannot be any real community of spirit between forces that produced symbols so different as that. Granted that both images are extravagances, are perversions of the pure creed, it must be a real divergence which could produce such opposite extravagances. The Buddhist is looking with a peculiar intentness inwards. The Christian is staring with a frantic intentness outwards. If we follow that clue steadily we shall find some interesting things.

A short time ago Mrs Besant,[1] in an interesting essay, announced that there was only one religion in the world, that all faiths were only versions or perversions of it, and that she was quite prepared to say what it was. According to Mrs Besant this universal Church is simply the universal self. It is the doctrine that we are really all one person; that there are no real walls of individuality between man and man. If I may put it so, she does not tell us to love our neighbours; she tells us to be our neighbours. That is Mrs Besant's thoughtful and suggestive description of the religion in which all men must find themselves in agreement. And I never heard of any suggestion in my life with which I more violently disagree. I want to love my neighbour not because he is I, but precisely because he is not I. I want to adore the world, not as one likes a looking-glass, because it is one's self, but as one loves a woman, because she is entirely different. If souls are separate love is possible. If souls are united love is obviously impossible. A man may be said loosely to love himself, but he can hardly fall in love with himself, or, if he does, it must be a monotonous courtship. If the world is full of real selves, they can be really unselfish selves. But upon Mrs Besant's principle the whole cosmos is only one enormously selfish person.

It is just here that Buddhism is on the side of modern pantheism and immanence. And it is just here that Christianity is on the side of humanity and liberty and love. Love desires personality; therefore love desires division. It is the instinct of Christianity to be glad that God has broken the universe into little pieces, because they are living pieces. It is her instinct to say 'little children love one another' rather than to tell one large person to love himself. This is the intellectual abyss between Buddhism and Christianity; that for the Buddhist or Theosophist personality is the fall of man, for the Christian it is the purpose of God, the whole point of his cosmic idea. The world-soul of the Theosophists asks man to love it only in order that man may throw himself into it. But the divine centre of Christianity actually threw man out of it in order that

1 Annie Besant (1847–1933) became president of the Theosophical Society in 1907.

he might love it. The oriental deity is like a giant who should have lost his leg or hand and be always seeking to find it; but the Christian power is like some giant who in a strange generosity should cut off his right hand, so that it might of its own accord shake hands with him. We come back to the same tireless note touching the nature of Christianity; all modern philosophies are chains which connect and fetter; Christianity is a sword which separates and sets free. No other philosophy makes God actually rejoice in the separation of the universe into living souls. But according to orthodox Christianity this separation between God and man is sacred, because this is eternal. That a man may love God it is necessary that there should be not only a God to be loved, but a man to love him. All those vague theosophical minds for whom the universe is an immense melting-pot are exactly the minds which shrink instinctively from that earthquake saying of our Gospels, which declare that the Son of God came not with peace but with a sundering sword. The saying rings entirely true even considered as what it obviously is; the statement that any man who preaches real love is bound to beget hate. It is as true of democratic fraternity as a divine love; sham love ends in compromise and common philosophy; but real love has always ended in bloodshed. Yet there is another and yet more awful truth behind the obvious meaning of this utterance of our Lord. According to Himself the Son was a sword separating brother and brother that they should for an aeon hate each other. But the Father also was a sword, which in the black beginning separated brother and brother, so that they should love each other at last.

This is the meaning of that almost insane happiness in the eyes of the mediaeval saint in the picture. This is the meaning of the sealed eyes of the superb Buddhist image. The Christian saint is happy because he has verily been cut off from the world; he is separate from things and is staring at them in astonishment. But why should the Buddhist saint be astonished at things? – since there is really only one thing, and that being impersonal can hardly be astonished at itself. There have been many pantheist poems suggesting wonder, but no really successful ones. The pantheist cannot wonder, for he cannot praise God or praise anything as really distinct from himself. Our immediate business here, however, is with the effect of this Christian admiration (which strikes outwards, towards a deity distinct from the worshipper) upon the general need for ethical activity and social reform. And surely its effect is sufficiently obvious. There is no real possibility of getting out of pantheism any special impulse to moral action. For pantheism implies in its nature that one thing is as good as another; whereas action implies in its nature that one thing is greatly preferable to another. Swinburne, in the high summer of his scepticism, tried in vain to wrestle with this difficulty. In *Songs before Sunrise*, written under the inspiration of Garibaldi and the revolt of Italy, he proclaimed the newer religion and the purer God which should wither up all the priests of the world:

> What doest thou now
> Looking Godward to cry
> I am I, thou art thou,
> I am low, thou art high,
> I am thou that thou seekest to find him, find
>   thou but thyself, thou art I.

Of which the immediate and evident deduction is that tyrants are as much the sons of God as Garibaldis ... The truth is that the western energy that dethrones tyrants has been directly due to the western theology that says 'I am I, thou art thou'.... The worshippers of Swinburne's god have covered Asia for centuries and have never dethroned a tyrant. The Indian saint may reasonably shut his eyes because he is looking at that which is I and Thou and We and They and It.... That external vigilance which has always been the mark of Christianity (the command that we should *watch* and pray) has expressed itself both in typical western orthodoxy and in typical western politics: but both depend on the idea of a divinity transcendent, different from ourselves, a deity that disappears. Certainly the most sagacious creeds may suggest that we should pursue God into deeper and deeper rings of the labyrinth of our own ego. But only we of Christendom have said that we should hunt God like an eagle upon the mountains: and we have killed all monsters in the chase.

Here again, therefore, we find that in so far as we value democracy and the self-renewing energies of the west, we are much more likely to find them in the old theology than the new. If we want reform, we must adhere to orthodoxy: especially in this

matter ... the matter of insisting on the immanent or the transcendent deity. By insisting specially on the immanence of God
we get introspection, self-isolation, quietism, social indifference –
Tibet. By insisting specially on the transcendence of God we get
wonder, curiosity, moral and political adventure, righteous indignation – Christendom. Insisting that God is inside man, man is
always inside himself. By insisting that God transcends man, man
has transcended himself.

If we take any other doctrine that has been called old-fashioned
we shall find the case the same. It is the same, for instance, in the
deep matter of the Trinity. Unitarians (a sect never to be mentioned without a special respect for their distinguished intellectual
dignity and high intellectual honour) are often reformers by the
accident that throws so many small sects into such an attitude. But
there is nothing in the least liberal or akin to reform in the substitution of pure monotheism for the Trinity. The complex God of the
Athanasian Creed may be an enigma for the intellect; but He is far
less likely to gather the mystery and cruelty of a Sultan than the
lonely god of Omar or Mahomet. The god who is a mere awful
unity is not only a king but an Eastern king. The *heart* of humanity,
especially of European humanity, is certainly much more satisfied
by the strange hints and symbols that gather round the Trinitarian
idea, the image of a council at which mercy pleads as well as justice,
the conception of a sort of liberty and variety existing even in the
inmost chamber of the world. For Western religion has always felt
keenly the idea 'it is not well for man to be alone'. The social
instinct asserted itself everywhere as when the Eastern idea of
hermits was practically expelled by the Western idea of monks.
So even asceticism became brotherly; and the Trappists were sociable even when they were silent. If this love of a living complexity
be our test, it is certainly healthier to have the Trinitarian religion
than the Unitarian. For to us Trinitarians (if I may say it with reverence) – to us God Himself is a society. It is indeed a fathomless
mystery of theology, and even if I were theologian enough to deal
with it directly, it would not be relevant to do so here. Suffice it to
say here that this triple enigma is as comforting as wine and open
as an English fireside; that this thing that bewilders the intellect
utterly quiets the heart: but out of the desert, from the dry places
and the dreadful suns, come the cruel children of the lonely God;

the real Unitarians who with scimitar in hand have laid waste the world. For it is not well for God to be alone.

Again, the same is true of that difficult matter of the danger of the soul, which has unsettled so many just minds. To hope for all souls is imperative; and it is quite tenable that their salvation is inevitable. It is tenable, but it is not specially favourable to activity or progress. Our fighting and creative society ought rather to insist on the danger of everybody, on the fact that every man is hanging by a thread or clinging to a precipice. To say that all will be well anyhow is a comprehensible remark: but it cannot be called the blast of a trumpet. Europe ought rather to emphasize possible perdition; and Europe always has emphasized it. Here its highest religion is at one with all its cheapest romances. To the Buddhist or the eastern fatalist existence is a science or a plan, which must end up in a certain way. But to a Christian existence is a *story*, which may end up in any way. In a thrilling novel (that purely Christian product) the hero is not eaten by cannibals; but it is essential to the existence of the thrill that he *might* be eaten by cannibals. The hero must (so to speak) be an eatable hero. So Christian morals have always said to the man, not that he would lose his soul, but that he must take care that he didn't. In Christian morals, in short, it is wicked to call a man 'damned': but it is strictly religious and philosophic to call him damnable.

All Christianity concentrates on the man at the cross-roads. The vast and shallow philosophies, the huge syntheses of humbug, all talk about ages and evolution and ultimate developments. The true philosophy is concerned with the instant. Will a man take this road or that? – that is the only thing to think about, if you enjoy thinking. The aeons are easy enough to think about, any one can think about them. The instant is really awful: and it is because our religion has intensely felt the instant, that it has in literature dealt much with battle and in theology dealt much with hell. It is full of *danger*, like a boy's book: it is at an immortal crisis. There is a great deal of real similarity between popular fiction and the religion of the western people. If you say that popular fiction is vulgar and tawdry, you only say what the dreary and well-informed say also about the images in the Catholic churches. Life (according to the faith) is very like a serial story in a magazine: life ends with the promise (or menace) 'to be continued in our next'. Also, with a noble vulgarity, life imitates the serial and leaves off at the exciting moment. For death is distinctly an exciting moment.

But the point is that a story is exciting because it has in it so strong an element of will, of what theology calls free will. You cannot finish a sum how you like. But you can finish a story how you like. When somebody discovered the Differential Calculus there was only one Differential Calculus he could discover. But when Shakespeare killed Romeo he might have married him to Juliet's old nurse if he had felt inclined. And Christendom has excelled in the narrative romance exactly because it has insisted on the theological free will. It is a large matter and too much to one side of the road to be discussed adequately here; but this is the real objection to that torrent of modern talk about treating crime as disease, about making a prison merely a hygienic environment like a hospital, of healing sin by slow scientific methods. The fallacy of the whole thing is that evil is a matter of active choice whereas disease is not. If you say that you are going to cure a profligate as you cure an asthmatic, my cheap and obvious answer is, 'Produce the people who want to be asthmatics as many people want to be profligates.' A man may lie still and be cured of a malady. But he must not lie still if he wants to be cured of a sin; on the contrary, he must get up and jump about violently. The whole point indeed is perfectly expressed in the very word which we use for a man in hospital; 'patient' is in the passive mood; 'sinner' is in the active. If a man is to be saved from influenza, he may be a patient. But if he is to be saved from forging, he must be not a patient but an *impatient*. He must be personally impatient with forgery. All moral reform must start in the active not the passive will.

Here again we reach the same substantial conclusion. In so far as we desire the definite reconstructions and the dangerous revolutions which have distinguished European civilization, we shall not discourage the thought of possible ruin; we shall rather encourage it. If we want, like the Eastern saints, merely to contemplate how right things are, of course we shall only say that they must go right. But if we particularly want to *make* them go right, we must insist that they may go wrong.

Lastly, this truth is yet again true in the case of the common modern attempts to diminish or to explain away the divinity of Christ. The thing may be true or not; that I shall deal with before

I end. But if the divinity is true it is certainly terribly revolutionary. That a good man may have his back to the wall is no more than we knew already; but that God could have His back to the wall is a boast for all insurgents for ever. Christianity is the only religion on earth that has felt that omnipotence made God incomplete. Christianity alone has felt that God, to be wholly God, must have been a rebel as well as a king. Alone of all creeds, Christianity has added courage to the virtues of the Creator. For the only courage worth calling courage must necessarily mean that the soul passes a breaking point – and does not break. In this indeed I approach a matter more dark and awful than it is easy to discuss; and I apologize in advance if any of my phrases fall wrong or seem irreverent touching a matter which the greatest saints and thinkers have justly feared to approach. But in that terrific tale of the Passion there is a distinct emotional suggestion that the author of all things (in some unthinkable way) went not only through agony, but through doubt. It is written, 'Thou shalt not tempt the Lord thy God'. No; but the Lord thy God may tempt Himself; and it seems as if this was what happened in Gethsemane. In a garden Satan tempted man: and in a garden God tempted God. He passed in some superhuman manner through our human horror of pessimism. When the world shook and the sun was wiped out of heaven, it was not at the crucifixion, but at the cry from the cross: the cry which confessed that God was forsaken of God. And now let the revolutionists choose a creed from all the creeds and a god from all the gods of the world, carefully weighing all the gods of inevitable recurrence and of unalterable power. They will not find another god who has himself been in revolt. Nay (the matter grows too difficult for human speech), but let the atheists themselves choose a god. They will find only one divinity who ever uttered their isolation; only one religion in which God seemed for an instant to be an atheist.

These can be called the essentials of the old orthodoxy, of which the chief merit is that it is the natural fountain of revolution and reform; and of which the chief defect is that it is obviously only an abstract assertion. Its main advantage is that it is the most adventurous and manly of all theologies. Its chief disadvantage is simply that it is a theology. It can always be urged against it that it is in its nature arbitrary and in the air. But it is not so high in the air but that great archers spend their whole lives in shooting arrows at it

– yes, and their last arrows; there are men who will ruin themselves and ruin their civilization if they may ruin also this old fantastic tale. This is the last and most astounding fact about this faith; that its enemies will use any weapon against it, the swords that cut their own fingers, and the firebrands that burn their own homes. Men who begin to fight the Church for the sake of freedom and human-ity end by flinging away freedom and humanity if only they may fight the Church. This is no exaggeration ... I know a man who has such a passion for proving that he will have no personal exist-ence after death that he falls back on the position that he has no personal existence now. He invokes Buddhism and says that all souls fade into each other ... I have known people who protested against religious education with arguments against any education, saying that the child's mind must grow freely or that the old must not teach the young. I have known people who showed that there could be no divine judgment by showing that there can be no human judgment, even for practical purposes. They burned their own corn to set fire to the church; they smashed their own tools to smash it; any stick was good enough to beat it with, though it were the last stick of their own dismembered furniture. We do not admire, we hardly excuse, the fanatic who wrecks this world for love of the other. But what are we to say of the fanatic who wrecks this world out of hatred of the other? He sacrifices the very exist-ence of humanity to the non-existence of God. He offers his victims not to the altar, but merely to assert the idleness of the altar and the emptiness of the throne. He is ready to ruin even that primary ethic by which all things live, for his strange and eternal vengeance upon some one who never lived at all.

And yet the thing hangs in the heavens unhurt. Its opponents only succeed in destroying all that they themselves justly hold dear. They do not destroy orthodoxy; they only destroy political and common courage sense. They do not prove that Adam was not responsible to God; how could they prove it? They only prove (from their premises) that the Czar is not responsible to Russia. They do not prove that Adam should not have been punished by God; they only prove that the nearest sweater should not be pun-ished by men. With their oriental doubts about personality they do not make certain that we shall have no personal life hereafter; they only make certain that we shall not have a very jolly or complete one here. . . . Not only is the faith the mother of all worldly energies, but its foes are the fathers of all worldly confusion. The secularists have not wrecked divine things; but the secularists have wrecked secular things, if that is any comfort to them. The Titans did not scale heaven; but they laid waste the world.

IX
AUTHORITY AND THE ADVENTURER

THE LAST chapter has been concerned with the contention that orthodoxy is not only (as is often urged) the only safe guardian of morality or order, but is also the only logical guardian of liberty, innovation and advance. If we wish to pull down the prosperous oppressor we cannot do it with the new doctrine of human perfectibility; we can do it with the old doctrine of Original Sin. If we want to uproot inherent cruelties or lift up lost populations we cannot do it with the scientific theory that matter precedes mind; we can do it with the supernatural theory that mind precedes matter. If we wish specially to awaken people to social vigilance and tireless pursuit of practice, we cannot help it much by insisting on the Immanent God and the Inner Light: for these are at best reasons for contentment; we can help it much by insisting on the transcendent God and the flying and escaping gleam; for that means divine discontent. If we wish particularly to assert the idea of a generous balance against that of a dreadful autocracy we shall instinctively be Trinitarian rather than Unitarian. If we desire European civilization to be a raid and a rescue, we shall insist rather that souls are in real peril than that their peril is ultimately unreal. And if we wish to exalt the outcast and the crucified, we shall rather wish to think that a veritable God was crucified, rather than a mere sage or hero. Above all, if we wish to protect the poor we shall be in favour of fixed rules and clear dogmas. The *rules* of a club are occasionally in favour of the poor member. The drift of a club is always in favour of the rich one.

And now we come to the crucial question which truly concludes the whole matter. A reasonable agnostic, if he has happened to agree with me so far, may justly turn round and say, 'You have found a practical philosophy in the doctrine of the Fall; very well. You have found a side of democracy now dangerously neglected wisely asserted in Original Sin; all right. You have found a truth in the doctrine of hell; I congratulate you. You are convinced that worshippers of a personal God look outwards and are progressive; I congratulate them. But even supposing that those doctrines do include those truths, why cannot you take the truths and leave the doctrines? Granted that all modern society is trusting the rich too much because it does not allow for human weakness; granted that orthodox ages have had a great advantage because (believing in the Fall) they did allow for human weakness, why cannot you simply allow for human weakness without believing in the Fall? If you have discovered that the idea of damnation represents a healthy idea of danger, why can you not simply take the idea of danger and leave the idea of damnation? If you see clearly the kernel of common sense in the nut of Christian orthodoxy, why cannot you simply take the kernel and leave the nut? Why cannot you (to use that cant phrase of the newspapers which I, as a highly scholarly agnostic, am a little ashamed of using), why cannot you simply take what is good in Christianity, what you can define as valuable, what you can comprehend, and leave all the rest, all the absolute dogmas that are in their nature incomprehensible?' This is the real question; this is the last question; and it is a pleasure to try to answer it.

The first answer is simply to say that I am a rationalist. I like to have some intellectual justification for my intuitions. If I am treating man as a fallen being it is an intellectual convenience to me to believe that he fell; and I find, for some odd psychological reason, that I can deal better with a man's exercise of free will if I believe that he has got it. But I am in this matter yet more definitely a rationalist. I do not propose to turn this book into one of ordinary Christian apologetics; I should be glad to meet at any other time the enemies of Christianity in that more obvious arena. Here I am only giving an account of my own growth in spiritual certainty. But I may pause to remark that the more I saw of the merely abstract arguments against the Christian cosmology the less I thought of them. I mean that having found the moral atmosphere of the Incarnation to be common sense, I then looked at the established intellectual arguments against the Incarnation and found them to be common nonsense. In case the argument should be thought to suffer from the absence of the ordinary apologetic I will here very briefly summarize my own arguments and conclusions on the purely objective or scientific truth of the matter.

If I am asked, as a purely intellectual question, why I believe in Christianity, I can only answer, 'For the same reason that an intelligent agnostic disbelieves in Christianity'. I believe in it quite rationally upon the evidence. But the evidence in my case, as in that of the intelligent agnostic, is not really in this or that alleged demonstration; it is in an enormous accumulation of small but unanimous facts. The secularist is not to be blamed because his objections to Christianity are miscellaneous and even scrappy; it is precisely such scrappy evidence that does convince the mind. I mean that a man may well be less convinced of a philosophy from four books, than from one book, one battle, one landscape, and one old friend. The very fact that the things are of different kinds increases the importance of the fact that they all point to one conclusion. Now, the non-Christianity of the average educated man today is almost always, to do him justice, made up of these loose but living experiences. I can only say that my evidences for Christianity are of the same vivid but varied kind as his evidences against it. For when I look at these various anti-Christian truths, I simply discover that none of them are true. I discover that the true tide and force of all the facts flows the other way. Let us take cases. Many a sensible modern man must have abandoned Christianity under the pressure of three such converging convictions as these: first, that men, with their shape, structure, and sexuality, are, after all, very much like beasts, a mere variety of the animal kingdom; second, that primeval religion arose in ignorance and fear; third, that priests have blighted societies with bitterness and gloom. Those three anti-Christian arguments are very different; but they are all quite logical and legitimate; and they all converge. The only objection to them (I discover) is that they are all untrue. If you leave off looking at books about beasts and men, if you begin to look at beasts and men then (if you have any humour or imagination, any sense of the frantic or the farcical) you will observe that the startling thing is not how like man is to the brutes, but how unlike he is. It is the monstrous scale of his divergence that requires an explanation. That man and brute are like is, in a sense, a truism; but that being so like they should then be so insanely unlike, that is the shock and the enigma. That an ape has hands is far less interesting to the philosopher than the fact that having hands he does next to nothing with them; does not play knuckle-bones or the violin; does not carve marble or carve mutton. People talk of barbaric architecture and debased art. But elephants do not build colossal temples of ivory even in a rococo style; camels do not paint even bad pictures, though equipped with the material of many camel's-hair brushes. Certain modern dreamers say that ants and bees have a society superior to ours. They have, indeed, a civilization; but that very truth only reminds us that it is an inferior civilization. Who ever found an ant-hill decorated with the statues of celebrated ants? Who has seen a bee-hive carved with the images of gorgeous queens of old? No; the chasm between man and other creatures may have a natural explanation, but it is a chasm. We talk of wild animals; but man is the only wild animal. It is man that has broken out. All other animals are tame animals; following the rugged respectability of the tribe or type. All other animals are domestic animals; man alone is ever undomestic, either as a profligate or a monk. So that this first superficial reason for materialism is, if anything, a reason for its opposite; it is exactly where biology leaves off that all religion begins.

It would be the same if I examined the second of the three chance rationalist arguments; the argument that all that we call divine began in some darkness and terror. When I did attempt to examine the foundations of this modern idea I simply found that there were none. Science knows nothing whatever about pre-historic man; for the excellent reason that he is pre-historic. A few professors choose to conjecture that such things as human sacrifice were once innocent and general and that they gradually dwindled; but there is no direct evidence of it, and the small amount of in-direct evidence is very much the other way. In the earliest legends we have, such as the tales of Isaac and of Iphigenia, human sacri-fice is not introduced as something old, but rather as something new; as a strange and frightful exception darkly demanded by the gods. History says nothing; and legends all say that the earth was kinder in its earliest time. There is no tradition of progress; but the whole human race has a tradition of the Fall. Amusingly enough, indeed, the very dissemination of this idea is used against its authenticity. Learned men literally say that this pre-historic calam-ity cannot be true because every race of mankind remembers it. I cannot keep pace with these paradoxes.

And if we took the third chance instance, it would be the same;

the view that priests darken and embitter the world. I look at the world and simply discover that they don't. Those countries in Europe which are still influenced by priests, are exactly the countries where there is still singing and dancing and coloured dresses and art in the open-air. Catholic doctrine and discipline may be walls; but they are the walls of a playground. Christianity is the only frame which has preserved the pleasure of Paganism. We might fancy some children playing on the flat grassy top of some tall island in the sea. So long as there was a wall round the cliff's edge they could fling themselves into every frantic game and make the place the noisiest of nurseries. But the walls were knocked down, leaving the naked peril of the precipice. They did not fall over; but when their friends returned to them they were all huddled in terror in the centre of the island; and their song had ceased.

Thus these three facts of experience, such facts as go to make an agnostic, are, in this view, turned totally round. I am left saying, 'Give me an explanation, first, of the towering eccentricity of man among the brutes; second, of the vast human tradition of some ancient happiness; third, of the partial perpetuation of such pagan joy in the countries of the Catholic Church.' One explanation, at any rate, covers all three: the theory that twice was the natural order interrupted by some explosion or revelation such as people now call 'psychic'. Once Heaven came upon the earth with a power or seal called the image of God, whereby man took command of Nature; and once again (when in empire after empire men had been found wanting) Heaven came to save mankind in the awful shape of a man. This would explain why the mass of men always look backwards; and why the only corner where they in any sense look forwards is the little continent where Christ has His Church. I know it will be said that Japan has become progressive. But how can this be an answer when even in saying 'Japan has become progressive', we really only mean, 'Japan has become European'? But I wish here not so much to insist on my own explanation as to insist on my original remark. I agree with the ordinary unbelieving man in the street in being guided by three or four odd facts all pointing to something; only when I came to look at the facts I always found they pointed to something else.

I have given an imaginary triad of such ordinary anti-Christian arguments; if that be too narrow a basis I will give on the spur of the moment another. These are the kind of thoughts which in combination create the impression that Christianity is something weak and diseased. First, for instance, that Jesus was a gentle creature, sheepish and unworldly, a mere ineffectual appeal to the world; second, that Christianity arose and flourished in the dark ages of ignorance, and that to these the Church would drag us back; third, that the people still strongly religious or (if you will) superstitious – such people as the Irish – are weak, unpractical, and behind the times. I only mention these ideas to affirm the same thing: that when I looked into them independently I found, not that the conclusions were unphilosophical, but simply that the facts were not facts. Instead of looking at books and pictures about the New Testament I looked at the New Testament. There I found an account, not in the least of a person with his hair parted in the middle or his hands clasped in appeal, but of an extraordinary being with lips of thunder and acts of lurid decision, flinging down tables, casting out devils, passing with the wild secrecy of the wind from mountain isolation to a sort of dreadful demagogy; a being who often acted like an angry god – and always like a god. Christ had even a literary style of his own, not to be found, I think, elsewhere; it consists of an almost furious use of the *a fortiori*. His 'how much more' is piled one upon another like castle upon castle in the clouds. The diction used *about* Christ has been, and perhaps wisely, sweet and submissive. But the diction used by Christ is quite curiously gigantesque; it is full of camels leaping through needles and mountains hurled into the sea. Morally it is equally terrific; he called himself a sword of slaughter, and told men to buy swords if they sold their coats for them. That he used other even wilder words on the side of non-resistance greatly increases the mystery; but it also, if anything, rather increases the violence. We cannot even explain it by calling such a being insane; for insanity is usually along one consistent channel. The maniac is generally a monomaniac. Here we must remember the difficult definition of Christianity already given; Christianity is a superhuman paradox whereby two opposite passions may blaze beside each other. The one explanation of the Gospel language that does explain it, is that it is the survey of one who from some supernatural height beholds some more startling synthesis.

I take in order the next instance offered: the idea that Christianity belongs to the Dark Ages. Here I did not satisfy myself with reading modern generalizations; I read a little history. And in history I found that Christianity, so far from belonging to the Dark Ages, was the one path across the Dark Ages that was not dark. It was the shining bridge connecting two shining civilizations. If any one says that the faith arose in ignorance and savagery the answer is simple: it didn't. It arose in the Mediterranean civilization in the full summer of the Roman Empire. The world was swarming with sceptics, and pantheism was as plain as the sun, when Constantine nailed the cross to the mast. It is perfectly true that afterwards the ship sank; but it is far more extraordinary that the ship came up again: repainted and glittering, with the cross still at the top. This is the amazing thing the religion did: it turned a sunken ship into a submarine. The ark lived under the load of waters; after being buried under the debris of dynasties and clans, we arose and remembered Rome. If our faith had been a mere fad of the fading empire, fad would have followed fad in the twilight, and if the civilization ever re-emerged (and many such have never re-emerged) it would have been under some new barbaric flag. But the Christian Church was the last life of the old society and was also the first life of the new. She took the people who were forgetting how to make an arch and she taught them to invent the Gothic arch. In a word, the most absurd thing that could be said of the Church is the thing we have all heard said of it. How can we say that the Church wishes to bring us back into the Dark Ages? The Church was the only thing that ever brought us out of them.

I added in this second trinity of objections an idle instance taken from those who feel such people as the Irish to be weakened or made stagnant by superstition. I only added it because this is a peculiar case of a statement of fact that turns out to be a statement of falsehood. It is constantly said of the Irish that they are impractical. But if we refrain for a moment from looking at what is said about them and look at what is *done* about them, we shall see that the Irish are not only practical, but quite painfully successful. The poverty of their country, the minority of their members are simply the conditions under which they were asked to work; but no other group in the British Empire has done so much with such conditions. The Nationalists were the only minority that ever succeeded in twisting the whole British Parliament sharply out of its path. The Irish peasants are the only poor men in these islands who have forced their masters to disgorge. These people, whom we call priest-ridden, are the only Britons who will not be squire-ridden. And when I came to look at the actual Irish character, the case was the same. Irishmen are best at the specially *hard* professions – the trades of iron, the lawyer, and the soldier. In all these cases, there-fore, I came back to the same conclusion: the sceptic was quite right to go by the facts, only he had not looked at the facts. The sceptic is too credulous; he believes in newspapers or even in encyclopaedias. Again the three questions left me with three very antagonistic ques-tions. The average sceptic wanted to know how I explained the namby-pamby note in the Gospel, the connection of the creed with mediaeval darkness and the political impracticability of the Celtic Christians. But I wanted to ask, and to ask with an earnestness amounting to urgency, 'What is this incomparable energy which appears first in one walking the earth like a living judgment and this energy which can die with a dying civilization and yet force it to a resurrection from the dead; this energy which last of all can inflame a bankrupt peasantry with so fixed a faith in justice that they get what they ask, while others go empty away; so that the most helpless island of the Empire can actually help itself?'

There is an answer: it is an answer to say that the energy is truly from outside the world; that it is psychic, or at least one of the results of a real psychical disturbance. The highest gratitude and respect are due to the great human civilizations such as the old Egyptian or the existing Chinese. Nevertheless it is no injustice for them to say that only modern Europe has exhibited incessantly a power of self-renewal recurring often at the shortest intervals and descending to the smallest facts of building or costume. All other societies die finally and with dignity. We die daily. We are always being born again with almost indecent obstetrics. It is hardly an exaggeration to say that there is in historic Christendom a sort of unnatural life: it could be explained as a supernatural life. It could be explained as an awful galvanic life working in what would have been a corpse. . . . That is the weird inspiration of our estate: you and I have no business to be here at all. We are all *revenants*; all living Christians are dead pagans walking about. Just as Europe was about to be gathered in silence to Assyria and

Babylon, something entered into its body. And Europe has had a strange life – it is not too much to say that it has had the *jumps* – ever since.

I have dealt at length with such typical triads of doubt in order to convey the main contention – that my own case for Christianity is rational; but it is not simple. It is an accumulation of varied facts, like the attitude of the ordinary agnostic. But the ordinary agnostic has got his facts all wrong. He is a non-believer for a multitude of reasons; but they are untrue reasons. He doubts because the Middle Ages were barbaric, but they weren't; because Darwinism is demonstrated, but it isn't; because miracles do not happen, but they do; because monks were lazy, but they were very industrious; because nuns are unhappy, but they are particularly cheerful; because Christian art was sad and pale, but it was picked out in peculiarly bright colours and gay with gold; because modern science is moving away from the supernatural, but it isn't, it is moving towards the supernatural with the rapidity of a railway train.

But among these million facts all flowing one way there is, of course, one question sufficiently solid and separate to be treated briefly, but by itself; I mean the objective occurrence of the supernatural. In another chapter I have indicated the fallacy of the ordinary supposition that the world must be impersonal because it is orderly. A person is just as likely to desire an orderly thing as a disorderly thing. But my own positive conviction that personal creation is more conceivable than material fate, is, I admit, in a sense, undiscussable. I will not call it a faith or an intuition, for those words are mixed up with mere emotion, it is strictly an intellectual conviction; but it is a *primary* intellectual conviction like the certainty of self or the good of living. Any one who likes, therefore, may call my belief in God merely mystical; the phrase is not worth fighting about. But my belief that miracles have happened in human history is not a mystical belief at all; I believe in them upon human evidences as I do in the discovery of America. Upon this point there is a simple logical fact that only requires to be stated and cleared up. Somehow or other an extraordinary idea has arisen that the disbelievers in miracles consider them coldly and fairly, while believers in miracles accept them only in connection with some dogma. The fact is quite the other way. The believers in miracles accept them (rightly or wrongly) because they have evidence for them. The disbelievers in miracles deny them (rightly or wrongly) because they have a doctrine against them. The open, obvious, democratic thing is to believe an old apple-woman when she bears testimony to a miracle, just as you believe an old apple-woman when she bears testimony to a murder. The plain, popular course is to trust the peasant's word about the ghost exactly as far as you trust the peasant's word about the landlord. Being a peasant he will probably have a great deal of healthy agnosticism about both. Still you could fill the British Museum with evidence uttered by the peasant, and given in favour of the ghost. If it comes to human testimony there is a choking cataract of human testimony in favour of the supernatural. If you reject it, you can only mean one of two things. You reject the peasant's story about the ghost either because the man is a peasant or because the story is a ghost story. That is, you either deny the main principle of democracy, or you affirm the main principle of materialism – the abstract impossibility of miracle. You have a perfect right to do so; but in that case you are the dogmatist. It is we Christians who accept all actual evidence – it is you rationalists who refuse actual evidence being constrained to do so by your creed. But I am not constrained by any creed in the matter, and looking impartially into certain miracles of mediaeval and modern times, I have come to the conclusion that they occurred. All argument against these plain facts is always argument in a circle. If I say, 'Mediaeval documents attest certain miracles as much as they attest certain battles', they answer, 'But mediaevals were superstitious'; if I want to know in what they were superstitious, the only ultimate answer is that they believed in the miracles. If I say 'a peasant saw a ghost', I am told, 'But peasants are so credulous.' If I ask, 'Why credulous?' the only answer is – that they see ghosts. Iceland is impossible because only stupid sailors have seen it; and the sailors are only stupid because they say they have seen Iceland. It is only fair to add that there is another argument that the unbeliever may rationally use against miracles, though he himself generally forgets to use it.

He may say that there has been in many miraculous stories a notion of spiritual preparation and acceptance: in short, that the miracle could only come to him who believed in it. It may be so, and if it is so how are we to test it? If we are inquiring whether certain results follow faith, it is useless to repeat wearily that (if they happen) they do follow faith. If faith is one of the conditions, those without faith have a most healthy right to laugh. But they have no right to judge. Being a believer may be, if you like, as bad as being drunk; still if we were extracting psychological facts from drunkards, it would be absurd to be always taunting them with having been drunk. Suppose we were investigating whether angry men really saw a red mist before their eyes. Suppose sixty excellent householders swore that when angry they had seen this crimson cloud: surely it would be absurd to answer 'Oh, but you admit you were angry at the time.' They might reasonably rejoin (in a stentorian chorus), 'How the blazes could we discover, without being angry, whether angry people see red?" So the saints and ascetics might rationally reply, 'Suppose that the question is whether believers can see visions – even then, if you are interested in visions it is no point to object to believers.' You are still arguing in a circle – in that old mad circle with which this book began.

The question of whether miracles ever occur is a question of common sense and of ordinary historical imagination: not of any final physical experiment. One may here surely dismiss that quite brainless piece of pedantry which talks about the need for 'scientific conditions' in connection with alleged spiritual phenomena. If we are asking whether a dead soul can communicate with a living it is ludicrous to insist that it shall be under conditions in which no two living souls in their senses would seriously communicate with each other. The fact that ghosts prefer darkness no more disproves the existence of ghosts than the fact that lovers prefer darkness disproves the existence of love. If you choose to say, 'I will believe that Miss Brown called her *fiancé* a periwinkle or any other endearing term, if she will repeat the word before seventeen psychologists', then I shall reply, 'Very well, if those are your conditions, you will never get the truth, for she certainly will not say it.' It is just as unscientific as it is unphilosophical to be surprised that in an unsympathetic atmosphere certain extraordinary sympathies do not arise. It is as if I said that I could not tell if there was a fog because the air was not clear enough; or as if I insisted on perfect sunlight in order to see a solar eclipse.

As a common-sense conclusion, such as those to which we come about sex or about midnight (well knowing that many details must in their own nature be concealed) I conclude that miracles do happen. I am forced to it by a conspiracy of facts: the fact that the men who encounter elves or angels are not the mystics and the morbid dreamers, but fishermen, farmers, and all men at once coarse and cautious; the fact that we all know men who testify to spiritualistic incidents but are not spiritualists; the fact that science itself admits such things more and more every day. Science will even admit the Ascension if you call it Levitation, and will very likely admit the Resurrection when it has thought of another word for it. I suggest the Regalvanization. But the strongest of all is the dilemma above mentioned, that these supernatural things are never denied except on the basis either of anti-democracy or of materialist dogmatism – I may say materialist mysticism. The sceptic always takes one of the two positions; either an ordinary man need not be believed, or an extraordinary event must not be believed. For I hope we may dismiss the argument against wonders attempted in the mere recapitulation of frauds, of swindling mediums or trick miracles. That is not an argument at all, good or bad. A false ghost disproves the reality of ghosts exactly as much as a forged banknote disproves the existence of the Bank of England – if anything, it proves its existence.

Given this conviction that the spiritual phenomena do occur (my evidence for which is complex but rational), we then collide with one of the worst mental evils of the age. The greatest disaster of the nineteenth century was this: that men began to use the word 'spiritual' as the same as the word 'good'. They thought that to grow in refinement and uncorporeality was to grow in virtue. When scientific evolution was announced, some feared that it would encourage mere animality. It did worse: it encouraged mere spirituality. It taught men to think that so long as they were passing from the ape they were going to the angel. But you can pass from the ape and go to the devil. . . . Between this sunken pride and the towering humilities of heaven there are, one must suppose, spirits of shapes and sizes. Man, in encountering them, must make much the same mistakes that he makes in encountering any other varied types in any other distant continent. It must be hard at first to know who is supreme and who is subordinate. If a shade arose from the under world, and stared at Piccadilly, that shade would not quite understand the idea of an ordinary closed carriage. He would suppose that the coachman on the box was a triumphant conqueror, dragging behind him a kicking and imprisoned captive. So, if we see spiritual facts for the first time, we may mistake who is uppermost. It is not enough to find the gods; they are obvious; we must find God, the real chief of the gods. We must have a long historic experience in supernatural phenomena – in order to discover which are really natural. In this light I find the history of Christianity, and even of its Hebrew origins, quite practical and clear. It does not trouble me to be told that the Hebrew god was one among many. I know he was, without any research to tell me so. Jehovah and Baal looked equally important, just as the sun and the moon looked the same size. It is only slowly that we learn that the sun is immeasurably our master, and the small moon only our satellite. Believing that there is a world of spirits, I shall walk in it as I do in the world of men, looking for the thing that I like and think good. Just as I should seek in a desert for clean water, or toil at the North Pole to make a comfortable fire, so I shall search the land of void and vision until I find something fresh like water, and comforting like fire; until I find some place in eternity, where I am literally at home. And there is only one such place to be found.

I have now said enough to show (to any one to whom such an explanation is essential) that I have in the ordinary arena of apologetics, a ground of belief. In pure records of experiment (if these be taken democratically without contempt or favour) there is evidence first, that miracles happen, and second that the nobler miracles belong to our tradition. But I will not pretend that this curt discussion is my real reason for accepting Christianity instead of taking the moral good of Christianity as I should take it out of Confucianism.

I have another far more solid and central ground for submitting to it as a faith, instead of merely picking up hints from it as a scheme. And that is this: that the Christian Church in its practical relation to my soul is a living teacher, not a dead one. It not only certainly taught me yesterday, but will almost certainly teach me tomorrow. Once I saw suddenly the meaning of the shape of the cross; some day I may see suddenly the meaning of the shape of the mitre. One fine morning I saw why windows were pointed; some fine morning I may see why priests were shaven. Plato has told you a truth; but Plato is dead. Shakespeare has startled you with an image; but Shakespeare will not startle you with any more.

But imagine what it would be to live with such men still living, to know that Plato might break out with an original lecture tomorrow, or that at any moment Shakespeare might shatter everything with a single song. The man who lives in contact with what he believes to be a living Church is a man always expecting to meet Plato and Shakespeare tomorrow at breakfast. He is always expecting to see some truth that he has never seen before. There is one only other parallel to this position; and that is the parallel of the life in which we all began. When your father told you, walking about the garden, that bees stung or that roses smelt sweet, you did not talk of taking the best out of his philosophy. When the bees stung you, you did not call it an entertaining coincidence. When the rose smelt sweet you did not say 'My father is a rude, barbaric symbol, enshrining (perhaps unconsciously) the deep delicate truths that flowers smell.' No: you believed your father, because you had found him to be a living fountain of facts, a thing that really knew more than you; a thing that would tell you truth tomorrow, as well as today. And if this was true of your father, it was even truer of your mother; at least it was true of mine, to whom this book is dedicated. Now, when society is in a rather futile fuss about the subjection of women, will no one say how much every man owes to the tyranny and privilege of women, to the fact that they alone rule education until education becomes futile: for a boy is only sent to be taught at school when it is too late to teach him anything. The real thing has been done already, and thank God it is nearly always done by women. Every man is womanized, merely by being born. They talk of the masculine woman; but every man is a feminized man. And if ever men walk to Westminster to protest against this female privilege, I shall not join their procession.

For I remember with certainty this fixed psychological fact; that the very time when I was most under a woman's authority, I was most full of flame and adventure. Exactly because when my mother said that ants bit they did bite, and because snow did come in winter (as she said); therefore the whole world was to me a fairyland of wonderful fulfilments, and it was like living in some Hebraic age, when prophecy after prophecy came true. I went out as a child into the garden, and it was a terrible place to me, precisely because I had a clue to it: if I had held no clue it would not have been terrible, but tame. A mere unmeaning wilderness is not even impressive. But the garden of childhood was fascinating, exactly because everything had a fixed meaning which could be found out in its turn. Inch by inch I might discover what was the object of the ugly shape called a rake; or form some shadowy conjecture as to why my parents kept a cat.

So, since I have accepted Christendom as a mother and not merely as a chance example, I have found Europe and the world once more like the little garden where I stared at the symbolic shapes of cat and rake; I look at everything with the old elvish ignorance and expectancy. This or that rite or doctrine may look as ugly and extraordinary as a rake; but I have found by experience that such things end somehow in grass and flowers. A clergyman may be apparently as useless as a cat, but he is also as fascinating, for there must be some strange reason for his existence. I give one instance out of a hundred; I have not myself any instinctive kinship with that enthusiasm for physical virginity, which has certainly been a note of historic Christianity. But when I look not at myself but at the world, I perceive that this enthusiasm is not only a note of Christianity, but a note of Paganism, a note of high human nature in many spheres. The Greeks felt virginity when they carved Artemis, the Romans when they robed the vestals, the worst and wildest of the great Elizabethan playwrights clung to the literal purity of a woman as to the central pillar of the world. Above all, the modern world (even while mocking sexual innocence) has flung itself into a generous idolatry of sexual innocence – the great modern worship of children. For any man who loves children will agree that their peculiar beauty is hurt by a hint of physical sex. With all this human experience, allied with the Christian authority, I simply conclude that I am wrong, and the church right; or rather that I am defective, while the church is universal. It takes all sorts to make a church; she does not ask me to be celibate. But the fact that I have no appreciation of the celibates, I accept like the fact that I have no ear for music. The best human experience is against me, as it is on the subject of Bach. Celibacy is one flower in my father's garden, of which I have not been told the sweet or terrible name. But I may be told it any day.

This, therefore, is, in conclusion, my reason for accepting the religion and not merely the scattered and secular truths out of the religion. I do it because the thing has not merely told this truth or that truth, but has revealed itself as a truth-telling thing. All other philosophies say the things that plainly seem to be true; only this philosophy has again and again said the thing that does not seem to be true, but is true. Alone of all creeds it is convincing where it is not attractive; it turns out to be right, like my father in the garden. Theosophists for instance will preach an obviously attractive idea like reincarnation; but if we wait for its logical results, they are spiritual superciliousness and the cruelty of caste. For if a man is a beggar by his own pre-natal sins, people will tend to despise the beggar. But Christianity preaches an obviously unattractive idea, such as original sin; but when we wait for its results, they are pathos and brotherhood, and a thunder of laughter and pity; for only with original sin we can at once pity the beggar and distrust the king. Men of science offer us health, an obvious benefit; it is only afterwards that we discover that by health, they mean bodily slavery and spiritual tedium. Orthodoxy makes us jump by the sudden brink of hell; it is only afterwards that we realize that jumping was an athletic exercise highly beneficial to our health. It is only afterwards that we realize that this danger is the root of all drama and romance. The strongest argument for the divine grace is simply its ungraciousness. The unpopular parts of Christianity turn out when examined to be the very props of the people. The outer ring of Christianity is a rigid guard of ethical abnegations and professional priests; but inside that inhuman guard you will find the old human life dancing like children, and drinking wine like men; for Christianity is the only frame for pagan freedom. But in the modern philosophy the case is opposite; it is its outer ring that is obviously artistic and emancipated; its despair is within.

And its despair is this, that it does not really believe that there is any meaning in the universe; therefore it cannot hope to find any romance; its romances will have no plots. A man cannot expect any adventures in the land of anarchy. But a man can expect any number of adventures if he goes travelling in the land of authority. One can find no meanings in a jungle of scepticism; but the man will find more and more meanings who walks through a forest of doctrine and design. Here everything has a story tied to its tail, like the tools or pictures in my father's house; for it is my father's house. I end where I began – at the right end. I have entered at least the gate of all good philosophy. I have come into my second childhood.

But this larger and more adventurous Christian universe has one final mark difficult to express; yet as a conclusion of the whole matter I will attempt to express it. All the real argument about religion turns on the question of whether a man who was born upside down can tell when he comes right way up. The primary paradox of Christianity is that the ordinary condition of man is not his sane or sensible condition; that the normal itself is an abnormality. That is the inmost philosophy of the Fall. . . . This is the prime paradox of our religion; something that we have never in any full sense known, is not only better than ourselves, but even more natural to us than ourselves. And there is really no test of this except the merely experimental one with which these pages began, the test of the padded cell and the open door. It is only since I have known orthodoxy that I have known mental emancipation. But, in conclusion, it has one special application to the ultimate idea of joy.

It is said that Paganism is a religion of joy and Christianity of sorrow; it would be just as easy to prove that Paganism is pure sorrow and Christianity pure joy. Such conflicts mean nothing and lead nowhere. Everything human must have in it both joy and sorrow; the only matter of interest is the manner in which the two things are balanced or divided. And the really interesting thing is this, that the pagan was (in the main) happier and happier as he approached the earth, but sadder and sadder as he approached the heavens. The gaiety of the best Paganism, as in the playfulness of Catullus or Theocritus, is, indeed, an eternal gaiety never to be forgotten by a grateful humanity. But it is all a gaiety about the facts of life, not about its origin. To the pagan the small things are as sweet as the small brooks breaking out of the mountain; but the broad things are as bitter as the sea. When the pagan looks at the very core of the cosmos he is struck cold. Behind the gods, who are merely despotic, sit the fates, who are deadly. Nay, the fates are worse than deadly; they are dead. And when rationalists say that the ancient world was more enlightened than the Christian, from their point of view they are right. For when they say 'enlightened' they mean darkened with incurable despair. It is profoundly true that the ancient world was more modern than the Christian. The common bond is in the fact that ancients and moderns have both been miserable about existence, about everything, while mediaevals were happy about that at least. I freely grant that the pagans, like the moderns, were only miserable about everything – they were quite jolly about everything else. I concede that the Christians of the Middle Ages were only at peace about everything – they were at war about everything else. But if the question turn on the primary pivot of the cosmos, then there was more cosmic contentment in the narrow and bloody streets of Florence than in the theatre of Athens or the open garden of Epicurus. Giotto lived in a gloomier town than Euripides, but he lived in a gayer universe.

The mass of men have been forced to be gay about the little things, but sad about the big ones. Nevertheless (I offer my last dogma defiantly) it is not native to man to be so. Man is more himself, man is more manlike, when joy is the fundamental thing in him, and grief the superficial. Melancholy should be an innocent interlude, a tender and fugitive frame of mind; praise should be the permanent pulsation of the soul. Pessimism is at best an emotional half-holiday; joy is the uproarious labour by which all things live. Yet, according to the apparent estate of man as seen by the pagan or the agnostic, this primary need of human nature can never be fulfilled. Joy ought to be expansive; but for the agnostic it must be contracted, it must cling to one corner of the world. Grief ought to be a concentration; but for the agnostic its desolation is spread through an unthinkable eternity. This is what I call being born upside down. The sceptic may truly be said to be topsy-turvy; for his feet are dancing upwards in idle ecstasies, while his brain is in the abyss. To the modern man the heavens are actually below the earth. The explanation is simple; he is standing on his head; which is a very weak pedestal to stand on. But when he has found his feet again he knows it. Christianity satisfies suddenly and perfectly man's ancestral instinct for being the right way up; satisfies it supremely in this; that by its creed joy becomes something gigantic and sadness something special and small. The vault above us is not deaf because the universe is an idiot; the silence is not the heartless silence of an endless and aimless world. Rather the silence around us is a small and pitiful stillness like the prompt stillness in a sick-room. We are perhaps permitted tragedy as a sort of merciful comedy: because the frantic energy of divine things would knock us down like a drunken farce. We can take our own tears more lightly than we could take the tremendous levities of the angels. So we sit perhaps in a starry chamber of silence, while the laughter of the heavens is too loud for us to hear.

Joy, which was the small publicity of the pagan, is the gigantic secret of the Christian. And as I close this chaotic volume I open again the strange small book from which all Christianity came; and I am again haunted by a kind of confirmation. The tremendous figure which fills the Gospels towers in this respect, as in every other, above all the thinkers who ever thought themselves tall. His pathos was natural, almost casual. The Stoics, ancient and modern, were proud of concealing their tears. He never concealed His tears; He showed them plainly on His open face at any daily sight, such as the far sight of His native city. Yet He concealed something. Solemn supermen and imperial diplomatists are proud of restraining their anger. He never restrained His anger. He flung furniture down the front steps of the Temple, and asked men how they expected to escape the damnation of Hell. Yet He restrained something. I say it with reverence; there was in that shattering personality a thread that must be called shyness. There was something that He hid from all men when He went up a mountain to pray. There was something that He covered constantly by abrupt silence or impetuous isolation. There was some one thing that was too great for God to show us when He walked upon our earth; and I have sometimes fancied that it was His mirth.

THE
EVERLASTING MAN

INTRODUCTION
THE PLAN OF THIS BOOK

T HERE are two ways of getting home; and one of them is to stay there. The other is to walk round the whole world till we come back to the same place; and I tried to trace such a journey in a story I once wrote. It is, however, a relief to turn from that topic to another story that I never wrote. Like every book I never wrote, it is by far the best book I have ever written. It is only too probable that I shall never write it, so I will use it symbolically here; for it was a symbol of the same truth. I conceived it as a romance of those vast valleys with sloping sides, like those along which the ancient White Horses of Wessex are scrawled along the flanks of the hills. It concerned some boy whose farm or cottage stood on such a slope, and who went on his travels to find something, such as the effigy and grave of some giant; and when he was far enough from home he looked back and saw that his own farm and kitchen-garden, shining flat on the hill-side like the colours and quarterings of a shield, were but parts of some such gigantic figure, on which he had always lived, but which was too large and too close to be seen. That, I think, is a true picture of the progress of any really independent intelligence today; and that is the point of this book.

The point of this book, in other words, is that the next best thing to being really inside Christendom is to be really outside it. And a particular point of it is that the popular critics of Christianity are not really outside it. They are on a debatable ground, in every sense of the term. They are doubtful in their very doubts. Their criticism has taken on a curious tone; as of a random and illiterate heckling. Thus they make current and anti-clerical cant as a sort of small-talk. They will complain of parsons dressing like parsons; as if we should be any more free if all the police who shadowed or collared us were plain-clothes detectives. Or they will complain that a sermon cannot be interrupted, and call a pulpit a coward's castle; though they do not call an editor's office a coward's castle. It would be unjust both to journalists and priests; but it would be much truer of journalists. The clergyman appears in person and could easily be kicked as he came out of church; the journalist conceals even his name so that nobody can kick him. They write wild and pointless articles and letters in the press about why the churches are empty, without even going there to find out if they are empty, or which of them are empty. Their suggestions are more vapid and vacant than the most insipid curate in a three-act farce, and move us to comfort him after the manner of the curate in the *Bab Ballads*;[1] 'Your mind is not so blank as that of Hopley Porter.' So we may truly say to the very feeblest cleric: 'Your mind is not so blank as that of Indignant Layman or Plain Man or Man in the Street, or any of your critics in the newspapers; for they have not the most shadowy notion of what they want themselves, let alone of what you ought to give them.' They will suddenly turn round and revile the Church for not having prevented the War, which they themselves did not want to prevent; and which nobody had ever professed to be able to prevent, except some of that very school of progressive and cosmo-politan sceptics who are the chief enemies of the Church. It was the anti-clerical and agnostic world that was always prophesy-ing the advent of universal peace; it is that world that was, or should have been, abashed and confounded by the advent of universal war. As for the general view that the Church was discredited by the War – they might as well say that the Ark was discredited by the Flood. When the world goes wrong, it proves rather that the Church is right. The Church is justified, not because her children do not sin, but because they do. But that marks their mood about the whole religious tradition: they are in a state of reaction against it. It is well with the boy when he lives on his father's land; and well with him again when he is far enough from it to look back on it and see it as a whole. But these people have got into an intermediate state, have fallen into an intervening valley from which they can see neither the heights beyond them nor the heights behind. They cannot get out of the penumbra of Christian controversy. They cannot be Christians and they cannot leave off being Anti-Christians. Their whole atmosphere is the atmosphere of a reaction: sulks, perversity, petty criticism. They still live in the shadow of the faith and have lost the light of the faith.

1 A collection of light verse by W. S. Gilbert, illustrated with his comic drawings.

INTRODUCTION 411

Now the best relation to our spiritual home is to be near enough to love it. But the next best is to be far enough away not to hate it. It is the contention of these pages that while the best judge of Christianity is a Christian, the next best judge would be something more like a Confucian. The worst judge of all is the man now most ready with his judgments; the ill-educated Christian turning gradually into the ill-tempered agnostic, entangled in the end of a feud of which he never understood the beginning, blighted with a sort of hereditary boredom with he knows not what, and already weary of hearing what he has never heard. He does not judge Christianity calmly as a Confucian would; he does not judge it as he would judge Confucianism. He cannot by an effort of fancy set the Catholic Church thousands of miles away in strange skies of morning and judge it as impartially as a Chinese pagoda. It is said that the great St Francis Xavier, who very nearly succeeded in setting up the Church there as a tower overtopping all pagodas, failed partly because his followers were accused by their fellow missionaries of representing the Twelve Apostles with the garb or attributes of Chinamen. But it would be far better to see them as Chinamen, and judge them fairly as Chinamen, than to see them as featureless idols merely made to be battered by iconoclasts; or rather as cockshies to be pelted by empty-handed cockneys. It would be better to see the whole thing as a remote Asiatic cult, the mitres of its bishops as the towering head-dresses of mysterious bonzes; its pastoral staffs as the sticks twisted like serpents carried in some Asiatic procession; to see the prayer-book as fantastic as the prayer-wheel and the Cross as crooked as the Swastika. Then at least we should not lose our temper as some of the sceptical critics seem to lose their temper, not to mention their wits. Their anti-clericalism has become an atmosphere, an atmosphere of negation and hostility from which they cannot escape. Compared with that, it would be better to see the whole thing as something belonging to another continent, or to another planet. It would be more philosophical to stare indifferently at bonzes than to be perpetually and pointlessly grumbling at bishops. It would be better to walk past a church as if it were a pagoda than to stand permanently in the porch, impotent either to go inside and help or to go outside and forget. For those in whom a mere reaction has thus become an obsession, I do seriously recommend the imaginative effort of conceiving the Twelve Apostles as Chinamen. In other words, I recommend these critics to try to do as much justice to Christian saints as if they were Pagan sages.

But with this we come to the final and vital point. I shall try to show in these pages that when we *do* make this imaginative effort to see the whole thing from the outside, we find that it really looks like what is traditionally said about it inside. It is exactly when the boy gets far enough off to see the giant that he sees that he really is a giant. It is exactly when we do at last see the Christian Church afar under those clear and level eastern skies that we see that it is really the Church of Christ. To put it shortly, the moment we are really impartial about it, we know why people are partial to it. But this second proposition requires more serious discussion; and I shall here set myself to discuss it.

As soon as I had clearly in my mind this conception of something solid in the solitary and unique character of the divine story, it struck me that there was exactly the same strange and yet solid character in the human story that had led up to it; because that human story also had a root that was divine. I mean that just as the Church seems to grow more remarkable when it is fairly compared with the common religious life of mankind, so mankind itself seems to grow more remarkable when we compare it with the common life of nature. And I have noticed that most modern history is driven to something like sophistry, first to soften the sharp transition from animals to men, and then to soften the sharp transition from heathens to Christians. Now the more we really read in a realistic spirit of those two transitions the sharper we shall find them to be. It is because the critics are *not* detached that they do not see this detachment; it is because they are not looking at things in a dry light that they cannot see the difference between black and white. It is because they are in a particular mood of reaction and revolt that they have a motive for making out that all the white is dirty grey and the black not so black as it is painted. I do not say there are not human excuses for their revolt; I do not say it is not in some ways sympathetic; what I say is that it is not in any way scientific. An iconoclast may be indignant; an iconoclast may be justly indignant; but an iconoclast is not impartial. And it is stark hypocrisy to pretend that nine-tenths of the higher critics and scientific evolutionists and professors of comparative religion are in the least impartial.

Why should they be impartial, what is being impartial, when the whole world is at war about whether one thing is a devouring superstition or a divine hope? I do not pretend to be impartial in the sense that the final act of faith fixes a man's mind because it satisfies his mind. But I do profess to be a great deal more impartial than they are; in the sense that I can tell the story fairly, with some sort of imaginative justice to all sides; and they cannot. I do profess to be impartial in the sense that I should be ashamed to talk such nonsense about the Lama of Tibet as they do about the Pope of Rome, or to have as little sympathy with Julian the Apostate as they have with the Society of Jesus. They are not impartial; they never by any chance hold the historical scales even; and above all they are never impartial upon this point of evolution and transition. They suggest everywhere the grey gradations of twilight, because they believe it is the twilight of the gods. I propose to maintain that whether or no it is the twilight of gods, it is not the daylight of men.

I maintain that when brought out into the daylight these two things look altogether strange and unique; and that it is only in the false twilight of an imaginary period of transition that they can be made to look in the least like anything else. The first of these is the creature called man and the second is the man called Christ. I have therefore divided this book into two parts: the former being a sketch of the main adventure of the human race in so far as it remained heathen; and the second a summary of the real difference that was made by it becoming Christian. Both motives necessitate a certain method, a method which is not very easy to manage, and perhaps even less easy to define or defend.

In order to strike, in the only sane or possible sense, the note of impartiality, it is necessary to touch the nerve of novelty. I mean that in one sense we see things fairly when we see them first. That, I may remark in passing, is why children generally have very little difficulty about the dogmas of the Church. But the Church, being a highly practical thing for working and fighting, is necessarily a thing for men and not merely for children. There must be in it for working purposes a great deal of tradition, of familiarity, and even of routine. So long as its fundamentals are sincerely felt, this may even be the saner condition. But when its fundamentals are doubted, as at present, we must try to recover the candour and wonder of the child; the unspoilt realism and objectivity of innocence.

Or if we cannot do that, we must try at least to shake off the cloud of mere custom and see the thing as new, if only by seeing it as unnatural. Things that may well be familiar so long as familiarity breeds affection had much better become unfamiliar when familiarity breeds contempt. For in connection with things so great as are here considered, whatever our view of them, contempt must be a mistake. Indeed contempt must be an illusion. We must invoke the most wild and soaring sort of imagination; the imagination that can see what is there.

The only way to suggest the point is by an example of something, indeed of almost anything, that has been considered beautiful or wonderful. George Wyndham[1] once told me that he had seen one of the first aeroplanes rise for the first time and it was very wonderful; but not so wonderful as a horse allowing a man to ride on him. Somebody else has said that a fine man on a fine horse is the noblest bodily object in the world. Now, so long as people feel this in the right way, all is well. The first and best way of appreciating it is to come of people with a tradition of treating animals properly; of men in the right relation to horses. A boy who remembers his father who rode a horse, who rode it well and treated it well, will know that the relation can be satisfactory and will be satisfied. He will be all the more indignant at the ill-treatment of horses because he knows how they ought to be treated; but he will see nothing but what is normal in a man riding on a horse. He will not listen to the great modern philosopher who explains to him that the horse ought to be riding on the man. He will not pursue the pessimist fancy of Swift and say that men must be despised as monkeys and horses worshipped as gods. And horse and man together making an image that is to him human and civilized, it will be easy, as it were, to lift horse and man together into something heroic or symbolical; like a vision of St George in the clouds. The fable of the winged horse will not be wholly unnatural to him: and he will know why Ariosto set many a Christian hero in such an airy saddle, and made him the rider of the sky. For the horse has really been lifted up along with the man in the wildest fashion in the very word we use when we speak 'chivalry'. The very name of the horse has been given to the highest mood and moment of the man; so that

1 George Wyndham (1863–1913), reforming Conservative Chief Secretary for Ireland.

we might almost say that the handsomest compliment to a man is to call him a horse.

But if a man has got into a mood in which he is *not* able to feel this sort of wonder, then his cure must begin right at the other end. We must now suppose that he has drifted into a dull mood, in which somebody sitting on a horse means no more than somebody sitting on a chair. The wonder of which Wyndham spoke, the beauty that made the thing seem an equestrian statue, the meaning of the more chivalric horseman, may have become to him merely a convention and a bore. Perhaps they have been merely a fashion; perhaps they have gone out of fashion; perhaps they have been talked about too much or talked about in the wrong way; perhaps it was then difficult to care for horses without the horrible risk of being horsy. Anyhow, he has got into a condition when he cares no more for a horse than for a towel-horse. His grandfather's charge at Balaclava seems to him as dull and dusty as the album containing such family portraits. Such a person has not really become enlightened about the album; on the contrary, he has only become blind with the dust. But when he has reached *that* degree of blindness, he will not be able to look at a horse or a horseman at all until he has seen the whole thing as a thing entirely unfamiliar and almost unearthly.

Out of some dark forest under some ancient dawn there must come towards us, with lumbering yet dancing motions, one of the very queerest of the prehistoric creatures. We must see for the first time the strangely small head set on a neck not only longer but thicker than itself, as the face of a gargoyle is thrust out upon a gutter-spout, the one disproportionate crest of hair running along the ridge of that heavy neck like a beard in the wrong place; the feet, each like a solid club of horn, alone amid the feet of so many cattle; so that the true fear is to be found in showing, not the cloven, but the uncloven hoof. Nor is it mere verbal fancy to see him thus as a unique monster; for in a sense a monster means what is unique, and he is really unique. But the point is that when we thus see him as the first man saw him, we begin once more to have some imaginative sense of what it meant when the first man rode him. In such a dream he may seem ugly, but he does not seem unimpressive; and certainly that two-legged dwarf who could get on top of him will not seem unimpressive. By a longer and more erratic road we shall come back to the same marvel of the man and the horse; and the marvel will be, if possible, even more marvellous. We shall have again a glimpse of St George; the more glorious because St George is not riding on the horse, but rather riding on the dragon.

In this example, which I have taken merely because it is an example, it will be noted that I do not say that the nightmare seen by the first man of the forest is either more true or more wonderful than the normal mare of the stable seen by the civilized person who can appreciate what is normal. Of the two extremes, I think on the whole that the traditional grasp of truth is the better. But I say that the truth is found at one or other of these two extremes, and is lost in the intermediate condition of mere fatigue and forgetfulness of tradition. In other words, I say it is better to see a horse as a monster than to see it only as a slow substitute for a motor-car. If we have got into *that* state of mind about a horse as something stale, it is far better to be frightened of a horse because it is a good deal too fresh.

Now, as it is with the monster that is called a horse, so it is with the monster that is called a man. Of course the best condition of all, in my opinion, is always to have regarded man as he is regarded in my philosophy. He who holds the Christian and Catholic view of human nature will feel certain that it is a universal and therefore a sane view, and will be satisfied. But if he has lost the sane vision, he can only get it back by something very like a mad vision; that is, by seeing man as a strange animal and realizing how strange an animal he is. But just as seeing the horse as a prehistoric prodigy ultimately led back to, and not away from, an admiration for the mastery of man, so the *really* detached consideration of the curious career of man will lead back to, and not away from, the ancient faith in the dark designs of God. In other words, it is exactly when we do see how queer the quadruped is that we praise the man who mounts him; and exactly when we do see how queer the biped is that we praise the Providence that made him.

In short, it is the purpose of this introduction to maintain this thesis: that it is exactly when we do regard man as an animal that we know he is not an animal. It is precisely when we do try to picture him as a sort of horse on its hind legs, that we suddenly realize that he must be something as miraculous as the winged horse that towered up into the clouds of heaven. All roads lead to Rome, all ways lead round again to the central and civilized philosophy, including this road through elfland and topsy-turvydom. But it may be that it is better never to have left the land of a reasonable tradition, where men ride lightly upon horses and are mighty hunters before the Lord.

So also in the specially Christian case we have to react against the heavy bias of fatigue. It is almost impossible to make the facts vivid, because the facts are familiar; and for fallen men it is often true that familiarity is fatigue. I am convinced that if we could tell the supernatural story of Christ word for word as of a Chinese hero, call him the Son of Heaven instead of the Son of God, and trace his rayed nimbus in the gold thread of Chinese embroideries or the gold lacquer of Chinese pottery, instead of in the gold leaf of our own old Catholic paintings, there would be a unanimous testimony to the spiritual purity of the story. We should hear nothing then of the injustice of substitution or the illogicality of atonement, of the superstitious exaggeration of the burden of sin or the impossible insolence of an invasion of the laws of nature. We should admire the chivalry of the Chinese conception of a god who fell from the sky to fight the dragons and save the wicked from being devoured by their own fault and folly. We should admire the subtlety of the Chinese view of life, which perceives that all human imperfection is in very truth a crying imperfection. We should admire the Chinese esoteric and superior wisdom, which said there are higher cosmic laws than the laws we know; we believe every common Indian conjurer who chooses to come to us and talk in the same style. If Christianity were only a new oriental fashion, it would never be reproached with being an old and oriental faith. I do not propose in this book to follow the alleged example of St Francis Xavier with the opposite imaginative intention, and turn the Twelve Apostles into Mandarins; not so much to make them look like natives as to make them look like foreigners. I do not propose to work what I believe would be a completely successful practical joke; that of telling the whole story of the Gospel and the whole history of the church in a setting of pagodas and pigtails; and noting with malignant humour how much it was admired as a heathen story, in the very quarters where it is condemned as a Christian story. But I do propose to strike wherever possible this note of what is new and strange, and for that reason the style even on so serious a subject may sometimes be deliberately grotesque and fanciful. I do desire to help the reader to see Christendom from the outside in the sense of seeing it as a whole, against the background of other historic things; just as I desire him to see humanity as a whole against the background of natural things. And I say that in both cases, when seen thus, they stand out from their background like supernatural things. They do *not* fade into the rest with the colours of impressionism; they stand out from the rest with the colours of heraldry; as vivid as a red cross on a white shield or a black lion on a ground of gold. So stands the Red Clay against the green field of nature, or the White Christ against the red clay of his race.

But in order to see them clearly we have to see them as a whole. We have to see how they developed as well as how they began; for the most incredible part of the story is that things which began thus should have developed thus. Anyone who chooses to indulge in mere imagination can imagine that other things might have happened or other entities evolved. Anyone thinking of what might have happened may conceive a sort of evolutionary equality; but anyone facing what did happen must face an exception and a prodigy. If there was ever a moment when man was only an animal, we can if we choose make a fancy picture of his career transferred to some other animal. An entertaining fantasia might be made in which elephants built in elephantine architecture, with towers and turrets like tusks and trunks, cities beyond the scale of any colossus. A pleasant fable might be conceived in which a cow had developed a costume, and put on four boots and two pairs of trousers. We could imagine a Supermonkey more marvellous than any Superman, a quadrumanous creature carving and painting with his hands and cooking and carpentering with his feet. But if we are considering what did happen, we shall certainly decide that man has distanced everything else with a distance like that of the astronomical spaces and a speed like that of the still thunderbolt of the light. And in the same fashion, while we can if we choose see the Church amid a mob of Mithraic or Manichean superstitions squabbling and killing each other at the end of the Empire, while we can if we choose imagine the Church killed in the struggle and some other chance cult taking its place, we shall be the more surprised (and possibly puzzled) if we meet it two thousand years afterwards rushing through the ages as the winged thunderbolt of thought and everlasting enthusiasm; a thing without rival or resemblance; and still as new as it is old.

II
THE RIDDLES OF THE GOSPEL

To UNDERSTAND the nature of this chapter, it is necessary to recur to the nature of this book. The argument which is meant to be the backbone of the book is of the kind called the *reductio ad absurdum*. It suggests that the results of assuming the rationalist thesis are more irrational than ours; but to prove it we must assume that thesis. Thus in the first section I often treated man as merely an animal, to show that the effect was more impossible than if he were treated as an angel. In the sense in which it was necessary to treat man merely as an animal, it is necessary to treat Christ merely as a man. I have to suspend my own beliefs, which are much more positive; and assume this limitation even in order to remove it. I must try to imagine what would happen to a man who did really read the story of Christ as the story of a man; and even of a man of whom he had never heard before. And I wish to point out that a really impartial reading of that kind would lead, if not immediately to belief, at least to a bewilderment of which there is really no solution except in belief. In this chapter, for this reason, I shall bring in nothing of the spirit of my own creed; I shall exclude the very style of diction, and even of lettering, which I should think fitting in speaking in my own person. I am speaking as an imaginary heathen human being, honestly, staring at the Gospel story for the first time.

Now it is not at all easy to regard the New Testament as a New Testament. It is not at all easy to realize the good news as new. Both for good and evil familiarity fills us with assumptions and associations; and no man of our civilization, whatever he thinks of our religion, can really read the thing as if he had never heard of it before. Of course it is in any case utterly unhistorical to talk as if the New Testament were a neatly bound book that had fallen from heaven. It is simply the selection made by the authority of the Church from a mass of early Christian literature. But apart from any such question, there is a psychological difficulty in feeling the

New Testament as new. There is a psychological difficulty in seeing those well-known words simply as they stand and without going beyond what they intrinsically stand for. And this difficulty must indeed be very great; for the result of it is very curious. The result of it is that most modern critics and most current criticism, even popular criticism, makes a comment that is the exact reverse of the truth. It is so completely the reverse of the truth that one could almost suspect that they had never read the New Testament at all.

We have all heard people say a hundred times over, for they seem never to tire of saying it, that the Jesus of the New Testament is indeed a most merciful and humane lover of humanity, but that the Church has hidden this human character in repellant dogmas and stiffened it with ecclesiastical terrors till it has taken on an inhuman character. This is, I venture to repeat, very nearly the reverse of the truth. The truth is that it is the image of Christ in the churches that is almost entirely mild and merciful. It is the image of Christ in the Gospels that is a good many other things as well. The figure in the Gospels does indeed utter in words of almost heart-breaking beauty his pity for our broken hearts. But they are very far from being the only sort of words that he utters. Nevertheless they are almost the only kind of words that the Church in its popular imagery ever represents him as uttering. That popular imagery is inspired by a perfectly sound popular instinct. The mass of the poor are broken, and the mass of the people are poor, and for the mass of mankind the main thing is to carry the conviction of the incredible compassion of God. But nobody with his eyes open can doubt that it is chiefly this idea of compassion that the popular machinery of the Church does seek to carry. The popular imagery carries a great deal to excess the sentiment of 'Gentle Jesus, meek and mild'. It is the first thing that the outsider feels and criticizes in a Pietà or a shrine of the Sacred Heart. As I say, while the art may be insufficient, I am not sure that the instinct is unsound. In any case there is something appalling, something that makes the blood run cold, in the idea of having a statue of Christ in wrath. There is something insupportable even to the imagination in the idea of turning the corner of a street or coming out into the spaces of a marketplace, to meet the petrifying petrifaction of *that* figure as it turned upon a generation of vipers, or that face as it looked at the face of a hypocrite. The Church can reasonably be justified therefore if she turns the most merciful face or aspect towards men; but it is certainly the most merciful aspect that she does turn. And the point is here that it is very much more specially and exclusively merciful than any impression that could be formed by a man merely reading the New Testament for the first time. A man simply taking the words of the story as they stand would form quite another impression; an impression full of mystery and possibly of inconsistency; but certainly not merely an impression of mildness. It would be intensely interesting; but part of the interest would consist in its leaving a good deal to be guessed at or explained. It is full of sudden gestures evidently significant except that we hardly know what they signify; of enigmatic silences; of ironical replies. The outbreaks of wrath, like storms above our atmosphere, do not seem to break out exactly where we should expect them, but to follow some higher weather-chart of their own. The Peter whom popular Church teaching presents is very rightly the Peter to whom Christ said in forgiveness, 'Feed my lambs.' He is not the Peter upon whom Christ turned as if he were the devil, crying in that obscure wrath, 'Get thee behind me, Satan.' Christ lamented with nothing but love and pity over Jerusalem which was to murder him. We do not know what strange spiritual atmosphere or spiritual insight led him to sink Bethsaida lower in the pit than Sodom. I am putting aside for the moment all questions of doctrinal inferences or expositions, orthodox or otherwise; I am simply imagining the effect on a man's mind if he did really do what these critics are always talking about doing; if he did really read the New Testament without reference to orthodoxy and even without reference to doctrine. He would find a number of things which fit in far less with the current unorthodoxy than they do with the current orthodoxy. He would find, for instance, that if there are any descriptions that deserved to be called realistic, they are precisely the descriptions of the supernatural. If there is one aspect of the New Testament Jesus in which he may be said to present himself eminently as a practical person, it is in the aspect of an exorcist. There is nothing meek and mild, there is nothing even in the ordinary sense mystical, about the tone of the voice that says 'Hold thy peace and come out of him.' It is much more like the tone of a very business-like lion-tamer or a strong-minded doctor dealing with a homicidal maniac. But this is only a side issue for the sake of illustration; I am not now raising these controversies; but considering the case of the imaginary man from the moon to whom the New Testament is new.

Now the first thing to note is that if we take it merely as a human story, it is in some ways a very strange story. I do not refer here to its tremendous and tragic culmination or to any implications involving triumph in that tragedy. I do not refer to what is commonly called the miraculous element; for on that point philosophies vary and modern philosophies very decidedly waver. Indeed the educated Englishman of today may be said to have passed from an old fashion, in which he would not believe in any miracles unless they were ancient, and adopted a new fashion in which he will not believe in any miracles unless they are modern. He used to hold that miraculous cures stopped with the first Christians and is now inclined to suspect that they began with the first Christian Scientists. But I refer here rather specially to unmiraculous and even to unnoticed and inconspicuous parts of the story. There are a great many things about it which nobody would have invented, for they are things that nobody has ever made any particular use of; things which if they were remarked at all have remained rather as puzzles. For instance, there is that long stretch of silence in the life of Christ up to the age of thirty. It is of all silences the most immense and imaginatively impressive. But it is not the sort of thing that anybody is particularly likely to invent in order to prove something; and nobody so far as I know has ever tried to prove anything in particular from it. It is impressive, but it is only impressive as a fact; there is nothing particularly popular or obvious about it as a fable. The ordinary trend of hero-worship and myth-making is much more likely to say the precise opposite. It is much more likely to say (as I believe some of the gospels rejected by the Church do say) that Jesus displayed a divine precocity and began his mission at a miraculously early age. And there is indeed something strange in the thought that he who of all humanity needed least preparation seems to have had most. Whether it was some mode of the divine humility, or some truth of which we see the shadow in the longer domestic tutelage of the higher creatures of the earth, I do not propose to speculate; I mention it simply as an example of the sort of thing that does in any case give rise to speculations, quite apart from recognized religious speculations. Now the whole story is full of these things. It is not by any means, as baldly presented in print, a story that it is easy to get to the bottom of. It is anything but what these people talk of as a simple Gospel. Relatively speaking, it is the Gospel that has the mysticism and the Church that has the rationalism. As I should put it, of course, it is the Gospel that is the riddle and the Church that is the answer. But whatever be the answer, the Gospel as it stands is almost a book of riddles.

First, a man reading the Gospel sayings would not find platitudes. If he had read even in the most respectful spirit the majority of ancient philosophers and of modern moralists, he would appreciate the unique importance of saying that he did not find platitudes. It is more than can be said even of Plato. It is much more than can be said of Epictetus[1] or Seneca or Marcus Aurelius or Apollonius of Tyana.[2] And it is immeasurably more than can be said of most of the agnostic moralists and the preachers of the ethical societies; with their songs of service and their religion of brotherhood. The morality of most moralists ancient and modern, has been one solid and polished cataract of platitudes flowing for ever and ever. That would certainly not be the impression of the imaginary independent outsider studying the New Testament. He would be conscious of nothing so commonplace and in a sense of nothing so continuous as that stream. He would find a number of strange claims that might sound like the claim to be the brother of the sun and moon; a number of very startling pieces of advice; a number of stunning rebukes; a number of strangely beautiful stories. He would see some very gigantesque figures of speech about the impossibility of threading a needle with a camel or the possibility of throwing a mountain into the sea. He would see a number of very daring simplifications of the difficulties of life; like the advice to shine upon everybody indifferently as does the sunshine or not to worry about the future any more than the birds. He would find on the other hand some passages of almost impenetrable darkness, so far as he is concerned, such as the moral of the parable of the Unjust Steward. Some of these things might strike him as fables and some as truths; but none as truisms. For instance, he would not find the ordinary platitudes in favour of peace. He would find several paradoxes in favour of peace. He would find

1 Greek stoic philosopher (c. AD55-c. 135).
2 Greek Neo-Pythagorean philosopher (c. AD15-c. 100).

several ideals of non-resistance, which taken as they stand would be rather too pacific for any pacifist. He would be told in one passage to treat a robber *not* with passive resistance, but rather with positive and enthusiastic encouragement, if the terms be taken literally; heaping up gifts upon the man who had stolen goods. But he would not find a word of all that obvious rhetoric against war which has filled countless books and odes and orations; not a word about the wickedness of war, the wastefulness of war, the appalling scale of the slaughter in war and all the rest of the familiar frenzy; indeed not a word about war at all. There is nothing that throws any particular light on Christ's attitude towards organized warfare, except that he seems to have been rather fond of Roman soldiers. Indeed it is another perplexity, speaking from the same external and human standpoint, that he seems to have got on much better with Romans than he did with Jews. But the question here is a certain tone to be appreciated by merely reading a certain text; and we might give any number of instances of it.

The statement that the meek shall inherit the earth is very far from being a meek statement. I mean it is not meek in the ordinary sense of mild and moderate and inoffensive. To justify it, it would be necessary to go very deep into history and anticipate things undreamed of then and by many unrealized even now; such as the way in which the mystical monks reclaimed the lands which the practical kings had lost. If it was a truth at all, it was because it was a prophecy. But certainly it was not a truth in the sense of a truism. The blessing upon the meek would seem to be a very violent statement; in the sense of doing violence to reason and probability. And with this we come to another important stage in the speculation. As a prophecy it really was fulfilled; but it was only fulfilled long afterwards. The monasteries were the most practical and prosperous estates and experiments in reconstruction after the barbaric deluge; the meek did really inherit the earth. But nobody could have known anything of the sort at the time – unless indeed there was one who knew. Something of the same thing may be said about the incident of Martha and Mary; which has been interpreted in retrospect and from the inside by the mystics of the Christian contemplative life. But it was not at all an obvious view of it; and most moralists, ancient and modern, could be trusted to make a rush for the obvious. What torrents of effortless eloquence would have flowed from them to swell any slight superiority on the part of Martha; what splendid sermons about the Joy of Service and the Gospel of Work and the World Left Better Than We Found It, and generally all the ten thousand platitudes that can be uttered in favour of taking trouble – by people who need take no trouble to utter them. If in Mary the mystic and child of love Christ was guarding the seed of something more subtle, who was likely to understand it at the time? Nobody else could have seen Clare and Catherine and Teresa shining above the little roof at Bethany. It is so in another way with that magnificent menace about bringing into the world a sword to sunder and divide. Nobody could have guessed then either how it could be fulfilled or how it could be justified. Indeed some freethinkers are still so simple as to fall into the trap and be shocked at a phrase so deliberately defiant. They actually complain of the paradox for not being a platitude.

But the point here is that if we *could* read the Gospel reports as things as new as newspaper reports, they would puzzle us and perhaps terrify us much *more* than the same things as developed by historical Christianity. For instance, Christ after a clear allusion to the eunuchs of eastern courts, said there would be eunuchs of the kingdom of heaven. If this does not mean the voluntary enthusiasm of virginity, it could only be made to mean something much more unnatural or uncouth. It is the historical religion that humanizes it for us by experience of Franciscans or of Sisters of Mercy. The mere statement standing by itself might very well suggest a rather dehumanized atmosphere; the sinister and inhuman silence of the Asiatic harem and divan. This is but one instance out of scores; but the moral is that the Christ of the Gospel might actually seem more strange and terrible than the Christ of the Church.

I am dwelling on the dark or dazzling or defiant or mysterious side of the Gospel words, not because they had not obviously a more obvious and popular side, but because this is the answer to a common criticism on a vital point. The freethinker frequently says that Jesus of Nazareth was a man of his time, even if he was in advance of his time; and that we cannot accept his ethics as final for humanity. The freethinker then goes on to criticize his ethics, saying plausibly enough that men cannot turn the other cheek, or that they must take thought for the morrow, or that the self-denial is too ascetic or the monogamy too severe. But the Zealots and the Legionaries did not turn the other cheek any more than we do, if so much. The Jewish traders and Roman tax-gatherers took thought for the morrow as much as we, if not more. We cannot pretend to be abandoning the morality of the past for one more suited to the present. It is certainly not the morality of another age, but it might be of another world.

In short, we can say that these ideals are impossible in themselves. Exactly what we cannot say is that they are impossible for us. They are rather notably marked by a mysticism which, if it be a sort of madness, would always have struck the same sort of people as mad. Take, for instance, the case of marriage and the relations of the sexes. It might very well have been true that a Galilean teacher taught things natural to a Galilean environment; but it is not. It might rationally be expected that a man in the time of Tiberius would have advanced a view conditioned by the time of Tiberius; but he did not. What he advanced was something quite different; something very difficult; but something no more difficult now than it was then. When, for instance, Mahomet made his polygamous compromise we may reasonably say that it was conditioned by a polygamous society. When he allowed a man four wives he was really doing something suited to the circumstances, which might have been less suited to other circumstances. Nobody will pretend that the four wives were like the four winds, something seemingly a part of the order of nature; nobody will say that the figure four was written for ever in stars upon the sky. But neither will anyone say that the figure four is an inconceivable ideal; that it is beyond the power of the mind of man to count up to four; or to count the number of his wives and see whether it amounts to four. It is a practical compromise carrying with it the character of a particular society. If Mahomet had been born in Acton in the nineteenth century, we may well doubt whether he would instantly have filled that suburb with harems of four wives apiece. As he was born in Arabia in the sixth century, he did in his conjugal arrangements suggest the conditions of Arabia in the sixth century. But Christ in his view of marriage does not in the least suggest the conditions of Palestine in the first century. He does not suggest anything at all, except the sacramental view of marriage as developed long afterwards by the Catholic Church. It was quite as difficult for people then as for people now. It was much more puzzling to people then than to people now. Jews and Romans and Greeks did not believe, and did not even understand enough to disbelieve, the mystical idea that the man and the woman had become one sacramental substance. We may think it an incredible or impossible ideal; but we cannot think it any more incredible or impossible than they would have thought it. In other words, whatever else is true, it is not true that the controversy has been altered by time. Whatever else is true, it is emphatically not true that the ideas of Jesus of Nazareth were suitable to his time, but are no longer suitable to our time. Exactly how suitable they were to his time is perhaps suggested in the end of his story.

The same truth might be stated in another way by saying that if the story be regarded as merely human and historical, it is extraordinary how very little there is in the recorded words of Christ that ties him at all to his own time. I do not mean the details of a period, which even a man of the period knows to be passing. I mean the fundamentals which even the wisest man often vaguely assumes to be eternal. For instance, Aristotle was perhaps the wisest and most wide-minded man who ever lived. He founded himself entirely upon fundamentals, which have been generally found to remain rational and solid through all social and historical changes. Still, he lived in a world in which it was thought as natural to have slaves as to have children. And therefore he did permit himself a serious recognition of a difference between slaves and free men. Christ as much as Aristotle lived in a world that took slavery for granted. He did not particularly denounce slavery. He started a movement that could exist in a world with slavery. But he started a movement that could exist in a world without slavery. He never used a phrase that made his philosophy depend even upon the very existence of the social order in which he lived. He spoke as one conscious that everything was ephemeral, including the things that Aristotle thought eternal. By that time the Roman Empire had come to be merely the *orbis terrarum*, another name for the world. But he never made his morality dependent on the existence of the Roman Empire or even on the existence of the world. 'Heaven and earth shall pass away; but my words shall not pass away.'

The truth is that when critics have spoken of the local limitations of the Galilean, it has always been a case of the local limitations of the critics. He did undoubtedly believe in certain things that one particular modern sect of materialists do not believe. But they were not things particularly peculiar to his time. It would be nearer the truth to say that the denial of them is quite peculiar to our time. Doubtless it would be nearer still to the truth to say merely that a certain solemn social importance, in the minority disbelieving them, is peculiar to our time. He believed, for instance, in evil spirits or in the psychic healing of bodily ills; but not because he was a Galilean born under Augustus. It is absurd to say that a man believed things because he was a Galilean under Augustus when he might have believed the same things if he had been an Egyptian under Tutenkamen or an Indian under Gengis Khan. But with this general question of the philosophy of diabolism or of divine miracles I deal elsewhere. It is enough to say that the materialists have to prove the impossibility of miracles against the testimony of all mankind, not against the prejudices of provincials in North Palestine under the first Roman Emperors. What they have to prove, for the present argument, is the presence in the Gospels of those particular prejudices of those particular provincials. And, humanly speaking, it is astonishing how little they can produce even to make a beginning of proving it.

So it is in this case of the sacrament of marriage. We may not believe in sacraments, as we may not believe in spirits, but it is quite clear that Christ believed in this sacrament in his own way and not in any current or contemporary way. He certainly did not get his argument against divorce from the Mosaic law or the Roman law or the habits of the Palestinian people. It would appear to his critics then exactly what it appears to his critics now; an arbitrary and transcendental dogma coming from nowhere save in the sense that it came from him. I am not at all concerned here to defend that dogma; the point here is that it is just as easy to defend it now as it was to defend it then. It is an ideal altogether outside time; difficult at any period; impossible at no period. In other words, if anyone says it is what might be expected of a man walking about in that place at that period, we can quite fairly answer that it is much *more* like what might be the mysterious utterance of a being beyond man, if he walked alive among men.

I maintain therefore that a man reading the New Testament frankly and freshly would *not* get the impression of what is now often meant by a human Christ. The merely human Christ is a made-up figure, a piece of artificial selection, like the merely evolutionary man. Moreover there have been too many of these human Christs found in the same story, just as there have been too many keys to mythology found in the same stories. Three or four separate schools of rationalism have worked over the ground and produced three or four equally rational explanations of his life. The first rational explanation of his life was that he never lived. And this in turn gave an opportunity for three or four different explanations; as that he was a sun-myth or a corn-myth, or any other kind of myth that is also a monomania. Then the idea that he was a divine being who did not exist gave place to the idea that he was a human being who did exist. In my youth it was the fashion to say that he was merely an ethical teacher in the manner of the Essenes, who had apparently nothing very much to say that Hillel or a hundred other Jews might not have said; as that it is a kindly thing to be kind and an assistance to purification to be pure. Then somebody said he was a madman with a Messianic delusion. Then others said he was indeed an original teacher because he cared about nothing but Socialism; or (as others said) about nothing but Pacifism. Then a more grimly scientific character appeared who said that Jesus would never have been heard of at all except for his prophecies of the end of the world. He was important merely as a Millenarian . . . and created a provincial scare by announcing the exact date of the crack of doom. Among other variants on the same theme was the theory that he was a spiritual healer and nothing else; a view implied by Christian Science, which has really to expound a Christianity without the Crucifixion in order to explain the curing of Peter's wife's mother or the daughter of a centurion. There is another theory that concentrates entirely on the business of diabolism and what it would call the contemporary superstition about demoniacs; as if Christ, like a young deacon taking his first orders, had got as far as exorcism and never got any further. Now each of these explanations in itself seems to me singularly inadequate; but taken together they do suggest something of the very mystery which they miss. There must surely have been something not only mysterious but many-sided about Christ if so many smaller Christs can be carved out of him. If the Christian Scientist is satisfied with him as a spiritual healer and the Christian Socialist is satisfied with him as a social reformer, so satisfied that they do not even expect him to be anything else, it looks as if he really covered rather more ground than they could be expected to expect. And it does seem to suggest that there might be more than they fancy in these other mysterious attributes of casting out devils or prophesying doom.

Above all, would not such a new reader of the New Testament stumble over something that would startle him much more than it startles us? I have here more than once attempted the rather impossible task of reversing time and the historic method; and in fancy looking forward to the facts, instead of backward through the memories. So I have imagined the monster that man might have seemed at first to the mere nature around him. We should have a worse shock if we really imagined the nature of Christ named for the first time. What should we feel at the first whisper of a certain suggestion about a certain man? Certainly it is not for us to blame anybody who should find that first wild whisper merely impious and insane. On the contrary, stumbling on that rock of scandal is the first step. Stark staring incredulity is a far more loyal tribute to that truth than a modernist metaphysic that would make it out merely a matter of degree. It were better to rend our robes with a great cry against blasphemy, like Caiaphas in the judgment, or to lay hold of the man as a maniac possessed of devils like the kinsmen and the crowd, rather than to stand stupidly debating fine shades of pantheism in the presence of so catastrophic a claim. There is more of the wisdom that is one with surprise in any simple person, full of the sensitiveness of simplicity, who should expect the grass to wither and the birds to drop dead out of the air, when a strolling carpenter's apprentice said calmly and almost carelessly, like one looking over his shoulder: 'Before Abraham was, I am.'

III

THE STRANGEST STORY IN
THE WORLD

... $\mathbf{E}$VEN in the matter of mere literary style, if we suppose our-selves thus sufficiently detached to look at it in that light, there is a curious quality to which no critic seems to have done justice. It had among other things a singular air of piling tower upon tower by the use of the *a fortiori*; making a pagoda of degrees like the seven heavens. I have already noted that almost inverted imaginative vision which pictured the impossible penance of the Cities of the Plain. There is perhaps nothing so perfect in all language or literature as the use of these three degrees in the par-able of the lilies of the field; in which he seems first to take one small flower in his hand and note its simplicity and even its impotence; then suddenly expands it in flamboyant colours into all the palaces and pavilions full of a great name in national legend and national glory; and then, by yet a third overturn, shrivels it to nothing once more with a gesture as if flinging it away '... and if God so clothes the grass that today is and tomorrow is cast into the oven – how much more....' It is like the building of a good Babel tower by white magic in a moment and in the movement of a hand; a tower heaved suddenly up to heaven on the top of which can be seen afar off, higher than we had fancied possible, the figure of man; lifted by three infinities above all other things, on a starry ladder of light logic and swift imagination. Merely in a literary sense it would be more of a masterpiece than most of the masterpieces in the librar-ies; yet it seems to have been uttered almost at random while a man might pull a flower. But merely in a literary sense also, this use of the comparative in several degrees has about it a quality which seems to me to hint of much higher things than the modern sug-gestion of the simple teaching of pastoral or communal ethics. There is nothing that really indicates a subtle and in the true sense a superior mind so much as this power of comparing a lower thing with a higher and yet that higher with a higher still; of thinking on three planes at once. There is nothing that wants the rarest sort of wisdom so much as to see, let us say, that the citizen is higher than the slave and yet that the soul is infinitely higher than the citizen or the city. It is not by any means a faculty that commonly belongs to these simplifiers of the Gospel; those who insist on what they call a simple morality and others call a sentimental morality. It is not at all covered by those who are content to tell everybody to remain at peace. On the contrary, there is a very striking example of it in the apparent inconsistency between Christ's sayings about peace and about a sword. It is precisely this power which perceives that while a good peace is better than a good war, even a good war is better than a bad peace. These far-flung comparisons are nowhere so common as in the Gospels; and to me they suggest something very vast. So a thing solitary and solid, with the added dimension of depth or height, might tower over the flat creatures living only on a plane.

This quality of something that can only be called subtle and superior, something that is capable of long views and even of double meanings, is not noted here merely as a counterblast to the commonplace exaggerations of amiability and mild idealism. It is also to be noted in connection with the more tremendous truth touched upon at the end of the last chapter. For this is the very last character that commonly goes with mere megalomania; especially such steep and staggering megalomania as might be involved in that claim. This quality that can only be called intellectual distinction is not, of course, an evidence of divinity. But it is an evidence of a probable distaste for vulgar and vainglorious claims to divinity. A man of that sort, if he were only a man, would be the last man in the world to suffer from that intoxication by one notion from nowhere in particular, which is the mark of the self-deluding sensationalist in religion. Nor is it even avoided by denying that Christ did make this claim. Of no such man as that, of no other prophet or philosopher of the same intellectual order, would it be even possible to pretend that he had made it. Even if the Church had mistaken his meaning, it would still be true that no other historical tradition except the Church had ever even made the same mistake. Mahomedans did not misunderstand Mahomet and suppose he was Allah. Jews did not misinterpret Moses and identify him with Jehovah. Why was this claim alone exaggerated unless this alone was made? Even if Christianity was one vast universal blunder, it is still a blunder as solitary as the Incarnation.

The purpose of these pages is to fix the falsity of certain vague and vulgar assumptions; and we have here one of the most false. There is a sort of notion in the air everywhere that all the religions are equal because all the religious founders were rivals; that they are all fighting for the same starry crown. It is quite false. The claim to that crown, or anything like that crown, is really so rare as to be unique. Mahomet did not make it any more than Micah or Malachi. Confucius did not make it any more than Plato or Marcus Aurelius. Buddha never said he was Brahma. Zoroaster no more claimed to be Ormuz than to be Ahriman. The truth is that, in the common run of cases, it is just as we should expect it to be, in common sense and certainly in Christian philosophy. It is exactly the other way. Normally speaking, the greater a man is, the less likely he is to make the very greatest claim. Outside the unique case we are considering, the only kind of man who ever does make that kind of claim is a very small man; a secretive or self-centred monomaniac. Nobody can imagine Aristotle claiming to be the father of gods and men, come down from the sky; though we might imagine some insane Roman Emperor like Caligula claiming it for him, or more probably for himself. Nobody can imagine Shakespeare talking as if he were literally divine; though we might imagine some crazy American crank finding it as a cryptogram in Shakespeare's works, or preferably in his own works. It is possible to find here and there human beings who make this supremely superhuman claim. It is possible to find them in lunatic asylums; in padded cells; possibly in strait waistcoats. But what is much more important than their mere materialistic fate in our very materialistic society, under very crude and clumsy laws about lunacy, the type we know as tinged with this, or tending towards it, is a diseased and disproportionate type; narrow yet swollen and morbid to monstrosity. It is by rather an unlucky metaphor that we talk of a madman as cracked; for in a sense he is not cracked enough. He is cramped rather than cracked; there are not enough holes in his head to ventilate it. This impossibility of letting in daylight on a delusion does sometimes cover and conceal a delusion of divinity. It can be found, not among prophets and sages and founders of religions, but only among a low set of lunatics. But this is exactly where the argument becomes intensely interesting; because the argument proves too much. For nobody supposes that Jesus of Nazareth was *that* sort of person. No modern critic in his five wits thinks that the preacher of the Sermon on the Mount was a horrible half-witted imbecile that might be scrawling stars on the walls of a cell. No atheist or blasphemer believes that the author of the Parable of the Prodigal Son was a monster with one mad idea like a cyclops with one eye. Upon any possible historical criticism, he must be put higher in the scale of human beings than that. Yet by all analogy we have really to put him there or else in the highest place of all.

In fact, those who can really take it (as I here hypothetically take it) in a quite dry and detached spirit, have here a most curious and interesting human problem. It is so intensely interesting, considered as a human problem, that it is in a spirit quite disinterested, so to speak, that I wish some of them had turned that intricate human problem into something like an intelligible human portrait. If Christ was simply a human character, he really was a highly complex and contradictory human character. For he combined exactly the two things that lie at the two extremes of human variation. He was exactly what the man with a delusion never is; he was wise; he was a good judge. What he said was always unexpected; but it was always unexpectedly magnanimous and often unexpectedly moderate. Take a thing like the point of the parable of the tares and the wheat. It has the quality that unites sanity and subtlety. It has not the simplicity of a madman. It has not even the simplicity of a fanatic. It might be uttered by a philosopher a hundred years old, at the end of a century of Utopias. Nothing could be less like this quality of seeing beyond and all round obvious things, than the condition of the egomaniac with the one sensitive spot on his brain. I really do not see how these two characters could be convincingly combined, except in the astonishing way in which the creed combines them. For until we reach the full acceptance of the fact as a fact, however marvellous, all mere approximations to it are actually further and further away from it. Divinity is great enough to be divine; it is great enough to call itself divine. But as humanity grows greater, it grows less and less likely to do so. God is God, as the Moslems say; but a great man knows he is not God, and the greater he is the better he knows it. That is the paradox; everything that is merely approaching to that point is merely receding from it. Socrates, the wisest man, knows that he knows nothing. A lunatic may think he is omniscience, and a fool may talk as if he were omniscient. But Christ is in another sense omniscient if he not only knows, but knows that he knows.

Even on the purely human and sympathetic side, therefore, the Jesus of the New Testament seems to me to have in a great many ways the note of something superhuman; that is of something human and more than human. But there is another quality running through all his teachings which seems to me neglected in most modern talk about them as teachings; and that is the persistent suggestion that he has not really come to teach. If there is one incident in the record which affects me personally as grandly and gloriously human, it is the incident of giving wine for the wedding-feast. That is really human in the sense in which a whole crowd of prigs, having the appearance of human beings, can hardly be described as human. It rises superior to all superior persons. It is as human as Herrick and as democratic as Dickens. But even in that story there is something else that has that note of things not fully explained; and in a way here very relevant. I mean the first hesitation, not on any ground touching the nature of the miracle, but on that of the propriety of working any miracles at all, at least at that stage; 'my time is not yet come'. What did that mean? At least it certainly meant a general plan or purpose in the mind, with which certain things did or did not fit in. And if we leave out that solitary strategic plan, we not only leave out the point of the story, but the story.

We often hear of Jesus of Nazareth as a wandering teacher; and there is a vital truth in that view in so far as it emphasizes an attitude towards luxury and convention which most respectable people would still regard as that of a vagabond. It is expressed in his own great saying about the holes of the foxes and the nests of the birds, and, like many of his great sayings, it is felt as less powerful than it is, through lack of appreciation of that great paradox by which he spoke of his own humanity as in some way collectively and representatively human; calling himself simply the Son of Man; that is, in effect, calling himself simply Man. It is fitting that the New Man or the Second Adam should repeat in so ringing a voice and with so arresting a gesture the great fact which came first in the original story; that man differs from the brutes by everything, even by deficiency; that he is in a sense less normal and even less native; a stranger upon the earth. It is well to speak of his wanderings in this sense and in the sense that he shared the drifting life of the most homeless and hopeless of the poor. It is assuredly well to remember that he would quite certainly have been moved on by the police and almost certainly arrested by the police, for having no visible means of subsistence. For our law has in it a turn of humour or touch of fancy which Nero and Herod never happened to think of; that of actually punishing homeless people for not sleeping at home.

But in another sense the word 'wandering' as applied to his life is a little misleading. As a matter of fact, a great many of the pagan sages and not a few of the pagan sophists might truly be described as wandering teachers. In some of them their rambling journeys were not altogether without a parallel in their rambling remarks. Apollonius of Tyana, who figured in some fashionable cults as a sort of ideal philosopher, is represented as rambling as far as the Ganges and Ethiopia, more or less talking all the time. There was actually a school of philosophers called the Peripatetics; and most even of the great philosophers give us a vague impression of having very little to do except to walk and talk. The great conversations which give us our glimpses of the great minds of Socrates or Buddha or even Confucius often seem to be parts of a never-ending picnic; and especially, which is the important point, to have neither beginning nor end. Socrates did indeed find the conversation interrupted by the incident of his execution. But it is the whole point, and the whole particular merit, of the position of Socrates that death was only an interruption and an incident. We miss the real moral importance of the great philosopher if we miss that point; that he stares at the executioner with an innocent surprise, and almost an innocent annoyance, at finding anyone so unreasonable as to cut short a little conversation for the elucidation of truth. He is looking for truth and not looking for death. Death is but a stone in the road which can trip him up. His work in life is to wander on the roads of the world and talk about truth for ever. Buddha, on the other hand, did arrest attention by one gesture; it was the gesture of renunciation, and therefore in a sense of denial. But by one dramatic negation he passed into a world of negation that was not dramatic; which he would have been the first to insist was not dramatic. Here again we miss the particular moral importance of the great mystic if we do not see the distinction; that it was his whole point that he had done with drama, which consists of desire and struggle and generally of defeat and disappointment. He passes into peace and lives to instruct others how to pass into it. Henceforth his life is that of the ideal philosopher; certainly a far more really ideal philosopher than Apollonius of Tyana; but still a philosopher in the sense that it is not his business to do anything but rather to explain everything; in his case, we might almost say, mildly and softly to explode everything. For the messages are basically different. Christ said 'Seek first the kingdom, and all these things shall be added unto you.' Buddha said 'Seek first the kingdom, and then you will need none of these things.'

Now compared to these wanderers the life of Jesus went as swift and straight as a thunderbolt. It was above all things dramatic; it did above all things consist in doing something that had to be done. It emphatically would not have been done, if Jesus had walked about the world for ever doing nothing except tell the truth. And even the external movement of it must not be described as a wandering in the sense of forgetting that it was a journey. This is where it was a fulfilment of the myths rather than of the philosophies; it is a journey with a goal and an object, like Jason going to find the Golden Fleece, or Hercules the golden apples of the Hesperides. The gold that he was seeking was death. The primary thing that he was going to do was to die. He was going to do other things equally definite and objective; we might almost say equally external and material. But from first to last the most definite fact is that he is going to die. No two things could possibly be more different than the death of Socrates and the death of Christ. We are meant to feel that the death of Socrates was, from the point of view of his friends at least, a stupid muddle and miscarriage of justice interfering with the flow of a humane and lucid, I had almost said a light philosophy. We are meant to feel that Death was the bride of Christ as Poverty was the bride of St Francis. We are meant to feel that his life was in that sense a sort of love-affair with death, a romance of the pursuit of the ultimate sacrifice. From the moment when the star goes up like a birthday rocket to the moment when the sun is extinguished like a funeral torch, the whole story moves on wings with the speed and direction of a drama, ending in an act beyond words.

Therefore the story of Christ is the story of a journey, almost in the manner of a military march; certainly in the manner of the quest of a hero moving to his achievement or his doom. It is a story that begins in the paradise of Galilee, a pastoral and peaceful land having really some hint of Eden, and gradually climbs the rising country into the mountains that are nearer to the storm-clouds and the stars, as to a Mountain of Purgatory. He may be met as if straying in strange places, or stopped on the way for discussion or dispute; but his face is set towards the mountain city. That is the meaning of that great culmination when he crested the ridge and stood at the turning of the road and suddenly cried aloud, lamenting over Jerusalem. Some light touch of that lament is in every patriotic poem; or if it is absent, the patriotism stinks with vulgarity. That is the meaning of the stirring and startling incident at the gates of the Temple, when the tables were hurled like lumber down the steps, and the rich merchants driven forth with bodily blows; the incident that must be at least as much of a puzzle to the pacifists as any paradox about non-resistance can be to any of the militarists. I have compared the quest to the journey of Jason, but we must never forget that in a deeper sense it is rather to be compared to the journey of Ulysses. It was not only a romance of travel but a romance of return; and of the end of a usurpation. No healthy boy reading the story regards the rout of the Ithacan suitors as anything but a happy ending. But there are doubtless some who regard the rout of the Jewish merchants and money-changers with that refined repugnance which never fails to move them in the presence of violence, and especially of violence against the well-to-do. The point here, however, is that all these incidents have in them a character of mounting crisis. In other words, these incidents are not incidental. When Apollonius the ideal philosopher is brought before the judgment-seat of Domitian[1] and vanishes by magic, the miracle is entirely incidental. It might have occurred at any time in the wandering life of the Tyanean; indeed, I believe it is doubtful in date as well as in substance. The ideal philosopher merely vanished, and resumed his ideal existence somewhere else for an

1 Roman emperor AD 81–96.

indefinite period. It is characteristic of the contrast perhaps that Apollonius was supposed to have lived to an almost miraculous old age. Jesus of Nazareth was less prudent in his miracles. When Jesus was brought before the judgment-seat of Pontius Pilate, he did not vanish. It was the crisis and the goal; it was the hour and the power of darkness. It was the supremely supernatural act, of all his miraculous life, that he did not vanish.

Every attempt to amplify that story has diminished it. The task has been attempted by many men of real genius and eloquence as well as by only too many vulgar sentimentalists and self-conscious rhetoricians. The tale has been retold with patronizing pathos by elegant sceptics and with fluent enthusiasm by boisterous best-sellers. It will not be retold here. The grinding power of the plain words of the Gospel story is like the power of mill-stones; and those who can read them simply enough will feel as if rocks had been rolled upon them. Criticism is only words about words; and of what use are words about such words as these? What is the use of word-painting about the dark garden filled suddenly with torchlight and furious faces? 'Are you come out with swords and staves as against a robber? All day I sat in your temple teaching, and you took me not.' Can anything be added to the massive and gathered restraint of that irony; like a great wave lifted to the sky and refusing to fall? 'Daughters of Jerusalem, weep not for me but weep for yourselves and for your children.' As the High Priest asked what further need he had of witnesses, we might well ask what further need we have of words. Peter in a panic repudiated him: 'and immediately the cock crew; and Jesus looked upon Peter, and Peter went out and wept bitterly'. Has anyone any further remarks to offer? Just before the murder he prayed for all the murderous race of men, saying, 'They know not what they do'; is there anything to say to that, except that we know as little what we say? Is there any need to repeat and spin out the story of how the tragedy trailed up the Via Dolorosa and how they threw him in haphazard with two thieves in one of the ordinary batches of execution; and how in all that horror and howling wilderness of desertion one voice spoke in homage, a startling voice from the very last place where it was looked for, the gibbet of the criminal; and he said to that nameless ruffian, 'This night shalt thou be with me in Paradise'? Is there anything to put after that but a full-stop? Or is anyone prepared to answer adequately that farewell gesture to all flesh which created for his Mother a new Son?

It is more within my powers, and here more immediately to my purpose, to point out that in that scene were symbolically gathered all the human forces that have been vaguely sketched in this story. As kings and philosophers and the popular element had been symbolically present at his birth, so they were more practically concerned in his death; and with that we come face to face with the essential fact to be realized. All the great groups that stood about the Cross represent in one way or another the great historical truth of the time; that the world could not save itself. Man could do no more. Rome and Jerusalem and Athens and everything else were going down like a sea turned into a slow cataract. Externally indeed the ancient world was still at its strongest; it is always at that moment that the inmost weakness begins. But in order to understand that weakness we must repeat what has been said more than once; that it was not the weakness of a thing originally weak. It was emphatically the strength of the world that was turned to weakness and the wisdom of the world that was turned to folly.

In this story of Good Friday it is the best things in the world that are at their worst. That is what really shows us the world at its worst. It was, for instance, the priests of a true monotheism and the soldiers of an international civilization. Rome, the legend, founded upon fallen Troy and triumphant over fallen Carthage, had stood for a heroism which was the nearest that any pagan ever came to chivalry. Rome had defended the household gods and the human decencies against the ogres of Africa and the hermaphrodite monstrosities of Greece. But in the lightning flash of this incident, we see great Rome, the imperial republic, going downward under her Lucretian doom. Scepticism has eaten away even the confident sanity of the conquerors of the world. He who is enthroned to say what is justice can only ask, 'What is truth?' So in that drama which decided the whole fate of antiquity, one of the central figures is fixed in what seems the reverse of his true rôle. Rome was almost another name for responsibility. Yet he stands for ever as a sort of rocking statue of the irresponsible. Man could do no more. Even the practical had become the impracticable. Standing between the pillars of his own judgment-seat, a Roman had washed his hands of the world.

There too were the priests of that pure and original truth that was behind all the mythologies like the sky behind the clouds. It was the most important truth in the world; and even that could not save the world. Perhaps there is something overpowering in pure personal theism; like seeing the sun and moon and sky come together to form one staring face. Perhaps the truth is too tremendous when not broken by some intermediaries divine or human; perhaps it is merely too pure and far away. Anyhow it could not save the world; it could not even convert the world. There were philosophers who held it in its highest and noblest form; but they not only could not convert the world, but they never tried. You could no more fight the jungle of popular mythology with a private opinion than you could clear away a forest with a pocket-knife. The Jewish priests had guarded it jealously in the good and the bad sense. They had kept it as a gigantic secret. As savage heroes might have kept the sun in a box, they kept the Everlasting in the tabernacle. They were proud that they alone could look upon the blinding sun of a single deity; and they did not know that they had themselves gone blind. Since that day their representatives have been like blind men in broad daylight, striking to right and left with their staffs, and cursing the darkness. But there has been that in their monumental monotheism that it has at least remained like a monument, the last thing of its kind, and in a sense motionless in the more restless world which it cannot satisfy. For it is certain that for some reason it cannot satisfy. Since that day it has never been quite enough to say that God is in his heaven and all is right with the world; since the rumour that God had left his heavens to set it right.

And as it was with these powers that were good, or at least had once been good, so it was with the element which was perhaps the best, or which Christ himself seems certainly to have felt as the best. The poor to whom he preached the good news, the common people who heard him gladly, the populace that had made so many popular heroes and demigods in the old pagan world, showed also the weaknesses that were dissolving the world. They suffered the evils often seen in the mob of the city, and especially the mob of the capital, during the decline of a society. The same thing that makes the rural population live on tradition makes the urban population live on rumour. Just as its myths at the best had been irrational, so its likes and dislikes are easily changed by base-less assertion that is arbitrary without being authoritative. Some brigand or other was artificially turned into a picturesque and popular figure and run as a kind of candidate against Christ. In all this we recognize the urban population that we know, with its newspaper scares and scoops. But there was present in this ancient population an evil more peculiar to the ancient world. We have noted it already as the neglect of the individual, even of the indi-vidual voting the condemnation and still more of the individual condemned. It was the soul of the hive; a heathen thing. The cry of this spirit also was heard in that hour, 'It is well that one man die for the people.' Yet this spirit in antiquity of devotion to the city and to the state had also been in itself and in its time a noble spirit. It had its poets and its martyrs; men still to be honoured for ever. It was failing through its weakness in not seeing the separate soul of a man, the shrine of all mysticism; but it was only failing as everything else was failing. The mob went along with the Sad-ducees and the Pharisees, the philosophers and the moralists. It went along with the imperial magistrates and the sacred priests, the scribes and the soldiers, that the one universal human spirit might suffer a universal condemnation; that there might be one deep, unanimous chorus of approval and harmony when Man was rejected of men.

There were solitudes beyond where none shall follow. There were secrets in the inmost and invisible part of that drama that have no symbol in speech; or in any severance of a man from men. Nor is it easy for any words less stark and single-minded than those of the naked narrative even to hint at the horror of exaltation that lifted itself above the hill. Endless expositions have not come to the end of it, or even to the beginning. And if there be any sound that can produce a silence, we may surely be silent about the end and the extremity; when a cry was driven out of that darkness in words dreadfully distinct and dreadfully unintelligible, which man shall never understand in all the eternity they have purchased for him; and for one annihilating instant an abyss that is not for our thoughts had opened even in the unity of the absolute; and God had been forsaken of God.

They took the body down from the cross and one of the few rich men among the first Christians obtained permission to bury it in a rock tomb in his garden; the Romans setting a military guard lest there should be some riot and attempt to recover the body. There was once more a natural symbolism in these natural proceedings; it was well that the tomb should be sealed with all the secrecy of ancient eastern sepulture and guarded by the authority of the Caesars. For in that second cavern the whole of that great and glorious humanity which we call antiquity was gathered up and covered over; and in that place it was buried. It was the end of a very great thing called human history; the history that was merely human. The mythologies and the philosophies were buried there, the gods and the heroes and the sages. In the great Roman phrase, they had lived. But as they could only live, so they could only die; and they were dead.

On the third day the friends of Christ coming at day-break to the place found the grave empty and the stone rolled away. In varying ways they realized the new wonder; but even they hardly realized that the world had died in the night. What they were looking at was the first day of a new creation, with a new heaven and a new earth; and in a semblance of the gardener God walked again in the garden, in the cool not of the evening but the dawn.

IV

THE WITNESS OF THE HERETICS

CHRIST founded the Church with two great figures of speech; in the final words to the Apostles who received authority to found it. The first was the phrase about founding it on Peter as on a rock; the second was the symbol of the keys. About the meaning of the former there is naturally no doubt in my own case; but it does not directly affect the argument here save in two more secondary aspects. It is yet another example of a thing that could only fully expand and explain itself afterwards, and even long afterwards. And it is yet another example of something the very reverse of simple and self-evident even in the language, in so far as it described a man as a rock when he had much more the appearance of a reed.

But the other image of the keys has an exactitude that has hardly been exactly noticed. The keys have been conspicuous enough in the art and heraldry of Christendom; but not everyone has noted the peculiar aptness of the allegory. We have now reached the point in history where something must be said of the first appearance and activities of the Church in the Roman Empire; and for that brief description nothing could be more perfect than that ancient metaphor. The Early Christian was very precisely a person carrying about a key, or what he said was a key. The whole Christian movement consisted in claiming to possess that key. It was not merely a vague forward movement, which might be better represented by a battering-ram. It was not something that swept along with it similar or dissimilar things, as does a modern social movement. As we shall see in a moment, it rather definitely refused to do so. It definitely asserted that there was a key and that it possessed that key and that no other key was like it; in that sense it was as narrow as you please. Only it happened to be the key that could unlock the prison of the whole world; and let in the white daylight of liberty.

The creed was like a key in three respects; which can be most conveniently summed up under this symbol. First, a key is above all things a thing with a shape. It is a thing that depends entirely upon keeping its shape. The Christian creed is above all things the philosophy of shapes and the enemy of shapelessness. That is where it differs from all that formless infinity, Manichean[1] or Buddhist, which makes a sort of pool of night in the dark heart of Asia; the ideal of uncreating all the creatures. That is where it differs also from the analogous vagueness of mere evolutionism; the idea of creatures constantly losing their shape. A man told that his solitary latchkey had been melted down with a million others into a Buddhistic unity would be annoyed. But a man told that his key was gradually growing and sprouting in his pocket, and branching into new wards or complications, would not be more gratified.

Second, the shape of a key is in itself a rather fantastic shape. A savage who did not know it was a key would have the greatest difficulty in guessing what it could possibly be. And it is fantastic because it is in a sense arbitrary. A key is not a matter of abstractions; in that sense a key is not a matter of argument. It either fits the lock or it does not. It is useless for men to stand disputing over it, considered by itself; or reconstructing it on pure principles of geometry or decorative art. It is senseless for a man to say he would like a simpler key; it would be far more sensible to do his best with a crowbar. And thirdly, as the key is necessarily a thing with a pattern, so this was one having in some ways a rather elaborate pattern. When people complain of the religion being so early complicated with theology and things of the kind, they forget that the world had not only got into a hole, but had got into a whole maze of holes and corners. The problem itself was a complicated problem; it did not in the ordinary sense merely involve anything so simple as sin. It was also full of secrets, of unexplored and unfathomable fallacies, of unconscious mental diseases, of dangers in all directions. If the faith had faced the world only with the platitudes about peace and simplicity some moralists would confine it to, it would not have had the faintest effect on that luxurious and labyrinthine lunatic asylum. What it did do we must now roughly describe; it is enough to say here that there was undoubtedly much about the key that seemed complex; indeed there was only one thing about it that was simple. It opened the door.

There are certain recognized and accepted statements in this matter which may for brevity and convenience be described as lies.

1 Manicheanism was a dualistic philosophy propounded by the Persian Manes, which held matter to be evil and mind to be good.

We have all heard people say that Christianity arose in an age of barbarism. They might just as well say that Christian Science arose in an age of barbarism. They may think Christianity was a symptom of social decay, as I think Christian Science a symptom of mental decay. They may think Christianity a superstition that ultimately destroyed a civilization, as I think Christian Science a superstition capable (if taken seriously) of destroying any number of civilizations. But to say that a Christian of the fourth or fifth centuries was a barbarian living in a barbarous time is exactly like saying that Mrs Eddy[1] was a Red Indian. And if I allowed my constitutional impatience with Mrs Eddy to impel me to call her a Red Indian, I should incidentally be telling a lie. We may like or dislike the imperial civilization of Rome in the fourth century; we may like or dislike the industrial civilization of America in the nineteenth century; but that they both were what we commonly mean by a civilization no person of commonsense could deny if he wanted to. This is a very obvious fact but it is also a very fundamental one; and we must make it the foundation of any further description of constructive Christianity in the past. For good or evil, it was pre-eminently the product of a civilized age, perhaps of an over-civilized age. This is the first fact apart from all praise or blame; indeed I am so unfortunate as not to feel that I praise a thing when I compare it to Christian Science. But it is at least desirable to know something of the savour of a society in which we are condemning or praising anything; and the science that connects Mrs Eddy with tomahawks or the Mater Dolorosa[2] with totems may for our general convenience be eliminated. The dominant fact, not merely about the Christian religion, but about the whole pagan civilization, was that which has been more than once repeated in these pages. The Mediterranean was a lake in the real sense of a pool; in which a number of different cults or cultures were, as the phrase goes, pooled. Those cities facing each other round the circle of the lake became more and more one cosmopolitan culture. On its legal and military side it was the Roman Empire; but it was very many-sided. It might be called superstitious in the sense that it contained a great number of varied superstitions; but by no possibility can any part of it be called barbarous.

1 Mary Baker Eddy (1821–1910), founder of the Christian Science religion.
2 The mother of sorrows, traditional title of the Blessed Virgin Mary.

In this level of cosmopolitan culture arose the Christian religion and the Catholic Church; and everything in the story suggests that it was felt to be something new and strange. Those who have tried to suggest that it evolved out of something much milder or more ordinary have found that in this case their evolutionary method is very difficult to apply. They may suggest that Essenes or Ebionites or such things were the seed; but the seed is invisible; the tree appears very rapidly full-grown; and the tree is something totally different. It is certainly a Christmas tree in the sense that it keeps the kindliness and moral beauty of the story of Bethlehem; but it was as ritualistic as the seven-branched candlestick, and the candles it carried were considerably more than were probably permitted by the first prayer-book of Edward the Sixth. It might well be asked, indeed, why any one accepting the Bethlehem tradition should object to golden or gilded ornament since the Magi themselves brought gold, why he should dislike incense in the church since incense was brought even to the stable. But these are controversies that do not concern me here. I am concerned only with the historical fact, more and more admitted by historians, that very early in its history this thing became visible to the civilization of antiquity; and that already the Church appeared as a Church; with everything that is implied in a Church and much that is disliked in a Church. We will discuss in a moment how far it was like other ritualistic or magical or ascetical mysteries in its own time. It was certainly not in the least like merely ethical and idealistic movements in our time. It had a doctrine; it had a discipline; it had sacraments; it had degrees of initiation; it admitted people and expelled people; it affirmed one dogma with authority and repudiated another with anathemas. If all these things be the marks of Antichrist, the reign of Antichrist followed very rapidly upon Christ.

Those who maintain that Christianity was not a Church but a moral movement of idealists have been forced to push the period of its perversion or disappearance further and further back. A bishop of Rome writes claiming authority in the very lifetime of St John the Evangelist; and it is described as the first papal aggression. A friend of the Apostles writes of them as men he knew and says they taught him the doctrine of the Sacrament; and Mr Wells can only murmur that the reaction towards barbaric blood-rites may have happened rather earlier than might be expected. The date of the Fourth Gospel, which at one time was steadily growing later and later, is now steadily growing earlier and earlier; until critics are staggered at the dawning and dreadful possibility that it might be something like what it professes to be. The last limit of an early date for the extinction of true Christianity has probably been found by the latest German professor . . . This learned scholar says that Pentecost was the occasion for the first founding of an ecclesiastical, dogmatic, and despotic Church utterly alien to the simple ideals of Jesus of Nazareth. This may be called, in a popular as well as a learned sense, the limit. What do professors of this kind imagine that men are made of? Suppose it were a matter of any merely human movement, let us say that of the conscientious objectors. Some say the early Christians were Pacifists; I do not believe it for a moment; but I am quite ready to accept the parallel for the sake of the argument. Tolstoy or some great preacher of peace among peasants has been shot as a mutineer for defying conscription; and a little while afterwards his few followers meet together in an upper room in remembrance of him. They never had any reason for coming together except that common memory; they are men of many kinds with nothing to bind them, except that the greatest event in all their lives was this tragedy of the teacher of universal peace. They are always repeating his words, revolving his problems, trying to imitate his character. The Pacifists meet at their Pentecost and are possessed of a sudden ecstasy of enthusiasm and wild rush of the whirlwind of inspiration, in the course of which they proceed to establish universal Conscription, to increase the Navy Estimates, to insist on everybody going about armed to the teeth and on all the frontiers bristling with artillery; the proceedings concluded with the singing of 'Boys of the Bulldog Breed' and 'Don't let them scrap the British Navy'. That is something like a fair parallel to the theory of these critics; that the transition from their idea of Jesus to their idea of Catholicism could have been made in the little upper room at Pentecost. Surely anybody's commonsense would tell him that enthusiasts, who only met through their common enthusiasm for a leader whom they loved, would not instantly rush away to establish everything that he hated. No, if the 'ecclesiastical and dogmatic system' is as old as Pentecost it is as old as Christmas. If we trace it back to such very early Christians we must trace it back to Christ.

We may begin then with these two negations. It is nonsense to say that the Christian faith appeared in a simple age; in the sense of an unlettered and gullible age. It is equally nonsense to say that the Christian faith was a simple thing; in the sense of a vague or childish or merely instinctive thing. Perhaps the only point in which we could possibly say that the Church fitted into the pagan world, is the fact that they were both not only highly civilized but rather complicated. They were both emphatically many-sided; but antiquity was then a many-sided hole, like a hexagonal hole waiting for an equally hexagonal stopper. In that sense only the Church was many-sided enough to fit the world. The six sides of the Mediterranean world faced each other across the sea and waited for something that should look all ways at once. The Church had to be both Roman and Greek and Jewish and African and Asiatic. In the very words of the Apostle of the Gentiles, it was indeed all things to all men. Christianity then was not merely crude and simple and was the very reverse of the growth of a barbaric time. But when we come to the contrary charge, we come to a much more plausible charge. It is very much more tenable that the Faith was but the final phase of the decay of civilization, in the sense of the excess of civilization; that this superstition was a sign that Rome was dying, and dying of being much too civilized. That is an argument much better worth considering; and we will proceed to consider it.

At the beginning of this book I ventured on a general summary of it, in a parallel between the rise of humanity out of nature and the rise of Christianity out of history. I pointed out that in both cases what had gone before might imply something coming after; but did not in the least imply what did come after. If a detached mind had seen certain apes it might have deduced more anthropoids; it would not have deduced man or anything within a thousand miles of what man has done. In short, it might have seen Pithecanthropus[1] or the Missing Link looming in the future, if possible almost as dimly and doubtfully as we see him looming in the past. But if it foresaw him appearing it would also foresee him disappearing, and leaving a few faint traces just as he has left a few faint traces; if they are traces. To foresee that Missing Link would

[1] Upright ape-man, the Java Man discovered in 1891 by the anthropologist Eugène Dubois.

not be to foresee Man, or anything like Man. Now this earlier explanation must be kept in mind; because it is an exact parallel to the true view of the Church; and the suggestion of it having evolved naturally out of the Empire in decay.

The truth is that in one sense a man might very well have predicted that the imperial decadence would produce something like Christianity. That is, something a little like and gigantically different. A man might very well have said, for instance, 'Pleasure has been pursued so extravagantly that there will be a reaction into pessimism. Perhaps it will take the form of asceticism; men will mutilate themselves instead of merely hanging themselves.' Or a man might very reasonably have said, 'If we weary of our Greek and Latin gods we shall be hankering after some eastern mystery or other; there will be a fashion in Persians or Hindoos.' Or a man of the world might well have been shrewd enough to say, 'Powerful people are picking up these fads; some day the court will adopt one of them and it may become official.' Or yet another and gloomier prophet might be pardoned for saying, 'The world is going downhill; dark and barbarous superstitions will return, it does not matter much which. They will all be formless and fugitive like dreams of the night.'

Now it is the intense interest of the case that all these prophecies were really fulfilled; but it was not the Church that fulfilled them. It was the Church that escaped from them, confounded them, and rose above them in triumph. In so far as it was probable that the mere nature of hedonism would produce a mere reaction of asceticism, it did produce a mere reaction of asceticism. It was the movement called Manichean and the Church was its mortal enemy. In so far as it would have naturally appeared at that point of history, it did appear; it did also disappear, which was equally natural. The mere pessimist reaction did come with the Manichees and did go with the Manichees. But the Church did not come with them or go with them; and she had much more to do with their going than with their coming. Or again, in so far as it was probable that even the growth of scepticism would bring in a fashion of eastern religion, it did bring it in; Mithras came from far beyond Palestine out of the heart of Persia, bringing strange mysteries of the blood of bulls. Certainly there was everything to show that some such fashion would have come in any case. But certainly there is nothing in the world to show that it would not have passed away in any case. Certainly an Oriental fad was something eminently fitted to the fourth or fifth century; but that hardly explains it having remained to the twentieth century, and still going strong. In short, in so far as things of the kind might have been expected then, things like Mithraism[1] were experienced then; but it scarcely explains our more recent experiences. And if we were still Mithraists merely because Mithraic head-dresses and other Persian apparatuses might be expected to be all the rage in the days of Domitian, it would almost seem by this time that we must be a little dowdy.

It is the same, as will be suggested in a moment, with the idea of official favouritism. In so far as such favouritism shown towards a fad was something that might have been looked for during the decline and fall of the Roman Empire, it was something that did exist in that Empire and did decline and fall with it. It throws no sort of light on the thing that resolutely refused to decline and fall; that grew steadily while the other was declining and falling; and which even at this moment is going forward with fearless energy, when another aeon has completed its cycle and another civilization seems almost ready to fall or to decline.

Now the curious fact is this; that the very heresies which the early Church is blamed for crushing testify to the unfairness for which she is blamed. In so far as something deserved the blame, it was precisely the things that she is blamed for blaming. In so far as something was merely a superstition, she herself condemned that superstition. In so far as something was a mere reaction into barbarism, she herself resisted it because it was a reaction into barbarism. In so far as something was a fad of the fading empire, that died and deserved to die, it was the Church alone that killed it. The Church is reproached for being exactly what the heresy was repressed for being. The explanations of the evolutionary historians and higher critics do really explain why Arianism[2] and Gnosticism[3] and Nestorianism[4] were born and also why they died. They do not explain

---

1 Mystery religion centred on the god Mithras.
2 The heresy of Arius (250–336) that the Son of God was created by God the Father.
3 An early Christian heresy that claimed to have superior knowledge of spiritual things, interpreting the Scriptures by a mystic philosophy.
4 Christological heresy named after Nestorius, Patriarch of Constantinople between 428 and 431.

why the Church was born or why she has refused to die. Above all, they do not explain why she should have made war on the very evils she is supposed to share.

Let us take a few practical examples of the principle; the principle that if there was anything that was really a superstition of the dying empire, it did really die with the dying empire; and certainly was not the same as the very thing that destroyed it. For this purpose we will take in order two or three of the most ordinary explanations of Christian origins among the modern critics of Christianity. Nothing is more common, for instance, than to find such a modern critic writing something like this: 'Christianity was above all a movement of ascetics, a rush into the desert, a refuge in the cloister, a renunciation of all life and happiness; and this was a part of a gloomy and inhuman reaction against nature itself, a hatred of the body, a horror of the material universe, a sort of universal suicide of the senses and even of the self. It came from an eastern fanaticism like that of the fakirs and was ultimately founded on an eastern pessimism, which seems to feel existence itself as an evil.'

Now the most extraordinary thing about this is that it is all quite true; it is true in every detail except that it happens to be attributed entirely to the wrong person. It is not true of the Church; but it is true of the heretics condemned by the Church. It is as if one were to write a most detailed analysis of the mistakes and misgovernment of the ministers of George the Third, merely with the small inaccuracy that the whole story was told about George Washington; or as if somebody made a list of the crimes of the Bolshevists with no variation except that they were all attributed to the Czar. The early Church was indeed very ascetic, in connection with a totally different philosophy; but the philosophy of a war on life and nature as such really did exist in the world, if the critics only knew where to look for it.

What really happened was this. When the Faith first emerged into the world, the very first thing that happened to it was that it was caught in a sort of swarm of mystical and metaphysical sects, mostly out of the East; like one lonely golden bee caught in a swarm of wasps. To the ordinary onlooker, there did not seem to be much difference, or anything beyond a general buzz; indeed in a sense there was not much difference, so far as stinging and being stung were concerned. The difference was that only one golden dot in all that whirring gold-dust had the power of going forth to make hives for all humanity; to give the world honey and wax or (as was so finely said in a context too easily forgotten) 'the two noblest things, which are sweetness and light'. The wasps all died that winter; and half the difficulty is that hardly anyone knows anything about them and most people do not know that they ever existed; so that the whole story of that first phase of our religion is lost. Or, to vary the metaphor, when this movement or some other movement pierced the dyke between the east and west and brought more mystical ideas into Europe, it brought with it a whole flood of other mystical ideas besides its own, most of them ascetical and nearly all of them pessimistic. They very nearly flooded and overwhelmed the purely Christian element. They came mostly from that region that was a sort of dim borderland between the eastern philosophies and the eastern mythologies, and which shared with the wilder philosophers that curious craze for making fantastic patterns of the cosmos in the shape of maps and genealogical trees. Those that are supposed to derive from the mysterious Manes are called Manichean; kindred cults are more generally known as Gnostic; they are mostly of a labyrinthine complexity, but the point to insist on is the pessimism; the fact that nearly all in one form or another regarded the creation of the world as the work of an evil spirit. Some of them had that Asiatic atmosphere that surrounds Buddhism; the suggestion that life is a corruption of the purity of being. Some of them suggested a purely spiritual order which had been betrayed by the coarse and clumsy trick of making such toys as the sun and moon and stars. Anyhow all this dark tide out of the metaphysical sea in the midst of Asia poured through the dykes simultaneously with the creed of Christ; but it is the whole point of the story that the two were not the same; that they flowed like oil and water. That creed remained in the shape of a miracle; a river still flowing through the sea. And the proof of the miracle was practical once more; it was merely that while all that sea was salt and bitter with the savour of death, of this one stream in the midst of it a man could drink.

Now that purity was preserved by dogmatic definitions and exclusions. It could not possibly have been preserved by anything else. If the Church had not renounced the Manicheans it might have become merely Manichean. If it had not renounced the Gnostics it might have become Gnostic. But by the very fact that it did renounce them it proved that it was not either Gnostic or Manichean. At any rate it proved that something was not either Gnostic or Manichean; and what could it be that condemned them, if it was not the original good news of the runners from Bethlehem and the trumpet of the Resurrection? The early Church was ascetic, but she proved that she was not pessimistic, simply by condemning the pessimists. The creed declared that man was sinful, but it did not declare that life was evil, and it proved it by damning those who did. The condemnation of the early heretics is itself condemned as something crabbed and narrow; but it was in truth the very proof that the Church meant to be brotherly and broad. It proved that the primitive Catholics were specially eager to explain that they did *not* think man utterly vile; that they did *not* think life incurably miserable; that they did *not* think marriage a sin or procreation a tragedy. They were ascetic because asceticism was the only possible purge of the sins of the world; but in the very thunder of their anathemas they affirmed for ever that their asceticism was not to be anti-human or anti-natural; that they did wish to purge the world and not destroy it. And nothing else except those anathemas could possibly have made it clear, amid a confusion which still confuses them with their mortal enemies. Nothing else but dogma could have resisted the riot of imaginative invention with which the pessimists were waging their war against nature; with their Aeons and their Demiurge, their strange Logos and their sinister Sophia. If the Church had not insisted on theology, it would have melted into a mad mythology of the mystics, yet further removed from reason or even from rationalism; and, above all, yet further removed from life and from the love of life. Remember that it would have been an inverted mythology, one contradicting everything natural in paganism; a mythology in which Pluto would be above Jupiter and Hades hang higher than Olympus; in which Brahma and all that has the breath of life would be subject to Sheeva,[1] shining with the eye of death.

That the early Church was itself full of an ecstatic enthusiasm for renunciation and virginity makes this distinction much more

1 Hindu god.

striking and not less so. It makes all the more important the place where the dogma drew the line. A man might crawl about on all fours like a beast because he was an ascetic. He might stand night and day on the top of a pillar and be adored for being an ascetic. But he could not say that the world was a mistake or the marriage state a sin without being a heretic. What was it that thus deliberately disengaged itself from eastern asceticism by sharp definition and fierce refusal, if it was not something with an individuality of its own; and one that was quite different? If the Catholics are to be confused with the Gnostics, we can only say it was not their fault if they are. And it is rather hard that the Catholics should be blamed by the same critics for persecuting the heretics and also for sympathizing with the heresy.

The Church was not a Manichean movement, if only because it was not a movement at all. It was not even merely an ascetical movement, because it was not a movement at all. It would be nearer the truth to call it the tamer of asceticism than the mere leader or loosener of it. It was a thing having its own theory of asceticism, its own type of asceticism, but most conspicuous at the moment as the moderator of other theories and types. This is the only sense that can be made, for instance, of the story of St Augustine. As long as he was a mere man of the world, a mere man drifting with his time, he actually was a Manichean. It really was quite modern and fashionable to be a Manichean. But when he became a Catholic, the people he instantly turned on and rent in pieces were the Manicheans. The Catholic way of putting it is that he left off being a pessimist to become an ascetic. But as the pessimists interpreted asceticism, it might be said that he left off being an ascetic to become a saint. The war upon life, the denial of nature, were exactly the things he had already found in the heathen world outside the Church, and had to renounce when he entered the Church. The very fact that St Augustine remains a somewhat sterner or sadder figure than St Francis or St Teresa only accentuates the dilemma. Face to face with the gravest or even grimmest of Catholics, we can still ask, 'Why did Catholicism make war on Manichees, if Catholicism was Manichean?'

Take another rationalistic explanation of the rise of Christendom. It is common enough to find another critic saying, 'Christianity did not really rise at all; that is, it did not merely rise from below; it was imposed from above. It is an example of the power of the executive, especially in despotic states. The Empire was really an Empire; that is, it was really ruled by the Emperor. One of the Emperors happened to become a Christian. He might just as well have become a Mithraist or a Jew or a Fire-Worshipper; it was common in the decline of the Empire for eminent and educated people to adopt these eccentric eastern cults. But when he adopted it it became the official religion of the Roman Empire; and when it became the official religion of the Roman Empire, it became as strong, as universal and as invincible as the Roman Empire. It has only remained in the world as a relic of that Empire; or, as many have put it, it is but the ghost of Caesar still hovering over Rome.' This also is a very ordinary line taken in the criticism of orthodoxy, to say that it was only officialism that ever made it orthodoxy. And here again we can call on the heretics to refute it.

The whole great history of the Arian heresy might have been invented to explode this idea. It is a very interesting history often repeated in this connection; and the upshot of it is in that in so far as there ever was a merely official religion, it actually died because it was merely an official religion; and what destroyed it was the real religion. Arius advanced a version of Christianity which moved, more or less vaguely, in the direction of what we should call Unitarianism; though it was not the same, for it gave to Christ a curious intermediary position between the divine and human. The point is that it seemed to many more reasonable and less fanatical; and among these were many of the educated class in a sort of reaction against the first romance of conversion. Arians were a sort of moderates and a sort of modernists. And it was felt that after the first squabbles this was the final form of rationalized religion into which civilization might well settle down. It was accepted by Divus Caesar himself and became the official orthodoxy; the generals and military princes drawn from the new barbarian powers of the north, full of the future, supported it strongly. But the sequel is still more important. Exactly as a modern man might pass through Unitarianism to complete agnosticism, so the greatest of the Arian emperors ultimately shed the last and thinnest pretence of Christianity; he abandoned even Arius and returned to Apollo. He was a Caesar of the Caesars; a soldier, a scholar, a man of large ambitions and ideals; another of the philosopher kings. It seemed to him as if at his signal the sun rose again. The oracles began to speak like birds beginning to sing at dawn; paganism was itself again; the gods returned. It seemed the end of that strange interlude of an alien superstition. And indeed it was the end of it, so far as there was a mere interlude of mere superstition. It was the end of it, in so far as it was the fad of an emperor or the fashion of a generation. If there really was something that began with Constantine, then it ended with Julian.[1]

But there was something that did not end. There had arisen in that hour of history, defiant above the democratic tumult of the Councils of the Church, Athanasius against the world. We may pause upon the point at issue; because it is relevant to the whole of this religious history, and the modern world seems to miss the whole point of it. We might put it this way. If there is one question which the enlightened and liberal have the habit of deriding and holding up as a dreadful example of barren dogma and senseless sectarian strife, it is this Athanasian question of the Co-Eternity of the Divine Son. On the other hand, if there is one thing that the same liberals always offer us as a piece of pure and simple Christianity, untroubled by doctrinal disputes, it is the single sentence, 'God is Love'. Yet the two statements are almost identical; at least one is very nearly nonsense without the other. The barren dogma is only the logical way of stating the beautiful sentiment. For if there be a being without beginning, existing before all things, was He loving when there was nothing to be loved? If through that unthinkable eternity He is lonely, what is the meaning of saying He is love? The only justification of such a mystery is the mystical conception that in His own nature there was something analogous to self-expression; something of what begets and beholds what it has begotten. Without some such idea, it is really illogical to complicate the ultimate essence of deity with an idea like love. If the moderns really want a simple religion of love, they must look for it in the Athanasian Creed. The truth is that the trumpet of true Christianity, the challenge of the charities and simplicities of Bethlehem or Christmas Day, never rang out more arrestingly and unmistakably than in the defiance of Athanasius to the cold compromise of the Arians. It was emphatically he who really was fighting for a God

1 Julian the Apostate, Roman emperor 361–3, rejected Christianity in favour of Neo-Platonic paganism.

of Love against a God of colourless and remote cosmic control; the God of the stoics and the agnostics. It was emphatically he who was fighting for the Holy Child against the grey deity of the Pharisees and the Sadducees. He was fighting for that very balance of beautiful interdependence and intimacy, in the very Trinity of the Divine Nature, that draws our hearts to the Trinity of the Holy Family. His dogma, if the phrase be not misunderstood, turns even God into a Holy Family.

That this purely Christian dogma actually for a second time rebelled against the Empire, and actually for a second time re-founded the Church in spite of the Empire, is itself a proof that there was something positive and personal working in the world, other than whatever official faith the Empire chose to adopt. This power utterly destroyed the official faith that the Empire did adopt. It went on its own way as it is going on its own way still. There are any number of other examples in which is repeated precisely the same process we have reviewed in the case of the Manichean and the Arian. A few centuries afterwards, for instance, the Church had to maintain the same Trinity, which is simply the logical side of love, against another appearance of the isolated and simplified deity in the religion of Islam. Yet there are some who cannot see what the Crusaders were fighting for; and some even who talk as if Christianity had never been anything but a form of what they call Hebraism coming in with the decay of Hellenism. Those people must certainly be very much puzzled by the war between the Crescent and the Cross. If Christianity had never been anything but a simpler morality sweeping away polytheism, there is no reason why Christendom should not have been swept into Islam. The truth is that Islam itself was a barbaric reaction against that very humane complexity that is really a Christian character; that idea of balance in the deity, as of balance in the family, that makes that creed a sort of sanity, and that sanity the soul of civilization. And that is why the Church is from the first a thing holding its own position and point of view, quite apart from the accidents and anarchies of its age. That is why it deals blows impartially right and left, at the pessimism of the Manichean or the optimism of the Pelagian. It was not a Manichean movement because it was not a movement at all. It was not an official fashion because it was not a fashion at all. It was something that could coincide with movements and fashions, could control them and could survive them.

So might rise from their graves the great heresiarchs to confound their comrades of today. There is nothing that the critics now affirm that we cannot call on these great witnesses to deny. The modern critic will say lightly enough that Christianity was but a reaction into asceticism and anti-natural spirituality, a dance of fakirs furious against life and love. But Manes[1] the great mystic will answer them from his secret throne and cry, 'These Christians have no right to be called spiritual; these Christians have no title to be called ascetics; they who compromised with the curse of life and all the filth of the family. Through them the earth is still foul with fruit and harvest and polluted with population. Theirs was no movement against nature, or my children would have carried it to triumph; but these fools renewed the world when I would have ended it with a gesture.' And another critic will write that the Church was but the shadow of the Empire, the fad of a chance Emperor, and that it remains in Europe only as the ghost of the power of Rome. And Arius the deacon will answer out of the darkness of oblivion: 'No, indeed, or the world would have followed my more reasonable religion. For mine went down before demagogues and men defying Caesar; and around my champion was the purple cloak and mine was the glory of the eagles. It was not for lack of these things that I failed.' And yet a third modern will maintain that the creed spread only as a sort of panic of hell-fire; men everywhere attempting impossible things in fleeing from incredible vengeance; a nightmare of imaginary remorse; and such an explanation will satisfy many who see something dreadful in the doctrine of orthodoxy. And then there will go up against it the terrible voice of Tertullian,[2] saying, 'And why then was I cast out; and why did soft hearts and heads decide against me when I proclaimed the perdition of all sinners; and what was this power that thwarted me when I threatened all backsliders with hell? For none ever went up that hard road so far as I; and mine was the *Credo Quia Impossibile*.'[3] Then there is the fourth suggestion that there was something of the

1 See note 1, p.445.
2 Tertullian (*c.*160–*c.* 220), often called the father of Latin Christianity, whose ascetic and rigourist views eventually led him to embrace the Montanist heresy.
3 I believe because it is impossible.

Semitic secret society in the whole matter; that it was a new invasion of the nomad spirit shaking a kindlier and more comfortable
paganism, its cities and its household gods; whereby the jealous
monotheistic races could after all establish their jealous God. And
Mahomet shall answer out of the whirlwind, the red whirlwind of
the desert, 'Who ever served the jealousy of God as I did or left him
more lonely in the sky? Who ever paid more honour to Moses and
Abraham or won more victories over idols and the images of
paganism? And what was this thing that thrust me back with the
energy of a thing alive; whose fanaticism could drive me from Sicily
and tear up my deep roots out of the rock of Spain? What faith was
theirs who thronged in thousands of every class and country crying
out that my ruin was the will of God; and what hurled great Godfrey as from a catapult over the wall of Jerusalem; and what
brought great Sobieski[1] like a thunderbolt to the gates of Vienna?
I think there was more than you fancy in the religion that has so
matched itself with mine.'

Those who would suggest that the faith was a fanaticism are
doomed to an eternal perplexity. In their account it is bound to
appear as fanatical for nothing, and fanatical against everything.
It is ascetical and at war with ascetics, Roman and in revolt against
Rome, monotheistic and fighting furiously against monotheism;
harsh in its condemnation of harshness; a riddle not to be explained even as unreason. And what sort of unreason is it that
seems reasonable to millions of educated Europeans through all
the revolutions of some sixteen hundred years? People are not
amused with a puzzle or a paradox or a mere muddle in the mind
for all that time. I know of no explanation except that such a thing
is not unreason but reason; that if it is fanatical it is fanatical for
reason and fanatical against all the unreasonable things. That is
the only explanation I can find of a thing from the first so detached
and so confident, condemning things that looked so like itself,
refusing help from powers that seemed so essential to its existence,
sharing on its human side all the passions of the age, yet always
at the supreme moment suddenly rising superior to them, never
saying exactly what it was expected to say and never needing to

1 John III Sobieski, king of Poland (1674–96), defeated the Turks in 1683 at the Battle
of Vienna.

unsay what it had said; I can find no explanation except that, like Pallas[1] from the brain of Jove, it had indeed come forth out of the mind of God, mature and mighty and armed for judgment and for war.

1 Athena, patron goddess of Athens, was born out of the head of Zeus.

V

THE ESCAPE FROM PAGANISM

THE MODERN missionary, with his palm-leaf hat and his umbrella, has become rather a figure of fun. He is chaffed among men of the world for the ease with which he can be eaten by cannibals and the narrow bigotry which makes him regard the cannibal culture as lower than his own. Perhaps the best part of the joke is that the men of the world do not see that the joke is against themselves. It is rather ridiculous to ask a man just about to be boiled in a pot and eaten, at a purely religious feast, why he does not regard all religions as equally friendly and fraternal. But there is a more subtle criticism uttered against the more old-fashioned missionary; to the effect that he generalizes too broadly about the heathen and pays too little attention to the difference between Mahomet and Mumbo-Jumbo. There was probably truth in this complaint, especially in the past; but it is my main contention here that the exaggeration is all the other way at present. It is the temptation of the professors to treat mythologies too much as theologies; as things thoroughly thought out and seriously held. It is the temptation of the intellectuals to take much too seriously the fine shades of various schools in the rather irresponsible metaphysics of Asia. Above all it is their temptation to miss the real truth implied in the idea of Aquinas contra Gentiles or Athanasius contra mundum.

If the missionary says, in fact, that he is exceptional in being a Christian, and that the rest of the races and religions can be collectively classified as heathen, he is perfectly right. He may say it in quite the wrong spirit, in which case he is spiritually wrong. But in the cold light of philosophy and history, he is intellectually right. He may not be right-minded, but he is right. He may not even have a right to be right, but he is right. The outer world to which he brings his creed really is something subject to certain generalizations covering all its varieties, and is not merely a variety of similar creeds. Perhaps it is in any case too much of a temptation to pride or hypocrisy to call it heathenry. Perhaps it would be better simply to call it humanity. But there are certain broad characteristics of what we call humanity while it remains in what we call heathenry. They are not necessarily bad characteristics; some of them are worthy of the respect of Christendom; some of them have been absorbed and transfigured in the substance of Christendom. But they existed before Christendom and they still exist outside Christendom, as certainly as the sea existed before a boat and all round a boat; and they have as strong and as universal and as unmistakable a savour as the sea.

For instance, all real scholars who have studied the Greek and Roman culture say one thing about it. They agree that in the ancient world religion was one thing and philosophy quite another. There was very little effort to rationalize and at the same time to realize a real belief in the gods. There was very little pretence of any such real belief among the philosophers. But neither had the passion or perhaps the power to persecute the other, save in particular and peculiar cases; and neither the philosopher in his school nor the priest in his temple seems ever to have seriously contemplated his own concept as covering the world. A priest sacrificing to Artemis[1] in Calydon did not seem to think that people would some day sacrifice to her instead of to Isis beyond the sea; a sage following the vegetarian rule of the Neo-Pythagoreans did not seem to think it would universally prevail and exclude the methods of Epictetus or Epicurus. We may call this liberality if we like; I am not dealing with an argument but describing an atmosphere. All this, I say, is admitted by all scholars; but what neither the learned nor the unlearned have fully realized, perhaps, is that this description is really an exact description of all non-Christian civilization today; and especially of the great civilizations of the East. Eastern paganism really is much more all of a piece, just as ancient paganism was much more all of a piece, than the modern critics admit. It is a many-coloured Persian Carpet as the other was a varied and tesselated Roman pavement; but the one real crack right across that pavement came from the earthquake of the Crucifixion.

The modern European seeking his religion in Asia is reading his religion into Asia. Religion there is something different; it is both

1 Artemis sent a monstrous boar to ravage Calydon in Aetolia because its king had failed to honour her in his religious rites.

more and less. He is like a man mapping out the sea as land; marking waves as mountains; not understanding the nature of its peculiar permanence. It is perfectly true that Asia has its own dignity and poetry and high civilization. But it is not in the least true that Asia has its own definite dominions of moral government, where all loyalty is conceived in terms of morality; as when we say that Ireland is Catholic or that New England was Puritan. The map is not marked out in religions, in our sense of churches. The state of mind is far more subtle, more relative, more secretive, more varied and changing, like the colours of the snake. The Moslem is the nearest approach to a militant Christian; and that is precisely because he is a much nearer approach to an envoy from western civilization. The Moslem in the heart of Asia almost stands for the soul of Europe. And as he stands between them and Europe in the matter of space, so he stands between them and Christianity in the matter of time. In that sense the Moslems in Asia are merely like the Nestorians in Asia. Islam, historically speaking, is the greatest of the Eastern heresies. It owed something to the quite isolated and unique individuality of Israel; but it owed more to Byzantium and the theological enthusiasm of Christendom. It owed something even to the Crusades. It owed nothing whatever to Asia. It owed nothing to the atmosphere of the ancient and traditional world of Asia, with its immemorial etiquette and its bottomless or bewildering philosophies. All that ancient and actual Asia felt the entrance of Islam as something foreign and western and warlike, piercing it like a spear.

Even where we might trace in dotted lines the domains of Asiatic religions, we should probably be reading into them something dogmatic and ethical belonging to our own religion. It is as if a European ignorant of the American atmosphere were to suppose that each 'state' was a separate sovereign state as patriotic as France or Poland; or that when a Yankee referred fondly to his 'home town' he meant he had no other nation, like a citizen of ancient Athens or Rome. As he would be reading a particular sort of loyalty into America, so we are reading a particular sort of loyalty into Asia. There are loyalties of other kinds; but not what men in the west mean by being a believer, by trying to be a Christian, by being a good Protestant or a practising Catholic. In the intellectual world it means something far more vague and varied by doubts and speculations. In the moral world it means something far more loose and drifting. A professor of Persian at one of our great universities, so passionate a partisan of the East as practically to profess a contempt for the West, said to a friend of mine: 'You will never understand oriental religions, because you always conceive religion as connected with ethics. This kind has really nothing to do with ethics.' We have most of us known some Masters of the Higher Wisdom, some Pilgrims upon the Path to Power, some eastern esoteric saints and seers, who had really nothing to do with ethics. Something different, something detached and irresponsible, tinges the moral atmosphere of Asia and touches even that of Islam. . . . It is even more vivid in such glimpses as we get of the genuine and ancient cults of Asia. Deeper than the depths of metaphysics, far down in the abysses of mystical meditations, under all that solemn universe of spiritual things, is a secret, an intangible and a terrible levity. It does not really very much matter what one does. Either because they do not believe in a devil, or because they do believe in a destiny, or because experience here is everything and eternal life something totally different, but for some reason they are totally different. I have read somewhere that there were three great friends famous in mediaeval Persia for their unity of mind. One became the responsible and respected Vizier of the Great King; the second was the poet Omar,[1] pessimist and epicurean, drinking wine in mockery of Mahomet; the third was the Old Man of the Mountain who maddened his people with hashish that they might murder other people with daggers. It does not really much matter what one does.

. . . But this sort of universalist cannot have what we call a character; it is what we call a chaos. He cannot choose; he cannot fight; he cannot repent; he cannot hope. He is not in the same sense creating something; for creation means rejection. He is not, in our religious phrase, making his soul. For our doctrine of salvation does really mean a labour like that of a man trying to make a statue beautiful; a victory with wings. For that there must be a final choice; for a man cannot make statues without rejecting stone. And there really is this ultimate unmorality behind the metaphysics of Asia. And the reason is that there has been nothing through all

1 Omar Khayyam (1048–1131), Persian poet, who wrote, 'Enjoy wine . . . and don't be afraid.'

those unthinkable ages to bring the human mind sharply to the point; to tell it that the time has come to choose. The mind has lived too much in eternity. The soul has been too immortal; in the special sense that it ignores the idea of mortal sin. It has had too much of eternity, in the sense that it has not had enough of the hour of death and the day of judgment. It is not crucial enough; in the literal sense that it has not had enough of the cross. That is what we mean when we say that Asia is very old. But strictly speaking Europe is quite as old as Asia; indeed in a sense any place is as old as any other place. What we mean is that Europe has not merely gone on growing older. It has been born again.

Asia is all humanity; as it has worked out its human doom. Asia, in its vast territory, in its varied populations, in its heights of past achievement and its depths of dark speculation, is itself a world; and represents something of what we mean when we speak of the world. It is a cosmos rather than a continent. It is the world as man has made it; and contains many of the most wonderful things that man has made. Therefore Asia stands as the one representative of paganism and the one rival to Christendom. But everywhere else where we get glimpses of that mortal destiny, they suggest stages in the same story. Where Asia trails away into the southern archipelagoes of the savages, or where a darkness full of nameless shapes dwells in the heart of Africa, or where the last survivors of lost races linger in the cold volcano of prehistoric America, it is all the same story; sometimes perhaps later chapters of the same story. It is men entangled in the forest of their own mythology; it is men drowned in the sea of their own metaphysics. Polytheists have grown weary of the wildest of fictions. Monotheists have grown weary of the most wonderful of truths. Diabolists here and there have such a hatred of heaven and earth that they have tried to take refuge in hell. It is the Fall of Man; and it is exactly that fall that was being felt by our own fathers at the first moment of the Roman decline. We also were going down that wide road; down that easy slope; following the magnificent procession of the high civilizations of the world.

If the Church had not entered the world then, it seems probable that Europe would be now very much what Asia is now. Something may be allowed for a real difference of race and environment, visible in the ancient as in the modern world. But after all we talk about the changeless East very largely because it has not suffered the great change. Paganism in its last phase showed considerable signs of becoming equally changeless. This would not mean that new schools or sects of philosophy would not arise; as new schools did arise in Antiquity and do arise in Asia. It does not mean that there would be no real mystics or visionaries; as there were mystics in Antiquity and are mystics in Asia. It does not mean that there would be no social codes, as there were codes in Antiquity and are codes in Asia. It does not mean that there could not be good men or happy lives, for God has given all men a conscience and conscience can give all men a kind of peace. But it does mean that the tone and proportion of all these things, and especially the proportion of good and evil things, would be in the unchanged West what they are in the changeless East. And nobody who looks at that changeless East honestly, and with a real sympathy, can believe that there is anything there remotely resembling the challenge and revolution of the Faith.

In short, if classic paganism had lingered until now, a number of things might well have lingered with it; and they would look very like what we call the religions of the East. There would still be Pythagoreans teaching reincarnation, as there are still Hindus teaching reincarnation. There would still be Stoics making a religion out of reason and virtue, as there are still Confucians making a religion out of reason and virtue. There would still be Neo-Platonists studying transcendental truths, the meaning of which was mysterious to other people and disputed even amongst themselves; as the Buddhists still study a transcendentalism mysterious to others and disputed among themselves. There would still be intelligent Apollonians apparently worshipping the sun-god but explaining that they were worshipping the divine principle; just as there are still intelligent Parsees apparently worshipping the sun but explaining that they are worshipping the deity. There would still be wild Dionysians dancing on the mountain as there are still wild Dervishes dancing in the desert. There would still be crowds of people attending the popular feasts of the gods, in pagan Europe as in pagan Asia. There would still be crowds of gods, local and other, for them to worship. And there would still be a great many more people who worshipped them than people who believed in them. Finally there would still be a very large number of people who did worship gods and did believe in gods; and who believed in gods and worshipped gods simply because they were demons. There would still be Levantines secretly sacrificing to Moloch[1] as there are still Thugs secretly sacrificing to Kalee.[2] There would still be a great deal of magic; and a great deal of it would be black magic. There would still be a considerable admiration of Seneca and a considerable imitation of Nero; just as the exalted epigrams of Confucius could coexist with the tortures of China. And over all that tangled forest of traditions growing wild or withering would brood the broad silence of a singular and even nameless mood; but the nearest name of it is nothing. All these things, good and bad, would have an indescribable air of being too old to die.

None of these things occupying Europe in the absence of Christendom would bear the least likeness to Christendom. Since the Pythagorean Metempsychosis would still be there, we might call it the Pythagorean religion as we talk about the Buddhist religion. As the noble maxims of Socrates would still be there, we might call it the Socratic religion as we talk about the Confucian religion. As the popular holiday was still marked by a mythological hymn to Adonis, we might call it the religion of Adonis as we talk about the religion of Juggernaut. As literature would still be based on the Greek mythology, we might call that mythology a religion, as we call the Hindu mythology a religion. We might say that there were so many thousands or millions of people belonging to that religion, in the sense of frequenting such temples or merely living in a land full of such temples. But if we called the last tradition of Pythagoras or the lingering legend of Adonis by the name of a religion, then we must find some other name for the Church of Christ.

If anybody says that philosophic maxims preserved through many ages, or mythological temples frequented by many people, are things of the same class and category as the Church, it is enough to answer quite simply that they are not. Nobody thinks they are the same when he sees them in the old civilization of Greece and Rome; nobody would think they were the same if that civilization had lasted two thousand years longer and existed at the present day; nobody can in reason think they are the same in the parallel

1 God to whom children were offered in sacrifice.
2 Hindu patron goddess of this Indian fraternity of robbers and murderers who preyed upon travellers and were suppressed by the British in the 1830s.

pagan civilization in the East, as it is at the present day. None of these philosophies or mythologies are anything like a Church; certainly nothing like a Church Militant. And, as I have shown elsewhere, even if this rule were not already proved, the exception would prove the rule. The rule is that pre-Christian or pagan history does not produce a Church Militant; and the exception, or what some would call the exception, is that Islam is at least militant if it is not Church. And that is precisely because Islam is the one religious rival that is *not* pre-Christian and therefore not in that sense pagan. Islam was a product of Christianity; even if it was a by-product; even if it was a bad product. It was a heresy or parody emulating and therefore imitating the Church. It is no more surprising that Mahomedanism had something of her fighting spirit than that Quakerism had something of her peaceful spirit. After Christianity there are any number of such emulations or extensions. Before it there are none.

The Church Militant is thus unique because it is an army marching to effect a universal deliverance. The bondage from which the world is thus to be delivered is something that is very well symbolized by the state of Asia as by the state of pagan Europe. I do not mean merely their moral or immoral state. The missionary, as a matter of fact, has much more to say for himself than the enlightened imagine, even when he says that the heathen are idolatrous and immoral. A touch or two of realistic experience about Eastern religion, even about Moslem religion, will reveal some startling insensibilities in ethics; such as the practical indifference to the line between passion and perversion. It is not prejudice but practical experience which says that Asia is full of demons as well as gods. But the evil I mean is in the mind. And it is in the mind wherever the mind has worked for a long time alone. It is what happens when all dreaming and thinking have come to an end in an emptiness that is at once negation and necessity. It sounds like an anarchy, but it is also a slavery. It is what has been called already the wheel of Asia; all those recurrent arguments about cause and effect or things beginning and ending in the mind, which make it impossible for the soul really to strike out and go anywhere or do anything. And the point is that it is not necessarily peculiar to Asiatics; it would have been true in the end of Europeans – if something had not happened. If the Church Militant had not been a thing marching, all men would have been marking time. If the Church Militant had not endured a discipline, all men would have endured a slavery.

What that universal yet fighting faith brought into the world was hope. Perhaps the one thing common to mythology and philosophy was that both were really sad; in the sense that they had not this hope even if they had touches of faith or charity. We may call Buddhism a faith; though to us it seems more like a doubt. We may call the Lord of Compassion a Lord of Charity, though it seems to us a very pessimist sort of pity. But those who insist most on the antiquity and size of such cults must agree that in all their ages they have not covered all their areas with that sort of practical and pugnacious hope. In Christendom hope has never been absent; rather it has been errant, extravagant, excessively fixed upon fugitive chances. Its perpetual revolution and reconstruction has at least been an evidence of people being in better spirits. Europe did very truly renew its youth like the eagles; just as the eagles of Rome rose again over the legions of Napoleon, or we have seen soaring but yesterday the silver eagle of Poland. But in the Polish case even revolution always went with religion. Napoleon himself sought a reconciliation with religion. Religion could never be finally separated even from the most hostile of the hopes; simply because it was the real source of the hopefulness. And the cause of this is to be found simply in the religion itself. Those who quarrel about it seldom even consider it in itself. There is neither space nor place for such a full consideration here; but a word may be said to explain a reconciliation that always recurs and still seems to require explanation.

There will be no end to the weary debates about liberalizing theology, until people face the fact that the only liberal part of it is really the dogmatic part. If dogma is incredible, it is because it is incredibly liberal. If it is irrational, it can only be in giving us more assurance of freedom than is justified by reason. The obvious example is that essential form of freedom which we call free-will. It is absurd to say that a man shows his liberality in denying his liberty. But it is tenable that he has to affirm a transcendental doctrine in order to affirm his liberty. There is a sense in which we might reasonably say that if man has a primary power of choice, he has in that fact a supernatural power of creation, as if he could raise the dead or give birth to the unbegotten. Possibly in that case a man must be a miracle; and certainly in that case he must be a miracle in order to be a man; and most certainly in order to be a free man. But it is absurd to forbid him to be a free man and do it in the name of a more free religion.

But it is true in twenty other matters. Anybody who believes at all in God must believe in the absolute supremacy of God. But in so far as that supremacy does allow of any degrees that can be called liberal or illiberal, it is self-evident that the illiberal power is the deity of the rationalists and the liberal power is the deity of the dogmatists. Exactly in proportion as you turn monotheism into monism you turn it into despotism. It is precisely the unknown God of the scientist, with his impenetrable purpose and his inevitable and unalterable law, that reminds us of a Prussian autocrat making rigid plans in a remote tent and moving mankind like machinery. It is precisely the God of miracles and of answered prayers who reminds us of a liberal and popular prince, receiving petitions, listening to parliaments and considering the cases of a whole people. I am not now arguing the rationality of this conception in other respects; as a matter of fact it is not, as some suppose, irrational; for there is nothing irrational in the wisest and most well-informed king acting differently according to the action of those he wishes to save. But I am here only noting the general nature of liberality, or of free or enlarged atmosphere of action. And in this respect it is certain that the king can only be what we call magnanimous if he is what some call capricious. It is the Catholic, who has the feeling that his prayers do make a difference, when offered for the living and the dead, who also has the feeling of living like a free citizen in something almost like a constitutional commonwealth. It is the monist who lives under a single iron law who must have the feeling of living like a slave under a sultan. Indeed I believe that the original use of the word *suffragium*, which we now use in politics for a vote, was that employed in theology about a prayer. The dead in Purgatory were said to have the suffrages of the living. And in this sense, of a sort of right of petition to the supreme ruler, we may truly say that the whole of the Communion of Saints, as well as the whole of the Church Militant, is founded on universal suffrage.

But above all, it is true of the most tremendous issue; of that tragedy which has created the divine comedy of our creed. Nothing short of the extreme and strong and startling doctrine of the divinity of Christ will give that particular effect that can truly stir the popular sense like a trumpet; the idea of the king himself serving in the ranks like a common soldier. By making that figure merely human we make that story much less human. We take away the point of the story which actually pierces humanity; the point of the story which was quite literally the point of a spear. It does not especially humanize the universe to say that good and wise men can die for their opinions; any more than it would be any sort of uproariously popular news in an army that good soldiers may easily get killed. It is no news that King Leonidas[1] is dead any more than that Queen Anne is dead; and men did not wait for Christianity to be men, in the full sense of being heroes. But if we are describing, for the moment, the atmosphere of what is generous and popular and even picturesque, any knowledge of human nature will tell us that no sufferings of the sons of men, or even of the servants of God, strike the same note as the notion of the master suffering instead of his servants. And this is given by the theological and emphatically not by the scientific deity. No mysterious monarch, hidden in his starry pavilion at the base of the cosmic campaign, is in the least like that celestial chivalry of the Captain who carries his five wounds in the front of battle.

What the denouncer of dogma really means is not that dogma is bad; but rather that dogma is too good to be true. That is, he means that dogma is too liberal to be likely. Dogma gives man too much freedom when it permits him to fall. Dogma gives even God too much freedom when it permits him to die. That is what the intelligent sceptics ought to say; and it is not in the least my intention to deny that there is something to be said for it. They mean that the universe is itself a universal prison; that existence itself is a limitation and a control; and it is not for nothing that they call causation a chain. In a word, they mean quite simply that they cannot believe these things; not in the least that they are unworthy of belief. We say, not lightly but very literally, that the truth has made us free. They say that it makes us so free that it cannot be the truth.

1 King of Sparta, the hero of the Battle of Thermopylae in 480 BC, at which the vastly outnumbered Greek forces repulsed the Persian invaders, only to be betrayed by a Greek traitor.

To them it is like believing in fairyland to believe in such freedom as we enjoy. It is like believing in men with wings to entertain the fancy of men with wills. It is like accepting a fable about a squirrel in conversation with a mountain to believe in a man who is free to ask or a God who is free to answer. This is a manly and a rational negation for which I for one shall always show respect. But I decline to show any respect for those who first of all clip the wings and cage the squirrel, rivet the chains and refuse the freedom, close all the doors of the cosmic prison on us with a clang of eternal iron, tell us that our emancipation is a dream and our dungeon a necessity; and then calmly turn round and tell us they have a freer thought and a more liberal theology.

The moral of all this is an old one; that religion is revelation. In other words, it is a vision, and a vision received by faith; but it is a vision of reality. The faith consists in a conviction of its reality. That, for example, is the difference between a vision and a day-dream. And that is the difference between religion and mythology. That is the difference between faith and all that fancy-work, quite human and more or less healthy, which we considered under the head of mythology. There is something in the reasonable use of the very word vision that implies two things about it; first that it comes very rarely, possibly that it comes only once; and secondly that it probably comes once and for all. A day-dream may come every day. A day-dream may be different every day. It is something more than the difference between telling ghost-stories and meeting a ghost.

But if it is not a mythology neither is it a philosophy. It is not a philosophy because, being a vision, it is not a pattern but a picture. It is not one of those simplifications which resolve everything into an abstract explanation; as that everything is recurrent; or everything is relative; or everything is inevitable; or everything is illusive. It is not a process but a story. It has proportions, of the sort seen in a picture or a story; it has not the regular repetitions of a pattern or a process; but it replaces them by being convincing as a picture or a story is convincing. In other words, it is exactly, as the phrase goes, like life. For indeed it is life. An example of what is meant here might well be found in the treatment of the problem of evil. It is easy enough to make a plan of life of which the background is black, as the pessimists do; and then admit a speck or two of star-dust more or less accidental, or at least in the literal sense insignifi-cant. And it is easy enough to make another plan on white paper, as the Christian Scientists do, and explain or explain away some-how such dots or smudges as may be difficult to deny. Lastly it is easiest of all, perhaps, to say as the dualists do, that life is like a chess-board in which the two are equal; and can as truly be said to consist of white squares on a black board or of black squares on a white board. But every man feels in his heart that none of these three paper plans is like life; that none of these worlds is one in which he can live. Something tells him that the ultimate idea of a world is not bad or even neutral; staring at the sky or the grass or the truths of mathematics or even a new-laid egg, he has a vague feeling like the shadow of that saying of the great Christian philo-sopher, St Thomas Aquinas, 'Every existence, as such, is good.' On the other hand, something else tells him that it is unmanly and debased and even diseased to minimize evil to a dot or even a blot. He realizes that optimism is morbid. It is if possible even more morbid than pessimism. These vague but healthy feelings, if he followed them out, would result in the idea that evil is in some way an exception but an enormous exception; and ultimately that evil is an invasion or yet more truly a rebellion. He does not think that everything is right or that everything is wrong, or that everything is equally right and wrong. But he does think that right has a right to be right and therefore a right to be there; and wrong has no right to be wrong and therefore no right to be there. It is the prince of the world; but it is also a usurper. So he will apprehend vaguely what the vision will give to him vividly; no less than all that strange story of treason in heaven and the great desertion by which evil damaged and tried to destroy a cosmos that it could not create. It is a very strange story and its proportions and its lines and colours are as arbitrary and absolute as the artistic composition of a picture. It is a vision which we do in fact symbolize in pictures by titanic limbs and passionate tints of plumage; all that abysmal vision of falling stars and the peacock panoplies of the night. But that strange story has one small advantage over the diagrams. It is like life.

Another example might be found, not in the problem of evil, but in what is called the problem of progress. One of the ablest agnostics of the age once asked me whether I thought mankind grew better or grew worse or remained the same. He was confident that the alternative covered all possibilities. He did not see that it only covered patterns and not pictures; processes and not stories. I asked him whether he thought that Mr Smith of Golder's Green got better or worse or remained exactly the same between the age of thirty and forty. It then seemed to dawn on him that it would rather depend on Mr Smith; and how he chose to go on. It had never occurred to him that it might depend on how mankind chose to go on; and that its course was not a straight line or an upward or downward curve, but a track like that of a man across a valley, going where he liked and stopping where he chose, going into a church or falling drunk in a ditch. The life of man is a story; an adventure story; and in our vision the same is true even of the story of God.

The Catholic faith is the reconciliation because it is the realization both of mythology and philosophy. It is a story and in that sense one of a hundred stories; only it is a true story. It is a philosophy and in that sense one of a hundred philosophies; only it is a philosophy that is like life. But above all, it is a reconciliation because it is something that can only be called the philosophy of stories. That normal narrative instinct which produced all the fairy tales is something that is neglected by all the philosophies — except one. The Faith is the justification of that popular instinct; the finding of a philosophy for it or the analysis of the philosophy in it. Exactly as a man in an adventure story has to pass various tests to save his life, so the man in this philosophy has to pass several tests and save his soul. In both there is an idea of free will operating under conditions of design; in other words, there is an aim and it is the business of a man to aim at it; we therefore watch to see whether he will hit it. Now this deep and democratic and dramatic instinct is derided and dismissed in all the other philosophies. For all the other philosophies avowedly end where they begin; and it is the definition of a story that it ends differently; that it begins in one place and ends in another. From Buddha and his wheel to Akhen Aten[1] and his disc, from Pythagoras with his abstraction of number to Confucius with his religion of routine,

1 Disc of the sun in ancient Egyptian mythology, the deity of the religion established by the Egyptian Pharaoh Amenhotep IV, who later took the name Akhenaten.

there is not one of them that does not in some way sin against the soul of a story. There is none of them that really grasps this human notion of the tale, the test, the adventure; the ordeal of the free man. Each of them starves the story-telling instinct, so to speak, and does something to spoil human life considered as a romance; either by fatalism (pessimist or optimist) and that destiny that is the death of adventure; or by indifference and that detachment that is the death of drama; or by a fundamental scepticism that dissolves the actors into atoms; or by a materialistic limitation blocking the vista of moral consequences; or a mechanical recurrence making even moral tests monotonous; or a bottomless relativity making even practical tests insecure. There is such a thing as a human story; and there is such a thing as the divine story which is also a human story; but there is no such thing as a Hegelian story or a Monist story or a relativist story or a determinist story; for every story, yes, even a penny dreadful or a cheap novelette, has something in it that belongs to our universe and not theirs. Every short story does truly begin with creation and end with a last judgment.

And *that* is the reason why the myths and the philosophers were at war until Christ came. That is why the Athenian democracy killed Socrates out of respect for the gods; and why every strolling sophist gave himself the airs of a Socrates whenever he could talk in a superior fashion of the gods; and why the heretic Pharaoh wrecked his huge idols and temples for an abstraction and why the priests could return in triumph and trample his dynasty under foot; and why Buddhism had to divide itself from Brahminism, and why in every age and country outside Christendom there has been a feud for ever between the philosopher and the priest. It is easy enough to say that the philosopher is generally the more rational; it is easier still to forget that the priest is always the more popular. For the priest told the people stories; and the philosopher did not understand the philosophy of stories. It came into the world with the story of Christ.

And this is why it had to be a revelation or vision given from above. Any one who will think of the theory of stories or pictures will easily see the point. The true story of the world must be told by somebody to somebody else. By the very nature of a story it cannot be left to occur to anybody. A story has proportions, variations, surprises, particular dispositions, which cannot be worked out by rule in the abstract, like a sum. We could not deduce whether or no Achilles would give back the body of Hector from a Pythagorean theory of number or recurrence; and we could not infer for ourselves in what way the world would get back the body of Christ, merely from being told that all things go round and round upon the wheel of Buddha. A man might perhaps work out a proposition of Euclid without having heard of Euclid; but he would not work out the precise legend of Eurydice without having heard of Eurydice. At any rate he would not be certain how the story would end and whether Orpheus was ultimately defeated. Still less could he guess the end of our story; or the legend of our Orpheus rising, not defeated, from the dead.

To sum up; the sanity of the world was restored and the soul of man offered salvation by something which did indeed satisfy the two warring tendencies of the past; which had never been satisfied in full and most certainly never satisfied together. It met the mythological search for romance by being a story and the philosophical search for truth by being a true story. That is why the ideal figure had to be a historical character, as nobody had ever felt Adonis or Pan to be a historical character. But that is also why the historical character had to be the ideal figure; and even fulfil many of the functions given to these other ideal figures; why he was at once the sacrifice and the feast, why he could be shown under the emblems of the growing vine or the rising sun. The more deeply we think of the matter the more we shall conclude that, if there be indeed a God, his creation could hardly have reached any other culmination than this granting of a real romance to the world. Otherwise the two sides of the human mind could never have touched at all; and the brain of man would have remained cloven and double; one lobe of it dreaming impossible dreams and the other repeating invariable calculations. The picture-makers would have remained for ever painting the portrait of nobody. The sages would have remained for ever adding up numerals that came to nothing. It was that abyss that nothing but an incarnation could cover; a divine embodiment of our dreams; and he stands above that chasm whose name is more than priest and older even than Christendom; Pontifex Maximus, the mightiest maker of a bridge.

But even with that we return to the more specially Christian symbol in the same tradition; the perfect pattern of the keys. This is a historical and not a theological outline, and it is not my duty here to defend in detail that theology, but merely to point out that it could not even be justified in design without being justified in detail – like a key. Beyond the broad suggestion of this chapter I attempt no apologetic about why the creed should be accepted. But in answer to the historical query of why it was accepted, and is accepted, I answer for millions of others in my reply; because it fits the lock; because it is like life. It is one among many stories; only it happens to be a true story. It is one among many philosophies; only it happens to be the truth. We accept it; and the ground is solid under our feet and the road is open before us. It does not imprison us in a dream of destiny or a consciousness of the universal delusion. It opens to us not only incredible heavens, but what seems to some an equally incredible earth, and makes it credible. This is the sort of truth that is hard to explain because it is a fact; but it is a fact to which we can call witnesses. We are Christians and Catholics not because we worship a key, but because we have passed a door; and felt the wind that is the trumpet of liberty blow over the land of the living.

VI

THE FIVE DEATHS OF THE FAITH

IT IS NOT the purpose of this book to trace the subsequent history of Christianity, especially the later history of Christianity; which involves controversies of which I hope to write more fully elsewhere. It is devoted only to the suggestion that Christianity, appearing amid heathen humanity, had all the character of a unique thing and even of a supernatural thing. It was not like any of the other things; and the more we study it the less it looks like any of them. But there is a certain rather peculiar character which marked it henceforward even down to the present moment, with a note on which this book may well conclude.

I have said that Asia and the ancient world had an air of being too old to die. Christendom has had the very opposite fate. Christendom has had a series of revolutions and in each one of them Christianity has died. Christianity has died many times and risen again; for it had a God who knew the way out of the grave. But the first extraordinary fact which marks this history is this: that Europe has been turned upside down over and over again; and that at the end of each of these revolutions the same religion has again been found on top. The Faith is always converting the age, not as an old religion but as a new religion. This truth is hidden from many by a convention that is too little noticed. Curiously enough, it is a convention of the sort which those who ignore it claim especially to detect and denounce. They are always telling us that priests and ceremonies are not religion and that religious organization can be a hollow sham; but they hardly realize how true it is. It is so true that three or four times at least in the history of Christendom the whole soul seemed to have gone out of Christianity; and almost every man in his heart expected its end. This fact is only masked in mediaeval and other times by that very official religion which such critics pride themselves on seeing through. Christianity remained the official religion of a Renaissance prince or the official religion of an eighteenth-century bishop, just as an ancient mythology remained the official religion of Julius Caesar or the Arian creed long remained the official religion of Julian the Apostate. But there was a difference between the cases of Julius and of Julian; because the Church had begun its strange career. There was no reason why men like Julius should not worship gods like Jupiter for ever in public and laugh at them for ever in private. But when Julian treated Christianity as dead, he found it had come to life again. He also found, incidentally, that there was not the faintest sign of Jupiter ever coming to life again. This case of Julian and the episode of Arianism is but the first of a series of examples that can only be roughly indicated here. Arianism, as has been said, had every human appearance of being the natural way in which that particular superstition of Constantine might be expected to peter out. All the ordinary stages had been passed through; the creed had become a respectable thing, had become a ritual thing, had then been modified into a rational thing; and the rationalists were ready to dissipate the last remains of it, just as they do today. When Christianity rose again suddenly and threw them, it was almost as unexpected as Christ rising from the dead. But there are many other examples of the same thing, even about the same time. The rush of missionaries from Ireland, for instance, has all the air of an unexpected onslaught of young men on an old world, and even on a Church that showed signs of growing old. Some of them were martyred on the coast of Cornwall; and the chief authority on Cornish antiquities told me that he did not believe for a moment that they were martyred by heathens but (as he expressed it with some humour) 'by rather slack Christians'.

Now if we were to dip below the surface of history, as it is not in the scope of this argument to do, I suspect that we should find several occasions when Christendom was thus to all appearance hollowed out from within by doubt and indifference, so that only the old Christian shell stood as the pagan shell had stood so long. But the difference is that in every such case, the sons were fanatical for the faith where the fathers had been slack about it. This is obvious in the case of the transition from the Renaissance to the Counter-Reformation. It is obvious in the case of a transition from the eighteenth century to the many Catholic revivals of our own time. But I suspect many other examples which would be worthy of separate studies.

The Faith is not a survival. It is not as if the Druids had managed somehow to survive somewhere for two thousand years. That is what might have happened in Asia or ancient Europe, in that indifference or tolerance in which mythologies and philosophies could live for ever side by side. It has not survived; it has returned again and again in this western world of rapid change and institutions perpetually perishing. Europe, in the tradition of Rome, was always trying revolution and reconstruction; rebuilding a universal republic. And it always began by rejecting this old stone and ended by making it the head of the corner; by bringing it back from the rubbish-heap to make it the crown of the capitol. Some stones of Stonehenge are standing and some are fallen; and as the stone falleth so shall it lie. There has not been a Druidic renaissance every century or two, with the young Druids crowned with fresh mistletoe, dancing in the sun on Salisbury Plain. Stonehenge has not been rebuilt in every style of architecture from the rude round Norman to the last rococo of the Baroque. The sacred place of the Druids is safe from the vandalism of restoration.

But the Church in the West was not in a world where things were too old to die; but in one in which they were always young enough to get killed. The consequence was that superficially and externally it often did get killed; nay, it sometimes wore out even without getting killed. And there follows a fact I find it somewhat difficult to describe, yet which I believe to be very real and rather important. As a ghost is the shadow of a man, and in that sense the shadow of life, so at intervals there passed across this endless life a sort of shadow of death. It came at the moment when it would have perished had it been perishable. It withered away everything that was perishable. If such animal parallels were worthy of the occasion, we might say that the snake shuddered and shed a skin and went on, or even that the cat went into convulsions as it lost only one of its nine-hundred-and-ninety-nine lives. It is truer to say, in a more dignified image, that a clock struck and nothing happened; or that a bell tolled for an execution that was everlastingly postponed.

What was the meaning of all that dim but vast unrest of the

twelfth century; when, as it has been so finely said, Julian stirred in his sleep? Why did there appear so strangely early, in the twilight of dawn after the Dark Ages, so deep a scepticism as that involved in urging nominalism[1] against realism? For realism against nominalism was really realism against rationalism, or something more destructive than what we call rationalism. The answer is that just as some might have thought the Church simply a part of the Roman Empire, so others later might have thought the Church only a part of the Dark Ages. The Dark Ages ended as the Empire had ended; and the Church should have departed with them, if she had been also one of the shades of night. It was another of those spectral deaths or simulations of death. I mean that if nominalism had succeeded, it would have been as if Arianism had succeeded, it would have been the beginning of a confession that Christianity had failed. For nominalism is a far more fundamental scepticism than mere atheism. Such was the question that was openly asked as the Dark Ages broadened into that daylight that we call the modern world. But what was the answer? The answer was Aquinas in the chair of Aristotle, taking all knowledge for his province; and tens of thousands of lads down to the lowest ranks of peasant and serf, living in rags and on crusts about the great colleges, to listen to the scholastic philosophy.

What was the meaning of all that whisper of fear that ran round the west under the shadow of Islam, and fills every old romance with incongruous images of Saracen knights swaggering in Norway or the Hebrides? Why were men in the extreme west, such as King John if I remember rightly, accused of being secretly Moslems, as men are accused of being secretly atheists? Why was there that fierce alarm among some of the authorities about the rationalistic Arab version of Aristotle? Authorities are seldom alarmed like that except when it is too late. The answer is that hundreds of people probably believed in their hearts that Islam would conquer Christendom; that Averroes was more rational than Anselm; that the Saracen culture was really, as it was superficially, a superior culture. Here again we should probably find a whole generation, the older generation, very doubtful and depressed and weary. The coming of Islam would only have been the coming of Unitarianism

[1] The philosophy that regards universals or abstract concepts as mere names without any corresponding realities.

a thousand years before its time. To many it may have seemed quite reasonable and quite probable and quite likely to happen. If so, they would have been surprised at what did happen. What did happen was a roar like thunder from thousands and thousands of young men, throwing all their youth into one exultant counter-charge; the Crusades. It was the sons of St Francis, the Jugglers of God, wandering singing over all the roads of the world; it was the Gothic going up like a flight of arrows; it was the waking of the world. In considering the war of the Albigensians, we come to the breach in the heart of Europe and the landslide of a new philo-sophy that nearly ended Christendom for ever. In that case the new philosophy was also a very old philosophy, it was pessimism. It was none the less like modern ideas because it was as old as Asia; most modern ideas are. It was the Gnostics returning; but why did the Gnostics return? Because it was the end of an epoch, like the end of the Empire; and should have been the end of the Church. It was Schopenhauer hovering over the future; but it was also Manich-aeus rising from the dead; that men might have death and that they might have it more abundantly.

It is rather more obvious in the case of the Renaissance, simply because the period is so much nearer to us and people know so much more about it. But there is more even in that example than most people know. Apart from the particular controversies which I wish to reserve for a separate study, the period was far more chaotic than those controversies commonly imply. When Pro-testants call Latimer a martyr to Protestantism, and Catholics reply that Campion was a martyr to Catholicism, it is often forgot-ten that many who perished in such persecutions could only be described as martyrs to atheism or anarchism or even diabolism. That world was almost as wild as our own; the men wandering about in it included the sort of man who says there is no God, the sort of man who says he is himself God, the sort of man who says something that nobody can make head or tail of. If we could have the *conversation* of the age following the Renaissance, we should probably be shocked by its shameless negations. The remarks attributed to Marlowe are probably pretty typical of the talk in many intellectual taverns. The transition from Pre-Reformation to Post-Reformation Europe was through a void of very yawning questions; yet again in the long run the answer was the same. It was one of those moments when, as Christ walked on the water, so was Christianity walking in the air.

But all these cases are remote in date and could only be proved in detail. We can see the fact much more clearly in the case when the paganism of the Renaissance ended Christianity and Christianity unaccountably began all over again. But we can see it most clearly of all in the case which is close to us and full of manifest and minute evidence; the case of the great decline of religion that began about the time of Voltaire. For indeed it is our own case; and we ourselves have seen the decline of that decline. The two hundred years since Voltaire do not flash past us at a glance like the fourth and fifth centuries or the twelfth and thirteenth centuries. In our own case we can see this oft-repeated process close at hand; we know how completely a society can lose its fundamental religion without abolishing its official religion; we know how men can all become agnostics long before they abolish bishops. And we know that also in this last ending, which really did look to us like the final ending, the incredible thing has happened again; the Faith has a better following among the young men than among the old. When Ibsen spoke of the new generation knocking at the door, he certainly never expected that it would be the church-door.

At least five times, therefore, with the Arian and the Albigensian, with the Humanist sceptic, after Voltaire and after Darwin, the Faith has to all appearance gone to the dogs. In each of these five cases it was the dog that died. How complete was the collapse and how strange the reversal, we can only see in detail in the case nearest to our own time.

A thousand things have been said about the Oxford Movement and the parallel French Catholic revival; but few have made us feel the simplest fact about it; that it was a surprise. It was a puzzle as well as a surprise; because it seemed to most people like a river turning backwards from the sea and trying to climb back into the mountains. To have read the literature of the eighteenth and nineteenth centuries is to know that nearly everybody had come to take it for granted that religion was a thing that would continually broaden like a river, till it reached an infinite sea. Some of them expected it to go down in a cataract of catastrophe, most of them expected it to widen into an estuary of equality and moderation; but all of them thought its returning on itself a prodigy as incredible as witchcraft. In other words, most moderate people thought that faith like freedom would be slowly broadened down; and some advanced people thought that it would be very rapidly broadened down, not to say flattened out. All that world of Guizot and Macaulay and the commercial and scientific liberality was perhaps more certain than any men before or since about the direction in which the world is going. People were so certain about the direction that they only differed about the pace. Many anticipated with alarm, and a few with sympathy, a Jacobin revolt that should guillotine the Archbishop of Canterbury or a Chartist riot that should hang the parsons on the lamp-posts. But it seemed like a convulsion in nature that the Archbishop instead of losing his head should be looking for his mitre; and that instead of diminishing the respect due to parsons we should strengthen it to the respect due to priests. It revolutionized their very vision of revolution; and turned their very topsy-turvydom topsy-turvy.

In short, the whole world being divided about whether the stream was going slower or faster, became conscious of something vague but vast that was going against the stream. Both in fact and figure there is something deeply disturbing about this, and that for an essential reason. A dead thing can go with the stream, but only a living thing can go against it. A dead dog can be lifted on the leaping water with all the swiftness of a leaping hound; but only a live dog can swim backwards. A paper boat can ride the rising deluge with all the airy arrogance of a fairy ship; but if the fairy ship sails up-stream it is really rowed by the fairies. And among the things that merely went with the tide of apparent progress and enlargement, there was many a demagogue or sophist whose wild gestures were in truth as lifeless as the movement of a dead dog's limbs wavering in the eddying water; and many a philosophy uncommonly like a paper boat, of the sort that it is not difficult to knock into a cocked hat. But even the truly living and even life-giving things that went with that stream did not thereby prove that they were living or life-giving. It was this other force that was unquestionably and unaccountably alive; the mysterious and un-measured energy that was thrusting back the river. That was felt to be like the movement of some great monster; and it was none the less clearly a living monster because most people thought it a prehistoric monster. It was none the less an unnatural, an incongruous, and to some a comic upheaval; as if the Great Sea Serpent had suddenly risen out of the Round Pond – unless we consider the Sea Serpent as more likely to live in the Serpentine. This flippant element in the fantasy must not be missed, for it was one of the clearest testimonies to the unexpected nature of the reversal. That age did really feel that a preposterous quality in prehistoric animals belonged also to historic rituals; that mitres and tiaras were like the horns or crests of antediluvian creatures; and that appealing to a Primitive Church was like dressing up as a Primitive Man.

The world is still puzzled by that movement; but most of all because it still moves. I have said something elsewhere of the rather random sort of reproaches that are still directed against it and its much greater consequences; it is enough to say here that the more such critics reproach it the less they explain it. In a sense it is my concern here, if not to explain it, at least to suggest the direction of the explanation; but above all, it is my concern to point out one particular thing about it. And that is that it had all happened before; and even many times before.

To sum up, in so far as it is true that recent centuries have seen an attenuation of Christian doctrine, recent centuries have only seen what the most remote centuries have seen. And even the modern example has only ended as the mediaeval and pre-mediaeval examples ended. It is already clear, and grows clearer every day, that it is not going to end in the disappearance of the diminished creed; but rather in the return of those parts of it that had really disappeared. It is going to end as the Arian compromise ended, as the attempts at a compromise with Nominalism and even with Albigensianism ended. But the point to seize in the modern case, as in all the other cases, is that what returns is not in that sense a simplified theology; not according to that view a purified theology; it is simply theology. It is that enthusiasm for theological studies that marked the most doctrinal ages; it is the divine science. An old Don with D. D. after his name may have become the typical figure of a bore; but that was because he was himself bored with his theology, not because he was excited about it. It was precisely because he was admittedly more interested in the Latin of Plautus than in the Latin of Augustine, in the Greek of Xenophon than in the Greek of Chrysostom. It was precisely because he was more interested in a dead tradition than in a decidedly living tradition. In short, it was precisely because he was himself a type of the time in which Christian faith was weak. It was not because men would not hail, if they could, the wonderful and almost wild vision of a Doctor of Divinity.

There are people who say they wish Christianity to remain as a spirit. They mean, very literally, that they wish it to remain as a ghost. But it is not going to remain as a ghost. What follows this process of apparent death is not the lingering of the shade; it is the resurrection of the body. These people are quite prepared to shed pious and reverential tears over the Sepulchre of the Son of Man; what they are not prepared for is the Son of God walking once more upon the hills of morning. These people, and indeed most people, were indeed by this time quite accustomed to the idea that the old Christian candle-light would fade into the light of common day. To many of them it did quite honestly appear like that pale yellow flame of a candle when it is left burning in daylight. It was all the more unexpected, and therefore all the more unmistakable, that the seven-branched candle-stick suddenly towered to heaven like a miraculous tree and flamed until the sun turned pale. But other ages have seen the day conquer the candle-light and then the candle-light conquer the day. Again and again, before our time, men have grown content with a diluted doctrine. And again and again there has followed on that dilution, coming as out of the darkness in a crimson cataract, the strength of the red original wine. And we only say once more today as has been said many times by our fathers: 'Long years and centuries ago our fathers or the founders of our people drank, as they dreamed, of the blood of God. Long years and centuries have passed since the strength of that giant vintage has been anything but a legend of the age of giants. Centuries ago already is the dark time of the second fermentation, when the wine of Catholicism turned into the vinegar of Calvinism. Long since that bitter drink has been itself diluted; rinsed out and washed away by the waters of oblivion and the wave of the world. Never did we think to taste again even that bitter tang of sincerity and the spirit, still less the richer and the sweeter strength of the purple vineyards in our dreams of the age of gold.

Day by day and year by year we have lowered our hopes and lessened our convictions; we have grown more and more used to seeing those vats and vineyards overwhelmed in the water-floods and the last savour and suggestion of that special element fading like a stain of purple upon a sea of grey. We have grown used to dilution, to dissolution, to a watering down that went on for ever. But "Thou hast kept the good wine until now." '

This is the final fact, and it is the most extraordinary of all. The faith has not only often died but it has often died of old age. It has not only been often killed but it has often died a natural death; in the sense of coming to a natural and necessary end. It is obvious that it has survived the most savage and the most universal persecutions from the shock of the Diocletian fury to the shock of the French Revolution. But it has a more strange and even a more weird tenacity; it has survived not only war but peace. It has not only died often but degenerated often and decayed often; it has survived its own weakness and even its own surrender. We need not repeat what is so obvious about the beauty of the end of Christ in its wedding of youth and death. But this is almost as if Christ had lived to the last possible span, had been a white-haired sage of a hundred and died of natural decay, and then had risen again rejuvenated, with trumpets and the rending of the sky. It was said truly enough that human Christianity in its recurrent weakness was sometimes too much wedded to the powers of the world; but if it was wedded it has very often been widowed. It is a strangely immortal sort of widow. An enemy may have said at one moment that it was but an aspect of the power of the Caesars; and it sounds as strange today as to call it an aspect of the power of the Pharaohs. An enemy might say that it was the official faith of feudalism; and it sounds as convincing now as to say that it was bound to perish with the ancient Roman villa. All these things did indeed run their course to its normal end; and there seemed no course for the religion but to end with them. It ended and it began again.

'Heaven and earth shall pass away, but my words shall not pass away.' The civilization of antiquity was the whole world: and men no more dreamed of its ending than of the ending of daylight. They could not imagine another order unless it were in another world. The civilization of the world has passed away and those words have not passed away. In the long night of the Dark Ages feudalism was so familiar a thing that no man could imagine himself without a lord: and religion was so woven into that network that no man would have believed they could be torn asunder. Feudalism itself was torn to rags and rotted away in the popular life of the true Middle Ages; and the first and freshest power in that new freedom was the old religion. Feudalism had passed away, and the words did not pass away. The whole mediaeval order, in many ways so complete and almost cosmic a home for man, wore out gradually in its turn: and here at least it was thought that the words would die. They went forth across the radiant abyss of the Renaissance and in fifty years were using all its light and learning for new religious foundations, new apologetics, new saints. It was supposed to have been withered up at last in the dry light of the Age of Reason; it was supposed to have disappeared ultimately in the earthquake of the Age of Revolution. Science explained it away; and it was still there. History disinterred it in the past; and it appeared suddenly in the future. Today it stands once more in our path; and even as we watch it, it grows.

If our social relations and records retain their continuity, if men really learn to apply reason to the accumulating facts of so crushing a story, it would seem that sooner or later even its enemies will learn from their incessant and interminable disappointments not to look for anything so simple as its death. They may continue to war with it, but it will be as they war with nature; as they war with the landscape, as they war with the skies. 'Heaven and earth shall pass away, but my words shall not pass away.' They will watch for it to stumble; they will watch for it to err; they will no longer watch for it to end. Insensibly, even unconsciously, they will in their own silent anticipations fulfil the relative terms of that astounding prophecy; they will forget to watch for the mere extinction of what has so often been vainly extinguished; and will learn instinctively to look first for the coming of the comet or the freezing of the star.

CONCLUSION
THE SUMMARY OF THIS BOOK

I HAVE taken the liberty once or twice of borrowing the excellent phrase about an Outline of History; though this study of a special truth and a special error can of course claim no sort of comparison with the rich and many-sided encyclopaedia of history, for which that name was chosen. And yet there is a certain reason in the reference; and a sense in which the one thing touches and even cuts across the other. For the story of the world as told by Mr Wells could here only be criticized as an outline. And, strangely enough, it seems to me that it is only wrong as an outline. It is admirable as an accumulation of history; it is splendid as a storehouse or treasury of history; it is a fascinating disquisition on history; it is most attractive as an amplification of history; but it is quite false as an outline of history. The one thing that seems to me quite wrong about it is the outline; the sort of outline that can really be a single line, like that which makes all the difference between a caricature of the profile of Mr Winston Churchill and of Sir Alfred Mond.[1] In simple and homely language, I mean the things that stick out; the things that make the simplicity of a silhouette. I think the proportions are wrong; the proportions of what is certain as compared with what is uncertain, of what played a great part as compared with what played a smaller part, of what is ordinary and what is extraordinary, of what really lies level with an average and what stands out as an exception.

I do not say it as a small criticism of a great writer, and I have no reason to do so; for in my own much smaller task I feel I have failed in very much the same way. I am very doubtful whether I have conveyed to the reader the main point I meant about the proportions of history, and why I have dwelt so much more on some things than others. I doubt whether I have clearly fulfilled the plan that I set out in the introductory chapter; and for that reason I add

1 Jewish industrialist, financier and politician (1868–1930).

these lines as a sort of summary in a concluding chapter. I do believe that the things on which I have insisted are more essential to an outline of history than the things which I have subordinated or dismissed. I do not believe that the past is most truly pictured as a thing in which humanity merely fades away into nature, or civilization merely fades away into barbarism, or religion fades away into mythology, or our own religion fades away into the religions of the world. In short I do not believe that the best way to produce an outline of history is to rub out the lines. I believe that, of the two, it would be far nearer the truth to tell the tale very simply, like a primitive myth about a man who made the sun and stars or a god who entered the body of a sacred monkey. I will therefore sum up all that has gone before in what seems to me a realistic and reasonably proportioned statement; the short story of mankind.

In the land lit by that neighbouring star, whose blaze is the broad daylight, there are many and very various things, motionless and moving. There moves among them a race that is in its relation to others a race of gods. The fact is not lessened but emphasized because it can behave like a race of demons. Its distinction is not an individual illusion, like one bird pluming itself on its own plumes; it is a solid and a many-sided thing. It is demonstrated in the very speculations that have led to its being denied. That men, the gods of this lower world, are linked with it in various ways is true; but it is another aspect of the same truth. That they grow as the grass grows and walk as the beasts walk is a secondary necessity that sharpens the primary distinction. It is like saying that a magician must after all have the appearance of a man; or that even the fairies could not dance without feet. It has lately been the fashion to focus the mind entirely on these mild and subordinate resemblances and to forget the main fact altogether. It is customary to insist that man resembles the other creatures. Yes; and that very resemblance he alone can see. The fish does not trace the fish-bone pattern in the fowls of the air; or the elephant and the emu compare skeletons. Even in the sense in which man is at one with the universe it is an utterly lonely universality. The very sense that he is united with all things is enough to sunder him from all.

Looking around him by this unique light, as lonely as the literal flame that he alone has kindled, this demigod or demon of the visible world makes that world visible. He sees around him a world of a certain style or type. It seems to proceed by certain rules or at least repetitions. He sees a green architecture that builds itself without visible hands; but which builds itself into a very exact plan or pattern, like a design already drawn in the air by an invisible finger. It is not, as is now vaguely suggested, a vague thing. It is not a growth or a groping of blind life. Each seeks an end; a glorious and radiant end, even for every daisy or dandelion we see in looking across the level of a common field. In the very shape of things there is more than green growth; there is the finality of the flower. It is a world of crowns. This impression, whether or no it be an illusion, has so profoundly influenced this race of thinkers and masters of the material world, that the vast majority have been moved to take a certain view of that world. They have concluded, rightly or wrongly, that the world had a plan as the tree seemed to have a plan; and an end and crown like the flower. But so long as the race of thinkers was able to think, it was obvious that the admission of this idea of a plan brought with it another thought more thrilling and even terrible. There was someone else, some strange and unseen being, who had designed these things, if indeed they were designed. There was a stranger who was also a friend; a mysterious benefactor who had been before them and built up the woods and hills for their coming, and had kindled the sunrise aganst their rising, as a servant kindles a fire. Now this idea of a mind that gives a meaning to the universe has received more and more confirmation within the minds of men, by meditations and experiences much more subtle and searching than any such argument about the external plan of the world. But I am concerned here with keeping the story in its most simple and even concrete terms; and it is enough to say here that most men, including the wisest men, have come to the conclusion that the world has such a final purpose and therefore such a first cause. But most men in some sense separated themselves from the wisest men, when it came to the treatment of that idea. There came into existence two ways of treating that idea; which between them made up most of the religious history of the world.

The majority, like the minority, had this strong sense of a second meaning in things; of a strange master who knew the secret of the world. But the majority, the mob or mass of men, naturally tended to treat it rather in the spirit of gossip. The gossip, like all gossip, contained a great deal of truth and falsehood. The world began to tell itself tales about the unknown being or his sons or servants or messengers. Some of the tales may truly be called old wives' tales; as professing only to be very remote memories of the morning of the world; myths about the baby moon or the half-baked mountains. Some of them might more truly be called travellers' tales; as being curious but contemporary tales brought from certain borderlands of experience; such as miraculous cures or those that bring whispers of what has happened to the dead. Many of them are probably true tales; enough of them are probably true to keep a person of real commonsense more or less conscious that there really is something rather marvellous behind the cosmic curtain. But in a sense it is only going by appearances; even if the appearances are called apparitions. It is a matter of appearances – and disappearances. At the most these gods are ghosts; that is, they are glimpses. For most of us they are rather gossip about glimpses. And for the rest, the whole world is full of rumours, most of which are almost avowedly romances. The great majority of the tales about gods and ghosts and the invisible king are told, if not for the sake of the tale, at least for the sake of the topic. They are evidence of the eternal interest of the theme; they are not evidence of anything else, and they are not meant to be. They are mythology or the poetry that is not bound in books – or bound in any other way.

Meanwhile the minority, the sages or thinkers, had withdrawn apart and had taken up an equally congenial trade. They were drawing up plans of the world; of the world which all believed to have a plan. They were trying to set forth the plan seriously and to scale. They were setting their minds directly to the mind that had made the mysterious world; considering what sort of a mind it might be and what its ultimate purpose might be. Some of them made that mind much more impersonal than mankind has generally made it; some simplified it almost to a blank; a few, a very few, doubted it altogether. One or two of the more morbid fancied that it might be evil and an enemy; just one or two of the more degraded in the other class worshipped demons instead of gods. But most of these theorists were theists: and they not only saw a moral plan in nature, but they generally laid down a moral plan for humanity. Most of them were good men who did good work: and they were remembered and reverenced in various ways. They were scribes; and their scriptures became more or less holy scriptures. They were law-givers; and their tradition became not only legal but ceremonial. We may say that they received divine honours, in the sense in which kings and great captains in certain countries often received divine honours. In a word, wherever the other popular spirit, the spirit of legend and gossip could come into play, it surrounded them with the more mystical atmosphere of the myths. Popular poetry turned the sages into saints. But that was all it did. They remained themselves; men never really forgot that they were men, only made into gods in the sense that they were made into heroes. Divine Plato, like Divus Caesar, was a title and not a dogma. In Asia, where the atmosphere was more mythological, the man was made to look more like a myth, but he remained a man. He remained a man of a certain special class or school of men, receiving and deserving great honour from mankind. It is the order or school of the philosophers; the men who have set themselves seriously to trace the order across any apparent chaos in the vision of life. Instead of living on imaginative rumours and remote traditions and the tail-end of exceptional experiences about the mind and meaning behind the world, they have tried in a sense to project the primary purpose of that mind *a priori*. They have tried to put on paper a possible plan of the world; almost as if the world were not yet made.

Right in the middle of all these things stands up an enormous exception. It is quite unlike anything else. It is a thing final like the trump of doom, though it is also a piece of good news; or news that seems too good to be true. It is nothing less than the loud assertion that this mysterious maker of the world has visited his world in person. It declares that really and even recently, or right in the middle of historic times, there did walk into the world this original invisible being; about whom the thinkers make theories and the mythologists hand down myths; the Man Who Made the World. That such a higher personality exists behind all things had indeed always been implied by all the best thinkers, as well as by all the most beautiful legends. But nothing of this sort had ever been implied in any of them. It is simply false to say that the other sages and heroes had claimed to be that mysterious master and maker, of whom the world had dreamed and disputed. Not one of them had ever claimed to be anything of the sort. Not one of their sects or schools had ever claimed that they had claimed to be anything of the sort. The most that any religious prophet had said was that he was the true servant of such a being. The most that any visionary had ever said was that men might catch glimpses of the glory of that spiritual being; or much more often of lesser spiritual beings. The most that any primitive myth had ever suggested was that the Creator was present at the Creation. But that the Creator was present at scenes a little subsequent to the supper-parties of Horace, and talked with tax-collectors and government officials in the detailed daily life of the Roman Empire, and that this fact continued to be firmly asserted by the whole of that great civilization for more than a thousand years – that is something utterly unlike anything else in nature. It is the one great startling statement that man has made since he spoke his first articulate word, instead of barking like a dog. Its unique character can be used as an argument against it as well as for it. It would be easy to concentrate on it as a case of isolated insanity; but it makes nothing but dust and nonsense of comparative religion.

It came on the world with a wind and rush of running messengers proclaiming that apocalyptic portent; and it is not unduly fanciful to say that they are running still. What puzzles the world, and its wise philosophers and fanciful pagan poets, about the priests and people of the Catholic Church is that they still behave as if they were messengers. A messenger does not dream about what his message might be, or argue about what it probably would be; he delivers it as it is. It is not a theory or a fancy but a fact. It is not relevant to this intentionally rudimentary outline to prove in detail that it is a fact; but merely to point out that these messengers do deal with it as men deal with a fact. All that is condemned in Catholic tradition, authority, and dogmatism and the refusal to retract and modify, are but the natural human attributes of a man with a message relating to a fact. I desire to avoid in this last summary all the controversial complexities that may once more cloud the simple lines of that strange story; which I have already called, in words that are much too weak, the strangest story in the world. I desire merely to mark those main lines and specially to mark where the great line is really to be drawn. The religion of the world, in its right proportions, is not divided into fine shades of mysticism or more or less rational forms of mythology. It is divided by the line between the men who are bringing that message and the men who have not yet heard it, or cannot yet believe it.

But when we translate the terms of that strange tale back into the more concrete and complicated terminology of our time, we find it covered by names and memories of which the very familiarity is a falsification. For instance, when we say that a country contains so many Moslems, we really mean that it contains so many monotheists; and we really mean, by that, that it contains so many men; men with the old average assumption of men – that the invisible ruler remains invisible. They hold it along with the customs of a certain culture and under the simpler laws of a certain law-giver; but so they would if their law-giver were Lycurgus or Solon. They testify to something which is a necessary and noble truth; but was never a new truth. Their creed is not a new colour; it is the neutral and normal tint that is the background of the many-coloured life of man. Mahomet did not, like the Magi, find a new star; he saw through his own particular window a glimpse of the great grey field of the ancient starlight. So when we say that the country contains so many Confucians or Buddhists, we mean it contains so many pagans whose prophets have given them another and rather vaguer version of the invisible power; making it not only invisible but almost impersonal. When we say that they also have temples and idols and priests and periodical festivals, we simply mean that this sort of heathen is enough of a human being to admit the popular element of pomp and pictures and feasts and fairy-tales. We only mean that Pagans have more sense than Puritans. But what the gods are supposed to *be*, what the priests are commissioned to *say*, is not a sensational secret like what those running messengers of the Gospel had to say. Nobody else except those messengers has any Gospel; nobody else has any good news; for the simple reason that nobody else has any news.

Those runners gather impetus as they run. Ages afterwards they still speak as if something had just happened. They have not lost the speed and momentum of messengers; they have hardly lost, as it were, the wild eyes of witnesses. In the Catholic Church, which is the cohort of the message, there are still those headlong acts of holiness that speak of something rapid and recent; a self-sacrifice that startles the world like a suicide. But it is not a suicide; it is not pessimistic; it is still as optimistic as St Francis of the flowers and birds. It is newer in spirit than the newest schools of thought; and it is almost certainly on the eve of new triumphs. For these men serve a mother who seems to grow more beautiful as new generations rise up and call her blessed. We might sometimes fancy that the Church grows younger as the world grows old.

For this is the last proof of the miracle; that something so supernatural should have become so natural. I mean that anything so unique when seen from the outside should only seem universal when seen from the inside. I have not minimized the scale of the miracle, as some of our milder theologians think it wise to do. Rather have I deliberately dwelt on that incredible interruption, as a blow that broke the very backbone of history. I have great sympathy with the monotheists, the Moslems, or the Jews, to whom it seems a blasphemy; a blasphemy that might shake the world. But it did not shake the world; it steadied the world. That fact, the more we consider it, will seem more solid and more strange. I think it a piece of plain justice to all the unbelievers to insist upon the audacity of the act of faith that is demanded of them. I willingly and warmly agree that it is, in itself, a suggestion at which we might expect even the brain of the believer to reel, when he realized his own belief. But the brain of the believer does not reel; it is the brains of the unbelievers that reel. We can see their brains reeling on every side and into every extravagance of ethics and psychology; into pessimism and the denial of life; into pragmatism and the denial of logic; seeking their omens in nightmares and their canons in contradictions; shrieking for fear at the far-off sight of things beyond good and evil, or whispering of strange stars where two and two make five. Meanwhile this solitary thing that seems at first so outrageous in outline remains solid and sane in substance. It remains the moderator of all these manias; rescuing reason from the Pragmatists exactly as it rescued laughter from the Puritans. I repeat that I have deliberately emphasized its intrinsically defiant and dogmatic character. The mystery is how anything so startling should have remained defiant and dogmatic and yet become perfectly normal and natural. I have admitted freely that, considering the incident in itself, a man who says he is God may be classed with a man who says he is glass. But the man who says he is glass is not a glazier making windows for all the world. He does not remain for after ages as a shining and crystalline figure, in whose light everything is as clear as crystal.

But this madness has remained sane. The madness has remained sane when everything else went mad. The madhouse has been a house to which, age after age, men are continually coming back as to a home. That is the riddle that remains; that anything so abrupt and abnormal should still be found a habitable and hospitable thing. I care not if the sceptic says it is a tall story; I cannot see how so toppling a tower could stand so long without foundation. Still less can I see how it could become, as it has become, the home of man. Had it merely appeared and disappeared, it might possibly have been remembered or explained as the last leap of the rage of illusion, the ultimate myth of the ultimate mood, in which the mind struck the sky and broke. But the mind did not break. It is the one mind that remains unbroken in the break-up of the world. If it were an error, it seems as if the error could hardly have lasted a day. If it were a mere ecstasy, it would seem that such an ecstasy could not endure for an hour. It has endured for nearly two thousand years; and the world within it has been more lucid, more level-headed, more reasonable in its hopes, more healthy in its instincts, more humorous and cheerful in the face of fate and death, than all the world outside. For it was the soul of Christendom that came forth from the incredible Christ; and the soul of it was common sense. Though we dared not look on His face we could look on His fruits; and by His fruits we should know Him. The fruits are solid and the fruitfulness is much more than a metaphor; and nowhere in this sad world are boys happier in apple-trees, or men in more equal chorus singing as they tread the vine, than under the fixed flash of this instant and intolerant enlightenment; the lightning made eternal as the light.

ST THOMAS AQUINAS

I

ON TWO FRIARS

LET ME at once anticipate comment by answering to the name of that notorious character, who rushes in where even the Angels of the Angelic Doctor might fear to tread. Some time ago I wrote a little book of this type and shape on St Francis of Assisi; and some time after (I know not when or how, as the song says, and certainly not why) I promised to write a book of the same size, or the same smallness on St Thomas Aquinas. The promise was Franciscan only in its rashness; and the parallel was very far from being Thomistic in its logic. You can make a sketch of St Francis: you could only make a plan of St Thomas, like the plan of a labyrinthine city. And yet in a sense he would fit into a much larger or a much smaller book. What we really know of his life might be pretty fairly dealt with in a few pages; for he did not, like St Francis, disappear in a shower of personal anecdotes and popular legends. What we know, or could know, or may eventually have the luck to learn, of his work, will probably fill even more libraries in the future than it has filled in the past. It was allowable to sketch St Francis in an outline; but with St Thomas everything depends on the filling up of the outline. It was even mediaeval in a manner to illuminate a miniature of the Poverello, whose very title is a diminutive. But to make a digest, in the tabloid manner, of the Dumb Ox of Sicily passes all digestive experiments in the matter of an ox in a tea-cup. But we must hope it is possible to make an outline of biography, now that anybody seems capable of writing an outline of history or an outline of anything. Only in the present case the outline is rather an outsize. The gown that could contain the colossal friar is not kept in stock.

I have said that these can only be portraits in outline. But the concrete contrast is here so striking, that even if we actually saw the two human figures in outline, coming over the hill in their friar's gowns, we should find that contrast even comic. It would be like seeing, even afar off, the silhouettes of Don Quixote and

Sancho Panza, or of Falstaff and Master Slender. St Francis was a lean and lively little man; thin as a thread and vibrant as a bowstring; and in his motions like an arrow from the bow. All his life was a series of plunges and scampers; darting after the beggar, dashing naked into the woods, tossing himself into the strange ship, hurling himself into the Sultan's tent and offering to hurl himself into the fire. In appearance he must have been like a thin brown skeleton autumn leaf dancing eternally before the wind; but in truth it was he that was the wind.

St Thomas was a huge heavy bull of a man, fat and slow and quiet; very mild and magnanimous but not very sociable; shy, even apart from the humility of holiness; and abstracted, even apart from his occasional and carefully concealed experiences of trance or ecstasy. St Francis was so fiery and even fidgety that the ecclesiastics, before whom he appeared quite suddenly, thought he was a madman. St Thomas was so stolid that the scholars, in the schools which he attended regularly, thought he was a dunce. Indeed, he was the sort of schoolboy, not unknown, who would much rather be thought a dunce than have his own dreams invaded, by more active or animated dunces. This external contrast extends to almost every point in the two personalities. It was the paradox of St Francis that while he was passionately fond of poems, he was rather distrustful of books. It was the outstanding fact about St Thomas that he loved books and lived on books; that he lived the very life of the clerk or scholar in *The Canterbury Tales*, who would rather have a hundred books of Aristotle and his philosophy than any wealth the world could give him. When asked for what he thanked God most, he answered simply, 'I have understood every page I ever read.' St Francis was very vivid in his poems and rather vague in his documents; St Thomas devoted his whole life to documenting whole systems of Pagan and Christian literature; and occasionally wrote a hymn like a man taking a holiday. They saw the same problem from different angles, of simplicity and subtlety; St Francis thought it would be enough to pour out his heart to the Mohammedans, to persuade them not to worship Mahound. St Thomas bothered his head with every hair-splitting distinction and deduction, about the Absolute or the Accident, merely to prevent them from misunderstanding Aristotle. St Francis was the son of a shopkeeper, or middle-class trader; and while his whole life was a revolt against the mercantile life of his father, he retained none the less, something of the quickness and social adaptability which makes the market hum like a hive. In the common phrase, fond as he was of green fields, he did not let the grass grow under his feet. He was what American millionaires and gangsters call a live wire. It is typical of the mechanistic moderns that, even when they try to imagine a live thing, they can only think of a mechanical metaphor from a dead thing. There is such a thing as a live worm; but there is no such thing as a live wire. St Francis would have heartily agreed that he was a worm; but he was a very live worm. Greatest of all foes to the go-getting ideal, he had certainly abandoned getting, but he was still going. St Thomas, on the other hand, came out of a world where he might have enjoyed leisure, and he remained one of those men whose labour has something of the placidity of leisure. He was a hard worker, but nobody could possibly mistake him for a hustler. He had something indefinable about him, which marks those who work when they need not work. For he was by birth a gentleman of a great house, and such repose can remain as a habit, when it is no longer a motive. But in him it was expressed only in its most amiable elements; for instance, there was possibly something of it in his effortless courtesy and patience. Every saint is a man before he is a saint; and a saint may be made of every sort or kind of man; and most of us will choose between these different types according to our different tastes. But I will confess that, while the romantic glory of St Francis has lost nothing of its glamour for me, I have in later years grown to feel almost as much affection, or in some aspects even more, for this man who unconsciously inhabited a large heart and a large head, like one inheriting a large house, and exercised there an equally generous if rather more absent-minded hospitality. There are moments when St Francis, the most unworldly man who ever walked the world, is almost too efficient for me.

St Thomas Aquinas has recently reappeared, in the current culture of the colleges and the salons, in a way that would have been quite startling even ten years ago. And the mood that has concentrated on him is doubtless very different from that which popularized St Francis quite twenty years ago.

The Saint is a medicine because he is an antidote. Indeed that is why the saint is often a martyr; he is mistaken for a poison because he is an antidote. He will generally be found restoring the world to sanity by exaggerating whatever the world neglects, which is by no means always the same element in every age. Yet each generation seeks its saint by instinct; and he is not what the people want, but rather what the people need. This is surely the very much mistaken meaning of those words to the first saints, 'Ye are the salt of the earth', which caused the Ex-Kaiser to remark with all solemnity that his beefy Germans were the salt of the earth; meaning thereby merely that they were the earth's beefiest and therefore best. But salt seasons and preserves beef, not because it is like beef; but because it is very unlike it. Christ did not tell his apostles that they were only the excellent people, or the only excellent people, but that they were the exceptional people; the permanently incongruous and incompatible people; and the text about the salt of the earth is really as sharp and shrewd and tart as the taste of salt. It is because they were the exceptional people, that they must not lose their exceptional quality. If salt lose its savour, wherewith shall it be salted?' is a much more pointed question than any mere lament over the price of the best beef. If the world grows too worldly, it can be rebuked by the Church; but if the Church grows too worldly, it cannot be adequately rebuked for worldliness by the world.

Therefore it is the paradox of history that each generation is converted by the saint who contradicts it most. St Francis had a curious and almost uncanny attraction for the Victorians; for the nineteenth-century English who seemed superficially to be most complacent about their commerce and their comon sense. Not only a rather complacent Englishman like Matthew Arnold, but even the English Liberals whom he criticized for their complacency, began slowly to discover the mystery of the Middle Ages through the strange story told in feathers and flames in the hagiographical pictures of Giotto. There was something in the story of St Francis that pierced through all those English qualities which are most famous and fatuous, to all those English qualities which are most hidden and human: the secret softness of heart; the poetical vagueness of mind; the love of landscape and of animals. St Francis of Assisi was the only mediaeval Catholic who really became popular in England on his own merits. It was largely because of a subconscious feeling that the modern world had neglected those particular merits. The English middle classes found their only missionary in the figure, which of all types in the world they most despised; an Italian beggar.

So, as the nineteenth century clutched at the Franciscan romance, precisely because it had neglected romance, so the twentieth century is already clutching at the Thomist rational theology, because it has neglected reason. In a world that was too stolid, Christianity returned in the form of a vagabond; in a world that has grown a great deal too wild, Christianity has returned in the form of a teacher of logic. In the world of Herbert Spencer men wanted a cure for indigestion; in the world of Einstein they want a cure for vertigo. In the first case, they dimly perceived the fact that it was after a long fast that St Francis sang the Song of the Sun and the praise of the fruitful earth. In the second case, they already dimly perceived that, even if they only want to understand Einstein, it is necessary first to understand the use of the understanding. They begin to see that, as the eighteenth century thought itself the age of reason, and the nineteenth century thought itself the age of common sense, the twentieth century cannot as yet even manage to think itself anything but the age of uncommon nonsense. In those conditions the world needs a saint; but above all, it needs a philosopher. And these two cases do show that the world, to do it justice, has an instinct for what it needs. The earth was really very flat, for those Victorians who most vigorously repeated that it was round, and Alverno of the Stigmata stood up as a single mountain in the plain. But the earth is an earthquake, a ceaseless and apparently endless earthquake, for the moderns for whom Newton has been scrapped along with Ptolemy. And for them there is something more steep and even incredible than a mountain; a piece of really solid ground; the level of the level-headed man. Thus in our time the two saints have appealed to two generations, an age of romantics and an age of sceptics; yet in their own age they were doing the same work; a work that has changed the world.

Again, it may be said truly that the comparison is idle, and does not fit in well even as a fancy; since the men were not properly even of the same generation or the same historic moment. If two friars are to be presented as a pair of Heavenly Twins, the obvious comparison is between St Francis and St Dominic. The relations of St Francis and St Thomas were, at nearest, those of uncle and nephew ... For if St Francis and St Dominic were the great twin brethren,

Thomas was obviously the first great son of St Dominic, as was his friend Bonaventure of St Francis. Nevertheless, I have a reason (indeed two reasons) for taking as a text the accident of two title-pages; and putting St Thomas beside St Francis, instead of pairing him off with Bonaventure the Franciscan. It is because the comparison, remote and perverse as it may seem, is really a sort of short cut to the heart of history; and brings us by the most rapid route to the real question of the life and work of St Thomas Aquinas. For most people now have a rough but picturesque picture in their minds of the life and work of St Francis of Assisi. And the shortest way of telling the other story is to say that, while the two men were thus a contrast in almost every feature, they were really doing the same thing. One of them was doing it in the world of the mind and the other in the world of the worldly. But it was the same great mediaeval movement; still but little understood. In a constructive sense, it was more important than the Reformation. Nay, in a constructive sense, it was the Reformation.

About this mediaeval movement there are two facts that must first be emphasized. They are not, of course, contrary facts, but they are perhaps answers to contrary fallacies. First, in spite of all that was once said about superstition, the Dark Ages and the sterility of Scholasticism, it was in every sense a movement of enlargement, always moving towards greater light and even greater liberty. Second, in spite of all that was said later on about progress and the Renaissance and forerunners of modern thought, it was almost entirely a movement of orthodox theological enthusiasm, unfolded from within. It was *not* a compromise with the world, or a surrender to heathens or heretics, or even a mere borrowing of external aids, even when it did borrow them. In so far as it did reach out to the light of common day, it was like the action of a plant which by its own force thrusts out its leaves into the sun; not like the action of one who merely lets daylight into a prison.

In short, it was what is technically called a Development in doctrine. But there seems to be a queer ignorance, not only about the technical, but the natural meaning of the word Development. The critics of Catholic theology seem to suppose that it is not so much an evolution as an evasion; that it is at best an adaptation. They fancy that its very success is the success of surrender. But that is not the natural meaning of the word Development. When we talk of a child being well-developed, we mean that he has grown bigger and stronger with his own strength; not that he is padded with borrowed pillows or walks on stilts to make him look taller. When we say that a puppy develops into a dog, we do not mean that his growth is a gradual compromise with a cat; we mean that he becomes more doggy and not less. Development is the expansion of all the possibilities and implications of a doctrine, as there is time to distinguish them and draw them out; and the point here is that the enlargement of mediaeval theology was simply the full comprehension of that theology. And it is of primary importance to realize this fact first, about the time of the great Dominican and the first Franciscan, because their tendency, humanistic and naturalistic in a hundred ways, was truly the development of the supreme doctrine, which was also the dogma of all dogmas. It is in this that the popular poetry of St Francis and the almost rationalistic prose of St Thomas appear most vividly as part of the same movement. They are both great growths of Catholic development, depending upon external things only as every living and growing thing depends on them; that is, it digests and transforms them, but continues in its own image and not in theirs. A Buddhist or a Communist might dream of two things which simultaneously eat each other, as the perfect form of unification. But it is not so with living things. St Francis was content to call himself the Troubadour of God; but not content with the God of the Troubadours. St Thomas did not reconcile Christ to Aristotle; he reconciled Aristotle to Christ.

Yes; in spite of the contrasts that are as conspicuous and even comic as the comparison between the fat man and the thin man, the tall man and the short; in spite of the contrast between the vagabond and the student, between the apprentice and the aristocrat, between the book-hater and the book-lover, between the wildest of all missionaries and the mildest of all professors, the great fact of mediaeval history is that these two great men were doing the same great work; one in the study and the other in the street. They were not bringing something new into Christianity, in the sense of something heathen or heretical into Christianity; on the contrary, they were bringing Christianity into Christendom. But they were bringing it back against the pressure of certain historic tendencies, which had hardened into habits in many great schools and authorities in the Christian Church; and they were using tools and

weapons which seemed to many people to be associated with heresy or heathenry. St Francis used Nature much as St Thomas used
Aristotle; and to some they seemed to be using a Pagan goddess
and a Pagan sage. What they were really doing, and especially what
St Thomas was really doing, will form the main matter of these
pages; but it is convenient to be able to compare him from the first
with a more popular saint; because we may thus sum up the substance of it in the most popular way. Perhaps it would sound too
paradoxical to say that these two saints saved us from Spirituality;
a dreadful doom. Perhaps it may be misunderstood if I say that St
Francis, for all his love of animals, saved us from being Buddhists;
and that St Thomas, for all his love of Greek philosophy, saved us
from being Platonists. But it is best to say the truth in its simplest
form; that they both reaffirmed the Incarnation, by bringing God
back to earth.

This analogy, which may seem rather remote, is really perhaps
the best practical preface to the philosophy of St Thomas. As we
shall have to consider more closely later on, the purely spiritual or
mystical side of Catholicism had very much got the upper hand in
the first Catholic centuries; through the genius of Augustine, who
had been a Platonist, and perhaps never ceased to be a Platonist;
through the transcendentalism of the supposed work of the Areo-
pagite; through the Oriental trend of the later Empire and something Asiatic about the almost pontifical kinghood of Byzantium;
all these things weighed down what we should now roughly call the
Western element; though it has as good a right to be called the
Christian element; since its common sense is but the holy familiarity of the word made flesh. Anyhow, it must suffice for the moment
to say that theologians had somewhat stiffened into a sort of Platonic pride in the possession of intangible and untranslatable truths
within; as if no part of their wisdom had any root anywhere in the
real world. Now the first thing that Aquinas did, though by no
means the last, was to say to these pure trancendentalists something
substantially like this.

'Far be it from a poor friar to deny that you have these dazzling
diamonds in your head, all designed in the most perfect mathematical shapes and shining with a purely celestial light; all there,
almost before you begin to think, let alone to see or hear or feel.
But I am not ashamed to say that I find my reason fed by my senses;

that I owe a great deal of what I think to what I see and smell and taste and handle; and that so far as my reason is concerned, I feel obliged to treat all this reality as real. To be brief, in all humility, I do not believe that God meant Man to exercise only that peculiar, uplifted and abstracted sort of intellect which you are so fortunate as to possess: but I believe that there is a middle field of facts which are given by the senses to be the subject matter of the reason; and that in that field the reason has a right to rule, as the representative of God in Man. It is true that all this is lower than the angels; but it is higher than the animals, and all the actual material objects Man finds around him. True, man also can be an object; and even a deplorable object. But what man has done man may do; and if an antiquated old heathen called Aristotle can help me to do it I will thank him in all humility.'

Thus began what is commonly called the appeal to Aquinas and Aristotle. It might be called the appeal to Reason and the Authority of the Senses. And it will be obvious that there is a sort of popular parallel to it in the fact that St Francis did not only listen for the angels, but also listened to the birds. And before we come to those aspects of St Thomas that were very severely intellectual, we may note that in him as in St Francis there is a preliminary practical element which is rather moral; a sort of good and straightforward humility; and a readiness in the man to regard even himself in some ways as an animal; as St Francis compared his body to a donkey. It may be said that the contrast holds everywhere, even in zoological metaphor, and that if St Francis was like that common or garden donkey who carried Christ into Jerusalem, St Thomas, who was actually compared to an ox, rather resembled that Apocalyptic monster of almost Assyrian mystery; the winged bull. But again, we must not let all that can be contrasted eclipse what was common; or forget that neither of them would have been too proud to wait as patiently as the ox and ass in the stable of Bethlehem.

There were of course, as we shall soon see, many other much more curious and complicated ideas in the philosophy of St Thomas; besides this primary idea of a central common sense that is nourished by the five senses. But at this stage, the point of the story is not only that this was a Thomist doctrine, but that it is a truly and eminently Christian doctrine. For upon this point modern writers write a great deal of nonsense; and show more than their normal ingenuity in missing the point. Having assumed without argument, at the start, that all emancipation must lead men away from religion and towards irreligion, they have just blankly and blindly forgotten what is the outstanding feature of the religion itself.

It will not be possible to conceal much longer from anybody the fact that St Thomas Aquinas was one of the great liberators of the human intellect. The sectarians of the seventeenth and eighteenth centuries were essentially obscurantists, and they guarded an obscurantist legend that the Schoolman was an obscurantist. This was wearing thin even in the nineteenth century; it will be impossible in the twentieth. It has nothing to do with the truth of their theology or his; but only with the truth of historical proportion, which begins to reappear as quarrels begin to die down. Simply as one of the facts that bulk big in history, it is true to say that Thomas was a very great man who reconciled religion with reason, who expanded it towards experimental science, who insisted that the senses were the windows of the soul and that the reason had a divine right to feed upon facts, and that it was the business of the Faith to digest the strong meat of the toughest and most practical of pagan philosophies. It is a fact, like the military strategy of Napoleon, that Aquinas was thus fighting for all that is liberal and enlightened, as compared with his rivals, or for that matter his successors and supplanters. Those who, for other reasons, honestly accept the final effect of the Reformation will none the less face the fact, that it was the Schoolman who was the Reformer; and that the later Reformers were by comparison reactionaries. I use the word not as a reproach from my own standpoint, but as a fact from the ordinary modern progressive standpoint. For instance, they riveted the mind back to the literal sufficiency of the Hebrew Scriptures; when St Thomas had already spoken of the Spirit giving grace to the Greek philosophies. He insisted on the social duty of works; they only on the spiritual duty of faith. It was the very life of the Thomist teaching that Reason can be trusted: it was the very life of Lutheran teaching that Reason is utterly untrustworthy.

Now when this fact is found to be a fact, the danger is that all the unstable opposition will suddenly slide to the opposite extreme. Those who up to that moment have been abusing the Schoolman as a dogmatist will begin to admire the Schoolman as a Modernist who diluted dogma. They will hastily begin to adorn his statue with all the faded garlands of progress, to present him as a man in advance of his age, which is always supposed to mean in agreement with our age; and to load him with the unprovoked imputation of having produced the modern mind. They will discover his attraction, and somewhat hastily assume that he was like themselves, because he was attractive. Up to a point this is pardonable enough; up to a point it has already happened in the case of St Francis. But it would not go beyond a certain point in the case of St Francis. Nobody, not even a Freethinker like Renan or Matthew Arnold, would pretend that St Francis was anything but a devout Christian, or had any other original motive except the imitation of Christ. Yet St Francis also had that liberating and humanizing effect upon religion; though perhaps rather on the imagination than the intellect. But nobody says that St Francis was loosening the Christian code, when he was obviously tightening it; like the rope round his friar's frock. Nobody says he merely opened the gates to sceptical science, or sold the pass to heathen humanism, or looked forward only to the Renaissance or met the Rationalists half way. No biographer pretends that St Francis, when he is reported to have opened the Gospels at random and read the great texts about Poverty, really only opened the *Aeneid* and practised the *Sors Virgiliana*[1] out of respect for heathen letters and learning. No historian will pretend that St Francis wrote *The Canticle of the Sun* in close imitation of a Homeric Hymn to Apollo or loved birds because he had carefully learned all the tricks of the Roman Augurs.

In short, most people, Christian or heathen, would now agree that the Franciscan sentiment was primarily a Christian sentiment, unfolded from within, out of an innocent (or, if you will, ignorant) faith in the Christian religion itself. Nobody, as I have said, says that St Francis drew his primary inspiration from Ovid. It would be every bit as false to say that Aquinas drew his primary inspiration from Aristotle. The whole lesson of his life, especially of his early life, the whole story of his childhood and choice of a career, shows that he was supremely and directly devotional; and that he passionately loved the Catholic worship long before he found he had to fight for it. But there is also a special and clinching instance

1 Oracular responses obtained by opening the works of Virgil at random.

of this, which once more connects St Thomas with St Francis. It seems to be strangely forgotten that both these saints were in actual fact imitating a Master, who was not Aristotle let alone Ovid, when they sanctified the senses or the simple things of nature; when St Francis walked humbly among the beasts or St Thomas debated courteously among the Gentiles.

Those who miss this, miss the point of the religion, even if it be a superstition; nay, they miss the very point they would call most superstitious. I mean the whole staggering story of the God-Man in the Gospels. A few even miss it touching St Francis and his unmixed and unlearned appeal to the Gospels. They will talk of the readiness of St Francis to learn from the flowers or the birds as something that can only point onward to the Pagan Renaissance. Whereas the fact stares them in the face; first, that it points backwards to the New Testament, and second that it points forward, if it points to anything, to the Aristotelian realism of the *Summa* of St Thomas Aquinas. They vaguely imagine that anybody who is humanizing divinity must be paganizing divinity; without seeing that the humanizing of divinity is actually the strongest and starkest and most incredible dogma in the Creed. St Francis was becoming more like Christ, and not merely more like Buddha, when he considered the lilies of the field or the fowls of the air; and St Thomas was becoming more of a Christian, and not merely more of an Aristotelian, when he insisted that God and the image of God had come in contact through matter with a material world. These saints were, in the most exact sense of the term, Humanists; because they were insisting on the immense importance of the human being in the theological scheme of things. But they were not Humanists marching along a path of progress that leads to Modernism and general scepticism; for in their very Humanism they were affirming a dogma now often regarded as the most superstitious Superhumanism. They were strengthening that staggering doctrine of Incarnation, which the sceptics find it hardest to believe. There cannot be a stiffer piece of Christian divinity than the divinity of Christ.

This is a point that is here very much to the point; that these men became more orthodox, when they became more rational or natural. Only by being thus orthodox could they be thus rational and natural. In other words, what may really be called a liberal theology was unfolded from within, from out of the original mysteries of Catholicism. But that liberality had nothing to do with liberalism; in fact it cannot even now coexist with liberalism.* The matter is so cogent, that I will take one or two special ideas of St Thomas to illustrate what I mean. Without anticipating the elementary sketch of Thomism that must be made later, the following points may be noted here.

For instance, it was a very special idea of St Thomas that Man is to be studied in his whole manhood; that a man is not a man without his body, just as he is not a man without his soul. A corpse is not a man; but also a ghost is not a man. The earlier school of Augustine and even of Anselm had rather neglected this, treating the soul as the only necessary treasure, wrapped for a time in a negligible napkin. Even here they were less orthodox in being more spiritual. They sometimes hovered on the edge of those Eastern deserts that stretch away to the land of transmigration; where the essential soul may pass through a hundred unessential bodies; reincarnated even in the bodies of beasts or birds. St Thomas stood up stoutly for the fact that a man's body is his body as his mind is his mind; and that *he* can only be a balance and union of the two. Now this is in some ways a naturalistic notion, very near to the modern respect for material things; a praise of the body that might be sung by Walt Whitman or justified by D. H. Lawrence: a thing that might be called Humanism or even claimed by Modernism. In fact, it may be Materialism; but it is the flat contrary of Modernism. It is bound up, in the modern view, with the most monstrous, the most material, and therefore the most miraculous of miracles. It is specially connected with the most startling sort of dogma, which the Modernist can least accept; the Resurrection of the Body.

Or again, his argument for Revelation is quite rationalistic; and on the other side, decidedly democratic and popular. His argument for Revelation is not in the least an argument against Reason. On the contrary, he seems inclined to admit that truth could be reached by a rational process, if only it were rational enough; and also long enough. Indeed, something in his character, which I have

* I use the world liberalism here in the strictly limited theological sense, in which Newman and other theologians use it. In its popular political sense, as I point out later, St Thomas rather tended to be a Liberal, especially for his time.

called elsewhere optimism, and for which I know no other approximate term, led him rather to exaggerate the extent to which all men would ultimately listen to reason. In his controversies, he always assumes that they will listen to reason. That is, he does emphatically believe that men can be convinced by argument; when they reach the end of the argument. Only his common sense also told him that the argument never ends. I might convince a man that matter as the origin of Mind is quite meaningless, if he and I were very fond of each other and fought each other every night for forty years. But long before he was convinced on his deathbed, a thousand other materialists would have been born, and nobody can explain everything to everybody. St Thomas takes the view that the souls of all the ordinary hard-working and simple-minded people are quite as important as the souls of thinkers and truth-seekers; and he asks how all these people are possibly to find time for the amount of reasoning that is needed to find truth. The whole tone of the passage shows both a respect for scientific enquiry and a strong sympathy with the average man. His argument for Revelation is not an argument against Reason; but it is an argument for Revelation. The *conclusion* he draws from it is that men must receive the highest moral truths in a miraculous manner; or most men would not receive them at all. His arguments are rational and natural; but his own deduction is all for the supernatural; and, as is common in the case of his argument, it is not easy to find any deduction except his own deduction. And when we come to that, we find it is something as simple as St Francis himself could desire; the message from heaven; the story that is told out of the sky; the fairytale that is really true.

It is plainer still in more popular problems like Free Will. If St Thomas stands for one thing more than another, it is what may be called subordinate sovereignties or autonomies. He was, if the flippancy may be used, a strong Home Ruler. We might even say he was always defending the independence of dependent things. He insisted that such a thing could have its own rights in its own region. It was his attitude to the Home Rule of the reason and even the senses; 'Daughter am I in my father's house; but mistress in my own.' And in exactly this sense he emphasized a certain dignity in Man, which was sometimes rather swallowed up in the purely theistic generalizations about God. Nobody would say he wanted to divide Man from God; but he did want to distinguish Man from God. In this strong sense of human dignity and liberty there is much that can be and is appreciated now as a noble humanistic liberality. But let us not forget that its upshot was that very Free Will, or moral responsibility of Man, which so many modern liberals would deny. Upon this sublime and perilous liberty hang heaven and hell, and all the mysterious drama of the soul. It is distinction and not division; but a man *can* divide himself from God, which, in a certain aspect, is the greatest distinction of all.

Again, though it is a more metaphysical matter, which must be mentioned later, and then only too slightly, it is the same with the old philosophical dispute about the Many and the One. Are things so different that they can never be classified; or so unified that they can never be distinguished? Without pretending to answer such questions here, we may say broadly that St Thomas comes down definitely on the side of Variety, as a thing that is real as well as Unity. In this, and questions akin to this, he often departs from the great Greek philosophers who were sometimes his models; and entirely departs from the great Oriental philosophers who are in some sense his rivals. He seems fairly certain that the difference between chalk and cheese, or pigs and pelicans, is not a mere illusion, or dazzle of our bewildered mind blinded by a single light; but is pretty much what we all feel it to be. It may be said that this is mere common sense; the common sense that pigs are pigs; to that extent related to the earthbound Aristotelian common sense; to a human and even a heathen common sense. But note that here again the extremes of earth and heaven meet. It is also connected with the dogmatic Christian idea of the Creation; of a Creator who created pigs, as distinct from a Cosmos that merely evolved them.

In all these cases we see repeated the point stated at the start. The Thomist movement in metaphysics, like the Franciscan movement in morals and manners, was an enlargement and a liberation, it was emphatically a growth of Christian theology from within; it was emphatically *not* a shrinking of Christian theology under heathen or even human influences. The Franciscan was free to be a friar, instead of being bound to be a monk. But he was more of a Christian, more of a Catholic, even more of an ascetic. So the Thomist was free to be an Aristotelian, instead of being bound to be an Augustinian. But he was even more of a theologian; more of

an orthodox theologian; more of a dogmatist, in having recovered
through Aristotle the most defiant of all dogmas, the wedding of
God with Man and therefore with Matter. Nobody can understand
the greatness of the thirteenth century, who does not realize that it
was a great growth of new things produced by a living thing. In
that sense it was really bolder and freer than what we call the
Renaissance, which was a resurrection of old things discovered in
a dead thing. In that sense mediaevalism was not a Renascence,
but rather a Nascence. It did not model its temples upon the tombs,
or call up dead gods from Hades. It made an architecture as new
as modern engineering: indeed it still remains the most modern
architecture. Only it was followed at the Renaissance by a more
antiquated architecture. In that sense the Renaissance might be
called the Relapse. Whatever may be said of the Gothic and the
Gospel according to St Thomas, they were not a Relapse. It was
a new thrust like the titanic thrust of Gothic engineering; and its
strength was in a God who makes all things new.

In a word, St Thomas was making Christendom more Christian
in making it more Aristotelian. This is not a paradox but a plain
truism, which can only be missed by those who may know what is
meant by an Aristotelian, but have simply forgotten what is meant
by a Christian. As compared with a Jew, a Moslem, a Buddhist, a
Deist, or most obvious alternatives, a Christian *means* a man who
believes that deity or sanctity has attached to matter or entered the
world of the senses. Some modern writers, missing this simple
point, have even talked as if the acceptance of Aristotle was a sort
of concession to the Arabs; like a Modernist vicar making a concession to the Agnostics. They might as well say that the Crusades were
a concession to the Arabs as say that Aquinas rescuing Aristotle
from Averrhoes was a concession to the Arabs. The Crusaders
wanted to recover the place where the body of Christ had been,
because they believed, rightly or wrongly, that it was a Christian
place. St Thomas wanted to recover what was in essence the body
of Christ itself; the sanctified body of the Son of Man which had
become a miraculous medium between heaven and earth. And
he wanted the body, and all its senses, because he believed, rightly
or wrongly, that it was a Christian thing. It might be a humbler or
homelier thing than the Platonic mind; that is why it was Christian.
St Thomas was, if you will, taking the lower road when he walked

in the steps of Aristotle. So was God, when He worked in the work-shop of Joseph.

Lastly, these two great men were not only united to each other but separated from most of their comrades and contemporaries by the very revolutionary character of their own revolution. In 1215, Dominic Guzman,[1] the Castilian, founded an Order very similar to that of Francis; and, by a most curious coincidence of history, at almost exactly the same moment as Francis. It was directed primarily to preaching the Catholic philosophy to the Albigensian heretics; whose own philosophy was one of the many forms of that Manichæanism with which this story is much concerned. It had its roots in the remote mysticism and moral detachment of the East; and it was therefore inevitable that the Dominicans should be rather more a brotherhood of philosophers, where the Franciscans were by comparison a brotherhood of poets. For this and other reasons, St Dominic and his followers are little known or under-stood in modern England; they were involved eventually in a reli-gious war, which followed on a theological argument; and there was something in the atmosphere of our country, during the last century or so, which made the theological argument even more incomprehensible than the religious war. The ultimate effect is in some ways curious; because St Dominic, even more than St Francis, was marked by that intellectual independence, and strict standard of virtue and veracity, which Protestant cultures are wont to regard as specially Protestant. It was of him that the tale was told, and would certainly have been told more widely among us if it had been told of a Puritan, that the Pope pointed to his gorgeous Papal Palace and said, 'Peter can no longer say "Silver and gold have I none"'; and the Spanish friar answered, 'No, and neither can he now say, "Rise and walk".'...

---

1 St Dominic (1170–1221), founder of the Order of Preachers, the Dominicans.

III
THE ARISTOTELIAN REVOLUTION

... **P**ERHAPS under the shadow of the storm that menaced all Friars, Bonaventure, the Franciscan, grew into so great a friendship with Thomas the Dominican, that their contemporaries compared them to David and Jonathan. The point is of some interest; because it would be quite easy to represent the Franciscan and the Dominican as flatly contradicting each other. The Franciscan may be represented as the Father of all the Mystics; and the Mystics can be represented as men who maintain that the final fruition or joy of the soul is rather a sensation than a thought. The motto of the Mystics has always been, 'Taste and see'. Now St Thomas also began by saying, 'Taste and see'; but he said it of the first rudimentary impressions of the human animal. It might well be maintained that the Franciscan puts Taste last and the Dominican puts it first. It might be said that the Thomist begins with something solid like the taste of an apple, and afterwards deduces a divine life for the intellect; while the Mystic exhausts the intellect first, and says finally that the sense of God is something like the taste of an apple. A common enemy might claim that St Thomas begins with the taste of fruit and St Bonaventure ends with the taste of fruit. But they are both right; if I may say so, it is a privilege of people who contradict each other in their cosmos to be both right. The Mystic is right in saying that the relation of God and Man is essentially a love-story; the pattern and type of all love-stories. The Dominican rationalist is equally right in saying that the intellect is at home in the topmost heavens; and that the appetite for truth may outlast and even devour all the duller appetites of man.

At the moment Aquinas and Bonaventure were encouraged in the possibility that they were both right; by the almost universal agreement that they were both wrong. It was in any case a time of wild disturbance, and, as is common in such times, those who were trying to put things right were most vigorously accused of putting things wrong. Nobody knew who would win in that welter; Islam, or the Manichees of the Midi; or the two-faced and mocking Emperor; or the Crusades; or the old Orders of Christendom. But some men had a very vivid feeling that everything was breaking up; and that all the recent experiments or excesses were part of the same social dissolution; and there were two things that such men regarded as signs of ruin; one was the awful apparition of Aristotle out of the East, a sort of Greek god supported by Arabian worshippers; and the other was the new freedom of the Friars. It was the opening of the monastery and the scattering of the monks to wander over the world. The general feeling that they wandered like sparks from a furnace hitherto contained; the furnace of the abnormal love of God: the sense that they would utterly unbalance the common people with the counsels of perfection; that they would drift into being demagogues; all this finally burst out in a famous book called *The Perils of the Latter Times*, by a furious reactionary, William de St Amour.[1] It challenged the French King and the Pope, so that they established an enquiry. And Aquinas and Bonaventure, the two incongruous friends, with their respectively topsy-turvy universes, went up to Rome together, to defend the freedom of the Friars.

Thomas Aquinas defended the great vow of his youth, for freedom and for the poor; and it was probably the topmost moment of his generally triumphant career, for he turned back the whole backward movement of his time. Responsible authorities have said that, but for him, the whole great popular movement of the Friars might have been destroyed. With this popular victory the shy and awkward student finally becomes a historical character and a public man. After that, he was identified with the Mendicant Orders. But while St Thomas may be said to have made his name in the defence of the Mendicant Orders against the reactionaries, who took the same view of them as his own family had taken, there is generally a difference between a man making his name and a man really doing his work. The work of Thomas Aquinas was yet to come; but less shrewd observers than he could already see that it was coming. Broadly speaking, the danger was the danger of the orthodox, or those who too easily identify the old order with the

1 Amour (*c.* 1200–72), published in 1256 *De Periculis Novissimorum Temporum*, a violent attack on the mendicant friars, which Pope Alexander IV ordered to be burned, at the same time excommunicating its author.

orthodox, forcing a final and conclusive condemnation of Aristotle. There had already been rash and random condemnations to that effect, issued here and there, and the pressure of the narrower Augustinians upon the Pope and the principal judges became daily more pressing. The peril had appeared, not unnaturally, because of the historical and geographical accident of the Moslem proximity to the culture of Byzantium. The Arabs had got hold of the Greek manuscripts before the Latins who were the true heirs of the Greeks. And Moslems, though not very orthodox Moslems, were turning Aristotle into a pantheist philosophy still less acceptable to orthodox Christians. This second controversy, however, requires more explanation than the first. As is remarked on an introductory page, most modern people do know that St Francis at least was a liberator of large sympathies; that, whatever their positive view of mediaevalism, the Friars were in a relative sense a popular movement, pointing to greater fraternity and freedom; and a very little further information would inform them that this was every bit as true of the Dominican as of the Franciscan Friars. Nobody now is particularly likely to start up in defence of feudal abbots or fixed and stationary monks, against such impudent innovators as St Francis and St Thomas. We may therefore be allowed to summarize briefly the great debate about the Friars, though it shook all Christendom in its day. But the greater debate about Aristotle presents a greater difficulty; because there are modern misconceptions about it which can only be approached with a little more elaboration.

Perhaps there is really no such thing as a Revolution recorded in history. What happened was always a Counter-Revolution. Men were always rebelling against the last rebels; or even repenting of the last rebellion. This could be seen in the most casual contemporary fashions, if the fashionable mind had not fallen into the habit of seeing the very latest rebel as rebelling against all ages at once. The Modern Girl with the lipstick and the cocktail is as much a rebel against the Woman's Rights Woman of the '80's, with her stiff stick-up collars and strict teetotalism, as the latter was a rebel against the Early Victorian lady of the languid waltz tunes and the album full of quotations from Byron; or as the last, again, was a rebel against a Puritan mother to whom the waltz was a wild orgy and Byron the Bolshevist of his age. Trace even the Puritan mother

back through history and she represents a rebellion against the
Cavalier laxity of the English Church, which was at first a rebel
against the Catholic civilization, which had been a rebel against
the Pagan civilization. Nobody but a lunatic could pretend that
these things were a progress; for they obviously go first one way
and then the other. But whichever is right, one thing is certainly
wrong; and that is the modern habit of looking at them only from
the modern end. For that is only to see the end of the tale; they
rebel against they know not what, because it arose they know not
when; intent only on its ending, they are ignorant of its beginning;
and therefore of its very being. The difference between the smaller
cases and the larger, is that in the latter there is really so huge a
human upheaval that men start from it like men in a new world;
and that very novelty enables them to go on very long; and generally to go on too long. It is because these things start with a vigorous
revolt that the intellectual impetus lasts long enough to make them
seem like a survival. An excellent example of this is the real story
of the revival and the neglect of Aristotle. By the end of the
mediaeval time, Aristotelianism did eventually grow stale. Only a
very fresh and successful novelty ever gets quite so stale as that.

When the moderns, drawing the blackest curtain of obscurant-
ism that ever obscured history, decided that nothing mattered
much before the Renaissance and the Reformation, they instantly
began their modern career by falling into a big blunder. It was the
blunder about Platonism. They found, hanging about the courts of
the swaggering princes of the sixteenth century (which was as far
back in history as they were allowed to go) certain anti-clerical artists and scholars who said they were bored with Aristotle and were
supposed to be secretly indulging in Plato. The moderns, utterly
ignorant of the whole story of the mediaevals, instantly fell into the
trap. They assumed that Aristotle was some crabbed antiquity and
tyranny from the black back of the Dark Ages, and that Plato was
an entirely new Pagan pleasure never yet tasted by Christian men.
... Of course, the story is exactly the other way round. If anything,
it was Platonism that was the old orthodoxy. It was Aristotelianism
that was the very modern revolution. And the leader of that
modern revolution was the man who is the subject of this book.

The truth is that the historical Catholic Church began by being
Platonist; by being rather too Platonist. Platonism was in that

very golden Greek air that was breathed by the first great Greek theologians. The Christian Fathers were much more like the Neo-Platonists than were the scholars of the Renaissance; who were only Neo-Neo-Platonists. For Chrysostom or Basil it was as ordinary and normal to think in terms of the Logos, or the Wisdom which is the aim of philosophers, as it is to any men of any religion today to talk about social problems or progress or the economic crisis throughout the world. St Augustine followed a natural mental evolution when he was a Platonist before he was a Manichean, and a Manichean before he was a Christian. And it was exactly in that last association that the first faint hint, of the danger of being *too* Platonist, may be seen.

From the Renaissance to the nineteenth century, the Moderns have had an almost monstrous love of the Ancients. In considering mediaeval life, they could never regard the Christians as anything but the pupils of the Pagans; of Plato in ideas, or Aristotle in reason and science. It was not so. On some points, even from the most monotonously modern standpoint, Catholicism was centuries ahead of Platonism or Aristotelianism. We can see it still, for instance, in the tiresome tenacity of Astrology. On that matter the philosophers were all in favour of superstition; and the saints and all such superstitious people were against superstition. But even the great saints found it difficult to get disentangled from this superstition. Two points were always put by those suspicious of the Aristotelianism of Aquinas; and they sound to us now very quaint and comic, taken together. One was the view that the stars are personal beings, governing our lives; the other the great general theory that men have one mind between them; a view obviously opposed to immortality; that is, to individuality. Both linger among the Moderns; so strong is still the tyranny of the Ancients. Astrology sprawls over the Sunday papers, and the other doctrine has its hundredth form in what is called Communism; or the Soul of the Hive.

For on one preliminary point, this position must not be misunderstood. When we praise the practical value of the Aristotelian Revolution, and the originality of Aquinas in leading it, we do not mean that the Scholastic philosophers before him had not been philosophers, or had not been highly philosophical, or had not been in touch with ancient philosophy. In so far as there was ever a bad break in philosophical history, it was not before St Thomas, or at the beginning of mediaeval history; it was after St Thomas and at the beginning of modern history. The great intellectual tradition that comes down to us from Pythagoras and Plato was never interrupted or lost through such trifles as the sack of Rome, the triumph of Attila or all the barbarian invasions of the Dark Ages. It was only lost after the introduction of printing, the discovery of America, the founding of the Royal Society and all the enlightenment of the Renaissance and the modern world. It was there, if anywhere, that there was lost or impatiently snapped the long thin delicate thread that had descended from distant antiquity; the thread of that unusual human hobby; the habit of thinking. This is proved by the fact that the printed books of this later period largely had to wait for the eighteenth century, or the end of the seventeenth century, to find even the names of the new philosophers; who were at the best a new kind of philosophers. But the decline of the Empire, the Dark Ages and the early Middle Ages, though too much tempted to neglect what was opposed to Platonic philosophy, had never neglected philosophy. In that sense St Thomas, like most other very original men, has a long and clear pedigree. He himself is constantly referring back to the authorities from St Augustine to St Anselm, and from St Anselm to St Albert, and even when he differs, he also defers.

A very learned Anglican once said to me, not perhaps without a touch of tartness, 'I can't understand why everybody talks as if Thomas Aquinas were the beginning of the Scholastic philosophy. I could understand their saying he was the end of it.' Whether or no the comment was meant to be tart, we may be sure that the reply of St Thomas would have been perfectly urbane. And indeed it would be easy to answer, with a certain placidity, that in his Thomist language, the end of a thing does not mean its destruction, but its fulfilment. No Thomist will complain, if Thomism is the end of our philosophy, in the sense in which God is the end of our existence. For that does not mean that we cease to exist, but that we become as perennial as the *philosophia perennis*. Putting this claim on one side, however, it is important to remember that my distinguished interlocutor was perfectly right, in that there had been whole dynasties of doctrinal philosophers before Aquinas, leading up to the day of the great revolt of the Aristotelians. Nor was even

ST THOMAS AQUINAS

that revolt a thing entirely abrupt and unforeseen. An able writer in the *Dublin Review* not long ago pointed out that in some respects the whole nature of metaphysics had advanced a long way since Aristotle, by the time it came to Aquinas. And that it is no disrespect to the primitive and gigantic genius of the Stagirite to say that in some respects he was really but a rude and rough founder of philosophy, compared with some of the subsequent subtleties of mediaevalism; that the Greek gave a few grand hints which the Scholastics developed into the most delicate fine shades. This may be an overstatement, but there is a truth in it. Anyhow, it is certain that even in Aristotelian philosophy, let alone Platonic philosophy, there was already a tradition of highly intelligent interpretation. If that delicacy afterwards degenerated into hair-splitting, it was none the less delicate hair-splitting; and work requiring very scientific tools.

What made the Aristotelian Revolution really revolutionary was the fact that it was really religious. It is the fact, so fundamental that I thought it well to lay it down in the first few pages of this book, that the revolt was largely a revolt of the most Christian elements in Christendom. St Thomas, every bit as much as St Francis, felt subconsciously that the hold of his people was slipping on the solid Catholic doctrine and discipline, worn smooth by more than a thousand years of routine; and that the Faith needed to be shown under a new light and dealt with from another angle. But he had no motive except the desire to make it popular for the salvation of the people. It was true, broadly speaking, that for some time past it had been too Platonist to be popular. It needed something like the shrewd and homely touch of Aristotle to turn it again into a religion of common sense. Both the motive and the method are illustrated in the war of Aquinas against the Augustinians.

First, it must be remembered that the Greek influence continued to flow from the Greek Empire; or at least from the centre of the Roman Empire which was in the Greek city of Byzantium, and no longer in Rome. That influence was Byzantine in every good and bad sense; like Byzantine art, it was severe and mathematical and a little terrible; like Byzantine etiquette, it was Oriental and faintly decadent. We owe to the learning of Mr Christopher Dawson[1]

---

1 Catholic historian of culture and religion (1889–1970).

much enlightenment upon the way in which Byzantium slowly stiffened into a sort of Asiatic theocracy, more like that which served the Sacred Emperor in China. But even the unlearned can see the difference, in the way in which Eastern Christianity flattened everything, as it flattened the faces of the images into icons. It became a thing of patterns rather than pictures; and it made definite and destructive war upon statues. Thus we see, strangely enough, that the East was the land of the Cross and the West was the land of the Crucifix. The Greeks were being dehumanized by a radiant symbol, while the Goths were being humanized by an instrument of torture. Only the West made realistic pictures of the greatest of all the tales out of the East. Hence the Greek element in Christian theology tended more and more to be a sort of dried-up Platonism; a thing of diagrams and abstractions; to the last indeed noble abstractions, but not sufficiently touched by that great thing that is by definition almost the opposite of abstraction: Incarnation. Their Logos was the Word; but not the Word made Flesh. In a thousand very subtle ways, often escaping doctrinal definition, this spirit spread over the world of Christendom from the place where the Sacred Emperor sat under his golden mosaics; and the flat pavement of the Roman Empire was at last a sort of smooth pathway for Mahomet. For Islam was the ultimate fulfilment of the Iconoclasts. Long before that, however, there was this tendency to make the Cross merely decorative like the Crescent; to make it a pattern like the Greek key or the Wheel of Buddha. But there is something passive about such a world of patterns, and the Greek Key does not open any door, while the Wheel of Buddha always moves round and never moves on.

Partly through these negative influences, partly through a necessary and noble asceticism which sought to emulate the awful standard of the martyrs, the earlier Christian ages had been excessively anti-corporeal and too near the danger-line of Manichean mysticism. But there was far less danger in the fact that the saints macerated the body than in the fact that the sages neglected it. Granted all the grandeur of Augustine's contribution to Christianity, there was in a sense a more subtle danger in Augustine the Platonist than even in Augustine the Manichee. There came from it a mood which unconsciously committed the heresy of dividing the substance of the Trinity. It thought of God too exclusively as a

Spirit who purifies or a Saviour who redeems; and too little as a Creator who creates. That is why men like Aquinas thought it right to correct Plato by an appeal to Aristotle; Aristotle who took things as he found them, just as Aquinas accepted things as God created them. In all the work of St Thomas the world of positive creation is perpetually present. Humanly speaking, it was he who saved the human element in Christian theology, if he used for convenience certain elements in heathen philosophy. Only, as has already been urged, the human element is also the Christian one.

The panic upon the Aristotelian peril, that had passed across the high places of the Church, was probably a dry wind from the desert. It was really filled rather with fear of Mahomet than fear of Aristotle. And this was ironic, because there was really much more difficulty in reconciling Aristotle with Mahomet than in reconciling him with Christ. Islam is essentially a simple creed for simple men; and nobody can ever really turn pantheism into a simple creed. It is at once too abstract and too complicated. There are simple believers in a personal God; and there are atheists more simple-minded than any believers in a personal God. But few can, in mere simplicity, accept a godless universe as a god. And while the Moslem, as compared with the Christian, had perhaps a less human God, he had if possible a more personal God. The will of Allah was very much of a will, and could not be turned into a stream of tendency. On all that cosmic and abstract side the Catholic was more accommodating than the Moslem – up to a point. The Catholic could admit at least that Aristotle was right about the impersonal elements of a personal God. Hence, we may say broadly of the Moslem philosophers, that those who became good philosophers became bad Moslems. It is not altogether unnatural that many bishops and doctors feared that the Thomists might become good philosophers and bad Christians. But there were also many, of the strict school of Plato and Augustine, who stoutly denied that they were even good philosophers. Between those rather incongruous passions, the love of Plato and the fear of Mahomet, there was a moment when the prospects of any Aristotelian culture in Christendom looked very dark indeed. Anathema after anathema was thundered from high places; and under the shadow of the persecution, as so often happens, it seemed for a moment that barely one or two figures stood alone in the storm-swept area.

They were both in the black and white of the Dominicans; for Albertus and Aquinas stood firm.

In that sort of combat there is always confusion; and majorities change into minorities and back again, as if by magic. It is always difficult to date the turn of the tide, which seems to be a welter of eddies; the very dates seeming to overlap and confuse the crisis. But the change, from the moment when the two Dominicans stood alone to the moment when the whole Church at last wheeled into line with them, may perhaps be found at about the moment when they were practically brought before a hostile but a not unjust judge. Stephen Tempier,[1] the Bishop of Paris, was apparently a rather fine specimen of the old fanatical Churchman, who thought that admiring Aristotle was a weakness likely to be followed by adoring Apollo. He was also, by a piece of bad luck, one of the old social conservatives, who had intensely resented the popular revolution of the Preaching Friars. But he was an honest man; and Thomas Aquinas never asked for anything but permission to address honest men. All around him there were other Aristotelian revolutionaries of a much more dubious sort. There was Siger,[2] the sophist from Brabant, who learned all his Aristotelianism from the Arabs; and had an ingenious theory about how an Arabian agnostic could also be a Christian. There were a thousand young men of the sort that had shouted for Abelard; full of the youth of the thirteenth century and drunken with the Greek wine of Stagira. Over against them, lowering and implacable, was the old Puritan party of the Augustinians; only too delighted to class the rationalistic Albert and Thomas with the equivocal Moslem metaphysicians.

It would seem that the triumph of Thomas was really a personal triumph. He withdrew not a single one of his propositions; though it is said that the reactionary Bishop did condemn some of them after his death. On the whole, however, Aquinas convinced most of his critics that he was quite as good a Catholic as they were. There was a sequel of squabbles between the Religious Orders, following upon this controversial crisis. But it is probably true to say that the fact, that a man like Aquinas had managed even partially

1 Tempier (d. 1279), condemned 219 philosophical and theological theses that were being disputed at the University of Paris in 1277.
2 Siger (*c.* 1240–80s) was a proponent of Averroism.

to satisfy a man like Tempier, was the end of the essential quarrel. What was already familiar to the few became familiar to the many; that an Aristotelian could really be a Christian. Another fact assisted in the common conversion. It rather curiously resembles the story of the translation of the Bible; and the alleged Catholic suppression of the Bible. Behind the scenes, where the Pope was much more tolerant than the Paris Bishop, the friends of Aquinas had been hard at work producing a new translation of Aristotle. It demonstrated that in many ways the heretical translation had been a very heretical translation. With the final consummation of this work, we may say that the great Greek philosophy entered finally into the system of Christendom. The process has been half humorously described as the Baptism of Aristotle.

We have all heard of the humility of the man of science; of many who were very genuinely humble; and of some who were very proud of their humility. It will be the somewhat too recurrent burden of this brief study that Thomas Aquinas really did have the humility of the man of science; as a special variant of the humility of the saint. It is true that he did not himself contribute anything concrete in the experiment or detail of physical science; in this, it may be said, he even lagged behind the last generation, and was far less of an experimental scientist than his tutor Albertus Magnus.[1] But for all that, he was historically a great friend to the freedom of science. The principles he laid down, properly under-stood, are perhaps the best that can be produced for protecting science from mere obscurantist persecution. For instance, in the matter of the inspiration of Scripture, he fixed first on the obvious fact, which was forgotten by four furious centuries of sectarian battle, that the meaning of Scripture is very far from self-evident; and that we must often interpret it in the light of other truths. If a literal interpretation is really and flatly contradicted by an obvious fact, why then we can only say that the literal interpretation must be a false interpretation. But the fact must really be an obvious fact. And unfortunately, nineteenth-century scientists were just as ready to jump to the conclusion that any guess about nature was an obvious fact, as were seventeenth-century sectarians to jump

1 St Albert the Great (1193/1206–80), a Dominican friar, taught St Thomas Aquinas at the University of Paris. He was famous for his knowledge of science, which he denied was in conflict with religion.

to the conclusion that any guess about Scripture was the obvious explanation. Thus, private theories about what the Bible ought to mean, and premature theories about what the world ought to mean, have met in loud and widely advertised controversy, especially in the Victorian time; and this clumsy collision of two very impatient forms of ignorance was known as the quarrel of Science and Religion.

But St Thomas had the scientific humility in this very vivid and special sense; that he was ready to take the lowest place; for the examination of the lowest things. He did not, like a modern specialist, study the worm as if it were the world; but he was willing to begin to study the reality of the world in the reality of the worm. His Aristotelianism simply meant that the study of the humblest fact will lead to the study of the highest truth. That for him the process was logical and not biological, was concerned with philosophy rather than science, does not alter the essential idea that he believed in beginning at the bottom of the ladder. But he also gave, by his view of Scripture and Science, and other questions, a sort of charter for pioneers more purely practical than himself. He practically said that if they could really prove their practical discoveries, the traditional interpretation of Scripture must give way before those discoveries. He could hardly, as the common phrase goes, say fairer than that. If the matter had been left to him, and men like him, there never would have been any quarrel between Science and Religion. He did his very best to map out two provinces for them, and to trace a just frontier between them.

It is often cheerfully remarked that Christianity has failed, by which is meant that it has never had that sweeping, imperial and imposed supremacy, which has belonged to each of the great revolutions, every one of which has subsequently failed. There was never a moment when men could say that every man was a Christian; as they might say for several months that every man was a Royalist or a Republican or a Communist. But if sane historians want to understand the sense in which the Christian character has succeeded, they could not find a better case than the massive moral pressure of a man like St Thomas, in support of the buried rationalism of the heathens, which had as yet only been dug up for the amusement of the heretics. It was, quite strictly and exactly, because a new kind of man was conducting rational enquiry in a new kind of way, that men forgot the curse that had fallen on the temples of the dead demons and the palaces of the dead despots; forgot even the new fury out of Arabia against which they were fighting for their lives; because the man who was asking them to return to sense, or to return to their senses, was not a sophist but a saint. Aristotle had described the magnanimous man, who is great and knows that he is great. But Aristotle would never have recovered his own greatness, but for the miracle that created the more magnanimous man; who is great and knows that he is small.

There is a certain historical importance in what some would call the heaviness of the style employed. It carries a curious impression of candour, which really did have, I think, a considerable effect upon contemporaries. The saint has sometimes been called a scep-tic. The truth is that he was very largely tolerated as a sceptic because he was obviously a saint. When he seemed to stand up as a stubborn Aristotelian, hardly distinguishable from the Arabian heretics, I do seriously believe that what protected him was very largely the prodigious power of his simplicity and his obvious good-ness and love of truth. Those who went out against the haughty confidence of the heretics were stopped and brought up all stand-ing, against a sort of huge humility which was like a mountain; or perhaps like that immense valley that is the mould of a mountain. Allowing for all mediaeval conventions, we can feel that with the other innovators, this was not always so. The others, from Abelard down to Siger of Brabant, have never quite lost, in the long process of history, a faint air of showing off. Nobody could feel for a moment that Thomas Aquinas was showing off. The very dulness of diction, of which some complain, was enormously convincing. He could have given wit as well as wisdom; but he was so prodi-giously in earnest that he gave his wisdom without his wit.

After the hour of triumph came the moment of peril. It is always so with alliances, and especially because Aquinas was fighting on two fronts. His main business was to defend the Faith against the abuse of Aristotle; and he boldly did it by supporting the use of Aristotle. He knew perfectly well that armies of atheists and anar-chists were roaring applause in the background at his Aristotelian victory over all he held most dear. Nevertheless, it was never the existence of atheists, any more than Arabs or Aristotelian pagans, that disturbed the extraordinary controversial composure of

Thomas Aquinas. The real peril that followed on the victory he had won for Aristotle was vividly presented in the curious case of Siger of Brabant; and it is well worth study, for anyone who would begin to comprehend the strange history of Christendom. It is marked by one rather queer quality; which has always been the unique note of the Faith, though it is not noticed by its modern enemies, and rarely by its modern friends. It is the fact symbolized in the legend of Antichrist, who was the double of Christ; in the profound proverb that the Devil is the ape of God. It is the fact that falsehood is never so false as when it is very nearly true. It is when the stab comes near the nerve of truth, that the Christian conscience cries out in pain. And Siger of Brabant, following on some of the Arabian Aristotelians, advanced a theory which most modern newspaper readers would instantly have declared to be the same as the theory of St Thomas. That was what finally roused St Thomas to his last and most emphatic protest. He had won his battle for a wider scope of philosophy and science; he had cleared the ground for a general understanding about faith and enquiry; an understanding that has generally been observed among Catholics, and certainly never deserted without disaster. It was the idea that the scientist should go on exploring and experimenting freely, so long as he did not claim an infallibility and finality which it was against his own principles to claim. Meanwhile the Church should go on developing and defining, about supernatural things, so long as she did not claim a right to alter the deposit of faith, which it was against her own principles to claim. And when he had said this, Siger of Brabant got up and said something so horribly like it, and so horribly unlike, that (like Antichrist) he might have deceived the very elect.

Siger of Brabant said this: the Church must be right theologically, but she can be wrong scientifically. There are two truths; the truth of the supernatural world, and the truth of the natural world, which contradicts the supernatural world. While we are being naturalists, we can suppose that Christianity is all nonsense; but then, when we remember that we are Christians, we must admit that Christianity is true even if it is nonsense. In other words, Siger of Brabant split the human head in two, like the blow in an old legend of battle; and declared that a man has two minds, with one of which he must entirely believe and with the other may utterly disbelieve. To many this would at least seem like a parody of Thomism. As a fact, it was the assassination of Thomism. It was not two ways of finding the same truth; it was an untruthful way of pretending that there are two truths. And it is extraordinarily interesting to note that this is the one occasion when the Dumb Ox really came out like a wild bull. When he stood up to answer Siger of Brabant, he was altogether transfigured, and the very style of his sentences, which is a thing like the tone of a man's voice, is suddenly altered. He had never been angry with any of the enemies who disagreed with him. But these enemies had attempted the worst treachery: they had made him agree with them.

Those who complain that theologians draw fine distinctions could hardly find a better example of their own folly. In fact, a fine distinction can be a flat contradiction. It was notably so in this case. St Thomas was willing to allow the one truth to be approached by two paths, precisely *because* he was sure there was only one truth. Because the Faith was the one truth, nothing discovered in nature could ultimately contradict the Faith. Because the Faith was the one truth, nothing really deduced from the Faith could ultimately contradict the facts. It was in truth a curiously daring confidence in the reality of his religion; and though some may linger to dispute it, it has been justified. The scientific facts, which were supposed to contradict the Faith in the nineteenth century, are nearly all of them regarded as unscientific fictions in the twentieth century. Even the materialists have fled from materialism; and those who lectured us about determinism in psychology are already talking about indeterminism in matter. But whether his confidence was right or wrong, it was specially and supremely a confidence that there is one truth which cannot contradict itself. And this last group of enemies suddenly sprang up, to tell him they entirely agreed with him in saying that there are two contradictory truths. Truth, in the mediaeval phrase, carried two faces under one hood; and these double-faced sophists practically dared to suggest that it was the Dominican hood.

So, in his last battle and for the first time, he fought as with a battle-axe. There is a ring in the words altogether beyond the almost impersonal patience he maintained in debate with so many enemies. 'Behold our refutation of the error. It is not based on documents of faith, but on the reasons and statements of the philosophers themselves. If then anyone there be who, boastfully taking pride in his supposed wisdom, wishes to challenge what we have written, let him not do it in some corner nor before children who are powerless to decide on such difficult matters. Let him reply openly if he dare. He shall find me then confronting him, and not only my negligible self, but many another whose study is truth. We shall do battle with his errors or bring a cure to his ignorance.'

The Dumb Ox is bellowing now; like one at bay and yet terrible and towering over all the baying pack. We have already noted why, in this one quarrel with Siger of Brabant, Thomas Aquinas let loose such thunders of purely moral passion; it was because the whole work of his life was being betrayed behind his back, by those who had used his victories over the reactionaries. The point at the moment is that this is perhaps his one moment of personal passion, save for a single flash in the troubles of his youth; and he is once more fighting his enemies with a firebrand. And yet, even in this isolated apocalypse of anger, there is one phrase that may be commended for all time to men who are angry with much less cause. If there is one sentence that could be carved in marble, as representing the calmest and most enduring rationality of his unique intelligence, it is a sentence which came pouring out with all the rest of this molten lava. If there is one phrase that stands before history as typical of Thomas Aquinas, it is that phrase about his own argument: 'It is not based on documents of faith, but on the reasons and statements of the philosophers themselves.' Would that all Orthodox doctors in deliberation were as reasonable as Aquinas in anger! Would that all Christian apologists would remember that maxim; and write it up in large letters on the wall, before they nail any theses there. At the top of his fury, Thomas Aquinas understands, what so many defenders of orthodoxy will not understand. It is no good to tell an atheist that he is an atheist; or to charge a denier of immortality with the infamy of denying it; or to imagine that one can force an opponent to admit he is wrong, by proving that he is wrong on somebody else's principles, but not on his own. After the great example of St Thomas, the principle stands, or ought always to have stood established; that we must either not argue with a man at all, or we must argue on his grounds and not ours. We may do other things *instead* of arguing, according to our views of what actions are morally permissible; but if we argue we must argue 'on the reasons and statements of the philosophers themselves'. This is the common sense in a saying attributed to a friend of St Thomas, the great St Louis, King of France, which shallow people quote as a sample of fanaticism; the sense of which is, that I must either argue with an infidel as a real philosopher can argue, or else 'thrust a sword through his body as far as it will go'. A real philosopher (even of the opposite school) will be the first to agree that St Louis was entirely philosophical. . . .

IV

A MEDITATION ON THE MANICHEES

THERE is one casual anecdote about St Thomas Aquinas which illuminates him like a lightning-flash, not only without but within. For it not only shows him as a character, and even as a comedy character, and shows the colours of his period and social background; but also, as if for an instant, makes a transparency of his mind. It is a trivial incident which occurred one day, when he was reluctantly dragged from his work, and we might almost say from his play. For both were for him found in the unusual hobby of thinking, which is for some men a thing much more intoxicating than mere drinking. He had declined any number of society invitations, to the courts of kings and princes, not because he was unfriendly, for he was not; but because he was always glowing within with the really gigantic plans of exposition and argument which filled his life. On one occasion, however, he was invited to the court of King Louis IX of France, more famous as the great St Louis, and for some reason or other, the Dominican authorities of his Order told him to accept; so he immediately did so, being an obedient friar even in his sleep; or rather in his permanent trance of reflection.

It is a real case against conventional hagiography that it sometimes tends to make all saints seem to be the same. Whereas in fact no men are more different than saints; not even murderers. And there could hardly be a more complete contrast, given the essentials of holiness, than between St Thomas and St Louis. St Louis was born a knight and a king; but he was one of those men in whom a certain simplicity, combined with courage and activity, makes it natural, and in a sense easy, to fulfil directly and promptly any duty or office, however official. He was a man in whom holiness and healthiness had no quarrel; and their issue was in action. He did not go in for thinking much, in the sense of theorizing much. But, even in theory, he had that sort of presence of mind, which belongs to the rare and really practical man when he has to think. He never said the wrong thing; and he was orthodox by instinct. In the old pagan proverb about kings being philosophers or philosophers kings, there was a certain miscalculation, connected with a mystery that only Christianity could reveal. For while it is possible for a king to wish very much to be a saint, it is not possible for a saint to wish very much to be a king. A good man will hardly be always dreaming of being a great monarch; but, such is the liberality of the Church, that she cannot forbid even a great monarch to dream of being a good man. But Louis was a straightforward soldierly sort of person who did not particularly mind being a king, any more than he would have minded being a captain or a sergeant or any other rank in his army. Now a man like St Thomas would definitely dislike being a king, or being entangled with the pomp and politics of kings; not only his humility, but a sort of subconscious fastidiousness and fine dislike of futility, often found in leisurely and learned men with large minds, would really have prevented him making contact with the complexity of court life. Also, he was anxious all his life to keep out of politics; and there was no political symbol more striking, or in a sense more challenging, at that moment, than the power of the King in Paris.

Paris was truly at that time an *aurora borealis*; a Sunrise in the North. We must realize that lands much nearer to Rome had rotted with paganism and pessimism and Oriental influences of which the most respectable was that of Mahound. Provence and all the South had been full of a fever of nihilism or negative mysticism, and from Northern France had come the spears and swords that swept away the unchristian thing. In Northern France also sprang up that splendour of building that shine like swords and spears: the first spires of the Gothic. We talk now of grey Gothic buildings; but they must have been very different when they went up white and gleaming into the northern skies, partly picked out with gold and bright colours; a new flight of architecture, as startling as flying-ships. The new Paris ultimately left behind by St Louis must have been a thing white like lilies and splendid as the oriflamme. It was the beginning of the great new thing: the nation of France, which was to pierce and overpower the old quarrel of Pope and Emperor in the lands from which Thomas came. But Thomas came very unwillingly, and, if we may say it of so kindly a man, rather sulkily. As he entered Paris, they showed him from the hill that splendour of new spires beginning, and somebody said something like, 'How grand it must be to own all this.' And Thomas Aquinas only muttered, 'I would rather have that Chrysostom MS. I can't get hold of.'

Somehow they steered that reluctant bulk of reflection to a seat in the royal banquet hall; and all that we know of Thomas tells us that he was perfectly courteous to those who spoke to him, but spoke little, and was soon forgotten in the most brilliant and noisy clatter in the world: the noise of French talking. What the Frenchmen were talking about we do not know; but they forgot all about the large fat Italian in their midst, and it seems only too possible that he forgot all about them. Sudden silences will occur even in French conversation; and in one of these the interruption came. There had long been no word or motion in that huge heap of black and white weeds, like motley in mourning, which marked him as a mendicant friar out of the streets, and contrasted with all the colours and patterns and quarterings of that first and freshest dawn of chivalry and heraldry. The triangular shields and pennons and pointed spears, the triangular swords of the Crusade, the pointed windows and the conical hoods, repeated everywhere that fresh French mediaeval spirit that did, in every sense, come to the point. But the colours of the coats were gay and varied, with little to rebuke their richness; for St Louis, who had himself a special quality of coming to the point, had said to his courtiers, 'Vanity should be avoided; but every man should dress well, in the manner of his rank, that his wife may the more easily love him.'

And then suddenly the goblets leapt and rattled on the board and the great table shook, for the friar had brought down his huge fist like a club of stone, with a crash that startled everyone like an explosion; and had cried out in a strong voice, but like a man in the grip of a dream, 'And *that* will settle the Manichees!'

The palace of a king, even when it is the palace of a saint, has its conventions. A shock thrilled through the court, and every one felt as if the fat friar from Italy had thrown a plate at King Louis, or knocked his crown sideways. They all looked timidly at the terrible seat, that was for a thousand years the throne of the Capets; and many there were presumably prepared to pitch the big black-robed beggarman out of the window. But St Louis, simple as he seemed, was no mere mediaeval fountain of honour or even fountain of mercy; but also the fountain of two eternal rivers; the irony and the courtesy of France. And he turned to his secretaries, asking them in a low voice to take their tablets round to the seat of the absent-minded controversialist, and take a note of the argument that had just occurred to him; because it must be a very good one and he might forget it. I have paused upon this anecdote, first, as has been said, because it is the one which gives us the most vivid snapshot of a great mediaeval character; indeed of two great mediaeval characters. But it also specially fitted to be taken as a type or a turning-point, because of the glimpse it gives of the man's main preoccupation; and the sort of thing that might have been found in his thoughts, if they had been thus surprised at any moment by a philosophical eavesdropper or through a psychological keyhole. It was not for nothing that he was still brooding, even in the white court of St Louis, upon the dark cloud of the Manichees.

This book is meant only to be the sketch of a man; but it must at least lightly touch, later on, upon a method and a meaning; or what our journalism has an annoying way of calling a message. A few very inadequate pages must be given to the man in relation to his theology and his philosophy; but the thing of which I mean to speak here is something at once more general and more personal even than his philosophy. I have therefore introduced it here, before we come to anything like technical talk about his philosophy. It was something that might alternatively be called his moral attitude, or his temperamental predisposition, or the purpose of his life so far as social and human effects were concerned: for he knew better than most of us that there is but one purpose in this life, and it is one that is beyond this life. But if we wanted to put in a picturesque and simplified form what he wanted for the world, and what was his work in history, apart from theoretical and theological definitions, we might well say that it really was to strike a blow and settle the Manichees.

The full meaning of this may not be apparent to those who do not study theological history; and perhaps even less apparent to those who do. Indeed it may seem equally irrelevant to the history and the theology. In history St Dominic and Simon de Montfort[1]

---

[1] Simon IV de Montfort (*c.* 1160–1218), led the crusade against the Manichean Cathar or Albigensian sect, dying at the siege of Toulouse. His son, Simon V de Montfort (1208?–65), who later led the baronial opposition to King Henry III of England, may also have taken part in the Albigensian crusades as a youth in the 1220s.

between them had already pretty well settled the Manichees. And in theology, of course, an encyclopaedic doctor like Aquinas dealt with a thousand other heresies besides the Manichean heresy. Nevertheless, it does represent his main position and the turn he gave to the whole history of Christendom.

I think it well to interpose this chapter, though its scope may seem more vague than the rest; because there is a sort of big blunder about St Thomas and his creed, which is an obstacle for most modern people in even beginning to understand them. It arises roughly thus. St Thomas, like other monks, and especially other saints, lived a life of renunciation and austerity; his fasts, for instance, being in marked contrast to the luxury in which he might have lived if he chose. This element stands high in his religion, as a manner of asserting the will against the power of nature, of thanking the Redeemer by partially sharing his sufferings, of making a man ready for anything as a missionary or martyr, and similar ideals. These happen to be rare in the modern industrial society of the West, outside his communion; and it is therefore assumed that they are the whole meaning of that communion. Because it is uncommon for an alderman to fast for forty days, or a politician to take a Trappist vow of silence, or a man about town to live a life of strict celibacy, the average outsider is convinced, not only that Catholicism is nothing except asceticism, but that asceticism is nothing except pessimism. He is so obliging as to explain to Catholics why they hold this heroic virtue in respect; and is ever ready to point out that the philosophy behind it is an Oriental hatred of anything connected with Nature, and a purely Schopenhauerian disgust with the Will to Live. . . . How marriage can be a sacrament if sex is a sin, or why it is the Catholics who are in favour of birth and their foes who are in favour of birth-control, I will leave the critic to worry out for himself. My concern is not with that part of the argument; but with another.

The ordinary modern critic, seeing this ascetic ideal in an authoritative Church, and not seeing it in most other inhabitants of Brixton or Brighton, is apt to say, 'This is the result of Authority; it would be better to have Religion without Authority.' But in truth, a wider experience outside Brixton or Brighton would reveal the mistake. It is rare to find a fasting alderman or a Trappist politician, but it is still more rare to see nuns suspended in the air on hooks or spikes; it is unusual for a Catholic Evidence Guild orator in Hyde Park to begin his speech by gashing himself all over with knives; a stranger calling at an ordinary presbytery will seldom find the parish priest lying on the floor with a fire lighted on his chest and scorching him while he utters spiritual ejaculations. Yet all these things are done all over Asia, for instance, by voluntary enthusiasts acting solely on the great impulse of Religion; of Religion, in their case, not commonly imposed by any immediate Authority; and certainly not imposed by this particular Authority. In short, a real knowledge of mankind will tell anybody that Religion is a very terrible thing; that it is truly a raging fire, and that Authority is often quite as much needed to restrain it as to impose it. Asceticism, or the war with the appetites, is itself an appetite. It can never be eliminated from among the strange ambitions of Man. But it can be kept in some reasonable control; and it is indulged in much saner proportion under Catholic Authority than in Pagan or Puritan anarchy. Meanwhile, the whole of this ideal, though an essential part of Catholic idealism when it is understood, is in some ways entirely a side issue. It is not the primary principle of Catholic philosophy; it is only a particular deduction from Catholic ethics. And when we begin to talk about primary philosophy, we realize the full and flat contradiction between the monk fasting and the fakir hanging himself on hooks.

Now nobody will begin to understand the Thomist philosophy, or indeed the Catholic philosophy, who does not realize that the primary and fundamental part of it is entirely the praise of Life, the praise of Being, the praise of God as the Creator of the World. Everything else follows a long way after that, being conditioned by various complications like the Fall or the vocation of heroes. The trouble occurs because the Catholic mind moves upon two planes; that of the Creation and that of the Fall. The nearest parallel is, for instance, that of England invaded; there might be strict martial law in Kent because the enemy had landed in Kent, and relative liberty in Hereford; but this would not affect the affection of an English patriot for Hereford or Kent, and strategic caution in Kent would not affect the love of Kent. For the love of England would remain, both of the parts to be redeemed by discipline and the parts to be enjoyed in liberty. Any extreme of Catholic asceticism is a wise, or unwise, precaution against the evil of the Fall; it is *never* a doubt about the good of the Creation. And *that* is where it really does differ, not only from the rather excessive eccentricity of the gentleman who hangs himself on hooks, but from the whole cosmic theory which is the hook on which he hangs. In the case of many Oriental religions, it really is true that the asceticism is pessimism; that the ascetic tortures himself to death out of an abstract hatred of life; that he does not merely mean to control Nature as he should, but to contradict Nature as much as he can. And though it takes a milder form than hooks in millions of the religious populations of Asia, it is a fact far too little realized, that the dogma of the denial of life does really rule as a first principle on so vast a scale. One historic form it took was that great enemy of Christianity from its beginnings: the Manichees.

What is called the Manichean philosophy has had many forms; indeed it has attacked what is immortal and immutable with a very curious kind of immortal mutability. It is like the legend of the magician who turns himself into a snake or a cloud; and the whole has that nameless note of irresponsibility, which belongs to much of the metaphysics and morals of Asia, from which the Manichean mystery came. But it is always in one way or another a notion that nature is evil; or that evil is at least rooted in nature. The essential point is that as evil has roots in nature, so it has rights in nature. Wrong has as much right to exist as right. As already stated this notion took many forms. Sometimes it was a dualism, which made evil an equal partner with good; so that neither could be called an usurper. More often it was a general idea that demons had made the material world, and if there were any good spirits, they were concerned only with the spiritual world. Later, again, it took the form of Calvinism, which held that God had indeed made the world, but in a special sense, made the evil as well as the good: had made an evil will as well as an evil world. On this view, if a man chooses to damn his soul alive, he is not thwarting God's will but rather fulfilling it. In these two forms, of the early Gnosticism and the later Calvinism, we see the superficial variety and fundamental unity of Manicheanism. The old Manicheans taught that Satan originated the whole work of creation commonly attributed to God. The new Calvinists taught that God originates the whole work of damnation commonly attributed to Satan. One looked back to the first day when a devil acted like a god, the other looked forward to a last day when a god acted like a devil. But both had the idea that the creator of the earth was primarily the creator of the evil, whether we call him a devil or a god.

Since there are a good many Manicheans among the Moderns, as we may remark in a moment, some may agree with this view, some may be puzzled about it, some may only be puzzled about why we should object to it. To understand the mediaeval controversy, a word must be said of the Catholic doctrine, which is as modern as it is mediaeval. That 'God looked on all things and saw that they were good' contains a subtlety which the popular pessimist cannot follow, or is too hasty to notice. It is the thesis that there are no bad things, but only bad uses of things. If you will, there are no bad things but only bad thoughts; and especially bad intentions. Only Calvinists can really believe that hell is paved with good intentions. That is exactly the one thing it cannot be paved with. But it is possible to have bad intentions about good things; and good things, like the world and the flesh have been twisted by a bad intention called the devil. But he cannot make *things* bad; they remain as on the first day of creation. The work of heaven alone was material; the making of a material world. The work of hell is entirely spiritual.

This error then had many forms; but especially, like nearly every error, it had two forms, a fiercer one which was outside the Church and attacking the Church, and a subtler one, which was inside the Church and corrupting the Church. There has never been a time when the Church was not torn between that invasion and that treason. It was so, for instance, in the Victorian time. Darwinian 'competition', in commerce or race conflict, was every bit as brazen an atheist assault, in the nineteenth century, as the Bolshevist No-God movement in the twentieth century. To brag of brute prosperity, to admire the most muddly millionaires who had cornered wheat by a trick, to talk about the 'unfit' (in imitation of the scientific thinker who would finish them off because he cannot even finish his own sentence – unfit for what?) – all that is as simply and openly Anti-Christian as the Black Mass. Yet some weak and worldly Catholics did use this cant in defence of Capitalism, in their first rather feeble resistance to Socialism. At least they did until the great Encyclical of the Pope on the Rights of Labour put a stop to all their nonsense. The evil is always both within and without the Church; but in a wilder form outside and a milder form inside. So it was, again, in the seventeenth century, when there was Calvinism outside and Jansenism inside. And so it was in the thirteenth century, when the obvious danger outside was in the revolution of the Albigensians; but the potential danger inside was in the very traditionalism of the Augustinians. For the Augustinians derived only from Augustine, and Augustine derived partly from Plato, and Plato was right, but not quite right. It is a mathematical fact that if a line be not perfectly directed towards a point, it will actually go further away from it as it comes nearer to it. After a thousand years of extension, the miscalculation of Platonism had come very near to Manicheanism.

Popular errors are nearly always right. They nearly always refer to some ultimate reality, about which those who correct them are themselves incorrect. It is a very queer thing that 'Platonic Love' has come to mean for the un-lettered something rather purer and cleaner than it means for the learned. Yet even those who realize the great Greek evil may well realize that perversity often comes out of the wrong sort of purity. Now it was the inmost lie of the Manichees that they identified purity with sterility. It is singularly contrasted with the language of St Thomas, which always connects purity with fruitfulness; whether it be natural or supernatural. And, queerly enough, as I have said, there does remain a sort of reality in the vulgar colloquialism that the affair between Sam and Susan is 'quite Platonic'. It is true that, quite apart from the local perversion, there was in Plato a sort of idea that people would be better without their bodies; that their heads might fly off and meet in the sky in merely intellectual marriage, like cherubs in a picture. The ultimate phase of this 'Platonic' philosophy was what inflamed poor D. H. Lawrence into talking nonsense, and he was probably unaware that the Catholic doctrine of marriage would say much of what he said, without talking nonsense. Anyhow, it is historically important to see that Platonic love did somewhat distort both human and divine love, in the theory of the early theologians. Many mediaeval men, who would indignantly deny the Albigensian doctrine of sterility, were yet in an emotional mood to abandon the body in despair; and some of them to abandon everything in despair.

In truth, this vividly illuminates the provincial stupidity of those who object to what they call 'creeds and dogmas'. It was precisely the creed and dogma that saved the sanity of the world. These people generally propose an alternative religion of intuition and feeling. If, in the really Dark Ages, there had been a religion of feeling, it would have been a religion of black and suicidal feeling. It was the rigid creed that resisted the rush of suicidal feeling. The critics of asceticism are probably right in supposing that many a Western hermit did *feel* rather like an Eastern fakir. But he could not really *think* like an Eastern fakir; because he was an orthodox Catholic. And what kept his thought in touch with healthier and more humanistic thought was simply and solely the Dogma. He could not deny that a good God had created the normal and natural world; he could not say that the devil had made the world; because he was not a Manichee. A thousand enthusiasts for celibacy, in the day of the great rush to the desert or the cloister, might have called marriage a sin, if they had only considered their individual ideals, in the modern manner, and their own immediate feelings about marriage. Fortunately, they had to accept the Authority of the Church, which had definitely said that marriage was not a sin. A modern emotional religion might at any moment have turned Catholicism into Manicheanism. But when Religion would have maddened men, Theology kept them sane.

In this sense St Thomas stands up simply as the great orthodox theologian, who reminded men of the creed of Creation, when many of them were still in the mood of mere destruction. It is futile for the critics of mediaevalism to quote a hundred mediaeval phrases that may be supposed to sound like mere pessimism, if they will not understand the central fact; that mediaeval men did not care about being mediaeval and did not accept the authority of a mood, because it was melancholy, but did care very much about orthodoxy, which is not a mood. It was because St Thomas could *prove* that his glorification of the Creator and His creative joy was more orthodox than any atmospheric pessimism, that he dominated the Church and the world, which accepted that truth as a test. But when this immense and impersonal importance is allowed for, we may agree that there was a personal element as well. Like most of the great religious teachers, he was fitted individually for the task that God had given him to do. We can if we like call that talent instinctive; we can even descend to calling it temperamental.

Anybody trying to popularize a mediaeval philosopher must use language that is very modern and very unphilosophical. Nor is this a sneer at modernity; it arises from the moderns having dealt so much in moods and emotions, especially in the arts, that they have developed a large but loose vocabulary, which deals more with atmosphere than with actual attitude or position. As noted else-where, even the modern philosophers are more like the modern poets; in giving an individual tinge even to truth, and often looking at all life through different coloured spectacles. To say that Schop-enhauer had the blues, or that William James had a rather rosier outlook, would often convey more than calling the one a Pessimist or the other a Pragmatist. This modern moodiness has its value, though the moderns overrate it; just as mediaeval logic had its value, though it was overrated in the later Middle Ages. But the point is that to explain the mediaevals to the moderns, we must often use this modern language of mood. Otherwise the character will be missed, through certain prejudices and ignorances about all such mediaeval characters. Now there is something that lies all over the work of St Thomas Aquinas like a great light; which is some-thing quite primary and perhaps unconscious with him, which he would perhaps have passed over as an irrelevant personal quality; and which can now only be expressed by a rather cheap journalistic term, which he would probably have thought quite senseless.

Nevertheless, the only working word for that atmosphere is Optimism. I know that the word is now even more degraded in the twentieth century than it was in the nineteenth century. Men talked lately of being Optimists about the issue of War; they talk now of being Optimists about the revival of Trade; they may talk tomor-row of being Optimists about the International Ping-pong Tourna-ment. But men in the Victorian time did mean a little more than that, when they used the word Optimist of Browning or Steven-son or Walt Whitman. And in a rather larger and more luminous sense than in the case of these men, the term was basically true of Thomas Aquinas. He did, with a most solid and colossal convic-tion, believe in Life; and in something like what Stevenson called the great theorem of the livableness of life. It breathes somehow in his very first phrases about the reality of Being. If the morbid

Renaissance intellectual is supposed to say, 'To be or not to be – that is the question', then the massive mediaeval doctor does most certainly reply in a voice of thunder, 'To be – that is the answer'. The point is important; many not unnaturally talk of the Renaissance as the time when certain men began to believe in Life. The truth is that it was the time when a few men, for the first time, began to disbelieve in Life. The mediaevals had put many restrictions, and some excessive restrictions, upon the universal human hunger and even fury for Life. Those restrictions had often been expressed in fanatical and rabid terms; the terms of those resisting a great natural force; the force of men who desired to live. Never until modern thought began, did they really have to fight with men who desired to die. That horror had threatened them in Asiatic Albigensianism, but it never became normal to them – until now.

But this fact becomes very vivid indeed, when we compare the greatest of Christian philosophers with the only men who were anything like his equals, or capable of being his rivals. They were people with whom he did not directly dispute; most of them he had never seen; some of them he had never heard of. Plato and Augustine were the only two with whom he could confer as he did with Bonaventure or even Averrhoes. But we must look elsewhere for his real rivals, and the only real rivals of the Catholic theory. They are the heads of great heathen systems; some of them very ancient, some very modern, like Buddha on the one hand or Nietzsche on the other. It is when we see his gigantic figure against this vast and cosmic background, that we realize, first, that he was the only optimist theologian, and second, that Catholicism is the only optimist theology. Something milder and more amiable may be made out of the deliquescence of theology, and the mixture of the creed with everything that contradicts it; but among consistent cosmic creeds, this is the only one that is entirely on the side of Life.

Comparative religion has indeed allowed us to compare religions – and to contrast them. Fifty years ago, it set out to prove that all religions were much the same; generally proving, alternately, that they were all equally worthy and that they were all equally worthless. Since then this scientific process has suddenly begun to be scientific, and discovered the depths of the chasms as well as the heights of the hills. It is indeed an excellent improvement that sincerely religious people should respect each other. But respect has discovered difference, where contempt knew only indifference. The more we really appreciate the noble revulsion and renunciation of Buddha, the more we see that intellectually it was the converse and almost the contrary of the salvation of the world by Christ. The Christian would escape from the world into the universe: the Buddhist wishes to escape from the universe even more than from the world. One would uncreate himself; the other would return to his Creation: to his Creator. Indeed it was so genuinely the converse of the idea of the Cross as the Tree of Life, that there is some excuse for setting up the two things side by side, as if they were of equal significance. They are in one sense parallel and equal; as a mound and a hollow, as a valley and a hill. There is a sense in which that sublime despair is the only alternative to that divine audacity. It is even true that the truly spiritual and intellectual man sees it as a sort of dilemma; a very hard and terrible choice. There is little else on earth that can compare with these for completeness. And he who will not climb the mountain of Christ does indeed fall into the abyss of Buddha.

The same is true, in a less lucid and dignified fashion, of most other alternatives of heathen humanity; nearly all are sucked back into that whirlpool of recurrence which all the ancients knew. Nearly all return to the one idea of returning. That is what Buddha described so darkly as the Sorrowful Wheel. It is true that the sort of recurrence which Buddha described as the Sorrowful Wheel, poor Nietzsche actually managed to describe as the Joyful Wisdom. I can only say that if bare repetition was his idea of Joyful Wisdom, I should be curious to know what was his idea of Sorrowful Wisdom. But as a fact, in the case of Nietzsche, this did not belong to the moment of his breaking out, but to the moment of his breaking down. It came at the end of his life, when he was near to mental collapse; and it is really quite contrary to his earlier and finer inspirations of wild freedom or fresh and creative innovation. Once at least he had tried to break out; but he also was only broken – on the wheel.

Alone upon the earth, and lifted and liberated from all the wheels and whirlpools of the earth, stands up the faith of St Thomas; weighted and balanced indeed with more than Oriental metaphysics and more than Pagan pomp and pageantry; but vitally and vividly alone in declaring that life is a living story, with a great beginning and a great close; rooted in the primeval joy of God and finding its fruition in the final happiness of humanity; opening with the colossal chorus in which the sons of God shouted for joy, and ending in that mystical comradeship, shown in a shadowy fashion in those ancient words that move like an archaic dance; 'For His delight is with the sons of men'.

It is the fate of this sketch to be sketchy about philosophy, scanty or rather empty about theology, and to achieve little more than a decent silence on the subject of sanctity. And yet it must none the less be the recurrent burden of this little book, to which it must return with some monotony, that in this story the philosophy did depend on the theology, and the theology did depend on the sanctity. In other words, it must repeat the first fact, which was emphasized in the first chapter: that this great intellectual creation was a Christian and Catholic creation and cannot be understood as anything else. It was Aquinas who baptized Aristotle, when Aristotle could not have baptized Aquinas; it was a purely Christian miracle which raised the great Pagan from the dead. And this is proved in three ways (as St Thomas himself might say), which it will be well to summarize as a sort of summary of this book.

First, in the life of St Thomas, it is proved in the fact that only his huge and solid orthodoxy could have supported so many things which then seemed to be unorthodox. Charity covers a multitude of sins; and in that sense orthodoxy covers a multitude of heresies; or things which are hastily mistaken for heresies. It was precisely because his personal Catholicism was so convincing, that his impersonal Aristotelianism was given the benefit of the doubt. He did not smell of the faggot because he did smell of the firebrand; of the firebrand he had so instantly and instinctively snatched up, under a real assault on essential Catholic ethics. A typically cynical modern phrase refers to the man who is so good that he is good for nothing. St Thomas was so good that he was good for everything; that his warrant held good for what others considered the most wild and daring speculations, ending in the worship of nothing. Whether or no he baptized Aristotle, he was truly the godfather of Aristotle, he was his sponsor; he swore that the old Greek would do no harm; and the whole world trusted his word.

Second, in the philosophy of St Thomas, it is proved by the fact that everything depended on the new Christian *motive* for the study of facts, as distinct from truths. The Thomist philosophy began with the lowest roots of thought, the senses and the truisms of the reason; and a Pagan sage might have scorned such things, as he scorned the servile arts. But the materialism, which is merely cynicism in a Pagan, can be Christian humility in a Christian. St Thomas was willing to begin by recording the facts and sensations of the material world, just as he would have been willing to begin by washing up the plates and dishes in the monastery. The point of his Aristotelianism was that even if common sense about concrete things really was a sort of servile labour, he must not be ashamed to be *servus servorum Dei*.[1] Among heathens the mere sceptic might become the mere cynic; Diogenes in his tub had always a touch of the tub-thumper; but even the dirt of the cynics was dignified into dust and ashes among the saints. If we miss that, we miss the whole meaning of the greatest revolution in history. There was a new *motive* for beginning with the most material, and even with the meanest things.

Third, in the theology of St Thomas, it is proved by the tremendous truth that supports all that theology; or any other Christian theology. There really was a new reason for regarding the senses, and the sensations of the body, and the experiences of the common man, with a reverence at which great Aristotle would have stared, and no man in the ancient world could have begun to understand. The Body was no longer what it was when Plato and Porphyry and the old mystics had left it for dead. It had hung upon a gibbet. It had risen from a tomb. It was no longer possible for the soul to despise the senses, which had been the organs of something that was more than man. Plato might despise the flesh; but God had not despised it. The senses had truly become sanctified; as they are blessed one by one at a Catholic baptism. 'Seeing is believing' was no longer the platitude of a mere idiot, or common individual, as in Plato's world; it was mixed up with real conditions of real belief. Those revolving mirrors that send messages to the brain of man, that light that breaks upon the brain, these had truly revealed to God himself the path to Bethany or the light on the high rock of Jerusalem. These ears that resound with common noises had reported also to the secret knowledge of God the noise of the crowd

1 Servant of the servants of God.

that strewed palms and the crowd that cried for Crucifixion. After the Incarnation had become the idea that is central in our civilization, it was inevitable that there should be a return to materialism, in the sense of the serious value of matter and the making of the body. When once Christ had risen, it was inevitable that Aristotle should rise again.

Those are three real reasons, and very sufficient reasons, for the general support given by the saint to a solid and objective philosophy. And yet there was something else, very vast and vague, to which I have tried to give a faint expression by the interposition of this chapter. It is difficult to express it fully, without the awful peril of being popular, or what the Modernists quite wrongly imagine to be popular; in short, passing from religion to religiosity. But there is a general tone and temper of Aquinas, which it is as difficult to avoid as daylight in a great house of windows. It is that *positive* position of his mind, which is filled and soaked as with sunshine with the warmth of the wonder of created things. There is a certain private audacity, in his communion, by which men add to their private names the tremendous titles of the Trinity and the Redemption; so that some nun may be called 'of the Holy Ghost'; or a man bear such a burden as the title of St John of the Cross. In this sense, the man we study may specially be called St Thomas of the Creator. The Arabs have a phrase about the hundred names of God; but they also inherit the tradition of a tremendous name unspeakable because it expresses Being itself, dumb and yet dreadful as an instant inaudible shout; the proclamation of the Absolute. And perhaps no other man ever came so near to calling the Creator by His own name, which can only be written I Am.

VI

THE APPROACH TO THOMISM

THE FACT that Thomism is the philosophy of common sense is itself a matter of common sense. Yet it wants a word of explanation, because we have so long taken such matters in a very uncommon sense. For good or evil, Europe since the Reformation, and most especially England since the Reformation, has been in a peculiar sense the home of paradox. I mean in the very peculiar sense that paradox was at home, and that men were at home with it. The most familiar example is the English boasting that they are practical *because* they are not logical. To an ancient Greek or a Chinaman this would seem exactly like saying that London clerks excel in adding up their ledgers, because they are not accurate in their arithmetic. But the point is not that it is a paradox; it is that parodoxy has become orthodoxy; that men repose in a paradox as placidly as in a platitude. It is not that the practical man stands on his head, which may sometimes be a stimulating if startling gymnastic; it is that he *rests* on his head; and even sleeps on his head. This is an important point, because the use of paradox is to awaken the mind. Take a good paradox, like that of Oliver Wendell Holmes: 'Give us the luxuries of life and we will dispense with the necessities.' It is amusing and therefore arresting; it has a fine air of defiance; it contains a real if romantic truth. It is all part of the fun that it is stated almost in the form of a contradiction in terms. But most people would agree that there would be considerable danger in basing the whole social system on the notion that necessaries are not necessary; as some have based the whole British Constitution on the notion that nonsense will always work out as common sense. Yet even here, it might be said that the invidious example has spread, and that the modern industrial system does really say, 'Give us luxuries like coal-tar soap, and we will dispense with necessities like corn.'

So much is familiar; but what is not even now realized is that not only the practical politics, but the abstract philosophies of the modern world have had this queer twist. Since the modern world began in the sixteenth century, nobody's system of philosophy has really corresponded to everybody's sense of reality; to what, if left to themselves, common men would call common sense. Each started with a paradox; a peculiar point of view demanding the sacrifice of what they would call a sane point of view. That is the one thing common to Hobbes and Hegel, to Kant and Bergson, to Berkeley and William James. A man had to believe something that no normal man would believe, if it were suddenly propounded to his simplicity; as that law is above right, or right is outside reason, or things are only as we think them, or everything is relative to a reality that is not there. The modern philosopher claims, like a sort of confidence man, that if once we will grant him this, the rest will be easy; he will straighten out the world, if once he is allowed to give this one twist to the mind.

It will be understood that in these matters I speak as a fool; or, as our democratic cousins would say, a moron; anyhow as a man in the street; and the only object of this chapter is to show that the Thomist philosophy is nearer than most philosophies to the mind of the man in the street. . . .

The Hegelian may say that an egg is really a hen, because it is a part of an endless process of Becoming; the Berkeleian may hold that poached eggs only exist as a dream exists; since it is quite as easy to call the dream the cause of the eggs as the eggs the cause of the dream; the Pragmatist may believe that we get the best out of scrambled eggs by forgetting that they ever were eggs, and only remembering the scramble. But no pupil of St Thomas needs to addle his brains in order adequately to addle his eggs; to put his head at any peculiar angle in looking at eggs, or squinting at eggs, or winking the other eye in order to see a new simplification of eggs. The Thomist stands in the broad daylight of the brotherhood of men, in their common consciousness that eggs are not hens or dreams or mere practical assumptions; but things attested by the Authority of the Senses, which is from God.

Thus, even those who appreciate the metaphysical depth of Thomism in other matters have expressed surprise that he does not deal at all with what many now think the main metaphysical question; whether we can prove that the primary act of recognition of any reality is real. The answer is that St Thomas recognized instantly, what so many modern sceptics have begun to suspect rather laboriously; that a man must either answer that question in the affirmative, or else never answer any question, never ask any question, never even exist intellectually, to answer or to ask. I suppose it is true in a sense that a man can be a fundamental sceptic, but he cannot be anything else; certainly not even a defender of fundamental scepticism. If a man feels that all the movements of his own mind are meaningless, then his mind is meaningless, and he is meaningless; and it does not mean anything to attempt to discover his meaning. Most fundamental sceptics appear to survive, because they are not consistently sceptical and not at all fundamental. They will first deny everything and then admit something, if for the sake of argument – or often rather of attack without argument. I saw an almost startling example of this essential frivolity in the professor of final scepticism, in a paper the other day. A man wrote to say that he accepted nothing but Solipsism, and added that he had often wondered it was not a more common philosophy. Now Solipsism simply means that a man believes in his own existence, but not in anybody or anything else. And it never struck this simple sophist, that if his philosophy was true, there obviously were no other philosophers to profess it.

To this question 'Is there anything?' St Thomas begins by answering 'Yes'; if he began by answering 'No', it would not be the beginning, but the end. That is what some of us call common sense. Either there is no philosophy, no philosophers, no thinkers, no thought, no anything; or else there is a real bridge between the mind and reality. But he is actually less exacting than many thinkers, much less so than most rationalist and materialist thinkers, as to what that first step involves; he is content, as we shall see, to say that it involves the recognition of Ens or Being as something definitely beyond ourselves. Ens is Ens: Eggs are eggs, and it is not tenable that all eggs were found in a mare's nest.

Needless to say, I am not so silly as to suggest that all the writings of St Thomas are simple and straightforward; in the sense of being easy to understand. There are passages I do not in the least understand myself; there are passages that puzzle much more learned and logical philosophers than I am; there are passages about which the greatest Thomists still differ and dispute. But that is a question of a thing being hard to read or understand: not hard to accept when understood. That is a mere matter of 'The Cat sat on the Mat' being written in Chinese characters; or 'Mary had a Little Lamb' in Egyptian hieroglyphics. The only point I am stressing here is that Aquinas is almost always on the side of simplicity, and supports the ordinary man's acceptance of ordinary truisms. For instance, one of the most obscure passages, in my very inadequate judgment, is that in which he explains how the mind is certain of an external object and not merely of an impression of that object; and yet apparently reaches it through a concept, though not merely through an impression. But the only point here is that he does explain that the mind is certain of an external object. It is enough for this purpose that his conclusion is what is called the conclusion of common sense; that it is his purpose to justify common sense; even though he justifies it in a passage which happens to be one of rather uncommon subtlety. The problem of later philosophers is that their conclusion is as dark as their demonstration; or that they bring out a result of which the result is chaos.

Unfortunately, between the man in the street and the Angel of the Schools, there stands at this moment a very high brick wall, with spikes on the top, separating two men who in many ways stand for the same thing. The wall is almost a historical accident; at least it was built a very long time ago, for reasons that need not affect the needs of normal men today; least of all the greatest need of normal men; which is for a normal philosophy. The first difficulty is merely a difference of form; not in the mediaeval but in the modern sense. There is first a simple obstacle of language; there is then a rather more subtle obstacle of logical method. But the language itself counts for a great deal; even when it is translated, it is still a foreign language; and it is, like other foreign languages, very often translated wrong. As with every other literature from another age or country, it carried with it an atmosphere which is beyond the mere translation of words, as they are translated in a traveller's phrase-book. For instance, the whole system of St Thomas hangs on one huge and yet simple idea; which does actually cover everything there is, and even everything that could possibly be. He represents this cosmic conception by the word *Ens*; and anybody who can read any Latin at all, however rudely, feels it to be the apt and fitting word; exactly as he feels it in a French word in a piece of good French prose. It ought to be a matter of logic; but it is also a matter of language.

Unfortunately there is no satisfying translation of the word *Ens*. The difficulty is rather verbal than logical, but it is practical. I mean that when the translator says in English 'being', we are aware of a rather different atmosphere. Atmosphere ought not to affect these absolutes of the intellect; but it does. The new psychologists, who are almost eagerly at war with reason, never tire of telling us that the very terms we use are coloured by our subconsciousness, with something we meant to exclude from our consciousness. And one need not be so idealistically irrational as a modern psychologist, in order to admit that the very shape and sound of words do make a difference, even in the baldest prose, as they do in the most beautiful poetry. We cannot quite prevent the imagination from remembering irrelevant associations even in the abstract sciences like mathematics. Jones Minimus, hustled from history to geometry, may for an instant connect the Angles of the isosceles triangle with the Angles of the Anglo-Saxon Chronicle; and even the mature mathematician, if he is as mad as the psychoanalyst hopes, may have in the roots of his subconscious mind something material in his idea of a root. Now it unfortunately happens that the word 'being', as it comes to a modern Englishman, through modern associations, has a sort of hazy atmosphere that is not in the short and sharp Latin word. Perhaps it reminds him of fantastic professors in fiction, who wave their hands and say, 'Thus do we mount to the ineffable heights of pure and radiant Being'; or, worse still, of actual professors in real life, who say, 'All Being is Becoming; and is but the evolution of Not-Being by the law of its Being.' Perhaps it only reminds him of romantic rhapsodies in old love stories; 'Beautiful and adorable being, light and breath of my very being.' Anyhow it has a wild and woolly sort of sound; as if only very vague people used it; or as if it might mean all sorts of different things.

Now the Latin word *Ens* has a sound like the English word *End*. It is final and even abrupt; it is nothing except itself. There was once a silly gibe against Scholastics like Aquinas, that they discussed whether angels could stand on the point of a needle. It is at least certain that this first word of Aquinas is as sharp as the point of a pin. For that also is, in an almost ideal sense, an End. But when we say that St Thomas Aquinas is concerned fundamentally with the idea of Being, we must not admit any of the cloudier generalizations that we may have grown used to, or even grown tired of, in the sort of idealistic writing that is rather rhetoric than philosophy. Rhetoric is a very fine thing in its place, as a mediaeval scholar would have willingly agreed, as he taught it along with logic in the schools; but St Thomas Aquinas himself is not at all rhetorical. Perhaps he is hardly even sufficiently rhetorical. There are any number of purple patches in Augustine; but there are no purple patches in Aquinas. He did on certain definite occasions drop into poetry; but he very seldom dropped into oratory. And so little was he in touch with some modern tendencies, that whenever he did write poetry, he actually put it into poems. There is another side to this, to be noted later. He very specially possessed the philosophy that inspires poetry; as he did so largely inspire Dante's poetry. And poetry without philosophy has only inspiration, or, in vulgar language, only wind. He had, so to speak, the imagination without the imagery. And even this is perhaps too sweeping. There is an image of his, that is true poetry as well as true philosophy; about the tree of life bowing down with a huge humility, because of the very load of its living fruitfulness; a thing Dante might have described so as to overwhelm us with the tremendous twilight and almost drug us with the divine fruit. But normally, we may say that his words are brief even when his books are long. I have taken the example of the word *Ens*, precisely because it is one of the cases in which Latin is plainer than plain English. And his style, unlike that of St Augustine and many Catholic Doctors, is always a penny plain rather than twopence coloured. It is often difficult to understand, simply because the subjects are so difficult that hardly any mind, except one like his own, can fully understand them. But he never darkens it by using words without knowledge, or even more legitimately, by using words belonging only to imagination or intuition. So far as his method is concerned, he is perhaps the one real Rationalist among all the children of men.

This brings us to the other difficulty; that of logical method. I have never understood why there is supposed to be something crabbed or antique about a syllogism; still less can I understand what anybody means by talking as if induction had somehow taken the place of deduction. The whole point of deduction is that true premises produce a true conclusion. What is called induction seems simply to mean collecting a larger number of true premises, or perhaps, in some physical matters, taking rather more trouble to see that they are true. It may be a fact that a modern man can get more out of a great many premises, concerning microbes or asteroids, than a mediaeval man could get out of a very few premises about salamanders and unicorns. But the process of deduction from the data is the same for the modern mind as for the mediaeval mind; and what is pompously called induction is simply collecting more of the data. And Aristotle or Aquinas, or anybody in his five wits, would of course agree that the conclusion could only be true if the premises were true; and that the more true premises there were the better. It was the misfortune of mediaeval culture that there were not enough true premises, owing to the rather ruder conditions of travel or experiment. But however perfect were the conditions of travel or experiment, they could only produce premises; it would still be necessary to deduce conclusions. But many modern people talk as if what they call induction were some magic way of reaching a conclusion, without using any of those horrid old syllogisms. But induction does not lead us to a conclusion. Induction only leads us to a deduction. Unless the last three syllogistic steps are all right, the conclusion is all wrong. Thus, the great nineteenth-century men of science, whom I was brought up to revere ('accepting the conclusions of science', it was always called), went out and closely inspected the air and the earth, the chemicals and the gases, doubtless more closely than Aristotle or Aquinas, and then came back and embodied their final conclusion in a syllogism. 'All matter is made of microscopic little knobs which are indivisible. My body is made of matter. Therefore my body is made of microscopic little knobs which are indivisible.' They were not wrong in the form of their reasoning; because it is the only way to reason. In this world there is nothing except a syllogism – and a fallacy. But of course these modern men knew, as the mediaeval men knew, that their conclusions would not be true unless their premises were true. And that is where the trouble began. For the men of science, or their sons and nephews, went out and took another look at the knobby nature of matter; and were surprised to find that it was not knobby at all. So they came back and completed the process with their syllogism; 'All matter is made of whirling protons and electrons. My body is made of matter. Therefore my body is made of whirling protons and electrons.' And that again is a good syllogism; though they may have to look at matter once or twice more, before we know whether it is a true premise and a true conclusion. But in the final process of truth there is nothing else except a good syllogism. The only other thing is a bad syllogism; as in the familiar fashionable shape; 'All matter is made of protons and electrons. I should very much like to think that mind is much the same as matter. So I will announce, through the microphone or the megaphone, that my mind is made of protons and electrons.' But that is not induction; it is only a very bad blunder in deduction. That is not another or new way of thinking; it is only ceasing to think.

What is really meant, and what is much more reasonable, is that the old syllogists sometimes set out the syllogism at length; and certainly that is not always necessary. A man can run down the three steps much more quickly than that; but a man cannot run down the three steps if they are not there. If he does, he will break his neck, as if he walked out of a fourth-storey window. The truth about this false antithesis of induction and deduction is simply this; that as premises or data accumulated, the emphasis and detail was shifted to them, from the final deduction to which they lead. But they did lead to a final deduction; or else they led to nothing. The logician had so much to say about electrons or microbes that he dwelt most on these data and shortened or assumed his ultimate syllogism. But if he reasoned rightly, however rapidly, he reasoned syllogistically.

As a matter of fact, Aquinas does not usually argue in syllogisms; though he always argues syllogistically. I mean he does not set out all the steps of the logic in each case; the legend that he does so is part of that loose and largely unverified legend of the Renaissance; that the Schoolmen were all crabbed and mechanical mediaeval bores. But he does argue with a certain austerity, and disdain of ornament, which may make him seem monotonous to anyone specially seeking the modern forms of wit or fancy. But all this has nothing to do with the question asked at the beginning of this chapter and needing to be answered at the end of it; the question of what he is arguing for. In that respect it can be repeated, most emphatically, that he is arguing for common sense. He is arguing for a common sense which would even now commend itself to most of the common people. He is arguing for the popular proverbs that seeing is believing; that the proof of the pudding is in the eating; that a man cannot jump down his own throat or deny the fact of his own existence. He often maintains the view by the use of abstractions; but the abstractions are no more abstract than Energy or Evolution or Space-Time; and they do not land us, as the others often do, in hopeless contradictions about common life. The Pragmatist sets out to be practical, but his practicality turns out to be entirely theoretical. The Thomist begins by being theoretical, but his theory turns out to be entirely practical. That is why a great part of the world is returning to it today.

Finally, there is some real difficulty in the fact of a foreign language; apart from the ordinary fact of the Latin language. Modern philosophical terminology is not always exactly identical with plain English; and mediaeval philosophical terminology is not at all identical even with modern philosophical terminology. It is not really very difficult to learn the meaning of the main terms; but their mediaeval meaning is sometimes the exact opposite of their modern meaning. The obvious example is in the pivotal word 'form'. We say nowadays, 'I wrote a formal apology to the Dean', or 'The proceedings when we wound up the Tip-Cat Club were purely formal'. But we mean that they were purely fictitious; and St Thomas, had he been a member of the Tip-Cat Club, would have meant just the opposite. He would have meant that the proceedings dealt with the very heart and soul and secret of the whole being of the Tip-Cat Club; and that the apology to the Dean was so essentially apologetic that it tore the very heart out in tears of true contrition. For 'formal' in Thomist language means actual, or possessing the real decisive quality that makes a thing itself. Roughly when he describes a thing as made out of Form and Matter, he very rightly recognizes that Matter is the more mysterious and indefinite and featureless element; and that what stamps anything with its own identity is its Form. Matter, so to speak, is not so much the solid as the liquid or gaseous thing in the cosmos; and in this most modern scientists are beginning to agree with him. But the form is the fact; it is that which makes a brick a brick, and a bust a bust, and not the shapeless and trampled clay of which either may be made. The stone that broke a statuette, in some

Gothic niche, might have been itself a statuette; and under chemical analysis, the statuette is only a stone. But such a chemical analysis is entirely false as a philosophical analysis. The reality, the thing that makes the two things real, is in the idea of the image and in the idea of the image-breaker. This is only a passing example of the mere idiom of the Thomist terminology; but it is not a bad prefatory specimen of the truth of Thomist thought. Every artist knows that the form is not superficial but fundamental; that the form is the foundation. Every sculptor knows that the form of the statue is not the outside of the statue, but rather the inside of the statue; even in the sense of the inside of the sculptor. Every poet knows that the sonnet-form is not only the form of the poem; but the poem. No modern critic who does not understand what the mediaeval Schoolman meant by form can meet the Schoolman as an intellectual equal.

VII
THE PERMANENT PHILOSOPHY

IT IS a pity that the word Anthropology has been degraded to the study of Anthropoids. It is now incurably associated with squabbles between prehistoric professors (in more senses than one) about whether a chip of stone is the tooth of a man or an ape; sometimes settled as in that famous case, when it was found to be the tooth of a pig. It is very right that there should be a purely physical science of such things; but the name commonly used might well, by analogy, have been dedicated to things not only wider and deeper, but rather more relevant. Just as, in America, the new Humanists have pointed out to the old Humanitarians that their humanitarianism has been largely concentrated on things that are *not* specially human, such as physical conditions, appetites, economic needs, environment and so on – so in practice those who are called Anthropologists have to narrow their minds to the materialistic things that are *not* notably anthropic. They have to hunt through history and pre-history something which emphatically is *not* *Homo Sapiens*, but is always in fact regarded as *Simius Insipiens*. *Homo Sapiens* can only be considered in relation to *Sapientia*; and only a book like that of St Thomas is really devoted to the intrinsic idea of *Sapientia*. In short, there ought to be a real study called Anthropology corresponding to Theology. In this sense St Thomas Aquinas, perhaps more than he is anything else, is a great anthropologist.

I apologize for the opening words of this chapter to all those excellent and eminent men of science, who are engaged in the real study of humanity in its relation to biology. But I rather fancy that they will be the last to deny that there has been a somewhat disproportionate disposition, in popular science, to turn the study of human beings into the study of savages. And savagery is not history: it is either the beginning of history or the end of it. I suspect that the greatest scientists would agree that only too many professors have thus been lost in the bush or the jungle; professors who wanted to study anthropology and never got any further than anthropophagy. But I have a particular reason for prefacing this suggestion of a higher anthropology by an apology to any genuine biologists who might seem to be included, but are certainly not included, in a protest against cheap popular science. For the first thing to be said about St Thomas as an anthropologist, is that he is really remarkably like the best sort of modern biological anthropologist; of the sort who would call themselves Agnostics. This fact is so sharp and decisive a turning point in history, that the history really needs to be recalled and recorded.

St Thomas Aquinas closely resembles the great Professor Huxley, the Agnostic who invented the word Agnosticism. He is like him in his way of starting the argument, and he is unlike everybody else, before and after, until the Huxleyan age. He adopts almost literally the Huxleyan definition of the Agnostic method; 'To follow reason as far as it will go'; the only question is – where does it go? He lays down the almost startlingly modern or materialist statement; 'Everything that is in the intellect has been in the senses'. This is where he began, as much as any modern man of science, nay, as much as any modern materialist who can now hardly be called a man of science; at the very opposite end of enquiry from that of the mere mystic. The Platonists, or at least the Neo-Platonists, all tended to the view that the mind was lit entirely from within; St Thomas insisted that it was lit by five windows, that we call the windows of the senses. But he wanted the light from without to shine on what was within. He wanted to study the nature of Man, and not merely of such moss and mushrooms as he might see through the window, and which he valued as the first enlightening experience of man. And starting from this point, he proceeds to climb the House of Man, step by step and story by story, until he has come out on the highest tower and beheld the largest vision.

In other words, he is an anthropologist, with a complete theory of Man, right or wrong. Now the modern Anthropologists, who called themselves Agnostics, completely failed to be Anthropologists at all. Under their limitations, they could not get a complete theory of Man, let alone a complete theory of nature. They began by ruling out something which they called the Unknowable. The incomprehensibility was almost comprehensible, if we could really understand the Unknowable in the sense of the Ultimate. But it rapidly became apparent that all sorts of things were Unknowable, which were exactly the things that a man has got to know. It is necessary to know whether he is responsible or irresponsible, perfect or imperfect, perfectible or unperfectible, mortal or immortal, doomed or free, not in order to understand God, but in order to understand Man. Nothing that leaves these things under a cloud of religious doubt can possibly pretend to be a Science of Man; it shrinks from anthropology as completely as from theology. Has a man free will; or is his sense of choice an illusion? Has he a conscience, or has his conscience any authority; or is it only the prejudice of the tribal past? Is there any real hope of settling these things by human reason; and has *that* any authority? Is he to regard death as final; and is he to regard miraculous help as possible? Now it is all nonsense to say that these are unknowable in any remote sense, like the distinction between the Cherubim and the Seraphim, or the Procession of the Holy Ghost. The Schoolmen may have shot too far beyond our limits in pursuing the Cherubim and Seraphim. But in asking whether a man can choose or whether a man will die, they were asking ordinary questions in natural history; like whether a cat can scratch or whether a dog can smell. Nothing calling itself a complete Science of Man can shirk them. And the great Agnostics did shirk them. They may have said they had no scientific evidence; in that case they failed to produce even a scientific hypothesis. What they generally did produce was a wildly unscientific contradiction. Most Monist moralists simply said that Man has no choice; but he must think and act heroically as if he had. Huxley made morality, and even Victorian morality, in the exact sense, supernatural. He said it had arbitrary rights above nature; a sort of theology without theism.

I do not know for certain why St Thomas was called the Angelic Doctor; whether it was that he had an angelic temper, or the intellectuality of an Angel; or whether there was a later legend that he concentrated on Angels – especially on the points of needles. If so, I do not quite understand how this idea arose; history has many examples of an irritating habit of labelling somebody in connection with something, as if he never did anything else. Who was it who began the inane habit of referring to Dr Johnson as 'our lexicographer'; as if he never did anything but write a dictionary? Why do most people insist on meeting the large and far-reaching mind of Pascal at its very narrowest point; the point at which it was sharpened into a spike by the spite of the Jansenists against the Jesuits? It is just possible, for all I know, that this labelling of Aquinas as a specialist was an obscure depreciation of him as a universalist. For that is a very common trick for the belittling of literary or scientific men. St Thomas must have made a certain number of enemies, though he hardly ever treated them as enemies. Unfortunately, good temper is sometimes more irritating than bad temper. And he had, after all, done a great deal of damage, as many mediaeval men would have thought; and, what is more curious, a great deal of damage to both sides. He had been a revolutionist against Augustine and a traditionalist against Averrhoes. He might appear to some to have tried to wreck that ancient beauty of the city of God, which bore some resemblance to the Republic of Plato. He might appear to others to have inflicted a blow on the advancing and levelling forces of Islam, as dramatic as that of Godfrey storming Jerusalem. It is possible that these enemies, by way of damning with faint praise, talked about his very respectable little work on Angels: as a man might say that Darwin was really reliable when writing on coral-insects; or that some of Milton's Latin poems were very creditable indeed. But this is only a conjecture, and many other conjectures are possible. And I am disposed to think that St Thomas really was rather specially interested in the nature of Angels, for the same reason that made him even more interested in the nature of Men. It was a part of that strong personal interest in things subordinate and semidependent, which runs through his whole system: a hierarchy of higher and lower liberties. He was interested in the problem of the Angel, as he was interested in the problem of the Man, because it was a problem; and especially because it was a problem of an intermediate creature. I do not pretend to deal here with this mysterious quality, as he conceives it to exist in that inscrutable intellectual being, who is less than God but more than Man. But it was this quality of a link in the chain, or a rung in the ladder, which mainly concerned the theologian, in developing his own particular theory of degrees. Above all, it is this which chiefly moves him, when he finds so fascinating the central mystery of Man. And for him the point is always that Man is not a balloon going up into the sky, nor a mole burrowing merely in the earth; but rather a thing like a tree, whose roots are fed from the earth, while its highest branches seem to rise almost to the stars.

I have pointed out that mere modern free-thought has left everything in a fog, including itself. The assertion that thought is free led first to the denial that will is free; but even about that there was no real determination among the Determinists. In practice, they told men that they must treat their will as free though it was not free. In other words, Man must live a double life; which is exactly the old heresy of Siger of Brabant about the Double Mind. In other words, the nineteenth century left everything in chaos; and the importance of Thomism to the twentieth century is that it may give us back a cosmos. We can give here only the rudest sketch of how Aquinas, like the Agnostics, beginning in the cosmic cellars, yet climbed to the cosmic towers.

Without pretending to span within such limits the essential Thomist idea, I may be allowed to throw out a sort of rough version of the fundamental question, which I think I have known myself, consciously or unconsciously since my childhood. When a child looks out of the nursery window and sees anything, say the green lawn of the garden, what does he actually know; or does he know anything? There are all sorts of nursery games of negative philosophy played round this question. A brilliant Victorian scientist delighted in declaring that the child does not see any grass at all; but only a sort of green mist reflected in a tiny mirror of the human eye. This piece of rationalism has always struck me as almost insanely irrational. If he is not sure of the existence of the grass, which he sees through the glass of a window, how on earth can he be sure of the existence of the retina, which he sees through the glass of a microscope? If sight deceives, why can it not go on deceiving? Men of another school answer that grass is a mere green impression on the mind; and that he can be sure of nothing except the mind. They declare that he can only be conscious of his own consciousness; which happens to be the one thing that we know the child is not conscious of at all. In that sense, it would be far truer to say that there is grass and no child, than to say that there is a conscious child but no grass. St Thomas Aquinas, suddenly intervening in this nursery quarrel, says emphatically that the child is aware of *Ens*. Long before he knows that grass is grass, or self is self, he knows that something is something. Perhaps it would be best to say very emphatically (with a blow on the table), 'There *is* an Is'. That is as much monkish credulity as St Thomas asks of us at the start. Very few unbelievers start by asking us to believe so little. And yet, upon this sharp pin-point of reality, he rears by long logical processes that have never really been successfully overthrown, the whole cosmic system of Christendom.

Thus, Aquinas insists very profoundly, but very practically, that there *instantly* enters, with this idea of affirmation, the idea of contradiction. It is instantly apparent, even to the child, that there cannot be both affirmation and contradiction. Whatever you call the thing he sees, a moon or a mirage or a sensation or a state of consciousness, when he sees it, he knows it is not true that he does not see it. Or whatever you call what he is supposed to be doing, seeing or dreaming or being conscious of an impression, he knows that if he is doing it, it is a lie to say he is not doing it. Therefore there has already entered *something* beyond even the first fact of being; there follows it like its shadow the first fundamental creed or commandment; that a thing cannot be and not be. Henceforth, in common or popular language, there is a false and true. I say in popular language, because Aquinas is nowhere more subtle than in pointing out that being is not strictly the same as truth; seeing truth must mean the appreciation of being by some mind capable of appreciating it. But in a general sense there has entered that primeval world of pure actuality, the division and dilemma that brings the ultimate sort of war into the world; the everlasting duel between Yes and No. This is the dilemma that many sceptics have darkened the universe and dissolved the mind, solely in order to escape. They are those who maintain that there is something that is both Yes and No. I do not know whether they pronounce it Yo.

The next step following on this acceptance of actuality or certainty, or whatever we call it in popular language, is much more difficult to explain in that language. But it represents exactly the point at which nearly all other systems go wrong, and in taking the third step abandon the first. Aquinas has affirmed that our first sense of fact is a fact; and he cannot go back on it without falsehood. But when we come to look at the fact or facts, as we know them, we observe that they have a rather queer character; which has made many moderns grow strangely and restlessly sceptical about them. For instance, they are largely in a state of change, from being one thing to being another; or their qualities are relative to other things; or they appear to move incessantly; or they appear to vanish entirely. At this point, as I say, many sages lose hold of the first principle of reality, which they would concede at first; and fall back on saying that there is nothing except change; or nothing except comparison; or nothing except flux; or in effect that there is nothing at all. Aquinas turns the whole argument the other way, keeping in line with his first realization of reality. There is no doubt about the being of being, even if it does sometimes look like becoming; that is because what we see is not the fulness of being; or (to continue a sort of colloquial slang) we never see being being as much as it can. Ice is melted into cold water and cold water is heated into hot water; it cannot be all three at once. But this does not make water unreal or even relative; it only means that its being is limited to being one thing at a time. But the fulness of being is everything that it can be; and without it the lesser or approximate forms of being cannot be explained as anything; unless they are explained away as nothing.

This crude outline can only at the best be historical rather than philosophical. It is impossible to compress into it the metaphysical proofs of such an idea; especially in the mediaeval metaphysical language. But this distinction in philosophy is tremendous as a turning point in history. Most thinkers, on realizing the apparent mutability of being, have really forgotten their own realization of the being, and believed only in the mutability. They cannot even say that a thing changes into another thing; for them there is no instant in the process at which it is a thing at all. It is only a change. It would be more logical to call it nothing changing into nothing, than to say (on these principles) that there ever was or will be a moment when the thing is itself. St Thomas maintains that the ordinary thing at any moment is something; but it is not everything that it could be. There is a fulness of being, in which it could be everything that it can be. Thus, while most sages come at last to nothing but naked change, he comes to the ultimate thing that is unchangeable, because it is all the other things at once. While they describe a change which is really a change in nothing, he describes a changelessness which includes the changes of everything. Things change because they are not complete; but their reality can only be explained as part of something that is complete. It is God.

Historically, at least, it was round this sharp and crooked corner that all the sophists have followed each other while the great Schoolman went up the high road of experience and expansion; to the beholding of cities, to the building of cities. They all failed at this early stage because, in the words of the old game, they took away the number they first thought of. The recognition of something, of a thing or things, is the first act of the intellect. But because the examination of a thing shows it is not a fixed or final thing, they inferred that there is nothing fixed or final. Thus, in various ways, they all began to see a thing as something thinner than a thing; a wave; a weakness; an abstract instability. St Thomas, to use the same rude figure, saw a thing that was thicker than a thing; that was even more solid than the solid but secondary facts he had started by admitting as facts. Since we know them to be real, any elusive or bewildering element in their reality cannot really be unreality; and must be merely their relation to the real reality. A hundred human philosophies, ranging over the earth from Nominalism to Nirvana and Maya, from formless evolutionism to mindless quietism, all come from this first break in the Thomist chain; the notion that, because what we see does not satisfy us or explain itself, it is not even what we see. That cosmos is a contradiction in terms and strangles itself; but Thomism cuts itself free. The defect we see, in what is, is simply that it is not all that is. God is more actual even than Man; more actual even than Matter; for God with all His powers at every instant is immortally in action.

A cosmic comedy of a very curious sort occurred recently; involving the views of very brilliant men, such as Mr Bernard Shaw and the Dean of St Paul's. Briefly, freethinkers of many sorts had often said they had no need of a Creation, because the cosmos had always existed and always would exist. Mr Bernard Shaw said he had become an atheist because the universe had gone on making itself from the beginning or without a beginning; Dean Inge later displayed consternation at the very idea that the universe could have an end. Most modern Christians, living by tradition where mediaeval Christians could live by logic or reason, vaguely felt that it was a dreadful idea to deprive them of the Day of Judgment. Most modern agnostics (who are delighted to have their ideas called dreadful) cried out all the more, with one accord, that the self-producing, self-existent, truly scientific universe had never needed to have a beginning and could not come to an end. At this very instant, quite suddenly, like the look-out man on a ship who shouts a warning about a rock, the *real* man of science, the expert who was examining the facts, announced in a loud voice that the universe *was* coming to an end. He had not been listening, of course, to the talk of the amateurs; he had been actually examining the texture of matter; and he said it was disintegrating: the world was apparently blowing itself up by a gradual explosion called energy; the whole business would certainly have an end and had presumably had a beginning. This was very shocking indeed; not to the orthodox, but rather specially to the unorthodox; who are rather more easily shocked. Dean Inge, who had been lecturing the orthodox for years on their stern duty of accepting all scientific discoveries, positively wailed aloud over this truly tactless scientific discovery; and practically implored the scientific discoverers to go away and discover something different. It seems almost incredible; but it is a fact that he asked what God would have to amuse Him, if the universe ceased. That is a measure of how much the modern mind needs Thomas Aquinas. But even without Aquinas, I can hardly conceive any educated man, let alone such a learned man, believing in God at all without assuming that God contains in Himself every perfection including eternal joy; and does not require the solar system to entertain him like a circus.

To step out of these presumptions, prejudices and private disappointments, into the world of St Thomas, is like escaping from a scuffle in a dark room into the broad daylight. St Thomas says, quite straightforwardly, that he himself believes this world has a beginning and end; because such seems to be the teaching of the Church; the validity of which mystical message to mankind he defends elsewhere with dozens of quite different arguments. Anyhow, the Church said the world would end; and apparently the Church was right; always supposing (as we are always supposed to suppose) that the latest men of science are right. But Aquinas says he sees no particular reason, in reason, why this world should not be a world without end; or even without beginning. And he is quite certain that, if it were entirely without end or beginning, there would still be exactly the same logical need of a Creator. Anybody who does not see that, he gently implies, does not really understand what is meant by a Creator.

For what St Thomas means is not a mediaeval picture of an old king; but this second step in the great argument about *Ens* or Being; the second point which is so desperately difficult to put correctly in popular language. That is why I have introduced it here in the particular form of the argument that there must be a Creator even if there is no Day of Creation. Looking at Being as it is now, as the baby looks at the grass, we see a second thing about it; in quite popular language, it *looks* secondary and dependent. Existence exists; but it is not sufficiently self-existent; and would never become so merely by going on existing. The same primary sense which tells us it is Being, tells us that it is not perfect Being; not merely imperfect in the popular controversial sense of containing sin or sorrow; but imperfect as Being; less actual than the actuality it implies. For instance, its Being is often only Becoming; beginning to Be or ceasing to Be; it implies a more constant or complete thing of which it gives in itself no example. That is the meaning of that basic mediaeval phrase, 'Everything that is moving is moved by another'; which, in the clear subtlety of St Thomas, means inexpressibly more than the mere Deistic 'somebody wound up the clock' with which it is probably often confounded. Anyone who thinks deeply will see that motion has about it an essential incompleteness, which approximates to something more complete.

The actual argument is rather technical; and concerns the fact that potentiality does not explain itself; moreover, in any case, unfolding must be of something folded. Suffice it to say that the mere modern evolutionists, who would ignore the argument, do not do so because they have discovered any flaw in the argument; for they have never discovered the argument itself. They do so because they are too shallow to see the flaw in their own argument; for the weakness of their thesis is covered by fashionable phraseology, as the strength of the old thesis is covered by old-fashioned phraseology. But for those who really think, there is always something really unthinkable about the whole evolutionary cosmos, as they conceive it; because it is something coming out of nothing; an ever-increasing flood of water pouring out of an empty jug. Those who can simply accept that, without even seeing the difficulty, are not likely to go so deep as Aquinas and see the solution of his difficulty. In a word, the world does not explain itself, and cannot do so merely by continuing to expand itself. But anyhow, it is absurd for the Evolutionist to complain that it is unthinkable for an admittedly unthinkable God to make everything out of nothing, and then pretend that it is *more* thinkable that nothing should turn itself into everything.

We have seen that most philosophers simply fail to philosophize about things because they change; they also fail to philosophize about things because they differ. We have no space to follow St Thomas through all these negative heresies; but a word must be said about Nominalism, or the doubt founded on the things that differ. Everyone knows that the Nominalist declared that things differ too much to be really classified; so that they are only labelled. Aquinas was a firm but moderate Realist, and therefore held that there really are general qualities; as that human beings are human, and other paradoxes. To be an extreme Realist would have taken him too near to being a Platonist. He recognized that individuality is real, but said that it coexists with a common character making some generalization possible; in fact, as in most things, he said exactly what all common sense would say, if no intelligent heretics had ever disturbed it. Nevertheless, they still continue to disturb it. I remember when Mr H. G. Wells had an alarming fit of Nominalist philosophy; and poured forth book after book to argue that everything is unique and untypical; as that a man is so much an individual that he is not even a man. It is a quaint and almost comic fact, that this chaotic negation especially attracts those who are always complaining of social chaos, and who propose to replace it by the most sweeping social regulations. It is the very men who say that nothing can be classified, who say that everything must be codified. Thus Mr Bernard Shaw said that the only golden rule is that there is no golden rule. He prefers an iron rule; as in Russia.

But this is only a small inconsistency in some moderns as individuals. There is a much deeper inconsistency in them as theorists in relation to the general theory called Creative Evolution. They seem to imagine that they avoid the metaphysical doubt about mere change by assuming (it is not very clear why) that the change will always be for the better. But the mathematical difficulty of finding a corner in a curve is not altered by turning the chart upside down, and saying that a downward curve is now an upward curve.

The point is that there is no point in the curve; no place at which we have a logical right to say that the curve has reached its climax, or revealed its origin, or come to its end. It makes no difference that they choose to be cheerful about it, and say, 'It is enough that there is always a beyond'; instead of lamenting, like the more realistic poets of the past, over the tragedy of mere Mutability. It is not enough that there is always a beyond; because it might be beyond bearing. Indeed the only defence of this view is that sheer boredom is such an agony, that any movement is a relief. But the truth is that they have never read St Thomas, or they would find, with no little terror, that they really agree with him. What they really mean is that change is not mere change; but is the unfolding of something; and if it is thus unfolded, though the unfolding takes twelve million years, it must be there already. In other words, they agree with Aquinas that there is everywhere potentiality that has not reached its end in act. But if it is a definite potentiality, and if it can only end in a definite act, why then there is a Great Being, in whom all potentialities already exist as a plan of action. In other words, it is impossible even to say that the change is for the better, unless the best exists somewhere, both before and after the change. Otherwise it is indeed mere change, as the blankest sceptics or the blackest pessimists would see it. Suppose two entirely new paths open before the progress of Creative Evolution. How is the evolutionist to know which Beyond is the better; unless he accepts from the past and present some standard of the best? By their superficial theory everything can change; everything can improve, even the nature of improvement. But in their submerged common sense, they do not really think that an ideal of kindness could change to an ideal of cruelty. It is typical of them that they will sometimes rather timidly use the word Purpose; but blush at the very mention of the word Person.

St Thomas is the very reverse of anthropomorphic, in spite of his shrewdness as an anthropologist. Some theologians have even claimed that he is too much of an agnostic; and has left the nature of God too much of an intellectual abstraction. But we do not need even St Thomas, we do not need anything but our own common sense, to tell us that if there has been from the beginning anything that can possibly be called a Purpose, it must reside in something that has the essential elements of a Person. There cannot be an intention hovering in the air all by itself, any more than a memory that nobody remembers or a joke that nobody has made. The only chance for those supporting such suggestions is to take refuge in blank and bottomless irrationality; and even then it is impossible to prove that anybody has any right to be unreasonable, if St Thomas has no right to be reasonable.

In a sketch that aims only at the baldest simplification, this does seem to me the simplest truth about St Thomas the philosopher. He is one, so to speak, who is faithful to his first love; and it is love at first sight. I mean that he immediately recognized a real quality in things; and afterwards resisted all the disintegrating doubts arising from the nature of those things. That is why I emphasize, even in the first few pages, the fact that there is a sort of purely Christian humility and fidelity underlying his philosophic realism. St Thomas could as truly say, of having seen merely a stick or a stone, what St Paul said of having seen the rending of the secret heavens, 'I was not disobedient to the heavenly vision'. For though the stick or the stone is an earthly vision, it is through them that St Thomas finds his way to heaven; and the point is that he is obedient to the vision; he does not go back on it. Nearly all the other sages who have led or misled mankind do, on one excuse or another, go back on it. They dissolve the stick or the stone in chemical solutions of scepticism, either in the medium of mere time and change; or in the difficulties of classification of unique units; or in the difficulty of recognizing variety while admitting unity. The first of these three is called debate about flux or formless transition; the second is the debate about Nominalism and Realism, or the existence of general ideas; the third is called the ancient metaphysical riddle of the One and the Many. But they can all be reduced under a rough image to this same statement about St Thomas. He is still true to the first truth and refusing the first treason. He will not deny what he has seen, though it be a secondary and diverse reality. He will not take away the numbers he first thought of, though there may be quite a number of them.

He has seen grass; and will not say he has not seen grass, because it today is and tomorrow is cast into the oven. That is the substance of all scepticism about change, transition, transformism and the rest. He will not say that there is no grass but only growth. If grass grows and withers, it can only mean that it is part of a greater thing, which is even more real; not that the grass is less real than it looks. St Thomas has a really logical right to say, in the words of the modern mystic, A. E.: 'I begin by the grass to be bound again to the Lord.'

He has seen grass and grain; and he will not say that they do not differ, because there is something common to grass and grain. Nor will he say that there is nothing common to grass and grain, because they do really differ. He will not say, with the extreme Nominalists, that because grain can be differentiated into all sorts of fruitage, or grass trodden into mire with any kind of weed, therefore there can be no *classification* to distinguish weeds from slime or to draw a fine distinction between cattle-food and cattle. He will not say with the extreme Platonists, on the other hand, that he saw the perfect fruit in his own head by shutting his eyes, *before* he saw any difference between grain and grass. He saw one thing and then another thing, and then a common quality; but he does not really pretend that he saw the quality before the thing.

He has seen grass and gravel; that is to say, he has seen things really different; things not classified together like grass and grain. The first flash of fact shows us a world of really strange things; not merely strange to us, but strange to each other. The separate things need have nothing in common except Being. Everything is Being; but it is not true that everything is Unity. It is here, as I have said, that St Thomas does definitely, one might say defiantly, part company with the Pantheist and Monist. All things are; but among the things that are is the thing called difference, quite as much as the thing called similarity. And here again we begin to be bound again to the Lord, not only by the universality of grass, but by the incompatibility of grass and gravel. For this world of different and varied beings is especially the world of the Christian Creator; the world of created things, like things made by an artist; as compared with the world that is only one thing, with a sort of shimmering and shifting veil of misleading change; which is the conception of so many of the ancient religions of Asia and the modern sophistries of Germany. In the face of these, St Thomas still stands stubborn in the same obstinate objective fidelity. He has seen grass and gravel; and he is not disobedient to the heavenly vision.

To sum up; the reality of things, the mutability of things, the diversity of things, and all other such things that can be attributed to things, is followed carefully by the mediaeval philosopher, without losing touch with the original point of the reality. There is no space in this book to specify the thousand steps of thought by which he shows that he is right. But the point is that, even apart from being right he is real. He is a realist in a rather curious sense of his own, which is a third thing, distinct from the almost contrary mediaeval and modern meanings of the word. Even the doubts and difficulties about reality have driven him to believe in more reality rather than less. The *deceitfulness* of things which has had so sad an effect on so many sages, has almost a contrary effect on this sage. If things deceive us, it is by being more real than they seem. As ends in themselves they always deceive us; but as things tending to a greater end, they are even more real than we think them. If they seem to have a relative unreality (so to speak) it is because they are potential and not actual; they are unfulfilled, like packets of seeds or boxes of fireworks. They have it in them to be more real than they are. And there is an upper world of what the Schoolman called Fruition, or Fulfilment, in which all this relative relativity becomes actuality; in which the trees burst into flower or the rockets into flame.

Here I leave the reader, on the very lowest rung of those ladders of logic, by which St Thomas besieged and mounted the House of Man. It is enough to say that by arguments as honest and laborious, he climbed up to the turrets and talked with angels on the roofs of gold. This is, in a very rude outline, his philosophy; it is impossible in such an outline to describe his theology. Anyone writing so small a book about so big a man, must leave out something. Those who know him best will best understand why, after some considerable consideration, I have left out the only important thing.

VIII
THE SEQUEL TO ST THOMAS

IT IS often said that St Thomas, unlike St Francis, did not permit in his work the indescribable element of poetry: As, for instance, that there is little reference to any pleasure in the actual flowers and fruit of natural things, though any amount of concern with the buried roots of nature. And yet I confess that, in reading his philosophy, I have a very peculiar and powerful impression analogous to poetry. Curiously enough, it is in some ways more analogous to painting, and reminds me very much of the effect produced by the *best* of the modern painters, when they throw a strange and almost crude light upon stark and rectangular objects, or seem to be groping for rather than grasping the very pillars of the subconscious mind. It is probably because there is in his work a quality which is Primitive, in the best sense of a badly misused word; but anyhow, the pleasure is definitely not only of the reason, but also of the imagination.

Perhaps the impression is connected with the fact that painters deal with things without words. An artist draws quite gravely the grand curves of a pig; because he is not thinking of the *word* pig. There is no thinker who is so unmistakably thinking about things and not being misled by the indirect influence of words, as St Thomas Aquinas. It is true in that sense that he has not the advantage of words, any more than the disadvantage of words. Here he differs sharply, for instance, from St Augustine who was, among other things a wit. He was also a sort of prose poet, with a power over words in their atmospheric and emotional aspect; so that his books abound with beautiful passages that rise in the memory like strains of music ... It is true that there is little or nothing of this kind in St Thomas; but if he was without the higher use of the mere magic of words, he was also free from that abuse of it, by mere sentimentalists or self-centred artists, which can become merely morbid and a very black magic indeed. And truly it is by some such comparison with the purely introspective intellectual, that we may find a hint about the real nature of the thing I describe, or rather fail to describe; I mean the elemental and primitive poetry that shines through all his thoughts; and especially through the thought with which all his thinking begins. It is the intense rightness of his sense of the relation between the mind and the real thing outside the mind.

That *strangeness* of things, which is the light in all poetry, and indeed in all art, is really connected with their otherness; or what is called their objectivity. What is subjective must be stale; it is exactly what is objective that is in this imaginative manner strange. In this the great contemplative is the complete contrary of that false contemplative, the mystic who looks only into his own soul, the selfish artist who shrinks from the world and lives only in his own mind. According to St Thomas, the mind acts freely of itself, but its freedom exactly consists in finding a way out to liberty and the light of day; to reality and the land of the living. In the subjectivist, the pressure of the world forces the imagination inwards. In the Thomist, the energy of the mind forces the imagination outwards, but because the images it seeks are real things. All their romance and glamour, so to speak, lies in the fact that they are real things; things *not* to be found by staring inwards at the mind. The flower is a vision because it is not only a vision. Or, if you will, it is a vision because it is not a dream. This is for the poet the strangeness of stones and trees and solid things; they are strange because they are solid. I am putting it first in the poetical manner, and indeed it needs much more technical subtlety to put it in the philosophical manner. According to Aquinas, the object becomes a part of the mind; nay, according to Aquinas, the mind actually becomes the object. But, as one commentator acutely puts it, it only becomes the object and does not create the object. In other words, the object *is* an object; it can and does exist outside the mind, or in the absence of the mind. And *therefore* it enlarges the mind of which it becomes a part. The mind conquers a new province like an emperor; but only because the mind has answered the bell like a servant. The mind has opened the doors and windows, because it is the natural activity of what is inside the house to find out what is outside the house. If the mind is sufficient to itself, it is insufficient for itself. For this feeding upon fact *is* itself; as an organ it has an object which is objective; this eating of the strange strong meat of reality.

Note how this view avoids both pitfalls; the alternative abysses of impotence. The mind is not merely receptive, in the sense that it absorbs sensations like so much blotting-paper; on that sort of softness has been based all that cowardly materialism, which conceives man as wholly servile to his environment. On the other hand, the mind is not purely creative, in the sense that it paints pictures on the windows and then mistakes them for a landscape outside. But the mind is active, and its activity consists in following, so far as the will chooses to follow, the light outside that does really shine upon real landscapes. That is what gives the indefinably virile and even adventurous quality to this view of life; as compared with that which holds that material inferences pour in upon an utterly helpless mind, or that which holds that psychological influences pour out and create an entirely baseless phantasmagoria. In other words, the essence of the Thomist common sense is that two agencies are at work; reality and the recognition of reality; and their meeting is a sort of marriage. Indeed it is very truly a marriage, because it is fruitful; the only philosophy now in the world that really is fruitful. It produces practical results, precisely because it is the combination of an adventurous mind and a strange fact.

. . . Anyhow, upon that marriage, or whatever it may be called, the whole system of St Thomas is founded; God made Man so that he was capable of coming in contact with reality; and those whom God hath joined, let no man put asunder.

Now, it is worthy of remark that it is the only working philosophy. Of nearly all other philosophies it is strictly true that their followers work in spite of them, or do not work at all. No sceptics work sceptically; no fatalists work fatalistically; all without exception work on the principle that it is possible to assume what it is not possible to believe. No materialist who thinks his mind was made up for him, by mud and blood and heredity, has any hesitation in making up his mind. No sceptic who believes that truth is subjective has any hesitation about treating it as objective.

Thus St Thomas's work has a constructive quality absent from almost all cosmic systems after him. For he is already building a house, while the newer speculators are still at the stage of testing the rungs of a ladder, demonstrating the hopeless softness of the unbaked bricks, chemically analysing the spirit in the spirit-level, and generally quarrelling about whether they can even make the tools that will make the house. Aquinas is whole intellectual aeons ahead of them, over and above the common chronological sense of saying a man is in advance of his age; he is ages in advance of our age. For he has thrown out a bridge across the abyss of the first doubt, and found reality beyond and begun to build on it. Most modern philosophies are not philosophy but philosophic doubt; that is, doubt about whether there can be any philosophy. If we accept St Thomas's fundamental act or argument in the acceptance of reality, the further deductions from it will be equally real; they will be things and not words. Unlike Kant and most of the Hegelians, he has a faith that is not merely a doubt about doubt. It is not merely what is commonly called a faith about faith; it is a faith about fact. From this point he can go forward, and deduce and develop and decide, like a man planning a city and sitting in a judgment-seat. But never since that time has any thinking man of that eminence thought that there is any real evidence for anything, not even the evidence of his senses, that was strong enough to bear the weight of a definite deduction.

From all this we may easily infer that this philosopher does not merely touch on social things, or even take them in his stride to spiritual things; though that is always his direction. He takes hold of them, he has not only a grasp of them, but a grip. As all his controversies prove, he was perhaps a perfect example of the iron hand in the velvet glove. He was a man who always turned his full attention to anything; and he seems to fix even passing things as they pass. To him even what was momentary was momentous. The reader feels that any small point of economic habit or human accident is for the moment almost scorched under the converging rays of a magnifying lens. It is impossible to put in these pages a thousandth part of the decisions on details of life that may be found in his work; it would be like reprinting the law-reports of an incredible century of just judges and sensible magistrates. We can only touch on one or two obvious topics of this kind.

I have noted the need to use modern atmospheric words for certain ancient atmospheric things; as in saying that St Thomas was what most modern men vaguely mean by an Optimist. In the same way, he was very much what they vaguely mean by a Liberal. I do not mean that any of his thousand political suggestions would suit any such definite political creed; if there are nowadays any definite political creeds. I mean, in the same sense, that he has a sort of atmosphere of believing in breadth and balance and debate. He may not be a Liberal by the extreme demands of the moderns for we seem always to mean by the moderns the men of the last century, rather than this. He was very much of a Liberal compared with the most modern of all moderns; for they are nearly all of them turning into Fascists and Hitlerites. But the point is that he obviously preferred the sort of decisions that are reached by deliberation rather than despotic action; and while, like all his contemporaries and co-religionists, he has no doubt that true authority may be authoritative, he is rather averse to the whole savour of its being arbitrary. He is much less of an Imperialist than Dante, and even his Papalism is not very Imperial. He is very fond of phrases like 'a mob of free men' as the essential material of a city; and he is emphatic upon the fact that law, when it ceases to be justice, ceases even to be law.

If this work were controversial, whole chapters could be given to the economics as well as the ethics of the Thomist system. It would be easy to show that, in this matter, he was a prophet as well as a philosopher. He foresaw from the first the peril of that mere reliance on trade and exchange, which was beginning about his time; and which has culminated in a universal commercial collapse in our time. He did not merely assert that Usury is unnatural, though in saying that he only followed Aristotle and obvious common sense, which was never contradicted by anybody until the time of the commercialists, who have involved us in the collapse. The modern world began by Bentham writing the Defence of Usury, and it has ended after a hundred years in even the vulgar newspaper opinion finding Finance indefensible. But St Thomas struck much deeper than that. He even mentioned the truth, ignored during the long idolatry of trade, that things which men produce only to sell are likely to be worse in quality than the things they produce in order to consume. Something of our difficulty about the fine shades of Latin will be felt when we come to his statement that there is always a certain *inhonestas* about trade. For *inhonestas* does not exactly mean dishonesty. It means approximately 'something unworthy', or, more nearly perhaps, 'something not quite handsome'. And he was right; for trade, in the modern sense, does mean selling something for a little more than it is worth, nor would the nineteenth-century economists have denied it. They would only have said that he was not practical; and this seemed sound while their view led to practical prosperity. Things are a little different now that it has led to universal bankruptcy.

Here, however, we collide with a colossal paradox of history. The Thomist philosophy and theology, quite fairly compared with other philosophies like the Buddhist or the Monist, with other theologies like the Calvinist or the Christian Scientist, is quite obviously a working and even a fighting system; full of common sense and constructive confidence; and therefore normally full of hope and promise. Nor is this hope vain or this promise unfulfilled. In this not very hopeful modern moment, there are no men so hopeful as those who are today looking to St Thomas as a leader in a hundred crying questions of craftsmanship and ownership and economic ethics. There is undoubtedly a hopeful and creative Thomism in our time. But we are none the less puzzled by the fact that this did not immediately follow on St Thomas's time. It is true that there was a great march of progress in the thirteenth century; and in some things, such as the status of the peasant, matters had greatly improved by the end of the Middle Ages. But nobody can honestly say that Scholasticism had greatly improved by the end of the Middle Ages. Nobody can tell how far the popular spirit of the Friars had helped the later popular mediaeval movements; or how far this great Friar, with his luminous rules of justice and his lifelong sympathy with the poor, may have indirectly contributed to the improvement that certainly occurred. But those who followed his method, as distinct from his moral spirit, degenerated with a strange rapidity; and it was certainly not in the Scholastics that the improvement occurred. Of some of the Scholastics we can only say that they took everything that was worst in Scholasticism and made it worse. They continued to count the steps of logic; but every step of logic took them further from common sense. They forgot how St Thomas had started almost as an agnostic; and seemed resolved to leave nothing in heaven or hell about which anybody could be agnostic. They were a sort of rabid rationalists, who would have left no mysteries in the Faith at all. In the earliest Scholasticism there is something that strikes a modern as fanciful and pedantic; but, properly understood, it has a fine spirit in its fancy. It is the spirit of freedom; and especially the spirit of free will. Nothing seems more quaint, for instance, than the speculations about what would have happened to every vegetable or animal or angel, if Eve had chosen *not* to eat the fruit of the tree. But this was originally full of the thrill of choice; and the feeling that she might have chosen otherwise. It was this detailed detective method that was followed, without the thrill of the original detective story. The world was cumbered with countless tomes, proving by logic a thousand things that can be known only to God. They developed all that was really sterile in Scholasticism, and left for us all that is really fruitful in Thomism.

There are many historical explanations. There is the Black Death, which broke the back of the Middle Ages; the consequent decline in clerical culture, which did so much to provoke the Reformation. But I suspect that there was another cause also; which can only be stated by saying that the contemporary fanatics, who controverted with Aquinas, left their own school behind them; and in a sense that school triumphed after all. The really narrow Augustinians, the men who saw the Christian life only as the narrow way, the men who could not even comprehend the great Dominican's exultation in the blaze of Being, or the glory of God in all his creatures, the men who continued to insist feverishly on every text, or even on every truth, that appeared pessimistic or paralysing, these gloomy Christians could not be extirpated from Christendom; and they remained and waited for their chance. The narrow Augustinians, the men who would have no science or reason or rational use of secular things, might have been defeated in controversy, but they had an accumulated passion of conviction. There was an Augustinian monastery in the North where it was near to explosion.

Thomas Aquinas had struck his blow; but he had not entirely settled the Manichees. The Manichees are not so easily settled; in the sense of settled forever. He had ensured that the main outline of the Christianity that has come down to us should be supernatural but not anti-natural; and should never be darkened with a false spirituality to the oblivion of the Creator and the Christ who was made Man. But as his tradition trailed away into less liberal or less creative habits of thought, and as his mediaeval society fell away and decayed through other causes, the thing against which he had made war crept back into Christendom. A certain spirit or element in the Christian religion, necessary and sometimes noble but always needing to be balanced by more gentle and generous elements in the Faith, began once more to strengthen, as the framework of Scholasticism stiffened or split. The Fear of the Lord, that is the beginning of wisdom, and therefore belongs to the beginnings, and is felt in the first cold hours before the dawn of civilization; the power that comes out of the wilderness and rides on the whirlwind and breaks the gods of stone; the power before which the eastern nations are prostrate like a pavement; the power before which the primitive prophets run naked and shouting, at once proclaiming and escaping from their god; the fear that is rightly rooted in the beginnings of every religion, true or false: the fear of the Lord, that is the beginning of wisdom; but not the end.

It is often remarked, as showing the ironical indifference of rulers to revolutions, and especially the frivolity of those who are called the Pagan Popes of the Renaissance, in their attitude to the Reformation, that when the Pope first heard of the first movements of Protestantism, which had started in Germany, he only said in an offhand manner that it was 'some quarrel of monks'. Every Pope of course was accustomed to quarrels among the monastic orders; but it has always been noted as a strange and almost uncanny negligence that he could see no more than this in the beginnings of the great sixteenth-century schism. And yet, in a somewhat more recondite sense, there is something to be said for what he has been blamed for saying. In one sense, the schismatics had a sort of spiritual ancestry even in mediaeval times.

It will be found earlier in this book; and it *was* a quarrel of monks. We have seen how the great name of Augustine, a name never mentioned by Aquinas without respect but often mentioned without agreement, covered an Augustinian school of thought naturally lingering longest in the Augustinian Order. The difference, like every difference between Catholics, was only a difference of emphasis. The Augustinians stressed the idea of the impotence of man before God, the omniscience of God about the destiny of man, the need for holy fear and the humiliation of intellectual pride, more than the opposite and corresponding truths of free will or human dignity or good works. In this they did in a sense continue the distinctive note of St Augustine, who is even now regarded as relatively the determinist doctor of the Church. But there is emphasis and emphasis; and a time was coming when emphasizing the one side was to mean flatly contradicting the other. Perhaps, after all, it did begin with a quarrel of monks; but the Pope was yet to learn how quarrelsome a monk could be. For there was one particular monk in that Augustinian monastery in the German forests, who may be said to have had a single and special talent for emphasis; for emphasis and nothing except emphasis; for emphasis with the quality of earthquake. He was the son of a slatecutter; a man with a great voice and a certain volume of personality; brooding, sincere, decidedly morbid; and his name was Martin Luther. Neither Augustine nor the Augustinians would have desired to see the day of that vindication of the Augustinian tradition; but in one sense, perhaps, the Augustinian tradition was avenged after all.

It came out of its cell again, in the day of storm and ruin, and cried out with a new and mighty voice for an elemental and emotional religion, and for the destruction of all philosophies. It had a peculiar horror and loathing of the great Greek philosophies, and of the scholasticism that had been founded on those philosophies. It had one theory that was the destruction of all theories; in fact it had its own theology which was itself the death of theology. Man could say nothing to God, nothing from God, nothing about God, except an almost inarticulate cry for mercy and for the supernatural help of Christ, in a world where all natural things were useless. Reason was useless. Will was useless. Man could not move himself an inch any more than a stone. Man could not trust what was in his head any more than a turnip. Nothing remained in earth or heaven, but the name of Christ lifted in that lonely imprecation; awful as the cry of a beast in pain.

We must be just to those huge human figures, who are in fact the hinges of history. However strong, and rightly strong, be our own controversial conviction, it must never mislead us into thinking that something trivial has transformed the world. So it is with that great Augustinian monk, who avenged all the ascetic Augustinians of the Middle Ages; and whose broad and burly figure has been big enough to block out for four centuries the distant human mountain of Aquinas. It is not, as the moderns delight to say, a question of theology. The Protestant theology of Martin Luther was a thing that no modern Protestant would be seen dead in a field with; or if the phrase be too flippant, would be specially anxious to touch with a barge-pole. That Protestantism was pessimism; it was nothing but bare insistence on the hopelessness of all human virtue, as an attempt to escape hell. That Lutheranism is now quite unreal; more modern phases of Lutheranism are rather more unreal; but Luther was not unreal. He was one of those great elemental barbarians, to whom it is indeed given to change the world. To compare those two figures bulking so big in history, in any philosophical sense, would of course be futile and even unfair. On a great map like the mind of Aquinas, the mind of Luther would be almost invisible. But it is not altogether untrue to say, as so many journalists have said without caring whether it was true or untrue, that Luther opened an epoch; and began the modern world.

He was the first man who ever consciously used his consciousness; or what was later called his Personality. He had as a fact a rather strong personality. Aquinas had an even stronger personality; he had a massive and magnetic presence; he had an intellect that could act like a huge system of artillery spread over the whole world; he had that instantaneous presence of mind in debate, which alone really deserves the name of wit. But it never occurred to him to use anything except his wits, in defence of a truth distinct from himself. It never occurred to Aquinas to use Aquinas as a weapon. There is not a trace of his ever using his personal advantages, of birth or body or brain or breeding, in debate with anybody. In short, he belonged to an age of intellectual unconsciousness, to an age of intellectual innocence, which was very intellectual. Now Luther did begin the modern mood of depending on things not merely intellectual. It is not a question of praise or blame; it matters little whether we say that he was a strong personality, or that he was a bit of a big bully. When he quoted a Scripture text, inserting a word that is not in Scripture, he was content to shout back at all hecklers: 'Tell them that Dr Martin Luther will have it so!' That is what we now call Personality. A little later it was called Psychology. After that it was called Advertisement or Salesmanship. But we are not arguing about advantages or disadvantages. It is due to this great Augustinian pessimist to say, not only that he did triumph at last over the Angel of the Schools, but that he did in a very real sense make the modern world. He destroyed Reason; and substituted Suggestion.

It is said that the great Reformer publicly burned the *Summa Theologica* and the works of Aquinas; and with the bonfire of such books this book may well come to an end. They say it is very difficult to burn a book; and it must have been exceedingly difficult to burn such a mountain of books as the Dominican had contributed to the controversies of Christendom. Anyhow, there is something lurid and apocalyptic about the idea of such destruction, when we consider the compact complexity of all that encyclopaedic survey of social and moral and theoretical things. All the close-packed definitions that excluded so many errors and extremes; all the broad and balanced judgments upon the clash of loyalties or the choice of evils; all the liberal speculations upon the limits of government or the proper conditions of justice; all the distinctions between the use and abuse of private property; all the rules and exceptions about the great evil of war; all the allowances for human weakness and all the provisions for human health; all this mass of mediaeval humanism shrivelled and curled up in smoke before the eyes of its enemy; and that great passionate peasant rejoiced darkly, because the day of the Intellect was over. Sentence by sentence it burned, and syllogism by syllogism; and the golden maxims turned to golden flames in that last and dying glory of all that had once been the great wisdom of the Greeks. The great central Synthesis of history, that was to have linked the ancient with the modern world, went up in smoke and, for half the world, was forgotten like a vapour.

For a time it seemed that the destruction was final. It is still expressed in the amazing fact that (in the North) modern men can still write histories of philosophy, in which philosophy stops with the last little sophists of Greece and Rome; and is never heard of again until the appearance of such a third-rate philosopher as Francis Bacon. And yet this small book, which will probably do nothing else, or have very little other value, will be at least a testimony to the fact that the tide has turned once more. It is four hundred years after; and this book, I hope (and I am happy to say I believe) will probably be lost and forgotten in the flood of better books about St Thomas Aquinas, which are at this moment pouring from every printing-press in Europe, and even in England and America. Compared with such books it is obviously a very slight and amateurish production; but it is not likely to be burned, and if it were, it would not leave even a noticeable gap in the pouring mass of new and magnificent work, which is now daily dedicated to the *philosophia perennis*; to the Everlasting Philosophy.

FATHER BROWN
STORIES

THE BLUE CROSS

Between the silver ribbon of morning and the green glittering ribbon of sea, the boat touched Harwich and let loose a swarm of folk like flies, among whom the man we must follow was by no means conspicuous – nor wished to be. There was nothing notable about him, except a slight contrast between the holiday gaiety of his clothes and the official gravity of his face. His clothes included a slight, pale grey jacket, a white waistcoat, and a silver straw hat with a grey-blue ribbon. His lean face was dark by contrast, and ended in a curt black beard that looked Spanish and suggested an Elizabethan ruff. He was smoking a cigarette with the seriousness of an idler. There was nothing about him to indicate the fact that the grey jacket covered a loaded revolver, that the white waistcoat covered a police card, or that the straw hat covered one of the most powerful intellects in Europe. For this was Valentin himself, the head of the Paris police and the most famous investigator of the world; and he was coming from Brussels to London to make the greatest arrest of the century.

Flambeau was in England. The police of three countries had tracked the great criminal at last from Ghent to Brussels, from Brussels to the Hook of Holland; and it was conjectured that he would take some advantage of the unfamiliarity and confusion of the Eucharistic Congress, then taking place in London. Probably he would travel as some minor clerk or secretary connected with it; but, of course, Valentin could not be certain; nobody could be certain about Flambeau.

It is many years now since this colossus of crime suddenly ceased keeping the world in a turmoil; and when he ceased, as they said after the death of Roland, there was a great quiet upon the earth. But in his best days (I mean, of course, his worst) Flambeau was a figure as statuesque and international as the Kaiser. Almost every morning the daily paper announced that he had escaped the consequences of one extraordinary crime by committing another.

He was a Gascon of gigantic stature and bodily daring; and the wildest tales were told of his outbursts of athletic humour; how he turned the *juge d'instruction* upside down and stood him on his head, 'to clear his mind'; how he ran down the Rue de Rivoli with a policeman under each arm. It is due to him to say that his fantastic physical strength was generally employed in such bloodless though undignified scenes; his real crimes were chiefly those of ingenious and wholesale robbery. But each of his thefts was almost a new sin, and would make a story by itself. It was he who ran the great Tyrolean Dairy Company in London, with no dairies, no cows, no carts, no milk, but with some thousand subscribers. These he served by the simple operation of moving the little milk-cans outside people's doors to the doors of his own customers. It was he who had kept up an unaccountable and close correspondence with a young lady whose whole letter-bag was intercepted, by the extraordinary trick of photographing his messages infinitesimally small upon the slides of a microscope. A sweeping simplicity, however, marked many of his experiments. It is said he once repainted all the numbers in a street in the dead of night merely to divert one traveller into a trap. It is quite certain that he invented a portable pillar-box, which he put up at corners in quiet suburbs on the chance of strangers dropping postal orders into it. Lastly, he was known to be a startling acrobat; despite his huge figure, he could leap like a grasshopper and melt into the treetops like a monkey. Hence the great Valentin, when he set out to find Flambeau, was perfectly well aware that his adventures would not end when he had found him.

But how was he to find him? On this the great Valentin's ideas were still in process of settlement.

There was one thing which Flambeau, with all his dexterity of disguise, could not cover, and that was his singular height. If Valentin's quick eye had caught a tall apple-woman, a tall grenadier, or even a tolerably tall duchess, he might have arrested them on the spot. But all along his train there was nobody that could be a disguised Flambeau, any more than a cat could be a disguised giraffe. About the people on the boat he had already satisfied himself; and the people picked up at Harwich or on the journey limited themselves with certainty to six. There was a short railway official travelling up to the terminus, three fairly short market gardeners picked up two stations afterwards, one very short widow lady going up

from a small Essex town, and a very short Roman Catholic priest
going up from a small Essex village. When it came to the last case,
Valentin gave it up and almost laughed. The little priest was so
much the essence of those Eastern flats; he had a face as round and
dull as a Norfolk dumpling; he had eyes as empty as the North Sea;
he had several brown-paper parcels which he was quite incapable
of collecting. The Eucharistic Congress had doubtless sucked out
of their local stagnation many such creatures, blind and helpless,
like moles disinterred. Valentin was a sceptic in the severe style of
France, and could have no love for priests. But he could have pity
for them, and this one might have provoked pity in anybody. He
had a large, shabby umbrella, which constantly fell on the floor.
He did not seem to know which was the right end of his return
ticket. He explained with a moon-calf simplicity to everybody in
the carriage that he had to be careful, because he had something
made of real silver 'with blue stones' in one of his brown-paper
parcels. His quaint blending of Essex flatness with saintly simplicity
continuously amused the Frenchman till the priest arrived (somehow) at Stratford with all his parcels, and came back for his
umbrella. When he did the last, Valentin even had the good nature
to warn him not to take care of the silver by telling everybody about
it. But to whomever he talked, Valentin kept his eye open for someone else, he looked out steadily for anyone, rich or poor, male or
female, who was well up to six feet; for Flambeau was four inches
above it.

He alighted at Liverpool Street, however, quite conscientiously
secure that he had not missed the criminal so far. He then went to
Scotland Yard to regularize his position and arrange for help in
case of need; he then lit another cigarette and went for a long stroll
in the streets of London. As he was walking in the streets and
squares beyond Victoria, he paused suddenly and stood. It was a
quaint, quiet square, very typical of London, full of an accidental
stillness. The tall, flat houses round looked at once prosperous
and uninhabited; the square of shrubbery in the centre looked as
deserted as a green Pacific islet. One of the four sides was much
higher than the rest, like a dais; and the line of this side was broken
by one of London's admirable accidents — a restaurant that looked
as if it had strayed from Soho. It was an unreasonably attractive
object, with dwarf plants in pots and long, striped blinds of lemon

yellow and white. It stood specially high above the street, and in the usual patchwork way of London, a flight of steps from the street ran up to meet the front door almost as a fire-escape might run up to a first-floor window. Valentin stood and smoked in front of the yellow-white blinds and considered them long.

The most incredible thing about miracles is that they happen. A few clouds in heaven do come together into the staring shape of one human eye. A tree does stand up in the landscape of a doubtful journey in the exact and elaborate shape of a note of interrogation. I have seen both these things myself within the last few days. Nelson docs die in the instant of victory; and a man named Williams does quite accidentally murder a man named Williamson; it sounds like a sort of infanticide. In short, there is in life an element of elfin coincidence which people reckoning on the prosaic may perpetually miss. As it has been well expressed in the paradox of Poe, wisdom should reckon on the unforeseen.

Aristide Valentin was unfathomably French; and the French intelligence is intelligence specially and solely. He was not 'a thinking machine'; for that is a brainless phrase of modern fatalism and materialism. A machine only *is* a machine because it cannot think. But he was a thinking man, and a plain man at the same time. All his wonderful successes, that looked like conjuring, had been gained by plodding logic, by clear and commonplace French thought. The French electrify the world not by starting any paradox, they electrify it by carrying out a truism. They carry a truism so far – as in the French Revolution. But exactly because Valentin understood reason, he understood the limits of reason. Only a man who knows nothing of motors talks of motoring without petrol; only a man who knows nothing of reason talks of reasoning without strong, undisputed first principles. Here he had no strong first principles. Flambeau had been missed at Harwich; and if he was in London at all, he might be anything from a tall tramp on Wimbledon Common to a tall toastmaster at the Hôtel Métropole. In such a naked state of nescience, Valentin had a view and a method of his own.

In such cases he reckoned on the unforeseen. In such cases, when he could not follow the train of the reasonable, he coldly and carefully followed the train of the unreasonable. Instead of going to the right places – banks, police stations, rendezvous – he systematically went to the wrong places; knocked at every empty house, turned down every *cul de sac*, went up every lane blocked with rubbish, went round every crescent that led him uselessly out of the way. He defended this crazy course quite logically. He said that if one had a clue this was the worst way; but if one had no clue at all it was the best, because there was just the chance that any oddity that caught the eye of the pursuer might be the same that had caught the eye of the pursued. Somewhere a man must begin, and it had better be just where another man might stop. Something about that flight of steps up to the shop, something about the quietude and quaintness of the restaurant, roused all the detective's rare romantic fancy and made him resolve to strike at random. He went up the steps, and sitting down at a table by the window, asked for a cup of black coffee.

It was half-way through the morning, and he had not breakfasted; the slight litter of other breakfasts stood about on the table to remind him of his hunger; and adding a poached egg to his order, he proceeded musingly to shake some white sugar into his coffee, thinking all the time about Flambeau. He remembered how Flambeau had escaped, once by a pair of nail scissors, and once by a house on fire; once by having to pay for an unstamped letter; and once by getting people to look through a telescope at a comet that might destroy the world. He thought his detective brain as good as the criminal's, which was true. But he fully realized the disadvantage. 'The criminal is the creative artist; the detective only the critic,' he said with a sour smile, and lifted his coffee cup to his lips slowly, and put it down very quickly. He had put salt in it.

He looked at the vessel from which the silvery powder had come; it was certainly a sugar-basin; as unmistakably meant for sugar as a champagne-bottle for champagne. He wondered why they should keep salt in it. He looked to see if there were any more orthodox vessels. Yes; there were two salt-cellars quite full. Perhaps there was some speciality in the condiment in the salt-cellars. He tasted it; it was sugar. Then he looked round at the restaurant with a refreshed air of interest, to see if there were any traces of that singular artistic taste which puts the sugar in the salt-cellars and the salt in the sugar-basin. Except for an odd splash of some dark fluid on one of the white-papered walls, the whole place appeared neat, cheerful and ordinary. He rang the bell for the waiter.

When that official hurried up, fuzzy-haired and somewhat

bleary-eyed at that early hour, the detective (who was not without
an appreciation of the simpler forms of humour) asked him to taste
the sugar and see if it was up to the high reputation of the hotel.
The result was that the waiter yawned suddenly and woke up.

'Do you play this delicate joke on your customers every morning?' inquired Valentin. 'Does changing the salt and sugar never
pall on you as a jest?'

The waiter, when this irony grew clearer, stammeringly assured
him that the establishment had certainly no such intention; it must
be a most curious mistake. He picked up the sugar-basin and looked
at it; he picked up the salt-cellar and looked at that, his face growing
more and more bewildered. At last he abruptly excused himself,
and hurrying away, returned in a few seconds with the proprietor.
The proprietor also examined the sugar-basin and then the salt-
cellar; the proprietor also looked bewildered.

Suddenly the waiter seemed to grow inarticulate with a rush of
words.

'I zink,' he stuttered eagerly, 'I zink it is those two clergymen.'

'What two clergymen?'

'The two clergymen,' said the waiter, 'that threw soup at the wall.'

'Threw soup at the wall?' repeated Valentin, feeling sure this
must be some singular Italian metaphor.

'Yes, yes,' said the attendant excitedly, and pointing at the dark
splash on the white paper; 'threw it over there on the wall.'

Valentin looked his query at the proprietor, who came to his
rescue with fuller reports.

'Yes, sir,' he said, 'it's quite true, though I don't suppose it has
anything to do with the sugar and salt. Two clergymen came in
and drank soup here very early, as soon as the shutters were taken
down. They were both very quiet, respectable people; one of
them paid the bill and went out; the other, who seemed a slower
coach altogether, was some minutes longer getting his things
together. But he went at last. Only, the instant before he stepped
into the street he deliberately picked up his cup, which he had
only half emptied, and threw the soup slap on the wall. I was in
the back room myself, and so was the waiter; so I could only rush
out in time to find the wall splashed and the shop empty. It didn't
do any particular damage, but it was confounded cheek; and
I tried to catch the men in the street. They were too far off

though; I only noticed they went round the next corner into Carstairs Street.'

The detective was on his feet, hat settled and stick in hand. He had already decided that in the universal darkness of his mind he could only follow the first odd finger that pointed; and this finger was odd enough. Paying his bill and clashing the glass doors behind him, he was soon swinging round into the other street.

It was fortunate that even in such fevered moments his eye was cool and quick. Something in a shop-front went by him like a mere flash; yet he went back to look at it. The shop was a popular green-grocer and fruiterer's, an array of goods set out in the open air and plainly ticketed with their names and prices. In the two most prominent compartments were two heaps, of oranges and of nuts respectively. On the heap of nuts lay a scrap of cardboard, on which was written in bold, blue chalk, 'Best tangerine oranges, two a penny.' On the oranges was the equally clear and exact description, 'Finest Brazil nuts, 4d. a lb.' M. Valentin looked at these two placards and fancied he had met this highly subtle form of humour before, and that somewhat recently. He drew the attention of the red-faced fruiterer, who was looking rather sullenly up and down the street, to this inaccuracy in his advertisements. The fruiterer said nothing, but sharply put each card into its proper place. The detective, leaning elegantly on his walking cane, continued to scrutinize the shop. At last he said, 'Pray excuse my apparent irrelevance, my good sir, but I should like to ask you a question in experimental psychology and the association of ideas.'

The red-faced shopman regarded him with an eye of menace; but he continued gaily, swinging his cane. 'Why,' he pursued, 'why are two tickets wrongly placed in a greengrocer's shop like a shovel hat that has come to London for a holiday? Or, in case I do not make myself clear, what is the mystical association which connects the idea of nuts marked as oranges with the idea of two clergymen, one tall and the other short?'

The eyes of the tradesman stood out of his head like a snail's; he really seemed for an instant likely to fling himself upon the stranger. At last he stammered angrily, 'I don't know what you 'ave to do with it, but if you're one of their friends, you can tell 'em from me that I'll knock their silly 'eads off, parsons or no parsons, if they upset my apples again.'

'Indeed?' asked the detective, with great sympathy. 'Did they upset your apples?'

'One of 'em did,' said the heated shopman; 'rolled 'em all over the street. I'd 'ave caught the fool but for havin' to pick 'em up.'

'Which way did these parsons go?' asked Valentin.

'Up that second road on the left-hand side, and then across the square,' said the other promptly.

'Thanks,' said Valentin, and vanished like a fairy. On the other side of the second square he found a policeman, and said, 'This is urgent, constable; have you seen two clergymen in shovel hats?'

The policeman began to chuckle heavily. 'I 'ave, sir; and if you arst me, one of 'em was drunk. He stood in the middle of the road that bewildered that—'

'Which way did they go?' snapped Valentin.

'They took one of them yellow buses over there,' answered the man; 'them that go to Hampstead.'

Valentin produced his official card and said very rapidly, 'Call up two of your men to come with me in pursuit,' and crossed the road with such contagious energy that the ponderous policeman was moved to almost agile obedience. In a minute and a half the French detective was joined on the opposite pavement by an inspector and a man in plain clothes.

'Well, sir,' began the former, with smiling importance, 'and what may—?'

Valentin pointed suddenly with his cane. 'I'll tell you on the top of that omnibus,' he said, and was darting and dodging across the tangle of the traffic. When all three sank panting on the top seats of the yellow vehicle, the inspector said, 'We could go four times as quick in a taxi.'

'Quite true,' replied their leader placidly, 'if we only had an idea of where we were going.'

'Well, where *are* you going?' asked the other, staring.

Valentin smoked frowningly for a few seconds; then, removing his cigarette, he said, 'If you *know* what a man's doing, get in front of him; but if you want to guess what he's doing, keep behind him. Stray when he strays; stop when he stops; travel as slowly as he. Then you may see what he saw and may act as he acted. All we can do is to keep our eyes skinned for a queer thing.'

'What sort of a queer thing do you mean?' asked the inspector.

'Any sort of queer thing,' answered Valentin, and relapsed into obstinate silence.

The yellow omnibus crawled up the northern roads for what seemed like hours on end; the great detective would not explain further, and perhaps his assistants felt a silent and growing doubt of his errand. Perhaps, also, they felt a silent and growing desire for lunch, for the hours crept long past the normal luncheon hour, and the long roads of the North London suburbs seemed to shoot out into length after length like an infernal telescope. It was one of those journeys on which a man perpetually feels that now at last he must have come to the end of the universe, and then finds he has only come to the beginning of Tufnell Park. London died away in draggled taverns and dreary scrubs, and then was unaccountably born again in blazing high streets and blatant hotels. It was like passing through thirteen separate vulgar cities all just touching each other. But though the winter twilight was already threatening the road ahead of them, the Parisian detective still sat silent and watchful, eyeing the frontage of the streets that slid by on either side. By the time they had left Camden Town behind, the policemen were nearly asleep; at least, they gave something like a jump as Valentin leapt erect, struck a hand on each man's shoulder, and shouted to the driver to stop.

They tumbled down the steps into the road without realizing why they had been dislodged; when they looked round for enlightenment they found Valentin triumphantly pointing his finger towards a window on the left side of the road. It was a large window, forming part of the long façade of a gilt and palatial public-house; it was the part reserved for respectable dining, and labelled 'Restaurant'. This window, like all the rest along the frontage of the hotel, was of frosted and figured glass; but in the middle of it was a big, black smash, like a star in the ice.

'Our cue at last,' cried Valentin, waving his stick; 'the place with the broken window.'

'What window? What cue?' asked his principal assistant. 'Why, what proof is there that this has anything to do with them?'

Valentin almost broke his bamboo stick with rage.

'Proof!' he cried. 'Good God! the man is looking for proof! Why, of course, the chances are twenty to one that it has *nothing* to do with them. But what else can we do? Don't you see we must either follow one wild possibility or else go home to bed?' He banged his way into the restaurant, followed by his companions, and they were soon seated at a late luncheon at a little table, and looking at the star of smashed glass from the inside. Not that it was very informative to them even then.

'Got your window broken, I see,' said Valentin to the waiter, as he paid his bill.

'Yes, sir,' answered the attendant, bending busily over the change, to which Valentin silently added an enormous tip. The waiter straightened himself with mild but unmistakable animation.

'Ah, yes, sir,' he said. 'Very odd thing, that, sir.'

'Indeed? Tell us about it,' said the detective with careless curiosity.

'Well, two gents in black came in,' said the waiter; 'two of those foreign parsons that are running about. They had a cheap and quiet little lunch, and one of them paid for it and went out. The other was just going out to join him when I looked at my change again and found he'd paid me more than three times too much. "Here," I says to the chap who was nearly out of the door, "you've paid too much." "Oh," he says, very cool, "have we?" "Yes," I says, and picks up the bill to show him. Well, that was a knock-out.'

'What do you mean?' asked his interlocutor.

'Well, I'd have sworn on seven Bibles that I'd put 4s. on that bill. But now I saw I'd put 14s., as plain as paint.'

'Well?' cried Valentin, moving slowly, but with burning eyes, 'and then?'

'The parson at the door he says, all serene, "Sorry to confuse your accounts, but it will pay for the window." "What window?" I says. "The one I'm going to break," he says, and smashed that blessed pane with his umbrella.'

All the inquirers made an exclamation; and the inspector said under his breath, 'Are we after escaped lunatics?' The waiter went on with some relish for the ridiculous story:

'I was so knocked silly for a second, I couldn't do anything. The man marched out of the place and joined his friend just round the corner. Then they went so quick up Bullock Street that I couldn't catch them, though I ran round the bars to do it.'

'Bullock Street,' said the detective, and shot up that thoroughfare as quickly as the strange couple he pursued.

Their journey now took them through bare brick ways like tunnels; streets with few lights and even with few windows; streets that seemed built out of the blank backs of everything and everywhere. Dusk was deepening, and it was not easy even for the London policemen to guess in what exact direction they were treading. The inspector, however, was pretty certain that they would eventually strike some part of Hampstead Heath. Abruptly one bulging and gas-lit window broke the blue twilight like a bull's-eye lantern; and Valentin stopped an instant before a little garish sweetstuff shop. After an instant's hesitation he went in; he stood amid the gaudy colours of the confectionery with entire gravity and bought thirteen chocolate cigars with a certain care. He was clearly preparing an opening; but he did not need one.

An angular, elderly young woman in the shop had regarded his elegant appearance with a merely automatic inquiry; but when she saw the door behind him blocked with the blue uniform of the inspector, her eyes seemed to wake up.

'Oh,' she said, 'if you've come about that parcel, I've sent it off already.'

'Parcel!' repeated Valentin; and it was his turn to look inquiring.

'I mean the parcel the gentleman left – the clergyman gentleman.'

'For goodness' sake,' said Valentin, leaning forward with his first real confession of eagerness, 'for Heaven's sake tell us what happened exactly.'

'Well,' said the woman, a little doubtfully, 'the clergymen came in about half an hour ago and bought some peppermints and talked a bit, and then went off towards the Heath. But a second after, one of them runs back into the shop and says, "Have I left a parcel?" Well, I looked everywhere and couldn't see one; so he says, "Never mind; but if it should turn up, please post it to this address," and he left me the address and a shilling for my trouble. And sure enough, though I thought I'd looked everywhere, I found he'd left a brown-paper parcel, so I posted it to the place he said. I can't remember the address now; it was somewhere in Westminster. But as the thing seemed so important, I thought perhaps the police had come about it.'

'So they have,' said Valentin shortly. 'Is Hampstead Heath near here?'

'Straight on for fifteen minutes,' said the woman, 'and you'll come right out on the open.' Valentin sprang out of the shop and began to run. The other detectives followed him at a reluctant trot.

The street they threaded was so narrow and shut in by shadows that when they came out unexpectedly into the void common and vast sky they were startled to find the evening still so light and clear. A perfect dome of peacock-green sank into gold amid the blackening trees and the dark violet distances. The glowing green tint was just deep enough to pick out in points of crystal one or two stars. All that was left of the daylight lay in a golden glitter across the edge of Hampstead and that popular hollow which is called the Vale of Health. The holiday makers who roam this region had not wholly dispersed: a few couples sat shapelessly on benches; and here and there a distant girl still shrieked in one of the swings. The glory of heaven deepened and darkened around the sublime vulgarity of man; and standing on the slope and looking across the valley, Valentin beheld the thing which he sought.

Among the black and breaking groups in that distance was one especially black which did not break – a group of two figures clerically clad. Though they seemed as small as insects, Valentin could see that one of them was much smaller than the other. Though the other had a student's stoop and an inconspicuous manner, he could see that the man was well over six feet high. He shut his teeth and went forward, whirling his stick impatiently. By the time he had substantially diminished the distance and magnified the two black figures as in a vast microscope, he had perceived something else; something which startled him, and yet which he had somehow expected. Whoever was the tall priest, there could be no doubt about the identity of the short one. It was his friend of the Harwich train, the stumpy little *curé* of Essex whom he had warned about his brown-paper parcels.

Now, so far as this went, everything fitted in finally and rationally enough. Valentin had learned by his inquiries that morning that a Father Brown from Essex was bringing up a silver cross with sapphires, a relic of considerable value, to show some of the foreign priests at the congress. This undoubtedly was the 'silver with blue stones'; and Father Brown undoubtedly was the little greenhorn in the train. Now there was nothing wonderful about the fact that what Valentin had found out Flambeau had also found out;

Flambeau found out everything. Also there was nothing wonderful in the fact that when Flambeau heard of a sapphire cross he should try to steal it; that was the most natural thing in all natural history. And most certainly there was nothing wonderful about the fact that Flambeau should have it all his own way with such a silly sheep as the man with the umbrella and the parcels. He was the sort of man whom anybody could lead on a string to the North Pole; it was not surprising that an actor like Flambeau, dressed as another priest, could lead him to Hampstead Heath. So far the crime seemed clear enough; and while the detective pitied the priest for his helplessness, he almost despised Flambeau for condescending to so gullible a victim. But when Valentin thought of all that had happened in between, of all that had led him to his triumph, he racked his brains for the smallest rhyme or reason in it. What had the stealing of a blue-and-silver cross from a priest from Essex to do with chucking soup at wallpaper? What had it to do with calling nuts oranges, or with paying for windows first and breaking them afterwards? He had come to the end of his chase; yet somehow he had missed the middle of it. When he failed (which was seldom), he had usually grasped the clue, but nevertheless missed the criminal. Here he had grasped the criminal, but still he could not grasp the clue.

The two figures that they followed were crawling like black flies across the huge green contour of a hill. They were evidently sunk in conversation, and perhaps did not notice where they were going; but they were certainly going to the wilder and more silent heights of the Heath. As their pursuers gained on them, the latter had to use the undignified attitudes of the deer-stalker, to crouch behind clumps of trees and even to crawl prostrate in deep grass. By these ungainly ingenuities the hunters even came close enough to the quarry to hear the murmur of the discussion, but no word could be distinguished except the word 'reason' recurring frequently in a high and almost childish voice. Once over an abrupt dip of land and a dense tangle of thickets, the detectives actually lost the two figures they were following. They did not find the trail again for an agonizing ten minutes, and then it led round the brow of a great dome of hill overlooking an amphitheatre of rich and desolate sunset scenery. Under a tree in this commanding yet neglected spot was an old ramshackle wooden seat. On this seat sat the two priests still in serious speech together. The gorgeous green and gold still clung to the darkening horizon; but the dome above was turning slowly from peacock-green to peacock-blue, and the stars detached themselves more and more like solid jewels. Mutely motioning to his followers, Valentin contrived to creep up behind the big branching tree, and, standing there in deathly silence, heard the words of the strange priests for the first time.

After he had listened for a minute and a half, he was gripped by a devilish doubt. Perhaps he had dragged the two English policemen to the wastes of a nocturnal heath on an errand no saner than seeking figs on its thistles. For the two priests were talking exactly like priests, piously, with learning and leisure, about the most aerial enigmas of theology. The little Essex priest spoke the more simply, with his round face turned to the strengthening stars; the other talked with his head bowed, as if he were not even worthy to look at them. But no more innocently clerical conversation could have been heard in any white Italian cloister or black Spanish cathedral.

The first he heard was the tail of one of Father Brown's sentences, which ended, '. . . what they really meant in the Middle Ages by the heavens being incorruptible.'

The taller priest nodded his bowed head and said:

'Ah, yes, these modern infidels appeal to their reason; but who can look at those millions of worlds and not feel that there may well be wonderful Universes above us where reason is utterly unreasonable?'

'No,' said the other priest; 'reason is always reasonable, even in the last limbo, in the lost borderland of things. I know that people charge the Church with lowering reason, but it is just the other way. Alone on earth, the Church makes reason really supreme. Alone on earth, the Church affirms that God Himself is bound by reason.'

The other priest raised his austere face to the spangled sky and said:

'Yet who knows if in that infinite universe—?'

'Only infinite physically,' said the little priest, turning sharply in his seat, 'not infinite in the sense of escaping from the laws of truth.'

Valentin behind his tree was tearing his fingernails with silent fury. He seemed almost to hear the sniggers of the English detectives whom he had brought so far on a fantastic guess only to listen to the metaphysical gossip of two mild old parsons. In his impatience he lost the equally elaborate answer of the tall cleric, and when he listened again it was again Father Brown who was speaking:

'Reason and justice grip the remotest and the loneliest star. Look at those stars. Don't they look as if they were single diamonds and sapphires? Well, you can imagine any mad botany or geology you please. Think of forests of adamant with leaves of brilliants. Think the moon is a blue moon, a single elephantine sapphire. But don't fancy that all that frantic astronomy would make the smallest difference to the reason and justice of conduct. On plains of opal, under cliffs cut out of pearl, you would still find a notice-board, "Thou shalt not steal".'

Valentin was just in the act of rising from his rigid and crouching attitude and creeping away as softly as might be, felled by the one great folly of his life. But something in the very silence of the tall priest made him stop until the latter spoke. When at last he did speak, he said simply, his head bowed and his hands on his knees:

'Well, I still think that other worlds may perhaps rise higher than our reason. The mystery of heaven is unfathomable, and I for one can only bow my head.'

Then, with brow yet bent and without changing by the faintest shade his attitude or voice, he added:

'Just hand over that sapphire cross of yours, will you? We're all alone and I could pull you to pieces like a straw doll.'

The utterly unaltered voice and attitude added a strange violence to that shocking change of speech. But the guarder of the relic only seemed to turn his head by the smallest section of the compass. He seemed still to have a somewhat foolish face turned to the stars. Perhaps he had not understood. Or, perhaps, he had understood and sat rigid with terror.

'Yes,' said the tall priest, in the same low voice and in the same still posture, 'yes, I am Flambeau.'

Then, after a pause, he said:

'Come, will you give me that cross?'

'No,' said the other, and the monosyllable had an odd sound.

Flambeau suddenly flung off all his pontifical pretensions. The great robber leaned back in his seat and laughed low but long.

'No,' he cried; 'you won't give it me, you proud prelate. You won't give it me, you little celibate simpleton. Shall I tell you why you won't give it me? Because I've got it already in my own breast-pocket.'

The small man from Essex turned what seemed to be a dazed face in the dusk, and said, with the timid eagerness of 'The Private Secretary':

'Are – are you sure?'

Flambeau yelled with delight.

'Really, you're as good as a three-act farce,' he cried. 'Yes, you turnip, I am quite sure. I had the sense to make a duplicate of the right parcel, and now, my friend, you've got the duplicate, and I've got the jewels. An old dodge, Father Brown – a very old dodge.'

'Yes,' said Father Brown, and passed his hand through his hair with the same strange vagueness of manner. 'Yes, I've heard of it before.'

The colossus of crime leaned over to the little rustic priest with a sort of sudden interest.

'*You* have heard of it?' he asked. 'Where have *you* heard of it?'

'Well, I mustn't tell you his name, of course,' said the little man simply. 'He was a penitent, you know. He had lived prosperously for about twenty years entirely on duplicate brown-paper parcels. And so, you see, when I began to suspect you, I thought of this poor chap's way of doing it at once.'

'Began to suspect me?' repeated the outlaw with increased intensity. 'Did you really have the gumption to suspect me just because I brought you up to this bare part of the heath?'

'No, no,' said Brown with an air of apology. 'You see, I suspected you when we first met. It's that little bulge up the sleeve where you people have the spiked bracelet.'

'How in Tartarus,' cried Flambeau, 'did you ever hear of the spiked bracelet?'

'Oh, one's little flock, you know!' said Father Brown, arching his eyebrows rather blankly. 'When I was a curate in Hartlepool, there were three of them with spiked bracelets. So, as I suspected you from the first, don't you see, I made sure that the cross should go safe, anyhow. I'm afraid I watched you, you know. So at last I saw you change the parcels. Then, don't you see, I changed them back again. And then I left the right one behind.'

'Left it behind?' repeated Flambeau, and for the first time there was another note in his voice beside his triumph.

'Well, it was like this,' said the little priest, speaking in the same unaffected way. 'I went back to that sweet-shop and asked if I'd left a parcel, and gave them a particular address if it turned up. Well, I knew I hadn't; but when I went away again I did. So, instead of running after me with that valuable parcel, they have sent it flying to a friend of mine in Westminster.' Then he added rather sadly, 'I learnt that, too, from a poor fellow in Hartlepool. He used to do it with handbags he stole at railway stations, but he's in a monastery now. Oh, one gets to know, you know,' he added, rubbing his head again with the same sort of a desperate apology. 'We can't help being priests. People come and tell us these things.'

Flambeau tore a brown-paper parcel out of his inner pocket and rent it in pieces. There was nothing but paper and sticks of lead inside it. He sprang to his feet with a gigantic gesture, and cried:

'I don't believe you. I don't believe a bumpkin like you could manage all that. I believe you've still got the stuff on you, and if you don't give it up – why, we're all alone, and I'll take it by force!'

'No,' said Father Brown simply, and stood up also, 'you won't take it by force. First, because I really haven't still got it. And, second, because we are not alone.'

Flambeau stopped in his stride forward.

'Behind that tree,' said Father Brown, pointing, 'are two strong policemen and the greatest detective alive. How did they come here, do you ask? Why, I brought them, of course! How did I do it? Why, I'll tell you if you like! Lord bless you, we have to know twenty such things when we work among the criminal classes! Well, I wasn't sure you were a thief, and it would never do to make a scandal against one of our own clergy. So I just tested you to see if anything would make you show yourself. A man generally makes a small scene if he finds salt in his coffee; if he doesn't, he has some reason for keeping quiet. I changed the salt and sugar, and you kept quiet. A man generally objects if his bill is three times too big. If he pays it, he has some motive for passing unnoticed. I altered your bill, and you paid it.'

The world seemed waiting for Flambeau to leap like a tiger. But he was held back as by a spell; he was stunned with the utmost curiosity.

'Well,' went on Father Brown, with lumbering lucidity, 'as you wouldn't leave any tracks for the police, of course somebody had to. At every place we went to, I took care to do something that would get us talked about for the rest of the day. I didn't do much harm – a splashed wall, spilt apples, a broken window; but I saved the cross, as the cross will always be saved. It is at Westminster by now. I rather wonder you didn't stop it with the Donkey's Whistle.'

'With the what?' asked Flambeau.

'I'm glad you've never heard of it,' said the priest, making a face. 'It's a foul thing. I'm sure you're too good a man for a Whistler. I couldn't have countered it even with the Spots myself; I'm not strong enough in the legs.'

'What on earth are you talking about?' asked the other.

'Well, I did think you'd know the Spots,' said Father Brown, agreeably surprised. 'Oh, you can't have gone so very wrong yet!'

'How in blazes do you know all these horrors?' cried Flambeau.

The shadow of a smile crossed the round, simple face of his clerical opponent.

'Oh, by being a celibate simpleton, I suppose,' he said. 'Has it never struck you that a man who does next to nothing but hear men's real sins is not likely to be wholly unaware of human evil? But, as a matter of fact, another part of my trade, too, made me sure you weren't a priest.'

'What?' asked the thief, almost gaping.

'You attacked reason,' said Father Brown. 'It's bad theology.'

And even as he turned away to collect his property, the three policemen came out from under the twilight trees. Flambeau was an artist and a sportsman. He stepped back and swept Valentin a great bow.

'Do not bow to me, *mon ami*,' said Valentin, with silver clearness. 'Let us both bow to our master.'

And they both stood an instant uncovered, while the little Essex priest blinked about for his umbrella.

THE QUEER FEET

If you meet a member of that select club, 'The Twelve True
Fishermen', entering the Vernon Hotel for the annual club dinner, you will observe, as he takes off his overcoat, that his evening
coat is green and not black. If (supposing that you have the star-
defying audacity to address such a being) you ask him why, he will
probably answer that he does it to avoid being mistaken for a
waiter. You will then retire crushed. But you will leave behind you
a mystery as yet unsolved and a tale worth telling.

If (to pursue the same vein of improbable conjecture) you were
to meet a mild, hard-working little priest, named Father Brown,
and were to ask him what he thought was the most singular luck
of his life, he would probably reply that upon the whole his best
stroke was at the Vernon Hotel, where he had averted a crime and,
perhaps, saved a soul, merely by listening to a few footsteps in a
passage. He is perhaps a little proud of this wild and wonderful
guess of his, and it is possible that he might refer to it. But since it
is immeasurably unlikely that you will ever rise high enough in the
social world to find 'The Twelve True Fishermen', or that you will
ever sink low enough among slums and criminals to find Father
Brown, I fear you will never hear the story at all unless you hear it
from me.

The Vernon Hotel, at which The Twelve True Fishermen held
their annual dinners, was an institution such as can only exist in an
oligarchical society which has almost gone mad on good manners.
It was that topsy-turvy product – an 'exclusive' commercial enterprise. That is, it was a thing which paid not by attracting people,
but actually by turning people away. In the heart of a plutocracy
tradesmen become cunning enough to be more fastidious than
their customers. They positively create difficulties so that their
wealthy and weary clients may spend money and diplomacy in
overcoming them. If there were a fashionable hotel in London
which no man could enter who was under six foot, society would

meekly make up parties of six-foot men to dine in it. If there were
an expensive restaurant which by a mere caprice of its proprietor
was only open on Thursday afternoon, it would be crowded on
Thursday afternoon. The Vernon Hotel stood, as if by accident,
in the corner of a square in Belgravia. It was a small hotel; and a
very inconvenient one. But its very inconveniences were considered as walls protecting a particular class. One inconvenience, in
particular, was held to be of vital importance: the fact that practically only twenty-four people could dine in the place at once. The
only big dinner table was the celebrated terrace table, which stood
open to the air on a sort of veranda overlooking one of the most
exquisite old gardens in London. Thus it happened that even the
twenty-four seats at this table could only be enjoyed in warm
weather; and this making the enjoyment yet more difficult made it
yet more desired. The existing owner of the hotel was a Jew named
Lever; and he made nearly a million out of it, by making it difficult
to get into. Of course he combined with this limitation in the scope
of his enterprise the most careful polish in its performance. The
wines and cooking were really as good as any in Europe, and the
demeanour of the attendants exactly mirrored the fixed mood of
the English upper class. The proprietor knew all his waiters like
the fingers on his hand; there were only fifteen of them all told.
It was much easier to become a Member of Parliament than to
become a waiter in that hotel. Each waiter was trained in terrible
silence and smoothness, as if he were a gentleman's servant. And,
indeed, there was generally at least one waiter to every gentleman
who dined.

The club of The Twelve True Fishermen would not have consented to dine anywhere but in such a place, for it insisted on a
luxurious privacy; and would have been quite upset by the mere
thought that any other club was even dining in the same building.
On the occasion of their annual dinner the Fishermen were in the
habit of exposing all their treasures, as if they were in a private
house, especially the celebrated set of fish knives and forks which
were, as it were, the insignia of the society, each being exquisitely
wrought in silver in the form of a fish, and each loaded at the hilt
with one large pearl. These were always laid out for the fish course,
and the fish course was always the most magnificent in that magnificent repast. The society had a vast number of ceremonies and

observances, but it had no history and no object; that was where it
was so very aristocratic. You did not have to be anything in order
to be one of the Twelve Fishers; unless you were already a certain
sort of person, you never even heard of them. It had been in existence twelve years. Its president was Mr Audley. Its vice-president
was the Duke of Chester.

If I have in any degree conveyed the atmosphere of this appalling hotel, the reader may feel a natural wonder as to how I came
to know anything about it, and may even speculate as to how so
ordinary a person as my friend Father Brown came to find himself
in that golden gallery. As far as that is concerned, my story is
simple, or even vulgar. There is in the world a very aged rioter
and demagogue who breaks into the most refined retreats with the
dreadful information that all men are brothers, and wherever this
leveller went on his pale horse it was Father Brown's trade to
follow. One of the waiters, an Italian, had been struck down with
a paralytic stroke that afternoon; and his Jewish employer, marvel-
ling mildly at such superstitions, had consented to send for the
nearest Popish priest. With what the waiter confessed to Father
Brown we are not concerned, for the excellent reason that the
cleric kept it to himself; but apparently it involved him in writing
out a note or statement for the conveying of some message or the
righting of some wrong. Father Brown, therefore, with a meek
impudence which he would have shown equally in Buckingham
Palace, asked to be provided with a room and writing materials.
Mr Lever was torn in two. He was a kind man, and had also that
bad imitation of kindness, the dislike of any difficulty or scene. At
the same time the presence of one unusual stranger in his hotel
that evening was like a speck of dirt on something just cleaned.
There was never any borderland or ante-room in the Vernon
Hotel, no people waiting in the hall, no customers coming in on
chance. There were fifteen waiters. There were twelve guests. It
would be as startling to find a new guest in the hotel that night as
to find a new brother taking breakfast or tea in one's own family.
Moreover, the priest's appearance was second-rate and his clothes
muddy; a mere glimpse of him afar off might precipitate a crisis in
the club. Mr Lever at last hit on a plan to cover, since he might
not obliterate, the disgrace. When you enter (as you never will) the
Vernon Hotel, you pass down a short passage decorated with a

few dingy but important pictures, and come to the main vestibule and lounge which opens on your right into passages leading to the public rooms, and on your left to a similar passage pointing to the kitchens and offices of the hotel. Immediately on your left hand is the corner of a glass office, which abuts upon the lounge – a house within a house, so to speak, like the old hotel bar which probably once occupied its place.

In this office sat the representative of the proprietor (nobody in this place ever appeared in person if he could help it), and just beyond the office, on the way to the servants' quarters, was the gentlemen's cloak-room, the last boundary of the gentlemen's domain. But between the office and the cloak-room was a small private room without other outlet, sometimes used by the proprietor for delicate and important matters, such as lending a duke a thousand pounds or declining to lend him sixpence. It is a mark of the magnificent tolerance of Mr Lever that he permitted this holy place to be for about half an hour profaned by a mere priest, scribbling away on a piece of paper. The story which Father Brown was writing down was very likely a much better story than this one, only it will never be known. I can merely state that it was very nearly as long, and that the last two or three paragraphs of it were the least exciting and absorbing.

For it was by the time he had reached these that the priest began a little to allow his thoughts to wander and his animal senses, which were commonly keen, to awaken. The time of darkness and dinner was drawing on; his own forgotten little room was without a light, and perhaps the gathering gloom, as occasionally happens, sharpened the sense of sound. As Father Brown wrote the last and least essential part of his document, he caught himself writing to the rhythm of a recurrent noise outside, just as one sometimes thinks to the tune of a railway train. When he became conscious of the thing he found what it was: only the ordinary patter of feet passing the door, which in a hotel was no very unlikely matter. Nevertheless, he stared at the darkened ceiling, and listened to the sound. After he had listened for a few seconds dreamily, he got to his feet and listened intently, with his head a little on one side. Then he sat down again and buried his brow in his hands, now not merely listening, but listening and thinking also.

The footsteps outside at any given moment were such as one

might hear in any hotel; and yet, taken as a whole, there was something very strange about them. There were no other footsteps. It was always a very silent house, for the few familiar guests went at once to their own apartments, and the well-trained waiters were told to be almost invisible until they were wanted. One could not conceive any place where there was less reason to apprehend anything irregular. But these footsteps were so odd that one could not decide to call them regular or irregular. Father Brown followed them with his finger on the edge of the table, like a man trying to learn a tune on the piano.

First, there came a long rush of rapid little steps, such as a light man might make in winning a walking race. At a certain point they stopped and changed to a sort of slow, swinging stamp, numbering not a quarter of the steps, but occupying about the same time. The moment the last echoing stamp had died away would come again the run or ripple of light, hurrying feet, and then again the thud of the heavier walking. It was certainly the same pair of boots, partly because (as has been said) there were no other boots about, and partly because they had a small but unmistakable creak in them. Father Brown had the kind of head that cannot help asking questions; and on this apparently trivial question his head almost split. He had seen men run in order to jump. He had seen men run in order to slide. But why on earth should a man run in order to walk? Or, again, why should he walk in order to run? Yet no other description would cover the antics of this invisible pair of legs. The man was either walking very fast down one-half of the corridor in order to walk very slow down the other half; or he was walking very slow at one end to have the rapture of walking fast at the other. Neither suggestion seemed to make much sense. His brain was growing darker and darker, like his room.

Yet, as he began to think steadily, the very blackness of his cell seemed to make his thoughts more vivid, he began to see as in a kind of vision the fantastic feet capering along the corridor in unnatural or symbolic attitudes. Was it a heathen religious dance? Or some entirely new kind of scientific exercise? Father Brown began to ask himself with more exactness what the steps suggested. Taking the slow step first; it certainly was not the step of the proprietor. Men of his type walk with a rapid waddle, or they sit still. It could not be any servant or messenger waiting for directions.

It did not sound like it. The poorer orders (in an oligarchy) sometimes lurch about when they are slightly drunk, but generally, and
especially in such gorgeous scenes, they stand or sit in constrained
attitudes. No; that heavy yet springy step, with a kind of careless
emphasis, not specially noisy, yet not caring what noise it made,
belonged to only one of the animals of this earth. It was a gentleman of western Europe, and probably one who had never worked
for his living.

Just as he came to this solid certainty, the step changed to the
quicker one, and ran past the door as feverishly as a rat. The listener
remarked that though this step was much swifter it was also much
more noiseless, almost as if the man were walking on tiptoe. Yet it
was not associated in his mind with secrecy, but with something
else – something that he could not remember. He was maddened
by one of those half-memories that make a man feel half-witted.
Surely he had heard that strange, swift walking somewhere.
Suddenly he sprang to his feet with a new idea in his head, and
walked to the door. His room had no direct outlet on the passage,
but let on one side into the glass office, and on the other into the
cloak-room beyond. He tried the door into the office, and found it
locked. Then he looked at the window, now a square pane full of
purple cloud cleft by livid sunset, and for an instant he smelt evil
as a dog smells rats.

The rational part of him (whether the wiser or not) regained its
supremacy. He remembered that the proprietor had told him that
he should lock the door, and would come later to release him. He
told himself that twenty things he had not thought of might explain
the eccentric sounds outside; he reminded himself that there was
just enough light left to finish his own proper work. Bringing his
paper to the window so as to catch the last stormy evening light,
he resolutely plunged once more into the almost completed record.
He had written for about twenty minutes, bending closer and
closer to his paper in the lessening light; then suddenly he sat
upright. He had heard the strange feet once more.

This time they had a third oddity. Previously the unknown man
had walked, with levity indeed and lightning quickness, but he had
walked. This time he ran. One could hear the swift, soft, bounding
steps coming along the corridor, like the pads of a fleeing and
leaping panther. Whoever was coming was a very strong, active

man, in still yet tearing excitement. Yet, when the sound had swept up to the office like a sort of whispering whirlwind, it suddenly changed again to the old slow, swaggering stamp.

Father Brown flung down his paper, and, knowing the office door to be locked, went at once into the cloak-room on the other side. The attendant of this place was temporarily absent, probably because the only guests were at dinner and his office was a sinecure. After groping through a grey forest of overcoats, he found that the dim cloak-room opened on the lighted corridor in the form of a sort of counter or half-door, like most of the counters across which we have all handed umbrellas and received tickets. There was a light immediately above the semi circular arch of this opening. It threw little illumination on Father Brown himself, who seemed a mere dark outline against the dim sunset window behind him. But it threw an almost theatrical light on the man who stood outside the cloak-room in the corridor.

He was an elegant man in very plain evening dress; tall, but with an air of not taking up much room; one felt that he could have slid along like a shadow where many smaller men would have been obvious and obstructive. His face, now flung back in the lamplight, was swarthy and vivacious, the face of a foreigner. His figure was good, his manners good-humoured and confident; a critic could only say that his black coat was a shade below his figure and manners, and even bulged and bagged in an odd way. The moment he caught sight of Brown's black silhouette against the sunset, he tossed down a scrap of paper with a number and called out with amiable authority, 'I want my hat and coat, please; I find I have to go away at once.'

Father Brown took the paper without a word, and obediently went to look for the coat; it was not the first menial work he had done in his life. He brought it and laid it on the counter; meanwhile, the strange gentleman who had been feeling in his waistcoat pocket, said, laughing, 'I haven't got any silver; you can keep this.' And he threw down half a sovereign, and caught up his coat.

Father Brown's figure remained quite dark and still; but in that instant he had lost his head. His head was always most valuable when he had lost it. In such moments he put two and two together and made four million. Often the Catholic Church (which is wedded to common sense) did not approve of it. Often he did not approve of it himself. But it was a real inspiration – important at rare crises – when whosoever shall lose his head the same shall save it.

'I think, sir,' he said civilly, 'that you have some silver in your pocket.'

The tall gentleman stared. 'Hang it,' he cried, 'if I choose to give you gold, why should you complain?'

'Because silver is sometimes more valuable than gold,' said the priest mildly; 'that is, in large quantities.'

The stranger looked at him curiously. Then he looked still more curiously up the passage towards the main entrance. Then he looked back at Brown again, and then he looked very carefully at the window beyond Brown's head, still coloured with the after-glow of the storm. Then he seemed to make up his mind. He put one hand on the counter, vaulted over as easily as an acrobat and towered above the priest, putting one tremendous hand upon his collar.

'Stand still,' he said, in a hacking whisper. 'I don't want to threaten you, but—'

'I do want to threaten you,' said Father Brown, in a voice like a rolling drum. 'I want to threaten you with the worm that dieth not, and the fire that is not quenched.'

'You're a rum sort of cloak-room clerk,' said the other.

'I am a priest, Monsieur Flambeau,' said Brown, 'and I am ready to hear your confession.'

The other stood gasping for a few moments, and then staggered back into a chair.

The first two courses of the dinner of The Twelve True Fishermen had proceeded with placid success. I do not possess a copy of the menu; and if I did it would not convey anything to anybody. It was written in a sort of super-French employed by cooks, but quite unintelligible to Frenchmen. There was a tradition in the club that the *hors d'œuvres* should be various and manifold to the point of madness. They were taken seriously because they were avowedly useless extras, like the whole dinner and the whole club. There was also a tradition that the soup course should be light and unpretend-ing – a sort of simple and austere vigil for the feast of fish that was to come. The talk was that strange, slight talk which governs the

British Empire, which governs it in secret, and yet would scarcely enlighten an ordinary Englishman even if he could overhear it. Cabinet Ministers on both sides were alluded to by their Christian names with a sort of bored benignity. The Radical Chancellor of the Exchequer, whom the whole Tory party was supposed to be cursing for his extortions, was praised for his minor poetry, or his saddle in the hunting field. The Tory leader, whom all Liberals were supposed to hate as a tyrant, was discussed and, on the whole, praised – as a Liberal. It seemed somehow that politicians were very important. And yet, anything seemed important about them except their politics. Mr Audley, the chairman, was an amiable, elderly man who still wore Gladstone collars; he was a kind of symbol of all that phantasmal and yet fixed society. He had never done anything – not even anything wrong. He was not fast; he was not even particularly rich. He was simply in the thing; and there was an end of it. No party could ignore him, and if he had wished to be in the Cabinet he certainly would have been put there. The Duke of Chester, the vice-president, was a young and rising politician. That is to say, he was a pleasant youth, with flat, fair hair and a freckled face, with moderate intelligence and enormous estates. In public his appearances were always successful and his principle was simple enough. When he thought of a joke he made it, and was called brilliant. When he could not think of a joke he said that this was no time for trifling, and was called able. In private, in a club of his own class, he was simply quite pleasantly frank and silly, like a schoolboy. Mr Audley, never having been in politics, treated them a little more seriously. Sometimes he even embarrassed the company by phrases suggesting that there was some difference between a Liberal and a Conservative. He himself was a Conservative, even in private life. He had a roll of grey hair over the back of his collar, like certain old-fashioned statesmen, and seen from behind he looked like the man the empire wants. Seen from the front he looked like a mild, self-indulgent bachelor, with rooms in the Albany – which he was.

As has been remarked, there were twenty-four seats at the terrace table, and only twelve members of the club. Thus they could occupy the terrace in the most luxurious style of all, being ranged along the inner side of the table, with no one opposite, commanding an uninterrupted view of the garden, the colours of which were still vivid, though evening was closing in somewhat luridly for the time of year. The chairman sat in the centre of the line, and the vice-president at the right-hand end of it. When the twelve guests first trooped into their seats it was the custom (for some unknown reason) for all the fifteen waiters to stand lining the wall like troops presenting arms to the king, while the fat proprietor stood and bowed to the club with radiant surprise, as if he had never heard of them before. But before the first chink of knife and fork this army of retainers had vanished, only the one or two required to collect and distribute the plates darting about in deathly silence. Mr Lever, the proprietor, of course had disappeared in convulsions of courtesy long before. It would be exaggerative, indeed irreverent, to say that he ever positively appeared again. But when the important course, the fish course, was being brought on, there was – how shall I put it? – a vivid shadow, a projection of his personality, which told that he was hovering near. The sacred fish course consisted (to the eyes of the vulgar) in a sort of monstrous pudding, about the size and shape of a wedding cake, in which some considerable number of interesting fishes had finally lost the shapes which God had given to them. The Twelve True Fishermen took up their celebrated fish knives and fish forks, and approached it as gravely as if every inch of the pudding cost as much as the silver fork it was eaten with. So it did, for all I know. This course was dealt with in eager and devouring silence; and it was only when his plate was nearly empty that the young duke made the ritual remark, 'They can't do this anywhere but here.'

'Nowhere,' said Mr Audley, in a deep bass voice, turning to the speaker and nodding his venerable head a number of times. 'Nowhere, assuredly, except here. It was represented to me that at the Café Anglais—'

Here he was interrupted and even agitated for a moment by the removal of his plate, but he recaptured the valuable thread of his thoughts. 'It was represented to me that the same could be done at the Café Anglais. Nothing like it, sir,' he said, shaking his head ruthlessly, like a hanging judge. 'Nothing like it.'

'Overrated place,' said a certain Colonel Pound, speaking (by the look of him) for the first time for some months.

'Oh, I don't know,' said the Duke of Chester, who was an optimist, 'it's jolly good for some things. You can't beat it at—'

A waiter came swiftly along the room, and then stopped dead. His stoppage was as silent as his tread; but all those vague and kindly gentlemen were so used to the utter smoothness of the unseen machinery which surrounded and supported their lives, that a waiter doing anything unexpected was a start and a jar. They felt as you and I would feel if the inanimate world disobeyed – if a chair ran away from us.

The waiter stood staring a few seconds, while there deepened on every face at table a strange shame which is wholly the product of our time. It is the combination of modern humanitarianism with the horrible modern abyss between the souls of the rich and poor. A genuine historic aristocrat would have thrown things at the waiter, beginning with empty bottles, and very probably ending with money. A genuine democrat would have asked him, with a comrade-like clearness of speech, what the devil he was doing. But these modern plutocrats could not bear a poor man near to them, either as a slave or as a friend. That something had gone wrong with the servants was merely a dull, hot embarrassment. They did not want to be brutal, and they dreaded the need to be benevolent. They wanted the thing, whatever it was, to be over. It was over. The waiter, after standing for some seconds rigid, like a cataleptic, turned round and ran madly out of the room.

When he reappeared in the room, or rather in the doorway, it was in company with another waiter, with whom he whispered and gesticulated with southern fierceness. Then the first waiter went away, leaving the second waiter, and reappeared with a third waiter. By the time a fourth waiter had joined this hurried synod, Mr Audley felt it necessary to break the silence in the interests of Tact. He used a very loud cough, instead of the presidential hammer, and said, 'Splendid work young Moocher's doing in Burmah. Now, no other nation in the world could have—'

A fifth waiter had sped towards him like an arrow, and was whispering in his ear, 'So sorry. Important! Might the proprietor speak to you?'

The chairman turned in disorder, and with a dazed stare saw Mr Lever coming towards them with his lumbering quickness. The gait of the good proprietor was indeed his usual gait, but his face was by no means usual. Generally it was a genial copper-brown; now it was a sickly yellow.

'You will pardon me, Mr Audley,' he said, with asthmatic breathlessness. 'I have great apprehensions. Your fish-plates, they are cleared away with the knife and fork on them!'

'Well, I hope so,' said the chairman, with some warmth.

'You see him?' panted the excited hotel keeper; 'you see the waiter who took them away? You know him?'

'Know the waiter?' answered Mr Audley indignantly. 'Certainly not!'

Mr Lever opened his hands with a gesture of agony. 'I never send him,' he said. 'I know not when or why he come. I send my waiter to take away the plates, and he find them already away.'

Mr Audley still looked rather too bewildered to be really the man the empire wants; none of the company could say anything except the man of wood – Colonel Pound – who seemed galvanized into an unnatural life. He rose rigidly from his chair, leaving all the rest sitting, screwed his eyeglass into his eye, and spoke in a raucous undertone as if he had half-forgotten how to speak. 'Do you mean,' he said, 'that somebody has stolen our silver fish service?'

The proprietor repeated the open-handed gesture with even greater helplessness; and in a flash all the men at the table were on their feet.

'Are all your waiters here?' demanded the Colonel, in his low, harsh accent.

'Yes; they're all here. I noticed it myself,' cried the young duke, pushing his boyish face into the inmost ring. 'Always count 'em as I come in; they look so queer standing up against the wall.'

'But surely one cannot exactly remember,' began Mr Audley, with heavy hesitation.

'I remember exactly, I tell you,' cried the duke excitedly. 'There never have been more than fifteen waiters at this place, and there were no more than fifteen tonight, I'll swear; no more and no less.'

The proprietor turned upon him, quaking in a kind of palsy of surprise. 'You say ... you say,' he stammered, 'that you see all my fifteen waiters?'

'As usual,' assented the duke. 'What is the matter with that?'

'Nothing,' said Lever, with a deepening accent, 'only you did not. For one of zem is dead upstairs.'

There was a shocking stillness for an instant in that room. It may be (so supernatural is the word death) that each of those idle men looked for a second at his soul, and saw it as a small dried pea. One of them – the duke, I think – even said with the idiotic kindness of wealth, 'Is there anything we can do?'

'He has had a priest,' said the Jew, not untouched.

Then, as to the clang of doom, they awoke to their own position. For a few weird seconds they had really felt as if the fifteenth waiter might be the ghost of the dead man upstairs. They had been dumb under that oppression, for ghosts were to them an embarrassment, like beggars. But the remembrance of the silver broke the spell of the miraculous; broke it abruptly and with a brutal reaction. The colonel flung over his chair and strode to the door. 'If there was a fifteenth man here, friends,' he said, 'that fifteenth fellow was a thief. Down at once to the front and back doors and secure everything; then we'll talk. The twenty-four pearls of the club are worth recovering.'

Mr Audley seemed at first to hesitate about whether it was gentlemanly to be in such a hurry about anything; but, seeing the duke dash down the stairs with youthful energy, he followed with a more mature motion.

At the same instant a sixth waiter ran into the room, and declared that he had found the pile of fish plates on a sideboard, with no trace of the silver.

The crowd of diners and attendants that tumbled helter skelter down the passages divided into two groups. Most of the Fishermen followed the proprietor to the front room to demand news of any exit. Colonel Pound, with the Chairman, the vice-president, and one or two others darted down the corridor leading to the servants' quarters, as the more likely line of escape. As they did so they passed the dim alcove or cavern of the cloak-room, and saw a short, black-coated figure, presumably an attendant, standing a little way back in the shadow of it.

'Hallo there!' called out the duke. 'Have you seen anyone pass?'

The short figure did not answer the question directly, but merely said, 'Perhaps I have got what you are looking for, gentlemen.'

They paused, wavering and wondering, while he quietly went to the back of the cloak-room, and came back with both hands full of shining silver, which he laid out on the counter as calmly as a salesman. It took the form of a dozen quaintly shaped forks and knives.

'You – you—' began the colonel, quite thrown off his balance at last. Then he peered into the dim little room and saw two things: first, that the short, black-clad man was dressed like a clergyman; and, second, that the window of the room behind him was burst, as if someone had passed violently through.

'Valuable things to deposit in a cloak-room, aren't they?' remarked the clergyman, with cheerful composure.

'Did – did you steal those things?' stammered Mr Audley, with staring eyes.

'If I did,' said the cleric pleasantly, 'at least I am bringing them back again.'

'But you didn't,' said Colonel Pound, still staring at the broken window.

'To make a clean breast of it, I didn't,' said the other, with some humour. And he seated himself quite gravely on a stool.

'But you know who did,' said the colonel.

'I don't know his real name,' said the priest placidly; 'but I know something of his fighting weight, and a great deal about his spiritual difficulties. I formed the physical estimate when he was trying to throttle me, and the moral estimate when he repented.'

'Oh, I say – repented!' cried young Chester, with a sort of crow of laughter.

Father Brown got to his feet, putting his hands behind him. 'Odd, isn't it,' he said, 'that a thief and a vagabond should repent, when so many who are rich and secure remain hard and frivolous, and without fruit for God or man? But there, if you will excuse me, you trespass a little upon my province. If you doubt the penitence as a practical fact, there are your knives and forks. You are The Twelve True Fishers, and there are all your silver fish. But He has made me a fisher of men.'

'Did you catch this man?' asked the colonel, frowning.

Father Brown looked him full in his frowning face. 'Yes,' he said, 'I caught him, with an unseen hook and an invisible line which is long enough to let him wander to the ends of the world, and still to bring him back with a twitch upon the thread.'

There was a long silence. All the other men present drifted away to carry the recovered silver to their comrades, or to consult the proprietor about the queer condition of affairs. But the grim-faced colonel still sat sideways on the counter, swinging his long, lank legs and biting his dark moustache.

At last he said quietly to the priest, 'He must have been a clever fellow, but I think I know a cleverer.'

'He was a clever fellow,' answered the other, 'but I am not quite sure of what other you mean.'

'I mean you,' said the colonel, with a short laugh. 'I don't want to get the fellow jailed; make yourself easy about that. But I'd give a good many silver forks to know exactly how you fell into this affair, and how you got the stuff out of him. I reckon you're the most up-to-date devil of the present company.'

Father Brown seemed rather to like the saturnine candour of the soldier. 'Well,' he said, smiling, 'I mustn't tell you anything of the man's identity, or his own story, of course; but there's no particular reason why I shouldn't tell you of the mere outside facts which I found out for myself.'

He hopped over the barrier with unexpected activity, and sat beside Colonel Pound, kicking his short legs like a little boy on a gate. He began to tell the story as easily as if he were telling it to an old friend by a Christmas fire.

'You see, colonel,' he said, 'I was shut up in that small room there doing some writing, when I heard a pair of feet in this passage doing a dance that was as queer as the dance of death. First came quick, funny little steps, like a man walking on tiptoe for a wager; then came slow, careless, creaking steps, as of a big man walking about with a cigar. But they were both made by the same feet, I swear, and they came in rotation; first the run and then the walk, and then the run again. I wondered at first idly and then wildly why a man should act these two parts at once. One walk I knew; it was just like yours, colonel. It was the walk of a well-fed gentleman waiting for something, who strolls about rather because he is physically alert than because he is mentally impatient. I knew that I knew the other walk, too, but I could not remember what it was. What wild creature had I met on my travels that tore along on tiptoe in that extraordinary style? Then I heard a clink of plates somewhere; and the answer stood up as plain as St Peter's. It was the walk of a waiter – that walk with the body slanted forward, the eyes looking down, the ball of the toe spurning away the ground, the coat tails and napkin flying. Then I thought for a minute and a half more. And I believe I saw the manner of the crime, as clearly as if I were going to commit it.'

Colonel Pound looked at him keenly, but the speaker's mild grey eyes were fixed upon the ceiling with almost empty wistfulness.

'A crime,' he said slowly, 'is like any other work of art. Don't look surprised; crimes are by no means the only works of art that come from an infernal workshop. But every work of art, divine or diabolic, has one indispensable mark – I mean, that the centre of it is simple, however much the fulfilment may be complicated. Thus, in *Hamlet*, let us say, the grotesqueness of the grave-digger, the flowers of the mad girl, the fantastic finery of Osric, the pallor of the ghost and the grin of the skull are all oddities in a sort of tangled wreath round one plain tragic figure of a man in black. Well, this also,' he said, getting slowly down from his seat with a smile, 'this also is the plain tragedy of a man in black. Yes,' he went on, seeing the colonel look up in some wonder, 'the whole of this tale turns on a black coat. In this, as in *Hamlet*, there are the rococo excrescences – yourselves, let us say. There is the dead waiter, who was there when he could not be there. There is the invisible hand that swept your table clear of silver and melted into air. But every clever crime is founded ultimately on some one quite simple fact – some fact that is not itself mysterious. The mystification comes in covering it up, in leading men's thoughts away from it. This large and subtle and (in the ordinary course) most profitable crime, was built on the plain fact that a gentleman's evening dress is the same as a waiter's. All the rest was acting, and thundering good acting, too.'

'Still,' said the colonel, getting up and frowning at his boots. 'I am not sure that I understand.'

'Colonel,' said Father Brown, 'I tell you that this archangel of impudence who stole your forks walked up and down this passage twenty times in the blaze of all the lamps, in the glare of all the eyes. He did not go and hide in dim corners where suspicion might have searched for him. He kept constantly on the move in the lighted corridors, and everywhere that he went he seemed to be there by right. Don't ask me what he was like; you have seen him yourself six or seven times tonight. You were waiting with all the other grand people in the reception room at the end of the passage there, with the terrace just beyond. Whenever he came among you gentlemen, he came in the lightning style of a waiter, with bent head, flapping napkin and flying feet. He shot out on to the terrace, did something to the table cloth, and shot back again towards the office and the waiters' quarters. By the time he had come under the eye of the office clerk and the waiters he had become another man in every inch of his body, in every instinctive gesture. He strolled among the servants with the absent-minded insolence which they have all seen in their patrons. It was no new thing to them that a swell from the dinner party should pace all parts of the house like an animal at the Zoo; they know that nothing marks the Smart Set more than a habit of walking where one chooses. When he was magnificently weary of walking down that particular passage he would wheel round and pace back past the office; in the shadow of the arch just beyond he was altered as by a blast of magic, and went hurrying forward again among the Twelve Fishermen, an obsequious attendant. Why should the gentlemen look at a chance waiter? Why should the waiters suspect a first-rate walking gentleman? Once or twice he played the coolest tricks. In the proprietor's private quarters he called out breezily for a syphon of soda water, saying he was thirsty. He said genially that he would carry it himself, and he did; he carried it quickly and correctly through the thick of you, a waiter with an obvious errand. Of course, it could not have been kept up long, but it only had to be kept up till the end of the fish course.

'His worst moment was when the waiters stood in a row; but even then he contrived to lean against the wall just around the corner in such a way that for that important instant the waiters thought him a gentleman, while the gentlemen thought him a waiter. The rest went like winking. If any waiter caught him away from the table, that waiter caught a languid aristocrat. He had only to time himself two minutes before the fish was cleared, become a swift servant, and clear it himself. He put the plates down on a sideboard, stuffed the silver in his breast pocket, giving it a bulgy look, and ran like a hare (I heard him coming) till he came to the cloak-room. There he had only to be a plutocrat again – a plutocrat called away suddenly on business. He had only to give his ticket to the cloak-room attendant, and go out again elegantly as he had come in. Only – only I happened to be the cloak-room attendant.'

'What did you do to him?' cried the colonel, with unusual intensity. 'What did he tell you?'

'I beg your pardon,' said the priest immovably, 'that is where the story ends.'

'And the interesting story begins,' muttered Pound. 'I think I understand his professional trick. But I don't seem to have got hold of yours.'

'I must be going,' said Father Brown.

They walked together along the passage to the entrance hall, where they saw the fresh, freckled face of the Duke of Chester, who was bounding buoyantly along towards them.

'Come along, Pound,' he cried breathlessly. 'I've been looking for you everywhere. The dinner's going again in spanking style, and old Audley has got to make a speech in honour of the forks being saved. We want to start some new ceremony, don't you know, to commemorate the occasion. I say, you really got the goods back, what do you suggest?'

'Why,' said the colonel, eyeing him with a certain sardonic approval. 'I should suggest that henceforward we wear green coats instead of black. One never knows what mistakes may arise when one looks so like a waiter.'

'Oh, hang it all!' said the young man, 'a gentleman never looks like a waiter.'

'Nor a waiter like a gentleman, I suppose,' said Colonel Pound, with the same lowering laughter on his face. 'Reverend sir, your friend must have been very smart to act the gentleman.'

Father Brown buttoned up his commonplace overcoat to the neck, for the night was stormy, and took his commonplace umbrella from the stand.

'Yes,' he said; 'it must be very hard work to be a gentleman; but, do you know, I have sometimes thought that it may be almost as laborious to be a waiter.'

And saying 'Good evening,' he pushed open the heavy doors of that palace of pleasures. The golden gates closed behind him, and he went at a brisk walk through the damp, dark streets in search of a penny omnibus.

THE WRONG SHAPE

CERTAIN of the great roads going north out of London continue far into the country a sort of attenuated and interrupted spectre of a street, with great gaps in the building, but preserving the line. Here will be a group of shops, followed by a fenced field or paddock, and then a famous public-house, and then perhaps a market garden or a nursery garden, and then one large private house, and then another field and another inn, and so on. If anyone walks along one of these roads he will pass a house which will probably catch his eye, though he may not be able to explain its attraction. It is a long, low house, running parallel with the road, painted mostly white and pale green, with a veranda and sun-blinds, and porches capped with those quaint sort of cupolas like wooden umbrellas that one sees in some old-fashioned houses. In fact, it is an old-fashioned house, very English and very suburban in the good old wealthy Clapham sense. And yet the house has a look of having been built chiefly for the hot weather. Looking at its white paint and sun-blinds one thinks vaguely of pugarees and even of palm trees. I cannot trace the feeling to its root; perhaps the place was built by an Anglo-Indian.

Anyone passing this house, I say, would be namelessly fascinated by it; would feel that it was a place about which some story was to be told. And he would have been right, as you shall shortly hear. For this is the story – the story of the strange things that did really happen in it in the Whitsuntide of the year 18—.

Anyone passing the house on the Thursday before Whit-Sunday at about half-past four p.m. would have seen the front door open, and Father Brown, of the small church of St Mungo, come out smoking a large pipe in company with a very tall French friend of his called Flambeau, who was smoking a very small cigarette. These persons may or may not be of interest to the reader, but the truth is that they were not the only interesting things that were displayed when the front door of the white-and-green house was opened. There are further peculiarities about this house, which must be described to start with, not only that the reader may understand this tragic tale, but also that he may realize what it was that the opening of the door revealed.

The whole house was built upon the plan of a T, but a T with a very long cross piece and a very short tail piece. The long cross piece was the frontage that ran along in face of the street, with the front door in the middle; it was two storeys high, and contained nearly all the important rooms. The short tail piece, which ran out at the back immediately opposite the front door, was one storey high, and consisted only of two long rooms, the one leading into the other. The first of these two rooms was the study in which the celebrated Mr Quinton wrote his wild Oriental poems and romances. The farther room was a glass conservatory full of tropical blossoms of quite unique and almost monstrous beauty, and on such afternoons as these was glowing with gorgeous sunlight. Thus when the hall door was open, many a passer-by literally stopped to stare and gasp; for he looked down a perspective of rich apartments to something really like a transformation scene in a fairy play: purple clouds and golden suns and crimson stars that were at once scorchingly vivid and yet transparent and far away.

Leonard Quinton, the poet, had himself most carefully arranged this effect; and it is doubtful whether he so perfectly expressed his personality in any of his poems. For he was a man who drank and bathed in colours, who indulged his lust for colour somewhat to the neglect of form – even of good form. This it was that had turned his genius so wholly to eastern art and imagery; to those bewildering carpets or blinding embroideries in which all the colours seem fallen into a fortunate chaos, having nothing to typify or to teach. He had attempted, not perhaps with complete artistic success, but with acknowledged imagination and invention, to compose epics and love stories reflecting the riot of violent and even cruel colour; tales of tropical heavens of burning gold or blood-red copper; of eastern heroes who rode with twelve-turbaned mitres upon elephants painted purple or peacock green; of gigantic jewels that a hundred negroes could not carry, but which burned with ancient and strange-hued fires.

In short (to put the matter from the more common point of view), he dealt much in eastern heavens, rather worse than most western hells; in eastern monarchs, whom we might possibly call maniacs; and in eastern jewels which a Bond Street jeweller (if the hundred staggering negroes brought them into his shop) might possibly not regard as genuine. Quinton was a genius, if a morbid one; and even his morbidity appeared more in his life than in his work. In temperament he was weak and waspish, and his health had suffered heavily from oriental experiments with opium. His wife – a handsome, hard-working, and, indeed, over-worked woman – objected to the opium, but objected much more to a live Indian hermit in white and yellow robes, whom her husband had insisted on entertaining for months together, a Virgil to guide his spirit through the heavens and the hells of the east.

It was out of this artistic household that Father Brown and his friend stepped on to the door-step; and to judge from their faces, they stepped out of it with much relief. Flambeau had known Quinton in wild student days in Paris, and they had renewed the acquaintance for a week-end; but apart from Flambeau's more responsible developments of late, he did not get on well with the poet now. Choking oneself with opium and writing little erotic verses on vellum was not his notion of how a gentleman should go to the devil. As the two paused on the doorstep, before taking a turn in the garden, the front garden gate was thrown open with violence, and a young man with a billycock hat on the back of his head tumbled up the steps in his eagerness. He was a dissipated-looking youth with a gorgeous red necktie all awry, as if he had slept in it, and he kept fidgeting and lashing about with one of those little jointed canes.

'I say,' he said breathlessly, 'I want to see old Quinton. I must see him. Has he gone?'

'Mr Quinton is in, I believe,' said Father Brown, cleaning his pipe, 'but I do not know if you can see him. The doctor is with him at present.'

The young man, who seemed not to be perfectly sober, stumbled into the hall; and at the same moment the doctor came out of Quinton's study, shutting the door and beginning to put on his gloves.

'See Mr Quinton?' said the doctor coolly. 'No, I'm afraid you can't. In fact, you mustn't on any account. Nobody must see him; I've just given him his sleeping draught.'

'No, but look here, old chap,' said the youth in the red tie, trying affectionately to capture the doctor by the lapels of his coat. 'Look here. I'm simply sewn up, I tell you. I—'

'It's no good, Mr Atkinson,' said the doctor, forcing him to fall back; 'when you can alter the effects of a drug I'll alter my decision,' and, settling on his hat, he stepped out into the sunlight with the other two. He was a bull-necked, good-tempered little man with a small moustache, inexpressibly ordinary, yet giving an impression of capability.

The young man in the billycock, who did not seem to be gifted with any tact in dealing with people beyond the general idea of clutching hold of their coats, stood outside the door, as dazed as if he had been thrown out bodily, and silently watched the other three walk away together through the garden.

'That was a sound, spanking lie I told just now,' remarked the medical man, laughing. 'In point of fact, poor Quinton doesn't have his sleeping draught for nearly half an hour. But I'm not going to have him bothered with that little beast, who only wants to borrow money that he wouldn't pay back if he could. He's a dirty little scamp, though he is Mrs Quinton's brother, and she's as fine a woman as ever walked.'

'Yes,' said Father Brown. 'She's a good woman.'

'So I propose to hang about the garden till the creature has cleared off,' went on the doctor, 'and then I'll go in to Quinton with the medicine. Atkinson can't get in, because I locked the door.'

'In that case, Dr Harris,' said Flambeau, 'we might as well walk round at the back by the end of the conservatory. There's no entrance to it that way but it's worth seeing, even from the outside.'

'Yes, and I might get a squint at my patient,' laughed the doctor, 'for he prefers to lie on an ottoman right at the end of the conservatory amid all those blood-red poinsettias; it would give me the creeps. But what are you doing?'

Father Brown had stopped for a moment, and picked up out of the long grass, where it had almost been wholly hidden, a queer, crooked Oriental knife, inlaid exquisitely in coloured stones and metals.

'What is this?' asked Father Brown, regarding it with some disfavour.

'Oh, Quinton's, I suppose,' said Dr Harris carelessly; 'he has all sorts of Chinese knickknacks about the place. Or perhaps it belongs to the mild Hindoo of his whom he keeps on a string.'

'What Hindoo?' asked Father Brown, still staring at the dagger in his hand.

'Oh, some Indian conjurer,' said the doctor lightly; 'a fraud, of course.'

'You don't believe in magic?' asked Father Brown without looking up.

'Oh crikey! magic!' said the doctor.

'It's very beautiful,' said the priest in a low, dreaming voice; 'the colours are very beautiful. But it's the wrong shape.'

'What for?' asked Flambeau, staring.

'For anything. It's the wrong shape in the abstract. Don't you ever feel that about Eastern art? The colours are intoxicatingly lovely; but the shapes are mean and bad – deliberately mean and bad. I have seen wicked things in a Turkey carpet.'

'*Mon Dieu!*' cried Flambeau, laughing.

'They are letters and symbols in a language I don't know; but I know they stand for evil words,' went on the priest, his voice growing lower and lower. 'The lines go wrong on purpose – like serpents doubling to escape.'

'What the devil are you talking about?' said the doctor with a loud laugh.

Flambeau spoke quietly to him in answer. 'The Father sometimes gets this mystic's cloud on him,' he said; 'but I give you fair warning that I have never known him have it except when there was some evil quite near.'

'Oh, rats!' said the scientist.

'Why, look at it,' cried Father Brown, holding out the crooked knife at arm's length, as if it were some glittering snake. 'Don't you see it is the wrong shape? Don't you see that it has no hearty and plain purpose? It does not point like a spear. It does not sweep like a scythe. It does not *look* like a weapon. It looks like an instrument of torture.'

'Well, as you don't seem to like it,' said the jolly Harris, 'it had better be taken back to its owner. Haven't we come to the end of this confounded conservatory yet? This house is the wrong shape, if you like.'

'You don't understand,' said Father Brown, shaking his head. 'The shape of this house is quaint – it is even laughable. But there is nothing *wrong* about it.'

As they spoke they came round the curve of glass that ended the conservatory, an uninterrupted curve, for there was neither door nor window by which to enter at that end. The glass, however, was clear, and the sun still bright, though beginning to set; and they could see not only the flamboyant blossoms inside, but the frail figure of the poet in a brown velvet coat lying languidly on the sofa, having, apparently, fallen half asleep over a book. He was a pale, slight man, with loose, chestnut hair and a fringe of beard that was the paradox of his face, for the beard made him look less manly. These traits were well known to all three of them; but even had it not been so, it may be doubted whether they would have looked at Quinton just then. Their eyes were riveted on another object.

Exactly in their path, immediately outside the round end of the glass building, was standing a tall man, whose drapery fell to his feet in faultless white, and whose bare, brown skull, face, and neck gleamed in the setting sun like splendid bronze. He was looking through the glass at the sleeper, and he was more motionless than a mountain.

'Who is that?' cried Father Brown, stepping back with a hissing intake of his breath.

'Oh, it is only that Hindoo humbug,' growled Harris; 'but I don't know what the deuce he's doing here.'

'It looks like hypnotism,' said Flambeau, biting his black moustache.

'Why are you unmedical fellows always talking bosh about hypnotism?' cried the doctor. 'It looks a deal more like burglary.'

'Well, we will speak to it, at any rate,' said Flambeau, who was always for action. One long stride took him to the place where the Indian stood. Bowing from his great height, which overtopped even the Oriental's, he said with placid impudence:

'Good evening, sir. Do you want anything?'

Quite slowly, like a great ship turning into a harbour, the great yellow face turned, and looked at last over its white shoulder. They were startled to see that its yellow eyelids were quite sealed, as in sleep. 'Thank you,' said the face in excellent English. 'I want nothing.' Then, half opening the lids, so as to show a slit of opalescent eyeball, he repeated, 'I want nothing.' Then he opened his eyes wide with a startling stare, said, 'I want nothing,' and went rustling away into the rapidly darkening garden.

'The Christian is more modest,' muttered Father Brown; 'he wants something.'

'What on earth was he doing?' asked Flambeau, knitting his black brows and lowering his voice.

'I should like to talk to you later,' said Father Brown.

The sunlight was still a reality, but it was the red light of evening, and the bulk of the garden trees and bushes grew blacker and blacker against it. They turned round the end of the conservatory, and walked in silence down the other side to get round to the front door. As they went they seemed to wake something, as one startles a bird, in the deeper corner between the study and the main building; and again they saw the white-robed fakir slide out of the shadow, and slip round towards the front door. To their surprise, however, he had not been alone. They found themselves abruptly pulled up and forced to banish their bewilderment by the appearance of Mrs Quinton, with her heavy golden hair and square pale face, advancing on them out of the twilight. She looked a little stern, but was entirely courteous.

'Good evening, Dr Harris,' was all she said.

'Good evening, Mrs Quinton,' said the little doctor heartily. 'I am just going to give your husband his sleeping draught.'

'Yes,' she said in a clear voice. 'I think it is quite time.' And she smiled at them, and went sweeping into the house.

'That woman's over-driven,' said Father Brown; 'that's the kind of woman that does her duty for twenty years, and then does something dreadful.'

The little doctor looked at him for the first time with an eye of interest. 'Did you ever study medicine?' he asked.

'You have to know something of the mind as well as the body,' answered the priest; 'we have to know something of the body as well as the mind.'

'Well,' said the doctor, 'I think I'll go and give Quinton his stuff.'

They had turned the corner of the front façade, and were approaching the front doorway. As they turned into it they saw the man in the white robe for the third time. He came so straight towards the front door that it seemed quite incredible that he had not just come out of the study opposite to it. Yet they knew that the study door was locked.

Father Brown and Flambeau, however, kept this weird contradiction to themselves, and Dr Harris was not a man to waste his thoughts on the impossible. He permitted the omnipresent Asiatic to make his exit, and then stepped briskly into the hall. There he found a figure which he had already forgotten. The inane Atkinson was still hanging about, humming and poking things with his knobby cane. The doctor's face had a spasm of disgust and decision, and he whispered rapidly to his companion, 'I must lock the door again, or this rat will get in. But I shall be out again in two minutes.'

He rapidly unlocked the door and locked it again behind him, just balking a blundering charge from the young man in the billycock. The young man threw himself impatiently on a hall chair. Flambeau looked at a Persian illumination on the wall; Father Brown, who seemed in a sort of daze, dully eyed the door. In about four minutes the door was opened again. Atkinson was quicker this time. He sprang forward, held the door open for an instant, and called out, 'Oh, I say, Quinton, I want—'

From the other end of the study came the clear voice of Quinton, in something between a yawn and a yell of weary laughter.

'Oh, I know what you want. Take it, and leave me in peace. I'm writing a song about peacocks.'

Before the door closed half a sovereign came flying through the aperture; and Atkinson, stumbling forward, caught it with singular dexterity.

'So that's settled,' said the doctor, and, locking the door savagely, he led the way out into the garden.

'Poor Leonard can get a little peace now,' he added to Father Brown; 'he's locked in all by himself for an hour or two.'

'Yes,' answered the priest; 'and his voice sounded jolly enough when we left him.' Then he looked gravely round the garden, and saw the loose figure of Atkinson standing and jingling the half-sovereign in his pocket, and beyond, in the purple twilight, the figure of the Indian sitting bolt upright upon a bank of grass with his face turned towards the setting sun. Then he said abruptly, 'Where is Mrs Quinton?'

'She has gone up to her room,' said the doctor. 'That is her shadow on the blind.'

Father Brown looked up, and frowningly scrutinized a dark outline at the gas-lit window.

'Yes,' he said, 'that is her shadow,' and he walked a yard or two and threw himself upon a garden seat.

Flambeau sat down beside him; but the doctor was one of those energetic people who live naturally on their legs. He walked away, smoking, into the twilight, and the two friends were left together.

'My father,' said Flambeau in French, 'what is the matter with you?'

Father Brown was silent and motionless for half a minute then he said: 'Superstition is irreligious, but there is something in the air of this place. I think it's that Indian – at least, partly.'

He sank into silence, and watched the distant outline of the Indian, who still sat rigid as if in prayer. At first sight he seemed motionless, but as Father Brown watched him he saw that the man swayed ever so slightly with a rhythmic movement, just as the dark tree-tops swayed ever so slightly in the little wind that was creeping up the dim garden paths and shuffling the fallen leaves a little.

The landscape was growing rapidly dark, as if for a storm, but they could still see all the figures in their various places. Atkinson was leaning against a tree, with a listless face; Quinton's wife was still at her window; the doctor had gone strolling round the end of the conservatory; they could see his cigar like a will-o'-the-wisp; and the fakir still sat rigid and yet rocking, while the trees above him began to rock and almost to roar. Storm was certainly coming.

'When that Indian spoke to us,' went on Brown in a conversational undertone, 'I had a sort of vision, a vision of him and all his universe. Yet he only said the same thing three times. When first he said, "I want nothing," it meant only that he was impenetrable, that Asia does not give itself away. Then he said again, "I want nothing," and I knew that he meant that he was sufficient to himself, like a cosmos, that he needed no God, neither admitted any sins. And when he said the third time, "I want nothing," he said it with blazing eyes. And I knew that he meant literally what he said; that nothing was his desire and his home; that he was weary for

nothing as for wine; that annihilation, the mere destruction of
everything or anything—'

Two drops of rain fell; and for some reason Flambeau started
and looked up, as if they had stung him. And the same instant the
doctor down by the end of the conservatory began running towards
them, calling out something as he ran.

As he came among them like a bombshell the restless Atkinson
happened to be taking a turn nearer to the house front; and the
doctor clutched him by the collar in a convulsive grip. 'Foul play!'
he cried; 'what have you been doing to him, you dog?'

The priest had sprung erect, and had the voice of steel of a
soldier in command.

'No fighting,' he cried coolly; 'we are enough to hold anyone we
want to. What is the matter, doctor?'

'Things are not right with Quinton,' said the doctor, quite white.
'I could just see him through the glass, and I don't like the way he's
lying. It's not as I left him, anyhow.'

'Let us go into him,' said Father Brown shortly. 'You can leave
Mr Atkinson alone. I have had him in sight since we heard
Quinton's voice.'

'I will stop here and watch him,' said Flambeau hurriedly. 'You
go in and see.'

The doctor and the priest flew to the study door, unlocked it,
and fell into the room. In doing so they nearly fell over the large
mahogany table in the centre at which the poet usually wrote; for
the place was lit only by a small fire kept for the invalid. In the
middle of this table lay a single sheet of paper, evidently left there
on purpose. The doctor snatched it up, glanced at it, handed it
to Father Brown, and crying, 'Good God, look at that!' plunged
towards the glass room beyond, where the terrible tropic flowers
still seemed to keep a crimson memory of the sunset.

Father Brown read the words three times before he put down
the paper. The words were, 'I die by my own hand; yet I die
murdered!' They were in the quite inimitable, not to say illegible,
handwriting of Leonard Quinton.

Then Father Brown, still keeping the paper in his hand, strode
towards the conservatory, only to meet his medical friend coming
back with a face of assurance and collapse. 'He's done it,' said
Harris.

They went together through the gorgeous unnatural beauty of cactus and azalea and found Leonard Quinton, poet and romancer, with his head hanging downward off his ottoman and his red curls sweeping the ground. Into his left side was thrust the queer dagger that they had picked up in the garden, and his limp hand still rested on the hilt.

Outside, the storm had come at one stride, like the night in Coleridge, and garden and glass roof were darkening with driving rain. Father Brown seemed to be studying the paper more than the corpse; he held it close to his eyes; and seemed trying to read it in the twilight. Then he held it up against the faint light, and, as he did so, lightning stared at them for an instant so white that the paper looked black against it.

Darkness full of thunder followed, and after the thunder Father Brown's voice said out of the dark, 'Doctor, this paper is the wrong shape.'

'What do you mean?' asked Doctor Harris, with a frowning stare.

'It isn't square,' answered Brown. 'It has a sort of edge snipped off at the corner. What does it mean?'

'How the deuce should I know?' growled the doctor. 'Shall we move the poor chap, do you think? He's quite dead.'

'No,' answered the priest; 'we must leave him as he lies and send for the police.' But he was still scrutinizing the paper.

As they went back through the study he stopped by the table and picked up a small pair of nail scissors. 'Ah,' he said with a sort of relief, 'this is what he did it with. But yet—' And he knitted his brows.

'Oh, stop fooling with that scrap of paper,' said the doctor emphatically. 'It was a fad of his. He had hundreds of them. He cut all his paper like that,' as he pointed to a stack of sermon paper still unused on another and smaller table. Father Brown went up to it and held up a sheet. It was the same irregular shape.

'Quite so,' he said. 'And here I see the corners that were snipped off.' And to the indignation of his colleague he began to count them.

'That's all right,' he said, with an apologetic smile. 'Twenty-three sheets cut and twenty-two corners cut off them. And as I see you are impatient we will rejoin the others.'

'Who is to tell his wife?' asked Dr Harris. 'Will you go and tell her now, while I send a servant for the police?'

'As you will,' said Father Brown indifferently. And he went out to the hall door.

Here also he found a drama, though of a more grotesque sort. It showed nothing less than his big friend Flambeau in an attitude to which he had long been unaccustomed, while upon the pathway at the bottom of the steps was sprawling with his boots in the air the amiable Atkinson, his billycock hat and walking-cane sent flying in opposite directions along the path. Atkinson had at length wearied of Flambeau's almost paternal custody, and had endeavoured to knock him down, which was by no means a smooth game to play with the Roi des Apaches, even after that monarch's abdication.

Flambeau was about to leap upon his enemy and secure him once more, when the priest patted him easily on the shoulder.

'Make it up with Mr Atkinson, my friend,' he said. 'Beg a mutual pardon and say "Good night". We need not detain him any longer.' Then, as Atkinson rose somewhat doubtfully and gathered his hat and stick and went towards the garden gate, Father Brown said in a more serious voice, 'Where is that Indian?'

They all three (for the doctor had joined them) turned involuntarily towards the dim grassy bank amid the tossing trees, purple with twilight, where they had last seen the brown man swaying in his strange prayers. The Indian was gone.

'Confound him,' said the doctor, stamping furiously. 'Now I know that it was that nigger that did it.'

'I thought you didn't believe in magic,' said Father Brown quietly.

'No more I did,' said the doctor, rolling his eyes. 'I only know that I loathed that yellow devil when I thought he was a sham wizard. And I shall loathe him more if I come to think he was a real one.'

'Well, his having escaped is nothing,' said Flambeau. 'For we could have proved nothing and done nothing against him. One hardly goes to the parish constable with a story of suicide imposed by witchcraft or auto-suggestion.'

Meanwhile Father Brown had made his way into the house, and now went to break the news to the wife of the dead man.

When he came out again he looked a little pale and tragic; but what passed between them in that interview was never known, even when all was known.

Flambeau, who was talking quietly with the doctor, was surprised to see his friend reappear so soon at his elbow; but Brown took no notice, and merely drew the doctor apart. 'You have sent for the police, haven't you?' he asked.

'Yes,' answered Harris. 'They ought to be here in ten minutes.'

'Will you do me a favour?' said the priest quietly. 'The truth is, I make a collection of these curious stories, which often contain, as in the case of our Hindoo friend, elements which can hardly be put into a police report. Now, I want you to write out a report of this case for my private use. Yours is a clever trade,' he said, looking at the doctor gravely and steadily in the face. 'I sometimes think that you know some details of this matter which you have not thought fit to mention. Mine is a confidential trade like yours, and I will treat anything you write for me in strict confidence. But write the whole.'

The doctor, who had been listening thoughtfully with his head a little on one side, looked the priest in the face for an instant, and said, 'All right,' and went into the study, closing the door behind him.

'Flambeau,' said Father Brown, 'there is a long seat there under the veranda, where we can smoke, out of the rain. You are my only friend in the world, and I want to talk to you. Or, perhaps, be silent with you.'

They established themselves comfortably in the veranda seat; Father Brown, against his common habit, accepted a good cigar and smoked it steadily in silence, while the rain shrieked and rattled on the roof of the veranda.

'My friend,' he said at length, 'this is a very queer case. A very queer case.'

'I should think it was,' said Flambeau, with something like a shudder.

'You call it queer, and I call it queer,' said the other, 'and yet we mean quite opposite things. The modern mind always mixes up two different ideas: mystery in the sense of what is marvellous, and mystery in the sense of what is complicated. That is half its difficulty about miracles. A miracle is startling; but it is simple. It is simple because it *is* a miracle. It is power coming directly from God (or the devil) instead of indirectly through nature or human wills. Now you mean that this business is marvellous because it is miraculous, because it is witchcraft worked by a wicked Indian. Understand, I do not say that it was not spiritual or diabolic. Heaven and hell only know by what surrounding influences strange sins come into the lives of men. But for the present my point is this: If it was pure magic, as you think, then it is marvellous; but it is not mysterious – that is, it is not complicated. The quality of a miracle is mysterious, but its manner is simple. Now, the manner of this business has been the reverse of simple.'

The storm that had slackened for a little seemed to be swelling again, and there came heavy movements as of faint thunder. Father Brown let fall the ash of his cigar and went on:

'There has been in this incident,' he said, 'a twisted, ugly, complex quality that does not belong to the straight bolts either of heaven or hell. As one knows the crooked track of a snail, I know the crooked track of a man.'

The white lightning opened its enormous eye in one wink, the sky shut up again, and the priest went on:

'Of all these crooked things, the crookedest was the shape of that piece of paper. It was crookeder than the dagger that killed him.'

'You mean the paper on which Quinton confessed his suicide,' said Flambeau.

'I mean the paper on which Quinton wrote, "I die by my own hand,"' answered Father Brown. 'The shape of that paper, my friend, was the wrong shape; the wrong shape, if ever I have seen it in this wicked world.'

'It only had a corner snipped off,' said Flambeau, 'and I understand that all Quinton's paper was cut that way.'

'It was a very odd way,' said the other, 'and a very bad way, to my taste and fancy. Look here, Flambeau, this Quinton – God receive his soul! – was perhaps a bit of a cur in some ways, but he really was an artist, with the pencil as well as the pen. His handwriting, though hard to read, was bold and beautiful. I can't prove what I say; I can't prove anything. But I tell you with the full force of conviction that he could never have cut that mean little piece off a sheet of paper. If he had wanted to cut down paper for some purpose of fitting in, or binding up, or what not, he would have made quite a different slash with the scissors. Do you remember the shape? It was a mean shape. It was a wrong shape. Like this. Don't you remember?'

And he waved his burning cigar before him in the darkness, making irregular squares so rapidly that Flambeau really seemed to see them as fiery hieroglyphics upon the darkness – hieroglyphics such as his friend had spoken of, which are undecipherable, yet can have no good meaning.

'But,' said Flambeau, as the priest put his cigar in his mouth again and leaned back, staring at the roof. 'Suppose somebody else did use the scissors. Why should somebody else, cutting pieces off his sermon paper, make Quinton commit suicide?'

Father Brown was still leaning back and staring at the roof, but he took his cigar out of his mouth and said, 'Quinton never did commit suicide.'

Flambeau stared at him. 'Why, confound it all,' he cried; 'then why did he confess to suicide?'

The priest leaned forward again, settled his elbows on his knees, looked at the ground, and said in a low distinct voice, 'He never did confess to suicide.'

Flambeau laid his cigar down. 'You mean,' he said, 'that the writing was forged?'

'No,' said Father Brown; 'Quinton wrote it all right.'

'Well, there you are,' said the aggravated Flambeau; 'Quinton wrote, "I die by my own hand," with his own hand on a plain piece of paper.'

'Of the wrong shape,' said the priest calmly.

'Oh, the shape be damned!' cried Flambeau. 'What has the shape to do with it?'

'There were twenty-three snipped papers,' resumed Brown unmoved, 'and only twenty-two pieces snipped off. Therefore one of the pieces had been destroyed, probably that from the written paper. Does that suggest anything to you?'

A light dawned on Flambeau's face, and he said, 'There was something else written by Quinton, some other words. "They will tell you I die by my own hand," or "Do not believe that—" '

'Hotter, as the children say,' said his friend. 'But the piece was hardly half an inch across; there was no room for one word, let alone five. Can you think of anything hardly bigger than a comma which the man with hell in his heart had to tear away as a testimony against him?'

'I can think of nothing,' said Flambeau at last.

'What about quotation marks?' said the priest, and flung his cigar far into the darkness like a shooting star.

All words had left the other man's mouth, and Father Brown said, like one going back to fundamentals:

'Leonard Quinton was a romancer, and was writing an Oriental romance about wizardry and hypnotism. He—'

At this moment the door opened briskly behind them and the doctor came out with his hat on. He put a long envelope into the priest's hands.

'That's the document you wanted,' he said, 'and I must be getting home. Good night.'

'Good night,' said Father Brown, as the doctor walked briskly to the gate. He had left the front door open, so that a shaft of gaslight fell upon them. In the light of this Brown opened the envelope and read the following words:

> DEAR FATHER BROWN, – *Vicisti Galilæe!* Otherwise, damn your eyes, which are very penetrating ones. Can it be possible that there is something in all that stuff of yours after all?
>
> I am a man who has ever since boyhood believed in Nature and in all natural functions and instincts, whether men called them moral or immoral. Long before I became a doctor, when I was a schoolboy keeping mice and spiders, I believed that to be a good animal is the best thing in the world. But just now I am shaken; I have believed in Nature; but it seems as if Nature could betray a man. Can there be anything in your bosh? I am really getting morbid.
>
> I loved Quinton's wife. What was there wrong in that? Nature told me to, and it's love that makes the world go round. I also thought, quite sincerely, that she would be happier with a clean animal like me than with that tormenting little lunatic. What was there wrong in that? I was only facing facts, like a man of science. She would have been happier.
>
> According to my own creed I was quite free to kill Quinton, which was the best thing for everybody, even himself. But as a healthy animal I had no notion of killing myself. I resolved, therefore, that I would never do it until I saw a chance that would leave me scot free. I saw that chance this morning.
>
> I have been three times, all told, into Quinton's study today. The

first time I went in he would talk about nothing but the weird tale, called 'The Curse of a Saint', which he was writing, which was all about how some Indian hermit made an English colonel kill himself by thinking about him. He showed me the last sheets, and even read me the last paragraph, which was something like this, 'The conqueror of the Punjab, a mere yellow skeleton, but still gigantic, managed to lift himself on his elbow and gasp in his nephew's ear, "I die by my own hand, yet I die murdered!"' It so happened, by one chance out of a hundred, that those last words were written at the top of a new sheet of paper. I left the room, and went out into the garden intoxicated with a frightful opportunity.

We walked round the house, and two more things happened in my favour. You suspected an Indian, and you found a dagger which the Indian might most probably use. Taking the opportunity to stuff it in my pocket I went back to Quinton's study, locked the door, and gave him his sleeping draught. He was against answering Atkinson at all, but I urged him to call out and quiet the fellow, because I wanted a clear proof that Quinton was alive when I left the room for the second time. Quinton lay down in the conservatory, and I came through the study. I am a quick man with my hands, and in a minute and a half I had done what I wanted to do. I had emptied all the first part of Quinton's romance into the fireplace, where it burnt to ashes. Then I saw that the quotation marks wouldn't do, so I snipped them off, and to make it seem likelier, snipped the whole quire to match. Then I came out with the knowledge that Quinton's confession of suicide lay on the front table, while Quinton lay alive, but asleep, in the conservatory beyond.

The last act was a desperate one; you can guess it: I pretended to have seen Quinton dead and rushed to his room. I delayed you with the paper; and, being a quick man with my hands, killed Quinton while you were looking at his confession of suicide. He was half-asleep, being drugged, and I put his own hand on the knife and drove it into his body. The knife was of so queer a shape that no one but an operator could have calculated the angle that would reach his heart. I wonder if you noticed this.

When I had done it the extraordinary thing happened. Nature deserted me. I felt ill. I felt just as if I had done something wrong. I think my brain is breaking up; I feel some sort of desperate pleasure in thinking I have told the thing to somebody; that I shall not have to be alone with it if I marry and have children. What is the matter with me? ... Madness ... or can one have remorse, just as if one were in Byron's poems! I cannot write any more.

— JAMES ERSKINE HARRIS.

Father Brown carefully folded up the letter and put it in his breast pocket just as there came a loud peal at the gate bell, and the wet waterproofs of several policeman gleamed in the road outside.

THE RESURRECTION OF
FATHER BROWN

THERE was a brief period during which Father Brown enjoyed, or rather did not enjoy, something like fame. He was a nine days' wonder in the newspapers; he was even a common topic of controversy in the weekly reviews; his exploits were narrated eagerly and inaccurately in any number of clubs and drawing-rooms, especially in America. Incongruous and indeed incredible as it may seem, to anyone who knew him, his adventures as a detective were even made the subject of short stories appearing in magazines.

Strangely enough, this wandering limelight struck him in the most obscure, or at least the most remote, of his many places of residence. He had been sent out to officiate, as something between a missionary and a parish priest, in one of those sections of the northern coast of South America, where strips of country still cling insecurely to European powers, or are continually threatening to become independent republics, under the gigantic shadow of President Monroe. The population was red and brown with pink spots; that is, it was Spanish-American, and largely Spanish-American-Indian, but there was a considerable and increasing infiltration of Americans of the northern sort — Englishmen, Germans and the rest. And the trouble seems to have begun when one of these visitors, very recently landed and very much annoyed at having lost one of his bags, approached the first building of which he came in sight — which happened to be the mission-house and chapel attached to it, in front of which ran a long veranda and a long row of stakes, up which were trained the black twisted vines, their square leaves red with autumn. Behind them, also in a row, a number of human beings sat almost as rigid as the stakes, and coloured in some fashion like the vines. For while their broad-brimmed hats were as black as their unblinking eyes, the complexions of many of them might have been made out of the dark red

644 FATHER BROWN STORIES

timber of those transatlantic forests. Many of them were smoking
very long, thin black cigars; and in all that group the smoke was
almost the only moving thing. The visitor would probably have
described them as natives, though some of them were very proud
of Spanish blood. But he was not one to draw any fine distinction
between Spaniards and Red Indians, being rather disposed to dismiss people from the scene when once he had convicted them of
being native to it.

He was a newspaper man from Kansas City, a lean, light-haired
man with what Meredith called an adventurous nose; one could
almost fancy it found its way by feeling its way and moved like the
proboscis of an ant-eater. His name was Snaith, and his parents,
after some obscure meditation, had called him Saul, a fact which
he had the good feeling to conceal as far as possible. Indeed, he
had ultimately compromised by calling himself Paul, though by
no means for the same reason that had affected the Apostle of the
Gentiles. On the contrary, so far as he had any views on such
things, the name of the persecutor would have been more appropriate; for he regarded organized religion with the conventional
contempt which can be learnt more easily from Ingersoll than from
Voltaire. And this was, as it happened, the not very important side
of his character which he turned towards the mission station and
the groups in front of the veranda. Something in their shameless
repose and indifference inflamed his own fury of efficiency; and, as
he could get no particular answer to his first questions, he began
to do all the talking himself.

Standing out there in the strong sunshine, a spick-and-span
figure in his Panama hat and neat clothes, his grip-sack held in a
steely grip, he began to shout at the people in the shadow. He began
to explain to them very loudly why they were lazy and filthy, and
bestially ignorant and lower than the beasts that perish, in case this
problem should have previously exercised their minds. In his
opinion, it was the deleterious influence of priests that had made
them so miserably poor and so hopelessly oppressed that they were
able to sit in the shade and smoke and do nothing.

'And a mighty soft crowd you must be at that,' he said, 'to be
bullied by these stuck-up josses because they walk about in their
mitres and their tiaras and their gold copes and other glad rags,
looking down on everybody else like dirt – being bamboozled by

crowns and canopies and sacred umbrellas like a kid at a pantomime; just because a pompous old High Priest of Mumbo-Jumbo
looks as if he was the lord of the earth. What about you? What do
you look like, you poor simps? I tell you, that's why you're way-
back in barbarism and can't read or write and—'

At this point the High Priest of Mumbo-Jumbo came in an undignified hurry out of the door of the mission-house, not looking
very like a lord of the earth, but rather like a bundle of black secondhand clothes buttoned round a short bolster in the semblance of a
guy. He was not wearing his tiara, supposing him to possess one,
but a shabby broad hat not very dissimilar from those of the Spanish
Indians, and it was thrust to the back of his head with a gesture of
botheration. He seemed just about to speak to the motionless
natives when he caught sight of the stranger and said quickly:

'Oh, can I be of any assistance? Would you like to come inside?'

Mr Paul Snaith came inside; and it was the beginning of a considerable increase of that journalist's information on many things.
Presumably his journalistic instinct was stronger than his prejudices, as, indeed, it often is in clever journalists; and he asked a
good many questions the answers to which interested and surprised
him. He discovered that the Indians could read and write, for the
simple reason that the priest had taught them; but that they did
not read or write any more than they could help, from a natural
preference for more direct communications. He learned that these
strange people, who sat about in heaps in the veranda without stirring a hair, could work quite hard on their own patches of land;
especially those of them who were more than half Spanish; and he
learned with still more astonishment that they all had patches of
land that were really their own. That much was part of a stubborn
tradition that seemed quite native to natives. But in that also the
priest had played a certain part, and by doing so had taken perhaps
what was his first and last part in politics, if it was only local politics.
There had recently swept through that region one of those fevers
of atheist and almost anarchist Radicalism which break out period-
ically in countries of the Latin culture, generally beginning in a
secret society and generally ending in a civil war and in very little
else. The local leader of the iconoclastic party was a certain Alvarez, a rather picturesque adventurer of Portuguese nationality but,
as his enemies said, of partly negro origin, the head of any number

of lodges and temples of initiation of the sort that in such places clothe even atheism with something mystical. The leader on the more conservative side was a much more commonplace person, a very wealthy man named Mendoza, the owner of many factories and quite respectable, but not very exciting. It was the general opinion that the cause of law and order would have been entirely lost if it had not adopted a more popular policy of its own, in the form of securing land for the peasants; and this movement had mainly originated from the little mission-station of Father Brown.

While he was talking to the journalist, Mendoza, the Conservative leader, came in. He was a stout, dark man, with a bald head like a pear and a round body also like a pear; he was smoking a very fragrant cigar, but he threw it away, perhaps a little theatrically, when he came into the presence of the priest, as if he had been entering church; and bowed with a curve that in so corpulent a gentleman seemed quite improbable. He was always exceedingly serious in his social gestures, especially towards religious institutions. He was one of those laymen who are much more ecclesiastical than ecclesiastics. It embarrassed Father Brown a good deal, especially when carried thus into private life.

'I think I am an anti-clerical,' Father Brown would say with a faint smile; 'but there wouldn't be half so much clericalism if they would only leave things to the clerics.'

'Why, Mr Mendoza,' exclaimed the journalist with a new animation, 'I think we have met before. Weren't you at the Trade Congress in Mexico last year?'

The heavy eyelids of Mr Mendoza showed a flutter of recognition, and he smiled in his slow way. 'I remember.'

'Pretty big business done there in an hour or two,' said Snaith with relish. 'Made a good deal of difference to you, too, I guess.'

'I have been very fortunate,' said Mendoza modestly.

'Don't you believe it!' cried the enthusiastic Snaith. 'Good fortune comes to the people who know when to catch hold; and you caught hold good and sure. But I hope I'm not interrupting your business?'

'Not at all,' said the other. 'I often have the honour of calling on the padre for a little talk. Merely for a little talk.'

It seemed as if this familiarity between Father Brown and a successful and even famous man of business completed the reconciliation between the priest and the practical Mr Snaith. He felt, it might be supposed, a new respectability clothe the station and the mission, and was ready to overlook such occasional reminders of the existence of religion as a chapel and a presbytery can seldom wholly avoid. He became quite enthusiastic about the priest's programme – at least on its secular and social side – and announced himself ready at any moment to act in the capacity of live wire for its communication to the world at large. And it was at this point that Father Brown began to find the journalist rather more troublesome in his sympathy than in his hostility.

Mr Paul Snaith set out vigorously to feature Father Brown. He sent long and loud eulogies on him across the continent to his newspaper in the Middle West. He took snapshots of the unfortunate cleric in the most commonplace occupations and exhibited them in gigantic photographs in the gigantic Sunday papers of the United States. He turned his sayings into slogans, and was continually presenting the world with 'A Message' from the reverend gentleman in South America. Any stock less strong and strenuously receptive than the American race would have become very much bored with Father Brown. As it was, he received handsome and eager offers to go on a lecturing tour in the States; and when he declined, the terms were raised with expressions of respectful wonder. A series of stories about him, like the stories of Sherlock Holmes, were, by the instrumentality of Mr Snaith, planned out and put before the hero with requests for his assistance and encouragement. As the priest found they had started, he could offer no suggestion except that they should stop. And this in turn was taken by Mr Snaith as the text for a discussion on whether Father Brown should disappear temporarily over a cliff, in the manner of Dr Watson's hero. To all these demands the priest had patiently to reply in writing, saying that he would consent on such terms to the temporary cessation of the stories and begging that a considerable interval might occur before they began again. The notes he wrote grew shorter and shorter; and as he wrote the last of them, he sighed.

Needless to say, this strange boom in the North reacted on the little outpost in the South where he had expected to live in so lonely an exile. The considerable English and American population already on the spot began to be proud of possessing so widely advertised a person. American tourists, of the sort who land with a loud demand for Westminster Abbey, landed on that distant coast with a loud demand for Father Brown. They were within measurable distance of running excursion trains named after him, and bringing crowds to see him as if he were a public monument. He was especially troubled by the active and ambitious new traders and shopkeepers of the place, who were perpetually pestering him to try their wares and to give them testimonials. Even if the testimonials were not forthcoming, they would prolong the correspondence for the purpose of collecting autographs. As he was a good-natured person they got a good deal of what they wanted out of him; and it was in answer to a particular request from a Frankfort wine-merchant named Eckstein that he wrote hastily a few words on a card, which were to prove a terrible turning-point in his life.

Eckstein was a fussy little man with fuzzy hair and pince-nez, who was wildly anxious that the priest should not only try some of his celebrated medicinal port, but should let him know where and when he would drink it, in acknowledging its receipt. The priest was not particularly surprised at the request, for he was long past surprise at the lunacies of advertisement. So he scribbled something down and turned to other business which seemed a little more sensible. He was again interrupted, by a note from no less a person than his political enemy Alvarez, asking him to come to a conference at which it was hoped that a compromise on an outstanding question might be reached; and suggesting an appointment that evening at a café just outside the walls of the little town. To this also he sent a message of acceptance by the rather florid and military messenger who was waiting for it; and then, having an hour or two before him, sat down to attempt to get through a little of his own legitimate business. At the end of the time he poured himself out a glass of Mr Eckstein's remarkable wine and, glancing at the clock with a humorous expression, drank it and went out into the night.

Strong moonlight lay on the little Spanish town, so that when he came to the picturesque gateway, with its rather rococo arch and the fantastic fringe of palms beyond it, it looked rather like a scene in a Spanish opera. One long leaf of palm with jagged edges, black against the moon, hung down on the other side of the arch, visible through the archway, and had something of the look of the jaw of a black crocodile. The fancy would not have lingered in his imagination but for something else that caught his naturally alert eye. The air was deathly still, and there was not a stir of wind; but he distinctly saw the pendent palm-leaf move.

He looked around him and realized that he was alone. He had left the last houses behind, which were mostly closed and shuttered, and was walking between two long blank walls built of large and shapeless but flattened stones, tufted here and there with the queer prickly weeds of that region – walls which ran parallel all the way to the gateway. He could not see the lights of the café outside the gate; probably it was too far away. Nothing could be seen under the arch but a wider expanse of large-flagged pavement, pale in the moon, with the straggling prickly pear here and there. He had a strong sense of the smell of evil; he felt queer physical oppression; but he did not think of stopping. His courage, which was considerable, was perhaps even less strong a part of him than his curiosity. All his life he had been led by an intellectual hunger for the truth, even of trifles. He often controlled it in the name of proportion; but it was always there. He walked straight through the gateway, and on the other side a man sprang like a monkey out of the tree-top and struck at him with a knife. At the same moment another man came crawling swiftly along the wall and, whirling a cudgel round his head, brought it down. Father Brown turned, staggered, and sank in a heap; but as he sank there dawned on his round face an expression of mild and immense surprise.

There was living in the same little town at this time another young American, particularly different from Mr Paul Snaith. His name was John Adams Race, and he was an electrical engineer, employed by Mendoza to fit out the old town with all the new conveniences. He was a figure far less familiar in satire and international gossip than that of the American journalist. Yet, as a matter of fact, America contains a million men of the moral type of Race to one of the moral type of Snaith. He was exceptional in being exceptionally good at his job, but in every other way he was very simple. He had begun life as a druggist's assistant in a Western village, and risen by sheer work and merit; but he still regarded his home town as the natural heart of the habitable world. He had been taught a very Puritan, or purely Evangelical, sort of Christianity from the Family Bible at his mother's knee; and in so far as he had time to have any religion, that was still his religion. Amid all the dazzling lights of the latest and even wildest discoveries, when he was at the very edge and extreme of experiment, working miracles of light and sound like a god creating new stars and solar systems, he never for a moment doubted that the things 'back home' were the best things in the world; his mother and the Family Bible and the quiet and quaint morality of his village. He had as serious and noble a sense of the sacredness of his mother as if he had been a frivolous Frenchman. He was quite sure the Bible religion was really the right thing; only he vaguely missed it wherever he went in the modern world. He could hardly be expected to sympathize with the religious externals of Catholic countries; and in a dislike of mitres and croziers he sympathized with Mr Snaith, though not in so cocksure a fashion. He had no liking for the public bowings and scrapings of Mendoza, and certainly no temptation to the masonic mysticism of the atheist Alvarez. Perhaps all that semi-tropical life was too coloured for him, shot with Indian red and Spanish gold. Anyhow, when he said there was nothing to touch his home town, he was not boasting. He really meant that there was somewhere something plain and unpretentious and touching, which he really respected more than anything else in the world. Such being the mental attitude of John Adams Race in a South American station, there had been growing on him for some time a curious feeling, which contradicted all his prejudices and for which he could not account. For the truth was this: that the only thing he had ever met in his travels that in the least reminded him of the old woodpile and the provincial proprieties and the Bible on his mother's knee was (for some inscrutable reason) the round face and black clumsy umbrella of Father Brown.

He found himself insensibly watching that commonplace and even comic black figure as it went bustling about; watching it with an almost morbid fascination, as if it were a walking riddle or contradiction. He had found something he could not help liking in the heart of everything he hated; it was as if he had been horribly tormented by lesser demons and then found that the Devil was quite an ordinary person.

Thus it happened that, looking out of his window on that moon-lit night, he saw the Devil go by, the demon of unaccountable blamelessness, in his broad black hat and long black coat, shuffling along the street towards the gateway, and saw it with an interest which he could not himself understand. He wondered where the priest was going, and what he was really up to; and remained gazing out into the moonlit street long after the little black figure had passed. And then he saw something else that intrigued him further. Two other men whom he recognized passed across his window as across a lighted stage. A sort of blue limelight of the moon ran in a spectral halo round the big bush of hair that stood erect on the head of little Eckstein, the wine-seller, and it outlined a taller and darker figure with an eagle profile and a queer old-fashioned and very top-heavy black hat, which seemed to make the whole outline still more bizarre, like a shape in a shadow panto-mime. Race rebuked himself for allowing the moon to play such tricks with his fancy; for on a second glance he recognized the black Spanish side-whiskers and high-featured face of Dr Calderon, a worthy medical man of the town, whom he had once found attend-ing professionally on Mendoza. Still, there was something in the way the men were whispering to each other and peering up the street that struck him as peculiar. On a sudden impulse he leapt over the low window-sill and himself went bareheaded up the road, following their trail. He saw them disappear under the dark arch-way, and a moment after there came a dreadful cry from beyond; curiously loud and piercing, and all the more blood-curdling to Race because it said something very distinctly in some tongue that he did not know.

The next moment there was a rushing of feet, more cries, and then a confused roar of rage or grief that shook the turrets and tall palm trees of the place; there was a movement in the mob that had gathered, as if they were sweeping backwards through the gateway. And then the dark archway resounded with a new voice, this time intelligible to him and falling with the note of doom, as someone shouted through the gateway:

'Father Brown is dead!'

He never knew what prop gave way in his mind, or why some-thing on which he had been counting suddenly failed him; but he ran towards the gateway and was just in time to meet his country-man, the journalist Snaith, coming out of the dark entrance, deadly pale and snapping his fingers nervously.

'It's quite true,' said Snaith, with something which for him approached to reverence. 'He's a goner. The doctor's been looking at him, and there's no hope. Some of these damned Dagos clubbed him as he came through the gate – God knows why. It'll be a great loss to the place.'

Race did not or perhaps could not reply, but ran on under the arch to the scene beyond. The small black figure lay where it had fallen on the wilderness of wide stones starred here and there with green thorn; and the great crowd was being kept back, chiefly by the mere gestures of one gigantic figure in the foreground. For there were many there who swayed hither and thither at the mere movement of his hand, as if he had been a magician.

Alvarez, the dictator and demagogue, was a tall, swaggering figure, always rather flamboyantly clad, and on this occasion he wore a green uniform with embroideries like silver snakes crawling all over it, with an order round his neck hung on a very vivid maroon ribbon. His close curling hair was already grey, and in contrast his complexion, which his friends called olive and his foes octoroon, looked almost literally golden, as if it were a mask moulded in gold. But his large-featured face, which was powerful and humorous, was at this moment properly grave and grim. He had been waiting, he explained, for Father Brown at the café, when he had heard a rustle and a fall and, coming out, had found the corpse lying on the flagstones.

'I know what some of you are thinking,' he said, looking round proudly, 'and if you are afraid of me – as you are – I will say it for you. I am an atheist; I have no god to call on for those who will not take my word. But I tell you in the name of every root of honour that may be left to a soldier and a man, that I had no part in this. If I had the men here that did it, I would rejoice to hang them on that tree.'

'Naturally we are glad to hear you say so,' said old Mendoza stiffly and solemnly, standing by the body of his fallen coadjutor. 'This blow has been too appalling for us to say what else we feel at present. I suggest that it will be more decent and proper if we remove my friend's body and break up this irregular meeting. I understand,' he added gravely to the doctor, 'that there is unfortunately no doubt.'

'There is no doubt,' said Dr Calderon.

John Race went back to his lodgings sad and with a singular

sense of emptiness. It seemed impossible that he should miss a man whom he never knew. He learned that the funeral was to take place next day; for all felt that the crisis should be past as quickly as possible, for fear of riots that were hourly growing more probable. When Snaith had seen the row of Red Indians sitting in the veranda, they might have been a row of ancient Aztec images carved in red wood. But he had not seen them as they were when they heard that the priest was dead.

Indeed they would certainly have risen in revolution and lynched the republican leader, if they had not been immediately blocked by the direct necessity of behaving respectfully to the coffin of their own religious leader. The actual assassins, whom it would have been most natural to lynch, seemed to have vanished into thin air. Nobody knew their names; and nobody would ever know whether the dying man had even seen their faces. That strange look of surprise that was apparently his last look on earth might have been the recognition of their faces. Alvarez repeated violently that it was no work of his, and attended the funeral, walking behind the coffin in his splendid silver and green uniform with a sort of bravado of reverence.

Behind the veranda a flight of stone steps scaled a very steep green bank, fenced by a cactus-hedge, and up this the coffin was laboriously lifted to the ground above, and placed temporarily at the foot of the great gaunt crucifix that dominated the road and guarded the consecrated ground. Below in the road were great seas of people lamenting and telling their beads – an orphan population that had lost a father. Despite all these symbols that were provocative enough to him, Alvarez behaved with restraint and respect; and all would have gone well – as Race told himself – had the others only let him alone.

Race told himself bitterly that old Mendoza had always looked like an old fool and had now very conspicuously and completely behaved like an old fool. By a custom common in simpler societies, the coffin was left open and the face uncovered, bringing the pathos to the point of agony for all those simple people. This, being consonant to tradition, need have done no harm; but some officious person had added to it the custom of the French free-thinkers, of having speeches by the graveside. Mendoza proceeded to make a speech – a rather long speech, and the longer it was, the longer and lower sank John Race's spirits and sympathies with the religious ritual involved. A list of saintly attributes, apparently of the most antiquated sort, was rolled out with the dilatory dulness of an after-dinner speaker who does not know how to sit down. That was bad enough; but Mendoza had also the ineffable stupidity to start reproaching and even taunting his political opponents. In three minutes he had succeeded in making a scene; and a very extra-ordinary scene it was.

'We may well ask,' he said, looking around him pompously, 'we may well ask where such virtues can be found among those who have madly abandoned the creed of their fathers. It is when we have atheists among us, atheist leaders, nay, sometimes even atheist rulers, that we find their infamous philosophy bearing fruit in crimes like this. If we ask who murdered this holy man, we shall assuredly find—'

Africa of the forests looked out of the eyes of Alvarez the hybrid adventurer; and Race fancied he could see suddenly that the man was after all a barbarian, who could not control himself to the end; one might guess that all his 'illuminated' transcendentalism had a touch of Voodoo. Anyhow, Mendoza could not continue, for Alvarez had sprung up and was shouting back at him and shouting him down, with infinitely superior lungs.

'Who murdered him?' he roared. 'Your God murdered him! His own God murdered him! According to you, he murders all his faithful and foolish servants – as he murdered *that* one,' and he made a violent gesture, not towards the coffin but the crucifix. Seeming to control himself a little, he went on in a tone still angry but more argumentative: 'I don't believe it, but you do. Isn't it better to have no God than one that robs you in this fashion? I, at least, am not afraid to say there is none. There is no power in all this blind and brainless universe that can hear your prayer or return your friend. Though you beg heaven to raise him, he will not rise. Though I dare heaven to raise him, he will not rise. Here and now I will put it to the test – I defy the God who is not there to waken the man who sleeps for ever.'

There was a shock of silence, and the demagogue had made his sensation.

'We might have known,' cited Mendoza in a thick gobbling voice, 'when we allowed such men as you—'

A new voice cut into his speech; a high and shrill voice with a Yankee accent.

'Stop! Stop!' cried Snaith the journalist, 'something's up! I swear I saw him move.'

He went racing up the steps and rushed to the coffin, while the mob below swayed with indescribable frenzies. The next moment he had turned a face of amazement over his shoulder and made a signal with his finger to Dr Calderon, who hastened forward to confer with him. When the two men stepped away again from the coffin, all could see that the position of the head had altered. A roar of excitement rose from the crowd and seemed to stop suddenly, as if cut off in mid-air; for the priest in the coffin gave a groan and raised himself on one elbow, looking with bleared and blinking eyes at the crowd.

John Adams Race, who had hitherto known only miracles of science, never found himself able in after years to describe the topsy-turvydom of the next few days. He seemed to have burst out of the world of time and space, and to be living in the impossible. In half an hour the whole of that town and district had been transformed into something never known for a thousand years; a mediaeval people turned to a mob of monks by a staggering miracle; a Greek city where the god had descended among men. Thousands prostrated themselves in the road, hundreds took vows on the spot; and even the outsiders, like the two Americans, were able to think and speak of nothing but the prodigy. Alvarez himself was shaken, as well he might be; and sat down, with his head upon his hands.

And in the midst of all this tornado of beatitude was a little man struggling to be heard. His voice was small and faint, and the noise was deafening. He made weak little gestures that seemed more those of irritation than anything else. He came to the edge of the parapet above the crowd, waving it to be quiet, with movements rather like the flap of the short wings of a penguin. There was some-thing a little more like a lull in the noise; and then Father Brown for the first time reached the utmost stretch of the indignation that he could launch against his children.

'Oh, you *silly* people,' he said in a high and quavering voice; 'Oh, you silly, *silly* people.'

Then he suddenly seemed to pull himself together, made a bolt for the steps with his more normal gait, and began hurriedly to descend.

'Where are you going, Father?' said Mendoza, with more than his usual veneration.

'To the telegraph office,' said Father Brown hastily. 'What? No, of course it's not a miracle. Why should there be a miracle? Miracles are not so cheap as all that.'

And he came tumbling down the steps, the people flinging themselves before him to implore his blessing.

'Bless you, bless you,' said Father Brown hastily. 'God bless you all and give you more sense.'

And he scuttled away with extraordinary rapidity to the telegraph office, where he wired to his Bishop's secretary, 'There is some mad story about a miracle here; hope his lordship not give authority. Nothing in it.'

As he turned away from this effort, he tottered a little with the reaction, and John Race caught him by the arm.

'Let me see you home,' he said; 'you deserve more than these people are giving you.'

John Race and the priest were seated in the presbytery; the table was still piled up with the papers with which the latter had been wrestling the day before; the bottle of wine and the emptied wine-glass still stood where he had left them.

'And now,' said Father Brown almost grimly, 'I can begin to think.'

'I shouldn't think too hard just yet,' said the American. 'You must be wanting a rest. Besides, what are you going to think about?'

'I have pretty often had the task of investigating murders, as it happens,' said Father Brown. 'Now I have got to investigate my own murder.'

'If I were you,' said Race, 'I should take a little wine first.'

Father Brown stood up and filled himself another glass, lifted it, looked thoughtfully into vacancy and put it down again. Then he sat down once more and said:

'Do you know what I felt like when I died? You may not believe it, but my feeling was one of overwhelming astonishment.'

'Well,' answered Race, 'I suppose you were astonished at being knocked on the head.'

Father Brown leaned over to him and said in a low voice:

'I was astonished at not being knocked on the head.'

Race looked at him for a moment as if he thought the knock on the head had been only too effective; but he only said, 'What do you mean?'

'I mean that when that man brought his bludgeon down with a great swipe, it stopped at my head and did not even touch it. In the same way, the other fellow made as if to strike me with a knife, but he never gave me a scratch. It was just like play-acting. I think it was. But then followed the extraordinary thing.'

He looked thoughtfully at the papers on the table for a moment and then went on:

'Though I had not even been touched with knife or stick, I began to feel my legs doubling up under me and my very life failing. I knew I was being struck down by something, but it was not by those weapons. Do you know what I think it was?'

And he pointed to the wine on the table.

Race picked up the wine-glass and looked at it and smelt it.

'I think you are right,' he said. 'I began as a druggist and studied chemistry. I couldn't say for certain without an analysis, but I think there's something very unusual in this stuff. There are drugs by which the Asiatics produce a temporary sleep that looks like death.'

'Quite so,' said the priest calmly. 'The whole of this miracle was faked, for some reason or other. That funeral scene was staged and timed. I think it is part of that raving madness of publicity that has got hold of Snaith; but I can hardly believe he would go quite so far, merely for that. After all, it's one thing to make copy out of me and run me as a sort of sham Sherlock Holmes, and—'

Even as the priest spoke his face altered. His blinking eyelids shut suddenly and he stood up as if he were choking. Then he put one wavering hand as if groping his way towards the door.

'Where are you going?' asked the other in some wonder.

'If you ask me,' said Father Brown, who was quite white, 'I was going to pray. Or rather, to praise.'

'I'm not sure I understand. What is the matter with you?'

'I was going to praise God for having so strangely and so incredibly saved me – saved me by an inch.'

'Of course,' said Race, 'I am not of your religion; but believe me,

I have religion enough to understand that. Of course you would thank God for saving you from death.'

'No,' said the priest. 'Not from death. From disgrace.'

The other sat staring; and the priest's next words broke out of him with a sort of cry.

'And if it had only been my disgrace! But it was the disgrace of all I stand for; the disgrace of the Faith that they went about to encompass. What it might have been! The most huge and horrible scandal ever launched against us since the last lie was choked in the throat of Titus Oates.'

'What on earth are you talking about?' demanded his companion.

'Well, I had better tell you at once,' said the priest; and sitting down, he went on more composedly: 'It came to me in a flash when I happened to mention Snaith and Sherlock Holmes. Now I happen to remember what I wrote about his absurd scheme; it was the natural thing to write, and yet I think they had ingeniously manoeuvred me into writing just those words. They were something like "I am ready to die and come to life again like Sherlock Holmes, if that is the best way." And the moment I thought of that, I realized that I had been made to write all sorts of things of that kind, all pointing to the same idea. I wrote, as if to an accomplice, saying that I would drink the drugged wine at a particular time. Now, don't you see?'

Race sprang to his feet still staring: 'Yes,' he said, 'I think I begin to see.'

'*They* would have boomed the miracle. Then *they* would have bust up the miracle. And what is the worst, they would have proved that *I* was in the conspiracy. It would have been *our* sham miracle. That's all there is to it; and about as near hell as you and I will ever be, I hope.'

Then he said, after a pause, in quite a mild voice:

'They certainly would have got quite a lot of good copy out of me.'

Race looked at the table and said darkly, 'How many of these brutes were in it?'

Father Brown shook his head. 'More than I like to think of,' he said; 'but I hope some of them were only tools. Alvarez might think that all's fair in war, perhaps; he has a queer mind. I'm very much afraid that Mendoza is an old hypocrite; I never trusted him, and he hated my action in an industrial matter. But all that will wait; I have only got to thank God for the escape. And especially that I wired at once to the Bishop.'

John Race appeared to be very thoughtful.

'You've told me a lot I didn't know,' he said at last, 'and I feel inclined to tell you the only thing you don't know. I can imagine how those fellows calculated well enough. They thought any man alive, waking up in a coffin to find himself canonized like a saint, and made into a walking miracle for everyone to admire, would be swept along with his worshippers and accept the crown of glory that fell on him out of the sky. And I reckon their calculation was pretty practical psychology, as men go. I've seen all sorts of men in all sorts of places; and I tell you frankly I don't believe there's one man in a thousand who could wake up like that with all his wits about him; and while he was still almost talking in his sleep, would have the sanity and the simplicity and the humility to—' He was much surprised to find himself moved, and his level voice wavering.

Father Brown was gazing abstractedly, and in a rather cock-eyed fashion, at the bottle on the table. 'Look here,' he said, 'what about a bottle of real wine?'

THE MIRACLE OF MOON CRESCENT

Moon Crescent was meant in a sense to be as romantic as its name; and the things that happened there were romantic enough in their way. At least it had been an expression of that genuine element of sentiment, historic and almost heroic, which manages to remain side by side with commercialism in the elder cities on the eastern coast of America. It was originally a curve of classical architecture really recalling that eighteenth-century atmosphere in which men like Washington and Jefferson had seemed to be all the more republicans for being aristocrats. Travellers faced with the recurrent query of what they thought of our city were understood to be specially answerable for what they thought of our Moon Crescent. The very contrasts that confuse its original harmony were characteristic of its survival. At one extremity or horn of the crescent its last windows looked over an enclosure like a strip of a gentleman's park with trees and hedges as formal as a Queen Anne garden. But immediately round the corner, the other windows, even of the same rooms, or rather 'apartments', looked out on the blank, unsightly wall of a huge warehouse attached to some ugly industry. The apartments of Moon Crescent itself were at that end remodelled on the monotonous pattern of an American hotel, and rose to a height, which, though lower than the colossal warehouse, would have been called a skyscraper in London. But the colonnade that ran round the whole frontage upon the street had a grey and weather-stained stateliness suggesting that the ghosts of the Fathers of the Republic might still be walking to and fro in it. The insides of the rooms, however, were as neat and new as the last New York fittings could make them, especially at the northern end between the neat garden and the blank warehouse wall. They were a system of very small flats, as we should say in England, each consisting of a sitting-room, bedroom, and bathroom, as identical as the hundred cells of a hive. In one of these the celebrated Warren Wynd sat at

his desk sorting letters and scattering orders with wonderful rapidity and exactitude. He could only be compared to a tidy
whirlwind.

Warren Wynd was a very little man with loose grey hair and a
pointed beard, seemingly frail but fierily active. He had very wonderful eyes, brighter than stars and stronger than magnets, which
nobody who had ever seen them could easily forget. And indeed
in his work as a reformer and regulator of many good works he had
shown at least that he had a pair of eyes in his head. All sorts of
stories and even legends were told of the miraculous rapidity with
which he could form a sound judgment, especially of human character. It was said that he selected the wife who worked with him
so long in so charitable a fashion, by picking her out of a whole
regiment of women in uniform marching past at some official
celebration, some said of the Girl Guides and some of the Women
Police. Another story was told of how three tramps, indistin-
guishable from each other in their community of filth and rags, had
presented themselves before him asking for charity. Without a
moment's hesitation he had sent one of them to a particular
hospital devoted to a certain nervous disorder, had recommended
the second to an inebriates' home, and had engaged the third at a
handsome salary as his own private servant, a position which he
filled successfully for years afterwards. There were, of course, the
inevitable anecdotes of his prompt criticisms and curt repartees
when brought in contact with Roosevelt, with Henry Ford, and
with Mrs Asquith and all other persons with whom an American
public man ought to have a historic interview, if only in the newspapers. Certainly he was not likely to be overawed by such personages; and at the moment here in question he continued very calmly
his centrifugal whirl of papers, though the man confronting him
was a personage of almost equal importance.

Silas T. Vandam, the millionaire and oil magnate, was a lean
man with a long, yellow face and blue-black hair, colours which
were the less conspicuous yet somehow the more sinister because
his face and figure showed dark against the window and the white
warehouse wall outside it; he was buttoned up tight in an elegant
overcoat with strips of astrachan. The eager face and brilliant eyes
of Wynd, on the other hand, were in the full light from the other
window overlooking the little garden, for his chair and desk stood

facing it; and though the face was preoccupied, it did not seem
unduly preoccupied about the millionaire. Wynd's valet or personal servant, a big, powerful man with flat fair hair, was standing
behind his master's desk holding a sheaf of letters; and Wynd's
private secretary, a neat, red-haired youth with a sharp face, had
his hand already on the door handle, as if guessing some purpose
or obeying some gesture of his employer. The room was not only
neat but austere to the point of emptiness; for Wynd, with characteristic thoroughness, had rented the whole floor above, and turned
it into a loft or storeroom, where all his other papers and possessions were stacked in boxes and corded bales.

'Give these to the floor-clerk, Wilson,' said Wynd to the servant
holding the letters, 'and then get me the pamphlet on the Minneapolis Night Clubs; you'll find it in the bundle marked G. I shall
want it in half an hour, but don't disturb me till then. Well, Mr
Vandam, I think your proposition sounds very promising; but
I can't give a final answer till I've seen the report. It ought to reach
me tomorrow afternoon, and I'll 'phone you at once. I'm sorry
I can't say anything more definite just now.'

Mr Vandam seemed to feel that this was something like a polite
dismissal; and his sallow, saturnine face suggested that he found a
certain irony in the fact.

'Well, I suppose I must be going,' he said.

'Very good of you to call, Mr Vandam,' said Wynd, politely; 'you
will excuse my not coming out, as I've something here I must fix at
once. Fenner,' he added to the secretary, 'show Mr Vandam to his
car, and don't come back again for half an hour. I've something
here I want to work out by myself; after that I shall want you.'

The three men went out into the hallway together, closing the
door behind them. The big servant, Wilson, was turning down
the hallway in the direction of the floor-clerk, and the other two
moving in the opposite direction towards the lift; for Wynd's apartment was high up on the fourteenth floor. They had hardly gone
a yard from the closed door when they became conscious that the
corridor was filled with a marching and even magnificent figure.
The man was very tall and broad-shouldered, his bulk being the
more conspicuous for being clad in white, or a light grey that
looked like it, with a very wide white panama hat and an almost
equally wide fringe or halo of almost equally white hair. Set in this

aureole his face was strong and handsome, like that of a Roman emperor, save that there was something more than boyish, something a little childish, about the brightness of his eyes and the beatitude of his smile.

'Mr Warren Wynd in?' he asked, in hearty tones.

'Mr Warren Wynd is engaged,' said Fenner; 'he must not be disturbed on any account. I may say I am his secretary and can take any message.'

'Mr Warren Wynd is not at home to the Pope or the Crowned Heads,' said Vandam, the oil magnate, with sour satire. 'Mr Warren Wynd is mighty particular. I went in there to hand him over a trifle of twenty thousand dollars on certain conditions, and he told me to call again like as if I was a call-boy.'

'It's a fine thing to be a boy,' said the stranger, 'and a finer to have a call; and I've got a call he's just got to listen to. It's a call out of the great good country out West, where the real American is being made while you're all snoring. Just tell him that Art Alboin of Oklahoma City has come to convert him.'

'I tell you nobody can see him,' said the red-haired secretary, sharply. 'He has given orders that he is not to be disturbed for half an hour.'

'You folks down East are all against being disturbed,' said the breezy Mr Alboin, 'but I calculate there's a big breeze getting up in the West that will have to disturb you. He's been figuring out how much money must go to this and that stuffy old religion; but I tell you any scheme that leaves out the new Great Spirit movement in Texas and Oklahoma, is leaving out the religion of the future.'

'Oh, I've sized up those religions of the future,' said the millionaire, contemptuously. 'I've been through them with a tooth-comb; and they're as mangy as yellow dogs. There was that woman called herself Sophia; ought to have called herself Sapphira, I reckon. Just a plum fraud. Strings tied to all the tables and tambourines. Then there were the Invisible Life bunch; said they could vanish when they liked, and they did vanish, too, and a hundred thousand of my dollars vanished with them. I knew Jupiter Jesus out in Denver; saw him for weeks on end; and he was just a common crook. So was the Patagonian Prophet; you bet he's made a bolt for Patagonia. No, I'm through with all that; from now on I only believe what I see. I believe they call it being an atheist.'

'I guess you got me wrong,' said the man from Oklahoma, almost eagerly. 'I guess I'm as much of an atheist as you are. No supernatural or superstitious stuff in our movement; just plain science. The only real right science is just health, and the only real right health is just breathing. Fill your lungs with the wide air of the prairie and you could blow all your old eastern cities into the sea. You could just puff away their biggest men like thistledown. That's what we do in the new movement out home: we breathe. We don't pray; we breathe.'

'Well, I suppose you do,' said the secretary, wearily. He had a keen, intelligent face which could hardly conceal the weariness; but he had listened to the two monologues with the admirable patience and politeness (so much in contrast with the legends of impatience and insolence) with which such monologues are listened to in America.

'Nothing supernatural,' continued Alboin, 'just the great natural fact behind all the supernatural fancies. What did the Jews want with a God except to breathe into man's nostrils the breath of life? We do the breathing into our own nostrils out in Oklahoma. What's the meaning of the very word Spirit? It's just the Greek for breathing exercises. Life, progress, prophecy; it's all breath.'

'Some would allow it's all wind,' said Vandam; 'but I'm glad you've got rid of the divinity stunt, anyhow.'

The keen face of the secretary, rather pale against his red hair, showed a flicker of some odd feeling suggestive of a secret bitterness.

'I'm not glad,' he said, 'I'm just sure. You seem to like being atheists; so you may be just believing what you like to believe. But I wish to God there were a God; and there ain't. It's just my luck.'

Without a sound or stir they all became almost creepily conscious at this moment that the group, halted outside Wynd's door, had silently grown from three figures to four. How long the fourth figure had stood there none of the earnest disputants could tell, but he had every appearance of waiting respectfully and even timidly for the opportunity to say something urgent. But to their nervous sensibility he seemed to have sprung up suddenly and silently like a mushroom. And indeed, he looked rather like a big, black mushroom, for he was quite short and his small, stumpy figure was eclipsed by his big, black clerical hat; the resemblance might have been more complete if mushrooms were in the habit of carrying umbrellas, even of a shabby and shapeless sort.

Fenner, the secretary, was conscious of a curious additional surprise at recognizing the figure of a priest; but when the priest turned up a round face under the round hat and innocently asked for Mr Warren Wynd, he gave the regular negative answer rather more curtly than before. But the priest stood his ground.

'I do really want to see Mr Wynd,' he said. 'It seems odd, but that's exactly what I do want to do. I don't want to speak to him. I just want to see him. I just want to see if he's there to be seen.'

'Well, I tell you he's there and can't be seen,' said Fenner, with increasing annoyance. 'What do you mean by saying you want to see if he's there to be seen? Of course he's there. We all left him there five minutes ago, and we've stood outside this door ever since.'

'Well, I want to see if he's all right,' said the priest.

'Why?' demanded the secretary, in exasperation.

'Because I have serious, I might say solemn, reasons,' said the cleric, gravely, 'for doubting whether he is all right.'

'Oh, Lord!' cried Vandam, in a sort of fury, 'not more superstitions.'

'I see I shall have to give my reasons,' observed the little cleric, gravely. 'I suppose I can't expect you even to let me look through the crack of a door till I tell you the whole story.'

He was silent a moment as in reflection, and then went on without noticing the wondering faces around him. 'I was walking outside along the front of the colonnade when I saw a very ragged man running hard round the corner at the end of the crescent. He came pounding along the pavement towards me, revealing a great, raw-boned figure and a face I knew. It was the face of a wild Irish fellow I once helped a little; I will not tell you his name. When he saw me he staggered, calling me by mine and saying, "Saints alive, it's Father Brown; you're the only man whose face could frighten me today." I knew he meant he'd been doing some wild thing or other, and I don't think my face frightened him much, for he was soon telling me about it. And a very strange thing it was. He asked me if I knew Warren Wynd, and I said no, though I knew he lived near the top of these flats. He said, "That's a man who thinks he's a saint of God; but if he knew what I was saying of him he should be ready to hang himself." And he repeated hysterically more than once, "Yes, ready to hang himself." I asked him if he'd done any harm to Wynd, and his answer was rather a queer one. He said, "I took a pistol and I loaded it with neither shot nor slug, but only with a curse." As far as I could make out, all he had done was to go down that little alley between this building and the big warehouse, with an old pistol loaded with a blank charge, and merely fire it against the wall, as if that would bring down the building. "But as I did it," he said, "I cursed him with the great curse, that the justice of God should take him by the hair and the vengeance of hell by the heels, and he should be torn asunder like Judas and the world know him no more." Well, it doesn't matter now what else I said to the poor, crazy fellow; he went away quieted down a little, and I went round to the back of the building to inspect. And sure enough, in the little alley at the foot of this wall there lay a rusty antiquated pistol; I know enough about pistols to know it had been loaded only with a little powder; there were the black marks of powder and smoke on the wall, and even the mark of the muzzle, but not even a dent of any bullet. He had left no trace of destruction; he had left no trace of anything, except those black marks and that black curse he had hurled into heaven. So I came back here to ask for this Warren Wynd and find out if he's all right.'

Fenner the secretary laughed. 'I can soon settle that difficulty for you. I assure you he's quite all right; we left him writing at his desk only a few minutes ago. He was alone in his flat; it's a hundred feet up from the street, and so placed that no shot could have reached him, even if your friend hadn't fired blank. There's no other entrance to this place but this door, and we've been standing outside it ever since.'

'All the same,' said Father Brown, gravely, 'I should like to look in and see.'

'Well, you can't,' retorted the other. 'Good Lord, you don't tell me you think anything of the curse.'

'You forget,' said the millionaire, with a slight sneer, 'the reverend gentleman's whole business is blessings and cursings. Come, sir, if he'd been cursed to hell, why don't you bless him back again? What's the good of your blessings if they can't beat an Irish larrykin's curse?'

'Does anybody believe such things now?' protested the Westerner.

'Father Brown believes a good number of things, I take it,' said Vandam, whose temper was suffering from the past snub and the present bickering. 'Father Brown believes a hermit crossed a river on a crocodile conjured out of nowhere, and then he told the crocodile to die, and it sure did. Father Brown believes that some blessed saint or other died, and had his dead body turned into three dead bodies, to be served out to three parishes that were all bent on figuring as his home-town. Father Brown believes that a saint hung his cloak on a sunbeam and another used his for a boat to cross the Atlantic. Father Brown believes the holy donkey had six legs and the house at Loreto flew through the air. He believes in hundreds of stone virgins winking and weeping all day long. It's nothing to him to believe that a man might escape through the keyhole or vanish out of a locked room. I reckon he doesn't take much stock of the laws of nature.'

'Anyhow, I have to take stock in the laws of Warren Wynd,' said the secretary, wearily, 'and it's his rule that he's to be left alone when he says so. Wilson will tell you just the same,' for the large servant who had been sent for the pamphlet, passed placidly down the corridor even as he spoke, carrying the pamphlet, but serenely passing the door. 'He'll go and sit on the bench by the floor clerk and twiddle his thumbs till he's wanted; but he won't go in before then; and nor will I. I reckon we both know which side our bread is buttered, and it'd take a good many of Father Brown's saints and angels to make us forget it.'

'As for saints and angels—' began the priest.

'It's all nonsense,' repeated Fenner. 'I don't want to say anything offensive, but that sort of thing may be very well for crypts and cloisters and all sorts of moonshiny places. But ghosts can't get through a closed door in an American hotel.'

'But men can open a door, even in an American hotel,' replied Father Brown, patiently. 'And it seems to me the simplest thing would be to open it.'

'It would be simple enough to lose me my job,' answered the secretary, 'and Warren Wynd doesn't like his secretaries so simple as that. Not simple enough to believe in the sort of fairy-tales you seem to believe in.'

'Well,' said the priest gravely, 'it is true enough that I believe in a good many things that you probably don't. But it would take a considerable time to explain all the things I believe in, and all the reasons I have for thinking I'm right. It would take about two seconds to open that door and prove I am wrong.'

Something in the phrase seemed to please the more wild and restless spirit of the man from the West.

'I'll allow I'd love to prove you wrong,' said Alboin, striding suddenly past them, 'and I will.'

He threw open the door of the flat and looked in. The first glimpse showed that Warren Wynd's chair was empty. The second glance showed that his room was empty also.

Fenner, electrified with energy in his turn, dashed past the other into the apartment.

'He's in his bedroom,' he said curtly, 'he must be.'

As he disappeared into the inner chamber, the other men stood in the empty outer room staring about them. The severity and simplicity of its fittings, which had already been noted, returned on them with a rigid challenge. Certainly in this room there was no question of hiding a mouse, let alone a man. There were no curtains and, what is rare in American arrangements, no cupboards. Even the desk was no more than a plain table with a shallow drawer and a tilted lid. The chairs were hard and high-backed skeletons. A moment after the secretary reappeared at the inner door, having searched the two inner rooms. A staring negation stood in his eyes and his mouth seemed to move in a mechanical detachment from it as he said sharply, 'He didn't come out through here?'

Somehow the others did not even think it necessary to answer that negation in the negative. Their minds had come up against something like the blank wall of the warehouse that stared in at the opposite window, gradually turning from white to grey as dusk slowly descended with the advancing afternoon. Vandam walked over to the window-sill against which he had leant half an hour before and looked out of the open window. There was no pipe or fire-escape, no shelf or foothold of any kind on the sheer fall to the little by-street below, there was nothing on the similar expanse of wall that rose many storeys above. There was even less variation on the other side of the street; there was nothing whatever but the wearisome expanse of whitewashed wall. He peered downwards, as if expecting to see the vanished philanthropist lying in a suicidal wreck on the path. He could see nothing but one small dark object which, though diminished by distance, might well be the pistol that the priest had found lying there. Meanwhile, Fenner had walked to the other window, which looked out from a wall equally blank and inaccessible, but looking out over a small ornamental park instead of a side street. Here a clump of trees interrupted the actual view of the ground; but they reached but a little way up the huge human cliff. Both turned back into the room and faced each other in the gathering twilight, where the last silver gleams of daylight on the shiny tops of desks and tables were rapidly turning grey. As if the twilight itself irritated him, Fenner touched the switch and the scene sprang into the startling distinctness of electric light.

'As you said just now,' said Vandam, grimly, 'there's no shot from down there could hit him, even if there was a shot in the gun. But even if he was hit with a bullet he wouldn't have just burst like a bubble.'

The secretary, who was paler than ever, glanced irritably at the bilious visage of the millionaire.

'What's got you started on those morbid notions? Who's talking about bullets and bubbles? Why shouldn't he be alive?'

'Why not indeed?' replied Vandam, smoothly. 'If you'll tell me where he is, I'll tell you how he got there.'

After a pause the secretary muttered, rather sulkily, 'I suppose you're right. We're right up against the very thing we were talking about. It'd be a queer thing if you or I ever came to think there was anything in cursing. But who could have harmed Wynd shut up in here?'

Mr Alboin, of Oklahoma, had been standing rather astraddle in the middle of the room, his white, hairy halo as well as his round eyes seeming to radiate astonishment. At this point he said, abstractedly, with something of the irrelevant impudence of an *enfant terrible*:

'You didn't cotton to him much, did you, Mr Vandam?'

Mr Vandam's long, yellow face seemed to grow longer as it grew more sinister, while he smiled and answered quietly:

'If it comes to these coincidences, it was you, I think, who said that a wind from the West would blow away our big men like thistledown.'

'I know I said it would,' said the Westerner, with candour; 'but all the same, how the devil could it?'

The silence was broken by Fenner saying with an abruptness amounting to violence:

'There's only one thing to say about this affair. It simply hasn't happened. It can't have happened.'

'Oh, yes,' said Father Brown out of the corner, 'it has happened all right.'

They all jumped; for the truth was they had all forgotten the insignificant little man who had originally induced them to open the door. And the recovery of memory went with a sharp reversal of mood; it came back to them with a rush that they had all dismissed him as a superstitious dreamer for even hinting at the very thing that had since happened before their eyes.

'Snakes!' cried the impetuous Westerner, like one speaking before he could stop himself. 'Suppose there were something in it, after all!'

'I must confess,' said Fenner, frowning at the table, 'that his reverence's anticipations were apparently well founded. I don't know whether he has anything else to tell us.'

'He might possibly tell us,' said Vandam, sardonically, 'what the devil we are to do now.'

The little priest seemed to accept the position in a modest, but matter-of-fact manner. 'The only thing I can think of,' he said, 'is first to tell the authorities of this place, and then to see if there were any more traces of my man who let off the pistol. He vanished round the other end of the Crescent where the little garden is. There are seats there, and it's a favourite place for tramps.'

Direct consultations with the headquarters of the hotel, leading to indirect consultations with the authorities of the police, occupied them for a considerable time; and it was already nightfall when they went out under the long, classical curve of the colonnade. The Crescent looked as cold and hollow as the moon after which it was named, and the moon itself was rising luminous but spectral behind the black tree-tops when they turned the corner by the little public garden. Night veiled much of what was merely urban and artificial about the place; and as they melted into the shadows of the trees they had a strange feeling of having suddenly travelled many hundred miles from their homes. When they had walked in silence for a little, Alboin, who really had something elemental about him, suddenly exploded.

'I give up,' he cried; 'I hand in my checks. I never thought I should come to such things; but what happens when the things come to you? I beg your pardon, Father Brown; I reckon I'll just come across, so far as you and your fairy-tales are concerned. After this, it's me for the fairy-tales. Why, you said yourself, Mr Vandam, that you're an atheist and only believe what you see. Well, what was it you did see? Or rather, what was it you didn't see?'

'I know,' said Vandam and nodded in a gloomy fashion.

'Oh, it's partly all this moon and trees that get on one's nerves,' said Fenner, obstinately. 'Trees always look queer by moonlight, with their branches crawling about. Look at that—'

'Yes,' said Father Brown, standing still and peering at the moon through a tangle of trees. 'That's a very queer branch up there.'

When he spoke again he only said:

'I thought it was a broken branch.'

But this time there was a catch in his voice that unaccountably turned his hearers cold. Something that looked rather like a dead branch was certainly dependent in a limp fashion from the tree that showed dark against the moon; but it was not a dead branch. When they came close to it to see what it was, Fenner sprang away again with a ringing oath. Then he ran in again and loosened a rope from the neck of a dingy little body dangling with drooping plumes of grey hair. Somehow he knew that the body was a dead body before he managed to take it down from the tree. A very long coil of rope was wrapped round and round the branches, and a comparatively short length of it hung from the fork of the branch to the body. A large garden tub was rolled a yard or so from under the feet, like the stool kicked away from the feet of a suicide.

'Oh, my God!' said Alboin, so that it seemed as much a prayer as an oath. 'What was it that man said about him? – "If he knew, he would be ready to hang himself." Wasn't that what he said, Father Brown?'

'Yes,' said Father Brown.

'Well,' said Vandam, in a hollow voice, 'I never thought to see or say such a thing. But what can one say except that the curse has worked?'

Fenner was standing with hands covering his face; and the

priest laid a hand on his arm and said, gently, 'Were you very fond of him?'

The secretary dropped his hands and his white face was ghastly under the moon.

'I hated him like hell,' he said; 'and if he died by a curse it might have been mine.'

The pressure of the priest's hand on his arm tightened; and the priest said, with an earnestness he had hardly yet shown:

'It wasn't your curse; pray be comforted.'

The police of the district had considerable difficulty in dealing with the four witnesses who were involved in the case. All of them were reputable, and even reliable people in the ordinary sense; and one of them was a person of considerable power and importance: Silas Vandam of the Oil Trust. The first police officer who tried to express scepticism about his story struck sparks from the steel of that magnate's mind very rapidly indeed.

'Don't you talk to me about sticking to the facts,' said the millionaire, with asperity. 'I've stuck to a good many facts before you were born, and a few of the facts have stuck to me. I'll give you the facts all right, if you've got the sense to take 'em down correctly.'

The policeman in question was youthful and subordinate, and had a hazy idea that the millionaire was too political to be treated as an ordinary citizen; so he passed him and his companions on to a more stolid superior, one Inspector Collins, a grizzled man with a grimly comfortably way of talking; as one who was genial but would stand no nonsense.

'Well, well,' he said, looking at the three figures before him with twinkling eyes, 'this seems to be a funny sort of a tale.'

Father Brown had already gone about his daily business; but Silas Vandam had suspended even the gigantic business of the markets for an hour or so to testify to his remarkable experience. Fenner's business as secretary had ceased in a sense with his employer's life; and the great Art Alboin, having no business in New York or anywhere else, except the spreading of the Breath of Life or religion of the Great Spirit, had nothing to draw him away at the moment from the immediate affair. So they stood in a row in the inspector's office, prepared to corroborate each other.

'Now I'd better tell you to start with,' said the inspector cheer-fully, 'that it's no good for anybody to come to me with any miracu-lous stuff. I'm a practical man and a policeman, and that sort of thing is all very well for priests and parsons. This priest of yours seems to have got you all worked up about some story of a dreadful death and judgment; but I'm going to leave him and his religion out of it altogether. If Wynd came out of that room, somebody let him out. And if Wynd was found hanging on that tree, somebody hung him there.'

'Quite so,' said Fenner, 'but as our evidence is that nobody let him out, the question is how could anybody have hung him there?'

'How could anybody have a nose on his face?' asked the inspector. 'He had a nose on his face, and he had a noose round his neck. Those are facts; and as I say, I'm a practical man and go by the facts. It can't have been done by a miracle, so it must have been done by a man.'

Alboin had been standing rather in the background; and indeed his broad figure seemed to form a natural background to the leaner and more vivacious men in front of him. His white head was bowed with a certain abstraction; but as the inspector said the last sen-tence, he lifted it, shaking his hoary mane in a leonine fashion, and looking dazed but awakened. He moved forward into the centre of the group, and they had a vague feeling that he was even vaster than before. They had been only too prone to take him for a fool or a mountebank; but he was not altogether wrong when he said that there was in him a certain depth of lungs and life, like a west wind stored up in its strength, which might some day puff lighter things away.

'So you're a practical man, Mr Collins,' he said, in a voice at once soft and heavy. 'It must be the second or third time you've mentioned in this little conversation that you are a practical man; so I can't be mistaken about that. And a very interesting little fact it is for anybody engaged in writing your life, letters, and table-talk, with portrait at the age of five, daguerreotype of your grandmother and views of the old home-town; and I'm sure your biographer won't forget to mention it, along with the fact that you had a pug nose with a pimple on it, and were nearly too fat to walk. And as you're a practical man, perhaps you would just go on practising till you've brought Warren Wynd to life again, and found out exactly how a practical man gets through a deal door. But I think you've got it wrong. You're not a practical man. You're a practical joke; that's what you are. The Almighty was having a bit of fun with us when he thought of you.'

With a characteristic sense of drama he went sailing towards the door before the astonished inspector could reply; and no after-recriminations could rob him of a certain appearance of triumph.

'I think you were perfectly right,' said Fenner. 'If those are practical men, give me priests.'

Another attempt was made to reach an official version of the event, when the official authorities fully realized who were the backers of the story, and what were the implications of it. Already it had broken out in the Press in its most sensationally and even shamelessly psychic form. Interviews with Vandam on his marvellous adventure, articles about Father Brown and his mystical intuitions, soon led those who feel responsible for guiding the public to wish to guide it into a wiser channel. Next time the inconvenient witnesses were approached in a more indirect and tactful manner. They were told, almost in an airy fashion, that Professor Vair was very much interested in such abnormal experiences; was especially interested in their own astonishing case. Professor Vair was a psychologist of great distinction; he had been known to take a detached interest in criminology; it was only some little time afterwards that they discovered that he was in any way connected with the police.

Professor Vair was a courteous gentleman, quietly dressed in pale grey clothes, with an artistic tie and a fair, pointed beard; he looked more like a landscape painter to anyone not acquainted with a certain special type of don. He had an air not only of courtesy, but of frankness.

'Yes, yes, I know,' he said smiling; 'I can guess what you must have gone through. The police do not shine in enquiries of a psychic sort, do they? Of course, dear old Collins said he only wanted the facts. What an absurd blunder! In a case of this kind we emphatically do *not* only want the facts. It is even more essential to have the fancies.'

'Do you mean,' asked Vandam gravely, 'that all that we call the facts were merely fancies?'

'Not at all,' said the professor; 'I only mean that the police are stupid in thinking they can leave out the psychological element in these things. Well, of course, the psychological element is everything in everything, though it is only just beginning to be understood. To begin with, take the element called personality. Now I have heard of this priest, Father Brown, before; and he is one of the most remarkable men of our time. Men of that sort carry a sort of atmosphere with them; and nobody knows how much his nerves and even his very senses are affected by it for the time being. People are hypnotized – yes, hypnotized; for hypnotism, like everything else, is a matter of degree; it enters slightly into all daily conversation; it is not necessarily conducted by a man in evening dress on a platform in a public hall. Father Brown's religion has always understood the psychology of atmospheres, and knows how to appeal to everything simultaneously; even for instance, to the sense of smell. It understands those curious effects produced by music on animals and human beings; it can—'

'Hang it,' protested Fenner, 'you don't think he walked down the corridor carrying a church organ?'

'He knows better than to do that,' said Professor Vair, laughing. 'He knows how to concentrate the essence of all these spiritual sounds and sights, and even smells, in a few restrained gestures; in an art or school of manners. He could contrive so to concentrate your minds on the supernatural by his mere presence, that natural things slipped off your minds to left and right, unnoticed. Now you know,' he proceeded with a return to cheerful good sense, 'that the more we study it the more queer the whole question of human evidence becomes. There is not one man in twenty who really observes things at all. There is not one man in a hundred who observes them with real precision; certainly not one in a hundred who can first observe, then remember, and finally describe. Scientific experiments have been made again and again, showing that men under a strain have thought a door was shut when it was open, or open when it was shut. Men have differed about the number of doors or windows in a wall just in front of them. They have suffered optical illusions in broad daylight. They have done this even without the hypnotic effect of personality; but here we have a very powerful and persuasive personality bent upon fixing only one picture on your minds; the picture of the wild, Irish rebel shaking his pistol at the sky and firing that vain volley, whose echoes were the thunders of heaven.'

'Professor,' cried Fenner, 'I'd swear on my deathbed that door never opened.'

'Recent experiments,' went on the professor, quietly, 'have suggested that our consciousness is not continuous, but is a succession of very rapid impressions like a cinema; it is possible that somebody or something may, so to speak, slip in or out between the scenes. It acts only in the instant while the curtain is down. Probably the patter of conjurers and all forms of sleight of hand depend on what we may call these black flashes of blindness between the flashes of sight. Now this priest and preacher of transcendental notions had filled you with a transcendental imagery; the image of the Celt like a Titan shaking the tower with his curse. Probably he accompanied it with some slight but compelling gesture, pointing your eyes and minds in the direction of the unknown destroyer below. Or perhaps something else happened, or somebody else passed by.'

'Wilson, the servant,' grunted Alboin, 'went down the hallway to wait on the bench, but I guess he didn't distract us much.'

'You never know how much,' replied Vair; 'it might have been that or more likely your eyes following some gesture of the priest as he told his tale of magic. It was in one of those black flashes that Mr Warren Wynd slipped out of his door and went to his death. That is the most probable explanation. It is an illustration of the new discovery. The mind is not a continuous line, but rather a dotted line.'

'Very dotted,' said Fenner, feebly. 'Not to say dotty.'

'You don't really believe,' asked Vair, 'that your employer was shut up in a room like a box?'

'It's better than believing that I ought to be shut up in a room like a padded cell,' answered Fenner. 'That's what I complain of in your suggestions, professor. I'd as soon believe in a priest who believes in a miracle, as disbelieve in any man having any right to believe in a fact. The priest tells me that a man can appeal to a God I know nothing about, to avenge him by the laws of some higher justice that I know nothing about. There's nothing for me to say except that I know nothing about it. But at least if the poor Paddy's prayer and pistol could be heard in a higher world, that higher world might act in some way that seems odd to us. But you ask me to disbelieve the facts of this world as they appear to my own five wits. According to you, a whole procession of Irishmen carrying blunderbusses may have walked through this room while we were talking, so long as they took care to tread on the blind spots in our minds. Miracles of the monkish sort, like materializing a crocodile or hanging a cloak on a sunbeam, seem quite sane compared to you.'

'Oh, well,' said Professor Vair, rather curtly, 'if you are resolved to believe in your priest and his miraculous Irishman, I can say no more. I'm afraid you have not had an opportunity of studying psychology.'

'No,' said Fenner dryly, 'but I've had an opportunity of studying psychologists.'

And bowing politely, he led his deputation out of the room and did not speak till he got into the street; then he addressed them rather explosively.

'Raving lunatics!' cried Fenner in a fume. 'What the devil do they think is to happen to the world if nobody knows whether he's seen anything or not? I wish I'd blown his silly head off with a blank charge, and then explained that I did it in a blind flash. Father Brown's miracle may be miraculous or no, but he said it would happen and it did happen. All these blasted cranks can do is to see a thing happen and then say it didn't. Look here, I think we owe it to the padre to testify to his little demonstration. We're all sane, solid men who never believed in anything. We weren't drunk. We weren't devout. It simply happened just as he said it would.'

'I quite agree,' said the millionaire. 'It may be the beginning of mighty big things in the spiritual line; but anyhow, the man who's in the spiritual line himself, Father Brown, has certainly scored over this business.'

A few days afterwards Father Brown received a very polite note signed Silas T. Vandam, and asking him if he could attend at a stated hour at the apartment which was the scene of the disappearance, in order to take steps for the establishment of that marvellous occurrence. The occurrence itself had already begun to break out in the newspapers, and was being taken up everywhere by the enthusiasts of occultism. Father Brown saw the flaring posters inscribed 'Suicide of Vanishing Man', and 'Man's Curse Hangs Philanthropist', as he passed towards Moon Crescent and mounted the steps on the way to the elevator. He found the little group much as he left it, Vandam, Alboin, and the secretary; but there was an entirely new respectfulness and even reverence in their tone towards himself. They were standing by Wynd's desk, on which lay a large paper and writing materials, as they turned to greet him.

'Father Brown,' said the spokesman, who was the white-haired Westerner, somewhat sobered with his responsibility, 'we asked you here in the first place to offer our apologies and our thanks. We recognize that it was you that spotted the spiritual manifestation from the first. We were hard-shell sceptics, all of us; but we realize now that a man must break that shell to get at the great things behind the world. You stand for those things; you stand for that super-normal explanation of things; and we have to hand it to you. And in the second place, we feel that this document would not be complete without your signature. We are notifying the exact facts to the Psychical Research Society because the newspaper accounts are not what you might call exact. We've stated how the curse was spoken out in the street; how the man was sealed up here in a room like a box; how the curse dissolved him straight into thin air, and in some unthinkable way materialized him as a suicide hoisted on a gallows. That's all we can say about it; but all that we know, and have seen with our own eyes. And as you were the first to believe in the miracle, we all feel that you ought to be the first to sign.'

'No, really,' said Father Brown, in embarrassment. 'I don't think I should like to do that.'

'You mean you'd rather not sign first?'

'I mean I'd rather not sign at all,' said Father Brown, modestly. 'You see, it doesn't quite do for a man in my position to joke about miracles.'

'But it was you who said it was a miracle,' said Alboin, staring.

'I'm so sorry,' said Father Brown; 'I'm afraid there's some mistake. I don't think I ever said it was a miracle. All I said was that it might happen. What you said was that it couldn't happen, because it would be a miracle if it did. And then it did. And so you said it was a miracle. But I never said a word about miracles or magic, or anything of the sort from beginning to end.'

'But I thought you believed in miracles,' broke out the secretary.

'Yes,' answered Father Brown, 'I believe in miracles. I believe in man-eating tigers, but I don't see them running about everywhere. If I want any miracles, I know where to get them.'

'I can't understand your taking this line, Father Brown,' said Vandam, earnestly. 'It seems so narrow; and you don't look narrow to me, though you are a parson. Don't you see, a miracle like this will knock all materialism endways? It will just tell the whole world in big print that spiritual powers can work and do work. You'll be serving religion as no parson ever served it yet.'

The priest had stiffened a little and seemed in some strange way clothed with unconscious and impersonal dignity, for all his stumpy figure. 'Well,' he said, 'you wouldn't suggest I should serve religion by what I know to be a lie. I don't know precisely what you mean by the phrase; and, to be quite candid, I'm not sure you do. Lying may be serving religion; I'm sure it's not serving God. And since you are harping so insistently on what I believe, wouldn't it be as well if you had some sort of notion of what it is?'

'I don't think I quite understand,' observed the millionaire, curiously.

'I don't think you do,' said Father Brown, with simplicity. 'You say this thing was done by spiritual powers. What spiritual powers? You don't think the holy angels took him and hung him on a garden tree, do you? And as for the unholy angels – no, no, no. The men who did this did a wicked thing, but they went no further than their own wickedness; they weren't wicked enough to be dealing with spiritual powers. I know something about Satanism, for my sins; I've been forced to know. I know what it is, what it practically always is. It's proud and it's sly. It likes to be superior; it loves to horrify the innocent with things half understood, to make children's flesh creep. That's why it's so fond of mysteries and initiations and secret societies and all the rest of it. Its eyes are turned inwards, and however grand and grave it may look, it's always hiding a small, mad smile.' He shuddered suddenly, as if caught in an icy draught of air. 'Never mind about them; they've got nothing to do with this, believe me. Do you think that poor, wild Irishman of mine, who ran raving down the street, who blurted out half of it when he first saw my face, and ran away for fear he should blurt out more, do you think Satan confides any secrets to him? I admit he joined in a plot, probably in a plot with two other men worse than himself; but for all that he was just in an everlasting rage when he rushed down the lane and let off his pistol and his curse.'

'But what on earth does all this mean?' demanded Vandam. 'Letting off a toy pistol and a twopenny curse wouldn't do what was done, except by a miracle. It wouldn't make Wynd disappear like a fairy. It wouldn't make him reappear a quarter of a mile away with a rope round his neck.'

'No,' said Father Brown, sharply, 'but what would it do?'

'And still I don't follow you,' said the millionaire gravely.

'I say, what would it do?' repeated the priest, showing, for the first time, a sort of animation verging on annoyance. 'You keep on repeating that a blank pistol-shot wouldn't do this, and wouldn't do that; that if that was all, the murder wouldn't happen or the miracle wouldn't happen. It doesn't seem to occur to you to ask what would happen. What would happen to you, if a lunatic let off a firearm without rhyme or reason right under your window? What's the very first thing that would happen?'

Vandam looked thoughtful. 'I guess I should look out of the window,' he said.

'Yes,' said Father Brown, 'you'd look out of the window. That's the whole story. It's a sad story, but it's finished now; and there were extenuating circumstances.'

'Why should looking out of the window hurt him?' asked Alboin. 'He didn't fall out, or he'd have been found in the lane.'

'No,' said Father Brown, in a low voice. 'He didn't fall. He rose.' There was something in his voice like the groan of a gong, a note of doom, but otherwise he went on steadily.

'He rose, but not on wings; not on the wings of any holy or unholy angels. He rose at the end of a rope, exactly as you saw him in the garden: a noose dropped over the head the moment it was poked out of the window. Don't you remember Wilson, that big servant of his, a man of huge strength, while Wynd was the lightest of little shrimps? Didn't Wilson go to the floor above to get a pamphlet, to a room full of luggage corded in coils and coils of rope? Has Wilson been seen since that day? I fancy not.'

'Do you mean,' asked the secretary, 'that Wilson whisked him clean out of his own window like a trout on a line?'

'Yes,' said the other, 'and let him down again out of the other window into the park, where the third accomplice hooked him on to a tree. Remember the lane was always empty; remember the wall opposite was quite blank; remember it was all over in five minutes after the Irishman gave the signal with the pistol. There were three of them in it, of course; and I wonder whether you can all guess who they were.'

They were all three staring at the plain, square window and the blank, white wall beyond; and nobody answered.

'By the way,' went on Father Brown, 'don't think I blame you for jumping to preternatural conclusions. The reason's very simple, really. You all swore you were hard-shelled materialists; and as a matter of fact you were all balanced on the very edge of belief – of belief in almost anything. There are thousands balanced on it today; but it's a sharp, uncomfortable edge to sit on. You won't rest till you believe something; that's why Mr Vandam went through new religions with a tooth-comb and Mr Alboin quotes Scripture for his religion of breathing exercises, and Mr Fenner grumbles at the very God he denies. That's where you all split; it's natural to believe in the supernatural. It never feels natural to accept only natural things. But though it wanted only a touch to tip you into preternaturalism about these things, these things really were only natural things. They were not only natural, they were almost un-naturally simple. I suppose there never was quite so simple a story as this.'

Fenner laughed and then looked puzzled. 'I don't understand one thing,' he said. 'If it was Wilson, how did Wynd come to have a man like that on such intimate terms? How did he come to be killed by a man he'd seen every day for years? He was famous as being a judge of men.'

Father Brown thumped his umbrella on the ground with an emphasis he rarely showed.

'Yes,' he said, almost fiercely. 'That was how he came to be killed. He was killed for just that. He was killed for being a judge of men.'

They all stared at him, but he went on, almost as if they were not there.

'What is any man that he should be a judge of men?' he demanded. 'These three were the tramps that once stood before him and were dismissed rapidly right and left to one place or another; as if for them there were no cloak of courtesy, no stages of intimacy, no free will in friendship. And twenty years has not exhausted the indignation born of that unfathomable insult in that moment when he dared to know them at a glance.'

'Yes,' said the secretary; 'I understand . . . and I understand how it is that you understand – all sorts of things.'

'Well, I'm blamed if I understand,' cried the breezy Western gentleman boisterously. 'Your Wilson and your Irishman seem to be just a couple of cut-throat murderers who killed their benefactor. I've no use for a black and bloody assassin of that sort in my morality, whether it's religion or not.'

'He was a black and bloody assassin, no doubt,' said Fenner, quietly. 'I'm not defending him; but I suppose it's Father Brown's business to pray for all men, even for a man like—'

'Yes,' assented Father Brown, 'it's my business to pray for all men, even for a man like Warren Wynd.'

THE DAGGER WITH WINGS

FATHER Brown, at one period of his life, found it difficult to hang his hat on a hat-peg without repressing a slight shudder. The origin of this idiosyncrasy was indeed a mere detail in much more complicated events; but it was perhaps the only detail that remained to him in his busy life to remind him of the whole business. Its remote origin was to be found in the facts which led Dr Boyne, the medical officer attached to the police force, to send for the priest on a particular frosty morning in December.

Dr Boyne was a big dark Irishman, one of those rather baffling Irishmen to be found all over the world, who will talk scientific scepticism, materialism and cynicism at length and at large, but who never dream of referring anything touching the ritual of religion to anything except the traditional religion of their native land. It would be hard to say whether their creed is a very superficial varnish or a very fundamental substratum; but most probably it is both, with a mass of materialism in between. Anyhow, when he thought that matters of that sort might be involved, he asked Father Brown to call, though he made no pretence of preference for that aspect of them.

'I'm not sure I want you, you know,' was his greeting. 'I'm not sure about anything yet. I'm hanged if I can make out whether it's a case for a doctor, or a policeman, or a priest.'

'Well,' said Father Brown with a smile, 'as I suppose you're both a policeman and a doctor, I seem to be rather in a minority.'

'I admit you're what politicians call an instructed minority,' replied the doctor. 'I mean I know you've had to do a little in our line as well as your own. But it's precious hard to say whether this business is in your line or ours, or merely in the line of the Commissioners in Lunacy. We've just had a message from a man living near here, in that white house on the hill, asking for protection against a murderous persecution. We've gone into the facts as far as we could, and perhaps I'd better tell you the story as it is supposed to have happened, from the beginning.

'It seems that a man named Aylmer, who was a wealthy land-owner in the West Country, married rather late in life and had three sons, Philip, Stephen and Arnold. But in his bachelor days, when he thought he would have no heir, he had adopted a boy whom he thought very brilliant and promising, who went by the name of John Strake. His origin seems to be vague: they say he was a foundling; some say he was a gipsy. I think the last notion is mixed up with the fact that Aylmer in his old age dabbled in all sorts of dingy occultism, including palmistry and astrology, and his three sons say that Strake encouraged him in it. But they said a great many other things besides that. They said Strake was an amazing scoundrel and especially an amazing liar; a genius in inventing lies on the spur of the moment and telling them so as to deceive a detective. But that might very well be a natural prejudice, in the light of what happened. Perhaps you can more or less imagine what happened. The old man left practically everything to the adopted son; and when he died the three real sons disputed the will. They said their father had been frightened into surrender and, not to put too fine a point on it, into gibbering idiocy. They said Strake had the strangest and most cunning ways of getting at him, in spite of the nurses and the family, and terrorizing him on his death-bed. Anyhow, they seemed to have proved something about the dead man's mental condition, for the courts set aside the will and the sons inherited. Strake is said to have broken out in the most dreadful fashion, and sworn he would kill all three of them, one after another, and that nothing could hide them from his vengeance. It is the third or last of the brothers, Arnold Aylmer, who is asking for police protection.'

'Third and last,' said the priest, looking at him gravely.

'Yes,' said Boyne. 'The other two are dead.'

There was a silence before he continued. 'That is where the doubt comes in. There is no proof they were murdered, but they might possibly have been. The eldest, who took up his position as squire, was supposed to have committed suicide in his garden. The second, who went into trade as a manufacturer, was knocked on the head by the machinery in his factory; he might very well have taken a false step and fallen. But if Strake did kill them, he is certainly very cunning in his way of getting to work and getting away. On the other hand, it's more than likely that the whole thing is a mania of conspiracy founded on a coincidence. Look here, what I want is this: I want somebody of sense, who isn't an official, to go up and have a talk with this Mr Arnold Aylmer, and form an impression of him. You know what a man with a delusion is like, and how a man looks when he is telling the truth. I want you to be the advance guard, before we take the matter up.'

'It seems rather odd,' said Father Brown, 'that you haven't had to take it up before. If there is anything in this business, it seems to have been going on for a good time. Is there any particular reason why he should send for you just now, any more than any other time?'

'That had occurred to me, as you may imagine,' answered Dr Boyne. 'He does give a reason, but I confess it is one of the things that make me wonder whether the whole thing isn't only the whim of some half-witted crank. He declares that all his servants have suddenly gone on strike and left him; so that he is obliged to call on the police to look after his house. And on making enquiries, I certainly do find that there has been a general exodus of servants from that house on the hill; and of course the town is full of tales, very one-sided tales I dare say. Their account of it seems to be that their employer had become quite impossible in his fidgets and fears and exactions; that he wanted them to guard the house like sentries or sit up like night nurses in a hospital; that they could never be left alone because he must never be left alone. So they all announced in a loud voice that he was a lunatic, and left. Of course that does not prove he is a lunatic; but it seems rather rum nowadays for a man to expect his valet or his parlour-maid to act as an armed guard.'

'And so,' said the priest with a smile, 'he wants a policeman to act as his parlour-maid because his parlour-maid won't act as a policeman.'

'I thought that rather thick, too,' agreed the doctor, 'but I can't take the responsibility of a flat refusal till I've tried a compromise. You are the compromise.'

'Very well,' said Father Brown simply. 'I'll go and call on him now if you like.'

The rolling country round the little town was sealed and bound with frost, and the sky was as clear and cold as steel except in the north-east, where clouds with lurid haloes were beginning to climb up the sky. It was against these darker and more sinister colours that the house on the hill gleamed with a row of pale pillars, forming a short colonnade of the classical sort. A winding road led up to it across the curve of the down, and plunged into a mass of dark bushes. Just before it reached the bushes, the air seemed to grow colder and colder, as if he were approaching an icehouse or the North Pole. But he was a highly practical person, never entertaining such fancies except as fancies. And he merely cocked his eye at the great livid cloud crawling up over the house, and remarked cheerfully:

'It's going to snow.'

Through a low ornamental iron gateway of the Italianate pattern he entered a garden having something of that desolation which only belongs to the disorder of orderly things. Deep green growths were grey with the faint powder of the frost, large weeds had fringed the fading pattern of the flower-beds as if in a ragged frame; and the house stood as if waist-high in a stunted forest of shrubs and bushes. The vegetation consisted largely of evergreens or very hardy plants; and though it was thus thick and heavy, it was too northern to be called luxuriant. It might be described as an Arctic jungle. So it was in some sense with the house itself, which had a row of columns and a classical façade, which might have looked out on the Mediterranean; but which seemed now to be withering in the wind of the North Sea. Classical ornament here and there accentuated the contrast; caryatides and carved masks of comedy or tragedy looked down from corners of the building upon the grey confusion of the garden paths; but the faces seemed to be frost-bitten. The very volutes of the capitals might have curled up with the cold.

Father Brown went up the grassy steps to a square porch flanked by big pillars and knocked at the door. About four minutes afterwards he knocked again. Then he stood still, patiently waiting with his back to the door and looked out on the slowly darkening landscape. It was darkening under the shadow of that one great continent of cloud that had come flying out of the north; and even as he looked out beyond the pillars of the porch, which seemed huge and black above him in the twilight, he saw the opalescent crawling rim of the great cloud as it sailed over the roof and bowed over the porch like a canopy. The grey canopy with its faintly coloured fringes seemed to sink lower and lower upon the garden beyond, until what had recently been a clear and pale-hued winter sky was left in a few silver ribbons and rags like a sickly sunset. Father Brown waited; and there was no sound within.

Then he betook himself briskly down the steps and round the house to look for another entrance. He eventually found one, a side door in the flat wall, and on this also he hammered and outside this also he waited. Then he tried the handle and found the door apparently bolted or fastened in some fashion; and then he moved along that side of the house, musing on the possibilities of the position, and wondering whether the eccentric Mr Aylmer had barricaded himself too deep in the house to hear any kind of summons; or whether perhaps he would barricade himself all the more, on the assumption that any summons must be the challenge of the avenging Strake. It might be that the decamping servants had only unlocked one door when they left in the morning, and that their master had locked that; but whatever he might have done it was unlikely that they, in the mood of that moment, had looked so carefully to the defences. He continued his prowl round the place; it was not really a large place, though perhaps a little pretentious; and in a few moments he found he had made the complete circuit. A moment after he found what he suspected and sought. The French window of one room, curtained and shadowed with creeper, stood open by a crack, doubtless accidentally left ajar, and he found himself in a central room, comfortably upholstered in a rather old-fashioned way, with a staircase leading up from it on one side and a door leading out of it on the other. Immediately opposite him was another door, with red glass let into it, a little gaudily for later tastes; something that looked like a red-robed figure in cheap stained glass. On a round table to the right stood a sort of aquarium – a great bowl full of greenish water, in which fishes and similar things moved about as in a tank; and just opposite it a plant of the palm variety with very large green leaves. All this looked so very dusty and early Victorian that the telephone, visible in the curtained alcove, was almost a surprise.

'Who is that?' a voice called out sharply and rather suspiciously from behind the stained-glass door.

'Could I see Mr Aylmer?' asked the priest apologetically.

The door opened and a gentleman in a peacock-green dressing-gown came out with an inquiring look. His hair was rather rough and untidy, as if he had been in bed or lived in a state of slowly getting up, but his eyes were not only awake but alert, and some would have said alarmed. Father Brown knew that the contradiction was likely enough in a man who had rather run to seed under the shadow either of a delusion or a danger. He had a fine aquiline face when seen in profile, but when seen full-face the first impression was of the untidiness and even the wilderness of his loose brown beard.

'I am Mr Aylmer,' he said, 'but I have got out of the way of expecting visitors.'

Something about Mr Aylmer's unrestful eye prompted the priest to go straight to the point. If the man's persecution was only a monomania, he would be the less likely to resent it.

'I was wondering,' said Father Brown softly, 'whether it is quite true that you never expect visitors.'

'You are right,' replied his host steadily, 'I always expect one visitor. And he may be the last.'

'I hope not,' said Father Brown, 'but at least I am relieved to infer that I do not look very like him.'

Mr Aylmer shook himself with a sort of savage laugh. 'You certainly do not,' he said.

'Mr Aylmer,' said Father Brown frankly, 'I apologize for the liberty, but some friends of mine have told me about your trouble, and asked me to see if I could do anything for you. The truth is, I have some little experience in affairs like this.'

'There are no affairs like this,' said Aylmer.

'You mean,' observed Father Brown, 'that the tragedies in your unfortunate family were not normal deaths?'

'I mean they were not even normal murders,' answered the other. 'The man who is hounding us all to death is a hell-hound, and his power is from hell.'

'All evil has one origin,' said the priest gravely. 'But how do you know they were not normal murders?'

Aylmer answered with a gesture which offered his guest a chair; then he seated himself slowly in another, frowning with his hands on his knees; but when he looked up his expression had grown milder and more thoughtful, and his voice was quite cordial and composed.

'Sir,' he said, 'I don't want you to imagine that I'm in the least an unreasonable person. I have come to these conclusions by reason, because unfortunately reason really leads there. I have read a great deal on these subjects; for I was the only one who inherited my father's scholarship in somewhat obscure matters, and I have since inherited his library. But what I tell you does not rest on what I have read but on what I have seen.'

Father Brown nodded, and the other proceeded, as if picking his words:

'In my elder brother's case I was not certain at first. There were no marks or footprints where he was found shot, and the pistol was left beside him. But he had just received a threatening letter, certainly from our enemy, for it was marked with a sign like a winged dagger, which was one of his infernal cabalistic tricks. And a servant said she had seen something moving along the garden wall in the twilight that was much too large to be a cat. I leave it there; all I can say is that if the murderer came, he managed to leave no traces of his coming. But when my brother Stephen died it was different; and since then I have known. A machine was working in an open scaffolding under the factory tower; I scaled the platform a moment after he had fallen under the iron hammer that struck him; I did not see anything else strike him, but I saw what I saw.

'A great drift of factory smoke was rolling between me and the factory tower; but through a rift of it I saw on the top of it a dark human figure, wrapped in what looked like a black cloak. Then the sulphurous smoke drove between us again; and when it cleared I looked up at the distant chimney. There was nobody there. I am a rational man, and I will ask all rational men how he had reached that dizzy unapproachable turret, and how he left it.'

He stared across at the priest with a sphinx-like challenge; then after a silence he said abruptly:

'My brother's brains were knocked out, but his body was not much damaged. And in his pocket we found one of those warning messages dated the day before and stamped with the flying dagger.

'I am sure,' he went on gravely, 'that the symbol of the winged dagger is not merely arbitrary or accidental. Nothing about that abominable man is accidental. He is all design; though it is indeed a most dark and intricate design. His mind is woven not only out of elaborate schemes but out of all sorts of secret languages and signs and dumb signals and wordless pictures which are the names of nameless things. He is the worst sort of man that the world knows: he is the wicked mystic. Now I don't pretend to penetrate all that is conveyed by this symbol; but it seems surely that it must have a relation to all that was most remarkable, or even incredible, in his movements as he had hovered round my unfortunate family. Is there no connexion between the idea of a winged weapon and the mystery by which Philip was struck dead on his own lawn without the lightest touch of any footprint having disturbed the dust or grass? Is there no connexion between the plumed poignard flying like a feathered arrow and that figure which hung on the far top of the toppling chimney, clad in a cloak for pinions?'

'You mean,' said Father Brown thoughtfully, 'that he is in a perpetual state of levitation.'

'Simon Magus did it,' replied Aylmer, 'and it was one of the commonest predictions of the Dark Ages that Antichrist would be able to fly. Anyhow, there was the flying dagger on the document; and whether or no it could fly, it could certainly strike.'

'Did you notice what sort of paper it was on?' asked Father Brown. 'Common paper?'

The sphinx-like face broke abruptly into a harsh laugh.

'You can see what they're like,' said Aylmer grimly, 'for I got one myself this morning.'

He was leaning back in his chair now, with his long legs thrust out from under the green dressing-gown, which was a little short for him, and his bearded chin pillowed on his chest. Without moving otherwise he thrust his hand deep in the dressing-gown pocket and held out a fluttering scrap of paper at the end of a rigid arm. His whole attitude was suggestive of a sort of paralysis, that was both rigidity and collapse. But the next remark of the priest had a curious effect of rousing him.

Father Brown was blinking in his short-sighted way at the paper presented to him. It was a singular sort of paper, rough without being common, as from an artist's sketch-book; and on it was drawn boldly in red ink a dagger decorated with wings like the rod of Hermes, with the written words, 'Death comes the day after this, as it came to your brothers.'

Father Brown tossed the paper on the floor and sat bolt upright in his chair.

'You mustn't let that sort of stuff stupefy you,' he said sharply. 'These devils always try to make us helpless by making us hopeless.'

Rather to his surprise, an awakening wave went over the prostrate figure, which sprang from its chair as if startled out of a dream.

'You're right, you're right!' cried Aylmer with a rather uncanny animation, 'and the devils shall find I'm not so hopeless after all, nor so helpless either. Perhaps I have more hope and better help than you fancy.'

He stood with his hands in his pockets, frowning down at the priest, who had a momentary doubt, during that strained silence, about whether the man's long peril had not touched the man's brain. But when he spoke it was quite soberly.

'I believe my unfortunate brothers failed because they used the wrong weapons. Philip carried a revolver, and that was how his death came to be called suicide. Stephen had police protection, but he also had a sense of what made him ridiculous; and he could not allow a policeman to climb up a ladder after him to a scaffolding where he stood only a moment. They were both scoffers, reacting into scepticism from the strange mysticism of my father's last days. But I always knew there was more in my father than they understood. It is true that by studying magic he fell at last under the blight of black magic: the black magic of this scoundrel Strake. But my brothers were wrong about the antidote. The antidote to black magic is not brute materialism or worldly wisdom. The antidote to black magic is white magic.'

'It rather depends,' said Father Brown, 'what you mean by white magic '

'I mean silver magic,' said the other, in a low voice, like one speaking of a secret revelation. Then after a silence he said, 'Do you know what I mean by silver magic? Pray excuse me a moment.'

He turned and opened the central door with the red glass and went into a passage beyond it. The house had less depth than Brown had supposed; instead of the door opening into interior rooms, the corridor it revealed ended in another door on the garden. The door of one room was on one side of the passage; doubtless, the priest told himself, the proprietor's bedroom, whence he had rushed out in his dressing-gown. There was nothing else on that side but an ordinary hat-stand with the ordinary dingy cluster of old hats and overcoats; but on the other side was something more interesting;

a very dark old oak sideboard laid out with some old silver, and overhung by a trophy or ornament of old weapons. It was by that that Arnold Aylmer halted, looking up at a long, antiquated pistol with a bell-shaped mouth.

The door at the end of the passage was barely open, and through the crack came a streak of white daylight. The priest had very quick instincts about natural things, and something in the unusual brilliancy of that white line told him what had happened outside. It was indeed what he had prophesied when he was approaching the house. He ran past his rather startled host and opened the door, to face something that was at once a blank and a blaze. What he had seen shining through the crack was not only the more negative whiteness of daylight but the positive whiteness of snow. All round, the sweeping fall of the country was covered with that shining pallor that seems at once hoary and innocent.

'Here is white magic anyhow,' said Father Brown in his cheerful voice. Then as he turned back into the hall he murmured, 'And silver magic too, I suppose,' for the white lustre touched the silver with splendour and lit up the old steel here and there in the darkling armoury. The shaggy head of the brooding Aylmer seemed to have a halo of silver fire, as he turned with his face in shadow and the outlandish pistol in his hand.

'Do you know why I choose this sort of old blunderbuss?' he asked. 'Because I can load it with this sort of bullet.'

He had picked up a small apostle spoon from the sideboard, and by sheer violence broke off the small figure at the top. 'Let us go back into the other room,' he added.

'Did you ever read about the death of Dundee?' he asked when they had reseated themselves. He had recovered from his momentary annoyance at the priest's restlessness. 'Graham of Claverhouse, you know, who persecuted the Covenanters and had a black horse that could ride straight up a precipice. Don't you know he could only be shot with a silver bullet, because he had sold himself to the Devil? That's one comfort about you; at least you know enough to believe in the Devil.'

'Oh, yes,' replied Father Brown, 'I believe in the Devil. What I don't believe in is the Dundee. I mean the Dundee of Covenanting legends, with his nightmare of a horse. John Graham was simply a seventeenth-century professional soldier, rather better than most.

If he dragooned them it was because he was a dragoon, but not a dragon. Now my experience is that it's not that sort of swaggering blade who sells himself to the Devil. The devil-worshippers I've known were quite different. Not to mention names, which might cause a social flutter, I'll take a man in Dundee's own day. Have you ever heard of Dalrymple of Stair?'

'No,' replied the other gruffly.

'You've heard of what he did,' said Father Brown, 'and it was worse than anything Dundee ever did; yet he escapes the infamy by oblivion. He was the man who made the Massacre of Glencoe. He was a very learned man and lucid lawyer, a statesman with very serious and enlarged ideas of statesmanship, a quiet man with a very refined and intellectual face. That's the sort of man who sells himself to the Devil.'

Aylmer half started from his chair with an enthusiasm of eager assent.

'By God, you are right,' he cried. 'A refined intellectual face! That is the face of John Strake.'

Then he raised himself and stood looking at the priest with a curious concentration. 'If you will wait here a little while,' he said, 'I will show you something.'

He went back through the central door, closing it after him; going, the priest presumed, to the old sideboard or possibly to his bedroom. Father Brown remained seated, gazing abstractedly at the carpet, where a faint red glimmer shone from the glass in the doorway. Once it seemed to brighten like a ruby and then darkened again, as if the sun of that stormy day had passed from cloud to cloud. Nothing moved except the aquatic creatures which floated to and fro in the dim green bowl. Father Brown was thinking hard.

A minute or two afterwards he got up and slipped quietly to the alcove of the telephone, where he rang up his friend Dr Boyne, at the official headquarters. 'I wanted to tell you about Aylmer and his affairs,' he said quietly. 'It's a queer story, but I rather think there's something in it. If I were you I'd send some men up here straight away; four or five men, I think, and surround the house. If anything does happen there'll probably be something startling in the way of an escape.'

Then he went back and sat down again, staring at the dark

carpet, which again glowed blood-red with the light from the glass door. Something in that filtered light set his mind drifting on certain borderlands of thought, with the first white daybreak before the coming of colour, and all that mystery which is alternately veiled and revealed in the symbol of windows and of doors.

An inhuman howl in a human voice came from beyond the closed doors, almost simultaneously with the noise of firing. Before the echoes of the shot had died away the door was violently flung open and his host staggered into the room, the dressing-gown half torn from his shoulder and the long pistol smoking in his hand. He seemed to be shaking in every limb, yet he was shaken in part with an unnatural laughter.

'Glory be to the White Magic!' he cried; 'Glory be to the silver bullet! The hell-hound has hunted once too often, and my brothers are avenged at last.'

He sank into a chair and the pistol slid from his hand and fell on the floor. Father Brown darted past him, slipped through the glass door and went down the passage. As he did so he put his hand on the handle of the bedroom door, as if half intending to enter; then he stooped a moment, as if examining something – and then he ran to the outer door and opened it.

On the field of snow, which had been so blank a little while before, lay one black object. At the first glance it looked a little like an enormous bat. A second glance showed that it was, after all, a human figure; fallen on its face, the whole head covered by a broad black hat having something of a Latin-American look; while the appearance of black wings came from the two flaps or loose sleeves of a very vast black cloak spread out, perhaps by accident, to their utmost length on either side. Both the hands were hidden, though Father Brown thought he could detect the position of one of them, and saw close to it, under the edge of the cloak, the glimmer of some metallic weapon. The main effect, however, was curiously like that of the simple extravagances of heraldry; like a black eagle displayed on a white ground. But by walking round it and peering under the hat the priest got a glimpse of the face, which was indeed what his host had called refined and intellectual; even sceptical and austere: the face of John Strake.

'Well, I'm jiggered,' muttered Father Brown. 'It really does look like some vast vampire, that has swooped down like a bird.'

'How else could he have come?' came a voice from the doorway; and Father Brown looked up to see Aylmer once more standing there.

'Couldn't he have walked?' replied Father Brown evasively.

Aylmer stretched out his arm and swept the white landscape with a gesture.

'Look at the snow,' he said in a deep voice that had a sort of roll and thrill in it. 'Is not the snow unspotted – pure as the white magic you yourself called it? Is there a speck on it for miles, save that one foul black blot that has fallen there? There are no footprints, but a few of yours and mine; there are none approaching the house from anywhere.'

Then he looked at the little priest for a moment with a concentrated and curious expression, and said:

'I will tell you something else. That cloak he flies with is too long to walk with. He was not a very tall man; and it would trail behind him like a royal train. Stretch it out over his body, if you like, and see.'

'What happened to you both?' asked Father Brown abruptly.

'It was too swift to describe,' answered Aylmer. 'I had looked out of the door and was turning back when there came a kind of rushing of wind all around me, as if I were being buffeted by a wheel revolving in mid-air. I spun round somehow and fired blindly; and then I saw nothing but what you see now. But I am morally certain you wouldn't see it, if I had not had a silver shot in my gun. It would have been a different body lying there in the snow.'

'By the way,' remarked Father Brown, 'shall we leave it lying there in the snow? Or would you like it taken into your room – I suppose that's your bedroom in the passage?'

'No, no,' replied Aylmer hastily, 'we must leave it there till the police have seen it. Besides, I've had as much of such things as I can stand for the moment. Whatever else happens, I'm going to have a drink. After that, they can hang me if they like.'

Inside the central apartment, between the palm plant and the bowl of fishes, Aylmer tumbled into a chair. He had nearly knocked the bowl over as he lurched into the room, but he had managed to find the decanter of brandy after plunging his hand rather blindly into several cupboards and corners. He did not at any time look like a methodical person, but at this moment his distraction must have been extreme. He drank with a long gulp and began to talk rather feverishly, as if to fill up a silence.

'I see you are still doubtful,' he said, 'though you have seen the thing with your own eyes. Believe me, there was something more behind the quarrel between the spirit of Strake and the spirit of the house of Aylmer. Besides, you have no business to be an unbeliever. You ought to stand for all the things these stupid people call super-stitions. Come now, don't you think there's a lot in those old wives' tales about luck and charms and so on, silver bullets included? What do you say about them as a Catholic?'

'I say I'm an agnostic,' replied Father Brown, smiling.

'Nonsense,' said Aylmer impatiently. 'It's your business to believe things.'

'Well, I do believe some things, of course,' conceded Father Brown; 'and therefore, of course, I don't believe other things.'

Aylmer was leaning forward, and looking at him with a strange intensity that was almost like that of a mesmerist.

'You do believe it,' he said. 'You do believe everything. We all believe everything, even when we deny everything. The deniers believe. The unbelievers believe. Don't you feel in your heart that these contradictions do not really contradict: that there is a cosmos that contains them all? The soul goes round upon a wheel of stars and all things return; perhaps Strake and I have striven in many shapes, beast against beast and bird against bird, and perhaps we shall strive for ever. But since we seek and need each other, even that eternal hatred is an eternal love. Good and evil go round in a wheel that is one thing and not many. Do you not realize in your heart, do you not believe behind all your beliefs, that there is but one reality and we are its shadows; and that all things are but aspects of one thing: a centre where men melt into Man and Man into God?'

'No,' said Father Brown.

Outside twilight had begun to fall, in that phase of such a snow-laden evening when the land looks brighter than the sky. In the porch of the main entrance, visible through a half-curtained window, Father Brown could dimly see a bulky figure standing. He glanced casually at the French windows through which he had originally entered, and saw they were darkened with two equally motionless figures. The inner door with the coloured glass stood slightly ajar; and he could see in the short corridor beyond, the ends of two long shadows, exaggerated and distorted by the level light of evening, but still like grey caricatures of the figures of men. Dr Boyne had already obeyed his telephone message. The house was surrounded.

'What is the good of saying no?' insisted his host, still with the same hypnotic stare. 'You have seen part of that eternal drama with your own eyes. You have seen the threat of John Strake to slay Arnold Aylmer by black magic. You have seen Arnold Aylmer slay John Strake by white magic. You see Arnold Aylmer alive and talking to you now. And yet you do not believe it.'

'No, I do not believe it,' said Father Brown, and rose from his chair like one terminating a visit.

'Why not?' asked the other.

The priest only lifted his voice a little, but it sounded in every corner of the room like a bell.

'Because you are not Arnold Aylmer,' he said. 'I know who you are. Your name is John Strake; and you have murdered the last of the brothers, who is lying outside in the snow.'

A ring of white showed round the iris of the other man's eyes; he seemed to be making, with bursting eyeballs, a last effort to mesmerize and master his companion. Then he made a sudden movement sideways; and even as he did so the door behind him opened and a big detective in plain clothes put one hand quietly on his shoulder. The other hand hung down, but it held a revolver. The man looked wildly round, and saw plain-clothes men in all corners of the quiet room.

That evening Father Brown had another and longer conversation with Dr Boyne about the tragedy of the Aylmer family. By that time there was no longer any doubt of the central fact of the case, for John Strake had confessed his identity and even confessed his crimes; only it would be truer to say that he boasted of his victories. Compared to the fact that he had rounded off his life's work with the last Aylmer lying dead, everything else, including existence itself, seemed to be indifferent to him.

'The man is a sort of monomaniac,' said Father Brown. 'He is not interested in any other matter; not even in any other murder. I owe him something for that; for I had to comfort myself with the reflection a good many times this afternoon. As has doubtless occurred to you, instead of weaving all that wild but ingenious romance about winged vampires and silver bullets, he might have put an ordinary leaden bullet into me, and walked out of the house. I assure you it occurred quite frequently to me.'

'I wonder why he didn't,' observed Boyne. 'I don't understand it; but I don't understand anything yet. How on earth did you discover it, and what in the world did you discover?'

'Oh, you provided me with very valuable information,' replied Father Brown modestly, 'especially the one piece of information that really counted. I mean the statement that Strake was a very inventive and imaginative liar, with great presence of mind in producing his lies. This afternoon he needed it; but he rose to the occasion. Perhaps his only mistake was in choosing a preternatural story; he had the notion that because I am a clergyman I should believe anything. Many people have little notions of that kind.'

'But I can't make head or tail of it,' said the doctor. 'You must really begin at the beginning.'

'The beginning of it was a dressing-gown,' said Father Brown simply. 'It was the one really good disguise I've ever known. When you meet a man in a house with a dressing-gown on, you assume quite automatically that he's in his own house. I assumed it myself, but afterwards queer little things began to happen. When he took the pistol down he clicked it at arm's length, as a man does to make sure a strange weapon isn't loaded; of course he would know whether the pistols in his own hall were loaded or not. I didn't like the way he looked for the brandy, or the way he nearly barged into the bowl of fishes. For a man who has a fragile thing of that sort as a fixture in his rooms gets a quite mechanical habit of avoiding it. But these things might possibly have been fancies; the first real point was this. He came out from the little passage between the two doors; and in that passage there's only one other door leading to a room; so I assumed it was the bedroom he had just come from. I tried the handle; but it was locked. I thought this odd; and looked through the keyhole. It was an utterly bare room, obviously deserted; no bed, no anything. Therefore he had not come from inside any room, but from outside the house. And when I saw that, I think I saw the whole picture.

'Poor Arnold Aylmer doubtless slept and perhaps lived upstairs, and came down in his dressing-gown and passed through the red glass door. At the end of the passage, black against the winter daylight, he saw the enemy of his house. He saw a tall bearded man in a broad-brimmed black hat and a large flapping black cloak. He did not see much more in this world. Strake sprang on him, throttling or stabbing him; we cannot be sure till the inquest. Then Strake, standing in the narrow passage between the hat-stand and the old sideboard and looking down in triumph on the last of his foes, heard something he had not expected. He heard footsteps in the parlour beyond. It was myself entering by the French windows.

'His masquerade was a miracle of promptitude. It involved not only a disguise but a romance – an impromptu romance. He took off his big black hat and cloak and put on the dead man's dressing-gown. Then he did a rather grisly thing; at least a thing that affects my fancy as more grisly than the rest. He hung the corpse like a coat on one of the hat-pegs. He draped it in his own long cloak, and found it hung well below the heels; he covered the head entirely with his own wide hat. It was the only possible way of hiding it in that little passage with the locked door; but it was really a very clever one. I myself walked past the hat-stand once without knowing it was anything but a hat-stand. I think that unconsciousness of mine will always give me a shiver.

'He might perhaps have left it at that; but I might have discovered the corpse at any minute; and, hung where it was, it was a corpse calling for what you might call an explanation. He adopted the bolder stroke of discovering it himself and explaining it himself.

'Then there dawned on this strange and frightfully fertile mind the conception of a story of substitution; the reversal of the parts. He had already assumed the part of Arnold Aylmer. Why should not his dead enemy assume the part of John Strake? There must have been something in that topsy-turvydom to take the fancy of that darkly fanciful man. It was like some frightful fancy-dress ball to which the two mortal enemies were to go dressed up as each other. Only the fancy-dress ball was to be a dance of death: and one of the dancers would be dead. That is why I can imagine that man putting it in his own mind, and I can imagine him smiling.'

Father Brown was gazing into vacancy with his large grey eyes, which, when not blurred by his trick of blinking, were the one notable thing in his face. He went on speaking simply and seriously:

'All things are from God; and above all, reason and imagination and the great gifts of the mind. They are good in themselves; and we must not altogether forget their origin even in their perversion. Now this man had in him a very noble power to be perverted; the power of telling stories. He was a great novelist; only he had twisted his fictive power to practical and to evil ends; to deceiving men with false fact instead of with true fiction. It began with his deceiving old Aylmer with elaborate excuses and ingeniously detailed lies; but even that may have been, at the beginning, little more than the tall stories and tarradiddles of the child who may say equally he has seen the King of England or the King of the Fairies. It grew strong in him through the vice that perpetuates all vices, pride; he grew more and more vain of his promptitude in producing stories, of his originality and subtlety in developing them. That is what the young Aylmers meant by saying that he could always cast a spell over their father; and it was true. It was the sort of spell that the story-teller cast over the tyrant in the Arabian Nights. And to the last he walked the world with the pride of a poet, and with the false yet unfathomable courage of a great liar. He could always produce more Arabian Nights if ever his neck was in danger. And today his neck was in danger.

'But I am sure, as I say, that he enjoyed it as a fantasy as well as a conspiracy. He set about the task of telling the true story the wrong way round: of treating the dead man as living and the live man as dead. He had already got into Aylmer's dressing-gown; he proceeded to get into Aylmer's body and soul. He looked at the corpse as if it were his own corpse lying cold in the snow. Then he spread-eagled it in that strange fashion to suggest the sweeping descent of a bird of prey, and decked it out not only in his own dark and flying garments but in a whole dark fairy-tale about the black bird that could only fall by the silver bullet. I do not know whether it was the silver glittering on the sideboard or the snow shining beyond the door that suggested to his intensely artistic temperament the theme of white magic and the white metal used against magicians. But whatever its origin, he made it his own like a poet; and did it very promptly, like a practical man. He completed the exchange and reversal of parts by flinging the corpse out on to the snow as the corpse of Strake. He did his best to work up a creepy conception of Strake as something hovering in the air everywhere, a harpy with wings of speed and claws of death; to explain the absence of footprints and other things. For one piece of artistic impudence I hugely admire him. He actually turned one of the contradictions in his case into an argument for it; and said that the man's cloak being too long for him proved that he never walked on the ground like an ordinary mortal. But he looked at me very hard while he said that; and something told me that he was at that moment trying a very big bluff.'

Dr Boyne looked thoughtful. 'Had you discovered the truth by then?' he asked. 'There is something very queer and close to the nerves, I think, about notions affecting identity. I don't know whether it would be more weird to get a guess like that swiftly or slowly. I wonder when you suspected and when you were sure.'

'I think I really suspected when I telephoned to you,' replied his friend. 'And it was nothing more than the red light from the closed door brightening and darkening on the carpet. It looked like a splash of blood that grew vivid as it cried for vengeance. Why should it change like that? I knew the sun had not come out; it could only be because the second door behind it had been opened and shut on the garden. But if he had gone out and seen his enemy then, he would have raised the alarm then; and it was some time afterwards that the fracas occurred. I began to feel he had gone out to do something ... to prepare something ... but as to when I was certain, that is a different matter. I knew that right at the end he was trying to hypnotize me, to master me by the black art of eyes like talismans and a voice like an incantation. That's what he used to do with old Aylmer, no doubt. But it wasn't only the way he said it, it was what he said. It was the religion and philosophy of it.'

'I'm afraid I'm a practical man,' said the doctor with gruff humour, 'and I don't bother much about religion and philosophy.'

'You'll never be a practical man till you do,' said Father Brown. 'Look here, doctor, you know me pretty well, I think you know I'm not a bigot. You know I know there are all sorts in all religions; good men in bad ones and bad men in good ones. But there's just one little fact I've learned simply as a practical man, an entirely practical point, that I've picked up by experience, like the tricks of an animal or the trademark of a good wine. I've scarcely ever met a criminal who philosophized at all, who didn't philosophize along those lines of orientalism and recurrence and reincarnation, and the wheel of destiny and the serpent biting its own tail. I have found merely in practice that there is a curse on the servants of that serpent; on their belly shall they go and the dust shall they eat; and there was never a blackguard or a profligate born who could not talk that sort of spirituality. It may not be like that in its real religious origins; but here in our working world it is the religion of rascals; and I knew it was a rascal who was speaking.'

'Why,' said Boyne, 'I should have thought that a rascal could pretty well profess any religion he chose.'

'Yes,' assented the other, 'he could profess any religion; that is he could pretend to any religion, if it was all a pretence. If it was mere mechanical hypocrisy and nothing else, no doubt it could be done by a mere mechanical hypocrite. Any sort of mask can be put on any sort of face. Anybody can learn certain phrases or state verbally that he holds certain views. I can go out into the street and state that I am a Wesleyan Methodist or a Sandemanian, though I fear in no very convincing accent. But we are talking about an artist; and for the enjoyment of the artist the mask must be to some extent moulded on the face. What he makes outside him must correspond to something inside him; he can only make his effects out of some of the materials of his soul. I suppose he could have said he was a Wesleyan Methodist; but he could never be an eloquent Methodist as he can be an eloquent mystic and fatalist. I am talking of the sort of ideal such a man thinks of if he really tries to be idealistic. It was his whole game with me to be as idealistic as possible; and whenever that is attempted by that sort of man, you will generally find it is that sort of ideal. That sort of man may be dripping with gore; but he will always be able to tell you quite sincerely that Buddhism is better than Christianity. Nay, he will tell you quite sincerely that Buddhism is more Christian than Christianity. That alone is enough to throw a hideous and ghastly ray of light on his notion of Christianity.'

'Upon my soul,' said the doctor, laughing, 'I can't make out whether you're denouncing or defending him.'

'It isn't defending a man to say he is a genius,' said Father Brown. 'Far from it. And it is simply a psychological fact that an artist will betray himself by some sort of sincerity. Leonardo da Vinci cannot draw as if he couldn't draw. Even if he tried, it will always be a strong parody of a weak thing. This man would have made something much too fearful and wonderful out of the Wesleyan Methodist.'

When the priest went forth again and set his face homeward, the cold had grown more intense and yet was somehow intoxicating. The trees stood up like silver candelabra of some incredibly cold Candlemas of purification. It was a piercing cold, like that silver sword of pure pain that once pierced the very heart of purity. But it was not a killing cold, save in the sense of seeming to kill all the mortal obstructions to our immortal and immeasurable vitality. The pale green sky of twilight, with one star like the star of Bethlehem, seemed by some strange contradiction to be a cavern of clarity. It was as if there could be a green furnace of cold which wakened all things to lifelike warmth, and that the deeper they went into those cold crystalline colours the more were they light like winged creatures and clear like coloured glass. It tingled with truth and it divided truth from error with a blade like ice; but all that was left had never felt so much alive. It was as if all joy were a jewel in the heart of an iceberg. The priest hardly understood his own mood as he advanced deeper and deeper into the green gloaming, drinking deeper and deeper draughts of that virginal vivacity of the air. Some forgotten muddle and morbidity seemed to be left behind, or wiped out as the snow had painted out the footprints of the man of blood. As he shuffled homewards through the snow, he muttered to himself, 'And yet he is right enough about there being a white magic, if he only knows where to look for it.'

THE DOOM OF THE DARNAWAYS

Two landscape-painters stood looking at one landscape, which was also a seascape, and both were curiously impressed by it, though their impressions were not exactly the same. To one of them, who was a rising artist from London, it was new as well as strange. To the other, who was a local artist, but with something more than a local celebrity, it was better known; but perhaps all the more strange for what he knew of it.

In terms of tone and form, as these men saw it, it was a stretch of sands against a stretch of sunset, the whole scene lying in strips of sombre colour, dead green and bronze and brown and a drab that was not merely dull but in that gloaming in some way more mysterious than gold. All that broke these level lines was a long building which ran out from the fields into the sands of the sea, so that its fringe of dreary weeds and rushes seemed almost to meet the seaweed. But its most singular feature was that the upper part of it had the ragged outlines of a ruin, pierced by so many wide windows and large rents as to be a mere dark skeleton against the dying light; while the lower bulk of the building had hardly any windows at all, most of them being blind and bricked up and their outlines only faintly traceable in the twilight. But one window at least was still a window; and it seemed strangest of all that it showed a light.

'Who on earth can live in that old shell?' exclaimed the Londoner, who was a big, bohemian-looking man, young but with a shaggy red beard that made him look older; Chelsea knew him familiarly as Harry Payne.

'Ghosts, you might suppose,' replied his friend Martin Wood. 'Well, the people who live there really are rather like ghosts.'

It was perhaps rather a paradox that the London artist seemed almost bucolic in his boisterous freshness and wonder, while the local artist seemed a more shrewd and experienced person, regarding him with mature and amiable amusement; indeed, the latter was altogether a quieter and more conventional figure, wearing darker clothes and with his square and stolid face clean-shaven.

'It is only a sign of the times, of course,' he went on, 'or of the passing of old times and old families with them. The last of the great Darnaways live in that house, and not many of the new poor are as poor as they are. They can't even afford to make their own top-storey habitable; but have to live in the lower rooms of a ruin, like bats and owls. Yet they have family portraits that go back to the Wars of the Roses and the first portrait-painting in England, and very fine some of them are; I happen to know, because they asked for my professional advice in overhauling them. There's one of them especially, and one of the earliest, but it's so good that it gives you the creeps.'

'The whole place gives you the creeps, I should think by the look of it,' replied Payne.

'Well,' said his friend, 'to tell you the truth, it does.'

The silence that followed was stirred by a faint rustle among the rushes by the moat; and it gave them, rationally enough, a slight nervous start when a dark figure brushed along the bank, moving rapidly and almost like a startled bird. But it was only a man walking briskly with a black bag in his hand: a man with a long sallow face and sharp eyes that glanced at the London stranger in a slightly darkling and suspicious manner.

'It's only Dr Barnet,' said Wood with a sort of relief. 'Good evening, Doctor. Are you going up to the house? I hope nobody's ill.'

'Everybody's always ill in a place like that,' growled the doctor; 'only sometimes they're too ill to know it. The very air of the place is a blight and a pestilence. I don't envy the young man from Australia.'

'And who,' asked Payne abruptly and rather absently, 'may the young man from Australia be?'

'Ah!' snorted the doctor, 'hasn't your friend told you about him? As a matter of fact I believe he is arriving today. Quite a romance in the old style of melodrama: the heir back from the Colonies to his ruined castle, all complete even down to an old family compact for his marrying the lady watching in the ivied tower. Queer old stuff, isn't it? But it really happens sometimes. He's even got a little money, which is the only bright spot there ever was in this business.'

'What does Miss Darnaway herself, in her ivied tower, think of the business?' asked Martin Wood dryly.

'What she thinks of everything else by this time,' replied the doctor. 'They don't think in this weedy old den of superstitions; they only dream and drift. I think she accepts the family contract and the colonial husband as part of the Doom of the Darnaways, don't you know. I really think that if he turned out to be a hump-backed negro with one eye and a homicidal mania, she would only think it added a finishing touch and fitted in with the twilight scenery.'

'You're not giving my friend from London a very lively picture of my friends in the country,' said Wood, laughing. 'I had intended taking him there to call; no artist ought to miss those Darnaway portraits if he gets the chance. But perhaps I'd better postpone it if they're in the middle of the Australian invasion.'

'Oh, do go in and see them, for the Lord's sake,' said Dr Barnet warmly. 'Anything that will brighten their blighted lives will make my task easier. It will need a good many colonial cousins to cheer things up, I should think; and the more the merrier. Come, I'll take you in myself.'

As they drew nearer to the house it was seen to be isolated like an island in a moat of brackish water which they crossed by a bridge. On the other side spread a fairly wide stony floor or embankment with great cracks across it, in which little tufts of weed and thorn sprouted here and there. This rock platform looked large and bare in the grey twilight, and Payne could hardly have believed that such a corner of space could have contained so much of the soul of a wilderness. This platform only jutted out on one side, like a giant door-step, and beyond it was the door; a very low-browed Tudor archway standing open but dark, like a cave.

When the brisk doctor led them inside without ceremony, Payne had, as it were, another shock of depression. He could have expected to find himself mounting to a very ruinous tower, by very narrow winding staircases; but in this case the first steps into the house were actually steps downwards. They went down several short and broken stairways into large twilit rooms which, but for their lines of dark pictures and dusty bookshelves, might have been the traditional dungeons beneath the castle moat. Here and there a candle in an old candlestick lit up some dusty accidental detail of a dead elegance; but the visitor was not so much impressed, or depressed, by this artificial light as by the one pale gleam of natural light. As he passed down the long room he saw the only window in that wall, a curious low oval window of a late-seventeenth-century fashion. But the strange thing about it was that it did not look out directly on any space of sky but only on a reflection of sky; a pale strip of daylight merely mirrored in the moat, under the hanging shadow of the bank. Payne had a memory of the Lady of Shalott who never saw the world outside except in a mirror. The lady of this Shalott not only in some sense saw the world in a mirror, but even saw the world upside-down.

'It's as if the house of Darnaway were falling literally as well as metaphorically,' said Wood in a low voice; 'as if it were sinking slowly into a swamp or a quicksand, until the sea goes over it like a green roof.'

Even the sturdy Dr Barnet started a little at the silent approach of the figure that came to receive them. Indeed, the room was so silent that they were all startled to realize that it was not empty. There were three people in it when they entered: three dim figures motionless in the dim room; all three dressed in black and looking like dark shadows. As the foremost figure drew nearer the grey light from the window, he showed a face that looked almost as grey as its frame of hair. This was old Vine, the steward, long left *in loco parentis* since the death of that eccentric parent, the last Lord Darnaway. He would have been a handsome old man if he had had no teeth. As it was he had one, which showed every now and then and gave him a rather sinister appearance. He received the doctor and his friends with a fine courtesy and escorted them to where the other two figures in black were seated. One of them seemed to Payne to give another appropriate touch of gloomy antiquity to the castle by the mere fact of being a Roman Catholic priest, who might have come out of a priest's hole in the dark old days. Payne could imagine him muttering prayers or telling beads, or tolling bells or doing a number of indistinct and melancholy things in that melancholy place. Just then he might be supposed to have been giving religious consolation to the lady; but it could hardly be supposed that the consolation was very consoling, or at any rate that it was very cheering. For the rest, the priest was personally insignificant enough, with plain and rather expressionless features; but the lady was a very different matter. Her face was very far from being plain or insignificant; it stood out from the darkness of her dress and hair and background with a pallor that was almost awful, but a beauty that was almost awfully alive. Payne looked at it as long as he dared; and he was to look at it a good deal longer before he died.

Wood merely exchanged with his friends such pleasant and polite phrases as would lead up to his purpose of revisiting the portraits. He apologized for calling on the day which he heard was to be one of family welcome; but he was soon convinced that the family was rather mildly relieved to have visitors to distract them or break the shock. He did not hesitate, therefore, to lead Payne through the central reception-room into the library beyond, where hung the portrait, for there was one which he was especially bent on showing, not only as a picture but almost as a puzzle. The little priest trudged along with them; he seemed to know something about old pictures as well as about old prayers.

'I'm rather proud of having spotted this,' said Wood. 'I believe it's a Holbein. If it isn't, there was somebody living in Holbein's time who was as great as Holbein.'

It was a portrait in the hard but sincere and living fashion of the period, representing a man clad in black trimmed with gold and fur, with a heavy, full, rather pale face but watchful eyes.

'What a pity art couldn't have stopped for ever at just that transition stage,' cried Wood, 'and never transitioned any more. Don't you see it's just realistic enough to be real? Don't you see the face speaks all the more because it stands out from a rather stiffer framework of less essential things? And the eyes are even more real than the face. On my soul, I think the eyes are too real for the face! It's just as if those sly, quick eyeballs were protruding out of a great pale mask.'

'The stiffness extends to the figure a little, I think,' said Payne. 'They hadn't quite mastered anatomy when mediaevalism ended, at least in the north. That left leg looks to me a good deal out of drawing.'

'I'm not so sure,' replied Wood quietly. 'Those fellows who painted just when realism began to be done, and before it began to be overdone, were often more realistic than we think. They put real details of portraiture into things that are thought merely conventional. You might say this fellow's eyebrows or eye-sockets are a little lop-sided; but I bet if you knew him you'd find that one of his eyebrows did really stick up more than the other. And I shouldn't wonder if he was lame or something, and that black leg was meant to be crooked.'

'What an old devil he looks!' burst out Payne suddenly. 'I trust his reverence will excuse my language.'

'I believe in the devil, thank you,' said the priest with an inscrutable face. 'Curiously enough there was a legend that the devil was lame.'

'I say,' protested Payne, 'you can't really mean that he was the devil; but who the devil was he?'

'He was the Lord Darnaway under Henry VII and Henry VIII,' replied his companion. 'But there are curious legends about him too; one of them is referred to in that inscription round the frame, and further developed in some notes left by somebody in a book I found there. They are both rather curious reading.'

Payne leaned forward, craning his head so as to follow the archaic inscription round the frame. Leaving out the antiquated lettering and spelling, it seemed to be a sort of rhyme running somewhat thus:

> In the seventh heir I shall return,
> In the seventh hour I shall depart,
> None in that hour shall hold my hand,
> And woe to her that holds my heart.

'It sounds creepy somehow,' said Payne, 'but that may be partly because I don't understand a word of it.'

'It's pretty creepy even when you do,' said Wood in a low voice. 'The record made at a later date, in the old book I found, is all about how this beauty deliberately killed himself in such a way that his wife was executed for his murder. Another note commemorates a later tragedy, seven successions later – under the Georges – in which another Darnaway committed suicide, having first thoughtfully left poison in his wife's wine. It's said that both suicides took place at seven in the evening. I suppose the inference is that he does really return with every seventh inheritor and makes things unpleasant, as the rhyme suggests, for any lady unwise enough to marry him.'

'On that argument,' replied Payne, 'it would be a trifle uncomfortable for the next seventh gentleman.'

Wood's voice was lower still as he said:

'The new heir will be the seventh.'

Harry Payne suddenly heaved up his great chest and shoulders like a man flinging off a burden.

'What crazy stuff are we all talking?' he cried. 'We're all educated men in an enlightened age, I suppose. Before I came into this damned dank atmosphere I'd never have believed I should be talking of such things, except to laugh at them.'

'You are right,' said Wood. 'If you lived long enough in this underground palace you'd begin to feel differently about things. I've begun to feel very curiously about that picture, having had so much to do with handling and hanging it. It sometimes seems to me that the painted face is more alive than the dead faces of the people living here; that it is a sort of talisman or magnet: that it commands the elements and draws out the destinies of men and things. I suppose you would call it very fanciful.'

'What is that noise?' cried Payne suddenly.

They all listened, and there seemed to be no noise except the dull boom of the distant sea; then they began to have the sense of something mingling with it; something like a voice calling through the sound of the surf, dulled by it at first, but coming nearer and nearer. The next moment they were certain: someone was shouting outside in the dusk.

Payne turned to the low window behind him and bent to look out. It was the window from which nothing could be seen except the moat with its reflection of bank and sky. But that inverted vision was not the same that he had seen before. From the hanging shadow of the bank in the water depended two dark shadows reflected from the feet and legs of a figure standing above upon the bank. Through that limited aperture they could see nothing but the two legs black against the reflection of a pale and livid sunset. But somehow that very fact of the head being invisible, as if in the clouds, gave something dreadful to the sound that followed; the voice of a man crying aloud what they could not properly hear or understand. Payne especially was peering out of the little window with an altered face, and he spoke with an altered voice:

'How queerly he's standing!'

'No, no,' said Wood, in a sort of soothing whisper. 'Things often look like that in reflection. It's the wavering of the water that makes you think that.'

'Think what?' asked the priest shortly.

'That his left leg is crooked,' said Wood.

Payne had thought of the oval window as a sort of mystical mirror; and it seemed to him that there were in it other inscrutable images of doom. There was something else beside the figure that he did not understand; three thinner legs showing in dark lines against the light, as if some monstrous three-legged spider or bird were standing beside the stranger. Then he had the less crazy thought of a tripod like that of the heathen oracles; and the next moment the thing had vanished and the legs of the human figure passed out of the picture.

He turned to meet the pale face of old Vine, the steward, with his mouth open, eager to speak, and his single tooth showing.

'He has come,' he said. 'The boat arrived from Australia this morning.'

Even as they went back out of the library into the central salon they heard the footsteps of the newcomer clattering down the entrance steps, with various items of light luggage trailed behind him. When Payne saw one of them, he laughed with a reaction of relief. His tripod was nothing but the telescopic legs of a portable camera, easily packed and unpacked; and the man who was carrying it seemed so far to take on equally solid and normal qualities. He was dressed in dark clothes, but of a careless and holiday sort; his shirt was of grey flannel, and his boots echoed uncompromisingly enough in those still chambers. As he strode forward to greet his new circle his stride had scarcely more than the suggestion of a limp. But Payne and his companions were looking at his face, and could scarcely take their eyes from it.

He evidently felt there was something curious and uncomfortable about his reception; but they could have sworn that he did not himself know the cause of it. The lady, supposed to be in some sense already betrothed to him, was certainly beautiful enough to attract him; but she evidently also frightened him. The old steward brought him a sort of feudal homage, yet treated him as if he were the family ghost. The priest still looked at him with a face which was quite indecipherable, and therefore perhaps all the more unnerving. A new sort of irony, more like the Greek irony, began to pass over Payne's mind. He had dreamed of the stranger as a devil, but it seemed almost worse that he was an unconscious destiny. He seemed to march towards crime with the monstrous innocence of Œdipus. He had approached the family mansion in so blindly buoyant a spirit as to have set up his camera to photograph his first sight of it; and even the camera had taken on the semblance of the tripod of a tragic pythoness.

Payne was surprised, when taking his leave a little while after, at something which showed that the Australian was already less unconscious of his surroundings. He said in a low voice:

'Don't go ... or come again soon. You look like a human being. This place fairly gives me the jumps.'

When Payne emerged out of those almost subterranean halls and came into the night air and the smell of the sea, he felt as if he had come out of that underworld of dreams in which events tumble on top of each other in a way at once unrestful and unreal. The arrival of the strange relative had been somehow unsatisfying and, as it were, unconvincing. The doubling of the same face in the old portrait and the new arrival troubled him like a two-headed monster. And yet it was not altogether a nightmare; nor was it that face, perhaps, that he saw most vividly.

'Did you say,' he asked of the doctor, as they strode together across the striped dark sands by the darkening sea, 'did you say that young man was betrothed to Miss Darnaway by a family compact or something? Sounds rather like a novel.'

'But an historical novel,' answered Dr Barnet. 'The Darnaways all went to sleep a few centuries ago, when things were really done that we all only read of in romances. Yes, I believe there's some family tradition by which second or third cousins always marry when they stand in a certain relation of age, in order to unite the property. A damned silly tradition, I should say; and if they often married in and in, in that fashion, it may account on principles of heredity for their having gone so rotten.'

'I should hardly say,' answered Payne a little stiffly, 'that they had all gone rotten.'

'Well,' replied the doctor, 'the young man doesn't *look* rotten, of course, though he's certainly lame.'

'The young man!' cried Payne, who was suddenly and unreasonably angry. 'Well, if you think the young lady looks rotten, I think
it's you who have rotten taste.'

The doctor's face grew dark and bitter. 'I fancy I know more
about it than you do,' he snapped.

They completed the walk in silence, each feeling that he had
been irrationally rude and had suffered equally irrational rudeness,
and Payne was left to brood alone on the matter, for his friend
Wood had remained behind to attend to some of his business in
connexion with the pictures.

Payne took very full advantage of the invitation extended by the
colonial cousin, who wanted somebody to cheer him up. During
the next few weeks he saw a good deal of the dark interior of the
Darnaway home; though it might be said that he did not confine
himself entirely to cheering up the colonial cousin. The lady's melancholy was of longer standing and perhaps needed more lifting;
anyhow, he showed a laborious readiness to lift it. He was not without a conscience, however, and the situation made him doubtful
and uncomfortable. Weeks went by and nobody could discover
from the demeanour of the new Darnaway whether he considered
himself engaged according to the old compact or no. He went
mooning about the dark galleries and stood staring vacantly at the
dark and sinister picture. The shades of that prison house were
certainly beginning to close on him, and there was little of his
Australian assurance left. But Payne could discover nothing upon
the point that concerned him most. Once he attempted to confide
in his friend Martin Wood, as he was pottering about in his capacity
of picture-hanger; but even out of him he got very little satisfaction.

'It seems to me you can't butt in,' said Wood shortly, 'because
of the engagement.'

'Of course I shan't butt in if there is an engagement,' retorted
his friend, 'but is there? I haven't said a word to her of course, but
I've seen enough of her to be pretty certain she doesn't think there
is, even if she thinks there may be. He doesn't say there is, or even
hint that there ought to be. It seems to me this shilly-shallying is
rather unfair on everybody.'

'Especially on you, I suppose,' said Wood a little harshly, 'but if
you ask me, I'll tell you what I think. I think he's afraid.'

'Afraid of being refused?' asked Payne.

'No, afraid of being accepted,' answered the other. 'Don't bite my head off – I don't mean afraid of the lady. I mean afraid of the picture.'

'Afraid of the picture!' repeated Payne.

'I mean afraid of the curse,' said Wood. 'Don't you remember the rhyme about the Darnaway doom falling on him and her?'

'Yes, but look here,' cried Payne. 'Even the Darnaway doom can't have it both ways. You tell me first that I mustn't have my own way because of the compact, and then that the compact mustn't have its own way because of the curse. But if the curse can destroy the compact, why should she be tied to the compact? If they're frightened of marrying each other, they're free to marry anybody else, and there's an end of it. Why should I suffer for the observance of something they don't propose to observe? It seems to me your position is very unreasonable.'

'Of course it's all a tangle,' said Wood rather crossly, and went on hammering at the frame of a canvas.

Suddenly, one morning, the new heir broke his long and baffling silence. He did it in a curious fashion, a little crude, as was his way, but with an obvious anxiety to do the right thing. He asked frankly for advice, not of this or that individual as Payne had done, but collectively as of a crowd. When he did speak, he threw himself on the whole company like a statesman going to the country. He called it 'a show-down'. Fortunately the lady was not included in this large gesture; and Payne shuddered when he thought of her feelings. But the Australian was quite honest; he thought the natural thing was to ask for help and for information, calling a sort of family council at which he put his cards on the table. It might be said that he flung down his cards on the table, for he did it with a rather desperate air, like one who had been harassed for days and nights by the increasing pressure of a problem. In that short time the shadows of that place of low windows and sinking pavements had curiously changed him and increased a certain resemblance that crept through all their memories.

The five men, including the doctor, were sitting round a table; and Payne was idly reflecting that his own light tweeds and red hair must be the only colours in the room, for the priest and the steward were in black, and Wood and Darnaway habitually wore dark grey suits that looked almost like black. Perhaps this incongruity had been what the young man had meant by calling him a human being. At that moment the young man himself turned abruptly in his chair and began to talk. A moment after the dazed artist knew that he was talking about the most tremendous thing in the world.

'Is there anything it it?' he was saying. 'That is what I've come to asking myself till I'm nearly crazy. I'd never have believed I should come to thinking of such things; but I think of the portrait and the rhyme and the coincidences or whatever you call them, and I go cold. Is there anything in it? Is there any Doom of the Darnaways or only a damned queer accident? Have I got a right to marry, or shall I bring something big and black out of the sky, that I know nothing about, on myself and somebody else?'

His rolling eye had roamed round the table and rested on the plain face of the priest, to whom he now seemed to be speaking. Payne's submerged practicality rose in protest against the problem of superstition being brought before that supremely superstitious tribunal. He was sitting next to Darnaway and struck in before the priest could answer.

'Well, the coincidences are curious, I admit,' he said, rather forcing a note of cheerfulness; 'but surely we—' and then he stopped as if he had been struck by lightning. For Darnaway had turned his head sharply over his shoulder at the interruption, and with the movement, his left eyebrow jerked up far above its fellow and for an instant the face of the portrait glared at him with a ghastly exaggeration of exactitude. The rest saw it; and all had the air of having been dazzled by an instant of light. The old steward gave a hollow groan.

'It is no good,' he said hoarsely, 'we are dealing with something too terrible.'

'Yes,' assented the priest in a low voice, 'we are dealing with something terrible; with the most terrible thing I know, and the name of it is nonsense.'

'What did you say?' said Darnaway, still looking towards him.

'I said nonsense,' repeated the priest. 'I have not said anything in particular up to now, for it was none of my business; I was only taking temporary duty in the neighbourhood and Miss Darnaway wanted to see me. But since you're asking me personally and point-blank, why, it's easy enough to answer. Of course there's no Doom of the Darnaways to prevent your marrying anybody you have any decent reason for marrying. A man isn't fated to fall into the small-est venial sin, let alone into crimes like suicide and murder. You can't be made to do wicked things against your will because your name is Darnaway, any more than I can because my name is Brown. The Doom of the Browns,' he added with relish – 'the Weird of the Browns would sound even better.'

'And you of all people,' repeated the Australian, staring, 'tell me to think like that about it.'

'I tell you to think about something else,' replied the priest cheer-fully. 'What has become of the rising art of photography? How is the camera getting on? I know it's rather dark downstairs, but those hollow arches on the floor above could easily be turned into a first-rate photographic studio. A few workmen could fit it out with a glass roof in no time.'

'Really,' protested Martin Wood, 'I do think you should be the last man in the world to tinker about with those beautiful Gothic arches, which are about the best work your own religion has ever done in the world. I should have thought you'd have had some feeling for that sort of art; but I can't see why you should be so uncommonly keen on photography.'

'I'm uncommonly keen on daylight,' answered Father Brown, 'especially in this dingy business; and photography has the virtue of depending on daylight. And if you don't know that I would grind all the Gothic arches in the world to powder to save the sanity of a single human soul, you don't know so much about my religion as you think you do.'

The young Australian had sprung to his feet like a man re-juvenated. 'By George, that's the talk,' he cried, 'though I never thought to hear it from that quarter. I'll tell you what, reverend sir, I'll do something that will show I haven't lost my courage after all.'

The old steward was still looking at him with quaking watch-fulness, as if he felt something fey about the young man's defiance. 'Oh,' he cried, 'what are you going to do now?'

'I am going to photograph the portrait,' replied Darnaway.

Yet it was barely a week afterwards that the storm of the catas-trophe seemed to swoop out of the sky, darkening that sun of sanity to which the priest had appealed in vain, and plunging the man-sion once more in the darkness of the Darnaway doom. It had been easy enough to fit up the new studio; and seen from inside it

looked very like any other such studio, empty except for the fulness
of the white light. A man coming from the gloomy rooms below
had more than normally the sense of stepping into a more than
modern brilliancy, as blank as the future. At the suggestion of
Wood, who knew the castle well and had got over his first aesthetic
grumblings, a small room remaining intact in the upper ruins was
easily turned into a dark room, into which Darnaway went out of
the white daylight to grope by the crimson gleams of a red lamp.
Wood said, laughing, that the red lamp had reconciled him to the
vandalism; as that blood-shot darkness was as romantic as an
alchemist's cave.

Darnaway had risen at daybreak on the day that he meant to
photograph the mysterious portrait, and had it carried up from the
library by the single corkscrew staircase that connected the two
floors. There he had set it up in the wide white daylight on a sort
of easel and planted his photographic tripod in front of it. He said
he was anxious to send a reproduction of it to a great antiquary
who had written on the antiquities of the house; but the others
knew that this was an excuse covering much deeper things. It was,
if not exactly a spiritual duel between Darnaway and the demoniac
picture, at least a duel between Darnaway and his own doubts. He
wanted to bring the daylight of photography face to face with that
dark masterpiece of painting; and to see whether the sunshine of
the new art would not drive out the shadows of the old.

Perhaps this was why he preferred to do it by himself, even if
some of the details seemed to take longer and involve more than
normal delay. Anyhow, he rather discouraged the few who visited
his studio during the day of the experiment, and who found him
focusing and fussing about in a very isolated and impenetrable
fashion. The steward had left a meal for him, as he refused to come
down; the old gentleman also returned some hours afterwards and
found the meal more or less normally disposed of but when he
brought it he got no more gratitude than a grunt. Payne went up
once to see how he was getting on, but finding the photographer
disinclined for conversation came down again. Father Brown had
wandered that way in an unobtrusive style, to take Darnaway a
letter from the expert to whom the photograph was to be sent. But
he left the letter on a tray, and whatever he thought of that great
glass-house full of daylight and devotion to a hobby, a world he

had himself in some sense created, he kept it to himself and came down. He had reason to remember very soon that he was the last to come down the solitary staircase connecting the floors, leaving a lonely man and an empty room behind him. The others were standing in the salon that led into the library, just under the great black ebony clock that looked like a titanic coffin.

'How was Darnaway getting on,' asked Payne, a little later, 'when you last went up?'

The priest passed a hand over his forehead. 'Don't tell me I'm getting psychic,' he said with a sad smile. 'I believe I'm quite dazzled with daylight up in that room and couldn't see things straight. Honestly, I felt for a flash as if there were something uncanny about Darnaway's figure standing before that portrait.'

'Oh, that's the lame leg,' said Barnet promptly. 'We know all about that.'

'Do you know,' said Payne abruptly, but lowering his voice, 'I don't think we do know all about it or anything about it. What's the matter with his leg? What was the matter with his ancestor's leg?'

'Oh, there's something about that in the book I was reading, in there, in the family archives,' said Wood. 'I'll fetch it for you,' and he stepped into the library just beyond.

'I think,' said Father Brown quietly, 'Mr Payne must have some particular reason for asking that.'

'I may as well blurt it out once and for all,' said Payne, but in a yet lower voice. 'After all, there is a rational explanation. A man from anywhere might have made up to look like the portrait. What do we know about Darnaway? He is behaving rather oddly—'

The others were staring at him in a rather startled fashion; but the priest seemed to take it very calmly.

'I don't think the old portrait's ever been photographed,' he said. 'That's why he wants to do it. I don't think there's anything odd about that.'

'Quite an ordinary state of things, in fact,' said Wood with a smile; he had just returned with the book in his hand. And even as he spoke there was a stir in the clockwork of the great dark clock behind him and successive strokes thrilled through the room up to the number of seven. With the last stroke there came a crash from the floor above that shook the house like a thunderbolt, and Father

Brown was already two steps up the winding staircase before the sound had ceased.

'My God!' cried Payne involuntarily; 'he is alone up there.'

'Yes,' said Father Brown without turning, as he vanished up the stairway. 'We shall find him alone.'

When the rest recovered from their first paralysis and ran helter-skelter up the stone steps and found their way to the new studio, it was true in that sense that they found him alone. They found him lying in a wreck of his tall camera, with its long splintered legs standing out grotesquely at three different angles; and Darnaway had fallen on top of it with one black crooked leg lying at a fourth angle along the floor. For the moment the dark heap looked as if he were entangled with some huge and horrible spider. Little more than a glance and a touch were needed to tell them that he was dead. Only the portrait stood untouched upon the easel, and one could fancy the smiling eyes shone.

An hour afterwards Father Brown, in helping to calm the confusion of the stricken household, came upon the old steward muttering almost as mechanically as the clock had ticked and struck the terrible hour. Almost without hearing them, he knew what the muttered words must be.

> In the seventh heir I shall return
> In the seventh hour I shall depart.

As he was about to say something soothing, the old man seemed suddenly to start awake and stiffen into anger; his mutterings changed to a fierce cry.

'You!' he cried, 'you and your daylight! Even you won't say now there is no doom for the Darnaways.'

'My opinion about that is unchanged,' said Father Brown mildly.

Then after a pause he added, 'I hope you will observe poor Darnaway's last wish and see the photograph is sent off.'

'The photograph!' cried the doctor sharply. 'What's the good of that? As a matter of fact, it's rather curious; but there isn't any photograph. It seems he never took it after all, after pottering about all day.'

Father Brown swung round sharply. 'Then take it yourselves,' he said. 'Poor Darnaway was perfectly right. It's most important that the photograph should be taken.'

As all the visitors, the doctor, the priest and the two artists trailed away in a black and dismal procession across the brown and yellow sands, they were at first more or less silent, rather as if they had been stunned. And certainly there had been something like a crack of thunder in a clear sky about the fulfilment of that forgotten superstition at the very time when they had most forgotten it; when the doctor and the priest had both filled their minds with rationalism as the photographer had filled his rooms with daylight. They might be as rationalistic as they liked; but in broad daylight, the seventh heir had returned, and in broad daylight, at the seventh hour he had perished.

'I'm afraid everybody will always believe in the Darnaway superstition now,' said Martin Wood.

'I know one who won't,' said the doctor sharply. 'Why should I indulge in superstition because somebody else indulges in suicide?'

'You think poor Mr Darnaway committed suicide?' asked the priest.

'I'm sure he committed suicide,' replied the doctor.

'It is possible,' agreed the other.

'He was quite alone up there, and he had a whole drug-store of poisons in the dark room. Besides, it's just the sort of thing that Darnaways do.'

'You don't think there's anything in the fulfilment of the family curse?'

'Yes,' said the doctor, 'I believe in one family curse and that is the family constitution. I told you it was heredity and they are all half mad. If you stagnate and breed in and brood in your own swamp like that, you're bound to degenerate whether you like it or not. The laws of heredity can't be dodged; the truths of science can't be denied. The minds of the Darnaways are falling to pieces, as their blighted old sticks and stones are falling to pieces, eaten away by the sea and the salt air. Suicide – of course he committed suicide; I daresay all the rest will commit suicide. Perhaps the best thing they could do.'

As the man of science spoke there sprang suddenly and with startling clearness into Payne's memory the face of the daughter of the Darnaways, a tragic mask pale against an unfathomable blackness, but itself of a blinding and more than mortal beauty. He opened his mouth to speak and found himself speechless.

'I see,' said Father Brown to the doctor, 'so you do believe in the superstition after all?'

'What do you mean – believe in the superstition? I believe in the suicide as a matter of scientific necessity.'

'Well,' replied the priest, 'I don't see a pin to choose between your scientific superstition and the other magical superstition. They both seem to end in turning people into paralytics, who can't move their own legs or arms or save their own lives or souls. The rhyme said it was the doom of the Darnaways to be killed, and the scientific textbook says it is the doom of the Darnaways to kill themselves. Both ways they seem to be slaves.'

'But I thought you said you believed in rational views of these things,' said Dr Barnet. 'Don't you believe in heredity?'

'I said I believed in daylight,' replied the priest in a loud and clear voice, 'and I won't choose between two tunnels of subterranean superstition that both end in the dark. And the proof of it is this: that you are all entirely in the dark about what really happened in that house.'

'Do you mean about the suicide?' asked Payne.

'I mean about the murder,' said Father Brown; and his voice, though only slightly lifted to a louder note, seemed somehow to resound over the whole shore. 'It was murder; but murder is of the will, which God made free.'

What the others said at the moment in answer to it Payne never knew. For the word had a rather curious effect on him; stirring him like the blast of a trumpet and yet bringing him to a halt. He stood still in the middle of the sandy waste and let the others go on in front of him; he felt the blood crawling through all his veins and the sensation that is called the hair standing on end; and yet he felt a new and unnatural happiness. A psychological process too quick and too complicated for himself to follow had already reached a conclusion that he could not analyse; but the conclusion was one of relief. After standing still for a moment he turned and went back slowly across the sands to the house of the Darnaways.

He crossed the moat with a stride that shook the bridge, descended the stairs and traversed the long rooms with a resounding tread, till he came to the place where Adelaide Darnaway sat haloed with the low light of the oval window, almost like some for-gotten saint left behind in the land of death. She looked up, and an expression of wonder made her face yet more wonderful.

'What is it?' she said. 'Why have you come back?'

'I have come for the Sleeping Beauty,' he said in a tone that had the resonance of a laugh. 'This old house went to sleep long ago, as the doctor said; but it is silly for you to pretend to be old. Come up into the daylight and hear the truth. I have brought you a word; it is a terrible word, but it breaks the spell of your captivity.'

She did not understand a word he said, but something made her rise and let him lead her down the long hall and up the stairs and out under the evening sky. The ruins of a dead garden stretched towards the sea, and an old fountain with the figure of a triton, green with rust, remained poised there, pouring nothing out of a dried horn into an empty basin. He had often seen that desolate outline against the evening sky as he passed, and it had seemed to him a type of fallen fortunes in more ways than one. Before long, doubtless, those hollow fonts would be filled, but it would be with the pale green bitter waters of the sea and the flowers would be drowned and strangled in seaweed. So, he had told himself, the daughter of the Darnaways might indeed be wedded, but she would be wedded to death and a doom as deaf and ruthless as the sea. But now he laid a hand on the bronze triton that was like the hand of a giant, and shook it as if he meant to hurl it over like an idol or an evil god of the garden.

'What do you mean?' she asked steadily. 'What is this word that will set us free?'

'The word is murder,' he said, 'and the freedom it brings is as fresh as the flowers of spring. No; I do not mean I have murdered anybody. But the fact that anybody can be murdered is itself good news, after the evil dreams you have been living in. Don't you understand? In that dream of yours everything that happened to you came from inside you; the doom of the Darnaways was stored up in the Darnaways; it unfolded itself like a horrible flower. There was no escape even by happy accident; it was all inevitable; whether it was Vine and his old wives' tales or Barnet and his new-fangled heredity. But this man who died was not the victim of a magic curse or an inherited madness. He was murdered; and for us that murder is simply an accident; yes, *requiescat in pace*, but a happy accident. It is a ray of daylight, because it comes from outside.'

She suddenly smiled. 'Yes, I believe I understand. I suppose you are talking like a lunatic, but I understand. But who murdered him?'

'I do not know,' he answered calmly, 'but Father Brown knows. And as Father Brown says, murder is at least done by the will, free as that wind from the sea.'

'Father Brown is a wonderful person,' she said after a pause. 'He was the only person who ever brightened my existence in any way at all until—'

'Until what?' asked Payne, and made a movement almost impetuous, leaning towards her and thrusting away the bronze monster so that it seemed to rock on its pedestal.

'Well, until you did,' she said and smiled again.

So was the sleeping palace awakened, and it is no part of this story to describe the stages of its awakening, though much of it had come to pass before the dark of that evening had fallen upon the shore. As Harry Payne strode homewards once more, across those dark sands that he had crossed in so many moods, he was at the highest turn of happiness that is given in this mortal life, and the whole red sea within him was at the top of its tide. He would have had no difficulty in picturing all that place again in flower and the bronze triton bright as a golden god and the fountain flowing with water or with wine. But all this brightness and blossoming had been unfolded for him by the one word 'murder', and it was still a word that he did not understand. He had taken it on trust, and he was not unwise; for he was one of those who have a sense of the sound of truth.

It was more than a month later that Payne returned to his London house to keep an appointment with Father Brown, taking the required photograph with him. His personal romance had prospered as well as was fitting under the shadow of such a tragedy, and the shadow itself therefore lay rather more lightly on him; but it was hard to view it as anything but the shadow of a family fatality. In many ways he had been much occupied, and it was not until the Darnaway household had resumed its somewhat stern routine, and the portrait had been restored to its place in the library, that he had managed to photograph it with a magnesium flare. Before sending it to the antiquary as originally arranged, he brought it to the priest who had so pressingly demanded it.

'I can't understand your attitude about all this, Father Brown,' he said. 'You act as if you had already solved the problem in some way of your own.'

The priest shook his head mournfully. 'Not a bit of it,' he answered. 'I must be very stupid but I'm quite stuck; stuck about the most practical point of all. It's a queer business; so simple up to a point, and then— Let me have a look at that photograph, will you?'

He held it close to his screwed, short-sighted eyes for a moment, and then said, 'Have you got a magnifying glass?'

Payne produced one, and the priest looked through it intently for some time and then said, 'Look at the title of that book at the edge of the bookshelf beside the frame: it's *The History of Pope Joan*. Now, I wonder . . . yes, by George; and the one above is something or other of Iceland. Lord! what a queer way to find it out! What a dolt and donkey I was not to notice it when I was there!'

'But what have you found out?' asked Payne impatiently.

'The last link,' said Father Brown, 'and I'm not stuck any longer. Yes, I think I know how that unhappy story went from first to last now.'

'But why?' insisted the other.

'Why, because,' said the priest with a smile, 'the Darnaway library contained books about Pope Joan and Iceland, not to mention another I see with the title beginning *The Religion of Frederick*, which is not so very hard to fill up.' Then, seeing the other's annoyance, his smile faded and he said more earnestly:

'As a matter of fact, this last point, though it is the last link, is not the main business. There were much more curious things in the case than that. One of them is rather a curiosity of evidence. Let me begin by saying something that may surprise you. Darnaway did not die at seven o'clock that evening. He had been already dead for a whole day.'

'Surprise is rather a mild word,' said Payne grimly, 'since you and I both saw him walking about afterwards.'

'No, we did not,' replied Father Brown quietly. 'I think we both saw him, or thought we saw him, fussing about with the focusing of his camera. Wasn't his head under that black cloak when you passed through the room? It was when I did. And that's why I felt there was something queer about the room and the figure. It wasn't that the leg was crooked, but rather that it wasn't crooked. It was dressed in the same sort of dark clothes; but if you see what you believe to be one man standing in the way that another man stands, you will think he's in a strange and strained attitude.'

'Do you really mean,' cried Payne with something like a shudder, 'that it was some unknown man?'

'It was the murderer,' said Father Brown. 'He had already killed Darnaway at daybreak and hid the corpse and himself in the dark room – an excellent hiding place, because nobody normally goes into it or can see much if he does. But he let it fall out on the floor at seven o'clock, of course, that the whole thing might be explained by the curse.'

'But I don't understand,' observed Payne. 'Why didn't he kill him at seven o'clock then, instead of loading himself with a corpse for fourteen hours?'

'Let me ask you another question,' said the priest. 'Why was there no photograph taken? Because the murderer made sure of killing him when he first got up, and before he could take it. It was essential to the murderer to prevent that photograph reaching the expert on the Darnaway antiquities.'

There was a sudden silence for a moment, and then the priest went on in a lower tone:

'Don't you see how simple it is? Why, you yourself saw one side of the possibility; but it's simpler even than you thought. You said a man might be faked to resemble an old picture. Surely it's simpler that a picture should be faked to resemble a man. In plain words, it's true in a rather special way that there was no doom of the Darnaways. There was no old picture; there was no old rhyme; there was no legend of a man who caused his wife's death. But there was a very wicked and a very clever man who was willing to cause another man's death in order to rob him of his promised wife.'

The priest suddenly gave Payne a sad smile, as if in reassurance. 'For the moment I believe you thought I meant you,' he said, 'but you were not the only person who haunted that house for sentimental reasons. You know the man, or rather you think you do. But there were depths in the man called Martin Wood, artist and antiquary, which none of his mere artistic acquaintances were likely to guess. Remember that he was called in to criticize and catalogue the pictures; in an aristocratic dustbin of that sort that practically means simply to tell the Darnaways what art treasures they had got. They would not be surprised at things turning up they had never noticed before. It had to be done well, and it was; perhaps he was right when he said that if it wasn't Holbein it was somebody of the same genius.'

'I feel rather stunned,' said Payne; 'and there are twenty things I don't see yet. How did he know what Darnaway looked like? How did he actually kill him? The doctors seem rather puzzled at present.'

'I saw a photograph the lady had which the Australian sent on before him,' said the priest, 'and there are several ways in which he could have learned things when the new heir was once recognized. We may not know these details; but they are not difficulties. You remember he used to help in the dark room; it seems to me an ideal place, say, to prick a man with a poisoned pin, with the poisons all handy. No, I say these were not difficulties. The difficulty that stumped me was how Wood could be in two places at once. How could he take the corpse from the dark room and prop it against the camera so that it would fall in a few seconds, without coming downstairs, when he was in the library looking out a book? And I was such a fool that I never looked at the books in the library; and it was only in this photograph, by very undeserved good luck, that I saw the simple fact of a book about Pope Joan.'

'You've kept your best riddle for the end,' said Payne grimly. 'What on earth can Pope Joan have to do with it?'

'Don't forget the book about the Something of Iceland,' advised the priest, 'or the religion of somebody called Frederick. It only remains to ask what sort of a man was the late Lord Darnaway.'

'Oh, does it?' observed Payne heavily.

'He was a cultivated, humorous sort of eccentric, I believe,' went on Father Brown. 'Being cultivated, he knew there was no such person as Pope Joan. Being humorous, he was very likely to have thought of the title of "The Snakes of Iceland" or something else that didn't exist. I venture to reconstruct the third title as *The Religion of Frederick the Great* – which also didn't exist. Now, doesn't it strike you that those would be just the titles to put on the backs of books that didn't exist; or in other words on a book-case that wasn't a book-case?'

'Ah!' cried Payne, 'I see what you mean now. There was some hidden staircase—'

'Up to the room Wood himself selected as a dark room,' said the priest nodding. 'I'm sorry. It couldn't be helped. It's dreadfully banal and stupid, as stupid as I have been on this pretty banal case. But we were mixed up in a real musty old romance of decayed gentility and a fallen family mansion; and it was too much to hope that we could escape having a secret passage. It was a priest's hole; and I deserve to be put in it.'

THE SONG OF THE FLYING FISH

THE SOUL of Mr Peregrine Smart hovered like a fly round one possession and one joke. It might be considered a mild joke, for it consisted merely of asking people if they had seen his goldfish. It might also be considered an expensive joke; but it is doubtful whether he was not secretly more attached to the joke than to the evidence of expenditure. In talking to his neighbours in the little group of new houses that had grown up round the old village green, he lost no time in turning the conversation in the direction of his hobby. To Dr Burdock, a rising biologist with a resolute chin and hair brushed back like a German's, Mr Smart made the easy transition. 'You are interested in natural history; have you seen my goldfish?' To so orthodox an evolutionist as Dr Burdock doubtless all nature was one; but at first sight the link was not close, as he was a specialist who had concentrated entirely upon the primitive ancestry of the giraffe. To Father Brown, from a church in the neighbouring provincial town, he traced a rapid train of thought which touched on the topics of 'Rome – St Peter – fisherman – fish – goldfish'. In talking to Mr Imlack Smith, the bank manager, a slim and sallow gentleman of dressy appearance but quiet demeanour, he violently wrenched the conversation to the subject of the gold standard, from which it was merely a step to goldfish. In talking to that brilliant Oriental traveller and scholar, Count Yvon de Lara (whose title was French and his face rather Russian, not to say Tartar), the versatile conversationalist showed an intense and intelligent interest in the Ganges and the Indian Ocean, leading naturally to the possible presence of goldfish in those waters. From Mr Harry Hartopp, the very rich but very shy and silent young gentleman who had recently come down from London, he had at last extorted the information that the embarrassed youth in question was *not* interested in fishing, and had then added, 'Talking about fishing, have you see my goldfish?'

The peculiar thing about the goldfish was that they were made of gold. They were part of an eccentric but expensive toy, said to have been made by the freak of some rich Eastern prince, and Mr Smart had picked it up at some sale or in some curiosity shop, such as he frequented for the purpose of lumbering up his house with unique and useless things. From the other end of the room it looked like a rather unusually large bowl containing rather unusually large living fish; a closer inspection showed it to be a huge bubble of beautifully blown Venetian glass, very thin and delicately clouded with faintly iridescent colour, in the tinted twilight of which hung grotesque golden fishes with great rubies for eyes. The whole thing was undoubtedly worth a great deal in solid material; how much more would depend upon the waves of lunacy passing over the world of collectors. Mr Smart's new secretary, a young man named Francis Boyle, though an Irishman and not credited with caution, was mildly surprised at his talking so freely of the gems of his collection to the group of comparative strangers who happened to have alighted in a rather nomadic fashion in the neighbourhood; for collectors are commonly vigilant and sometimes secretive. In the course of settling down to his new duties, Mr Boyle found he was not alone in this sentiment, and that in others it passed from a mild wonder to a grave disapproval.

'It's a wonder his throat isn't cut,' said Mr Smart's valet, Harris, not without a hypothetical relish, almost as if he had said, in a purely artistic sense, 'It's a pity.'

'It's extraordinary how he leaves things about,' said Mr Smart's head clerk, Jameson, who had come up from the office to assist the new secretary, 'and he won't even put up those ramshackle old bars across his ramshackle old door.'

'It's all very well with Father Brown and the doctor,' said Mr Smart's housekeeper, with a certain vigorous vagueness that marked her opinions, 'but when it comes to foreigners, I call it tempting providence. It isn't only the Count, either; that man at the bank looks to me much too yellow to be English.'

'Well, that young Hartopp is English enough,' said Boyle good-humouredly, 'to the extent of not having a word to say for himself.'

'He thinks the more,' said the housekeeper. 'He may not be exactly a foreigner, but he is not such a fool as he looks. Foreign is as foreign does, I say,' she added darkly.

Her disapproval would probably have deepened if she had heard the conversation in her master's drawing-room that afternoon, a conversation of which the goldfish were the text, though the offensive foreigner tended more and more to be the central figure. It was not that he spoke so very much; but even his silences had something positive about them. He looked the more massive for sitting in a sort of heap on a heap of cushions, and in the deepening twilight his wide Mongolian face seemed faintly luminous, like a moon. Perhaps his background brought out something atmospherically Asiatic about his face and figure, for the room was a chaos of more or less costly curiosities, amid which could be seen the crooked curves and burning colours of countless Eastern weapons, Eastern pipes and vessels, Eastern musical instruments and illuminated manuscripts. Anyhow, as the conversation proceeded, Boyle felt more and more that the figure seated on the cushions and dark against the twilight had the exact outline of a huge image of Buddha.

The conversation was general enough, for all the little local group were present. They were, indeed, often in the habit of dropping in at each other's houses, and by this time constituted a sort of club, of people coming from the four or five houses standing round the green. Of these houses Peregrine Smart's was the oldest, largest, and most picturesque; it straggled down almost the whole of one side of the square, leaving only room for a small villa, inhabited by a retired colonel named Varney, who was reported to be an invalid, and certainly was never seen to go abroad. At right angles to these stood two or three shops that served the simpler needs of the hamlet, and at the corner the inn of the Blue Dragon, at which Mr Hartopp, the stranger from London, was staying. On the opposite side were three houses, one rented by the Count de Lara, one by Dr Burdock, and the third still standing empty. On the fourth side was the bank, with an adjoining house for the bank manager, and a line of fence enclosing some land that was let for building. It was thus a very self-contained group, and the comparative emptiness of the open ground for miles round it threw the members more and more on each other's society. That afternoon one stranger had indeed broken into the magic circle; a hatchet-faced fellow with fierce tufts of eyebrow and moustache, and so shabbily dressed that he must have been a millionaire or a duke if he had really (as was alleged) come down to do business with the old collector. But he was known, at the Blue Dragon at least, as Mr Harmer.

To him had been recounted anew the glories of the gilded fish and the criticisms regarding their custody.

'People are always telling me I ought to lock them up more carefully,' observed Mr Smart, cocking an eyebrow over his shoulder at the dependant who stood there holding some papers from the office. Smart was a round-faced, round-bodied little old man, rather like a bald parrot. 'Jameson and Harris and the rest are always at me to bar the doors as if it were a mediaeval fortress, though really these rotten old rusty bars are too mediaeval to keep anybody out, I should think. I prefer to trust to luck and the local police.'

'It is not always the best bars that keep people out,' said the Count. 'It all depends on who's trying to get in. There was an ancient Hindu hermit who lived naked in a cave and passed through the three armies that encircled the Mogul and took the great ruby out of the tyrant's turban, and went back unscathed like a shadow. For he wished to teach the great how small are the laws of space and time.'

'When we really study the small laws of space and time,' said Dr Burdock dryly, 'we generally find out how those tricks are done. Western science has let in daylight on a good deal of Eastern magic. Doubtless a great deal can be done with hypnotism and suggestion, to say nothing of sleight-of-hand.'

'The ruby was not in the royal tent,' observed the Count in his dreamy fashion, 'but he found it among a hundred tents.'

'Can't all that be explained by telepathy?' asked the doctor sharply.

The question sounded the sharper because it was followed by a heavy silence, almost as if the distinguished Oriental traveller had, with imperfect politeness, gone to sleep.

'I beg your pardon,' he said, rousing himself with a sudden smile. 'I had forgotten we were talking with words. In the East we talk with thoughts, and so we never misunderstand each other. It is strange how you people worship words and are satisfied with words. What difference does it make to a thing that you now call it telepathy, as you once called it tomfoolery? If a man climbs into the sky on a mango-tree, how is it altered by saying it is only levitation, instead of saying it is only lies. If a mediaeval witch waved a wand and turned me into a blue baboon, you would say it was only atavism.'

The doctor looked for a moment as if he might say that it would not be so great a change after all. But before his irritation could find that or any other vent, the man called Harmer interrupted gruffly:

'It's true enough those Indian conjurers can do queer things, but I notice they generally do them in India. Confederates, perhaps, or merely mass psychology. I don't think those tricks have ever been played in an English village, and I should say our friend's goldfish were quite safe.'

'I will tell you a story,' said de Lara in his motionless way, 'which happened not in India, but outside an English barrack in the most modernized part of Cairo. A sentinel was standing inside the grating of an iron gateway looking out between the bars on to the street. There appeared outside the gate a beggar, barefoot and in native rags, who asked him, in English that was startlingly distinct and refined, for a certain official document kept in the building for safety. The soldier told the man, of course, that he could not come inside; and the man answered, smiling, "What is inside and what is outside?" The soldier was still staring scornfully through the iron grating when he gradually realized that, though neither he nor the gate had moved, he was actually standing in the street and looking in at the barrack yard, where the beggar stood still and smiling and equally motionless. Then, when the beggar turned towards the building, the sentry awoke to such sense as he had left, and shouted a warning to all the soldiers within the gated enclosure to hold the prisoner fast. "You won't get out of there anyhow," he said vindictively. Then the beggar said in his silver voice, "What is outside and what is inside?" And the soldier, still glaring through the same bars, saw that they were once more between him and the street, where the beggar stood free and smiling with a paper in his hand.'

Mr Imlack Smith, the bank manager, was looking at the carpet with his dark sleek head bowed, and he spoke for the first time.

'Did anything happen about the paper?' he asked.

'Your professional instincts are correct, sir,' said the Count with grim affability. 'It was a paper of considerable financial importance. Its consequences were international.'

'I hope they don't occur often,' said young Hartopp gloomily.

'I do not touch the political side,' said the Count serenely, 'but only the philosophical. It illustrates how the wise man can get behind time and space and turn the levers of them, so to speak, so that the whole world turns round before our eyes. But it is so hard for you people to believe that spiritual powers are really more powerful than material ones.'

'Well,' said old Smart cheerfully, 'I don't profess to be an authority on spiritual powers. What do you say, Father Brown?'

'The only thing that strikes me,' answered the little priest, 'is that all the supernatural acts we have yet heard of seem to be thefts. And stealing by spiritual methods seems to me much the same as stealing by material ones.'

'Father Brown is a Philistine,' said the smiling Smith.

'I have a sympathy with the tribe,' said Father Brown. 'A Philistine is only a man who is right without knowing why.'

'All this is too clever for me,' said Hartopp heartily.

'Perhaps,' said Father Brown with a smile, 'you would like to speak without words, as the Count suggests. He would begin by saying nothing in a pointed fashion, and you would retort with a burst of taciturnity.'

'Something might be done with music,' murmured the Count dreamily. 'It would be better than all these words.'

'Yes, I might understand that better,' said the young man in a low voice.

Boyle had followed the conversation with curious attention, for there was something in the demeanour of more than one of the talkers that seemed to him significant or even odd. As the talk drifted to music, with an appeal to the dapper bank manager (who was an amateur musician of some merit), the young secretary awoke with a start to his secretarial duties, and reminded his employer that the head clerk was still standing patiently with the papers in his hand.

'Oh, never mind about those just now, Jameson,' said Smart rather hurriedly. 'Only something about my account; I'll see Mr Smith about it later. You were saying that the 'cello, Mr Smith '

But the cold breath of business had sufficed to disperse the fumes of transcendental talk, and the guests began one after another to say farewell. Only Mr Imlack Smith, bank manager and musician, remained to the last; and when the rest were gone he and his host went into the inner room, where the goldfish were kept, and closed the door.

The house was long and narrow, with a covered balcony running along the first floor, which consisted mostly of a sort of suite of rooms used by the householder himself, his bedroom and dressing-room, and an inner room in which his very valuable treasures were sometimes stored for the night instead of being left in the rooms below. This balcony, like the insufficiently barred door below it, was a matter of concern to the housekeeper and the head clerk and the others who lamented the carelessness of the collector; but in truth that cunning old gentleman was more careful than he seemed. He professed no great belief in the antiquated fastenings of the old house, which the housekeeper lamented to see rusting in idleness, but he had an eye to the more important point of strategy. He always put his favourite goldfish in the room at the back of his bedroom for the night and slept in front of it, as it were, with a pistol under his pillow. And when Boyle and Jameson, awaiting his return from the *tête-à-tête*, at length saw the door open and their employer reappear, he was carrying the great glass bowl as reverently as if it had been the relic of a saint.

Outside, the last edges of the sunset still clung to the corners of the green square; but inside a lamp had already been kindled; and in the mingling of the two lights the coloured globe glowed like some monstrous jewel and the fantastic outlines of the fiery fishes seemed to give it indeed something of the mystery of a talisman, like strange shapes seen by a seer in the crystal of doom. Over the old man's shoulder the olive face of Imlack Smith stared like a sphinx.

'I am going up to London tonight, Mr Boyle,' said old Smart, with more gravity than he commonly showed. 'Mr Smith and I are catching the six-forty-five. I should prefer you, Jameson, to sleep upstairs in my room tonight; if you put the bowl in the back room as usual, it will be quite safe then. Not that I suppose anything could possibly happen.'

'Anything may happen anywhere,' said the smiling Mr Smith. 'I think you generally take a gun to bed with you. Perhaps you had better leave it behind in this case.'

Peregrine Smart did not reply, and they passed out of the house on to the road round the village green.

The secretary and the head clerk slept that night as directed in their employer's bedroom. To speak more strictly, Jameson, the head clerk, slept in a bed in the dressing-room, but the door stood open between, and the two rooms running along the front were practically one. Only the bedroom had a long French window giving on the balcony and an entrance at the back into the inner apartment where the goldfish bowl had been placed for safety. Boyle dragged his bed right across so as to bar this entrance, put the revolver under his pillow, and then undressed and went to bed, feeling that he had taken all possible precautions against an impossible or improbable event. He did not see why there should be any particular danger of normal burglary; and as for the spiritual burglary that figured in the traveller's tales of the Count de Lara, if his thoughts ran on them so near to sleep it was because they were such stuff as dreams are made of. They soon turned into dreams with intervals of dreamless slumber. The old clerk was a little more restless than usual; but after fussing about a little longer and repeating some of his favourite regrets and warnings, he also retired to his bed in the same manner and slept. The moon brightened and grew dim again above the green square and the grey blocks of houses in a solitude and silence that seemed to have no human witness; and it was when the white cracks of daybreak had already appeared in the corners of the grey sky that the thing happened.

Boyle, being young, was naturally both the healthier and the heavier sleeper of the two. Though active enough when he was once awake, he always had a load to lift in waking. Moreover, he had dreams of the sort that cling to the emerging mind like the dim tentacles of an octopus. They were a medley of many things, including his last look from the balcony across the four grey roads and the green square. But the pattern of them changed and shifted and turned dizzily, to the accompaniment of a low grinding noise, which sounded somehow like a subterranean river, and may have been no more than old Mr Jameson snoring in the dressing-room. But in the dreamer's mind all that murmur and motion was vaguely connected with the words of the Count de Lara, about a wisdom that could hold the levers of time and space and turn the world. In the dream it seemed as if a vast murmuring machinery under the world were really moving whole landscapes hither and thither, so that the ends of the earth might appear in a man's front-garden, or his own front-garden be exiled beyond the sea.

The first complete impressions he had were the words of a song, with a rather thin metallic accompaniment; they were sung in a foreign accent and a voice that was still strange and yet faintly familiar. And yet he could hardly feel sure that he was not making up poetry in his sleep.

> Over the land and over the sea
> My flying fishes will come to me,
> For the note is not of the world that wakes them,
> But in—

He struggled to his feet and saw that his fellow guardian was already out of bed; Jameson was peering out of the long window on to the balcony and calling out sharply to someone in the street below.

'Who's that?' he called out sharply. 'What do you want?'

He turned to Boyle in agitation, saying, 'There's somebody prowling about just outside. I knew it wasn't safe. I'm going down to bar that front door, whatever they say.'

He ran downstairs in a flutter and Boyle could hear the clattering of the bars upon the front door; but Boyle himself stepped out upon the balcony and looked out on the long grey road that led up to the house, and he thought he was still dreaming.

Upon that grey road leading across that empty moor and through that little English hamlet, there had appeared a figure that might have stepped straight out of the jungle or the bazaar – a figure out of one of the Count's fantastic stories; a figure out of the *Arabian Nights*. The rather ghostly grey twilight which begins to define and yet to discolour everything when the light in the east has ceased to be localized, lifted slowly like a veil of grey gauze and showed him a figure wrapped in outlandish raiment. A scarf of a strange sea-blue, vast and voluminous, went round the head like a turban, and then again round the chin, giving rather the general character of a hood; so far as the face was concerned it had the effect of a mask. For the raiment round the head was drawn close as a veil; and the head itself was bowed over a queer-looking musical instrument made of silver or steel, and shaped like a deformed or crooked violin. It was played with something like a silver comb, and the notes were curiously thin and keen. Before Boyle could open his mouth, the same haunting alien accent came from under the shadow of the burnous, singing words of the same sort:

> As the golden birds go back to the tree
> My golden fishes return to me.
> Return—

'You've no right here,' called out Boyle in exasperation, hardly knowing what he said.

'I have a right to the goldfish,' said the stranger, speaking more like King Solomon than an unsandalled Bedouin in a ragged blue cloak. 'And they will come to me. Come!'

He struck his strange fiddle as his voice rose sharply on the word. There was a pang of sound that seemed to pierce the mind, and then there came a fainter sound, like an answer: a vibrant whisper. It came from the dark room behind where the bowl of goldfish was standing.

Boyle turned towards it; and, even as he turned, the echo in the inner room changed to a long, tingling sound like an electric bell, and then to a faint crash. It was still a matter of seconds since he had challenged the man from the balcony; but the old clerk had already regained the top of the stairs, panting a little, for he was an elderly gentleman.

'I've locked up the door, anyhow,' he said.

'The stable door,' said Boyle out of the darkness of the inner room.

Jameson followed him into that apartment and found him staring down at the floor, which was covered with a litter of coloured glass like the curved bits of a broken rainbow.

'What do you mean by the stable door?' began Jameson

'I mean that the steed is stolen,' answered Boyle. 'The flying steeds. The flying fishes our Arab friend outside has just whistled to like so many performing puppies.'

'But how could he?' exploded the old clerk, as if such events were hardly respectable.

'Well, they're gone,' said Boyle shortly. 'The broken bowl is here, which would have taken a long time to open properly, but only a second to smash. But the fish are gone, God knows how, though I think our friend ought to be asked.'

'We are wasting time,' said the distracted Jameson. 'We ought to be after him at once.'

'Much better be telephoning the police at once,' answered Boyle. 'They ought to outstrip him in a flash with motors and telephones that go a good deal farther than we should ever get, running through the village in our nightgowns. But it may be there are things even the police cars and wires won't outstrip.'

While Jameson was talking to the police station through the telephone in an agitated voice, Boyle went out again on to the balcony and hastily scanned that grey landscape of daybreak. There was no trace of the man in the turban, and no other sign of life, except some faint stirrings an expert might have recognized in the hotel of the Blue Dragon. Only Boyle, for the first time, noted consciously something that he had all along been noting unconsciously. It was like a fact struggling in the submerged mind and demanding its own meaning. It was simply the fact that the grey landscape had never been entirely grey; there was one gold spot amid its stripes of colourless colour, a lamp lighted in one of the houses on the other side of the green. Something, perhaps irrational, told him that it had been burning through all the hours of the darkness and was only fading with the dawn. He counted the houses, and his calculation brought out a result which seemed to fit in with something, he knew not what. Anyhow, it was apparently the house of the Count Yvon de Lara.

Inspector Pinner had arrived with several policemen, and done several things of a rapid and resolute sort, being conscious that the very absurdity of the costly trinkets might give the case considerable prominence in the newspapers. He had examined everything, measured everything, taken down everybody's deposition, taken everybody's fingerprints, put everybody's back up, and found himself at the end left facing a fact which he could not believe. An Arab from the desert had walked up the public road and stopped in front of the house of Mr Peregrine Smart, where a bowl of artificial goldfish was kept in an inner room; he had then sung or recited a little poem, and the bowl had exploded like a bomb and the fishes vanished into thin air. Nor did it soothe the inspector to be told by a foreign Count, in a soft, purring voice, that the bounds of experience were being enlarged.

Indeed, the attitude of each member of the little group was characteristic enough. Peregrine Smart himself had come back from London the next morning to hear the news of his loss. Naturally he admitted a shock; but it was typical of something sporting and spirited in the little old gentleman, something that always made his small strutting figure look like a cock sparrow's, that he showed more vivacity in the search than depression at the loss. The man named Harmer, who had come to the village on purpose to buy the goldfish, might be excused for being a little testy on learning they were not there to be bought. But in truth his rather aggressive moustache and eyebrows seemed to bristle with something more definite than disappointment, and the eyes that darted over the company were bright with a vigilance that might well be suspicion. The sallow face of the bank manager, who had also returned from London though by a later train, seemed again and again to attract those shining and shifting eyes like a magnet. Of the two remaining figures of the original circle, Father Brown was generally silent when he was not spoken to, and the dazed Hartopp was often silent even when he was.

But the Count was not a man to let anything pass that gave an apparent advantage to his views. He smiled at his rationalistic rival, the doctor, in the manner of one who knows how it is possible to be irritating by being ingratiating.

'You will admit, doctor,' he said, 'that at least some of the stories you thought so improbable look a little more realistic today than they did yesterday. When a man as ragged as those I described is able, by speaking a word, to dissolve a solid vessel inside the four walls of the house he stands outside, it might perhaps be called an example of what I said about spiritual powers and material barriers.'

'And it might be called an example of what I said,' said the doctor sharply, 'about a little scientific knowledge being enough to show how the tricks are done.'

'Do you really mean, doctor,' asked Smart in some excitement, 'that you can throw any scientific light on this mystery?'

'I can throw light on what the Count calls a mystery,' said the doctor, 'because it is not a mystery at all. That part of it is plain enough. A sound is only a wave of vibration, and certain vibrations can break glass, if the sound is of a certain kind and the glass of a certain kind. The man did not stand in the road and think, which the Count tells us is the ideal method when Orientals want a little chat. He sang out what he wanted, quite loud, and struck a shrill note on an instrument. It is similar to many experiments by which glass of special composition has been cracked.'

'Such as the experiment,' said the Count lightly, 'by which several lumps of solid gold have suddenly ceased to exist.'

'Here comes Inspector Pinner,' said Boyle. 'Between ourselves,

I think he would regard the doctor's natural explanation as quite as much of a fairy tale as the Count's preternatural one. A very sceptical intellect, Mr Pinner's, especially about me. I rather think I am under suspicion.'

'I think we are all under suspicion,' said the Count.

It was the presence of this suspicion in his own case that led Boyle to seek the personal advice of Father Brown. They were walking round the village green together, some hours later in the day, when the priest, who was frowning thoughtfully at the ground as he listened, suddenly stopped.

'Do you see that?' he asked. 'Somebody's been washing the pavement here – just this little strip of pavement outside Colonel Varney's house. I wonder whether that was done yesterday.'

Father Brown looked rather earnestly at the house, which was high and narrow, and carried rows of striped sun-blinds of gay but already faded colours. The chinks or crannies that gave glimpses of the interior looked all the darker; indeed, they looked almost black in contrast with the façade thus golden in the morning light.

'That is Colonel Varney's house, isn't it?' he asked. 'He comes from the East, too, I fancy. What sort of man is he?'

'I've never even seen him,' answered Boyle. 'I don't think anybody's seen him, except Dr Burdock, and I rather fancy the doctor doesn't see him more than he need.'

'Well, I'm going to see him for a minute,' said Father Brown.

The big front door opened and swallowed the small priest, and his friend stood staring at it in a dazed and irrational manner, as if wondering whether it would ever open again. It opened in a few minutes, and Father Brown emerged, still smiling, and continued his slow and puttering progress round the square of roads. Sometimes he seemed to have forgotten the matter in hand altogether, for he would make passing remarks on historical and social questions, or on the prospects of development in the district. He remarked on the soil used for the beginning of a new road by the bank; he looked across the old village green with a vague expression.

'Common land. I suppose people ought to feed their pigs and geese on it, if they had any pigs or geese; as it is, it seems to feed nothing but nettles and thistles. What a pity that what was supposed to be a sort of large meadow has been turned into a small and petty wilderness. That's Dr Burdock's house opposite, isn't it?'

'Yes,' answered Boyle, almost jumping at this abrupt postscript.

'Very well,' answered Father Brown, 'then I think we'll go indoors again.'

As they opened the front door of Smart's house and mounted the stairs, Boyle repeated to his companion many details of the drama enacted there at daybreak.

'I suppose you didn't doze off again?' asked Father Brown, 'giving time for somebody to scale the balcony while Jameson ran down to secure the door.'

'No,' answered Boyle. 'I am sure of that. I woke up to hear Jameson challenging the stranger from the balcony; then I heard him running downstairs and putting up the bars, and then in two strides I was on the balcony myself.'

'Or could he have slipped in between you from another angle? Are there any other entrances besides the front entrance?'

'Apparently there are not,' said Boyle gravely.

'I had better make sure, don't you think?' asked Father Brown apologetically, and scuttled softly downstairs again. Boyle remained in the front bedroom gazing rather doubtfully after him. After a comparatively brief interval the round and rather rustic visage appeared again at the head of the stairs, looking rather like a turnip ghost with a broad grin.

'No. I think that settles the matter of entrances,' said the turnip ghost, cheerfully. 'And now I think, having got everything in a tight box, so to speak, we can take stock of what we've got. It's rather a curious business.'

'Do you think,' asked Boyle, 'that the Count, or the colonel, or any of these Eastern travellers have anything to do with it? Do you think it is – preternatural?'

'I will grant you this,' said the priest gravely, 'if the Count, or the colonel, or any of your neighbours did dress up in Arab masquerade and creep up to this house in the dark – then it *was* preternatural.'

'What do you mean? Why?'

'Because the Arab left no footprints,' answered Father Brown. 'The colonel on the one side and the banker on the other are the nearest of your neighbours. That loose red soil is between you and the bank, it would print off bare feet like a plaster cast and probably leave red marks everywhere. I braved the colonel's curry-seasoned temper to verify the fact that the front pavement was washed yesterday and not today; it was wet enough to make wet footprints all along the road. Now, if the visitor were the Count or the doctor in the houses opposite, he might possibly, of course, have come across the common. But he must have found it exceedingly uncomfortable with bare feet, for it is, as I remarked, one mass of thorns and thistles and stinging nettles. He would surely have pricked himself and probably left traces of it. Unless, as you say, he was a preternatural being.'

Boyle looked steadily at the grave and indecipherable face of his clerical friend.

'Do you mean that he was?' he asked, at length.

'There is one general truth to remember,' said Father Brown after a pause. 'A thing can sometimes be too close to be seen, as, for instance, a man cannot see himself. There was a man who had a fly in his eye when he looked through the telescope, and he discovered that there was a most incredible dragon in the moon. And I am told that if a man hears the exact reproduction of his own voice it sounds like the voice of a stranger. In the same way, if anything is right in the foreground of our life we hardly see it, and if we did we might think it quite odd. If the thing in the foreground got into the middle distance, we should probably think it had come from the remote distance. Just come outside the house again for a moment. I want to show you how it looks from another standpoint.'

He had already risen, and as they descended the stairs, he continued his remarks in a rather groping fashion as if he were thinking aloud.

'The Count and the Asiatic atmosphere all come in, because, in a case like this, everything depends on the preparation of the mind. A man can reach a condition in which a brick, falling on his head, will seem to be a Babylonian brick, carved with cuneiform and dropped from the Hanging Gardens of Babylon, so that he will never even look at the brick and see it is of one pattern with the bricks of his own house. So in your case—'

'What does this mean?' interrupted Boyle, staring and pointing at the entrance. 'What in the name of wonder does it mean? The door is barred again.'

He was staring at the front door, by which they had entered but a little while before, and across which stood once more the great dark bands of rusty iron which had once, as he had said, locked the stable door too late. There was something darkly and dumbly ironic in those old fastenings, closing behind them and imprisoning them as if of their own motion.

'Oh, those!' said Father Brown casually. 'I put up those bars myself, just now. Didn't you hear me?'

'No,' answered Boyle, staring. 'I heard nothing.'

'Well, I rather thought you wouldn't,' said the other equably. 'There's really no reason why anybody upstairs should hear those bars being put up. A sort of hook fits easily into a sort of hole. When you're quite close you hear a dull click; but that's all. The only thing that makes any noise a man could hear upstairs, is this.'

And he lifted the bar out of its socket and let it fall with a clang at the side of the door.

'It does make a noise if you *unbar* the door,' said Father Brown gravely, 'even if you do it pretty carefully.'

'You mean—'

'I mean,' said Father Brown, 'that what you heard upstairs was Jameson opening the door and not shutting it. And now let's open the door ourselves and go outside.'

When they stood outside in the street, under the balcony, the little priest resumed his previous explanation as coolly as if it had been a chemical lecture.

'I was saying that a man may be in the mood to look for something very distant, and not realize that it is something very close, something very close to himself, perhaps something very like himself. It was a strange and outlandish thing that you saw when you looked down at this road. I suppose it never occurred to you to consider what he saw when he looked up at that balcony?'

Boyle was staring at the balcony and did not answer, and the other added:

'You thought it very wild and wonderful that an Arab should come through civilized England with bare feet. You did not remember that at the same moment you had bare feet yourself.'

Boyle at last found words, and it was to repeat words already spoken.

'Jameson opened the door,' he said mechanically.

'Yes,' assented his friend. 'Jameson opened the door and came out into the road in his night-clothes, just as you came out on the balcony. He caught up two things that you had seen a hundred times: the length of old blue curtain that he wrapped round his head, and the Oriental musical instrument you must have often seen in that heap of Oriental curiosities. The rest was atmosphere and acting, very fine acting, for he is a very fine artist in crime.'

'Jameson!' exclaimed Boyle incredulously. 'He was such a dull old stick that I never even noticed him.'

'Precisely,' said the priest, 'he was an artist. If he could act a wizard or a troubadour for six minutes, do you think he could not act a clerk for six weeks?'

'I am still not quite sure of his object,' said Boyle.

'His object has been achieved,' replied Father Brown, 'or very nearly achieved. He had taken the goldfish already, of course, as he had twenty chances of doing. But if he had simply taken them, everybody would have realized that he had twenty chances of doing it. By creating a mysterious magician from the end of the earth, he set everybody's thoughts wandering far afield to Arabia and India, so that you yourself can hardly believe that the whole thing was so near home. It was too close to you to be seen.'

'If this is true,' said Boyle, 'it was an extraordinary risk to run, and he had to cut it very fine. It's true I never heard the man in the street say anything while Jameson was talking from the balcony, so I suppose that was all a fake. And I suppose it's true that there was time for him to get outside before I had fully woken up and got out on to the balcony.'

'Every crime depends on somebody not waking up too soon,' replied Father Brown, 'and in every sense most of us wake up too late. I, for one, have woken up much too late. For I imagine he's bolted long ago, just before or just after they took his finger-prints.'

'You woke up before anybody else, anyhow,' said Boyle, 'and I should never have woken up in that sense. Jameson was so correct and colourless that I forgot all about him.'

'Beware of the man you forget,' replied his friend; 'he is the one man who has you entirely at a disadvantage. But I did not suspect him, either, until you told me how you had heard him barring the door.'

'Anyhow, we owe it all to you,' said Boyle warmly.

'You owe it all to Mrs Robinson,' said Father Brown with a smile.

'Mrs Robinson?' questioned the wondering secretary. 'You don't mean the housekeeper?'

'Beware of the woman you forget, and even more,' answered the other. 'This man was a very high-class criminal; he had been an excellent actor, and therefore he was a good psychologist. A man like the Count never hears any voice but his own; but this man could listen, when you had all forgotten he was there, and gather exactly the right materials for his romance and know exactly the right note to strike to lead you all astray. But he made one bad mistake in the psychology of Mrs Robinson, the housekeeper.'

'I don't understand,' answered Boyle, 'what she can have to do with it.'

'Jameson did not expect the doors to be barred,' said Father Brown. 'He knew that a lot of men, especially careless men like you and your employer, could go on saying for days that something ought to be done, or might as well be done. But if you convey to a woman that something ought to be done, there is always a dreadful danger that she will suddenly do it.'

THE RED MOON OF MERU

Everyone agreed that the bazaar at Mallowood Abbey (by kind permission of Lady Mounteagle) was a great success; there were roundabouts and swings and side-shows which the people greatly enjoyed; I would also mention the Charity; which was the excellent object of the proceedings, if any of them could tell me what it was.

However, it is only with a few of them that we are here concerned; and especially with three of them, a lady and two gentlemen, who passed between two of the principal tents or pavilions, their voices high in argument. On their right was the tent of the Master of the Mountain, that world-famous fortune-teller by crystals and chiromancy; a rich purple tent, all over which were traced, in black and gold, the sprawling outlines of Asiatic gods waving any number of arms like octopods. Perhaps they symbolized the readiness of divine help to be had within; perhaps they merely implied that the ideal being of a pious palmist would have as many hands as possible. On the other side stood the plainer tent of Phroso the Phrenologist; more austerely decorated with diagrams of the heads of Socrates and Shakespeare, which were apparently of a lumpy sort. But these were presented merely in black and white, with numbers and notes, as became the rigid dignity of a purely rationalistic science. The purple tent had an opening like a black cavern, and all was fittingly silent within. But Phroso the Phrenologist, a lean, shabby, sunburnt person, with an almost improbably fierce black moustache and whiskers, was standing outside his own temple, and talking, at the top of his voice, to nobody in particular, explaining that the head of any passer-by would doubtless prove, on examination, to be every bit as knobbly as Shakespeare's. Indeed, the moment the lady appeared between the tents, the vigilant Phroso leapt on her and offered, with a pantomime of old-world courtesy, to feel her bumps.

She refused with civility that was rather like rudeness; but she must be excused, because she was in the middle of an argument.

She also had to be excused, or at any rate was excused, because she was Lady Mounteagle. She was not a nonentity, however, in any sense; she was at once handsome and haggard, with a hungry look in her deep, dark eyes and something eager and almost fierce about her smile. Her dress was bizarre for the period; for it was before the Great War had left us in our present mood of gravity and recollection. Indeed, the dress was rather like the purple tent; being of a semi-oriental sort, covered with exotic and esoteric emblems. But everyone knew that the Mounteagles were mad; which was the popular way of saying that she and her husband were interested in the creeds and culture of the East.

The eccentricity of the lady was a great contrast to the conventionality of the two gentlemen, who were braced and buttoned up in all the stiffer fashion of that far-off day, from the tips of their gloves to their bright top hats. Yet even here there was a difference; for James Hardcastle managed at once to look correct and distinguished, while Tommy Hunter only looked correct and commonplace. Hardcastle was a promising politician; who seemed in society to be interested in everything except politics. It may be answered gloomily that every politician is emphatically a promising politician. But to do him justice, he had often exhibited himself as a performing politician. No purple tent in the bazaar, however, had been provided for him to perform in.

'For my part,' he said, screwing in the monocle that was the only gleam in his hard, legal face, 'I think we must exhaust the possibilities of mesmerism before we talk about magic. Remarkable psychological powers undoubtedly exist, even in apparently backward peoples. Marvellous things have been done by fakirs.'

'Did you say done by fakers?' asked the other young man, with doubtful innocence.

'Tommy, you are simply silly,' said the lady. 'Why will you keep barging in on things you don't understand? You're like a schoolboy screaming out that he knows how a conjuring trick is done. It's all so Early Victorian – that schoolboy scepticism. As for mesmerism, I doubt whether you can stretch it to—'

At this point, Lady Mounteagle seemed to catch sight of somebody she wanted; a black stumpy figure standing at a booth where children were throwing hoops at hideous table ornaments. She darted across and cried:

'Father Brown, I've been looking for you. I want to ask you something. Do you believe in fortune-telling?'

The person addressed looked rather helplessly at the little hoop in his hand and said at last:

'I wonder in which sense you are using the word "believe". Of course, if it's all a fraud—'

'Oh, but the Master of the Mountain isn't a bit of a fraud,' she cried. 'He isn't a common conjurer or a fortune-teller at all. It's really a great honour for him to condescend to tell fortunes at my parties; for he's a great religious leader in his own country; a Prophet and a Seer. And even his fortune-telling isn't vulgar stuff about coming into a fortune. He tells you great spiritual truths about yourself, about your ideals.'

'Quite so,' said Father Brown. 'That's what I object to. I was just going to say that if it's all a fraud, I don't mind it so much. It can't be much more of a fraud than most things at fancy bazaars; and there, in a way, it's a sort of practical joke. But if it's a religion and reveals spiritual truths – then it's all as false as hell and I wouldn't touch it with a barge pole.'

'That is something of a paradox,' said Hardcastle, with a smile.

'I wonder what a paradox is,' remarked the priest in a ruminant manner. 'It seems to me obvious enough. I suppose it wouldn't do very much harm if somebody dressed up as a German spy, and pretended to have told all sorts of lies to the Germans. But if a man is trading in the *truth* with the Germans – well! So I think if a fortune-teller is trading in *truth* like that—'

'You really think,' began Hardcastle grimly.

'Yes,' said the other; 'I think he is trading with the enemy.'

Tommy Hunter broke into a chuckle. 'Well,' he said, 'if Father Brown thinks they're good so long as they're frauds, I should think he'd consider this copper-coloured prophet a sort of saint.'

'My cousin Tom is incorrigible,' said Lady Mounteagle. 'He's always going about showing up adepts, as he calls it. He only came down here in a hurry when he heard the Master was to be here, I believe. He'd have tried to show up Buddha or Moses.'

'Thought you wanted looking after a bit,' said the young man, with a grin on his round face. 'So I toddled down. Don't like this brown monkey crawling about.'

'There you go again!' said Lady Mounteagle. 'Years ago, when

I was in India, I suppose we all had that sort of prejudice against brown people. But now I know something about their wonderful spiritual powers, I'm glad to say I know better.'

'Our prejudices seem to cut opposite ways,' said Father Brown. 'You excuse his being brown because he is Brahminical; and I excuse his being Brahminical because he is brown. Frankly I don't care for spiritual powers much myself. I've got much more sympathy with spiritual weaknesses. But I can't see why anybody should dislike him merely because he is the same beautiful colour as copper, or coffee, or nut-brown ale, or those jolly peat-streams in the North. But then,' he added, looking across at the lady and screwing up his eyes, 'I suppose I'm prejudiced in favour of anything that's called brown.'

'There now!' cried Lady Mounteagle with a sort of triumph. 'I knew you were only talking nonsense!'

'Well,' grumbled the aggrieved youth with the round face. 'When anybody talks sense you call it schoolboy scepticism. When's the crystal-gazing going to begin?'

'Any time you like, I believe,' replied the lady. 'It isn't crystal-gazing, as a matter of fact, but palmistry; I suppose you would say it was all the same sort of nonsense.'

'I think there is a *via media* between sense and nonsense,' said Hardcastle, smiling. 'There are explanations that are natural and not at all nonsensical; and yet the results are very amazing. Are you coming in to be operated on? I confess I am full of curiosity.'

'Oh, I've no patience with such nonsense,' spluttered the sceptic, whose round face had become rather a red face with the heat of his contempt and incredulity. 'I'll let you waste your time on your mahogany mountebank; I'd rather go and throw at coconuts.'

The Phrenologist, still hovering near, darted at the opening.

'Heads, my dear sir,' he said, 'human skulls are of a contour far more subtle than that of coconuts. No coconut can compare with your own most—'

Hardcastle had already dived into the dark entry of the purple tent; and they heard a low murmur of voices within. As Tom Hunter turned on the Phrenologist with an impatient answer, in which he showed a regrettable indifference to the line between natural and preternatural sciences, the lady was just about to continue her little argument with the little priest, when she stopped in some surprise.

James Hardcastle had come out of the tent again, and in his grim face and glaring monocle, surprise was even more vividly depicted.

'He's not there,' remarked the politician abruptly. 'He's gone. Some aged nigger, who seems to constitute his *suite*, jabbered something to me to the effect that the Master had gone forth rather than sell sacred secrets for gold.'

Lady Mounteagle turned radiantly to the rest. 'There now,' she cried. 'I told you he was a cut above anything you fancied! He hates being here in a crowd; he's gone back to his solitude.'

'I am sorry,' said Father Brown gravely. 'I may have done him an injustice. Do you know where he has gone?'

'I think so,' said his hostess equally gravely. 'When he wants to be alone, he always goes to the cloisters, just at the end of the left wing, beyond my husband's study and private museum, you know. Perhaps you know this house was once an abbey.'

'I have heard something about it,' answered the priest, with a faint smile.

'We'll go there, if you like,' said the lady, briskly. 'You really ought to see my husband's collection; or the Red Moon at any rate. Haven't you ever heard of the Red Moon of Meru? Yes, it's a ruby.'

'I should be delighted to see the collection,' said Hardcastle quietly, 'including the Master of the Mountain, if that prophet is one exhibit in the museum.' And they all turned towards the path leading to the house.

'All the same,' muttered the sceptical Thomas, as he brought up the rear, 'I should very much like to know what the brown beast *did* come here for, if he didn't come to tell fortunes.'

As he disappeared, the indomitable Phroso made one more dart after him, almost snatching at his coat-tails.

'The bump—' he began.

'No bump,' said the youth, 'only a hump. Hump I always have when I come down to see Mounteagle.' And he took to his heels to escape the embrace of the man of science.

On their way to the cloisters, the visitors had to pass through the long room that was devoted by Lord Mounteagle to his remarkable private museum of Asiatic charms and mascots. Through one open door, in the length of the wall opposite, they could see the Gothic arches and the glimmer of daylight between them, marking the square open space, round the roofed border of which the monks had walked in older days. But they had to pass something that seemed at first sight rather more extraordinary than the ghost of a monk.

It was an elderly gentleman, robed from head to foot in white, with a pale green turban, but a very pink and white English complexion and the smooth white moustaches of some amiable Anglo-Indian colonel. This was Lord Mounteagle, who had taken his Oriental pleasures more sadly, or at least more seriously, than his wife. He could talk of nothing whatever, except Oriental religion and philosophy; and had thought it necessary even to dress in the manner of an Oriental hermit. While he was delighted to show his treasures, he seemed to treasure them much more for the truths supposed to be symbolized in them than for their value in collections, let alone cash. Even when he brought out the great ruby, perhaps the only thing of great value in the museum, in a merely monetary sense, he seemed to be much more interested in its name than in its size, let alone its price.

The others were all staring at what seemed a stupendously large red stone, burning like a bonfire seen through a rain of blood. But Lord Mounteagle rolled it loosely in his palm without looking at it; and staring at the ceiling, told them a long tale about the legendary character of Mount Meru, and how in the Gnostic mythology it had been the place of the wrestling of nameless primeval powers.

Towards the end of the lecture on the Demiurge of the Gnostics (not forgetting its connexion with the parallel concept of Manichæus) even the tactful Mr Hardcastle thought it time to create a diversion. He asked to be allowed to look at the stone; and as evening was closing in, and the long room with its single door was steadily darkening, he stepped out in the cloister beyond, to examine the jewel by a better light. It was then that they first became conscious, slowly and almost creepily conscious, of the living presence of the Master of the Mountain.

The cloister was on the usual plan, as regards its original structure; but the line of Gothic pillars and pointed arches that formed the inner square was linked together all along by a low wall, about waist high, turning the Gothic doors into Gothic windows and giving each a sort of flat window-sill of stone. This alteration was probably of ancient date; but there were other alterations of a quainter sort, which witnessed to the rather unusual individual ideas of Lord and Lady Mounteagle. Between the pillars hung thin curtains, or rather veils, made of beads or light canes, in a continental or southern manner; and on these again could be traced the lines and colours of Asiatic dragons or idols, that contrasted with the grey Gothic framework in which they were suspended. But this, while it further troubled the dying light of the place, was the least of the incongruities of which the company, with very varying feelings, became aware.

In the open space surrounded by the cloisters, there ran, like a circle in a square, a circular path paved with pale stones and edged with some sort of green enamel like an imitation lawn. Inside that, in the very centre, rose the basin of a dark green fountain, or raised pond, in which water-lilies floated and goldfish flashed to and fro; and high above these, its outline dark against the dying light, was a great green image. Its back was turned to them and its face so completely invisible in the hunched posture that the statue might almost have been headless. But in that mere dark outline in the dim twilight, some of them could see instantly that it was the shape of no Christian thing.

A few yards away, on the circular path, and looking towards the great green god, stood the man called the Master of the Mountain. His pointed and finely finished features seemed moulded by some skilful craftsman as a mask of copper. In contrast with this, his dark grey beard looked almost blue like indigo; it began in a narrow tuft on his chin, and then spread outwards like a great fan or the tail of a bird. He was robed in peacock green and wore on his bald head a high cap of uncommon outline: a head-dress none of them had ever seen before; but it looked rather Egyptian than Indian. The man was standing with staring eyes: wide open, fish-shaped eyes, so motionless that they looked like the eyes painted on a mummy-case. But though the figure of the Master of the Mountain was singular enough, some of the company, including Father Brown, did not look at him; they still looked at the dark green idol at which he himself was looking.

'This seems a queer thing,' said Hardcastle, frowning a little, 'to set up in the middle of an old abbey cloister.'

'Now, don't tell me you're going to be silly,' said Lady Mounteagle. 'That's just what we meant; to link up the great religions of

East and West; Buddha and Christ. Surely you must understand that all religions are really the same.'

'If they are,' said Father Brown mildly, 'it seems rather unnecessary to go into the middle of Asia to get one.'

'Lady Mounteagle means that they are different aspects or facets, as there are of this stone,' began Hardcastle; and becoming interested in the new topic, laid the great ruby down on the stone sill or ledge under the Gothic arch. 'But it does not follow that we can mix the aspects in one artistic style. You may mix Christianity and Islam, but you can't mix Gothic and Saracenic, let alone real Indian.'

As he spoke, the Master of the Mountain seemed to come to life like a cataleptic, and moved gravely round another quarter segment of the circle, and took up his position outside their own row of arches, standing with his back to them and looking now towards the idol's back. It was obvious that he was moving by stages round the whole circle, like a hand round a clock; but pausing for prayer or contemplation.

'What *is* his religion?' asked Hardcastle, with a faint touch of impatience.

'He says,' replied Lord Mounteagle, reverently, 'that it is older than Brahminism and purer than Buddhism.'

'Oh,' said Hardcastle, and continued to stare through his single eyeglass, standing with both his hands in his pockets.

'They say,' observed the nobleman in his gentle but didactic voice, 'that the deity called the God of Gods is carved in a colossal form in the cavern of Mount Meru

Even his lordship's lecturing serenity was broken abruptly by the voice that came over his shoulder. It came out of the darkness of the museum they had just left, when they stepped out into the cloister. At the sound of it the two younger men looked first incredulous, then furious, and then almost collapsed into laughter.

'I hope I do not intrude,' said the urbane and seductive voice of Professor Phroso, that unconquerable wrestler for the truth, 'but it occurred to me that some of you might spare a little time for that much despised science of Bumps, which—'

'Look here,' cried the impetuous Tommy Hunter, 'I haven't got any bumps; but you'll jolly well have some soon, you—'

Hardcastle mildly restrained him as he plunged back through

the door; and for the moment all the group had turned again and were looking back into the inner room.

It was at that moment that the thing happened. It was the impetuous Tommy, once more, who was the first to move, and this time to better effect. Before anyone else had seen anything, when Hardcastle had barely remembered with a jump that he had left the gem on the stone sill, Tommy was across the cloister with the leap of a cat and, leaning with his head and shoulders out of the aperture between two columns, had cried out in a voice that rang down all the arches, 'I've got him!'

In that instant of time, just after they turned, and just before they heard his triumphant cry, they had all seen it happen. Round the corner of one of the two columns, there had darted in and out again a brown or rather bronze-coloured hand, the colour of dead gold; such as they had seen elsewhere. The hand had struck as straight as a striking snake; as instantaneous as the flick of the long tongue of an ant-eater. But it had licked up the jewel. The stone slab of the window-sill shone bare in the pale and fading light.

'I've got him,' gasped Tommy Hunter; 'but he's wriggling pretty hard. You fellows run round him in front – he can't have got rid of it, anyhow.'

The others obeyed, some racing down the corridor and some leaping over the low wall, with the result that a little crowd, consisting of Hardcastle, Lord Mounteagle, Father Brown, and even the undetachable Mr Phroso of the bumps, had soon surrounded the captive Master of the Mountain, whom Hunter was hanging on to desperately by the collar with one hand, and shaking every now and then in a manner highly insensible to the dignity of Prophets as a class.

'Now we've got him, anyhow,' said Hunter, letting go with a sigh. 'We've only got to search him. The thing must be here.'

Three-quarters of an hour later, Hunter and Hardcastle, their top-hats, ties, gloves, slips and spats somewhat the worse for their recent activities, came face to face in the cloister and gazed at each other.

'Well,' asked Hardcastle with restraint, 'have you any views on the mystery?'

'Hang it all,' replied Hunter, 'you can't call it a mystery. Why, we all saw him take it ourselves.'

'Yes,' replied the other, 'but we didn't all see him lose it ourselves. And the mystery is, where has he lost it so that we can't
find it?'

'It must be somewhere,' said Hunter. 'Have you searched the
fountain and all round that rotten old god there?'

'I haven't dissected the little fishes,' said Hardcastle, lifting his
eyeglass and surveying the other. 'Are you thinking of the ring of
Polycrates?'

Apparently the survey, through the eyeglass, of the round face
before him, convinced him that it covered no such meditation on
Greek legend.

'It's not on him, I admit,' repeated Hunter, suddenly, 'unless he's
swallowed it.'

'Are we to dissect the Prophet, too?' asked the other smiling. 'But
here comes our host.'

'This is a most distressing matter,' said Lord Mounteagle, twisting his white moustache with a nervous and even tremulous hand.
'Horrible thing to have a theft in one's house, let alone connecting
it with a man like the Master. But, I confess, I can't quite make
head or tail of the way in which he is talking about it. I wish you'd
come inside and see what you think.'

They went in together, Hunter falling behind and dropping into
conversation with Father Brown, who was kicking his heels round
the cloister.

'You must be very strong,' said the priest pleasantly. 'You held
him with one hand; and he seemed pretty vigorous, even when we
had eight hands to hold him, like one of those Indian gods.'

They took a turn or two round the cloister, talking; and then they
also went into the inner room, where the Master of the Mountain
was seated on a bench, in the capacity of a captive, but with more
of the air of a king.

It was true, as Lord Mounteagle said, that his air and tone were
not very easy to understand. He spoke with a serene, and yet secretive sense of power. He seemed rather amused at their suggestions
about trivial hiding-places for the gem; and certainly he showed
no resentment whatever. He seemed to be laughing, in a still unfathomable fashion, at their efforts to trace what they had all seen
him take.

'You are learning a little,' he said, with insolent benevolence, 'of the laws of time and space; about which your latest science is a thousand years behind our oldest religion. You do not even know what is really meant by hiding a thing. Nay, my poor little friends, you do not even know what is meant by *seeing* a thing; or perhaps you would see this as plainly as I do.'

'Do you mean it is here?' demanded Hardcastle harshly.

'Here is a word of many meanings, also,' replied the mystic. 'But I did not say it was here. I only said I could see it.'

There was an irritated silence, and he went on sleepily.

'If you were to be utterly, unfathomably, silent, do you think you might hear a cry from the other end of the world? The cry of a worshipper alone in those mountains, where the original image sits, itself like a mountain. Some say that even Jews and Moslems might worship that image; because it was never made by man. Hark! Do you hear the cry with which he lifts his head and sees, in that socket of stone that has been hollow for ages, the one red and angry moon that is the eye of the mountain?'

'Do you really mean,' cried Lord Mounteagle, a little shaken, 'that you could make it pass from here to Mount Meru? I used to believe you had great spiritual powers, but—'

'Perhaps,' said the Master, 'I have more than you will ever believe.'

Hardcastle rose impatiently and began to pace the room with his hands in his pockets.

'I never believed so much as you did; but I admit that powers of a certain type may . . . Good God!'

His high, hard voice had been cut off in mid-air, and he stopped staring; the eyeglass fell out of his eye. They all turned their faces in the same direction; and on every face there seemed to be the same suspended animation.

The Red Moon of Meru lay on the stone window-sill, exactly as they had last seen it. It might have been a red spark blown there from a bonfire, or a red rose petal tossed from a broken rose; but it had fallen in precisely the same spot where Hardcastle had thoughtlessly laid it down.

This time Hardcastle did not attempt to pick it up again; but his demeanour was somewhat notable. He turned slowly and began to stride about the room again; but there was in his movements something masterful, where before it had been only restless.

Finally, he brought himself to a standstill in front of the seated Master, and bowed with a somewhat sardonic smile.

'Master,' he said, 'we all owe you an apology; and, what is more important, you have taught us all a lesson. Believe me, it will serve as a lesson as well as a joke. I shall always remember the very remarkable powers you really possess, and how harmlessly you use them. Lady Mounteagle,' he went on, turning towards her, 'you will forgive me for having addressed the Master first; but it was to you I had the honour of offering this explanation some time ago. I may say that I explained it before it had happened. I told you that most of these things could be interpreted by some kind of hypnotism. Many believe that this is the explanation of all those Indian stories about the mango plant and the boy who climbs a rope thrown into the air. It does not really happen; but the spectators are mesmerized into imagining that it happened. So we were all mesmerized into imagining this theft had happened. That brown hand coming in at the window, and whisking away the gem, was a momentary delusion; a hand in a dream. Only, having seen the stone vanish, we never looked for it where it was before. We plunged into the pond and turned every leaf of the water lilies; we were almost giving emetics to the goldfish. But the ruby has been here all the time.'

And he glanced across at the opalescent eyes and smiling bearded mouth of the Master, and saw that the smile was just a shade broader. There was something in it that made the others jump to their feet with an air of sudden relaxation and general, gasping relief.

'This is a very fortunate escape for us all,' said Lord Mounteagle, smiling rather nervously. 'There cannot be the least doubt it is as you say. It has been a most painful episode and I really don't know what apologics '

'I have no complaints,' said the Master of the Mountain, still smiling. 'You have never touched Me at all.'

While the rest went off rejoicing, with Hardcastle for the hero of the hour, the little Phrenologist with the whiskers sauntered back towards his preposterous tent. Looking over his shoulder he was surprised to find Father Brown following him.

'Can I feel your bumps?' asked the expert, in his mildly sarcastic tone.

'I don't think you want to feel any more, do you?' said the priest good-humouredly. 'You're a detective, aren't you?'

'Yep,' replied the other. 'Lady Mounteagle asked me to keep an eye on the Master, being no fool, for all her mysticism; and when he left his tent, I could only follow by behaving like a nuisance and a monomaniac. If anybody had come into my tent, I'd have had to look up Bumps in an encyclopaedia.'

'Bumps, What Ho She; see Folk-Lore,' observed Father Brown, dreamily. 'Well, you were quite in the part in pestering people – at a bazaar.'

'Rum case, wasn't it?' remarked the fallacious Phrenologist. 'Queer to think the thing was there all the time.'

'Very queer,' said the priest.

Something in his voice made the other man stop and stare.

'Look here!' he cried. 'What's the matter with you? What are you looking like that for? Don't you *believe* that it was there all the time?'

Father Brown blinked, rather as if he had received a buffet; then he said slowly and with hesitation, 'No ... the fact is ... I can't – I can't quite bring myself to believe it.'

'You're not the sort of chap,' said the other shrewdly, 'who'd say that without reason. Why don't you think the ruby had been there all the time?'

'Only because I put it back myself,' said Father Brown.

The other man stood rooted to the spot, like one whose hair was standing on end. He opened his mouth without speech.

'Or rather,' went on the priest, 'I persuaded the thief to let me put it back. I told him what I'd guessed and showed him there was still time for repentance. I don't mind telling you in professional confidence; besides, I don't think the Mounteagles would prosecute, now they've got the thing back, especially considering who stole it.'

'Do you mean the Master?' asked the late Phroso.

'No,' said Father Brown, 'the Master didn't steal it.'

'But I don't understand,' objected the other. 'Nobody was outside the window except the Master; and a hand certainly came from outside.'

'The hand came from outside, but the thief came from the inside,' said Father Brown.

'We seem to be back among the mystics again. Look here, I'm

a practical man; I only wanted to know if it is all right with the ruby—'

'I knew it was all wrong,' said Father Brown, 'before I even knew there was a ruby.'

After a pause he went on thoughtfully. 'Right away back in that argument of theirs, by the tents, I knew things were going wrong. People will tell you that theories don't matter and that logic and philosophy aren't practical. Don't you believe them. Reason is from God, and when things are unreasonable there is something the matter. Now, that quite abstract argument ended with something funny. Consider what the theories were. Hardcastle was a trifle superior and said that all things were perfectly possible; but they were mostly done merely by mesmerism, or clairvoyance; scientific names for philosophical puzzles, in the usual style. But Hunter thought it all sheer fraud and wanted to show it up. By Lady Mounteagle's testimony, he not only went about showing up fortune-tellers and such like, but he had actually come down specially to confront this one. He didn't often come; he didn't get on with Mounteagle, from whom, being a spendthrift, he always tried to borrow; but when he heard the Master was coming, he came hurrying down. Very well. In spite of that, it was Hardcastle who went to consult the wizard and Hunter who refused. He said he'd waste no time on such nonsense; having apparently wasted a lot of his life on proving it to be nonsense. That seems inconsistent. He thought in this case it was crystal-gazing; but he found it was palmistry.'

'Do you mean he made that an excuse?' asked his companion, puzzled.

'I thought so at first,' replied the priest, 'but I know now it was not an excuse, but a reason. He really was put off by finding it was a palmist, because—'

'Well,' demanded the other impatiently.

'Because he didn't want to take his glove off,' said Father Brown.

'Take his glove off?' repeated the inquirer.

'If he had,' said Father Brown mildly, 'we should all have seen that his hand was painted pale brown already. . . . Oh, yes, he did come down specially because the Master was here. He came down very fully prepared.'

'You mean,' cried Phroso, 'that it was Hunter's hand, painted brown, that came in at the window? Why, he was with us all the time!'

'Go and try it on the spot and you'll find it's quite possible,' said the priest. 'Hunter leapt forward and leaned out of the window; in a flash he could tear off his glove, tuck up his sleeve, and thrust his hand back round the other side of the pillar, while he gripped the Indian with the other hand and hallooed out that he'd caught the thief. I remarked at the time that he held the thief with one hand, where any sane man would have used two. But the other hand was slipping the jewel into his trouser pocket.'

There was a long pause and then the ex-Phrenologist said slowly, 'Well, that's a staggerer. But the thing stumps me still. For one thing, it doesn't explain the queer behaviour of the old magician himself. If he was entirely innocent, why the devil didn't he say so? Why wasn't he indignant at being accused and searched? Why did he only sit smiling and hinting in a sly way what wild and wonderful things he could do?'

'Ah!' cried Father Brown, with a sharp note in his voice: 'there you come up against it! Against everything these people don't and won't understand. All religions are the same, says Lady Mounteagle. Are they, by George! I tell you some of them are so different that the best man of one creed will be callous, where the worst man of another will be sensitive. I told you I didn't like spiritual power, because the accent is on the word power. I don't say the Master would steal a ruby; very likely he wouldn't; very likely he wouldn't think it worth stealing. It wouldn't be specially his temptation to take jewels; but it would be his temptation to take credit for miracles that didn't belong to him any more than the jewels. It was to *that* sort of temptation, to *that* sort of stealing that he yielded today. He liked us to think that he had marvellous mental powers that could make a material object fly through space; and even when he hadn't done it, he allowed us to think he had. The point about private property wouldn't occur primarily to him at all. The question wouldn't present itself in the form, "Shall I *steal* this pebble?" but only in the form, "Could I make a pebble vanish and reappear on a distant mountain?" The question of *whose* pebble would strike him as irrelevant. That is what I mean by religions being different. He is very proud of having what he calls spiritual powers. But what he calls spiritual doesn't mean what we call moral. It means rather

mental; the power of the mind over matter; the magician control-
ling the elements. Now we are not like that, even when we are no
better; even when we are worse. We, whose fathers at least were
Christians, who have grown up under those mediaeval arches even
if we bedizen them with all the demons of Asia – we have the very
opposite ambition and the very opposite shame. We should all
be anxious that nobody should think we had done it. He was actually anxious that everybody should think he had – even when he
hadn't. He actually stole the credit of stealing. While we were all
casting the crime from us like a snake, he was actually luring it to
him like a snake-charmer. But snakes are not pets in this country!
Here the traditions of Christendom tell at once under a test like
this. Look at old Mounteagle himself, for instance! Ah, you may be
as Eastern and esoteric as you like, and wear a turban and a long
robe and live on messages from Mahatmas; but if a bit of stone is
stolen in your house, and your friends are suspected, you will jolly
soon find out that you're an ordinary English gentleman in a fuss.
The man who really did it would never want us to think he did it,
for he also was an English gentleman. He was also something very
much better; he was a Christian thief. I hope and believe he was a
penitent thief.'

'By your account,' said his companion laughing, 'the Christian
thief and the heathen fraud went by contraries. One was sorry he'd
done it and the other was sorry he hadn't.'

'We mustn't be too hard on either of them,' said Father Brown.
'Other English gentlemen have stolen before now, and been
covered by legal and political protection; and the West also has
its own way of covering theft with sophistry. After all, the ruby is
not the only kind of valuable stone in the world that has changed
owners; it is true of other precious stones; often carved like cameos
and coloured like flowers.'

The other looked at him inquiringly; and the priest's finger was
pointed to the Gothic outline of the great Abbey.

'A great graven stone,' he said, 'and that was also stolen.'

THE CHIEF MOURNER OF MARNE

A BLAZE of lightning blanched the grey woods, tracing all the wrinkled foliage down to the last curled leaf, as if every detail were drawn in silver-point or graven in silver. The same strange trick of lightning by which it seems to record millions of minute things in an instant of time, picked out everything, from the elegant litter of the picnic spread under the spreading tree to the pale lengths of winding road, at the end of which a white car was waiting. In the distance a melancholy mansion with four towers like a castle, which in the grey evening had been but a dim and distant huddle of walls like a crumbling cloud, seemed to spring into the foreground, and stood up with all its embattled roofs and blank and staring windows. And in this, at least, the light had something in it of revelation. For to some of those grouped under the tree that castle was, indeed, a thing faded and almost forgotten, which was to prove its power to spring up again in the foreground of their lives.

The light also clothed for an instant, in the same silver splendour, at least one human figure that stood up as motionless as one of the towers. It was that of a tall man standing on a rise of ground above the rest, who were mostly sitting on the grass or stooping to gather up the hamper and crockery. He wore a picturesque short cloak or cape clasped with a silver clasp and chain, which blazed like a star when the flash touched it; and something metallic in his motionless figure was emphasized by the fact that his closely curled hair was of the burnished yellow that can be really called gold; and had the look of being younger than his face, which was handsome in a hard aquiline fashion, but looked, under the strong light, a little wrinkled and withered. Possibly it had suffered from wearing a mask of make-up, for Hugo Romaine was the greatest actor of his day. For that instant of illumination the golden curls and ivory mask and silver ornament made his figure gleam like that of a man in armour; the next instant his figure was a dark and even black silhouette against the sickly grey of the rainy evening sky.

But there was something about its stillness, like that of a statue, that distinguished it from the group at his feet. All the other figures around him had made the ordinary involuntary movement at the unexpected shock of light; for though the skies were rainy it was the first flash of the storm. The only lady present, whose air of carrying grey hair gracefully, as if she were really proud of it, marked her a matron of the United States, unaffectedly shut her eyes and uttered a sharp cry. Her English husband, General Outram, a very stolid Anglo-Indian with a bald head and black moustache and whiskers of antiquated pattern, looked up with one stiff movement and then resumed his occupation of tidying up. A young man of the name of Mallow, very big and shy, with brown eyes like a dog's, dropped a cup and apologized awkwardly. A third man, much more dressy, with a resolute head, like an inquisitive terrier's, and grey hair brushed stiffly back, was no other than the great newspaper proprietor, Sir John Cockspur; he cursed freely, but not in an English idiom or accent, for he came from Toronto. But the tall man in the short cloak stood up literally like a statue in the twilight; his eagle face under the full glare had been like the bust of a Roman Emperor, and the carved eyelids had not moved.

A moment after, the dark dome cracked across with thunder, and the statue seemed to come to life. He turned his head over his shoulder and said casually:

'About a minute and a half between the flash and the bang, but I think the storm's coming nearer. A tree is not supposed to be a good umbrella for the lightning, but we shall want it soon for the rain. I think it will be a deluge.'

The young man glanced at the lady a little anxiously and said: 'Can't we get shelter anywhere? There seems to be a house over there.'

'There is a house over there,' remarked the general, rather grimly; 'but not quite what you'd call a hospitable hotel.'

'It's curious,' said his wife sadly, 'that we should be caught in a storm with no house near but that one, of all others.'

Something in her tone seemed to check the younger man, who was both sensitive and comprehending; but nothing of that sort daunted the man from Toronto.

'Why, what's the matter with it?' he asked. 'Looks rather like a ruin.'

'That place,' said the general dryly, 'belongs to the Marquis of Marne.'

'Gee!' said Sir John Cockspur. 'I've heard all about that bird, anyhow; and a queer bird, too. Ran him as a front-page mystery in the *Comet* last year. "The Nobleman Nobody Knows".'

'Yes, I've heard of him, too,' said young Mallow in a low voice. 'There seem to be all sorts of weird stories about why he hides himself like that. I've heard that he wears a mask because he's a leper. But somebody else told me quite seriously that there's a curse on the family; a child born with some frightful deformity that's kept in a dark room.'

'The Marquis of Marne has three heads,' remarked Romaine gravely. 'Once in every three hundred years a three-headed nobleman adorns the family tree. No human being dares approach the accursed house except a silent procession of hatters, sent to provide an abnormal number of hats. But' – and his voice took one of those deep and terrible turns, that could cause such a thrill in the theatre – 'my friends, *those hats are of no human shape.*'

The American lady looked at him with a frown and a slight air of distrust, as if that trick of voice had moved her in spite of herself.

'I don't like your ghoulish jokes,' she said; 'and I'd rather you didn't joke about this, anyhow.'

'I hear and obey,' replied the actor; 'but am I, like the Light Brigade, forbidden even to reason why?'

'The reason,' she replied, 'is that he isn't the Nobleman Nobody Knows. I know him myself, or, at least, I knew him very well when he was an attaché at Washington thirty years ago, when we were all young. And he didn't wear a mask, at least, he didn't wear it with me. He wasn't a leper, though he may be almost as lonely. And he had only one head and only one heart, and that was broken.'

'Unfortunate love affair, of course,' said Cockspur. 'I should like that for the *Comet.*'

'I suppose it's a compliment to us,' she replied thoughtfully, 'that you always assume a man's heart is broken by a woman. But there are other kinds of love and bereavement. Have you never read "In Memoriam"? Have you never heard of David and Jonathan? What broke poor Marne up was the death of his brother; at least, he was really a first cousin, but had been brought up with him like a brother, and was much nearer than most brothers. James Mair, as the marquis was called when I knew him, was the elder of the two, but he always played the part of worshipper, with Maurice Mair as a god. And by his account, Maurice Mair was certainly a wonder. James was no fool and very good at his own political job; but it seems that Maurice could do that and everything else; that he was a brilliant artist and amateur actor and musician, and all the rest of it. James was very good-looking himself, long and strong and strenuous, with a high-bridged nose; though I suppose the young people would think he looked very quaint with his beard divided into two bushy whiskers in the fashion of those Victorian times. But Maurice was clean-shaven, and, by the portraits shown to me, certainly quite beautiful; though he looked a little more like a tenor than a gentleman ought to look. James was always asking me again and again whether his friend was not a marvel, whether any woman wouldn't fall in love with him, and so on, until it became rather a bore, except that it turned so suddenly into a tragedy. His whole life seemed to be in that idolatry; and one day the idol tumbled down, and was broken like any china doll. A chill caught at the seaside, and it was all over.'

'And after that,' asked the young man, 'did he shut himself up like this?'

'He went abroad at first,' she answered; 'away to Asia and the Cannibal Islands and Lord knows where. These deadly strokes take different people in different ways. It took him in the way of an utter sundering or severance from everything, even from tradition and as far as possible from memory. He could not bear a reference to the old tie; a portrait or an anecdote or even an association. He couldn't bear the business of a great public funeral. He longed to get away. He stayed away for ten years. I heard some rumour that he had begun to revive a little at the end of the exile; but when he came back to his own home he relapsed completely. He settled down into religious melancholia, and that's practically madness.'

'The priests got hold of him, they say,' grumbled the old general. 'I know he gave thousands to found a monastery, and lives himself rather like a monk – or, at any rate, a hermit. Can't understand what good they think that will do.'

'Goddarned superstition,' snorted Cockspur; 'that sort of thing ought to be shown up. Here's a man that might have been useful to the Empire and the world, and these vampires get hold of him and suck him dry. I bet with their unnatural notions they haven't even let him marry.'

'No, he has never married,' said the lady. 'He was engaged when I knew him, as a matter of fact, but I don't think it ever came first with him, and I think it went with the rest when everything else went. Like Hamlet and Ophelia – he lost hold of love because he lost hold of life. But I knew the girl; indeed, I know her still. Between ourselves, it was Viola Grayson, daughter of the old admiral. She's never married, either.'

'It's infamous! It's infernal!' cried Sir John, bounding up. 'It's not only a tragedy, but a crime. I've got a duty to the public, and I mean to see all this nonsensical nightmare ... in the twentieth century—'

He was almost choked with his own protest, and then, after a silence, the old soldier said:

'Well, I don't profess to know much about those things, but I think these religious people need to study a text which says, "Let the dead bury their dead." '

'Only, unfortunately, that's just what it looks like,' said his wife with a sigh. 'It's just like some creepy story of a dead man burying another dead man, over and over again for ever.'

'The storm has passed over us,' said Romaine, with a rather inscrutable smile. 'You will not have to visit the inhospitable house after all.'

She suddenly shuddered.

'Oh, I'll never do that again!' she exclaimed.

Mallow was staring at her.

'Again! Have you tried it before?' he cried.

'Well, I did once,' she said, with a lightness not without a touch of pride, 'but we needn't go back on all that. It's not raining now, but I think we'd better be moving back to the car.'

As they moved off in procession, Mallow and the general brought up the rear; and the latter said abruptly, lowering his voice:

'I don't want that little cad Cockspur to hear, but as you've asked you'd better know. It's the one thing I can't forgive Marne; but I suppose these monks have drilled him that way. My wife, who had been the best friend he ever had in America, actually came to that house when he was walking in the garden. He was looking at the ground like a monk, and hidden in a black hood that was really as ridiculous as any mask. She had sent her card in, and stood there in his very path. And he walked past her without a word or a glance, as if she had been a stone. He wasn't human; he was like some horrible automaton. She may well call him a dead man.'

'It's all very strange,' said the young man rather vaguely. 'It isn't like – like what I should have expected.'

Young Mr Mallow, when he left that rather dismal picnic, took himself thoughtfully in search of a friend. He did not know any monks, but he knew one priest, whom he was very much concerned to confront with the curious revelations he had heard that afternoon. He felt he would very much like to know the truth about the cruel superstition that hung over the house of Marne, like the black thundercloud he had seen hovering over it.

After being referred from one place to another, he finally ran his friend Father Brown to earth in the house of another friend, a Roman Catholic friend with a large family. He entered somewhat abruptly to find Father Brown sitting on the floor with a serious expression, and attempting to pin the somewhat florid hat belonging to a wax doll on to the head of a teddy bear.

Mallow felt a faint sense of incongruity; but he was far too full of his problem to put off the conversation if he could help it. He was staggering from a sort of set-back in a subconscious process that had been going on for some time. He poured out the whole tragedy of the house of Marne as he had heard it from the general's wife, along with most of the comments of the general and the newspaper proprietor. A new atmosphere of attention seemed to be created with the mention of the newspaper proprietor.

Father Brown neither knew nor cared that his attitudes were comic or commonplace. He continued to sit on the floor, where his large head and short legs made him look very like a baby playing with toys. But there came into his great grey eyes a certain expression that has been seen in the eyes of many men in many centuries through the story of nineteen hundred years; only the men were not generally sitting on floors, but at council tables, or on the seats of chapters or the thrones of bishops and cardinals; a far-off watchful look, heavy with the humility of a charge too great for men. Something of that anxious and far-reaching look is found in the eyes of sailors and of those who have steered through so many storms the ship of St Peter.

'It's very good of you to tell me this,' he said. 'I'm really awfully grateful, for we may have to do something about it. If it were only people like you and the general, it might be only a private matter; but if Sir John Cockspur is going to spread some sort of scare in his papers – well, he's a Toronto Orangeman, and we can hardly keep out of it.'

'But what will you say about it?' asked Mallow anxiously.

'The first thing I should say about it,' said Father Brown, 'is that, as you tell it, it doesn't sound like life. Suppose, for the sake of argument, that we are all pessimistic vampires blighting all human happiness. Suppose I'm a pessimistic vampire.' He scratched his nose with the teddy bear, became faintly conscious of the incongruity, and put it down. 'Suppose we do destroy all human and family ties. Why should we entangle a man again in an old family tie just when he showed signs of getting loose from it? Surely it's a little unfair to charge us both with crushing such affection and encouraging such infatuation. I don't see why even a religious maniac should be that particular sort of monomaniac, or how religion could increase that mania, except by brightening it with a little hope.'

Then he said, after a pause: 'I should like to talk to that general of yours.'

'It was his wife who told me,' said Mallow.

'Yes,' replied the other, 'but I'm more interested in what he didn't tell you than in what she did.'

'You think he knows more than she does?'

'I think he knows more than she says,' answered Father Brown. 'You tell me he used a phrase about forgiving everything except the rudeness to his wife. After all, what else was there to forgive?'

Father Brown had risen and shaken his shapeless clothes, and stood looking at the young man with screwed up eyes and a slightly quizzical expression. The next moment he had turned, and picking up his equally shapeless umbrella and large shabby hat, went stumping down the street.

He plodded through a variety of wide streets and squares till he came to a handsome old-fashioned house in the West End, where he asked the servant if he could see General Outram. After some little palaver he was shown into a study, fitted out less with books than with maps and globes, where the bald-headed, black-whiskered Anglo-Indian sat smoking a long, thin, black cigar and playing with pins on a chart.

'I am sorry to intrude,' said the priest, 'and all the more because I can't help the intrusion looking like interference. I want to speak to you about a private matter, but only in the hope of keeping it private. Unfortunately, some people are likely to make it public. I think, general, that you know Sir John Cockspur.'

The mass of black moustache and whisker served as a sort of mask for the lower half of the old general's face; it was always hard to see whether he smiled, but his brown eyes often had a certain twinkle.

'Everybody knows him, I suppose,' he said. 'I don't know him very well.'

'Well, you know everybody knows whatever he knows,' said Father Brown, smiling, 'when he thinks it convenient to print it. And I understand from my friend Mr Mallow, whom, I think, you know, that Sir John is going to print some scorching anti-clerical articles founded on what he would call the Marne Mystery. "Monks Drive Marquis Mad" etc.'

'If he is,' replied the general, 'I don't see why you should come to me about it. I ought to tell you I'm a strong Protestant.'

'I'm very fond of strong Protestants,' said Father Brown. 'I came to you because I was sure you would tell the truth. I hope it is not uncharitable to feel less sure of Sir John Cockspur.'

The brown eyes twinkled again, but the general said nothing.

'General,' said Father Brown, 'suppose Cockspur or his sort were going to make the world ring with tales against your country and your flag. Suppose he said your regiment ran away in battle or your staff were in the pay of the enemy. Would you let anything stand between you and the facts that would refute him? Wouldn't you get on the track of the truth at all costs to anybody? Well, I have a regiment, and I belong to an army. It is being discredited by what I am certain is a fictitious story; but I don't know the true story. Can you blame me for trying to find it out?'

The soldier was silent, and the priest continued:

'I have heard the story Mallow was told yesterday, about Marne retiring with a broken heart through the death of his more than brother. I am sure there was more in it than that. I came to ask you if you know any more.'

'No,' said the general shortly; 'I cannot tell you any more.'

'General,' said Father Brown with a broad grin, 'you would have called me a Jesuit if I had used that equivocation.'

The soldier laughed gruffly, and then growled with much greater hostility.

'Well, I won't tell you, then,' he said. 'What do you say to that?'

'I only say,' said the priest mildly, 'that in that case I shall have to tell you.'

The brown eyes stared at him; but there was no twinkle in them now. He went on:

'You compel me to state, less sympathetically perhaps than you could, why it is obvious that there is more behind. I am quite sure the marquis has better cause for his brooding and secretiveness than merely having lost an old friend. I doubt whether priests have anything to do with it; I don't even know if he's a convert or merely a man comforting his conscience with charities; but I'm sure he's something more than a chief mourner. Since you insist, I will tell you one or two of the things that made me think so.

'First, it was stated that James Mair was engaged to be married, but somehow became unattached again after the death of Maurice Mair. Why should an honourable man break off his engagement merely because he was depressed by the death of a third party? He's much more likely to have turned for consolation to it; but, anyhow, he was bound in decency to go through with it.'

The general was biting his black moustache, and his brown eyes had become very watchful and even anxious; but he did not answer.

'A second point,' said Father Brown, frowning at the table. 'James Mair was always asking his lady friend whether his cousin Maurice was not very fascinating, and whether women would not admire him. I don't know if it occurred to the lady that there might be another meaning to that inquiry.'

The general got to his feet and began to walk or stamp about the room.

'Oh, damn it all,' he said, but without any air of animosity.

'The third point,' went on Father Brown, 'is James Mair's curious manner of mourning – destroying all relics, veiling all portraits, and so on. It does sometimes happen, I admit; it might mean mere affectionate bereavement. But it might mean something else.'

'Confound you,' said the other, 'how long are you going on piling this up?'

'The fourth and fifth points are pretty conclusive,' said the priest calmly, 'especially if you take them together. The first is that Maurice Mair seems to have had no funeral in particular, considering he was a cadet of a great family. He must have been buried hurriedly; perhaps secretly. And the last point is that James Mair instantly disappeared to foreign parts; fled, in fact, to the ends of the earth.

'And so,' he went on, still in the same soft voice, 'when you would blacken my religion to brighten the story of the pure and perfect affection of two brothers, it seems—'

'Stop!' cried Outram in a tone like a pistol shot. 'I must tell you more, or you will fancy worse. Let me tell you one thing to start with. It was a fair fight.'

'Ah,' said Father Brown, and seemed to exhale a huge breath.

'It was a duel,' said the other. 'It was probably the last duel fought in England, and it is long ago now.'

'That's better,' said Father Brown. 'Thank God; that's a great deal better.'

'Better than the ugly things you thought of, I suppose?' said the general gruffly. 'Well, it's all very well for you to sneer at the pure and perfect affection; but it was true for all that. James Mair really was devoted to his cousin, who'd grown up with him like a younger brother. Elder brothers and sisters do sometimes devote themselves to a child like that, especially when he's a sort of infant phenomenon. But James Mair was the sort of simple character in whom even hate is in a sense unselfish. I mean that even when his tenderness turns to rage it is still objective, directed outwards to its object; he isn't conscious of himself. Now poor Maurice Mair was just the opposite. He was far more friendly and popular; but his success had made him live in a house of mirrors. He was first in every sort of sport and art and accomplishment; he nearly always won and took his winning amiably. But if ever by any chance he lost, there was just a glimpse of something not so amiable; he was a little jealous. I needn't tell you the whole miserable story of how he was a little jealous of his cousin's engagement; how he couldn't keep his restless vanity from interfering. It's enough to say that one of the few things in which James Mair was admittedly ahead of him was marksmanship with a pistol; and with that the tragedy ended.'

'You mean the tragedy began,' replied the priest. 'The tragedy of the survivor. I thought he did not need any monkish vampires to make him miserable.'

'To my mind he's more miserable than he need be,' said the general. 'After all, as I say, it was a ghastly tragedy, but it was a fair fight. And Jim had great provocation.'

'How do you know all this?' asked the priest.

'I know it because I saw it,' answered Outram stolidly. 'I was James Mair's second, and I saw Maurice Mair shot dead on the sands before my very eyes.'

'I wish you would tell me more about it,' said Father Brown reflectively. 'Who was Maurice Mair's second?'

'He had a more distinguished backing,' replied the general grimly. 'Hugo Romaine was his second; the great actor, you know. Maurice was mad on acting and had taken up Romaine (who was then a rising but still a struggling man), and financed the fellow and his ventures in return for taking lessons from the professional in his own hobby of amateur acting. But Romaine was then, I suppose, practically dependent on his rich friend, though he's richer now than any aristocrat. So his serving as second proves very little about what he thought of the quarrel. They fought in the English fashion, with only one second apiece; I wanted at least to have a surgeon, but Maurice boisterously refused it, saying the fewer people who knew, the better, and at the worst we could immediately get help. "There's a doctor in the village not half a mile away," he said; "I know him and he's got the fastest horse in the country. He could be brought here in no time; but there's no need to bring him here till we know." Well we all knew that Maurice ran most risk, as the pistol was not his weapon; so when he refused aid nobody liked to ask for it. The duel was fought on a flat stretch of sand on the east coast of Scotland; and both the sight and sound of it were masked from the hamlets inland by a long rampart of sandhills patched with rank grass; probably part of the links, though in those days no Englishman had heard of golf. There was one deep, crooked cranny in the sandhills through which we came out on the sands. I can see them now; first a wide strip of dead yellow, and beyond, a narrower strip of dark red; a dark red that seemed already like the long shadow of a deed of blood.

'The thing itself seemed to happen with horrible speed; as if a whirlwind had struck the sand. With the very crack of sound Maurice Mair seemed to spin like a teetotum and pitch upon his face like a ninepin. And queerly enough, while I'd been worrying about him up to that moment, the instant he was dead all my pity was for the man who killed him; as it is to this day and hour. I knew that with that, the whole huge terrible pendulum of my friend's lifelong love would swing back; and that whatever cause others might find to pardon him, he would never pardon himself for ever and ever. And so somehow the really vivid thing, the picture that burns in my memory so that I can't forget it, is not that of the catastrophe, the smoke and the flash and the falling figure. That seemed to be all over, like the noise that wakes a man up. What I saw, what I shall always see, is poor Jim hurrying across towards his fallen friend and foe, his brown beard looking black against the ghastly pallor of his face, with its high features cut out against the sea; and the frantic gestures with which he waved me to run for the surgeon in the hamlet behind the sandhills. He had dropped his pistol as he ran; he had a glove in one hand and the loose and fluttering fingers of it seemed to elongate and emphasize his wild pantomime of pointing or hailing for help. That is the picture that really remains with me; and there is nothing else in that picture, except the striped background of sands and sea and the dark, dead body lying still as a stone and the dark figure of the dead man's second standing grim and motionless against the horizon.'

'Did Romaine stand motionless?' asked the priest. 'I should have thought he would have run even quicker towards the corpse.'

'Perhaps he did when I had left,' replied the general. 'I took in that undying picture in an instant and the next instant I had dived among the sandhills, and was far out of sight of the others. Well, poor Maurice had made a good choice in the matter of doctors; though the doctor came too late, he came quicker than I should have thought possible. This village surgeon was a very remarkable man, red-haired, irascible, but extraordinarily strong in promptitude and presence of mind. I saw him but for a flash as he leapt on his horse and went thundering away to the scene of death, leaving

me far behind. But in that flash I had so strong a sense of his personality that I wished to God he had really been called in before the
duel began; for I believe on my soul he would have prevented it
somehow. As it was, he cleaned up the mess with marvellous swiftness; long before I could trail back to the seashore on my two feet,
his impetuous practicality had managed everything; the corpse
was temporarily buried in the sandhills and the unhappy homicide
had been persuaded to do the only thing he could do – to flee for
his life. He slipped along the coast till he came to a port and
managed to get out of the country. You know the rest; poor Jim
remained abroad for many years; later, when the whole thing had
been hushed up or forgotten, he returned to his dismal castle and
automatically inherited the title. I have never seen him from that
day to this, and yet I know what is written in red letters in the
inmost darkness of his brain.'

'I understand,' said Father Brown, 'that some of you have made
efforts to see him?'

'My wife never relaxed her efforts,' said the general. 'She refuses
to admit that such a crime ought to cut a man off for ever; and
I confess I am inclined to agree with her. Eighty years before it
would have been thought quite normal; and really it was man-
slaughter rather than murder. My wife is a great friend of the unfortunate lady who was the occasion of the quarrel; and she has an
idea that if Jim would consent to see Viola Grayson once again,
and receive her assurance that old quarrels are buried, it might
restore his sanity. My wife is calling a sort of council of old friends
tomorrow, I believe. She is very energetic.'

Father Brown was playing with the pins that lay beside the
general's map; he seemed to listen rather absent-mindedly. He had
the sort of mind that sees things in pictures; and the picture which
had coloured even the prosaic mind of the practical soldier took
on tints yet more significant and sinister in the more mystical mind
of the priest. He saw the dark red desolation of sand, the very hue
of Aceldama, and the dead man lying in a dark heap, and the
slayer, stooping as he ran, gesticulating with a glove in demented
remorse, and always his imagination came back to the third thing
that he could not yet fit into any human picture: the second of the
slain man standing motionless and mysterious, like a dark statue
on the edge of the sea. It might seem to some a detail; but for

him it was that stiff figure that stood up like a standing note of interrogation.

Why had not Romaine moved instantly? It was the natural thing for a second to do, in common humanity, let alone friendship. Even if there were some double dealing or darker motive not yet understood, one would think it would be done for the sake of appearances. Anyhow, when the thing was all over, it would be natural for the second to stir long before the other second had vanished beyond the sandhills.

'Does this man Romaine move very slowly?' he asked.

'It's queer you should ask that,' answered Outram, with a sharp glance. 'No, as a matter of fact he moves very quickly when he moves at all. But, curiously enough, I was just thinking that only this afternoon I saw him stand exactly like that, during the thunderstorm. He stood in that silver-clasped cape of his, and with one hand on his hip, exactly in every line as he stood on those bloody sands long ago. The lightning blinded us all, but he did not blink. When it was dark again he was standing there still.'

'I suppose he isn't standing there now?' inquired Father Brown. 'I mean, I suppose he moved sometime?'

'No, he moved quite sharply when the thunder came,' replied the other. 'He seemed to have been waiting for it, for he told us the exact time of the interval ... is anything the matter?'

'I've pricked myself with one of your pins,' said Father Brown. 'I hope I haven't damaged it.' But his eyes had snapped and his mouth abruptly shut.

'Are you ill?' inquired the general, staring at him.

'No,' answered the priest, 'I'm only not quite so stoical as your friend Romaine. I can't help blinking when I see light.'

He turned to gather up his hat and umbrella; but when he had got to the door he seemed to remember something and turned back. Coming up close to Outram, he gazed up into his face with a rather helpless expression, as of a dying fish, and made a motion as if to hold him by the waistcoat.

'General,' he almost whispered, 'for God's sake don't let your wife and that other woman insist on seeing Marne again. Let sleeping dogs lie, or you'll unleash all the hounds of hell.'

The general was left alone with a look of bewilderment in his brown eyes, as he sat down again to play with his pins.

Even greater, however, was the bewilderment which attended the successive stages of the benevolent conspiracy of the general's wife, who had assembled her little group of sympathizers to storm the castle of the misanthrope. The first surprise she encountered was the unexplained absence of one of the actors in the ancient tragedy. When they assembled by agreement at a quiet hotel quite near the castle, there was no sign of Hugo Romaine, until a belated telegram from a lawyer told them that the great actor had suddenly left the country. The second surprise, when they began the bombardment by sending up word to the castle with an urgent request for an interview, was the figure which came forth from those gloomy gates to receive the deputation in the name of the noble owner. It was no such figure as they would have conceived suitable to those sombre avenues or those almost feudal formalities. It was not some stately steward or major-domo, nor even a dignified butler or tall and ornamental footman. The only figure that came out of the cavernous castle doorway was the short and shabby figure of Father Brown.

'Look here,' he said, in his simple, bothered fashion. 'I told you you'd much better leave him alone. He knows what he's doing and it'll only make everybody unhappy.'

Lady Outram, who was accompanied by a tall and quietly dressed lady, still very handsome, presumably the original Miss Grayson, looked at the little priest with cold contempt.

'Really, sir,' she said, 'this is a very private occasion, and I don't understand what you have to do with it.'

'Trust a priest to have to do with a private occasion,' snarled Sir John Cockspur. 'Don't you know they live behind the scenes like rats behind a wainscot burrowing their way into everybody's private rooms? See how he's already in possession of poor Marne.' Sir John was slightly sulky, as his aristocratic friends had persuaded him to give up the great scoop of publicity in return for the privilege of being really inside a society secret. It never occurred to him to ask himself whether *he* was at all like a rat in a wainscot.

'Oh, that's all right,' said Father Brown, with the impatience of anxiety. 'I've talked it over with the marquis and the only priest he's ever had anything to do with; his clerical tastes have been much exaggerated. I tell you he knows what he's about; and I do implore you all to leave him alone.'

'You mean to leave him to this living death of moping and going mad in a ruin!' cried Lady Outram, in a voice that shook a little. 'And all because he had the bad luck to shoot a man in a duel more than a quarter of a century ago. Is that what you call Christian charity?'

'Yes,' answered the priest stolidly, 'that is what I call Christian charity.'

'It's about all the Christian charity you'll ever get out of these priests,' cried Cockspur bitterly. 'That's their only idea of pardoning a poor fellow for a piece of folly; to wall him up alive and starve him to death with fasts and penances and pictures of hell fire. And all because a bullet went wrong.'

'Really, Father Brown,' said General Outram, 'do you honestly think he deserves this? Is that your Christianity?'

'Surely the true Christianity,' pleaded his wife more gently, 'is that which knows all and pardons all; the love that can remember – and forget.'

'Father Brown,' said young Mallow, very earnestly, 'I generally agree with what you say; but I'm hanged if I can follow you here. A shot in a duel, followed instantly by remorse, is not such an awful offence.'

'I admit,' said Father Brown dully, 'that I take a more serious view of his offence.'

'God soften your hard heart,' said the strange lady, speaking for the first time. 'I am going to speak to my old friend.'

Almost as if her voice had raised a ghost in that great grey house, something stirred within and a figure stood in the dark doorway at the top of the great stone flight of steps. It was clad in dead black, but there was something wild about the blanched hair and something in the pale features that was like the wreck of a marble statue.

Viola Grayson began calmly to move up the great flight of steps; and Outram muttered in his thick black moustache: 'He won't cut her dead as he did my wife, I fancy.'

Father Brown, who seemed in a collapse of resignation, looked up at him for a moment.

'Poor Marne has enough on his conscience,' he said. 'Let us acquit him of what we can. At least he never cut your wife.'

'What do you mean by that?'

'He never knew her,' said Father Brown.

As they spoke, the tall lady proudly mounted the last step and came face to face with the Marquis of Marne. His lips moved, but something happened before he could speak.

A scream rang across the open space and went wailing away in echoes along those hollow walls. By the abruptness and agony with which it broke from the woman's lips it might have been a mere inarticulate cry. But it was an articulated word; and they all heard it with a horrible distinctness.

'Maurice!'

'What is it, dear?' cried Lady Outram, and began to run up the steps; for the other woman was swaying as if she might fall down the whole stone flight. Then she faced about and began to descend, all bowed and shrunken and shuddering. 'Oh, my God,' she was saying. 'Oh, my God . . . it isn't Jim at all . . . it's Maurice!'

'I think, Lady Outram,' said the priest gravely, 'you had better go with your friend.'

As they turned, a voice fell on them like a stone from the top of the stone stair, a voice that might have come out of an open grave. It was hoarse and unnatural, like the voices of men who are left alone with wild birds on desert islands. It was the voice of the Marquis of Marne, and it said: 'Stop!'

'Father Brown,' he said, 'before your friends disperse I authorize you to tell them all I have told you. Whatever follows, I will hide from it no longer.'

'You are right,' said the priest, 'and it shall be counted to you.'

'Yes,' said Father Brown quietly to the questioning company afterwards. 'He has given me the right to speak; but I will not tell it as he told me, but as I found it out for myself. Well, I knew from the first that the blighting monkish influence was all nonsense out of novels. Our people might possibly in certain cases encourage a man to go regularly into a monastery, but certainly not to hang about in a mediaeval castle. In the same way, they certainly wouldn't want him to dress up as a monk when he wasn't a monk. But it struck me that he might himself want to wear a monk's hood or even a mask. I had heard of him as a mourner, and then as a murderer; but already I had hazy suspicions that his reason for hiding might not only be concerned with what he was, but with who he was.

'Then came the general's vivid description of the duel; and the most vivid thing in it to me was the figure of Mr Romaine in the background; it was vivid because it was in the background. Why did the general leave behind him on the sand a dead man, whose friend stood yards away from him like a stock or a stone? Then I heard something, a mere trifle, about a trick habit that Romaine has of standing quite still when he is waiting for something to happen; as he waited for the thunder to follow the lightning. Well, that automatic trick in this case betrayed everything. Hugo Romaine, on that old occasion, also was waiting for something.'

'But it was all over,' said the general. 'What could he have been waiting for?'

'He was waiting for the duel,' said Father Brown.

'But I tell you I saw the duel!' cried the general.

'And I tell you you didn't see the duel,' said the priest.

'Are you mad?' demanded the other. 'Or why should you think I am blind?'

'Because you were blinded – that you might not see,' said the priest. 'Because you are a good man and God had mercy on your innocence, and he turned your face away from that unnatural strife. He set a wall of sand and silence between you and what really happened on that horrible red shore, abandoned to the raging spirits of Judas and of Cain.'

'Tell us what happened!' gasped the lady impatiently.

'I will tell it as I found it,' proceeded the priest. 'The next thing I found was that Romaine, the actor, had been training Maurice Mair in all the tricks of the trade of acting. I once had a friend who went in for acting. He gave me a very amusing account of how his first week's training consisted entirely of falling down; of learning how to fall flat without a stagger, as if he were stone dead.'

'God have mercy on us!' cried the general, and gripped the arms of his chair as if to rise.

'Amen,' said Father Brown. 'You told me how quickly it seemed to come; in fact, Maurice fell before the bullet flew and lay perfectly still, waiting. And his wicked friend and teacher stood also in the background, waiting.'

'We are waiting,' said Cockspur, 'and I feel as if I couldn't wait.'

'James Mair, already broken with remorse, rushed across to the fallen man and bent over to lift him up. He had thrown away his pistol like an unclean thing; but Maurice's pistol still lay under his hand and it was undischarged. Then as the elder man bent over the younger, the younger lifted himself on his left arm and shot the elder through the body. He knew he was not so good a shot; but there was no question of missing the heart at that distance.'

The rest of the company had risen and stood staring down at the narrator with pale faces. 'Are you sure of this?' asked Sir John at last, in a thick voice.

'I am sure of it,' said Father Brown, 'and now I leave Maurice Mair, the present Marquis of Marne, to your Christian charity. You have told me something today about Christian charity. You seemed to me to give it almost too large a place; but how fortunate it is for poor sinners like this man that you err so much on the side of mercy, and are ready to be reconciled to all mankind.'

'Hang it all,' exploded the general, 'if you think I'm going to be reconciled to a filthy viper like that, I tell you I wouldn't say a word to save him from hell. I said I could pardon a regular decent duel, but of all the treacherous assassins—'

'He ought to be lynched,' cried Cockspur excitedly. 'He ought to burn alive like a nigger in the States. And if there is such a thing as burning for ever, he jolly well—'

'I wouldn't touch him with a barge pole myself,' said Mallow.

'There is a limit to human charity,' said Lady Outram, trembling all over.

'There is,' said Father Brown dryly, 'and that is the real difference between human charity and Christian charity. You must forgive me if I was not altogether crushed by your contempt for my uncharitableness today; or by the lectures you read me about pardon for every sinner. For it seems to me that you only pardon the sins that you don't really think sinful. You only forgive criminals when they commit what you don't regard as crimes, but rather as conventions. So you tolerate a conventional duel, just as you tolerate a conventional divorce. You forgive because there isn't anything to be forgiven.'

'But, hang it all,' cried Mallow, 'you don't expect us to be able to pardon a vile thing like this?'

'No,' said the priest, 'but *we* have to be able to pardon it.'

He stood up abruptly and looked round at them.

'We have to touch such men, not with a barge pole, but with a benediction,' he said. 'We have to say the word that will save them from hell. We alone are left to deliver them from despair when your human charity deserts them. Go on your own primrose path pardoning all your favourite vices and being generous to your fashionable crimes; and leave us in the darkness, vampires of the night, to console those who really need consolation; who do things really indefensible, things that neither the world nor they themselves can defend; and none but a priest will pardon. Leave us with the men who commit the mean and revolting and real crimes; mean as St Peter when the cock crew, and yet the dawn came.'

'The dawn,' repeated Mallow doubtfully. 'You mean hope – for *him*?'

'Yes,' replied the other. 'Let me ask you one question. You are great ladies and men of honour and secure of yourselves; you would never, you can tell yourselves, stoop to such squalid treason as that. But tell me this. If any of you had so stooped, which of you, years afterwards, when you were old and rich and safe, would have been driven by conscience or confessor to tell such a story of yourself? You say you could not commit so base a crime. Could you confess so base a crime?'

The others gathered their possessions together and drifted by twos and threes out of the room in silence. And Father Brown, also in silence, went back to the melancholy castle of Marne.

THE SCANDAL OF FATHER BROWN

IT WOULD not be fair to record the adventures of Father Brown, without admitting that he was once involved in a grave scandal. There still are persons, perhaps even of his own community, who would say that there was a sort of blot upon his name. It happened in a picturesque Mexican road-house of rather loose repute, as appeared later; and to some it seemed that for once the priest had allowed a romantic streak in him, and his sympathy for human weakness, to lead him into loose and unorthodox action. The story in itself was a simple one; and perhaps the whole surprise of it consisted in its simplicity.

Burning Troy began with Helen; this disgraceful story began with the beauty of Hypatia Potter. Americans have a great power, which Europeans do not always appreciate, of creating institutions from below; that is by popular initiative. Like every other good thing, it has its lighter aspects; one of which, as has been remarked by Mr Wells and others, is that a person may become a public institution without becoming an official institution. A girl of great beauty or brilliancy will be a sort of uncrowned queen, even if she is not a Film Star or the original of a Gibson Girl. Among those who had the fortune, or misfortune, to exist beautifully in public in this manner, was a certain Hypatia Hard, who had passed through the preliminary stage of receiving florid compliments in society paragraphs of the local press, to the position of one who is actually interviewed by real pressmen. On War and Peace and Patriotism and Prohibition and Evolution and the Bible she had made her pronouncements with a charming smile; and if none of them seemed very near to the real grounds of her own reputation, it was almost equally hard to say what the grounds of her reputation really were. Beauty, and being the daughter of a rich man, are things not rare in her country; but to these she added whatever it is that attracts the wandering eye of journalism. Next to none of her admirers had even seen her, or even hoped to do so; and none of them could possibly derive any sordid benefit from her father's wealth. It was simply a sort of popular romance, the modern substitute for mythology; and it laid the first foundations of the more turgid and tempestuous sort of romance in which she was to figure later on; and in which many held that the reputation of Father Brown, as well as of others, had been blown to rags.

It was accepted, sometimes romantically, sometimes resignedly, by those whom American satire has named the Sob Sisters, that she had already married a very worthy and respectable business man of the name of Potter. It was even possible to regard her for a moment as Mrs Potter, on the universal understanding that her husband was only the husband of Mrs Potter.

Then came the Great Scandal, by which her friends and enemies were horrified beyond their wildest hopes. Her name was coupled (as the queer phrase goes) with a literary man living in Mexico; in status an American, but in spirit a very Spanish American. Unfortunately his vices resembled her virtues, in being good copy. He was no less a person than the famous or infamous Rudel Romanes; the poet whose works had been so universally popularized by being vetoed by libraries or prosecuted by the police. Anyhow, her pure and placid star was seen in conjunction with this comet. He was of the sort to be compared to a comet, being hairy and hot; the first in his portraits, the second in his poetry. He was also destructive; the comet's tail was a trail of divorces, which some called his success as a lover and some his prolonged failure as a husband. It was hard on Hypatia; there are disadvantages in conducting the perfect private life in public; like a domestic interior in a shop-window. Interviewers reported doubtful utterances about Love's Larger Law of Supreme Self-Realization. The Pagans applauded. The Sob Sisterhood permitted themselves a note of romantic regret; some having even the hardened audacity to quote from the poem of Maud Mueller, to the effect that of all the words of tongue or pen, the saddest are 'It might have been'. And Mr Agar P. Rock, who hated the Sob Sisterhood with a holy and righteous hatred, said that in this case he thoroughly agreed with Bret Harte's emendation of the poem: 'More sad are those we daily see; it is, but it hadn't ought to be.'

For Mr Rock was very firmly and rightly convinced that a very large number of things hadn't ought to be. He was a slashing and savage critic of national degeneration, on the *Minneapolis Meteor*, and a bold and honest man. He had perhaps come to specialize too much in the spirit of indignation, but it had had a healthy enough origin in his reaction against sloppy attempts to confuse right and wrong in modern journalism and gossip. He expressed it first in the form of a protest against an unholy halo of romance being thrown round the gunman and the gangster. Perhaps he was rather too much inclined to assume, in robust impatience, that all gangsters were Dagos and that all Dagos were gangsters. But his prejudices, even when they were a little provincial, were rather refreshing after a certain sort of maudlin and unmanly hero-worship, which was ready to regard a professional murderer as a leader of fashion, so long as the pressmen reported that his smile was irresistible or his tuxedo was all right. Anyhow, the prejudices did not boil the less in the bosom of Mr Rock, because he was actually in the land of the Dagos when this story opens; striding furiously up a hill beyond the Mexican border, to the white hotel, fringed with ornamental palms, in which it was supposed that the Potters were staying and that the mysterious Hypatia now held her court. Agar Rock was a good specimen of a Puritan, even to look at; he might even have been a virile Puritan of the seventeenth century, rather than the softer and more sophisticated Puritan of the twentieth. If you had told him that his antiquated black hat and habitual black frown, and fine flinty features, cast a gloom over the sunny land of palms and vines, he would have been very much gratified. He looked to right and left with eyes bright with universal suspicions. And, as he did so, he saw two figures on the ridge above him, outlined against the clear sub-tropical sunset; figures in a momentary posture which might have made even a less suspicious man suspect something.

One of the figures was rather remarkable in itself. It was poised at the exact angle of the turning road above the valley, as if by an instinct for the site as well as the attitude of statuary. It was wrapt in a great black cloak, in the Byronic manner, and the head that rose above it in swarthy beauty was remarkably like Byron's. This man had the same curling hair and curling nostrils; and he seemed to be snorting something of the same scorn and indignation against the world. He grasped in his hand a rather long cane or walking-stick, which having a spike of the sort used for mountaineering, carried at the moment a fanciful suggestion of a spear. It was rendered all the more fanciful by something comically contradictory in the figure of the other man, who carried an umbrella. It was indeed a new and neatly-rolled umbrella, very different, for instance, from Father Brown's umbrella: and he was neatly clad like a clerk in light holiday clothes; a stumpy stoutish bearded man; but the prosaic umbrella was raised and even brandished at an acute angle of attack. The taller man thrust back at him, but in a hasty defensive manner; and then the scene rather collapsed into comedy; for the umbrella opened of itself and its owner almost seemed to sink behind it, while the other man had the air of pushing his spear through a great grotesque shield. But the other man did not push it, or the quarrel, very far; he plucked out the point, turned away impatiently and strode down the road; while the other, rising and carefully refolding his umbrella, turned in the opposite direction towards the hotel. Rock had not heard any of the words of the quarrel, which must have immediately preceded this brief and rather absurd bodily conflict; but as he went up the road in the track of the short man with the beard, he revolved many things. And the romantic cloak and rather operatic good looks of the one man, combined with the sturdy self-assertion of the other, fitted in with the whole story which he had come to seek; and he knew that he could have fixed those two strange figures with their names: Romanes and Potter.

His view was in every way confirmed when he entered the pillared porch and heard the voice of the bearded man raised high in altercation or command. He was evidently speaking to the manager or staff of the hotel, and Rock heard enough to know that he was warning them of a wild and dangerous character in the neighbourhood.

'If he's really been to the hotel already,' the little man was saying, in answer to some murmur, 'all I can say is that you'd better not let him in again. Your police ought to be looking after a fellow of that sort, but anyhow, I won't have the lady pestered with him.'

Rock listened in grim silence and growing conviction; then he slid across the vestibule to an alcove where he saw the hotel register and turning to the last page, saw 'the fellow' had indeed been to the hotel already. There appeared the name of 'Rudel Romanes', that romantic public character, in very large and florid foreign lettering; and after a space under it, rather close together, the names of Hypatia Potter and Ellis T. Potter, in a correct and quite American handwriting.

Agar Rock looked moodily about him, and saw in the surroundings and even the small decorations of the hotel everything that he hated most. It is perhaps unreasonable to complain of oranges growing on orange-trees, even in small tubs; still more of their only growing on threadbare curtains or faded wallpapers as a formal scheme of ornament. But to him those red and golden moons, decoratively alternated with silver moons, were in a queer way the quintessence of all moonshine. He saw in them all that sentimental deterioration which his principles deplored in modern manners, and which his prejudices vaguely connected with the warmth and softness of the South. It annoyed him even to catch sight of a patch of dark canvas, half-showing a Watteau shepherd with a guitar, or a blue tile with a commonplace design of a Cupid on a dolphin. His common sense would have told him that he might have seen these things in a shop-window on Fifth Avenue; but where they were, they seemed like a taunting siren voice of the Paganism of the Mediterranean. And then suddenly, the look of all these things seemed to alter, as a still mirror will flicker when a figure has flashed past it for a moment; and he knew the whole room was full of a challenging presence. He turned almost stiffly, and with a sort of resistance, and knew that he was facing the famous Hypatia, of whom he had read and heard for so many years.

Hypatia Potter, *née* Hard, was one of those people to whom the word 'radiant' really does apply definitely and derivatively. That is, she allowed what the papers called her Personality to go out from her in rays. She would have been equally beautiful, and to some tastes more attractive, if she had been self-contained; but she had always been taught to believe that self-containment was only selfishness. She would have said that she had lost Self in Service; it would perhaps be truer to say that she had asserted Self in Service; but she was quite in good faith about the service. Therefore her outstanding starry blue eyes really struck outwards, as in the old metaphor that made eyes like Cupid's darts, killing at a distance; but with an abstract conception of conquest beyond any mere coquetry. Her pale fair hair, though arranged in a saintly halo, had a look of almost electric radiation. And when she understood that the stranger before her was Mr Agar Rock, of the *Minneapolis Meteor*, her eyes took on themselves the range of long searchlights, sweeping the horizon of the States.

But in this the lady was mistaken; as she sometimes was. For Agar Rock was not Agar Rock of the *Minneapolis Meteor*. He was at that moment merely Agar Rock; there had surged up in him a great and sincere moral impulse, beyond the coarse courage of the interviewer. A feeling profoundly mixed of a chivalrous and national sensibility to beauty, with an instant itch for moral action of some definite sort, which was also national, nerved him to face a great scene; and to deliver a noble insult. He remembered the original Hypatia, the beautiful Neo-Platonist, and how he had been thrilled as a boy by Kingsley's romance in which the young monk denounces her for harlotries and idolatries. He confronted her with an iron gravity and said:

'If you'll pardon me, Madam, I should like to have a word with you in private.'

'Well,' she said, sweeping the room with her splendid gaze, 'I don't know whether you consider this place private.'

Rock also gazed round the room and could see no sign of life less vegetable than the orange-trees, except what looked like a large black mushroom, which he recognized as the hat of some native priest or other, stolidly smoking a black local cigar, and otherwise as stagnant as any vegetable. He looked for a moment at the heavy, expressionless features, noting the rudeness of that peasant type from which priests so often come, in Latin and especially Latin-American countries; and lowered his voice a little as he laughed.

'I don't imagine that Mexican padre knows our language,' he said. 'Catch those lumps of laziness learning any language but their own. Oh, I can't swear he's a Mexican; he might be anything; mongrel Indian or nigger, I suppose. But I'll answer for it he's not an American. Our ministries don't produce that debased type.'

'As a matter of fact,' said the debased type, removing his black cigar, 'I'm English and my name is Brown. But pray let me leave you if you wish to be private.'

'If you're English,' said Rock warmly, 'you ought to have some normal Nordic instinct for protesting against all this nonsense.

Well, it's enough to say now that I'm in a position to testify that there's a pretty dangerous fellow hanging round this place; a tall fellow in a cloak, like those old pictures of crazy poets.'

'Well, you can't go much by that,' said the priest mildly; 'a lot of people round here use those cloaks, because the chill strikes very suddenly after sunset.'

Rock darted a dark and doubtful glance at him; as if suspecting some evasion in the interests of all that was symbolized to him by mushroom hats and moonshine. 'It wasn't only the cloak,' he growled, 'though it was partly the way he wore it. The whole look of the fellow was theatrical, down to his damned theatrical good looks. And if you'll forgive me, Madam, I strongly advise you to have nothing to do with him, if he comes bothering here. Your husband has already told the hotel people to keep him out—'

Hypatia sprang to her feet and, with a very unusual gesture, covered her face, thrusting her fingers into her hair. She seemed to be shaken, possibly with sobs, but by the time she had recovered they had turned into a sort of wild laughter.

'Oh, you are all too funny,' she said, and, in a way very unusual with her, ducked and darted to the door and disappeared.

'Bit hysterical when they laugh like that,' said Rock uncomfortably; then, rather at a loss, and turning to the little priest: 'as I say, if you're English, you ought really to be on my side against these Dagos, anyhow. Oh, I'm not one of those who talk tosh about Anglo-Saxons; but there is such a thing as history. You can always claim that America got her civilization from England.'

'Also, to temper our pride,' said Father Brown, 'we must always admit that England got her civilization from Dagos.'

Again there glowed in the other's mind the exasperated sense that his interlocutor was fencing with him, and fencing on the wrong side, in some secret and evasive way; and he curtly professed a failure to comprehend.

'Well, there was a Dago, or possibly a Wop, called Julius Caesar,' said Father Brown; 'he was afterwards killed in a stabbing match; you know these Dagos always use knives. And there was another one called Augustine, who brought Christianity to our little island; and really, I don't think we should have had much civilization without those two.'

'Anyhow, that's all ancient history,' said the somewhat irritated journalist, 'and I'm very much interested in modern history. What I see is that these scoundrels are bringing Paganism to our country, and destroying all the Christianity there is. Also destroying all the common sense there is. All settled habits, all solid social order, all the way in which the farmers who were our fathers and grand-fathers did manage to live in the world, melted into a hot mush by sensations and sensualities about film-stars who are divorced every month or so, and make every silly girl think that marriage is only a way of getting divorced.'

'You are quite right,' said Father Brown. 'Of course I quite agree with you there. But you must make some allowances. Perhaps these Southern people are a little prone to that sort of fault. You must remember that Northern people have other kinds of faults. Perhaps these surroundings do encourage people to give too rich an impor-tance to mere romance. . . .'

The whole integral indignation of Agar Rock's life rose up within him at the word.

'I hate Romance,' he said, hitting the little table before him. 'I've fought the papers I worked for for forty years about the infer-nal trash. Every blackguard bolting with a bar-maid is called a romantic elopement or something; and now our own Hypatia Hard, a daughter of decent people, may get dragged into some rotten romantic divorce case, that will be trumpeted to the whole world as happily as a royal wedding. This mad poet Romanes is hanging round her; and you bet the spotlight will follow him, as if he were any rotten little Dago who is called the Great Lover on the films. I saw him outside; and he's got the regular spotlight face. Now my sympathies are with decency and common sense. My sym-pathies are with poor Potter, a plain straightforward broker from Pittsburgh, who thinks he has a right to his own home. And he's making a fight for it, too. I heard him hollering at the management, telling them to keep that rascal out; and quite right too. The people here seem a sly and slinky lot; but I rather fancy he's put the fear of God into them already.'

'As a matter of fact,' said Father Brown, 'I rather agree with you about the manager and the men in this hotel; but you mustn't judge all Mexicans by them. Also I fancy the gentleman you speak of has not only hollered, but handed round dollars enough to get the whole staff on his side. I saw them locking doors and whispering most excitedly. By the way, your plain straightforward friend seems to have a lot of money.'

'I've no doubt his business does well,' said Rock. 'He's quite the best type of sound business-man. What do you mean?'

'I fancied it might suggest another thought to you,' said Father Brown; and, rising with rather heavy civility, he left the room.

Rock watched the Potters very carefully that evening at dinner; and gained some new impressions, though none that disturbed his deep sense of the wrong that probably threatened the peace of the Potter home. Potter himself proved worthy of somewhat closer study; though the journalist had at first accepted him as prosaic and unpretentious, there was a pleasure in recognizing finer lines in what he considered the hero or victim of a tragedy. Potter had really rather a thoughtful and distinguished face, though worried and occasionally petulant. Rock got an impression that the man was recovering from an illness; his faded hair was thin but rather long, as if it had been lately neglected, and his rather unusual beard gave the onlooker the same notion. Certainly he spoke once or twice to his wife in a rather sharp and acid manner, fussing about tablets or some detail of digestive science; but his real worry was doubtless concerned with the danger from without. His wife played up to him in the splendid if somewhat condescending manner of a Patient Griselda; but her eyes also roamed continually to the doors and shutters, as if in half-hearted fear of an invasion. Rock had only too good reason to dread, after her curious outbreak, the fact that her fear might turn out to be only half-hearted.

It was in the middle of that night that the extraordinary event occurred. Rock, imagining himself to be the last to go up to bed, was surprised to find Father Brown still tucked obscurely under an orange-tree in the hall, and placidly reading a book. He returned the other's farewell without further words, and the journalist had his foot on the lowest step of the stair, when suddenly the outer door sprang on its hinges and shook and rattled under the shock of blows planted from without; and a great voice louder than the blows was heard violently demanding admission. Somehow the journalist was certain that the blows had been struck with a pointed stick like an alpenstock. He looked back at the darkened lower floor, and saw the servants of the hotel sliding here and there to see that the doors were locked; and not unlocking them. Then he slowly mounted to his room, and sat down furiously to write his report.

He described the siege of the hotel; the evil atmosphere; the shabby luxury of the place; the shifty evasions of the priest; above all, that terrible voice crying without, like a wolf prowling round the house. Then, as he wrote, he heard a new sound and sat up suddenly. It was a long repeated whistle, and in his mood he hated it doubly, because it was like the signal of a conspirator and like the love-call of a bird. There followed an utter silence, in which he sat rigid; then he rose abruptly; for he had heard yet another noise. It was a faint swish followed by a sharp rap or rattle; and he was almost certain that somebody was throwing something at a window. He walked stiffly downstairs, to the floor which was now dark and deserted; or nearly deserted. For the little priest was still sitting under the orange shrub, lit by a low lamp; and still reading his book.

'You seem to be sitting up late,' he said harshly.

'Quite a dissipated character,' said Father Brown, looking up with a broad smile, 'reading *Economics of Usury* at all wild hours of the night.'

'The place is locked up,' said Rock.

'Very thoroughly locked up,' replied the other. 'Your friend with the beard seems to have taken every precaution. By the way, your friend with the beard is a little rattled; I thought he was rather cross at dinner.'

'Natural enough,' growled the other, 'if he thinks savages in this savage place are out to wreck his home life.'

'Wouldn't it be better,' said Father Brown, 'if a man tried to make his home life nice inside, while he was protecting it from the things outside.'

'Oh, I know you will work up all the casuistical excuses,' said the other; 'perhaps he was rather snappy with his wife; but he's got the right on his side. Look here, you seem to me to be rather a deep dog. I believe you know more about this than you say. What the devil is going on in this infernal place? Why are you sitting up all night to see it through?'

'Well,' said Father Brown patiently, 'I rather thought my bedroom might be wanted.'

'Wanted by whom?'

'As a matter of fact, Mrs Potter wanted another room,' explained

Father Brown with limpid clearness. 'I gave her mine, because I could open the window. Go and see, if you like.'

'I'll see to something else first,' said Rock grinding his teeth. 'You can play your monkey tricks in this Spanish monkey-house, but I'm still in touch with civilization.' He strode into the telephone-booth and rang up his paper; pouring out the whole tale of the wicked priest who helped the wicked poet. Then he ran upstairs into the priest's room, in which the priest had just lit a short candle, showing the windows beyond wide open.

He was just in time to see a sort of rude rope-ladder unhooked from the window-sill and rolled up by a laughing gentleman on the lawn below. The laughing gentleman was a tall and swarthy gentleman, and was accompanied by a blonde but equally laughing lady. This time, Mr Rock could not even comfort himself by calling her laughter hysterical. It was too horribly genuine; and rang down the rambling garden-paths as she and her troubadour disappeared into the dark thickets.

Agar Rock turned on his companion a face of final and awful justice; like the Day of Judgment.

'Well, all America is going to hear of this,' he said. 'In plain words, you helped her to bolt with that curly-haired lover.'

'Yes,' said Father Brown, 'I helped her to bolt with that curly-haired lover.'

'You call yourself a minister of Jesus Christ,' cried Rock, 'and you boast of a crime.'

'I have been mixed up with several crimes,' said the priest gently. 'Happily for once this is a story without a crime. This is a simple fireside idyll; that ends with a glow of domesticity.'

'And ends with a rope-ladder instead of a rope,' said Rock. 'Isn't she a married woman?'

'Oh, yes,' said Father Brown.

'Well, oughtn't she to be with her husband?' demanded Rock.

'She is with her husband,' said Father Brown.

The other was startled into anger. 'You lie,' he said. 'The poor little man is still snoring in bed.'

'You seem to know a lot about his private affairs,' said Father Brown plaintively. 'You could almost write a life of the Man with a Beard. The only thing you don't seem ever to have found out about him is his name.'

'Nonsense,' said Rock. 'His name is in the hotel book.'

'I know it is,' answered the priest, nodding gravely, 'in very large letters; the name of Rudel Romanes. Hypatia Potter, who met him here, put her name boldly under his, when she meant to elope with him; and her husband put his name under that, when he pursued them to this place. He put it very close under hers, by way of protest. Then Romanes (who has pots of money, as a popular misanthrope despising men) bribed the brutes in this hotel to bar and bolt it and keep the lawful husband out. And I, as you truly say, helped him to get in.'

When a man is told something that turns things upside-down; that the tail wags the dog; that the fish has caught the fisherman; that the earth goes round the moon; he takes some little time before he even asks seriously if it is true. He is still content with the consciousness that it is the opposite of the obvious truth. Rock said at last, 'You don't mean that little fellow is the romantic Rudel we're always reading about; and that curly-haired fellow is Mr Potter of Pittsburgh.'

'Yes,' said Father Brown. 'I knew it the moment I clapped eyes on both of them. But I verified it afterwards.'

Rock ruminated for a time and said at last: 'I suppose it's barely possible you're right. But how did you come to have such a notion, in the face of the facts?'

Father Brown looked rather abashed; subsided into a chair, and stared into vacancy, until a faint smile began to dawn on his round and rather foolish face.

'Well,' he said, 'you see – the truth is, I'm not romantic.'

'I don't know what the devil you are,' said Rock roughly.

'Now *you* are romantic,' said Father Brown helpfully. 'For instance, you see somebody looking poetical, and you assume he is a poet. Do you know what the majority of poets look like? What a wild confusion was created by that coincidence of three good-looking aristocrats at the beginning of the nineteenth century: Byron and Goethe and Shelley! Believe me, in the common way, a man may write, "Beauty has laid her flaming lips on mine", or whatever that chap wrote, without being himself particularly beautiful. Besides, do you realize how *old* a man generally is by the time his fame has filled the world? Watts painted Swinburne with a halo of hair; but Swinburne was bald before most of his last American or Australian admirers had heard of his hyacinthine locks. So was D'Annunzio. As a fact, Romanes still has rather a fine head, as you will see if you look at it closely; he looks like an intellectual man; and he is. Unfortunately, like a good many other intellectual men, he's a fool. He's let himself go to seed with selfishness and fussing about his digestion. So that the ambitious American lady who thought it would be like soaring to Olympus with the Nine Muses to elope with a poet, found that a day or so of it was about enough for her. So that when her husband came after her, and stormed the place, she was delighted to go back to him.'

'But her husband,' queried Rock. 'I am still rather puzzled about her husband.'

'Ah, you've been reading too many of your erotic modern novels,' said Father Brown; and partly closed his eyes in answer to the protesting glare of the other. 'I know a lot of stories start with a wildly beautiful woman wedded to some elderly swine in the stock market. But why? In that, as in most things, modern novels are the very reverse of modern. I don't say it never happens; but it hardly ever happens now except by her own fault. Girls nowadays marry whom they like; especially spoilt girls like Hypatia. And whom do they marry? A beautiful wealthy girl like that would have a ring of admirers; and whom would she choose? The chances are a hundred to one that she'd marry very young and choose the handsomest man she met at a dance or a tennis-party. Well, ordinary business-men are sometimes handsome. A young god appeared (called Potter) and she wouldn't care if he was a broker or a burglar. But, given the environment, you will admit it's more likely he would be a broker; also, it's quite likely that he'd be called Potter. You see, you are so incurably romantic that your whole case was founded on the idea that a man looking like a young god, couldn't be called Potter. Believe me, names are not so appropriately distributed.'

'Well,' said the other, after a short pause, 'and what do you suppose happened after that?'

Father Brown got up rather abruptly from the seat in which he had collapsed; the candlelight threw the shadow of his short figure across the wall and ceiling, giving an odd impression that the balance of the room had been altered.

'Ah,' he muttered, 'that's the devil of it. That's the real devil. Much worse than the old Indian demons in this jungle. You thought I was only making out a case for the loose ways of these Latin Americans – well, the queer thing about you' – and he blinked owlishly at the other through his spectacles – 'the queerest thing about you is that in a way you're right.

'You say down with romance. I say I'd take my chance in fighting the genuine romances – all the more because they are precious few, outside the first fiery days of youth. I say – take away the Intellectual Friendships; take away the Platonic Unions; take away the Higher Laws of Self-fulfilment and the rest, and I'll risk the normal dangers of the job. Take away the love that isn't love, but only pride and vainglory and publicity and making a splash; and we'll take our chance of fighting the love that is love, when it has to be fought, as well as the love that is lust and lechery. Priests know young people will have passions, as doctors know they will have measles. But Hypatia Potter is forty if she is a day, and she cares no more for that little poet than if he were her publisher or her publicity man. That's just the point – he was her publicity man. It's your newspapers that have ruined her; it's living in the limelight; it's wanting to see herself in the headlines, even in a scandal if it were only sufficiently psychic and superior. It's wanting to be George Sand, her name immortally linked with Alfred de Musset. When her real romance of youth was over, it was the sin of middle age that got hold of her; the sin of intellectual ambition. She hasn't got any intellect to speak of but you don't need any intellect to be an intellectual.'

'I should say she was pretty brainy in one sense,' observed Rock reflectively.

'Yes; in one sense,' said Father Brown. 'In only one sense. In a business sense. Not in any sense that has anything to do with these poor lounging Dagos down here. You curse the Film Stars and tell me you hate romance. Do you suppose the Film Star, who is married for the fifth time, is misled by any romance? Such people are very practical; more practical than you are. You say you admire the simple solid Business Man. Do you suppose that Rudel Romanes isn't a Business Man? Can't you see he knew, quite as well as she did, the advertising advantages of this last grand affair with a famous beauty. He also knew very well that his hold on it was pretty insecure; hence his fussing about and bribing servants to lock doors. But what I mean to say, first and last, is that there'd be a lot less scandal if people didn't idealize sin and pose as sinners. These poor Mexicans may seem sometimes to live like beasts, or rather sin like men; but they don't go in for Ideals. You must at least give them credit for that.'

He sat down again, as abruptly as he had risen, and laughed apologetically. 'Well, Mr Rock,' he said, 'that is my complete confession; the whole horrible story of how I helped a romantic elopement. You can do what you like with it.'

'In that case,' said Rock, rising, 'I will go to my room and make a few alterations in my report. But, first of all, I must ring up my paper and tell them I've been telling them a pack of lies.'

Not much more than half an hour had passed, between the time when Rock had telephoned to say the priest was helping the poet to run away with the lady, and the time when he telephoned to say that the priest had prevented the poet from doing precisely the same thing. But in that short interval of time was born and enlarged and scattered upon the winds the Scandal of Father Brown. The truth is still half an hour behind the slander; and nobody can be certain when or where it will catch up with it. The garrulity of pressmen and the eagerness of enemies had spread the first story through the city, even before it appeared in the first printed version. It was instantly corrected and contradicted by Rock himself, in a second message stating how the story had really ended; but it was by no means certain that the first story was killed. A positively incredible number of people seemed to have read the first issue of the paper and not the second. Again and again, in every corner of the world, like a flame bursting from blackened ashes, there would appear the old tale of the Brown Scandal, or Priest Ruins Potter Home. Tireless apologists of the priest's party watched for it, and patiently tagged after it with contradictions and exposures and letters of protest. Sometimes the letters were published in the papers; and sometimes they were not. But still nobody knew how many people had heard the story without hearing the contradiction. It was possible to find whole blocks of blameless and inno-cent people who thought the Mexican Scandal was an ordinary recorded historical incident like the Gunpowder Plot. Then some-body would enlighten these simple people, only to discover that the old story had started afresh among a few quite educated people, who would seem the last people on earth to be duped by it. And so the two Father Browns chase each other round the world for ever; the first a shameless criminal fleeing from justice; the second a martyr broken by slander, in a halo of rehabilitation. But neither of them is very like the real Father Brown, who is not broken at all; but goes stumping with his stout umbrella through life, liking most of the people in it; accepting the world as his companion, but never as his judge.

THE QUICK ONE

THE STRANGE story of the incongruous strangers is still remembered along that strip of the Sussex coast, where the large and quiet hotel called the Maypole and Garland looks across its own gardens to the sea. Two quaintly assorted figures did, indeed, enter that quiet hotel on that sunny afternoon; one being conspicuous in the sunlight, and visible over the whole shore, by the fact of wearing a lustrous green turban, surrounding a brown face and a black beard; the other would have seemed to some even more wild and weird, by reason of his wearing a soft black clergyman's hat with a yellow moustache and yellow hair of leonine length. He at least had often been seen preaching on the sands or conducting Band of Hope services with a little wooden spade; only he had certainly never been seen going into the bar of an hotel. The arrival of these quaint companions was the climax of the story, but not the beginning of it; and, in order to make a rather mysterious story as clear as possible, it is better to begin at the beginning.

Half an hour before those two conspicuous figures entered the hotel, and were noticed by everybody, two other very inconspicuous figures had also entered it, and been noticed by nobody. One was a large man, and handsome in a heavy style, but he had a knack of taking up very little room, like a background; only an almost morbidly suspicious examination of his boots would have told anybody that he was an Inspector of Police in plain clothes; in very plain clothes. The other was a drab and insignificant little man, also in plain clothes, only that they happened to be clerical clothes; but nobody had ever seen *him* preaching on the sands.

These travellers also found themselves in a sort of large smoking-room with a bar, for a reason which determined all the events of that tragic afternoon. The truth is that the respectable hotel called the Maypole and Garland was being 'done-up'. Those who had liked it in the past were moved to say that it was being done down;

or possibly done in. This was the opinion of the local grumbler, Mr Raggley, the eccentric old gentleman who drank cherry brandy in a corner and cursed. Anyhow, it was being carefully stripped of all the stray indications that it had once been an English inn; and being busily turned, yard by yard and room by room, into something resembling the sham palace of a Levantine usurer in an American film. It was, in short, being 'decorated'; but the only part where the decoration was complete, and where customers could yet be made comfortable, was this large room leading out of the hall. It had once been honourably known as a Bar Parlour and was now mysteriously known as a Saloon Lounge, and was newly 'decorated', in the manner of an Asiatic Divan. For Oriental ornament pervaded the new scheme; and where there had once been a gun hung on hooks, and sporting prints and a stuffed fish in a glass case, there were now festoons of Eastern drapery and trophies of scimitars, tulwars and yataghans, as if in unconscious preparation for the coming of the gentleman with the turban. The practical point was, however, that the few guests who did arrive had to be shepherded into this lounge, now swept and garnished, because all the more regular and refined parts of the hotel were still in a state of transition. Perhaps that was also the reason why even those few guests were somewhat neglected, the manager and others being occupied with explanations or exhortations elsewhere. Anyhow, the first two travellers who arrived had to kick their heels for some time unattended.

The bar was at the moment entirely empty, and the Inspector rang and rapped impatiently on the counter; but the little clergyman had already dropped into a lounge seat and seemed in no hurry for anything. Indeed his friend the policeman, turning his head, saw that the round face of the little cleric had gone quite blank, as it had a way of doing sometimes; he seemed to be staring through his moonlike spectacles at the newly decorated wall.

'I may as well offer you a penny for your thoughts,' said Inspector Greenwood, turning from the counter with a sigh, 'as nobody seems to want my pennies for anything else. This seems to be the only room in the house that isn't full of ladders and whitewash; and this is so empty that there isn't even a potboy to give me a pot of beer.'

'Oh ... my thoughts are not worth a penny, let alone a pot of beer,' answered the cleric, wiping his spectacles, 'I don't know why . . . but I was thinking how easy it would be to commit a murder here.'

'It's all very well for you, Father Brown,' said the Inspector good-humouredly. 'You've had a lot more murders than your fair share; and we poor policemen sit starving all our lives, even for a little one. But why should you say . . . Oh I see, you're looking at all those Turkish daggers on the wall. There are plenty of things to commit a murder *with*, if that's what you mean. But not more than there are in any ordinary kitchen: carving-knives or pokers or what not. That isn't where the snag of a murder comes in.'

Father Brown seemed to recall his rambling thoughts in some bewilderment; and said that he supposed so.

'Murder is always easy,' said Inspector Greenwood. 'There can't possibly be anything more easy than murder. I could murder you at this minute – more easily than I can get a drink in this damned bar. The only difficulty is committing a murder without committing oneself as a murderer. It's this shyness about owning up to a murder; it's this silly modesty of murderers about their own master-pieces, that makes the trouble. They will stick to this extraordinary fixed idea of killing people without being found out; and that's what restrains them, even in a room full of daggers. Otherwise every cutler's shop would be piled with corpses. And that, by the way, explains the one kind of murder that really *can't* be prevented. Which is why, of course, we poor bobbies are always blamed for not preventing it. When a madman murders a King or a President, it can't be prevented. You can't make a King live in a coal-cellar, or carry about a President in a steel box. Anybody can murder him who does not mind being a murderer. That is where the madman is like the martyr – sort of beyond this world. A real fanatic can always kill anybody he likes.'

Before the priest could reply, a joyous band of bagmen rolled into the room like a shoal of porpoises; and the magnificent bellow of a big, beaming man, with an equally big and beaming tie-pin, brought the eager and obsequious manager running like a dog to the whistle, with a rapidity which the police in plain clothes had failed to inspire.

'I'm sure I'm very sorry, Mr Jukes,' said the manager, who wore a rather agitated smile and a wave or curl of very varnished hair across his forehead. 'We're rather understaffed at present; and I had to attend to something in the hotel, Mr Jukes.'

Mr Jukes was magnanimous, but in a noisy way; and ordered drinks all round, conceding one even to the almost cringing manager. Mr Jukes was a traveller for a very famous and fashionable wine and spirits firm; and may have conceived himself as lawfully the leader in such a place. Anyhow, he began a boisterous monologue, rather tending to tell the manager how to manage his hotel; and the others seemed to accept him as an authority. The policeman and the priest had retired to a low bench and small table in the background, from which they watched events, up to that rather remarkable moment when the policeman had very decisively to intervene.

For the next thing that happened, as already narrated, was the astonishing apparition of a brown Asiatic in a green turban, accompanied by the (if possible) more astonishing apparition of a Non-conformist minister; omens such as appear before a doom. In this case there was no doubt about evidence for the portent. A taciturn but observant boy cleaning the steps for the last hour (being a leisurely worker), the dark, fat, bulky bar-attendant, even the diplomatic but distracted manager, all bore witness to the miracle.

The apparitions, as the sceptics say, were due to perfectly natural causes. The man with the mane of yellow hair and the semi-clerical clothes was not only familiar as a preacher on the sands, but as a propagandist throughout the modern world. He was no less a person than the Rev. David Pryce-Jones, whose far-resounding slogan was Prohibition and Purification for Our Land and the Britains Overseas. He was an excellent public speaker and organizer; and an idea had occurred to him that ought to have occurred to Prohibitionists long ago. It was the simple idea that, if Prohibition is right, some honour is due to the Prophet who was perhaps the first Prohibitionist. He had corresponded with the leaders of Mahommedan religious thought, and had finally induced a distinguished Moslem (one of whose names was Akbar and the rest an untranslatable ululation of Allah with attributes) to come and lecture in England on the ancient Moslem veto on wine. Neither of them certainly had been in a public-house bar before; but they had come there by the process already described; driven from the genteel tea-rooms, shepherded into the newly-decorated saloon. Probably all would have been well, if the great Prohibitionist, in his innocence, had not advanced to the counter and asked for a glass of milk.

The commercial travellers, though a kindly race, emitted involuntary noises of pain; a murmur of suppressed jests was heard, as 'Shun the bowl', or 'Better bring out the cow'. But the magnificent Mr Jukes, feeling it due to his wealth and tie-pin to produce more refined humour, fanned himself as one about to faint, and said pathetically, 'They know they can knock me down with a feather. They know a breath will blow me away. They know my doctor says I'm not to have these shocks. And they come and drink cold milk in cold blood, before my very eyes.'

The Rev. David Pryce-Jones, accustomed to deal with hecklers at public meetings, was so unwise as to venture on remonstrance and recrimination, in this very different and much more popular atmosphere. The Oriental total abstainer abstained from speech as well as spirits; and certainly gained in dignity by doing so. In fact, so far as he was concerned, the Moslem culture certainly scored a silent victory; he was obviously so much more of a gentleman than the commercial gentlemen, that a faint irritation began to arise against his aristocratic aloofness; and when Mr Pryce-Jones began to refer in argument to something of the kind, the tension became very acute indeed.

'I ask you, friends,' said Mr Pryce-Jones, with expansive platform gestures, 'why does our friend here set an example to us Christians in truly Christian self-control and brotherhood? Why does he stand here as a model of true Christianity, of real refinement, of genuine gentlemanly behaviour, amid all the quarrels and riots of such places as these? Because, whatever the doctrinal differences between us, at least in his soil the evil plant, the accursed hop or vine, has never—'

At this crucial moment of the controversy it was that John Raggley, the stormy petrel of a hundred storms of controversy, red-faced, white-haired, his antiquated top-hat on the back of his head, his stick swinging like a club, entered the house like an invading army.

John Raggley was generally regarded as a crank. He was the sort of man who writes letters to the newspaper, which generally do not appear in the newspaper; but which do appear afterwards as pamphlets, printed (or misprinted) at his own expense; and circulated to a hundred wastepaper baskets. He had quarrelled alike with the Tory squires and the Radical County Councils; he hated Jews; and he distrusted nearly everything that is sold in shops, or even in hotels. But there was a backing of facts behind his fads; he knew the county in every corner and curious detail; and he was a sharp observer. Even the manager, a Mr Wills, had a shadowy respect for Mr Raggley, having a nose for the sort of lunacy allowed in the gentry; not indeed the prostrate reverence which he had for the jovial magnificence of Mr Jukes, who was really good for trade, but at least a disposition to avoid quarrelling with the old grumbler, partly perhaps out of fear of the old grumbler's tongue.

'And you will have your usual, Sir,' said Mr Wills, leaning and leering across the counter.

'It's the only decent stuff you've still got,' snorted Mr Raggley, slapping down his queer and antiquated hat. 'Damn it, I sometimes think the only English thing left in England is cherry brandy. Cherry brandy does taste of cherries. Can you find me any beer that tastes of hops, or any cider that tastes of apples, or any wine that has the remotest indication of being made out of grapes? There's an infernal swindle going on now in every inn in the country, that would have raised a revolution in any other country. I've found out a thing or two about it, I can tell you. You wait till I can get it printed, and people will sit up. If I could stop our people being poisoned with all this bad drink—'

Here again the Rev. David Pryce-Jones showed a certain failure in tact; though it was a virtue he almost worshipped. He was so unwise as to attempt to establish an alliance with Mr Raggley, by a fine confusion between the idea of bad drink and the idea that drink is bad. Once more he endeavoured to drag his stiff and stately Eastern friend into the argument, as a refined foreigner superior to our rough English ways. He was even so foolish as to talk of a broad theological outlook; and ultimately to mention the name of Mahomet, which was echoed in a sort of explosion.

'God damn your soul!' roared Mr Raggley, with a less broad theological outlook. 'Do you mean that Englishmen mustn't drink English beer, because wine was forbidden in a damned desert by that dirty old humbug Mahomet?'

In an instant, the Inspector of Police had reached the middle of the room with a stride. For, the instant before that, a remarkable change had taken place in the demeanour of the Oriental gentleman, who had hitherto stood perfectly still, with steady and shining eyes. He now proceeded, as his friend had said, to set an example in truly Christian self-control and brotherhood by reaching the wall with the bound of a tiger, tearing down one of the heavy knives hanging there and sending it smack like a stone from a sling, so that it stuck quivering in the wall exactly half an inch above Mr Raggley's ear. It would undoubtedly have stuck quivering in Mr Raggley, if Inspector Greenwood had not been just in time to jerk the arm and deflect the aim. Father Brown continued in his seat, watching the scene with screwed-up eyes and a screw of something almost like a smile at the corners of his mouth, as if he saw something beyond the mere momentary violence of the quarrel.

And then the quarrel took a curious turn; which may not be understood by everybody, until men like Mr John Raggley are better understood than they are. For the red-faced old fanatic was standing up and laughing uproariously as if it were the best joke he had ever heard. All his snapping vituperation and bitterness seemed to have gone out of him; and he regarded the other fanatic, who had just tried to murder him, with a sort of boisterous benevolence.

'Blast your eyes,' he said, 'you're the first man I've met in twenty years!'

'Do you charge this man, Sir?' said the Inspector, looking doubtful.

'Charge him, of course not,' said Raggley. 'I'd stand him a drink if he were allowed any drinks. I hadn't any business to insult his religion; and I wish to God all you skunks had the guts to kill a man, I won't say for insulting your religion, because you haven't got any, but for insulting anything – even your beer.'

'Now he's called us all skunks,' said Father Brown to Greenwood, 'peace and harmony seem to be restored. I wish that teetotal lecturer could get himself impaled on his friend's knife; it was he who made all the mischief.'

As he spoke, the odd groups in the room were already beginning to break up; it had been found possible to clear the commercial room for the commercial travellers, and they adjourned to it, the potboy carrying a new round of drinks after them on a tray. Father Brown stood for a moment gazing at the glasses left on the counter; recognizing at once the ill-omened glass of milk, and another which smelt of whisky; and then turned just in time to see the parting between those two quaint figures, fanatics of the East and West. Raggley was still ferociously genial; there was still something a little darkling and sinister about the Moslem, which was perhaps natural; but he bowed himself out with grave gestures of dignified reconciliation; and there was every indication that the trouble was really over.

Some importance, however, continued attached, in the mind of Father Brown at least, to the memory and interpretation of those last courteous salutes between the combatants. Because, curiously enough, when Father Brown came down very early next morning, to perform his religious duties in the neighbourhood, he found the long saloon bar, with its fantastic Asiatic decoration, filled with a dead white light of daybreak in which every detail was distinct; and one of the details was the dead body of John Raggley bent and crushed into a corner of the room, with the heavy-hilted crooked dagger rammed through his heart.

Father Brown went very softly upstairs again and summoned his friend the Inspector; and the two stood beside the corpse, in a house in which no one else was as yet stirring.

'We mustn't either assume or avoid the obvious,' said Greenwood after a silence, 'but it is well to remember, I think, what I was saying to you yesterday afternoon. It's rather odd, by the way, that I should have said it – yesterday afternoon.'

'I know,' said the priest, nodding with an owlish stare.

'I said,' observed Greenwood, 'that the one sort of murder we can't stop is murder by somebody like a religious fanatic. That brown fellow probably thinks that if he's hanged, he'll go straight to Paradise for defending the honour of the Prophet.'

'There is that, of course,' said Father Brown. 'It would be very reasonable, so to speak, of our Moslem friend to have stabbed him. And you may say we don't know of anybody else yet, who could at all reasonably have stabbed him. But ... but I was thinking....' And his round face suddenly went blank again and all speech died on his lips.

'What's the matter now?' asked the other.

'Well, I know it sounds funny,' said Father Brown in a forlorn voice. 'But I was thinking . . . I was thinking, in a way, it doesn't much matter who stabbed him.'

'Is this the New Morality?' asked his friend. 'Or the old Casuistry, perhaps. Are the Jesuits really going in for murder?'

'I didn't say it didn't matter who murdered him,' said Father Brown. 'Of course the man who stabbed him might possibly be the man who murdered him. But it might be quite a different man. Anyhow, it was done at quite a different time. I suppose you'll want to work on the hilt for finger-prints; but don't take too much notice of them. I can imagine other reasons for other people sticking this knife in the poor old boy. Not very edifying reasons, of course, but quite distinct from the murder. You'll have to put some more knives into him, before you find out about that.'

'You mean—' began the other, watching him keenly.

'I mean the autopsy,' said the priest, 'to find the real cause of death.'

'You're quite right, I believe,' said the Inspector, 'about the stabbing, anyhow. We must wait for the doctor; but I'm pretty sure he'll say you're right. There isn't blood enough. This knife was stuck in the corpse when it had been cold for hours. But why?'

'Possibly to put the blame on the Mahommedan,' answered Father Brown. 'Pretty mean, I admit, but not necessarily murder. I fancy there are people in this place trying to keep secrets, who are not necessarily the murderers.'

'I haven't speculated on that line yet,' said Greenwood. 'What makes you think so?'

'What I said yesterday, when we first came into this horrible room. I said it would be easy to commit a murder here. But I wasn't thinking about all those stupid weapons, though you thought I was. About something quite different.'

For the next few hours the Inspector and his friend conducted a close and thorough investigation into the goings and comings of everybody for the last twenty-four hours, the way the drinks had been distributed, the glasses that were washed or unwashed, and every detail about every individual involved, or apparently not involved. One might have supposed they thought that thirty people had been poisoned, as well as one.

It seemed certain that nobody had entered the building except by the big entrance that adjoined the bar; all the others were blocked in one way or another by the repairs. A boy had been cleaning the steps outside this entrance; but he had nothing very clear to report. Until the amazing entry of the Turk in the turban, with his teetotal lecturer, there did not seem to have been much custom of any kind, except for the commercial travellers who came in to take what they called 'quick ones'; and they seemed to have moved together, like Wordsworth's Cloud; there was a slight difference of opinion between the boy outside and the men inside about whether one of them had not been abnormally quick in obtaining a quick one, and come out on the doorstep by himself; but the manager and the barman had no memory of any such independent individual. The manager and the barman knew all the travellers quite well, and there was no doubt about their movements as a whole. They had stood at the bar chaffing and drinking; they had been involved, through their lordly leader, Mr Jukes, in a not very serious altercation with Mr Pryce-Jones; and they had witnessed the sudden and very serious altercation between Mr Akbar and Mr Raggley. Then they were told they could adjourn to the Commercial Room, and did so, their drinks being borne after them like a trophy.

'There's precious little to go on,' said Inspector Greenwood. 'Of course a lot of officious servants must do their duty as usual, and wash out all the glasses, including old Raggley's glass. If it weren't for everybody else's efficiency, we detectives might be quite efficient.'

'I know,' said Father Brown, and his mouth took on again the twisted smile. 'I sometimes think criminals invented hygiene. Or perhaps hygienic reformers invented crime; they look like it, some of them. Everybody talks about foul dens and filthy slums in which crime can run riot; but it's just the other way. They are called foul, not because crimes are committed, but because crimes are discovered. It's in the neat, spotless, clean and tidy places that crime can run riot; no mud to make footprints; no dregs to contain poison; kind servants washing out all traces of the murder; and the murderer killing and cremating six wives and all for want of a little Christian dirt. Perhaps I express myself with too much warmth – but look here. As it happens, I do remember one glass, which has doubtless been cleaned since, but I should like to know more about it.'

'Do you mean Raggley's glass?' asked Greenwood.

'No; I mean Nobody's glass,' replied the priest. 'It stood near that glass of milk and it still held an inch or two of whisky. Well, you and I had no whisky. I happen to remember that the manager, when treated by the jovial Jukes, had "a drop of gin". I hope you don't suggest that our Moslem was a whisky-drinker disguised in a green turban; or that the Rev. David Pryce-Jones managed to drink whisky and milk together, without noticing it.'

'Most of the commercial travellers took whisky,' said the Inspector. 'They generally do.'

'Yes; and they generally see they get it too,' answered Father Brown. 'In this case, they had it all carefully carted after them to their own room. But this glass was left behind.'

'An accident, I suppose,' said Greenwood, doubtfully. 'The man could easily get another in the Commercial Room afterwards.'

Father Brown shook his head. 'You've got to see people as they are. Now these sort of men – well, some call them vulgar and some common, but that's all likes and dislikes. I'd be content to say that they are mostly simple men. Lots of them very good men, very glad to go back to the missus and the kids; some of them might be blackguards; might have had several missuses; or even murdered several missuses. But most of them are simple men; and, mark you, just the least tiny little bit drunk. Not much; there's many a duke or don at Oxford drunker; but when that sort of man is at that stage of conviviality, he simply can't help noticing things, and noticing them very loud. Don't you observe that the least little incident jerks them into speech; if the beer froths over, they froth over with it, and have to say, "Whoa, Emma", or, "Doing me proud, aren't you?" Now I should say it's flatly impossible for five of these festive beings to sit round a table in the Commercial Room, and have only four glasses set before them, the fifth man being left out, without making a shout about it. Probably they would all make a shout about it. Certainly *he* would make a shout about it. He wouldn't wait, like an Englishman of another class, till he could get a drink quietly later. The air would resound with things like, "And what about little me?" or, "Here, George, have I joined the Band of Hope?" or, "Do you see any green in my turban, George?" But the barman heard no such complaints. I take it as certain that the glass of whisky left behind had been nearly emptied by somebody else; somebody we haven't thought about yet.'

'But can you think of any such person?' asked the other.

'It's because the manager and the barman won't hear of any such person, that you dismiss the one really independent piece of evidence; the evidence of that boy outside cleaning the steps. He says that a man, who may well have been a bagman, but who did not, in fact, stick to the other bagmen, went in and came out again almost immediately. The manager and the barman never saw him; or say they never saw him. But he got a glass of whisky from the bar somehow. Let us call him, for the sake of argument, The Quick One. Now you know I don't often interfere with your business, which I know you do better than I should do it, or should want to do it. I've never had anything to do with setting police machinery at work, or running down criminals, or anything like that. But, for the first time in my life, I want to do it now. I want you to find The Quick One; to follow The Quick One to the ends of the earth; to set the whole infernal official machinery at work like a drag-net across the nations, and jolly well recapture The Quick One. Because he is the man we want.'

Greenwood made a despairing gesture. 'Has he face or form or any visible quality except quickness?' he inquired.

'He was wearing a sort of Inverness cape,' said Father Brown, 'and he told the boy outside he must reach Edinburgh by next morning. That's all the boy outside remembers. But I know your organization has got on to people with less clue than that.'

'You seem very keen on this,' said the Inspector, a little puzzled.

The priest looked puzzled also, as if at his own thoughts; he sat with knotted brow and then said abruptly:

'You see, it's so easy to be misunderstood. All men matter. You matter. I matter. It's the hardest thing in theology to believe.'

The Inspector stared at him without comprehension; but he proceeded.

'We matter to God – God only knows why. But that's the only possible justification of the existence of policemen.' The policeman did not seem enlightened as to his own cosmic justification. 'Don't you see, the law really is right in a way, after all. If all men matter, all murderers matter. That which He has so mysteriously created, we must not suffer to be mysteriously destroyed. But—'

He said the last word sharply, like one taking a new step in decision.

'*But*, when once I step off that mystical level of equality I don't see that most of your important murders are particularly important. You are always telling me that this case and that is important. As a plain, practical man of the world, I must realize that it is the Prime Minister who has been murdered. As a plain, practical man of the world, I don't think that the Prime Minister matters at all. As a mere matter of human importance, I should say he hardly exists at all. Do you suppose if he and the other public men were shot dead tomorrow, there wouldn't be other people to stand up and say that every avenue was being explored, or that the Government had the matter under the gravest consideration? The masters of the modern world don't matter. Even the real masters don't matter much. Hardly anybody you ever read about in a newspaper matters at all.'

He stood up, giving the table a small rap: one of his rare gestures; and his voice changed again.

'But Raggley did matter. He was one of a great line of some half a dozen men who might have saved England. They stand up stark and dark like disregarded sign-posts, down all that smooth descending road which has ended in this swamp of merely commercial collapse. Dean Swift and Dr Johnson and old William Cobbett; they had all without exception the name of being surly or savage, and they were all loved by their friends, and they all deserved to be. Didn't you see how that old man, with the heart of a lion, stood up and forgave his enemy as only fighters can forgive? He jolly well *did* do what that greasy temperance lecturer talked about; he set an example to us Christians and was a model of Christianity. And when there is foul and secret murder of a man like that – then I do think it matters, matters so much that even the modern machinery of police will be a thing that any respectable person may make use of ... Oh, don't mention it. And so, for once in a way I really do want to make use of you.'

And so, for some stretch of those strange days and nights, we might almost say that the little figure of Father Brown drove before him into action all the armies and engines of the police forces of the Crown, as the little figure of Napoleon drove the batteries and the battle-lines of the vast strategy that covered

Europe. Police stations and post offices worked all night; traffic was stopped, correspondence was intercepted, inquiries were made in a hundred places, in order to track the flying trail of that ghostly figure, without face or name, with an Inverness cape and an Edinburgh ticket.

Meanwhile, of course, the other lines of investigation were not neglected. The full report of the post-mortem had not yet come in; but everybody seemed certain that it was a case of poisoning. This naturally threw the primary suspicion upon the cherry brandy; and this again naturally threw the primary suspicion on the hotel.

'Most probably on the manager of the hotel,' said Greenwood gruffly. 'He looks a nasty little worm to me. Of course it might be something to do with some servant, like the barman; he seems rather a sulky specimen, and Raggley might have cursed him a bit, having a flaming temper, though he was generally generous enough afterwards. But, after all, as I say, the primary responsibility, and therefore the primary suspicion, rests on the manager.'

'Oh, I knew the primary suspicion would rest on the manager,' said Father Brown. 'That was why I didn't suspect him. You see, I rather fancied somebody else must have known that the primary suspicion would rest on the manager; or the servants of the hotel. That is why I said it would be easy to kill anybody in the hotel. . . . But you'd better go and have it out with him, I suppose.'

The Inspector went; but came back again after a surprisingly short interview, and found his clerical friend turning over some papers that seemed to be a sort of *dossier* of the stormy career of John Raggley.

'This is a rum go,' said the Inspector. 'I thought I should spend hours cross-examining that slippery little toad there, for we haven't legally got a thing against him. And instead of that, he went to pieces all at once, and I really think he's told me all he knows in sheer funk.'

'I know,' said Father Brown. 'That's the way he went to pieces when he found Raggley's corpse apparently poisoned in his hotel. That's why he lost his head enough to do such a clumsy thing as decorate the corpse with a Turkish knife, to put the blame on the nigger, as he would say. There never is anything the matter with him but funk; he's the very last man that ever would really stick a knife into a live person. I bet he had to nerve himself to stick it into a dead one. But he's the very first person to be frightened of being charged with what he didn't do; and to make a fool of himself, as he did.'

'I suppose I must see the barman too,' observed Greenwood.

'I suppose so,' answered the other. 'I don't believe myself it was any of the hotel people – well, because it was made to look as if it *must* be the hotel people. . . . But look here, have you seen any of this stuff they've got together about Raggley? He had a jolly interesting life; I wonder whether anyone will write his biography.'

'I took a note of everything likely to affect an affair like this,' answered the official. 'He was a widower; but he did once have a row with a man about his wife; a Scotch land-agent then in these parts; and Raggley seems to have been pretty violent. They say he hated Scotchmen; perhaps that's the reason. . . . Oh, I know what you are smiling grimly about. A Scotchman. . . . Perhaps an Edinburgh man.'

'Perhaps,' said Father Brown. 'It's quite likely, though, that he did dislike Scotchmen, apart from private reasons. It's an odd thing, but all that tribe of Tory Radicals, or whatever you call them, who resisted the Whig mercantile movement, all of them did dislike Scotchmen. Cobbett did; Dr Johnson did; Swift described their accent in one of his deadliest passages; even Shakespeare has been accused of the prejudice. But the prejudices of great men generally have something to do with principles. And there was a reason, I fancy. The Scot came from a poor agricultural land, that became a rich industrial land. He was able and active; he thought he was bringing industrial civilization from the north; he simply didn't know that there had been for centuries a rural civilization in the south. His own grandfather's land was highly rural but not civilized. . . . Well, well; I suppose we can only wait for more news.'

'I hardly think you'll get the latest news out of Shakespeare and Dr Johnson,' grinned the police officer. 'What Shakespeare thought of Scotchmen isn't exactly evidence.'

Father Brown cocked an eyebrow, as if a new thought had surprised him. 'Why, now I come to think of it,' he said, 'there might be better evidence, even out of Shakespeare. He doesn't often mention Scotchmen. But he was rather fond of making fun of Welshmen.'

The Inspector was searching his friend's face; for he fancied he recognized an alertness behind its demure expression.

'By Jove,' he said. 'Nobody thought of turning the suspicions *that* way, anyhow.'

'Well,' said Father Brown, with broad-minded calm, 'you started by talking about fanatics; and how a fanatic could do anything. Well, I suppose we had the honour of entertaining, in this bar-parlour yesterday, about the biggest and loudest and most fat-headed fanatic in the modern world. If being a pig-headed idiot with one idea is the way to murder, I put in a claim for my reverend brother Pryce-Jones, the Prohibitionist, in preference to all the fakirs in Asia, and it's perfectly true, as I told you, that his horrible glass of milk was standing side by side on the counter with the mysterious glass of whisky.'

'Which you think was mixed up with the murder,' said Greenwood staring. 'Look here, I don't know whether you're really serious or not.'

Even as he was looking steadily in his friend's face, finding something still inscrutable in its expression, the telephone rang stridently behind the bar. Lifting the flap in the counter Inspector Greenwood passed rapidly inside, unhooked the receiver, listened for an instant, and then uttered a shout; not addressed to his interlocutor, but to the universe in general. Then he listened still more attentively and said explosively at intervals, 'Yes, yes.... Come round at once; bring him round if possible.... Good piece of work. ... Congratulate you.'

Then Inspector Greenwood came back into the outer lounge, like a man who has renewed his youth, sat down squarely on his seat, with his hands planted on his knees, stared at his friend, and said:

'Father Brown, I don't know how you do it. You seem to have known he was a murderer before anybody else knew he was a man. He was nobody; he was nothing; he was a slight confusion in the evidence; nobody in the hotel saw him; the boy on the steps could hardly swear to him; he was just a fine shade of doubt founded on an extra dirty glass. But we've got him, and he's the man we want.'

Father Brown had risen with the sense of the crisis, mechanically clutching the papers destined to be so valuable to the biographer of Mr Raggley; and stood staring at his friend. Perhaps this gesture jerked his friend's mind to fresh confirmations.

'Yes, we've got The Quick One. And very quick he was, like quicksilver, in making his get-away; we only just stopped him – off on a fishing trip to Orkney, he said. But he's the man, all right; he's the Scotch land-agent who made love to Raggley's wife; he's the man who drank Scotch whisky in this bar and then took a train for Edinburgh. And nobody would have known it but for you.'

'Well, what I meant,' began Father Brown, in a rather dazed tone; and at that instant there was a rattle and rumble of heavy vehicles outside the hotel; and two or three other and subordinate policemen blocked the bar with their presence. One of them, invited by his superior to sit down, did so in an expansive manner, like one at once happy and fatigued; and he also regarded Father Brown with admiring eyes.

'Got the murderer, sir, oh yes,' he said; 'I know he's a murderer, 'cause he bally nearly murdered me. I've captured some tough characters before now; but never one like this – hit me in the stomach like the kick of a horse and nearly got away from five men. Oh, you've got a real killer this time, Inspector.'

'Where is he?' asked Father Brown, staring.

'Outside in the van, in handcuffs,' replied the policeman, 'and, if you're wise, you'll leave him there – for the present.'

Father Brown sank into a chair in a sort of soft collapse; and the papers he had been nervously clutching were shed around him, shooting and sliding about the floor like sheets of breaking snow. Not only his face, but his whole body, conveyed the impression of a punctured balloon.

'Oh . . . Oh,' he repeated, as if any further oath would be inadequate. 'Oh . . . I've done it again.'

'If you mean you've caught the criminal again,' began Greenwood. But his friend stopped him with a feeble explosion, like that of expiring soda-water.

'I mean,' said Father Brown, 'that it's always happening; and really, I don't know why. I always try to say what I mean. But everybody else means such a lot by what I say.'

'What in the world is the matter now?' cried Greenwood, suddenly exasperated.

'Well, I say things,' said Father Brown in a weak voice, which could alone convey the weakness of the words. 'I say things, but everybody seems to know they mean more than they say. Once I saw a broken mirror and said "Something has happened," and they all answered, "Yes, yes, as you truly say, two men wrestled and one ran into the garden," and so on. I don't understand it, "Something happened", and "Two men wrestled", don't seem to me at all the same; but I dare say I read old books of logic. Well, it's like that here. You seem to be all certain this man is a murderer. But I never said he was a murderer. I said he was the man we wanted. He is. I want him very much. I want him frightfully. I want him as the one thing we haven't got in the whole of this horrible case – a witness!'

They all stared at him, but in a frowning fashion, like men trying to follow a sharp new turn of the argument; and it was he who resumed the argument.

'From the first minute I entered that big empty bar or saloon, I knew that what was the matter with all this business was emptiness; solitude; too many chances for anybody to be alone. In a word, the absence of witnesses. All we knew was that when we came in, the manager and the barman were not in the bar. But when *were* they in the bar? What chance was there of making any sort of time-table of when anybody was anywhere? The whole thing was blank for want of witnesses. I rather fancy the barman or somebody was in the bar just before we came; and that's how the Scotchman got his Scotch whisky. He certainly didn't get it after we came. But we can't begin to inquire whether anybody in the hotel poisoned poor Raggley's cherry brandy, till we really know who was in the bar and when. Now I want you to do me another favour, in spite of this stupid muddle, which is probably all my fault. I want you to collect all the people involved in this room – I think they're all still available, unless the Asiatic has gone back to Asia – and then take the poor Scotchman out of his handcuffs, and bring him in here, and let him tell us who did serve him with whisky, and who was in the bar, and who else was in the room, and all the rest. He's the only man whose evidence can cover just that period when the crime was done. I don't see the slightest reason for doubting his word.'

'But look here,' said Greenwood. 'This brings it all back to the hotel authorities; and I thought you agreed that the manager isn't the murderer. Is it the barman, or what?'

'I don't know,' said the priest blankly. 'I don't know for certain even about the manager. I don't know anything about the barman. I fancy the manager might be a bit of a conspirator, even if he wasn't a murderer. But I do know there's one solitary witness on earth who may have seen something; and that's why I set all your police dogs on his trail to the ends of the earth.'

The mysterious Scotchman, when he finally appeared before the company thus assembled, was certainly a formidable figure; tall, with a hulking stride and a long sardonic hatchet face, with tufts of red hair; and wearing not only an Inverness cape but a Glengarry bonnet. He might well be excused for a somewhat acrid attitude; but anybody could see he was of the sort to resist arrest, even with violence. It was not surprising that he had come to blows with a fighting fellow like Raggley. It was not even surprising that the police had been convinced, by the mere details of capture, that he was a tough and a typical killer. But he claimed to be a perfectly respectable farmer in Aberdeenshire, his name being James Grant; and somehow not only Father Brown, but Inspector Greenwood, a shrewd man with a great deal of experience, was pretty soon convinced that the Scot's ferocity was the fury of innocence rather than guilt.

'Now what we want from you, Mr Grant,' said the Inspector gravely, dropping without further parley into tones of courtesy, 'is simply your evidence on one very important fact. I am greatly grieved at the misunderstanding by which you have suffered, but I am sure you wish to serve the ends of justice. I believe you came into this bar just after it opened, at half-past five, and were served with a glass of whisky. We are not certain what servant of the hotel, whether the barman or the manager or some subordinate, was in the bar at that time. Will you look round the room, and tell me whether the bar-attendant who served you is present here.'

'Aye, he's present,' said Mr Grant, grimly smiling, having swept the group with a shrewd glance. 'I'd know him anywhere; and ye'll agree he's big enough to be seen. Do ye have all your inn-servants as grand as yon?'

The Inspector's eye remained hard and steady, and his voice colourless and continuous; the face of Father Brown was a blank; but on many other faces there was a cloud; the barman was not particularly big and not at all grand; and the manager was decidedly small.

'We only want the barman identified,' said the Inspector calmly. 'Of course we know him; but we should like you to verify it independently. You mean . . . ?' And he stopped suddenly.

'Weel, there he is plain enough,' said the Scotchman wearily; and made a gesture, and with that gesture the gigantic Jukes, the prince of commercial travellers, rose like a trumpeting elephant; and in a flash had three policemen fastened on him like hounds on a wild beast.

'Well, all that was simple enough,' said Father Brown to his friend afterwards. 'As I told you, the instant I entered the empty bar-room, my first thought was that, if the barman left the bar unguarded like that, there was nothing in the world to stop you or me or anybody else lifting the flap and walking in, and putting poison in any of the bottles standing waiting for customers. Of course, a practical poisoner would probably do it as Jukes did, by substituting a poisoned bottle for the ordinary bottle; that could be done in a flash. It was easy enough for him, as he travelled in bottles, to carry a flask of cherry brandy prepared and of the same pattern. Of course, it requires one condition; but it's a fairly common condition. It would hardly do to start poisoning the beer or whisky that scores of people drink, it would cause a massacre. But when a man is well known as drinking only one special thing, like cherry brandy, that isn't very widely drunk, it's just like poisoning him in his own home. Only it's a jolly sight safer. For practically the whole suspicion instantly falls on the hotel, or somebody to do with the hotel; and there's no earthly argument to show that it was done by anyone out of a hundred customers that might come into the bar; even if people realized that a customer could do it. It was about as absolutely anonymous and irresponsible a murder as a man could commit.'

'And why exactly did the murderer commit it?' asked his friend.

Father Brown rose and gravely gathered the papers which he had previously scattered in a moment of distraction.

'May I recall your attention,' he said smiling, 'to the materials of the forthcoming Life and Letters of the Late John Raggley? Or, for that matter, to his own spoken words? He said in this very bar that he was going to expose a scandal about the management of hotels; and the scandal was the pretty common one of a corrupt agreement between hotel proprietors and a salesman who took and gave secret commissions, so that his business had a monopoly of all the drink sold in the place. It wasn't even an open slavery like an ordinary tied house; it was a swindle at the expense of everybody the manager was supposed to serve. It was a legal offence. So the ingenious Jukes, taking the first moment when the bar was empty, as it often was, stepped inside and made the exchange of bottles; unfortunately at that very moment a Scotchman in an Inverness cape came in harshly demanding whisky. Jukes saw his only chance was to pretend to be the barman and serve the customer. He was very much relieved that the customer was a Quick One.'

'I think you're rather a Quick One yourself,' observed Greenwood; 'if you say you smelt something at the start, in the mere air of an empty room. Did you suspect Jukes at all at the start?'

'Well, he sounded rather rich somehow,' answered Father Brown vaguely. 'You know when a man has a rich voice. And I did sort of ask myself why he should have such a disgustingly rich voice, when all those honest fellows were fairly poor. But I think I knew he was a sham when I saw that big shining breast-pin.'

'You mean because it was sham?' asked Greenwood doubtfully.

'Oh, no; because it was genuine,' said Father Brown.

THE BLAST OF THE BOOK

PROFESSOR Openshaw always lost his temper, with a loud bang, if anybody called him a Spiritualist; or a believer in Spiritualism. This, however, did not exhaust his explosive elements; for he also lost his temper if anybody called him a disbeliever in Spiritualism. It was his pride to have given his whole life to investigating Psychic Phenomena; it was also his pride never to have given a hint of whether he thought they were really psychic or merely phenomenal. He enjoyed nothing so much as to sit in a circle of devout Spiritualists and give devastating descriptions of how he had exposed medium after medium and detected fraud after fraud: for indeed he was a man of much detective talent and insight, when once he had fixed his eye on an object, and he always fixed his eye on a medium, as a highly suspicious object. There was a story of his having spotted the same Spiritualistic mountebank under three different disguises: dressed as a woman, a white-bearded old man, and a Brahmin of a rich chocolate brown. These recitals made the true believers rather restless, as indeed they were intended to do; but they could hardly complain, for no Spiritualist denies the existence of fraudulent mediums; only the Professor's flowing narrative might well seem to indicate that all mediums were fraudulent.

But woe to the simple-minded and innocent Materialist (and Materialists as a race are rather innocent and simple-minded) who, presuming on this narrative tendency, should advance the thesis that ghosts were against the laws of nature, or that such things were only old superstitions; or that it was all tosh, or, alternatively, bunk. Him would the Professor, suddenly reversing all his scientific batteries, sweep from the field with a cannonade of unquestionable cases and unexplained phenomena, of which the wretched rationalist had never heard in his life, giving all the dates and details, stating all the attempted and abandoned natural explanations; stating everything, indeed, except whether he, John Oliver

Openshaw, did or did not believe in Spirits; and that neither Spiritualist nor Materialist could ever boast of finding out.

Professor Openshaw, a lean figure with pale leonine hair and hypnotic blue eyes, stood exchanging a few words with Father Brown, who was a friend of his, on the steps outside the hotel where both had been breakfasting that morning and sleeping the night before. The Professor had come back rather late from one of his grand experiments, in general exasperation, and was still tingling with the fight that he always waged alone and against both sides.

'Oh, I don't mind you,' he said laughing. 'You don't believe in it even if it's true. But all these people are perpetually asking me what I'm trying to prove. They don't seem to understand that I'm a man of science. A man of science isn't trying to prove anything. He's trying to find out what will prove itself.'

'But he hasn't found out yet,' said Father Brown.

'Well, I have some little notions of my own, that are not quite so negative as most people think,' answered the Professor, after an instant of frowning silence; 'anyhow, I've begun to fancy that if there is something to be found, they're looking for it along the wrong line. It's all too theatrical; it's showing off, all their shiny ectoplasm and trumpets and voices and the rest; all on the model of old melodramas and mouldy historical novels about the Family Ghost. If they'd go to history instead of historical novels, I'm beginning to think they'd really find something. But not Apparitions.'

'After all,' said Father Brown, 'Apparitions are only Appearances. I suppose you'd say the Family Ghost is only keeping up appearances.'

The Professor's gaze, which had commonly a fine abstracted character, suddenly fixed and focused itself as it did on a dubious medium. It had rather the air of a man screwing a strong magnifying-glass into his eye. Not that he thought the priest was in the least like a dubious medium; but he was startled into attention by his friend's thought following so closely on his own.

'Appearances!' he muttered, 'crikey, but it's odd you should say that just now. The more I learn, the more I fancy they lose by merely looking for appearances. Now if they'd look a little into Disappearances—'

'Yes,' said Father Brown, 'after all, the real fairy legends weren't so very much about the appearance of famous fairies; calling up

Titania or exhibiting Oberon by moonlight. But there were no end of legends about people *disappearing*, because they were stolen by the fairies. Are you on the track of Kilmeny or Thomas the Rhymer?'

'I'm on the track of ordinary modern people you've read of in the newspapers,' answered Openshaw. 'You may well stare; but that's my game just now; and I've been on it for a long time. Frankly, I think a lot of psychic appearances could be explained away. It's the disappearances I can't explain, unless they're psychic. These people in the newspapers who vanish and are never found – if you knew the details as I do . . . and now only this morning I got confirmation; an extraordinary letter from an old missionary, quite a respectable old boy. He's coming to see me at my office this morning. Perhaps you'd lunch with me or something; and I'd tell the results – in confidence.'

'Thanks; I will – unless,' said Father Brown modestly, 'the fairies have stolen me by then.'

With that they parted and Openshaw walked round the corner to a small office he rented in the neighbourhood; chiefly for the publication of a small periodical, of psychical and psychological notes of the driest and most agnostic sort. He had only one clerk, who sat at a desk in the outer office, totting up figures and facts for the purposes of the printed report; and the Professor paused to ask if Mr Pringle had called. The clerk answered mechanically in the negative and went on mechanically adding up figures; and the Professor turned towards the inner room that was his study. 'Oh, by the way, Berridge,' he added, without turning round, 'if Mr Pringle comes, send him straight in to me. You needn't interrupt your work; I rather want those notes finished tonight if possible. You might leave them on my desk tomorrow, if I am late.'

And he went into his private office, still brooding on the problem which the name of Pringle had raised; or rather, perhaps, had ratified and confirmed in his mind. Even the most perfectly balanced of agnostics is partially human; and it is possible that the missionary's letter seemed to have greater weight as promising to support his private and still tentative hypothesis. He sat down in his large and comfortable chair, opposite the engraving of Montaigne; and read once more the short letter from the Rev. Luke Pringle, making the appointment for that morning. No man knew better than Professor Openshaw the marks of the letter of the crank; the crowded details; the spidery handwriting; the unnecessary length and repetition. There were none of these things in this case; but a brief and businesslike typewritten statement that the writer had encountered some curious cases of Disappearance, which seemed to fall within the province of the Professor as a student of psychic problems. The Professor was favourably impressed; nor had he any unfavourable impression, in spite of a slight movement of surprise, when he looked up and saw that the Rev. Luke Pringle was already in the room.

'Your clerk told me I was to come straight in,' said Mr Pringle apologetically, but with a broad and rather agreeable grin. The grin was partly masked by masses of reddish-grey beard and whiskers; a perfect jungle of a beard, such as is sometimes grown by white men living in the jungles; but the eyes above the snub nose had nothing about them in the least wild or outlandish. Openshaw had instantly turned on them that concentrated spotlight or burning-glass of sceptical scrutiny which he turned on many men to see if they were mountebanks or maniacs; and, in this case, he had a rather unusual sense of reassurance. The wild beard might have belonged to a crank, but the eyes completely contradicted the beard; they were full of that quite frank and friendly laughter which is never found in the faces of those who are serious frauds or serious lunatics. He would have expected a man with those eyes to be a Philistine, a jolly sceptic, a man who shouted out shallow but hearty contempt for ghosts and spirits; but anyhow, no professional humbug could afford to look as frivolous as that. The man was buttoned up to the throat in a shabby old cape, and only his broad limp hat suggested the cleric; but missionaries from wild places do not always bother to dress like clerics.

'You probably think all this is another hoax, Professor,' said Mr Pringle, with a sort of abstract enjoyment, 'and I hope you will forgive my laughing at your very natural air of disapproval. All the same, I've got to tell my story to somebody who knows, because it's true. And, all joking apart, it's tragic as well as true. Well, to cut it short, I was missionary in Nya-Nya, a station in West Africa, in the thick of the forests, where almost the only other white man was the officer in command of the district, Captain Wales; and he and I grew rather thick. Not that he liked missions; he was, if I may say so, thick in many ways; one of those square-headed, square-shouldered men of action who hardly need to think, let alone believe. That's what makes it all the queerer. One day he came back to his tent in the forest, after a short leave, and said he had gone through a jolly rum experience, and didn't know what to do about it. He was holding a rusty old book in a leather binding, and he put it down on a table beside his revolver and an old Arab sword he kept, probably as a curiosity. He said this book had belonged to a man on the boat he had just come off; and the man swore that nobody must open the book, or look inside it; or else they would be carried off by the devil, or disappear, or something. Wales said this was all nonsense, of course; and they had a quarrel; and the upshot seems to have been that this man, taunted with cowardice or superstition, actually did look into the book; and instantly dropped it; walked to the side of the boat—'

'One moment,' said the Professor, who had made one or two notes. 'Before you tell me anything else. Did this man tell Wales where he had got the book, or who it originally belonged to?'

'Yes,' replied Pringle, now entirely grave. 'It seems he said he was bringing it back to Dr Hankey, the Oriental traveller now in England, to whom it originally belonged, and who had warned him of its strange properties. Well, Hankey is an able man and a rather crabbed and sneering sort of man; which makes it queerer still. But the point of Wales's story is much simpler. It is that the man who had looked into the book walked straight over the side of the ship, and was never seen again.'

'Do you believe it yourself?' asked Openshaw after a pause.

'Well, I do,' replied Pringle. 'I believe it for two reasons. First, that Wales was an entirely unimaginative man; and he added one touch that only an imaginative man could have added. He said that the man walked straight over the side on a still and calm day; but there was no splash.'

The Professor looked at his notes for some seconds in silence; and then said: 'And your other reason for believing it?'

'My other reason,' answered the Rev. Luke Pringle, 'is what I saw myself.'

There was another silence, until he continued in the same matter-of-fact way. Whatever he had, he had nothing of the eagerness with which the crank, or even the believer, tries to convince others.

'I told you that Wales put down the book on the table beside the sword. There was only one entrance to the tent; and it happened that I was standing in it, looking out into the forest, with my back to my companion. He was standing by the table grumbling and growling about the whole business; saying it was tomfoolery in the twentieth century to be frightened of opening a book; asking why the devil he shouldn't open it himself. Then some instinct stirred in me and I said that he had better not do that, it had better be returned to Dr Hankey. "What harm could it do?" he said rest-lessly. "What harm did it do?" I answered obstinately. "What happened to your friend on the boat?" He didn't answer; indeed I didn't know what he could answer; but I pressed my logical advantage in mere vanity. "If it comes to that," I said, "what is your version of what really happened on the boat?" Still he didn't answer; and I looked round and saw that he wasn't there.

'The tent was empty. The book was lying on the table; open, but on its face, as if he had turned it downwards. But the sword was lying on the ground near the other side of the tent; and the canvas of the tent showed a great slash, as if somebody had hacked his way out with the sword. The gash in the tent gaped at me; but showed only the dark glimmer of the forest outside. And when I went across and looked through the rent I could not be certain whether the tangle of the tall plants and the undergrowth had been bent or broken; at least not farther than a few feet. I have never seen or heard of Captain Wales from that day.

'I wrapped the book up in brown paper, taking good care not to look at it; and I brought it back to England, intending at first to return it to Dr Hankey. Then I saw some notes in your paper suggesting a hypothesis about such things; and I decided to stop on the way and put the matter before you, as you have a name for being balanced and having an open mind.'

Professor Openshaw laid down his pen and looked steadily at the man on the other side of the table; concentrating in that single stare all his long experience of many entirely different types of hum-bug, and even some eccentric and extraordinary types of honest men. In the ordinary way, he would have begun with the healthy hypothesis that the story was a pack of lies. On the whole he did incline to assume that it was a pack of lies. And yet he could not fit the man into his story; if it were only that he could not see that sort of liar telling that sort of lie. The man was not trying to look honest on the surface, as most quacks and impostors do; somehow, it seemed all the other way; as if the man *was* honest, in spite of something else that was merely on the surface. He thought of a good man with one innocent delusion; but again the symptoms were not the same; there was even a sort of virile indifference; as if the man did not care much about his delusion, if it was a delusion.

'Mr Pringle,' he said sharply, like a barrister making a witness jump, 'where is this book of yours now?'

The grin reappeared on the bearded face which had grown grave during the recital.

'I left it outside,' said Mr Pringle. 'I mean in the outer office. It was a risk, perhaps; but the less risk of the two.'

'What do you mean?' demanded the Professor. 'Why didn't you bring it straight in here?'

'Because,' answered the missionary, 'I knew that as soon as you saw it, you'd open it – before you had heard the story. I thought it possible you might think twice about opening it – after you'd heard the story.'

Then after a silence he added, 'There was nobody out there but your clerk; and he looked a stolid steady-going specimen, immersed in business calculations.'

Openshaw laughed unaffectedly. 'Oh, Babbage,' he cried, 'your magic tomes are safe enough with him, I assure you. His name's Berridge – but I often call him Babbage; because he's so exactly like a Calculating Machine. No human being, if you can call him a human being, would be less likely to open other people's brown-paper parcels. Well, we may as well go and bring it in now; though I assure you I will consider seriously the course to be taken with it. Indeed, I tell you frankly,' and he stared at the man again, 'that I'm not quite sure whether we ought to open it here and now, or send it to this Dr Hankey.'

The two had passed together out of the inner into the outer office; and even as they did so, Mr Pringle gave a cry and ran forward towards the clerk's desk. For the clerk's desk was there; but not the clerk. On the clerk's desk lay a faded old leather book, torn out of its brown-paper wrappings, and lying closed, but as if it had just been opened. The clerk's desk stood against the wide window that looked out into the street; and the window was shattered with a huge ragged hole in the glass; as if a human body had been shot through it into the world without. There was no other trace of Mr Berridge.

Both the two men left in the office stood as still as statues; and then it was the Professor who slowly came to life. He looked even more judicial than he had ever looked in his life, as he slowly turned and held out his hand to the missionary.

'Mr Pringle,' he said, 'I beg your pardon. I beg your pardon only for thoughts that I have had; and half-thoughts at that. But nobody could call himself a scientific man and not face a fact like this.'

'I suppose,' said Pringle doubtfully, 'that we ought to make some inquiries. Can you ring up his house and find out if he has gone home?'

'I don't know that he's on the telephone,' answered Openshaw, rather absently; 'he lives somewhere up Hampstead way, I think. But I suppose somebody will inquire here, if his friends or family miss him.'

'Could we furnish a description,' asked the other, 'if the police want it?'

'The police!' said the Professor, starting from his reverie. 'A description. . . . Well, he looked awfully like everybody else, I'm afraid, except for goggles. One of those clean-shaven chaps. But the police . . . look here, what *are* we to do about this mad business?'

'I know what I ought to do,' said the Rev. Mr Pringle firmly, 'I am going to take this book straight to the only original Dr Hankey, and ask him what the devil it's all about. He lives not very far from here, and I'll come straight back and tell you what he says.'

'Oh, very well,' said the Professor at last, as he sat down rather wearily; perhaps relieved for the moment to be rid of the responsibility. But long after the brisk and ringing footsteps of the little missionary had died away down the street, the Professor sat in the same posture, staring into vacancy like a man in a trance.

He was still in the same seat and almost in the same attitude, when the same brisk footsteps were heard on the pavement without and the missionary entered, this time, as a glance assured him, with empty hands.

'Dr Hankey,' said Pringle gravely, 'wants to keep the book for an hour and consider the point. Then he asks us both to call, and he will give us his decision. He specially desired, Professor, that you should accompany me on the second visit.'

Openshaw continued to stare in silence; then he said, suddenly: 'Who the devil is Dr Hankey?'

'You sound rather as if you meant he was the devil,' said Pringle, smiling, 'and I fancy some people have thought so. He had quite a reputation in your own line; but he gained it mostly in India, studying local magic and so on, so perhaps he's not so well known here. He is a yellow skinny little devil with a lame leg, and a doubtful temper; but he seems to have set up in an ordinary respectable practice in these parts, and I don't know anything definitely wrong about him – unless it's wrong to be the only person who can possibly know anything about all this crazy affair.'

Professor Openshaw rose heavily and went to the telephone; he rang up Father Brown, changing the luncheon engagement to a dinner, that he might hold himself free for the expedition to the house of the Anglo-Indian doctor; after that he sat down again, lit a cigar and sank once more into his own unfathomable thoughts.

Father Brown went round to the restaurant appointed for dinner, and kicked his heels for some time in a vestibule full of mirrors and palms in pots; he had been informed of Openshaw's afternoon engagement, and, as the evening closed in dark and stormy round the glass and the green plants, guessed that it had produced something unexpected and unduly prolonged. He even wondered for a moment whether the Professor would turn up at all; but when the Professor eventually did, it was clear that his own more general guesses had been justified. For it was a very wild-eyed and even wild-haired Professor who eventually drove back with Mr Pringle from the expedition to the North of London, where suburbs are still fringed with heathy wastes and scraps of common, looking more sombre under the rather thunderstorm sunset. Nevertheless, they had apparently found the house, standing a little apart though within hail of other houses; they had verified the brass-plate duly engraved, 'J. I. Hankey, M.D., M.R.C.S.' Only they did not find J. I. Hankey, M.D., M.R.C.S. They found only what a nightmare whisper had already subconsciously prepared them to find: a commonplace parlour with the accursed volume lying on the table, as if it had just been read; and beyond, a back door burst open and a faint trail of footsteps that ran a little way up so steep a garden-path that it seemed that no lame man could have run up so lightly. But it was a lame man who had run; for in those few steps there was the misshapen unequal mark of some sort of surgical boot; then two marks of that boot alone (as if the creature had hopped) and then nothing. There was nothing further to be learnt from Dr J. I. Hankey, except that he had made his decision. He had read the oracle and received the doom.

When the two came into the entrance under the palms, Pringle put the book down suddenly on a small table, as if it burned his fingers. The priest glanced at it curiously; there was only some rude lettering on the front with a couplet:

> They that looked into this book
> Them the Flying Terror took;

and underneath, as he afterwards discovered, similar warnings in Greek, Latin and French. The other two had turned away with a natural impulsion towards drinks, after their exhaustion and bewilderment; and Openshaw had called to the waiter, who brought cocktails on a tray.

'You will dine with us, I hope,' said the Professor to the missionary; but Mr Pringle amiably shook his head.

'If you'll forgive me,' he said, 'I'm going off to wrestle with this book and this business by myself somewhere. I suppose I couldn't use your office for an hour or so?'

'I suppose – I'm afraid it's locked,' said Openshaw in some surprise.

'You forget there's a hole in the window.' The Rev. Luke Pringle gave the very broadest of all his broad grins and vanished into the darkness without.

'A rather odd fellow, that, after all,' said the Professor, frowning.

He was rather surprised to find Father Brown talking to the waiter who had brought the cocktails, apparently about the waiter's most private affairs; for there was some mention of a baby who was now out of danger. He commented on the fact with some surprise, wondering how the priest came to know the man; but the former only said, 'Oh, I dine here every two or three months, and I've talked to him now and then.'

The Professor, who himself dined there about five times a week, was conscious that he had never thought of talking to the man; but his thoughts were interrupted by a strident ringing and a summons to the telephone. The voice on the telephone said it was Pringle; it was rather a muffled voice, but it might well be muffled in all those bushes of beard and whisker. Its message was enough to establish identity.

'Professor,' said the voice, 'I can't stand it any longer. I'm going to look for myself. I'm speaking from your office and the book is in front of me. If anything happens to me, this is to say good-bye. No – it's no good trying to stop me. You wouldn't be in time anyhow. I'm opening the book now. I . . .'

Openshaw thought he heard something like a sort of thrilling or shivering yet almost soundless crash; then he shouted the name of Pringle again and again; but he heard no more. He hung up the receiver, and, restored to a superb academic calm, rather like the calm of despair, went back and quietly took his seat at the dinner-table. Then, as coolly as if he were describing the failure of some small silly trick at a séance, he told the priest every detail of this monstrous mystery.

'Five men have now vanished in this impossible way,' he said. 'Every one is extraordinary; and yet the one case I simply can't get over is my clerk, Berridge. It's just because he was the quietest creature that he's the queerest case.'

'Yes,' replied Father Brown, 'it was a queer thing for Berridge to do, anyway. He was awfully conscientious. He was always so jolly careful to keep all the office business separate from any fun of his own. Why, hardly anybody knew he was quite a humorist at home and—'

'Berridge!' cried the Professor. 'What on earth are you talking about? Did you know him?'

'Oh no,' said Father Brown carelessly, 'only as you say I know the waiter. I've often had to wait in your office, till you turned up, and of course I passed the time of day with poor Berridge. He was rather a card. I remember he once said he would like to collect valueless things, as collectors did the silly things they thought valuable. You know the old story about the woman who collected valueless things.'

'I'm not sure I know what you're talking about,' said Openshaw. 'But even if my clerk was eccentric (and I never knew a man

I should have thought less so), it wouldn't explain what happened to him; and it certainly wouldn't explain the others.'

'What others?' asked the priest.

The Professor stared at him and spoke distinctly, as if to a child: 'My dear Father Brown, Five Men have disappeared.'

'My dear Professor Openshaw, no men have disappeared.'

Father Brown gazed back at his host with equal steadiness and spoke with equal distinctness. Nevertheless, the Professor required the words repeated, and they were repeated as distinctly.

'I say that no men have disappeared.'

After a moment's silence, he added, 'I suppose the hardest thing is to convince anybody that o + o + o = o. Men believe the oddest things if they are in a series; that is why Macbeth believed the three words of the three witches; though the first was something he knew himself; and the last something he could only bring about himself. But in your case the middle term is the weakest of all.'

'What do you mean?'

'You saw nobody vanish. You did not see the man vanish from the boat. You did not see the man vanish from the tent. All that rests on the word of Mr Pringle, which I will not discuss just now. But you'll admit this; you would never have taken his word yourself, *unless* you had seen it confirmed by your clerk's disappearance; just as Macbeth would never have believed he would be king, if he had not been confirmed in believing he would be Cawdor.'

'That may be true,' said the Professor, nodding slowly. 'But *when* it was confirmed, I knew it was the truth. You say I saw nothing myself. But I did; I saw my own clerk disappear. Berridge did disappear.'

'Berridge did not disappear,' said Father Brown. 'On the contrary.'

'What the devil do you mean by "on the contrary"?'

'I mean,' said Father Brown, 'that he never disappeared. He appeared.'

Openshaw stared across at his friend, but the eyes had already altered in his head, as they did when they concentrated on a new presentation of a problem. The priest went on:

'He appeared in your study, disguised in a bushy red beard and buttoned up in a clumsy cape, and announced himself as the Rev. Luke Pringle. And you had never noticed your own clerk enough to know him again, when he was in so rough-and-ready a disguise.'

'But surely,' began the Professor.

'Could you describe him for the police?' asked Father Brown. 'Not you. You probably knew he was clean-shaven and wore tinted glasses; and merely taking off those glasses was a better disguise than putting on anything else. You had never seen his eyes any more than his soul; jolly laughing eyes. He had planted his absurd book and all the properties; then he calmly smashed the window, put on the beard and cape and walked into your study; knowing that you had never looked at him in your life.'

'But why should he play me such an insane trick?' demanded Openshaw.

'Why, *because* you had never looked at him in your life,' said Father Brown; and his hand slightly curled and clinched, as if he might have struck the table, if he had been given to gesture. 'You called him the Calculating Machine, because that was all you ever used him for. You never found out even what a stranger strolling into your office could find out, in five minutes' chat: that he was a character; that he was full of antics; that he had all sorts of views on you and your theories and your reputation for "spotting" people. Can't you understand his itching to prove that you couldn't spot your own clerk? He has nonsense notions of all sorts. About collecting useless things, for instance. Don't you know the story of the woman who bought the two most useless things: an old doctor's brass-plate and a wooden leg? With those your ingenious clerk created the character of the remarkable Dr Hankey; as easily as the visionary Captain Wales. Planting them in his own house—'

'Do you mean that place we visited beyond Hampstead was Berridge's own house?' asked Openshaw.

'Did *you* know his house – or even his address?' retorted the priest. 'Look here, don't think I'm speaking disrespectfully of you or your work. You are a great servant of truth and you know I could never be disrespectful to that. You've seen through a lot of liars, when you put your mind to it. But don't *only* look at liars. Do, just occasionally, look at honest men – like the waiter.'

'Where is Berridge now?' asked the Professor, after a long silence.

'I haven't the least doubt,' said Father Brown, 'that he is back in your office. In fact, he came back into your office at the exact moment when the Rev. Luke Pringle read the awful volume and faded into the void.'

There was another long silence and then Professor Openshaw laughed; with the laugh of a great man who is great enough to look small. Then he said abruptly:

'I suppose I do deserve it; for not noticing the nearest helpers I have. But you must admit the accumulation of incidents was rather formidable. Did you *never* feel just a momentary awe of the awful volume?'

'Oh that,' said Father Brown. 'I opened it as soon as I saw it lying there. It's all blank pages. You see, I am not superstitious.'

THE GREEN MAN

A YOUNG man in knickerbockers, with an eager sanguine profile, was playing golf against himself on the links that lay parallel to the sand and sea, which were all growing grey with twilight. He was not carelessly knocking a ball about, but rather practising particular strokes with a sort of microscopic fury; like a neat and tidy whirlwind. He had learned many games quickly, but he had a disposition to learn them a little more quickly than they can be learnt. He was rather prone to be a victim of those remarkable invitations by which a man may learn the Violin in Six Lessons – or acquire a perfect French accent by a Correspondence Course. He lived in the breezy atmosphere of such hopeful advertisement and adventure. He was at present the private secretary of Admiral Sir Michael Craven, who owned the big house behind the park abutting on the links. He was ambitious, and had no intention of continuing indefinitely to be private secretary to anybody. But he was also reasonable, and he knew that the best way of ceasing to be a secretary was to be a good secretary. Consequently he was a very good secretary, dealing with the ever-accumulating arrears of the Admiral's correspondence with the same swift centripetal concentration with which he addressed the golf ball. He had to struggle with the correspondence alone and at his own discretion at present; for the Admiral had been with his ship for the last six months; and, though now returning, was not expected for hours, or possibly days.

With an athletic stride, the young man, whose name was Harold Harker, crested the rise of turf that was the rampart of the links and, looking out across the sands to the sea, saw a strange sight. He did not see it very clearly; for the dusk was darkening every minute under stormy clouds; but it seemed to him, by a sort of momentary illusion, like a dream of days long past or a drama played by ghosts, out of another age in history.

The last of the sunset lay in long bars of copper and gold above the last dark strip of sea that seemed rather black than blue. But blacker still against this gleam in the west, there passed in sharp outline, like figures in a shadow pantomime, two men with three-cornered cocked hats and swords; as if they had just landed from one of the wooden ships of Nelson. It was not at all the sort of hallucination that would have come natural to Mr Harker, had he been prone to hallucinations. He was of the type that is at once sanguine and scientific; and would be more likely to fancy the flying-ships of the future than the fighting-ships of the past. He therefore very sensibly came to the conclusion that even a futurist can believe his eyes.

His illusion did not last more than a moment. On the second glance, what he saw was unusual but not incredible. The two men who were striding in single file across the sands, one some fifteen yards behind the other, were ordinary modern naval officers; but naval officers wearing that almost extravagant full-dress uniform which naval officers never do wear if they can possibly help it; only on great ceremonial occasions such as the visits of Royalty. In the man walking in front, who seemed more or less unconscious of the man walking behind, Harker recognized at once the high-bridged nose and spike-shaped beard of his own employer the Admiral. The other man following in his tracks he did not know. But he did know something about the circumstances connected with the ceremonial occasion. He knew that when the Admiral's ship put in at the adjacent port, it was to be formally visited by a Great Personage; which was enough, in that sense, to explain the officers being in full dress. But he did also know the officers; or at any rate the Admiral. And what could have possessed the Admiral to come on shore in that rig-out, when one could swear he would seize five minutes to change into mufti or at least into undress uni-form, was more than his secretary could conceive. It seemed some-how to be the very last thing he would do. It was indeed to remain for many weeks one of the chief mysteries of this mysterious busi-ness. As it was, the outline of these fantastic court uniforms against the empty scenery, striped with dark sea and sand, had something suggestive of comic opera; and reminded the spectator of *Pinafore*.

The second figure was much more singular; somewhat sin-gular in appearance, despite his correct lieutenant's uniform, and still more extraordinary in behaviour. He walked in a strangely irregular and uneasy manner; sometimes quickly and sometimes slowly; as if he could not make up his mind whether to overtake the Admiral or not. The Admiral was rather deaf and certainly heard no footsteps behind him on the yielding sand; but the foot-steps behind him, if traced in the detective manner, would have given rise to twenty conjectures from a limp to a dance. The man's face was swarthy as well as darkened with shadow and every now and then the eyes in it shifted and shone, as if to accent his agita-tion. Once he began to run and then abruptly relapsed into a swag-gering slowness and carelessness. Then he did something which Mr Harker could never have conceived any normal naval officer in His Britannic Majesty's Service doing, even in a lunatic asylum. He drew his sword.

It was at this bursting-point of the prodigy that the two passing figures disappeared behind a headland on the shore. The staring secretary had just time to notice the swarthy stranger, with a resumption of carelessness, knock off a head of sea-holly with his glittering blade. He seemed then to have abandoned all idea of catching the other man up. But Mr Harold Harker's face became very thoughtful indeed; and he stood there ruminating for some time before he gravely took himself inland, towards the road that ran past the gates of the great house and so by a long curve down to the sea.

It was up this curving road from the coast that the Admiral might be expected to come, considering the direction in which he had been walking, and making the natural assumption that he was bound for his own door. The path along the sands, under the links, turned inland just beyond the headland and solidifying itself into a road, returned towards Craven House. It was down this road, therefore, that the secretary darted, with characteristic impetu-osity, to meet his patron returning home. But the patron was apparently not returning home. What was still more peculiar, the secretary was not returning home either; at least until many hours later; a delay quite long enough to arouse alarm and mystification at Craven House.

Behind the pillars and palms of that rather too palatial country house, indeed, there was expectancy gradually changing to uneasi-ness. Gryce the butler, a big bilious man abnormally silent below as well as above stairs, showed a certain restlessness as he moved

about the main front-hall and occasionally looked out of the side
windows of the porch, on the white road that swept towards the
sea. The Admiral's sister Marion, who kept house for him, had her
brother's high nose with a more sniffy expression; she was voluble,
rather rambling, not without humour, and capable of sudden
emphasis as shrill as a cockatoo. The Admiral's daughter Olive was
dark, dreamy, and as a rule abstractedly silent, perhaps melancholy; so that her aunt generally conducted most of the conversation, and that without reluctance. But the girl also had a gift of
sudden laughter that was very engaging.

'I can't think why they're not here already,' said the elder lady.
'The postman distinctly told me he'd seen the Admiral coming
along the beach; along with that dreadful creature Rook. Why in
the world they call him Lieutenant Rook—'

'Perhaps,' suggested the melancholy young lady, with a momentary brightness, 'perhaps they call him Lieutenant because he is a
Lieutenant.'

'I can't think why the Admiral keeps him,' snorted her aunt, as
if she were talking of a housemaid. She was very proud of her
brother and always called him the Admiral; but her notions of a
commission in the Senior Service were inexact.

'Well, Roger Rook is sulky and unsociable and all that,' replied
Olive, 'but of course that wouldn't prevent him being a capable
sailor.'

'Sailor!' cried her aunt with one of her rather startling cockatoo
notes, 'he isn't my notion of a sailor. The Lass that Loved a Sailor,
as they used to sing when I was young. . . . Just think of it! He's not
gay and free and whatsitsname. He doesn't sing chanties or dance
a hornpipe.'

'Well,' observed her niece with gravity, 'the Admiral doesn't
very often dance a hornpipe.'

'Oh, you know what I mean – he isn't bright or breezy or anything,' replied the old lady. 'Why, that secretary fellow could do
better than that.'

Olive's rather tragic face was transfigured by one of her good
and rejuvenating waves of laughter.

'I'm sure Mr Harker would dance a hornpipe for you,' she said,
'and say he had learnt it in half an hour from the book of instruc-
tions. He's always learning things of that sort.'

She stopped laughing suddenly and looked at her aunt's rather strained face.

'I can't think why Mr Harker doesn't come,' she added.

'I don't care about Mr Harker,' replied the aunt, and rose and looked out of the window.

The evening light had long turned from yellow to grey and was now turning almost to white under the widening moonlight, over the large flat landscape by the coast; unbroken by any features save a clump of sea-twisted trees round a pool and beyond, rather gaunt and dark against the horizon, the shabby fishermen's tavern on the shore that bore the name of the Green Man. And all that road and landscape was empty of any living thing. Nobody had seen the figure in the cocked hat that had been observed, earlier in the evening, walking by the sea; or the other and stranger figure that had been seen trailing after him. Nobody had even seen the secretary who saw them.

It was after midnight when the secretary at last burst in and aroused the household; and his face, white as a ghost, looked all the paler against the background of the stolid face and figure of a big Inspector of Police. Somehow that red, heavy, indifferent face looked, even more than the white and harassed one, like a mask of doom. The news was broken to the two women with such consideration or concealments as were possible. But the news was that the body of Admiral Craven had been eventually fished out of the foul weeds and scum of the pool under the trees; and that he was drowned and dead.

Anybody acquainted with Mr Harold Harker, secretary, will realize that, whatever his agitation, he was by morning in a mood to be tremendously on the spot. He hustled the Inspector, whom he had met the night before on the road down by the Green Man, into another room for private and practical consultation. He questioned the Inspector rather as the Inspector might have questioned a yokel. But Inspector Burns was a stolid character; and was either too stupid or too clever to resent such trifles. It soon began to look as if he were by no means so stupid as he looked; for he disposed of Harker's eager questions in a manner that was slow but methodical and rational.

'Well,' said Harker (his head full of many manuals with titles like *Be a Detective in Ten Days*). 'Well, it's the old triangle, I suppose. Accident, Suicide or Murder.'

'I don't see how it could be accident,' answered the policeman. 'It wasn't even dark yet and the pool's fifty yards from the straight road that he knew like his own doorstep. He'd no more have got into that pond than he'd go and carefully lie down in a puddle in the street. As for suicide, it's rather a responsibility to suggest it, and rather improbable too. The Admiral was a pretty spry and successful man and frightfully rich, nearly a millionaire in fact; though of course that doesn't prove anything. He seemed to be pretty normal and comfortable in his private life too; he's the last man I should suspect of drowning himself.'

'So that we come,' said the secretary, lowering his voice with the thrill, 'I suppose we come to the third possibility.'

'We won't be in too much of a hurry about that,' said the Inspector, to the annoyance of Harker, who was in a hurry about everything. 'But naturally there are one or two things one would like to know. One would like to know about his property, for instance. Do you know who's likely to come in for it? You're his private secretary; do you know anything about his will?'

'I'm not so private a secretary as all that,' answered the young man. 'His solicitors are Messrs Willis, Hardman and Dyke, over in Suttford High Street; and I believe the will is in their custody.'

'Well, I'd better get round and see them pretty soon,' said the Inspector.

'Let's get round and see them at once,' said the impatient secretary.

He took a turn or two restlessly up and down the room and then exploded in a fresh place.

'What have you done about the body, Inspector?' he asked.

'Dr Straker is examining it now at the Police Station. His report ought to be ready in an hour or so.'

'It can't be ready too soon,' said Harker. 'It would save time if we could meet him at the lawyer's.' Then he stopped and his impetuous tone changed abruptly to one of some embarrassment.

'Look here,' he said, 'I want ... we want to consider the young lady, the poor Admiral's daughter, as much as possible just now. She's got a notion that may be all nonsense; but I wouldn't like to disappoint her. There's some friend of hers she wants to consult, staying in the town at present. Man of the name of Brown; priest or parson of some sort; she's given me his address. I don't take much stock in priests or parsons, but—'

The Inspector nodded. 'I don't take any stock in priests or parsons; but I take a lot of stock in Father Brown,' he said. 'I happened to have to do with him in a queer sort of society jewel case. He ought to have been a policeman instead of a parson.'

'Oh, all right,' said the breathless secretary as he vanished from the room. 'Let him come to the lawyer's too.'

Thus it happened that, when they hurried across to the neighbouring town to meet Dr Straker at the solicitor's office, they found Father Brown already seated there, with his hands folded on his heavy umbrella, chatting pleasantly to the only available member of the firm. Dr Straker also had arrived, but apparently only at that moment, as he was carefully placing his gloves in his top-hat and his top-hat on a side-table. And the mild and beaming expression of the priest's moonlike face and spectacles, together with the silent chuckles of the jolly old grizzled lawyer, to whom he was talking, were enough to show that the doctor had not yet opened his mouth to bring the news of death.

'A beautiful morning after all,' Father Brown was saying. 'That storm seems to have passed over us. There were some big black clouds, but I notice that not a drop of rain fell.'

'Not a drop,' agreed the solicitor toying with a pen; he was the third partner, Mr Dyke; 'there's not a cloud in the sky now. It's the sort of day for a holiday.' Then he realized the newcomers and looked up, laying down the pen and rising. 'Ah, Mr Harker, how are you? I hear the Admiral is expected home soon.' Then Harker spoke, and his voice rang hollow in the room.

'I am sorry to say we are the bearers of bad news. Admiral Craven was drowned before reaching home.'

There was a change in the very air of the still office, though not in the attitudes of the motionless figures; both were staring at the speaker as if a joke had been frozen on their lips. Both repeated the word 'drowned' and looked at each other, and then again at their informant. Then there was a small hubbub of questions.

'When did this happen?' asked the priest.

'Where was he found?' asked the lawyer.

'He was found,' said the Inspector, 'in that pool by the coast, not far from the Green Man, and dragged out all covered with green scum and weeds so as to be almost unrecognizable. But Dr Straker here has— What is the matter, Father Brown? Are you ill?'

'The Green Man,' said Father Brown with a shudder. 'I'm so sorry . . . I beg your pardon for being upset.'

'Upset by what?' asked the staring officer.

'By his being covered with green scum, I suppose,' said the priest, with a rather shaky laugh. Then he added rather more firmly, 'I thought it might have been seaweed.'

By this time everybody was looking at the priest, with a not unnatural suspicion that he was mad; and yet the next crucial surprise was not to come from him. After a dead silence, it was the doctor who spoke.

Dr Straker was a remarkable man, even to look at. He was very tall and angular, formal and professional in his dress; yet retaining a fashion that has hardly been known since Mid-Victorian times. Though comparatively young, he wore his brown beard very long and spreading over his waistcoat; in contrast with it, his features, which were both harsh and handsome, looked singularly pale. His good looks were also diminished by something in his deep eyes that was not squinting, but like the shadow of a squint. Everybody noticed these things about him, because the moment he spoke, he gave forth an indescribable air of authority. But all he said was:

'There is one more thing to be said, if you come to details, about Admiral Craven being drowned.' Then he added reflectively, 'Admiral Craven was not drowned.'

The Inspector turned with quite a new promptitude and shot a question at him.

'I have just examined the body,' said Dr Straker, 'the cause of death was a stab through the heart with some pointed blade like a stiletto. It was after death, and even some little time after, that the body was hidden in the pool.'

Father Brown was regarding Dr Straker with a very lively eye, such as he seldom turned upon anybody; and when the group in the office began to break up, he managed to attach himself to the medical man for a little further conversation, as they went back down the street. There had not been very much else to detain them except the rather formal question of the will. The impatience of the young secretary had been somewhat tried by the professional etiquette of the old lawyer. But the latter was ultimately induced, rather by the tact of the priest than the authority of the policeman, to refrain from making a mystery where there was no mystery at all. Mr Dyke admitted, with a smile, that the Admiral's will was a very normal and ordinary document, leaving everything to his only child Olive; and that there really was no particular reason for concealing the fact.

The doctor and the priest walked slowly down the street that struck out of the town in the direction of Craven House. Harker had plunged on ahead of him with all his native eagerness to get somewhere; but the two behind seemed more interested in their discussion than their direction. It was in rather an enigmatic tone that the tall doctor said to the short cleric beside him:

'Well, Father Brown, what do you think of a thing like this?'

Father Brown looked at him rather intently for an instant and then said: 'Well, I've begun to think of one or two things; but my chief difficulty is that I only knew the Admiral slightly; though I've seen something of his daughter.'

'The Admiral,' said the doctor with a grim immobility of feature, 'was the sort of man of whom it is said that he had not an enemy in the world.'

'I suppose you mean,' answered the priest, 'that there's something else that will not be said.'

'Oh, it's no affair of mine,' said Straker hastily but rather harshly. 'He had his moods, I suppose. He once threatened me with a legal action about an operation; but I think he thought better of it. I can imagine his being rather rough with a subordinate.'

Father Brown's eyes were fixed on the figure of the secretary striding far ahead; and as he gazed he realized the special cause of his hurry. Some fifty yards farther ahead the Admiral's daughter was dawdling along the road towards the Admiral's house. The secretary soon came abreast of her; and for the remainder of the time Father Brown watched the silent drama of two human backs as they diminished into the distance. The secretary was evidently very much excited about something; but if the priest guessed what it was, he kept it to himself. When he came to the corner leading to the doctor's house, he only said briefly, 'I don't know if you have anything more to tell us.'

'Why should I?' answered the doctor very abruptly; and striding off, left it uncertain whether he was asking why he should have anything to tell, or why he should tell it.

Father Brown went stumping on alone, in the track of the two young people; but when he came to the entrance and avenues of the Admiral's park, he was arrested by the action of the girl, who turned suddenly and came straight towards him; her face unusually pale and her eyes bright with some new and as yet nameless emotion.

'Father Brown,' she said in a low voice, 'I must talk to you as soon as possible. You must listen to me, I can't see any other way out.'

'Why certainly,' he replied, as coolly as if a gutter-boy had asked him the time. 'Where shall we go and talk?'

The girl led him at random to one of the rather tumbledown arbours in the grounds; and they sat down behind a screen of large ragged leaves. She began instantly, as if she must relieve her feelings or faint.

'Harold Harker,' she said, 'has been talking to me about things. Terrible things.'

The priest nodded and the girl went on hastily. 'About Roger Rook. Do you know about Roger?'

'I've been told,' he answered, 'that his fellow-seamen call him The Jolly Roger, because he is never jolly; and looks like the pirate's skull and crossbones.'

'He was not always like that,' said Olive in a low voice. 'Something very queer must have happened to him. I knew him well when we were children; we used to play over there on the sands. He was harum-scarum and always talking about being a pirate; I dare say he was the sort they say might take to crime through reading shockers; but there was something poetical in his way of being piratical. He really was a Jolly Roger then. I suppose he was the last boy who kept up the old legend of really running away to sea; and at last his family had to agree to his joining the Navy. Well . . .'

'Yes,' said Father Brown patiently.

'Well,' she admitted, caught in one of her rare moments of mirth. 'I suppose poor Roger found it disappointing. Naval officers so seldom carry knives in their teeth or wave bloody cutlasses and black flags. But that doesn't explain the change in him. He just stiffened; grew dull and dumb, like a dead man walking about. He always avoids me; but that doesn't matter. I supposed some great grief that's no business of mine had broken him up. And now – well, if what Harold says is true, the grief is neither more nor less than going mad; or being possessed of a devil.'

'And what does Harold say?' asked the priest.

'It's so awful I can hardly say it,' she answered. 'He swears he saw Roger creeping behind my father that night; hesitating and then drawing his sword . . . and the doctor says father was stabbed with a steel point. . . . I *can't* believe Roger Rook had anything to do with it. His sulks and my father's temper sometimes led to quarrels; but what are quarrels? I can't exactly say I'm standing up for an old friend; because he isn't even friendly. But you can't help feeling sure of some things, even about an old acquaintance. And yet Harold swears that he—'

'Harold seems to swear a great deal,' said Father Brown.

There was a sudden silence; after which she said in a different tone:

'Well, he does swear other things too. Harold Harker proposed to me just now.'

'Am I to congratulate you, or rather him?' inquired her companion.

'I told him he must wait. He isn't good at waiting.' She was caught again in a ripple of her incongruous sense of the comic: 'He said I was his ideal and his ambition and so on. He has lived in the States; but somehow I never remember it when he is talking about dollars; only when he is talking about ideals.'

'And I suppose,' said Father Brown very softly, 'that it is because you have to decide about Harold that you want to know the truth about Roger.'

She stiffened and frowned, and then equally abruptly smiled, saying, 'Oh, you know too much.'

'I know very little, especially in this affair,' said the priest gravely. 'I only know who murdered your father.' She started up and stood staring down at him stricken white. Father Brown made a wry face as he went on: 'I made a fool of myself when I first realized it; when they'd just been asking where he was found, and went on talking about green scum and the Green Man.'

Then he also rose; clutching his clumsy umbrella with a new resolution, he addressed the girl with a new gravity.

'There is something else that I know, which is the key to all these riddles of yours; but I won't tell you yet. I suppose it's bad news; but it's nothing like so bad as the things you have been fancying.' He buttoned up his coat and turned towards the gate. 'I'm going to see this Mr Rook of yours. In a shed by the shore, near where Mr Harker saw him walking. I rather think he lives there.' And he went bustling off in the direction of the beach.

Olive was an imaginative person; perhaps too imaginative to be safely left to brood over such hints as her friend had thrown out; but he was in rather a hurry to find the best relief for her broodings. The mysterious connexion between Father Brown's first shock of enlightenment and the chance language about the pool and the inn, hag-rode her fancy in a hundred forms of ugly symbolism. The Green Man became a ghost trailing loathsome weeds and walking the countryside under the moon; the sign of the Green Man became a human figure hanging as from a gibbet; and the tarn itself became a tavern, a dark subaqueous tavern for the dead sailors. And yet he had taken the most rapid method to overthrow all such nightmares, with a burst of blinding daylight which seemed more mysterious than the night.

For before the sun had set, something had come back into her life that turned her whole world topsy-turvy once more; something she had hardly known that she desired until it was abruptly granted; something that was, like a dream, old and familiar, and yet remained incomprehensible and incredible. For Roger Rook had come striding across the sands, and even when he was a dot in the distance, she knew he was transfigured; and as he came nearer and nearer, she saw that his dark face was alive with laughter and exultation. He came straight towards her, as if they had never parted, and seized her shoulders saying: 'Now I can look after you, thank God.'

She hardly knew what she answered; but she heard herself questioning rather wildly why he seemed so changed and so happy.

'Because I am happy,' he answered. 'I have heard the bad news.'

All parties concerned, including some who seemed rather unconcerned, found themselves assembled on the garden path leading to Craven House, to hear the formality, now truly formal, of the lawyer's reading of the will; and the probable, and more practical, sequel of the lawyer's advice upon the crisis. Besides the grey-haired solicitor himself, armed with the testamentary document, there was the Inspector armed with more direct authority touching the crime, and Lieutenant Rook in undisguised attendance on the lady; some were rather mystified on seeing the tall figure of the doctor, some smiled a little on seeing the dumpy figure of the priest. Mr Harker, that Flying Mercury, had shot down to the lodge-gates to meet them, led them back on to the lawn, and then dashed ahead of them again to prepare their reception. He said he would be back in a jiffy; and anyone observing his piston-rod of energy could well believe it; but, for the moment, they were left rather stranded on the lawn outside the house.

'Reminds me of somebody making runs at cricket,' said the Lieutenant.

'That young man,' said the lawyer, 'is rather annoyed that the law cannot move quite so quickly as he does. Fortunately Miss Craven understands our professional difficulties and delays. She has kindly assured me that she still has confidence in my slowness.'

'I wish,' said the doctor, suddenly, 'that I had as much confidence in his quickness.'

'Why, what do you mean?' asked Rook, knitting his brows; 'do you mean that Harker is too quick?'

'Too quick and too slow,' said Dr Straker, in his rather cryptic fashion. 'I know one occasion at least when he was not so very quick. Why was he hanging about half the night by the pond and the Green Man, before the Inspector came down and found the body? Why did he meet the Inspector? Why should he expect to meet the Inspector outside the Green Man?'

'I don't understand you,' said Rook. 'Do you mean that Harker wasn't telling the truth?'

Dr Straker was silent. The grizzled lawyer laughed with grim good humour.

'I have nothing more serious to say against the young man,' he said, 'than that he made a prompt and praiseworthy attempt to teach me my own business.'

'For that matter, he made an attempt to teach me mine,' said the Inspector, who had just joined the group in front. 'But that doesn't matter. If Dr Straker means anything by his hints, they do matter. I must ask you to speak plainly, doctor. It may be my duty to question him at once.'

'Well, here he comes,' said Rook, as the alert figure of the secretary appeared once more in the doorway.

At this point Father Brown, who had remained silent and inconspicuous at the tail of the procession, astonished everybody very much; perhaps especially those who knew him. He not only walked rapidly to the front, but turned facing the whole group with an arresting and almost threatening expression, like a sergeant bringing soldiers to the halt.

'Stop!' he said almost sternly. 'I apologize to everybody; but it's absolutely necessary that I should see Mr Harker first. I've got to tell him something I know; and I don't think anybody else knows; something he's got to hear. It may save a very tragic misunderstanding with somebody later on.'

'What on earth do you mean?' asked old Dyke the lawyer.

'I mean the bad news,' said Father Brown.

'Here, I say,' began the Inspector indignantly; and then suddenly caught the priest's eye and remembered strange things he had seen in other days. 'Well, if it were anyone in the world but you, I should say of all the infernal cheek—'

But Father Brown was already out of hearing, and a moment afterwards was plunged in talk with Harker in the porch. They walked to and fro together for a few paces and then disappeared into the dark interior. It was about twelve minutes afterwards that Father Brown came out alone.

To their surprise he showed no disposition to re-enter the house, now that the whole company were at last about to enter it. He threw himself down on the rather rickety seat in the leafy arbour, and as the procession disappeared through the doorway, lit a pipe and proceeded to stare vacantly at the long ragged leaves about his head and to listen to the birds. There was no man who had a more hearty and enduring appetite for doing nothing.

He was apparently in a cloud of smoke and a dream of abstraction, when the front-doors were once more flung open and two or three figures came out helter-skelter, running towards him, the daughter of the house and her young admirer Mr Rook being easily winners in the race. Their faces were alight with astonishment; and the face of Inspector Burns, who advanced more heavily behind them, like an elephant shaking the garden, was inflamed with some indignation as well.

'What *can* all this mean?' cried Olive, as she came panting to a halt. 'He's gone!'

'Bolted!' said the Lieutenant explosively. 'Harker's just managed to pack a suitcase and bolted! Gone clean out of the back door and over the garden-wall to God knows where. What *did* you say to him?'

'Don't be silly!' said Olive, with a more worried expression. 'Of course you told him you'd found him out, and now he's gone. I never could have believed he was wicked like that!'

'Well!' gasped the Inspector, bursting into their midst. 'What have you done now? What have you let me down like this for?'

'Well,' repeated Father Brown, 'what have I done?'

'You have let a murderer escape,' cried Burns, with a decision that was like a thunderclap in the quiet garden; 'you have *helped* a murderer to escape. Like a fool I let you warn him; and now he is miles away.'

'I have helped a few murderers in my time, it is true,' said Father Brown; then he added, in careful distinction, 'not, you will understand, helped them to commit the murder.'

'But you knew all the time,' insisted Olive. 'You guessed from the first that it must be he. That's what you meant about being upset by the business of finding the body. That's what the doctor meant by saying my father might be disliked by a subordinate.'

'That's what I complain of,' said the official indignantly. 'You knew even then that he was the—'

'You knew even then,' insisted Olive, 'that the murderer was—'

Father Brown nodded gravely. 'Yes,' he said. 'I knew even then that the murderer was old Dyke.'

'Was *who*?' repeated the Inspector and stopped amid a dead silence; punctuated only by the occasional pipe of birds.

'I mean Mr Dyke, the solicitor,' explained Father Brown, like one explaining something elementary to an infant class. 'That gentleman with grey hair who's supposed to be going to read the will.'

They all stood like statues staring at him, as he carefully filled his pipe again and struck a match. At last Burns rallied his vocal powers to break the strangling silence with an effort resembling violence.

'But, in the name of heaven, *why*?'

'Ah, why?' said the priest and rose thoughtfully, puffing at his pipe. 'As to why he did it. . . . Well, I suppose the time has come to tell you, or those of you who don't know, the fact that is the key of all this business. It's a great calamity; and it's a great crime; but it's not the murder of Admiral Craven.'

He looked Olive full in the face and said very seriously:

'I tell you the bad news bluntly and in few words; because I think you are brave enough, and perhaps happy enough, to take it well. You have the chance, and I think the power, to be something like a great woman. You are not a great heiress.'

Amid the silence that followed it was he who resumed his explanation.

'Most of your father's money, I am sorry to say, has gone. It went by the financial dexterity of the grey-haired gentleman named Dyke, who is (I grieve to say) a swindler. Admiral Craven was murdered to silence him about the way in which he was swindled. The fact that he was ruined and you were disinherited is the single simple clue, not only to the murder, but to all the other mysteries in this business.' He took a puff or two and then continued.

'I told Mr Rook you were disinherited and he rushed back to help you. Mr Rook is a rather remarkable person.'

'Oh, chuck it,' said Mr Rook with a hostile air.

'Mr Rook is a monster,' said Father Brown with scientific calm. 'He is an anachronism, an atavism, a brute survival of the Stone Age. If there was one barbarous superstition we all supposed to be utterly extinct and dead in these days, it was that notion about honour and independence. But then I get mixed up with so many dead superstitions. Mr Rook is an extinct animal. He is a plesiosaurus. He did not want to live on his wife or have a wife who could call him a fortune-hunter. Therefore he sulked in a grotesque manner and only came to life again, when I brought him the good news that you were ruined. He wanted to work for his wife and not be kept by her. Disgusting, isn't it? Let us turn to the brighter topic of Mr Harker.

'I told Mr Harker you were disinherited and he rushed away in a sort of panic. Do not be too hard on Mr Harker. He really had better as well as worse enthusiasms; but he had them all mixed up. There is no harm in having ambitions; but he had ambitions and called them ideals. The old sense of honour taught men to suspect success; to say, "This is a benefit; it may be a bribe." The new nine-times-accursed nonsense about Making Good teaches men to identify being good with making money. That was all that was the matter with him; in every other way he was a thoroughly good fellow, and there are thousands like him. Gazing at the stars and rising in the world were all Uplift. Marrying a good wife and marrying a rich wife were all Making Good. But he was not a cynical scoundrel; or he would simply have come back and jilted or cut you as the case might be. He could not face you; while you were there, half of his broken ideal was left.

'I did not tell the Admiral; but somebody did. Word came to him somehow, during the last grand parade on board, that his friend the family lawyer had betrayed him. He was in such a towering passion that he did what he could never have done in his senses; came straight on shore in his cocked hat and gold lace to catch the criminal; he wired to the police station, and that was why the Inspector was wandering round the Green Man. Lieutenant Rook followed him on shore because he suspected some family trouble and had half a hope he might help and put himself right. Hence his hesitating behaviour. As for his drawing his sword when he dropped behind and thought he was alone, well that's a matter of imagination. He was a romantic person who had dreamed of swords and run away to sea; and found himself in a service where he wasn't even allowed to wear a sword except about once in three years. He thought he was quite alone on the sands where he played as a boy. If you don't understand what he did, I can only say, like Stevenson, "you will never be a pirate". Also you will never be a poet; and you have never been a boy.'

'I never have,' answered Olive gravely, 'and yet I think I understand.'

'Almost every man,' continued the priest musing, 'will play with anything shaped like a sword or dagger, even if it is a paper-knife. That is why I thought it so odd when the lawyer didn't.'

'What do you mean?' asked Burns, 'didn't what?'

'Why, didn't you notice,' answered Brown, 'at that first meeting in the office, the lawyer played with a pen and not with a paper-knife; though he had a beautiful bright steel paper-knife in the pattern of a stiletto? The pens were dusty and splashed with ink; but the knife had just been cleaned. But he did not play with it. There are limits to the irony of assassins.'

After a silence the Inspector said, like one waking from a dream: 'Look here . . . I don't know whether I'm on my head or my heels; I don't know whether you think you've got to the end; but I haven't got to the beginning. Where do you get all this lawyer stuff from? What started you out on that trail?'

Father Brown laughed curtly and without mirth.

'The murderer made a slip at the start,' he said, 'and I can't think why nobody else noticed it. When you brought the first news of the death to the solicitor's office, nobody was supposed to know anything there, except that the Admiral was expected home. When you said he was drowned, I asked when it happened and Mr Dyke asked where the corpse was found.'

He paused a moment to knock out his pipe and resumed reflectively:

'Now when you are simply told of a seaman, returning from the sea, that he has been drowned, it is natural to assume that he has been drowned at sea. At any rate, to allow that he may have been drowned at sea. If he had been washed overboard, or gone down with his ship, or had his body "committed to the deep", there would be no reason to expect his body to be found at all. The moment that man asked where it was found, I was sure he knew where it was found. Because he had put it there. Nobody but the murderer need have thought of anything so unlikely as a seaman being drowned in a land-locked pool a few hundred yards from the sea. That is why I suddenly felt sick and turned green, I dare say; as green as the Green Man. I never *can* get used to finding myself suddenly sitting beside a murderer. So I had to turn it off by talking in parables; but the parable meant something, after all. I said that the body was covered with green scum, but it might just as well have been seaweed.'

It is fortunate that tragedy can never kill comedy and that the two can run side by side; and that while the only acting partner of the business of Messrs Willis, Hardman and Dyke blew his brains out

when the Inspector entered the house to arrest him, Olive and
Roger were calling to each other across the sands at evening, as
they did when they were children together.

THE CRIME OF THE COMMUNIST

THREE men came out from under the low-browed Tudor arch in the mellow façade of Mandeville College, into the strong evening sunlight of a summer day which seemed as if it would never end; and in that sunlight they saw something that blasted like lightning; well-fitted to be the shock of their lives.

Even before they had realized anything in the way of a catastrophe, they were conscious of a contrast. They themselves, in a curious quiet way, were quite harmonious with their surroundings. Though the Tudor arches that ran like a cloister round the College gardens had been built four hundred years ago, at that moment when the Gothic fell from heaven and bowed, or almost crouched, over the cosier chambers of Humanism and the Revival of Learning – though they themselves were in modern clothes (that is in clothes whose ugliness would have amazed any of the four centuries) yet something in the spirit of the place made them all at one. The gardens had been tended so carefully as to achieve the final triumph of looking careless; the very flowers seemed beautiful by accident, like elegant weeds; and the modern costumes had at least any picturesqueness that can be produced by being untidy. The first of the three, a tall, bald, bearded maypole of a man, was a familiar figure in the Quad in cap and gown; the gown slipped off one of his sloping shoulders. The second was very square-shouldered, short and compact, with a rather jolly grin, commonly clad in a jacket, with his gown over his arm. The third was even shorter and much shabbier, in black clerical clothes. But they all seemed suitable to Mandeville College; and the indescribable atmosphere of the two ancient and unique Universities of England. They fitted into it and they faded into it; which is there regarded as most fitting.

The two men seated on garden chairs by a little table were a sort of brilliant blot on this grey-green landscape. They were clad mostly in black and yet they glittered from head to heel, from their burnished top-hats to their perfectly polished boots. It was dimly felt as an outrage that anybody should be so well-dressed in the well-bred freedom of Mandeville College. The only excuse was that they were foreigners. One was an American, a millionaire named Hake, dressed in the spotlessly and sparklingly gentlemanly manner known only to the rich of New York. The other, who added to all these things the outrage of an astrakhan overcoat (to say nothing of a pair of florid whiskers) was a German Count of great wealth, the shortest part of whose name was Von Zimmern. The mystery of this story, however, is not the mystery of why they were there. They were there for the reason that commonly explains the meeting of incongruous things; they proposed to give the College some money. They had come in support of a plan supported by several financiers and magnates of many countries, for founding a new Chair of Economics at Mandeville College. They had inspected the College with that tireless conscientious sightseeing of which no sons of Eve are capable except the American and the German. And now they were resting from their labours and looking solemnly at the College gardens. So far so good.

The three other men, who had already met them, passed with a vague salutation; but one of them stopped; the smallest of the three, in the black clerical clothes.

'I say,' he said, with rather the air of a frightened rabbit, 'I don't like the look of those men.'

'Good God! Who could?' ejaculated the tall man, who happened to be the Master of Mandeville. 'At least we have some rich men who don't go about dressed up like tailors' dummies.'

'Yes,' hissed the little cleric, 'that's what I mean. Like tailors' dummies.'

'Why, what do you mean?' asked the shorter of the other men, sharply.

'I mean they're like horrible waxworks,' said the cleric in a faint voice. 'I mean they don't move. Why don't they move?'

Suddenly starting out of his dim retirement, he darted across the garden and touched the German Baron on the elbow. The German Baron fell over, chair and all, and the trousered legs that stuck up in the air were as stiff as the legs of the chair.

Mr Gideon P. Hake continued to gaze at the College gardens with glassy eyes; but the parallel of a waxwork confirmed the impression that they were like eyes made of glass. Somehow the rich sunlight and the coloured garden increased the creepy impression of a stiffly dressed doll; a marionette on an Italian stage. The small man in black, who was a priest named Brown, tentatively touched the millionaire on the shoulder, and the millionaire fell sideways, but horribly all of a piece, like something carved in wood.

'*Rigor mortis*,' said Father Brown, 'and so soon. But it does vary a good deal.'

The reason the first three men had joined the other two men so late (not to say too late) will best be understood by noting what had happened just inside the building, behind the Tudor archway, but a short time before they came out. They had all dined together in Hall, at the High Table; but the two foreign philanthropists, slaves of duty in the matter of seeing everything, had solemnly gone back to the chapel, of which one cloister and a staircase remained un-examined; promising to rejoin the rest in the garden, to examine as earnestly the College cigars. The rest, in a more reverent and right-minded spirit, had adjourned as usual to the long narrow oak table, round which the after-dinner wine had circulated, for all any-body knew, ever since the College had been founded in the Middle Ages by Sir John Mandeville, for the encouragement of telling stories. The Master, with the big fair beard and the bald brow, took the head of the table, and the squat man in the square jacket sat on his left; for he was the Bursar or business man of the College. Next to him, on that side of the table, sat a queer-looking man with what could only be called a crooked face; for its dark tufts of moustache and eyebrow, slanting at contrary angles, made a sort of zig-zag, as if half his face were puckered or paralysed. His name was Byles; he was the lecturer in Roman History, and his political opinions were founded on those of Coriolanus, not to mention Tarquinius Superbus. This tart Toryism, and rabidly reactionary view of all current problems, was not altogether unknown among the more old-fashioned sort of dons; but in the case of Byles there was a suggestion that it was a result rather than a cause of his acerbity. More than one sharp observer had received the impression that there was something really wrong with Byles; that some secret or some great misfortune had embittered him; as if that half-withered face had really been blasted like a storm-stricken tree. Beyond him again sat Father Brown and at the end of the table a Professor of Chemistry, large and blond and bland, with eyes that were sleepy

and perhaps a little sly. It was well known that this natural philosopher regarded the other philosophers, of a more classical tradition, very much as old fogies. On the other side of the table, opposite
Father Brown, was a very swarthy and silent young man, with a
black pointed beard, introduced because somebody had insisted on
having a Chair of Persian; opposite the sinister Byles was a very
mild-looking little Chaplain, with a head like an egg. Opposite the
Bursar, and at the right hand of the Master, was an empty chair;
and there were many there who were glad to see it empty.

'I don't know whether Craken is coming,' said the Master, not
without a nervous glance at the chair, which contrasted with the
usual languid freedom of his demeanour. 'I believe in giving people
a lot of rope myself; but I confess I've reached the point of being
glad when he is here, merely because he isn't anywhere else.'

'Never know what he'll be up to next,' said the Bursar cheerfully,
'especially when he's instructing the young.'

'A brilliant fellow, but fiery of course,' said the Master, with a
rather abrupt relapse into reserve.

'Fireworks are fiery, and also brilliant,' growled old Byles, 'but
I don't want to be burned in my bed so that Craken can figure as
a real Guy Fawkes.'

'Do you really *think* he would join a physical force revolution, if
there were one?' asked the Bursar smiling.

'Well, *he* thinks he would,' said Byles sharply. 'Told a whole hall
full of undergraduates the other day that nothing now could avert
the Class War turning into a real war, with killing in the streets of
the town; and it didn't matter, so long as it ended in Communism
and the victory of the working class.'

'The Class War,' mused the Master, with a sort of distaste mellowed by distance, for he had known William Morris long ago and
been familiar enough with the more artistic and leisurely Socialists.
'I never can understand all this about the Class War. When I was
young, Socialism was supposed to mean saying that there are no
classes.'

''Nother way of saying that Socialists are no class,' said Byles
with sour relish.

'Of course, you'd be more against them than I should,' said the
Master thoughtfully, 'but I suppose my Socialism is almost as old-
fashioned as your Toryism. Wonder what our young friends really

think. What do you think, Baker?' he said abruptly to the Bursar on his left.

'Oh, I *don't* think, as the vulgar saying is,' said the Bursar laughing. 'You must remember I'm a very vulgar person. I'm not a thinker. I'm only a business man; and as a business man I think it's all bosh. You can't make men equal and it's damned bad business to pay them equal; especially a lot of them not worth paying for at all. Whatever it is, you've got to take the practical way out, because it's the only way out. It's not our fault if nature made everything a scramble.'

'I agree with you there,' said the Professor of Chemistry, speaking with a lisp that seemed childish in so large a man. 'Communism pretends to be oh so modern; but it is not. Throw-back to the superstitions of monks and primitive tribes. A scientific government, with a really ethical responsibility to posterity, would be always looking for the line of promise and progress; not levelling and flattening it all back into the mud again. Socialism is sentimentalism; and more dangerous than a pestilence, for in that at least the fittest would survive.'

The Master smiled a little sadly. 'You know you and I will never feel quite the same about differences of opinion. Didn't somebody say up here, about walking with a friend by the river, "Not differing much, except in opinion"? Isn't that the motto of a university? To have hundreds of opinions and not be opinionated. If people fall here, it's by what they are, not what they think. Perhaps I'm a relic of the eighteenth century; but I incline to the old sentimental heresy, "For forms of faith let graceless zealots fight; he can't be wrong whose life is in the right." What do you think about that, Father Brown?'

He glanced a little mischievously across at the priest and was mildly startled. For he had always found the priest very cheerful and amiable and easy to get on with; and his round face was mostly solid with good humour. But for some reason the priest's face at this moment was knotted with a frown much more sombre than any the company had ever seen on it; so that for an instant that commonplace countenance actually looked darker and more ominous than the haggard face of Byles. An instant later the cloud seemed to have passed; but Father Brown still spoke with a certain sobriety and firmness.

'I don't believe in that, anyhow,' he said shortly. 'How can his life be in the right, if his whole view of life is wrong? That's a modern muddle that arose because people didn't know how much views of life can differ. Baptists and Methodists knew they didn't differ very much in morality; but then they didn't differ very much in religion or philosophy. It's quite different when you pass from the Baptists to the Anabaptists; or from the Theosophists to the Thugs. Heresy always does affect morality, if it's heretical enough. I suppose a man may honestly believe that thieving isn't wrong. But what's the good of saying that he honestly believes in dishonesty?'

'Damned good,' said Byles with a ferocious contortion of feature, believed by many to be meant for a friendly smile. 'And that's why I object to having a Chair of Theoretical Thieving in this College.'

'Well, you're all very down on Communism, of course,' said the Master, with a sigh. 'But do you really think there's so much of it to be down on? Are any of your heresies really big enough to be dangerous?'

'I think they have grown so big,' said Father Brown gravely, 'that in some circles they are already taken for granted. They are actually unconscious. That is, without conscience.'

'And the end of it,' said Byles, 'will be the ruin of this country.'

'The end will be something worse,' said Father Brown.

A shadow shot or slid rapidly along the panelled wall opposite, as swiftly followed by the figure that had flung it; a tall but stooping figure with a vague outline like a bird of prey; accentuated by the fact that its sudden appearance and swift passage were like those of a bird startled and flying from a bush. It was only the figure of a long-limbed, high-shouldered man with long drooping moustaches, in fact, familiar enough to them all; but something in the twilight and candlelight and the flying and streaking shadow connected it strangely with the priest's unconscious words of omen; for all the world as if those words had indeed been an augury, in the old Roman sense; and the sign of it the flight of a bird. Perhaps Mr Byles might have given a lecture on such Roman augury; and especially on that bird of ill-omen.

The tall man shot along the wall like his own shadow until he sank into the empty chair on the Master's right, and looked across at the Bursar and the rest with hollow and cavernous eyes. His hanging hair and moustache were quite fair, but his eyes were so deep-set that they might have been black. Everyone knew, or could guess, who the newcomer was; but an incident instantly followed that sufficiently illuminated the situation. The Professor of Roman History rose stiffly to his feet and stalked out of the room, indicating with little *finesse* his feelings about sitting at the same table with the Professor of Theoretical Thieving, otherwise the Communist, Mr Craken.

The Master of Mandeville covered the awkward situation with nervous grace. 'I was defending you, or some aspects of you, my dear Craken,' he said smiling, 'though I am sure you would find me quite indefensible. After all, I can't forget that the old Socialist friends of my youth had a very fine ideal of fraternity and comradeship. William Morris put it all in a sentence, "Fellowship is heaven; and lack of fellowship is hell." '

'Dons as Democrats; see headline,' said Mr Craken rather disagreeably. 'And is Hard-Case Hake going to dedicate the new Commercial Chair to the memory of William Morris?'

'Well,' said the Master, still maintaining a desperate geniality, 'I hope we may say, in a sense, that all our Chairs are Chairs of good-fellowship.'

'Yes; that's the academic version of the Morris maxim,' growled Craken. ' "A Fellowship is heaven; and lack of a Fellowship is hell." '

'Don't be so cross, Craken,' interposed the Bursar briskly. 'Take some port. Tenby, pass the port to Mr Craken.'

'Oh well, I'll have a glass,' said the Communist Professor a little less ungraciously. 'I really came down here to have a smoke in the garden. Then I looked out of the window and saw your two precious millionaires were actually blooming in the garden; fresh, innocent buds. After all, it might be worth while to give them a bit of my mind.'

The Master had risen under cover of his last conventional cordiality, and was only too glad to leave the Bursar to do his best with the Wild Man. Others had risen, and the groups at the table had begun to break up; and the Bursar and Mr Craken were left more or less alone at the end of the long table. Only Father Brown continued to sit staring into vacancy with a rather cloudy expression.

'Oh, as to that,' said the Bursar. 'I'm pretty tired of them myself, to tell the truth; I've been with them the best part of a day going into facts and figures and all the business of this new Professorship. But look here, Craken,' and he leaned across the table and spoke with a sort of soft emphasis, 'you really needn't cut up so rough about this new Professorship. It doesn't really interfere with your subject. You're the only Professor of Political Economy at Mandeville and, though I don't pretend to agree with your notions, everybody knows you've got a European reputation. This is a special subject they call Applied Economics. Well, even today, as I told you, I've had a hell of a lot of Applied Economics. In other words, I've had to talk business with two business men. Would you particularly want to do that? Would you envy it? Would you stand it? Isn't that evidence enough that there is a separate subject and may well be a separate Chair?'

'Good God,' cried Craken with the intense invocation of the atheist. 'Do you think I don't want to apply Economics? Only, when we apply it, you call it red ruin and anarchy; and when you apply it, I take the liberty of calling it exploitation. If only you fellows would apply Economics, it's just possible that people might get something to eat. We are the practical people, and that's why you're afraid of us. That's why you have to get two greasy Capitalists to start another Lectureship; just because I've let the cat out of the bag.'

'Rather a wild cat, wasn't it,' said the Bursar smiling, 'that you let out of the bag?'

'And rather a gold-bag, wasn't it,' said Craken, 'that you are tying the cat up in again?'

'Well, I don't suppose we shall ever agree about all that,' said the other. 'But those fellows have come out of their chapel into the garden; and if you want to have your smoke there, you'd better come.' He watched with some amusement his companion fumbling in all his pockets till he produced a pipe, and then, gazing at it with an abstracted air, Craken rose to his feet, but even in doing so, seemed to be feeling all over himself again. Mr Baker the Bursar ended the controversy with a happy laugh of reconciliation. 'You are the practical people, and you will blow up the town with dynamite. Only you'll probably forget the dynamite, as I bet you've forgotten the tobacco. Never mind, take a fill of mine. Matches?' He threw a tobacco-pouch and its accessories across the table; to be caught by Mr Craken with that dexterity never forgotten by a cricketer, even when he adopts opinions generally regarded as not cricket. The two men rose together; but Baker could not forbear remarking, 'Are you really the only practical people? Isn't there anything to be said for the Applied Economics, that remembers to carry a tobacco-pouch as well as a pipe?'

Craken looked at him with smouldering eyes; and said at last, after slowly draining the last of his wine:

'Let's say there's another sort of practicality. I dare say I do forget details and so on. What I want you to understand is this' – he automatically returned the pouch; but his eyes were far away and jet-burning, almost terrible – 'because the inside of our intellect has changed, because we really have a new idea of right, we shall do things you think really wrong. And they will be very practical.'

'Yes,' said Father Brown, suddenly coming out of his trance. 'That's exactly what I said.'

He looked across at Craken with a glassy and rather ghastly smile, saying: 'Mr Craken and I are in complete agreement.'

'Well,' said Baker, 'Craken is going out to smoke a pipe with the plutocrats; but I doubt whether it will be a pipe of peace.'

He turned rather abruptly and called to an aged attendant in the background. Mandeville was one of the last of the very old-fashioned Colleges; and even Craken was one of the first of the Communists; before the Bolshevism of today. 'That reminds me,' the Bursar was saying, 'as you won't hand round your peace pipe, we must send out the cigars to our distinguished guests. If they're smokers they must be longing for a smoke; for they've been nosing about in the chapel since feeding-time.'

Craken exploded with a savage and jarring laugh. 'Oh, I'll take them their cigars,' he said. 'I'm only a proletarian.'

Baker and Brown and the attendant were all witnesses to the fact that the Communist strode furiously into the garden to confront the millionaires; but nothing more was seen or heard of them until, as is already recorded, Father Brown found them dead in their chairs.

It was agreed that the Master and the priest should remain to guard the scene of tragedy, while the Bursar, younger and more rapid in his movements, ran off to fetch doctors and policemen. Father Brown approached the table on which one of the cigars had burned itself away all but an inch or two; the other had dropped from the hand and been dashed out into dying sparks on the crazy-pavement. The Master of Mandeville sat down rather shakily on a sufficiently distant seat and buried his bald brow in his hands. Then he looked up at first rather wearily; and then he looked very startled indeed and broke the stillness of the garden with a word like a small explosion of horror.

There was a certain quality about Father Brown which might sometimes be called blood-curdling. He always thought about what he was doing and never about whether it was done; he would do the most ugly or horrible or undignified or dirty things as calmly as a surgeon. There was a certain blank, in his simple mind, of all those things commonly associated with being superstitious or sentimental. He sat down on the chair from which the corpse had fallen, picked up the cigar the corpse had partially smoked, carefully detached the ash, examined the butt-end and then stuck it in his mouth and lit it. It looked like some obscene and grotesque antic in derision of the dead; and it seemed to him to be the most ordinary common sense. A cloud floated upwards like the smoke of some savage sacrifice and idolatry; but to Father Brown it appeared a perfectly self-evident fact that the only way to find out what a cigar is like is to smoke it. Nor did it lessen the horror for his old friend, the Master of Mandeville, to have a dim but shrewd guess that Father Brown was, upon the possibilities of the case, risking his own life.

'No; I think that's all right,' said the priest, putting the stump down again. 'Jolly good cigars. Your cigars. Not American or German. I don't think there's anything odd about the cigar itself; but they'd better take care of the ashes. These men were poisoned somehow with the sort of stuff that stiffens the body quickly.... By the way, there goes somebody who knows more about it than we do.'

The Master sat up with a curiously uncomfortable jolt; for indeed the large shadow which had fallen across the pathway preceded a figure which, however heavy, was almost as soft-footed as a shadow. Professor Wadham, eminent occupant of the Chair of Chemistry, always moved very quietly in spite of his size, and there was nothing odd about his strolling in the garden; yet there seemed something unnaturally neat in his appearing at the exact moment when chemistry was mentioned.

Professor Wadham prided himself on his quietude; some would say his insensibility. He did not turn a hair on his flattened flaxen head, but stood looking down at the dead men with a shade of something like indifference on his large froglike face. Only when he looked at the cigar-ash, which the priest had preserved, he touched it with one finger; then he seemed to stand even stiller than before; but in the shadow of his face his eyes for an instant seemed to shoot out telescopically like one of his own microscopes. He had certainly realized or recognized something; but he said nothing.

'I don't know where anyone is to begin in this business,' said the Master.

'I should begin,' said Father Brown, 'by asking where these unfortunate men had been most of the time today.'

'They were messing about in my laboratory for a good time,' said Wadham, speaking for the first time. 'Baker often comes up to have a chat, and this time he brought his two patrons to inspect my department. But I think they went everywhere; real tourists. I know they went to the chapel and even into the tunnel under the crypt, where you have to light candles; instead of digesting their food like sane men. Baker seems to have taken them everywhere.'

'Were they interested in anything particular in your department?' asked the priest. 'What were you doing there just then?'

The Professor of Chemistry murmured a chemical formula beginning with 'sulphate', and ending with something that sounded like 'silenium'; unintelligible to both his hearers. He then wandered wearily away and sat on a remote bench in the sun, closing his eyes, but turning up his large face with heavy forbearance.

At this point, by a sharp contrast, the lawns were crossed by a brisk figure travelling as rapidly and as straight as a bullet; and Father Brown recognized the neat black clothes and shrewd dog-like face of a police-surgeon whom he had met in the poorer parts of the town. He was the first to arrive of the official contingent.

'Look here,' said the Master to the priest, before the doctor was within earshot, 'I must know something. Did you mean what you said about Communism being a real danger and leading to crime?'

'Yes,' said Father Brown smiling rather grimly, 'I have really noticed the spread of some Communist ways and influences; and, in one sense, this is a Communist crime.'

'Thank you,' said the Master. 'Then I must go off and see to something at once. Tell the authorities I'll be back in ten minutes.'

The Master had vanished into one of the Tudor archways at just about the moment when the police-doctor had reached the table and cheerfully recognized Father Brown. On the latter's suggestion that they should sit down at the tragic table, Dr Blake threw one sharp and doubtful glance at the big, bland and seemingly somnolent chemist, who occupied a more remote seat. He was duly informed of the Professor's identity, and what had so far been gathered of the Professor's evidence; and listened to it silently while conducting a preliminary examination of the dead bodies. Naturally, he seemed more concentrated on the actual corpses than on the hearsay evidence, until one detail suddenly distracted him entirely from the science of anatomy.

'What did the Professor say he was working at?' he inquired.

Father Brown patiently repeated the chemical formula he did not understand.

'*What?*' snapped Dr Blake, like a pistol-shot. 'Gosh! This is pretty frightful!'

'Because it's poison?' inquired Father Brown.

'Because it's piffle,' replied Dr Blake. 'It's simply nonsense. The Professor is quite a famous chemist. Why is a famous chemist deliberately talking nonsense?'

'Well, I think I know that one,' answered Father Brown mildly. 'He is talking nonsense, because he is telling lies. He is concealing something; and he wanted specially to conceal it from these two men and their representatives.'

The doctor lifted his eyes from the two men and looked across at the almost unnaturally immobile figure of the great chemist. He might almost have been asleep; a garden butterfly had settled upon him and seemed to turn his stillness into that of a stone idol. The large folds of his froglike face reminded the doctor of the hanging skins of a rhinoceros.

'Yes,' said Father Brown, in a very low voice. 'He is a wicked man.'

'God damn it all!' cried the doctor, suddenly moved to his very depths. 'Do you mean that a great scientific man like that deals in murder?'

'Fastidious critics would have complained of his dealing in

murder,' said the priest dispassionately. 'I don't say I'm very fond of people dealing in murder in that way myself. But what's much more to the point – I'm sure that *these* poor fellows were among his fastidious critics.'

'You mean they found his secret and he silenced them?' said Blake frowning. 'But what in hell was his secret? How could a man murder on a large scale in a place like this?'

'I have told you his secret,' said the priest. 'It is a secret of the soul. He is a bad man. For heaven's sake don't fancy I say that because he and I are of opposite schools or traditions. I have a crowd of scientific friends; and most of them are heroically disinterested. Even of the most sceptical, I would only say they are rather irrationally disinterested. But now and then you do get a man who is a materialist, in the sense of a beast. I repeat he's a bad man. Much worse than—' And Father Brown seemed to hesitate for a word.

'You mean much worse than the Communist?' suggested the other.

'No; I mean much worse than the murderer,' said Father Brown.

He got to his feet in an abstracted manner; and hardly realized that his companion was staring at him.

'But didn't you mean,' asked Blake at last, 'that this Wadham is the murderer?'

'Oh, no,' said Father Brown more cheerfully. 'The murderer is a much more sympathetic and understandable person. He at least was desperate; and had the excuses of sudden rage and despair.'

'Why,' cried the doctor, 'do you mean it was the Communist after all?'

It was at this very moment, appropriately enough, that the police officials appeared with an announcement that seemed to conclude the case in a most decisive and satisfactory manner. They had been somewhat delayed in reaching the scene of the crime, by the simple fact that they had already captured the criminal. Indeed, they had captured him almost at the gates of their own official residence. They had already had reason to suspect the activities of Craken the Communist during various disorders in the town; when they heard of the outrage they felt it safe to arrest him; and found the arrest thoroughly justified. For, as Inspector Cook radiantly explained to dons and doctors on the lawn of Mandeville garden, no sooner was the notorious Communist searched, than it was found that he was actually carrying a box of poisoned matches.

The moment Father Brown heard the word 'matches', he jumped from his seat as if a match had been lighted under him.

'Ah,' he cried, with a sort of universal radiance, 'and now it's all clear.'

'What do you mean by all clear?' demanded the Master of Mandeville, who had returned in all the pomp of his own officialism to match the pomp of the police officials now occupying the College like a victorious army. 'Do you mean you are convinced now that the case against Craken is clear?'

'I mean that Craken is cleared,' said Father Brown firmly, 'and the case against Craken is cleared away. Do you really believe Craken is the kind of man who would go about poisoning people with matches?'

'That's all very well,' replied the Master, with the troubled expression he had never lost since the first sensation occurred. 'But it was you yourself who said that fanatics with false principles may do wicked things. For that matter, it was you yourself who said that Communism is cropping up everywhere and Communistic habits spreading.'

Father Brown laughed in a rather shamefaced manner

'As to the last point,' he said, 'I suppose I owe you all an apology. I seem to be always making a mess of things with my silly little jokes.'

'Jokes!' repeated the Master, staring rather indignantly.

'Well,' explained the priest, rubbing his head. 'When I talked about a Communist habit spreading, I only meant a habit I happen to have noticed about two or three times even today. It is a Communist habit by no means confined to Communists. It is the extraordinary habit of so many men, especially Englishmen, of putting other people's matchboxes in their pockets without remembering to return them. Of course, it seems an awfully silly little trifle to talk about. But it does happen to be the way the crime was committed.'

'It sounds to me quite crazy,' said the doctor.

'Well, if almost any man may forget to return matches, you can bet your boots that Craken would forget to return them. So the poisoner who had prepared the matches got rid of them on to Craken, by the simple process of lending them and not getting them back. A really admirable way of shedding responsibility; because Craken himself would be perfectly unable to imagine where he had got them from. But when he used them quite innocently to light the cigars he offered to our two visitors, he was caught in an obvious trap; one of those too obvious traps. He was the bold bad Revolutionist murdering two millionaires.'

'Well, who else would want to murder them?' growled the doctor.

'Ah, who indeed?' replied the priest; and his voice changed to much greater gravity. 'There we come to the other thing I told you; and that, let me tell you, was not a joke. I told you that heresies and false doctrines had become common and conversational; that everybody was used to them; that nobody really noticed them. Did you think I meant *Communism* when I said that? Why, it was just the other way. You were all as nervous as cats about Communism; and you watched Craken like a wolf. Of course, Communism is a heresy; but it isn't a heresy that you people take for granted. It is Capitalism you take for granted; or rather the vices of Capitalism disguised as a dead Darwinism. Do you recall what you were all saying in the Common Room, about life being only a scramble, and nature demanding the survival of the fittest, and how it doesn't matter whether the poor are paid justly or not? Why *that* is the heresy that you have grown accustomed to, my friends; and it's every bit as much a heresy as Communism. That's the anti-Christian morality or immorality that you take quite naturally. And that's the immorality that has made a man a murderer today.'

'What man?' cried the Master, and his voice cracked with a sudden weakness.

'Let me approach it another way,' said the priest placidly. 'You all talk as if Craken ran away; but he didn't. When the two men toppled over, he ran down the street, summoned the doctor merely by shouting through the window, and shortly afterwards was trying to summon the police. That was how he was arrested. But doesn't it strike you, now one comes to think of it, that Mr Baker the Bursar is rather a long time looking for the police?'

'What is he doing then?' asked the Master sharply.

'I fancy he's destroying papers; or perhaps ransacking these men's rooms to see they haven't left us a letter. Or it may have something to do with our friend Wadham. Where does he come in? That is really very simple and a sort of joke too. Mr Wadham is experimenting in poisons for the next war; and has something of which a whiff of flame will stiffen a man dead. Of course, he had nothing to do with killing these men; but he did conceal his chemical secret for a very simple reason. One of them was a Puritan Yankee and the other a cosmopolitan Jew; and those two types are often fanatical Pacifists. They would have called it planning murder and probably refused to help the College. But Baker was a friend of Wadham and it was easy for him to dip matches in the new material.'

Another peculiarity of the little priest was that his mind was all of a piece, and he was unconscious of many incongruities; he would change the note of his talk from something quite public to something quite private, without any particular embarrassment. On this occasion, he made most of the company stare with mystification, by beginning to talk to one person when he had just been talking to ten; quite indifferent to the fact that only the one could have any notion of what he was talking about.

'I'm sorry if I misled you, doctor, by that maundering metaphysical digression on the man of sin,' he said apologetically. 'Of course it had nothing to do with the murder; but the truth is I'd forgotten all about the murder for the moment. I'd forgotten everything, you see, but a sort of vision of that fellow, with his vast unhuman face, squatting among the flowers like some blind monster of the Stone Age. And I was thinking that some men are pretty monstrous, like men of stone; but it was all irrelevant. Being bad inside has very little to do with committing crimes outside. The worst criminals have committed no crimes. The practical point is why did the practical criminal commit this crime. Why did Baker the Bursar want to kill these men? That's all that concerns us now. The answer is the answer to the question I've asked twice. Where were these men most of the time, apart from nosing in chapels or laboratories? By the Bursar's own account, they were talking business with the Bursar.

'Now, with all respect to the dead, I do not exactly grovel before the intellect of these two financiers. Their views on economics and ethics were heathen and heartless. Their views on Peace were tosh. Their views on Port were even more deplorable. But one thing they did understand; and that was business. And it took them a remarkably short time to discover that the business man in charge of the funds of this College was a swindler. Or shall I say, a true follower of the doctrine of the unlimited struggle for life and the survival of the fittest.'

'You mean they were going to expose him and he killed them before they could speak,' said the doctor frowning. 'There are a lot of details I don't understand.'

'There are some details I'm not sure of myself,' said the priest frankly. 'I suspect all that business of candles underground had something to do with abstracting the millionaires' own matches, or perhaps making sure they had no matches. But I'm sure of the main gesture, the gay and careless gesture of Baker tossing his matches to the careless Craken. That gesture was the murderous blow.'

'There's one thing I don't understand,' said the Inspector. 'How did Baker know that Craken wouldn't light up himself then and there at the table and become an unwanted corpse?'

The face of Father Brown became almost heavy with reproach; and his voice had a sort of mournful yet generous warmth in it.

'Well, hang it all,' he said, 'he was only an atheist.'

'I'm afraid I don't know what you mean,' said the Inspector, politely.

'He only wanted to abolish God,' explained Father Brown in a temperate and reasonable tone. 'He only wanted to destroy the Ten Commandments and root up all the religion and civilization that had made him, and wash out all the common sense of ownership and honesty; and let his culture and his country be flattened out by savages from the ends of the earth. That's all he wanted. You have no right to accuse him of anything beyond that. Hang it all, everybody draws the line somewhere! And you come here and calmly suggest that a Mandeville Man of the old generation (for Craken was of the old generation, whatever his views) would have begun to smoke, or even strike a match, while he was still drinking the College Port, of the vintage of '08 – no, no; men are not so utterly without laws and limits as all that! I was there; I saw him; he had not finished his wine, and you ask me why he did not *smoke*! No such anarchic question has ever shaken the arches of Mandeville College.... Funny place, Mandeville College. Funny place, Oxford. Funny place, England.'

'But you haven't anything particular to do with Oxford?' asked the doctor curiously.

'I have to do with England,' said Father Brown. 'I come from there. And the funniest thing of all is that even if you love it and belong to it, you still can't make head or tail of it.'

THE VAMPIRE OF THE VILLAGE

AT THE twist of a path in the hills, where two poplars stood up like pyramids dwarfing the tiny village of Potter's Pond, a mere huddle of houses, there once walked a man in a costume of a very conspicuous cut and colour, wearing a vivid magenta coat and a white hat tilted upon black ambrosial curls, which ended with a sort of Byronic flourish of whisker.

The riddle of why he was wearing clothes of such fantastic antiquity, yet wearing them with an air of fashion and even swagger, was but one of the many riddles that were eventually solved in solving the mystery of his fate. The point here is that when he had passed the poplars he seemed to have vanished; as if he had faded into the wan and widening dawn or been blown away upon the wind of morning.

It was only about a week afterwards that his body was found a quarter of a mile away, broken upon the steep rockeries of a terraced garden leading up to a gaunt and shuttered house called The Grange. Just before he had vanished, he had been accidentally overheard apparently quarrelling with some bystanders, and especially abusing their village as 'a wretched little hamlet'; and it was supposed that he had aroused some extreme passions of local patriotism and eventually been their victim. At least the local doctor testified that the skull had suffered a crushing blow that might have caused death, though probably only inflicted with some sort of club or cudgel. This fitted in well enough with the notion of an attack by rather savage yokels. But nobody ever found any means of tracing any particular yokel; and the inquest returned a verdict of murder by some persons unknown.

A year or two afterwards the question was reopened in a curious way; a series of events which led a certain Dr Mulborough, called by his intimates Mulberry in apt allusion to something rich and fruity about his dark rotundity and rather empurpled visage, travelling by train down to Potter's Pond, with a friend whom he had often consulted upon problems of the kind. In spite of the somewhat port-winy and ponderous exterior of the doctor, he had a shrewd eye and was really a man of very remarkable sense; which he considered that he showed in consulting a little priest named Brown, whose acquaintance he had made over a poisoning case long ago. The little priest was sitting opposite to him, with the air of a patient baby absorbing instruction; and the doctor was explaining at length the real reasons for the journey.

'I cannot agree with the gentleman in the magenta coat that Potter's Pond is only a wretched little hamlet. But it is certainly a very remote and secluded village; so that it seems quite outlandish, like a village of a hundred years ago. The spinsters are really spinsters – damn it, you could almost imagine you saw them spin. The ladies are not just ladies. They are gentlewomen; and their chemist is not a chemist, but an apothecary; pronounced potecary. They do just admit the existence of an ordinary doctor like myself to assist the apothecary. But I am considered rather a juvenile innovation, because I am only fifty-seven years old and have only been in the county for twenty-eight years. The solicitor looks as if he had known it for twenty-eight thousand years. Then there is the old Admiral, who is just like a Dickens illustration; with a house full of cutlasses and cuttle-fish and equipped with a telescope.'

'I suppose,' said Father Brown, 'there are always a certain number of Admirals washed up on the shore. But I never understood why they get stranded so far inland.'

'Certainly no dead-alive place in the depths of the country is complete without one of these little creatures,' said the doctor. 'And then, of course, there is the proper sort of clergyman; Tory and High Church in a dusty fashion dating from Archbishop Laud; more of an old woman than any of the old women. He's a white-haired studious old bird, more easily shocked than the spinsters. Indeed, the gentlewomen, though Puritan in their principles, are sometimes pretty plain in their speech; as the real Puritans were. Once or twice I have known old Miss Carstairs-Carew use expressions as lively as anything in the Bible. The dear old clergyman is assiduous in reading the Bible; but I almost fancy he shuts his eyes when he comes to those words. Well, you know I'm not particularly modern. I don't enjoy this jazzing and joy-riding of the Bright Young Things—'

'The Bright Young Things don't enjoy it,' said Father Brown. 'That is the real tragedy.'

'But I am naturally rather more in touch with the world than the people in this prehistoric village,' pursued the doctor. 'And I had reached a point when I almost welcomed the Great Scandal.'

'Don't say the Bright Young Things have found Potter's Pond after all,' observed the priest, smiling.

'Oh, even our scandal is on old-established melodramatic lines. Need I say that the clergyman's son promises to be our problem? It would be almost irregular, if the clergyman's son were quite regular. So far as I can see, he is very mildly and almost feebly irregular. He was first seen drinking ale outside the Blue Lion. Only it seems he is a poet, which in those parts is next door to being a poacher.'

'Surely,' said Father Brown, 'even in Potter's Pond that cannot be the Great Scandal.'

'No,' replied the doctor gravely. 'The Great Scandal began thus. In the house called The Grange, situated at the extreme end of The Grove, there lives a Lady. A Lonely Lady. She calls herself Mrs Maltravers (that is how we put it); but she only came a year or two ago and nobody knows anything about her. "I can't think why she wants to live here," said Miss Carstairs-Carew; "we do not visit her."'

'Perhaps that's why she wants to live there,' said Father Brown.

'Well, her seclusion is considered suspicious. She annoys them by being good-looking and even what is called good style. And all the young men are warned against her as a vamp.'

'People who lose all their charity generally lose all their logic,' remarked Father Brown. 'It's rather ridiculous to complain that she keeps herself to herself, and then accuse her of vamping the whole male population.'

'That is true,' said the doctor. 'And yet she is really rather a puzzling person. I saw her and found her intriguing; one of those brown women, long and elegant and beautifully ugly, if you know what I mean. She is rather witty, and though young enough certainly gives me an impression of what they call – well, experience. What the old ladies call a Past.'

'All the old ladies having been born this very minute,' observed Father Brown. 'I think I can assume she is supposed to have vamped the parson's son.'

'Yes, and it seems to be a very awful problem to the poor old parson. She is supposed to be a widow.'

Father Brown's face had a flash and spasm of his rare irritation. 'She is supposed to be a widow as the parson's son is supposed to be the parson's son, and the solicitor is supposed to be a solicitor and you are supposed to be a doctor. Why in thunder shouldn't she be a widow? Have they one speck of *prima facie* evidence for doubting that she is what she says she is?'

Dr Mulborough abruptly squared his broad shoulders and sat up.

'Of course you're right again,' he said. 'But we haven't come to the Scandal yet. . . . Well, the Scandal is that she is a widow.'

'Oh,' said Father Brown; and his face altered and he said something soft and faint, that might almost have been 'My God!'

'First of all,' said the doctor, 'they have made one discovery about Mrs Maltravers. She is an actress.'

'I fancied so,' said Father Brown. 'Never mind why. I had another fancy about her, that would seem even more irrelevant.'

'Well, at that instant it was scandal enough that she was an actress. The dear old clergyman of course is heartbroken, to think that his white hairs should be brought in sorrow to the grave by an actress and adventuress. The spinsters shriek in chorus. The Admiral admits he has sometimes been to a theatre in town; but objects to such things in what he calls "our midst". Well, of course I've no particular objection of that kind. This actress is certainly a lady, if a bit of a Dark Lady, in the manner of the Sonnets; the young man is very much in love with her; and I am no doubt a sentimental old fool in having a sneaking sympathy with the misguided youth who is sneaking round the Moated Grange; and I was getting into quite a pastoral frame of mind about this idyll, when suddenly the thunderbolt fell. And I, who am the only person who ever had any sympathy with these people, am sent down to be the messenger of doom.'

'Yes,' said Father Brown, 'and why *were* you sent down?'

The doctor answered with a sort of groan:

'Mrs Maltravers is not only a widow, but she is the widow of Mr Maltravers.'

'It sounds a shocking revelation, as you state it,' acknowledged the priest seriously.

'And Mr Maltravers,' continued his medical friend, 'was the man who was apparently murdered in this very village a year or two ago; supposed to have been bashed on the head by one of the simple villagers.'

'I remember you told me,' said Father Brown. 'The doctor, or some doctor, said he had probably died of being clubbed on the head with a cudgel.'

Dr Mulborough was silent for a moment in frowning embarrassment, and then said curtly, 'Dog doesn't eat dog, and doctors don't bite doctors, not even when they are mad doctors. I shouldn't care to cast any reflection on my eminent predecessor in Potter's Pond, if I could avoid it; but I know you are really safe for secrets. And, speaking in confidence, my eminent predecessor at Potter's Pond was a blasted fool; a drunken old humbug and absolutely incompetent. I was asked, originally by the Chief Constable of the County (for I've lived a long time in the county, though only recently in the village) to look into the whole business; the depositions and reports of the inquest and so on. And there simply isn't any question about it. Maltravers may have been hit on the head; he was a strolling actor passing through the place; and Potter's Pond probably thinks it is all in the natural order that such people should be hit on the head. But whoever hit him on the head did not kill him; it is simply impossible for the injury, as described, to do more than knock him out for a few hours. But just lately I have managed to turn up some other facts bearing on the matter; and the result of it is pretty grim.'

He sat louring at the landscape as it slid past the window, and then said more curtly:

'I am coming down here, and asking your help, because there's going to be an exhumation. There is very strong suspicion of poison.'

'And here we are at the station,' said Father Brown cheerfully. 'I suppose your idea is that poisoning the poor man would naturally fall among the household duties of his wife.'

'Well, there never seems to have been anyone else here who had any particular connection with him,' replied Mulborough, as they alighted from the train. 'At least there is one queer old crony of his, a broken-down actor, hanging round; but the police and the local solicitor seem convinced he is an unbalanced busybody; with some *idée fixe* about a quarrel with an actor who was his enemy; but who certainly wasn't Maltravers. A wandering accident, I should say, and certainly nothing to do with the problem of the poison.'

Father Brown had heard the story. But he knew that he never knew a story until he knew the characters in the story. He spent the next two or three days in going the rounds, on one polite excuse or another, to visit the chief actors of the drama. His first interview with the mysterious widow was brief but bright. He brought away from it at least two facts; one that Mrs Maltravers sometimes talked in a way which the Victorian village would call cynical; and, second, that like not a few actresses, she happened to belong to his own religious communion.

He was not so illogical (nor so unorthodox) as to infer from this alone that she was innocent of the alleged crime. He was well aware that his old religious communion could boast of several distinguished poisoners. But he had no difficulty in understanding its connection, in this sort of case, with a certain intellectual liberty which these Puritans would call laxity; and which would certainly seem to this parochial patch of an older England to be almost cosmopolitan. Anyhow, he was sure she could count for a great deal, whether for good or evil. Her brown eyes were brave to the point of battle, and her enigmatic mouth, humorous and rather large, suggested that her purposes touching the parson's poetical son, whatever they might be, were planted pretty deep.

The parson's poetical son himself, interviewed amid vast village scandal on a bench outside the Blue Lion, gave an impression of pure sulks. Hurrel Horner, son of the Rev. Samuel Horner, was a square-built young man in a pale grey suit with a touch of something arty in a pale green tie, otherwise mainly notable for a mane of auburn hair and a permanent scowl. But Father Brown had a way with him in getting people to explain at considerable length why they refused to say a single word. About the general scandalmongering in the village, the young man began to curse freely. He even added a little scandalmongering of his own. He referred bitterly to alleged past flirtations between the Puritan Miss Carstairs-Carew and Mr Carver the solicitor. He even accused that legal character of having attempted to force himself upon the acquaintance of Mrs Maltravers. But when he came to speak of his own father, whether out of an acid decency or piety, or because his anger was too deep for speech, he snapped out only a few words.

'Well, there it is. He denounces her day and night as a painted adventuress; a sort of barmaid with gilt hair. I tell him she's not; you've met her yourself, and you know she's not. But he won't even meet her. He won't even see her in the street or look at her out of a window. An actress would pollute his house and even his holy presence. If he is called a Puritan he says he's proud to be a Puritan.'

'Your father,' said Father Brown, 'is entitled to have his views respected, whatever they are; they are not views I understand very well myself. But I agree he is not entitled to lay down the law about a lady he has never seen and then refuse even to look at her, to see if he is right. That is illogical.'

'That's his very stiffest point,' replied the youth. 'Not even one momentary meeting. Of course, he thunders against my other theatrical tastes as well.'

Father Brown swiftly followed up the new opening, and learnt much that he wanted to know. The alleged poetry, which was such a blot on the young man's character, was almost entirely dramatic poetry. He had written tragedies in verse which had been admired by good judges. He was no mere stage-struck fool; indeed he was no fool of any kind. He had some really original ideas about acting Shakespeare; it was easy to understand his having been dazzled and delighted by finding the brilliant lady at the Grange. And even the priest's intellectual sympathy so far mellowed the rebel of Potter's Pond that at their parting he actually smiled.

It was that smile which suddenly revealed to Father Brown that the young man was really miserable. So long as he frowned, it might well have been only sulks; but when he smiled it was somehow a more real revelation of sorrow.

Something continued to haunt the priest about that interview with the poet. An inner instinct certified that the sturdy young man was eaten from within, by some grief greater even than the conventional story of conventional parents being obstacles to the course of true love. It was all the more so, because there were not any obvious alternative causes. The boy was already rather a literary and dramatic success; his books might be said to be booming. Nor did he drink or dissipate his well-earned wealth. His notorious revels at the Blue Lion reduced themselves to one glass of light ale; and he seemed to be rather careful with his money. Father Brown thought of another possible complication in connection with Hurrel's large resources and small expenditure; and his brow darkened.

The conversation of Miss Carstairs-Carew, on whom he called next, was certainly calculated to paint the parson's son in the darkest colours. But as it was devoted to blasting him with all the special vices which Father Brown was quite certain the young man did not exhibit, he put it down to a common combination of Puritanism and gossip. The lady, though lofty, was quite gracious, however, and offered the visitor a small glass of port-wine and a slice of seed-cake, in the manner of everybody's most ancient great-aunts, before he managed to escape from a sermon on the general decay of morals and manners.

His next port of call was very much of a contrast; for he disappeared down a dark and dirty alley, where Miss Carstairs-Carew would have refused to follow him even in thought; and then into a narrow tenement made noisier by a high and declamatory voice in an attic. . . . From this he re-emerged, with a rather dazed expression, pursued on to the pavement by a very excited man with a blue chin and a black frock-coat faded to bottle-green, who was shouting argumentatively:

'He did not disappear! Maltravers never disappeared! He appeared; he appeared dead and I've appeared alive. But where's all the rest of the company? Where's that man, that monster, who deliberately stole my lines, crabbed my best scenes and ruined my career? I was the finest Tubal that ever had trod the boards. He acted Shylock – he didn't need to act much for that! And so with the greatest opportunity of my whole career. I could show you press-cuttings on my rendering of Fortinbras—'

'I'm quite sure they were splendid and very well-deserved,' gasped the little priest. 'I understood the company had left the village before Maltravers died. But it's all right. It's quite all right.' And he began to hurry down the street again.

'He was to act Polonius,' continued the unquenchable orator behind him. Father Brown suddenly stopped dead.

'Oh,' he said very slowly, 'he was to act Polonius.'

'That villain Hankin!' shrieked the actor. 'Follow his trail. Follow him to the ends of the earth! Of course he'd left the village;

trust him for that. Follow him – find him; and may the curses—'
But the priest was again hurrying away down the street.

Two much more prosaic and perhaps more practical interviews followed this melodramatic scene. First the priest went into the bank, where he was closeted for ten minutes with the manager; and then paid a very proper call on the aged and amiable clergyman. Here again all seemed very much as described, unaltered and seemingly unalterable; a touch or two of devotion from more austere traditions, in the narrow crucifix on the wall, the big Bible on the bookstand and the old gentleman's opening lament over the increasing disregard of Sunday; but all with a flavour of gentility that was not without its little refinements and faded luxuries.

The clergyman also gave his guest a glass of port; but accompanied by an ancient British biscuit instead of seed-cake. The priest had again the weird feeling that everything was almost too perfect, and that he was living a century before his time. Only on one point the amiable old parson refused to melt into any further amiability; he meekly but firmly maintained that his conscience would not allow him to meet a stage player. However, Father Brown put down his glass of port with expressions of appreciation and thanks; and went off to meet his friend the doctor by appointment at the corner of the street; whence they were to go together to the offices of Mr Carver, the solicitor.

'I suppose you've gone the dreary round,' began the doctor, 'and found it a very dull village.'

Father Brown's reply was sharp and almost shrill.

'Don't call your village dull. I assure you it's a very extraordinary village indeed.'

'I've been dealing with the only extraordinary thing that ever happened here, I should think,' observed Dr Mulborough. 'And even that happened to somebody from outside. I may tell you they managed the exhumation quietly last night; and I did the autopsy this morning. In plain words, we've been digging up a corpse that's simply stuffed with poison.'

'A corpse stuffed with poison,' repeated Father Brown rather absently. 'Believe me, your village contains something much more extraordinary than that.'

There was abrupt silence, followed by the equally abrupt pulling of the antiquated bell-pull in the porch of the solicitor's house; and they were soon brought into the presence of that legal gentleman, who presented them in turn to a white-haired, yellow-faced gentleman with a scar, who appeared to be the Admiral.

By this time the atmosphere of the village had sunk almost into the subconsciousness of the little priest; but he was conscious that the lawyer was indeed the sort of lawyer to be the adviser of people like Miss Carstairs-Carew. But though he was an archaic old bird, he seemed something more than a fossil. Perhaps it was the uniformity of the background; but the priest had again the curious feeling that he himself was transplanted back into the early nineteenth century, rather than that the solicitor had survived into the early twentieth. His collar and cravat contrived to look almost like a stock as he settled his long chin into them; but they were clean as well as clean-cut; and there was even something about him of a very dry old dandy. In short, he was what is called well-preserved, even if partly by being petrified.

The lawyer and the Admiral, and even the doctor, showed some surprise on finding that Father Brown was rather disposed to defend the parson's son against the local lamentations on behalf of the parson.

'I thought our young friend rather attractive, myself,' he said. 'He's a good talker and I should guess a good poet; and Mrs Maltravers, who is serious about that at least, says he's quite a good actor.'

'Indeed,' said the lawyer. 'Potter's Pond, outside Mrs Maltravers, is rather more inclined to ask if he is a good son.'

'He is a good son,' said Father Brown. 'That's the extraordinary thing.'

'Damn it all,' said the Admiral. 'Do you mean he's really fond of his father?'

The priest hesitated. Then he said, 'I'm not quite so sure about that. That's the other extraordinary thing.'

'What the devil do you mean?' demanded the sailor with nautical profanity.

'I mean,' said Father Brown, 'that the son still speaks of his father in a hard unforgiving way; but he seems after all to have done more than his duty by him. I had a talk with the bank manager, and as we were inquiring in confidence into a serious crime,

under authority from the police, he told me the facts. The old
clergyman has retired from parish work; indeed, this was never
actually his parish. Such of the populace, which is pretty pagan, as
goes to church at all, goes to Dutton-Abbot, not a mile away. The
old man has no private means, but the son is earning good money;
and the old man is well looked after. He gave me some port of
absolutely first-class vintage; I saw rows of dusty old bottles of it;
and I left him sitting down to a little lunch quite *recherché* in an old-
fashioned style. It must be done on the young man's money.'

'Quite a model son,' said Carver, with a slight sneer.

Father Brown nodded, frowning, as if revolving a riddle of his
own; and then said:

'A model son. But rather a mechanical model.'

At this moment a clerk brought in an unstamped letter for the
lawyer; a letter which the lawyer tore impatiently across after a
single glance. As it fell apart, the priest saw a spidery, crazy
crowded sort of handwriting and the signature of 'Phoenix Fitzgerald'; and made a guess which the other curtly confirmed.

'It's that melodramatic actor that's always pestering us,' he said.
'He's got some fixed idea of an old feud with some dead and gone
fellow mummer of his, which can't have anything to do with the
case. We all refuse to see him, except the doctor, who did see him;
and the doctor says he's mad.'

'Yes,' said Father Brown, pursing his lips thoughtfully. 'I should
say he's mad. But of course there can't be any doubt that he's right.'

'Right?' cried Carver sharply. 'Right about what?'

'About this being connected with the old theatrical company,'
said Father Brown. 'Do you know the first thing that stumped me
about this story? It was that notion that Maltravers was killed by
villagers because he insulted their village. It's extraordinary what
coroners can get jurymen to believe; and journalists, of course, are
quite incredibly credulous. They can't know much about English
rustics. I'm an English rustic myself; at least I was grown, with
other turnips, in Essex. Can you imagine an English agricultural
labourer idealizing and personifying his village, like the citizen of
an old Greek city state; drawing the sword for its sacred banner,
like a man in the tiny mediaeval republic of an Italian town? Can
you hear a jolly old gaffer saying, "Blood alone can wipe out one
spot on the escutcheon of Potter's Pond"? By St George and the

Dragon, I only wish they would! But, as a matter of fact, I have a more practical argument for the other notion.'

He paused for a moment, as if collecting his thoughts, and then went on:

'They misunderstood the meaning of those few last words poor Maltravers was heard to say. He wasn't telling the villagers that the village was only a hamlet. He was talking to an actor; they were going to put on a performance in which Fitzgerald was to be Fortinbras, the unknown Hankin to be Polonius, and Maltravers, no doubt, the Prince of Denmark. Perhaps somebody else wanted the part or had views on the part; and Maltravers said angrily, "You'd be a miserable little Hamlet"; that's all.'

Dr Mulborough was staring; he seemed to be digesting the suggestion slowly but without difficulty. At last he said, before the others could speak:

'And what do you suggest that we should do now?'

Father Brown rose rather abruptly; but he spoke civilly enough. 'If these gentlemen will excuse us for the moment, I propose that you and I, doctor, should go round at once to the Horners. I know the parson and his son will both be there just now. And what I want to do, doctor, is this. Nobody in the village knows yet, I think, about your autopsy and its result. I want you simply to tell both the clergyman and his son, while they are there together, the exact fact of the case; that Maltravers died by poison and not by a blow.'

Dr Mulborough had reason to reconsider his incredulity when told that it was an extraordinary village. The scene which ensued, when he actually carried out the priest's programme, was certainly of the sort in which a man, as the saying is, can hardly believe his eyes.

The Rev. Samuel Horner was standing in his black cassock, which threw up the silver of his venerable head; his hand rested at the moment on the lectern at which he often stood to study the Scriptures, now possibly by accident only; but it gave him a greater look of authority. And opposite to him his mutinous son was sitting asprawl in a chair, smoking a cheap cigarette with an exceptionally heavy scowl; a lively picture of youthful impiety.

The old man courteously waved Father Brown to a seat, which he took and sat there silent, staring blandly at the ceiling.

But something made Mulborough feel that he could deliver his important news more impressively standing up.

'I feel,' he said, 'that you ought to be informed, as in some sense the spiritual father of this community, that one terrible tragedy in its record has taken on a new significance; possibly even more terrible. You will recall the sad business of the death of Maltravers; who was adjudged to have been killed with the blow of a stick, probably wielded by some rustic enemy.'

The clergyman made a gesture with a wavering hand. 'God forbid,' he said, 'that I should say anything that might seem to palliate murderous violence in any case. But when an actor brings his wickedness into this innocent village, he is challenging the judgment of God.'

'Perhaps,' said the doctor gravely. 'But anyhow it was not so that the judgment fell. I have just been commissioned to conduct a post mortem on the body; and I can assure you, first, that the blow on the head could not conceivably have caused the death; and, second, that the body was full of poison, which undoubtedly caused death.'

Young Hurrel Horner sent his cigarette flying and was on his feet with the lightness and swiftness of a cat. His leap landed him within a yard or so of the reading-desk.

'Are you certain of this?' he gasped. 'Are you absolutely certain that that blow could not cause death?'

'Absolutely certain,' said the doctor.

'Well,' said Hurrel, 'I almost wish this one could.'

In a flash before anyone could move a finger, he had struck the parson a stunning crack on the mouth, dashing him backwards like a disjointed black doll against the door.

'What are you doing?' cried Mulborough, shaken from head to foot with the shock and mere sound of the blow. 'Father Brown, what is this madman doing?'

But Father Brown had not stirred; he was still staring serenely at the ceiling.

'I was waiting for him to do that,' said the priest placidly. 'I rather wonder he hasn't done it before.'

'Good God,' cried the doctor. 'I know we thought he was wronged in some ways; but to strike his father; to strike a clergyman and a non-combatant—'

'He has not struck his father; and he has not struck a clergyman,' said Father Brown. 'He has struck a blackmailing blackguard of an actor dressed up as a clergyman, who has lived on him like a leech for years. Now he knows he is free of the blackmail, he lets fly; and I can't say I blame him much. More especially as I have very strong suspicions that the blackmailer is a poisoner as well. I think, Mulborough, you had better ring up the police.'

They passed out of the room uninterrupted by the two others, the one dazed and staggered, the other still blind and snorting and panting with passions of relief and rage. But as they passed, Father Brown once turned his face to the young man; and the young man was one of the very few human beings who have seen that face implacable.

'He was right there,' said Father Brown. 'When an actor brings his wickedness into this innocent village, he challenges the judgment of God.'

'Well,' said Father Brown, as he and the doctor again settled themselves in a railway carriage standing in the station of Potter's Pond. 'As you say, it's a strange story; but I don't think it's any longer a mystery story. Anyhow, the story seems to me to have been roughly this. Maltravers came here, with part of his touring company; some of them went straight to Dutton-Abbot, where they were all presenting some melodrama about the early nineteenth century; he himself happened to be hanging about in his stage dress, the very distinctive dress of a dandy of that time. Another character was an old-fashioned parson, whose dark dress was less distinctive and might pass as being merely old-fashioned. This part was taken by a man who mostly acted old men; had acted Shylock and was afterwards going to act Polonius.

'A third figure in the drama was our dramatic poet, who was also a dramatic performer, and quarrelled with Maltravers about how to present Hamlet, but more about personal things, too. I think it likely that he was in love with Mrs Maltravers even then; I don't believe there was anything wrong with them; and I hope it may now be all right with them. But he may very well have resented Maltravers in his conjugal capacity; for Maltravers was a bully and likely to raise rows. In some such row they fought with sticks, and the poet hit Maltravers very hard on the head, and, in the light of the inquest, had every reason to suppose he had killed him.

'A third person was present or privy to the incident, the man acting the old parson; and he proceeded to blackmail the alleged murderer, forcing from him the cost of his upkeep in some luxury as a retired clergyman. It was the obvious masquerade for such a man in such a place, simply to go on wearing his stage clothes as a retired clergyman. But he had his own reason for being a very retired clergyman. For the true story of Maltravers' death was that he rolled into a deep undergrowth of bracken, gradually recovered, tried to walk towards a house, and was eventually overcome, not by the blow, but by the fact that the benevolent clergyman had given him poison an hour before, probably in a glass of port. I was beginning to think so, when I drank a glass of the parson's port. It made me a little nervous. The police are working on that theory now; but whether they will be able to prove that part of the story, I don't know. They will have to find the exact motive; but it's obvious that this bunch of actors was buzzing with quarrels and Maltravers was very much hated.'

'The police may prove something now they have got the suspicion,' said Dr Mulborough. 'What I don't understand is why you ever began to suspect. Why in the world should you suspect that very blameless black-coated gentleman?'

Father Brown smiled faintly. 'I suppose in one sense,' he said, 'it was a matter of special knowledge; almost a professional matter, but in a peculiar sense. You know our controversialists often complain that there is a great deal of ignorance about what our religion is really like. But it is really more curious than that. It is true, and it is not at all unnatural, that England does not know much about the Church of Rome. But England does not know much about the Church of England. Not even as much as I do. You would be astonished at how little the average public grasps about the Anglican controversies; lots of them don't really know what is meant by a High Churchman or a Low Churchman, even on the particular points of practice, let alone the two theories of history and philosophy behind them. You can see this ignorance in any newspaper; in any merely popular novel or play.

'Now the first thing that struck me was that this venerable cleric had got the whole thing incredibly mixed up. No Anglican parson could be so wrong about every Anglican problem. He was supposed to be an old Tory High Churchman; and then he boasted of being a Puritan. A man like that might personally be rather Puritanical; but he would never call it being a Puritan. He professed a horror of the stage; he didn't know that High Churchmen generally don't have that special horror, though Low Churchmen do. He talked like a Puritan about the Sabbath; and then he had a crucifix in his room. He evidently had no notion of what a very pious parson ought to be, except that he ought to be very solemn and venerable and frown upon the pleasures of the world.

'All this time there was a subconscious notion running in my head; something I couldn't fix in my memory; and then it came to me suddenly. This is a Stage Parson. That is exactly the vague venerable old fool who would be the nearest notion a popular playwright or play-actor of the old school had of anything so odd as a religious man.'

'To say nothing of a physician of the old school,' said Mulborough good-humouredly, 'who does not set up to know much about being a religious man.'

'As a matter of fact,' went on Father Brown, 'there was a plainer and more glaring cause for suspicion. It concerned the Dark Lady of the Grange, who was supposed to be the Vampire of the Village. I very early formed the impression that this black blot was rather the bright spot of the village. She was treated as a mystery; but there was really nothing mysterious about her. She had come down here quite recently, quite openly, under her own name, to help the new inquiries to be made about her own husband. He hadn't treated her too well; but she had principles, suggesting that something was due to her married name and to common justice. For the same reason, she went to live in the house outside which her husband had been found dead. The other innocent and straightforward case, besides the Vampire of the Village, was the Scandal of the Village, the parson's profligate son. He also made no disguise of his profession or past connection with the acting world. That's why I didn't suspect him as I did the parson. But you'll already have guessed a real and relevant reason for suspecting the parson.'

'Yes, I think I see,' said the doctor, 'that's why you bring in the name of the actress.'

'Yes, I mean his fanatical fixity about not seeing the actress,' remarked the priest. 'But he didn't really object to seeing her. He objected to her seeing him.'

'Yes, I see that,' assented the other.

'If she had seen the Rev. Samuel Horner, she would instantly have recognized the very unreverend actor Hankin, disguised as a sham parson with a pretty bad character behind the disguise. Well, that is the whole of this simple village idyll, I think. But you will admit I kept my promise; I have shown you something in the village considerably more creepy than a corpse; even a corpse stuffed with poison. The black coat of a parson stuffed with a blackmailer is at least worth noticing and my live man is much deadlier than your dead one.'

'Yes,' said the doctor, settling himself back comfortably in the cushions. 'If it comes to a little cosy company on a railway journey, I should prefer the corpse.'

POEMS

WINE AND WATER

Old Noah he had an ostrich farm and fowls on the largest scale,
He ate his egg with a ladle in a egg-cup big as a pail,
And the soup he took was Elephant Soup and the fish he took
    was Whale,
But they all were small to the cellar he took when he set out
    to sail,
And Noah he often said to his wife when he sat down to dine,
'I don't care where the water goes if it doesn't get into the wine.'

The cataract of the cliff of heaven fell blinding off the brink
As if it would wash the stars away as suds go down a sink,
The seven heavens came roaring down for the throats of hell
    to drink,
And Noah he cocked his eye and said, 'It looks like rain, I think,
The water has drowned the Matterhorn as deep as a Mendip
    mine,
But I don't care where the water goes if it doesn't get into
    the wine.'

But Noah he sinned, and we have sinned; on tipsy feet we trod,
Till a great big black teetotaller was sent to us for a rod,
And you can't get wine at a P. S. A., or chapel, or Eisteddfod,
For the Curse of Water has come again because of the wrath
    of God,
And water is on the Bishop's board and the Higher Thinker's
    shrine,
But I don't care where the water goes if it doesn't get into
    the wine.

ANTICHRIST, OR THE REUNION OF CHRISTENDOM: AN ODE

'A bill which has shocked the conscience of every
Christian community in Europe.'

MR F. E. SMITH,
ON THE WELSH DISESTABLISHMENT BILL

Are they clinging to their crosses,
    F. E. Smith,
Where the Breton boat-fleet tosses,
    Are they, Smith?
Do they, fasting, trembling, bleeding,
    Wait the news from this our city?
Groaning 'That's the Second Reading!'
    Hissing 'There is still Committee!'
If the voice of Cecil falters,
    If McKenna's point has pith,
Do they tremble for their altars?
    Do they, Smith?

Russian peasants round their pope
    Huddled, Smith,
Hear about it all, I hope,
    Don't they, Smith?
In the mountain hamlets clothing
    Peaks beyond Caucasian pales,
Where Establishment means nothing
    And they never heard of Wales,
Do they read it all in Hansard
    With a crib to read it with –
'Welsh Tithes: Dr Clifford Answered.'
    Really, Smith?

In the lands where Christians were,
       F. E. Smith,
In the little lands laid bare,
       Smith, O Smith!
Where the Turkish bands are busy,
      And the Tory name is blessed
Since they hailed the Cross of Dizzy
      On the banners from the West!
Men don't think it half so hard if
      Islam burns their kin and kith,
Since a curate lives in Cardiff
      Saved by Smith.

It would greatly, I must own,
      Soothe me, Smith!
If you left this theme alone,
      Holy Smith!
For your legal cause or civil
      You fight well and get your fee;
For your God or dream or devil
      You will answer, not to me.
Talk about the pews and steeples
      And the Cash that goes therewith!
But the soul of Christian peoples . . .
      Chuck it, Smith!

ELEGY IN A COUNTRY CHURCHYARD

The men that worked for England
They have their graves at home:
And bees and birds of England
About the cross can roam.

But they that fought for England,
Following a falling star,
Alas, alas for England
They have their graves afar.

And they that rule in England,
In stately conclave met,
Alas, alas for England
They have no graves as yet.

LEPANTO

White founts falling in the courts of the sun,
And the Soldan of Byzantium is smiling as they run;
There is laughter like the fountains in that face of all men feared,
It stirs the forest darkness, the darkness of his beard,
It curls the blood-red crescent, the crescent of his lips,
For the inmost sea of all the earth is shaken with his ships.
They have dared the white republics up the capes of Italy,
They have dashed the Adriatic round the Lion of the Sea,
And the Pope has cast his arms abroad for agony and loss,
And called the kings of Christendom for swords about the Cross,
The cold queen of England is looking in the glass;
The shadow of the Valois is yawning at the Mass;
From evening isles fantastical rings faint the Spanish gun,
And the Lord upon the Golden Horn is laughing in the sun.

Dim drums throbbing, in the hills half heard,
Where only on a nameless throne a crownless prince has stirred,
Where, risen from a doubtful seat and half attainted stall,
The last knight of Europe takes weapons from the wall,
The last and lingering troubadour to whom the bird has sung,
That once went singing southward when all the world was young,
In that enormous silence, tiny and unafraid,
Comes up along a winding road the noise of the Crusade.
Strong gongs groaning as the guns boom far,
Don John of Austria is going to the war,
Stiff flags straining in the night-blasts cold
In the gloom black-purple, in the glint old-gold,
Torchlight crimson on the copper kettle-drums,
Then the tuckets, then the trumpets, then the cannon, and
        he comes.
Don John laughing in the brave beard curled,
Spurning of his stirrups like the thrones of all the world,
Holding his head up for a flag of all the free.
Love-light of Spain – hurrah!
Death-light of Africa!
Don John of Austria
Is riding to the sea.

Mahound is in his paradise above the evening star,
(*Don John of Austria is going to the war.*)
He moves a mighty turban on the timeless houri's knees,
His turban that is woven of the sunset and the seas.
He shakes the peacock gardens as he rises from his ease,
And he strides among the tree-tops and is taller than the trees,
And his voice through all the garden is a thunder sent to bring
Black Azrael and Ariel and Ammon on the wing.
Giants and the Genii,
Multiple of wing and eye,
Whose strong obedience broke the sky
When Solomon was king.

They rush in red and purple from the red clouds of the morn,
From temples where the yellow gods shut up their eyes in scorn;
They rise in green robes roaring from the green hells of the sea
Where fallen skies and evil hues and eyeless creatures be;
On them the sea-valves cluster and the grey sea-forests curl,
Splashed with a splendid sickness, the sickness of the pearl;
They swell in sapphire smoke out of the blue cracks of the
          ground, –
They gather and they wonder and give worship to Mahound.
And he saith, 'Break up the mountains where the hermit-folk
          can hide,
And sift the red and silver sands lest bone of saint abide,
And chase the Giaours flying night and day, not giving rest,
For that which was our trouble comes again out of the west.
We have set the seal of Solomon on all things under sun,
Of knowledge and of sorrow and endurance of things done,
But a noise is in the mountains, in the mountains, and I know
The voice that shook our palaces – four hundred years ago:
It is he that saith not 'Kismet'; it is he that knows not Fate;
It is Richard, it is Raymond, it is Godfrey in the gate!
It is he whose loss is laughter when he counts the wager worth,
Put down your feet upon him, that our peace be on the earth.'
For he heard drums groaning and he heard guns jar,
(*Don John of Austria is going to the war.*)
Sudden and still – hurrah!
Bolt from Iberia!

Don John of Austria
Is gone by Alcalar.

St Michael's on his mountain in the sea-roads of the north
(*Don John of Austria is girt and going forth.*)
Where the grey seas glitter and the sharp tides shift
And the sea folk labour and the red sails lift.
He shakes his lance of iron and he claps his wings of stone;
The noise is gone through Normandy; the noise is gone alone;
The North is full of tangled things and texts and aching eyes
And dead is all the innocence of anger and surprise,
And Christian killeth Christian in a narrow dusty room,
And Christian dreadeth Christ that hath a newer face of doom,
And Christian hateth Mary that God kissed in Galilee,
But Don John of Austria is riding to the sea.
Don John calling through the blast and the eclipse
Crying with the trumpet, with the trumpet of his lips,
Trumpet that sayeth ha!
Domino gloria!
Don John of Austria
Is shouting to the ships.

King Philip's in his closet with the Fleece about his neck
(*Don John of Austria is armed upon the deck.*)
The walls are hung with velvet that is black and soft as sin,
And little dwarfs creep out of it and little dwarfs creep in.
He holds a crystal phial that has colours like the moon,
He touches, and it tingles, and he trembles very soon,
And his face is as a fungus of a leprous white and grey
Like plants in the high houses that are shuttered from the day,
And death is in the phial, and the end of noble work,
But Don John of Austria has fired upon the Turk.
Don John's hunting, and his hounds have bayed –
Booms away past Italy the rumour of his raid
Gun upon gun, ha! ha!
Gun upon gun, hurrah!
Don John of Austria
Has loosed the cannonade.

The Pope was in his chapel before day or battle broke,
(*Don John of Austria is hidden in the smoke.*)
The hidden room in man's house where God sits all the year,
The secret window whence the world looks small and very dear.
He sees as in a mirror on the monstrous twilight sea
The crescent of his cruel ships whose name is mystery;
They fling great shadows foe-wards, making Cross and Castle dark,
They veil the plumèd lions on the galleys of St Mark;
And above the ships are palaces of brown, black-bearded chiefs,
And below the ships are prisons, where with multitudinous griefs,
Christian captives sick and sunless, all a laboring race repines
Like a race in sunken cities, like a nation in the mines.
They are lost like slaves that swat, and in the skies of morning hung
The stair-ways of the tallest gods when tyranny was young.
They are countless, voiceless, hopeless as those fallen or fleeing on
Before the high Kings' horses in the granite of Babylon.
And many a one grows witless in his quiet room in hell
Where a yellow face looks inward through the lattice of his cell,
And he finds his God forgotten, and he seeks no more a sign –
(*But Don John of Austria has burst the battle-line!*)
Don John pounding from the slaughter-painted poop,
Purpling all the ocean like a bloody pirate's sloop,
Scarlet running over on the silvers and the golds,
Breaking of the hatches up and bursting of the holds,
Thronging of the thousands up that labour under sea
White for bliss and blind for sun and stunned for liberty.
Vivat Hispania!
Domino Gloria!
Don John of Austria
Has set his people free!

Cervantes on his galley sets the sword back in the sheath
(*Don John of Austria rides homeward with a wreath.*)
And he sees across a weary land a straggling road in Spain,
Up which a lean and foolish knight forever rides in vain,
And he smiles, but not as Sultans smile, and settles back the
        blade . . .
(*But Don John of Austria rides home from the Crusade.*)

THE SECRET PEOPLE

Smile at us, pay us, pass us; but do not quite forget.
For we are the people of England, that never have spoken yet.
There is many a fat farmer that drinks less cheerfully,
There is many a free French peasant who is richer and sadder
　　　than we.
There are no folk in the whole world so helpless or so wise.
There is hunger in our bellies, there is laughter in our eyes;
You laugh at us and love us, both mugs and eyes are wet:
Only you do not know us. For we have not spoken yet.

The fine French kings came over in a flutter of flags and dames.
We liked their smiles and battles, but we never could say their
　　　names.
The blood ran red to Bosworth and the high French lords went
　　　down;
There was naught but a naked people under a naked crown.
And the eyes of the King's Servants turned terribly every way,
And the gold of the King's Servants rose higher every day.
They burnt the homes of the shaven men, that had been quaint
　　　and kind,
Till there was no bed in a monk's house, nor food that man
　　　could find.
The inns of God where no man paid, that were the wall of
　　　the weak,
The King's Servants ate them all. And still we did not speak.

And the face of the King's Servants grew greater than the King:
He tricked them, and they trapped him, and stood round him
　　　in a ring.
The new grave lords closed round him, that had eaten the
　　　abbey's fruits,
And the men of the new religion, with their bibles in their boots,
We saw their shoulders moving, to menace or discuss,
And some were pure and some were vile, but none took heed
　　　of us.
We saw the King as they killed him, and his face was proud
　　　and pale;
And a few men talked of freedom, while England talked of ale.

A war that we understood not came over the world and woke
Americans, Frenchmen, Irish; but we knew not the things
    they spoke.
They talked about rights and nature and peace and the
    people's reign:
And the squires, our masters, bade us fight; and never scorned
    us again.
Weak if we be for ever, could none condemn us then;
Men called us serfs and drudges; men knew that we were men.
In foam and flame at Trafalgar, on Albeura plains,
We did and died like lions, to keep ourselves in chains.
We lay in living ruins; firing and fearing not
The strange fierce face of the Frenchman who knew for what
    they fought,
And the man who seemed to be more than man we strained
    against and broke;
And we broke our own rights with him. And still we never spoke.

Our patch of glory ended; we never heard guns again.
But the squire seemed struck in the saddle; he was foolish, as if
    in pain.
He leaned on a staggering lawyer, he clutched a cringing Jew,
He was stricken; it may be, after all, he was stricken at Waterloo.
Or perhaps the shades of the shaven men, whose spoil is in
    his house,
Come back in shining shapes at last to spoil his last carouse:
We only know the last sad squires ride slowly towards the sea,
And a new people takes the land: and still it is not we.

They have given us into the hand of new unhappy lords,
Lords without anger and honour, who dare not carry their
    swords.
They fight by shuffling papers; they have bright dead alien eyes;
They look at our labour and laughter as a tired man looks
    at flies.
And the load of their loveless pity is worse than the ancient
    wrongs,
Their doors are shut in the evening; and they know no songs.

We hear men speaking for us of new laws strong and sweet,
Yet is there no man speaketh as we speak in the street.
It may be we shall rise the last as Frenchmen rose the first,
Our wrath come after Russia's wrath and our wrath be the worst.
It may be we are meant to mark with our riot and our rest
God's scorn for all men governing. It may be beer is best.
But we are the people of England; and we have not spoken yet.
Smile at us, pay us, pass us. But do not quite forget.

THE ROLLING ENGLISH ROAD

Before the Roman came to Rye or out to Severn strode,
The rolling English drunkard made the rolling English road.
A reeling road, a rolling road, that rambles round the shire,
And after him the parson ran, the sexton and the squire;
A merry road, a mazy road, and such as we did tread
The night we went to Birmingham by way of Beachy Head.

I knew no harm of Bonaparte and plenty of the Squire,
And for to fight the Frenchman I did not much desire;
But I did bash their baggonets because they came arrayed
To straighten out the crooked road an English drunkard made,
Where you and I went down the lane with ale-mugs in our hands,
The night we went to Glastonbury by way of Goodwin Sands.

His sins they were forgiven him; or why do flowers run
Behind him; and the hedges all strengthening in the sun?
The wild thing went from left to right and knew not which
      was which,
But the wild rose was above him when they found him in
      the ditch.
God pardon us, nor harden us; we did not see so clear
The night we went to Bannockburn by way of Brighton Pier.

My friends, we will not go again or ape an ancient rage,
Or stretch the folly of our youth to be the shame of age,
But walk with clearer eyes and ears this path that wandereth,
And see undrugged in evening light the decent inn of death;
For there is good news yet to hear and fine things to be seen,
Before we go to Paradise by way of Kensal Green.

THE DONKEY

When fishes flew and forests walked
    And figs grew upon thorn,
Some moment when the moon was blood
    Then surely I was born.

With monstrous head and sickening cry
    And ears like errant wings,
The devil's walking parody
    On all four-footed things.

The tattered outlaw of the earth,
    Of ancient crooked will;
Starve, scourge, deride me: I am dumb,
    I keep my secret still.

Fools! For I also had my hour;
    One far fierce hour and sweet:
There was a shout about my ears,
    And palms before my feet.

MARCUS AURELIUS
Meditations

GABRIEL GARCÍA MÁRQUEZ
The General in His Labyrinth
Love in the Time of Cholera
One Hundred Years of Solitude

ANDREW MARVELL
The Complete Poems

W. SOMERSET MAUGHAM
Collected Stories
The Skeptical Romancer (US only)

CORMAC McCARTHY
The Border Trilogy

HERMAN MELVILLE
The Complete Shorter Fiction
Moby Dick

JOHN STUART MILL
On Liberty and Utilitarianism

JOHN MILTON
The Complete English Poems

YUKIO MISHIMA
The Temple of the
Golden Pavilion

MARY WORTLEY MONTAGU
Letters

MICHEL DE MONTAIGNE
The Complete Works

THOMAS MORE
Utopia

TONI MORRISON
Beloved
Song of Solomon

ALICE MUNRO
Carried Away: A Selection of
Stories

MURASAKI SHIKIBU
The Tale of Genji

VLADIMIR NABOKOV
Lolita
Pale Fire
Pnin
Speak, Memory

V. S. NAIPAUL
Collected Short Fiction (US only)
A House for Mr Biswas

R. K. NARAYAN
Swami and Friends
The Bachelor of Arts
The Dark Room
The English Teacher
(in 1 vol.)
Mr Sampath – The Printer of
Malgudi
The Financial Expert
Waiting for the Mahatma
(in 1 vol.)

IRÈNE NÉMIROVSKY
David Golder
The Ball
Snow in Autumn
The Courilof Affair
(in 1 vol.)

FLANN O'BRIEN
The Complete Novels

FRANK O'CONNOR
The Best of Frank O'Connor

GEORGE ORWELL
Animal Farm
Nineteen Eighty-Four
Essays
Burmese Days, Keep the Aspidistra
Flying, Coming Up for Air
(in 1 vol.)

THOMAS PAINE
Rights of Man
and Common Sense

ORHAN PAMUK
My Name is Red

BORIS PASTERNAK
Doctor Zhivago

SYLVIA PLATH
The Bell Jar (US only)

PLATO
The Republic
Symposium and Phaedrus

EDGAR ALLAN POE
The Complete Stories

MARCO POLO
The Travels of Marco Polo

MARCEL PROUST
In Search of Lost Time
(in 4 vols, UK only)